Effective Instruction
for Special Education

Effective Instruction for Special Education

> Third Edition <

Margo A. Mastropieri
Thomas E. Scruggs

pro·ed
An International Publisher

8700 Shoal Creek Boulevard
Austin, Texas 78757-6897
800/897-3202   Fax 800/397-7633
www.proedinc.com

An International Publisher

© 1987, 1994, 2002 by PRO-ED, Inc.
8700 Shoal Creek Boulevard
Austin, Texas 78757-6897
800/897-3202   Fax 800/397-7633
www.proedinc.com

Library of Congress Cataloging-in-Publication Data

Mastropieri, Margo A., 1951–
    Effective instruction for special education / Margo A. Mastropieri, Thomas E.
Scruggs.—3rd ed.
        p.   cm.
    Includes bibliographical references (p.) and index.
    ISBN 0-89079-882-6
    1. Handicapped—Education—United States.   2. Effective teaching—United States.
3. Teachers of handicapped children—Training of—United States.   4. Special
education—United States.   I. Title.

LC4031.M35   2002
371.9'0973—dc21
                                                                    2001048151

This book is designed in Goudy and Frutiger.

Printed in the United States of America

1   2   3   4   5   6   7   8   9   10   06   05   04   03   02

Contents

List of Tables and Figures

Tables

Figures

Preface

This book is intended to provide practical information relevant to the instruction of students with mild disabilities, whether in self-contained, resource, or general education classroom (inclusive) settings. It is meant to be useful to preservice or inservice special educators or general education teachers concerned with the instruction of students in inclusive settings. We have tried to base the information included in this book on the most relevant research available on effective teaching methods in special education; however, we also have tried to present research-based information through the perspective of practitioners in special education.

Although several high-quality books on teaching methods exist, we have attempted to write a book that would address directly the actual practice of teaching and include step-by-step examples of effective teaching methods. To accomplish this, we first have described general principles of effective instruction, followed by more specific details associated with instruction in specific academic areas. We have included throughout examples of possible sequences of objectives and excerpts of possible teacher dialogue relevant to particular objectives. We do not intend to suggest by this that the sequence of objectives should be invariant or that teachers necessarily should deliver lessons from prepared scripts. We have provided such examples as models of possible sequences only, although we feel that employing instruction that closely resembles such models is likely to result in higher levels of achievement.

The reader also will notice that we have referred only infrequently to specific categories of exceptionality—including labels such as learning disabilities, emotional disturbance or behavioral disorders, or mild mental retardation. We do not mean to deny the value of labels for some purposes—for example, placement, research, advocacy, compliance, or external funding. However, the practices we suggest are likely to be effective with all such types of students, although some sections of the book can be emphasized more for classes involving specific categorical areas. For a methods class in learning disabilities, for example, instructors may wish to emphasize chapters dealing with basic skills instruction in academic areas and curriculum-based measurement. For a methods class in behavioral disorders, instructors may wish to emphasize sections dealing with the collection of behavioral data, behavior management, and social skills instruction. For a class in mental retardation, instructors may wish to emphasize sections dealing with life skills and vocational education. We feel, however, that all chapters have relevance to all of these areas of exceptionality. For example, research has indicated that many students classified as having learning disabilities exhibit relative deficits in social functioning. Likewise, students with behavior problems often exhibit academic deficiencies that can inhibit independent functioning in general education classes. Similarly, students with mental retardation often exhibit deficiencies in academic and social functioning. We feel, therefore, that the special education teacher needs skills in all these areas of teaching, although the relative emphasis may vary from student to student.

Although we have tried to provide as practical an orientation as is possible in a textbook, we would like to add our belief that supervised practice with children in instructional settings implementing these procedures is invaluable in developing effective teaching practices. In our own experiences with earlier versions of this book, we combined instructional classroom presentations with supervised practica in implementing these strategies. During these practicum-teaching sessions, specific teaching behaviors were observed directly by supervisors. Practicum students found videotape feedback of their teaching sessions particularly helpful in self-evaluation.

We feel that didactic instruction in effective teaching practices, coupled with supervised experience, can optimize both preservice and inservice teacher preparation.

We have tried to be sparing in the use of textual citations, in response to comments we frequently have heard that highly referenced material can disrupt the flow of a textbook and inhibit comprehension. For those who are interested in supporting information (and we hope that many will be), we have included major supporting references at the end of each chapter. Instructors may wish to assign some of these primary and secondary sources as supplementary materials for students at the master's level.

We have made numerous changes in this third edition, in addition to our general updating of references. We have added additional material on curriculum-based measurement, portfolio and performance assessment, and high-stakes testing. We have added supplemental material on behavior management and a variety of teaching and learning strategies in literacy, math, study skills, social skills, and vocational education, as these strategies reflect newer developments from the research literature. We have maintained our previous emphasis on the importance of meaning and how active thinking can be used to enhance learning, and we have added additional information on the importance of peer mediation and how group approaches can be particularly valuable in promoting learning objectives. Finally, we have changed our previous orientation from movement toward *mainstreaming* in general education settings, where students were expected to function independently after sufficient training in special education settings, to movement toward more inclusive settings, where students may still receive support relevant to their special needs as they progress toward more independent functioning. In support of this perspective, we have added an Inclusion Feature in each chapter, which describes applications of the information in the chapter in inclusive settings. We have also added a Technology Feature, which describes technological applications for the information in each chapter.

Finally, we have modified and added to our list of relevant curricular materials and software at the end of appropriate chapters, and we have included a list of publishers' addresses and Web sites in Appendix B. We do not mean by this to imply an unqualified endorsement of these materials or publishers; however, we felt that beginning teachers typically are unfamiliar with many curricular materials and software, and we decided to provide them with a starting place in their search for appropriate classroom materials. When these materials are used, we hope teachers will monitor their effectiveness with particular students in particular teaching situations.

We would like to dedicate this third edition to our parents, Dorothy and Francis Mastropieri, Janet Scruggs, and the memory of Edward B. Scruggs, who provided unconditional support of our own development and professional goals. We thank Pat Addison, Director of Special Education, Fairfax County Public Schools, for her support. We also thank Don Hammill and Jim Patton at PRO-ED for making this new edition possible, and the editorial assistance of Robin Spencer and Martin Wilson.

Chapter 1

꙳   ꙳   ꙳

Teacher Effectiveness

This book is concerned with effective teaching. Effective teaching refers to those things you can do as a teacher that can increase achievement and improve social behavior of your students. Research has repeatedly demonstrated that the type of behavior teachers exhibit can have a significant impact on student learning. In fact, the type of skills teachers exhibit can make the difference between student success and failure. This book is intended to describe these teaching skills.

Research has not always addressed effective teaching behaviors. Many years ago, researchers examined the influence of variables such as teacher personality, intelligence level, and style of dress in determining teacher effectiveness. Over time, researchers studied other variables, such as teaching methods (e.g., look-say vs. phonics methods for teaching reading) and the value of different types of curriculum (e.g., textbook vs. hands-on) in increasing achievement.

In the past few decades, researchers began to focus on behaviors exhibited by teachers that were linked to student achievement gains. This research was important because it addressed what teachers could do to maximize student learning. More recently, the roles of variables such as meaningfulness, concreteness, and active thinking have been investigated. These variables also have been found to be associated positively with student learning.

As a result of this research, several myths about teaching have been dispelled. It has been demonstrated conclusively that teachers do make a difference in student learning and that teachers who learn and practice certain teaching skills are more effective than teachers who do not. The notion that anyone can teach effectively also has been refuted. It is now known that skilled teachers can manipulate their behavior to make critical differences in student learning. This fact is as true for special education as it is for "regular" education.

It has been found that effective teaching practices are strongly related to achievement of students with mild disabilities (including learning disabilities, mild mental retardation, and behavior disorders; Englert, 1983, 1984; Rosenshine, 1997; Sindelar, Smith, Harriman, Hale, & Wilson, 1986). These practices include maximizing student engagement with instruction, asking direct and appropriate questions related to instructional objectives, and monitoring responses. Studies such as these support the notion that special educators can increase the amount of time spent on academic tasks and can improve instruction by (a) actively engaging students on task during instruction; (b) presenting information in clear, concise ways; (c) asking students questions relevant to the instructional objectives; (d) keeping students actively involved in relevant instructional activities; and (e) monitoring students' performance. These and related variables are known as the teacher effectiveness variables.

Teacher Effectiveness Variables

The important teacher effectiveness variables include time-on-task, content covered, delivery of instruction, questioning and feedback, guided and independent practice, and formative evaluation. Table 1.1 provides an overview of these variables. Overall, these variables are referred to as "alterable" variables because they are concerned with things teachers can do, or alter, in their teaching to increase student learning. In contrast, "nonalterable" variables, such as the teacher's gender or age, are not considered effective teaching variables because they are not alterable. Rosenshine and Stevens (1986; see also Rosenshine, 1997) have reviewed many of these variables and referred to them as "direct instruction." Overall, such instructional considerations have repeatedly been shown to increase learning, an important goal of special education.

Despite its successes, there have been criticisms of the effective instruction model (see Pressley & McCormick, 1995, for a discussion). It has been suggested that the model is overly teacher driven, relies too much on knowledge transmission by direct instruction, and is overly concerned with student academic achievement. Furthermore, many elements of direct instruction have been characterized as dull, repetitive, monotonous, or even punitive for students. However, we suggest that teacher effectiveness variables such as time-on-task are of great importance regardless of the approach to instruction being employed. (It is difficult to make a case for "off-task" behavior under any circumstances!) And although academic achievement is not the only purpose of schooling, it can be of critical importance to students enrolled in special education, especially those lacking the basic skills that will allow them to succeed independently in general education (inclusive) classrooms. Finally, even in situations when a lot of time spent on academic skill building is necessary, teachers can ensure that learning can be fun and exciting. Implementation of the teacher effectiveness components can help ensure that students find school an enjoyable and successful experience.

Time-on-Task

Time-on-task can be defined as the amount of time students spend on a particular task. However, the time-on-task can be subdivided into allocated time and engaged time. Researchers

Table 1.1. General Teacher Effectiveness Variables

Variable	Description
Time-on-task (engaged)	Time students are *actually working* on specific tasks (not simply scheduled or allocated time)
Content covered	Amount of information presented to students in a given time period
Scope and sequence	Total amount of content to be covered and order of presentation
Objectives	Description of behavioral outcomes of instruction
Pacing	Rate at which objectives are met
Providing information	Teacher delivery of content
Questioning	Prompting of overt student responses relevant to instructional objectives
Feedback	Teacher consequation of student responses
Guided and independent practice	Provision of opportunities for students to practice learned information in supervised and unsupervised conditions
Formative evaluation	Continuous assessment of learner progress toward prespecified goals and objectives

asked teachers to specify the amounts of time taken (allocated) for each academic subject during each day. At the same time, they observed the teachers' classrooms to determine how much time the students actually spent engaged in instructional activities. Although the amount of allocated time for instruction was similar for all teachers, researchers found that the amount of time students were actually engaged in relevant activities varied considerably from teacher to teacher and was consistently less than the amount of allocated time for all teachers. In a study of special education resource rooms, Haynes and Jenkins (1986) reported that only 44% of the allocated time, on average, was spent actively engaged in relevant instruction. It also was found that engaged time-on-task was directly related to higher levels of student achievement. Similarly, Leinhardt, Zigmond, and Cooley (1981) reported that many self-contained special education learning disabilities teachers spent an average of only 16 minutes a day directly teaching students reading skills. When you are thinking of how to increase the achievement of your students in your classroom, a very good place to start is increasing engaged time-on-task.

What are students doing when they are actively engaged in instruction? Engaged time-on-task activities involve active participation of students in areas that are directly relevant to instructional objectives. These activities include eye contact with the teacher, active attending to teacher presentation, direct responding to teacher questions, and active engagement with relevant instructional materials. The findings of engaged time-on-task research have been consistently clear: The more actively students participate in the instructional activities, the more they will learn. These findings are particularly important for special education because virtually all students referred for special education services exhibit academic deficiencies and, therefore, have the greatest need for effective, time-efficient instruction.

When students are not actively engaged in instruction, they are not learning. These ineffi-

cient activities do not involve active student participation and are not directly relevant to instructional objectives. These activities include sharpening a pencil, passing out and handing in papers, listening to teachers making general announcements, and taking bathroom breaks. In addition, verbal off-task behaviors include any teacher or student conversation not directly relevant to instructional objectives. Finally, inefficient classroom management includes time spent on disciplinary actions such as reprimanding or lecturing students for classroom misbehavior. All of the above off-task activities may be necessary at some point during the school day—it is hard to imagine a classroom in which time is never spent sharpening pencils or reminding students of class rules. However, the most effective teachers have learned how to minimize these activities so that the time spent actively engaged in instruction is maximized. Ideally, if a teacher allocates 60 minutes to reading instruction, this time should include 60 minutes of active engagement in reading instruction. Passing out papers and making announcements may be necessary activities, but they should not be included as part of the engaged instructional time. Research also has demonstrated that the least effective teachers spend excessive amounts of time attempting to manage classroom behaviors. Table 1.2 presents additional information regarding on-task behaviors. Behavior management techniques are described in more detail in Chapter 4.

Teachers can determine the amount of allocated versus engaged time-on-task in their own classrooms. First, write down the time periods designated for specific academic subjects. Enlist a teacher, aide, volunteer, or another person to observe directly the amount of time actually spent on those academic activities, using observation procedures described in Chapter 3 (see the Procedures for Collecting Formative Data section). Aim for 100% engaged time during allocated times so that time spent off task during these periods is minimized. Then, analyze the time that was spent off task and make decisions to decrease those activities that detracted from the engaged

Table 1.2. Engaged On-Task Behavior

---

1. Direct eye contact between student and teacher during teacher presentation.
2. A student answer to a teacher's question that is directly relevant to the instructional objective.
3. Students actively drilling one another on math facts using flash cards.
4. Students writing answers on a worksheet that is directly relevant to the instructional objective.
5. Student requesting clarification of a written chapter review question.
6. Students attending by making eye contact and responding appropriately during guided practice activity.
7. Students appropriately using math manipulative materials to learn math concepts and solve math problems.
8. Students appropriately using science materials to test scientific hypotheses.

---

time activities. The following sections describe some examples of off-task behaviors and corresponding strategies to minimize them. Additional off-task behaviors are given in Table 1.3.

The following case study provides an example of a teacher evaluating and modifying engagement rates to increase achievement.

Scenario for Evaluating Time-on-Task

Ms. M evaluated her formative data from the previous several weeks of instruction and felt that the rate of recent progress was inadequate to fulfill long-term objectives for many of her students. From examination of her scheduling records, she determined that she could not schedule additional instructional time during her already crowded day. As a consequence, she solicited the help of the consulting teacher from the district office to help her evaluate her level of engaged time-on-task.

The consulting teacher, Ms. C, came to her classroom on 3 consecutive days for three different classroom activities. During each visit, Ms. C used an interval recording procedure (see Chapter 3) to record the engaged on-task behaviors of three students that Ms. M had designated as representative of her class. Ms. C further divided the observational times into beginning, middle, and end of the instructional periods. Ms. C found that the overall engagement rate was 74%. Furthermore, it was found that engage-ment rates during the middle of lessons were very high (near 100%); however, rates of engagement were lower during early parts of lessons (76%) and lowest (52%) at the end of lessons. Ms. M then instituted a program to enhance engaged time-on-task at the beginning and end of class. This included strict limits for transition, a different seating arrangement in which two of the more distractible students were separated, and a token system for rewarding prompt and accurate completion of independent practice activities. In addition, Ms. M modified her instructional procedures to include higher levels of questioning during the beginning of lessons and higher levels of observation and contact with students during independent practice activities. Several weeks later, a reevaluation demonstrated that on-task engagement had risen to 94%, and academic progress had greatly increased. In addition, Ms. M's own record keeping indicated that classroom disruption had greatly decreased.

Transitional Activities

Research has indicated that transitions constitute a major source of student off-task behavior. *Transition* refers to students moving from one class, group, or subject to another. During this time, behaviors such as sharpening a pencil, using the restroom, obtaining drinks from the water fountain, and socializing inappropriately may occur. These activities are problematic if they in-

Table 1.3. Off-Task Behavior During Different Instructional Activities

Activities	Behavior	Example
	Teacher Off-Task	
During Instruction	Unnecessary digression	Talk about personal experiences.
	Description of academic information not directly relevant to instructional objectives	Discussion about different kinds of cars during the solving of miles-per-hour word problems.
	Classroom management	Lecturing inappropriate behavior during spelling class.
During Seatwork	Unnecessary wait time	Teacher has misplaced worksheets.
	Unnecessary interruptions	Teacher disrupts entire class to reprimand one student.
	Inappropriate assignments	Students provided with a worksheet that is not relevant to instructional objective or at the correct level of difficulty.
During Transitions	Unnecessary wait time	Teacher is late returning from break.
	Mismanagement	Directions for student behavior not clearly specified.
	Student Off-Task	
During Instruction	Unnecessary digression	Student comments about a recent television program.
	Lack of attention	Student looks out window during instruction.
	Inappropriate social behavior	Student pokes neighbor.
During Seatwork	Unnecessary disruptions	Student requests to go to restroom or nurse's office.
	Lack of sustained engagement with task	Student spends time looking for eraser in desk.
	Inappropriate social behavior	Student writes and passes notes to neighbors.
During Transitions	Procrastination	Student lingers in hallway after bell has rung.
	Inappropriate social behavior	Student unnecessarily pushes peers.

terfere with engaged time. Because some transition activities are necessary, teachers can plan for them to occur during prespecified times, rather than during a supposed engaged-time activity. In addition, teachers can create expectations that students will move from one activity to another quickly, quietly, and efficiently. You also can enforce efficient transitions positively by awarding points, tokens, or stickers (see Chapter 4) for prompt transitions, or you can simply inform the students that time lost in transition will be made up during free time. More specific examples of transition behaviors are given in Table 1.4.

Table 1.4. Decreasing Transitional Time

Transitional Time	Procedures	Possible Off-Task Behavior
Before school	Sharpen pencils	Socializing before transitional activities are completed
	Obtain drinks from water fountain	
	Use restroom	"Hanging out" too long on the playground
	Organize class materials	
	Be seated prior to bell	Standing in the hallways
Between academic periods	Put away last period's materials	Not putting away materials
	Hand in completed assignment	Unnecessary talking
	Get out appropriate text materials	Unnecessary moving around in classroom
	Be prepared with pencil, paper, and notebook	
	Move to appropriate seat	Not sitting in the appropriate place
	Be seated prior to bell	
Classroom to outdoor activity	Stay seated until bell rings	Getting ready before bell rings
	Put away all work materials after the bell rings	Leaving work on desk
	Hand in completed assignments	Leaving classroom furniture in a disorganized state
	Use restroom	
	Obtain drinks from water fountain	Pencils, papers, etc., left out that will have to be put away later
	Sharpen pencils	
	Obtain coats	
	Line up by the door	
Outdoor to classroom activity (prior to final bell)	Obtain drinks	Tardy to class
	Use restroom	Coat not hung up
	Sharpen pencils	Inappropriate socializing
	Obtain appropriate materials (e.g., texts, paper, pencils)	Playing with ball, etc., inside the classroom
	Sit in appropriate place	

Inappropriate Verbalizations

Another major source of off-task behavior is inappropriate verbal behavior, by students or teachers, that is not directly related to instructional objectives. Inappropriate verbalizations include describing personal experiences, digressing to inappropriate subjects, and questioning students on information that is irrelevant to the instructional objectives. You can monitor this behavior by tape-recording your lessons. In relistening to the recording, you can evaluate the appropriateness of classroom verbalizations. With such feedback, teachers can more easily remind themselves or their students when they are getting verbally off task. This is another area in which teacher expectations play an important role. If you clearly communicate the expectation that discussions should remain directly relevant to the lesson, your students will be more likely to exhibit appropriate verbalizations.

Inappropriate Social Behavior

Any inappropriate social behavior constitutes a major threat to effective instruction. When students exhibit behaviors such as teasing, arguing, fighting, or any other type of disruptive behavior, it not only detracts from engaged time-on-task but can also create a classroom atmosphere that is less conducive to learning. Teachers should not be overly punitive; neither should they waste classroom time with lengthy lectures on classroom behavior. Disruptive behavior should be dealt with effectively and efficiently so that time lost in behavior management is minimized. Again, the expectation of a serious classroom environment can be especially helpful. More specific details on classroom management are provided in Chapter 4.

Whenever you encounter a learning problem, in a particular student or in your classroom as a whole, one of the first things to consider is the amount of engaged time-on-task and how you can increase it. Some strategies for maximizing time-on-task are given in Table 1.5. When you are able to effectively maximize engaged time-on-task, you can consider other important teacher effectiveness variables, such as content covered.

Content Covered

Content covered refers to the amount of academic content to which students have been exposed throughout the school year. In part, the amount of content covered is determined by the length of the school day, the length of the school year, and the amount of time the student is placed in special services. However, these variables reflect only opportunities to cover content; to maximize content coverage, teachers need to attend carefully to the scope and sequence of all curricular materials, prioritize objectives within content areas, and pace instruction so that the amount of content covered throughout the year can be maximized.

Curriculum

A critical consideration in effective teaching is the choice of curricular material or curriculum

Table 1.5. Strategies for Maximizing Engaged Time-on-Task

1. Verbally praise students who exhibit on-task behavior. It is particularly important to praise students who are less often on task. This is part of a general "catch them being good" strategy.

2. Provide rewards (tokens, free time, privileges) for rapid, accurate completion of academic tasks.

3. Frequently question students regarding their knowledge of the content being covered. Students' minds are more likely to wander when they do not understand the content being covered.

4. If possible, schedule conceptually more difficult material (e.g., math or reading) earlier in the day, more routine tasks (e.g., handwriting practice) toward the end of the day.

5. Set an egg timer to ring at random intervals. If all students are on task when the timer rings, reward the class as a whole (e.g., with an additional minute of recess).

6. Select materials that make learning as concrete, meaningful, and interesting as possible. Heightening task interest generally increases engagement.

adaptation that most easily will facilitate learning. Curricula are most likely to meet the learning needs of students with mild disabilities if they are *directly relevant* to learning objectives, are *carefully sequenced* and include step-by-step presentations, provide sufficient *redundancy* in content covered, and contain relevant activities for *evaluation* of student progress. In addition, curricular materials should make learning as concrete and as meaningful as possible. Information that is concrete and meaningful is much easier to learn than information that is abstract and unrelated to students' experiences. When selecting instructional materials, be certain that they are meaningful and relevant for all students, including both male and female students and students from different ethnic or cultural backgrounds. To the extent that curricular materials do not contain all these elements, special education teachers must make adaptations so that these variables are included.

Scope and Sequence

Scope and sequence refers to the amount of content that will be covered and the order in which it will be presented. All academic areas of instruction should be presented with respect to a scope and sequence. In this way, teachers can set goals for the amount of content to be covered in a year and monitor progress toward meeting these goals throughout the school year. In special education, scope and sequence may parallel those used in general education settings. Because a major goal of special education is to integrate students into general education classrooms, it may be necessary to design a scope and sequence in which some content is covered at a faster rate than in general education settings so that students can meet the ultimate objective of catching up.

Special education teachers may also want to determine which components of the regular education scope and sequences are critical for passing school district and state competency tests. In special education settings, it also is important to prioritize objectives, so that unnecessary objec-

tives can be deleted and more important objectives emphasized. More time can be allocated to the most important components.

Objectives

All instruction is based on objectives. *Objective* describes the behavioral outcome of instruction. In other words, it specifies what a student will be able to do at the end of the instructional period. Objectives describe the behavior, the content and conditions under which a student's performance will be assessed, and the criteria for acceptable performance. For example, statements such as "The student will orally read 100 Dolch sight words from a list in 1 minute with 90% accuracy" or "The student will list in writing six precipitating causes of the Civil War in order of importance with 100% accuracy" are behavioral objectives.

Because the amount of content covered consists of behavioral objectives, it is important to maximize the number of objectives covered during a school year. Objectives will be discussed in more detail in Chapter 2.

Pacing

Pacing refers to the rate at which objectives are met within a particular scope and sequence of instruction. Given relevant and carefully specified objectives within a well-planned scope and sequence, the pacing of instruction will ensure that a sufficient amount of appropriate instruction is delivered. You can ensure that you will cover all appropriate instructional objectives throughout a year if you carefully plan and monitor the pace at which you move through these objectives. If your present pace appears too slow, it may be important to accelerate the pace by increasing time-on-task, allocating additional time to instruction, or eliminating less important aspects of the content covered.

Scope and sequence, objectives, and pacing are all means by which the amount of content covered can be maximized. Scope and sequence and objectives can ensure that time is spent on relevant and critical content, and optimal pacing can ensure that content covered is maximized.

Delivery of Information: The SCREAM Variables

Delivery of information is critical to effective teaching. Like other aspects of education, delivery of instruction has several components, each of which is necessary for teaching effectiveness. Three of these components are providing information, questioning, and offering feedback.

Most instruction begins with teacher-delivered presentations. For these presentations to be effective, several elements of teacher behavior must be included. These elements can be represented by the acronym SCREAM:

- S = structure
- C = clarity
- R = redundancy
- E = enthusiasm
- A = appropriate rate
- M = maximized engagement

First, teacher presentations must provide *structure*. Lessons are structured when teachers obtain students' attention and provide an overview of the lesson, including a description of lesson objectives; when they provide outlines of lesson materials and indicate transitional points in the lesson; when they emphasize critical components of the lesson; and when they summarize and review as the lesson proceeds. It is also important that students are made aware of the structure of lessons, so they know what is to be done and how it will be done.

Second, teacher presentations must provide *clarity*. Clarity involves speaking clearly and directly to the point of the objectives, avoiding unclear or vague terminology, and providing relevant, concrete examples. All verbalizations must be directly pertinent to the lesson objective. Fur-

thermore, clear presentations address only one objective at a time.

It has been seen that teacher presentations are limited in clarity when they include vague or unnecessary words. Smith and Land (1981) reported that the overuse of vague words lowered student achievement, as seen in the following presentation in which vague language is italicized:

> This mathematics lesson *might* enable you to understand a *little* more about *some things* we *usually* call number patterns. *Maybe* before we get to *probably* the main idea of the lesson, you should review a few prerequisite concepts. *Actually*, the first concept you need to review is positive integers. *As you know*, a positive integer is any whole number greater than zero. (p. 38)

Tape-record a sample of your presentations, and review the tapes to determine if you need to eliminate such vague or unnecessary words or other threats to clarity.

A third important component of teacher presentations is *redundancy*. Repetition of key elements of a lesson, particularly important concepts and rules, is related to higher levels of achievement. Unlike unnecessary or irrelevant repetition, which can be a threat to clarity, appropriate redundancy is an important aid to student learning and helps communicate the most significant elements of the lesson.

Fourth, teacher presentations must be made with *enthusiasm*. Enthusiasm helps maintain student attention and provides a positive attitude toward learning. Although enthusiasm is consistently related to affective outcomes, such as attitude toward school, it also is related to school achievement at the higher grade levels. Research has shown that enthusiasm—including body movement, gestures, facial expressiveness, vocal inflections, open acceptance of student ideas, and an overall sense of energy—can improve classroom behavior and raise achievement as much as 50% (Brigham, Scruggs, & Mastropieri, 1992).

Fifth, information must be presented at an *appropriate rate*. Although the speed of delivery depends on the nature of the content and the students' level of prior knowledge, the type of basic skills instruction typically provided in special education is delivered most effectively at a rapid pace. This helps maintain student attention and the momentum of the lesson and interacts well with enthusiasm variables.

Finally, in special education settings, teachers must *maximize engagement* by providing for active participation by students. This must be encouraged throughout the presentation and is described later. By providing structure, clarity, redundancy, enthusiasm, and an appropriate pace and by maximizing engagement, teachers can ensure that information has been provided effectively and efficiently.

Questioning

Delivering information is only one part of instruction. Some type of questioning must take place, enabling teachers to provide immediate practice and evaluation of student learning. Most teachers' questions should elicit thoughtful and correct answers, and all questions should elicit some type of substantive response. A general rule of thumb to maximize learning is to elicit at least 80% correct responding. If most students respond incorrectly to teacher questioning, or if many questions yield no response at all, then teachers should modify their instruction. For the type of basic skills instruction that frequently occurs in special education settings, high rates of correct responding to rapid teacher questioning are desirable. For higher level content or when students are asked to generalize, apply, or make decisions based on their learning, teachers will need to ask questions that require slower, more thoughtful responses and for which more than a single answer may be correct.

Also, for basic skills instruction, questions are frequently delivered on a low cognitive level (e.g., "What is the *i* before *e* rule?"). *Low cognitive level* refers to questioning that requires direct,

literal responses to recently presented information. Again, for evaluation or application objectives, higher level questioning may be appropriate (e.g., "How could you use the *i* before *e* rule to spell the word *receive?*").

For activities intended to promote inferential reasoning, higher level questioning is appropriate. Questions such as "Why does it make sense that mossy algae generally grow on the north side of trees?" and "Why do anteaters have long front claws?" are examples of questions designed to promote active thinking and reasoning. These types of questions are delivered at a slower rate, so that students have time to think and consider the question carefully. If answers are not immediately found, additional coaching and questioning can help activate students' relevant prior knowledge about the topic (e.g., moss, trees, and the position of the sun, or what anteaters eat).

Sometimes students fail to respond to a question because they do not understand it. For this reason, clarity of questioning is of particular importance. Regardless of the level of the question, it should be phrased in such a way that the meaning of the question and the type of expected response are clear.

Finally, teachers should question students equally. They should employ procedures of questioning that guarantee that the most assertive and the most reticent students, males and females, and students from different cultural backgrounds will be questioned equally. Outside observers or audiotape recordings can help ensure that all of your students are receiving equal attention. Sometimes it may be helpful to require choral responding, in which all students answer at the same time on a signal from the teacher. This procedure allows many more students to practice responding, although teachers must be sure that students are not simply copying peer responses. Whether students should be allowed to call out answers depends on the classroom. Generally, if students are motivated and enthusiastic, allowing students to call out answers will not relate to achievement. However, if students are generally reticent and slow to volunteer answers, it can be helpful to encourage open responding.

It can be seen, then, that the type of questions teachers ask and the ways in which they ask them are of critical importance to student achievement. Questioning procedures will be described in more detail in Chapters 5 through 8.

Feedback

Teacher feedback should be modified based on the type of question, the level of the students, and the correctness of the response. Responses can be correct, partially correct, or incorrect. Just as there are better and worse ways of asking questions, there are better and worse ways of providing feedback to students' correct responses. Teacher feedback should be overt, so that all students in the class will know whether the response was correct. Overt feedback may take the form of repeating the correct response ("Columbus is the capital of Ohio, correct!"), making more elaborations on the response ("That's right,

we carry the 1, which means we add 1 to the 10s column"), or simply acknowledging the correct answer with a smile or head nod. However, overt responding should be more limited during rapidly paced drill activities. Although it is important to be positive with correct responses, effusive or overelaborate praise is unnecessary and, in some cases, may have an embarrassing or inhibiting effect, particularly at the secondary level. Nevertheless, teacher feedback for correct responses should be prompt, direct, and positive. Additional information on positive feedback is provided in Table 1.6, and additional information on the use of verbal praise is given in Table 1.7 (summarized from Brophy, 1981).

Feedback to partially correct responses should first acknowledge the correct aspect of the response. Teachers should then provide prompts to elicit the complete response or rephrase the question ("Yes, Africa is a noun, but it is a special kind of noun—what kind of noun is it?"). If this fails, teachers can provide the answer or call on

Table 1.6. Feedback to Student Responses

Response	Feedback
Correct	Overt acknowledgment ("That is correct.")
	Not overly elaborate; appropriate to response.
	Should be more limited during rapid-paced drill activities.
Partially correct	Acknowledge correct aspect of response.
	Provide prompt or rephrase question.
	Provide answer or call on another student if necessary.
	Repeat question later in the lesson.
Incorrect	State simply that the response is incorrect.
	Do not prod or probe students who obviously do not know the answer.
	State correct response or call on another student.
	Do not criticize the student unless incorrect response is due to inattention, lack of effort, or refusal to follow directions; be judicious with criticism.
Lack of overt response	Question further to determine source of nonresponding.
	Elicit an overt response, even if "don't know" is most appropriate.
	When response is overt—correct or incorrect—respond as described above.

Table 1.7. Use of Effective Praise

1. Praise should be used to reinforce specific student behaviors. It should not be given in a random or unsystematic fashion. Students should know that it is a specific behavior of theirs that is being praised.

2. Praise should specify exactly what the student has done to merit praise (e.g., "Billy, you did a good job of getting in your seat quickly and opening your book to the correct page"). If students know *exactly* what behaviors were praiseworthy, they will be more likely to repeat them than if the praise is ambiguous (e.g., "Good work, Billy").

3. Praise should sound genuine and believable. Refrain from monotonous or routine-sounding praise, and vary language used to praise.

4. Praise should describe specific performance criteria (e.g., "You got over 90% correct") and relate the achievement to the student's previous performance (e.g., "This is your best work yet!").

5. Praise should be delivered for noteworthy effort. If a task was easy for the student to accomplish, the praise may be devalued or interpreted as a sign that modest efforts are encouraged.

6. Praise should demonstrate the relationship between hard work and achievement (e.g., "Aren't you glad you worked so hard on that project?") rather than luck or low level of task difficulty (e.g., "You're lucky you got that right," or "See, it was easy to do").

7. Praise should promote a sense of personal satisfaction in achievement (e.g., "You should be proud of yourself that you have completed such a difficult assignment so well").

Note. Adapted from "Teacher Praise: A Functional Analysis," by J. E. Brophy, 1981, *Review of Educational Research, 51,* 5–32.

another student. If a student gives the correct answer, the teacher should ask the same question later in the lesson to determine whether the students have mastered the content.

Feedback to incorrect responses in most cases should consist simply of a statement that the response was incorrect. Although clueing, coaching, prompting, and reminding may be helpful in eliciting a correct response, continuous prodding of students for answers they obviously do not know is often counterproductive ("Are you sure you can't remember?"). Instead, teachers should either call on another student or state the correct response. It is rarely helpful to criticize a student for an incorrect response; however, in certain cases in which lack of a correct response reflects inattention, refusal to follow directions, or an obvious lack of preparation, some form of negative feedback may help to reinforce the attitude that appropriate levels of effort are expected. If such feedback is necessary, it is important that it be used in the context of a generally positive classroom environment.

Lack of overt responses can lead to uncertainty in the classroom atmosphere. If a response is not delivered promptly, teachers should question further to determine whether the answer is unknown, the question is unclear, or the student did not hear the question ("Shawn, did you understand the question? Can you think of the answer?"). In this context, a prompt "don't know" response may be the most appropriate. It is important to note that a response must be rendered overtly before feedback can be provided. Feedback delivered in the absence of a response presumes knowledge of the student's intention, which may or may not be accurate.

Responding to unsolicited questions and comments that are relevant to the subject is important, especially at the higher grade levels. If a comment is not completely relevant, the teacher should restate it in such a way that the student's comment is accepted and its relevance to the lesson is made explicit. The teacher can either directly answer the student's questions or redirect them to the class. Such an approach indicates to students that their contributions are valued.

Presentation, questioning, and feedback are three components necessary for truly effective teaching. When relevant information has been presented effectively, students are usually given practice activities to reinforce learning.

Guided and Independent Practice Activities

Practice activities can be guided or independent. Guided practice is done under the direct supervision of the teacher, to ensure students are clear on the relevant concepts and procedures. Then, students work on practice activities independently. Practice activities should not be used as a vehicle for consuming time; neither should they be the dominant component of instruction. Students in general, and special education students in particular, do not learn new content efficiently through worksheets or other types of practice activities. However, practice activities can function as important supplements to instruction, serve to reinforce previous learning, and provide opportunities for independent work.

Teachers should be careful to select practice activities that directly reflect instructional objectives. In addition, such activities must be on the appropriate level of difficulty. Because practice activities are undertaken independently and feedback is often not immediate, it is important that such seatwork be completed with a very high rate of success. It also is important that students understand directions and formats. Teachers should carefully specify exactly what students are expected to do and provide practice and feedback on examples. Finally, because many students easily tire of worksheet activities, the teacher should be careful to select materials that are motivating and interesting and to provide positive feedback for work that is completed quickly, accurately, and neatly. Some strategies for maximizing the effectiveness of practice activities are provided in Figure 1.1. Further discussion of different types of practice activities and their uses appears in the Guided Practice and Independent Practice subsections of this chapter and in Chapters 5 through 8.

Many software programs can be used for practice activities. Advantages of computer software

are that they may be motivating for students and that they can provide immediate feedback for student responses. A disadvantage is that they might not reflect exactly the class instructional objectives. More information on software programs is provided throughout this text.

Formative Evaluation

Anyone who has been to school is familiar with end-of-year achievement tests. Such tests are *summative* because they provide a summary statement of the year's learning. Unlike summative evaluation, *formative* evaluation techniques gather information on a regular basis throughout the year. For example, daily or weekly quizzes (or probes) can provide teachers with valuable information on student progress and performance. Such information can assist teachers in making optimal instructional decisions for the design and delivery of their lessons.

In many cases, student performance can be placed on a chart or other graphic display so that students' rate of progress can be determined. In other cases, permanent products such as handwriting samples, tape recordings of reading performances, or science reports can be saved systematically in a portfolio to provide later feedback with current performance levels. Research has shown that such formative evaluation techniques are helpful in raising levels of student achievement. Ideally, formative evaluation should be based directly on instructional materials and the curriculum being used. The integration of assessment techniques with curriculum has been referred to as curriculum-based assessment.

Formative evaluation is helpful because it allows teachers to alter their instructional procedures based on student performance. When instruction is planned initially, it should follow a scope and sequence of objectives to be mastered throughout the year. Formative evaluation techniques can reveal to teachers whether those objectives are being met at an appropriate pace. If this pace is insufficient, the content covered throughout the year will be inadequate. If

Rules for Both Guided and Independent Practice

1. All activities must be directly relevant to the instructional objective.

   Example A: If the instructional objective covers long division, then all practice activities must require students to practice long division.

   Example B: If the objective requires the learning of the causes of the Civil War, then all activities must require students to learn (by identifying, locating, writing, or reflecting on) those causes.

2. All activities must allow students many opportunities to practice responding with the correct answers.

3. Students must be provided with corrective feedback.

Guided Practice

1. Guided practice activities allow teachers to interact with students and to provide students with immediate corrective feedback.

   Example A: Everyone got that answer correct!

   Example B: The correct answer is. . . .
   Remember the steps are. . . .

2. During guided practice activities, teachers can actively involve all of the students in responding.

   Example A: When I say go, everyone write the answer on his or her paper.

   Example B: Everyone who wrote this . . . , hold up his or her paper.

   Example C: When I say go, everyone who thinks he or she has the answer put his or her hand up.

   Example D: Everyone who has the answer put his or her thumbs up.

   Example E: When I say go, turn to your neighbor on your left. Left-side partners, say the answer as quickly and as accurately as you can. Right-side partners, listen and provide corrective feedback. Ready? Go.

   Example F: Everyone write the solution to the problem on the blackboard. Ready? Go.

3. Guided practice activities allow teachers to monitor and to verify whether students have "caught on" to the new instructional objective. Teachers can provide additional information if necessary.

4. When students respond at a high level of accuracy (e.g., 85% to 95%) they are ready to try some relevant independent practice.

Independent Practice

1. Independent practice activities allow students to become firm at responding accurately.

2. Independent practice activities can be used to build accurate and more rapid responding.

3. Independent practice activities can be used to facilitate overlearning.

4. Independent practice activities can include review of previously mastered content.

5. Independent practice activities can be used to facilitate application, generalization, and maintenance of skills.

Figure 1.1. Strategies for maximizing the effectiveness of guided and independent practice activities.

formative evaluation techniques reveal an insufficient rate of progress, the teacher will need to decide what modifications to make to improve the rate of learning. Generally, these decisions will reflect one of the critical variables discussed in this chapter. The most obvious example is to increase the amount of engaged time spent learning the objective. Another might be to increase the pace at which content is covered during lessons. A third might be to improve the quality of the teacher presentation by modifying presentation variables (e.g., structure, clarity, redundancy). It also might be possible to alter the rate and type of teacher questioning and feedback. In addition, variation in seatwork and practice activities might be called for. Through careful monitoring and manipulation of these variables, teachers can better ensure accurate mastery of intended objectives. Examples of formative evaluation techniques are provided in Table 1.8, and examples of strategies for making decisions based on formative data are provided in Table 1.9.

Multicultural Issues

The use of the effective instruction variables will result in successful learning if the instruction is sensitive to the needs of culturally and linguistically diverse students. Surveys of students and meetings with family and community members can help identify particular cultural needs and interests, which can then be incorporated into the class curriculum. Generally, all students should feel that their particular cultural background is valued and supported and is an important component of the classroom.

Some specific recommendations for teaching multicultural and linguistically diverse students, summarized from the work of Franklin (1992) and Cummins (1989), are given in Table 1.10 (see also New Zealand Department of Education, 1988, cited in Cummins, 1989). As can be seen in Table 1.10, most of these variables are important considerations for any classroom. Although earlier teacher effectiveness research de-emphasized such "nonalterable" variables as

Table 1.8. Some Formative Evaluation Techniques

Behavior	Possible Formative Evaluation Procedures
Math facts	Daily rate of correct versus error responses per minute plotted on graph paper.
Handwriting	Handwriting samples collected regularly and evaluated with respect to a specified standard for comparison.
Inappropriate behavior	Number of disciplinary referrals per week for prespecified behaviors.
Oral reading expression	Tape-recorded oral reading samples compared with a recorded standard of reading expression.
Out of seat	Daily number of out-of-seat occurrences plotted on graph paper.
Decoding CVC words	Oral reading rate of correctly and incorrectly read "nonsense" CVC words plotted on graph paper.
State history facts	Cumulative number of facts correctly stated on criterion-referenced tests measured against number of facts needed to pass school competency test.
Spelling	Number of words spelled correctly on weekly and monthly (cumulative) spelling tests.

Table 1.9. Strategies for Effective Instructional Decision Making
Based on Student Progress and Performance

If student progress and performance is good

1. Maintain instruction

2. Possibly increase pace of instruction

If student progress and performance is inadequate

1. Verify student has necessary preskills

2. Verify instructional objective is at the correct level of learning for

   a. acquisition
   b. fluency
   c. application
   d. generalization

3. Alter teacher effectiveness variables:

   a. increase time-on-task
   b. increase or alter teacher presentation
   c. increase or alter guided practice activities
   d. increase or alter independent practice activities
   e. check to ensure appropriateness of formative evaluation procedure

---

teacher personality, it has become clear that establishing and maintaining a warm, positive, accepting classroom environment is an important prerequisite to the other teacher effectiveness variables. For example, maximizing time-on-task or content coverage is of little use in a hostile or confrontational classroom atmosphere. On the other hand, teachers who create warm, supportive, caring classroom environments are more likely to receive the active cooperation of all students.

Students from culturally diverse backgrounds may identify less strongly with the school and classroom environment, so it is essential that teachers do all they can to make all students feel welcome and important. This is particularly important for students in special education, most of whom may have experienced failures in school and who may be less likely to invest themselves in classroom learning.

Baker et al. (1982) listed eight components of a warm and accepting classroom atmosphere: (1) collecting personal information, (2) using positive body language, (3) using a personal ap-

proach to student interaction, (4) giving honest praise, (5) spending time each day with the student, (6) expressing affection, (7) reducing grading pressure, and (8) giving students time to answer questions. By creating a positive and personal atmosphere, increasing contacts with family and community members, and including culturally relevant and meaningful instructional materials, teachers can effectively accommodate cultural and linguistic diversity in their classrooms. Additional information concerning multicultural issues is provided in subsequent chapters.

A Model for Delivery of Instruction

This section describes how teachers should deliver classroom instruction. A general model of teacher-led instruction of a daily lesson is described. This model includes the following teacher functions: (a) daily review, (b) presentation, (c) guided practice, (d) independent

Table 1.10. Recommendations for Teaching Multicultural and Linguistically Diverse Students

1. Create and maintain a positive, accepting, supportive classroom environment.
2. Vary the format of classroom instruction and increase classroom energy.
3. Increase verbal interaction and promote open-ended, divergent thinking.
4. Use resources, materials, and activities that are realistic to learners' cultural environment.
5. Maximize person-to-person interaction.
6. Use cooperative group activities when appropriate, and encourage positive student interactions.
7. Use bilingual or multilingual signs in school and classrooms.
8. Display pictures representing different cultures in school.
9. Use books and other printed material in different languages when appropriate.
10. Employ paraprofessionals who can tutor students in their primary language.
11. Encourage parental involvement in class and school activities.
12. Encourage students to use their primary language in class and school activities.
13. Encourage meaningful use of English, rather than precise grammar.
14. Integrate language use across content areas, rather than teaching language as an isolated subject.
15. Emphasize higher level cognitive skills.
16. Consider local circumstances and individual needs when adapting methods and materials.

Note. Adapted from Franklin (1992) and Cummins (1989).

practice, (e) weekly and monthly reviews, and (f) formative evaluation. An example of a lesson that incorporates most of these components is included in Figure 1.2.

Daily Review

Each lesson should begin with a daily review. During this time, teachers have an opportunity to monitor and adjust instruction based on student performance and to provide corrective feedback to students. In addition, this time allows the students an opportunity for overlearning facts, rules, procedures, and concepts.

There are many effective components to daily review. Ask questions about information previously covered to determine whether the information needs to be retaught. This type of questioning should parallel the formative evaluation of the previous lesson. If you find that students respond accurately at the end of one lesson but not at the beginning of the next lesson, there may be a problem with retention of initial learning. Using this information, you can make decisions about the optimal level of difficulty for students and monitor and adjust their instruction accordingly. Repeated review and questioning of previously learned material (overlearning), for example, can be very beneficial for long-term retention.

Another important component of daily review concerns handling of previously assigned homework. Homework can be reviewed by several methods. It may be helpful to quiz students at the beginning of class on material from the previous homework assignment. It also may be helpful for students to check each other's homework papers. In special education settings, however, students must be taught the specific procedures for checking homework. The students also can review homework in small-group settings. Of

Time	Component	Materials	Examples
9:00	*Daily review*	Overhead projector	"Last week we started talking about different kinds of words. Who remembers what kinds of words we talked about?" [Student response.] "Correct. One kind of word was a *noun*. [Write on board.] Tell us what a noun is, Juan…"
9:08	*Presentation of material to be learned*	Overhead projector	"Today we're going to learn about another kind of word. This word is called an *adjective* [Write on board.] Everybody say adjective with me. Ready? [Signal.] Adjective. Adjective. Good."
			"…I think you're beginning to get the idea of what an adjective is. Now watch what I write this time. [Write.] 'A sour apple.' Everybody, which word is the adjective? [Signal.] Good, *sour* is the adjective. Sue, what was the rule we said that tells you why *sour* is an adjective?"
9:20	*Guided practice*	Worksheets	"Now, everybody take a worksheet and we can practice finding adjectives together. Read the first sentence, Fred. [Fred reads.] So, in that sentence, everybody circle the adjective, and we'll see who can get it right."
9:30	*Independent practice*	Worksheets	"Does anyone have a question about how to find adjectives? Tell us again what we're going to do, Julie. [Julie responds.] OK, everybody go back to your desk quietly and finish your worksheet."
9:40	*Formative evaluation*	Test	"Everybody stop, make sure your name is on the worksheet, and pass it in. I'm going to pass out a 2-minute timing so you can show how much you've learned about adjectives. Don't turn the paper over until I tell you. Now, when I say 'go,' turn over the paper and circle as many adjectives as you can in 2 minutes. Bill, what are you going to do? [Responds.] Correct. Now, is everybody ready?"

Figure 1.2. Model for sample 45-minute lesson on identifying adjectives.

course, the homework assignments must be directly relevant to the instructional objectives to be beneficial. Homework is a type of independent practice activity, which is discussed further in Chapters 5 through 8.

Students should generate summaries of material from homework assignments and previously learned content. Students can either prepare questions and ask them of the class or provide written summaries of the previous lesson (if students have adequate writing skills). Above all, encourage students to ask questions about previously covered material that they may not understand.

Presentation of Material To Be Learned

Research has shown that the most effective teachers spend more time on the presentation of new content. However, time is not the only variable of importance in the effectiveness of presentations. For presentations to be clear and effective, teachers must first engage the students' attention and

1. clarify the goals and main points to be covered,

2. include step-by-step presentation of new material,

3. provide modeling and demonstrations of new procedures,

4. monitor student understanding and adjust instruction accordingly,

5. provide corrective feedback, and

6. consider the needs of culturally and linguistically diverse students.

When presenting new information, begin by gaining the attention of all students, and clearly state the overall goals and specific objectives of the lesson. Provide an overview of the main points to be covered in the lesson. In some cases, it may be helpful to write these main points on the blackboard or overhead projector. As the main points are covered, focus on one specific point at a time. This is critical in promoting a clear understanding of the presentation. It is also important to keep all verbalizations relevant to the specific objectives that will be covered. Although providing examples is helpful, such examples need to be clearly relevant to the presentation. Finally, use language that is clear and direct, avoiding words and phrases such as "sort of," "you know," "pretty much," "maybe," and "I guess." In special education settings, it is critical that the level of vocabulary used is appropriate for the students' comprehension level.

Step-by-step presentations are also critical to clear presentations. Subdivide material into component steps that can be easily understood by students. The material should be well organized and presented so that one step is mastered before the next step is presented. Directions should be clear and explicit. The subdivision of a larger task into smaller and more easily understood tasks is referred to as *task analysis* and is discussed further in Chapter 2 (see the Designing Instruction section).

Modeling and demonstrations are necessary to promote understanding of new content. When appropriate, directly perform the skill or process that is being taught. Include explicit and over-emphasized demonstration. When examples are presented, they should be concrete and directly relevant to the content being taught. Concrete examples are particularly important in special education settings where students may not catch on easily to novel concepts or discriminations. In such instances, provide a variety of relevant examples and nonexamples so that students will be able to discriminate the examples from the nonexamples (e.g., "This is an example of a rhombus. Is this next shape a rhombus?").

Monitoring and adjusting instruction is a necessary component of clear presentations. It is not always possible to predict what will be easily understood by a group of students. It is also sometimes difficult to know whether students have understood what was presented. Consequently, teachers should elicit active responses from students throughout the presentation. This is usually done by asking direct questions that are relevant to the presentation objectives. You can also require students to summarize the information presented. Try to involve all students all of the time, or most students most of the time. Simple questioning that requires all students to respond chorally or by hand raising can provide teachers with immediate feedback on student understanding. Another technique for monitoring students' understanding is having students pair off and verbally summarize information to each other. All of these procedures can provide a teacher with an immediate assessment of a student's level of understanding and can assist the teacher in making instructional decisions, such as whether to proceed to a new step or to review the last step.

Finally, corrective feedback is a critical component. During presentation and guided practice, teachers should frequently question students to monitor their understanding of the content being taught. The corrective feedback students are given on their responses at this point plays an important role in the amount students learn. Corrective feedback can be oral or written, but during teacher presentation and guided practice, it typically is oral. Often the type of feedback depends on the type of response, as described previously.

Guided Practice

Immediately following teacher presentation, students are asked to practice learned information. Such practice is designed to develop consistent and accurate responding under the direct observation of the teacher. Guided practice usually takes the form of teacher-led, small-group questions and answers or immediate teacher monitoring of written student responses. Teachers can incorporate all of the examples described for facilitating students' active participation into guided practice activities. Initially, practice takes place with high levels of teacher involvement. During this time, responses need to be as overt (observable) as possible, so that teachers can easily monitor students' behavior.

In addition, questions should be delivered at a high frequency and be directly relevant to the content. Responses to these questions are evaluated for understanding of the content. When necessary, teachers provide additional explanations, modeling, or demonstrations of relevant skills.

Finally, teachers must ensure that all students have participated and received feedback. Guided practice activities are intended to lead to independent performance. Therefore, continue with guided practice until all students are responding at a high rate of accuracy (usually above 80%).

Independent Practice

Independent practice usually follows guided practice and typically takes the form of some type of independent seatwork. It is important to remember that students must have achieved a high level of accuracy in guided practice before they can move to independent practice. Independent practice provides students with opportunities to integrate what they have learned with previous content, develop fluency in the execution of new skills, and apply and generalize newly acquired information. In independent practice activities, students' work is initially slower and more hesitant than in guided practice activities, but it should be as accurate as guided practice. As students develop fluency (accuracy plus rate of responding), responses become more confident and more automatic. The advantage of fluid, automatic responses is that they allow students to concentrate on learning new skills or applying learned skills to new situations. For example, students who are automatic at reading decoding skills can concentrate on comprehension, whereas students who are fluent at math facts and algorithms can concentrate on solving more complex problems.

Sometimes seatwork activities are employed simply to consume time. This is unfortunate because students who are managed effectively can benefit greatly from seatwork activities. For students to benefit, teachers should present material that is directly relevant to the lesson objectives. It also is important that students have exhibited sufficient accuracy during guided practice to ensure their successful functioning in independent activities. Finally, seatwork should follow guided practice activities directly, and teachers should guide students through the first few problems or examples.

Teachers can manage effectively the level of engagement during seatwork by establishing general procedural guidelines for seatwork activities so that students know what they are expected to do, how to obtain extra help, and what to do on completion of the assignment. In special education settings, teachers are often engaged in other activities such as delivering small-group instruction, whereas some students are completing seatwork assignments. In such cases, teachers can arrange seating so that they can observe the entire classroom at a glance. However, if teachers are not engaged in instruction, they should circulate among students to provide feedback, answer questions, and monitor student engagement.

Several alternatives can replace or supplement the typical paper-and-pencil, worksheet type of independent seatwork activity. First, independent seatwork can be replaced by additional teacher-led practice. This can be accomplished by a teacher or a paraprofessional (aide, volunteer, or parent). Such teacher-led practice may be beneficial in special education settings where students may be in need of more direct feedback and in which smaller class sizes allow the opportunity for group responses.

Another alternative to independent practice is the use of peers in tutoring or cooperative learning situations. In peer tutoring, one student is selected to monitor the performance of another student. If "tutors" are not on a higher academic level than their respective "tutees," tutors must be able to recognize or identify inappropriate responses. Flash cards are helpful when tutors may be unsure of correct responses, such as multiplication facts or new vocabulary. Tutoring dyads (pairs) of similar abilities can easily exchange roles to ensure that both members of the pair are receiving practice experience and feedback. If, on the other hand, tutors are selected because their academic skills are higher than those of the tutees, care must be taken to ensure that tutors also receive opportunities for practice and feedback. The fact that tutors are sometimes seen to gain from the tutoring process does not mean that they will always gain or that what they gain will be directly relevant to their instructional objectives.

A closely related activity, cooperative learning, involves small groups of students who cooperate on the completion of seatwork activities (e.g., Slavin, Madden, & Leavey, 1984a). These groups are composed of students of different abilities who work together in competition with other cooperative groups in their classroom. Groups that work most efficiently are given rewards for their performance.

Other types of independent practice activities can incorporate the use of computers and other audiovisual aids. Many of these devices provide immediate feedback to student responses. For the practice to be relevant, however, the computer software programs must match instructional objectives.

Weekly and Monthly Reviews

As mentioned earlier, daily review is critical for teachers to monitor and adjust instruction. It is also necessary to use cumulative reviews on weekly and monthly bases. These reviews provide information on how well students retain important content. Retention is critical, especially when successive content builds on facts and concepts covered previously. Teachers need to incorporate student performance on these daily, weekly, and monthly reviews into their formative evaluation plans. If reviews are done properly, teachers are better able to monitor and adjust instruction to include more thorough periodic reviews and reteaching.

Formative Evaluation

Formative evaluation is a continuous monitoring system that can be used to assess students' performance and progress. In addition, the information obtained from formative evaluation can be used to adjust instructional procedures if necessary. It has been shown that 1- and 2-minute samples of students' work are sufficient to document performance in some areas. Chapter 3 provides more information on specific formative evaluation procedures.

Effective Special Education: Using the "Pass" Variables

Special education teachers can be effective if they always remember to employ the "PASS" variables in their teaching:

- P = prioritize objectives
- A = adapt instruction
- S = systematically teach (SCREAM)
- S = systematically evaluate

First, *prioritize* objectives, emphasizing the most important objectives and de-emphasizing or eliminating less critical objectives. These most important objectives should receive the most intense instruction. Second, *adapt* instruction to meet the needs of the learners. These adaptations could include more time-on-task, more concrete materials, specific learning and memory strategies, specialized apparatus or learning materials, or modification of the physical environment. The adaptations should reflect the interaction of the curriculum and the characteristics of the individual student. Third, special education teachers should remember to "SCREAM" when they *systematically present* information to students. These variables (structure, clarity, redundancy, enthusiasm, appropriate pace, and maximized engagement) are critical to special education teaching effectiveness. Finally, special education teachers should be certain to *systematically evaluate* progress toward specific educational objectives and be prepared to reprioritize and readapt when striving to ensure that all students experience success.

Summary

- *Effective instruction* refers to the things teachers can do that are most highly related to successful achievement in special education. These behaviors are referred to as alterable variables because they can be modified by teachers to increase learning.

- Important teacher effectiveness variables include time-on-task, content covered, delivery of information, guided and independent practice activities, and formative evaluation. These variables are important to consider when designing instruction.

- A model for delivery of daily lessons includes daily review, presentation of material, guided practice, independent practice, weekly and monthly reviews, and formative evaluation. These components include teacher effectiveness variables and provide a general framework for the delivery of daily lessons.

- Effective instruction in special education involves use of the PASS variables. These variables are as follows: prioritize objectives, adapt instruction, systematically teach using the SCREAM variables, and systematically evaluate learning.

Relevant Research

Much of the research on teacher effectiveness is summarized in Wittrock's (1986) edited work on research on teaching. Chapters of the Wittrock book that deal directly with the variables described in Chapter 1 are authored by Brophy and Good (1986), Rosenshine and Stevens (1986), Doyle (1986), Walberg (1986), and Biddle and Anderson (1986). Some of the most important original research in this area was conducted by Anderson, Evertson, and Brophy (1979); Anderson, Evertson, and Emmer (1980); Berliner and Rosenshine (1977); Brophy (1979); Good and Grouws (1979); Robbins (1986); Rosenshine (1983); and Stallings and Krasavage (1986). Much of the research cited above involved "average" students, although the research involving lower achieving students, younger students, and students of lower socioeconomic status is more relevant to special education. Research replicating these findings on special education populations is reported by Englert (1983, 1984), Haynes and Jenkins (1986), Leinhardt et al. (1981), Sindelar et al. (1986), and Wilson and Wesson (1986). Larrivee (1985) describes research on teacher effectiveness in inclusive settings, that is, general education classrooms that include students with disabilities. Swanson and Hoskyn (2000) describe a meta-analysis of intervention research that provides general support for the direct instruction model for students with learning disabilities. Gleason, Carnine, and Vala (1991) have studied the pace of introducing new information. Mastropieri (1989) describe an application of teacher effectiveness research in a special education teacher preparation program, and Scruggs and Mastropieri (1993b) describe the importance of field-based experiences. The positive effects of teacher enthusiasm in special education settings are documented by Brigham, Scruggs, and Mastropieri (1992). The positive effects of higher order questioning are described by Scruggs, Mastropieri, Sullivan, and Hesser (1993); Scruggs, Mastropieri, and Sullivan (1994); and Sullivan, Mastropieri, and Scruggs (1995). Issues of teaching multicultural and linguistically diverse students are described in Volume 59, Issue 2 (Obiakor, Patton, & Ford, 1992) and Volume 56, Issue 2 (Figueroa, Fradd, & Correa, 1989) of *Exceptional Children*. Particularly useful are articles by Cummins (1989) and Franklin (1992). A recent textbook by Winzer and Mazurek (1998) provides many suggestions for special education teaching in multicultural contexts. In addition, much of the research validating effective instructional practices has been conducted in multicultural settings. Research in multicultural special education settings has provided specific support for teacher enthusiasm (Brigham, Scruggs, & Mastropieri, 1992), cooperative group learning (Brigham, Bakken, Scruggs, & Mastropieri, 1992), and use of relevant, meaningful materials (Scruggs, Mastropieri, Bakken, & Brigham, 1993). Support for the facilitative effects of a positive classroom atmosphere for special education students is given by Mastropieri, Scruggs, and Bohs (1994) and in Scruggs and Mastropieri (1994d). Finally, much of the literature on special education teacher effectiveness is summarized in Volume 52, Issue 6 of *Exceptional Children* (Algozzine & Meheady, 1986), particularly in articles by Bickel and Bickel (1986); Morsink, Soar, Soar, and Thomas (1986); and Reid (1986). An updated review on teacher effectiveness variables in special education was written by Rosenshine (1997). Discussion of the PASS variables and their application in inclusive settings is provided by Scruggs and Mastropieri (1995c) and Mastropieri and Scruggs (1997a, 1997b, 2000).

Successful Inclusive Teaching Strategies

Researchers who have studied teachers who successfully include students with disabilities in their classrooms have identified some common key factors (Larrivee, 1985; Scruggs & Mastropieri, 1994d; Mastropieri et al., 1998). Research has shown that effective teaching strategies can be very beneficial for teaching in inclusive classrooms. Key factors for effective inclusive teaching include the following:

- Effective classroom management strategies
    effective transitions
    use of positive comments
    consistent implementation of rules and consequences
    maximized academic time-on-task

- Appropriate academic tasks
    appropriate level of difficulty
    tasks modified to meet the abilities of students
    students can complete tasks successfully

- Instructional feedback
    positive feedback
    corrective feedback
    continuous feedback

- Supportive classroom environment
    open, accepting environment for all students
    use of positive, supporting comments
    welcomes students into classroom
    welcomes individual differences

Maximizing Time by Using Computer-Assisted Record Keeping

Many noninstructional tasks teachers have are time-consuming. Such tasks include creating a system for recording and maintaining student grades, attendance, and performance in classes; organizing and recording information from student portfolios; organizing and maintaining records of communications with parents, including phone numbers, e-mail addresses, and street addresses; and maintaining records of instruction, among many others. The amount of record keeping increases when students with disabilities are included in general education classes. For example, writing Individualized Education Programs (IEPs), maintaining careful records of progress on IEP objectives, and documenting instructional practices are all necessary. Teachers who successfully reduce record-keeping time develop some effective record-keeping strategies using computer-assisted technology, including the following:

- Software for maintaining grades, records, names, and addresses
    database programs such as Microsoft Access, ClarisWorks, or Microsoft Works

    spreadsheet programs such as Microsoft Excel, ClarisWorks, or Microsoft Works

    commercially available programs such as Grade Machine (Misty City Software: http://www.mistycity.com)

- Software for developing templates for communication
    word-processing programs such as Microsoft Word, ClarisWorks, Microsoft Works, Novell Wordperfect, Microsoft Powerpoint

- Software for graphics
    Print Shop by Broderbund, Creative Writer by Microsoft, SuperPrint by Scholastic

- Communication software for e-mail
    Netscape or Microsoft Outlook for establishing an address book of names and e-mail addresses

- Software to help with time management organizes daily goals, establishes priorities, and keeps track of accomplishments on a daily and weekly basis

- Check out Web sites for other software that may meet your particular needs. Search engines such as Yahoo, Excite, Infoseek, Google, and AskJeeves can assist in locating links to many software publishers relevant to educators and parents.

Chapter 2

❦   ❦   ❦

Designing Effective Instruction

For effective instruction to occur, teachers must design lessons carefully and systematically. In special education, federal law (Individuals with Disabilities Education Act [IDEA]) requires that all instruction be based on prespecified goals and objectives (U.S. Department of Education, 1998). Individual goals and objectives for each student are specified on Individualized Education Programs (IEPs), which must be reviewed at least annually. An example of a portion of an IEP is provided in Appendix A.

Instruction for students is designed on the basis of goals and objectives from the IEP. This is accomplished by prioritizing objectives from the scope and sequence and by developing and implementing instructional guidelines. To develop such guidelines, teachers must carefully consider all the teacher effectiveness variables discussed in the last chapter. These variables include time-on-task, content covered, delivering information, questioning, feedback, practice activities, and formative evaluation.

When developing instructional objectives, it is important to attend not only to the level of the content presented but also to the level of knowledge that is expected from the learner. For example, anyone who has taken tests realizes that multiple-choice questions are generally easier to answer than short-answer or fill-in-the-blank questions. This is partly because identifying correct answers is easier than producing correct answers. Therefore, objectives and their corresponding lessons need to specify the level of learning that is expected. In addition, the performance criteria must be specified. Prior to the lesson, teachers should know not only the target objective of the lesson but also that students are expected to respond with a given level of accuracy (e.g., 80%) on a specific evaluation measure. When the performance criteria are clearly specified, teachers have a clearer idea of how instruction should be designed and presented.

The Individualized Education Program

The IEP includes a number of components, including the following:

- a statement of the student's current level of educational functioning, including how the student's disability affects involvement and progress in the general education (inclusive) classroom;

- a description of when service will be initiated and the frequency and duration of services;

- a statement of long-term, annual goals;

- a statement of how annual goals will be measured, how progress will be monitored, and how parents will be kept informed;

- a list of short-term objectives related to the annual goals, relevant to the needs for participation in the general education classroom, and meeting other needs resulting from the disability;

- a statement of special and related service needs, needed program modifications, and needed support for school personnel;

- a statement of any needed modifications on state or district tests or alternative assessments to be administered;

- for all students 14 years old or older, a statement of transition services.

When completed, the IEP is signed by members of the multidisciplinary team (parents, teachers, and other relevant personnel, including social workers and school nurses).

Types of Objectives

A fundamental component of the IEP is the instructional objective. IEP objectives can be divided into general and specific, or long- and short-term objectives. Long-term objectives typically refer to the skills the student needs to perform more effectively in the general education classroom or a less restrictive environment. These objectives include general statements such as, "Student will improve reading performance to the appropriate grade-equivalent level, as measured by achievement tests." This overall objective describes the global skills the student needs to acquire to function at an average level in that general education classroom. However, it does not specify the precise skills the student needs to master to read at the appropriate grade level. These skills are specified in the short-term objectives, which describe the prerequisite steps students must take to meet the long-term objective. In the reading example, a short-term objective may include a statement such as, "Student will read word samples from grade-equivalent passages with 100% accuracy." In another example, the long-term objective for social behavior might be, "Student will exhibit appropriate verbal behavior according to school rules at all times." One of the corresponding short-term objectives might be, "Student will produce appropriate verbal responses to teacher questions in all cases," and "In a role-playing situation, the student will respond appropriately to teacher feedback and questions for 20 examples."

Common Elements of Objectives

As can be seen by the above examples and those in Table 2.1, all objectives have certain common elements. This is true whether objectives are short or long term and whether they deal with reading, math, or social skills. These common components include (a) the behavior to be exhibited, (b) the conditions (circumstances) under which the behavior is to be exhibited, and (c) the performance criteria. Often an objective will take the following form: "Given 20 division problems, including 2-digit divisors and 3-digit dividends, the student will compute answers and remainders at a criterion of 90% accuracy in less than 5 minutes." In this example, note that the computation of the answers to the division problems specifies the *behavior to be exhibited*. The be-

Table 2.1. Sample Behavioral Objectives

Area	Student Behavior	Conditions	Performance Criteria
Reading	Oral reading	100-word passage from appropriate reading level	In 1 minute with 100% accuracy
Handwriting	Copying	Lowercase letters A–K	With 100% accuracy
Spelling	Oral spelling	50 Dolch words	With 90% accuracy
Arithmetic	Computation	50 single-digit addition problems	In 1 minute with 90% accuracy
Language	Identification	20 instances of *on* and *in* from pictures	With 90% accuracy
Social Behavior	Ignoring	Teasing of others	9 times out of 10

havior is an observable, measurable performance of the student. By this definition, behaviors include oral reading, walking, talking, and permanent products such as handwriting samples. Covert operations such as thinking are not considered behaviors because they are not directly observable; however, these covert operations often are necessary for the execution of the behavior. In the final analysis, teachers can directly evaluate only observable behaviors.

The second critical component of an objective is the specified *conditions* under which the behavior will occur. In the example on long division, the objective specifies that the student has been provided with 20 division problems of a certain type. These problems constitute the circumstances under which the behavior will be performed. Circumstances also may include paper, pencil, a desk, a quiet environment, and teacher directions; however, space considerations may preclude the inclusion of such implicit conditions. Care must be taken, however, to ensure that all necessary conditions are specified and that there is general agreement regarding implicit conditions.

The final component of an objective is the performance *criteria* to be exhibited. When stating the performance criteria, it is necessary to include accuracy and perhaps fluency criteria. In the division example, an accuracy criterion of 90% is specified, as is a rate of four problems per minute. Such criteria should be based on overall performance goals expected of all students at their respective age and grade levels. One way of establishing such criteria is to determine performance levels of regular education students who have been identified by their teachers as competent at that skill. For example, if special education teachers were uncertain about the performance criteria for the division objective, they could ask regular educators at that grade level to identify several students competent in long division whose rate and accuracy on those 20 division problems could provide a basis for performance criteria. In addition to the general education classroom criteria, teachers also need to ensure that the performance criteria for one objective

lead to easy mastery of the next objective. Research has shown that students who have thoroughly mastered one objective can learn the next objective more easily when the scope and sequence follows an established hierarchy of skill development. However, it also must be remembered that spending too much time on one objective can interfere with the amount of content covered throughout the school year, as discussed in Chapter 1.

In summary, IEPs describe individual student goals and objectives. Objectives must include the behaviors to be assessed, conditions for assessing the behavior, and performance criteria. Objectives not only are a critical component of IEP assessment but also provide the basis for instructional design that considers the expected levels of student learning.

Levels of Learning

Identification and Production

Academic or social behavior can be exhibited in either identification or production formats. *Identification* refers to student performances such as matching, multiple choice, true/false, pointing, and selecting. Identification is usually important in the very early stages of learning that require the mastery of basic discriminations. For example, in the initial stages of reading instruction, students must be able to identify certain letters. At the higher grade levels, identification of novel concepts is often a necessary first step toward developing understanding of those concepts. Identification also is important when the amount of content being taught is large and when objective tests of the multiple-choice type represent the only practical means for assessing the learning of a large number of students. Some tasks, furthermore, may require learning only at the identification level, for example, identification of the meanings of different traffic lights. In many cases, however, students ultimately must be required to *produce* appropriate responses. For example, although it may be a necessary prerequisite for students to identify appropriate playground interactions, they must ultimately be able to produce appropriate playground interactions to function successfully in inclusive settings. *Production* refers to a student's observable rendition of task-relevant behavior. Such production tasks include oral reading, writing, speaking, computing, and performing. Table 2.2 provides some additional examples of identification and production tasks. Before instruction can proceed effectively, it is important to determine whether student behavior is expected to occur at the identification or production level.

Acquisition and Fluency

Just as identification and production reflect the type of behavior specified, acquisition and fluency reflect the performance criteria of those behaviors. Basically, *acquisition* refers to an accuracy criterion. Teaching on an acquisition level is oriented toward achieving higher levels of accuracy without regard for the rate of performance. For example, in teaching regrouping in simple addition, the initial emphasis may be on accurate performance. Also, teaching any basic

discrimination, such as *b* versus *d*, may require an accuracy criterion during acquisition. For such levels of initial learning, rate of performance is not as important as correct performance.

Once novel concepts or facts have been acquired, the next stage of instruction usually involves some type of fluency training. It may not be sufficient for students simply to decode a reading passage accurately if it takes them too long to do so. Once accurate responding has been established, it is generally necessary to establish fluency, as assessed by accuracy plus rate criteria. The student who is fluent at reading, then, not only reads at the same level of accuracy as other competent students but also at a similar rate. In most of the basic skill areas that are covered in special education classes, the attainment of both accuracy and fluency levels is critical. Table 2.3 provides some examples of accuracy and fluency criteria.

Application and Generalization

Application and generalization follow acquisition and fluency. *Application* refers to students exhibiting a critical skill in an appropriate context. For example, it is of little use for students

Table 2.2. Identification and Production Tasks

Area	Student Identification	Student Production
Reading	Points to vowels.	Orally reads vowels.
	Chooses which of four sentences represents main idea of passage.	Reads passage and states the "main idea."
Handwriting	Identifies correct cursive formation of capital S.	Writes cursive capital S.
Spelling	Given four choices, identifies correct spelling of "lamb."	Orally spells "lamb" correctly.
Arithmetic	Identifies regrouping problem.	Computes problem with regrouping.
Language	Identifies correct noun/verb agreement.	Orally produces sentences with correct noun/verb agreement.
Social Behavior	Points out students who are sharing a classroom toy.	Shares classroom toys.

Table 2.3. Accuracy and Fluency Criteria

Behavior	Accuracy Criteria (% correct)	Fluency Rate Criteria
Reading CVC+e words	90	40 correct per min
Answering comprehension questions	90	5 correct per min
Orally answering "+8" facts	100	50 correct per min
Printing capital letters	100	20 correct per min
Spelling *ou* words	100	10 correct per min
Writing sentences	100	6 correct in 30 min
Saying "thank you"	90*	10 times when appropriate during a day

*appropriate times

to be able to multiply three-digit numbers accurately and fluently if they cannot use these skills to solve word problems. Once basic skills have been mastered, students must be taught to apply them in intended contexts. For another example, social skills training often is conducted in the context of role playing in which students are required to produce appropriate social responses in contrived settings. For this learning to be of real importance, however, students need to apply those appropriate social behaviors in their classroom. *Application* refers not only to the behavior that is exhibited but also to the conditions under which it is to be exhibited (i.e., the applied context).

Generalization as used here is similar to application but refers to a broader and more global domain of conditions, which are generally outside the immediate control of the special education teacher. For example, assume that a student has been taught to take turns appropriately in a role-play playground setting and has attained accuracy and fluency levels of performance (i.e., the student exhibits "turn-taking" behavior accurately and in a timely fashion). In this instance, application would refer to exhibiting turn-taking skills on the playground under "real" circumstances. Generalization would refer to the demonstration of these skills in a different but still appropriate context, such as taking turns getting on a school bus. In an academic example, stu-

dents may learn to compute division problems accurately and fluently on worksheets. Application would refer to their performance of these skills in response to classroom word problems. Generalization would refer to the use of these skills in an inclusive classroom (i.e., a general education classroom that includes students with disabilities) or in determining the price of one slice of a whole pizza eaten with friends at a restaurant outside the school setting.

Some type of application or generalization is the end goal of special education. In most cases, it is important for teachers to directly teach the application of acquired basic skills and facts in their intended contexts. Generalization, however, is a more complex phenomenon that resists precise definition in many instances. Most people agree, however, that generalization can occur across settings, time, stimuli, and behaviors. Although appropriate generalization is nearly always desirable, it has proven to be much more difficult to teach than application.

Summary of Levels of Learning

Attention to different levels of learning is critical in instructional design for special education. *Identification* and *production* refer to different behaviors that may be expected from students in specific content areas. Whenever instruction is designed, teachers should consider whether students must produce a correct response or whether identification is a more appropriate objective. In addition, performance criteria should be assessed at various levels. *Acquisition* refers to accuracy criteria only, whereas *fluency* refers to accuracy plus rate of performance criteria. Fluency is of particular importance in basic skill areas such as reading, writing, and arithmetic. *Application* and *generalization* refer to the context in which these skills are applied. An example of an application task is when students are trained to use their decoding skills on an unfamiliar reading passage. *Generalization*, as used here, is somewhat broader and refers to the use of learned skills in untrained situations, such as the use of appropriate social skills in a grocery store. Table 2.4 provides examples of application and generalization, and Table 2.5 describes strategies for promoting generalization summarized from Stokes and Baer (1977) and from Scruggs and Mastropieri (1984c, 1994c).

Levels of learning are important considerations in designing instruction, in that it specifies *to what extent* something is to be learned. In addition to levels of learning, however, it is also important to attend to *what* will be learned and the type of learning it represents. Consideration of the type of learning is critical for optimal design of instruction.

Types of Learning

Most learning that takes place in school settings can be classified by type of learning. These include (a) discrimination learning, (b) factual learning, (c) rule learning, (d) procedural learning, (e) conceptual learning, and (f) problem-solving and thinking skills. Examples of these types of learning are found in Table 2.6. These are described separately in the sections that follow.

Discrimination Learning

Discrimination learning refers to learning that one stimulus is different from another stimulus or set of stimuli. One of the more obvious examples in special education is in learning to discriminate

Table 2.4. Application and Generalization Tasks

Behavior (acquisition/fluency)	Application	Generalization
Passages read correctly from reading textbook.	Reads correctly in classroom literature book.	Reads correctly in mainstream history textbook.
Long-division algorithms computed on worksheet.	Computes long-division word problems in class.	Computes long-division word problems on mainstream achievement test.
Roman numerals on worksheet.	Solves classroom problems that include Roman numerals.	Reads Roman numerals on museum during field trip.
Role-plays "please" and "thank you."	Says "please" and "thank you" to neighboring student.	Says "please" and "thank you" to physical education teacher.
Spells *kn* words correctly on spelling test.	Spells *kn* words correctly on sentence writing.	Spells *kn* words correctly in mainstream homework assignment.
Role-plays ignoring inappropriate behavior.	Ignores teasing of neighboring student.	Ignores teasing on school bus.

Table 2.5. Strategies for Promoting Generalization

1. *Train sufficient examples.* Teach students to respond correctly to a number of different examples.

2. *Train loosely.* Allow a wide variety of acceptable responses and conditions, and do not rely exclusively on overly structured situations.

3. *Use "indiscriminable contingencies."* Set up situations in which students are less certain exactly *when* their appropriate behavior will be rewarded. This will make them more likely to display appropriate social and academic behavior at all times.

4. *Use role-play activities.* Set up situations that are likely to occur in external settings (e.g., use of appropriate social skills during job interviews), and have students act out the roles of different participants.

5. *Train specific strategies.* Teach students the necessary procedures for accomplishing specific tasks in other environments or circumstances.

6. *Promote self-monitoring.* Teach students how to monitor and regulate their behavior in a variety of situations.

7. *Reinforce generalization.* Provide explicit, positive feedback when behavior is successfully generalized. Discuss with the student how this was accomplished, and encourage future generalization efforts.

8. *Retrain.* Directly reteach the desired social or academic behavior in the generalization setting or conditions, or in as many as possible.

Note. Adapted from Stokes and Baer (1977) and Scruggs and Mastropieri (1984c, 1994c).

Table 2.6. Types of Learning

Type of Learning	Reading	Arithmetic	Social
Discrimination	*p* vs. *q*	+ vs. −	cooperate vs. compete
Factual			
Associative	*l* = "ell"	5 + 2 = 7	Laughing at other people is rude.
Serial list	a, b, c, d, e . . .	2, 4, 6, 8, 10, 12 . . .	School song or motto.
Rule	If two vowels appear together, say the long sound of the first vowel.	To divide fractions, invert and multiply.	Do unto others as you would have others do unto you.
Concept	vowel	prime number	courtesy
Procedure	1. Read title 2. Self-question 3. Skim passage 4. Self-question 5. Read carefully 6. Answer questions	1. Count decimal places in division. 2. Move decimal point in divisor that many places to the right, insert caret. 3. Place decimal point directly above caret in quotient.	1. Walk quietly in line. 2. Take tray, utensils, and napkins. 3. Put lunch on tray. 4. Take carton of milk. 5. Walk quietly to lunch table.

between reversible letters, such as *b* and *d*. Such reversal problems are commonly reported in students with learning disabilities or reading disabilities. However, such reversals are also commonly observed in nearly all beginning readers. A student has learned a *b/d* discrimination when he or she can correctly identify the *b* from the *d*. In later stages of learning, students will be required to write (produce) a *b* or *d* correctly. Other examples of discrimination tasks include learning differences between or among stimuli when more than one is presented, such as colors (e.g., "Point to the red ball"), shapes (e.g., "Show me the triangle"), arithmetic symbols (e.g., "Which one means add?"), and appropriate social responses (e.g., "Which student said the right thing?"). Once students have learned to accurately discriminate sets of stimuli, they generally will need to learn to produce individual stimuli fluently. Discrimination learning may be the initial stage of other types of learning, particularly concept learning, and should not be considered exclusive from the types of learning that follow. When planning instruction, it is important to attend carefully to discrimination learning, particularly at the earliest stages of skill development or in the introduction of new content when, for example, initial discriminations between different types of minerals may be difficult. Discrimination plays a role in many types of learning that follow.

Factual Learning

Factual learning refers to making and establishing basic associations. Typically, factual learning follows a stimulus-response pattern. An obvious example of factual learning is in the acquisition of foreign language vocabulary. In learning that the Spanish word *casa* means *house*, students are provided with the stimulus term *casa* and are expected to produce the response *house*. Because an association must be made between *casa* and *house*, this type of factual learning is known as *associative*. In basic skill areas, factual learning includes the acquisition of basic math facts, such

as $5 + 3 = 8$, and basic decoding skills, such as learning appropriate sound–symbol relationships. Students can be required to produce a relevant fact when asked or to identify the correct fact in, for example, a multiple-choice format. Although accuracy, application, and generalization of a learned fact are important, particularly in test-taking situations, the fluency rate expected may vary in importance. For example, math facts should be learned to a high rate of fluency; however, a rapid rate of responding may be of less importance in some content-area learning.

Factual learning is so pervasive in schools, on all levels, that efficient factual learning is critical for school success. One potential problem with the teaching of facts is that it is sometimes possible for students to answer factual questions correctly without comprehending the content. Many undergraduate students, for example, can recall memorizing facts from textbooks without any real understanding of the information being tested. Although such memorizing may be helpful in increasing test scores, it may not increase learning in any real sense. However, this associative stage may represent the first step in catching on to important content and, in this sense, is a critical component of learning. For example, in studying statistics, students might simply memorize the fact that r^2 is equivalent to "the proportion of variance accounted for" and be able to produce (or identify) such a response on a test. Although learning this fact may represent an important first step, it is also important for this fact to be "understood" (i.e., that underlying concepts be learned). Understanding of this type can be assessed in application or generalization tasks, in which students are required to use the fact in some novel context. In other instances, factual learning may require only one response. For example, it may be important to know that the capital of Maryland is Annapolis. Given that a student understands what is meant by capital, learning that Annapolis is the capital of Maryland may be the only objective. In some cases, students may need to learn facts in a specified sequence, such as the days of the week ("Sunday, Monday, Tuesday . . ."), the months in a year

("January, February, March . . ."), or the letters of the alphabet ("a, b, c . . ."). This type of factual learning is referred to as *serial-list* learning. In other instances, factual learning represents the prerequisite building blocks for concept learning, which is described later in this chapter.

Rule Learning

Learning rules is critical for success in school. Many times students are referred to special education because they lack an understanding of rules. For example, a student may have failed to learn the application of inconsistent rules found in reading. A second example may be the lack of acquisition of classroom rules for social behavior. An example of a rule is as follows: "When two vowels go walking (appear together), the first one does the talking (says its name)." Here is another example: "In classroom situations, raise your hand and wait to be called upon before speaking."

Rules appear across all skill and content areas. In some areas, however, rules are inconsistent. Inconsistent rules have unpredictable exceptions. These are particularly common in reading and spelling. For example, the *i* before *e* rule lists as an exception when these vowels appear after the letter *c*. However, the word *financier* is itself an exception to this exception, subject to a different rule. Such inconsistent rules can be particularly difficult for students in special education.

In contrast, rules in mathematics are typically highly consistent. For example, when dividing fractions, the rule that specifies that the divisor be inverted is constant. Most rules in mathematics can be taught without respect to inconsistencies.

Many rules follow an if–then paradigm. This is often true in social behavior, which can be of particular difficulty for special education students. Such rules may vary from situation to situation and also may be applied inconsistently. For example, the rule, "If you are not in your seat when the bell rings, then you will be given a tardy slip," may be inconsistently applied by different teachers and even by the same teacher.

Although it is important for teachers to be as consistent as possible, it is also important for students to understand sources of inconsistency.

Rule learning can incorporate knowledge of facts and discriminations. For example, the "in-seat" rule above presumes that students can discriminate in-seat from out-of-seat and have learned the meaning of "tardy slip." Such facts and discriminations must be mastered prior to learning the relevant rules. In some cases, facts and rules can be combined sequentially in procedural learning.

Procedural Learning

Many activities in school require the execution of a series of behaviors in a specific sequence. This type of learning is referred to as *procedural learning*. Procedural learning, such as the procedures involved in long division, is very common in mathematics. In long division, students must execute a series of steps to accurately compute the solution of the problem. To execute this procedure, students must know the underlying facts and understand the rules that constitute the specific steps.

Procedures are also common in reading comprehension and study skills. To read and study effectively, students must learn to execute a series of steps to maximize their understanding of a passage, such as prereading/skimming, identifying critical information, executing appropriate learning strategies, reviewing, and self-questioning. To be effective, students must execute such strategies in sequence and require the use of procedural learning.

Students who are taught to use a learning strategy independently (such as the *cover, copy,* and *compare* strategy for learning spelling words) must use a three-step procedure. First, students must *recognize* the situation for which a particular strategy is appropriate. Second, students must *recall* the steps of the strategy in correct order. Finally, students must correctly *execute* the strategy for the specific task. Many different learning strategies are presented throughout this book, but students using these strategies independently must always use this three-part recognize–recall–execute procedure.

Other important procedural tasks are commonly found in vocational areas. For example, many students in special education are taught assembly tasks according to a certain procedural sequence. Finally, knowledge of procedures is important for general school functioning. Students must learn daily routines, such as entering a school cafeteria, many of which must be performed in sequence. In some cases, daily schedules are variable, and such schedules may be particularly difficult for students with disabilities. To a large extent, the application of learned skills represents a knowledge of relevant procedures. It is important for special education students to be taught skills and the procedures by which they are applied.

Conceptual Learning

Concepts form an integral component of all knowledge. Although it is difficult to define precisely, we know *conceptual learning* has occurred when a student can provide a correct response to a novel instance of the concept. For instance, while learning colors, students may have learned that a certain pencil is red. However, it cannot be determined that students have mastered the concept of red until they can identify red flowers, red crayons, and red chairs that they have not seen previously. Likewise, students may have learned that a specific geometric form has been given the name "triangle." However, students have not mastered the concept of *triangle* until they have demonstrated that they can identify or produce many forms of triangles. At the higher grade levels, students learn more complex concepts, such as "amphibian." To have mastered this concept thoroughly, students must have first acquired concepts for frog, toad, salamander, and newt. The knowledge of such a concept must be assessed across a wider domain of instances than simpler concepts such as red or triangle.

Some concepts can be taught through rule learning or through discrimination-learning paradigms. Many concepts follow the if–then rule-learning paradigm. Using the previously described triangle example, an if–then rule can be applied, as in the statement, "If a geometric figure has three straight sides that enclose a space, then it is a triangle." Students demonstrate knowledge of this concept by applying the rule in novel instances. As another example, students could be taught the following rule to learn the concept *insect*: "If an animal has six legs and three body segments (head, abdomen, thorax), it is an insect." Students who have learned this rule can also learn to apply it to different types of animals.

Concepts also can be taught through discrimination-learning paradigms. In such cases, students are provided with multiple instances and noninstances of the concept until they can identify the appropriate features in novel instances. A common use of this paradigm is in the teaching of locative prepositions. *Locative prepositions* refer to spatial orientation and include prepositions such as *above, below, on, in,* and *behind.* These concepts are difficult to teach with rule-learning paradigms and in special education are typically taught by means of instances and noninstances. For example, to teach the concept *on,* students could be shown a cup that in some cases is *on* the table and in some cases is *not on* the table. After students have been provided with sufficient examples, they should be able to identify or produce instances of the concept *on.* To identify the concept, students should respond correctly to the following question: "Is the cup/spoon/fork on the table?" To produce an example of the concept, students should respond appropriately to the following command: "Put the cup/spoon/fork on the table." Other concepts resist precise or simple definitions and generally are taught through discriminations of instances and noninstances. Such concepts include *freedom, justice,* and *appropriate.* In such cases, instances and noninstances are provided by statements, such as, "Running may be appropriate on the playgrounds, but it is not appropriate in the halls."

In many cases, concepts are taught by the provision of rules and examples. To teach the concept *fish*, teachers may first introduce a general rule: "If an animal lives in the water and has gills and scales, then it is a fish." After students have demonstrated knowledge and familiarity with the rule, they are taught to apply the rule to various instances and noninstances. For example: "This animal is a dolphin. It lives in the water. It does not have gills, and it does not have scales. Is it a fish?"

Concepts are an integral component of school learning. Concepts are interrelated with other types of learning such as factual learning and generally are taught through the use of rules and discriminations of instances and noninstances.

Concepts can range from very simple (e.g., *red, triangle*) to complex (e.g., *torque, covalent bonding*). The more complex concepts build on simpler concepts and require more prerequisite knowledge. Nevertheless, several considerations can facilitate acquisition of any concept. First, initially emphasize the critical features of the concept and describe less relevant attributes later. Second, link the new concept to things that students already know. Third, provide lots of examples of the new concept and include instances as well as noninstances.

Problem-Solving and Thinking Skills

Problem-solving and thinking skills are different from the types of learning described earlier. *Problem solving*, as used here, refers to students finding an answer or a solution in the absence of an immediate strategy or means for solving the problem. To this extent, it refers less to strategy-based math problem solving than it does to constructing proofs in geometry, such as the Pythagorean theorem, or solving the "magic square" problem (insert the numbers 1 through 9 into a nine-chambered square such that all the diagonals, rows, and columns all have the same sum). However, problem solving can occur on less formal tasks, such as finding the simplest solution to the following problem:

$$\frac{375 + 375 + 375 + 375 + 375}{5}.$$

Or it could be used in finding a way to keep the newts from using the water heater to crawl out of the classroom aquarium.

Thinking skills is a broader term and includes the use of active reasoning in solving problems or in acquiring or understanding new concepts. Thinking skills and problem solving are involved with the processes of learning more than the products of learning (such as facts and concepts). Nevertheless, there is good reason for considering thinking skills and problem solving in special education. Most students with mild disabilities are not active reasoners (they frequently have been characterized as "passive learners"); however, it has been argued that information is not truly learned (i.e., at the application and generalization levels) until it has been actively elaborated on, questioned, and reasoned through. Therefore, instructional activities that promote active reasoning through new information are likely to serve application and generalization objectives. Furthermore, there is reason to believe that students who have been encouraged to use thinking skills and problem-solving strategies will ultimately become more thoughtful, reflective learners.

Thinking skills and problem solving are best taught through modeling, prompting, and active coaching. It may be a good general policy to not answer some student questions until the students have demonstrated that they have actively thought about the question themselves. Usually some prior knowledge must be brought to bear on the task, and teachers can help prompt the retrieval of this relevant information, as seen in the following dialogue:

STUDENT: Look at the picture of this anteater. Why does it have such long claws on its front feet?

TEACHER: Can you think of a reason?

STUDENT: No.

TEACHER: Well, what do we know about anteaters?

STUDENT: I know they eat ants.

TEACHER: Good! They eat ants. And where do ants live?

STUDENT: In holes in the ground?

TEACHER: Right! So why does it make sense that anteaters have long front claws?

STUDENT: Oh! So they can dig for ants!

TEACHER: Exactly.

Research has shown that when students with mild disabilities are coached through reasoning activities such as this one, they learn more, remember more, and understand better than if they were just provided the answer by the teacher. However, students with mild disabilities may need very structured coaching to arrive at the correct conclusion.

Thinking skills or problem-solving strategies are acquired best with reference to a specific subject. Such skills do not transfer easily across knowledge domains, and the best thinking usually occurs within a content that is already very familiar to students.

Summary of Types of Learning

Types of learning can be subdivided into learning of discriminations, facts, rules, procedures, concepts, and problem-solving and thinking skills. It is important to note that these categories are not mutually exclusive and that many learning tasks include several different types of learning. Nevertheless, types of learning play an important role in the design of instruction and lend themselves to more appropriate delivery systems. If you know what types of learning you are eliciting in your instruction, it is easier to determine the best approaches to teaching. Understanding types and levels of learning provides important implications for instructional design.

Application to Instructional Design

Everything covered up to this point needs to be considered during the design and delivery of instruction. Effective instructional design strategies incorporate all of the important teaching and learning variables:

- Teacher effectiveness variables
  - engaged time-on-task
  - content covered
  - teacher presentation
  - questioning
  - feedback
  - guided and independent practice
  - formative evaluation.
- Instructional objectives
  - behavior
  - conditions
  - performance criteria
- Levels of learning
  - identification
  - production
  - accuracy and fluency
  - application and generalization
- Types of learning
  - discrimination learning
  - factual learning
  - rule learning
  - procedural learning
  - conceptual learning
  - problem-solving and thinking skills

It is important to consider all the above information on teaching and learning whenever designing instruction.

Designing Instruction

Design of instruction involves the systematic examination and organization of all curricular and teaching variables. Effective instructional design incorporates

- specification of long-term objectives,

- development of specific short-term objectives and sequencing of skills,

- selection of appropriate materials and instructional procedures, and

- specification of decision-making systems and evaluation procedures.

Each of these is described in the following sections.

Specification of Long-Term Objectives

When designing any instruction, first specify the content that should be learned by the end of the instructional sequence. An instructional sequence could consist of content that will be covered in a unit, quarter, semester, or year. It is important to clearly state long-term objectives so that you can continue to monitor progress toward mastery of these objectives as the year progresses.

Long-term objectives may include statements such as, "Students will count eight coins to a specific value, given pennies, nickels, dimes, quarters, half dollars, and silver dollars with 100% accuracy in less than 30 seconds." Another example of a long-term objective is the following: "Student will exhibit school-appropriate behavior during cafeteria lunch period without prompting for 3 consecutive weeks." Long-term objectives for special education students typically are derived from students' IEPs. However, the IEP objectives usually can be subdivided into several levels of long-term objectives. To maximize instructional efficiency, teachers should link such long-term objectives to the district curriculum scope and sequences. In addition, curriculum materials should link instructional procedures with these instructional objectives. When curricular materials are linked to long-

term objectives, appropriate curriculum-based assessment can be more readily implemented.

Specification of Short-Term Objectives

Short-term objectives provide the behavior, conditions, and performance criteria that form the framework of daily lessons. The subdivision of long-term objectives is sometimes referred to as *task analysis* (task analysis can also be applied within short-term objectives, as needed). Task analysis is the subdivision and sequencing of instructional steps at the optimal level of difficulty for students. Similarly, *conceptual analysis* refers to the subdivision and sequencing of instructional steps necessary to teach concepts. The optimal size of the instructional step is often determined by teachers based on previous formative evaluation data. Teachers need clearly specified short-term objectives to attend appropriately to the essential components of instruction.

Short-term objectives are similar in format to long-term objectives but generally describe very specifically the components of individual lessons. An example of a specific short-term objective, derived from the above long-term objective on coin counting, is as follows: "Student will identify the following coins: penny, nickel, dime, and quarter, with 100% accuracy." Another possible short-term objective could be the following: "Student will count from 1 to 20 nickels with 100% accuracy at a rate of 1 nickel per second."

Task analysis procedures also can be applied and short-term objectives specified in the area of social behavior. For the long-term objectives for cafeteria functioning presented earlier, cafeteria skills could be broken into tasks involving the procedures of going through cafeteria lines, seating, cleanup, and appropriate social behavior in cafeteria settings. When such a task analysis is complete, short-term objectives could include the following: "Given a cafeteria setting, student will exhibit appropriate social behaviors while standing in cafeteria line for 3 consecutive weeks to a

100% criterion. Appropriate social behavior as defined here includes speaking in a tone of voice that does not carry intelligibly for more than 5 feet and refraining from teasing or making inappropriate physical contact with other students."

Like long-term objectives, short-term objectives are typically derived from IEPs, although they are often stated on a higher level of specificity than is appropriate to individual lesson presentations. For efficient delivery of instruction, these objectives should be implemented with appropriate curriculum materials. A key to meeting short- and long-term objectives is selecting the most appropriate materials and instructional procedures.

Selection of Appropriate Materials and Instructional Procedures

Once objectives have been clearly specified, it should be easy to identify the types and levels of learning required. Teachers should be able to state whether they expect students to identify or produce correct responses, whether they expect learning to be produced at a level of accuracy or fluency, and whether students are expected to apply or generalize learned information. Objectives should clearly state the level of learning that is expected. In addition, teachers should be aware of the type of learning that is expected to be produced. For example, many of the initial tasks in a coin-counting curriculum require fluent production of factual responses ("this is a nickel, this is a penny"). Later on, students may need to employ rules and procedures for counting coins at specified levels of accuracy or fluency ("3 nickels [count by 5s] = 5, 10, 15 cents, plus 2 pennies [count on by 1s] = 16, 17 cents"). In previous lessons, discrimination of one type of coin from another, as assessed in identification tasks, may have been necessary. For other learners, teaching relevant concepts such as "money" may be important.

Once you have clearly determined what is to be taught, the next step is to identify the most appropriate materials and instructional proce-

dures. Instructional procedures refer to the manner in which instruction is implemented. For example, discrimination knowledge of the type needed for identification of specific coins typically is first taught in special education through a series of instances and noninstances (e.g., "This is a nickel. This is *not* a nickel. Is this a nickel?") and feedback on match-to-sample tasks (e.g., "Point to the nickel in this group of four coins"). For serial-list factual learning of the type used to teach counting by 5s, rehearsal is often used ("5, 10, 15, 20. . . . Now you say it"). To teach application of the procedural information involved in cafeteria line behaviors, teachers typically use repeated teacher-led modeling, prompting, and feedback (e.g., "First I pick up my tray, then I pick up a napkin, knife, fork, and spoon and put them on a tray. Now you do it.").

The type of teaching procedure may also reflect the level of learning. For example, teaching to accuracy criteria may include prompting and feedback for deliberate, careful work, whereas teaching to fluency criteria may involve prompting and reinforcement for rapid and efficient performance. Similarly, although teaching to application levels, teachers may employ more deliberate models and demonstrations, and generalization instruction may involve explicit instructions prior to the execution of the expected behavior (e.g., "Now tell me what you are going to do when you get to the playground"). Some further examples of instructional procedures are given in Table 2.7.

In addition, it is important that teachers carefully link instructional objectives and instructional procedures to specific instructional materials. Materials should be selected because they are directly relevant to instructional objectives. If available materials are not relevant to the instructional objectives or appropriate to learner characteristics (e.g., reading level), teachers should adapt existing materials or create new materials that are directly relevant to instructional objectives. If students are taught in special education settings, curricular materials and corresponding objectives should resemble as closely as possible those used in general education class-

Table 2.7. Instructional Implications for Different Types of Learning and Levels of Learning

Objective	Instructional Strategies*
Type of Learning	
Discriminations	Presentation of instances and noninstances. Using models, prompts, and feedback.
Factual	Rehearsal and repetition, using drill-and-practice techniques; teaching meaningful elaborations; presenting information in manageable chunks.
Rules	Drill and practice; application of examples.
Concepts	Presentation of instances and noninstances; provision of rules; provision of multiple examples.
Procedures	Drill and practice; application activities; modeling, prompting, and feedback.
Level of Learning	
Acquisition	Models; demonstrations; slow pace; reinforce accuracy.
Fluency	Fast pace; reinforce speed of accurate responding; alter reinforcement procedures.
Application	Multiple examples; modeling, prompting, and feedback.
Generalization	Prompts; provision of rules; role-play; multiple examples.

*Models, direct questions, and feedback can always be employed.

rooms. In fact, if a specific curriculum is used districtwide, teachers can more easily develop districtwide objectives and corresponding curriculum-based assessment materials that can be shared across teachers within school districts. Additional information on designing curriculum-based measures is presented in Chapter 3. Selection, evaluation, and adaptation of curriculum materials are discussed in Chapters 5 through 8.

Tables of Specifications

When designing a unit of instruction, it may be helpful to construct a table of specifications. A table of specifications subdivides content and behavior and can actually be a composite of the task/conceptual analysis, the expected levels of behavior (learning), the types of learning (e.g., discriminations, facts, rules, procedures), the performance criteria, and the conditions under which the behavior is expected to occur. In other words, a table of specifications organizes behavioral objectives. Some educators (e.g., Bloom,

Hastings, & Madaus, 1971; Howell & Kaplan, 1980) have proposed that these tables be used to design test items. The purpose of using tables of specifications is to enable teachers to evaluate their students' work more systematically. This table of specifications also can function as a record-keeping and lesson-planning device because the combination of subdivisions of behavior and subdivisions of content forms tasks or instructional objectives. Table 2.8 provides an example of a table of specifications for beginning reading decoding instruction. Content is arranged in order down the vertical axis, and behavior is arranged in order across the horizontal axis. For instance, the table of specifications subdivides the basic tasks involved in decoding skills into

1. consonants,

2. vowels,

3. CVC words (consonant-vowel-consonant words, such as *cat*),

4. CVCE words (consonant-vowel-consonant-silent *e* words, such as *cake*),

5. CCVC words (consonant-consonant-vowel-consonant words, such as *slap*).

The levels of behavior and learning are subdivided along the horizontal axis into (a) identification behavior at an acquisition level, (b) production behavior at an acquisition level, (c) production behavior at a fluency level, (d) production behavior at an application level, and (e) production behavior at a generalization level. As seen from Table 2.8, each cell can be made to represent an instructional objective that specifies the tasks and behaviors required. For the objectives to be complete, teachers need to supply the conditions under which the behavior is desired and the performance criteria that are considered necessary for success. For example, consider cell 1A. Here the content, consonants, is combined with the acquisition level of identification behavior. This means that an instructional objective similar to the following can be generated at the intersection of that content and behavior: "Students will correctly point to (notice that *point to* is an identification level of be-

havior) the correct consonant (the content level) from a list of 10 distractor consonants with 100% accuracy after hearing the teacher say either the consonant name or sound." Note that the performance criterion of 100% has been incorporated into the objective and that only accuracy, not fluency behavior, is emphasized.

Now, consider cell 1B. This cell designates the same content (consonants) but at a different level of behavior. This time the objective is as follows: "Students will correctly say (produce) the consonant name and/or sound upon teacher request with 100% accuracy." Note that the only change was the substitution of production behavior for the identification behavior used in cell 1A. In addition, notice that the objective for cell 1C would add fluency criteria to the objective that was designed for cell 1B, as in the following: "Given a list of consonants, students will say each sound or name each sound accurately within 1 second upon teacher request." Notice that cell 1D alters the behavior to the application level. A good example of the objective might be as follows: "Given a listing of words containing

Table 2.8. Table of Specifications for Initial Reading Decoding

CONTENT	BEHAVIOR				
	Identification	Production			
	A. Acquisition	B. Acquisition	C. Fluency	D. Application	E. Generalization
1. Consonants	1A	1B	1C	1D	1E
2. Vowels (short)	2A	2B	2C	2D	2E
3. CVC words (cat, pat, mat)	3A	3B	3C	3D	3E
4. CVCE words (cake)	4A	4B	4C	4D	4E
5. CCVC words (blab)	5A	5B	5C	5D	5E

Sample Objectives:

1A   Students will point to the correct consonant from a list of 10 distractor consonants with 100% accuracy after hearing the teacher say either the consonant name or sound.

2B   Students will correctly say the vowel name and short sound upon request with 100% accuracy.

3C   Given a list of CVCE words, students will read each word accurately within 1 second.

4D   Given a passage from the reading series, students will orally read the passage and pronounce each CVCE word accurately.

5E   Given a passage from the weekly newspaper, students will pronounce all CCVC words correctly.

CVC (consonant-vowel-consonant) letter patterns, the student will accurately say (produce) all the consonant sounds." Typically, when this objective is expected, teachers also will have introduced instruction on vowels; consequently, the application level of behavior would incorporate the correct reading of the entire CVC word. Cell 1E adds the generalization component to the objective. A good generalization objective might be similar to the following: "Given a newspaper, a basal reader, or a common product label, students will be able to say the consonant sounds and/or names."

Incorporating all of the instructional objectives above, teachers can design lessons to teach students each objective. Sometimes it may be desirable to subdivide the amount of the content included in each objective into either smaller or larger chunks. In other words, based on the students' needs, teachers may find that they need to cover fewer consonants in a lesson. In fact, most teachers probably introduce only a few, rather than all, consonants at a time. In addition, teachers may find that their students can proceed to producing the behaviors rather than spending the time on practicing identification. Teachers may feel that it is most useful to use a table of specifications as a framework for instruction to help conceptualize what needs to be taught, to what level, and the most appropriate instructional sequence. As will be seen throughout the remainder of this text, it is assumed that teacher judgment will play a critical role in the design and delivery of effective instruction; the consideration of levels of learning and sequence of skills can be very helpful in exercising this judgment.

Evaluation Procedures and Decision Making

Formative evaluation, discussed in Chapter 3, is critical for teachers to use to determine whether their instruction is having the desired effect. It is not enough to be able to say that students seem to be learning; it is important for teachers to develop certain standards by which they can determine whether their students are learning at a rate sufficient for them to meet their long-term objectives. To accomplish this, you must specify the steps necessary for meeting long-term objectives and determine the rate at which content should be covered. If content is not being mastered at an appropriate rate, you must modify your instructional procedures to increase the rate of learning.

To modify instructional procedures effectively, carefully examine your current instructional conditions. These conditions include

1. amount of engaged time on task;

2. rate at which content is covered;

3. instructional procedures, including review activities, type and length of teacher presentation, questioning and feedback procedures, type and length of practice activities, method of instructional delivery, and type of classroom management;

4. curriculum materials and objectives;

5. instructional strategies used, such as rehearsal or elaborations;

6. procedures to increase motivation, such as verbal praise, class privileges, or tangibles; and

7. evaluation procedures.

First, determine if each of these aspects is acceptably accounted for in current lessons. If they are not, design and add the missing element(s) to the planning and delivery of lessons. If all elements are accounted for, determine whether any element can be altered to increase the rate of learning. The most obvious modification is to increase the amount of engaged time-on-task. However, the overall engaged time may be optimal, but specific allocations of engaged time may not be optimal. For example, you may find that students are spending more time than necessary on independent practice activities, but time allocated to teacher presentation of new content is insufficient. Or, you may find that time allocations are optimal, but students are still not catching on to new content at a sufficient rate. If this is the case, it may be necessary to modify the type of instructional strategy. It could also be that the instructional procedures may have become monotonous, and, consequently, student motivation has decreased. In such a case, it may be important to change the type of instructional presentation or reinforcement procedures. Such changes could include, for example, using different learning strategies, using videotape or videodisk presentations, providing "hands-on" activities, using peers to teach or reinforce each other, allowing students to set their own goals, having randomly assigned groups participate in gamelike activities, or offering students more choices in instructional procedures.

Finally, it is important to evaluate the evaluation procedures themselves. It could be, for example, that students are really learning, but the evaluation procedures being used are not sensitive enough to the learning that is occurring. For example, a measure of "number of words correctly spelled" may indicate that progress is not being made, but a measure of correctly spelled letter sequences would reveal that students are making progress in spelling. It is also possible that the evaluation procedure being used does not match the level of behavior specified in the objectives. For example, it could be that students are being taught simply to identify correct and incorrect grammar and are making progress on this. But when they are asked to produce correct grammar in written products for evaluation, it does not appear that they are making progress because their instruction is not yet on the production level.

Task Analysis and Meaningfulness

Effective special education teachers are highly skilled at subdividing learning and behavioral tasks, as well as curriculum elements, into component parts. There are some important advantages to this type of task-analytic teaching. First,

it allows teachers to know exactly what they are teaching and what learners are expected to learn. Second, it allows for direct, objective evaluation of learner progress. Third, it allows teachers and students to proceed along a specified sequence of task difficulty. Finally, it allows teachers to specify precisely where difficulty occurs and determine exactly what appropriate remedial techniques should be applied. This type of teaching, based on task analysis, specific objectives, and continuous monitoring of progress toward larger goals and objectives, is commonly employed in special education and, when correctly applied, has been highly successful.

Nevertheless, there are some potential disadvantages to this model. The tables of specifications described previously and used throughout this text are intended as guidelines to facilitate decision making in special education. However, as tasks are broken down into subcomponents, they may become less meaningful to learners and, as such, more difficult to teach. Research over the past several years has demonstrated the necessity of preserving meaning in curriculum. Therefore, teachers should consider carefully the role of meaningfulness of the curriculum when applying table of specifications objectives. For example, when particular phonics rules are taught, learners always should be aware of the purpose of learning these rules. In addition, they should apply them to words and the meanings of those words as soon as possible. Likewise, when early math skills or facts are taught, students should be aware of the purpose of the instruction and begin to apply this new learning in meaningful, problem-solving contexts as soon as possible. Finally, teachers should integrate learning across traditional discipline areas as application and generalization objectives. For instance, reading and language arts should employ similar materials whenever possible. Students can, for example, write stories from books they have read or employ their math skills on vocational tasks. Overall, the most effective instruction uses careful task analysis techniques without sacrificing the meaningfulness of the learning tasks.

Summary

- Instructional design encompasses all of the important teaching variables. Appropriate instructional design is based on long- and short-term objectives and incorporates both levels (identification/production, accuracy, fluency, application, and generalization) and types (discrimination, fact, rule, concept, procedural) of learning as well as teacher effectiveness variables.

- An effectively designed instructional sequence includes goals and objectives, appropriate instructional methods and materials, and effective procedures for evaluating the success of instruction.

- A table of specifications subdivides content along the lines of levels of learning and the content to be taught and provides an optimal sequence of instruction. Tables of specifications are helpful as a model for conceptualizing what will be taught and the sequence in which it will be taught.

- Formative evaluation can be used to demonstrate progress toward long-term goals and objectives, and analysis of instructional variables can inform instructional decision making when the rate of progress does not seem adequate.

- When using task analysis to break down and sequence elements of instruction, it is important that the overall purpose and meaning of the learning is not lost. Use real, meaningful examples whenever possible, and teach for application and generalization objectives.

Relevant Research and Resources

Research

Much of Chapter 2 is concerned with establishing a model for instructional design. This model is based on previously applied and validated models of instructional design. One of the classic and most widely used texts on instructional objectives is that of Mager (1962). The model of discriminating levels of learning is based generally on the model provided by Haring, Lovitt, Hansen, and Eaton (1978). A review of research on types of learning is provided by Scruggs (1988) and Scruggs and Mastropieri (1984a). Much of the research that validates the application of this model is described at the end of Chapter 1. Problems in generalization of learned behavior and strategies for facilitating generalization outcomes are described by Scruggs and Mastropieri (1984c, 1994c) and Stokes and Baer (1977). Information on tables of specifications is provided by Bloom et al. (1971) and Howell and Kaplan (1980). Some new versions of tables of specifications and discussion of teacher decision making are presented by Howell and Davidson (1997). Information on instructional design is provided by Gagne (1965, 1970) and Gagne and Briggs (1974). Texts on curriculum-based assessment include Howell and Davidson (1997) and Salvia and Hughes (1990). Smith (1990a, 1990b) has described uses and issues associated with IEPs. Majsterek, Wilson, and Mandlebaum (1990) provide guidelines for evaluating IEP software.

Computer Software and Technology

Software that may be helpful in generating student IEPs is available from LinguiSystems (IEP Companion Software and LD Teacher's IEP Companion Software) and from EBSCO Curriculum Materials (1990). Curriculum Associates publishes Goals and Objectives Writer Software for creating, editing, and printing IEPs. Teacher Time Savers (Visions, distributed by Learning Services) can be used for organizing and planning instructional activities. See Appendix B for a list of addresses of producers and distributors of software and curricular materials.

Universal Design

Universal design is a concept that applies an approach of designing materials with the goals of access and use by all individuals. As such, universal design embraces an inclusive approach to the design of curriculum materials. An architectural example of a universal design is the design of "curb cuts" or the cuts made in sidewalk curbs to allow wheelchairs accessibility. However, curb cuts also enhance the use of sidewalks for all of us, including those on bicycles, pulling carts, pushing baby carriages, and even walkers and joggers. In other words, the universal design enhances accessibility for all, without stigmatizing any individual group. Universal design features may include the following (see Orkwis & McLane, 1998, for additional details):

- Multiple ways of presenting information so the content can be seen or heard in a variety of formats
  Digital text offers a variety of alternative formats, including changing the font size and color and background color or transforming written text into spoken text.

- Multiple ways for accommodating student expression so students have options for demonstrating their knowledge
  Reduce motor barriers by allowing alternatives such as writing, speaking, drawing, and illustrating.

- Multiple ways of engaging students in class activities to ensure all students participate
  Think along the continuums of novelty-familiarity and supporting-challenging.

For additional resources on applying universal design to curriculum materials contact the following:

- Center for Applied Special Technology (CAST; www.cast.org)
- Adaptive Environments Center (www.adaptenv.org)
- Center for Design and Business (www.centerdesignbusiness.org)
- Center for Universal Design (www.design.ncsu.edu/cud)

TECHNOLOGY FEATURE

Individualized Education Program (IEP) Software

Because all students with disabilities have Individualized Education Programs (IEPs), it is necessary to become familiar with your school district's particular IEP forms. Many districts have forms available electronically or as templates in word-processing programs. Templates of forms repeatedly used save valuable time. If templates are unavailable, it may be worthwhile to construct some. It may also be worthwhile to examine commercially available IEP software programs to determine whether any of these programs contain features that could assist you in maintaining records of student progress. As with any software program, there are usually features that prove valuable to you and features that seem cumbersome. The *Journal of Special Education Technology* contains some excellent reviews of various IEP software that are available commercially. After comparing and contrasting features of programs, an informed decision can be made as to the value of such a program in meeting specific needs. Some available programs include the following:

- *The IEP Planner* is available from Rodan Associates.
- *Talley Goals and Objectives Writer* is available form Curriculum Associates.
- *Brigance CIBS* contains a database of goals and objectives and is available from Curriculum Associates.

Chapter 3

᠀᠀᠀   ᠀᠀᠀   ᠀᠀᠀

Monitoring Student Progress

All effective instruction is based on instructional decision making informed by evaluation. Evaluation, which includes both *summative* and *formative* evaluation, is a critical component of effective instruction. Summative evaluation is typically given only once or twice during a school year, whereas formative evaluation is given frequently throughout the year, and instructional decisions are made on the basis of these measures. Another important distinction is between *norm-referenced* and *criterion-referenced* measures (see Table 3.1). Norm-referenced tests compare student scores to those of other students, whereas criterion-referenced tests compare student scores to a performance criterion.

A variety of procedures for collecting information for both types of tests also has been developed. These procedures include development of permanent products, such as *probes* and paper-and-pencil tasks, and recording of behavior through procedures that include direct observation, continuous recording, time sampling, and duration and event recording. A probe is a relatively short test, such as 20 multiplication problems, or a 1-minute timed reading. Once completed by students, the written result can be considered a permanent product. Permanent products can be collected, saved in a portfolio, and referred to over time. Record-keeping techniques can be used to successfully monitor student progress and inform instructional decision making. Such techniques include a variety of tables and graphic displays. Each of these evaluation procedures is presented in this chapter.

Reliability and Validity

To be valuable, all tests must possess *reliability* and *validity*. Reliability refers to the consistency or dependability of a test across time or across

Table 3.1. Features of Norm-Referenced and Criterion-Referenced Tests

Features	Norm-Referenced Tests	Criterion-Referenced Tests
Compares	Observed behavior to behavior of others.	Behavior to an existing standard (criterion).
Form of information	Percentiles and grade equivalents.	Proportions of standards mastered.
Common uses	Helpful for classifying and labeling students.	Helpful for designing and delivering instruction.
	Can be used to help evaluate educational programs.	Can be used to help evaluate specific educational treatments.
Limitations	Must be reliable and valid.	Must be reliable and valid.
Frequency of usage	Commonly administered once or twice a year.	Commonly administered frequently throughout the year.

items, and validity refers to the extent a test measures what it is intended to measure. Reliability is assessed by *test–retest* or *internal consistency* methods. Test–retest reliability describes whether a test provides similar results over a 2- or 3-week period. Test scores should be stable over relatively short periods of time, or the test is not very reliable. Reliability would be considered very low, for example, if the same achievement test were administered 2 weeks apart and yielded dramatically different results (e.g., 30th percentile scores and 90th percentile scores for the first and second test administrations, respectively).

Internal consistency describes whether all test items are measuring the same "construct," such as personality, intelligence, or reading achievement. In determining internal consistency, statistical procedures are used to determine whether, for example, all of the odd-numbered items are highly related to all of the even-numbered items. For example, if students scored at the eighth-grade level on the odd-numbered items and at the second-grade level on the even-numbered items on a test, that test would have low internal consistency. The teacher can determine the reliability of norm-referenced tests by examining the tests' technical manuals. Acceptable total-test reliability coefficients (scores) should be in the .80s and .90s (subtest reliability scores are sometimes lower). When scores are lower than that, tests should be viewed as suspect.

Validity helps to determine whether tests are measuring what they purport or intend to measure. Validity, for example, refers to whether tests are actually measuring constructs such as intelligence or reading achievement. Validity is typically determined by assessing performance on one test with performance on a highly related test. If both tests are considered valid, scores obtained on both tests will be comparable. For example, suppose that two reading comprehension tests are available. If both tests have high validity (both are true measures of reading comprehension), students' performance on both tests should be very similar. Again, test validity coefficients should be available in the technical manuals that accompany tests. Both high reliability and validity are necessary prerequisites for tests to be considered adequate for use (for other methods of assessing reliability and validity, see Overton, 1996; Salvia & Ysseldyke, 1998). It is important to examine the reliability and validity coefficients of a test prior to its use and to be certain that placement and instructional decisions are made on the basis of tests with adequate reliability and validity.

Norm-Referenced Tests

Norm-referenced tests are tests that have been given to a large, representative sample of students. Because all students took the test under the same conditions (e.g., the same directions, materials, time limits), the test is referred to as *standardized* (other types of tests can also be standardized). The scores of individual students are then compared with the scores of this larger normative sample, and the results are interpreted on a comparative basis. In other words, if a student scored higher than 90% of the students of the same age in the standardization sample, we can say the student scored at the 90th percentile. If a student achieved a score that is typical of fourth graders in the standardization sample, we can say the student scored at the fourth-grade level. Intelligence tests, personality tests, achievement tests, and competency tests are typically norm-referenced tests. Such tests provide valuable information on an individual student's performance as it compares with the performance of the general populations. These test results allow educators to make judgments concerning how well their student, classroom, school, or state is doing in relation to other students, classrooms, schools, and states. The results can be used to assist in making policy decisions, such as the type of curricular materials or the type of inservice teacher training programs that could be implemented.

Norm-referenced tests have been used mostly as summative evaluation measures. In other words, norm-referenced tests are usually administered only at the beginning or the end of the school year. When used in such a manner, the results summarize students' performance up to a certain point rather than assist in guiding effective instruction throughout the school year. However, as will be discussed later, any test can be normed (even criterion-referenced tests); therefore, it is incorrect to assume that all norm-referenced tests are summative tests.

Criterion-Referenced Tests

Criterion-referenced tests are tests that assess performance in relation to a particular criterion or curriculum. Criterion-referenced tests typically correspond to a particular set of skills or a specific curriculum. Therefore, a score on this type of test specifies how much of the curriculum or skill has been mastered, regardless of how well all the other students have performed. These types of tests can provide teachers with information on how well students have mastered the content covered to date, how rapidly content is being covered and mastered, how many students have mastered the objectives to date, and which students have not mastered which objectives. Many of the "high-stakes" tests that have been implemented in most states in recent years are criterion-referenced tests, in that a particular criterion (e.g., 70%) is set for acceptable scoring, even though many are based on standardized norm-referenced tests (Frase-Blunt, 2000).

Criterion-referenced tests can be administered on a formative basis (regularly or continuously), rather than on a yearly or summative basis. If criterion-referenced tests are designed to correspond with a specific curriculum, they are referred to as *curriculum-based* tests. Sometimes these tests are used as placement tests at the beginning of the school term or year. In other words, teachers can administer a curriculum-based U.S. history pretest to determine where in

the U.S. history curriculum they should begin to introduce new content. For example, if all students have previously learned and mastered the content of the discovery of America and pre–Revolutionary War units but not the Revolutionary War unit, instruction may not need to address the first two issues and can begin at the Revolutionary War unit. Such curriculum-based tests can be used to monitor students' progress throughout instruction and guide instructional practices throughout the year. For example, suppose a series of tests that correspond to the entire U.S. history curriculum had been developed. Assume that the items on these tests directly assess all content that is considered necessary to know on completion of the U.S. history course. Then, as content was introduced and covered, formative tests could be administered to determine students' progress in mastering that particular content. In addition, as mentioned in previous chapters, teachers could keep systematic records of their own teaching performance during these lessons, such as engaged time-on-task, types of guided and independent practice activities, and types of questioning and feedback activities. Results on the formatively administered curriculum-based tests can provide teachers with information on student progress and teaching effectiveness, and effective instructional decisions can be made based on actual data (records or performance).

Many special educators have suggested that most evaluation should be curriculum based (Deno, 1986; Fuchs & Fuchs, 1986a, 1986b; Fuchs, Fuchs, Hamlett, Phillips, & Bentz, 1994). It makes sense to link the scope and sequence of the objectives in specific content areas with curriculum-based tests. Some school districts have developed curriculum-based tests to match their curriculum areas. Such tests can assist teachers not only in linking their instruction to curriculum but also in guiding the instructional decision-making process.

Curriculum-based measurement (CBM) also should have good reliability and validity and have standardized administration procedures. In other words, CBM should reveal similar scores for students across brief time intervals (gains in learning notwithstanding), and CBM scores should be related to other measures of achievement in the same subject area. Although CBM scores are not always normed, it is possible to collect data recording how students typically perform throughout the year. It would be very useful for teachers to know, for example, that seventh-grade students have mastered half of the necessary objectives in an entire content area and that most seventh graders typically reach that point in mastery of the curriculum at about the midpoint of the school year.

Curriculum-based tests can also be designed to match IEP objectives and can then be used to designate when those objectives have been met. Ideally, IEP objectives will correspond closely to general education objectives and will, therefore, help ensure students' access to the general education curriculum.

Curriculum-based measurement can be devised for virtually any curriculum area, ranging from reading and writing to vocational skill areas to the social skills area. The first consideration in developing a series of curriculum-based tests is to define precisely the curriculum in terms of specific behavioral objectives and into a scope and sequence (or order in which the objectives should be met). Once this is completed, individual tests are designed to match each objective or series of objectives. Because objectives already specify the expected behavior, the conditions under which the behavior should be performed, and the performance criteria, designing a test is simply a matter of generating a pool of items that test each objective. It is critical that the behavior, conditions, and performance criteria in the objective match those of the test items. In other words, if the objective specifies production behavior at the fluency level of learning, then test items for this objective must also require production behavior at the fluency level of learning. If application or generalization behavior is specified in the objective, then test items also need to assess application or generalization.

Constructing a Curriculum-Based Measure

The first step in constructing a curriculum-based assessment is to select a target curriculum area. It is generally a good idea to begin with a content area that most of the students take. Typically, special educators select reading first; however, any content area is suitable. For the remainder of this discussion, assume that a reading series such as *Reading Mastery* (Engelmann & Bruner, 1995) has been selected.

The second step involves the random selection of reading passages from the targeted reading series. Any passage can be chosen if it contains typical reading material. It is generally wise to avoid selecting passages that contain an overabundance of dialogue or atypical material such as poems. Each passage should contain at least 100 words, although at some of the lower reading levels, such as the primer and preprimer levels, it may be necessary to use shorter passages.

If the purpose of designing curriculum-based measures includes both placement and monitoring progress, a minimum of 10 passages should be selected from the beginning third of a level, 10 from the middle third of a level, and 10 from the final third of a level. If teachers find that their long-term goals for most of their students consistently fall within a particular third of a level, it is recommended that two or three times as many passages be selected from that portion of the text. At present, there is no standard for a precise number of passages, but it is important that an adequate number be selected so that a sufficient number of different, randomly selected measures can be administered while progress is being monitored.

Once the passages have been chosen, two copies of each passage should be made and each copy labeled. A good labeling system includes a symbol representing the curriculum series (e.g., RM if Reading Mastery were selected), a symbol representing the level of the text, a symbol identifying the particular section of the level (e.g., B for beginning third, M for middle third, and

F for final third), and a number representing the ordinal relation of the passage within a particular level for each test (1, 2, 3, etc.). If the labeling system is implemented at the beginning, time and effort are saved later.

Mark off each labeled 100-word passage with slash marks (/). If the 100-word passage ends in the middle of a sentence, place a bracket ( ]) at the end of that sentence. Recall that two photocopies of each passage were made. One copy will be the teacher's copy; the other will be the student's copy. Some teachers like to count the number of words per line for each passage and write that number along the left side of the passage on the teacher's copy. As will be discussed later, this may or may not be necessary.

Some educators consider the process of test construction for reading to be complete at this time; however, other educators have emphasized that each passage should also include approximately five comprehension and recall items. It has been recommended that the comprehension items include the following:

1. Three factual or literal recall items. (Factual recall items require students to answer with information that is explicitly stated in the passage, e.g., "What is the name of Anna's store?")

2. One sequential factual item. (Sequential factual items require students to respond with information that is explicitly stated but also requires thinking about the order of the events in the passage, e.g., "What was the first thing Gilbert did after he took the fish?")

3. One inferential recall item. (Inferential items require students to respond with information that is not stated explicitly but rather is implied or implicit within the text, e.g., "How do you think Carlos felt when he heard the whistle blow?")

Specific examples of how to construct these types of questions are discussed in Chapter 5. However, if comprehension items are desired, both the questions and appropriate responses should be written on the teacher's copy of the tests. These types of questions can provide information on students' recall.

Administering a Curriculum-Based Measure

If the curriculum-based test is being used for initial placement, randomly select a passage from the third of the text level in which the student is expected to function well. If, however, the test is being used to monitor student progress, randomly select a passage from the section of the text that contains the long-term objective for that student (e.g., the last part of the text). Then, place the student's copy in front of the student and place the teacher's copy in front of the teacher. (Acetate can be placed over the teacher's copy so tests can be reused.) Say to the student, "When I say 'go,' begin reading aloud at the top of this page. [Point] Try to read each word all the way down to this slash mark. [Point] Ready? Go." Begin timing the student with a stopwatch. Make a slash mark at the end of 1 minute, stop timing, and record the total amount of time in seconds taken to read the 100-word selection. During the reading, circle any decoding errors that the student makes. If comprehension questions accompany the passage, teachers should now verbally ask students to answer each item. Responses can be recorded as correct or incorrect.

Scoring a Curriculum-Based Measure

If a student reads a 100-word selection for time, you can compute the number of words read correctly (reading accuracy) per minute. Suppose a particular student read 90 of 100 words correctly in 95 seconds. To compute the student's reading accuracy rate per minute, first determine accuracy by taking the total number of words read correctly (90) and dividing that number by the number of seconds (in this case, 90/95 = .95 words per second). Second, determine reading accuracy per minute by multiplying the accuracy percentage by 60 seconds (.95 words per second × 60 seconds = 57 correct words per minute). The number or errors per minute is the number of errors divided by the number of seconds, multiplied by 60 (in the present case, 10/95 = .105, × 60 = 6.3 errors per minute).

If, on the other hand, you stop the student after 1 minute, you simply count the number of words read correctly within that 1 minute. For example, if a student reads 88 words correctly, with 12 errors, in 1 minute, the student reads 88 words correctly per minute and makes 12 errors per minute on that level passage. Advantages of this procedure are that the student is required to read for only 1 minute, and the teacher does not have to perform as many calculations to determine the accuracy rate per minute. One disadvantage, however, is that a 1-minute reading may not be appropriate from some readers or some reading passages.

After either procedure, graph the student's performance. Teachers are better able to observe students' performance and progress over time when the data are displayed on a graph or chart, such as the one presented in Figure 3.1. To monitor progress effectively, teachers should administer one of these curriculum-based tests once or twice a week. Recall that it was recommended that the tests be randomly selected from the long-term goal level of the text. For instance, the long-term goal may be that the student read a selection from the final part of the text at a rate of 150 words per minute and 95% accuracy. This can be indicated on the chart at the appropriate date. As the student progresses, the teacher can determine whether the student is likely to meet the long-term goal at the present rate of learning. If the learning progress does not seem to be adequate, the teacher can then make instructional decisions based on the effective instruction variables to increase learning growth.

In many instances, students can be taught to graph their own performance data. This not only

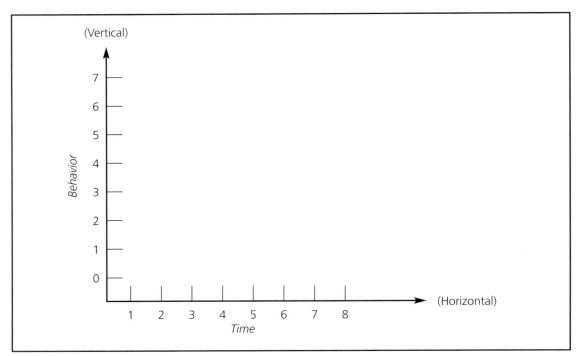

Figure 3.1. Typical layout of a chart reporting behavioral data.

saves teachers time but also helps students become aware of their own progress toward long-term goals.

When initial placement in the curriculum series is the major purpose of assessment, teachers should assess student performance at several different levels over time. Although there is no absolute criterion for placement in the reading curriculum, and many special cases exist, it is often useful to select an instructional level of at least 80 words per minute and about 90% accuracy (see also Chapter 5).

Similar procedures can be established for all curricular domains. In some school districts, educators have worked cooperatively to develop measures for specific content areas.

Little research currently exists to document the optimal length of curriculum-based tests. Many educators advocate short, frequent tests rather than longer, infrequent tests. The main advantage of short, frequent tests is better knowledge of daily to weekly student performance and progress, which, in turn, may help keep students and teachers on top of their performance. More specific information regarding the design of formative tests and associated decision-making rules and error analysis procedures is presented in each content area chapter.

Portfolio and Performance Assessment

Portfolio and performance-based assessment are each highly relevant to curriculum-based assessment. Student portfolios include permanent products from the student's work throughout the school year, including audiotapes of oral reading, samples of written work, samples of laboratory booklets and notes, summaries of student performance, copies of summative exams, teacher observations, and videotapes of student presentations or demonstrations. All these products should be evaluated with respect to some predetermined standard (performance criteria) so that progress throughout the school year can be documented and instruction can be modified if satisfactory progress is not being made.

For example, a student's handwriting portfolio may include samples of handwriting, written under formal and informal conditions and collected over time. These can be compared with a sample of handwriting that represents the student's long-term goal, and decisions can be made regarding the rate of progress in, for example, letter formation, alignment, and spacing. A reading portfolio could contain records of progress from curriculum-based measurement. But it could also include dated tape recordings of the student's oral reading (e.g., to evaluate progress in inflection or intonation); a log of books the student has read throughout the year, along with student reviews; and a checklist of reading skills the student has mastered. Through such means, teachers can gain greater insights into the entire reading process (see Wesson & King, 1996).

Portfolios can also address student social behavior. For example, in addition to charts of progress on social behaviors described later in this chapter, teachers could also include videotapes of the student during cooperative group activities, a log of disciplinary referrals, a description of the student's after-school activities, records of interviews with the student, and observations of the student's performance in the cafeteria. Portfolios such as these can provide different types of useful information in a variety of contexts.

Performance assessment refers to assessment of student performance with respect to a specific (usually "hands-on") curriculum. Performance assessment is particularly appropriate for hands-on science, math, social studies, or vocational curricula. In a performance assessment, students demonstrate what they have learned using "real" materials, rather than paper and pencil. They can, for example, complete electrical circuits in science, solve math problems using base 10 blocks, construct a model of an urban center, or solve a problem using drafting materials.

Performance assessment can be particularly useful in special education settings, where many students have difficulties with paper-and-pencil tasks and also may exhibit problems with test-taking skills (see Chapter 9) used on traditional tests. Performance assessment allows students to exhibit their acquired skills (on the application or generalization level) without overemphasis on language or literacy skills when these are not primarily being tested. For example, instead of describing the difference between series and parallel electrical circuits, students could be given the appropriate materials and asked to construct series and parallel circuits. As with portfolio assessment, teachers must evaluate performance assessment results with respect to specific performance criteria.

Procedures for Collecting Formative Data

Much data (information) collected in classroom situations are referred to as behavioral data, meaning observable activity that the student engages in. Generally, such data are collected one of two ways, which are described in this section. One way of collecting data is by direct observation of student behaviors. Another way involves the scoring of permanent products—such things as completed worksheets, written products, and recorded student responses.

Direct Observation

Direct observation procedures are generally employed for behaviors that are easily observed in classroom situations and for which there is no written product. However, for such observations to be accurate and systematic, it is important for the target behavior to be precisely defined, or *operationalized*, prior to observation. After a target behavior is operationalized, teachers select one of several procedures appropriate for observing and recording these behaviors.

Operationalizing Behavior

If a target behavior is not described precisely enough, it may not be recorded accurately. For instance, on-task behavior might be defined differently by different people, which could result in different operational descriptions. *On task* can be defined as "students visually or manually engaged with classroom materials." Such a description effectively operationalizes the behavior so that it can be observed and recorded accurately. Although different observers might define *on task* differently, the above definition describes *on task* in such a way that different individuals could record the occurrence of the behavior similarly.

Different definitions of *on task* may exist, however, depending on the characteristics of the task and the expectations placed on the student. For instance, during a handwriting activity, it may be appropriate for students' eyes and hands to be in contact with writing materials at all times (except to ask relevant questions or attend to teacher feedback). During a writing composition activity, however, students may need to reflect on their writing without being physically in contact with writing materials. Any operationalization of this type of on-task behavior needs to reflect the specific task demands. Furthermore, some students may have enough initial difficulty staying on task to make a less restrictive definition necessary at first. Such an operationalization could be "hands, feet, and eyes directed away from other students and all verbalization directly relevant to the task." In all cases, it is important for teachers to specify precisely the nature of the behavior to be observed. Additional examples of operational definitions are provided in Table 3.2. Teachers know that the behavior has been effectively operationalized when two different observers, or raters, independently record the same behavior of the same student. This is known as *interrater reliability*.

Recording Procedures

Once behavior has been operationalized, it cannot be recorded until an appropriate recording

Table 3.2. Operational Definitions

Behavior	Sample Operational Definition*
Talking out	Student speaks to another student, the class in general, or the teacher without being called upon.
On task	Student's eyes engaged on teacher or task. Manual engagement with classroom materials and writing utensils when appropriate.
Teasing	Student verbally referring to another student in a derogatory manner; inappropriate and unsolicited physical contact with another student.
Verbal courtesy	Student says "please" upon making a request and "thank you" upon receiving a favorable response to a request.
Arguing	Student questions a teacher's direction or judgement with expressions such as "Why?", "For what?", "No, I didn't," and "So?"
Good sitting	Student in seat with feet flat on the floor in front of desk and sitting up straight with body centered with respect to the desk and arms on desktop.
Daydreaming	Student's eyes looking away from academic task and not directly focused on any classroom object or person; no normal engagement with academic task.
Positive social interaction	Verbal exchange in which student comments favorably on another student or positively describes a shared experience, and in which student's comments receive favorable verbal response.

*Other definitions are also possible.

procedure has been chosen. These procedures include (a) continuous records, (b) duration recording, (c) interval recording, and (d) time sampling. Examples of these procedures are in Table 3.3.

Continuous Records

Sometimes teachers wish to have a record of all behavior that a student exhibits during a specific period. For instance, a teacher may know that a certain student often has problems getting along with other students during recess periods but does not know specifically what is happening during these periods that is related to the problem. Such descriptive records of all student behavior are called *continuous records*.

When teachers take continuous records, they record all observed behavior exhibited by a specific student during a specific time period. All behaviors recorded are also described with respect to the time the behavior occurred. A con-

tinuous record may be written somewhat like the following:

10:09 a.m.	Student takes one worksheet, passes remaining worksheets to student seated in back.
10:10 a.m.	Student takes pencil from desk and begins writing on worksheet.
10:12 a.m.	Student looks around the classroom, makes a face at another student (who does not respond), returns to work.
10:15 a.m.	Student opens desk and manipulates objects in desk.
10:17 a.m.	Upon prompt from teacher, student returns to work.
10:20 a.m.	Student still working.
10:21 a.m.	Student begins kicking the desk in front of student. Student in front whispers, "Stop it."
10:22 a.m.	Student replies, "What?" and returns to work.

Table 3.3. Sample Recording Procedures

Recording Procedure	Circumstances	Examples
Event	Behaviors are discrete.	Swearing
	Behaviors last similar amounts of time.	Homework assignments completed
	Knowledge of total frequency is desired.	Tardy to class
		Says "please"
Duration	Behaviors vary in length.	Out of seat
	Knowledge of total time is desired.	Off task
	An observer's total attention is available.	Minutes in transition
		Time in restroom
		Tantruming
Interval	Behaviors may vary in length.	Sitting quietly
	Total duration is not as important as estimate of percent of total time.	On task
		Appropriate social interaction
Time Sampling	Total duration is not as important as estimate of percent of total time.	On task
		Time spent in various activities
	Several students are observed at one time.	In seat
	Behaviors vary in length.	Cooperative play

Such a record can be helpful when detailed knowledge of student behavior is desired. Continuous records can also be helpful in certain circumstances to demonstrate that IEP objectives have been met. For example, suppose a student had the following IEP objective: "Student will ignore inappropriate teasing by others 90% of the time." Continuous records could help indicate when teasing occurred and exactly how the student responded.

One difficulty with continuous recording, as with many of the observation procedures described in this chapter, is that it demands the undivided attention of the observer. If the teacher is also the observer, the observation process can detract from other equally important classroom activities. However, some procedures for making the observation process less demanding of teachers' time include the use of peers, classroom aides, volunteers, other teachers, or school personnel in the collection of observational data. If such observers are used, however, they need to understand exactly how the behavior is operationalized and how it is to be recorded. Another way of making observations more efficient is by using videotape recording equipment. Not only can behavior be observed and recorded at a later date, but target students can be shown their own behavior on tape. If the behavior is largely oral, such as talking out of turn, the behavior could be recorded on audiotape for later entry into a continuous record.

Continuous records can be helpful when teachers want more information regarding a range of student behaviors. The procedures that follow are appropriate when teachers want detailed information on specific, operationalized behaviors.

Frequency Recording

Sometimes it is important to know the number of times a particular behavior is occurring. For instance, teachers may want information regarding the number of times specific students speak without raising their hands. To record this type of behavior, teachers can simply tally the number of occurrences of talking out of turn. If the time of observation is not the same each day, the behavior must be divided by the amount of time in the observation. For example, if students "talked out" 10 times in 1 hour on a given day and 15 times in 2 hours the following day, their rate of talking out decreased the second day (10 times per hour versus 7.5 times per hour). On the other hand, if the amount of observation time remains constant, no calculations are necessary.

Other behaviors that may lend themselves to this type of *frequency recording* include questions, trips to the bathroom, homework assignments completed, temper tantrums, socially appropriate verbalizations, or occasions that students are out-of-seat. It is important to note that frequency recording provides no information regarding the level of intensity of the behavior or the length of time the behavior was exhibited (e.g., in the case of temper tantrums). For instance, in counting the frequency of out-of-seat behaviors, it is important that such behaviors are generally about the same duration (length of time), such as the amount of time to get a drink or sharpen a pencil. For frequency recording to accurately represent target behaviors, the behaviors being tallied must all be highly similar. For example, out-of-seat behavior may occur for 30 seconds during one event and 30 minutes during the next. If this problem occurs, some other recording procedure may be more efficient.

Duration Recording

Duration recording is used when teachers are interested in the length of time over which a behavior occurs. For instance, teachers may not be interested simply in whether a student was out-

of-seat but also in the total length of time a student was out-of-seat. To conduct duration recording, the targeted behavior is operationalized (e.g., out-of-seat is defined as the seat of the student's pants not being in direct contact with the seat of the desk), and the teacher measures the amount of out-of-seat time exhibited using a stopwatch or other timing device. Such a procedure can be effective when the frequency of events is less important than the total time of occurrence of the behavior. The use of duration recording is appropriate when teachers would rather know how much time the student was out-of-seat than know how many times the student was out-of-seat. Other classroom behaviors that may be suitable for duration recording are minutes tardy, minutes off task, and minutes engaged socializing with peers.

Interval Recording

Some teachers or other personnel may wish to record the behavior of several students at one time. This type of recording can be very difficult if event or duration procedures are used. One alternative is the use of *interval recording*. To use interval recording, the teacher must first operationalize the behavior to be observed. For instance, *kicking* could be operationalized as "student's foot striking the forward desk, delivered with sufficient force to register sound at a radius of 20 feet." (Other operational definitions of *kicking* are, of course, possible.) The observer then sets an interval for which the occurrence or nonoccurrence of the behavior is to be recorded. As an example, suppose the interval is 15 seconds. Using a clock or stopwatch, the observer records whether the behavior (in this case, kicking) occurs during the interval. This occurrence or nonoccurrence is then recorded on a recording sheet that was developed prior to the observation session (see Figure 3.2). During interval recording, the total number of occurrences is not noted as it is in event recording. Only the fact that the behavior has occurred at all during the interval is noted. If the behavior does not occur,

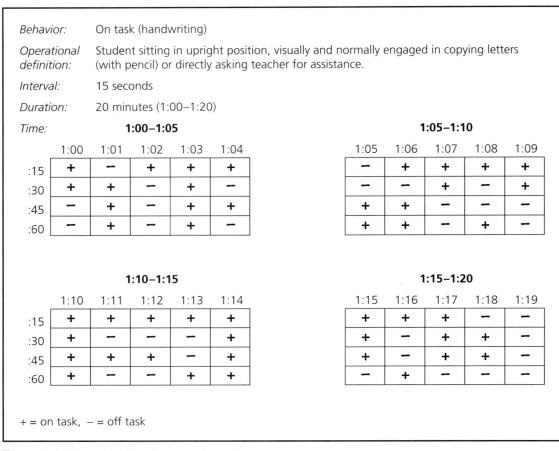

Behavior: On task (handwriting)

Operational definition: Student sitting in upright position, visually and normally engaged in copying letters (with pencil) or directly asking teacher for assistance.

Interval: 15 seconds

Duration: 20 minutes (1:00–1:20)

Time: **1:00–1:05**

	1:00	1:01	1:02	1:03	1:04
:15	+	−	+	+	+
:30	+	+	−	+	−
:45	−	+	−	+	+
:60	−	+	−	+	−

1:05–1:10

	1:05	1:06	1:07	1:08	1:09
:15	−	+	+	+	+
:30	−	−	+	−	+
:45	+	+	−	−	−
:60	+	+	−	+	−

1:10–1:15

	1:10	1:11	1:12	1:13	1:14
:15	+	+	+	+	+
:30	+	−	−	−	+
:45	+	+	+	−	+
:60	+	−	−	+	+

1:15–1:20

	1:15	1:16	1:17	1:18	1:19
:15	+	+	+	−	−
:30	+	−	+	+	−
:45	+	−	+	+	−
:60	−	+	−	−	−

+ = on task, − = off task

Figure 3.2. Recording sheet for interval recording.

the observer records a zero or another figure denoting nonoccurrence and moves on to the next interval, but this is a cumbersome procedure because it requires the observer to observe both the student and the clock. Another possibiltiy is to tape-record a series of quiet beeps or clicks at the end of each interval. With headphones, the observer can hear these beeps and know when each interval has ended.

Interval recording can be helpful when the behaviors being observed are variable in duration. For example, *talking out* could be operationalized as "any verbalization directed toward another student without explicit permission from the teacher." Such talking-out behavior could conceivably occur either as a simple exclamation or an extended discussion. Using interval recording procedures, the observer simply records whether the behavior has occurred during each interval. Occurrence of the behavior across several intervals may suggest extended conversation, whereas separate, distinct occurrences are recorded in separate intervals.

Interval data are generally summarized as percent data. For example, if 240 intervals of 15 seconds are recorded (i.e., a 60-minute sample), and the student exhibited talking-out behavior during 90 intervals, the corresponding score could be summarized as 37.5% (90/240) of total intervals. Generally, the reliability of such observations is computed as interobserver reliability. In the case of interval recording, two observers would independently observe the same behavior in the same student at the same time. If the behavior has been well operationalized and the observations are accurate, the two observers should agree on most observations. Usually, such agreement is recorded as the following:

$$\frac{\text{Number of agreements}}{\substack{\text{Total number of observations} \\ \text{(Agreements and disagreements)}}}$$

The resulting proportion is then expressed as a percentage. For instance, in the above example, if two observers agreed on 220 of the 240 items but disagreed on 20 items, the corresponding interrater reliability could be computed as

$$\frac{220}{220 + 20} = \frac{220}{240} = 91.7\%.$$

Generally, reliability over 90% is considered acceptable, but attempts should be made to resolve any inconsistencies or disagreements in observations. In some cases, however, reliability figures can be misleading. For example, what if the 20 disagreements described previously represented the only instances of occurrence of the behavior—that is, if the student was only off task during 20 of 240 intervals, and these were the same 20 for which there was no agreement? The observation obviously was not reliable (i.e., observers never agreed on occurrences), and yet the reliability coefficient would be relatively high. In such cases, it may be important to compute reliability of observation of occurrences separately, particularly if the behavior occurs only rarely.

As stated earlier, one advantage of interval recording is that several students can be observed at one time. If three students are being observed, for example, observers may first direct their attention primarily to the student who is most likely to exhibit the target behavior. Once this behavior has been exhibited, the student need not be observed for the remainder of the interval, and the observer can focus entirely on the other two students for the remainder of the interval. With interval recording, it is also possible to record several different behaviors for one student. For instance, intervals could be scored as on task (+), off-task verbal (−v), off-task motor (−m), or off-task daydreaming (−d). This type of recording can determine more precisely what students are doing when they are off task.

Time Sampling

The last recording procedure discussed here is *time sampling*. Like interval recording, this procedure provides only an estimate (sample) of relevant behavior. However, in most cases, time-sampling procedures can provide reliable and accurate information.

Like interval-recording procedures, time sampling involves setting time intervals that can be noted with clocks, stopwatches, or tape-recorded sounds. Unlike interval recording, however, observed behavior is recorded only at the instance of the time sample. For instance, if out-of-seat behavior is observed using a time-sampling procedure with samples taken at the end of every 1-minute period, only the behavior observed at the instance the second hand (or beep) registers the 1-minute mark is recorded. Although less behavior is directly observed this way, it is possible to record many different students at one time. With longer sampling periods, it is possible to assess an entire classroom at a time. For example, to give themselves a better idea of how students are spending their time, teachers could record what activities different students are engaged in at the end of every 10th minute during a free-time activity.

Time-sampling procedures make use of recording sheets similar to those used in interval recording. Data are also usually summarized as percentages of "times sampled." Reliability is also computed using generally the same procedures as interval recording. Although time-sampling procedures typically involve observing and recording of a smaller sample of behavior per student, many teachers find this method very practical for routine classroom use.

Summary of Observational Recording Procedures

Continuous records; event, duration, and interval recording; and time-sampling procedures are all used to gain an objective measure of student behavior. Objective evidence is often more useful to teachers than subjective impressions of a student's personality or attitude. For instance, it may be more valuable for teachers to know that a student was off task for 40% of a math period than to hear someone's perception that the student has a "bad attitude" or suffers from "math anxiety." Off-task information, if appropriately combined with other relevant behavioral information, can lead teachers directly to making appropriate interventions to change such behavior. For instance, if off-task data were combined with information that the student was performing at a very low level of accuracy on math problems, such information could lead teachers to believe that the difficulty level of the problems was not appropriate. On the other hand, unconfirmed subjective pronouncements about the student's attitude may not be reliable or valid and may be of little use in planning interventions.

In addition to the accuracy of recorded information, it is important to remember that students often behave differently when they know they are being observed. Particularly at first, observers must be unobtrusive so that students are not aware that they are being directly observed. If observation becomes more a part of normal classroom routine, however, students are likely to take less and less notice of these procedures.

Finally, it should be noted that observational procedures are only helpful if they directly reflect classroom objectives and are specifically relevant to IEP objectives. For instance, if a student's IEP objectives state that a student will "be out-of-seat no more than four times during the day at prespecified periods, and with teacher approval," observational recording is necessary to demonstrate whether the student has met or is making progress toward meeting the objective.

On many occasions, a teacher's judgment can accurately reflect student behavior. On other occasions, however, a teacher's perception may not be accurate. In special education (or regular education), some students exhibit behaviors that teachers regard as annoying or offensive. As familiarity with the student increases, teachers may begin to react less strongly to the behavior. It may appear to the teacher that the student's behavior is improving when, in fact, the teacher is simply becoming more accustomed to it. In such cases, observational data provide opportunities for more objective evaluation.

Graphic Display of Data

Teachers can collect a large amount of data over a school year. For these data to be meaningful, however, it is usually necessary to present the data on some type of chart. Charts typically consist of a vertical and a horizontal axis with data displayed between the axes. Usually, the occurrence of behavior is specified on the vertical axis, and the horizontal axis reflects the passage of time (see Figure 3.1). The rest of this section will describe the use of several types of graphic displays.

One way in which data can be presented is in a bar chart. For example, a graphic presentation could display how many weekly homework assignments were completed. In some cases, it may be more helpful to present the percentage of homework assignments completed because the total number of assignments may vary. Figure 3.3 shows how both sources of information can be included in one graphic display.

In other presentations, it may be more efficient to represent a data point with a dot, as in Figure 3.4. These dots can be connected to suggest possible trends in the data, such as the increase of desirable behaviors (e.g., rate of division problems solved correctly) or the decrease

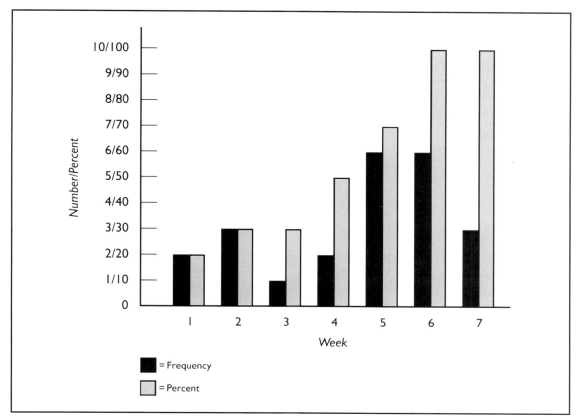

Figure 3.3. Example of a bar chart displaying both frequency and percentage data on completion of weekly homework assignments.

of undesirable behaviors (e.g., number of talk-outs). Such data displays can be enormously helpful in determining whether students have met (or are meeting) IEP objectives.

Validating Intervention Effectiveness

In most cases, IEP objectives do not specify *how* an objective is to be met. The type of treatment (intervention) used to meet the objective is usually a decision made by the special education teacher. It may also be important to determine whether the observed learning or behavior change was really due to the intervention, rather than some other reason. Interventions and charts

can be constructed to demonstrate this. First, collect preintervention observational data and record it in what is known as a *baseline phase*, as shown in the first part of Figure 3.5. A baseline phase documents the occurrence of the behavior prior to the intervention. For example, you may think that a student's late arrival to class each day is a problem. Observe and record the minutes the student is late each day for a certain period of time (e.g., 6 days). If this information suggests that tardiness is a problem, you can implement an intervention. An intervention for tardiness could involve positive reinforcement, such as tokens (e.g., poker chips) for prompt entry into the classroom. These tokens could be redeemable at a later date for prizes or privileges. The intervention could also involve punishment, such as

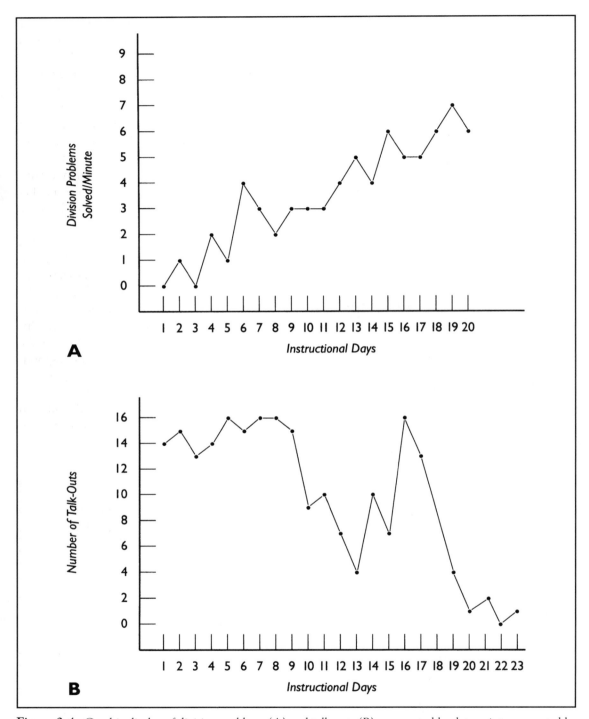

Figure 3.4. Graphic display of division problems (A) and talk-outs (B) represented by data points connected by lines to show trends.

informing the student that all class time lost through tardiness will be made up during recess, free time, or after school.

On the day the intervention is to begin, the teacher draws a vertical line and labels the intervention, as in Figure 3.5, and begins to collect data. If the resulting data look like those in the second part of Figure 3.5, the teacher may conclude that the intervention was effective. Looking at the chart in Figure 3.5, it does seem likely that the treatment succeeded. If you want to be more certain that the treatment and not some other event was responsible for the change in behavior, you can attempt to show control over the behavior by first returning to baseline, in which the intervention is not used (you stop attending to the behavior and no longer administer rewards or punishment). Then, reinstate the intervention at a later date, as in Figure 3.6. If the recorded behavior varies with treatment phase, as shown in Figure 3.6, it can be more safely concluded that the treatment was responsible for the behavior change. This type of demonstration of experimental control over behavior, sometimes referred to as *behavior modification* or *applied behavior analysis*, has been demonstrated to be helpful in special education settings. The type of experimental design described above is referred to as a *reversal* (or ABAB) design because the intervention is reversed in the return-to-baseline phase.

In some cases, however, it is not possible or desirable to return to baseline. Such cases include those in which learned behavior cannot be unlearned (behavioral "trapping"), such as with multiplication tables. For practical reasons, behavior that is highly destructive should not be returned to higher levels of intensity. In such cases, experimental control can be demonstrated with use of the *multiple baseline*, as shown in Figure 3.7, which depicts the use of a token reinforcement system for learning math facts. The baseline phases are of different lengths for different students, but the fact that each student increases in learning after implementation of the token system suggests that students are responding to the treatment and not something else.

Teachers do not always need to demonstrate experimental control over student behaviors. In most cases, it is sufficient to demonstrate that

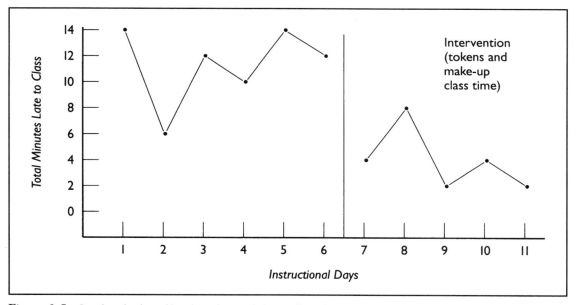

Figure 3.5. Graphic display of baseline data and data collected on minutes late to class after intervention using tokens and make-up time.

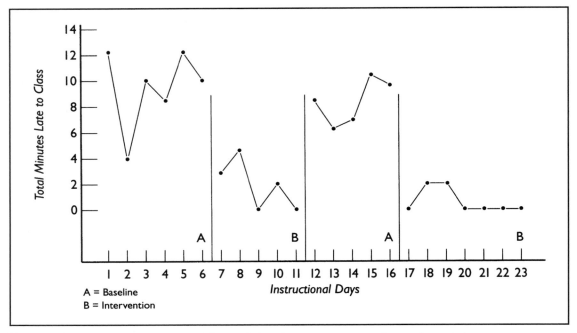

Figure 3.6. Graphic display of reversal (ABAB) data showing experimental control over behavior.

progress is being made and that objectives are being met at a satisfactory rate. In some cases, however, teachers may be uncertain of the effectiveness of a specific treatment or may wish to be more certain that a specific treatment is effective before using it with other students. In such cases, it may be helpful to employ reversal or multiple baseline designs.

Summary of Graphic Presentation of Data

Graphic presentations of permanent products or behavioral observations can be very helpful in determining whether instruction is effective. Although summative data are also helpful, teachers cannot afford to wait until the end of the school year to determine whether treatment has been effective. Graphic data displays, one type of formative evaluation, can provide this important information. Teachers need to decide for themselves how much time must be devoted to collection of student performance data. Research

has supported the contention that records of student performance should be taken regularly (e.g., twice a week per subject or skill area) and examined frequently to make effective decisions about instruction. Teachers should be able to judge when changes in instruction are necessary or not necessary. Whether data should be collected, charted, and evaluated daily may depend on a consideration of the task, the learner, and other responsibilities of the teacher. It is known, however, that careful, accurate, and regular collection of student performance data and the use of these data in making instructional decisions are a critical component of effective teaching.

Multicultural Issues

At least two issues in special education evaluation and assessment are directly relevant to multicultural and linguistically diverse students. First, students from multicultural and linguistically diverse backgrounds may be *overrepresented* in some special education settings (Artiles &

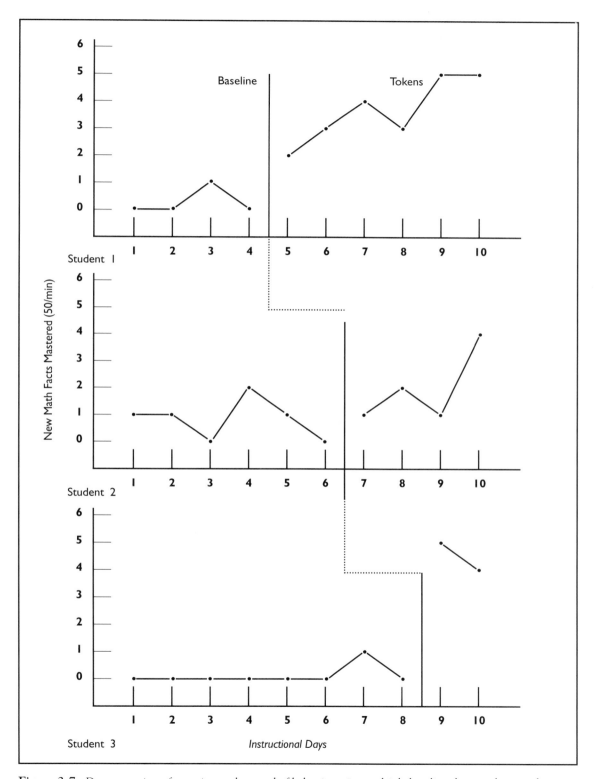

Figure 3.7. Demonstration of experimental control of behavior using multiple baseline data on three students.

Trent, 1994; MacMillan & Reschly, 1998). Overrepresentation means that a larger than expected proportion of students from a particular culturally or linguistically diverse group may be assigned special education. A discussion of the assessment procedures used for determining classification of students with respect to a particular category of disability (e.g., learning disabilities) is beyond the scope of this book. However, the concern that some groups may be overrepresented in special education suggests that special educators, as members of multidisciplinary referral teams, should help ensure that special education classification is the best possible educational option for individual students from multicultural or linguistically diverse backgrounds. Regular education classrooms also should be accommodating of student diversity; students should not be placed in special education programs simply because their culturally based cognitive or behavioral patterns are incompatible with rigid "monocultural" classroom instructional models (Artiles & Zamora-Durán, 1997; Franklin, 1992). Consider the information provided in Chapter 1 and throughout this text for suggestions for teaching effectively in multicultural contexts. In addition, maintain open communication between yourself and your students and their families and implement suggestions for addressing the needs of all students.

Another important issue involves fairness in assessment of academic progress. Assessment should be based on culturally relevant and meaningful curriculum materials that are in turn meaningfully associated with relevant instructional objectives. Fair assessment is best made on relevant curriculum to determine whether acceptable progress is being made and to inform instructional decision making.

Summary

- Evaluation is a critical component of effective instruction. Different types of evaluation are used for different purposes. Summative

evaluation is given only once or twice per school year, whereas formative evaluation is given frequently throughout the year. Norm-referenced tests compare student scores with those of other students, whereas criterion-referenced tests compare student scores to a performance criterion.

- Criterion-referenced tests designed to correspond with a specific curriculum are referred to as *curriculum-based tests*. Curriculum-based tests can assist teachers in linking their instruction to curriculum and in guiding instructional decision making.

- Portfolio assessment refers to the collection of student products throughout the school year, including audiotapes of student reading, samples of written work, laboratory booklets and notes, videotapes of student presentations, and teacher observations. Performance assessment refers to assessment of student performance with respect to actual materials rather than on a paper-and-pencil test.

- Direct observation of student behavior can also be helpful in monitoring progress and guiding intervention decisions. Recording procedures include event recording, duration recording, interval recording, and time sampling. Descriptive accounts of all student behaviors are referred to as *continuous records*.

- Observational data are best displayed on graphs and charts that represent behavior on the vertical axis and time on the horizontal axis. Specific designs, such as reversal and multiple baseline designs, can be employed to determine whether interventions are having the desired effects.

- Special educators, as members of multidisciplinary referral teams, should help ensure that special education is the best possible educational option for individual students from multicultural or linguistically diverse backgrounds. Obtaining relevant and unbiased student data is very important in making placement decisions that are helpful and fair. Assessment should be based on culturally relevant and meaningful curriculum materials associated with relevant instructional objectives.

Relevant Research and Resources

Research

Additional information on norm-referenced tests, criterion-referenced tests, and basic issues of reliability and validity is provided by Salvia and Ysseldyke (1998) and Overton (1996). Discussion of the implications of high-stakes testing for students with disabilities is provided by Frase-Blunt (2000). Implications of using criterion-referenced assessment are described by Popham and Husek (1969). An issue of *Exceptional Children* (Vol. 52, No. 3; Tucker, 1986) was devoted to curriculum-based assessment. Articles by Deno (1986); Germann and Tindal (1986); Fuchs and Fuchs (1986a); Marston and Magnusson (1986); Peterson, Heistad, Peterson, and Reynolds (1986); Gickling and Thompson (1986); and Blankenship (1986) are of particular interest and describe supporting research data. In the same issue, Galagan (1986) describes what he terms the "legal imperative" of the use of curriculum-based assessment in special education.

L. S. Fuchs (1986) reviews research supporting the use of formative evaluation procedures, and a meta-analysis of the effectiveness of formative evaluation is provided by Fuchs and Fuchs (1986b). Individual research reports on the effectiveness of curriculum-based assessment can be found in Deno, Marston, and Mirkin (1982); Deno, Mirkin, and Chiang (1982); Fuchs, Deno, and Marston (1983); Fuchs and Fuchs (1986a); and Fuchs, Deno, and Mirkin (1984). Applications of curriculum-based measurement are given by L. S. Fuchs (1987); Fuchs, Fuchs, Allinder, and Hamlett (1992); Fuchs et al. (1994); Fuchs, Fuchs, Hamlett, and Stecker (1991); and Fuchs, Fuchs, Hamlett, and Whinnery (1991). Texts on curriculum-based measurement are provided by Howell and Morehead (1987) and Howell and Nolet (1999). Wesson and King (1996) describe the implications of portfolio assessment in special education, and important information about

the uses of performance assessment is provided by L. S. Fuchs (1994). Woodward, Monroe, and Baxter (2001) discuss the utility of performance assessment in mathematics.

Description of direct observational systems is provided by Alberto and Troutman (1998), and additional information on graphing observational data is provided by Tawney and Gast (1984). This text also describes experimental designs that are helpful in validating behavioral interventions. Multicultural issues relative to assessment and placement are described in Artiles and Trent (1994); Artiles and Zamora-Durán (1997); Anderson and Webb-Johnson (1995); Ford, Obiakor, and Patton (1995); and MacMillan and Reschly (1998).

Materials

Curriculum Associates publishes the *Brigance Diagnostic Comprehensive Inventory of Basic Skills–Revised* and the *Inventory of Essential Skills*, which can be useful in criterion-referenced testing. A Spanish version of *Assessment of Basic Skills* is also available. Many curriculum-based performance or portfolio assessments must be developed by teachers to target specific classroom activities. However, *Full Option Science System* (*Encyclopedia Britannica*, distributed by Delta Education) and *Science and Technology for Children* (National Science Resources Center) seem very suitable for many students with mild disabilities and include materials for performance assessment of science learning.

Computer Software and Technology

Teachers may want to become familiar with some of the many word-processing programs, database programs, spreadsheet programs, and graphics programs, such as New Print Shop and Printmaster (distributed by The Learning Company), which can be adapted to record, store, and graph student performance data. Software has also become available for scoring norm-referenced tests, including the KeyMath–R ASSIST (American Guidance Service) and WRMT–R ASSIST (for the *Woodcock Reading Mastery Tests–Revised*; American Guidance Service). Sopris West produces !Observe: A Behavior Recording and Reporting Software Program for collecting and tracking data for functional behavioral assessments or designing behavior management interventions. Software is also avail-able for grading and record keeping, distributed by Learning Systems, including Grade Machine (Misty City Software), Grade Quick (Jackson), Micrograde (Chariot Software), and praesto-GRADE (Aptus Technologies), which can be used for rubrics and authentic assessment. The Portfolio Builder (Visions, distributed by Learning Systems) can be used by teachers or students to create student portfolios. See Appendix B for a list of addresses of producers and distributors of software and curricular materials.

Grading Policies and Practices for Students in Inclusive Classes

Given the recent emphases on inclusion, graduation requirements, and accountability as measured by state competency testing, grading policies and practices for students with disabilities have gained more attention. Grading policies and practices for students with disabilities in inclusive environments are important and controversial, and they lack common standards. Polloway, Epstein, Bursuck, Roderique, et al. (1994) and Bursuck et al. (1996) completed national surveys on grading policies and practices for students with disabilities. Polloway and colleagues reported that 64.9% of the schools reported grading policies, and 60% of those districts included modifications in grading practices within their policies for students with disabilities. Bursuck et al. reported on specific grading adaptations that teachers implemented. Most commonly reported adaptations included the following:

- assigning grades on IEP goals and objectives
- assigning grades on improvement
- providing separate grades for process and products
- giving multiple grades (for tests and for effort)
- adjusting grading weights for individuals (e.g., weighting tests less than projects for some students)
- assigning grades on meeting individual academic or behavioral contracts
- adjusting grading scales

Challenges remain regarding the evolution of grading practices for students with disabilities within inclusive environments. Be sure to determine your school district's policies on grading.

Using Curriculum-Based Measurement Software

Curriculum-based measurement (CBM) is a great way to monitor student progress (e.g., Fuchs et al., 1994). Computerized curriculum-based measurement software, developed by Lynn and Doug Fuchs and their colleagues, is available from PRO-ED. Fuchs and their colleagues have demonstrated though numerous research studies that teachers who use curriculum-based measurement have students who make significantly more academic progress. In their research in inclusive classrooms, teachers who provided regular instruction but required students to work at computers independently once each week to take assessments in reading, math, or spelling had greater academic achievement gains. The CBM requires minimal time ranging from 2 to 6 minutes depending on the test and student level. The software records student progress and generates individual student and classwide performance feedback.

Allinder, Bolling, Oats, and Gagnon (2000) demonstrated that when teachers also implemented some self-monitoring procedure that was structured to guide them in making better instructional decisions based on the student data, achievement gains were even greater. Specific procedures for using the CBM software in their study included the following:

- Teachers and students were instructed on how to use the CBM software:
    how to operate the software
    how to select the correct probe (test)
    how to record the data
    how to save the data

- Students
    were taught a test-taking strategy in which they were taught to skip items they did not know how to do because the test was based on the end-of-year goal,

    took the 3 to 5 minute probes twice weekly,

    examined their immediate test scores on the screen in graphic form indicating the number of digits correct

- Teachers were given decision rules, including the following:
    progress is sufficient to meet end-of-year goal, keep goal as is;

    progress is sufficient to meet end-of-year goal, raise student goal;

    progress is insufficient to meet end-of-year goal, implement an instructional change.
        Strategies for instructional decision making included strategies taught, amount of instructional time, student–teacher ratio, materials, and motivational strategies.

- Self-monitoring instructions for teachers included the following:
    complete a more detailed analysis of skills students completed (e.g., Did the students perform well during the previous 2 weeks? What skill should be targeted for the next 2 weeks? How will the teacher target the skill?)

Chapter 4

ϧ   ϧ   ϧ

Classroom Management

Effective classroom management is a critical component of effective teaching. Research has shown that the teachers who are the most effective in managing classroom behavior are also usually the most effective in improving classroom achievement. The reasons for this are obvious. Teachers who spend much of their day lecturing students on their behavior or continually exhorting students to "be quiet," "sit down," or "keep your hands to yourself" are losing valuable instructional time. If student achievement is to be maximized, it is critical for the classroom atmosphere to be friendly and cheerful but also businesslike and work oriented. The classroom atmosphere set by teachers gives a strong message to students regarding what is expected of them. Students with emotional or behavioral disorders may have been referred to special education precisely because general education teachers have had difficulty managing their behavior. In this regard, these students may prove to be particularly challenging. It must also be remembered that some students who have been classified as having learning disabilities or mild mental retardation and students who have a history of school failure also may present classroom behavior problems. The techniques for managing classroom behaviors are similar across all categories of special education; however, the level of intensity of the behavioral problems exhibited may vary from student to student or from classroom to classroom.

The first section of this chapter describes basic behavioral terminology. Next, applications of behavior management principles to the management of individual behavior are described. Following that, procedures for the management of whole classrooms are discussed. Finally, methods for room arrangement and scheduling relevant to effective classroom management are described.

Behavioral Terminology

Behavior is usually defined as the directly observable movements of a student (or other organism). Behavior is what we observe, measure, and intervene upon. Behavior is often changed by applying contingencies (consequences). In behavior management, these contingencies are often applied as *consequent events,* that is, after the behavior has been exhibited. Contingencies are intended to alter the future exhibition of the behavior.

Reinforcement and Punishment

Generally, the most effective contingency used in changing or modifying behavior is positive reinforcement. Positive reinforcement is any desirable consequent event that serves to increase the desired behavior. What is reinforcing to one student may not be reinforcing to another student, simply because the preferences of individuals differ. Generally, positive reinforcement includes social reinforcers (e.g., verbal praise), tangible reinforcers (e.g., stickers and awards), and primary reinforcers (e.g., candy). It is important to remember, however, that whether or not something serves as a reinforcer depends on whether it increases future behavior and not simply whether it seems to be desirable. For example, the teacher may feel that public social praise could be used to increase a certain student's on-task behavior. The teacher could then use statements such as, "I like the way you are working so hard on your assignment," to positively reinforce on-task behavior. If the on-task behavior does not increase as a result of using this praise (perhaps because the student is embarrassed by it), it cannot be said to function as a positive reinforcer.

Negative reinforcement, on the other hand, refers to undesirable consequent events that result in increased levels of future behavior. Negative reinforcement, which should not be confused with punishment (described below), involves the presentation of an undesirable stimulus that can be controlled by exhibition of the target behavior. A good example of negative reinforcement is the buzzer used in cars to remind riders to buckle seat belts. One buckles the seat belt not out of expectation of positive consequences but to stop the negative consequences of the buzzer. Another good example of negative reinforcement is nagging. Parents often nag children to clean up their rooms. Children comply not out of the expectation of a reward but to stop the parents' nagging. Similarly, infants often use crying as a negative reinforcement for parental attention. Parents attend to the infants so that they will stop crying. Although the examples given above show how negative reinforcement can be used, it is almost never the best treatment in classroom situations. Most of the time, it is better to use positive reinforcement to change behavior in the classroom. A classroom situation in which negative reinforcement is often used is lining up to go to the cafeteria or recess. The teacher informs the class that they will wait in line as long as it takes for everyone to stand quietly and behave appropriately. Standing in line is used as a negative reinforcement for appropriate behavior. Students know that if they behave appropriately as a group, they will not have to continue standing and waiting. Although using such contingencies may sometimes be necessary, it is

also possible to provide positive reinforcement, such as an additional few minutes of playground time, for prompt and efficient lining up.

In contrast to positive and negative reinforcement, both of which serve to increase behavior, punishment refers to consequent events that are intended to decrease future behavior. Although positive reinforcement is more desirable and effective as a means of behavior management, punishment may sometimes be necessary, particularly when the behavior is infrequent and more positive methods have failed. Different types of reinforcement and punishment are described in Table 4.1.

Schedules of Reinforcement

Teachers need to attend not only to the types of reinforcement used but also to schedules of reinforcement. Schedules of reinforcement refer to the rate at which reinforcement is delivered. For example, in the initial stages of behavior change, it may be necessary to use *continuous reinforcement* with some students. Reinforcement is continuous when it follows every observed instance of the target behavior. For example, every time students arrive in class before the tardy bell rings, they are provided with a reward, such as a sticker or token that counts toward other prizes or privileges. Reinforcement can also be applied on an interval basis. *Interval reinforcement* refers to the time intervals during which reinforcement is provided. *Fixed interval reinforcement* is reinforcement that is provided at regular, known intervals. For example, students are provided with reinforcement for being on task at fixed 5-minute intervals. This type of reinforcement tends to result in increased levels of performance immediately preceding the established interval. In contrast, *variable interval reinforcement* is provided at differing time intervals that are unknown to the student. Reinforcement could be delivered after 5 minutes, then after 8 minutes, and then after 1 minute for on-task behavior. Use of variable intervals of reinforcement can provide higher

Table 4.1. Consequent Events

Consequent Event	Description	Examples
Positive reinforcement	Provision of reward to increase desired behavior	Verbal praise
		Tokens, exchangeable for trinkets
		Privileges, such as leaving seat without permission
		Free time
		Longer recess
		Popcorn parties at end of week
Negative reinforcement	Cessation of negative event to increase desired behavior	Nagging
		Teasing, such as "chicken," "fraidy-cat"
		Staying in from recess until a specific assignment is completed
Punishment	Provision of negative consequences to decrease undesirable behavior	Verbal criticism
		Time-out
		Loss of privileges
		Overcorrection, such as cleaning every student's desk for writing on own desk
		Response cost, such as loss of earned tokens

and more consistent levels of performance than use of fixed intervals of reinforcement.

In addition to interval schedules, some reinforcement is applied on a ratio basis. *Ratio reinforcement* refers to the number of responses required for reinforcement and is often applied to behavioral events. For example, students are given positive reinforcement for every third time a homework assignment is completed accurately. This is an example of a *fixed ratio* schedule of reinforcement. Like a variable interval schedule, a *variable ratio* schedule applies to a schedule of reinforcement that is not fixed. For example, students are reinforced on the 3rd, 11th, and 8th occasion of homework completion. This type of schedule also tends to produce higher and more consistent levels of behavior than a fixed ratio schedule.

Managing Individual Student Behavior

Teachers, in general, and special education teachers, in particular, need to remain aware of the fact that classrooms are composed of individuals. These individuals often have different needs and may respond differently to the same treatment. The following section describes procedures that can be applied to individuals to manage appropriate classroom behavior.

Rules, Praise, and Ignoring

A necessary prerequisite to good classroom behavior is an awareness of the expectations for classroom behavior. Expectations should be directly and clearly communicated by posted classroom rules and teacher reminders. If students show problems discriminating between acceptable and unacceptable behaviors (e.g., acceptable and unacceptable tone of voice), they must be taught these discriminations (by explicit provision of instances and noninstances) before they can be expected to produce the desired behavior. Provision of rules for classroom behavior and student understanding of the rules are necessary prerequisites for behavior management.

Rules are often ineffective, however, if they are not supported by contingencies or are inconsistently enforced. Research has shown that provision of rules alone may have little effect on student behavior. One way rules can be enforced is through the use of praise and ignoring. Social praise for following classroom rules (e.g., "I like the way Jimmy has kept his hands to himself this period") can be effective in emphasizing that students are expected to follow rules. Teachers should seek out opportunities to provide social praise, particularly for students whose behavior is typically not praiseworthy. This type of activity is referred to as "catch them being good." Generally, this is a more effective way of positively changing behavior than frequent nagging or criticism. Likewise, teachers can choose to ignore one student's inappropriate behavior while praising another student's good behavior. For example, if Tyler is off task but Ramona is on task, the teacher could say, "I like the way Ramona is working hard and staying on task." Frequently, this statement of praise for Ramona will also help Tyler increase his on-task behavior.

In addition to using rules and praise, it is often helpful to ignore some types of inappropriate student behavior. Of course, behavior that is potentially harmful to other students must be attended to immediately. For many behaviors, however, the teacher can ignore the undesirable behavior and instead respond positively to another student who is exhibiting a positive instance of the behavior. If behavior is shown to decrease after it is ignored, the process is referred to as *extinction*.

Teachers can also unintentionally extinguish positive behaviors if they forget to reward them. Be careful that you attend to positive behaviors of your students so that they will continue.

Reprimands

Although it is important to be positive with students as often as possible, sometimes negative feedback in the form of reprimands is helpful in maintaining classroom behavior. Reprimands can alert the student that you disapprove of the behavior that was exhibited and that you expect better behavior in the future. When delivering reprimands, however, it is best if they are not considered a form of punishment, in that your scorn or your unpleasant, hostile, or aggressive manner is intended to inhibit future occurrences of the behavior. Such teacher behavior can create resentment on the part of the student, inhibit future communication, and contribute to an unpleasant classroom environment.

Kerr and Nelson (1998) have reviewed research on reprimands and identified the circumstances under which reprimands are most effective. Soft reprimands may be more effective in controlling disruptive behaviors than loud reprimands. When possible, speak in tones audible only to the disruptive student, rather than loudly so that the entire class hears. Do not raise your voice unless it seems absolutely necessary because such a strategy can be harmful to the classroom atmosphere and can lose its effectiveness over time. Stand near the student being reprimanded, but be sure to respect the student's personal space. Do not point your finger or insist that the student return eye contact because these actions can be viewed as hostile and aggressive. Finally, do not insist on having the last word. Allow the student some face-saving posturing if the student generally complies with your request.

If your reprimands are not effective in reducing future occurrences of the behavior (e.g., the student continues to talk out in class), do not continue to issue reprimands. Instead, plan for more intensive consequences (e.g., loss of privileges for talking out or a reward for discontinuing talk-outs).

Direct Appeal, Proximity, and Public Posting of Behavior

Direct appeal, proximity, and public posting of behavior are procedures that are simple to implement and often very successful at changing inappropriate behaviors. In implementing *direct appeal*, meet individually with a student who is misbehaving and ask that student to try hard to behave appropriately. For example, assume one student (Robbie) has been very disruptive by teasing another student (Wanda) repeatedly during social studies class. After class, ask Robbie to remain and speak directly to him regarding the problem. During the discussion, state something such as the following:

> Robbie, it has been difficult for you to complete your work during social studies because you have been teasing and bothering Wanda. I want you to try especially hard tomorrow to complete all of your work. If I see you start to tease Wanda, I will signal you with my hand like this. [Demonstrate hand signal] When you see that signal, it will remind you to get back to work and to leave Wanda alone. Do you think you can do this?

Proximity is another procedure that often results in appropriate behavior change. When you see a student acting inappropriately, walk over to that student. Usually the teacher's close appearance acts as a sufficient reminder to the student, and the inappropriate behavior ceases. Many times teachers can combine proximity with a signal (such as establishing eye contact) that serves as a reminder for the student.

Finally, improve classroom behavior by using *public posting* of good students' behavior. Place a chart that includes all students' names and spaces for inserting their positive accomplishments prominently in the classroom. Each day,

praise students by reading the names of some of the accomplished students to the class. The accomplishments can vary and include behaviors such as working hard, completing a task, and putting forth extra effort. In addition, you can select the biggest accomplishment for the week, such as the Super Effort Award.

Tangible Reinforcement

Social praise or the granting of privileges can function as positive reinforcement in managing a student's behavior. Sometimes, however, social praise is insufficient, and a more tangible type of reinforcement is required. *Tangible reinforcements* include things such as stickers, stars, toys, or *primary reinforcers* such as food and drink. Although many teachers do not like the idea of providing tangible rewards for behavior that is expected in general education settings without reward, in some instances the provision of tangible reinforcement can represent an important first step toward meeting long-term goals. In some cases, students have learned patterns of behavior that are at first difficult to change. Tangible reinforcement may be helpful in making some of these initial changes. Survey students' preferences and interests to select reinforcers that are appropriate for all students, including those from culturally and linguistically diverse groups. Tangible reinforcement can also be paired with social praise. In this way, students learn that the social praise is also important, and over time the tangible reinforcements can be faded out and replaced with social praise. Later, the reinforcement can be faded out, for example, by moving from continuous reinforcement to different levels of variable ratio or variable interval schedules.

One way to build in fading of tangible reinforcement is through the use of a *token system*. Token systems make use of things such as points or chips that are redeemable at a later date for actual tangible rewards. For example, a recording sheet, such as the one in Figure 4.1, is developed that describes a series of target behaviors for each period. As seen in Figure 4.1, a student can earn points for starting each period efficiently, working hard (on task), staying seated, not talking out of turn, finishing work, and cleaning up. The student is given from 0 to 5 points at the end of each period, depending on the level of appropriate behavior exhibited. Points are totaled at the end of the day and added to points previously earned. Students may use these points to "purchase" more tangible reinforcers, such as toys and games. It may be necessary at first for students to be able to purchase reinforcers for a relatively small number of points. As inappropriate behaviors come under greater levels of control, however, the "price" of reinforcers should be increased so that students must exhibit higher and higher levels of appropriate behavior to purchase tangible reinforcers. As students begin to exhibit higher levels of behavior control, their performance can also be monitored less closely.

Tangible reinforcers are often included as reward components of individual *behavioral contracts*. A contract is a signed agreement between students and teachers specifying certain behavioral outcomes and rewards. In designing a contract, the teacher and student meet, select an obtainable behavioral goal, specify the conditions and time for meeting the goal, specify the reward, and sign and date the contract. Contracts can be very effective at increasing positive academic and social behavior.

Tangible reinforcement has been shown to exert powerful control over many behaviors in special education settings. However, tangible reinforcement should be used only if milder forms of reinforcement do not prove successful.

Punishment

It would be nice if all classroom behavior could be managed through the use of positive reinforcement alone. Almost any special education teacher will agree, however, that some degree of punishment also is necessary to maintain order and keep the classroom functioning efficiently.

Period	Starting	Working Hard	In-Seat	No Talk-outs	Finish/ Cleanup	Total
1. Reading	1	0	1	1	0	3
2. Math	1	1	1	1	1	5
3. Recess	1	1	1	1	1	5
4. Writing	1	0	1	0	1	3
5. Lunch	1	1	1	1	1	5
6. Science	1	0	0	0	0	1
7. Spelling	1	1	1	1	1	5
8. Recess	1	1	1	1	1	5
9. Class Meeting Social Skills	1	1	1	0	1	4
Totals	9	6	8	6	7	36

Figure 4.1. Sample classroom recording sheet for token systems.

This does not mean that teachers should be negative in any way toward their students. Although a stern, direct reprimand may sometimes be helpful in communicating expectations, excessive criticism can be very harmful to a classroom environment. As with any intervention, whenever punishment is used, formative data should be collected so that the consequences of using punishment can be evaluated. The following sections describe three types of punishment: time-out, response cost, and overcorrection.

Time-out

Time-out is sometimes referred to as "time out from positive reinforcement" and so defined may not be a literal example of punishment. In most cases, however, time-out serves as an undesirable condition that is intended to decrease future behaviors and, as such, can be considered punishment. Time-out, then, like any administration of punishment, must be considered in the context of the procedures and principles of the school environment.

Time-out generally refers to some type of separation of the student from the normal classroom environment and is usually applied following a disruptive event for which time-out was prespecified as a consequence (i.e., the student was aware that time-out would be a consequence of a specific behavior). Sometimes time-out is used to provide a cooling-off period when students may have lost control of their tempers.

Although time-out is described as a unitary situation, it can be applied at several different levels. The mildest level, sometimes referred to as *contingent attention time-out*, involves removing a student from the immediate classroom activity but allowing the student to observe other students involved in the activity. In a higher level of time-out, the student is required to turn away from observing the classroom activities.

Some special education classrooms are equipped with time-out rooms in which students are completely isolated from the rest of the class, a procedure referred to as *exclusionary time-out*.

Before using time-out procedures, several considerations should be made. First, it should be established through formative evaluation of student behavior that reinforcement and milder levels of punishment have not been effective. Exclusionary time-out is then regarded as necessary, if not desirable. Second, exclusionary time-out should be brief. Five or 10 minutes is usually the maximum limit for such exclusionary procedures. Finally, most states—and common sense—require that lights be turned on and the door to a time-out room be unlocked. Exclusionary time-out, although considered a form of punishment, should be regarded as a type of intensive, formal feedback for misbehavior and a brief period for a student to reflect on this misbehavior. It should not be considered a type of incarceration.

Finally, as students leave the time-out room, they should be "debriefed" concerning the reasons they were put in time-out and given appropriate behavioral alternatives for the future. Students should be able to state why they earned a time-out, who was hurt by their behavior, and what they could do differently in the future. If loss of privileges (e.g., recess) is associated with time-out, these contingencies should also be specified. On the other hand, if students are consistently praised for positive competing behaviors (e.g., positive statements rather than teasing), disruptive behaviors requiring time-out may decrease. As with any type of punishment, the student should be made aware that it is the behavior and not the student that is unwelcome in the classroom. The following is an example of a debriefing procedure:

TEACHER: Your time-out is over. Before you go back to the classroom, we must discuss what happened. Why were you sent to time-out?

STUDENT: I was bad.

TEACHER: Can you tell me what you did?

STUDENT: Johnny made faces at me so I threw my pencil at him.

TEACHER: Were you sent to time-out because Johnny made faces?

STUDENT: No.

TEACHER: You were sent to time-out because you threw something at another student.

STUDENT: Yes.

TEACHER: Do you know why I cannot allow students to throw things?

STUDENT: Somebody might get hurt.

TEACHER: That's right. Somebody might get hurt. And some day that somebody might be you. Now, what can you do the next time you think Johnny is making faces?

STUDENT: Ignore him.

TEACHER: That's right. If you ignore him, he will stop. What else can you do if you think you are not going to be able to ignore him?

STUDENT: Tell you.

TEACHER: You can come and tell me, and I will make sure you don't get in trouble and also that no one teases you. Can you do that next time?

STUDENT: OK.

TEACHER: Just remember, you don't have to throw things. You can *ignore* and you can *tell me*. And remember, it's the *behavior* I don't like. But I like you and I know you can do better. Can't you?

STUDENT: Yes.

TEACHER: Good. Now let's go back to class and show everybody how well you can behave.

Overcorrection and Response Cost

Overcorrection refers to requiring compensation beyond the level of behavior. For example, a student who has defaced one desktop with crayon is required to clean all desks in the classroom. Overcorrection also refers to the overlearning of appropriate behaviors. For instance, a student who throws food in the lunchroom is required to spend a longer period of time appropriately carrying a tray of food to and from a lunch table.

Response cost involves the removal of previously earned rewards, such as tokens. For example, a student who misbehaves during one school period not only earns no points for that period but also loses points previously earned that day. When response cost is used, it is important that students are made aware that their previously earned tokens can be taken away under specific circumstances. Like all punishment procedures, it is important to be certain that more positive efforts are not effective before implementing overcorrection or response cost procedures.

Self-Monitoring

Self-monitoring refers to evaluation, recording, and reinforcement of behaviors by the student. Basically, teaching self-monitoring involves teaching the student to use the same principles that the teacher uses to modify his or her behavior. First, a student is taught to operationalize a target behavior, for example, teasing. Then the student is taught to record instances of teasing in his or her own behavior. Finally, the student is taught how to reward himself or herself for exhibiting predetermined criteria of behavior after confirmation by the teacher.

An example of how self-monitoring can be used is given in the following case study. Self-monitoring procedures such as these can be helpful for students who are overly active in class or who have problems maintaining attention. Self-monitoring can be an effective procedure for helping students to function appropriately in general education or inclusive settings. Training in self-instruction and attribution training, two components of self-monitoring, is described in the following section.

Self-Monitoring Scenario

Ms. S had a student (Jill) who had a great deal of difficulty keeping herself on task during independent practice activities. Furthermore, the student often maintained that she had been working consistently throughout the period. Ms. S's judgment told her that Jill was probably off task much more often than the student realized. It also seemed that when Jill was off task, she was usually watching some other student. In order to increase Jill's on-task behavior, as well as her awareness of her own behavior, Ms. S provided Jill with a self-monitoring sheet. This sheet showed a stick figure drawing of a student working at a desk and another picture of a student looking around the room. Below these figures were boxes and time intervals as shown below:

Ring	On-task	Off-task
1	☐	☐
2	☐	☐
3	☐	☐
4	☐	☐
5	☐	☐
6	☐	☐
7	☐	☐
8	☐	☐
9	☐	☐
10	☐	☐

Jill was told that a timer would ring at random intervals and that Jill should check the box that described what she was doing at that moment, regardless of what she had just done or what she felt she was about to do. Ms. S then set the timer to ring at random intervals, on a variable interval of about 5 minutes. At first, Ms. S monitored each of Jill's self-recordings. At the end of the first period, Jill was forced to admit she was visually off task considerably more frequently than she had thought. Ms. S then told her to continue her self-recording, and Ms. S would do the same. When Jill achieved 9 out of 10 on-task checks on three consecutive self-monitoring sheets and her observations agreed with her teacher's observations, she would be entitled to 15 minutes with her favorite library book. Ms. S found that Jill's self-monitored on-task behavior went from 30% to 90% in a very short period of time and that Jill became much more capable of monitoring her own behavior.

Self-Instruction Training

Self-instructions or self-questions are self-directed statements that function as guidelines for students to follow throughout a problem-solving process. Each self-instruction represents one step toward the solution of the problem. Researchers typically have used a format that includes five self-instructions, beginning with the definition of the problem or a statement such as, "What should I do?" The second statement examines all potential solutions by asking, "What are all the possible options?" The third statement focuses attention to the problem at hand. A sample self-question or statement might be, "I'd better think about my goal for right now." The fourth statement enables the student to select the best solution by asking a question or making a statement similar to the following: "I think the best solution is. . . ." The fifth and final statement builds in self-reinforcing or coping statements. Statements such as "I chose the right answer" or "Oops, I made a mistake, but next time I'll get the right answer" are examples of self-reinforcement and coping statements, respectively. This series of problem-solving statements assists students in (a) identifying the problem and its attributes, (b) generating strategies or series of steps to solve the problem, (c) examining all possible solution options, (d) implementing the optimal solution, and (e) rewarding themselves on completion of the solution.

A major goal of training in self-instruction is for students to internalize the self-instructions so that they are able to think through solutions to all problems. Generally, researchers and clinicians recommend that the following sequence of self-instructional procedures be implemented with all students:

1. The teacher models the task performance and overtly verbalizes the steps while the student observes and listens.

2. The student executes the task and overtly verbalizes all steps.

3. The teacher models the task while whispering the self-instruction.

4. The student executes the task and whispers the steps.

5. The teacher models the task again but this time uses *covert* self-instructional steps.

6. The student implements the procedure using covert self-instructional steps.

Teachers often add a self-monitoring component to self-instructional procedures. In other words, worksheets that list the questions or self-statements in sequential order are placed on a student's desk. During the initial implementation procedures, students can check off each question or statement as they think through the problem. As the procedures become more automatic, the monitoring sheet can be removed. Examples of questions that could appear on a self-monitoring checklist are as follows:

1. What should I do?
2. What are all the possible solutions?
3. What is my goal for now?
4. What is the best solution?
5. Did my solution work?

Procedures such as these can be beneficial for decreasing inattentive behavior and increasing performance on academic tasks. Further applica-

tions of self-instruction and self-monitoring are discussed in the content area chapters.

Reinforcement and punishment procedures are helpful tools for managing the behavior of individual students. It is also of great importance that students begin to understand that the rewards and consequences they receive are the result of decisions that they have made about their own behavior. Teaching students to attribute positive and negative consequences to their own decision making is known as *attribution training*.

Attribution Training

Many students fail to attribute their classroom behavior to effort or choice on their own part. They can be said to have an *external locus of control* because they feel that people or events external to themselves are in control of their success or failure in the classroom. Students who are said to have an *internal locus of control* feel that they themselves are in control and that they can make the decisions about conduct that will enable them to succeed. The purpose of attribution training is to teach students to attribute success or failure in the classroom to decisions they make themselves.

Negative attributions attribute success or failure to external forces. Examples are "I got sent to the office because the teacher doesn't like me," "Those other boys got me in trouble," and "I got rewarded because the teacher felt sorry for me." Positive attributions, on the other hand, attribute success or failure to forces the student can control. Examples of positive attributions are "I lost points because I didn't control my talking" or "I get to take a 'happy-gram' home because I ignored the other students when they tried to tease me." Whenever students are given feedback on their classroom behavior, either positive or negative, teachers should be certain that the students realize they are in control of the behaviors they choose to exhibit and the consequences these behaviors will receive. Teachers should not accept negative attributions, which attempt to place the cause of success or failure on others.

The dialogue presented earlier provides an example of a student's attempt to use a negative attribution and the teacher's refusal to accept it. Likewise, when students have a good day, teachers should remind them of the positive decisions they made that contributed to their success. For example, "Very good, Charles! You got all your points this period because you ignored Kimberly and focused on finishing your work!"

Attribution training is also very helpful for academic learning, in which student success or failure is attributed to effort and execution of appropriate learning/study strategies. Attribution training for academic learning is discussed further in Chapter 9.

Confrontations

Confrontations occur when students openly defy you, challenge your authority, or are aggressively noncompliant. Confrontations with aggressive students are among the greatest concerns of teachers. Canter and Canter (1993) have provided several recommendations for dealing with confrontations in an effective manner and for reducing their probability of occurring in the future.

1. The most important strategy is to create a positive classroom environment with open communication. If students perceive their teacher to be positive and accepting, as well as open to suggestions, and that classroom rules are fair and consistently enforced, confrontations are less likely to occur in the first place.

2. When confrontations do occur, be sure to remain calm. Breathe deeply, count to 10, and do not allow yourself to be drawn into a shouting match with the student. Loud and threatening remarks usually only intensify the confrontation, create resentment in the long term, and can lead some students to feel heroic by standing up to your threats. Use a calm, deliberate tone of voice and remind yourself, "This isn't about me." Do not interpret the situation as completely personal. Your maintenance of a calm attitude will help defuse the situation.

3. When possible, speak to the student privately and not in front of an audience of the student's peers. Acknowledge the student's feelings but maintain your desire that class rules be obeyed (e.g., "I understand you don't like it, but the assignment does need to be completed this period. Is there some other way I can help you with it?"). Express your interest in seeing the student succeed. Look for a face-saving solution.

4. Do not insist on having the last word. If the student ultimately complies with your requests, a little face-saving posturing on the part of the student may be allowable. What really matters ultimately is that rules are observed and order is enforced. Speak to the student later, if needed, when responses are likely to be less emotional.

5. In some cases, it may be wise to ignore the behavior for the moment and address it later when the student has calmed down. Such cases include behavior that is very much out of character for that particular student or seems particularly volatile or threatening.

6. Have a plan for confrontations that seem likely to become threatening to the safety of yourself or your students. Be aware ahead of time of how and when to call for additional support, and be aware of school policy on safety issues.

Confrontations can be very unpleasant experiences, but with careful planning and skillful handling, confrontations can be much less of a problem. Above all, the most important strategy is to create a positive, supportive, problem-solving environment that is unlikely to lead to confrontations.

Group Management Techniques

All of the techniques described to manage an individual's behavior can be adapted to modify group behavior. These techniques are especially beneficial for teachers. Recall that the major difficulty new teachers have in keeping students engaged on task is classroom management. Most of the techniques described in the previous section for use with individuals will be described for application with small and large groups of students. In addition, several techniques for large groups of students have been developed and found to be extremely effective in managing classroom behavior. Modifications of a classroom-level system have been used, as well as assertive discipline procedures on both classroom and schoolwide bases.

Motivation

The best overall strategy for managing classroom behavior is to create an environment in which students are motivated to learn and do not wish to create disturbances. In such environments, teachers and students are partners in a situation that is positive and beneficial for all. Both classroom behavior and academic learning can be greatly improved with motivational strategies.

Researchers often distinguish between *extrinsic* and *intrinsic* motivation. Extrinsic motivation generally refers to rewards or reinforcements given to students who work well and complete assignments accurately. In these cases, students work diligently not because they find the task satisfying but because of what they will earn if they work hard. Intrinsic motivation generally refers to efforts students put into tasks because they enjoy the learning activities or feel good about what they are learning. Overall, students are more intrinsically motivated to participate in experiential learning activities, such as those found in hands-on science experiments, than they are to participate in activities intended to improve basic skills functioning, such as learning spelling words. Unfortunately, in special education, basic skills learning is much more common, and therefore teachers often must rely on more external means of motivating students. But regardless of the learning activity, there are many ways to increase student motivation. Table 4.2 lists some general recommendations.

Motivation can be increased in your classroom by increasing the role students play in

Table 4.2. Strategies for Increasing Motivation

1. *Be as positive as possible.* Students work harder to gain rewards than they do to avoid punishment. Teachers can tape-record their interactions with students to ensure they are being positive whenever possible.

2. *Teach enthusiastically.* Use a rapid pace, varied inflection, and positive tone of voice. Use animated eye movements, frequent gestures, dramatic body movements, and emotive facial expression. Use variety in choice of words, and openly and positively accept ideas or suggestions made by students.

3. *Use exciting demonstrations and examples.* Show students how exciting learning can be.

4. *Choose topics and activities that interest students.* Even for basic skills learning, choose application examples that reflect student interest. For example, for math application activities, calculate data from the Indianapolis 500.

5. *Set realistic expectations* that you think students can meet, and be very positive when they meet them.

6. *Monitor progress toward goals,* and let students know how much progress they are making. When students set their own goals, they may be more motivated to achieve them.

7. *Intensify rewards,* using a variety of social and promotional rewards (e.g., public posting of achievement) and special class privileges in addition to more tangible awards.

8. *Promote positive attributions.* Students are more motivated, and more likely to succeed in the future, when they attribute their success to their own persistence of effort.

classroom decisions and in their own learning. These techniques are intended to increase the students' sense of ownership in the classroom and class activities; as a result, the students become more interested in participating. Survey students about class schedules, seating assignments, class activities, and class rules, and incorporate their input whenever possible. Ask students which rules seem fair and unfair, and what changes would improve the class atmosphere. When possible, give students options in selecting instructional activities, and ask students what type of rewards they would like to work for. Include students in *goal setting* for their own work. For example, ask students to set a goal for how many problems they will solve in a period, their reading rate at the end of the week, or the length of a paper they are writing. When the task is completed, compare the result with the goal that was set, provide feedback, and set a new goal for the future. Overall, attempts to include students in instructional and classroom decisions and to help set their own realistic learning goals will increase the motivation students feel to succeed in your classroom.

Rules, Praise, and Ignoring

Classroom rules should be simple. Rules should be discussed with the entire class, and instances and noninstances of the rules should be covered. Ideally, rules should be posted in clear view of the entire room. Rules should be stated positively rather than negatively. An example of a positively stated rule is "Good, courteous student behavior is expected at all times." "Misbehavior such as teasing and poking is not tolerated" is an example of a negatively stated rule. Because teachers should emphasize positive student behaviors, it is better to write the rules positively.

Rules, praise, and ignoring have been discussed previously as individual management techniques. The following case study provides an example of how a teacher used praise and ignoring of talkouts as a group management technique.

 ## Praise and Ignoring Scenario

Mr. L noticed that he was having more and more difficulty controlling talk-outs in his classroom. He wanted an objective evaluation of talk-outs in his classroom but was unable to find any school personnel with time to spare to do it. Besides, he was concerned that the presence of an outside observer in the classroom would change the class behavior in some way. As a result, unknown to his class, he tape-recorded several different class periods. After school, he prepared a table of all the talk-outs that had appeared on the tapes, including his own or other students' responses after each talk-out. What he found was that he was attending verbally (albeit negatively) to almost every talk-out, and in most cases, so were other students. Mr. L found that this attention seemed to be reinforcing talk-outs, rather than inhibiting them. He also found that many students (in fact, the majority) never talked out and also received almost no attention from him. Mr. L decided to change his teaching style so that he attended positively to students when they did not talk out and ignored students when they did talk out. Analysis of these recordings showed that all students but one had virtually eliminated their inappropriate talking-out. For the student who had not, he implemented a token system, whereby the student earned his recess minutes by making positive contributions in class. After this intervention, his tape-recordings showed him that instances of talk-outs had been virtually eliminated.

New teachers should (a) determine what school rules and consequences exist; (b) make their own system parallel with that of the school; (c) clearly communicate these rules and consequences to students, parents, and school administrators; (d) consistently praise appropriate behavior; and (e) consistently administer negative consequences, when necessary. Remember that positive comments should be used rather than negative ones and that consistency is a key to good classroom management. Other specific techniques, which are described in the next section, can be implemented in conjunction with rules, praise, and ignoring to establish excellent classroom management.

Class Contingencies

Research has shown that classwide contingencies, both positive and negative, can improve classroom behavior. These procedures can help teachers to enlist the support of students in promoting desired classwide responses. For example, suppose a classroom goal is to achieve a certain performance level in overall good behavior. Teachers can designate a class reward, such as a group popcorn party, a group movie, or an extra free period, that is dependent on the group's overall performance. Many times better-behaved students will help the behavior of weaker students by providing them with verbal reminders and prompts. In such cases, the class as a whole benefits from the appropriate behaviors. Conversely, the class as a whole does not receive the positive reward if the goal is not met. If such procedures are used, it is critical that the goals be realistic ones for the group. Students will soon recognize unobtainable goals and stop trying.

Another technique that has been successful in some classrooms consists of variations of the following scenario. Teachers state that every time they catch students doing something well, they will put a marble (or chip or paper clip) into a jar on their desk (in full view of all class members). Conversely, every time something inappropriate is seen, one marble or chip will be taken out of the jar. When the jar is full, the entire class will receive a reward, similar to the ones described earlier. As the jar becomes full, all students tend to remind one another of good behaviors and to self-monitor their own behaviors better in anticipation of the group reward. In resource room programs, where different students are present each period, teachers can label a separate jar for each period and thus have several group competitions simultaneously. In a self-contained classroom setting, the teacher can designate specific periods or times of the day that "count" and others that do not.

The Good Behavior Game (Brigham, Bakken, et al., 1992; Harris & Sherman, 1973) can promote cooperative behavior management within a class. Students are assigned to groups, and points are awarded to groups for prespecified behaviors by individuals. At the end of the activity, the group with the most points wins. In this type of behavior management system, students can be working individually or in cooperative groups.

These techniques can be combined with other forms of behavior management. Self-management and self-monitoring periods can be implemented and rewarded when performance is in accordance with specified rules. Extra privileges can be delivered to those students who effectively follow through with their respective self-monitoring plans.

Finally, teachers can use these procedures to reinforce different levels of learning with the class. Extra privileges assigned for good group work can provide the incentives necessary to keep progress at a desired rate.

Token Systems

Token systems can also be implemented on a groupwide basis. In such cases, the general rules for obtaining and exchanging tokens will be the same for the entire class. However, teachers occasionally may need to keep certain behaviors of some individuals on a continuous reinforcement schedule, whereas the behaviors of others are on a ratio or interval reinforcement schedule. In any event, teachers need to document the effectiveness of the reinforcement schedules that are being used.

Token systems or general point systems can be used most effectively when teachers have a classroom aide available to assist in recording behavior and awarding the tokens or points. An aide can be trained to carry a clipboard, pencil, and stopwatch and to accurately record student behaviors. Because many classrooms have either a part-time or full-time aide or a classroom volunteer, these procedures can be easily implemented in many settings.

Tokens can be awarded for appropriate social behaviors, such as attending behavior, appropriate tone of voice, and appropriate social interactions, as well as for academic task completion and performance. Academic performance should be rewarded only if students possess the academic knowledge necessary to complete the task. Reinforcement alone cannot be a substitute for instruction; it can, however, supplement instruction. Variations on token and point systems have been extremely effective in shaping desired behaviors and responses.

Level Systems

Level systems are variations on Hewett's (1968) original "engineered classroom." Level systems consist of a series of steps or levels that have corresponding rights, responsibilities, and privileges associated with them. Level systems have been successfully implemented in separate-setting schools, self-contained settings, and resource settings at both the elementary and secondary levels.

To design and implement a level system, teachers must first prioritize the expected behaviors (social and academic) and assign "levels" representing higher levels of classroom privileges. For example, assume that a situation with a low level of monitoring and a high level of privileges is assigned Level 5 and that a situation with continuous monitoring and no privileges is assigned Level 1. Levels 2, 3, and 4 are assigned behaviors and privileges arranged in a continuum between Levels 1 and 5. For instance, Level 2 could require students to sit in their seats during work periods and follow class rules, as in Level 1; however, Level 2 students would be

allowed to get up and go to the water fountain on their own after their assignments were completed. Each succeeding level adds not only more privileges but also more student responsibilities. Many teachers have successfully implemented level systems and prefer them to token or point systems. In addition, it is easier to implement self-monitoring procedures as a natural component of level systems than token or point systems.

After designing each level, teachers must clearly define criteria for passing from one level to another. Sometimes teachers incorporate the mastery of both social and academic behaviors to a specified criterion prior to moving students up a level. Conversely, when students fail to maintain adequate performance at their current level assignment, they can be moved down a level. This type of system affords teachers flexibility in assigning privileges. In addition, levels of independence assigned can be monitored with respect to the expectations of the general education classroom. This does not mean that students should be seen as having to "earn" their way into an inclusive setting; however, it may be very helpful to view the behaviors of individual students within the context of behavioral expectations in inclusive settings. As with any of the procedures described, teachers must carefully monitor the programs and student progress to ensure that the program is progressing effectively and efficiently.

Assertive Discipline

Lee Canter's (e.g., 1990, 2001) Assertive Discipline programs have been implemented and adopted by school districts across the country. They operate best on a schoolwide basis, in which all teachers and building administrators use the same rules and contingencies. One of the major assumptions of assertive discipline programs is that all students and their parents are carefully informed of all the rules and contingencies. Once the ground rules have been established, if a student disobeys a rule during class, no discussion takes place. The teacher simply writes the student's name on the blackboard. If a second infraction occurs, the teacher places a check mark next to the name. If a third occurs, the teacher writes a second check mark on the board. Typically, from this point on, variations of the assertive discipline program are implemented. In some cases, after two check marks, students miss 10 minutes of their recess period. In other cases, students are immediately removed to a time-out area, which is occasionally the classroom next door or the vice principal's office. In most cases, after a certain number of infractions have occurred, the student's parents are called and asked to follow through with a reprimand at home.

Most teachers find some adaptation of the program successful because the process eliminates the opportunity for discussion on the student's part. There is no opportunity for the student to say, "You're always picking on me!" or "Lawrence started it!" In any event, an assertive discipline program can be successful only if it is consistently implemented and all of the ground rules are understood prior to implementation. It is also important to implement positive goals so that the program does not become overly punitive. Additional guidelines for assertive discipline (summarized from Canter, 2001) are shown in Figure 4.2. Schools interested in implementing

---

1. Give expectations for teaching and learning

2. Provide rules:
   a. follow directions
   b. do not leave room without permission
   c. keep hands and feet to self
   d. no swearing or teasing

3. Corrective Actions:
   a. first time a student breaks a rule—reminder
   b. second time—5 minutes working away from group
   c. third time—10 minutes working away from group
   d. fourth time—phone to parents/guardians
   e. fifth time—send to principal
      severe clause—send to principal

4. Positive feedback:
   a. verbal recognition
   b. positive contact with parents/guardians
   c. special privileges
   d. tangible rewards

Schoolwide Implementation

Rules are schoolwide, with specific rules for playground, lunchroom, assembly, and hallway behaviors. They are implemented similarly by all teachers.

Discipline Card

Students who prove to be a behavior problem for several teachers may be issued a discipline card. All infractions made throughout the day are noted by each teacher, and corrective actions are administered by the final teacher.

Figure 4.2. Guidelines for introduction of assertive discipline to students. *Note.* From *Assertive Discipline*, by L. Canter, 2001, Santa Monica, CA: Lee Canter & Associates. Copyright 2001 by Lee Canter & Associates. Reprinted with permission.

these procedures should acquire all the necessary training materials.

Behavior Management Lessons

Good behavior can be taught to students using the same instructional delivery systems that are used to teach lessons in reading and other academic content areas. First, identify the behavior management plan that will be implemented. Second, identify the objectives to be covered and estimate the number of lessons necessary to teach the management plan. Then, design lessons to teach students the rules for that management plan using the variables for effective instruction. Figure 4.3 provides a sample behavioral contract. Once students completely understand the management plan being implemented, they will be more likely to behave appropriately.

Scheduling

One of the first and most difficult tasks that confront special education teachers every fall is the scheduling of their students, a task that must be completed rapidly at the beginning of each new year. Because the situations encountered in self-contained classrooms, resource or "pull-out programs," and inclusive classrooms are different, each is described separately in the sections that follow.

Self-Contained Classrooms

Generally, self-contained classrooms at the elementary level consist of students with learning disabilities, behavioral disorders, or mild mental disabilities who spend all or most of their academic day with a special education teacher. Similar programs are sometimes referred to as *extended resource* programs because students attend nonacademic periods such as lunch, physical education, and recess with typical age peers, although they receive all their academic work with a special education teacher. Many times students in self-contained settings also attend nonacademic periods with their age-appropriate peers. In either case, special educators are directly responsible for scheduling and teaching all academic subjects. Because classroom scheduling usually revolves around the entire school's schedule,

---

During the school year, I promise to follow these rules. If I follow these rules in the resource room, a token will be given to me each day. At the end of the week, if I have 4 to 5 tokens I will get 15 minutes of free time.

I, Vinnie Smith, promise to

1. follow the class rules;

2. talk only when the teacher gives permission;

3. touch other students' materials only when they give me permission; and

4. begin my assignment on time.

If I do not follow these rules, I may lose class privileges.

Vinnie Smith (student)   *Jennifer De la Vega (teacher)*

Figure 4.3. Sample behavioral contract, written by Jennifer De la Vega. (Used courtesy of Jennifer De la Vega.)

most programs share more commonalties than differences in overall schedules. Typically, an opening exercises period contains morning announcements and some type of short academic exercise. Reading is often scheduled for the first hour, during which students are divided into three or more groups based on ability. During this hour, these reading ability groups may need attention by one teacher and one aide. Each group's activities might also be subdivided into three 20-minute periods, including (a) 20 minutes of instruction with the teacher, (b) 20 minutes of instruction and/or guided practice with the aide, and (c) 20 minutes of independent practice and/or peer tutoring practice. This breakdown allows for maximal use of teachers and aides during the reading hour.

Following reading, many teachers schedule a restroom/water fountain break, followed by an arithmetic period. Again, ability groupings can be made, and instruction can follow some version of the reading period format. A recess and lunch period usually follows. After lunch, many teachers include a social skills period for the entire group, a language (written and oral) period, and a science and social studies period. Typically, physical education, art, and music classes are interspersed on weekly and biweekly bases.

Teachers in self-contained classrooms at both the elementary and secondary levels can usually determine their own schedules. Scheduling becomes more difficult, however, when they attempt to reintegrate their students into inclusive general education classes. This is discussed in more detail in Chapter 12.

Pull-out Programs

Elementary resource teachers probably have more difficult scheduling demands than teachers in self-contained classrooms. If scheduling has not been completed by the building administrators, resource teachers must not only adequately schedule all of their students but also satisfy the scheduling needs of regular educators. Because most students attend resource rooms for reading and math instruction, an optimal first step is to complete ability grouping for all students in those skill areas. In addition, to maintain good rapport with regular educators, resource teachers must consider regular classroom schedules when attempting to "pull out" resource students. Because it is almost impossible to please everyone 100% of the time, remember to be as pleasant as possible during communications regarding scheduling.

Once students have been assigned time periods for the resource room, it is critical to determine the daily routine for each student. Consider the teacher effectiveness variables, especially active participation and formative evaluation, during the routine design of daily formats. An example of a resource room schedule is given in Figure 4.4.

Because most secondary programs now use computerized scheduling, secondary resource teachers may not have to complete their own scheduling. At the secondary level, guidance counselors can assist in scheduling by having students sign up for third-hour reading and fourth-hour study skills. Optimal scheduling is discussed in more detail in Chapter 12.

Effective scheduling, like effective behavior management, requires thoughtful planning and good interpersonal skills. Generally, it is important to design schedules with the intention of providing the best possible service to the largest number of students, particularly because this service relates to other activities in the school day. In many cases, special education services constitute the most important part of the student's school day. However, care must be taken to ensure that all of a student's needs during a school day are being met.

Inclusive Classrooms

One potentially great advantage of fully inclusive classrooms is that there may not be scheduling complications per se. That is, if all instruction is delivered in the inclusive classroom, there is no need for concern about the best time to remove individual students with special needs

Time	Instructional Group (led by teacher)	Guided/Independent Practice Group (monitored by paraprofessional)
8:30–9:00	Reading Level I	Reading Level II
9:00–9:30	Reading Level II	Reading Level I
9:30–10:00	Reading Level III	Reading Level IV
10:00–10:30	Reading Level IV	Reading Level III
10:30–10:40	Recess/Break	Recess/Break
10:40–11:00	Math Level I	Math Level II
11:00–11:20	Math Level II	Math Level I
11:20–11:40	Math Level III	Math Level IV
11:40–12:00	Math Level IV	Math Level III
12:00–12:30	LUNCH BREAK	LUNCH BREAK
12:30–1:00	Language Arts Level I	Language Arts Level II
1:00–1:30	Language Arts Level II	Language Arts Level I
1:30–2:00	Social Skills (all levels)	open*
2:00–2:30	Study Skills Level I	open*
2:30–3:00	Study Skills Level II	open*

*Paraprofessional is available to assist with the main instructional group or to work with other small groups on an as-needed basis.

Figure 4.4. Daily resource room schedule.

from this setting. The student is not removed, and presumably the schedule of instruction follows the schedule for the entire classroom. However, complications may emerge even in inclusive classrooms. First, an individual student may need some specialized curriculum instruction in a particular subject area, and it will be necessary for an appropriate teacher to be there to work with the student. Second, a student may need to work on an area that is not a part of the general education curriculum. Examples of this could include social skills training or reading instruction at the higher grade levels when reading is no longer part of the curriculum. Finally, a student may need instruction in an area specifically related to a particular disability, such as speech therapy or Braille instruction, which is not usually a part of the general education curriculum. In such cases, classroom adaptations can be made (e.g., by "curriculum overlapping" or "multilevel curriculum instruction"; see Snell & Brown, 1993), but they may call for careful consideration of students' needs and the availability of appropriate instructional personnel. Such scheduling, however, will be oriented toward where teachers and other instructional personnel (rather than students) need to be at different times of the day. During all times of the day in inclusive classrooms, however, it is necessary for appropriate school personnel to be available to support individual students in meeting IEP goals.

Multicultural Issues

Students from some multicultural backgrounds may be referred disproportionally for behavior problems (Townsend, 2000). Some researchers (e.g., Anderson, 1992) have argued that differences in cultural backgrounds, particularly with respect to language usage, can result in misunderstandings that are interpreted incorrectly by teachers as behavior problems. Teachers of students from multicultural or linguistically diverse backgrounds should be certain that judgments made about students' classroom behavior are not based on misunderstandings about the use of language or on overly rigid notions about how all students should behave. Certainly, classroom behavioral expectations should be the same for all students, regardless of background. However, teachers should be certain that their behavioral expectations do not favor, consciously or unconsciously, students from one particular cultural background. Teachers should consider the diversity in their classroom when establishing behavioral expectations. Establishing and maintaining dialogue with students, parents, and community members can help establish fair and appropriate behavioral standards.

Summary

- Positive reinforcement is a desired consequent event that increases desired behavior. Negative reinforcement is the presentation of an undesirable stimulus that is stopped when target behavior is exhibited. Punishment is an aversive consequent event that reduces target behavior. Although negative reinforcement and punishment can be effective in changing behavior, positive reinforcement is the most effective.

- Simple posting of classroom rules is unlikely to improve student behavior. However, techniques such as praising positive behavior and ignoring inappropriate behavior can have positive effects. Direct appeal, proximity, and public posting of behavior can also have beneficial effects.

- Tangible reinforcements such as stickers, stars, toys, food, or drink can be used at early stages of shaping behavior or when weaker reinforcers have not been effective. Token systems can be used by giving tokens to students for good behavior. The tokens can later be exchanged for desired items or privileges.

- Punishment is less effective than positive reinforcement but may be helpful in some instances. Time-out, overcorrection, and re-

sponse cost are different types of punishment. Monitor the effects of punishment and ensure that more positive methods are not feasible before using punishment.

- Self-monitoring includes self-evaluation, recording, and reinforcement of behavior by the student and involves teaching the student to use the same principles the teacher uses to modify the student's own behavior. Self-monitoring can be helpful in promoting independence.

- Class contingencies, classwide token systems, level systems, and assertive discipline can be used for class or schoolwide behavior management. Behavior management systems and their functions can be presented to students in lessons similar to academic lessons.

- In some cases, differences in cultural backgrounds can result in misunderstandings about behavior problems. Teachers should be certain that their behavioral expectations do not favor students from one particular cultural background. Teachers should consider the diversity in their classroom when establishing behavioral expectations.

Relevant Research

Information on basic behavioral terminology is provided in several texts, including Alberto and Troutman (1998) and Martin and Pear (1998). These texts also provide details of behavioral techniques used in classroom management. Schedules of reinforcement are also described in these texts but were first described by Ferster and Skinner (1957). A discussion of behavioral methodology is provided by Scruggs (1992).

Published studies on effective management techniques for classroom behavior now number literally in the hundreds, only some of which can be mentioned here. Support for the relative effectiveness of positive reinforcement is provided by Mastropieri and Scruggs (1985–1986); Scruggs, Mastropieri, Cook, and Escobar (1986); and Scruggs and Mastropieri (1994c). An early and widely cited study on rules, praise, and ignoring is by Madsen, Becker, and Thomas (1968), and similar support for the use of these variables in classroom behavior management is given by Becker, Madsen, and Arnold (1967); Broden, Bruce, and Mitchell (1970); O'Leary, Kaufman, Kass, and Drabman (1970); Hachett (1975); and Mitchell and Crowell (1973). A review of research on teacher reprimands is provided by Kerr and Nelson (1998). The effectiveness of tangible reinforcement, including token systems, in special education classrooms is documented by Baker, Stanish, and Frazer (1972) and Jenkins and Gorrafa (1974). Forness and MacMillan (1972), however, caution against the overuse of tangible reinforcement. Punishment procedures are reviewed by MacMillan, Forness, and Trumball (1973) and Hewett and Forness (1984). Time-out interventions are validated by Spencer and Gray (1973), and time-out intervention for students with behavioral disorders is reviewed by Rutherford and Nelson (1982). Positive support for the use of a level system is provided by Mastropieri, Jenne, and Scruggs (1988), and positive support for the Good Behavior Game is given by Harris and Sherman (1973) and Brigham, Bakken, et al. (1992). Self-monitoring procedures are validated by Levendoski and Cartledge (2000). Kendall and Braswell (1985) provide a thorough review of cognitive-behavioral interventions with special education students, and Kerr and Nelson (1998) review successful strategies in that area. The effectiveness of group contingencies is reported by Wolf, Hanley, and King (1970) and Greenwood, Hops, and Delquadri (1974) and reviewed by Liton and Pumroy (1975). Successful self-management and self-monitoring research is reported by DiGangi and Maag (1992); Hughes, Ruhl, and Misra (1989); Shores, Gunter, and Jack (1993); DiGangi, Maag, and Rutherford (1991); Prater, Joy, Chilman, Temple, and Miller (1991); and Etscheidt (1991). Finally, a comprehensive review of self-recording research is reported by Lloyd and Landrum (1990), and a review of self-management research is reported by Nelson, Smith, Young, and Dodd (1991).

Information about the Assertive Discipline program can be found in Canter (1990), and suggestions for dealing with aggressive or confrontational students are provided in Canter and Canter (1993). Strategies for increasing motivation in special education and other settings have been reviewed by Dev (1997) and Ford (1995). Multicultural considerations in discipline are discussed by Townsend (2000), and a discussion of behavioral interventions used with diverse students is provided by Ishii-Jordan (2000).

Peer Assistants in Inclusive Environments

Peer assistants can help students with disabilities in inclusive environments remain on task during class. A peer can sometimes provide a gentle reminder to a student who has difficulties attending to the task. Often this reminder will be sufficient to assist some students with getting back to the task. In setting up a peer assistant program, attend to the following:

- Select peers who want to be peer assistants rather than simply assigning students to the role.

- Train peer assistants in the role.
  Be specific about what the assistant is to do and is *not* to do. (Caution: Some peers do too much for the students with disabilities—some too little.)

- Prepare the students with disabilities for working with a peer assistant.
  Review what the peer assistant will be doing.

- Role-play with the peer assistants and the student with disabilities the tasks they will be doing together.

- Monitor the situation carefully.
  If either the peer assistant or the student with disabilities feels uncomfortable, you may need to make a change.

Recruiting Positive Teacher Attention

Students with disabilities can be taught to be more proactive in general education classes. Research has demonstrated that when students with disabilities are given instruction in how to recruit teacher attention in positive ways, teachers provide students with more positive feedback and view them more positively. For example, Alber et al. (1999) taught students with disabilities how to recruit positive teacher attention in general education classes. In a special education setting, students were taught to raise their hands, wait patiently for recognition from teachers, and ask questions or make statements using a proper tone of voice. Students were then initially prompted to use the recruitment procedures in their inclusive classes. Their data revealed the following:

- Students recruited teacher attention at a higher rate than before training.
- Teachers rewarded students with more praise.
- Teachers provided more instructional feedback on an individual basis.
- Students' independent work accuracy rates increased substantially.

These findings appear promising and worthy of exploration with all students with disabilities in inclusive classes.

Using Videotapes as Self-Monitoring Devices

Some students who are working to improve their social skills can benefit from seeing actual videotapes of their social behavior during classes. Check with your school regarding obtaining permission from both the school and the parents to use videotaping in your class. Once permission is obtained, arrange the camera on a tripod in a location that can view the entire room or focus on particular students and record the class. Privately view the tape and edit segments for target students to see.

- Select segments that demonstrate appropriate social skills.
  Show these segments to target students and explain that this is the social behavior that is expected.

- Select segments that demonstrate inappropriate social behavior.
  Show those segments as noninstances of appropriate social behavior.

  Use these segments as teaching situations. Stop the tape and say, for example, "Stop and think about what might have been another way of handling that situation that would have been more socially appropriate."

- Select segments that demonstrate improvement in students' social skills and show them to reinforce those improvements.
  These segments can be used to document progress and shown to parents and administrators to demonstrate improvements.

Chapter 5

❧　　❧　　❧

Reading

Reading is one of the most important academic skills students learn during their years in school. Reading ability is very important for most instructional activities. For example, a student with reading problems typically cannot be expected to succeed without substantial adaptations in a history class because most information in history classes is conveyed through textbooks. In special education, students commonly exhibit serious deficits in reading skills. These deficits may make it more difficult for students to participate in other general education courses that emphasize reading skills, including science, drama, history, geography, English, foreign languages, health, civics, language arts, and, possibly, areas such as art and physical education. Although adaptations can be employed to facilitate learning in inclusive classrooms that normally require reading, students should nevertheless develop independent reading skills whenever possible.

There are many ways to teach reading, and there has been much debate over the best methods. Some educators have maintained that reading should be taught using a code-emphasis (phonics) approach. This approach teaches students to use word-attack skills to decode familiar and unfamiliar words. Other educational leaders have argued for a meaning-emphasis approach in teaching reading. This approach stresses the building of sight words and the use of contextual clues in deciphering unfamiliar words. In reality, however, there are few code-emphasis programs that do not also incorporate meaningfulness, and there are few meaning-emphasis programs that do not also teach decoding skills. In most cases, the issue of reading instruction concerns the degree of emphasis teachers should place on word-attack versus meaning. Because many students with disabilities are deficient in *phonemic awareness*—that is, the knowledge of speech sounds (phonemes) and how they are combined to form words—and in the use of the orthographic structure of language (letters) in aiding word recognition, research in special education has generally supported the effectiveness of code-emphasis programs. However, it is also critically important that the meaning of words and passages be emphasized at all stages of the teaching process and that students learn to read a variety of materials. In addition, research has shown that specific instructional strategies have been effective in promoting reading comprehension, an area sometimes neglected in special education settings. Although phonics instruction has been shown to be of critical importance, it should not be taught to the exclusion of the central purpose of reading—the extraction of meaning from written text.

This chapter first provides an overview of reading instruction that incorporates the application of effective teaching practices described in previous chapters, including maximizing engaged time-on-task, pacing, questioning, feedback, practice activities, and formative evaluation. The sections that follow describe practices for teaching phonetic analysis. The final section of the chapter describes strategies for improving reading comprehension.

A meaning-based approach referred to as *whole language* has been widely promoted for reading instruction. Advocates of this approach recommend (a) de-emphasis of phonics instruction in favor of emphasis on meaning and context in learning new words; (b) use of a wide variety of reading materials, including authentic literature; and (c) integration of reading, writing, and other language arts activities (Five, 1992). Although the latter two components can be very useful in helping students meet application and generalization objectives, at least some direct instruction in phonics and phonemic awareness is very likely to be necessary for students with mild disabilities. In addition, research has suggested that students with reading disabilities and other struggling readers already overuse context cues (because they lack word-attack skills) and frequently read words incorrectly when they try to guess the word based on context. Therefore, an approach that places great emphasis on context cues as a word-reading strategy may not be helpful for many problem readers. At present little, if any, convincing research supports the exclusive use of the whole-language approach with students with mild disabilities (e.g., Gersten & Dimino, 1993; Mather, 1992; Pressley & Rankin, 1994). In fact, some research (e.g., Rudenga, 1992) suggests that the whole-language approach, without other support, may not meet the needs of these students. Therefore, teachers who wish to rely exclusively on this method should be very careful to collect formative data that document its effectiveness with individual students. Snider (1997) has shown that students with learning disabilities can make progress in whole-language classrooms if they are also receiving explicit phonics instruction from special education teachers at the same time.

Teaching Reading: An Overview

Teaching reading is one of the most important activities of a special education teacher. Many students enter special education with a history of failure in reading. To maximize student learning during reading instruction, teachers should attend carefully to the components of reading instruction. The section that follows describes strategies for (a) selecting a reading program, (b) initial assessment and placement, (c) grouping for instruction, (d) teaching new information, (e) monitoring guided and independent practice, and (f) monitoring and adjusting instruction based on formative evaluation data.

Selecting a Reading Program

The reading programs that have been most successful in special education have generally emphasized phonics or word-attack skills. These programs are easily identified by their systematic use of controlled letters and letter combinations that repeat the same sounds. In this approach, students are provided with repeated practice on words containing similar letters and similar sounds. For example, when introducing the sound *ound*, as in *found*, a code-emphasis program provides a reading passage containing several different instances of the sound by using words such as *pound*, *bound*, *found*, *sound*, and *mound*. Exceptions to this pronunciation (e.g., *wound*, meaning injury) typically do not appear until much later in the program. In addition, sound patterns are not introduced until all individual sounds in the pattern have been covered. For example, *cat* would not be introduced until the three separate sounds, *c*, *a*, and *t*, had all been introduced. Examples of code- and meaning-emphasis programs are given in Figure 5.1.

Although code-emphasis programs may differ with respect to specific formats, use of illustrations, and the sequence in which skills are taught, they share the common feature of introducing specific sounds and word patterns in a systematic and controlled fashion and avoiding exceptions to phonetic rules when rules are first being learned.

Once a code-emphasis reading series has been identified, other features need to be considered before selecting a specific series. It may be impossible to locate a series that addresses all of the features listed below; however, when one or

Reading Passages	Explanation
Code Emphasis	
Dan ran to the big hill. He ran up the big hill. On top of the hill he ran to a big pit. He sat on top of the pit. In the pit he saw a dog. The dog was sad.	Includes sight words *the* and *to*, but all other words are regular pronunciations of short vowels (e.g., *Dan, ran, hill, pit, dog*).
Meaning Emphasis	
Dan thought he would like to know what was on top of the great hill behind his house. One day he climbed up to look for himself. He found a small dog caught in a pit.	Reads more like conversation but contains phonetic irregularities (e.g., three *ou* words [*thought, would, house*] that are all pronounced differently).

Figure 5.1. Code versus meaning emphasis in reading passages.

more of these features are lacking in a series, teachers need to supplement the deficits with other material.

1. *Interest level.* Has the series sacrificed interest level for phonetic regularity?

2. *Age appropriateness.* Are poorer readers likely to be insulted by content intended for younger students?

3. *Breadth of reading activities.* Does the series provide sufficient examples of reading under different formats, such as fiction, nonfiction, poetry, and current events?

4. *Compatibility with district's scope and sequence.* Does the series scope and sequence provide instruction on the skills that are emphasized in general education classrooms?

5. *Sufficient opportunity for practice.* Does the series provide sufficient practice for students with learning problems, particularly at fluency and mastery levels?

6. *Comprehension instruction.* Does the series emphasize particular comprehension strategies and skills?

7. *Validation data.* Does the series provide some evidence that it has been successfully implemented with students with disabilities?

8. *Instructional component.* Does the series provide teachers with specific instructional guidelines that correspond with the teacher effectiveness literature?

9. *Evaluation component.* Does the series provide a format by which student performance and instruction can be monitored and adjusted on a regular basis?

10. *Diversity.* Does the series provide sufficient representation of diverse cultures and gender roles?

No series will possess all of the above features, and in some cases, one or two of these features may be of little concern. For example, if the materials are used only with primary-age students, then a lower interest level may be appropriate. However, prior to adopting a series, all of the above questions need to be answered satisfactorily. Eventually, it is the teacher's responsibility to incorporate all of the above features into reading instruction. For example, if a series does not provide adequate comprehension instruction, teachers will have to supplement the series with reading comprehension instruction. If the series does not provide sufficient breadth of reading activities, teachers will need to obtain additional materials. Likewise, if a series does not include a formative evaluation component, teachers will need to develop an appropriate evaluation system on their own.

In many cases, teachers do not have the luxury of selecting their own reading programs. When this occurs, selection must be made from existing district materials. Teachers must then select the materials that contain most of the above features. Any features that are lacking should be supplemented by teachers. Probably the greatest problem encountered in the use of existing school district materials is that such materials may not provide controlled skill development and vocabulary. In such cases, teachers must adapt instruction to emphasize the phonetic regularities that do exist and de-emphasize the irregularities. Even with such adaptations, instructional materials may be far from optimal. Teachers can use other means to acquire phonetically based materials, such as contacting district libraries or the libraries of other districts and nearby universities. Publishers will often provide sample materials to teachers on request.

Reading Assessment

When students enter special education settings, their teachers typically have access to their assessment data, including evaluations of reading ability. Assessment data are usually normative, which means the scores compare a student's functioning with that of other students in terms of percentiles or grade equivalents. Such information is useful in determining the nature and extent of the academic deficiency and in assisting in special education placement decisions. Furthermore, normative data may provide some general insights into the student's reading abilities. Typical normative data, however, do not provide information helpful in placing the student along the continuum of scope and sequence objectives.

Curriculum-Based Assessment

To determine a student's level within a reading program, teachers must implement curriculum-based assessment. Curriculum-based assessment,

as described in Chapter 3, refers to the direct evaluation of a student's skills with respect to an instructional curriculum. Given that the curriculum objectives parallel those of the district's scope and sequence, as well as those of the IEP, a curriculum-based assessment simply locates the instructional starting place. For example, if the desired level of fluency is defined as 120 words per minute read orally with no errors, teachers should find the latest place in the curriculum at which this level of performance can be achieved. The first section of the curriculum at which this level of performance is not achieved is the optimal place to begin instruction. As another example, if successful reading comprehension, defined as answering correctly four recall questions and one inferential question per page, is desired, then an appropriate level to start is the point in the curriculum at which the student fails to meet these criteria. As stated earlier, such performance criteria should be determined by the evaluation of performance levels commonly observed in inclusive settings. These can be obtained by consultation with regular classroom teachers or similar evaluation of more typical students' performances.

It is important for teachers to develop standardized curriculum-based assessment procedures. To do this, teachers should select samples from passages of relatively low, moderate, and high difficulty from each level in their reading series. Performance criteria for decoding and comprehension should also be established for each level. As teachers develop a set of assessment devices, they will begin to have a systematic procedure for instructional placement in their reading curriculum. These procedures assist teachers in making instructional grouping decisions.

Although reading rates vary from school to school and vary with the difficulty of the reading material, some examples may be of interest. The following are reading rates per minute for students in the Minneapolis public schools, from Fuchs and Deno (1992):

Fall, Grade 2: 54.82 words per minute
Fall, Grade 3: 89.67 words per minute

Fall, Grade 4: 92.89 words per minute
Fall, Grade 5: 75.38 words per minute
Fall, Grade 6: 131.00 words per minute

Instructional Grouping

Curriculum-based assessment provides important information for instructional grouping. Instructional grouping is necessary to maximize teaching effectiveness. Although groups of mixed student ability are sometimes recommended, grouping students by skill level in reading instruction allows all students to work on skills they need to learn. When students are matched appropriately for instruction, the potential for all students to be engaged on task is maximized.

Instructional grouping is achieved by scheduling students together who perform at similar levels with respect to a specific curriculum. The more similarly the students perform, the more efficient the instructional group. In practice, however, it is not always easy to schedule perfectly matched instructional groups. Although instructional grouping is a way of maximizing instructional performance, it is also important to attend carefully to the instructional needs of individual students, particularly those whose performance is somewhat higher or lower than the majority of the group. Formative evaluation can help to ensure that all individuals are meeting instructional goals.

Once groups have been formed, teachers must ensure that assignment to groups remains dynamic and flexible. Research has shown that instructional groups have a tendency to remain static and stationary with respect to individual group membership. This is not always in the students' best interests. Group performance over time is a dynamic process, and this process should be carefully attended to by teachers. Membership within groups should be changed whenever performance warrants it. For example, if a student seems to progress more rapidly through the curriculum than other members of the group and seems insufficiently challenged, the student should be moved to a more appropriate instructional group. In other cases, it may be advisable to move a student from one group to another simply for the purpose of morale or group dynamics. Although research has shown that a student may benefit from being in a group with somewhat better readers, more caution should be applied in placing a student in a group with poorer readers.

The optimal number of students to be placed in a group cannot be precisely specified, but some considerations can be taken into account. These include

1. total number of students needing instruction,

2. ability of students to work independently,

3. total time allocated for reading instruction, and

4. instructional resources available, including space, materials, and aides, tutors, or other paraprofessionals (e.g., parents, volunteers).

All of the above factors should be considered when deciding the size of instructional groups. Generally, groups of two seem inefficient, but groups larger than eight may be cumbersome. Just as assignment to group membership should be dynamic, assignment of group size should also be dynamic. If the size of a group appears problematic, it should be adjusted accordingly.

Reading Instruction

Chapter 1 presented the important components of effective instruction. These include (a) daily review, (b) presentation of objectives and material to be learned, (c) guided practice, (d) independent practice, (e) weekly and monthly reviews, and (f) formative evaluation. These functions are described with respect to reading instruction. During reading lessons, teachers should emphasize that the purpose of reading is comprehension and enjoyment. When decoding skills and oral reading fluency are primary objectives, teachers must make extra efforts to show students that understanding is the underlying objective. This can be accomplished by making statements reiterating that the purpose of reading is to understand what the printed letters mean and by always including comprehension questions in lessons, such as "What does that mean?" "Can you think of another way to say that?" and "Can you use that word in a sentence?" A sample reading lesson is given in Figure 5.2.

Daily Review

Each reading lesson should begin with a review of the content covered in the previous lesson and a review of the purpose of reading. For example, if the previous lesson emphasized discrimination of words containing *b* and *d*, the

Component	Examples
1. *Daily Review*	"Yesterday we learned some new words and their meanings from our book. Let's go over them together. What is this word? [Point to board.] Good. And what does [that word] mean? Can you think of a sentence using [that word]? . . . Who remembers how [that word] was used in the story? . . ."
2. *State Purpose*	"Today we are going to learn some more new words. These words all have *r*s in them. First, we are going to learn how to say the words and what they mean. Then, we will practice using the words when we read our stories and when we write the words, their pronunciations, and their meanings in our reading logs."
3. *Deliver Information*	"These three letters plus *r*—[write on board] *ir, ur* and *er*—all make the /r/ sound when they are together. When we see these letters in words we know that we should make the /r/ sound. Everybody, say the sound with me. [Signal.] . . . Good. Now look at the words that I have on the overhead. Most of these words have those letters plus *r*. How do we say the sound of those letters plus *r*? Let's go over this list together. The first word is [say word]; repeat after me. [Signal.] Now let's go over the definitions of each of these words that contain the special letters plus *r*. Does anyone know the meaning of the first word?" [Call on students and provide definitions when necessary.] . . .
4. *Guided Practice*	"Now I want you to get with your tutoring partners. I have a set of flash cards containing these words, their pronunciations, and their meanings. Each of you should take a turn as the tutor and as the tutee. Remember to use the correct tutoring behaviors and to record each other's performance. . . ."
5. *Independent Practice*	"Good job working hard during tutoring. It looks like everyone has learned our new words. Stay with your partners, put the flash cards away, and take out your books. We are going to read and discuss the third chapter of our book. This chapter contains many of the words that have the /r/ sound we have just practiced. The students who were the last ones to be tutors will read first to their partners. After a page, switch roles. You should help each other with the new words. Jot down the words that you have trouble saying. We'll discuss the chapter together. . . ."
6. *Formative Evaluation*	"When you think you can say each of the new words, use each one in a sentence, and tell me what happened in Chapter 3. Raise your hand and I will let you take your quiz."

Figure 5.2. Sample reading lesson on *r*-controlled vowels.

next lesson should begin with a review of this discrimination and direct questioning of students to determine whether the discrimination has been mastered. Comprehension questions on the meanings of those words should also be included. If the discrimination is not found to be firm, additional instruction should be provided. For another example, if students had previously been taught a rule for decoding consonant–vowel–consonant–silent *e* (CVCE; e.g., *kite*) words, the rule should be reviewed prior to proceeding to the next lesson. Review not only provides the teacher with an opportunity to determine whether the information has been acquired, but it also provides students an opportunity for overlearning previously acquired information. Overlearning activities promote long-term retention and help set the stage for future learning activities. If homework has been assigned, this is the time to emphasize the importance of the homework and to check it to ensure that assignments have been completed accurately.

Presentation of Material To Be Learned

Presentation of new content in reading should follow the teacher presentation model presented in Chapter 1. When introducing new content, such as new letter sounds or a comprehension monitoring procedure, teachers must first state the objectives and main points to be covered. That is, in the case of a letter sound, teachers make it explicitly clear that the lesson's goal is to learn that letter sound. Similarly, teachers would make it clear that a specific procedure for monitoring comprehension will be learned. Next, teachers should include a step-by-step presentation of the new material. In the above examples, teachers would provide the letter and corresponding sound or present the comprehension-monitoring strategy in a step-by-step fashion. Next, teachers should model and demonstrate the new skill. Finally, after repeated questioning and practice, teachers should monitor students' understanding and adjust instruction accord-

ingly. These procedures will be described in more detail later in this chapter.

Guided Practice

In reading instruction, guided practice often takes the form of students reading orally in small-group settings. Oral reading can be either from word lists or passages of story books that contain instances of the material previously introduced. A major goal of teachers at this point in instruction is to maximize engaged time-on-task for all students. This is done by ensuring that all students actively participate, even when they are not reading aloud. There are several means by which teachers can ensure that all students are covertly participating while one student is reading aloud. The most obvious method is to call on students to read in a random, rather than a systematic, manner (e.g., left to right across the group). If students can deduce that they will not soon be asked to read, they are less likely to attend to the reading passage. Students also can be reinforced with praise, points, or tokens for knowing the correct place in the reading passage when called on. When asking questions, the teacher should mention the student's name after, rather than before, the question is asked (e.g., "What do you think the character is going to do next. . . . Ramon?"). If students think they might be called on, they are more likely to think actively about the answer. Another active participation strategy is to have all students respond simultaneously after a teacher's signal. It is also helpful to occasionally have all students orally read simultaneously. Likewise, teachers can ask questions that require all students to respond with their thumbs (or hands) up or down (e.g., "Do you think the bear will see them? Thumbs up for yes or thumbs down for no.").

Students can also read to each other in pairs rather than one at a time. Teachers can monitor the performance of several pairs of students with little difficulty. This activity can be very helpful in large groups that contain students of different reading levels.

Generally, it should be assumed that any procedure that facilitates or reinforces the active participation of all students at all times is likely to maximize learning. It is easy to understand how a reading group of four students, all of whom are actively engaged in reading, will be four times as effective as a similar group in which only one student at a time is on task. The most critical aspect of guided practice is to provide students with many opportunities to respond correctly. Guided practice is most appropriate when students have been introduced to new skills and are in the process of strengthening these newly acquired skills. Although errors are expected at this stage, teachers need to provide immediate corrective feedback so that only correct responses are strengthened. When students are responding at a high level of accuracy, guided practice is less necessary, and instruction can proceed to a more independent level.

Independent Practice

Independent practice in reading typically takes the form of independent seatwork, which may consist of silent reading with written responses to questions and completion of workbooks or worksheets. Independent practice is not as closely monitored by teachers, because they are often engaged with other students in instruction or guided practice. When students are engaged in independent practice, activities should closely parallel the goals of the lesson and be directly relevant to the guided practice activities that were previously completed. The teacher should reinforce quick, quiet, and accurate performance. Finally, independent practice activities need to be evaluated regularly. If a student is not performing accurately, additional guided practice or reteaching may be necessary. Conversely, if students are consistently exhibiting superior performance, they may need to proceed through the curriculum at a faster pace.

Independent practice can provide opportunities for overlearning in a context removed from a teacher-directed group setting. This may include developing mastery of skills. Independent practice is also helpful as a context for reinforcing independent study and work habits. It also provides an opportunity for students to develop a sense of responsibility for their own learning. However, research has generally shown that special education students learn at a slower rate from independent seatwork than they do from teacher-led instruction and guided practice. Although some benefits can be gained from independent practice, it is important for teachers to maximize the time spent in direct, teacher-led instructional contexts.

An alternative to the seatwork activity described earlier is the use of peer tutoring. Research has shown that special education students can function effectively as tutors and often gain fluency building skills in the process. In addition, tutoring has sometimes been seen to improve students' attitudes toward school and the content areas being tutored. Tutoring may also prove advantageous in that it provides students with additional practice in active responding. If peer tutors are employed, however, teachers must ensure that tutors use appropriate feedback procedures and that formative data are collected to ensure that both tutor and tutee benefit from the process. Because effective reading instruction demands a great deal of independent reading practice, tutoring can be an effective means of reaching this goal. Figure 5.3 presents additional information on peer tutoring, summarized from Scruggs, Mastropieri, and Richter (1985) and Scruggs and Mastropieri (1998).

One effective type of peer tutoring is known as classwide peer tutoring (CWPT; e.g., Delquadri, Greenwood, Whorton, Carta, & Hall, 1986). In this model, the entire class is divided into tutoring pairs of students of higher and lower ability and takes turns reading to each other. In a variation known as peer-assisted learning strategies (PALS; e.g., Fuchs, Fuchs, Mathes, & Simmons, 1997; Fuchs, Fuchs, & Burish, 2000), students can also ask each other "who," "what," "where," "why," and "when" questions or questions such as, "What is the most important *what* or *who* in the text?" and "What

---

Procedures for Peer Tutoring Programs

1. Select pairs that are likely to work well together.

2. For drill-and-practice activities using flash cards, students can be of similar ability. If a great deal of correction is likely or judgment is called for, however, the tutor should be of higher ability.

3. When acting as tutors, students should use the same teaching procedures as the teacher, except that they should not introduce new content. Correction of errors should be immediate and positive and require restatement of the correct response by the tutee (e.g., "No, the word is pronounced _____. You say it. [Response.] Good.").

4. Even though research has shown that tutors can often learn from tutoring, they should not be overused in this capacity. Formative evaluation should be used to show that all students' objectives are being met.

5. All tutoring activities should be relevant to specific instructional objectives.

Potential Benefits of Tutoring

1. Tutees can gain the benefits of additional individual engaged time-on-task (e.g., greater levels of accuracy and/or fluency).

2. Students who are accurate in a skill can gain fluency by acting as a tutor.

3. Students who are engaged in tutoring can gain a sense of responsibility for themselves and others and can gain improved attitudes toward the class and the content area taught (e.g., reading). However, tutoring may not fulfill global, more difficult-to-measure constructs such as self-esteem.

4. Formative evaluation can determine whether the above potential benefits have, in fact, been realized.

Figure 5.3. Peer tutoring. *Note.* Adapted from Scruggs and Mastropieri (1998).

is the most important thing about the *what* or *who* in the text?" Students can also ask each other main idea or sequencing questions (e.g., "What is the first thing you learned?" "What is the second thing you learned?"). In these cases, it is important to develop a "tutoring checklist," so all students know exactly what their responsibilities are.

Another alternative to worksheet activities is computer-assisted instruction (CAI). Like peer tutoring, CAI provides students with immediate feedback. In addition, a tutor is not required, and several contemporary programs include collection of performance data. One drawback of CAI is that computers at present are unable to monitor students' oral reading performance directly. CAI can be helpful in providing practice with feedback on word-attack skills and reading comprehension.

Weekly and Monthly Reviews

In special education, it is critical to continuously review previously covered material to ensure long-term retention of the material. For this reason, teachers should review acquired reading skills on a weekly, monthly, and daily basis. For example, weekly and monthly reviews of phonics rules or comprehension skills learned to date help to make these skills more concrete and reinforce students' knowledge of the overall scope, sequence, and purposes of reading instruction. To enhance students' confidence in their progress, teachers can provide students with examples of their previous levels of performance. For example, students can be required to keep alphabet books, dictionaries, or daily logs that contain records of new letters, sounds, words, meanings, books read, and strategies learned during reading.

These logs can become part of a student's portfolio and can document the amount of learning that has occurred. It is also helpful to record learning gains on graphs or charts and by playing audiotapes or videotapes of students' previous reading performances.

Formative Evaluation

As in all areas of instruction, formative data should be collected regularly, graphed, and used to guide the instructional decision-making process. Chapter 3 describes how to develop and administer curriculum-based formative evaluation in reading.

Chapter 3 also presents information on how to design, administer, and use curriculum-based measures (CBM) to monitor progress in reading. Research results have indicated that students will exhibit greater performance under the following conditions:

1. Teachers administer CBM at least twice a week.

2. Teachers select CBM based on students' long-term goals.

3. Teachers examine the results of the CBM and make relevant instructional decisions based on performance data (e.g., increase time on task, alter instructional grouping).

For example, students can be administered timed readings of 100-word selections that reflect long-term objectives from their curricular materials twice a week. Teachers can record reading rate, number and type of reading errors (decoding, omission, insertion, etc.), and comprehension scores (answers to factual and inferential questions about the passage). Examination of these data recorded over time can provide important information on student progress and instructional needs.

This section has presented an overview of reading instruction and described components common to all aspects of reading instruction. In any reading program, at any stage of instruction, it is important to review previous material, present new information clearly and concisely, provide guided practice on new material, provide independent practice activities, and periodically review cumulative information. It is also necessary to collect formative data and to regularly monitor and adjust instruction in accordance with formative data. At all times, it is important to maintain very high rates of on-task engagement.

The remainder of this chapter is devoted to applications of these procedures to specific areas of reading instruction. The next section discusses strategies for teaching phonemic awareness, word-attack skills (phonics), and reading fluency, and the last section discusses strategies for improving reading comprehension.

Teaching Phonemic Awareness

Phonemes are the smallest units of speech that make a difference to meaning, and there are 44 in the English language. For example, the phonemes /r/, /a/, /t/ make up the word *rat*. *Phonemic awareness* is the understanding that every spoken word can be thought of as a sequence of phonemes (Snow, Burns, & Griffin, 1998). Research has demonstrated that phonemic awareness is a strong predictor of early reading ability and that students with specific reading difficulties very frequently are weak in phonemic awareness. Fortunately, research has also demonstrated that students who are weak in phonemic awareness can be effectively trained in these skills and can realize significant gains in reading ability as a result.

Phonemic awareness training programs can teach such things as letter names and their sounds, classifying sounds as similar or different (e.g., /t/, /p/), creating rhymes, dividing words into phonemes, and creating new words using different phonemes. The following are some examples of phonemic awareness activities:

- Phoneme discrimination, such as, "Tell me if these words have different sounds: *pat–pat* (no); *tap–tack* (yes)."

- Segmenting sounds, such as, "How many sounds are in the word *cup*? Everybody, count the sounds together, /c/, /u/, /p/. How many sounds? Yes, three, that's correct."

- Rhyming, such as, "Tell me some words that rhyme with *can*. Let's see how many we can think of. Now, tell me some make-believe words that rhyme with *can* (e.g., *nan*)."

- Sound blending, such as, "Tell me what word I am saying: /p/, /e/, /t/."

- Identification of beginning sounds, such as the following: "What is the first sound in *dog*? That's right, /d/. Now tell me if these two words have same first sound: *pop–mop*. No, that's correct. They don't. Now, what about these? Do they have the same first sound: *net–neck*? Yes, that's right, they do both begin with /n/."

- Identifying middle and end sounds, using procedures described for identifying beginning sounds.

As students gain fluency with phonemic awareness skills, they can begin to learn that phonemes can be represented by letters, and these letters can be combined to make words. This is the beginning of phonics instruction as it applies to reading.

Teaching Phonics Skills

As stated earlier in this chapter, most research indicates that children with learning difficulties learn to read most easily under instruction that is systematic, well paced, and phonetic in orientation. If teachers provide intensive instruction and practice on critical word-attack skills, most students with learning difficulties can learn to read.

It was also stated earlier in this chapter that good word-attack skills are only one part of the total reading process. Without such skills, however, most special education students will not learn to read effectively. During phonics instruction, it is also important to emphasize meaning. At the earliest stages of reading instruction, students are primarily concerned with "cracking the code" of reading, but teachers need to emphasize the meaning of the printed words.

Word-attack or phonics instruction can be divided into several different components. These include (a) letter–sound correspondences, (b) sound blending, (c) phonics rule learning, and (d) learning of irregular sight words. Examples of these components are shown in Table 5.1, and they are described separately in the following sections.

Letter–Sound Correspondence

Letter–sound correspondence, or the learning of sound–symbol relationships, is the first major step in the reading process. During this component of reading instruction, students are taught that written language is composed of individual letter symbols and that the clues to the reading process are in these symbols. This initial concept about decoding should develop as students learn more about sound–symbol relationships.

Fact Learning

Letter–sound correspondence is one form of fact learning; that is, to learn that the letter *b* is associated with the *buh* sound (/b/) is to learn a fact. There is no general rule that will tell a student what sound a certain letter represents. These sounds and corresponding letters must simply be memorized, and the more time students spend actively practicing these sounds, the faster they will learn. Students also must learn to discriminate different letters, especially ones that differ only in spatial orientation, such as *b* and *d*.

Table 5.1. Phonics Examples

Phonics Components	Examples
Letter–sound correspondence	*a* as in hat
	b as in bat
	c as in cat
	d as in dog
Sound blending	cat = cuh-a-tuh
	hill = huh-iii-luh
Long vowels	
CVC+e	*o* as in vote
	a as in bake
vowel digraphs	*ea* as in beat
	ai as in bait
	oe as in toe
Diphthongs	*oi* as in voice
	ou as in sound
	ow as in brown
Consonant blends	*br* as in break
	bl as in black
	gr as in ground
	scr as in script
Long and short *oo*	
Long *oo*	*oo* as in too
	oo as in tool
Short *oo*	*oo* as in book
	oo as in cook
r-controlled vowels	*ur* as in hurt
	ir as in shirt
	er as in water
	ar as in star
	or as in actor

Such discriminations are necessary for accurate reading.

Sound Versus Names

The teaching of sound–symbol correspondence should not be confused with learning the names of the letters of the alphabet (e.g., *a, bee, cee, dee,* etc.). Many students enter school having learned their ABCs as a serial list, but many of them have no idea what these letter names represent. Their parents have simply reinforced

them for reciting them in the correct sequence. In fact, research has not demonstrated that learning to recite the alphabet is helpful in learning to read. However, in some cases, it may promote early success and improve a student's attitude toward learning to read, and it has been seen that letter identification is a strong early predictor of early reading ability. To this extent, learning the alphabet can contribute to overall familiarity with letters and make learning letter sounds less difficult.

Most Common Sound

When learning letter–sound correspondence, students must learn the most common sound associated with each letter first. Most consonants, other than *c* and *g*, have highly regular sounds associated with them. Vowel sounds are usually taught by providing the most common short sounds associated with them (e.g., *a* as in *apple, e* as in *bed, i* as in *bitter,* etc.). Letters are usually introduced one at a time after a review of previously learned letters. Students can be grouped easily for letter–sound knowledge because there are only a certain number of letters to be learned. When grouping for instruction or while delivering instruction, teachers need to determine the rate (fluency) at which students can identify letters, as well as their level of accuracy. At any given time during the instructional process, students should be able to read a list of letters previously taught at a rate of 100 or more per minute. Such automaticity of responding is necessary so that students can concentrate on other reading skills at a later date.

Teaching Letter Sounds

As stated earlier in this chapter, a reading lesson should begin with a review of previously learned information. In the case of letter sounds, the teacher should first review any previous learning and homework assignments (e.g., relevant phonics worksheets or records of guided practice with parents or sibling tutors). Next, the teacher should clearly state the objective for the day's lesson (e.g., "Today we are going to learn two new letter sounds"). Students can be asked to repeat this information on cue to ensure attention (e.g., "What are we going to learn, everybody?" [Signal]). When the teacher feels the group understands the purpose of the lesson, the first letter can be displayed or drawn on the board while the teacher says, "The letter sound we are going to learn today is /m/. [Point] Everybody say it with me: /m/." The students should repeat the letter sound on cue from the teacher, both as a group and individually, until the teacher feels the initial part of the association has been established. Students should then be given practice in discriminating the letter from other, previously learned letters. This can be done both as an identification task (e.g., "Point to the letter that makes the /m/ sound") and as a production task (e.g., "Read these letters as I point them out to you"). Students can also be familiarized with the physiology of sound production if they have not learned this earlier with phonemic awareness training ("Can you make the /m/ sound if you are holding your nose? Why not?"). It is important that students learn to read the individual letter first, then learn to read it in the context of previously learned information. It is also important to include reading sounds in the context of words, words in sentences, and sentences in stories as early and as often as possible. This will help reinforce that the purpose of reading is comprehension, not simply saying sounds of letters or reading words in isolation. If students begin to forget previous information, instruction may be proceeding too rapidly. If students always know all previously and presently introduced content, instruction may be proceeding too slowly. Daily probes (timings) of previously and presently taught information can help determine the optimal rate of instruction. An example of a probe sheet used to assess decoding skills could include a list of the letters and words being taught or even short passages containing the target information.

Like instruction in other areas, lessons should be positive and rapidly paced, allow for much overt student responding, and allow for a high level of correct responses. Errors should be acknowledged but not emphasized unless an error was due to carelessness, inattention, or flippancy. At such moments, teachers need to emphasize paying attention and putting forth effort.

Sequence of Instruction

In most cases, the sequence of introducing new letter sounds, word patterns, and words will parallel the curriculum. The teacher's guide that accompanies the reading series will generally identify which new letter sounds, word patterns, and words are being introduced. Teachers should be overt about introducing the new sound (even if the text is not) and make sure that the sounds are applied correctly in any application or generalization exercises (e.g., reading the new sound in context of words, sentences, and paragraphs).

Special Problems

Sometimes students will exhibit difficulty learning letter sounds. At such times, it is important to conduct an error analysis to try to determine the source of difficulty and attempt to correct it. Usually, letter–sound correspondence errors involve errors of discrimination learning or fact learning.

Many beginning readers, as well as students with learning difficulties, have problems *discriminating* between letters that differ only in orientation in space (*b* versus *d*, and *p* versus *q*). To avoid such problems initially, teachers should not introduce such letters consecutively. Several letters should be taught between the introduction of *b* and *d*, and sufficient practice should be provided to ensure that the first letter sound is completely mastered before the second is introduced. If difficulties persist, direct teaching of the discrimination may be necessary. Relevant activities include identification tasks in which students circle the *b*s in a random series of *b*s and *d*s. Formative data, such as the daily percentage of *b*s and *d*s correctly read, will help the teacher determine whether the student is making progress. In general, increasing engaged time-on-task helps develop the discrimination. In addition, some type of mnemonic (memory-enhancing) elaboration may prove helpful. For example, the student can be told to visualize a poster bed viewed from the side as a reminder that the *b* has the vertical line on the left side and the *d* has the vertical line on the right side. As with any mnemonic, however, the teacher must be careful to ensure that the students understand the purpose of the strategy and that the strategy is helping to reinforce learning.

Sometimes students exhibit difficulty remembering previously learned letter sounds as *facts*. In this case, errors are not simply the substitution of letters with similar appearances but rather covert errors (e.g., "I don't know") or confusion with dissimilar letters (e.g., *s* for *t*). In these cases, the student must be provided with additional practice on problem letter sounds. If the group as a whole is having difficulty, it may also be helpful to slow the pace of instruction or increase time-on-task variables. Providing the student with a tutor for a few extra minutes a day or enlisting the aid of parents or siblings in the evenings may also be helpful. Finally, some recent research has suggested that a letter–sound mnemonic may be helpful in the initial acquisition and retention of letter–sound correspondence. For example, showing a picture of the initial letter sound (e.g., a picture of a flower for *f*) has not been found to be particularly helpful in teaching the association between the sound /f/ and the letter *f*. However, making the *f* represent a flower

may be helpful in reinforcing the sound–symbol relationship. In any case, formative data can help determine whether instruction is producing a desired effect.

In some cases, students may have difficulty with auditory discrimination, that is, the ability to discriminate between similar-sounding phonemes. In these cases, the speech–language teacher may be able to help with appropriate assessments and intervention strategies.

Letter–sound correspondence is a principal component of the reading process and is taught by factual and discrimination paradigms, using procedures common to all effective teaching, including review of previous learning, statement of goals, introduction of new content, guided practice, independent practice, and weekly and monthly review. Generally, individual letter sounds are not taught independently but are taught in conjunction with other reading skills such as sound blending real words, which is described below.

Sound Blending

As students learn the sounds of individual letters, they must also learn to blend these sounds together to produce the sounds of letter combinations. This procedure, which is necessary in learning how to read words, must be taught overtly. *Sound blending* should begin as soon as students have learned enough letter sounds to begin to pronounce vowel–consonant (VC) pairs, such as *am* and *at*, or consonant–vowel–consonant (CVC) trigrams, such as *cat*, *big*, and *tan*. Students can also be taught to decode nonsense CVC trigrams such as *biv*, *lub*, and *pom*. The occasional use of nonsense words can help ensure that students are attending to the letter sounds and sound-blending procedure and have not simply memorized individual sight words. However, because nonsense words are devoid of meaning, they should be used sparingly.

Teaching Sound Blending

As in all lessons, students should first be informed of the purpose of the lesson (e.g., "We are now going to learn to read some new words").

Students are then asked to provide the sounds of the individual letters (e.g., "Everybody, what is this sound? [Point to *c*] What is this sound? [Point to *a*] What is this sound? [Point to *t*]"). Students are then asked to blend them along with the teacher (e.g., "Everybody, say them together with me: kuh-aaa-tuh. What's the word? [Response] Good! The word is *cat*. What does cat mean?"). Students should repeat this procedure several times with the teacher, as a group and individually, to ensure the word is learned accurately. As they learn new trigrams, the students should practice all words together to ensure that they learn to make appropriate discriminations between trigrams with different letter sounds. Teachers can help by providing students with flash cards or probe sheets on which appropriate CVC trigrams have been written and by timing students' responses to verify that the skills can be produced with fluency. Again, it is important to emphasize the meanings of the new words, too. Although teachers must use judgment when determining appropriate rates, 60 correct responses per minute is a good minimum rate to aim for before proceeding.

When students have produced sound-blending skills accurately and fluently, the teacher can assess the students for application of these skills by having them read the words in a passage from the curriculum materials. Again, the goal should be for the students to read these materials at accuracy and fluency rates similar to those of normally achieving students who are using similar materials. During story and passage reading, teachers also should emphasize the meaning of the information. After fluency practice, students can be asked to think about what happened in the story, describe what the story was about, predict what could happen next, and reread as necessary to confirm their answers. Students should not proceed to a new reading passage until they have read the current passage accurately and fluently. Just as a music teacher would not ask a pupil to sight-read a new piece on the piano each day, a reading teacher should allow the student time to develop the appropriate reading skills for the passage, when needed.

Onsets and Rimes

Stahl (1992), describing the work of Treiman (1985) and Adams (1990), presented the teaching of onsets and rimes as an alternative to the teaching of some individual phonics rules. The *onset* is the part of the syllable before the vowel, and the *rime* is the part of the syllable from the vowel onward. This also can be a useful strategy in promoting written language.

Analysis of phonic regularities by Adams (1990) indicated that rimes are much more regular than individual letters and combinations of letters. For example, the digraph *ea*, supposedly pronounced as long "e," is often irregular. However, with the exceptions of –*ead* (bead, head), –*eaf* (sheaf, deaf), and –*ear* (dear, bear), it is very regular. The rime –*ean*, for example, is almost always pronounced with the long "e" sound. In addition, rimes such as –*ack*, –*ing*, –*ide*, –*ight*, –*oke*, and –*ump* are very regular in pronunciation and are found in a large number of words.

Instruction based on these principles is used in several successful reading programs, including the Benchmark School, a school in Pennsylvania for children with reading difficulties that was recognized in 1986 for Excellence in Education by the U.S. Department of Education (Gaskins et al., 1988). When students encounter unfamiliar words (e.g., *wheat*), they are encouraged to compare them with words that are familiar to them (e.g., *meat*) to help their decoding and then to cross-check to ensure the new word as read makes sense in the passage.

Formative Data

Data can be collected on sound blending and word reading in several ways. Teachers can ask students to read lists of trigrams containing letters that have been learned and time the reading rate for both correct and incorrect responses. These data can be displayed on a graph or chart. Graphic presentations are helpful in determining whether students are making progress in acquiring reading skills. Students' reading logs also can be updated regularly to contain newly learned materials.

Another method for collecting formative data is the use of tape recordings. If tape recordings of reading performance are made regularly, they can provide another measure of reading progress. Reading performance data collected from tape recordings can also be quantified by recording the rate of correct versus incorrect performances and can also allow for evaluation of qualities such as expressiveness and phrasing. Tapes made previously can be played back to students to provide them with additional feedback on their progress. When students have read a specific passage to a prespecified level of fluency, they should move on to the next lesson. If the passage has not been read fluently, however, additional practice should be provided.

Special Problems

Sometimes individual students will demonstrate difficulty with sound blending. At such times, it may seem simpler to teach the words as sight words rather than sound blending. Giving in to this temptation should be avoided, however, because a firm knowledge of sound blending is much more likely to serve the student's long-term reading needs. The first thing a teacher can do when sound-blending problems are encountered is to analyze the task carefully. The teacher may be teaching too much information too rapidly, or the student may not have sufficiently mastered individual letter sounds. In the latter case, it is necessary to go back to letter–sound instruction until the student demonstrates a high rate of fluency on letter sounds. If difficulties in blending letter sounds persist, the teacher will need to intensify the instruction, either by increasing the total time-on-task or by providing more intensive one-on-one instruction, directed by either the teacher or another student who is deemed "expert" in sound blending. If motivation appears to be a problem, the teacher should make an effort to increase incentives to learn, either by additional teacher praise and attention or by awarding points or tokens redeemable for awards or privileges.

Phonics Rule Learning

Blends

After students have mastered letter sounds and sound blending, they must learn a series of rules for the correct pronunciation of groups of letters. The simplest examples are consonant blends because these are special cases of sound blending. Because sounds derived from consonant blends are regular and directly reflect the sounds of the letters, they are generally taught after CVC blending. Examples of consonant blends are *br*, *str*, and *bl*. Consonant blends are different from previously covered blending in that there are only a certain number of blends, and the sequence is invariant. For instance, one cannot pronounce blends such as *lpf* or *mtl*. Blends are introduced one at a time in the context of words, and opportunities for practice and feedback (both on individual blends and in the context of other blends) are provided. Ultimately, consonant blends should be recognized and pronounced as readily as individual letter sounds.

Diphthongs

Diphthongs are vowel pairs that produce two merged sounds. The diphthongs include *oi*, *ow*, and *ou* (as in *oil*, *owl*, and *foul*). These sounds are regular and should be taught as separate phonics facts and practiced in the contexts of words and their meanings.

Other Phonics Rules

Many word-attack strategies include the application of explicit rules for decoding. One of the first rules to be taught is the rule governing the pronunciation of CVC + *e* (CVCE) words. Such CVCE words include *hope, tape,* and *bite.* This rule states that in CVCE patterns, the internal vowel is pronounced with the long sound (i.e., it says its name), and the final *e* is silent. Students must be taught to (a) repeat the rule from memory, (b) discriminate a letter pattern that calls for application of the rule, and (c) correctly apply the rule to the letter pattern. If all three of these rule-learning components are not in place, it is unlikely that the word can be read correctly. When rules such as the CVC + *e* rule are taught, as in other word-attack skills, they should first be explicitly introduced (e.g., "Today we are going to learn a new rule"). Next, the rule should be explained and practiced with the group as a whole. After this, students should be given guided and independent practice in identifying CVCE patterns and in applying the rule. Students should be able to easily discriminate words such as *hop* from words such as *hope* and to clearly explain the rule that governs their pronunciation. An example of teaching the CVCE rule is the following:

TEACHER (T): How do you say this word? [Points.]

STUDENT (S): Hop.

T: Hop. Good. Now, watch me. [Writes an *e* at the end.] Now the word is *hope.* How do you say it?

S: Hope.

T: Good, hope. Now here's the rule: when you add *e* to a word like *hop,* you don't pronounce the *e,* but the *o* says its name. So, you say *ō* instead of *ŏ.* How do you say the word?

S: Hope.

T: Good, you say hope. What's the rule?

S: If you add *e,* you say *o.*

T: Right, if you add *e* to a word like *hop,* the vowel says its name. Let's try it with another word. How do you read this word? [Writes *cap.*]

S: Cap.

T: Cap, good. Now, I'm going to add an *e.* [Adds *e.*] How do you read it now?

S: Cape.

T: Correct, cape. How did you know to say cape?

S: Because you said it says its name.

T: What says its name?

S: The *a.*

T: Right, the *vowel* says its name, in this case, the *a.* Now let's try some more. Then let's review what these words mean.

Another important phonics rule governs the pronunciation of vowel *digraphs,* that is, double vowels that make a single sound, such as those in *hail, each,* and *reason.* In this case, the instructional procedures parallel those for other rule-learning situations.

When students have demonstrated accurate and fluent identification and production of phonics rules, they should be provided with guided opportunities to master these rules by learning to apply them in the context of reading passages. At all levels of learning, collection of formative data can help ensure that all learning objectives are being met.

When vowels are followed by *r* or *l,* the pronunciation may change. These vowels are referred to as *r-controlled* or *l-controlled* vowels. Examples of *r*-controlled vowels are found in *car, girl,* and *urn. All* and *stall* have *l*-controlled vowels. A lesson describing the teaching of *r*-controlled vowels is provided in Figure 5.2.

Special Problems

Research has shown that many special education students have difficulty with rule learning. Generally, when problems occur, task-and-error analysis shows that the problem lies in (a) recall of the rule, (b) identification of the relevant letter patterns, or (c) correct application of the rule. The source of the error can be uncovered by questioning (e.g., "What kind of word is this? What is the rule you use for this kind of word? How should you read this word?"). Students should then be given additional guided practice on the difficult components. Sometimes, rules can be stated in a way that aids in their recall. A familiar example is the rhyme, "When two vowels go walking, the first one does the talking." Although this rhyme is easy to memorize, it is critical that students know what is meant by "vowels," "go walking," "first one," and "does the talking." Otherwise, memorizing the rhyme will be of little use to students.

Teachers should introduce phonics rules as they are introduced in the curriculum materials. A good reading program will consist of regularly sequenced word-attack skills and include a great deal of practice on each new skill. If the new skills to be taught are not provided explicitly in the teacher's guide, the teacher must determine the requirements of the new task and introduce them in reading lessons.

Remember, when teaching phonics, that rules should not come to dominate reading instruction. In many cases, rule understanding will come with repeated exposure to word patterns in context. As recommended by Stahl (1992), reading instruction should focus on "words, not rules." If students begin to perceive that reading instruction consists primarily of memorizing and reciting rules, reading instruction is less likely to be successful.

Irregular Sight Words

Unfortunately, many words in the English language cannot be pronounced by the accurate application of word-attack skills. These exceptions include words such as *heir, was, one, two,* and *research* and are found at all levels of reading difficulty. In general, it is wise to avoid the introduction of irregular words until regular phonics rules have been learned and mastered.

Irregular sight words must be taught as facts; that is, learning how to read the word *through* is only useful for reading that individual word. This is very different from learning individual phonics rules that can be applied to a large number of individual words. When teaching irregular words, it is best not to elaborate on the nature of the words other than to state that these special words must be read in a special way. They are taught by using extended drill and practice, using flash cards, writing on the blackboard, or picking them out of reading passages.

If students demonstrate difficulty in learning specific sight words, the teacher should first determine whether the word was ever explicitly taught. Often sight words that a student has never encountered appear in a new reading passage. In this case, a student with good word-attack skills will attempt a phonetic reading of the word or attempt to deduce the sound of the word through contextual cues. If a sight word has not been taught, explicit instruction should be provided. Unless they are teaching students how to use contextual cues to read new words, however, teachers should not surprise students with unfamiliar irregular words. Teachers should be able to identify new sight words in reading passages and teach them to accuracy and fluency before students are asked to apply them in context.

If a student is having trouble reading sight words that have been previously taught, additional drill and practice must be provided. In some cases, teachers may decide that too many new words have been introduced in too short a time period and, consequently, may reduce the pace of instruction. Another approach is to increase the amount of time-on-task in active responding to the sight words. This can be provided either by the teacher, an aide, a parent, or a peer tutor who is familiar enough with the words to provide corrective feedback. If individuals other than the teacher deliver instruction, care must be taken to ensure that specific objectives are being met because the teacher may not be able to observe all of the instruction. In all cases, formative data can help to determine whether objectives are being met.

Summary of Phonics Instruction

In the preceding section, phonics or decoding instruction was divided into letter–sound correspondence, sound blending, phonics rule learning, and irregular sight words. These components were described with respect to the teaching of relevant facts, rules, discriminations, and procedures. Although phonics instruction has been divided into several components, it must be remembered that the overall goal is to tie all these components into clear, efficient reading of text. Providing guided practice of all previously learned skills on reading passages is an opportunity to ensure that all previously learned skills have been effectively integrated. If problems occur, teachers should be able to identify the source of the problem and provide corrective instruction.

Although good decoding skills are critical for the reading success of special education students, these skills alone do not guarantee that students will become competent readers. To become competent readers, students also need to develop skills for comprehending what they read.

Reading Comprehension

Reading comprehension is the ultimate goal of reading instruction. All of the phonics and decoding skills discussed previously are necessary prerequisites for successful reading comprehension. In the past, little instruction in reading comprehension took place in classroom settings. However, recent research has advanced our understanding not only of what processes occur during reading comprehension but also of how to facilitate the explicit instruction of reading comprehension. It is now generally agreed that

reading comprehension involves an interaction of several variables, including the learner, the background (or prior knowledge of the topic and schema) of the reader, the strategies (or metacognitive skills) the learner possesses, and the text material itself. In addition, it is known that readers employ strategies to facilitate comprehension before, during, and after reading. In the following sections, each of these variables is described and discussed in relation to how reading comprehension can be taught.

The Learner

The reading level of the learner must be determined. As mentioned previously, after completion of a curriculum-based assessment, learners can be placed at an appropriate level of difficulty in the text material. It is important to match the learner with the appropriate difficulty level and to maximize the learner's attentional and motivational levels. Teachers can maximize attention and motivation by stressing their importance to instruction or by manipulating classroom contingencies based on performance. Ultimately, teachers want students to be accountable for their own learning; therefore, a combination of teacher emphasis and contingencies may be used initially, followed by a fading out of the contingencies.

Prior Knowledge and Schema

Research has shown that the amount and type of background knowledge students bring to reading passages influence the amount and type of information that is recalled or comprehended. This is sometimes referred to as prior knowledge or *schema*. Schemata (plural) are considered to be networks of conceptual knowledge about the world in which one lives. This conceptual knowledge assists people in understanding and thinking about events encountered in reading. For example, the phrase "I am going to a birthday party" evokes a birthday knowledge system or schema, which includes concepts of birthday cake, candles, and gift-wrapped presents. Even if a more detailed description of the birthday party is missing from the reading passage, most readers would be able to describe a birthday party scenario without much difficulty. Likewise, on encountering a passage that describes a highway scene with an ambulance and blocked-off traffic, most readers would be able to describe an accident schema.

Prior knowledge can be directly evoked by teacher questioning. For example, immediately prior to reading a passage about beavers, the teacher can ask students to discuss and elaborate on what they already know about beavers. Activation of prior knowledge can lead to enhanced comprehension of the passages. As the students read the passages, the teacher can remind or ask students to describe how the passage interacts with students' prior knowledge as discussed before reading the passage. Such schemata, or meaningfully oriented clusters of information, allow readers to interact with elements in the text material. Typically, readers tend to form hypotheses about the text based on the schemata or prior knowledge they bring with them. These hypotheses are usually refined after the reading of a story has been completed. For example, when introducing a book about dinosaurs, the teacher could say, "This book is about dinosaurs. Everyone, think about what you know about dinosaurs. [Pause for thinking time.] What things do you know about dinosaurs, Markeisha?" Students can then form hypotheses about the book, and on completing the book the teacher could say, "Who remembers what they predicted would happen in this book? Were you right? How did your predictions change? What new information do you have about dinosaurs?" This interactive view of the reading process relies on two components. First, readers construct hypotheses based on their schemata and the text. Second, readers refine those hypotheses to comprehend, interpret, and evaluate the text material. For refinement of hypotheses to take place, readers must employ comprehension-monitoring strategies. A table of specifications for comprehension

monitoring is given in Table 5.2. Such strategies are also referred to as metacognitive strategies.

Metacognitive Strategies

Comprehension-Monitoring Skills

Comprehension monitoring refers to the ability to monitor understanding of text as it is being read. Comprehension monitoring can include understanding (a) individual words, (b) particular sentences, (c) relationships among sentences, and (d) the entire text or story. Recently, numerous types of self-monitoring and self-questioning strategies have been taught to students, and, when the strategies have been used effectively, students' comprehension performance has improved. Several of these strategies will be described briefly. As in all the instruction techniques, students should learn to identify these new strategies prior to producing them.

Self-Questioning

Self-questioning is a global strategy that can encompass many of the more specific strategies. In its basic form, self-questioning simply means asking questions of oneself while reading. In the initial teaching stages, students are usually required to state their self-questions aloud so that teachers can monitor their performance. As students become more proficient at self-questioning, they are sometimes required to use a self-monitoring sheet and either check off or write down the questions when they ask them. Ultimately, when students consistently and accurately employ the self-questioning strategies, even the self-monitoring sheets can be phased out. A simple example of a self-questioning strategy is teaching students to ask themselves, "Do I understand what I just read?" If students are able to answer affirmatively, they can proceed with reading the passage. However, if they answer negatively, they are required to go back and reread the passage until they are able to answer correctly. An ex-

Table 5.2. Table of Specifications for Reading Comprehension

	BEHAVIOR				
	Identification	Production			
CONTENT	*A. Acquisition*	*B. Acquisition*	*C. Fluency*	*D. Application*	*E. Generalization*
1. *Who, what, when, where, how, why*	1A	1B	1C	1D	1E
2. *Facts and details*	2A	2B	2C	2D	2E
3. *Titles*	3A	3B	3C	3D	3E
4. *Sequencing events*	4A	4B	4C	4D	4E
5. *Paraphrasing and summarizing*	5A	5B	5C	5D	5E
6. *Main ideas*	6A	6B	6C	6D	6E
7. *Inferences*	7A	7B	7C	7D	7E
8. *Predictions*	8A	8B	8C	8D	8E
9. *Deductions*	9A	9B	9C	9D	9E

Behavioral Objectives:

1A   After reading a paragraph and being given multiple-choice questions, students will circle the correct answer to questions like the following: "Who was in the story?" and "When did the story take place?" All questions will be answered correctly.

2B   After reading two paragraphs, students will write every fact and detail that occurred in those paragraphs with 100% accuracy.

3C   After reading a story, students will immediately be able to provide an appropriate title for the story (within 15 seconds).

4D   After reading a story in the basal reading series, students will be able to successfully sequence all the events.

6E   After reading Chapter 7 in their free-time books, students will be able to tell the main ideas of all the stories.

ample of this type of self-monitoring strategy is given in Figure 5.4 (see also Graves, 1986).

Paraphrasing and Summarizing

Another strategy that can be incorporated into self-questioning is paraphrasing. Paraphrasing is simply restating in one's own words what was just read. Paraphrasing can be used for words, sentences, paragraphs, or entire stories. Teachers also can ask students to summarize a story. In this case, a summary would be similar to a paraphrase. The critical aspect of this task is for students to restate in their own words what they have read. Summarization strategies can involve students asking themselves, "Who or what is the

passage about?" and "What happened in the passage?" Summarization can also include deleting unnecessary information, finding a higher order (superordinate) term to describe a list of actions or items, and identifying or inventing a paragraph topic sentence.

Sequencing Events

Another strategy, which is best used near the end of a story, is sequencing the events that have occurred. This task is particularly helpful when the chronological order of events is important to remember. For example, students may be required to know the events that occurred first, second, and third in a story (e.g., the sequence of events that

		Yes	No
Paragraph 1	Do I understand what I read? If yes, continue reading. If no, reread the part I just read.	☐	☐
Paragraph 2	Do I understand what I read? If yes, continue reading. If no, reread the part I just read.	☐	☐
Paragraph 3	Do I understand what I read? If yes, continue reading. If no, reread what I just read.	☐	☐
Paragraph 4	Do I understand what I read? If yes, continue reading. If no, reread what I just read.	☐	☐

Figure 5.4. Sample self-monitoring sheet. *Note.* This model can be adapted to prompt students concerning specific information (e.g., Why did the bird fall out of the tree? Where did Jose go after school?).

led to the U.S. involvement in Vietnam). In the initial stages of learning sequencing, instruction may take the form of requiring students to identify which of two events occurred first. Later, the production of events would be required, and, finally, students may be required to sequence all the major events silently through self-questioning.

Main Ideas

Main ideas of sentences, paragraphs, and stories need to be identified and produced by students. A main idea is a condensed one- or two-sentence version of the passage. When students are asked to generate the best title of a passage, they are being required to name a main idea. Typically, this skill is the first step required prior to summarizing entire passages. A sample lesson on main idea instruction is given in Figure 5.5.

Some researchers have hypothesized that students should be taught to identify the main idea in pictures before being required to identify the main idea in paragraphs or groups of sentences. If these types of activities are practiced first, teachers can be sure that students really understand what a main idea is. As in any identification stage

of instruction, students can be required to select the best main idea from several choices. After mastery of the identification-stage objectives, students can be required to produce the main idea of illustrations. Instruction can then proceed to requiring students to identify and produce main ideas, first from sentences and then from paragraphs and increasingly larger reading selections.

Following Directions

The ability to follow directions accurately is a necessary prerequisite for most comprehension activities. Directions can be written or verbal but must be followed correctly if the task is to be completed.

Identifying and Producing Who, What, When, Where, How, and Why

Literal recall refers to the factual (stated) information contained in passages. Answers to who, what, when, where, how, and why questions are usually stated explicitly in passages, and their recall is therefore considered literal. The successful

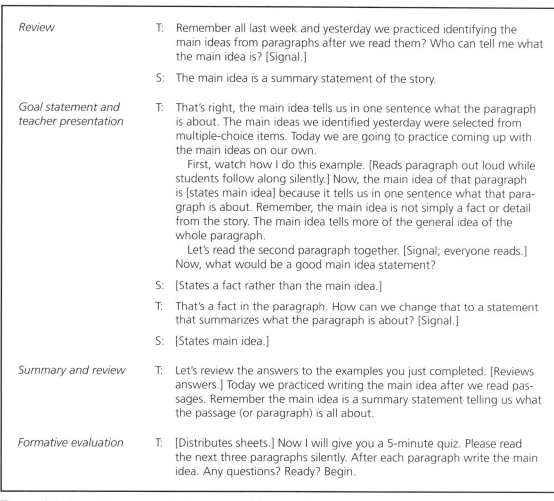

Review — T: Remember all last week and yesterday we practiced identifying the main ideas from paragraphs after we read them? Who can tell me what the main idea is? [Signal.]

S: The main idea is a summary statement of the story.

Goal statement and teacher presentation — T: That's right, the main idea tells us in one sentence what the paragraph is about. The main ideas we identified yesterday were selected from multiple-choice items. Today we are going to practice coming up with the main ideas on our own.
First, watch how I do this example. [Reads paragraph out loud while students follow along silently.] Now, the main idea of that paragraph is [states main idea] because it tells us in one sentence what that paragraph is about. Remember, the main idea is not simply a fact or detail from the story. The main idea tells more of the general idea of the whole paragraph.
Let's read the second paragraph together. [Signal; everyone reads.] Now, what would be a good main idea statement?

S: [States a fact rather than the main idea.]

T: That's a fact in the paragraph. How can we change that to a statement that summarizes what the paragraph is about? [Signal.]

S: [States main idea.]

Summary and review — T: Let's review the answers to the examples you just completed. [Reviews answers.] Today we practiced writing the main idea after we read passages. Remember the main idea is a summary statement telling us what the passage (or paragraph) is all about.

Formative evaluation — T: [Distributes sheets.] Now I will give you a 5-minute quiz. Please read the next three paragraphs silently. After each paragraph write the main idea. Any questions? Ready? Begin.

Figure 5.5. Sample lesson to teach the concept of the main idea.

recall of answers to these questions means that students have recalled or comprehended important information from passages. Students can be required to go back to the narrative and locate precisely where the answers to questions are located. Sometimes these answers are referred to as the major facts and details of passages. An example of a self-monitoring sheet for such facts and details is given in Figure 5.6.

Understanding Vocabulary

To fully comprehend a passage, students must understand the meaning of the vocabulary words contained in the passage. Sometimes vocabulary meanings can be determined by understanding the context in which they are used. Students could be asked, for example, to replace the word with a word or phrase they already know and determine whether the words make sense in this context. Other times, new words can be figured out from word-analysis skills, such as decoding the prefix, suffix, or root words (e.g., "You know what *interested* means. So what do you think *disinterested* means?"). In some instances, the exact meaning may not be necessary for complete understanding of the passage, but in other instances, students may need to ask someone else the meaning or look it up in a dictionary or glossary.

Paragraph 1

1. Can I tell where this story takes place?
   ☐ Yes   ☐ No
   If yes, where? _____
   If no, read paragraph.

Paragraph 2

2. Can I tell who is in this story?
   ☐ Yes   ☐ No
   If yes, who? _____
   If no, reread paragraph.

Paragraph 3

3. Can I tell what the con man gave the robber?
   ☐ Yes   ☐ No
   If yes, what? _____
   If no, reread paragraph.

4. Can I tell who dressed in the robe?
   ☐ Yes   ☐ No
   If yes, who? _____
   If no, reread paragraph.

Paragraph 4

5. Can I tell who has the robe?
   ☐ Yes   ☐ No
   If yes, who? _____
   If no, reread paragraph.

6. Can I tell who has the core?
   ☐ Yes   ☐ No
   If yes, who? _____
   If no, reread paragraph.

Figure 5.6 Self-monitoring sheet designed to accompany a specific reading story, by DeAnn Umbower and Mary Taylor. (Used courtesy of DeAnn Umbower and Mary Taylor.)

Highlighting

Highlighting typically refers to underlining or highlighting with a colored marker the major points, events, or characters in a narrative. Sometimes students are not allowed to write in texts, but at other times it is permissible. It may be necessary to teach students how to identify the components that need highlighting. Further information on text highlighting is found in Chapter 9.

Recalling Nonexplicit Information

Information is not always stated explicitly, but answers can be deduced or inferred from the facts that are presented. Deductions are made based on knowledge of a general rule and follow logically from that rule. For example, after reading a passage that first presents general information on the hibernation of bears during the winter months and then presents information on a particular bear, readers could deduce that the particular bear would also hibernate during the winter months. Sometimes the general rule or premise is stated explicitly in the text, but other times readers may need to already possess the appropriate prior knowledge of the general rule. In either case, once the general rule is known, a specific instance or fact usually can be deduced based on the knowledge and application of that rule. Teachers can assist students in identifying specific rules and in deducing the correct, but not explicitly stated, information.

Another type of information that is not explicitly stated in texts is called inferential information. Inferential comprehension is made by taking all of the specifically stated facts into consideration and then using that information to infer the answer. A question such as "How did Maria feel?" is an inferential question. To answer the question effectively, readers must refer to specifically stated facts and details, such as, "It was her birthday party" and "She had her favorite cake and ice cream," to infer that Maria was excited and happy, rather than sad and disappointed. Teachers can assist students in recognizing inferential questions and locating the specific facts that will aid them in inferring the correct answer. A sample lesson on inferential comprehension is excerpted in Figure 5.7.

Typically, comprehension of information that is not explicitly stated is the most difficult aspect of reading comprehension for students with learning difficulties. With specific, direct instruction and practice using the principles of teacher effectiveness in these areas, however, special education students can make progress.

Imagery

Imagery is the imagining of a picture of what has occurred. Occasionally, imagery has successfully augmented students' ability to recall information from prose passages. Typically, students are told to imagine and think about events in a story. After such instructions, students think about the events and make up a picture in their minds to facilitate recall of those events later on. Teachers can help students by asking direct questions about the images they have created (e.g., "How big is the pond? Is it cloudy or sunny? Are there houses on the pond?"). Imagery has been more successful with older students than younger students.

Previewing and Reviewing Activities

Previewing the material prior to reading can help activate prior knowledge and schemata. A preview can consist of examining the title, major subheadings, summaries, and illustrations included in the stories. Previewing allows readers to get ready for the topic through self-questioning, such as, "Do I know anything about this topic?" or "Is it related to something else I know?" In addition, taking time to review the material on completion can facilitate recall. For example, students can ask questions such as, "Can I summarize the story? Do I know the correct sequence of events? Can I answer all the who, what, when, where, how, and why questions?" Both previewing and reviewing activities can facilitate recall.

Uses of Metacognitive Skills

Recall that this section's premise is that reading comprehension involves an interaction of learners with their schemata strategies and metacognitive skills. Metacognitive skills enable the reader to determine which of the previously mentioned skills are appropriate for the type of reading. In other words, sophisticated readers not only successfully employ all of the skills presented but, more important, independently know when to execute the particular skills.

Successful readers consciously and spontaneously employ strategies to recall the sequence of events, summarize passages as they read, or

Review	T: Remember that we have been practicing reading passages, thinking about what was happening in those passages, and answering questions such as who was in the story and when and where the story took place. Remember that whenever we've had comprehension questions to answer we've been able to go back to the passage and locate the answer. Let's do an example together. Everybody read the passage in your book silently with me. [Signal.] Raise your hand when you have the following answers: Who? What? Where? When? Now, raise your hand when you can locate the answer for each of the following questions. . . .
State goal and teacher presentation	T: Today we are going to read passages and learn how to answer comprehension questions for which you can't go back to the passage and find the exact answer. In order to answer questions like these, you need to have read the passage and thought about what was happening in that passage just like before. However, you also have to infer or try to figure out the answer from the information that was provided in that passage. Let me give you an example. [Teacher reads passage.] Now can we answer the following question: How did Cindy feel? That information is not stated exactly in the story. However, we can figure out the answer from the information that was presented. First, we know that the score in the volleyball game was a tie. We also know that Cindy's first serve was an ace. Do you know what an ace means?
	S: Cindy's team scored another point because no one could return her serve.
	T: Right. We also know that Cindy's second serve was another ace and she smiled. How did Cindy feel? Who can figure out how she felt and why she felt that way? *[Teacher presents several similar examples.]*
Guided practice	T: [Distributes papers.] Now we are going to practice answering some similar questions. [Teacher leads students, providing corrective feedback as necessary.]
Independent practice *(This step should be followed by formative evaluation.)*	T: Since you have all done well on these, I want you to try the next ones by yourselves. Ready? Begin.

Figure 5.7. Lesson on teaching inferential comprehension skills.

deduce outcomes and make predictions based on the reading passages. Because poor readers are less likely to execute these tasks, direct teaching and practice of these skills using modeling, prompting, feedback, and formative evaluation are necessary. In addition, teaching verbal self-questioning can assist in this process. Table 5.3 presents an adaptation of a reading comprehension taxonomy summarized from Baumann (1986). Notice that this taxonomy subdivides reading comprehension skills in a fashion similar to that found in Table 5.2. Teachers need to

Table 5.3. Taxonomy of Reading Comprehension

I. Literal Recall
    A. Details
    B. Main Ideas
    C. Sequences
    D. Comparisons
    E. Cause and Effect Relationships
    F. Character Traits

II. Inferential Recall
    A. Supporting Details
    B. Main Ideas
    C. Sequences
    D. Comparisons
    E. Cause and Effect Relationships
    F. Character Traits

III. Evaluation and Judgment
    A. Reality and Fantasy
    B. Fact or Opinion
    C. Adequacy of Validity
    D. Appropriateness
    E. Worth, Desirability, or Acceptability

IV. Appreciation
    A. Emotional Response to Content
    B. Identification with Characters
    C. Reactions to Language
    D. Imagery

Note. Adapted from Baumann (1986).

identify the most important aspects of reading comprehension for their students and determine the optimal sequence of instruction.

Before, During, and After Reading

As mentioned earlier, many of the strategies that students can be taught to facilitate reading comprehension are employed at three distinct times: before, during, and after reading. Table 5.4 presents a summary listing of many strategies that teachers can teach their students to use at each of these time periods. As with all instruction, the collection of formative data can help determine whether instructional objectives are being met.

Text Material

The particular text material used can either augment or detract from reading comprehension instruction. It is important to take the following features into consideration when selecting text material: (a) readability; (b) sequencing of skills and context; (c) type of print; (d) type of illustrations; (e) type of diagrams, maps, and/or charts; (f) types of stories, passages, and poems; (g) types of practice activities; (h) amount and type of supplemental practice/workbook activities; and (i) type of instructional practice and guidance on reading comprehension. More detailed information on text and supplementing textual materials with text-embedded adjunct aids, such as maps and advance organizers, is presented in Chapter 9. Overall, choose text that is at the appropriate reading level and that allows sufficient opportunities for practicing reading comprehension activities that include literal and inferential questioning. Select a wide variety of reading materials, including "authentic" literature (as distinguished from contrived, basal-type stories), to the extent that students are able to read this material fluently. A variety of reading material can help students meet application and generalization objectives and also can help students develop an appreciation and enjoyment of books and reading. All the comprehension strategies discussed in this chapter can be used with a variety of materials.

Putting It All Together: Reading Comprehension Instruction

In special education, students typically need explicit direct instruction on many or all of the components discussed up to this point. Once the reading material and students have been matched, specific objectives for teaching all of the comprehension monitoring skills need to be developed and taught using the teacher effectiveness model. In addition, students can be taught directly how to use their prior knowledge and how to activate it during reading. For example,

Table 5.4. Comprehension Strategies Undertaken Before, During, and After Reading

Before Reading	During Reading	After Reading
Examine Text	*Summarize Key Issues*	*Summarize Entire Selection*
1. preview organization	1. determine main ideas	1. integrate information
2. examine charts, illustrations	2. organize main ideas	2. concisely summarize all elements of text
Mobilize Prior Knowledge	*Make Predictions*	*Determine Achievement*
1. Examine/think about content	1. generate hypotheses	1. confirm/refute predictions
2. examine/think about vocabulary	2. refine predictions	2. answer questions
Determine Purpose of Reading	*Clarify Hypotheses*	*Apply Learning*
1. select strategies	1. confirm hypotheses	1. study information
2. generate questions	2. refute hypotheses	2. rehearse information

assume a lesson's objective is to introduce deductive-reasoning strategies and to review the steps for recalling facts and details from reading passages. As in all lessons, teachers would first review procedures for recalling facts and details from passages. When it is determined that the review was sufficient, teachers would introduce deductive reasoning, probably by stating the rules of deductive reasoning and providing positive and negative examples. During this instruction, teachers would use examples to model, prompt, and provide corrective feedback on the use of deductive reasoning. All students would be actively engaged during this teacher presentation and student participation activity. When it is determined that students are ready for a guided practice activity, teachers would go through several step-by-step examples with the entire group prior to allowing students to practice on their own. Teachers would then carefully circulate among the students and provide immediate corrective feedback on their performances. When it is determined that the skill has been practiced to an extent that the students are executing it accurately, they would be ready to receive an independent practice activity. Finally, near the end of the lesson, teachers could require students to

complete a short assignment on the skill to have a measure of their daily performance.

Eventually, reading comprehension instruction can involve a more complex group process, such as the reciprocal teaching model proposed by Palincsar and Brown (1984). Throughout this model, various reading comprehension questions and strategies are discussed verbally, and all students take turns participating as group leader in a dialogue. The major strategies practiced in reciprocal teaching include (a) summarizing, (b) question generating, (c) clarifying, and (d) predicting. Summarizing facilitates students' ability to identify and integrate the most salient parts of the text. Question generating provides students with the opportunity to pose questions about the text and to self-test. Students are taught to clarify text content so that they become aware that many aspects of the text, such as vocabulary or new concepts, can influence comprehension. Finally, students are taught to make predictions about what will happen next in the text. Making predictions is thought to assist students in (a) understanding a purpose for reading, (b) using the structure of the text (e.g., subheadings), and (c) confirming or refuting their hypotheses. The critical aspects necessary for success appear to be direct teaching, modeling, and guided practice in the effective use of summarizing, question generating, clarifying, and predicting.

As mentioned previously, in the past teachers concentrated more on the teaching of decoding skills than on the teaching of comprehension skills. However, in special education, it is necessary to emphasize the instruction of both, so that students meet the ultimate objective of reading—deriving meaning from print.

This section has discussed the skills and procedures necessary to teach reading comprehension. It was stressed that reading comprehension is the end goal of reading and that it involves the interaction of the learner, the learner's prior knowledge and schemata, the learner's metacognitive abilities and use of comprehension-monitoring skills, and the text itself. It was emphasized that (a) the learners and texts must be matched at the appropriate difficulty level, (b) the learners' attention and motivation on the task are critical, (c) the learners must be instructed to activate their prior knowledge and schemata on topics being covered, (d) direct instruction using the teacher effectiveness model takes place on all comprehension-monitoring skills, and (e) the learners must be provided with ample guided and independent practice at executive comprehension-monitoring strategies. Finally, learners should use these comprehension skills over a wide variety of printed materials, including newspapers, magazines, literature, lab manuals, and trade books.

Special Problems

Sometimes special education teachers encounter students, particularly at the upper elementary or secondary level, who have struggled unsuccessfully with reading skills for many years. Because of this history of failure, they may be particularly unwilling to continue to work on skill acquisition (either phonics or comprehension skills), even though this may be the approach most likely to lead to literacy development. If this mo-

tivational problem seems so severe that the student appears to prefer accepting failure to making an effort, it may be helpful to try a different approach. In the authors' own experience, particularly recalcitrant learners may be successfully motivated to try an approach similar to what has been named "language experience." Using this method, students dictate stories in their own words to the teacher or into a tape recorder. The stories can be about the students' own lives or about a special interest, such as basketball. The teacher or aide then transcribes the stories on the word processor and meets with the students individually to read the stories they have "written." Students who have had little success with reading may be positively encouraged by seeing their own stories in print and may be positively motivated to learn how to read them. Because the stories are in the students' own language, there should be little difficulty with vocabulary. Similarly, inferring, predicting, and using context cues should hold little difficulty. As students read the passages successfully, they can create an "anthology" of their own writings.

The drawback of this method is that it essentially compels the teacher, at least at first, to abandon the type of sequenced skill acquisition that typically is very helpful for students with reading disabilities. Furthermore, because the passages may be learned simply as sight words, generalization of reading skills may be limited. Teachers who choose to employ this approach are advised to introduce relevant skills as soon as possible, as students gain interest in and ownership of their own reading skills, and to validate the method's effectiveness using formative evaluation.

In other cases, students have met with years of failure attempting to learn word-attack skills, or they do not appear to be developmentally able to understand the complexities of a phonics-based program. When other approaches have not been successful, a sight-word reading program such as the *Edmark Reading Program* may be useful. Before implementing such a program, however, be certain that a more generalizable code-emphasis program will not be effective.

Summary

- Curriculum materials for reading instruction tend to favor either a meaning-emphasis or code-emphasis approach to learning. Many students with reading difficulties benefit from the structure and regularity of a code-emphasis approach. Careful consideration of reading materials and curriculum-based measurement can help ensure the selection of appropriate materials.

- Instruction in reading can incorporate the important elements of lessons, including daily review, presentation of objective and material to be learned, guided practice, independent practice, weekly and monthly reviews, and formative evaluation.

- Many students with special needs lack phonemic awareness, or the understanding that words are composed of phonemes. Phonemic awareness can be taught through activities such as phoneme discrimination, segmenting sounds, rhyming, and sound blending.

- Phonics skills can be taught systematically and can include lessons in letter-sound correspondence, sound blending, phonics rule learning, and learning of irregular sight words.

- Reading comprehension instruction can include a number of different skills, including summarizing and paraphrasing, sequencing, identifying the main idea, following directions, identifying details, understanding vocabulary, and making inferences. Students can employ comprehension strategies before, during, and after reading. Self-questioning strategies promote independent strategy use.

Relevant Research and Resources

Research

Reviews of the issues involved in whole-language reading instruction for students with learning disabilities are presented by Mather (1992), Gersten and Dimino (1993), and Pressley and Rankin (1994) (for another view, see Five, 1992). Research on the teaching of reading is reviewed by Calfee and Drum (1986), Paris and Oka (1989), and Weisberg (1988), whereas Ciborowski (1992) and Gaskins and Elliot (1991) describe comprehensive implementation procedures for reading instruction. Much of the research related to all aspects of identifying and preventing reading difficulties in young children is described by Snow et al. (1998). Ball (1996) provides a review on phonological awareness and learning disabilities. Research documenting the positive effects of phonemic awareness training is described by a number of researchers, including Williams (1980); Ball and Blachman (1991); O'Conner, Jenkins, and Slocum (1995); O'Conner, Jenkins, Leicester, and Slocum (1993); Vadasy, Jenkins, Antil, Wayne, and O'Conner (1997); and Jenkins, Vadasy, Firebaugh, and Profilet (2000).

Support for the role of a code-emphasis approach to reading is described by Stahl and Miller (1989), and Adams (1990). For reviews of the failures of psycholinguistic and perceptual-motor approaches to teaching reading, see Kavale and Forness (1985). Evaluation of engaged time-on-task in special education studies is made by Haynes and Jenkins (1986); Leinhardt et al. (1981); and Zigmond, Vallecorsa, and Leinhardt (1980). Support for a direct instructional, phonics-based approach to reading instruction in special education is provided by many researchers, such as Hendrickson, Roberts, and Shores (1978); Pany and Jenkins (1978); Pany, Jenkins, and Schreck (1982); Pflaum and Bryan (1982); Roberts and Deutsch-Smith (1980); Schworm (1979); Stein and Goldman (1980); Blackman, Burger, Tan, and Weiner (1982); and Meyer (1982). Fluency-developing activities are described by Bos (1982), Weinstein and Cooke (1992), and Mastropieri, Leinhart, and Scruggs (1999).

A variety of strategy instruction studies have been completed over the past decades, and all have reported positive effects for training students with mild disabilities in the strategies, including the following: the effects of peers and adaptations of reciprocal teaching (Bruce & Chan, 1991; Englert & Mariage, 1991; Palincsar & Brown, 1984; Rosenshine & Meister, 1994; Speece, MacDonald, Kilsheimer, & Krist, 1997), repeated readings (O'Shea, Sindelar, & O'Shea, 1987), word identification strategies (Lenz & Hughes, 1990), peer previewing (Salend & Nowak, 1988), variations of summarization and self-monitoring (Malone & Mastropieri, 1992), paraphrasing (Jenkins, Heliotis, Stein, & Haynes, 1987), summarization (Gajria & Salvia, 1992), summarization and attributional retraining (Borkowski, Weyhing, & Carr, 1988), vocabulary instruction and interactive instruction (Bos & Anders, 1990a, 1990b), self-questioning (Griffey, Zigmond, & Leinhardt, 1988; Simmonds, 1992), informed strategy training (Rottman & Cross, 1990), and program variations (Jenkins & Jewell, 1993; O'Conner, Jenkins, Cole, & Mills, 1993). Studies investigating the effects of imagery are described by Chan, Cole, and Morris (1990); Clark, Deshler, Schumaker, Alley, and Warner (1984); Ferro and Pressley (1991); and Rose, Cundick, and Higbee (1983). Studies investigating the effects of various types of text structure include Bacon and Carpenter (1989); Simmons, Kameenui, and Darch (1988); Pickering, Pickering, and Buchanan (1988); and Gurney, Gersten, Dimino, and Carnine (1990). Reports of the benefits of attribution and strategy training are described by Borkowski et al. (1988) and Fulk and Mastropieri (1990). Wong (1979, 1980), Wong and Wong (1986), and Wong and Jones (1982) provide additional information on teaching reading comprehension in special education settings. Wong (1986b) provides a review of special education research on metacognition, whereas Palincsar and Brown (1984) and Graves (1986) provide additional support for the use of metacomprehension training as a facilitator of prose recall. Vellutino (1979) provides a review of research on reading problems. Spatial organizer research is provided by Mastropieri and Peters (1987), whereas activating prior knowledge research is provided by Gaffney (1984) and Snider (1989). Support for the use of

mnemonic illustrations in reading is presented by Scruggs, Mastropieri, McLoone, Levin, and Morrison (1987) and Mastropieri, Scruggs, and Levin (1987a). Additional information on self-monitoring in reading is provided by Hallahan, Marshall, and Lloyd (1981). Much of the above reading comprehension research is reviewed and synthesized by Mastropieri and Scruggs (1997a) and Mastropieri, Scruggs, Bakken, and Whedon (1996). For a discussion of a meaning-based approach to reading literature and writing in middle school inclusive classes, see Morocco, Hindin, Mata-Aguilar, and Clark-Chiarelli (2001).

Tutoring interventions in reading are described by Osguthorpe and Scruggs (1986); Scruggs, Mastropieri, and Richter (1985); Scruggs and Richter (1985); Cook, Scruggs, Mastropieri, and Casto (1985-1986); Scruggs and Osguthorpe (1986); Scruggs, Mastropieri, Tolfa, and Osguthorpe (1986); Mastropieri, Spencer, Scruggs, and Talbott (2000); and Scruggs and Mastropieri (1998). Vadasy, Jenkins, and Pool (2000) describe the use of peer tutors in phonological and early reading skills. Research on classwide peer tutoring and peer-assisted learning strategies is described by Delquadri et al. (1986); Utley, Mortweet, and Greenwood (1997); Fuchs et al. (1997); Mathes and Fuchs (1993); and Fuchs, Fuchs, and Burish (2000). Computer-assisted phonological instruction is described by Wise and Olson (1995) and Olson, Wise, Ring, and Johnson (1997). Studies investigating the effects of computers and reading decoding, fluency, and/or comprehension are described by Swanson and Trahan (1992); Torgesen, Waters, Cohen, and Torgesen (1988); and Cohen, Torgesen, and Torgesen (1988).

Curricular Materials

Phonemic awareness training materials include *Phonological Awareness Training for Reading* (PRO-ED) and *CLUES for Phonemic Awareness* (Curriculum Associates); some activities for developing phonemic awareness are described by Fischer (1993). Code-based reading series include the following: *Reading Mastery* and *Corrective*

Reading Decoding (SRA/McGraw-Hill), *Merrill Linguistic Readers* (Charles E. Merrill Publishing), *Angling for Words* series (Academic Therapy), and *SRA Open Court* (SRA/McGraw-Hill). SRA/McGraw-Hill also publishes the supplementary materials *SRA Reading Labs* and the *Specific Skills Series* for reading comprehension. These latter materials can be helpful as practice activities; however, be careful that students have learned and are applying relevant strategies while using these materials. Curriculum Associates provides *CLUES for Better Reading* to build reading comprehension skills. Sight-word reading programs include the *Edmark Reading Program* (Edmark) and the *The Essential Sight Words Program* (PRO-ED). Other reading materials published by Globe Fearon include the *Globe Readers' Collection* and *Be a Better Reader*. For older readers, Globe Fearon publishes *Basic English*.

Books that have low readability levels but high interest can be obtained from Globe Fearon (Pacemaker Classics, Uptown, Downtown series), Lakeshore Learning Materials, and LinguiSystems (the *Abridged & Accessible Classics Activity Program* and *Victory*). PRO-ED distributes many high-interest, low-vocabulary books, such as the *High Noon* series. SRA/McGraw-Hill also publishes the series *Learning Through Literature*, which can be used to integrate literature learning in reading programs, and the *Open Court* series, which contains phonics and literature materials. Steck-Vaughn produces *Multicultural Stories*. LinguiSystems also publishes materials that attempt to combine skill-based and whole-language approaches to reading instruction. Reading lists of books that can be used by beginning readers have been published by advocates of Reading Recovery (Clay & Watson, 1987). Similarly, Allyn & Bacon publishes a listing of regularly patterned books that can be used in teaching reading when attempting to control the vocabulary and word patterns. These lists include books such as those published by the Philomel

Books, including *The Very Hungry Caterpillar* (Carle, 1987). These literature, trade, and picture books can be integrated into reading programs for students with disabilities.

Computer Software and Technology

Computer programs that are commercially available can be used for practice activities for students with mild disabilities. Many programs have been developed, and availability of new programs will undoubtedly increase in the future. Okolo, Bahr, and Reith (1993) have provided a comprehensive review of computer-based instruction in special education. Programs can usually be classified as drill and practice, games, tutorials, problem solving, simulations, or production programs. Teachers are encouraged to evaluate the programs to determine suitability for meeting students' needs and IEP objectives. Some programs currently available for basic reading practice are Stickybear's Reading Fun Park, Stickybear's ABC Deluxe, and Stickybear's Reading Room Deluxe (Optimum Resource); First Phonics and Consonant Blends and Digraphs (Sunburst); Learn to Read with Phonics (The Learning Company); Phonics Mastery (Gamco); and Reading Blaster (Optimum Resource). The Learning Company also produces the Reader Rabbit series. Practice on reading comprehension is provided in Stickybear Reading Comprehension (Optimum Resource), Reading Concepts, Reading for Critical Thinking, Undersea Reading for Meaning, and Captain Zog's Main Idea (Gamco). Mindplay produces the reading tutorial program My Reading Coach. Don Johnston Developmental Equipment produces the high-interest, low-vocabulary Start-to-Finish books with audiocassettes and CD. See Appendix B for a list of addresses of producers and distributors of software and curricular materials.

Assisting Students with Reading Difficulties

Learning content from textbooks becomes increasingly important as students progress through school. The switch from learning to read to learning from reading is challenging for many students with disabilities. Several approaches can assist students who are experiencing difficulties reading grade-level materials, many of which can be implemented within inclusive environments. Some approaches include providing students with reading instruction and practice to improve reading abilities; others involve reducing the reading level demands so students can focus on content. It might be optimal to include both approaches whenever possible.

- Provide additional opportunities for practicing reading and reading comprehension strategies.
    - Provide additional instruction as necessary on reading skills.
    - Peer assistants or tutors can be used to provide more reading opportunities.
    - Cooperative learning groups can allow students to share the reading.

- Provide reading materials that cover similar content but are written on lower reading levels.
    - Many textbooks and trade books can be located that present similar content but are written on lower reading levels.

    - Some materials (e.g., Mesa, Arizona science materials) provide a variety of reading levels within a single grade-level science material.

- Provide audiotape versions of text.
    - Obtain copies of audiotaped texts from the Library of Congress (www.loc.gov) and the American Printing House for the Blind.

    - Provide reading materials in a digital format and use a program such as CAST eReader (see www.cast.org to download a free trial version of the software) that enables students to transform the electronic text into spoken voice and use visual highlighting or enables students to read along or listen to the text. The eReader can be used with Web pages, word-processing documents, texts, and newspapers. Such digital formats will be more suitable for students with visual disabilities as well as reading difficulties. Scan reading materials into digital formats or acquire them from some of the increasingly available sources, including the following:
        - Electric Library (www.elibrary.com)
        - Electronic Newspapers, Magazines, and Journals (www.lib.ncsu.edu:80/stacks)
        - Alex Catalog of Electronic Texts (http://sunsite.berkeley.edu/alex/)
        - Children's Literature Web Guide (www.acs.ucalgary.ca/~dkbrown)
        - Internet Public Library (www.ipl.org/)
        - On-Line Books Page (http://digital.library.upenn.edu/books/)
        - Project Gutenberg (www.gutenberg.net)
        - Literature Online (http://lion.chadwyck.com)

TECHNOLOGY FEATURE

WiggleWorks

Advances in technology have assisted students with disabilities with reading tasks. Wiggle-Works (Scholastic Inc., www.scholastic.com) was developed to include universal design features by researchers at the Center for Applied Special Technology (CAST; www.cast.org). Universal design features make curriculum accessible to all students, including those with disabilities. For example, the WiggleWorks program is a beginning early literacy system that involves multimedia, including books and computer-assisted technology. The series consists of 72 books in paperback and CD formats, and students can interact by reading, speaking, writing, and listening. The specific universal design features that are embedded within the WiggleWorks program include the following (see www.cast.org and www. scholastic.com for additional details):

- Information that can be represented in multiple ways. In WiggleWorks, the font size and color of text can be altered to meet the needs of students.

- Expression options are available. For example, students can "write" by recording their voice, typing, drawing, or placing words from word lists into text.

- Students can read along while text is read to them using the CDs.

- Various alternative methods for engaging students with the curriculum are built into the program. For example, reading aloud, reading silently, writing, and alterations in the text fonts and colors can ensure that students with disabilities can interact with the materials.

Chapter 6

✦   ✦   ✦

Oral and Written Language

Many students enrolled in special education exhibit difficulty in oral and written language. Therefore, systematic, high-quality instruction must be delivered in these areas to ensure that students' development in language arts skills parallel advances they are making in reading and other skill areas.

Oral and written language involves a series of interrelated skills. Four major components of language arts are discussed in this chapter: (a) oral language, (b) handwriting, (c) spelling, and (d) written composition. The application and generalization of these language skills are critical to overall success in school.

Oral Language

Special education teachers encounter a wide range of variability in the spoken, or oral, language abilities of their students. Nearly all students classified as having moderate to severe disabilities are in need of language training. However, many students with mild disabilities, including students with learning disabilities, behavior disorders, or mild mental retardation, do not exhibit severe spoken language problems, and some may not have oral language development included in their IEP objectives. Furthermore, students who do exhibit serious language problems are often referred to specially trained speech and language teachers for remediation.

Many students with mild disabilities, however, do exhibit difficulties in some aspects of oral language. Kavale and Forness (1987) completed a critical analysis of research on subtyping in learning disabilities and reported that 60% of the students with learning disabilities exhibited some type of language problem. Consequently, teachers may wish to provide some language instruction for these students. Some published materials that provide scope and sequence for several aspects of language development are available for this type of instruction. When using these materials, teachers should choose the aspects of the materials that most directly correspond to specific instructional objectives.

Most language training for students with mild disabilities includes instruction in phonological production, listening comprehension skills, vocabulary development, syntactical and morphological skills, and semantics (Polloway & Smith, 1999). In all aspects of language training, teachers must attend to the receptive (identification) versus expressive (production) functions of language use as well as to the general accuracy, fluency, application, and generalization levels of learning. Some materials, for example, attend mainly to training receptive vocabulary at the accuracy stage of learning. Although this in itself is a worthwhile objective, teachers must make certain that the chosen materials teach all of what the student needs to learn. If the material does not, additional lessons must be developed or otherwise acquired by the teacher.

Phonological Production

Students can exhibit problems in producing appropriate speech patterns. Some problems include (a) articulation problems, (b) voice disorders, and (c) speech dysfluencies. Articulation disorders are problems in pronunciation, in which sounds can be omitted, added, distorted (e.g., lisping), or substituted (e.g., "wun" for "run"). Voice disorders affect the volume, pitch, or quality of voice and include speech that is strained, hoarse, breathy, or nasal. Dysfluencies interrupt the natural flow or rhythm of speech, the most common type is stuttering (Moore & Hicks, 1994; Schwartz, 1994).

Special education teachers usually collaborate with speech or language therapists to promote appropriate speech patterns. Teachers can assist by referring students for speech–language services, modeling and reinforcing appropriate phonological production when necessary, and supporting the therapy provided by the speech–language therapist. Teachers and speech therapists form interdisciplinary teams to provide services to students with problems in phonological production.

Listening Comprehension Skills

Teachers can help students improve their listening comprehension skills at all age levels, as listening comprehension skills begin at a very early age and continue to develop throughout the individual's life. Develop particular activities to cultivate students' attention to their own comprehension by enforcing and practicing specific skill areas. Examples of listening comprehension skills include the following:

- restating or summarizing information the students have just heard;

- stating a main idea from a story they have listened to;

- restating a sequence of events in a story or procedures to be followed;

- following directions, by restating and then implementing directions;

- interpreting the meaning of stories or poems they have heard;

- listening to discriminate fact from opinion (Polloway & Smith, 1999).

As listening skills develop, students learn skills for attending to language that will also contribute to the development of reading comprehension skills.

Vocabulary Development

Students with vocabulary deficiencies should receive training both on whole words and meaningful word parts, such as common prefixes and suffixes with standard meanings (e.g., *anti-*). Generally, vocabulary words that are directly meaningful and relevant to the students' lives and school experiences should be taught. During acquisition, students should first learn to identify word meanings. If students have acquired relevant concepts, this is often accomplished by rehearsal. For example, if a student is learning that *corridor* is another word for *hall*, *corridor* can be taught as a fact. That is, whatever was previously associated with *hall* can now be associated with *corridor*. However, if a student is acquiring the vocabulary word *pugnacious* but has not learned the relevant concept, the student must first be taught this concept, usually by provision of a verbal description or rule followed by presentation of instances or noninstances (e.g., "Children who are aggressive fight with and bully other children. What do aggressive children do? [Answer] Good. In this picture [show picture], is the boy being aggressive?"). Once they have learned the concept of *aggressive*, students can be taught synonyms (words with similar meaning) as facts (e.g., "Another word for *aggressive* is *pugnacious*"). Once students have acquired accuracy and fluency levels of performance with vocabulary words, they can learn to apply the new words to their own expressive vocabularies. This can be accomplished by asking students to use words in contextual sentences (e.g., "Say, 'She is an aggressive student,' using a different word for *aggressive*"). Also, students should be reinforced for using the new words spontaneously in classroom conversation. As in the acquisition of spelling words, vocabulary words should be overlearned and assessed frequently and cumulatively to ensure that words are not being forgotten. It is also helpful to compile a list of vocabulary words learned to use for review, training, and feedback for students as well as for teachers' records. Teachers can also evaluate the rate of acquiring vocabulary words with respect to IEP goals and objectives. If, for example, a student has learned 15 new vocabulary words in the first 3 months of school and an IEP objective states that the student will learn 200 new words over the year, this objective will probably not be met without more intensive, faster-paced instruction.

Special Problems

If students have difficulty learning new vocabulary words, teachers should first ascertain whether relevant concepts are being mastered. If not, conceptual learning should be intensified. If relevant concepts have been acquired (i.e., if the student can explain the concept but cannot produce the appropriate vocabulary word), additional drill and practice should be provided, perhaps using a peer tutor. If students initially acquire vocabulary word meanings but do not retain them over time, more overlearning activities may be indicated. It is also helpful to use new words as often as possible during class, especially when students show difficulty in applying the word in novel contexts.

One helpful method of learning new vocabulary words is *elaboration* of the new word, through root words, similar words, or acoustic cues. One elaboration strategy that has received much research attention is the mnemonic *keyword method*. In the keyword method, the new vocabulary word is first changed into another word that is concrete and already familiar. For example, to learn that a dahlia is a type of flower, the word *dahlia* is first recoded to the keyword *doll*. *Doll* is a good keyword for *dahlia* because it sounds like the first part of *dahlia* and is easily pictured. The learner is then shown (or asked to imagine) a picture of the keyword and the referent interacting; in this case, the student perhaps can picture a doll sniffing a flower. It is important

that the keyword be associated with the referent in the picture and not simply pictured with it. Thus, although a picture containing a doll and a flower may not be sufficient to facilitate the association, a doll sniffing, picking, or otherwise interacting with the flower is more likely to facilitate the association. Finally, the retrieval process should be explicitly described to the student: "When you hear the word *dahlia*, remember the keyword *doll*, remember the picture of the doll, and think of what else was in the picture. The doll sniffing the flower means that dahlia is a kind of flower." Additional examples of the keyword method are given in Table 6.1, and Figure 6.1 presents a sample lesson for instructing students using this method.

The keyword method can be very helpful in vocabulary learning as well as in learning facts in content areas such as science and social studies. Other applications of the keyword method are discussed in the chapters that follow. For vocabulary learning, however, it must be emphasized that research has supported the use of the keyword method for the initial acquisition of vocabulary words. Other strategies are necessary to develop fluency and production of the new vocabulary words.

Syntactic and Morphological Skills

Students typically enter school settings with well-developed oral language skills, which were acquired at home or in other extracurricular environments. Therefore, the teaching of syntax (i.e., grammar, or the rules of language) and morphology (i.e., the system of building meaning in words, such as the use of the morpheme *-ed*, meaning past tense) may depend on a careful error analysis of specific students' spoken language. This can be done by obtaining a *language sample*. Tape-record a conversation with a particular student, transcribe the student's dialogue and look for a pattern of errors in the student's grammar. Students may then be grouped with respect to identified instructional needs and taught

Table 6.1. Examples of the Keyword Method for Learning Vocabulary

Vocabulary Word (Meaning)	Keyword	Picture or Image
Dahlia (flower)	doll	A *doll* sniffing a *flower.*
Viaduct (bridge)	duck	A *duck* walking on a *bridge.*
Marmalade (jam)	mama	A *mama* spreading *jam* for her child.
Toreador (bullfighter)	tornado	A *bullfighter* fighting a *tornado.*
Barrister (lawyer)	bear	A *bear* acting like a *lawyer.*
Celebrate (honor with a festive occasion)	celery	A *festive occasion* in which *celery* is served.
Persuade (convince)	purse	One woman *convincing* another to buy a *purse.*
Orbit (travel around a heavenly body)	rabbit	A *rabbit traveling* around the earth.
Beacon (signal light)	bacon	A *signal light* shining on a pan of *bacon.*
Oxalis (clover-like plant)	oxen	*Oxen* eating *clover-like plants.*
Vituperation (abusive speech)	viper	*Viper* engaging in *abusive speech.*
Jodhpurs (riding breeches)	joggers	*Joggers* wearing *riding* breeches.
Dirigible (blimp)	deer	A *deer* with a *blimp* tied to its antlers.
Corsair (pirate)	core	A *pirate* eating an apple *core.*

specific syntactic skills. Some published materials are available for developing such skills and also provide a scope and sequence for the development of these skills. When using these materials, the teacher should be certain that specific student objectives are being addressed. In other words, any training in syntax should address student deficiencies observed in those specific skills. Much syntax training involves a type of rule learning in that students must first be able to identify specific grammatical rules that apply to specific situations. It should also be obvious that syntax must be learned to a level at which performance is fluent and easily applied to spontaneous oral language.

Syntax and morphology can be subdivided into literally hundreds of areas. Major areas of

instruction include subject–verb agreement, verb tense, pronoun usage, sentence structure, adjective usage, and adverb usage. For lessons in subject–verb agreement, for example, the teacher can begin by reviewing previous learning and stating the lesson's objective: "We are going to learn how to say some new sentences." The teacher then displays a picture and provides modeling for subject–verb agreement: "Look at this picture. The cows run. You say it. [Signal]." After this sentence has been acquired, the teacher presents the discrimination: "Now, look at this new picture. The cow *runs*. You say it. [Signal]." When the discrimination has been mastered, the teacher should promote fluent, unmodeled responses using a variety of stimulus cards. Students can be given guided and inde-

Today I'm going to help you learn some new vocabulary words. I want you to try hard, because at the end of our session, I will give you a quiz to see how well you remember the meanings of the words. I am going to teach you using a special method of remembering.

The first thing I am going to teach you is a keyword for each new vocabulary word. A keyword is a little word that sounds like part of the new vocabulary word and is easily pictured. For example, the keyword for *jodhpurs* is *joggers*. What is the keyword for *jodhpurs*? Good. Now I'm going to show you a picture that will help you remember the meaning of *jodhpurs*. [Show illustration.] The keyword for *jodhpurs* is *joggers*. Jodhpurs are riding breeches. Remember this picture of joggers wearing riding breeches. Remember this picture of what? [Signal.] And jodhpurs means what? [Signal.]

Jodhpurs are riding breeches made loose and full above the knees and close-fitting below them.

JODHPURS (joggers)

[Remove illustration.] Now, when I ask you the meaning of the word, you need to do the following things. For example, if I said, "What does *jodhpurs* mean?" or "What are jodhpurs?" first you should think back to the keyword for *jodhpurs*. That is [answer]. Good. Then, you need to think back to what else was happening in that picture, which was [answer]. Good! Joggers wearing riding breeches. Therefore, we know that jodhpurs are riding breeches. Let's try the next example.

(continues)

Figure 6.1. Sample instructions for teaching new vocabulary words with the keyword method.

pendent practice with workbooks, computers, or other instructional aides. The final goal, of course, is to develop correct subject–verb agreement in spontaneous spoken language. Progress toward objectives can be assessed by taking regular oral language samples, transcribing them, and evaluating the extent to which instructed syntactic features have been mastered. Teachers must also reinforce the use of correct syntax throughout the day.

Syntax and morphology also can be taught in the context of everyday language usage. Some examples of teaching methods include correcting a student's errors, expanding short or incomplete utterances, and asking a student to complete statements begun by the teacher. Teachers

The keyword for *oryx* is *ore*. What is the keyword for *oryx*? [Answer.] Good. Now I'm going to show you a picture that will help you remember the meaning of *oryx*. [Show illustration.] The keyword for *oryx* is *ore*. Oryx are a type of antelope with long horns that project backwards. Remember this picture of a type of antelope pulling ore out of a mine. Remember this picture of what? [Signal.] And *oryx* means what? [Signal.]

An oryx is any of a group of large African antelopes with long, straight horns projecting backwards.

ORYX (ore)

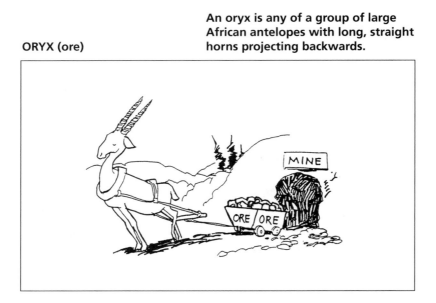

[Remove illustration.] If I said, "What does *oryx* mean?" or "What is an oryx?" first remember what the keyword for *oryx* is. [Answer.] Good! Then, you need to think back to the picture that has the ore in it and then think back to what else was happening in that picture. [Answer.] Good. Therefore, *oryx* means a type of antelope because the keyword for oryx is ore and the picture has a type of antelope pulling ore out of a mine. Do you have any questions?

Figure 6.1. *Continued.*

can also ask students to retell stories they have just heard, in their own words, or to engage in sentence-combining activities, in which they make one sentence from two or more smaller sentences (Polloway & Smith, 1999).

Dialect

In some instances, students deviate from Standard English not because of inappropriate language development but because they speak a different dialect. Often, different dialects consist of language patterns that are regular within themselves but differ from Standard English in many syntactical, morphological, and phonological respects. Some argue that the language in the public schools and the mainstream United States is Standard English and that all students should learn this way of speaking. Others argue that different dialects are necessary for cultural identity and should not be suppressed. A good policy for an individual teacher is to determine the school or district policy on dialect issues and to teach according to this standard. In the long run, it seems best to let the community decide how its children's educational needs, including issues involving dialect, can best be served.

Special Problems

In some instances, students have particular problems with syntax. Such problems should be addressed by careful task and error analyses, followed by more intensive instruction and additional time-on-task. With respect to syntax, morphology, or other issues relevant to oral language, the speech and language teacher may be able to provide assistance.

Semantics

Semantics, which deals with meaning in language, is the most important aspect of language in regard to how language is expressed and understood. With respect to semantics, expressive language reflects the individual's ability to be understood, and receptive language reflects the individual's ability to understand oral language. Training intended to facilitate language in the form of listening comprehension is commonly thought to be highly related to reading comprehension.

Typically, when teaching semantic understanding, teachers read sentences or paragraphs and question students on their meaning. These questions initially involve basic factual recall (e.g., "Who bought the sausage at the store?") and later advance to inferential and deductive reasoning based on the sentences heard. In this type of instruction, students are taught to solve analogies and syllogisms. Analogies are statements that require understanding of relationships between words (e.g., "*Bear* is to *cub* as *cow* is to . . ."). Syllogisms are the basic elements of deductive reasoning and contain a major premise (e.g., "All humans are mortal"), a minor premise (e.g., "Socrates is human"), and a conclusion (e.g., "Therefore, Socrates is mortal").

When teachers teach semantic usage, their specification of objectives and sequences of teaching should be as systematic and explicit as any in any other instructional area. Previous information is first reviewed (e.g., "Yesterday, what did we say were the four *wh–* questions?"). Second, the purpose of the lesson is explicitly stated (e.g., "Today we are going to answer some different *wh–* questions"), followed by teacher-directed instruction (e.g., "Yesterday, Fred walked to town to use the telephone. You say it. [Signal] Now, who walked? [Fred] Where did he walk? [Town] When did he walk there? [Yesterday] Why did he walk there? [To use the telephone]"). Students then receive guided and individual practice on the lesson, and formative data are collected on their performance. As with syntax, the overall goal is comprehension of the meaning of spoken language in everyday usage.

Curriculum Materials

A number of commercially produced language development materials are available, several of which are listed at the end of this chapter. Because commercial language programs often address many different aspects of language functioning, it is important to ensure that the program selected addresses directly the needs of individual students. If not, the program should be changed or amended. For example, the *Language for Learning* program (SRA/McGraw-Hill) employs a very directive, teacher-led drill-and-practice approach to learning such skill areas of early language (K–2) as *identity* (e.g., polars, prepositions, pronouns, comparatives–superlatives), *action* (e.g., same–different, categories, verb tense), and *parts* (e.g., or, all, one, none). In contrast, the *Peabody Language Development Kits* (American Guidance Service) uses a somewhat less structured, storytelling-type format to cover a variety of subject areas (e.g., absurdities, body parts, places, emotions, parts and wholes) and skill areas (e.g., assembling, sequencing, matching, pantomiming, describing). The effectiveness of both of these sets of materials has been supported by research; however, teachers must determine which program is best for the needs of individual students.

Special Problems

When students exhibit difficulty understanding the meaning of spoken language, teachers first need to determine whether students are attending appropriately. In many cases, attention—not receptive semantic language—is the problem. In these cases, students should be prompted and reinforced for attending. Often, it is not sufficient simply to ask the students to repeat what was just said. Students must demonstrate that they actively processed the information by restating the previous statement in different words or by answering comprehension-type questions.

If attention is not a problem, teachers next need to assess whether relevant vocabulary is understood. If not, vocabulary instruction or the use of simpler vocabulary is needed. If students understand the vocabulary, teachers must then determine whether the difficulty involves literal recall or the ability to make deductions or inferences based on what was heard. Specific instructions in the area of difficulty should then be provided.

Students may also exhibit difficulty expressing meaning in spoken language. Teachers should try to determine what the students are attempting to communicate by questioning the student and then should model the appropriately verbalized sentence. If expressive vocabulary is a problem, these words should be taught. Overall, expressive semantic difficulties should be regularly evaluated and carefully monitored to ensure that progress is being made. With any case of persistent speech or language problems, the speech and language teacher should be consulted.

Sometimes, a student's expressive language is semantically correct yet notable because of its bizarre content. If a student's expressive language persistently reflects a different perspective on reality than typically expressed by others (e.g., repeated expression of unrealistic fears and fantasies accompanied by apparent lack of understanding of how these statements are received by others), this may be evidence of serious psychological problems for which more specific professional help may be necessary. It is, of course, not up to the special education teacher to make such a diagnosis. However, teachers should record incidents of aberrant speech and be careful to reinforce more socially appropriate patterns of language. A continuous record of instances of bizarre speech and a listing of antecedent and consequent events may prove helpful in these cases. In addition, special education teachers should consult with their respective school psychologists for advice in working with students who exhibit bizarre speech patterns.

Handwriting

Handwriting is a very important skill for students to master. It has been argued that students can use word processors in place of learning good handwriting skills; however, most students will not have continual access to computers to assist them with their writing. It has also been seen that papers of students with poor handwriting and spelling are rated lower by teachers for composition quality. Furthermore, handwriting problems can interfere with other composing processes and constrain overall writing development. Research has revealed that handwriting problems are greatest among students who have academic difficulties.

Some have suggested that handwriting skills can be allowed to develop "naturally" and that no specific skill instruction is necessary. It has been argued that exposure to reading and writing for "real" purposes is the best way to develop handwriting, with "on-the-spot" instruction as needed (i.e., specific assistance on skill areas as they are encountered in context). Although this may be true for some learners, empirical evidence does not support the idea that natural approaches are sufficient for many students to develop good handwriting skills. Furthermore, "on-the-spot" instruction may address established or developing problems insufficiently for special needs students (Graham, 1999).

There has been a debate in handwriting instruction as to whether manuscript (printing) or cursive (handwriting) should be taught first. Many schools tend to introduce manuscript in kindergarten or first grade and cursive in second or third grade; however, some schools have introduced cursive first. In addition, some schools have adopted a particular handwriting system, such as *D'Nealian Handwriting* (Thurber & Jordan, 1981), *Better Handwriting for You* (Noble, 1966), or *Zaner-Bloser Handwriting: Basic Skills and Applications* (Barbe, Lucas, Hackney, Braun, & Wasylyk, 1987). It is recommended that special educators adopt the systems that are used in their school districts. Even though cursive writing is more regular and consistent, research has shown that the initial use of manuscript writing has several advantages, including (a) being easier for young children to learn, (b) facilitating learning to read and spell, (c) not being detrimental to learning cursive writing, and (d) being generally more legible than cursive writing. Nevertheless, most students will develop their own style of writing regardless of the script style they are taught.

The most successful handwriting instruction combines appropriate materials, direct instruction, distributed practice, and self-monitoring strategies. The following sections discuss handwriting assessment and instruction for acquisition, fluency, and application levels of learning. Instruction procedures for manuscript and cursive writing are combined here because the teaching behaviors and practice activities differ only in whether the letters are manuscript or cursive in form.

Handwriting Assessment/ Error Analysis

In both cursive and manuscript forms, handwriting can be informally assessed very easily. Several formal published handwriting assessment measures exist, such as the *Test of Written Language*

–Third Edition (Hammill & Larsen, 1996) and the *Zaner-Bloser Evaluation Scale* (1986). Teachers should use a scope and sequence that includes both manuscript and cursive letter formations for assessing and instructing handwriting. In addition, handwriting instruction and assessment should follow a sequence from easy to difficult. In other words, the sequence of instruction should proceed as follows: (a) tracing models, (b) tracing faded-out models, (c) copying close models, (d) copying models from the blackboard, and (e) writing from memory as shown in Figure 6.2. Likewise, assessment should proceed from producing individual letters, words, sentences, and paragraphs to producing short narratives.

Student behavior critical to the handwriting process can be examined. It is recommended that teachers check the following student behaviors:

1. Is the student holding the pencil correctly?

2. Is the student positioning the paper correctly?

3. Are the student's posture and sitting position conducive to good handwriting?

4. Is the student motivated during handwriting exercises?

5. Is the student consistently using the same hand during writing exercises?

Occasionally, a slight modification in one of these behaviors will dramatically improve a student's handwriting.

An analysis of the student's handwriting can also lead to appropriate instructional strategies. Teachers can attend to the following aspects of the student's handwritten products.

1. letter formation

2. letter size

3. letter alignment

4. letter spacing

5. letter orientation

6. letter omissions, additions, and/or substitutions

Task	Example
Tracing models	Student traces over:
	cat
Tracing faded-out models	Student traces over:
	cat
Copying close models	Student copies:
	cat
Copying models from blackboard	Same as copying close models, except from blackboard:
Writing from memory	No model.

Figure 6.2. Letter-copying sequence.

7. rate or speed at which handwriting is completed

These considerations are discussed in relation to instruction at the acquisition, fluency, and application levels in the following sections.

Acquisition Instruction

For young students, beginning handwriting instruction can focus on the fundamentals of writing and practice in the physical skills of handwriting. This can include exercises involving free scribbling, exercises to promote left–right orientation, and the writing of basic strokes for straight lines, circles, curved lines, and diagonal lines. During acquisition instruction of letter writing, the major goal is for students to produce accurately all of the letters in isolation and in combinations that form words and sentences, without regard to fluency. This stage of handwriting instruction corresponds to the letter identification stage in reading. Typically, students begin to trace letter shapes. Because handwriting is a production task, it is assumed that students can accurately identify all of the letters and can discriminate among difficult letters. However, because the first stage in writing is tracing models, teachers can use this stage to reinforce the similarities and differences among many letter shapes (e.g., *b* and *d*, *p* and *q*). Teachers should use the same instructional procedures for teaching difficult letter discriminations that were discussed in Chapter 5. During this stage, it is critical for teachers to model, demonstrate, and provide corrective feedback on the correct posture and pencil and paper positioning because this is the stage in which good and bad habits are formed. Provide models of the order, number, and direction of strokes for each new letter. A sample sequence for instruction is given in Figure 6.3.

Have students practice the following steps for forming specific letters: (a) tracing entire letters, (b) completing letters that consist of dashed lines, (c) copying letters from close and distant models, and (d) producing letters without using models. Corrective feedback is critical. Students need to be provided with sufficient practice opportunities to acquire these skills with 100% accuracy. Although "neatness" with 100% accuracy is a somewhat subjective standard, teachers can assist students in evaluating their own performances by clearly stating the evaluation standards. Standards, which typically include letter size, letter shape, letter orientation, and letter closure, can be displayed with the use of models. One particularly effective self-checking procedure is the use of transparent overlays that accurately display all the critical attributes of the letters and are available for students to superimpose over their completed work. This self-checking process helps students to recognize and correct their own errors and has been shown to improve writing performance.

In teaching students handwriting, teachers should (a) design an instructional objective that matches the students' ability to the instructional materials and performance criteria used and (b) use the teacher effectiveness variables during the design and delivery of the lesson. Teacher presentation should be clear and concise, and modeling demonstration and feedback should be given. Students' active participation should involve all students all of the time, and all students should have many opportunities to

Sequence	Groups	Examples
1.	point	*i t*
2.	loop	*e l f*
3.	circle	*o p q g*
4.	mound	*m n*

Figure 6.3. Instructional sequence for cursive letters.

practice newly learned letters, first under the teacher's guidance and then independently. Optimal practice activities are directly related to the objective. In other words, all involve practice in writing (tracing or copying) the letters to be mastered.

For independent practice during acquisition, self-instruction procedures and self-correction procedures can be added to increase handwriting accuracy. Self-instruction components include the following:

1. Student says aloud the letters or words that need to be written.

2. Student names the letters that need to be written.

3. Student repeats each letter name as it is written down.

4. Student describes verbally the motions of the pencil while forming the letter (e.g., verbal description for writing the letter *a:* "Start at the middle line; go around, down to the bottom line; back up to the beginning; retrace down to the bottom line." [Graham, 1983, p. 233]).

Self-correction procedures require students first to identify their own errors by circling incorrectly formed letters and then to produce accurately formed letters. A combination of self-instruction, self-correction, and the teacher effectiveness variables can be quite successful in promoting good handwriting.

The key to success at this level is a sufficient amount of guided and independent practice. When students can accurately produce all the letters without a model, instruction can proceed to fluency-building activities. Formative evaluation can help to determine whether students need more or less time-on-task. An example of an acquisition lesson is given in Figure 6.4.

Fluency Instruction

The goal during fluency instruction is to increase the rate at which students are able to accurately

produce manuscript and/or cursive letters. Again, it is important to reinforce good posture, pencil holding, and paper position during these instructional periods. Teachers can spend their review time reinforcing accuracy of letter formations, good posture, and positioning. During the teacher presentation phase, teachers should stress fluency while maintaining accuracy. This type of instruction requires a great deal of practice activity. Teachers can also reinforce good independent work habits during these practice activities. Because fluency instruction emphasizes the rate at which students can write accurately, practice activities should involve extra incentives for fast yet accurate completion. During this phase of instruction, teachers may want to alter reinforcers to maintain student motivation. Most activities during this phase will be independent practice activities that require handwriting and emphasize speed as well as accuracy.

Application and Generalization Instruction

Application instruction in handwriting refers to instruction aimed at allowing students opportunities to apply their handwriting skills to a variety of tasks. This instruction can be combined with instructional assignments in other areas, such as creative writing, homework assignments, and mathematics work. Once students have become fluent in handwriting, they can be reminded that they are expected to demonstrate these skills on all written work. This is also an opportune time to remind students to use self-correction procedures. At times it may be necessary to remind, prompt, and correct minor problem areas.

Special Problems

Most handwriting problems reflect insufficient task analysis, insufficient engaged time-on-task, or content that has been covered too rapidly. If motor or other problems are so severe that hand-

Lesson Section	Teacher Dialogue
Review	Last week we started to learn cursive writing. What was the group of letters we learned last week, everybody? [Signal.] Correct, the *e* group. The *e* group was letters *e, h,* and *l.* Everybody write cursive *e, h,* and *l* on a piece of paper.
State purpose	Today we are going to learn two letters of the *i* group. These letters are *i* and *t.*
Present information	Everybody watch me write an *i* on the board. [Writes.] Do you see how I did it? I start at the line, go up, and come back down. What did I do last, Raymond? [Answers.] Correct, I put a dot on the *i.*
Guided practice	I'm going to give you a worksheet now to practice the letters *i* and *t.* On the first line, you write right over the letters. What do you do on the first line, George? [Answers.] Good. Write right over the letters on the first line. Everybody try it.
Independent practice	I can see everyone is doing very well on the letters *i* and *t.* Now I want you to go back to your desks and write *i* and *t* slowly and neatly, just like we practiced. Write each letter 25 times.
Formative evaluation	Everybody hand in your papers now, and I'll tell you how well you did.

Figure 6.4. Excerpts from a sample acquisition lesson.

writing problems affect other skill areas, it may be wise to substitute a typewriter or word processor for essential writing activities while continuing to practice handwriting as much as time allows. If students have a problem with pencil grip, use large pencils, grip enhancers that slip over pencils, tape or rubber bands, or a practice golf ball to make pencils easier to grip.

Further analysis of handwriting problems may indicate that the total number of letters being miswritten is fewer than expected. Research has shown that only four symbols—*a, e, r,* and *t*—account for about half of all misformed cursive letters. Additional attention to these letters, or other specific letter misformations identified through error analysis, can bring about disproportionate gains in handwriting performance.

Left-handed writers may be more at risk for handwriting problems. For manuscript writing, place paper directly in front of the student; for cursive writing, place it on an opposite slant. Typically, the student's hand position is curved, with the hand resting on the little finger. Smudging can be a problem, so use a pencil with hard lead.

Spelling

In some ways, spelling is a more difficult activity than reading. Reading requires students to recognize letters and letter patterns and recall corresponding sounds, which are then verbalized. In spelling, students are required to *produce* the corresponding letters. Recall of the correct spelling of words requires a type of serial-list learning (i.e., recall of letters in a series) in the context of application of phonics rules.

Ideally, spelling should be regarded as an essential element of a well-integrated literacy curriculum and incorporated within the general study of written and spoken language. Students should learn to spell words as they learn to read them. Generally, it is inappropriate to give students spelling words that are not a part of their reading vocabulary. Like reading instruction, spelling instruction in special education should progress systematically along a continuum of phonic analysis and sight-word skills with high levels of engaged time-on-task devoted to practicing the spelling words. Employ a variety of methods and materials for spelling activities, and include spelling in regular meaningful writing activities. Add more difficult or irregular words as they are introduced into the reading program.

Training

An example of parts of a spelling lesson is given in Figure 6.5. Like any other lesson, teachers should review previous material and explicitly state the purpose of the lesson (e.g., "Today we are going to learn three new spelling words taken from your reader"). The teacher then presents the first word and models the spelling. If the word is a CVC word, such as *cat* or some other highly regular word, the teacher should review the component sounds by asking, for example,

Lesson Section	Teacher Dialogue
Review	We have been learning how to spell four *oa* words. Can you remember what those four words were, Mary? [Mary responds.] Yes, the words were: *soap, goat, boat,* and *float.* Now, let's all spell them together. Everybody ready? Everyone spell *boat.* [Signal.] Good. B-O-A-T. Boat. . . .
State purpose	Today we are going to learn three more *oa* words and one word that is *not* an *oa* word. . . .
Present information	Everyone watch while I write them one at a time on the board. The first word is [writes] *coat.* Everyone, spell it with me. [Signal.] C-O-A-T. Good. Coat. . . .
	Now, the last word we are going to learn has the *oh* sound, but it is not an *oa* word. This word is *pour.* Watch while I write it. [Writes.] OK, let's all spell it together: P-O-U-R. Now, you spell it for me, Bob. [Spells.] Good. What is different about this word, Mary? [Answers.] Right, it is not spelled with *oa;* it is spelled with what, George? [Answers.] Right, it is spelled with *ou.* . . .
Guided practice	Now, everybody write these words on the paper I am giving you. I want you to study these words using the study strategy you have used before. Remember, look at the word and spell it, cover the word and spell it, then check your spelling. If you are right, go to the next word. What do you do if you are wrong, George? [Answers.] Good. If you are wrong, study the word again. When you think you know the four words, ask me or ask your neighbor to give you a written test. . . .
Independent practice	OK, everybody go back to your desks now and study the four words from today plus the four words from before. In 10 minutes you will all take a test.
Formative evaluation	OK, everybody put your words away and take out a clean piece of paper. Get ready to spell all eight words.

Figure 6.5. Excerpts from a sample daily spelling lesson on one-syllable *oa* words.

"What letter makes the /k/ sound? What letter makes the /t/ sound? What letter makes the /a/ sound?" When letter sounds are clearly understood, students should be asked to spell the word orally (e.g., "Everybody, how do you spell *cat*? [Signal]"). Students who have had previous training in phonemic awareness should find these exercises very familiar; in fact, phonemic awareness training has shown to promote skill in beginning spelling. If phonics rules other than letter–sound correspondence are used, these rules should be explicitly stated, and their use in spelling the word should be described. It is also helpful to group words with similar spellings and those that follow similar rules. If irregular words are being taught, teachers should simply state the spelling and ask students to repeat it. A possible table of specifications for spelling is given in Table 6.2.

Guided Practice

Once students understand the initial process of spelling new words, guided practice should be provided. Practice can take the form of small-group oral rehearsal of new words or active monitoring of tutor pairs using flash cards. It is also helpful to provide frequent written tests of new spelling words, especially when students check their own work after the test and immediately correct errors. These errors should then be the focus of additional practice.

Independent Practice

When students begin to demonstrate accuracy in spelling performance, they should receive additional independent practice to develop fluency and promote overlearning for long-term retention. Several types of independent practice activities can be helpful. One obvious approach is to provide flash cards to pairs of students on the same spelling level who can drill each other on the words and record levels of accuracy or fluency performance. It is also helpful to teach students a strategy for independent study of spelling

words: (a) read and spell the word, (b) cover the word, (c) copy the word, (d) check the word and correct if necessary, and (e) retest errors or, if correct, move to the next word. This word study procedure is known as "cover, copy, compare" (Murphy, Hern, Williams, & McLaughlin, 1990; see also Graham, 1999). When students have performed this procedure accurately, they can repeat the procedure saying as well as writing the spelling word. Students who are studying independently should be provided with specific goals relative to their abilities (e.g., "You should be able to spell these four words by the end of class"), and their performances should be evaluated. It can also be helpful for students to set their own goals for each study session or for a week of studying. Goal setting can help them become more invested in their own learning and more carefully attend to their own learning.

In general, having students copy spelling words or use words in various workbook or practice activities, such as matching shapes, unscrambling letters, or locating them in word-search activities, is less likely to enforce learning than is direct drill and practice. Some of these activities may be helpful in meeting other objectives, however, such as developing handwriting skills by copying. A list of spelling activities that are supported by research (Graham, 1999; Loomer, 1982) is provided in Table 6.3.

Evaluation

As stated earlier, spelling activities should parallel progress made in reading. Many spelling curriculum materials show little relation to reading materials. In such cases, the teacher should select words carefully to match the reading sequence. It is also helpful to attend to school scope and sequence to ensure that students are meeting school objectives. Students should be retested frequently on words covered to date to ensure that spelling words are not forgotten. Teachers can compile a list of spelling words learned to date to provide students and teachers with information on student progress and to

Table 6.2. Table of Specifications for Spelling

CONTENT	Identification	Production			
	A. Acquisition	B. Acquisition	C. Fluency	D. Application	E. Generalization
1. CV words	1A	1B	1C	NA	NA
2. CVC words	2A	2B	2C	NA	NA
3. CVC+e words	3A	3B	3C	3D	3E
4. Words with internal vowel digraphs:					
(1) oa	4(1)A	4(1)B	4(1)C	4(1)D	4(1)E
(2) ou	4(2)A	4(2)B	4(2)C	4(2)D	4(2)E
(3) ae	4(3)A	4(3)B	4(3)C	4(3)D	4(3)E
(4) ie	4(4)A	4(4)B	4(4)C	4(4)D	4(4)E
(5) ei	4(5)A	4(5)B	4(5)C	4(5)D	4(5)E
5. Words with diphthongs:					
(1) oi	5(1)A	5(1)B	5(1)C	5(1)D	5(1)E
(2) ou	5(2)A	5(2)B	5(2)C	5(2)D	5(2)E
(3) ow	5(3)A	5(3)B	5(3)C	5(3)D	5(3)E
6. Words with two-letter initial blends:					
(1) st	6(1)A	6(1)B	6(1)C	6(1)D	6(1)E
(2) sp	6(2)A	6(2)B	6(2)C	6(2)D	6(2)E
(3) sl	6(3)A	6(3)B	6(3)C	6(3)D	6(3)E
(4) br	6(4)A	6(4)B	6(4)C	6(4)D	6(4)E
(5) bl	6(5)A	6(5)B	6(5)C	6(5)D	6(5)E
7. Words with three-letter initial blends:					
(1) str	7(1)A	7(1)B	7(1)C	7(1)D	7(1)E
(2) spr	7(2)A	7(2)B	7(2)C	7(2)D	7(2)E

NA = not applicable

Sample Objectives:

2A   Given 20 pictures representing CVC words, student will correctly identify each correct spelling from four choices with 100% accuracy.

3B   Student will correctly spell, in writing, 20 orally presented CVC+e words.

4(2)C Student will correctly spell, in writing, 10 orally presented words containing the vowel digraph *ou* with 100% accuracy in 1 minute.

6(3)D Student will correctly spell all words containing the initial blend *bl* in journal entries.

7(2)E Student will correctly spell all words containing the initial blend *spr* in inclusive class written assignments.

Table 6.3. Spelling Techniques Supported by Research

Students learn to spell more effectively when they:

- Increase engaged learning time
- Use self-monitoring strategies
- Check their own spelling and make corrections
- Use study strategies, such as cover, copy, and compare
- Use learning strategies such as clustering, rehearsal, and elaboration
- Study similar words together
- Frequently review previously learned words

Note. Adapted from Graham (1999) and Loomer (1982).

compare this progress with the student's IEP objectives.

Special Problems

If students present problems in learning spelling words, teachers should use error analysis to determine whether the errors are due to a lack of understanding of a phonics rule. If this is the problem, the rule should be retaught and its relevance to the spelling word made explicit. If the student exhibits understanding of relevant phonics rules, additional drill and practice should be provided. If retention of previously learned words is a problem, the student should engage in more overlearning activities or move more slowly through the curriculum, perhaps by limiting the number of words learned at a time. Another possibility is to provide additional time-on-task through tutors, self-study, or homework assignments. Because spelling is rarely regarded by special education students as a self-reinforcing activity, teachers may also want to ensure that sufficient motivation has been provided for spelling performance. To this end, some type of goal setting, described previously, in which the learners help set their own daily, weekly, and monthly spelling goals, may be helpful. Keep records of learning progress and share them with students. Use gamelike formats, peer tutoring, computer-assisted instruction, and reinforcement to keep students interested in building their spelling skills.

Finally, research has supported the use of a spelling mnemonic, particularly at the upper elementary or secondary levels. Spelling mnemonics are useful in cases in which memory of phonics rules is not helpful for recall of, usually, one difficult part of a word. For example, some students have difficulty remembering the vowels that appear in the word *cemetery*, although recall of the consonants does not pose a problem. In this case, the student can be provided with or asked to generate an interactive sentence, such as "She screamed, 'E-E-E' as she walked by the cemetery," to help recall the vowels. For another example, to remember the spelling word *villain*, the sentence, "The *villain* had a *villa* in the town," could be used. For such an elaboration to be helpful, however, the student must know the meaning, as well as the spelling, of all words in the elaborative sentence. Mnemonics are useful when the student has overall knowledge of the spelling but is having difficulty on just one or two letters. Additional examples of the use of mnemonics (Shefter, 1976; Suid, 1990) are given in Table 6.4 (see also Dowling, 1995, for more mnemonic spellings).

Written Language

Written language or composition requires the use of almost all of the skills covered in this text. Written language is an application of oral language that requires mastery of preskills, including reading, handwriting, spelling, thinking, syntax,

Table 6.4. Spelling Mnemonics

Word	Example
privilege	Special priVILEges are VILE.
laboratory	A LABORatory is for LABOR.
judgment	GM (General Motors) made a judGMent.
stationery	LettERs are written on stationERy.
bargain	You GAIN from a barGAIN.
feminist	The feMINIst would not wear a MINI skirt.
revelant	The ANT was relevANT to the science class.
obedient	If you are not obeDIEnt, you will DIE.
sacrilegious	SacRILEgious people RILE me.
grammar	Bad gramMAR will MAR your reputation.

Note. Adapted from Shefter (1976) and Suid (1990).

and semantics. Successful writing skills are among the most difficult skills to acquire because they require the application of so many prerequisite skills. In addition, good writing instruction has rarely taken place in classrooms. Traditionally, teachers distributed blank paper to students and issued directions such as, "Write what you did on your summer vacation." More recently, however, research has identified the elements of high-quality writing instruction. Several formal and informal writing assessment measures are also available. It is recommended that special education teachers identify district-level objectives and curriculum materials in the area of writing and adjust their objectives accordingly.

As in most other curriculum areas, researchers recently have begun to emphasize the role of meaning in the writing process. This is accomplished by teaching such necessary skills as writing mechanics within the context of written products that are meaningful to learners. Furthermore, the integration of writing with other relevant academic activities has been emphasized. This means that students should be encouraged to read what they and other students have written, write about books or passages they have read, and engage in relevant, interactive dialogue about what they and others have read and written. The most effective special education teachers conduct efficient, skill-based instruction while emphasizing application and generalized use of these skills in meaningful and motivating contexts.

Examination of Written Products

Assessment procedures for formal and informal writing share common elements. Typically, students' written language is subdivided into common elements, which are shown in Table 6.5.

Students' performance on these elements can also vary as a function of student and situation variables such as the (a) particular assignment and purpose of writing, (b) amount and type of teacher directions, (c) amount of time allocated for the task, (d) background knowledge, and (e) motivation and attention given to the task. Several samples of students' written products should be evaluated in terms of both the elements listed above and student and situation variables. Once these evaluations are collected, an error analysis can be completed to determine specific subskill areas that need instruction or reteaching.

Table 6.5. Common Elements of Written Language

1. *Mechanics*
   a. capitalization
   b. penmanship
   c. punctuation
   d. format
   e. spelling
   f. error monitoring

2. *Grammar or syntax*
   a. subject–verb agreement
   b. verb tense
   c. pronoun usage
   d. sentence structure
   e. adjective usage
   f. adverb usage

3. *Semantics*
   a. language usage
   b. vocabulary usage

4. *Organization*
   a. sequencing of ideas
   b. sequencing of sentences
   c. sequencing of paragraphs

5. *Content*
   a. relevance to topic
   b. breadth and depth of knowledge displayed
   c. originality
   d. degree of documentation

6. *Type of writing*
   a. declarative
   b. narrative
   c. expository
   d. letters

7. *Sophistication of writing*
   a. sentence length
   b. sentence variation
   c. sentence complexity
   d. sophistication of ideas

Instructional Strategies

This aim of this text is to present the teacher effectiveness model as a framework for incorporating all instruction, and this section presents that model as it is used with writing instruction. Sample lessons are presented first, based on the error analysis or examination of students' written products. Second, specific instructional strategies to increase sentence complexity or sophistication of writing are discussed. Third, prewriting strategies are discussed, followed by postwriting strategies. Finally, instruction in specific types of writing is presented.

Sample Lesson Designed from an Error Analysis

Using the method of examining writing products, teachers can determine very specific instructional needs. For example, if students consistently produce incorrect subject–verb agreement in their compositions, whether the tasks are timed or untimed, then a decision would be made to reteach correct subject–verb agreement. First, the teacher would develop an instructional objective or series of objectives reflecting the content to be taught. In this case, a good example is "Students will identify correct subject–verb agreement in sentences with 100% accuracy," followed by "Students will write the correct subject–verb agreement in sentences with 100% accuracy." A fluency (rate) application and a generalization objective, such as, "Students will consistently use the correct subject–verb agreement in all of their writing assignments," are then specified. Notice that the first instructional objective emphasizes the identification of the correct grammar, followed by the production of the correct forms in contrived formats (accuracy and rate), and finally the application or generalization objective.

After specifying the objectives, the teacher can design the instructional lesson using all of the teacher effectiveness variables. An example of each in the context of teaching subject–verb agreement is presented below.

1. *Review.* Teacher begins the lesson with a review of subjects and verbs. During this time, students respond to the teacher's questions, thus providing the teacher with information on how well past content has been retained. The decision can then be made to either introduce new content or reinstruct old content.

2. *Teacher presentation.* Teacher verbally presents the lesson's objective, tells students the rules for subject–verb agreement, provides examples and nonexamples, and requires all students to participate in responding to direct questions on the rule and examples of the rule. Teacher provides corrective feedback to students during the presentation and keeps the pace of instruction moving rapidly enough to ensure that all students are participating.

3. *Guided practice.* During this portion of the lesson, students are actively engaged in a practice activity that is guided by the teacher. This ensures that students practice correct subject–verb agreements.

4. *Independent practice.* Once it is determined that students are able to practice subject–verb agreement activities successfully, the teacher allows students to continue to practice independently. However, the teacher continues to monitor students' work.

5. *Formative evaluation.* After students complete the independent practice activity, the teacher can give students a 1- or 2-minute quiz to verify their mastery of subject–verb agreement. The quiz should include several items that match the specific objective covered in the lesson. In this case, because subject–verb agreement is being reintroduced, the teacher can decide whether more or less time is needed on this task.

The amount of engaged time-on-task; the type of teacher presentation, questioning, and feedback; the type and amount of guided practice and independent practice; and student performance can now be examined to determine if and how instruction should be monitored and adjusted.

Any pattern of deficiencies in students' written composition can be analyzed and reinstructed using the above model. Again, it is recommended that teachers use districtwide objectives and scope and sequences to maximize access to the general education curriculum. Most important, systematic analysis of students' errors should be combined with effective instruction in those deficit areas.

Increasing Sentence Complexity

Many students with mild disabilities write very simple sentences consisting of a subject and a verb. To analyze the complexity of a student's writing, the teacher can conduct a T-unit analysis (see McGill-Franzen, 1979). A T-unit, or *minimal terminal unit*, is a main clause or a main clause and its accompanying subordinate clause. The number of words used per T-unit can be calculated (see Figure 6.6). Typically, the higher the number of words per T-unit, the more sophisticated the writing. The teacher can analyze the students' writing to determine the average T-unit length. If the T-unit length is low, teachers should teach sentence-combining activities. Through examples and practice, sentence-combining activities teach students how to write sentences that contain main clauses and subordinate clauses. For example, consider the following series of simple sentences:

> Su-Hsiang went outside. (3 words, 1 T-unit)
> She looked at the flowers. (5 words, 1 T-unit)
> The flowers were dry. (4 words, 1 T-unit)
> She got some water. (4 words, 1 T-unit)
> She watered the flowers. (4 words, 1 T-unit)

Using sentence-combining activities that incorporate the combination of simple sentences to form a major clause and subordinate clauses by using words such as *when, whether, or,* and *however,* the above example can be rewritten to look like the following:

We have our summer vacations at the ocean. I like swimming in the water when the waves are big. Making sand castles is fun. I like walking along the water, and I like looking for shells. I like everything we do at the ocean.

Sentence	Number of words	Number of T-units
We have our summer vacations at the ocean.	8	1
I like swimming in the water when the waves are big.	11	1
Making sand castles is fun.	5	1
I like walking along the water, and I like looking for shells.	12	2
I like everything we do at the ocean.	8	1
Total	44	6

Total T-units: 6
Total words: 44
Words/T-units: 7.3

Figure 6.6. Calculation of T-units.

Su-Hsiang went outside to look at the flowers. (8 words, 1 T-unit)

Because the flowers were dry, she got some water and watered the flowers. (13 words, 1 T-unit)

Specific instruction and practice can be completed using sentence-combining activities. Again, specific objectives and the teacher effectiveness variables should be incorporated into sentence-combining instruction.

Prewriting Strategies

Specific instruction also needs to be conducted on prewriting strategies. Nothing is more frustrating than to sit down with a blank piece of paper, a pencil, and no ideas about what to do or how to start doing it. To avoid this problem, specific instruction and practice can be given in the following areas:

1. brainstorming topic ideas
2. methods for getting started
3. narrowing topics
4. outlining major subheadings
5. outlining minor details
6. organizing ideas
7. writing first drafts
8. researching topics

Adequate instruction, including guided and independent practice, should be provided on all of the above prewriting strategies. Some examples for prewriting strategies are given in Figure 6.7.

Postwriting Strategies

Adequate instruction should to be implemented on postwriting strategies. Effective use of postwriting strategies can make the difference between

Assignment: Write a persuasive paper on a school policy.

1. What is a school policy? (If you don't know, try to find out.)

2. List as many school policies as you can.

3. Which of these policies do you feel most strongly about?

4. Are you in favor of it or opposed to it?

5. List as many arguments as you can think of.

6. Can you think of any more?

7. List the arguments in order of importance to you.

8. What would happen if your ideas were accepted?

Figure 6.7. Prewriting strategies.

an excellent paper and a less-than-adequate paper. Postwriting strategies include the following:

1. proofreading for spelling, mechanics, and general format

2. proofreading for adequate organization of ideas and content coverage

3. revising based on (1) and (2) above

4. editing and handing in assignments on time

Very specific error-monitoring and self-monitoring strategies can be combined not only to assist students in locating and correcting errors but also to ensure that checking skills are completed. Figure 6.8 contains a self-monitoring sheet for the story grammar strategy for organizing and sequencing ideas in narrative prose or stories (see Harris & Graham, 1996). At this point in the process, peers can be very useful in reviewing manuscripts, identifying the positive features of a student's written product, and recommending revisions.

Word processors are becoming more widely available for students' use. Some word-processing programs contain spell-check features, which check for spelling errors, and counters, which tally total words and sentences. Computer programs such as these can be invaluable for use in guided and independent practice activities for

students. However, as with any instruction, their ultimate efficacy will depend on teachers' collection of formative data and teachers' judgments as to whether objectives have been mastered. MacArthur (1996) has described the uses of technology in promoting the writing processes of students with learning disabilities.

Specific Types of Written Products

Writing is an application of many skills. In addition, there are many purposes for writing, the form for each of which needs to be explicitly instructed. For example, students may be required to write any of the following:

1. personal letters

2. thank you notes

3. letters to manufacturers requesting exchanges of merchandise

4. research reports

5. persuasive arguments or opinion essays

6. compare–contrast essays

7. creative prose

8. poetry

9. technical manuals

	Yes	No
Did I use the story grammar strategy (3-W, 2-What, 2-How)?	☐	☐
Did I include:		
• *Who* the main character and other characters are?	☐	☐
• *When* the story takes place?	☐	☐
• *Where* the story takes place?	☐	☐
• *What* the main character wants to do?	☐	☐
• *What* happens when the main character tries to do it?	☐	☐
• *How* the story ends?	☐	☐
• *How* the characters feel at the end?	☐	☐

Figure 6.8. Story grammar self-monitoring sheet. *Note.* Adapted from *Making the Writing Process Work: Strategies for Composing and Self-Regulating,* by K. Harris and S. Graham, 1996. Cambridge, MA: Brookline Books. Adapted with permission.

All of these are easier to write if a concrete model is provided (see Figure 6.9). Be careful, however, that overreliance on a model does not inhibit creativity of ideas in the later stages of writing. All types of writing should be instructed using the proposed teacher effectiveness model, and students' performance should be monitored. Special educators should determine regular education goals and objectives in writing and adjust them accordingly for their special needs students.

Harris and Graham (1996) proposed the use of the TREE strategy for planning a simple opinion essay: note *T*opic sentence, note *R*easons, *E*xamine reasons (are they convincing?), and note *E*nding. For writing simple stories, Harris and Graham recommended the SPACE strategy: note *S*etting, *P*urpose, *A*ction, *C*onclusion, and *E*motions. Each of these strategies can also be adapted to postwriting strategies.

Wong, Butler, Ficzere, and Kuperis (1997) developed a model that was very effective at helping students write "compare–contrast" essays. First, students were taught to generate topics and brainstorm different ways of comparing and contrasting these topics. For example, for the topic of concerts, students could create categories of "rock concerts" and "school concerts."

They then develop a list of features on which comparisons and contrasts of rock concerts and school concerts could be made. In this case, students could identify the goals, the content, and people's dress and demeanor as three relevant features. Then a table is created for each of these features, listing different ideas for each feature and whether the two categories are similar or different with respect to each idea (e.g., under content, whether the type of music is the same or different). This information is summarized in a student helper sheet, and students use this to compose a first draft of the essay.

Collaborative Writing

Researchers have recently begun to recommend student interaction and collaboration in writing. Students have improved the quality of their writing and their attitudes toward writing when they engage in collaborative activities with other students under teacher supervision. Students can meet in pairs or groups to brainstorm ideas, plan and organize written products, monitor and encourage progress toward task completion, and proofread and revise each other's work, perhaps

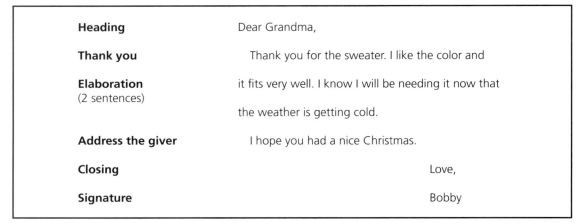

Heading	Dear Grandma,
Thank you	Thank you for the sweater. I like the color and
Elaboration (2 sentences)	it fits very well. I know I will be needing it now that the weather is getting cold.
Address the giver	I hope you had a nice Christmas.
Closing	Love,
Signature	Bobby

Figure 6.9. Model thank-you note.

using self-monitoring checklists. Although it is important to ensure that individual students have mastered the competencies necessary for independent writing, it also can be very helpful and rewarding to teach writing as a collaborative, interactive process.

Englert and Mariage (1996) described a peer-questioning activity ("Sharing Chair") to help primary-grade students expand their ideas for writing. A student reads his or her story ideas to a group of students, who ask questions about the meaning of the story. Answers to these questions can provide ideas for story development or can be incorporated in text revisions. Also, peer-questioning activities promote the idea that writers are writing for an audience, and they should consider the needs and interests of the audience when writing. Mariage (2000) described an example with "Gerry," a third-grade student with learning disabilities, sharing his one-sentence journal entry and soliciting feedback from nine other students, part of which follows:

GERRY: Today I made a sand castle with Byron. Any comments or questions? Marky?

MARK: Was it big?

GERRY: Yeah.

MARK: How big?

GERRY: Big. About this big, about as big as this chair. Hannah?

NATHAN: What does it look like?

GERRY: Um, um, I forgot. I think Byron knows. (to Byron) How big? What did the sand castle look like?

BYRON: (Comes to the front of room and stands next to Gerry). Well, it was about like this (shows about two feet high). It took up a lot of sand.

GERRY: Any more comments or questions? (Mariage, 2000, p. 96)

Although Gerry was one of the lower functioning students in the class, he had opportunities to interact with peers and develop his thinking toward communicating better with his audience. Mariage (2000) concluded,

As this story illustrates, Gerry's simple one-sentence story generates 10 questions from his audience and allows him to make verbal contact with six different classmates and his teacher. Over time, this contact in positive and appropriate ways with peers becomes part of the normative feature of the event and reinforces the conversational conventions that foster social competence. (p. 98)

Special Problems

When students exhibit difficulty with written language, teachers must determine where the difficulties lie. First, teachers may wish to determine whether the problem is primarily due to insufficient ability to manipulate paper and pencil. If this is the case, provision of fluency-building activities in handwriting or adaptations to improve pencil grip may be desirable. In addition, teachers may wish to determine whether the problem is due primarily to insufficient ability to generate novel ideas. To determine if this is the case, teachers can require students to write titles and descriptions of illustrations. A series of pictures depicting a story can be presented to the students, and students can be asked to write down the sequence of events from the illustrations. By implementing this type of procedure, teachers eliminate the generation of novel ideas from the writing task. Teachers can then determine how accurately students can describe a sequence of events in writing.

A more precise evaluation of students' ability to use proper grammar, including sentence structure and punctuation, can also be made. Composition instruction can then proceed with the aid of such illustrations. The illustrations can eventually be phased out from instruction and replaced by verbal story starters. For example, a teacher writes, "This morning when I woke up, I found a crumpled-up old paper bag by the side of my bed. What could be in it? Did I hear something move inside? Cautiously, I looked inside and found . . ." Given this "starter," many students find it easier to write. Students can also be encouraged to develop their own story starters. In other cases, students can be encouraged to write about recent personal experiences.

Some teachers have found that requiring students to write on a daily basis in journals or logs greatly facilitates the performance of reluctant writers. Some teachers choose not to read or evaluate these written products so that students will write more freely and learn to enjoy writing more. Many teachers set aside a regular time for writing. This frequent practice sometimes enables students to gain confidence in writing. In addition, it may be beneficial for teachers to add self-correction components to writing instruction. During self-correction activities, students can be required to identify their errors and then produce the correct responses. When self-correction is explicitly taught, students may be better able to generalize error-monitoring strategies to their independent work.

Summary

- Effective instruction in oral and written language is based on (a) determining specific instructional objectives from a larger task analysis or scope and sequence and (b) designing effective lessons based on the teacher effectiveness variables. If teachers use the specified instructional model for delivery of instruction, they will be better able to monitor and adjust instruction based on student performance in each area.

- Oral language training for students with mild disabilities includes instruction in phonological production, listening comprehension skills, vocabulary development, syntactical and morphological skills, and semantics. Carefully sequenced instruction can be very effective in each of these areas.

- Handwriting can be an important preskill for a number of writing activities. Initial writing instruction can include free scribbling, left-to-right orientation, and the basics of letter formation. Letter and word writing can develop from a carefully arranged sequence of objectives. A number of skills, including pencil grip, seating, and paper position, are needed to develop handwriting.

- Spelling instruction should parallel progress in reading, be incorporated into an overall program of written language, employ a variety of methods and materials, and include regular, meaningful writing activities. Students should use self-monitoring strategies, check their own spelling and make corrections, frequently review previously learned words, and use learning strategies such as rehearsal and elaboration.

- Written language incorporates skills from nearly all other language areas. Teachers should teach in areas of difficulty identified from error analysis, in addition to providing instruction in prewriting, writing, and post-writing strategies. Specific models can be provided for specific types of writing. In addition, students should use specific writing strategies for specific types of writing, such as story grammar, opinion papers, and compare–contrast essays.

Relevant Research and Resources

Research

Oral language. Disorders in speech production are reviewed by Moore and Hicks (1994) and Schwartz (1994). The general effectiveness of a direct instruction approach to oral language with children from lower income groups is described by Gersten, Woodward, and Darch (1986), who have also described similar interventions with students with disabilities. Lloyd, Cullinan, Heins, and Epstein (1980) provide support for direct instruction procedures in improving the oral and written language of students with learning disabilities. Use of the keyword method in facilitating initial acquisition of vocabulary words is supported in research described by Condus, Marshall, and Miller (1986); McLoone, Scruggs, Mastropieri, and Zucker (1986); Mastropieri, Scruggs, Levin, Gaffney, and McLoone (1985); Mastropieri, Scruggs, and Levin (1985a); Scruggs, Mastropieri, and Levin (1985); Mastropieri, Scruggs, and Fulk (1990); Fulk, Mastropieri, and Scruggs (1992); Mastropieri (1988); and Scruggs and Laufenberg (1986). Carlisle (1993) reviews literature on vocabulary learning and reading disabilities. Additional suggestions for oral language training in special education are given by Bording, McLaughlin, and Williams (1984); Minskoff (1982); and Fisher, White, and Fisher (1984), whereas Bos and Anders (1987, 1990a, 1990b) describe an interactive process for facilitating vocabulary learning. Polloway and

Smith (1999) provide an excellent text on language instruction for students with disabilities.

Handwriting. Reviews of handwriting research are provided by Graham and Weintraub (1996) and Graham (1999), and relevant issues are described by Graham (1992). The use of task analysis, overlearning, monitoring, and verbal cues in handwriting is described by Hagen (1983). Self-instruction and self-correction techniques are evaluated by Graham (1983); Kosiewicz, Hallahan, Lloyd, and Graves (1982); and Robin, Armel, and O'Leary (1975). Other techniques for improving handwriting performance are suggested by Connell (1983), Hanover (1983), and Ruedy (1983).

Spelling. An overview of effective spelling practice is provided by Loomer (1982). Most of these techniques have been validated on students with learning disabilities, behavioral disorders, and mild mental retardation. Research on spelling in special education is reviewed by Graham (1992, 1999). Error analysis procedures are described by Ganschow (1984). Time-on-task as an important variable is discussed by Gerber (1984). The importance of list length and cumulative rehearsal/distributed practice is demonstrated by Gettinger, Bryant, and Fayne (1982); Gettinger (1984); Neef, Iwata, and Page (1980); and Weaver (1984). Gettinger et al. (1982) demonstrate the importance of grouping words with similar spellings. Self-monitoring and self-checking procedures are validated by Beck, Matson, and Kazdin (1983). Effective tutoring procedures are described by Higgins (1982) and Reith, Polsgrove, and Eckert (1984). Rehearsal techniques are described by Weaver (1984), and cognitive approaches are described by Wong (1986a) and Englert, Hiebert, and Stewart (1985). Fuchs et al. (1992) review research on curriculum-based measurement in spelling for students with learning and behavioral disabilities. Finally, validation of the spelling mnemonic, albeit with students without disabilities, is reported by Negin

(1978). Initial results that support a time delay procedure are presented by Stevens and Schuster (1987). Reviews of research on spelling interventions for students with learning disabilities are provided by Gordon, Vaughn, and Schumm (1993); Fulk and Stormont-Spurgin (1995); and Graham (1999).

Written language. Additional information on assessment of written language is provided by Isaacson (1984, 1985a, 1985b) and Thomas, Englert, and Gregg (1987). An issue of *Learning Disabilities Research & Practice* (Vol. 6, No. 4), edited by Graham and MacArthur (1991), was devoted to writing. Reviews of research on writing instruction for students with mild disabilities are provided by Graham (1982), Isaacson (1987), and Wong (1998). Additional information on teaching strategies is given by Moran (1983); Nutter and Safran (1984); Weygant (1981); Giordano (1984); Walmsley (1984); Bridge and Hiebert (1985); Graham and Harris (1987); Hillocks (1984); Englert (1990); Englert and Mariage (1991); MacArthur, Graham, and Schwartz (1991); Zaragoza and Vaughn (1992); Graham, MacArthur, Schwartz, and Page-Voth (1992); Wong, Wong, and Blenkinsop (1989); and Dowis and Schloss (1992). The effective use of peers as collaborators in writing is described by MacArthur, Schwartz, and Graham (1991); Wong, Wong, Darlington, and Jones (1991); Englert et al. (1991); Englert and Mariage (1996); Mariage (2000); and Englert, Berry, and Dunsmore (2001). The use of computers in the writing process is described by Hine, Goldman, and Cosden (1990); Malouf, Wizer, Pilato, and Grogan (1990); and MacArthur (1996). Curriculum-based measurement and the assessment of writing are discussed by Parker, Tindal, and Hasbrouck (1991); Deno, Marston, and Mirkin (1982); and Tindal and Parker (1989). Five (1992) describes the integration of students with mild disabilities into a collaborative class writing program. Harris and Graham (1996) wrote an outstanding book on teaching writing. Their research is reviewed by Graham, Harris, MacArthur, and Schwartz (1991).

Curricular Materials

Commercially available curricular materials exist in the language development area. A sample of these materials include *Peabody Language Development Kits* (American Guidance Service), *Language for Learning* and *Language Roundup* (SRA/McGraw-Hill), and *Clinical Language Intervention Program* (Psychological Corporation). Other language materials include *Language Resource Activity Kit*, *Practicing Independent Concepts for Language*, and *Predictable Stories for Language* (PRO-ED).

Handwriting materials include *D'Nealian Handwriting* (Scott, Foresman, Thurber, & Jordan, 1981), *Cursive Writing Program* (SRA/McGraw-Hill), and *Zaner-Bloser Handwriting* (Zaner-Bloser; Barbe et al. 1987). Curriculum Associates produces *Handwriting: A Fresh Start*, a remedial handwriting program for Grade 3 to adult. Spelling curriculum materials include *Morphographic Spelling* (SRA/McGraw-Hill), *Recipe for Spelling*, and the *Stetson Spelling Program* (PRO-ED). *Spelling Power* (Curriculum Associates) includes books and CDs. Curriculum Associates also produces *Palabra Lista*, the Spanish *QUICK-WORD* handbooks, *QUICK-WORD Dictionary of Classroom Words*, and *QUICK-WORD Literature Guide for Everyday Readers*. Spelling is also included in the *Angling for Words* series (Academic Therapy). Mnemonic spelling strategies are provided by Shefter (1976), Suid (1990), and Dowling (1995).

Materials are also available to facilitate written communication. These include *Success in Writing* (Globe Fearon), *Let's Write* (Zaner-Bloser), *Springboards for Writing, Teaching Written Expression* (Academic Therapy), and *Capitalization and Punctuation* and *Lessons in Writing Sentences* (Curriculum Associates). Curriculum Associates also produces the *Language Skills* series for developing fundamental writing skills and *Writing Portfolios*, which incorporates the writing process and the use of student-centered portfolios. Educational Activities produces *How to Write for Everyday Living*.

Computer Software and Technology

Computer software is also available for supplementing instruction in the language area. One vocabulary learning program is Words Around Me (Edmark). Several word-processing programs are available, and teachers should select programs based on availability at their schools. Most programs contain spell-check components, and many programs also contain grammar checks (e.g., Microsoft Word). MindPlay distributes Author! Author!, Ace Reporter, Ace Detective, Ace Publisher, and Ace Explorer. Sunburst produces Growing as a Writer and Write On! Plus: Literature Studies. The Essential Language series, including Paragraph Power and Responsive Writing, Writing Renegades, and Precision Writing, is available from Gamco Industries. Optimum Resource distributes Stickybear Spelling, and I Love Spelling (DK Interactive Learning, distributed by Learning Services) is an interactive, motivational approach to spelling. A special needs section is included in the teacher's guide.

Finally, word prediction software programs are available. These programs predict the word after the author has typed a letter or a couple of letters. A listing of word options is displayed, and the author selects the correct option. According to Heinisch and Hecht (1993), more than 15 word prediction programs are available, including Predict It and Co:Writer® 4000 (Don Johnston Developmental Equipment) and KeyWiz (Words +). See Appendix B for a list of addresses of producers and distributors of software and curricular materials.

Writing Strategies That Work in Inclusive Classes

Writing can be problematic for some students with disabilities. Recent research has demonstrated the positive effects of teaching students in inclusive classes the use of self-regulation strategies combined with strategies for writing compositions (e.g., De La Paz, 1999; De La Paz, Owen, Harris, & Graham, 2000). Susan De La Paz and her colleagues taught middle school students with and without disabilities self-regulated strategy development, which teaches students how to write essays using a series of sequenced steps beginning with the planning process and culminating with editing the final version (see also Harris & Graham, 1996). In one of these studies, teachers used these techniques to prepare their students for the state competency tests in writing.

General education teachers taught students the following self-regulation strategy:

- PLAN
    Pay attention to the prompt
    List the main ideas
    Add supporting details
    Number your ideas

- WRITE
    Work from your plan to develop your thesis statement
    Remember your goals
    Include transition words for each of your paragraphs
    Try to use different kinds of sentences
    Use exciting, interesting, $100,000 words

Steps were learned and practiced independently. During instruction, students were provided with cue cards that contained "starter ideas or sentences for writing their paragraphs." One example for "how to start with an attention getter" included the following: "Use a series of questions; Use a series of statements; Use a brief funny story; Use a mean or angry statement; Start with the opposite opinion of what you believe" (De La Paz et al., 2000, p. 102). Performance on essays indicated that all levels of middle school students, including high achievers, low achievers, and students with learning disabilities, received some benefits from the strategy instruction.

TECHNOLOGY FEATURE

Use of Word Processing, Speech Synthesis, and Word Prediction

Advances in technology have improved the writing performance of students with disabilities. Several researchers have assessed the effects of several types of word-processing software that contain word prediction and speech synthesis components with students with disabilities and reported on the positive benefits associated with using technology, especially when combined with strategic writing instruction (e.g., MacArthur, 1998). Some of the many types of hardware and software available to assist students with disabilities are listed:

- Hardware
  AlphaSmart 2000 (Intelligent Peripheral Devices, Inc.) is a small portable keyboard designed for students to use for word processing. Advantages are the low cost, small size, the ease of use for word processing and editing, and ease with printing.

- Keyboarding software
  KidKeys (Davidson and Associates)
  Mavis Beacon Teaches Typing for Kids (Mindscape)
  Read, Write and Type (The Learning Company)

- Software for independent writing
  Co: Writer (Don Johnston Incorporated) includes a word prediction components feature, which predicts the word based on the first few letters typed. Word choices are supplied that are correct in grammar and spelling.

  Write: Outloud (Don Johnston Incorporated) is a talking word processor that includes a spell checker.

  KidWorks Deluxe (Davidson & Associates) reads back stories that students have written.

Software that supports a process approach to writing:
  The Ultimate Writing and Creativity Center (The Learning Company)
  The Writing Workshop (Milliken Publishing)
  Student Writing and Research Center (The Learning Company)

Chapter 7

❧　　　❧　　　❧

Mathematics

Like reading and written language, mathematics is one of the essential basic skill areas. Understanding of mathematics and the applications of mathematics are necessary for functioning in the world of work as well as for independent living. All children are expected to learn the vocabulary, concepts, computational skills, procedures, algorithms, and problem-solving strategies essential for successful mastery of mathematics. Mathematics includes but is not limited to arithmetic. Arithmetic includes basic addition, subtraction, multiplication and division operations, and algorithms (or step-by-step procedures used for solving more complex computation problems). Mathematics is broader in definition, including arithmetic as well as numeration, number systems, fractions, decimals, problem solving, geometry, measurement, time, money, algebra, calculus, and interpretation of charts, tables, and graphs.

Reform in mathematics education was initiated by the National Council of Teachers of Mathematics (NCTM) and resulted in the establishment of curriculum and evaluation standards for school mathematics, first in 1989 and then revised in 2000 as *Principles and Standards for School Mathematics* (NCTM, 2000). The 2000 NCTM standards include both content and process standards, which are intended to be implemented from kindergarten to Grade 12. The content standards refer to the content students should learn and include number and operations, algebra, geometry, measurement, data analysis, and probability. The process standards refer to ways of acquiring and using content knowledge and include problem solving, reasoning and proof, communication, connections, and representation (NCTM, 2000).

Unfortunately, in the 1989 version, the NCTM made virtually no reference to students with disabilities or how their special needs should be addressed (Rivera, 1998a). The 2000 standards state, "Students with special educational needs must have the opportunities and support they require to attain a substantial understanding of important mathematics" (p. 4). Although this represents a substantial improvement, little specific information is presented regarding how these opportunities and support are to be provided. The challenge, then, is to offer instruction that provides access to the general education curriculum, including NCTM standards where appropriate, but that also allows students to acquire the skills and strategies necessary for successful mathematics functioning. As suggested by the NCTM (2000),

> Students with special learning needs in mathematics must be supported both by their classroom teachers and by special education staff. Special-needs educators responsible for mathematics instruction should participate in mathematics professional development, which will allow them to collaborate with classroom teachers in assessing and analyzing students' work in order to plan instruction. (p. 368)

Various educational approaches have been recommended in teaching mathematics. Some educators have proposed the direct teaching of basic skills that emphasize the mastery of math facts and operations, as well as problem solving.

Others (including the NCTM) have proposed using inductive techniques that emphasize a reasoning and problem-solving approach—using concrete manipulatives, learner construction of mathematical ideas, and use of calculators and computers—and that emphasize the interrelatedness of mathematical concepts. The debate in the approach to mathematics instruction is similar to the debate in various approaches to teaching reading (see Chapter 5). In reality, the skills emphasized in each approach are considered essential for a thorough understanding and generalization of mathematics. In special education, research has generally supported the effectiveness of programs that emphasize a direct instruction approach toward the teaching of all areas, including basic math facts, vocabulary, concepts, and problem-solving strategies. It is critical for special educators to use the teacher effectiveness variables in the delivery of mathematics instruction and, in addition, to examine the type of learner behavior expected (identification, production, and application), the level of learning (acquisition and fluency), and the type of learning (discriminations, facts, rules, procedures, and concepts) to design an optimal set of instructional strategies. However, it is also critical that students understand underlying mathematical concepts and that they learn to reason mathematically, using problem-solving and thinking skills. It is not enough that they memorize math facts or that they mechanically apply strategies to solve problems they do not really understand. To this extent, use of manipulative materials, real-world problems, and a variety of problem representations can be helpful.

Research has documented that very little instructional time is allocated to mathematics in the classroom. In fact, many elementary-age students spend less than 20 minutes a day engaged in relevant mathematics instruction. Students with mild disabilities desperately need excellent instruction in all areas of mathematics. Chapter 11 presents examples of the importance of mathematics skills in daily living. Students with special needs require excellent instruction in all areas of mathematics, especially in areas that emphasize the generalization and application of skills related to math.

This chapter first provides an overview of mathematics instruction, including the selection of a mathematics program, mathematics assessment and error analysis, instructional grouping, and the use of the teacher effectiveness variables. The sections that follow describe practices for teaching beginning, intermediate, and higher level math skills.

Teaching Mathematics: An Overview

The teaching of mathematics is a critical activity for the special educator. As mentioned earlier, most special needs students enter special education programs with specific skill deficiencies in mathematics. This section describes strategies for selecting a mathematics program, providing initial assessment and placement, using general error analysis, grouping for instruction, presenting new information, delivering guided and independent practice activities, and monitoring and adjusting instruction based on formative evaluation data.

Selecting a Mathematics Program

School districts typically adopt a particular series for instruction in mathematics. Most series divide the teaching of specific facts, concepts, and algorithms into various grade levels. The series usually provides student textbooks, student workbooks, and a teacher's guide. In addition, several remedial math programs have been published and are widely available, along with supplemental programs that are designed to provide additional practice in specific skill areas. (Several are listed at the end of this chapter.) Before selecting a specific mathematics series, teachers should determine the district's scope and sequence for math skills and then consider the following features:

1. *Scope and sequence of math skills.* Has the series clearly identified a scope and sequence of objectives that matches the district's scope and sequence? Is the content organized so that prerequisite skills are taught prior to the applications of those skills? Are skills that could be easily confused with one another introduced separately or simultaneously?

2. *Breadth of mathematics activities.* Does the series provide sufficient examples of math problems under different formats, such as vertical problems, horizontal problems, word problems, and applications to real-world situations?

3. *Concreteness and meaningfulness.* Does the series make mathematics learning as concrete and as meaningful as possible? Are a sufficient number of real-world problems and examples provided?

4. *Sufficient opportunities for practice.* Does the series provide sufficient guided and independent practice activities for students with learning problems, particularly at the fluency and generalization levels? Does the series present sufficient types of formats within the practice activities, and are reviews that cover previously learned skills included?

5. *Strategy instruction.* Does the series provide the teacher with specific cognitive strategies for learning and applying new facts, rules, concepts, and procedures?

6. *Instructional component.* Does the series provide the teacher with specific instructional guidelines and formats for introducing new facts, rules, concepts, and procedures that correspond with the teacher effectiveness literature?

7. *Evaluation component.* Does the series provide a format by which student performance and progress can be monitored and adjusted on a regular basis? Does the series provide a placement test?

8. *Validation data.* Does the series provide some evidence that it has been successfully implemented with special education students?

9. *Diversity.* Does the series provide sufficient representation of diverse cultures and gender roles?

Probably no material will possess all of the features listed above; however, prior to selecting a math series, all of the above questions need to be answered satisfactorily. It will be up to the teacher to supplement the series in any areas of deficit. For example, if a series does not provide adequate strategy instruction for solving word problems, then teachers will need to supplement the series by providing students with specific strategy instructions and corresponding guided and independent practice activities. Likewise, if the series lacks sufficient practice activities, teachers will have to supplement it by providing additional relevant exercises.

Teachers must often select and use a math program from existing district materials. In such a case, teachers must select a program that addresses as many of the above features as possible and supplement their instruction with any missing features. The most frequently encountered problems include (a) material presented on too abstract a level with insufficient examples, (b) insufficient relevant practice activities, (c) inadequate strategic instructions, (d) insufficient instructions for the introduction of new concepts, (e) insufficient application and generalization examples (including practice using different formats), and (f) insufficient formative evaluation procedures. Teachers must adapt their instructional procedures to accommodate such inadequacies.

Mathematics Assessment

When students enter special education programs for mathematics instruction, they typically have been tested for current level of functioning or performance in math. This current level of performance is usually expressed as a grade equivalent score, a percentile score, or a stanine score from a norm-referenced test. This overall score provides information concerning how these students are performing in relation to all other students of that age and grade level. Although this information can be beneficial in determining the need for special education services, it usually does not provide information regarding specific skills the students have or have not mastered in relation to the curriculum materials used in a particular school. As mentioned in Chapter 5, it is recommended that special educators administer curriculum-based assessment to determine where along the scope and sequence of objectives in the curriculum the student needs to begin instruction.

Curriculum-Based Assessment and Instructional Grouping

Although many diagnostic tests are available and some can provide teachers with an analysis of skills students possess and lack, use of such tests should be linked to curriculum materials being used in the classroom. Otherwise, teachers should begin to develop their own curriculum-based tests to determine where along the curriculum students need instruction. As was emphasized in Chapter 5, when district objectives match curriculum objectives, and students' IEP objectives are based on these objectives, curriculum-based assessment locates the starting point for instruction. For example, assume that a specific mathematics series has been adopted for use. Next, assume that a series of curriculum-based tests that correspond with the adopted math series has been developed. The first step in implementing this assessment procedure involves selecting the test at the approximate skill level (first, second, third, etc.) of the new student. After completing the administration and scoring of the test, the teacher can identify specific skills that have or have not been mastered in relation to the curriculum. Appropriate placement for instructional purposes can then be completed.

Procedures such as these can also assist teachers in making instructional grouping decisions. Refer to the previous example, but instead of administering the test to one student, administer the test to all students who are required to receive mathematics instruction in the special education setting. After scoring all of the tests,

teachers can determine how to form their instructional groups based on an examination of students' mastery of specific math skills.

Periodic administration of such curriculum-based measures can provide teachers with the following information:

1. Are the originally formed instructional groups still optimal?

2. Are the students mastering the skills at an appropriate rate?

3. Are students retaining previously mastered skills?

4. Are the students' skills applicable to inclusive mathematics classes or appropriate to the general education curriculum?

These curriculum-based assessment procedures can become an integral part of the instructional process. The tests focus attention on the specific mathematics skills students need to master and, therefore, assist teachers in designing and delivering instruction at levels appropriate for specific students. (For a discussion of all of the factors that need to be taken into consideration when forming instructional groups, see Chapter 5.) In addition, teachers can obtain valuable information regarding students' mathematics performance by using the error analysis procedures described in the next section.

Error Analysis

Mathematics is well suited for use in error analysis procedures. As mentioned previously, error analysis is a technique that is used to analyze students' errors in an attempt to determine patterns in those errors. For example, typical systematic errors could include any of the following:

1. *Incorrect fact.* The student consistently recalls a fact incorrectly (e.g., $7 \times 8 = 57$).

2. *Incorrect operation.* The student executes the incorrect operation (e.g., consistently per-

forms addition when the operation should be multiplication).

3. *Incorrect execution of procedures.* The student applies the steps to an algorithm incorrectly. The procedure may not be known or may be executed in the wrong sequence, or a necessary step may be omitted (e.g., the steps necessary to execute a long-division problem or subtraction with borrowing).

4. *No pattern errors.* The responses are incorrect but appear to be random.

5. *Combinations of incorrect facts and incorrectly employed operations and/or algorithms.*

The first step in completing an error analysis is to obtain a sample of the student's work. Recent classroom assignments, classroom tests, or survey or curriculum-based tests may be used. Second, the work is corrected. The student's errors are then categorized by error type, using the classification suggested above. Special educators can also develop an informal checklist that incorporates all possible operations, facts, and algorithms. This checklist can be used to monitor students' progress toward mastery. Figure 7.1 pre-

sents a sample error analysis checklist. When students make errors, teachers should be able to determine the reason for those errors. It will probably be necessary to provide instruction in those areas. It is important to note that simply because a student appears to make an error, it does not necessarily mean that the student does not know that particular fact, operation, or algorithm. It may simply be a careless error. In fact, after completing an error analysis and determining specific error patterns, teachers can verify whether such errors are in need of remediation by asking students to explain the steps and procedures they used to arrive at their answers. That is why it is important to monitor instruction based on student performance data that are collected continuously.

Teacher Effectiveness and Mathematics Instruction

As in all of the areas addressed in this book, the teacher effectiveness variables can be combined with the content of mathematics instruction to

Content Area	Addition	Subtraction	Multiplication	Division
Basic fact knowledge (0–20)	8 + 7 — 14	12 − 9 — 	7 × 6 — 45	81 ÷ 9 = 7
Basic operation knowledge	15 + 4 — 11	17 − 9 — 26	6 × 6 — 12	9 ÷ 3 = 27
Basic procedural knowledge (regrouping, long-division steps)	27 + 6 — 213	53 − 36 — 23	25 × 44 — 80 80 — 160	1R95 32⟌63 63 — 32 — 95

Note: Only the major breakdowns are provided in this example. Additional subdivisions should be added as necessary.

Figure 7.1. An error-analysis checklist.

maximize student achievement gains. The model that is presented next is based in part on teacher effectiveness research in mathematics, which was conducted over a period of several years and demonstrated very impressive achievement gains in mathematics for the participating students. What follows is an example of an application of the teacher effectiveness functions during a mathematics lesson.

Daily Review

Each mathematics lesson should begin with a review of the content covered in the previous lesson. For example, assume a series of lessons and objectives on money was being covered. In addition, presume that lesson objectives covering the identification and naming values of all coins have been introduced and practiced previously and that the present lesson objective requires students to name values of different groups of coins. The lesson review would cover the identification and naming values of coins in isolation. Direct teacher questioning similar to the following would be appropriate. The teacher holds up a penny or an illustration of a penny and says, "What coin is this? [Signal response] How much is a penny worth? [Signal response]." Eventually, all of the coins that had been previously practiced would be reviewed. Corrective feedback would be provided if necessary, and, based on student performance, teachers would know whether those objectives had been mastered. If homework worksheets had been assigned as an independent practice activity, this would be the appropriate time to check students' performance for understanding.

Presentation of New Material

Presentation of the new content should parallel the procedures outlined in Chapter 1. Teachers must first clarify the goals and main objectives for the day's lesson. In this example, the teacher could say, "We have all learned how to identify pennies, nickels, dimes, quarters, half dollars, and silver dollars and how to tell the value of those coins. Today we are going to learn how to name (i.e., count the value of) different combinations of those same coins." The teacher would present several examples in a step-by-step fashion using the model–lead–test approach. In the present example, the teacher could say, "See this? [Point to nickel on blackboard] What is it? How much is it worth? What is this? [Point to a penny] How much is it worth? Now, one nickel and one penny are worth 6 cents together, because one nickel equals 5 cents and one penny equals 1 cent, and 5 cents plus 1 cent equals 6 cents. When you are asked to tell the value of several coins, first you determine the value of each coin, then you add all the values together." The teacher tells the students the procedures to use to determine the values of several coins and simultaneously presents an illustration. Next, the teacher should present another example and lead the students through the procedures by asking students, "What is the first thing to do in adding coins together? What do you do after you determine the value of each coin?" Another example should then be provided. This format should be followed until it is determined that students are ready for a guided practice activity.

Guided Practice

Recall that the major goal of guided practice is to ensure that all of the students have opportunities to practice the new skills correctly and frequently with teacher feedback and monitoring. All teacher questions should be directly relevant to the instructional objective—in this case, relevant to adding values of different groups of coins. All or most of the students should participate in all or most of the guided practice activity. During the above lesson, the teacher might continue to present examples and require students to respond orally on signal. Students could also be required to solve problems individually, write the responses on individual slates, and hold up their slates on cue. Throughout this activity, student performance can be monitored, and teachers can provide immediate corrective feedback whenever necessary. If students require additional review on the procedure, teachers can easily re-present the information just presented. Students need the opportunity to practice the newly introduced skills under constant teacher monitoring. This helps to ensure that students are practicing the skills correctly. When students have learned the new skill and are executing it accurately, teachers can proceed to independent practice activities.

Independent Practice

Independent practice in mathematics often consists of paper-and-pencil tasks that students are required to execute on their own. It is critical for teachers to initially guide students during this activity. In fact, it is recommended that teachers lead students through the first few examples to ensure that students understand the task demands. It is also important for teachers to monitor students' independent practice by circulating around the room. If students appear to be having difficulty, teachers can provide immediate corrective feedback and reinstruct the essential components of the new skill.

During this stage of the lesson, quick and accurate performance needs to be reinforced. Teachers can use independent practice activities to reinforce good, independent study behaviors. Most important, however, teachers need to ensure that such activities are directly relevant to the lesson's main objective. In the present example, most items on the practice activity should require students to practice adding and naming values of various groups of coins. Other items could require students to exhibit previously taught skills. These activities allow students opportunities to (a) practice the newly introduced skill, (b) become fluent at the new skill, and (c) overlearn the skill so that teaching applications of the skill can proceed.

Several alternatives to the typical seatwork activity provide viable independent practice activities too. Peer tutoring, computer-assisted instruction, and various other audiovisual aids (e.g., tape recorders) are all valuable procedures that, when implemented and monitored carefully, can be effective alternatives to independent seatwork. However, as in any procedure, teachers need to ensure that (a) the activities are directly relevant to the instructional objectives and (b) student performance is carefully monitored.

Weekly and Monthly Reviews

In special education settings, it is especially important to review previously taught skills. This is necessary to ensure long-term retention and to allow for easier application and generalization of those skills. Weekly and monthly reviews can be built into the introduction of new skills. Such reviews can also document the progress of mastering IEP objectives. Reviews can be implemented using the procedures described for introducing new skills. In addition, such review sessions can be optimal times for implementing peer tutoring. At these times, it is important to inform students of their progress.

Formative Evaluation

In all instruction, teachers may implement formative evaluation near the end of the independent practice activity. A short test requiring students to execute the skills just practiced can assist teachers in adjusting their instruction based on students' performance. Remember that decisions to alter instructional procedures can include (a) increasing time-on-task, (b) reintroducing new skills, (c) conducting additional model–lead–test procedures, (d) adding more concrete and meaningful examples, (e) having additional guided practice, and (f) having additional independent practice. In order to be valid, however, decisions must be based on student performance data.

This section presented a very general overview of mathematics instruction and described the components of instruction necessary for all math skills. It is important to document student progress and evaluate instruction based on that progress. Good instruction incorporates clear teacher presentations and active student participation in guided and independent practice activities that are directly relevant to instructional objectives. The remainder of this chapter presents specific strategies for teaching beginning, intermediate, and higher level mathematics skills.

Beginning Math

Beginning mathematics includes skills and concepts in numeration, counting, one-to-one correspondence, equivalence, signs and symbols, addition concepts, addition facts, multidigit addition without regrouping, column addition, subtraction concepts, and multidigit subtraction without regrouping. Table 7.1 presents possible specifications for beginning math skills, and each area is discussed separately in the sections that follow. Teachers are again reminded to consult their districts' math scope and sequence. District objectives may vary from those presented in Table 7.1. It is also important to point out that each content area listed can be further subdivided into its own table of specifications.

Numeration

One of the first skills students learn when they enter school is counting. Many students, in fact, have already mastered counting skills before they start school. Basically, counting involves *serial-list learning* (e.g., learning series such as 1, 2, 3, etc.), much like learning the letters of the alphabet. Learning to count has little value unless students are also given instruction in the underlying concepts of numeration, which include one-to-one correspondence and equivalence. Although all components of numeration should be mastered, these components are discussed separately in the following sections.

Counting

As stated earlier, counting involves serial-list learning and constitutes factual information. However, for students who are just learning to count, there is much more involved than this. To count, students must order the number names in the correct sequence, establish a correspondence between number names and counted objects, and understand that the last number counted represents the total number of the objects counted. The procedures of counting include assigning a number word (e.g., "three") to each counted object, separating the entire domain of objects into those that have been counted and those that remain to be counted, and physically keeping track of the counting by pointing, moving the objects, or eye tracking (Van Luit & Schopman, 2000). Problems with counting could occur in any of these conceptual or procedural areas.

Different aspects of counting should be addressed in early numeracy. *Subitizing* refers to enumerating small numbers of objects (i.e., five or fewer) without directly counting them. *Acoustic counting* is saying numbers in sequence. *Point counting* refers to pointing to objects while saying each number name. When done correctly, pointing and counting are said to be *synchronized*. *Resultative counting* involves understanding that the order in which the items are counted is irrelevant to obtaining the correct total number of items. *Counting on* is the ability to start counting with a number other than 1 (and is a good introduction to adding), and *skip counting* or "count-bys" are the procedures of counting by 2s, 4s, 5s, and so on. (Val Luit & Schopman, 2000).

Counting is usually taught by providing direct drill and practice in all these areas to develop acquisition and fluency. Teachers first review any previously learned procedures and concepts and then teach the new information to be learned in short segments. For example, a teacher could review counting from 1 to 5, determine whether all students have learned this sequence, and then introduce the next three numbers: 6, 7, and 8.

Table 7.1. Table of Specifications for Beginning Math Skills

	BEHAVIOR				
	Identification	Production			
CONTENT	A. Acquisition	B. Acquisition	C. Fluency	D. Application	E. Generalization
1. *Counting*					
a. rote 1–10	1aA	1aB	1aC	1aD	1aE
b. rote 1–20 and higher	1bA	1bB	1bC	1bD	1bE
c. counting beginning at numbers other than 1	1cA	1cB	1cC	1cD	1cE
d. count-bys 10, 5, etc.	1dA	1dB	1dC	1dD	1dE
e. count backwards	1eA	1eB	1eC	1eD	1eE
2. *Symbol skills*					
a. writes and identifies symbols 1–5, 6–10, teens, etc.	2aA	2aB	2aC	2aD	2aE
b. draws lines for numeration (2 = **//**)	2bA	2bB	2bC	2bD	2bE
c. signs (+, −, =)	2cA	2cB	2cC	2cD	2cE
d. reads and writes equations	2dA	2dB	2dC	2dD	2dE
3. *Operations*					
a. single-digit addition	3aA	3aB	3aC	3aD	3aE
b. single-digit subtraction	3bA	3bB	3bC	3bD	3bE
c. story problems	3cA	3cB	3cC	3cD	3cE
d. column addition	3dA	3dB	3dC	3dD	3dE
4. *Facts*					
a. +1 facts	4aA	4aB	4aC	4aD	4aE
b. +2 facts	4bA	4bB	4bC	4bD	4bE

(*continues*)

Table 7.1. *Continued.*

	BEHAVIOR				
	Identification	**Production**			
CONTENT	*A. Acquisition*	*B. Acquisition*	*C. Fluency*	*D. Application*	*E. Generalization*
5. *Concepts/ vocabulary*					
a. one-to-one correspondence	5aA	5aB	5aC	5aD	5aE
b. equality	5bA	5bB	5bC	5bD	5bE
c. add, more than	5cA	5cB	5cC	5cD	5cE
d. subtract, less than	5dA	5dB	5dC	5dD	5dE

Sample Objectives:

1aA Student will correctly point to the target digit (1–10) from a list of five distractor digits after hearing the teacher say the number.

2aB Students will correctly write the symbol for the digits (1–10) after hearing the teacher say the number.

3cD Students will correctly execute 10 simple story problems involving basic addition facts after hearing and/or reading the problems.

5cE Students will correctly use and apply the concept of addition to real problems involving buying candy at the store.

"Okay, we all know how to count to 5. Now we're going to learn to count to 8. Listen to me do it: 1, 2, 3, 4, 5, 6, 7, 8. Everybody say 6, 7, 8 with me. [Signal and repeat if necessary] Good! Once more. [Signal] Okay, now let's all count together from 1 to 8. [Signal] Now, you do it. [Signal]" Provide corrective feedback as necessary.

Usually, many repetitions are required to learn counting fluently, and continuous monitoring on progress charts can be helpful in determining whether students are making satisfactory progress. It is also important to ensure that counting skills are learned cumulatively; that is, at any stage, students can go back to the first number and count consecutively to the last number learned. In most cases, students should eventually learn to count at a fluency rate of more than 100 numbers per minute. In addition, students should receive instruction in all aspects of counting described previously, including skip counting and count-ons. For example, students can be taught early on to count by 10s, 2s, and 5s or to count three numbers higher than 6 in a manner similar to that just described. This, too, involves serial-list learning and is factual information. Individual student needs and abilities can determine the amount of new information to be presented at one time. Often during this type of instruction, it is a good idea for the teacher to set the pace for student responding by either clapping or snapping fingers whenever a response is desired.

As counting skills are gained, it is important for students to learn to associate each number with its respective symbol (i.e., 1 = one, 2 = two, 3 = three). This type of factual learning is associative and can be taught concurrently with counting skills by means of drill and practice with flash cards. Many students come to school knowing their numbers, but complete knowledge in this area should not be taken for granted. To be sure that associative components are being mastered, teachers should avoid always presenting number symbols in sequence. "Okay, now we are going to practice some numbers we learned last week. Everybody, what is this number? [Display 3; signal] Three, that's right. Now, what is this number? [Display 6; signal] Six, that's right." As students become fluent, they should be able to read these numbers almost as fast as they can count.

One-to-One Correspondence

One-to-one correspondence means that a student can apply counting and numeration skills to a set of similarly classified objects and that different objects (e.g., pennies, beads) can be matched with respect to quantity. In other words, a student, when asked, should be able to apply counting and numeration skills to items that he or she has not counted before, such as a group of blocks, boxes, or pennies. This application task ensures that the student has acquired the concept of one-to-one correspondence—that is, that numbers can be applied, one to each thing, to determine how many there are. As with other concepts, the test of acquisition is passed when counting skills can be applied to objects the student has not classified and counted before (e.g., "Charles, tell us how many chairs are in this classroom"). When students can apply skills in a variety of specific tasks, teachers rate whether these skills can be generalized across other teachers, classroom settings, objects, or combinations. If not, teachers should prompt, reward, or reteach the counting skill in the new context.

Equivalence

Equivalence is a functional concept in mathematics that asserts that different sets with the same number of objects in them are in some way equivalent. As a concept, equivalence is tested in application tasks involving instances of the concept. For example, two sets of pennies can be placed side by side to show that they are equivalent. The teacher then can count each set and demonstrate that the numbers are equal. Following that positive example of "these two groups of pennies are equal," a negative example can be shown. In the present example, one penny could be removed and the teacher would say, "These two groups are not equal." Students can then be tested on these examples for understanding. Additional examples (e.g., pencils) can be used in a similar fashion. The equal sign (=) can be intro-

duced here as an associative fact. As students begin to identify equivalence, they can be asked to determine equivalent numbers of different objects (e.g., "Here are six erasers. Show me the same number of pencils."). Once students have demonstrated this ability, independent practice activities, such as relevant worksheets, can help to reinforce this concept. Similarly, the concepts *more than* and *less than* can be introduced. The concepts are taught by provision of a general rule and specific instances and noninstances, practiced and assessed by means of novel examples (e.g., "Does this row have *more* pennies than that row? Does it have *less* [or fewer] pennies? Good, this row has *less*, or fewer, pennies than that row.") Teachers must use the students' responses to determine whether additional practice activities on instances and noninstances are required for thorough understanding.

Signs, Symbols, and Shapes

As students develop skills in math, they must learn the symbols that will direct them to the operations they will be conducting. Students may have already learned the equal sign (=) from equivalence lessons. As the need for new symbol identification arises, these symbols should be taught as simple associative facts. For example: [Display +]. "What does this symbol tell you to do? [Signal] Right, it tells you to add." It is not generally helpful to teach symbols before they are needed.

Shapes, such as triangles, squares, and circles, are usually introduced in the primary grades as an initial stage of geometry. However, students usually do not make practical use of such information (other than identification) until several years later. Learning shapes is a form of concept learning, in that students must be able to identify a novel instance of the concept and discriminate it from noninstances. For example, when teaching what a triangle is, teachers could provide a rule and show how it could be applied. Consider the following example:

A triangle is a closed shape with *three straight sides*. How many straight sides? [Signal] Three. That's right. So if it has three straight sides, it is a triangle. That means [point to shape] this is a triangle, and this is a triangle, and this is not a triangle. Is this a triangle? [Signal] Yes. Why is this a triangle, Shawna? Right, because it has three straight sides. Why is this a triangle, Chico? Because it has three straight sides. Is this a triangle, Christina? Why not? Right, because it has four straight sides.

Teachers can determine that the concept has been mastered when students can accurately identify a large number of triangles and describe relevant attributes.

When students begin to display knowledge of different shapes, teachers can introduce the initial concepts involved in fractions. Shapes are often employed in teaching initial fraction concepts because they are familiar, concrete, and easily divided. Teachers can select a circle and present it to the class as a single, whole thing. The circle can then be divided into two equal pieces, each of which constitutes ½ of a circle—the 1 representing the number of shaded-in pieces and the 2 representing the total number of pieces. As concepts, fractions must be taught using precise, multiple examples, and students must eventually demonstrate their ability to describe fractions they have not seen previously. Again, formative data recording the type and value of the fractions correctly identified can be helpful in determining whether the information is being learned efficiently.

Addition and Subtraction Facts

When students have mastered all necessary preskills, they usually begin to learn the basic addition and subtraction facts. This type of learning, involving the memorization of a large number of abstract facts, is often a long and tedious process for students with mild disabilities, particularly for many of those who have been described as having mild mental retardation.

The learning of basic addition and subtraction facts is associative, and there is little alternative but to provide as much direct drill and practice as possible to ensure that basic facts are being learned. It is important to collect formative data to determine whether sufficient progress is being made.

Several things need to be considered when teaching addition and subtraction facts. First, the teacher must make an effort to make this portion of the school day at least as enjoyable as any other portion of the school day. This can be done by a genuine attitude of enthusiasm on the part of the teacher and by communicating to the students that, although the task is not easy, it is nonetheless rewarding and something they should take pride in. Gamelike activities, computer-assisted instruction, goal setting, attribution training, and positive feedback are all ways to promote motivation in math fact learning. Teachers should also be prompt to reward students for effort and progress and convey to students the importance of the task.

Second, teachers should carefully sequence instruction and use formative data to determine that content is not being covered too quickly or slowly. Small chunks of content can be covered and mastered prior to the addition of new facts. New math facts, as they are introduced, do not require elaborate explanations; the most important aspect of the task is usually the use of rapid-paced, fluency-building activities that lead to a high percentage (80%–90%) of correct responses. To maximize the total number of opportunities for correct responding, teachers can employ peer tutors with flash cards, drill and practice provided by computer software (some handheld calculators provide this practice), or an independent study strategy in which the student self-prompts with a flash card, answers, and self-evaluates by examining the reverse side of the flash card. Students or tutors can learn to provide themselves with a series of trials (on facts for which they are 80%–90% accurate) and to evaluate their performance on each trial. Such student-collected (or tutor-collected) data can help ensure on-task behavior and allow the teacher to evaluate progress. The teacher can also test periodically to ensure accuracy of self- or tutor-provided data.

As math facts are learned to fluency levels, they should be reviewed periodically to be certain they are not being forgotten as new facts are introduced. The overall goal of math fact instruction is automatic, fluent responses to problems.

Strategies for Addition and Subtraction Facts

Generally, facts in mathematics are taught using procedures similar to those used in any other type of factual learning. Math facts may prove to be difficult for students with mild disabilities to remember because of the abstract nature of numbers. If students demonstrate particular difficulty acquiring relevant facts, remedial procedures usually involve provision of additional engaged time for learning and smaller or more carefully sequenced steps. If no additional time is available during the school day, teachers can try to enlist the aid of parents or older siblings to provide additional practice at home. Teachers can also attempt to ensure that high engagement rates are operating at relevant times and that the student is properly motivated and has not become discouraged. If the student appears to be developing a negative attitude toward learning math facts, efforts must be made to manipulate the curriculum so that a very high rate of accurate responding is produced and the student is rewarded for maintaining that high level of performance, even if such manipulation requires slowing the pace of instruction.

Two additional methods have been proposed for assisting students' acquisition of math facts. Thornton and Toohey (1985; see also Bley & Thornton, 1989) compiled a system of strategic computation. These include "count-ons" for +1, +2, and +3 facts, in which the student starts with the larger number and counts on 1, 2, or 3 additional numbers (e.g., for 5 + 3, "five . . . six, seven, *eight*"). Another is "zeros," which employs

the simple rule of adding by 0. The "doubles" strategy is more complicated and involves thinking of pictures for adding doubles. For instance, the 2 + 2 fact employs a car picture, with two front and two back (= 4) tires. The 3 + 3 fact employs a picture of a grasshopper, with three legs on each side, and the 4 + 4 fact employs a picture of a spider. Five plus five uses a picture of two hands, 6 + 6 an egg carton, and 7 + 7 a pack of crayons. For facts that are "near doubles" (e.g., 5 + 6), students think of a double fact (e.g., 5 + 5) and add the remainder. So, in this case, 5 + 6 = (5 + 5) + 1 = 10 + 1 = 11. The "nines" strategy employs addition by 10 and then subtracting 1 (e.g., 9 + 5 = [10 + 5] −1 = 15 − 1 = 14).

Similarly, strategies for subtraction facts include "count-backs" for −1, −2, −3 facts (e.g., for 8 − 3, "eight . . . seven, six, *five*") and "zero" facts, which involve subtracting zero from a number (e.g., 7 − 0), or subtracting two numbers whose difference is zero (e.g., 7 − 7 = 0). An additional 15 facts are referred to as "count-ups," in which the answer can be determined by counting up from the subtrahend to the minuend, when the difference is 1, 2, or 3 (e.g., for 11 − 8, "nine, ten, eleven," counting 3). "New doubles" are those subtraction facts that reveal doubles in the difference and subtrahend (e.g., 6 − 3 = 3). These strategies can be helpful for students who have learned addition concepts but are having difficulty remembering facts. Developing a chart or list of math facts learned and facts remaining to be learned can help develop motivation.

Stein, Silbert, and Carnine (1997) recommended the teaching of math facts in "number families." That is, rather than teaching 5 + 3 = 8 as a separate fact, teach at the same time all the number facts that employ the numbers 5, 3, and 8. Those facts are 5 + 3 = 8, 3 + 5 = 8, 8 − 3 = 5, and 8 − 5 = 3. Teaching number families together allows students to learn clusters of related facts, and improve their conceptual understanding of numbers.

Another method for learning to compute facts is Touch Math (Innovative Learning Concepts; Bullock, Pierce, & McClelland, 1987, 1989).

The system involves placing dots that represent quantity on numbers, for which students can later use imagery. For example, the number 1 has one dot in the middle of the number; 2 has a dot on the top and on the bottom left side of the number; 3 has dots on top, middle, and bottom left; four dots in a square pattern are placed on the number 4; and so on. For numbers 6 through 9, encircled dots, or *double touches*, are used. Six has three double touches, 7 has three double and one single touch (dot), and so on. Students are taught (e.g., when adding) to start with the higher number and count the additional numbers of dots on the other addend (number to be added). In this way, Touch Math is a type of number line in which the markers are integrated into the physical structure of the numbers. For subtraction, students start with the minuend value and count backwards on the subtrahend. (For multiplication, students use "count-bys" [e.g., 3s], where each touch of the multiplier represents a count-by of the multiplicand [e.g., 3, 6, 9, 12 for 3×4]. For division, students count up from 0 by count-bys of the divisor and write tally marks as they count. When they reach the dividend value, the number of tally marks represents the quotient.) More complete information for using Touch Math is presented by Bullock et al. (1987).

These strategies can be helpful in facilitating early math fact use. However, because they focus on strategies for computation rather than problem solving, effort must be made to ensure they are applied in relevant mathematical reasoning contexts.

Special Problems

There may come a time when teachers begin to regard the teaching of hundreds of math facts as hopeless for particular students. Math facts can appear to be a bewildering array of nonending, meaningless problems to many students, who appear completely incapable of learning more than a few at a time, only to forget those as soon as new facts are introduced. On the other hand, special education teachers typically are trained

not to "give up" on any student. We do not intend to recommend any specific procedures for determining when the teaching of facts may not be beneficial or may be premature. Nevertheless, the dominant focus of mathematics should be on reasoning and problem solving, not memorizing facts. There are, in fact, alternatives to the learning of math facts, such as the use of calculators, fact tables, and number lines, and teachers may choose to employ these alternatives when memorization of facts does not seem to be a viable alternative. Before taking such a step, teachers should be certain that they have data that document insufficient learning progress over a significant period of time and over several documented attempts to remedy the problem. In addition, teachers should have the agreement of a principal or special education coordinator that such an alternative seems productive. Finally, teachers should not presume that the student will *never* learn math facts; renewed attempts to teach such information should be made at a later, specified date. The decision to discontinue the drill on math facts for the time being should be made only because this drill is thought to inhibit overall mathematics learning at the present time. If calculators are to be employed for use in calculating math facts, however, students must be trained in their effective use, with modeling, practice, and feedback (Horton, Lovitt, & White, 1992). A useful activity guide for learning to use calculators is *Calculator Companions* (Learning Resources; Duffie, Rutherford, & Schectman, 1990).

Addition and Subtraction Concepts

It is very possible to learn math facts without understanding what they mean. Ginsburg (1998a, 1998b) described a case of a first-grader who was able to answer addition problems correctly but who could not describe what the "+" symbol meant in the problem $3 + 4 = ?$. When asked about the "=" sign, the following conversation took place:

TOBY:	. . . it tells you three plus four, three plus four, so it's telling you, that, um, I think, the, um, the end is coming up—the end.
INTERVIEWER:	The end is coming up—what do you mean, the end is coming up?
TOBY:	Like, if you have equals, and so you have seven, then. [She is gesturing to the problem on the table]. So if you do three plus four equals seven, that would be right. (Ginsburg, 1998a, p. 42)

As facts are being learned, students must be taught relevant concepts and meanings associated with addition and subtraction. Without instruction in the meaning of addition and subtraction, students will have difficulty applying math facts to problem-solving activities. Knowledge of math concepts per se, however, cannot be expected to facilitate fluency in math facts, although such knowledge can facilitate comprehension of the meaning of math facts.

Addition and subtraction concepts are generally communicated through manipulation of concrete objects and use of count-ons. For example, a teacher may say,

> I have three paper clips. See, one, two, three. If I *add* two more paper clips, how many will I have? Count with me: four, *five*. If I add two paper clips to three paper clips, I will have five paper clips altogether. Now you try it. If you have four paper clips and add three, how many will you have altogether? [Prompt and provide feedback].

Such activities in addition and subtraction can reinforce the relevant concepts for students. Figure 7.2 presents some strategies for teaching addition concepts. As with other concepts, a general rule or procedure is demonstrated, and students are prompted to demonstrate knowledge of the concept using novel instances. When students can effectively add and subtract quantities of real objects in a variety of instances and explain the meaning, evidence of concept acquisition has been provided. It is important to re-

member, however, that such conceptual instruction is unlikely to facilitate the automatic recall of facts at a fluency level necessary for later complex operations. Conceptual understanding of such processes can lead students to determine the answers to addition and subtraction problems through other means, such as number lines or finger counting. A number line is simply a horizontal line with consecutive numbers marked off on it. To add 4 and 3, for example, students place their pencils on the number 4 and then, using count-ons, move three more places to the right, to the spot indicated as 7. To subtract, students place their pencils on the number indicating the minuend (the number from which another number is to be subtracted) and move the number of places to the left indicated by the subtrahend (the number to be subtracted), which will indicate the difference. Although such means provide evidence that relevant concepts have been mastered, they are long and tedious means for arriving at solutions. Optimal mathematics instruction involves an appropriate combination of factual and conceptual learning.

Special Problems

If students demonstrate persistent difficulties in acquiring simple math concepts, attempts should be made to enhance simple discriminations and provide additional instances, noninstances, and practice. For instance, if a student has difficulty learning what a triangle is, the teacher should simplify the initial discrimination by pairing triangles of similar shape and size only with circles. As the student becomes proficient with this discrimination, other more similar shapes, such as squares, can be employed with different types of triangles. If students have difficulty with the concept of resultative counting, they can count the same number of objects in many different sequences to demonstrate the total number is always the same. If students demonstrate difficulty learning *less than* or *more than*, initial discriminations can be simplified in the same way. For example, students can be shown two

Initial Procedures

1. Sets of lines

$$||||\quad|||\quad=\quad|||||||$$
$$4\qquad 3\qquad=\qquad 7$$

2. Sets of dots

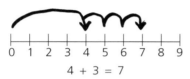

$$4\quad+\quad 3\quad=\quad 7$$

3. Number lines

```
      ⌒⌒⌒⌒
   ⌒       ↓  ↓  ↓
 ├──┼──┼──┼──┼──┼──┼──┼──┼──┼──┤
 0  1  2  3  4  5  6  7  8  9
          4 + 3 = 7
```

4. Manipulatives
   Objects such as pennies, buttons, beans, fingers

Prerequisite Skills

1. One-to-one correspondence
2. Counting
3. Equivalence
4. Plus sign

Possible Fading Techniques

4 + 3 = 7　　four plus 5, 6, 7, = 7
•••

(Student draws dots under second digit.)

Figure 7.2. Strategies for teaching addition concepts.

sets of the same objects that vary greatly in number (e.g., 2 versus 20 pennies). As the students gain accuracy in making this type of discrimination, objects and number differences can be varied. In addition, a wide variety of manipulative math materials are available to assist in math concept development. As in all other cases, collection of formative evaluation data can be very helpful in determining whether students are acquiring important concepts. Because mathematics can be regarded as an essentially hierarchical sequence of skills, a firm foundation of initial facts and concepts is critical for later skill development.

Early Problem Solving

As students become familiar with computation in addition and subtraction, they can be exposed to problem-solving strategies. Show a word prob-

lem with pennies, for example: "Here are 3 pennies. If I spend 2, how many would we have left?" Using flash cards, teachers can begin to introduce word problems. Display, for example, the card 8 − 2, and say, "Eight minus two: If you saw 8 birds in a tree, and 2 flew away, how many birds would be left?" As you begin to write problems out, add information such as,

$$\begin{array}{r} 5 \text{ blocks} \\ -\ 3 \text{ blocks} \\ \hline 2 \text{ blocks} \end{array}$$

These can begin to become more complex, such as

$$\begin{array}{r} 6 \text{ cookies} \\ -\ 3 \text{ cookies eaten} \\ \hline \text{cookies are left} \end{array}$$

Finally, more elaborate sentences can be written, such as the following:

Arlene had 3 library books.
She checked out 2 more.

Now she has ____ library books.

Miller and Mercer (1993) have referred to this procedure as a graduated word problem sequence strategy, including concrete, semiconcrete, and abstract levels of instruction. If students learn to do this type of problem, traditional word problems should be a less difficult step.

Problems Learning Math Vocabulary

Some students may have difficulty with mathematics procedures because they do not understand relevant vocabulary and therefore do not understand teacher explanations. In such cases, increase direct teaching and practice, peer tutors with flash cards, or relevant guided practice activities to promote relevant vocabulary knowledge. In addition, use of mnemonic techniques may be helpful. For example, to remember that the multiplier is the bottom number of a multiplication problem, teachers can present a mnemonic keyword (see Chapter 5) for multiplier ("pliers") and show a picture in which an open pair of pliers represents the multiplication sign, displayed next to the multiplier. For multiplicand, the keyword *hand* could be shown pointing to the appropriate number. Similarly, divisors can be shown wearing *visors* (keyword for divisor), and *quotation marks* (keyword for quotient) can be placed around quotients. These visual keyword prompts can be removed as students remember the terms or learn to use imagery to prompt themselves.

Intermediate Math

In this section, it is assumed that students have learned the skills described in the previous section to fluency, application, and generalization levels. Figures 7.3 and 7.4 present the typical instructional sequence for addition and subtraction problems. The next set of skills taught generally includes place value, regrouping in addition and subtraction, multiplication and division facts and algorithms (procedures), measurement, and the solving of word problems.

Place Value

Place value refers to a student's ability to identify the relative value of numbers depending on their positions in a series. The concept of place value in our system revolves around the concept of base 10; that is, whenever we reach a factor of 10 in counting (10, 100, 1,000, etc.), we reflect this distinction by a change in place value.

The overall concept of place value in a base 10 system can be communicated by use of commercially available block materials or simple teacher-made materials. Blocks are composed of *units* (one single block), *longs* (composed of 10 units in a single line), *flats* (composed of a 10 × 10 ten-flat block of units), or *cubes* (composed of 1,000, or 10 × 10 × 10 units). Teachers can use these blocks to illustrate that groups of 10 or 100 blocks can be traded in for higher units. Teachers can model this procedure for counting or arithmetic tasks and ask their students to use the blocks. Concepts of place value can be learned when students are able to manipulate the blocks correctly in novel instances. Figure 7.5 demonstrates place value for the number 126. If 6 more units were added (126 + 6), they would be added to the units column. The 12 units are traded for 1 long (10) and 2 units. The long is placed in the appropriate column, making the sum 1 flat (= 100), 3 longs (= 30), and 2 units (= 2), or 132.

Manipulatives such as these can be helpful in facilitating the learning of a concept by making it more concrete. However, this does not necessarily mean that students will be able to independently apply such learning to operations on written numbers. For students to demonstrate that whole numbers should be lined up along similar rows of place values (1s above 1s, 10s

Skills	Examples	
1. Adding single-digit numbers	$3 + 2 =$	$\begin{array}{r} 4 \\ + \quad 3 \\ \hline \end{array}$
2. Adding single- or double-digit numbers together (no regrouping)	$\begin{array}{r} 23 \\ + \quad 5 \\ \hline \end{array}$	$\begin{array}{r} 16 \\ + \quad 11 \\ \hline \end{array}$
3. Adding three single-digit numbers	$\begin{array}{r} 2 \\ 4 \\ + \quad 1 \\ \hline \end{array}$	$\begin{array}{r} 5 \\ 1 \\ + \quad 3 \\ \hline \end{array}$
4. Adding multidigits together (no regrouping)	$\begin{array}{r} 123 \\ + 412 \\ \hline \end{array}$	$\begin{array}{r} 473 \\ + \quad 15 \\ \hline \end{array}$
5. Adding 2-digit numbers with regrouping in 1s column	$\begin{array}{r} 48 \\ + \quad 19 \\ \hline \end{array}$	$\begin{array}{r} 67 \\ + \quad 5 \\ \hline \end{array}$
6. Adding multidigit numbers with regrouping in 1s to 10s and/or 10s to 100s columns	$\begin{array}{r} 489 \\ + \quad 19 \\ \hline \end{array}$	$\begin{array}{r} 357 \\ + 261 \\ \hline \end{array}$
7. Adding multidigit numbers in columns with and without regrouping	$\begin{array}{r} 78 \\ 22 \\ + \quad 13 \\ \hline \end{array}$	$\begin{array}{r} 688 \\ 123 \\ + 437 \\ \hline \end{array}$

Figure 7.3. Typical teaching sequence for addition problems.

above 10s, etc.) or that sums of 10 or larger will involve regrouping of places, examples will need to be directly modeled, prompted, and corrected.

Regrouping

Understanding of place value is important for developing skill in regrouping. *Regrouping*, sometimes referred to as carrying in addition or borrowing in subtraction, refers to making use of higher order columns when values exceed the relevant factor of 10 on a particular column. Although conceptual understanding of place value is important, regrouping is basically a rule-governed procedural task and should be taught as such. As with any procedure, students must learn to (a) discriminate instances when the proce-

dure is applicable from noninstances, (b) retrieve relevant procedural information, and (c) successfully execute the procedure. For example, in the simple regrouping problem

$$\begin{array}{r} 19 \\ + \quad 3 \\ \hline \end{array}$$

students are first taught that regrouping (i.e., carrying) will be necessary. ([Show problem] "Look at this problem. What does the sign tell us to do? [Signal] That's right, it tells us to add. So, which number do we add first? Good, we add the number in the right (1s) column. So, we first add which two numbers? That's right, the 9 and the 3. What's the sum? Twelve, right. Now, I am going to tell you something new. If the numbers add to 10 or more, you write the 1s number under the 1s column and write the 10s number

Skills	Examples	
1. Basic facts (0–10)	9 − 6	7 − 4 =
2. Subtracting a single- or double-digit number from a double-digit number without regrouping	19 − 6	37 − 12
3. Subtracting a single- or double-digit number from a double-digit number with regrouping from 10s to 1s	23 − 7	52 − 29
4. Subtracting multidigit numbers from multidigit numbers with regrouping from 10s to 1s and/or 100s to 10s	703 − 192	821 − 473
5. Subtracting involving all levels of regrouping	91,998 − 8,729	7,503 − 4,767

Figure 7.4. Typical teaching sequence for subtraction problems.

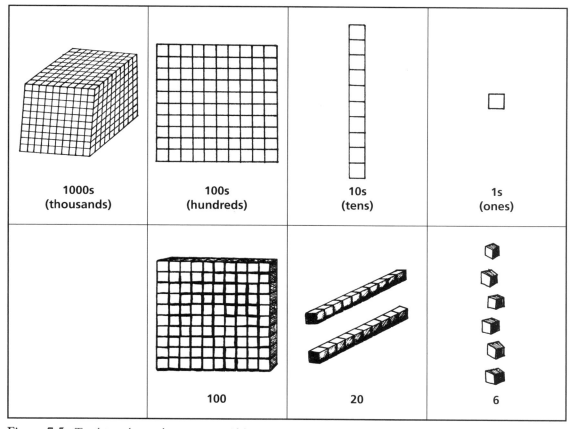

Figure 7.5. Teaching place value concepts: *126.*

above the 10s column. [Model procedure] See, 9 + 3 equals 12, so I write the 2 *under* the 9 and 3, and I write the 1 *over* the 1 in the 10s place. Now, I add the numbers in the 10s column: 1 and the 1 and write down the 2. Let's do it again with another problem. [Repeat procedure].")

Stein et al. (1997) recommended an intermediate step, *renaming*, to be employed before regrouping. That is, in the sum 17 + 9, the sum in the 1s column, 16, is renamed as 10 and 6, so that the 10 can be written in the 10 column and the 6 written below the 1s column. Similar procedures are used to teach regrouping (i.e., borrowing in subtraction).

After each procedure has been modeled, students must be given guided practice and feedback along every step. First, they must identify when the numbers in the 1s place sum to a value greater than 9. Then, they must remember the steps to execute. Finally, they must execute these steps accurately to compute the correct answer. As can be seen, students may at first perceive regrouping as a highly complex task requiring many different operations. When introducing this or any other procedure, the teacher must teach the separate steps carefully and determine that students have mastered each step before moving on. Figure 7.6 presents specific steps for teaching re-

Prerequisite Skills	Rule	Example	Procedures
Addition facts Place value 3-digit column addition	If, after adding two or more digits in a single column, the sum equals a 2-digit number, then regrouping must be completed.	26 + 17	Add the two digits in the 1s column (6 + 7 = 13)
Vocabulary used in lesson (e.g., 1s column, sum, etc.)	Students must *recognize* (identify) that regrouping is necessary.	2|6 + 1|7 3	13 = one 10 and three 1s, and the 10 *cannot* be in the 1s column
Concept of regrouping	Student must *retrieve* the appropriate steps for regrouping.	1 26 + 17	Place the one 10 at the top of the 10s column and
	Students must *execute* the steps in the procedure.	1 26 + 17 3	Place the ones under the 1s column
		$1 + 2 = 3 \begin{cases} 1 \\ 26 \\ + 17 \\ \hline 3 \end{cases}$	Add the first two numbers in the 10s column
		$3 \begin{cases} 1 \\ 26 \\ (3 + 1) + 17 \\ \hline 43 \end{cases}$	Add the sum of the first two numbers to the last number and write the sum under the 10s column

Figure 7.6. Strategies to teach addition with regrouping.

grouping in addition. Teachers may find it beneficial to have students fluently recognize when the procedure is called for prior to practicing the execution of the specific procedures. In addition, during the acquisition level of instruction, it may be necessary to write the steps necessary to execute the procedures on a separate sheet of paper. Students can then check off each step as it is executed. Many teachers have also successfully used graph paper instead of blank paper during the initial instruction periods. Graph paper helps students line up the numbers appropriately.

When students begin to exhibit high rates of correct responses, they can begin independent practice activities, usually in the form of worksheets. Because many commercially available worksheets do not contain sufficient examples of practice at all difficulty levels, special education teachers may need to construct their own worksheets. When students are completing worksheets independently, it is important that they be encouraged to work quickly, accurately, and efficiently. Students should have specific goals set for them (e.g., "By the end of the period, you should have finished these three pages") and be supervised frequently enough to ensure they do not practice errors. When students exhibit consistently high levels of fluent responding, they should be provided with opportunities to generalize these skills to other situations. This will be discussed further in the section on word problems.

Multiplication and Division Concepts

Students enrolled in special education classes often have difficulty at first in understanding the meaning of multiplication and division. These concepts should be taught using specific, concrete examples. Commercially produced materials are available, but teachers can also develop their own materials using classroom materials such as paper clips. Using such objects, arrangements that portray multiplication or division concepts can be made. For example, the operation 3 × 2 can be demonstrated with the use of three groups

of paper clips containing two paper clips per group. Students can then count the paper clips by 1s, 2s, or 3s to arrive at the total of 6. (Count-bys are also used in Touch Math to convey multiplication and division concepts.) As with any concept, students can be said to have acquired it when they can demonstrate novel instances (e.g., "Using these pennies, show me what 4 × 3 means"). Similarly, division concepts can be taught by removing prespecified groups from a total and showing the answer in number of groups. For example, for the problem 6 ÷ 3, students can be shown a group of six erasers while groups of three are removed. Because two groups of three can be removed, the answer is 2. Again students have acquired the concept when they can apply it to novel instances.

Multiplication and Division Facts

The first facts to be learned in multiplication or division involve signs and terminology. For multiplication, students must be able to identify the × sign as representing multiplication and also learn such vocabulary as *multiplier, multiplicand,* and *product.* If such terms are not learned to a fluency level, communication with the student about multiplication will be difficult. For division, students must learn the division sign and the terms *divisor, dividend,* and *quotient.* If relevant division concepts have been learned, these terms will be easier to teach. Figures 7.7 and 7.8 present the typical instructional sequence for multiplication and division problems.

Teaching number facts in multiplication and division is similar to teaching number facts in addition and subtraction in that high levels of drill and practice are required for fluent performance. Again, teacher-led drill can be supplemented with computer programs, tutors, programmable calculators, and family involvement. Multiplication facts generally are taught first to fluency levels (at least 50 facts per minute from flash cards) before division facts are taught (unless facts are taught as number families).

Skills	Examples
1. Count by 5s, 2s, etc.	5 10 15 20 25 30 35 40 45 50
2. Basic facts (0–9)	9 × 3 7 × 7
3. Single-digit factor times double-digit without regrouping	22 × 3 31 × 7
4. Single-digit factor times double-digit factor with regrouping	27 × 4 58 × 6
5. Single-digit factor times multidigit factor with or without regrouping	672 × 9 235 × 6
6. Multidigit factors times multidigit factors with or without regrouping	672 × 89 23 ×32

Figure 7.7. Typical instructional sequence for multiplication problems.

Learning multiplication facts can be facilitated by preteaching relevant counting skills. For example, students who have learned to count by 2s (i.e., 2, 4, 6, 8, etc.) have already established a set of responses for learning the 2s tables. As students learn their multiplication tables, progress can be displayed on charts so that students can be made more aware of their progress.

Division facts can be taught after multiplication tables have been learned. If multiplication facts have been learned to fluency levels, division facts should be acquired much more quickly, because the number patterns have already been learned in one sense (e.g., $2 \times 3 = 6$ is highly similar to $6 \div 2 = 3$). If students have clearly learned the similarities between multiplication and division concepts, division facts will be more meaningful. Use of number families, as described by Stein et al. (1997), would involve teaching together the multiplication and division facts: $3 \times 4 = 12$, $4 \times 3 = 12$, $12 \div 4 = 3$, and $12 \div 3 = 4$.

Because division facts may be learned more rapidly than multiplication facts, teachers may be tempted to cover division facts too quickly. Although learning should proceed more quickly, it may not. The same procedures to carefully evaluate and monitor progress should be employed in division as in any other aspect of mathematics learning. Again, facts are learned through repeated drill and practice, coupled with motivational and confidence-building activities, a positive attitude, and continuous measurement and evaluation of progress.

Multiplication and Division Procedures

Procedural learning relevant to computations in multiplication and long division is viewed by many students as a complex and unrewarding task. If teachers appropriately analyze the tasks, provide sufficient appropriate instruction, and maintain a confident, positive attitude, procedural tasks can be regarded as rewarding and productive. Procedural learning, as stated earlier, involves three components: (a) identification of when the procedure is necessary, (b) recall of the

Skills	Examples
1. Basic facts (0–9)	$3\overline{)21}$ $18 \div 2 =$
2. Single-digit divisor and quotient with remainder	$\overset{\text{R}}{2\overline{)19}}$ $\overset{\text{R}}{3\overline{)22}}$
3. Single-digit divisor with multidigit dividend with and without remainders	$\overset{\text{R}}{3\overline{)345}}$ $2\overline{)68}$
4. Estimation and rounding skills to the nearest 10	$76 = 80$ $74 = 70$
5. Double-digit divisors with dividends requiring estimation	$28\overline{)6800}$
6. Multidigit divisors with multidigit dividends	$365\overline{)49{,}850}$

Figure 7.8. Typical instructional sequence for division problems.

steps in the procedure, and (c) accurate execution of the steps in the procedure. To teach these procedures efficiently, teachers must carefully attend to all three steps. In multiplication, for example, a number of instances that call for specific procedures must be identified: Does the multiplier (bottom number) have more than one digit? If so, the student must be able to execute the procedure for double-digit multiplication. Does the product of each fact contain more than one digit? If so, students must execute the regrouping procedure. A good first step to such instruction is to ensure that students have fluent ability to identify when procedures are necessary. This can be facilitated by providing practice on the identification step only. For example, students can be given sets of multiplication problems and asked to indicate instances in which regrouping procedures are necessary.

When students have demonstrated the ability to identify cases in which procedures are necessary, they should be taught to recall the steps involved in the execution of the specific procedure. Then steps are learned as a serial list. For example, in a long-division problem, one procedure involves (a) estimating a product, (b) completing and writing down the product under the appropriate portion of the dividend, (c) bringing down the next number, and (d) repeating the procedure as necessary. This procedure is a complex one, and students need to develop fluency in being able to describe the necessary steps in sequence. In order to do this, direct drill and practice are necessary.

Finally, when students can identify when a procedure is called for and list the steps involved, they should learn to effectively execute the procedure to obtain the correct answer. Because students are able to state the steps required, it should not be assumed that they will be able to execute the steps without difficulty. Direct teaching and guided practice are necessary to ensure that this final step can be carried out. Ultimately, students should be able to carry out all steps of mathematics procedures fluently and without hesitation. Figure 7.9 presents the specific steps and procedures for teaching multidigit multiplication. Graph paper can be used during acquisition instruction to assist students in proper alignment of the digits. Teachers may also find it helpful to list these steps on the blackboard and on students' individual monitoring sheets. Initially, students can be required to check off each step as it is implemented. Some teachers have found it

Prerequisite Skills	Rule	Example	Procedures
Multiplication facts Place value Regrouping Addition facts	In completing multidigit multiplication problems, always begin multiplying by using the multiplier in the 1s column and multiply all the numbers in the multiplicand from right to left.	27 × 32 ――― 54	Multiply all the top numbers by the number in the lower 1s column (2 × 7 = 14, write down the four, carry the 1. 2 × 2 = 4, + 1 = 5; write down the 5)
	Proceed to the digit in the 10s column of the multiplier and complete the same process.	27 × 32 ――― 54 0	Place a zero in the 1s column under the 4, because we are now going to multiply by 10s
	Each time write the answer under the multiplier. After completing all multiplication, draw a line under the last row of numbers and add the columns to obtain your answer.	**2** 27 × 32 ――― 54 810	Multiply all the top numbers by the number in the lower 10s column (3 × 7 = 21, write down the 1 next to the 0, carry the 2. 3 × 2 = 6, + 2 = 8; write 8 next to the one)
		27 × 32 ――― 54 + 810	Draw a line under 810, and place an addition sign next to 810
		27 × 32 ――― 54 + 810 ――― + 864	Add the columns, just like an addition problem (4 + 0 = 4, write down the 4. 5 + 1 = 6, write down the 6. 8 + 0 = 8, write down the 8)
			The answer is the bottom number, in this case, 864

Figure 7.9. Strategies to teach multidigit multiplication.

beneficial to add additional prompts and cues, such as color codes, for steps during acquisition instruction. Once the skills have been acquired, these extra prompts can be removed. Again, formative evaluation techniques are helpful in determining whether students are computing problems at an adequate rate.

Measurement

Most measurement tasks at the intermediate level involve (a) conceptual and factual learning of units of equivalence and (b) procedures involved in making measurements (i.e., the application of measurement facts). First, concepts of equivalence can be demonstrated by use of measuring instruments. For example, two pint containers can be shown to fill one quart container. When students can demonstrate such operations reliably in novel situations, they have acquired the concept. Measurement facts can be taught using drill-and-practice techniques similar to those used in teaching multiplication and division tables. Finally, students can be shown, through modeling, prompting, and feedback, the procedure for measuring different units of length, volume, time, and so on. In these cases, it is also important to reinforce knowledge of relevant facts and concepts.

Word Problems

Any amount of mathematics instruction is of little use unless students can use knowledge of concepts, facts, and procedures to solve problems. Word problems can be considered application tasks that involve the use of previous learning.

In most cases, solving a word problem involves the three steps previously described in executing any procedure. After reading or listening to a problem, students must first determine which major procedure (i.e., operation) is called for to solve the problem. Students should be readily able to describe any problem as calling for addition, subtraction, multiplication, or division. They then need to retrieve the steps needed to execute the general procedure—for example, that one particular number must be divided by another and the quotient expressed with respect to a particular unit (e.g., pies, dollars, books, hours). Finally, the entire procedure must be accurately executed. Of course, the execution of this procedure (division) will involve, in turn, identification, recall, and execution of other procedures related to the division operation.

It may be helpful to teach these steps separately. For instance, students can be shown examples of word problems in which they are asked simply to indicate whether addition, subtraction, multiplication, or division is called for. Figure 7.10 presents a sample set of strategies to teach students typical *clue words* for problem solving. Clue words are not best used in isolation but in the context of other information gathered from the word problem; that is, simply because the word *altogether* is in the problem does not guarantee that it will be an addition problem. Also, many problems do not fit this simple model. When students have mastered this objective, they can be given problems in which they are asked to indicate the operation and describe the steps necessary to execute the general procedure. Finally, if these two steps have been

Operation	Clue Word	Example
Addition	altogether both together in all	How much did it cost altogether?
Subtraction	left	How many are left?
Multiplication	Tells one, asks for quantity.	Boxes. Each one weighs 3 lbs. How much do 5 boxes weigh?
Division	Tells quantity, asks for one (how much each).	Five equal boxes weigh 15 lbs. How much does one weigh?

Figure 7.10. Strategies for clue-word problem solving.

mastered, students can be asked to execute the procedures and solve the problem. Ultimately, students should be able to reason their way through two-part problems and problems for which obvious clue words are not included. Students can be said to have generalized this learning when they can solve similar problems in other classrooms or in nonschool settings (e.g., dividing the cost of a pizza). Figure 7.11 provides a strategy for thinking through word problems (Shiah, Mastropieri, Scruggs, & Fulk, 1995).

Montague (1992) trained students to use a strategy for solving word problems with seven steps, including read, paraphrase, visualize, hypothesize, estimate, compute, and check. When attempting to determine the nature of a word problem and the appropriate operation for its solution, show students how to visualize a problem, draw a picture, and identify and highlight important cue words and phrases (Case, Harris, & Graham, 1992). For example, consider the following problem:

> To build his cabin, James must carry 18 logs across the river in his canoe. He can only carry 3 logs at a time. How many trips must he make?

Students can circle or highlight words such as *carry, 18 logs,* and *3 logs at a time.* The words *18 logs* can be annotated as "tells a quantity." Students can visualize James carrying logs in his

canoe, draw a picture of James carrying logs in his canoe, or draw a sketch representing groups of 3 logs as James makes several trips. Through these steps, students can arrive at an appropriate mathematical operation for solving the problem (in this case, division) and also be able to check if the obtained answer makes sense. For example, if a student mistakenly multiplies and arrives at an answer of 54, reviewing these same strategies can reveal that 54 is not sensible because it is more than the total number of logs.

Peer and Cooperative Group Learning

Strategies that can be applied at any point in the math curriculum involve the use of peers, either as tutors or in cooperative groups. Peers can be used to study math facts from flash cards, check each other's work, or reinforce newly acquired concepts. In cooperative learning groups, students can work collectively on problem-solving activities or on worksheets in guided practice activities. As with all peer-mediated activities, teachers should ensure that students can apply appropriate social skills to group situations and that individual as well as group progress is being made. Careful attention to curriculum demands as they affect individual learners and to group dynamics can help ensure that peer and group learning activities are successful.

Cooperative learning has also been widely recommended as a strategy for inclusive classrooms. In such situations, cooperative groups of students with differing skill levels (including students with disabilities) work together to learn skills and complete mathematics (or other subject area) assignments. Because each group as a whole is approximately equal, groups can compete fairly with each other to complete assignments, gain new skill levels, or solve particular problems. In such situations, higher achieving students are motivated to help lower achieving students so that the group as a whole will succeed. However, as with any cooperative group situation, teachers must ensure that all students

---

1. *Read* the problem.
2. *Think* about the problem.
3. *Decide* the operation sign.
4. *Write* math sentence.
5. *Compute* the problem.
6. *Label* the answer.
7. *Check* the problem.

Figure 7.11. Strategy for math problem solving. *Note.* Adapted from Shiah, Mastropieri, Scruggs, and Fulk (1995).

have learned appropriate social skills for this type of interaction. In addition, in inclusive classrooms, it is also important to ensure that regular class peers know how to interact with and effectively assist students with disabilities. For example, it is important that peers do not simply do the work for lower achieving students but that they help them to understand the content to be learned. In these situations, it is particularly important to gather formative data on the progress of individual students.

Problems in Intermediate Math

Problems in mathematics fact learning on the intermediate level may parallel those that appear on the lower levels. When such problems occur, the solution is generally found in careful task analysis and increased drill and practice, whether teacher led or monitored by computers, calculators, peers, or family members. The decision to replace learning of multiplication and division tables with calculators or printed tables of facts should be made in conjunction with administrative personnel and only after repeated attempts to facilitate fact learning have been documented.

There is one procedure that has been helpful for learning ×9 tables, shown in Figure 7.12. In addition, many students can easily count by 5s and use this knowledge to facilitate learning of ×5 tables. Students who have a firm knowledge of addition facts and the concept of multiplication (as should all students learning multiplication tables) should be able to easily solve ×2 tables (e.g., $5 \times 2 = 5 + 5$). Finally, the answer to ×1 and ×0 problems should be obvious to students who know relevant concepts. If the student, then, can determine ×0, ×1, ×2, ×5, and ×9 tables and apply relevant equivalence concepts (commutativity, e.g., $3 \times 6 = 6 \times 3$), there will be only 15 facts left to learn! Such an approach may make the task of learning multiplication facts more bearable for some students.

The 15 facts referred to in the previous paragraph are 3×3, 4, 6, 7, and 8; 4×4, 6, 7, and 8; 6×6, 7, and 8; 7×7 and 8; and 8×8. These can all be learned using a mnemonic technique known as the "pegword method." This method replaces a rhyming name for each number: 1 is *bun*, 2 is *shoe*, 3 is *tree*, 4 is *door*, and so on to 10 is *hen*. For numbers higher than 10, use 12 is *elf*, 18 is *aiding* (e.g., with an ambulance), 20 is *twin*, 30 is *dirty* or *thirsty*, 40 is *party*, 50 is *gifty* (i.e., gift wrapped), and 60 is *witchy*. Teachers can create pictures for each of the strategies. For example, for $3 \times 3 = 9$, students can say, "Tree to tree is line" and be shown (or think of) a line between two (different, not "twin") trees. For $3 \times 4 = 12$, students can say, "Tree door is elf" and be shown

---

1. Hold hands out with palms facing downward in front of you.

2. Number your fingers 1 to 10 from left to right (e.g., little finger on your left hand is number 1, thumb on you right hand is 6, while little finger on right hand is 10).

3. For a given 9s problem (e.g., $9 \times 4 =$), select the number that is not 9 (i.e., 4), count over on your fingers, beginning with number 1 (your left hand little finger) to that digit. In this example, you should count over to the index finger, or 4th finger on your left hand. Then, bend that finger down.

4. The number of fingers to the left of the bent finger represents the number of 10s in the answer, while the number of fingers to the right of the bent finger represents the number of 1s in the answer. In the case of 9×4, since three fingers are to the left and six fingers are to the right, the correct answer is 36. In the case of 9×5, the left thumb is bent. Four fingers are to the left and five are to the right of the bent thumb. The answer, then, is 45.

Figure 7.12. Steps for calculating 9s tables.

a picture of an elf behind a door in a tree. For $4 \times 8 = 32$, students can say, "Door to gate, dirty shoe" and be shown a picture of someone kicking a door and a gate with a dirty shoe. For $7 \times 8 = 56$, they can say, "Heaven's gate holds gifty sticks." Examples of all 15 strategies are provided by Mastropieri and Scruggs (1991).

Higher Level Math

The mathematics learning described in this section is advanced relative to the skills covered in the previous sections. This section will describe the teaching of fractions, decimals, ratios, geometry, and algebra.

Fractions and Decimals

Concepts relevant to fractions have been described previously. The concept to be taught with respect to decimals is that the numbers represent 10ths, 100ths, 1,000ths, and so on.

Students have mastered this concept when they can identify such proportions in novel instances. The distinction between fractions and decimals is in notation and in procedural operations more than in concepts, which are essentially the same. Actually, decimals can be regarded as a special case of fractions.

Once basic concepts and vocabulary are understood, instruction usually involves teaching procedures for computation of decimals and fractions. Addition of fractions with like denominators follows a simple rule: Leave the denominators constant and add the numerators. Beyond this simple application, procedures become more and more complex. In more complex procedures, it is helpful to teach the three steps to procedural learning for each new procedure. Students, for example, must learn to identify when the sum of two or more fractions results in a numerator that is greater than the denominator. This identification should access the retrieval of the appropriate procedure: (a) divide the numerator by the denominator, (b) record the quotient as the whole

number, and (c) record the remainder as the numerator of the original fraction. Finally, students should demonstrate the ability to execute such a procedure.

A different set of procedures is necessary for reducing fractions. In executing the procedure, students should first attempt to identify the largest number that can be divided into both numerator and denominator. Students should master the identification step of this procedure to the extent that any fraction is automatically evaluated to determine whether it can be reduced. Figure 7.13 presents a sample lesson on the instruction of concepts in fractions. Figure 7.14 presents specific strategies and procedures for instruction in the operations of fractions.

Decimal operations are generally less complex than fractions if students have mastered all of the relevant preskills. For addition and subtraction, students must learn to arrange numbers vertically with reference to the decimal point rather than the digit placed farthest to the right. The decimal point is then added to its proper position in the sum or difference. Similarly, simple rules govern the placement of decimal points in products and quotients. Although such rules are basically simple, students should understand *why* they are performing these operations as well as *how* such operations are performed. Figure 7.15 presents strategies for instruction in operations involving decimals, and Figure 7.16 presents a sample lesson using self-monitoring in decimal operations instruction. These relevant concepts can be enforced both prior to and during the instruction of specific procedures.

Instruction of ratio and proportion concepts and procedures generally involves application of fraction knowledge. An example that is typically used for building the concept of ratios is recipes. Students can be shown how, in order to prepare a meal for twice as many people as specified in the recipe, a proportion of 2:1 must be followed for each ingredient. Students can be said to understand the concept when they can adapt proportion concepts to novel tasks, such as different recipes calling for different proportions. Finally, students need to apply previously learned skills

Component	Examples
Daily review	Last week in math we practiced addition and subtraction of whole numbers. Everyone write one addition problem and one subtraction problem. . . .
State objective and teacher presentation	Today, we are going to learn about fractions. Fractions are parts of whole numbers or units.
	[Draw a circle.] This is a circle in a whole unit.
	[Shade in half of the circle.] This shaded part *represents* one of the two parts or one-half of the whole circle.
	[Draw another circle, shade in a small portion—less than half.] This shaded part is not *half* of the circle.
	[Point to first circle.] This shaded part is *half*.
	[Point to second circle.] This is not half.
	Is this half?
	Here is a whole glass of water [show]. I can divide this glass in *two* [draw a line through middle and pour out the top part], and I will have one-half left. How much will I have left, Robert?
	Continue with several additional examples of whole versus half.
Guided practice	[Worksheets with the following examples are on all students' desks.]
	Now, we are going to practice some more items. Everyone put his or her finger on number 1. Look across at the three examples. Circle the one that is only half. Everyone hold his or her paper up when you've completed the first example. . . .
Independent practice	[Worksheets similar to the one used during guided practice are distributed.] Now, everyone, this sheet is just like the one we completed. Everyone put his or her finger on number 1. Circle the picture that shows half. Good. Now do the same for all the rest of the items on this page. . . .
	[Collect when done; review.] Today, we . . . .
Formative evaluation	[Teacher distributes a similar sheet.] Okay, now when I say go, everybody begin this sheet just like the last one we completed. Any questions? Go. [After 1 minute.] Stop and hand in your papers.

Figure 7.13. Sample lesson for teaching initial fraction concepts.

in conjunction with proportions. It should not be assumed that students are able to execute proportion and ratio operations until they have exhibited this ability in several different cases. When students do so, teachers should make sure that all steps of the procedure are understood.

Problems in Fractions and Decimals

If students have mastered the necessary preskills, they should have little difficulty acquiring concepts relevant to fractions and decimals. If such problems are observed, demonstrations of

Skill Area	Prerequisite Skills	Rules	Procedures	Example
Addition of fractions with like denominators	Addition Fraction concepts Fraction vocabulary	If the denominators are identical, add the numerators.	Read the problem.	$\dfrac{3}{8} + \dfrac{2}{8}$
			If the denominators are equal (are the same number), just add the numerators.	$3 + 2 = 5$
			Write the sum of the numerators as your new numerator and carry over your denominator to the denominator spot.	$\dfrac{3}{8} + \dfrac{2}{8} = \dfrac{5}{8}$
			Read your answer.	$\dfrac{5}{8}$
Subtraction of fractions with like denominators	All of above plus subtraction	If the denominators are identical, subtract the numerators.	Read the problem.	$\dfrac{3}{8} - \dfrac{2}{8}$
			If the denominators are equal, just subtract the numerators.	$3 - 2 = 1$
			Write the difference of the numerators as your new numerator, and write the same denominator as your new denominator.	$\dfrac{3}{8} - \dfrac{2}{8} = \dfrac{1}{8}$
			Read your answer.	$\dfrac{1}{8}$
Multiplication of fractions	All of the above	Multiply the numerator by numerator to form a new numerator and multiply the denominator by denominator.	Read the problem.	$\dfrac{1}{3} \times \dfrac{2}{5}$
			Multiply the two numerators.	$1 \times 2 = 2$

(continues)

Figure 7.14. Strategies for teaching fractions.

Skill Area	Prerequisite Skills	Rules	Procedures	Example
			Write the product as the new numerator.	$\frac{1}{3} \times \frac{2}{5} = \frac{2}{}$
			Multiply the two denominators.	$3 \times 5 = 15$
			Write the product as the new denominator.	$\frac{1}{3} \times \frac{2}{5} = \frac{2}{15}$
			Read the answer.	$\frac{2}{15}$
Division of fractions	All of the above plus division	If you see a fraction problem that requires division, invert the second fraction and then use the multiplication rule (i.e., multiply the numerators and multiply the denominators).	Read the problem.	$\frac{1}{3} \div \frac{2}{5}$
			Invert the second fraction (turn it upside down).	$\frac{2}{5} \rightarrow \frac{5}{2}$
			Change the sign from division to multiplication.	$\frac{1}{3} \times \frac{5}{2}$
			Multiply the numerators.	$1 \times 5 = 5$
			Write the product as the new numerator.	$\frac{1}{3} \times \frac{5}{2} = \frac{5}{}$
			Multiply the denominators.	$3 \times 2 = 6$
			Write the product as the new denominator.	$\frac{1}{3} \times \frac{5}{2} = \frac{5}{6}$
			Read the answer.	$\frac{5}{6}$

Note. Other skills involving fractions include some of the following: using mixed fractions in all operations, finding lowest common multiples, finding greatest common factors, and reducing fractions. As above, all skills need to be task analyzed and sequenced.

Figure 7.14. *Continued.*

Operations	Rules	Examples
Addition	Line up the decimals in the addends and place the decimal in line in the sum.	$21.1 + 3.1$ $\begin{array}{r} 21.1 \\ +\ 3.1 \\ \hline 24.2 \end{array}$
Subtraction	Same as addition.	$35.01 - 19.10$ $\begin{array}{r} 35.01 \\ -\ 19.10 \\ \hline 15.91 \end{array}$
Multiplication	Count the number of digits to the right of the decimal point in both the multiplier and multiplicand.	$\begin{array}{r} 3.1 \leftarrow 3 \\ \times\ .22 \leftarrow \\ \hline 62 \\ 62 \\ \hline \end{array}$
	Leave that many decimal places in the product.	$3 \rightarrow\ .682$
Division	Move decimal in divisor to the right of the last number.	$.20\,\overline{\smash{)}660.}$
		$.20.\,\overline{\smash{)}\ }$
	Move decimal in dividend an equivalent number of spaces to right.	$.20.\,\overline{\smash{)}660.00.}$

Figure 7.15. Strategies for operations involving decimals.

relevant concepts should be made more concrete. As very specific, concrete examples are mastered, they can be enhanced by presentation of different, less concrete examples. Generally, the more opportunities students have to manipulate or operate on specific examples, the more likely they are to master the concept.

In general, students who are fluent on basic math facts should have little difficulty learning computation procedures. One source of difficulty that is frequently encountered is reduction of fractions after initial calculations because it is not easy to specify an exact procedure that students can use in every instance. Some general guidelines can be reinforced, however, and are pre-

sented below as questions the student should ask of any fraction.

1. Can the denominator be divided by the numerator (e.g., 4/8 = 1/2)?

2. Do the numerator and denominator both end in 0? If so, divide by 10 (e.g., 20/30 = 2/3).

3. Do the numerator and denominator end in 0 or 5? If so, divide by 5 (e.g., 15/20 = 3/4).

4. Can the numerator and denominator be divided by 3 (e.g., 3/9 = 1/3)?

If these steps are practiced over a period of time, reduction of fractions may become a less

Review	Remember how we have practiced doing long division? Look at this example with me.

$$20 \overline{\smash{)}100}$$

Everyone compute the answer with me . . . .

State objective and teacher presentation	Today we are going to learn what to do when we have decimals in the divisor. We can't divide when there is a decimal in the divisor. These are examples of decimals in the devisor:

$$1.20 \overline{\smash{)}878} \qquad .7 \overline{\smash{)}82} \qquad .11 \overline{\smash{)}211}$$

Are these examples of decimals in the divisors?

$$.10 \overline{\smash{)}82} \ \text{[Yes]} \qquad 10 \overline{\smash{)}82} \ \text{[No]}$$

$$1.9 \overline{\smash{)}77} \ \text{[Yes]} \qquad 19 \overline{\smash{)}77} \ \text{[No]}$$

You must complete the following steps before you compute a division problem:

First, look at the divisor to see whether or not it contains a decimal.

Second, if there is no decimal in the divisor, divide as usual.

Third, if there is a decimal, move the decimal to the right of the last number in the divisor.

Fourth, move the decimal in the dividend an equivalent number of spaces to the right.

Fifth, now divide as usual.

Everybody watch me as I use those steps to help me divide. [Proceed through several examples.]

Now, when you see a division problem, go through the following steps on the self-monitoring sheet below:

Self-Monitoring Sheet for Division Involving Decimals

First, look at the divisor to see whether or not it contains a decimal.

Second, if there is no decimal, divide as usual.

Third, if there is a decimal, move the decimal to the right of the last number in the divisor.

Fourth, move the decimal in the dividend an equivalent number of spaces to the right.

Fifth, now, divide as usual.

Figure 7.16. Sample lesson for using self-monitoring instructions in teaching division involving decimals.

difficult task. Similar procedures applied to multiplication problems before computation reduce the need for later reduction:

$$\frac{2}{5} \times \frac{15}{16} = \frac{\overset{1}{\cancel{2}}}{\cancel{5}} \times \frac{\overset{3}{\cancel{15}}}{\cancel{16}} = \frac{3}{8}$$

Geometry

Basic geometry concepts involving shape have been described previously. Many of the operations in basic geometry involve the application of a formula, which is essentially a rule-learning task. For example, for students to compute the area (A) of a square, they must be able to retrieve the relevant formula ($A = B^2$). This formula involves the concept of the area of a square, which can be demonstrated by drawing a grid of the unit of measurement on the square and counting the square units represented. Computing the area from a formula also involves the knowledge that $B^2 = B \times B$, and the B stands for the length of any side of the square. When students have learned these concepts, they must learn the appropriate formula as a fact. Finally, they must learn to apply the formula to the particular area being computed. For example, when computing the area of a square with a side of 3 feet, students

must first retrieve the appropriate formula ($A = B^2$) and apply it to the specific instance (i.e., $A = 3^2 = 3 \times 3 = 9$). Students must attend to every step in the sequence to arrive at the correct answer.

Similar procedures are necessary for the computation of areas of other shapes, although the formulas are somewhat more complex. In addition, for computations involving circles, students must also learn that the symbol π equals approximately $3\frac{1}{7}$ or 3.14 and that this number must be substituted in appropriate equations. Also, a number of other symbolic notations must be learned as facts (and concepts) before they can be applied to computation problems. These include such notations as $r =$ radius, $b =$ base, $h =$ height, and so on. Careful task and conceptual analysis will help determine exactly what students already know and what they must be taught to perform particular operations in geometry.

Higher levels of geometry instruction typically involve deductive-reasoning paradigms, and many special education students experience difficulty using this kind of reasoning in problem-solving activities. Teachers should first be certain that students have mastered all of the relevant rules, concepts, and facts. A series of deductive reasoning steps can then be executed, based on all known information, to lead to the solution. For example, consider Figure 7.17 and the following problem: Given that a, b, and c are

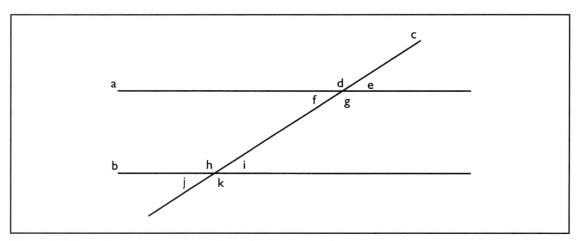

Figure 7.17. Problem requiring the use of prior knowledge and deductive reasoning.

straight lines, *a* is parallel to *b*, and angle *d* ($\angle$ *d*) is 120°, what does $\angle$ *k* equal?

To approach this problem, students must first have demonstrated knowledge of the concepts of *straight line* and *parallel*. They must also know the fact that all straight lines equal 180°. Using this information, they must apply it to a procedure for determining the value of $\angle$ *k*. This procedure involves a series of deductions based on prior knowledge. Given sufficient practice in solving similar problems, however, students will begin to recognize the deductive steps that lead to the following solution:

1. line c = 180°

2. $\angle$ d = 120°

3. $\angle$ f = 180° − 120° = 60°

4. *a* ∥ *b*

5. $\angle$ *f* = *j* = 60°

6. $\angle$ k = 180° − 60° = 120°

Many special education students have difficulty with this type of deductive reasoning, often because they are not certain how to proceed. Students should be given many instances for each type of solution so that prior knowledge of procedures can cue the student in problem solving. Students should then be taught a general procedure for solving such problems. This procedure involves first writing down everything that is known about the problem and, second, listing information that is not known but can be computed. Students should then examine all of this information with respect to prior experience with similar problems to determine the steps for the solution. As with other problem-solving strategies of this type, students should carefully reflect on what information is known or can be calculated and whether any information can be added to the original list. Frequently, efforts to increase the amount of known information can lead to a correct solution. Carefully structured teacher questioning, prompting, and coaching can help guide the students' thinking.

"Big Ideas"

Carnine (1998) described the importance of teaching "big ideas" in mathematics, providing students with an idea of more general themes, rather than a large number of formulae and problem solutions. For example, it can be seen that all volume formulae are derived from the "big idea" of the product of the area of the base and a multiple of the height. This is preferable to individually teaching the separate formulae for calculating volumes of, for example, rectangular prism, rectangular wedge, rectangular cylinder, triangular pyramid, conic pyramid, and sphere. For example, in figures in which the sides go straight up, such as a rectangular prism or cylinder, the formula is the area of the base × height (b × h). For figures that come to a point, including pyramids and cones, the formula is the area of the base × ⅓ of the height (b × ⅓h). Teaching students that a number of different formulae can be derived from one simple principle can enforce the general concept as well as specific applications.

Problems in Geometry

A number of materials are commercially available for reinforcing geometry concepts. Most difficulties students exhibit with geometry involve problems with vocabulary, formulae, or application to specific procedures. Careful task and error analysis should be employed in addition to questioning students to determine the exact nature of the problem. When problems are identified, they should be approached by additional drill and practice on specific facts and procedures, using a pace appropriate to the instructional sequence. If problems occur in geometry problem solving when essential vocabulary and concepts are well understood, high levels of guided practice are necessary. Because difficulties in this area can be a source of great frustration, it is particularly helpful to provide assistance in a manner that maintains a high level of correct responding.

Algebra

Introduction to algebra can begin very early in mathematics instruction. For example, students can be introduced to algebraic notations with problems such as

$$2 + 3 = x$$

as an alternative to

$$\begin{array}{r} 2 \\ + 3 \end{array}$$

A different set of operations, of course, is required when students are asked to solve problems such as $2 + x = 5$. Although some students are able to use reasoning or trial-and-error approaches to solve such problems, instruction in these kinds of solutions requires teaching of equivalence concepts and specific procedures for problem solving. First, students must be made aware that the equal sign (=) means that values on either side are identical and that overall operations applied to one side must be applied to the other. These concepts can be demonstrated through the use of real numbers or objects. Students must then be taught that operations should be employed to isolate x, or the unknown value, on one side of the equation. The other side, if free of unknowns, will reveal the answer. For example, to solve $2 + x = 5$ for the value of x, students must first determine that x can be isolated by subtracting the value 2 from both sides of the equation, an operation that results in $x = 3$, the answer.

As problems become more complicated, students must demonstrate knowledge of operational procedures; that is, for $5x + 2 = 12$, subtraction must be performed first, followed by division by 5 to produce the solution, 2.

Once solutions have been determined, students should be encouraged to check work for accuracy by substituting obtained values for unknown symbols. Manipulative materials, such as algebra tiles (available from Delta Education), can be very useful in enforcing early algebra concepts. Algebra tiles include materials to represent positive and negative integers, as well as unknown elements in algebraic equations.

Problem-Solving Strategies

Hutchinson (1993) described a strategy for helping students solve algebra problems. For example, consider the following problem:

> A man walks 6 km farther than his son. If the total distance walked by both is 32 km, how far did each walk? (Hutchinson, 1993, p. 38)

Students were provided with a structured worksheet, for which students needed to fill in the following components:

- Goal:
- What I don't know:
- What I know:
- Kind of problem:
- Equation:
- Solving the equation:
- Solution:
- Compare with goal.
- Check (p. 40).

Students were also asked to use a self-questioning procedure, including the following self-questions:

1. Have I read and understood each sentence?

2. Have I got the whole picture, a representation, for this problem?

3. Have I written down my representation on the worksheet? (p. 39)

Students also asked self-questions for writing and solving the equation. In the present instance, students need to determine that the man's son walked x km, and the man, who walked 6 km farther, walked $x + 6$ km. Using the worksheet questions, then, students could identify the goal, the unknowns, the knowns, the type of problem, and the equation. The two distances represented, then, are x km and $x + 6$ km, totaled 32 km, and can be written in the equation:

$$x + (x + 6) = 32$$

Using a problem solution strategy, students can arrive at the correct answer:

$$x + (x + 6) = 32$$
$$2x + 6 = 32$$
$$2x + 6 \,(-6) = 32 - 6$$
$$2x = 26$$
$$x = 13$$

So, the man walked $x + 6 = 19$ km, and his son walked $x = 13$ km.

For related examples of algebra strategy instruction, see Maccini and Hughes (2000) and Lang (2001).

Problems in Algebra

Once they learn relevant concepts, students have little difficulty solving very simple algebra problems. As problems become more complex and higher levels of deductions are required, however, problem solving can present great difficulties. When this point is reached, it is important to go back to the level of problems that did not present difficulty and reteach the more complex procedures using smaller steps and increased levels of direct teaching and guided practice. If peer or other tutors are employed, it must first be determined that algebraic procedures are being taught the same way by all tutors and the teachers. When students have overlearned a very specific set of procedures, the next one should be introduced. If such a teaching strategy seriously hampers the rate of curriculum covered, teachers should determine whether the content learned will be sufficiently useful or whether different, more practical content should be covered.

Functional Math

As can be seen in the preceding pages, higher level mathematics skills involve application of all previously learned skills on a higher concep-

tual level. Thus, many special education students, particularly those characterized as having mild mental retardation, can exhibit persistent difficulty in acquiring these skills. How far (or whether) to proceed with instruction in these areas is a decision that involves consideration of (a) the level of difficulty exhibited, (b) realistic educational goals for the student, and (c) instructional alternatives involving more practical applications that may ultimately prove more useful for the student. It is generally not sufficient, however, to perceive that a specific student will have difficulty learning a specific content. If preskills have been mastered, it should be documented that the student exhibits persistent difficulties over time and through instructional adaptations to the extent that specific instructional alternatives should be considered. Such considerations have taken on increasing importance in states that have mandated high-stakes testing as a requirement for graduation.

Rather than entering classes for advanced mathematics, many students receive instruction that places more emphases on practical application of basic skills, which is referred to as *functional math* (Patton, Cronin, Bassett, & Koppel, 1998). Topics in fuctional math include using the calendar, writing checks and keeping bank accounts, computing household expenses, making purchases, paying bills, and completing tax forms. The extent of emphasis that needs to be placed on functional math depends on consideration of the needs of the individual students. Many students are typically assumed, correctly or incorrectly, to be able to acquire these skills without explicit instruction; however, without functional math skills, the goal of independent living will be much more difficult to attain. A relevant textbook in this area is *Practical Mathematics for Consumers* (Staudacher & Turner, 1994). It may be helpful to examine the skill areas covered in such materials and be certain that students already have relevant skills, or that these skills are covered in existing curriculum materials. If not, it may be very useful to supplement instruction with lessons in functional math.

Summary

- Competence in mathematics is required for employment as well as independent living. Learning in mathematics is facilitated by careful selection of the scope and sequence of objectives, appropriate curriculum, and application of effective teaching variables.

- Beginning math skills, such as numeration, counting, one-to-one correspondence, and equivalence, are critical for later mathematics learning. Attention to conceptual, factual, and procedural learning is critically important at this early level.

- Basic number and operation concepts, including addition and subtraction, are enforced by direct teaching, use of number lines, and use of manipulatives.

- Students with special learning needs often have great difficulty learning basic facts. It is important to teach math facts as efficiently as possible so that students will have time to devote to conceptual, procedural, and problem-solving elements of math instruction. Learning of math facts can be enforced through drill and practice, peer mediation, appropriate software, and independent study strategies. Specific strategies also promote recall of math facts. Place value and regrouping concepts can be enforced with manipulatives, and procedures can be enforced with specific instructional strategies.

- Solving word problems is a very important part of mathematics learning. It can be enforced with a concrete to semiconcrete to abstract teaching sequence that can begin very early in the introduction of fact learning and number concepts. Problem solving can also be promoted by self-monitoring strategies and the use of clue words, highlighting, visualizing, pictures, and other problem solving strategies. Cooperative group activities can help facilitate problem solving.

- Manipulative materials can be helpful in promoting concepts of fractions and decimals. Relevant procedures are taught by direct instruction, guided practice, and self-monitoring strategies.

- Early algebra concepts can be introduced early in mathematics instruction. Manipulative materials such as algebra tiles can enforce relevant concepts, and strategy and self-monitoring instruction can promote effective problem solving.

- It is important to ensure that relevant practical skills in math, including budgeting, banking, money management, and paying taxes, are being learned in math instruction. Such skills are essential for independent living as well as functioning effectively at work.

Relevant Research and Resources

Research

Overviews of mathematics instruction are written by Romberg and Carpenter (1986), Baroody and Hume (1991), and Mayer (1993). Good and Grouws (1979) and Carpenter (1985) provide extensive information on the effective teaching model for mathematics. The National Council of Teachers of Mathematics (NCTM) has presented standards for teaching mathematics (NCTM, 2000). Special education perspectives on an earlier version of these standards are provided by Rivera (1998a). General reviews of mathematics instruction in special education are provided by Mastropieri, Scruggs, and Shiah (1991) and Mastropieri, Bakken, and Scruggs (1991) and are found in Rivera (1998b). Woodward et al. (2001) discuss the utility of performance assessment in mathematics.

Jordan and Montani (1996) review cognitive and developmental perspectives on mathematical difficulties in young children. Problems of early numeracy skills and a description of an early numeracy program are described by Van Luit and Schopman (2000). Applications of the direct instruction model for at-risk learners are reviewed by Gersten et al. (1986). Books that present information relevant to teaching mathematics to students with special needs include Stein et al.

(1997); Baroody (1989); Bley and Thornton (1989); Cawley, Fitzmaurice-Hayes, and Shaw (1988); Cawley (1984); and Rivera (1998b). Instructional design issues in mathematics, including the teaching of "big ideas," are discussed by Carnine (1998). Scott (1993) describes the positive effects of Touch Math with students with mild disabilities. The effects of the use of computers on mathematics learning are presented by Mastropieri, Scruggs, and Shiah (1997); Shiah et al. (1995); and Trifiletti, Frith, and Armstrong (1984). The use of calculators is described by Horton et al. (1992). Reviews of research on teaching money skills are provided by Browder and Grasso (1999). A strategic intervention for improving computation for students with learning disabilities is described by Naglieri and Johnson (2000). Strategy training research in which special education students have been successfully taught procedures for problem solution is reported by Fleischner, Nuzum, and Marzola (1987); Englert, Culatta, and Hein (1987); Cullinan, Lloyd, and Epstein (1981); Lloyd, Saltzman, and Kauffinan (1981); Rivera and Smith (1987); and Rivera, Smith, Goodwin, and Bryant (1998). Various approaches and strategies for solving problems are described by Bottge and Hasselbring (1993); Case et al. (1992); Garnett (1992); Thornton and Toohey (1985); Montague, Bos, and Doucette (1991); Skinner, Bamberg, Smith, and Powell (1993); Wilson and Sindelar (1991); Montague (1998); and Montague, Warger, and Morgan (2000). Lucangeli, Cornoldi, and Tellarini (1998) describe metacognition and learning disabilities in mathematics. Montague and Applegate (1993) provide an analysis on problem-solving analyses of students with mild disabilities, and the effects of teaching math problems through a sequence of concrete to abstract procedures is described by Mercer and Miller (1992) and Miller and Mercer (1993). Grobecker (2000) describes some difficulties of students with learning disabilities in conceptualizing fractions, as well as the benefits of specific questioning and manipulative materials. The effects of strategy training on higher level mathematics problem solving are described by Zawaiza and Gerber (1993). Hutchinson (1993), Maccini and Hughes (2000), and Lang (2001) describe problem-solving strategies for algebra, and a review of algebra instruction for students with learning disabilities is provided by Maccini, McNaughton, and Ruhl (1999). Some self-instruction training techniques in special education are described by Leon and Pepe (1983). Peer-mediated instructional techniques and cooperative learning approaches are described by Slavin, Madden and Leavey (1984a, 1984b) and Beirne-Smith (1991). For some concerns about the effectiveness of cooperative learning as an inclusion strategy, see Tateyama-Sniezek (1990). A life skills approach to math instruction is described by Patton et al. (1998).

Curricular Materials

Examples of math materials with clear scope and sequences that are targeted for students with mild disabilities include *DISTAR Arithmetic K–3*, *Corrective Mathematics Program*, and *Connecting Math Concepts* (SRA/McGraw-Hill). *The Touch Math Program* (Innovative Learning Concepts) is available for teaching basic addition, subtraction, multiplication, and division. The *Practical Arithmetic* series, *Success in Math*, and *Pacemaker Curriculum: Algebra* are available from Globe Fearon, and PRO-ED produces *Real Life Math* and *Counting Money*. Curriculum Associates produces a number of materials relevant to math instruction, including *Strategies to Achieve Math Success* and *Math the Write Way*, which prepares students to write mathematically. The *Quick-Math Handbook* provides an easy reference to key math terms and procedures and frequently used formulae, and *Math: Connecting with the Standards* provides hands-on math activities focused on the NCTM 2000 standards.

Manipulative materials are available from Delta Education and include items such as the base 10 blocks, algebra tiles, and associated worksheet materials. Creative Publications also produces math and science manipulatives, including fraction pieces, tangrams, learning links, linker cubes, play money, money stamps, pattern blocks, attribute blocks, and geoboards, as does Summit Learning. Many of these items can be acquired as components of math manipulative kits for various age and ability levels, including Cuisenaire rods. Finally, calculators that can be used on the overhead projector (Calc-u-vue) and matching student solar-powered calculators are available from Learning Resources and Delta Education. A textbook for functional math is provided by Staudacher and Turner (1994).

Computer Software and Technology

Computer software in mathematics has become widely available. Many programs could be used as supplements for practice activities for basic fact acquisition and some for problem-solving activities. Some basic math skill programs include Number Facts series (Gamco Industries) and Math Blaster (Optimum Resource). Problem-solving programs that are available include Math Problem Solver series (Curriculum Associates), Word Problem Square Off series, Math Word Problem series (Gamco), and Stickybear Math Word Problem Solving (Optimum Resource). Optimum Resource also distributes Stickybear Math Splash and Stickybear Math Town. Sunburst produces Math Connections: Algebra, Pre-Algebra World, and Fraction Attraction. DK Interactive Learning distributes I Love Math, an interactive, motivational program. Edmark produces the Mighty Math series, as well as Zoo Zillions, Astro Algebra, and Cosmic Geometry. Gamco distributes the Math Concepts series and Money Challenge/Discover Time. See Appendix B for a list of addresses of producers and distributors of software and curricular materials.

INCLUSION FEATURE

Peer Assistants in Math

Math can be an extremely difficult academic task for many students with disabilities. Some research has indicated that peers can help students with disabilities improve their performance in math (e.g., Slavin, 1997). Cooperative learning and peer tutoring have been successfully implemented in math classes. In cooperative learning, students with and without disabilities are placed in heterogeneous cooperative groups of three to five students, with usually only one student with disabilities per group. During the cooperative learning, students help one another complete their math assignments, and group contingencies or rewards are distributed to students based on the entire group's performance, including the average of their member's learning. In this way, individual accountability becomes an important factor for the group. It is in the best interest of the group to help each individual member perform well. It is hypothesized that group contingencies motivate students to do a good job of explaining concepts and skills to their partners during math.

Other researchers have investigated whether the size of the group during such learning activities appears to influence performance among students (Fuchs, Fuchs, Kazdan, et al., 2000). These findings indicated that pairs of students performed consistently higher academically than small groups. When implementing some form of peer groupings in math, consider the following:

- Arranging groups
    select students who will work well together
    maintain groups of two when possible

- Preparing students to work with partners or in small groups
    establish social behavior rules and responsibilities
    establish academic task rules and responsibilities
        teach students roles and responsibilities when working with partners
        and in small groups

- Arrange contingency rewards that include individual accountability

- Monitor student and partner and group performances

Using Multimedia and Contextualized Problems to Teach Math

Contextualized problems have their basis in life and appear as real-life problems to students. Recent research has shown that when students with disabilities are taught contextualized math problems using multimedia, their performance is enhanced significantly (e.g., Goldman, & Hasselbring, 1997; Hasselbring & Moore, 1996). These researchers and their colleagues developed a video-based series called *The Adventures of Jasper Woodbury* and *Ben's Pet Project* that cover content areas in math, including algebra, geometry, trip planning, and statistics by using real-life, interesting stories. The content is presented on a CD-ROM to ensure that students can replay any episodes. *Ben's Pet Project* begins with Ben reading and hearing information about a lumber sale in the background. Ben and his friend later visit a pet store and think about purchasing a pet. Later they have to determine whether they will have enough money to purchase the pet and a cage for the pet. The story proceeds in an interesting manner, and students become engaged in problem solving by gathering all the facts. Moreover, as in real life, not all the facts are supplied neatly in the video, and students must select relevant from irrelevant facts. To solve the problems, students must identify all the subproblems and understand where and how to use procedural knowledge. Findings have indicated that students taught using anchored approaches such as these have outperformed their control counterparts (Botte & Hasselbring, 1993).

Chapter 8

ℑ   ℑ   ℑ

Science and Social Studies

The teaching of science and social studies is often given a lower priority in special education. Because many special education students are greatly in need of basic skills remediation, the additional time required to teach basic reading, math, and language often replaces time conventionally allotted to areas such as geography, history, or zoology. It is true that basic skills are of primary importance; however, it is also true that special education students have as great a need as anyone else to learn about the world around them. Time should be allocated to ensure that all students acquire not only basic skills but also a knowledge of, and curiosity about, their world.

Curriculum specialists have long advocated specialized teaching procedures for science and social studies. Science specialists have often recommended teaching by the discovery or inquiry method—that is, that teachers act as facilitators to the students' own "scientific discoveries" of basic principles. Such techniques, it is argued, provide an experiential basis to science and provide insight into scientific methods. Similarly, social studies curriculum specialists have advocated Socratic inquiry methods in which students are prompted to use their own reasoning to arrive at relevant concepts, relationships, and ethical or moral principles. Although each of these approaches has its particular strengths, it should be remembered that instructional procedures should reflect instructional objectives; that is, if specific deductive reasoning strategies are the instructional objectives, then deductive reasoning strategies should be taught. If learning scientific procedures is the objective, then scientific procedures should be taught. Likewise, if moral reasoning is

an objective, that is what should be taught. However, content area instruction, including science, history, and geography, also includes as objectives the learning of factual information (including classification systems), concepts, rules, and procedures, as does any other content area. Furthermore, these learning tasks must also be taught initially through accuracy levels to fluency, application, and generalization levels of learning. Teachers must consult with school administration and teaching personnel to help determine the most appropriate instructional objectives for their students.

A final issue for consideration concerns the primary setting for content area instruction. Some special education students who exhibit great difficulty on basic skills tasks, such as reading age-appropriate material independently, note taking and study skills, and writing skills, may receive science and social studies instruction in a special education setting. Other students may receive instruction in an inclusive classroom and additional help in study skills or other areas from the special education teacher. The distinction here is between a special educator in a primary role of delivering content area information or in a secondary, supportive role of providing assistance in study skills. Consultation with parents, other teachers, administrators, and students themselves, as well as an objective evaluation of necessary prerequisite skills, can help determine the best placement for the student and the optimal role of the special education teacher.

Science and social studies comprise content areas of enormous variety, and it is certainly beyond the scope of this chapter to cover more than the basic elements of science and social studies instruction. This chapter will, however, provide a general overview of typical science and social studies content, followed by some procedures for delivery of instruction in these specific areas.

Science

Most science content can be divided into *life science*, which is the study of living things and includes botany, zoology, and anatomy; and *earth and physical science*, which is the study of physical concepts and laws and includes geology, paleontology, chemistry, physics, electricity, and astronomy. These two areas are described separately.

Life Science

Life science is fundamentally concerned with classification and description of living things, their interaction, and their environments. Concept learning and fact learning play important roles in teaching life science. For instance, a fundamental distinction made in the classification of living things is between plants and animals

(excluding, for the moment, fungi, protists, and prokaryotes). These two *kingdoms* are actually concepts and must be taught as such. As described in previous chapters, concepts can be said to have been acquired when the learner can independently identify novel instances and noninstances of the concept. In this case, the students have acquired the concepts of plants and animals when they can accurately identify plants or animals that they have not seen before. Concepts are usually taught by providing a general rule or set of rules and providing sufficient practice on identifying instances or noninstances of the concept.

Animals

The early discrimination between plants and animals is a relatively simple one that can usually be acquired simply by provision of instances and noninstances. More difficult concepts and definitions may require the provision of rules for aiding the discrimination. Table 8.1 provides a table of specifications for the classification of animals. Note that this is a very general table that can be modified to address the needs of specific students

Table 8.1. Table of Specifications for Classification of Vertebrate Animals

| | BEHAVIOR | | | | |
| | Identification | Production | | | |
CONTENT	A. Acquisition	B. Acquisition	C. Fluency	D. Application	E. Generalization
1. *Fish*	1A	1B	1C	1D	1E
2. *Amphibian*	2A	2B	2C	2D	2E
3. *Reptile*	3A	3B	3C	3D	3E
4. *Mammal*	4A	4B	4C	4D	4E
5. *Bird*	5A	5B	5C	5D	5E

Sample Objectives:

1A   Given 20 drawings containing one fish and four nonfish animal distractors, student will correctly circle the fish in all cases.

2B   Student will orally provide a correct definition of amphibian and describe common characteristics.

3C   Within 30 seconds, student will orally provide a definition of reptile and describe common characteristics of reptiles.

4D   Student will describe mammals and their characteristics after reading classroom materials about mammals.

5E   Student will identify birds and describe relevant characteristics of birds on a class field trip.

(e.g., the table can be expanded to include more detailed information). For example, a major discrimination within the animal kingdom is between *vertebrates* and *invertebrates*. Students must be first taught that the vocabulary word *vertebrate* means backbone and refers to an internal skeleton. Specific rules can be of help in promoting the early discrimination between vertebrates and invertebrates. For example, if an organism looks like a bug, worm, shellfish, or octopus, it is probably an invertebrate. One way of getting across the concept of vertebrates so that students can make appropriate discriminations is simply to teach the five classifications of vertebrates: fish, amphibian, reptile, mammal, and bird. However, before this is done, it is simpler to provide general instances and noninstances of vertebrates until students have learned the concept in a general way. At first it might be helpful to display pictures or drawings of vertebrates in which the skeletons can be seen.

When students have learned the basic discrimination between invertebrates and vertebrates, they can begin to learn about different kinds of vertebrates and invertebrates. It may be easier to start with vertebrates because these animals are likely to be more well known to students than invertebrates. As stated earlier, the five classifications of vertebrates are fish, amphibian, reptile, mammal, and bird. The learning of this serial list may be promoted by the provision of a mnemonic, first-letter strategy—in this case, the acronym FARM-B (F for fish, A for amphibian, R for reptile, and so on). They should be told to remember FARM-B for classification of vertebrates because most farm animals, such as cows, chickens, and horses, are vertebrates.

Following learning of the serial list, students must master the five classification concepts so that they can discriminate between the different kinds of vertebrates and state the important attributes or characteristics associated with each classification. For example, attributes of fish are that they (a) are cold blooded, (b) breathe through gills, (c) have scales, and (d) live in the water. Drill-and-practice techniques and the provision of multiple examples are helpful in learning these attributes. In addition, students should be regularly assessed on their ability to discriminate between different types of vertebrates and to state reasons for making the discriminations. For example, students can be provided a worksheet containing pictures of different kinds of vertebrates and asked to write the type of vertebrate beneath each picture. If students possess fluent writing ability, they can be asked to state why they classified each animal as a certain type of vertebrate. If students have not yet learned writing skills, they can be asked to state their reasons orally. Pictures, books, media, and living examples can also be very helpful. Drill and practice, cumulative review, and frequent formative data collection procedures will facilitate learning and allow the teacher to make instructional decisions. Extended discussion of individual animals, their behavior and characteristics, can also help enforce relevant concepts.

When students have learned about the classification and characteristics of vertebrates, they can learn about invertebrates. For example, a distinction can be made between *mollusks*, including animals with soft bodies such as small snails, bivalves (such as clams), and squidlike animals, and *arthropods*, including animals with jointed legs such as spiders, crabs, lobsters, and insects. Students should be taught to discriminate between mollusks and arthropods in the same manner as they were taught to discriminate between types of vertebrates: Many instances and noninstances of each concept should be provided, along with rules to guide the discrimination between mollusks and arthropods. Finally, guided and independent practice on making such discriminations should be provided, and formative data should be collected. Excerpts from a possible lesson are provided in Figure 8.1. When these discriminations have been learned, further subdivisions, such as the division of arthropods into arachnids (spiders) and insects, are taught. Because spiders and some insects are similar in appearance, provision of specific rules is necessary to promote understanding; that is, spiders have eight legs and two body parts, whereas insects have six legs and three body parts. In all

Component	Examples
Daily review	"Last month, we learned about vertebrates. Tell me what a vertebrate is, Michelle. [Answers.] Correct. A vertebrate has an internal skeleton. Now, last week we started talking about invertebrates. What is an invertebrate, Robert?"
State purpose	"Today we will learn about two kinds of invertebrates. One kind is called a mollusk. Everyone say it with me. [Signal.] Mollusk. The other kind . . ."
Deliver information	"Many mollusks have shells and live in the sea, like clams. [Show picture.] Some have shells and live on land, like snails. [Show picture.] Some live in the sea and don't have shells, like the octopus. [Show picture.] But, except for the shell, they all have soft bodies. What do they all have? [Signal.] . . ."
	"Now, the other kind of invertebrate I want to tell you about is the arthropod. Arthropods are animals like insects, spiders, and centipedes—like the animals in these pictures. [Show pictures.] Remember, animals that look like bugs are called arthropods. Hard-shelled sea animals are also called arthropods, like these crabs and lobsters. [Show picture.] But all arthropods have jointed legs. What do all arthropods have? [Signal.] Correct. All arthropods have jointed legs, like these. [Show pictures.] . . ."
	"Now lets try some more examples. [Show picture.] Is this animal an arthropod or a mollusk, Mary? [Answers.] Correct, it is a mollusk. How do you know it is a mollusk, Robert? . . . [Present several additional examples and question entire class.]"
Guided practice	"Now I'm going to give everybody a worksheet, and we can do this one together. First, look at picture number one. Now, everybody write the letter *M* under the picture if it is a mollusk and *A* if it is an arthropod. Do it now, and we'll check your answers together . . ."
	"How do we know if an animal is a mollusk? [Signal for class response.] Correct. How do we know if an animal is an arthropod? [Signal for class response.] Correct. . . . Now, what is the answer to number one?"
Independent practice	"Now that we've gone over the directions and samples for the new worksheet, I want everyone to do these by themselves at their desks. . . ."
Formative evaluation	"Everybody clear your desk and we'll have a little test on arthropods and mollusks."

Figure 8.1. Lesson on mollusks and arthropods.

instruction, it is critical to observe the principles of effective instruction used in previous areas: review, introduction, presentation, guided practice, independent practice, and formative evaluation. Again, presentation and discussion of individual spiders and insects, their behavior and characteristics, can help promote learning of relevant concepts.

Observational and Experiential Learning

Few educators would recommend that life sciences be taught simply as a list of facts and concepts without provision of observation or experience with the plants and animals being studied. There are three major methods of providing experience outside of the regular curriculum materials: media presentations, outside activities, and exhibiting animals in the classroom.

Media Presentations

Films, videotapes and videodisks, and the Internet can be extremely helpful in showing students a number of living things that they may not have had an opportunity to see for themselves. In addition, media presentations can be used to increase interest and curiosity about living things. All media presentations should enhance prespecified objectives for the science unit. Teachers should preview media presentations and become familiar with the machinery used to present the information. Class time should not be wasted with an irrelevant film, nor should class time be lost because the teacher is not familiar with instructional media equipment. If instructional media are to be used, the teacher should be able to specify the objectives involved in the presentation and the procedures by which the objectives can be evaluated. For instance, if the objective of presenting a particular videotape is to provide specific information on the distinction between frogs and toads and to provide several attributes unique to each type of amphibian, determine prior to the presentation what types of questions students should be able to answer at the end of the presentation. In addition, students should be made aware of the purpose of the presentation and the information they are expected to acquire. For example, a teacher could introduce the filmstrip by saying the following: "We have been learning about different types of amphibians. What do we know about amphibians? [Solicit responses and provide feedback.] Today we are going to see a filmstrip about two kinds of amphibians, frogs and toads. Who can tell us something about frogs and toads? [Solicit responses and provide feedback.] When the filmstrip is over, you should be able to tell me three ways of telling frogs and toads apart. Are you ready? [Show filmstrip.]" When the filmstrip is over, the teacher can determine, through verbal questioning or a worksheet activity, whether the information has been learned.

One particular shortcoming of media presentations in special education is that new information is typically presented only once, and students have no opportunity to practice the information. Make sure that important information has been practiced to the point where it will be remembered. Media presentations can be interesting and enriching experiences but are, in themselves, no guarantee that the information will be remembered. Additional instructional activities, possibly including repeated presentations, may be necessary to ensure learning and retention.

Outside Activities

In some cases, teachers may wish to take their students to a nearby field, pond, or other natural community to observe animals in their natural habitat or to collect specimens of insects or other animals. Such activities can be very helpful in extending the experiential base needed to make learned information more meaningful. However, as with media presentations, it is important that (a) objectives relevant to the activity be developed, (b) students be informed of the objectives, (c) activities be carefully planned and specified ahead of time, and (d) means be developed for evaluating whether objectives have been met. For example, "to observe a pond community" is an objective that has not been specified carefully enough and does not lend itself to more than the simplest evaluation of outcomes. Finally, such an objective does not impart to students a clear idea of what behavior is expected of them. If, however, the objective is for students to record their observations in a notebook; collect as many observations as possible of insects, arachnids, and amphibians; and classify them correctly, students and teachers are both aware of the purpose and expectations of the visit.

An activity such as the one just described can be regarded as a generalization activity in that classroom knowledge is being applied in a real-world setting. To this end, outside activities should be carefully specified and evaluated. It should also be remembered that outside activities are typically less structured and familiar to students than routine classroom activities and, as such, have potential for aggravating behavioral problems. To avoid such a situation, teachers should be certain that students are aware of the behavior expected of them as well as the consequences for appropriate and inappropriate behavior.

Classroom Exhibits

Teachers may wish to exhibit, or allow their students or community to exhibit, animals from other settings. A wide variety of animals appropriate for classroom display is available from biological supply companies. Students may benefit experientially from the direct contact that such exhibits provide. As with other experiential activities, however, objectives for these activities should be specified ahead of time, along with the procedures by which these objectives can be monitored. Exhibits can be highly effective supplements to instruction; however, they should not be considered replacements for direct teaching of important concepts, facts, and rules.

Before obtaining animals for the classroom, a number of considerations should be made, including the following:

- Check out any restrictions your school might have about classroom animals.

- Consider the specific characteristics of animals before they are acquired. For example, hamsters are generally nocturnal and may not be particularly active during school hours. Reptiles must be kept warm or they will not eat, and they may catch "colds" and die. Newts will have difficulty detecting food if the water is not kept clean. Crayfish are susceptible to diseases that can spread rapidly among other crayfish.

- Some students have allergies to specific animals, so be sure to acquire animals that will not cause allergic reactions.

- If you order animals from a supply catalogue, make sure the outside weather is appropriate for the animal and that someone will be available to attend to the animals as soon as they are received. Consider the season of the year (e.g., butterflies cannot be released in northern climates during the winter).

- Some animals require live food, so consider the implications of this on your class. Also, some students may be prone to abuse animals, so be sure the animals are well protected. Protect animals also from student "kindness" (e.g., many fish die from overfeeding by well-meaning students).

One positive use of classroom exhibits is the demonstration of life cycles. Insects such as butterflies and amphibians such as frogs can provide very useful demonstrations of life cycles. When employing such exhibits, however, be certain that the observational experiences are paired with appropriate instruction targeted toward specific objectives; students will not necessarily learn all relevant information about life cycles simply because certain animals have been in the classroom.

Another typical experiential activity is the use of animals as classroom pets. Newts, fish, hamsters, rabbits, guinea pigs, and birds are frequently seen in classrooms. Such pets are not only a common source of enjoyment for students but can also provide opportunities for observation of the growth and behavior patterns of particular animals over time. Classroom pets can also form the basis for procedural learning of the care and feeding of such animals. Important activities necessary for the care of the animal can be divided among the students, who can gain important insights concerning their own responsibilities to such animals. As with other activities, however, objectives should be clearly specified, and procedures for evaluating such activities should be developed.

Plants

Instruction in classification and characteristics of plants can parallel instruction in animal life. As in the previous section, major classification systems of plant life are taught using procedures for promoting discrimination learning and concept learning. In addition, attributes of specific types of plants can be taught as facts. Enhancement of classroom learning can be achieved through media presentations, and outdoor activities can do much to enhance knowledge of plant life, particularly when such activities are undertaken with respect to specific instructional objectives (see Figure 8.2). Finally, plants of many different kinds can be raised in the classroom and cared for over time by all students assuming different roles. Growing plants from seeds can also be a rewarding learning activity. As in any special education instruction, objectives should parallel the scope and sequence of objectives in the regular classroom to as great an extent as possible.

When acquiring classroom plants, be sure that they will be able to grow appropriately in the environment provided. Plants frequently die from overwatering, so be sure to implement a watering schedule suited to the plant. When raising plants from seeds, consider the germination period of the plant, so that sufficient growth can be observed over the course of the relevant academic unit. Use glass terrariums, plastic bags, or hydroponic environments when appropriate to facilitate observation of root development. Remember, plants can promote development of molds, so consider whether this might create allergy problems for some students.

Anatomy

Anatomy is the study of the structure and function of the human body. The study of anatomy is important to special education because of the relationship between anatomy and other areas

Component	Examples
Daily review	"We have been learning about oak, maple, and walnut leaves. [Hold up leaf.] Which kind of leaf is this one, Bill? . . ."
State purpose	"Today we are going to go outside, and I want each student to find three oak leaves from different trees, three maple leaves from different trees, and three walnut leaves from different trees. What are you going to do, Mary? . . ."
Provide information	"The first thing I want you to do when we start is to get your coats on. Then we will leave the classroom and the building quietly. Then I want everyone to follow me to the trees . . ."
Guided practice	[Outside] "Now, everyone look on the ground under this tree and see if you can find a maple leaf. Show me when you've found one . . ."
Independent practice	"Okay, now everyone finish by yourself: collect three maple, three oak, and three walnut leaves from different trees. . . ."
Formative evaluation	[Classroom] "Everybody put your leaves on the table in groups, and I'll check them. . . ."

Figure 8.2. Plant lesson with outdoor application activity.

such as health, nutrition, and physical education. The study of anatomy is also relevant to sex education, although this is a controversial topic in some school districts and should be taught only with the approval of the school administration and parent groups.

Anatomy is concerned with the structure and function of different organs and organ systems of the human body. Usually, one organ system (e.g., respiratory, circulatory, nervous, digestive, or reproductive) is studied at a time. Unlike the study of plants and animals, organ systems do not form a particular hierarchy of classification. In addition, the study of anatomy is finite in that there is only one example of a particular organ. Because of this, anatomy is more likely to emphasize the learning of facts rather than concepts, rules, or discriminations. For example, there is only one instance (in the human species) of a pancreas, but there are many different instances of amphibians. Teaching about amphibians, then, requires the teaching of rules, discriminations, and instances and noninstances of the concept *amphibian*. Teaching about the pancreas, however, requires the teaching of facts regarding the structure and function of this organ.

A typical anatomy lesson would be taught using the same teacher effectiveness principles described in this and previous chapters. After the review of previous instruction, the teacher specifies the overall objective for the present lesson (e.g., "Today we are going to learn about the circulatory system of the human body") and the specific objectives (e.g., "We will learn the parts of the heart and how they work together to keep the blood flowing"). Following the introduction, the teacher presents the information to be learned, questions students, and provides feedback on their responses. Following this, a guided practice activity is provided; for example, students label the parts of a human heart on a worksheet. Students can complete such activities independently once they have reached a certain level of accuracy (about 90%). Generalization of this information can be developed by having students assemble a commercial model of a human heart and describe the relevant anatomical details as they

do so. They could also draw and label parts of a heart from memory or identify similar parts in a cow's or sheep's heart. Future lessons on the circulatory system could focus on the structure and function of blood and the blood vessels. For a related health activity, students could learn about cholesterol, its effects on the circulatory system, and what dietary changes can prevent cholesterol problems. Students can also receive lessons on the effect of cigarette smoking on the circulatory system. As in other areas in the life sciences, instructional media and models can be helpful in making the information more concrete and in enriching the experiential basis of learning. As with other uses of instructional media, however, teachers should be careful to demonstrate that specific objectives are being met by the presentation of such instructional media. Finally, the scope and sequence of instructional objectives should follow a specific table of specifications that parallels the district scope and sequence of objectives. The extent to which students have met these objectives should be documented by formative evaluation techniques.

Earth and Physical Sciences

Earth and physical sciences are generally more abstract and further removed from students' everyday experience than life sciences and, consequently, may be more difficult to learn than life sciences, particularly for students who exhibit difficulty with abstract thinking. Teachers, then, should make the information as concrete as possible and incorporate evaluation techniques that address whether students demonstrate real understanding of the information being taught. For example, for students to demonstrate that they understand principles of electricity, they should not only be able to recite the principles but also be able to describe how a specific wiring diagram would be expected to produce a specific effect.

The earth and physical sciences include such fields of study as geology, astronomy, electricity, chemistry, and physics. The remainder of this section will describe geology and astronomy.

Geology

Geology is the study of the history and structure of the earth as recorded in rocks. It encompasses the earth's structure, function, composition, surface features, and history. The study of fossils in the rocks, as well as the life forms they describe, is referred to as paleontology and can be studied in a manner similar to the life sciences. Geology instruction can involve the classification and description of various rocks and minerals. *Minerals* are homogeneous crystalline substances, such as gold or quartz, whereas *rocks* are composed of different types of mineral or nonmineral substances. Generally, students can be taught the different classifications of rocks (igneous, metamorphic, sedimentary) and their specific attributes, including common or specific uses of different rocks and minerals. Instruction in this area generally parallels instruction in life sciences; that is, initial classifications and discriminations are taught using discrimination, concept, and rule learning. They are also tested similarly in that students are expected to identify novel instances of such types of rocks as igneous or sedimentary. Specific types of rocks and minerals (e.g., quartz, feldspar, turquoise) can be described with respect to specific attributes (such as common colors or streaks, hardness, luster, and use). The overall purpose of instruction is to teach students about the composition of the earth and the ways rocks and minerals have been used in the world around them. A sample lesson is excerpted in Figure 8.3.

Another important aspect of geology is the overall composition and character of the earth itself. Instruction includes the composition of rocks and minerals in the different layers of the earth and the interaction of these layers, which is responsible for volcanoes, earthquakes, and mountain formation. Relevant to the "big ideas" strategies described in Chapter 7 for teaching volume formulae in mathematics, "big ideas" can be applied to unifying concepts in science. Woodward and Noell (1992) described the principle of *convection*, which refers to the roughly circular flow of molecules when they are heated. Once the principle of convection is understood,

Component	Examples
Daily review	"Last Tuesday we talked about igneous rocks. Tell me what igneous rocks are, Arnold . . . ."
State purpose	"Today we are going to study sedimentary rocks . . ."
Delivery of information	"A sedimentary rock is one that is made of material that has settled at the bottom of an ocean or lake. It starts out as small particles, like sand, that get cemented together under pressure and through time. Look at the screen, and I'll show you some examples of sedimentary rock . . ."
Guided practice	"Now I'm going to show you some specimens, and each of you write whether each specimen is a sedimentary or igneous rock. When you have written each answer, we will check them together."
Independent practice	"Now turn to page 156 in your book. You will see a number of rocks pictured. Number your paper from 1 to 20 and write an *I* if the rock is igneous, and write an *S* if the rock sedimentary. . . ."
Formative evaluation	"All right, trade papers with your neighbor, and we will check your work."

Figure 8.3. Sample lesson on rocks.

it can be applied to understand relevant concepts involving plate tectonics, earthquakes, volcanic activity, and mountain building near coastal regions. Finding ways of combining concepts into "big ideas" can be a particularly effective strategy in special education, where students may feel overwhelmed with seemingly endless details in the array of material to be learned.

Astronomy

Astronomy is the study of the stars, planets, and other extraterrestrial phenomena such as comets, asteroids, and meteorites. One difficulty in teaching astronomy is that much of the information must be conveyed through pictures rather than direct observation. Heavenly bodies that can be directly observed, including planets, constellations, the Milky Way, and the moon in different phases, cannot usually be seen during school hours and must be simulated in some way. Pictures, models, and media presentations, including videotape and videodisk, can be helpful in providing information. The Internet can also provide a great deal of relevant information about astronomy. The NASA/Goddard Space Flight Center has a Web page that also includes links to student activities and curriculum for teachers and can be reached at www.gsfc.nasa.gov/education/education_home.html.

Basic concepts and discriminations (e.g., meteor versus meteorite, star versus planet, galaxy versus nebula) can be taught using the procedures described throughout this book, including rule learning and provision of sufficient instances and noninstances of specific concepts. Again, a detailed table of specifications and formative evaluation procedures can ensure that objectives are being met.

Hands-On Science

Many professional science organizations today recommend the use of "hands-on" curriculum materials for teaching science. These materials de-emphasize the use of textbooks and paper-and-pencil activities in favor of direct manipulation of scientific phenomena brought into the classroom. For example, students observe cell structure with microscopes, grow plants under varying conditions and record growth rates, observe and record the properties of various rocks and minerals, create series and parallel electrical circuits and construct electric motors and telegraphs, predict and record the movement of a pendulum under different conditions, and re-create landforms in miniature. Instead of simply reading about science, students are provided with the opportunity to interact directly with science materials using scientific methods.

It has been argued that hands-on science activities are particularly helpful for younger students and for students with mild disabilities because these activities place less emphasis on basic skills such as reading and writing, present information at a high level of concreteness and meaningfulness, and can be highly motivating for students who are often uninspired by textbooks and worksheets. Furthermore, research has suggested that students with mild disabilities learn more with hands-on science materials and prefer them over the use of traditional textbook and worksheet activities. Including students with mild disabilities into cooperative groups of normally achieving students doing hands-on science may be more successful than placing students with mild disabilities into inclusive science classes that use traditional curriculum materials. Because of the amount of materials required in hands-on science approaches, it is usually necessary for students to work in groups and share materials. Sometimes different roles are assigned to group members, and different roles can be matched to individual strengths and interests. In the Full Option Science System (FOSS; Britannica), each group consists of four members: the "reader," the "recorder," the "getter," and the "starter." Other models are more flexible, using smaller or larger groups when appropriate and planning for more helping or tutoring roles. These cooperative group situations potentially are more accommodating for many students with special needs than approaches requiring independent work on textbooks and worksheets.

Mastropieri et al. (1998) described the application of a hands-on unit on ecosystems in an inclusive fourth-grade science class, which contained a number of students with disabilities. Students met in cooperative groups and constructed interactive terrariums and aquariums ("eco-columns"), each of which contained plant and animal life, using the *Science and Technology for Children* (STC) materials (distributed by Carolina Biological Supply Company). The terrariums and aquariums were interconnected, so that water evaporating from the aquarium passed through the terrarium and then condensed as "rain," which fell onto the plants in the terrarium and drained back into the aquarium. Crickets in the terrarium and guppies in the aquarium fed on the plants and controlled their growth. The "eco-columns" were then paired for scientific experiments to test the effects of different amounts of fertilizer, acidic "rain," and road salt on the ecosystems. Students made predictions, recorded observations, and drew conclusions about the results of their experiments. After the unit was over, students were tested, and their scores were compared with students in other fourth-grade classes who had studied the same ecosystems content from textbooks. Students in the hands-on class far outperformed students in the other classes on tests of factual learning as well as tests of application and generalization of learned content. Furthermore, students with disabilities scored at about the middle (rather than the bottom) of the inclusive, hands-on science class. Students in this class also reported much higher levels of enjoyment of science and interest in science learning.

Proponents of hands-on science often emphasize teaching "process" skills over the teaching of facts. These process skills include such things as observing, classifying, predicting, inferring, and hypothesizing. As applied to real-world tasks, experience using these process skills could be very

beneficial to students with mild disabilities. For instance, students can be presented with deflated balloons placed on each side of a balance. They can then be asked whether they think air weighs anything and asked to predict what would happen if one of the balloons were inflated and then replaced on one side of the balance. When they complete the activity, students describe their observations and explain why the outcome was different from or the same as what they had predicted. Such activities, appropriately structured, could help students develop their thinking skills and become more confident in their own ability to understand and explain the world around them.

However, there are also some potential drawbacks to the use of these materials. Students who have not learned appropriate social behavior may interact inappropriately with science materials or with other students in cooperative group situations. Furthermore, if, as sometimes occurs, unstructured "discovery" activities are employed with these materials, some students with mild disabilities may not be able to move through the activities or the reasoning processes as rapidly as their regular class peers.

Nevertheless, with appropriate modifications, these potential drawbacks often can be overcome. Teachers can determine the social skills prerequisites for such learning and ensure that individual special needs students have learned these skills. Also, if the activities are sufficiently rewarding, students' participation can be made contingent on appropriate behavior. Likewise, if questioning is carefully structured, students can be coached through thinking processes, by teachers or trained peers, and led to make their own conclusions, rather than simply becoming confused or waiting for other students to answer. Research has suggested that such coaching, if done carefully, can increase learning and retention. For example, the teacher may have just pointed out from a picture or video that camels have two long sets of eyelashes. Rather than simply providing an explanation and asking the student to repeat it, the teacher may choose to coach the student through the explanation, using strategies for promoting thinking skills, as shown in the following dialogue:

TEACHER: Why do you think camels may have two sets of eyelashes?

STUDENT: I don't know . . .

TEACHER: Well, let's think it through, using information we already know. What do you know about camels?

STUDENT: They don't have to drink much water, 'cause they live in the desert.

TEACHER: Good! And what's it like in the desert?

STUDENT: Hot, dry.

TEACHER: Hot, dry, what else?

STUDENT: It's sandy and windy.

TEACHER: Sandy and windy, good. So, if it's sandy and windy in the desert, why do you think camels have two sets of eyelashes?

STUDENT: Oh! To keep the sand out of their eyes.

TEACHER: Exactly.

Research has suggested that students with mild disabilities learn, comprehend, and remember information better if they are coached to think it through themselves than if they simply are told the information. However, the coaching must be carefully structured and adapted to meet the needs of individual learners.

Finally, additional time may be required to allow students with mild disabilities to repeat science activities and practice the necessary skills (e.g., measuring, using specific apparatus such as microscopes). It is important that individual students' contributions are carefully monitored to ensure that all students are meeting their personal objectives.

Several different versions of hands-on science materials are currently available and are listed at the end of this chapter. Some things to look for in choosing hands-on science curriculum mate-

rials are clear, explicit description of classroom activities; sufficient information for teachers; and evaluation materials that help teachers determine that target information and skills are being acquired. It is also important to ensure that the materials help students meet objectives relevant to the general education curriculum, particularly if they will be taking state competency tests in these areas. When employing these activities, it is helpful to be certain that students understand all rules and activity expectations before they begin handling the materials. It may also be found that some activities are learned best when they are undertaken more than once. With the first presentation, students can concentrate on mastering the required manipulative skills. With additional presentations of the same or only slightly modified activity, students can concentrate more on the underlying concepts being studied. Mastropieri and Scruggs (1994a) have listed specific recommendations for teaching the various units covered with hands-on science activities.

Social Studies

Social studies involves the study of people and their institutions and encompasses such areas as state and local history, U.S. history, world history, and geography, as well as constitution, government, civics, and political science. Most people consider a basic knowledge and understanding of history, geography, and government essential to public education. This section will consider these three areas in turn.

History

History in secondary schools is usually subdivided into state and local, United States, and world history content areas. Some students are not enrolled in inclusive classes and must, therefore, learn history content in special education classrooms. Special education teachers should consult with regular classroom teachers and administrators to determine the optimal scope and sequence of objectives for the students. If these objectives have not been clearly specified in general education classes, special education teachers should adapt objectives from existing textbooks and other classroom materials. Students in special classes should pass through content as similar as possible to that used in general education classes in the appropriate grade levels, so that they will be more likely to function independently when they do enter inclusive classes.

Much of what is taught in history classes involves learning of facts and concepts. Although it is very important to analyze, synthesize, and evaluate historical events and situations, in most cases, historical facts and concepts comprise a significant component of the content taught and tested.

Students with serious reading problems will not be able to learn historical information from age-appropriate textbooks without accommodations. They can benefit, however, from clear teacher presentation of relevant information, as well as from visual information such as pictures from textbooks, filmstrips, videotapes, and films. After review, introduction, presentation questions, and feedback on historical information, guided and independent practice activities can be implemented. Students can be asked to match names of historical figures with accomplishments or to write brief answers to short written questions. Finally, as in all lessons, formative data can be collected on student progress. Excerpts from a sample lesson in U.S. history are given in Figure 8.4.

Component	Examples
Daily review	"Last week we were talking about the events that led to the War of 1812 between America and England. What were some of these events, Ed? . . ."
State purpose	"Today we are going to learn some more reasons why the War of 1812 was fought. . . ."
Provide information	"After the Revolutionary War, the Americans gained control of land west of the Appalachian Mountains. [Show on map.] However, the many Indian tribes that lived there became resentful of the encroachment of their lands. . . ."
	"Why did the Indians become resentful, Terry? [Answers.] Good. The white settlers were coming into their lands and beginning to destroy some of their hunting grounds. . . ."
	"The English in Canada saw this resentment develop and encouraged the Indians to attack the settlers. . . ."
	"These events led to the Battle of Tippecanoe, where the Indians were defeated by the army of William Henry Harrison. After the battle, many white American settlers felt there would never be peace with the Indians as long as the British were in Canada. Now, let's summarize what I said and write the points on the board. What did I say first, Bill? . . ."
Guided practice	"Now let's all read about these events in the chapter and answer some questions together. . . ."
Independent practice	"Now, finish the questions by yourself. . . ."
Formative evaluation	"When you finish, turn the papers in, and I'll tell you how well you did."

Figure 8.4. Sample history lesson.

In some school systems, mastery of basic facts and concepts associated with history and government is a requirement necessary for graduation and is evaluated on state competency tests. If this is the case, teachers should place specific emphasis on the mastery of those particular facts. In any case, access to the general education curriculum is a requirement of IDEA.

Geography

Geography deals with the natural features, climate, products, and inhabitants of different regions of the world. Again, special education teachers should attempt to incorporate objectives from the general education curriculum into their own scope and sequence of objectives.

Geography instruction involves the frequent use of maps—both to describe physical features of different regions and to show relationships between regions, whether in size or in proximity. For this reason, teachers should be certain that students fully understand the relevance and meaning of maps. To develop such understanding, teachers might start with a map of the classroom, so that students can match exactly the map features with classroom features. Students can be asked to construct their own symbols for chairs, desks, tables, and so on. When students have demonstrated this ability, maps of the school and the local community can be constructed. As the maps become larger and larger, students can begin to study broader areas, such as their state, region, or country.

Geography, of course, involves much more than the study of maps. Geography is also the study of the peoples who inhabit different regions of the earth. Again, the more meaningful the information is made, the more likely it is to be remembered. For example, it may be helpful to describe certain concepts, such as *fall line* (the point on a river near a coast beyond which ships cannot navigate). When students have learned this, as well as relevant geographical features (e.g., Appalachian piedmont, Atlantic coastal plain, major rivers), they should be able to identify the location of many eastern cities in the United States on a topographical map (e.g., Trenton, Philadelphia, Baltimore, Washington, Richmond, Augusta), rather than simply being told their location. This process is similar to the teaching of "big ideas" in math and science.

Textbook pictures and instructional media can be very helpful in enforcing relevant concepts. Additional drill-and-practice techniques can reinforce these facts and help ensure that they will be remembered. The National Geographic Society has a Web site (www.nationalgeographic.com/kids/index/html) that includes features, information, and activities for children.

Government

Constitution and government courses are often required for graduation from secondary schools, so teachers should ensure that students learn the necessary information. Much of this content is factual, so strategies for enhancing factual learning are appropriate. For example, in learning the organizational structure of the U.S. government, students must learn, among other things, that there are three major branches of government (executive, legislative, judicial), that each branch is associated with specific functions, that the executive branch consists of a president and the president's cabinet, that the legislative branch consists of the two houses of Congress (Senate and House of Representatives, with two senators per state and representatives based on state population), and that the judicial branch consists of the nine-member Supreme Court and the lower federal courts.

Courses in government can seem overwhelming to special education students who exhibit difficulty with memory and study skills. To cover the most information possible, teachers should first be certain that all of the information presented is essential to the objectives (remember "prioritize," from the PASS variables covered in Chapter 1). Teaching unnecessary facts not only consumes instructional time but also can make the learning of necessary facts more difficult. Second, teachers should provide careful sequencing of information, intensive drill and practice, and overlearning opportunities so that information will be retained. Third, efforts should be made to ensure that the information is presented in as meaningful a way as possible. To this end, media presentations that address specific objectives, models of government buildings, and pictures from textbooks can be helpful. Situations in which students act out various governmental roles or lifestyles of specific periods or create clothing and prepare foods from time periods and cultures can also be helpful in promoting comprehension. Discussing "executive," "legislative," and "judicial" functions in classroom, school, or home situations may help develop relevant concepts. Finally, formative data collection procedures can provide the teacher with information concerning how well the information is being learned.

Generalization tasks in this content area may take the form of producing correct responses on state competency tests taken outside the class; thus, preparing students to take such tests is important (see Chapter 9). Other generalization tasks include applying learned information to discussions about current events or issues, writing letters to specific government officials to acquire a Social Security number, and completing federal and state income tax forms. Additional generalization examples are provided in Chapter 11.

Special Problems and Strategies

Table 8.2 indicates many of the problems that are commonly encountered in science and social studies instruction. As seen in the table, some of these problems may involve lack of attention or poor social behavior. For these problems, some type of self-monitoring procedure may be helpful. If listening, note-taking, or test-taking skills are a problem, the student should be given instruction in these skills (see Chapter 9). Chapter 9 also provides suggestions for helping the student prepare research papers, if such skills are thought to be lacking. In a great number of cases, however, students may have difficulty learning and retaining factual information of the type that frequently appears on tests. Research has identified learning and memory problems as major factors contributing to failures in inclusive classrooms. Table 8.3 lists some techniques to use for improving memory for content area information. In the section that follows, we discuss organizational and mnemonic techniques in more detail.

Table 8.2. Problems in Content Area Instruction

Problem	Instructional Procedures
Paying attention	• Reteach preskills. • Teach listening and note-taking skills. • Teach self-monitoring procedures. • Monitor and reinforce attending.
Social behavior	• Be certain academic prerequisites are met. • Teach social skills. • Reinforce social behavior. • Teach self-monitoring procedures.
Factual learning	• Increase time-on-task for learning. • Make information more meaningful. • Teach organizational strategies. • Teach mnemonic strategies.
Study skills	• Teach skills outlined in Chapter 10.
Report writing	• Teach skills outlined in Chapter 10.

Table 8.3. Recommendations for Improving Memory

1. *Increase attention.* Students will certainly not remember what they have not attended to in the first place.

2. *Use external memory.* Whenever possible, have the student write things down, write on calendars, use checklists, or use stickers to help remember things.

3. *Enhance meaningfulness.* Relate new information to things the student already knows. Use lots of familiar examples when introducing new concepts.

4. *Use pictures or imagery.* Things are better remembered when they are pictured or imaged. Make sure students study pictures carefully and can describe all relevant details.

5. *Minimize irrelevant or interfering information.* Avoid digressions, and place most emphasis on the most important aspects of a topic.

6. *Promote active manipulation.* Use concrete examples of real things whenever possible, and encourage students to actively manipulate these examples. Have them describe their experiences during and after the activity.

7. *Promote active learning.* Prompt students to think about new facts and concepts for themselves (e.g., "Why do you think vultures have no feathers on their heads? What do you know about vultures that might help you figure this out?"). Encourage them to think of novel instances of new concepts ("Who can think of another example of a first-class lever?").

8. *Increase practice.* Find additional opportunities, even if only for a few minutes, for students to go over the important information again and gain additional engaged time-on-task.

9. *Use organizational strategies.* Material that is clearly presented in a well-organized format is easier to remember than material that is not well organized.

10. *Use mnemonic strategies.* Mnemonic strategies, when appropriate, have been extremely effective for students with mild disabilities.

Note. Adapted from *Guidelines for Effective Mainstreaming in Science*, by M. A. Mastropieri and T. E. Scruggs, 1993, West Lafayette, IN: Purdue Research Foundation. Adapted with permission.

Organizational Strategies

There are a variety of techniques for organizing content area information to enhance learning and memory. One of the simplest, outlining, should always be used because it conforms to the "structure" component of the SCREAM teacher presentation variables. Clear, direct, and simple outlines presented on an overhead projector or on the blackboard can help direct a teacher presentation and keep students informed of the organization and pace of the presentation. Some researchers have promoted the use of advance organizers, in which overall information is organized, at a higher level of abstraction, prior to the presentation of information. This strategy is intended to promote activation of prior knowledge and organized thinking about the concepts to be covered.

More complex organizational techniques involve spatial organization. This can be done in a "relationship" chart in which the things being studied (e.g., plants, minerals, rivers) are listed down the left side of the chart and attributes or characteristics of these things are listed across the top. For content that contains superordinate and subordinate concepts, a "relationship map" or "web" can be used (Bos & Anders, 1990a, 1990b). In this case, superordinate concepts and their descriptors are placed in a central location and enclosed in a circle or rectangle. Related concepts are clustered together and placed in "subordinate" circles or boxes, as can be seen in Figure 8.5.

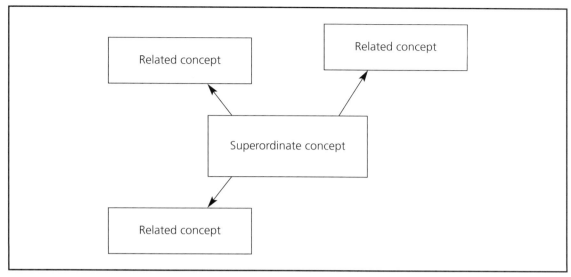

Figure 8.5. Related concepts cluster.

Sometimes such a spatial arrangement of content information is referred to as a "visual spatial display" (Darch & Carnine, 1986). "Concept diagrams" (Bulgren, Schumaker, & Deshler, 1988) list a new concept at the top of the chart, beneath which are definitions, characteristics, or attributes that are organized into *sometimes, always,* or *never* present. Below this can be instances and noninstances of the concept, organized into separate lists. For example, under the concept "monarchy," heredity power of kings or queens is always present, a female ruler is sometimes present, and free elections of rulers are never present. An instance could be France under Louis XIV in the 18th century, and a noninstance could be the Soviet Union under Stalin in the 20th century. Some researchers (e.g., Bos & Anders, 1990a, 1990b) have recommended an interactive teaching model in which the teacher and students collaborate in spatially organizing the content.

Englert and Mariage (1991) described the "POSSE" strategy. The letters in the acronym POSSE stand for predicting ideas, organizing predicted ideas, searching text structure, summarizing main ideas, and evaluating comprehension. Students are first taught to predict what information would be in the text, list it, and write relevant questions. For example, before reading about snakes, readers describe what they know about snakes and ask questions about what they do not know (Englert, Tarrant, Mariage, & Oxer, 1994). In the second step, students organize their thoughts in semantically related groups and present them in a visual display in which subordinate concepts are circled and placed around a superordinate concept. In the search and summarize steps, students study the text, identify main ideas, generate questions, and create another organizational diagram. Finally, they evaluate by comparing, clarifying, and predicting information learned from reading. They generate questions and record the answers on think sheets.

In general, information that is well organized is better understood and better remembered than information that is not. In some cases, spatial placement of target information (e.g., the meat eaters are all on the right side of the diagram) can help facilitate recall. However, although students with mild disabilities can remember the spatial placement of familiar information (e.g., tiger, rhinoceros), they are less likely to remember the spatial placement of unfamiliar information (e.g., rhodochrosite, ornitholestes). Teachers should ensure that information is meaningful and familiar before using spatial organizing strategies.

Independent Text Study Strategies

Many students with special learning needs can benefit from explicit instruction on strategies for studying expository text material, such as that found in science and social studies textbooks. Many of these strategies are described in Chapter 5 as reading comprehension strategies and in Chapter 7 as strategies for reading for later retrieval. These include strategies such as summarizing and sequencing, self-monitoring, and structured multiple readings of text. In addition, the organizational strategies described previously can also be adapted to independent study strategies. One strategy that seems particularly helpful for textbooks considers the structure of expository text (Bakken, Mastropieri, & Scruggs, 1997). Using this strategy, the student identifies the text structure of individual paragraphs. These can include time–order, cause–effect, compare–contrast, enumeration, sequence, classification, or main idea (Cook & Mayer, 1988). Then, structure-specific strategies are used to enhance recall. For example, if a main idea structure is identified, students identify and write down the main idea (e.g., photosynthesis), along with supporting statements. If an enumeration is identified, students write down the several items that are enumerated (e.g., a list of rivers in Germany). If a sequence structure is identified, students note the items in the specific order required (e.g., a sequence of steps in a scientific investigation or the sequence in which food passes through the digestive tract). Such use of text structure can be very beneficial for students with special learning needs.

Mnemonic Strategies

Some mnemonic techniques were discussed previously in the reading, language arts, and mathematics chapters. However, mnemonic strategies can be particularly effective for increasing content area learning and memory (Scruggs & Mastropieri, 2000). Mnemonic techniques have been very thoroughly researched in special education and have been employed successfully with students with learning disabilities, behavioral disorders, and mild mental disabilities across a variety of content areas and age levels. Three particularly effective mnemonic techniques are the keyword method, the pegword method, and letter strategies.

The Keyword Method

The keyword method was introduced in Chapter 6 in the context of vocabulary learning. However, the keyword method can also be very helpful for making content area information easier to remember. For example, to teach students to remember that the patriot Thomas Paine wrote the pamphlet, *Common Sense,* urging Americans to fight the British, teachers can create a keyword, such as *pain,* that sounds like Paine and can be pictured. A picture is then created (see Figure 8.6) of Thomas Paine having a pain from writing *Common Sense.* A woman in the picture says, "If you had common sense, you'd stop writing," to remind students of the name of the pamphlet.

Likewise, to help students remember that Antonie van Leeuwenhoek was an early microscope scientist, teachers can create the keyword *glue on hook* for *Leeuwenhoek* and show a picture of an early microscope being held in place with glue on a hook. To help students remember that George M. Cohan wrote the patriotic World War I song, "Over There," teachers can picture a child with an ice cream *cone* (keyword for Cohan). When asked where he bought it, the child points to an ice cream stand and sings, "Over there," as in Figure 8.7.

Keywords can also be used for word parts, which can be combined to form scientific terms. For example, to teach that *paleo-* means old, show a picture of old people carrying *pails* (keyword for *paleo–*). To teach that *-ology* means "the study of," show a picture of an owl (keyword for *–ology*) studying. To teach that zo- means animals, show a picture of animals in a zoo (keyword for zo–). Students can learn to apply these word

Figure 8.6. Thomas Paine (pain) wrote "Common Sense." From *Teaching Students Ways to Remember: Strategies for Learning Mnemonically,* by M. A. Mastropieri and T. E. Scruggs, 1991, Cambridge, MA: Brookline Books. Reprinted with permission.

parts to understand larger terms: paleontology = the study of old things; paleozoic era = the age of old animals, before dinosaurs; and zoology = the study of animals.

Keywords can also build on one another. To teach that the core of the earth is composed of iron and nickel, show an apple *core* (keyword for core) made with irons (for ironing clothes) and (5-cent) nickels. To teach that the earth's mantle is made of rock, show a *man* (keyword for mantle) made of solid rock. Indicate the earth's crust by drawing *crusts* of bread on the earth's mountains, plains and ocean floors. These pictures can then be combined in one illustration that shows the relative positions of these parts of the earth, as shown in Figure 8.8.

Keywords can also be used to show multiple attributes. To show that the Cenozoic era was characterized by the growth of mammals, the origin of humans, and ice ages, show a picture of a caveman (humans) with other mammals in an ice-age scene. The caveman is shown flipping a *cent,* keyword for *Cenozoic* (new animals) era.

Keywords have also been shown to help spatial learning, such as recall of map features. For example, a tiger (keyword for *Fort Ticonderoga*) placed correctly on a map may facilitate learning of the location of Fort Ticonderoga, more than just providing the name in the appropriate location.

Finally, keywords can be used as both the stimulus (question) and the response (answer) terms. For example, to help students remember that the capital of Arkansas is Little Rock, teachers can show students a picture of Noah's *Ark* (keyword for Arkansas) landing on a *little rock* (keyword for Little Rock). To help students remember that Frankfort is the capital of Kentucky, show a picture of dogs in a *kennel* (keyword for Kentucky) eating *frankfurters* (keyword for Frankfort).

Figure 8.7. George M. Cohan (cone) wrote "Over There." From *Teaching Students Ways to Remember: Strategies for Learning Mnemonically,* by M. A. Mastropieri and T. E. Scruggs, 1991, Cambridge, MA: Brookline Books. Reprinted with permission.

The Pegword Method

The pegword method, first mentioned in Chapter 7, creates rhyming proxies for numbers (e.g., *one* is *bun, two* is *shoe*, etc.) and is useful for linking new information to numbers. For instance, to help students remember that a wheelbarrow is an example of a second-class lever, show a picture of a wheelbarrow with the wheel resting against a shoe (pegword for *two*, or *second*). To promote recall of Newton's first law of motion—that an object at rest tends to stay at rest—picture a bun (pegword for one) at rest (e.g., lying in bed). To help students remember that the 19th amendment to the U.S. Constitution guaranteed women the right to vote, show a picture of a woman outfitted as a knight (19 = "knighting") going to a voting booth.

Pegwords can also be combined with keywords. For example, to teach that the mineral wolframite is number 4 on the Mohs hardness scale, show a picture of a *wolf* (keyword for wolframite) looking in a *door* (pegword for 4). To promote recall of the multiple facts that wolframite, in addition to being hardness level 4, is often black in color and is used as a source of tungsten filaments in light bulbs, show a black wolf looking in a door and turning on a light. Research has shown that students with mild disabilities can remember color cues in mnemonic pictures, either literally (e.g., an orange *crocodile* = the mineral crocoite, which is orange in color) or symbolically (e.g., a green broccoli = the dinosaur brachiosaurus is herbivorous [green color]).

Letter Strategies

Letter strategies are very often used by secondary and college students to help them remember lists or categories of information. In one type of letter strategy, the acronym, each letter of the word

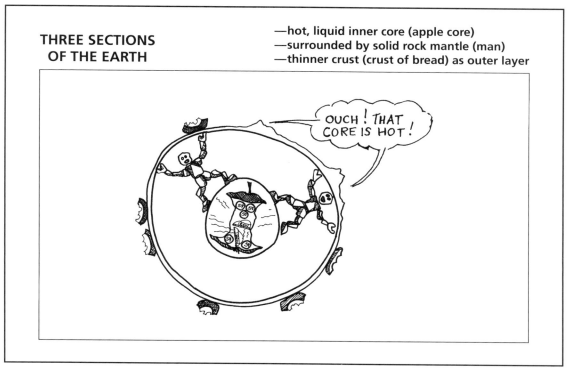

THREE SECTIONS OF THE EARTH

—hot, liquid inner core (apple core)
—surrounded by solid rock mantle (man)
—thinner crust (crust of bread) as outer layer

Figure 8.8. Parts of the earth: core (apple core), mantle (man), crust (crust of bread). From *Teaching Students Ways to Remember: Strategies for Learning Mnemonically*, by M. A. Mastropieri and T. E. Scruggs, 1991, Cambridge, MA: Brookline Books. Reprinted with permission.

stands for another word in a list. This strategy has already been introduced in this book in listing teacher presentation elements as the SCREAM variables (structure, clarity, redundancy, etc.). A common example of an acronym is HOMES to describe the names of the Great Lakes (Huron, Ontario, Michigan, etc.). For more examples, ROY G. BIV is often used to help students remember the colors of the spectrum of visible light (red, orange, yellow, etc.), and FARM-B can be used to remember the five classes of vertebrates (fish, amphibians, reptiles, etc.).

Acronyms can also be used in conjunction with keywords or pegwords. For example, to remember the countries associated with the World War I–era Central Powers Alliance, show a picture of children playing tag in Central Park. *Central Park* is the keyword for Central Powers, and *TAG* stands for Turkey, Austria-Hungary, and Germany. Likewise, to remember the freedoms guaranteed by the first amendment to the U.S.

Constitution, think of a singer who *raps* about *buns*. Bun is the pegword for one, or first, amendment, and RAPS stands for the freedoms of religion, assembly, press, and speech guaranteed by that amendment.

Acronyms are also used to list steps in cognitive strategies or routines to be executed by students. Some of these strategies are described in Chapter 9 and include SQ3R (for survey, question, read, recite, review) and OARWET (for overview, achieve, read, write, evaluate, test).

Some lists of information are difficult to transform into meaningful acronyms. However, other letter strategies can also be helpful. For example, a meaningful acronym cannot be constructed from the names of the planets of the solar system, but an *acrostic* is possible: "My very educated mother just served us nine pizzas" stands for Mercury, Venus, Earth, and so on, in their usual order. Likewise, a similar mnemonic letter strategy, "King Philip's class ordered a family of gentle spaniels," can promote recall of classifications in life science (in order: kingdom, phylum, class, order, family, genus, species). In this case, each term is represented by more than one letter.

One important consideration to make when using first-letter strategies is that all information in the list to be learned is familiar. It does little good, for example, to teach the acronym HOMES if students are not sufficiently familiar with the names of the Great Lakes that one letter can prompt their recall. In addition, it may be helpful to link the acronym to the category being remembered (e.g., homes pictured on lakes to help students remember that HOMES is a strategy for remembering the Great Lakes and not some other list).

Using Mnemonic Strategies

Mnemonic strategies have been demonstrated to be very effective in promoting memory of students with special learning needs. The following are some things to consider when using mnemonic strategies:

1. Mnemonic strategies have not been seen to inhibit comprehension; however, whenever associative–factual information is taught, teachers must require application and generalization levels of learning to ensure that the information is comprehended. Because mnemonics are essentially verbal learning strategies, it is important to ensure that students have had relevant learning experiences to enforce awareness of the concepts represented by the words.

2. There is no guarantee that a particular mnemonic strategy will be helpful. Test students for recall of the strategies as well as recall of facts. If a particular strategy does not appear to be working, even if it is a well-constructed mnemonic, discontinue its use.

3. As effective as mnemonic strategies are, they nevertheless will require practice to ensure their effectiveness. Teachers can use drill and practice, tutoring or cooperative group learning, or relevant teacher-constructed worksheets to provide sufficient task engagement. When ques-

tioning students, it is also helpful for teachers to ask first for the target information and second how the student remembered the information.

4. Many teachers express concern about their ability to draw mnemonic pictures; however, even very simple drawings have been effective. Some recommended alternatives include the following: (a) draw simple stick figures, (b) use cut-outs from magazines, (c) employ an artistically talented student to draw pictures, (d) ask students to draw their own pictures, (e) help students create mental images, and (f) use clip art software. If imagery is used, have students carefully think through all the relevant details of their image and have them describe it in detail. Additional practice probably will be necessary if mental images are substituted for pictures.

5. Given all the information students need to learn and remember in school, creation of sufficient mnemonics to cover school content in a variety of subject areas may at first appear to be an impossible task. Collect just a few good mnemonic strategies at first for information students need to know but easily forget (e.g., states and capitals, order of U.S. presidents). Add to these strategies a little at a time, enlisting the help of students and other teachers. More complete information for constructing and using mnemonics and more examples are provided in Mastropieri and Scruggs (1991).

Summary

- Science and social studies are critically important content areas and should not be overlooked, even when emphasizing basic skills instruction.

- Science content includes life science and earth and physical science. These areas involve the teaching of important discriminations, facts, and concepts, for which use of the effective teaching variables are critical. Teaching "big ideas" can be helpful in promoting science learning.

- Observational and experiential learning includes media presentations, outside activities, and classroom exhibits. These are important in promoting meaningfulness of the content. When observational and experiential learning are used, they should address specific objectives and be included in the general scope and sequence of the curriculum.

- Hands-on science is recommended by professional science organizations and may be particularly beneficial in special education. Hands-on science promotes meaningful learning, improves the concreteness of the subject being learned, and is associated with higher achievement and better attitudes toward science than traditional textbook learning. Hands-on science is also useful as a strategy for promoting learning in inclusive classrooms. Relative disadvantages of hands-on learning are a potential for inappropriate social behavior and problems with learning based on discovery or independent insight. Specific strategies can address these potential problems.

- Social studies involves the study of history, geography, and government and can be taught by direct instruction, activities and examples, media presentations, and the teaching of "big ideas."

- Special problems in learning and memory of science and social studies content can be addressed by teaching study skills, use of organizational strategies, and use of mnemonic strategies.

- Mnemonic strategies include the keyword method, the pegword method, and letter strategies. They have been shown to be very effective in promoting memory objectives in students with special needs.

Relevant Research and Resources

Research

Comprehensive reviews of science education intervention research for students with disabilities are given by Mastropieri and Scruggs (1992) and

Scruggs, Mastropieri, and Boon (1998). An issue of *Remedial and Special Education* (Cawley, 1994) was devoted entirely to science education and students with disabilities. Various approaches to content area instruction are described by Scruggs and Mastropieri (1993a, 1993b) and Mastropieri and Scruggs (1994b, 1996). Parmar and Cawley (1993) describe science textbook recommendations for teaching students with disabilities.

Research in content area instruction has focused on teaching strategies such as effective teaching variables (Kinder & Bursuck, 1993); text adaptations, precision teaching, and framed outlines (Lovitt, Rudsit, Jenkins, Pious, & Benedetti, 1985, 1986); interactive semantic feature analysis (Bos & Anders, 1987, 1990a, 1990b); content area enhancement strategies (Bulgren, Deshler, & Schumaker, 1993, 1997; Bulgren, Schumaker, & Deshler, 1988, 1994; Hudson, Lignugaris-Kraft, & Miller, 1993; Lenz, Bulgren, & Hudson, 1990); critical thinking maps (Idol, 1987); MULTIPASS and SOS (Schumaker, Deshler, Alley, Warner, & Denton, 1982); concept routines (Bulgren et al. 1988); POSSE strategy (Englert & Mariage, 1991; Englert et al., 1994); vocabulary strategies (Mastropieri et al., 1990); spatial learning (Brigham, 1992a, 1992b; Brigham, Scruggs, & Mastropieri, 1995; Scruggs, Mastropieri, Brigham, & Sullivan, 1992); and visual spatial strategies (Darch & Carnine, 1986). Models and procedures for content area instruction are provided by Nolet and Tindal (1993) and by Woodward and Noell (1992). Text structure processing strategies are described by Bakken et al., (1997), and Cook and Mayer (1988).

The effectiveness of activities-based instruction in science is described by Mastropieri, Scruggs, and Magnusen (1999); Scruggs and Mastropieri (1994b); and Scruggs, Mastropieri, Bakken, and Brigham (1993). Adaptations of science activities for students with disabilities are described by Mastropieri and Scruggs (1994a, 1995, 1996) and Scruggs and Mastropieri (1994a, 1995a, 1995b). Successful applications of hands-on science in inclusive settings are described by Bay, Staver, Bryan, and Hale (1992); Mastropieri et al., (1998); and Mastropieri and

Scruggs (1994b). Cautions about student scientific preconceptions are raised by Scruggs, Mastropieri, and Wolfe (1995), and possible concerns with overreliance on learner insight or discovery for all types of learners are described by Mastropieri, Scruggs, and Butcher (1997) and Mastropieri, Scruggs, Boon, and Carter (2001).

Mastropieri, Scruggs, and Levin (1983); Scruggs and Mastropieri (1984c, 1985); Mastropieri and Peters (1987); and Scruggs and Mastropieri (1984b) provide information on the use of pictures in facilitating recall of content area information. Support for the use of mnemonic illustrations in enhancing content area information is provided by Mastropieri (1985, 1988); Mastropieri and Scruggs (1984b); Mastropieri, Scruggs, and Levin (1983, 1985a, 1985b, 1986, 1987a, 1987b); Scruggs, Mastropieri, Levin, and Gaffney (1985); Mastropieri, Scruggs, McLoone, and Levin (1985); Scruggs, Mastropieri, Levin, McLoone, et al. (1985); Scruggs, Mastropieri, and Levin (1986, 1987); Veit, Scruggs, and Mastropieri (1986); Scruggs, Mastropieri, McLoone, et al. (1987); Scruggs and Mastropieri (1984d, 1992c); Scruggs and Laufenberg (1986); and Laufenberg and Scruggs (1986). Studies involving content area classroom applications of mnemonic instruction are described in King-Sears, Mercer, and Sindelar (1992); Mastropieri, Emerick, and Scruggs (1988); Mastropieri, Sweda, and Scruggs (2000); Mastropieri and Scruggs (1988, 1989a, 1989b, 1989c, 1989d, 1998a, 1998b); Scruggs and Mastropieri (1989a, 1989b, 1992a); Mastropieri, Scruggs, Bakken, and Brigham (1992); and Mastropieri, Scruggs, Whittaker, and Bakken (1994). Descriptions of the model of reconstructive elaborations as applied to content area learning are described by Mastropieri and Scruggs (1989b, 1989c, 1989d, 1991), and comprehensive research syntheses are presented by Mastropieri and Scruggs (1989a) and Scruggs and Mastropieri (1990a, 1990b, 2000).

Research investigating the coaching of thinking skills related to content area instruction, such as the "camel's eyelashes" example, has been conducted by Sullivan et al. (1995), and similar research on coached elaborations is reported by Scruggs, Mastropieri, Sullivan, and Hesser (1993) and Scruggs et al. (1994). Support for the use of advance organizers is provided by Lenz, Alley, and Schumaker (1987), and support for the use of learning strategies is provided by Deshler, Ellis, and Lenz (1996) and Ellis, Lenz, and Sabornie (1987). Wong (1985) presents suggestions for facilitating content area learning. Several comprehensive reviews on cognitive strategy instruction that can be applied to content area instruction are written by Pressley and Associates (1990), Gaskins and Elliot (1991), Ciborowski (1992), and Pressley, Scruggs, and Mastropieri (1989). The integration of thinking skills and strategy training is discussed by Scruggs and Mastropieri (1993c), and the utility of meaning-based approaches for enhancing understanding in science and social studies is described by Palincsar, Magnusson, Collins, and Cutter (2001) and Ferretti, MacArthur, and Okolo (2001).

Curriculum Materials

Commercial materials representing both textbook- and activities-oriented (hands-on science) approaches to instruction can be used with students with mild disabilities. Many of the programs integrate science and math activities. *SAVI/SELPH* (Lawrence Hall of Science, University of California, Berkeley) presents activities-based science curricular materials that were originally developed to meet the needs of students with disabilities. Lawrence Hall of Science also produces *Great Explorations in Math and Science (GEMS)*, *Marine Activities Resources and Education (MARE)*, and *Outdoor Biology Instructional System (OBIS)*. Other activities-based programs that might need modifications to meet students' needs include those distributed by Delta Education (*Delta Science Modules*, *Science Curriculum Improvement Study—3*, and *Full Option Science System*), and by Carolina Biological Supply (*Science and Technology for Children*). AIMS (AIMS Education Foundation) is an activity-based program that integrates math and science. Creative

Publications also distributes manipulative materials and kits in science, such as *Windows on Beginning Science*. Materials intended to facilitate critical thinking in science include *Critical Thinking in Science* (Critical Thinking Press & Software) and *SRA Real Science* (SRA/McGraw-Hill). An excellent resource for teachers that lists all science materials is *Science for Children: Resources for Teachers* (National Science Resources Center [NSRC]). Steck-Vaughn produces the *Science World* series and the *Animals by Habitat* series, and Globe Fearon publishes the *General Science* series.

Social studies materials include *The World We Share* (Curriculum Associates), *America's History: Land of Liberty,* and the *20 Events* series (Steck-Vaughn). Other low-readability social studies textbooks are published by Globe Fearon and include *Pacemaker Curriculum: History and Geography, One Nation, Many People,* and *World Myths and Legends I and II*. American Guidance Service publishes *AGS World Geography*. Creative Publications produces *Critical Thinking in Social Studies*. The *Rainbow Program* (Curriculum Associates) incorporates books, CDs, and audiocassettes to introduce children K–2 to different places and peoples in the world.

Computer Software and Technology

Computer software and technologically advanced materials have become available in science and social studies. Many programs can be used as supplements for practice activities, and some programs can be used as major components of the curriculum. For example, the Bank Street College of Education developed several multimedia curriculum programs that integrate science, social studies, language, and math. *The Voyage of the Mimi* and *The Second Voyage of the Mimi* (distributed by Sunburst) combine video or videodisk, computer software, and print materials. The Learning Company distributes *Where in the World Is Carmen San Diego, Oregon Trail,* and *Amazon Trail*. Steck-Vaughn produces the CD *Decades of Change* and the "Primary Source" video collection with CNN/Turner Learning. Additional software programs that are available in science include the following: Learning Services distributes Amazing Animals, My Amazing Human Body, and Earth Quest (DK Interactive Learning), which include special needs information in the teachers' guides. Don Johnston Developmental Equipment produces software for virtual "hands-on" experiences in a safe environment, including Thinkin' Science and Virtual Labs: Electricity.

Social studies programs that are available include States and Capitals and Space Commander: A States and Capitals Game (Gamco Industries) and Trading Post and Solve It! American History Mysteries 1492–1865 (Sunburst Communications). The Carmen San Diego software mentioned earlier includes relevant geography information. See Appendix B for a list of addresses of producers and distributors of software and curricular materials.

Designing Modified Practice Activities for Students in Inclusive Classes

Some students with disabilities who are included in general education science and social studies classes may require modified practice activities. The major idea underlying modifications is allowing students with disabilities to practice the same learning objective as other students while minimizing aspects of the activity that hinder students' ability to complete that practice effectively. Think of modifications as existing along a continuum ranging from minor to major adaptations and along another continuum of various format modifications. Think about the potential difficulty of the task and then think of possible modifications to minimize that difficulty while maintaining the prioritized objectives for the lesson in the modified practice activity for students with disabilities.

Potential Difficulty	Potential Modification
Task requires extensive writing	Reduce the written demands of the task by making part of the task an identification task rather than a production task. This may mean rewriting some items into multiple-choice, matching, or short-answer formats in lieu of longer essay formats, or even providing the use of word processors to facilitate the writing process.
Task requires extensive reading	Provide an alternative method for silent reading by providing, for example, a tape-recorded version of material or a peer assistant who can share the reading.
Task requires completion of numerous problems	Select several relevant examples for the students with disabilities to complete; if they complete them successfully, it may be unnecessary for them to complete the entire task. Remember that the processing of information for many students with disabilities can be twice as long as that as general education students.
Task requires extensive sustained attention	Break tasks into shorter segments. Allow breaks in between segments. Alternate types of tasks by including a reading activity followed by a writing activity, followed by an activity that requires movement around the class.

Using Inspiration Software for Studying Science and Social Studies

Inspiration software is a graphic organizer tool that can be used to develop charts for organizing concepts in science and social studies. These graphic organizers can be used as study guides for lessons in science and social studies for students with disabilities.

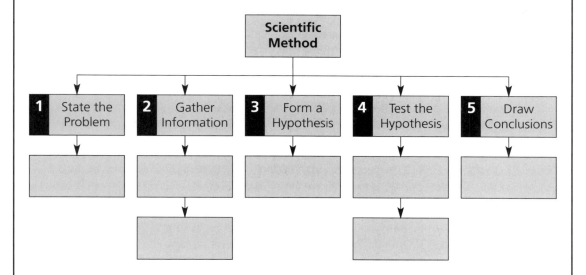

How to use this template

1. Type the steps taken while conducting a scientific inquiry into the subsymbols associated with the appropriate stage of the procedure.
2. Add subsymbols as necessary using the Create tools.
3. For additional help, read the Notes text associated with each step.

Benefits of using the Scientific Method template

Using a template such as this helps students understand scientific method at the same time they are actually involved in it. Student experiments will also be uniform in format, making comparison easier.

This diagram created using Inspiration® by Inspiration Software, Inc.

The scientific method example is a template from the Inspiration 6 software. Illustrations or text can be inserted in any box. Organizers can be completed using the software. Teachers can choose to have students fill in printed versions of the organizers while completing activities or complete them using computers after finishing the activities.

Chapter 9

❧   ❧   ❧

Study Skills

As students advance from elementary to secondary educational settings, the demands for independent learning skills increase. A special education student at the junior high school or high school level frequently attends inclusive content area classes for which a specific set of skills is needed. It is important to emphasize that these study skills are different from the basic skills remediation techniques that have been covered previously. As a separate set of skills, they must be taught separately.

Ideally, study skills instruction involves teaching the student how to independently apply the techniques that teachers have been applying all along. To this extent, much of study skills instruction is procedural in nature and requires the student to (a) *recognize* instances in which the specific procedure (study skill or strategy) is called for, (b) *recall* the steps involved in executing the procedure, and (c) *execute* the procedure. Students who have mastered basic skills and who have learned effective study skills are well on their way to becoming independent learners.

Study skills involve a wide range of independent behaviors that cover a variety of school-related situations. In this chapter, study skills are subdivided into the following general areas: (a) listening and note taking, (b) homework, (c) reading for later retrieval, (d) test taking, (e) library skills, (f) report writing, and (g) independent projects.

Listening and Note Taking

Listening and note-taking skills are the behaviors a student should exhibit during classroom instruction. Research has shown that students on both elementary and secondary levels spend a substantial amount of their time listening. In secondary schools, the ability to listen efficiently may make the difference between passing and failing a particular course. Unfortunately, many students with disabilities and attention deficit disorders have listening skills that are not well developed (Deshler et al., 1996).

Although many teachers believe that good listening is a naturally developed ability, research has demonstrated that good listening skills can be taught. In most cases, these skills are critical for special education students.

Listening skills have common elements that distinguish them from other skills or abilities. First, listening can be distinguished from paying attention, which may involve behaviors such as good posture and eye contact. Neither can it be said that listening is the same as intelligence in that good listeners are "bright" but poor listeners are "not bright." Good listening involves specific cognitive effort and applies active thinking to classroom lecture information. Active-thinking skills are described in the following sections, and a possible table of specifications for listening and note taking is given in Table 9.1.

Determining the Purpose

The first thing effective listeners must do in a lecture situation is to determine their purpose for listening. If students are certain of their purpose, they are more likely to set and meet relevant goals. For example, the purpose for listening might be (and often is) to obtain the information

Table 9.1. Table of Specifications for Listening and Note Taking

	BEHAVIOR				
	Identification	Production			
CONTENT	A. Acquisition	B. Acquisition	C. Fluency	D. Application	E. Generalization
1. Determines purpose of presentation	1A	1B	1C	1D	1E
2. Determines plan of organization	2A	2B	2C	2D	2E
3. Summarizes and relates main ideas (1) oral (2) written	3(1)A 3(2)A	3(1)B 3(2)B	3(1)C 3(2)C	3(1)D 3(2)D	3(1)E 3(2)E

Sample Objectives:

1A　Given teacher statements during a lecture in a role-play situation, student orally identifies purpose statement four of five times.

2B　Given teacher statements during a lecture in a role-play situation, student accurately states plan for organization of information in four of five instances.

3(1)C　Given a role-play, teacher-lecture situation, student orally summarizes the main idea and relates main ideas of lecture within 2 minutes of the presentation.

3(2)D　Student accurately summarizes and relates main idea of class lecture, in writing, in four of five cases.

3(2)E　Student accurately summarizes and relates main idea of an inclusive class lecture, in writing, in four of five cases.

necessary for an upcoming test. The lecture may be the sole source of such information, or it may serve to highlight important information from a textbook. On the other hand, the purpose for listening might be to learn directions for completing an assignment. In this case, listeners need to understand all of the procedures necessary and relevant for completing the assignment. Effective lecturers, of course, always state the purpose of the presentation. If the purpose is not clearly stated, students must ask the speaker to clarify the purpose of the lecture.

Finally, when the presentation has ended, students should determine whether the purpose has been achieved. If, for example, the speaker's purpose was to inform students of specific factual information that will be tested later, students must determine whether they have been provided with this information. If they have not or if there is any uncertainty, students should request re-statement or clarification. If the speaker's purpose was to provide directions for an assignment, students should determine whether they now have all the information they need to complete the assignment. If they do not, asking for clarification or further information is necessary.

Determining a Plan of Organization

Once the purpose of the presentation is clear, students should determine how the information presented should be organized. Teachers who employ effective teaching practices, of course, are explicit about how information is to be organized. If the overall organization of the presentation is not explicitly stated, students should attempt to determine the speaker's overall plan of organization. This can be accomplished by (a) recognizing the speaker's main points, (b) noting supporting details or examples of these main points, (c) following sequences of ideas, and (d) attending to transitional words or phrases. To be good listeners, students should acquire skills for identifying the overall organization of the presentation and taking notes that emphasize this organization. However, when the overall organization is not apparent to students, the speaker should be asked to clarify the organization.

Student note taking should clearly reflect the purpose and organization of the presentation. Notes should be clear and legible (see handwriting, in Chapter 6) and provide room for later elaboration. Notes should indicate the main points of the presentation, and supporting points or examples should be clearly related to the main points. Points that appear to be of particular importance from the speaker's presentation (e.g., possible test questions) should be highlighted in the notes. Note takers should also be able to discriminate between information that is important and relevant to the main ideas being discussed and information that is not. Excluding less relevant or irrelevant information from notes can be as important as including relevant information.

It is important to remember that it is possible to take too many notes as well as to take too few notes. Notes should be succinct and to the point and should not take time away from active listening. Finally, notes should be read as soon as possible after class so that ambiguous or carelessly written sections can be rewritten.

Summarizing and Relating Main Ideas

Throughout the presentation, students should summarize the main points being covered and relate these main ideas to their own experiences. Summarizing and relating should be done both mentally and on paper. Summarizing provides additional rehearsal of the speaker's main points and organizational plan, whereas relating main ideas to the student's experience makes informa-

tion more meaningful and ties it to information already in the student's long-term memory, which facilitates later retrieval.

Finally, the entire presentation should be summarized. A teacher using effective teaching variables will be certain to do this, but students should, nevertheless, make sure that all important points have been summarized, asking questions when needed. Students' notes should reflect this overall summary of the information presented.

The LINKS Strategy

Suritsky and Hughes (1996) described the LINKS strategy for listening and notetaking. The letters of LINKS stand for listen, identify cues, note, keywords, and stack information into outline format. Listening and identifing cues are strategies for identifying important information from teacher cues. Students are also taught to write individual important words rather than complete sentences, abbreviate words and eliminate punctuation, cross out rather than erase errors, allow extra space to add additional information, and use synonyms.

Students should practice this strategy until they become fluent. The strategy also teaches students to use two columns for note taking. In the left-hand column, they write main ideas, and in the right-hand column, they write supporting details.

Homework

Homework can be assigned at any grade level and increases in amount and complexity as the grade levels increase (Polloway, Epstein, Bursuck, Jayanthi, & Comblad, 1994). However, Polloway, Foley, and Epstein (1992) reported that students with learning disabilities may have 2½ times as much difficulty completing homework assignments, so it is important that students are given appropriate homework assignments and training in how to complete homework.

In special education settings, assigned homework may best be considered an extended form of independent practice activity; students have had guided practice on the task and may also have had some independent practice. The homework assignment is intended to help build fluency in cases in which responses are mostly correct and it seems unlikely that students will be inappropriately practicing error responses. If students are given worksheet-type activities as homework, teachers should ensure that directions are clearly understood and that students complete the first few examples independently and accurately. Of course, homework assignments should reflect specific instructional objectives.

Sometimes homework assignments represent application or generalization tasks that cannot easily be completed in class, or assignments are given in inclusive classes in which a higher level of independent learning is expected. In these cases, the homework completion skills are procedural in nature and involve the student executing a specific routine to fulfill task requirements. In such cases, it may be beneficial to have the student create and complete a self-monitoring checklist in which all subtasks and subroutines are listed in order. As with any independent assignment, the teacher should review the product as soon as possible after completion and deliver feedback. If the task has not been completed satisfactorily, it may be necessary to review the self-monitoring sheet to determine the reason. Some students with mild disabilities may be less likely to complete tasks independently, so teachers in these cases should enlist parent or peer assistance and reinforce task completion.

Reading for Later Retrieval

Teachers frequently make a reading assignment by simply saying, "Read Chapter 12 for Monday," without providing additional information concerning the manner in which the chapter is to be read or the purpose for the reading exercise. When this occurs, the student must determine the purpose of the reading assignment by questioning the teacher, questioning other students, or thinking back to similar assignments. (Although it may seem appropriate to question the teacher, some teachers may resent being asked too many questions by the same student. It is important for students to determine how much questioning a specific teacher is willing to accept.) Once the purpose of the reading assignment is determined, the best method of studying for the test can be determined.

Several strategies have been suggested to facilitate comprehension and memory of text. These methods commonly involve procedures in which mnemonic first-letter cues are provided. All of the methods require proceeding through the reading assignment several times, typically skimming, reading in depth, and reviewing. One of the most commonly proposed methods is referred to as SQ3R (for survey, question, read, recite, review). Other similar strategies have been proposed, including PQRST (preview, question, read, state, test), Triple S (scan, search, summarize), and OARWET (overview, achieve, read, write, evaluate, test), or the POSSE strategy discussed in Chapter 8. Use of any of these acronyms may be helpful to students. In general, however, all of these strategies suggest that students preview, read, think about, and review text material. In addition, most include self-questioning and answering to enforce major points of the reading assignment. These procedures are described below.

Prereading

The purpose of prereading activities is to develop (a) a general idea of the content to be studied and (b) an *advance organizer* that will allow students to organize information more efficiently when it is studied. During prereading activities, students look over the entire passage and activity, considering how it is organized and what the main points are. Students should look at the title, subheadings, graphs, charts, any other illustrative materials, headings, introductory sections, and summary sections. All of these sections should give the reader an idea of what is being covered in the text. During prereading, students should question themselves on the general points covered in the material. At this stage, questions such as, "What is this chapter about? How is it organized? What specific points are being emphasized?" are appropriate for students to ask themselves. It is also helpful to review the student's own prior knowledge about the subject at this point and think of questions that may be answered in the text. An excerpt from a lesson on prereading is given in Figure 9.1.

Reading

During this stage, students should carefully and deliberately read through the entire assignment. Introduction and summary sections should be read most carefully; less important points should be read more quickly. As the student reads, he or she should take notes on the main points. Important parts can also be highlighted in the book. If the teacher has identified any points of the assignment as particularly important (e.g., "Pay particular attention to the section on the Missouri Compromise"), these should also be highlighted. If written responses to questions about the reading assignment are required, these should be considered while the passage is being read, rather than after it has been read. A major threat to comprehension is the use of new or unfamiliar vocabulary. As students read, they should note any words with which they are unfamiliar. If they are unable to determine the meaning of these words through the use of context cues or knowledge of root words, a dictionary or glossary should be consulted. Students should realize that without an understanding of key vocabulary words, comprehension of the passage will be difficult if not impossible.

Lesson Component	Examples
Daily review	"We have been reading textbook information for meaning. What are the rules we discussed, George? . . ."
State purpose	"Today I am going to tell you what to do before you start to read carefully. . . ."
Deliver information	"Before you read carefully, look over the whole passage. First, look at the title, subheadings, graphs, pictures, and other illustrations. Second, read the introduction and summary. Third, ask yourself: What is this passage about? What is the main idea and how is it organized? When you can answer these questions, you are ready to read the whole passage carefully. Now, let's go over the steps again. . . ."
Guided practice	"Now, let's practice on Chapter 4 of your history book. Let's preread the chapter together. What do you do first, Bill? . . ."
Independent practice	"I think you all have the idea now. I want everybody to preread Chapter 5 of your textbook. It should take you no longer than 5 minutes. . . ."
Formative evaluation	"OK, close your book and answer this self-questioning sheet about the chapter. When you're done, we'll check your work. . . ."

Figure 9.1. A prereading lesson.

Throughout the reading stage, students should continue to monitor their comprehension (e.g., "Do I understand what I am reading?"), should not allow their minds to wander during the reading (radio and TV are often distracting influences), and should continue to question themselves regarding the author's main purpose throughout the assignment. Use of text structure strategies, described in Chapter 8, could also be helpful during the reading stage.

Many textbooks contain illustrations that are intended to facilitate learning. Students should be taught to study these illustrations carefully. While studying each illustration, they should ask themselves questions such as, "What section of the text does the illustration describe? What is the relevance/purpose of the illustration? Can I describe the important parts of the illustration without looking at it?" Such questions can ensure that students will benefit from text illustrations.

Review

After the reading stage, students should briefly skim the entire assignment again, including their own notes, and ask themselves questions concerning the passage. Appropriate questions include the following: "What was the main purpose of the assignment? What was the overall organization? What were the main points? What is likely to appear on the next test?" It is generally best to review the assignment immediately after completion and then review again a day or so later to evaluate comprehension. Students can restate the passage to themselves in their own words and answer questions that could be generated from the text.

Attribution

Once students have learned a particular strategy for reading comprehension or recall, they must effectively apply it and generalize its use to appropriate contexts. To facilitate generalization, teachers can encourage their students with attri-

bution training. Attribution was first discussed in Chapter 4 in the context of behavior management. Teachers who emphasize strategy attribution help students attribute their academic successes to effort and to appropriate and effective strategy execution. Likewise, when students fail, teachers help the students attribute the failure to inadequate or inappropriate strategy use, when appropriate. In general, attribution training attempts to help students make positive attributions such as, "I succeeded because I tried hard and used the correct strategy," or "I failed because I didn't plan my time wisely," and to avoid negative attributions such as, "I failed because I am stupid," or "I succeeded because I got lucky." Helping students attribute success or failure to things that are within their own control empowers them and helps them assume more responsibility for their work (Borkowski et al., 1988).

Study for Tests

Once information from the text has been thoroughly read and comprehended, it can often be committed to memory for later recall on tests. Before beginning to memorize information, students should have demonstrated (at least to themselves) that they thoroughly understand and comprehend the relevant information. Next, students should know what type of information is likely to be tested as well as how it will be tested. For example, if factual recall is expected and multiple-choice formats are to be employed, as is often the case, this information should tell students to focus on facts with the intention of *identifying* rather than *producing* correct answers. If, on the other hand, more conceptual information will be asked on an essay-type test, students should focus their study on general themes, elaborating these themes, and relating them to other concepts. Practice writing essay-type answers can also be helpful.

As stated previously, information is more easily remembered if it is meaningful to the learner. Therefore, any type of elaboration the student can provide that serves to make the information more meaningful is likely to improve the recall of this information. In many cases, students can make information more meaningful by relating it to other things they have learned or to events in their own lives. Analogies of this type are helpful in promoting understanding of school-related concepts. In addition, self-questioning procedures of the type described in Chapter 5 are helpful.

Using strategies for organizing information from notes and text can also be very helpful in preparing for tests. Some of these organizational strategies were discussed in Chapter 8. Students who have been involved in "interactive teaching" models, in which organizational charts and maps are created in collaboration with students and the teacher, will be more likely to create such charts and maps independently.

Overlearning and drill are also likely to improve recall. Important information can be recited again and again until a high level of fluency is attained and then overlearned to improve long-term retention. One disadvantage of self-instructional drill-and-practice routines is that they can seem dull and repetitive to the learner. This can be ameliorated somewhat by employing short (10- to 15-minute) intensive drill-and-practice routines over a longer period of time, employing goal setting, and recording progress on a chart or graph to improve motivation.

Finally, memory for many kinds of factual information can be improved by means of the mnemonic strategies discussed in previous chapters. The keyword method can be particularly helpful in learning terminology and new vocabulary, as well as lists of information. The pegword method can be useful in learning numbered or ordered information or facts that come in a specified series. In some cases, first-letter clues can be helpful in learning serial lists or information that can be clustered.

Researchers have described several strategies for promoting independent generation of mnemonic strategies. Essentially, students must first identify the important information that they think they may have difficulty remembering. Once they have identified unfamiliar terms, names, places, dates, and so on, they must determine what type of strategy is most appropriate. They must then reconstruct the unfamiliar information using the relevant mnemonic (keyword, pegword, or letter strategy). Then they must depict it in a meaningful way with the associated information, practice the strategy, and monitor their recall. King-Sears et al. (1992) described the "IT FITS" strategy for using the keyword method:

- **I**dentify the term (e.g., the scientific term *ranidae*)

- **T**ell the definition of the term (*ranidae* = frogs)

- **F**ind a keyword (keyword for *ranidae* = "rainy day")

- **I**magine the definition interacting with the keyword (frogs sitting in the rain)

- **T**hink about the definition interacting with the keyword (frogs sitting in the rain)

- **S**tudy the mnemonic strategy (*ranidae* → "rainy day" → frogs in the rain → frogs)

Students will probably have the most difficulty independently creating keywords because this is a production task that requires insight and analysis of speech sounds. It may be helpful for students to say the syllables separately to themselves and determine whether any of these syllables remind them of familiar words. Rhyming dictionaries, some of which are available online, may also be helpful. Scruggs and Mastropieri (1992a) used classroom brainstorming strategies to create class-generated keywords. It seems likely that such classroom strategy creation could be a valuable step toward independent strategy use.

Test-Taking Skills

Research has shown that students with mild disabilities, particularly students with learning disabilities or behavioral disorders, can be taught strategies for improving their performance on tests. These strategies represent application skills for previously learned information. In other words, students not only need to learn and remember important content area information but also must be able to apply this knowledge in appropriate test-taking situations. A thorough description of test-taking skills in a wide variety of areas is provided by Hughes (1996) and Scruggs and Mastropieri (1992d). Some of this information is summarized below.

Test-taking skills that can be employed in nearly every test-taking situation include (a) using time wisely, (b) reading all directions and questions carefully, (c) attempting to answer every question, and (d) actively reasoning through each test item. Students should also be taught to ask for clarification whenever any aspect of the test process is not fully understood. In addition to these general test-taking strategies, specific strategies can be employed with different types of tests. These can be divided into test-taking strategies appropriate for *objective* tests (multiple choice, true/false, matching) and strategies appropriate for *written* tests (short answer and essay). An example of a lesson on test-taking skills is given in Figure 9.2.

Objective Tests

The following section discusses strategies that can be employed in answering objective test questions. Objective test items include multiple choice, true–false, and matching items. Multiple-

Lesson Component	Examples
Daily review	"Last week we talked about answering multiple-choice questions on a test. What was one important rule for answering multiple-choice questions, Bill? . . ."
State purpose	"Today I am going to teach you the SNOW strategy to answer essay questions. . . ."
Providing information and guided practice	"The first thing you do is *study* the question carefully and be sure you understand what it means. Let's take some examples from your history class. . . ."
	"The second thing you do is *note* down everything you can think of about the question. Let's practice on the example question on the Bill of Rights. . . ."
	"Now the third thing you do is *organize* what you have written into an outline. How can we organize the Bill of Rights ideas, Mary? . . ."
	"When you have your outline, the last step is to *write* the answer. What are all the steps, Richard? . . ."
Independent practice	"Now I'm going to give you two practice essay questions. These are questions just like you might get on your history test next week. I want you to do the first three steps: (1) *study* the question carefully, (2) *note* down everything you can think of about the question, and (3) *organize* your thoughts into an outline. . . ."
Formative evaluation	"When you finish, we'll look at your outlines and see how well you did. . . ."

Figure 9.2. Test-taking skills lesson.

choice tests usually include a *stem* (the main part of the item) and several *options* from which the test taker must choose the most appropriate answer to the information presented in the stem. True–false items are statements (usually statements of fact) that the test taker must characterize as true or false. Matching items are presented in two columns, and the test taker is required to match each partial statement in one column with information in the second column. The purpose of test-taking strategies for objective tests is to maximize use of the knowledge that students have, rather than to help students guess the correct answer when they clearly do not know the answer. The following strategies can be used to maximize complete or partial knowledge of the content being tested.

1. *Be familiar with test formats.* Sometimes students perform poorly on tests not because they do not know the information but because they are unfamiliar with the format demands of the particular test. For example, group-administered reading decoding tests may require students to choose one of four options that includes a sound most like the one indicated in the stem (see number 4 in this list). Although students may have learned how to read these letter sounds in context (the real purpose of the test), they may not be able to apply word-attack knowledge to this particular format. When test formats are known in advance, provide students opportunities to practice applying their knowledge on these formats (using, of course, different items from those that will appear on the test). Test publishers often publish practice tests to help familiarize students with test formats. Students with special needs may need instruction and feedback on how to respond appropriately to these practice tests. In addition, teachers can create their own worksheets using specific test formats.

2. *Respond to the intention of the test makers.* Answers to objective test items should reflect the level of instruction and learning addressed in the course. For example, consider the following test item:

▶ During the occupation of Boston, the British received their most severe losses at Bunker Hill.

(True or False)

Some students may answer "False," arguing that the Battle of Bunker Hill was in fact fought on Breed's Hill. The wise test taker, however, would choose an answer based on the level of information addressed in the class. If, after reflection, the answer still appears ambiguous, the student should address the ambiguity directly (e.g., by questioning the teacher or explaining the issue in a written comment on the test).

3. *Anticipate the answer, then look for it.* A careful evaluation of the meaning of the question can help the student avoid error in choosing an answer. Although students may not anticipate exactly the answer called for, logical characteristics can be anticipated. Such anticipation can prevent students from being misled by an incorrect item choice.

4. *Consider all alternatives.* Because students (particularly students with mild disabilities) frequently jump at the first plausible option, test makers may place an attractive decoy prior to the correct answer. This will not be a problem if the student examines all items individually. For example, consider the following test item:

▶ [Choose the word that contains the underlined sound]:

Cough

(a) call
(b) ghost
(c) fox
(d) gone

Some students may be tempted to choose the first word that begins the same as the stem word (a) or contains the same letters as the underlined sound (b). Students who carefully consider all choices are more likely to answer the item correctly.

5. *Use logical reasoning.* If the exact answer is not known for certain, use of partial knowledge

to eliminate unlikely alternatives can increase the probability of a correct response. For example, consider the following test item:

► The Whisky Rebellion occurred as a direct result of:

   (a) objection to Jefferson's embargo
   (b) British occupation of distilleries
   (c) Washington's tax policies
   (d) westward expansion into Indian territory

If the student knows that the Whiskey Rebellion took place during Washington's administration, he or she can choose between (c) and (d), improving the probability of a correct response from 25% to 50%.

6. *Look for specific determiners.* Statements that contain the words *always* and *never* (rather than, for example, *usually* or *rarely*) should be taken literally. These items are often false because few statements allow for no exceptions. However, they are not necessarily false. Students should carefully consider the content as well as the intent of the test maker.

In addition to the above-mentioned strategies, a number of other strategies exist but should not be directly taught. These strategies rely entirely on flaws in test construction. Poorly constructed tests often contain cues in test items that can be used to the test taker's advantage, even with no accompanying knowledge of the content. For example, on poorly constructed tests, items with the following characteristics provide cues to the correct answer:

1. The *longest* answer is usually correct.

2. The correct answer will not be the *first* or *last* option.

3. The correct answer will not contain extreme words such as *stupid* or *nonsense*.

4. The correct answer will not be a flippant remark or an absurd idea.

5. The correct answer will be the most carefully qualified option.

6. The correct answer will be a sentence bearing familiar phraseology or technical language.

There are three arguments against the use of such cues in test taking. First, time is best used in active examination of the content of test items; second, guessing on the basis of any partial knowledge is better than presupposing a test flaw. Finally, developing reliance on such strategies could prove detrimental when taking standardized objective tests, which contain few, if any, such flaws. The overall purpose of teaching test-taking skills is to maximize the validity of students' test performances by providing strategies that maximize the application of partial and complete knowledge. Teaching students to use tricks for correctly guessing the answers is not a purpose of these strategies. In fact, if consistent flaws in test items are found, the teacher who develops or uses these tests should be alerted to these flaws.

Written Tests

Sentence Completion Tests

Short-answer tests generally involve sentence completion items or answers in which one to three sentences are expected. Strategies for one-to three-sentence answers are included in those described for essay questions in the next section. Selected strategies for sentence completion items include the following:

1. If otherwise unsure, *guess.* Sentence completion items rarely involve a penalty for incorrect answers. In addition, students may be closer to the correct answer than they think they are.

2. Use *partial knowledge.* Students should respond to a sentence completion question with information they do have. An example is the following item:

▶ Constantinople fell to the Turks in
_____.

(Answer: 1453)

If the exact date is not known, the answer "the 15th century" may earn partial credit. On the other hand, if the student knows that the instructor requires precise answers, he or she should attempt a "best-guess" answer.

3. Make the sentence sound *logical* and *consistent*. The part of the sentence that is presented contains cues that restrict possible answers. For example, the item

▶ An important use of magnesium is
_____.

restricts the answer possibilities to those considered (by the test maker) to be important. Such a cue should restrict possible answers.

Other strategies that are useful for evaluating sentence completion items include the use of grammatical cues and consideration of the length of the answer blank. These cues should be taught only as they interact with partial knowledge of the content of the test item.

Short-Answer and Essay Tests

In general, short-answer and essay questions are the most difficult to answer, and as with any other type of test question, there is no substitute for knowledge of the content. However, students are rarely presented with a test question about which they have absolutely no information. The strategies to be taught, then, will involve developing a careful understanding of the question and organizing and presenting known information in a manner that maximizes the resulting test score. The first four steps presented here correspond to the SNOW strategy mentioned in Figure 9.2.

1. *Study the question carefully*. The best written answer to a test question is useless unless the major purpose of the question is carefully considered and addressed. If there are different parts or sub-questions in a question, they must be addressed directly. Underlining or circling important words or terms in the question can help students to think clearly about the answer. Questions also often provide cues on the expected length of the answer. A longer-than-expected answer not only is unnecessary but also takes time away from answering other questions.

2. As students read the essay question, they should immediately *write down the points that first occur to them*. Often, the first few minutes of the test provide the best opportunities for recall of factual information. Later in the test period, as students begin to tire, time is better spent organizing and elaborating than attempting to retrieve new factual information.

3. *Organize information before writing*. Once the facts about each question have been noted, the test taker should organize them prior to writing. A good way to do this is to note major points and then decide the order in which they should be presented. Secondary points should be included under appropriate major points.

4. *Write directly to the point of the question*. If the answer is well known to the test takers, they should directly answer the major stated purpose of the question in the first sentence. The remainder of the answer should be devoted to providing evidence that directly supports the answer, written in a clear, concise, and well-organized form.

5. *Answer every question*. Often, questions for which the test taker has only partial understanding are given. Because examiners nearly always give partial credit for partial information, test takers should provide the information they do have that is directly related to the content being asked. Long-winded answers that provide irrelevant factual information are usually not helpful.

6. *Use time wisely*. Students should schedule enough time to answer each question. If time begins to run out, however, students should answer remaining essay questions using an outline form. Because many graders evaluate the number of important points covered, such answers may still earn many points.

Finally, considerations such as neatness and legibility of handwriting can be of critical importance in maximizing a test score.

Library Skills

Any student enrolled in inclusive classes will frequently be called on to use the school library or to consult other reference materials. Although many students are able to learn these skills by themselves and know how and when to ask for help, students receiving special education services often exhibit difficulty using the library unless they are explicitly taught the specific procedures involved in library use. Generally speaking, the optimal setting for such instruction is the library itself, where appropriate skills can be practiced using real library materials. In this section, specific library skills will be described separately, followed by appropriate instructional procedures. These skills include (a) use of reference books, (b) use of periodical indexes, and (c) use of database indexes. Finally, techniques for teaching students how to prepare research papers will be described.

Reference Books

Reference books commonly found in libraries include dictionaries, encyclopedias, biographical sources, and almanacs. Students should understand the different purposes served by each type of reference book and should be able to describe when each type of book is employed. Students should be taught the purpose of each type of reference book as factual information; that is, dictionaries are typically used for looking up the pronunciation, meanings, spellings, or histories (etymology) of specific words, whereas encyclopedias are commonly used to gain factual information on topics. This can be taught by examples, modeling, and drill. Students should then be able to identify which type of reference

book should be used to answer different types of questions. For example, if a teacher asks, "Where would you go to find out how to pronounce a word?" students should be able to answer "dictionary." Students should then be able to use reference books to find answers to specific questions, such as, "Who discovered New Zealand?" or "How is *chthonic* pronounced?" Before this can be done, however, students must know how to look up information that is organized alphabetically.

Finding Alphabetically Organized Information

Looking up items that have been organized in alphabetical order is a common source of frustration and discouragement for many special education students. However, if approached systematically, these skills can be mastered. A necessary prerequisite skill, of course, is learning the alphabet. Teachers should be certain that students are fluent and automatic in this serial-list skill and do not simply produce the letters of the alphabet in correct serial order. They must also be able to start at any given place in the alphabet and produce all letters that follow. If students need to know whether *i* comes before *q*, they should not need to start at the beginning of the alphabet but should be able to start with the letter *i* or *q* and recite forward to determine the answer. If these preskills are mastered, looking up words or topics is much less difficult.

When students know the word to be investigated and know the appropriate reference material, it is important that they know the correct spelling of the word. (An exception is when students use a dictionary for determining the spelling of a particular word. In this case, the student determines the *most likely* spelling of several possibilities.) Once the correct spelling is determined, looking up the word is a matter of comparing the word to the reference order, one letter at a time. For instance, in looking up the word *bird* in an encyclopedia, students may enact the following procedures:

1. First, find the volume that contains all words starting with the letter *b.*

2. Then, find the section of the volume that contains words starting with *bi.* To do this, open the volume and compare the first two letters of those words (usually printed at the top of the page) with *bi.* For instance, if the book is opened to a word starting with *bl,* the student should determine that *i* comes before *l* and proceed backward to the *bi* words.

3. The student should then examine the third letter of the words until *bir* words are found. After this, finding the one word spelled *bird* should not be difficult.

This skill will seem less frustrating if students are encouraged to concentrate, at least at first, on accuracy of task completion rather than speed (fluency). It is also helpful to start on simple words (like *bird*) and move to more complicated words as the task becomes easier for students.

Periodical Searches

Information from periodicals can be more informative, current, and interesting than information gained from other sources. In some cases, periodical references may be the only source of current information, such as new developments in current events or new archeological discoveries. Students will need skills in accessing periodical sources through electronic databases, such as Infotrac or ProQuest. ProQuest contains Periodical Abstracts in newspaper, periodical, and peer-reviewed databases. These databases provide reference information for the source (e.g., magazine title, issue number, date) and an abstract, or brief summary, of the article. In some cases, the full text of the article is available. Although these databases are not difficult to use, basic facility with computers and the mouse is necessary. The librarian can provide specific information on the databases that are available and how they can be used. The special educator then can provide task analysis and guided practice until students have achieved independent skill. Once relevant articles are found, students should be sure to write down (a) the name of the periodical, (b) the date published, (c) the title of the article, and (d) the page numbers. Once these have been noted, the student should know the procedures for locating the periodical. Students should not only be familiarized with the exact procedure for locating magazines in the school library, but they should also be taught how to ask for needed information so that they would be able to use any library. When students have demonstrated ability to employ skills necessary for using periodical searches, they should be taught additional library skills.

Report Writing

Choosing a Topic

One problem common to many students is selecting a topic for a research paper. If students have difficulty selecting a topic, they lose valuable time necessary for writing a paper. They also lose time if their initial choice of a topic is not well thought out and they must choose a more appropriate topic. Finding an appropriate topic usually involves three main considerations: (a) personal interest, (b) the student's own ability and experience level, and (c) time limits necessary for completion. If these three criteria are met, students should have little difficulty preparing for the paper.

To find an appropriate topic, students should be taught to "brainstorm" different ideas and then find the one that seems to meet the above considerations the best. This skill can be developed by direct teaching of topic finding. Teachers can present a general topic area to students (e.g., trees) and direct them to prepare a list of possible topics that are interesting, within the student's ability, and appropriate to a specified time limit. Students should prepare a list, consider all possibilities, and decide on one topic. Activities such as these can make it easier for students to choose topics for assignments in inclusive classes.

Finding Information

Once the topic is selected, students should prepare a list of information needed from the library. If students know very little about a particular topic, they will need to obtain further information before they can prepare the list. Usually, general information on a particular topic can be obtained in an encyclopedia or book.

Before going to the library, students should prepare a list of information that will be needed to write the paper. In addition to the information needed, this list should contain the sources where such information can be found. Students can then enter the library with knowledge of (a) the purpose of the library visit, (b) the procedures necessary for fulfilling the purpose, and (c) criteria necessary to meet the purpose.

Writing the Paper

Students should begin by writing an outline for the paper, once enough information has been gathered for such an outline. In the outline, students can note what further information will be required and how it can be obtained. Further trips to the library can then be made to acquire specific pieces of information. All information should be collected neatly on note cards that include the source of the information.

If library skills are used systematically and purposefully and students have mastered necessary subskills (e.g., reading for meaning, writing, note taking), writing the research paper should not be a difficult task. In writing the paper, students should first make sure that the topic is carefully outlined and that necessary information is neatly organized within the outline. Writing the paper should then be approached as a series of small tasks, each referring to a part of the outline, rather than one enormous project. Students can monitor their own progress by checking each section off a list when it is completed. Overall, written reports should follow a clear central purpose and a well-defined, consistent outline. Additional information on writing is given in Chapter 6.

Special Problems

Students who have been referred for special services may exhibit great difficulty preparing written reports or research papers. In a sense, preparing an independent written product requires the highest levels of school functioning. To this extent, some students may be well into school before necessary prerequisite skills have been learned. On the other hand, it is not unusual for third and fourth graders to be assigned a written report that is several pages long. In some cases, tasks can be simplified by having students report on magazine, encyclopedia articles, or a field trip experience.

In the case of students with mild disabilities, students may at first need a great deal of attention (similar to guided practice) on every step of the process before they are able to proceed independently on later projects. After a few papers have been completed with teacher involvement, it should be easier for students to write independently, particularly if the student has become familiar with all of the important procedural steps.

Students who have become accustomed to structured special education environments may exhibit problems generalizing social behavior appropriate to the library setting. This may be particularly true of students with behavioral disorders. Compared with special education classrooms, libraries can be seen as highly distracting, unstructured, and requiring a high degree of self-control skills. To minimize potential problems in library settings, teachers should make all students aware of the purpose of the library visit beforehand. Students should also know the procedures they are to employ in the library and the consequences for breaking library rules. Many times, problems that occur in library visits can be attributed to a lack of clear purpose in the visit. Finally, if problems are anticipated, it may be helpful to bring students to the library in small numbers when other students are not present. On the other hand, students can sometimes benefit from the appropriate modeling of library-related behaviors provided by regular class students.

A final concern for any low-achieving student is an understanding of plagiarism. Students who are discouraged and frustrated at the prospect of writing a research paper are more likely to be tempted to copy whole sections from other authors' works. Students must be familiarized with the ethical and legal implications of plagiarism; perhaps even more important, students must be provided with the skills needed to paraphrase or cite the work of others without copying it and to derive satisfaction in a truly independent effort well done.

Independent Projects

Sometimes students are assigned projects to complete independently. Such projects are most common in science and are executed somewhat differently than a written report, although a written report or presentation may be a component of the project. Figure 9.3 provides a checklist for completing science projects.

Summary

- Listening and note-taking skills are critical for students in secondary classes. Students must learn to determine the purpose of a teacher presentation, ask clarifications when unsure, determine a plan of organization for the information, summarize, and relate main ideas.

- Homework can be considered an important extension of independent practice activities. Checklists and support of parents and peers can be helpful in promoting homework completion.

- An important part of study skills is reading for later retrieval. Such study includes pre-reading activities, reading, and review of text

☐	1. Identify general area of interest (e.g., plants, goldfish) through discussion, reading, and brainstorming.
☐	2. Identify the specific question to be investigated (e.g., the effects of salt on plant growth) through discussion, reading, and brainstorming.
☐	3. Identify specific methods for addressing the question (e.g., adding different amounts of salt to the water of different plants), and confirm the methods with the teacher.
☐	4. Obtain necessary equipment and/or supplies.
☐	5. Conduct the experiment, and keep records of procedures and progress.
☐	6. Observe and record findings (e.g., plant growth).
☐	7. Summarize Steps 1–6 above.
☐	8. Organize summaries for class presentation. Decide on exhibits, charts, or diagrams to be displayed. Practice the presentation and get feedback.
☐	9. Present the entire project and its findings to the class.

Figure 9.3. Checklist for preparing science projects. *Note.* Adapted from *Guidelines for Effective Mainstreaming in Science*, by M. A. Mastropieri and T. E. Scruggs, 1993, West Lafayette, IN: Purdue Research Foundation. Adapted with permission.

material. Attribution of learning and achievement to the use of appropriate study skills can be helpful in maintaining independent use of study skills.

- Studying for tests should be done with specific reference to the type of test that will be given. Elaboration, organization, overlearning, and mnemonic study strategies, such as the IT-FITS strategy, can be useful in learning and remembering information for tests.

- Test-taking skills refer to the application of knowledge to a specific testing format. Helpful strategies for taking tests include using time wisely, reading test information carefully, answering each question, and actively reasoning through each item. Other strategies can be applied to specific test formats and include eliminating choices known to be incorrect, considering the intention of the test maker, and writing directly to the point of the question.

- Library skills are important for successful completion of independent papers and projects. They include skills for looking up alphabetical information and effectively searching databases.

- Important steps for report writing include choosing a topic, finding relevant information, writing the report, and monitoring progress.

Relevant Research and Resources

Much of the important research on study skills training with adolescents with learning disabilities has been conducted by Don Deshler, Jean Schumaker, and their colleagues at the University of Kansas Center for Research on Learning and is described in Deshler et al. (1996). Deshler and Schumaker (1990) describe their learning strategies model and develop numerous training packages in the strands of acquisition, storage, and expression of knowledge. Additional proce-

dures on study skills are provided in Carman and Adams (1977), Alverman (1983), and Devine (1981). Generalization skills are discussed by Mastropieri and Scruggs (1984a) and Scruggs and Mastropieri (1984c, 1994c).

Specific research applications of test-taking skills training with students with mild disabilities are provided by Lee and Alley (1981); Hughes (1996); Scruggs, Bennion, and Lifson (1985a, 1985b); Scruggs and Jenkins (1985); Scruggs and Lifson (1985, 1986); Lifson, Scruggs, and Bennion (1984); Scruggs and Mastropieri (1986); Scruggs, Mastropieri, and Veit (1986); Scruggs, Mastropieri, Tolfa, and Jenkins (1985); Osguthorpe and Scruggs (1986); Scruggs (1985a, 1985b); and Scruggs and Tolfa (1985). A meta-analysis of test-taking skills training is provided by Scruggs, White, and Bennion (1986). Reviews on test-taking skills are provided by Scruggs and Mastropieri (1988) and Hughes (1996). Scruggs and Mastropieri (1992d) have provided a book on test-taking skills training.

Transfer of learning and self-instruction research are provided by Borkowski and Varnhagen (1984), Wong (1985), Wong and Wong (1986), and Brown, Campione, and Barclay (1979). Research cited in the science and social studies chapter can also be cited as evidence supporting the efficacy of various learning and study strategies. Test-taking strategies are described in detail by Scruggs and Mastropieri (1988, 1992d), and comprehensive procedures to use in teaching mnemonic strategies are presented in Mastropieri and Scruggs (1991). Polloway et al. (1992) provide a discussion on the issues of homework between normally achieving students and students with disabilities. Texts by Pressley and Associates (1990), Gaskins and Elliot (1991), and Ciborowski (1992) provide useful information on the implementation of strategy-based instruction, and Mastropieri and Scruggs (1994a) provide detailed guidelines for facilitating school success. Strategies for training generalized use of the keyword method are validated by Fulk et al. (1992), McLoone et al. (1986), Scruggs and Mastropieri (1992a), and King-Sears et al. (1992).

Curricular Materials

The University of Kansas Center for Research in Learning Disabilities has produced numerous learning strategies packages. Some of the specific training modules include the *Word Identification Strategy*, the *Paraphrasing Strategy*, the *FIRST-Letter Mnemonic Strategy*, and the *Sentence Writing Strategy*. Contact the University of Kansas Center for Research in Learning Disabilities for procedures for participating in their training sessions and obtaining training materials. Curriculum Associates produces the *Organization Skills* program emphasizing organizational and study skills, as well as *30 Lessons in Notetaking* and *30 Lessons in Outlining, Skills for School Success*, and *Advanced Skills for School Success*. *Graphic Organizers for Reading*, also from Curriculum Associates, helps students organize and summarize their reading, Grades 2–8. *You Can Take Charge!* study skills are available from Zaner-Bloser. American Guidance Service publishes the *Test-Taking Tips and Strategies* video series and the *Taking the (T)error out of Testing* materials, and Curriculum Associates publishes *Test Ready*. SRA/McGraw-Hill publishes *Scoring High*, developed for specific achievement tests and specific content areas. The *Bad Speller's Dictionary* (Random House) and the *Misspeller's Dictionary* (Simon & Schuster) are available for checking written products for spelling errors when the correct spelling is unknown.

Computer Software and Technology

Software programs have also become available in the area of test-taking skills and study skills. Two examples are Study to Succeed for general study skills and Test-Taking Made Easy for test-taking skills (Lawrence Productions). Inspiration Software (Inspiration Software, distributed by Learning Services) can be used by students to organize thinking by producing concept maps and other graphic organizers. See Appendix B for a list of addresses of producers and distributors of software and curricular materials.

Cooperative Homework Teams in Math

Math homework is often an extremely difficult activity for students with disabilities. Sometimes the homework is completed and turned in, but other times it is not. Sometimes students forget to complete their homework; other times they may forget how to complete their math homework. In attempts to improve the math homework completion of students with learning disabilities and emotional disabilities, O'Melia and Rosenberg (1997) assessed the use of cooperative homework teams with middle school students with disabilities in math classes. Cooperative homework teams

- consisted of three to four students,

- met for approximately the first 10 minutes of each class,

- were encouraged to help one another,

- had an assigned "checker" who collected and graded the homework and turned in the homework and grades to the teacher, and

- were assigned points and awards for weekly accomplishments.

At the study's conclusion, students in the cooperative homework team condition had significantly higher homework completion and accuracy rates than students in the condition without cooperative homework teams. Advantages of the cooperative homework teams include

- extra motivation working with peers,

- more immediate feedback on their homework on a daily basis, and

- incentives provided to cooperative homework teams for succeeding.

TECHNOLOGY FEATURE

Teaching Students to Complete Multimedia Projects

Multimedia refers to the integration of text, graphics, sound, animation, illustrations, photographs, and video. Combining those features into multimedia authoring tools enables students to complete multimedia projects. Multimedia projects allow more options for researching, combining, synthesizing, and presenting information and, as such, appear ideally suited to the learning needs of students with disabilities. First, students study materials presented in a variety of formats, including text, movie, graphics, and animation. Students can focus in-depth learning using formats that are more readily comprehensible to them. For example, video components may provide more understanding than written text for students with reading difficulties. Then students can put together a project using all available multimedia components. Creating multimedia projects allows students to select from all media formats, rather than emphasizing only a written product. Researchers have demonstrated that students with disabilities can be successful when they create multimedia projects in social studies (Ferretti & Okolo, 1996; Okolo, Cavalier, Ferretti, & MacArthur, 2000). In Okolo and Ferretti's research, students with learning disabilities participated in cooperative learning groups within an inclusive class environment and successfully completed projects on the American Revolutionary War.

Many software programs lend themselves to the creation of multimedia projects.

- Microsoft Powerpoint is a simple program that students can use to develop projects that can be shown using the computer or printed out in hard copy. Students can insert text, illustrations, animations, and sound effects to create multimedia projects.

- HyperStudio (Roger Wagner Publishing) is a multimedia authoring software program that can be used to develop multimedia projects, including text, illustrations, sound, and videos.

Chapter 10

Social Skills

Researchers have documented that many special education students, including students with behavioral disorders, learning disabilities, and mental retardation, exhibit deficits in age-appropriate social skills (Kavale & Forness, 1995; Kavale, Mathur, Forness, Rutherford, & Quinn, 1997). Some educators have suggested that many of the current inclusion efforts are made more challenging because special education students lack appropriate and acceptable social behavior. Other educators have indicated that appropriate social skills are necessary for success in all aspects of life. For example, research indicates that many former special education students who are now young adults lose their jobs not primarily due to their competence at executing the required job-related skills but due to their poor social skills. Many are fired for neglecting to follow directions or not asking for clarification of directions, as well as forgetting to call in sick and being unable to receive and execute suggestions for improvement. Social skills can, therefore, be considered critical for success in school, at home, and at work.

Researchers have addressed ways to increase positive social behaviors. This chapter is intended to present the major issues surrounding social skills instruction. First, social skills are defined; second, specific procedures for assessing social skills are presented; and third, instructional procedures that fit within the teacher effectiveness model are described, with a discussion of training generalization of social skills.

Definition of Social Skills

The area of social skills has resisted precise definition simply because so many educators and researchers have adopted specific definitions to meet their particular needs during specific situations. Most definitions emphasize that social skills are those behaviors necessary for successful interactions at home, at school, and in the community. Some educators refer to social skills as social competence and refer to the socially competent individual as one who can function adequately in his or her environment by meeting goals without disrupting others. Social skills can, therefore, be considered a collection of behaviors in a learner's repertoire of skills that enables him or her to interact successfully in the environment. So defined, many specific skills have been identified as social skills (see Table 10.1).

The degree to which individuals execute the social skills presented in Table 10.1 influences how well they interact with, get along with, and are accepted by their peers and others in the environment. The list is not exhaustive; it does, however, provide a general listing of the skills that are most commonly reported as social skills and those that appear in many published social skills programs.

A major problem in the social skills area is the lack of a definite scope and sequence or a hierarchy of social skills. It is much easier for a special

Table 10.1. Specific Social Skills

Content Area	Component Skills
Conversation skills	Joining a conversation Interrupting a conversation Starting a conversation Maintaining a conversation Ending a conversation Use of appropriate tone of voice Use of appropriate distance and eye contact
Assertiveness skills	Asking for clarifications Making requests Denying requests Negotiating requests Exhibiting politeness
"Play" interaction skills (e.g., making friends)	Sharing with others Inviting others to play Encouraging others Praising others
Problem-solving and coping skills	Staying calm and relaxed Listing possible solutions Choosing the best solution Taking responsibility for self Handling name calling and teasing Staying out of trouble
Self-help skills	Good grooming (clean, neat) Good dressing (wearing clothes that fit) Good table manners Good eating behaviors
Classroom task-related behaviors	On-task behavior Attending to tasks Completing tasks Following directions Trying your best
Self-related behaviors	Giving positive feedback to self Expressing feelings Accepting negative feedback Accepting consequences
Job interview skills	Being prepared (dress, attitude, etc.) Being attentive Listening skills Asking for clarification Thinking prior to speaking

educator to conduct a curriculum-based assessment, identify specific skill deficits, and instruct students in reading, language, or mathematics than it is in social skills. The next section presents procedures recommended for assessing and prioritizing social skills.

Social Skills Assessment

The purpose of social skills assessment is similar to that in the academic areas; that is, assessment first identifies students with particular social skills deficits. Second, assessment identifies where along a continuum of objectives instruction needs to begin. Finally, ongoing formative evaluation provides information on student performance and progress along that continuum of objectives (Cartledge & Milburn, 1995).

Typical social skills assessment procedures include the following methods: (a) sociometric measures, (b) teacher ratings, (c) role-play tests, and (d) naturalistic or direct observation. In the following sections, each procedure is briefly described, followed by a task-analytical model of assessment that is linked to a specific social skills curriculum area.

Sociometric Measures

Sociometric measures are intended to assess interpersonal attraction or degree of social acceptance among the sampled populations. Three of the most common sociometric techniques include (a) the peer nomination method, (b) the rating scale, and (c) the paired comparison method. The peer nomination method requires students to name specific classmates who meet a particular social criterion. For example, all of the students in Ms. Hunt's classroom could be asked to write down the names of (a) the three classmates they most like to do things with and (b) the three classmates they least like to do things with. A student's score is the total number of "nominations," based on either the positive or the negative criteria. The resulting totals can be viewed

as an indication of social acceptance (positive nominations) or social rejection (negative nominations). Some researchers have suggested that the nomination method actually provides a measure of "best friendship," which can be viewed as similar to social acceptance.

The rating scale method requires students to rank all of their classmates on a numerical scale according to a social criterion. In the above example, students would be provided with a listing of all their classmates and a Likert-type rating scale. The rating scale could range from 1 to 5, with 1 equal to *never play with* and 5 equal to *play with a lot*. Students would be required to circle the number that best represents their feelings toward each classmate. A student's measure of social acceptance or rejection is the average rating from all their classmates.

The paired comparison method is a variation of the rating scale technique. Students are presented with one classmate and all possible pairings with other classmates. Each time, students must select the "most liked" or "least liked" peer. Measures of social acceptance or rejection are derived by totaling the number of times each student is selected for all pairings.

The advantages of sociometric measures include (a) administration ease and (b) quick identification or screening of a student's acceptance or rejection by peers. The disadvantages, however, include (a) lack of identification of specific social skill deficits, (b) lack of use as a continuous monitoring evaluation measure (because the measure does not identify specific social skill deficits and it is not necessarily sensitive to students' social skill changes), and (c) lack of identification of students who are neither intensely liked nor disliked, but simply tolerated, and yet lack appropriate social skills.

Teacher Ratings

Teacher ratings are intended to provide information relevant to students' particular strengths and weaknesses in social skills. The most common type of teacher rating scale lists social behaviors and requires teachers to identify "how well" or "how frequently" students exhibit those behaviors appropriately. Many social skills packages have begun to include teacher checklists as accompanying screening devices.

The advantages of teacher ratings include (a) ease of administration, (b) reliance on teachers' expertise and daily experience with students, and (c) fair utility as a screening device. Typically, however, such devices lack necessary reliability and validity data. If the teacher rating scale is linked directly to a social skills curriculum, it can be used as a formative evaluation device to monitor students' progress. Unfortunately, many widely used teacher rating scales are not linked to specific curricular materials.

Role-Play Tests

Role-play tests, or analogue observations, are intended to assess a student's ability to execute appropriate social behaviors in contrived settings. Various scenarios are presented to the student, and the student's responses are evaluated for the appropriateness of specific social behaviors. Many researchers have developed their own role-play tests because certain social behaviors are difficult to observe in natural settings. For example, it is virtually impossible to assess whether a student possesses appropriate conversation skills when observing the student during a history lecture. To provide the student with opportunities to execute specific social skills, researchers have designed and used various role-play scenarios.

The advantages of role-play tests include (a) the ability to assess specific social skills in controlled settings and (b) the ability to determine whether the student has acquired the social skill, is fluent at performing the skill, has generalized the skill, or is at the acquisition level of learning. The disadvantages, however, include (a) lack of normative data, including reliability and validity, and (b) lack of direct correspondence between contrived scenarios and naturalistic settings with respect to demonstrated competencies.

Naturalistic or Direct Observation

Direct observation procedures can be employed in natural settings to determine which social behaviors are appropriate. As described in Chapter 3, various observation techniques can be employed to determine the frequency of appropriate and inappropriate social behaviors and the quality of such behaviors. In addition, continuous records can be used to analyze the antecedents and consequences of social interactions.

To be successful, direct observation procedures must meet several prerequisites. First, the specific social skills must be operationally defined (see Chapter 3). Second, observers must be trained to a criterion performance. Third, reliability of observations should be assessed frequently. Finally, the behaviors targeted must be high-frequency behaviors, or contrived settings must be constructed to evaluate low-frequency behaviors. In addition, if direct observation procedures are tailored to correspond to specific social skills instructional objectives, then these observation procedures can be used to monitor progress continuously throughout instruction.

All of the social skills assessment procedures discussed have limitations, some of which are more serious than others. Major limitations include (a) lack of reliability and validity data, (b) lack of social norms, and (c) lack of a direct correspondence with curriculum materials. To be effective, social skills assessments must identify behaviors that can be changed to improve social skills (Walker, Colvin, & Ramsey, 1995). Teachers should select a simple, reliable screening device and use a task-analytical, curriculum-based assessment procedure similar to the one described in the next section.

Task-Analytical/Curriculum-Based Assessment

Procedures for specifying skill sequences, levels of learning and behaviors, and performance criteria can be identified in the social skills area, just as they can be specified in academic skill areas such as reading and mathematics. Once these sequences are established, teachers can implement systematic instruction using the teacher effectiveness variables. The instructional sequences will assist teachers in ensuring mastery and generalization of social skills.

The most difficult tasks that teachers face are selecting a specific social skills curriculum and specifying performance criteria. The latter is difficult because the acceptable standards for social behaviors tend to be based on subjective rather than objective criteria. For example, what one teacher considers appropriate classroom behavior may be considered inappropriate by another teacher. However, special educators can begin to develop such standards for their students based on a composite of the performance criteria enforced by the regular classroom educators in their particular schools. Special educators can distribute questionnaires to general education teachers that contain items such as the following: (a) What are your classroom rules and regulations? (b) What are the materials that students need to bring to class to be considered prepared for class? (c) What are the standards for acceptable behavior in terms of entering and exiting the classroom, requesting permission to use the restrooms, sharpening pencils, requesting assistance on assignments, and leaving their seats/ desks? Responses to these and other relevant items can assist special educators in developing standards for performance criteria for social behaviors.

The issue of selecting a social skills curriculum is equally challenging. Many social skills training packages have been published, some of which appear well organized and some of which lack sufficient instructional procedures, guided and independent practice activities, and formative evaluation procedures. In addition, many social skills programs are targeted for a particular population (e.g., preschool, elementary, or secondary levels). A checklist for evaluating published social skills materials is provided in

Figure 10.1. Examples of social skills materials are the *Getting Along with Others* series and the *Skillstreaming* series, both published by Research Press. It is recommended, however, that teachers use task analysis skills to subdivide the content along particular social skills domains of behavior and to combine that subdivision with the levels of learning, behavior, and performance criteria to form a table of specifications. The specifications can be used to generate assessment objectives and instruction objectives. For example, assume that one major goal in social skills training is to improve conversation skills. A task analysis on conversation skills might reveal the following subskills:

1. appropriate eye contact
2. appropriate distance
3. appropriate tone of voice
4. starting a conversation
5. maintaining a conversation
6. interrupting a conversation
7. joining a conversation
8. ending a conversation

These subskills can be combined with the following levels of behavior, learning, and conditions:

1. identification of appropriate behavior

2. production of appropriate behavior in a role-play situation (first at the acquisition level, followed by the fluency level)

3. production of appropriate behavior spontaneously in the special education setting (first at the acquisition level, followed by a fluent production)

4. generalization/production of appropriate behavior in a regular class setting

5. generalization/production of appropriate behavior at lunch, recess, and home

6. execution of appropriate behavior at all times

By combining the content subdivisions listed along the left vertical axis and the levels of

Title:

Authors:

Publishers:

Cost:

Target Population:

Brief Description of Materials:

Scope and sequence available? If so, describe briefly.

Pre–post social skills assessment measures included?

Amount and types of practice activities (e.g., modeling, role-playing, rehearsal, homework) included?

Criteria for acceptable performance of objectives and skills included?

Generalization training included?

Efficacy data included?

How modifiable are the materials for different age or ability levels?

In 100 words or less, write your impression of the materials:

Figure 10.1. Social skills materials evaluation.

learning, behavior, and conditions listed across the top horizontal axis, a table of specifications that has as its overall goal improving conversation skills is formed. Each cell within the table can be used to generate individual behavioral objectives for assessment and instructional purposes. Teachers will have designated specific standards for each objective. Typically, a trials-to-criterion approach has been used to demonstrate mastery of social–behavioral objectives.

Another instructional goal in social skills or table of specifications that could be widely used with special education students, especially students with behavioral disorders, is improvement of classroom task-related behaviors. Task analysis of the general goal could yield the following subskills:

1. attending to tasks
2. following directions
3. asking for clarifications
4. completing tasks
5. staying on task
6. putting forth best effort

The breakdown of levels of learning, behavior, and conditions may be identical to those in Table 10.2. Again, this analysis provides the special educator with a more ecologically valid assessment and instructional plan.

It is important to note that all subskill areas need to be operationally defined. An excellent method to use with students is the provision of several relevant, concrete examples and several irrelevant examples.

In summary, it is recommended that this task-analytical approach toward summary skills be combined with levels of learning, behavior, and conditions to form curriculum-based social skill assessment devices. In the assessment of any social skills, it must first be determined whether the student recognizes that certain social behaviors are called for. For example, prior to exhibiting appropriate conversational skills, the student

Table 10.2. Table of Specifications for Conversation Skills

| | BEHAVIOR | | | | |
| | Identification | Production | | | |
CONTENT	*A. Acquisition*	*B. Acquisition*	*C. Fluency*	*D. Application*	*E. Generalization*
1. *eye contact*	1A	1B	1C	1D	1E
2. *tone of voice*	2A	2B	2C	2D	2E
3. *appropriate distance*	3A	3B	3C	3D	3E
4. *starting a conversation*	4A	4B	4C	4D	4E
5. *maintaining conversation*	5A	5B	5C	5D	5E
6. *interrupting conversation*	6A	6B	6C	6D	6E
7. *joining a conversation*	7A	7B	7C	7D	7E
8. *ending a conversation*	8A	8B	8C	8D	8E

Sample Objectives:

1A Students will identify appropriate eye contact from inappropriate eye contact 10 out of 10 times after viewing role-plays on a videotape.

4B Students will start a conversation appropriately 10 out of 10 times during role-play situations.

5C Students will maintain a conversation appropriately 10 out of 10 times in the special education setting.

6D Students will interrupt conversations appropriately during recess.

7E Students will join conversations appropriately at home.

must be able to identify the fact that this situation calls for appropriate conversational skills. Finally, when planning social skills assessment and instruction, teachers should ensure that considerations are given to cultural and ethnic diversity. The next section describes how these devices can be used for planning and delivering of social skills instruction.

Design and Delivery of Social Skills Instruction

Social skills instruction involves teaching the student to apply all of the skills being directly taught. To this extent, much of social skills instruction is procedural in nature and requires the student to *recognize* instances in which specific social skills are called for, as well as noninstances. Students must then *recall* the steps necessary to

execute the skill and, finally, *execute* the procedure effectively and efficiently in a variety of settings and situations.

Design and delivery of social skills instruction include all of the teacher effectiveness variables emphasized throughout this text, including (a) daily review, (b) presentation of material to be learned, (c) guided practice, (d) independent practice, (e) weekly and monthly reviews, and (f) formative evaluation. These teaching functions are presented in this section as used with social skills content. A sample lesson is excerpted in Figure 10.2.

Daily Review

Each social skills lesson should begin with a review of the content previously covered. It is also appropriate to review the homework assignment at this time. If the previous lesson emphasized

Review	"Last week we practiced the appropriate way to have eye contact with someone during a conversation. Can you all turn to your partner and show me appropriate eye contact? [Signal.] Good, everyone seems to remember that appropriate eye contact means holding your head up and looking your partner directly in the eyes."
Goal statement and teacher presentation	"Today we are going to practice identifying the appropriate tone to use during conversations. Watch the video monitor while I play some examples for you. [Video presents several examples (i.e., "This is an appropriate tone of voice") and several nonexamples (i.e., "This is *not* an appropriate tone of voice").] Remember, an appropriate tone of voice is not too loud or too soft, and it is interpreted as one showing interest in speaking with your partner." [Show several additional examples and nonexamples.]
Guided practice	"Now, we are going to select the examples that show us an appropriate tone of voice. [Turn on video for additional examples and nonexamples.] Is this appropriate? [Signal.]" [Provide corrective feedback as necessary throughout the presentation of several instances and noninstances.]
Independent practice	[Student continues with similar activity that requires individual responding on paper.]
Formative evaluation	[Teacher uses a similar practice activity but collects examples to grade and score later.]

Figure 10.2. Sample lesson for teaching social skills.

the identification of appropriate eye contact and tone of voice in conversations, the next lesson should begin with a review that includes discrimination practice of instances and noninstances of appropriate eye contact and tone of voice. If these subtasks cannot be accurately identified, additional practice emphasizing examples and nonexamples of each subtask should be introduced. These review procedures provide teachers with opportunities to assess students' performance and provide students with opportunities for overlearning previously acquired information.

Presentation of New Content

Teachers first need to clarify the goals and main objectives to be covered. If the lesson's major objectives include producing appropriate eye contact during conversations and producing the appropriate tone of voice during conversations in role-play situations, teachers could explicitly state the following to the students:

> Yesterday, we practiced telling when appropriate eye contact and tone of voice were used in talking. Remember, when you watched people talking you could tell appropriate eye contact from inappropriate eye contact, and you could tell appropriate tone of voice from inappropriate tone of voice. Today, we are going to practice using appropriate eye contact and tone of voice during conversations.

Next, teachers should provide a step-by-step presentation of the new material. Teachers can model and demonstrate several examples of appropriate eye contact and tone of voice during a role-play conversation. Additional explanations of why the examples are appropriate should be supplied, and noninstances should be interspersed among the examples to verify students' understanding of the concepts. After several minutes of this modeling, demonstration, and questioning, teachers should ask students to practice these two behaviors in role-play scenarios. Two students could be selected to model the appropriate eye contact and tone of voice for the rest of the students. With most students, teachers should supply scripted scenarios in which students play the roles of various characters. Supplying scripts allows students to concentrate on producing the correct responses (i.e., appropriate eye contact and tone of voice), rather than wasting time and effort thinking of topics for conversation.

Guided Practice

After students have modeled several examples for the class and teachers have monitored their performances and provided immediate corrective feedback, all students can be paired off and provided with scripted scenarios for practice exercises.

The major goal during guided practice is to allow all of the students as many opportunities as possible to practice accurately executing the new skill. This can be accomplished in several ways. For example, teachers can tell everyone to begin executing Scenario A and simultaneously wander around to specific pairs and provide immediate corrective feedback. Teachers could also have pairs practice different scenarios and then randomly call on pairs to demonstrate the appropriate skills for the class. Observers from the class could be required to critique the demonstrations; if the demonstrations were inappropriate, the observers could explain how the models could be altered to be appropriate. Teachers can involve all of the observers by asking the group to respond by signaling with hands or thumbs up or down about the correctness of the demonstration. All accurate responses should be reinforced with praise.

In general, activities that are directly relevant to the objective and that require active participation by all students are most likely to maximize the learning. During guided practice, errors are expected, and it is mandatory for teachers to provide immediate corrective feedback. Usually, a model–lead–test approach is an acceptable procedure to use in correcting students' errors. Teachers must be sure students have mastered the objective to the required level of proficiency before allowing them to practice independently.

Independent Practice

Independent practice activities need to be directly relevant to instructional objectives. Independent practice is usually not monitored as closely as guided practice by teachers, who may frequently be reading to another instructional group while students complete independent practice activities. It is a challenge to design independent practice activities for many of the social skills objectives. Because the production of the appropriate behavior is the desired response (e.g., the production of appropriate eye contact and tone of voice), traditional paper-and-pencil activities are often inappropriate. However, scripted scenarios can be presented on worksheets, and students can be required to execute the scenarios appropriately with a peer. Similar scenarios should be sent home as independent practice activities. In addition, teachers can begin to emphasize the importance of these behaviors throughout the day (i.e., during all interpersonal interactions). Although this objective will be emphasized more in the progression of skill development, it is appropriate for teachers to explain to students that these skills will be used in all conversations.

The most successful social skills training interventions have employed many practice activities, including homework assignments. When practice activities are designed to be executed in different scenarios, in different settings, and with different people, teachers provide practice that should help students to generalize and apply the desired behaviors to other settings. During such practice activities, accurate responses should be reinforced.

Weekly and Monthly Reviews

As in all content areas, special educators need to provide for weekly and monthly reviews of all social skills objectives covered. This type of formal review demonstrates to students the amount of progress they have made while providing opportunities for practice in applying previously learned skills to new situations. This overlearn-ing and generalization practice appears to be necessary for special education students to function independently in inclusive settings. Teachers can present these review periods as challenges for the students. Many students appear quite surprised by the amount of ground that they have covered.

Formative Evaluation

As with all lessons, teachers should include a short assessment at the end of each session to determine whether students have mastered the lesson's objectives. In social skills training, a short scenario or two that require all students to produce the responses can be given at the end of the lesson. Teachers record whether students respond correctly. These student performance data are then used to make an instructional decision regarding the next session. Based on student performance, the following variables can be altered for the next lesson:

1. increase or decrease engaged time-on-task

2. increase or decrease teacher presentation

3. increase or decrease number and type of examples and nonexamples

4. increase or decrease guided practice activities

5. increase or decrease corrective feedback

6. increase or decrease independent practice activities

7. increase or decrease cumulative review

8. alter one or more of 1 through 7 above

9. alter the formative evaluation

Any of the variables listed above can be manipulated in making an instructional decision based on actual performance data. Teachers can also decide that only two or three students need additional engaged time-on-task and, therefore, can insert another practice activity for those particular students. In any event, it is necessary to administer a formative evaluation measure and to use that information to guide future instructional sessions.

'On-the-Spot' Social Skills Instruction

Because social skills are exhibited in all situations, teachers may find it especially beneficial to incorporate "on-the-spot" instructional sessions in addition to the regularly scheduled sessions. In other words, as inappropriate and appropriate social behaviors occur throughout the day, it is good practice to emphasize newly practiced social skills to students. For instance, teachers can positively reinforce students who exhibit appropriate social skills in the cafeteria. Teachers can provide additional instruction and require students to practice social skills that are considered appropriate. A teacher might provide the on-the-spot instruction after observing a student exhibiting an inappropriate skill by stating, "Remember how we learned the correct way of getting someone's attention? Let's try doing it that way now."

This section has provided an example that illustrates how the teacher effectiveness variables can be used in the design, delivery, and evaluation of social skills instruction. Important features in designing social skills instruction include the following:

(a) instructional objectives be clearly specified;

(b) teachers present relevant information through models of instances and noninstances of skills;

(c) relevant guided practice activities involve all students;

(d) teachers monitor and adjust instruction based on student performance;

(e) relevant independent practice activities, including homework, be assigned;

(f) daily, weekly, and monthly reviews be included; and

(g) formative evaluation procedures be implemented to assess ongoing performance.

Generalization

Trained social skills are of little use if students do not generalize their use to other situations or settings. It is important to remember that students are most likely to generalize learned behaviors when generalization is specifically programmed. Several strategies may be helpful in promoting generalization of social skills (see also Elksnin, 1994):

1. Develop activities to be as realistic as possible.

2. Ensure that students have completely mastered the skills before generalization is expected. Students are unlikely to generalize behaviors they have not mastered in the training sessions.

3. Demonstrate how generalized social skills can help maximize social success and minimize failure. If students come to understand that social skills are in their own best interest, they will be more likely to generalize them.

4. Involve peers, parents, and school personnel in the training. Other individuals can help prompt appropriate social skills in different situations as students are being trained.

5. At first, the primary trainer can accompany students into different settings to monitor, prompt, and reinforce appropriate social behavior.

6. Teach students to monitor and evaluate their own use of social skills in different situations. Provide reinforcement for effective self-management.

7. Give "homework" assignments to implement specific social skills in situations outside school.

8. Periodically retrain and reinforce good social skills over time.

It is also helpful to promote positive attributions for students using social skills. Statements such as, "Do you see how well that social skill [e.g., praising others] worked for you?" can be helpful in promoting generalization.

Ensure Training Is Effective

Despite the importance of appropriate social skills, some comprehensive reviews of social skills training have suggested that such training often produces only modest gains in students' social behavior (Forness & Kavale, 1996; Kavale et al., 1997; Vaughn, McIntosh, & Hogan, 1990). When training social skills, teachers should specifically operationalize the desired behavior and carefully monitor progress. Positive social behavior can be realized through effective instruction, persistent effort, and problem solving.

Summary

- Researchers have documented that many special education students exhibit deficits in age-appropriate social skills. Overall school functioning and inclusion efforts can be made more successful when students learn to demonstrate acceptable social behavior.

- Social skills assessment is similar to assessment in the academic areas; that is, assessment first identifies students with particular social skills deficits. Next, assessment helps determine where along a continuum of objectives instruction needs to begin. Formative evaluation provides information on student performance and progress along that continuum of objectives.

- Social skills assessment procedures can include the following methods: (a) sociometric measures, (b) teacher ratings, (c) role-play tests, and (d) naturalistic or direct observation.

- Procedures for specifying skill sequences, levels of learning and behaviors, and performance criteria can be identified in the social skills area, just as they can be in academic skill areas. Once these sequences are delineated, teachers can implement systematic instruction using the teacher effectiveness variables.

- Many published social skills training materials are available and vary greatly in quality.

Choose materials that are well organized and provide sufficient instructional procedures, guided and independent practice activities, and formative evaluation procedures.

- Teachers should use task analysis to subdivide content along particular social skills domains of behavior and combine that subdivision with the levels of learning, behavior, and performance criteria to form a table of specifications.

- Design and delivery of social skills instruction include all of the teacher effectiveness variables, including (a) daily review, (b) presentation of material to be learned, (c) guided practice, (d) independent practice, (e) weekly and monthly reviews, and (f) formative evaluation.

- Because social skills are exhibited in all situations, teachers should incorporate "on-the-spot" instructional sessions in addition to the regularly scheduled sessions. As inappropriate and appropriate social behaviors occur throughout the day, it is good practice to emphasize newly practiced social skills to students.

- Trained social skills are of little benefit if students do not generalize their use to other situations or settings. Learned behaviors, including social skills, are most likely to generalize when generalization is specifically programmed.

Relevant Research and Resources

Research

Reviews of social competence and skills are provided by Cartledge and Milburn (1995), Forness and Kavale (1996), Kavale et al. (1997), Salzberg et al. (1988), Sullivan and Mastropieri (1994), Vaughn et al. (1990), and Zaragoza, Vaughn, and McIntosh (1991). Gresham, Sugai, and Horner (2001) discuss some of the modest effects of some social skills training and provide suggestions for designing and implementing effective social skills training interventions. Reviews related to social competence and social skills include those on cognitive–behavioral interventions and self-management (Ager & Cole, 1991; Nelson et al., 1991). Walker et al. (1995) describe strategies for improving social skills, and Cartledge (1996) has provided a text on social skills instruction and cultural diversity.

Social skills training has received substantial research attention over the past several decades (Gresham, 1981, 1982, 1984; Gresham & Lemanek, 1983; Keogh, 1981). Interest in the area of social skills training can be attributed to the problems in inclusion efforts (Gresham, 1981) and to the fact that special educators have historically spent more time instructing students in basic skill areas, such as reading, and assumed that social skills did not need explicit instruction. In addition, research has revealed that most students with mild disabilities exhibit deficiencies in social competence when compared with their normally achieving peers. Consequently, in the past decade, numerous investigations using students with disabilities have been conducted to determine the optimal type of social skills training to ameliorate these deficiencies in social skills. Many variables have been examined over the years in studies on social skills training, including the following:

1. Instructional procedures employed, including the following:

(a) use of multiple intervention strategies such as direct instruction, modeling, and role rehearsal (Vaughn, Ridley, & Cox, 1983); direct instruction, modeling, role rehearsal, prompting, and feedback (LeGreca & Mesibov, 1981; Matson et al., 1980); direct instruction, modeling, role-playing, role rehearsal, feedback, and self-monitoring (Thorkildsen, 1984); games and self-reporting (Amerikaner & Summerline, 1982); reinforcement of some type in combination with other intervention strategies (Schloss,

Schloss, & Harris, 1984; Thorkildsen, 1984; Walker et al., 1983); and use of homework activities in combination with other strategies (Thorkildsen, 1984); and

(b) use of single intervention strategies such as modeling (Donahue & Bryan, 1983) and contracting (Lanunziata, Hill, & Krause, 1981).

2. Behaviors targeted for improvement, including the following:

(a) greeting and joining a conversation (Le-Greca & Mesibov, 1981);

(b) peer interaction, such as helping others, playing with others, and assertiveness (Evers & Schwartz, 1973; Moore, Cartledge, & Heckaman, 1994);

(c) facial expressions and verbalizations for positive and negative situations (Kazdin, Esveldt-Dawson, & Matson, 1983);

(d) providing positive and negative feedback, solving problems, resisting peer pressure, negotiating, and following instructions (Hazel, Schumaker, Sherman, & Sheldon, 1982; Schumaker & Ellis, 1982);

(e) providing compliments, appropriate requests, tone of voice, eye contact, and body posture (Matson et al., 1980);

(f) appropriate social play (Strain & Wiegerink, 1976);

(g) appropriate response to instruction (Warrenfeltz et al., 1981) and eliciting positive teacher attention (Alber, Heward, & Hippler, 1999);

(h) positive social behavior (Ragland, Kerr, & Strain, 1981) and anger management (Presley & Hughes, 2000); and

(i) transition goals and self-determination (Agran, Blanchard, & Wehmeyer (2000).

3. Instructional settings in which social skills training typically occurs:

(a) public schools (Amerikaner & Summerline, 1982; Donahue & Bryan, 1983, Evers &

Schwartz, 1973; Thorkildsen, 1984; Walker et al., 1983),

(b) residential treatment centers (Kazdin et al., 1983; Matson et al., 1980),

(c) clinical settings (Cooke & Apolloni, 1976), and

(d) multiple settings (Hazel et al., 1982; Ragland et al., 1981).

4. Type of trainers employed, including the following:

(a) trained experimenters or therapists (Hazel et al., 1982; Schloss et al., 1984),

(b) classroom teacher (Schumaker & Ellis, 1982; Strain & Wiegerink, 1976), and

(c) peer tutors (Lancioni, 1982; Ragland et al., 1981), including students with emotional disabilities as tutors of social skills (Blake, Wang, Cartledge, & Gardner, 2000).

5. Instructional format, including the following:

(a) small-group instructional sessions (Amerikaner & Summerline, 1982; Cooke & Apolloni, 1976; Evers & Schwartz, 1973),

(b) individual instructional sessions (Donahue & Bryan, 1983; Hazel et al., 1982; Thorkildsen, 1984), and

(c) combinations of small-group and individual sessions (Matson et al., 1980).

6. Duration of social skills training programs, ranging from

(a) shorter number of training sessions (1 to 5) (Donahue & Bryan, 1983),

(b) medium number of training sessions (6 to 15 sessions) (Amerikaner & Summerline, 1982; Ford et al., 1995), and

(c) larger number of training sessions (more than 15) (Strain & Wiegerink, 1976; Thorkildsen, 1984).

7. Type of students, including students with

(a) learning disabilities (Schumaker & Ellis, 1982),

(b) mental retardation (Lancioni, 1982), and

(c) behavioral disorders (Kiburz, Miller, & Morrow, 1984).

8. Age of the students, including the following:

(a) preschoolers (Mastropieri & Scruggs, 1985–1986; Strain & Wiegerink, 1976),

(b) elementary-age students (Amerikaner & Summerline, 1982),

(c) preadolescent students (Bierman & Furman, 1984), and

(d) adolescent students (Schumaker & Ellis, 1982).

Curricular Materials

Social skills curricular materials have become widely available. It is recommended that teachers carefully evaluate the programs to ensure they will meet the needs of their students. The *Walker Social Skills Curriculum,* including the *ACCEPTS Program* (A Curriculum for Children's Effective Peer and Teacher Skills) and the *ACCESS Program* (Adolescent Curriculum for Communication and Effective Social Skills), *Personal Power: Student Effectiveness Training, Developing Appropriate Teacher Interaction Skills, Gaining Self-Control,* and *Peer Interaction Skills* are available from PRO-ED. *Getting Along with Others: Teaching Social Effectiveness to Children, Skillstreaming the Elementary School Child, Skillstreaming the Adolescent, Teaching Prosocial Behavior to Antisocial Youth,* and *ASSET: A Social Skills Program for Adolescents* are available from Research Press. *The Solution Book* is available from SRA/McGraw-Hill. American Guidance Service distributes *Social Skills on the Job* for secondary and adult learners and *Working Together:*

Building Children's Social Skills Through Folk Literature, a multicultural approach to social skills.

Computer Software and Technology

Several of the programs listed as curricular materials have optional video and/or audio compo-

nents (e.g., *The Walker Social Skills Curriculum*). In addition, some researchers have developed videodisk programs for social skills training (e.g., Thorkildsen, 1984). See Appendix B for a list of addresses of producers and distributors of software and curricular materials.

INCLUSION FEATURE

Stop and Think Sheet
for Improving Social Skills

Some students with disabilities are taught self-intructions to monitor their own social skills improvement by using self-monitoring sheets. Once students have been taught to identify the problem, focus their attention on correcting the problem, plan a response, and practice evaluating their responses, they can implement the procudure using self-monitoring in inclusive classes. Self-monitoring sheets can be used in inclusive classes to help students remember, think, and implement the correct steps for targeted areas of social skills improvement. The example is designed to help a student remember to stop and think before interrupting others and before saying inappropriate things during class discussions and conversations. Each time the student talks in class, he or she is told to stop and think through the following sequence of steps and place a check in the yes or no column, indicating whether he or she successfully monitored speaking out and speaking appropriately in class. Initially, teachers can complete the same checklist and compare recording the results with the student to ensure that the student is accurately marking his or her efforts. Rewards can be established if, for example, the student can successfully record yes marks for the day or week.

"Stop and Think" Self-Monitoring Sheet

	Yes	No
Did I stop before talking?	☐	☐
Did I think before talking?	☐	☐
Did I think what I was going to say was appropriate?	☐	☐
Did I raise my hand before talking?	☐	☐
Did I successfully contribute to the class discussion?	☐	☐
Enter total number of yes and no responses	_____	_____

TECHNOLOGY FEATURE

Social Skills Media

Many students with disabilities can profit from social skills instruction. Social skills instruction can be a challenging area for many teachers. Many programs, including videos, are available commercially that can help build teachers' and parents' understanding of the basic need for social skills instruction. For example, Richard Lavoie is the lead presenter in three videos distributed by WETA:

- Last One Picked . . . First One Picked On: Learning Disabilities and Social Skills (1994)

- Learning Disabilities and Discipline with Richard Lavoie: When the Chips Are Down . . . Strategies for Improving Children's Behavior (1997)

- How Difficult Can This Be? The F.A.T. City Workshop (1989)

All three tapes present excellent information on learning disabilities in a format that is enjoyable yet makes powerful statements about the learning needs of these students. Some teachers have reported showing these tapes to their secondary-age students and indicated that the content appeared to increase students' understanding of learning disabilities.

Chapter 11

✦   ✦   ✦

Teaching for Transition: Life Skills, Career, and Vocational Education

Remediation of deficits in academic and social functioning is a primary responsibility of special education teachers. The overall goal of special education, however, is successful independent functioning in inclusive environments. Ultimately, this means successful functioning in postschool environments, the domain of adult living. Recently, a great deal of attention has been paid to the importance of preparing students for the transition from school to occupational and independent living environments.

Such instruction should not be put off until a year or two before the student is expected to graduate. Orientation of the student to the world of work and adult living should begin early in the elementary school years and should be integrated into all aspects of the school curriculum at all grade levels. In fact, all students with disabilities who have IEPs are now required to have Individual Transition Plans (ITPs) when they reach 14 years of age, which are intended to facilitate transition from school to community, vocational programs, college, or employment (Asselin, Todd-Allen, & DeFur, 1998).

One important feature of transitional education to which all teachers should attend is the relevance of the adopted curricular materials to independent living skills (Patton et al., 1998). This relevance should be made explicitly clear to students. For example, it is important to teach students the basic skills and operations in mathematics so that they will ultimately be able to use these skills in solving word problems. However, an important purpose of learning to solve word

problems in school is to be able to solve practical math problems in home or occupational environments. If this final generalization step is not learned, the preceding steps will prove to be of little value outside of a school setting. Likewise, many other content or curricular areas have direct relevance to adult functioning, and this relevance should be made explicit to students.

In this chapter, several different aspects of life skills, career, and vocational education will be considered. Although everything taught in school should be relevant to everyday living, the following sections will focus on content with obvious and immediate importance to adult living. These sections will describe life skills, career, and vocational education, respectively.

Life Skills

Life skills instruction typically refers to those skills that are relevant to independent, day-to-day living. Instruction includes personal finance, health and fitness, and leisure activities, each of which is considered separately here (Cronin & Patton, 1993).

Personal Finance

Personal finance is often included within mathematics curricula and includes all aspects of saving, spending, and budgeting money. Students who have been taught effective skills for personal finance stand a far greater chance of success in life than those who have not been taught these skills. Aspects of personal finance appropriate for instruction in special education settings are described in the following sections.

Budget Balancing

Lessons on personal finance can be started with instruction in developing a personal budget. Students can be taught the distinction between "gross salary" and "take-home pay." Simulated paychecks can be used to illustrate income tax withholding, as well as Social Security, insurance, and other deductions.

When students have learned to compute monthly take-home pay, they should be shown how to budget their resources so that they can live most efficiently. Many consumer specialists suggest that an expenditure of 25% to 33% of monthly take-home income on housing is desirable. Students should estimate their future incomes based on salaries or wages advertised in the help wanted section of the newspaper, from library research, or from information obtained from the guidance counselor's office. Once they have computed their approximate take-home pay, students should check the newspaper listings for available housing and determine where they could live given a rent of approximately one-third of their income.

If students plan to live alone, of course, the cost for housing would likely be much higher than if they arranged to share a house or apartment. Also, students may consider living with parents or guardians until a specific amount of money is saved, which could be put toward a car, for example. Regardless, students should be taught to consider the specific economic consequences of various forms of living arrangements (see Figure 11.1).

Similar considerations can be made for budgeting food. Local TV news stations frequently report on the cost of groceries to the average shopper. These costs can be compared with the cost of eating out in restaurants, and estimates

Income	
Gross monthly wages	$820.00
Less deductions and withholding	−220.00
Net income	$600.00
Expenses	
Rent	$220.00
Utilities	70.00
Food	90.00
Transportation (bus)	20.00
Clothing	50.00
Personal (toothpaste, etc.)	15.00
Medical	35.00
Entertainment	40.00
Subtotal	$540.00
Savings	+ 60.00
Total	$600.00

Figure 11.1. Monthly budget.

can be made of the proportion of monthly income spent on food. Finally, students should consider the amount of monthly income remaining after expenditures for housing and food for other expenses such as clothing, transportation (including car payments, bus fares, parking charges, and car maintenance), home furnishings, medical expenses, entertainment and recreational costs, and savings. Expenses can be estimated by asking students what type and level of goods and services they desire and determining the costs of these goods and services from newspapers, television, and library sources.

Students can also be introduced to various form of budgeting, including computer software that can be used to budget income. As with other instructional activities in special education, it is not sufficient to simply "introduce" students to practices for managing personal finance. Budgeting should be practiced on a regular basis until students' responses are automatic and likely to be carried into the transitional environment.

Using a Checkbook

A critical skill for independent living is managing checking accounts. Typically, students with mild disabilities have acquired math skills appropriate for such computation by the time they reach high school, but they may need practice on the specific aspects of check writing and correctly subtracting the amount of the check from the checking account balance. These procedures can best be taught by acquiring facsimiles of checkbooks and providing instruction, guided practice, and independent practice on aspects of check writing. Figure 11.2 provides some excerpts from a lesson on check writing.

Credit

Any student who is preparing to enter the world of independent living should be aware of the possible consequences of using various forms of credit. It is important for students to learn how to compute additional expenses incurred by finance charges and to consider such additional charges when making purchases on credit. Students can become efficient at such computation through the provision of problems in math classes that use real-world examples (e.g., computing the total cost of an automobile purchased on credit and comparing it with the price of purchasing the same vehicle without finance charges). Finally, students should be informed of the consequences of obligating too much monthly income to installment payments, as well as the consequences of failing to meet such obligations.

Purchasing Goods and Services

Because many students enrolled in special education settings are not likely to earn large salaries immediately upon graduation from high school,

Component	Examples
Daily review	"Last week we learned the names of the parts of a check. Look at this example. What is the name of this part of the check? . . ."
State objective and teacher presentation	"Today we are going to practice writing checks. [Show overhead transparency of a blank check.] Everyone look up at this example with me. We are going to write out a check to Dr. Sydney for $35.63. First, I write in today's date in the date spot. [Write in date.] Then, I find the part of the check that says *Pay to the order of,* and I write in Dr. Sydney. Next, I find the enclosed box with the dollar sign, and I write in the amount of the check, in this case, $35.63. Then . . . Let's practice several additional examples together. . . ."
Guided practice	"Now, I want each of you to practice writing the following checks to your neighbor. [Distribute checks worksheets and circulate around room.] Let's check the first example together. . . ."
Independent practice	[Worksheets similar to the ones just completed are distributed.] "This activity is exactly like the one we just finished. This time I want you to work independently. If you have any questions, raise your hand and I will come to your desk. . . ."
Formative evaluation	"You have three minutes to complete this activity. You are expected to fill in the appropriate information on these two checks. Ready, begin. . . ."

Figure 11.2. Sample lesson on check writing.

it is important for them to learn how to obtain the greatest value for the income they do earn. For this reason, students should learn how to make sensible purchases, shop for values, find and use coupons, and comparison shop. Lessons that could be taught in this area include the relative merit of generic "store" brands versus established brand names, as well as how to interpret misleading advertising (e.g., that a particular brand of toothpaste will make one more popular among peers).

Health and Fitness

Health and physical fitness are arguably among the most important concerns in any life skills curriculum. Instruction in health and fitness has three major components: (a) an information component that communicates facts about health and fitness, (b) an attitude component that strives to impress upon students the importance of health concerns so that the informational component will be implemented, and (c) development of habits of good health and fitness.

The most important information about good health is not difficult to learn; basic facts concerning regular checkups, proper diet, avoidance of alcohol and drugs, weight regulation, and regular exercise can be communicated in a relatively small number of lessons. Developing optimal attitudes about health and fitness can take much longer, however, and developing appropriate health habits is most difficult of all.

Appropriate attitudes toward fitness and health should be modeled by the teacher. Teachers who are themselves overweight, out of shape, or otherwise unhealthy due to personal negligence may have less credibility with students concerning health habits. Teachers should practice good health habits and actively communicate the importance of doing so to their students. Information concerning the harmful effects of drugs, alcohol, and tobacco can be acquired from organizations such as the American Cancer Society and is best communicated by adult models who do not themselves abuse these substances. Finally, appropriate habits can be promoted by encouragement from physical education teachers and by support of exercise programs in the classroom settings. Teachers can help students conduct formative evaluation of their physical progress (e.g., number of chin-ups or times for running 400 meters) and encourage them to set personal goals and take personal satisfaction in meeting these goals. Encouragement and support of physical fitness help to promote a positive attitude in the independent living environment.

Leisure Activities

Many students with mild disabilities are less able to enumerate options available to them than are their more average peers. This relative shortcoming applies as much to leisure activities as it does to employment options or living alternatives. Even though a basic function of school is to provide training relevant to the world of work, effective use of leisure time is also important in the development of the whole person. Some relevant information on leisure activities can be provided in academic classes (e.g., promotion of reading for enjoyment provided in reading or English classes). Other options for leisure-time activities can be taught separately. Students should be taught about the various social, service, or athletic organizations that exist in a community and how to become a member of these organizations. Likewise, it may be profitable to acquaint students with community recreational facilities, such as public parks, lakes, swimming pools, and athletic facilities. Community organizations can alert the teacher to the variety of public facilities that are available for leisure activities. As is true of health and fitness, it is important to encourage the appropriate attitudes toward constructive leisure activities so that individuals actively pursue these activities as adults and do not resign themselves to watching television as their major leisure activity.

Some of the major topics in life skills instruction have been outlined. Many additional related areas can be incorporated into a life skills curriculum. Related areas include personal identity and values clarification, dealing with conflict and disappointment, dating and marriage, home repairs, buying and using medicines, voting and political activity, and finding new friends (see Cronin & Patton, 1993). Which topics should be included in a life skills curriculum can be determined by interacting with guidance counselors, administrative personnel, parent–teacher organizations, and community service personnel. Decisions concerning life skills curricula should be a function of the total school and community orientation toward such training (e.g., some communities have very specific views concerning sex education in the schools). It is also important to determine what life skills are currently being taught in the existing regular education curriculum. As with content area and other types of instruction, care should be taken to ensure that (a) regular class instruction is not a preferable alternative and (b) the scope and sequence of life skills instruction parallels as closely as possible the objectives addressed in the general education classroom.

Career Education

A distinction is often made between vocational education, which is concerned with specific job-related training, and career education, which is concerned with a more general orientation to the world of work and can begin in elementary school (Grubb, 1996). Although many different components could conceivably be included in a career education curriculum, the following four major components will be considered here: (a) developing appropriate attitudes and habits related to work, (b) developing appropriate work-related social skills, (c) developing awareness of occupational alternatives, and (d) developing awareness of individual career preferences through career counseling and vocational assessment. Each component will be considered separately in the following sections.

Attitudes and Habits

It is important for every person to develop a generally positive attitude toward work and effective, goal-oriented work habits. Students in school should learn to work hard and take pride in their accomplishments. If their achievement or ability is below average in some areas, as is often the case in special education, students should nonetheless take pride in what they do achieve, as well as the amount of progress they are able to make. If these attitudes are thoroughly internalized with respect to school tasks, they are more likely to generalize to work-related tasks in the outside world.

It is difficult to influence attitudes and habits through direct instruction in individual lessons. Although students may be taught to recite the types of habits and attitudes that are desirable and linked to success, it is another matter altogether to adopt these attitudes and habits as their own, as reflected in classroom behavior. This process, which can take years, can be promoted through the establishment of a classroom atmosphere that, although warm and friendly, is nonetheless businesslike and achievement oriented. Students should be continually encouraged to put forth their best efforts and be rewarded for doing so. In many cases, student performance may not meet expectations, but students should be aware that their level of effort can always meet expectations. To this end, teacher praise for effort (e.g., "You should be proud of yourself for all the hard work you put into that assignment. Not everyone would have stuck with it the way you did.") can be helpful. Such statements deliver a message to students that hard work and persistent efforts are valuable in and of themselves. On the other hand, it is equally important to recognize when students are not working up to their potential and to deliver appropriate feedback. In such cases, lower-than-expected effort should be acknowledged, and specific behaviors that the student can improve should be pointed out with statements such as, "I am sorry to see that you didn't try very hard on that assignment.

I noted you spent a lot of time looking out the window and going up to the pencil sharpener. I know you can do better work than this and that you can work much harder than you worked last period." It is important to end these statements on an encouraging note regarding higher expectations for the child. It is also important to note when the student is not working hard because the assignment is too difficult or is not clearly understood.

As students progress in school, they should be made as responsible as possible for their own work because independent work will be expected of them on most jobs. Students who are used to teachers watching their every move will be poorly prepared for occupations in which the level of supervision is considerably lower. If appropriate work habits and positive attitudes are encouraged throughout school, students are far more likely to be successful outside of school.

Social Skills

Research has indicated that individuals are much less likely to lose their jobs because of lack of ability or intelligence than they are to lose them because of a lack of appropriate job-related social skills (Salzberg, Lignugaris-Kraft, & McCuller, 1988). Employees who have good attitudes, work habits, and social skills are likely to be well liked by their employers. When they do exhibit performance deficits, they are likely to receive additional feedback or training. On the other hand, employees who exhibit poor work habits, bad attitudes, and poor social skills are not likely to be well liked by their employers. When such workers exhibit performance deficits, they are likely to be fired because these performance deficits can be used as an excuse to get rid of an unpopular employee.

There are several areas of appropriate job-related social skills instruction. Students should be encouraged to exhibit good interpersonal skills with their teachers as a prerequisite to exhibiting good social skills with their future employers. To this end, students should be encouraged to exhibit many of the same skills that effective teachers exhibit toward students; that is, students should learn to interact with teachers as individual human beings. Polite social conversation that acknowledges the teacher–student relationship can be helpful in promoting good interpersonal relations. Likewise, conversation and behavior that suggest that the student is considerate of the teacher's needs can help to develop an atmosphere in which teachers and students alike are more comfortable. Students who practice such behaviors have an advantage over students who do not; the same is true of employer–employee relationships. Although excessively attentive or obsequious behavior is generally not appreciated by employers or teachers, and although peers do not respect a teacher's pet, students in special education classes often have the opposite problem. Some students are slow to realize that teacher–student relationships have as much to do with the student as they do with the teacher. The same will be true of employer–employee relations, so teachers are wise to point out and reinforce student behavior that facilitates positive teacher–student relations.

Job-related social skills instruction can also be incorporated into social skills training (see Chapter 10). As students approach the age at which they are likely to enter the job market, the relevance of social skills training to employment should be made explicit. Students can be taught to ask questions and show an interest in performing competently on their jobs. In addition, students need to learn to ask for clarification when they do not understand directions. Many performance difficulties on the job site can be attributed to unclear or poorly understood directions. Jobs that are not well understood cannot be competently executed, so clarity in directions should be ensured before the task is begun. Likewise, interpersonal skills with peers are also important, particularly because many jobs require cooperative effort. Asking for help, doing one's share, and acknowledging assistance (e.g., by saying "thank you") are all important aspects of good peer relations on the job. Students should also be encouraged to use what they have learned about teasing, name-calling, and gossiping when they arrive on the job site. These behaviors are even less likely to be tolerated at work than they were at school. A possible table of specifications for job-related social skills is presented in Table 11.1.

Finally, job-related social skills can be promoted during any vocational instruction students receive in school. Employer–employee relations can be modeled through execution of assigned projects, and good peer relations can be stressed

on projects that require cooperative effort. Again, appropriate social behaviors in classes can be stressed as being of at least equal importance as appropriate vocational skills.

Occupational Alternatives

Most of us, at one time or another, have been asked, "What do you want to do for a living?" or "What would you like to do when you grow up?" Children often answer with the occupations of a favorite adult or an occupation that appears

Table 11.1. Table of Specifications for Job-Related Social Skills

CONTENT	BEHAVIOR				
	Identification	**Production**			
	A. Acquisition	**B. Acquisition**	**C. Fluency**	**D. Application**	**E. Generalization**
1. *Conversation skills* (1) with employer	1(1)A	1(1)B	1(1)C	1(1)D	1(1)E
(2) with co-worker	1(2)A	1(2)B	1(2)C	1(2)D	1(2)E
(3) with customers	1(3)A	1(3)B	1(3)C	1(3)D	1(3)E
2. *Task-related skills* (1) asking for clarification	2(1)A	2(1)B	2(1)C	2(1)D	2(1)E
(2) asking for assistance	2(2)A	2(2)B	2(2)C	2(2)D	2(2)E
(3) volunteering to assist	2(3)A	2(3)B	2(3)C	2(3)D	2(3)E
3. *Personal appearance* (1) appropriate grooming	3(1)A	3(1)B	3(1)C	3(1)D	3(1)E
(2) appropriate dress	3(2)A	3(2)B	3(2)C	3(2)D	3(2)E

Sample Objectives:

1(1)A   Students will identify the scenarios that exhibit an employee having appropriate conversation skills with an employer 10 out of 10 times.

2(2)C   Students will ask for assistance in completing job-related tasks as often as appropriate during all of the role-play scenarios.

3(1)E   Students will come to work after they have showered and neatly combed their hair.

glamorous on television. A mature and practical vocational decision, however, depends on careful consideration of occupational alternatives.

Students are unlikely to acquire this information on their own. Good career education includes systematic instruction in the many different types of employment available. Students should also be informed of which occupations are most widely represented in their immediate geographical area. As students grow older and learn more about their own interests and abilities, they are more likely to make informed career choices for themselves, based on a thorough knowledge of career alternatives.

The school guidance counselor or staff development office should be able to supply information on occupational alternatives that can be transmitted to the class as factual information using instructional procedures similar to those described earlier. In addition, adults from the community can be asked to come to class and describe their occupations to the students. As with any "community speaker" activity, it is important for the speaker, the teacher, and the students to understand the objectives of the activity and how those objectives will be evaluated. Asking the speaker to submit a brief outline of his or her presentation can give students some advance information on the topic.

Another source of information on occupations is through media presentations such as slide presentations, filmstrips, films, and videotapes. These may be available from the guidance counselor, school district office, or local library. Again, when these materials are used, it is important to specify the objectives beforehand.

A final consideration in teaching about career alternatives is that information should be cumulative; that is, student awareness of career alternatives should increase over time and not be forgotten. To facilitate cumulative recall, students can be required to compile a permanent record of career information (e.g., a career notebook in which information relevant to specific careers, students' notes, and information cut out from magazines or scrapbooks can be included). Such a notebook could be used for periodic review

regarding career options. In addition, any new information that the student receives on a particular occupation can be inserted into the appropriate space on an ongoing basis.

Making Specific Career Choices

Aspects of career education covered to this point include development of appropriate work habits and attitudes, development of job-related social skills, and development of knowledge of career alternatives. This section discusses developing awareness of individual career preferences. Two important considerations in making career decisions are that such choices be informed and realistic. Informed choice means that the individual is well aware not only of career alternatives but also of the specific demands of those particular careers. In addition to personal interest level, other aspects of particular career choices to be considered include level of salary, regularity, length of hours, working conditions (including social as well as physical environment), and amount of training necessary. Students should be well informed on all these aspects of specific careers before they consider them seriously.

Realistic career choices are those for which the student shows potential ability and those for which sufficient employment demand exists. For example, many high school–age students may express a desire to be a professional athletes or musicians. These choices may provide information regarding the student's perceived need for attention or popularity, but in most cases, they reflect neither informed nor realistic choices. To make a realistic career choice, students must understand their own level of ability with respect to the choice and the general likelihood of obtaining employment in that particular field. Students can easily underestimate as well as overestimate their own level of ability, so some type of objective feedback can be helpful. Records of previous student performance in vocationally relevant courses, as well as performance on vocational aptitude tests, can be useful materials for providing this kind of feedback. Finally, published interest inventories can be used to identify students' general interests. As with any other tests, however, vocational aptitude and interest tests are only as useful as their reliability and validity data. This means that if a student expresses interest in animal husbandry, this interest should also be apparent 2 weeks later (reliability). Likewise, if a vocational aptitude test discriminates between people with high versus low aptitude for automobile mechanics, the test maker should supply data that indicate that persons scoring high on this test become better automobile mechanics than persons scoring low on this test (validity).

Most schools employ counselors whose job, in part, is to help students make informed and reasonable career choices. It is important for special education teachers to work closely with these personnel to ensure that each student makes informed and reasonable career choices. One possible avenue to career decisions is encouraging students to find related employment on either a part-time basis after school hours or as part of a work-study program incorporated into the school day. Although it is unlikely that students will be able to find exactly the type of employment they are interested in, they may find employment that shares some common characteristics. For example, if a career they are considering involves a good deal of contact with the public, students may find part-time employment that involves contact with the public and then evaluate their reactions to this aspect of their career alternative.

Vocational Education

Vocational education is usually taken to mean direct training in career-related skills. Students are taught the skills they will use in their chosen field. Typical vocational areas include agricultural education, business education, family and consumer science, marketing education, trade and industrial education, and technology education (Sarkees-Wircenski & Scott, 1995). These areas of instruction require well-equipped instructional settings and trained instructors who are proficient in the vocational skills being taught. States are required

to provide for the special needs of students with disabilities in vocational education, according to the Carl Perkins Vocational Education Act of 1984 (Asselin et al., 1998).

Vocational instruction is often an area of difficulty in the special education setting. Although many special education students can benefit from vocational instruction, relatively few special education teachers have extensive knowledge of vocational education. Likewise, few vocational education teachers have extensive knowledge of special education procedures. Nevertheless, special education teachers can do much to ensure that students receive high-quality, relevant vocational training. The section that follows focuses on issues of curriculum planning, instructional techniques, placement, and follow-up.

Curriculum Planning

One important consideration in planning vocational curricula is which vocational training area specific students should be placed in. As stated earlier, several techniques can be employed to help students identify vocational preferences. Special education teachers, however, should attempt to determine which skill areas are most likely to result in employment. This requires an evaluation of several factors. Are sufficient job opportunities available in the community? Many legitimate vocational skill areas are unlikely to result in employment unless the potential employee is prepared to move to another part of the country. For students who intend to to reside in the same geographical area after graduation, this is an important consideration. Information on the potential job market can be gathered by examining the classified section of the local newspaper, contacting the local chamber of commerce, and contacting potential employers.

Another consideration to be made in determining areas for vocational instruction is the level of competition for particular jobs. If employment exists but is highly competitive, students with disabilities may have difficulty obtaining employment even when adequately trained.

It may be more practical to counsel students to enroll in training in areas that are less competitive. A final consideration involves evaluating the attitudes of potential employers toward individuals with mild disabilities. In many cases, employers are more than willing to make certain allowances (e.g., accommodating a low reading ability or a slower rate of initial learning) in return for good work habits, positive attitudes, and good social skills. Other employers may be reluctant to make special allowances of any kind and may, in fact, be somewhat hostile to the idea of hiring workers with mild disabilities. In some cases, these attitudes can be changed, either through education or through provision of positive examples. In other cases, it may be wiser to look elsewhere for positive employment opportunities. It may be helpful to compile a notebook or other record of possible employment alternatives and add to it over time as more information is gained. In addition, previous successes can help with future placements. If employers have had successful experiences with individuals with disabilities in the past, they are more likely to hire individuals from such programs in the future.

When potential employers and relevant vocational areas are identified, it is wise to consult with employers regarding the skills they value most and to ensure that these skills are included in the vocational curriculum. Specific training in these skills can increase the probability of later employment.

Vocational Instruction

If the special education teacher is qualified to provide instruction in one or more vocational area, he or she may be the primary vocational skills instructor of special education students. However, it should first be determined that students cannot be taught effectively in an inclusive environment. In most cases, special education students are taught vocational skills by the vocational education teacher, and the special education teacher acts as a consultant. In this capacity, special education teachers should learn as much as possible about the areas being taught so that they can provide helpful feedback based on knowledge of special education as well as on knowledge of particular students. If time permits, the special education teacher can work as a co-teacher in vocational education classes to ensure the success of their students. Special education teachers can provide valuable information regarding instructional features such as careful task analysis, positive practice, behavioral contingencies, feedback and reinforcement, and formative evaluation, many of which may not be included as regular components of inclusive vocational instruction. To communicate effectively with the vocational education teacher, however, special education teachers need to learn as much as possible about the vocational skills being taught.

If students exhibit persistent difficulties with particular vocational areas, additional teacher attention may be required. As with any other content area, teachers should carefully task-analyze the content, isolate the particular areas of difficulty, and provide additional instruction in those particular areas.

Special education teachers can help establish necessary modifications in instruction for students with special needs. A checklist can be created that lists areas of possible concern in vocational settings—such as access, movement, safety, mobility judgment, measurement, counting, or strength—and how modifications can be made in these areas. Safety in vocational settings is a particular concern for students with special needs. Special education and vocational education teachers should establish requirements for safety and monitor these requirements carefully (Sarkees-Wircenski & Scott, 1995).

Students with special needs in vocational settings can benefit greatly from careful specification of the competencies required and documentation of progress toward the acquisition of those competencies. In bricklayer construction, for example, students need to acquire skills spreading mortar, laying brick to a line, building a brick corner, cutting brick and block, and determining spacing for standard-size brick. Systematic checklists of these competencies and criteria for mastery can be very helpful (Sarkees-Wircenski & Scott, 1995). Formative evaluation can document progress toward completion of objectives.

Many vocational texts and manuals are written beyond the reading levels of many students enrolled in special education. In these cases, materials can be supplemented with teacher-directed instruction and with help developing chapter outlines. Students can review audio-taped versions of text as homework assignments. Rewriting some sections to make them more readable and comprehensible to students also may be beneficial.

Often, students exhibit difficulty because they have failed to master important technical vocabulary (e.g., wheel alignment, steering axis inclination angle, steering knuckle). Almost any vocational area has its own unique terminology, and students who do not master this terminology will be unable to learn any new information that uses it. Special education teachers can acquire a list of relevant vocabulary words from the vocational teacher and ensure that these words have been mastered. A technical terms tabulation sheet can list all necessary technical terms, how they will be presented (e.g., text, lecture, demonstration, audiovisual presentation), and criteria for mastery (Sarkees-Wircenski & Scott, 1995). Additional teacher- or tutor-led drill and practice is likely to be beneficial. In some cases, use of the keyword mnemonic technique described earlier or other verbal elaborations may prove helpful. In any case, teachers should ensure that students not only can define relevant vocabulary but also have made it part of their working vocabulary (e.g., in communicating with the vocational teacher). In addition, knowledge of specific facts (e.g., torque specifications) is necessary for success in vocational areas. If such knowledge is not acquired efficiently, additional practice provided by teachers or tutors may be helpful. Checklists can also be used to monitor progress in these areas.

Much vocational learning is procedural in nature (e.g., remove and diagnose condition of spark plugs). If difficulty is noticed in mastering procedural aspects of vocational skills training, teachers can employ relevant teaching strategies: modeling, prompting, and evaluating student performance on each step in the task. If tasks involve a particularly long sequence of operations, teachers should introduce the task a few steps at a time and, as previously learned steps are mastered, gradually add additional steps. It should also be remembered that *application* of procedural information is necessary. For example, it is not sufficient for students to simply be able to recite the steps necessary to complete a particular assembly task; ultimately, it will be necessary for students to actually execute these steps in the appropriate setting. To meet this objective, additional hands-on training may be necessary.

Placement and Follow-Up

After students have learned specific vocational skills, appropriate job placement is necessary. In some cases, the training provided is really *prevocational* in that placement is into a vocational or technical school. Students will have been taught skills appropriate for this type of placement (e.g., independent behaviors at work stations, appropriate social skills, and adequate levels of basic skills and prerequisite vocational knowledge).

Regardless of the exact nature of the placement, the teachers need to determine that a specific placement is appropriate to the ability and skill level of the individual and that potential support services are available if problems arise. If time permits, teachers can include themselves as a potential resource. Openness and an honest appraisal of students' abilities can ensure that placement will be successful.

Once students graduate from school and obtain employment, they are no longer directly the responsibility of the school. However, periodic follow-up through mail, telephone, or personal visits can ensure that placements are successful and that vocational education programs are effective. Although teachers do not have the time or resources to make a major impact on outside placements, they can nonetheless evaluate sources of failure in placements and take steps to ensure that similar failures do not occur again. For example, if students are found to be lacking in specific skills, instruction on these skills can be included or intensified in the school curriculum in the future.

Finally, a notebook or other permanent record is helpful in documenting, over time, which placements have been most successful, along with probable reasons for success. Likewise, placements that were less successful can also provide useful information for future training and programming. Although special education teachers should not feel personally responsible for every failure or success of each student after he or she leaves the school, they should take some satisfaction in knowing that they did everything reasonably possible to promote success in their students' transitions to adult life.

Summary

- Orientation to the world of work and adult living should begin early in the elementary school years and should be integrated into all aspects of the school curriculum. All students with disabilities who have IEPs are required to have ITPs when they reach 14 years of age, which are intended to facilitate transition from school to community, vocational programs, college, or employment.

- Life skills instruction refers to those skills relevant to independent, day-to-day living. Instruction includes personal finance, health and fitness, and leisure activities. Critical skills for independent living include managing checking accounts, using various forms of credit, making sensible purchases, and shopping for best values.

- Health and physical fitness are among the most important concerns in any life skills curriculum. Instruction in health and fitness has three major components: (a) facts about health and fitness, (b) values concerning the importance of health concerns, and (c) development of habits of good health and fitness.

- Students should be introduced to the various social, service, or athletic organizations that exist in a community and how to become a member of these organizations. Students can also become acquainted with community recreational facilities, such as public parks, lakes, swimming pools, and athletic facilities.

- A career education curriculum includes four major components: (a) developing appropriate attitudes and habits related to work, (b) developing appropriate work-related social skills, (c) developing awareness of occupational alternatives, and (d) developing individual career preferences through career counseling and vocational assessment.

- Typical vocational education areas include agricultural education, business education, family and consumer science, marketing education, trade and industrial education, and technology education. Curriculum planning, instructional techniques, and placement and follow-up are important in supporting vocational education for students with special needs.

- Special education teachers can provide valuable information regarding instructional features such as careful task analysis, positive practice, behavioral contingencies, feedback and reinforcement, and formative evaluation, many of which may not be included as regular components of inclusive vocational instruction.

- Periodic follow-up through mail, telephone, or personal visits can ensure that placements are successful and that vocational education programs are effective.

Relevant Research and Resources

Research

In 1992, *Learning Disability Quarterly* devoted a special issue (Vol. 15, Issue 4) to employment of individuals with learning disabilities. Brown and

Gerber (1992), Gerber (1992), Reiff and DeFur (1992), and Mellard and Hazel (1992) discuss issues surrounding social competence and developing independence. Jacobs and Hendricks (1992) and Grossman (1992) address job opportunities. Zigmond (1990) presents issues surrounding a reconceptualization of secondary programs for students with learning disabilities; Okolo (1988) addresses environmental issues in vocational settings for adolescents with mild disabilities; and Trapani (1990) discusses transition goals for adolescents with learning disabilities, including social competence, social skills, and secondary curriculum. Several researchers have addressed vocational assessment issues, including reliability and validity (Greenan & Browning, 1989; Rojewski & Greenan, 1992) and curriculum-based assessment for vocational education (Schloss, Smith, & Schloss, 1990). Grossman (1992) addresses legal issues surrounding employment for individuals with disabilities.

Knowles (1978) provides specific important information on potential life problems of the adult learner. Cronin and Patton (1993) provide an excellent text on life skills instruction. A text on career education is provided by Grubb (1996). Further information on career education in special education is found in Brolin (1978, 1989), Clark (1979), and Phelps and Lutz (1977). Many of these sources also provide information on vocational education. Sarkees-Wircenski and Scott (1995) provide a very thorough text on vocational education for individuals with special needs, as well as effective teaching strategies that are appropriate for a number of vocational training areas. Bender, Brannan, and Verhoven (1984) have written an informative text on leisure education. Additional information on several aspects of life skills instruction, career education and vocational education—including assessment and evaluation, particularly as these areas apply to students with mental retardation—can be found in Polloway and Patton (1997); Beirne-Smith, Ittenbach, and Patton (1998); and Patton et al. (1998). Miller and Schloss (1983) provide a comprehensive text on career and vocational education for students with disabilities. Volume 9, Issue 6 (November/December, 1986) of *Remedial and Special Education* is devoted to employment issues.

A historical overview of transition and federally sponsored initiatives is described by Rusch and Phelps (1987). A statewide study of transition services for students with mild disabilities is described by Benz and Halpern (1987). Interagency collaboration models for transition are provided by Johnson, Bruininks, and Thurlow (1987). Issues concerning transition are described by Edgar (1987), Knowlton and Clark (1987), and Asselin et al. (1998). Agran et al. (2000) describe procedures for promoting transition goals and self-determination. Lanford and Cary (2000) discuss the issue of graduation requirements for students with disabilities.

Curricular Materials

Various curricular materials have been published in the area of daily living skills and transition. It is critical that teachers evaluate these materials, because materials range dramatically from focusing on skills and levels for students with severe disabilities to those with mild disabilities. Bender and Valletutti (1982) have published a curriculum guide for transition for adolescents. The *Employability Skills Inventory* is published by Curriculum Associates. *Vocational Entry-Skills for Secondary and Adult Students* is distributed by Academic Therapy. Opportunities for Learning distributes *Me and Jobs* and *Exploring Careers*, and the *Life Skills Workshop* is distributed by LinguiSystems. Educational Activities produces *How to Write for Everyday Living* and *Math for Everyday Living*. Brolin (1989) has published a competency-based approach to career education. Cronin and Patton (1993) have authored a guide for integrating life skills instruction into the curriculum for students with special needs. James Stanfield produces a variety of materials relevant to the school-to-life transition, including the *Transitions Curriculum*, and the *LifeSmart* video curriculum, including *JobSmart, PeopleSmart, DateSmart, MoneySmart,* and *SafetySmart* programs. James Stanfield also produces the *First Job Survival Skills* series and the *Cooperative Living Program.*

Computer Software and Technology

Some of the technology mentioned in the social skills chapter (see Chapter 10) is suitable for teaching transition skills. Word-processing programs are available (see Chapter 6) and would also be helpful for teaching students transition skills. Educational Activities produces the *Getting Ahead on the Job* video and video CD. See Appendix B for a list of addresses of producers and distributors of software and curricular materials.

Graduation Standards and Requirements

Graduation from high school is an important event in students' lives, especially for many students with disabilities. With the implementation of statewide competency testing and newer standards of learning, issues surrounding graduation have become increasingly controversial. Many states and school districts are struggling to define fair, effective policies for graduation requirements for all students. Students with disabilities are required to meet all graduation requirements established by the local school districts. Key factors for students with disabilities appear to be involvement of family and modifications that may be written into students' IEPs. Many recent court rulings have set precedence for the establishment of graduation requirements. As states begin to implement newer minimum competency testing standards that are linked to high school graduation, expect to see even more case law appearing. Some of the major factors regarding graduation are listed next (see Lanford & Cary, 2000, for additional details pertaining to recent court rulings).

Graduation Standards

- Local school districts
    - set graduation standards
    - set the graduation credit requirements
    - establish grading procedures
    - can establish modified grading procedures for all students
    - establish attendance requirements
    - establish requirements for high school diplomas
    - can establish standards for regular and nonstandard diplomas

Multimedia Occupational Vocational Transitioning Planning

Career planning is important for all students, especially for students with disabilities. Many aptitude surveys and tests are available to help you assist students in determining their interests. Some of these surveys are available in CD-ROM formats that enable students to revisit aspects of interest. For example, the Career IQ and Interest test assesses six broad areas, including general ability, verbal aptitude, numeric aptitude, spatial aptitude, perceptual aptitude, and manual dexterity.

Other databases that help students evaluate their study skills and learning needs for college are available on the World Wide Web. For example, the Center for Learning at Muskingum College in Ohio has developed a database that can be accessed by anyone using the Internet (http://www.ldonline.org/ld_indepth/postsecondary/muskingum.html). The database contains information on learning assessment and learning strategies instruction. The Learning Strategies section provides information on memory, time management, and writing, as well as an alphabetical index of strategies. There are also specific academic area strategies, including English, history, and math. Finally, an extensive reference list is included.

Chapter 12

❧   ❧   ❧

Consultation and Collaboration

he preceding chapters emphasized the implementation of the teacher effectiveness variables in skill and content areas ranging from reading to social skills instruction. Research has demonstrated that teachers can make a great difference in student achievement when these instructional variables are consciously manipulated. Improving academic progress facilitates the inclusion process for special education students. There is, however, another equally important role that special educators must play—the role of the *consultant teacher*. Special educators need to develop exceptional interpersonal skills to effectively communicate with (a) parents, (b) regular educators, (c) building administrators, (d) school special services personnel (e.g., psychologist), and (e) community support personnel (e.g., probation officers, mental health workers). In addition, many school districts have adopted service delivery models that require special educators not only to directly teach students with mild and moderate disabilities several hours a day but also to consult and work with regular educators for the remainder of the school day. Because both teaching and consulting skills are necessary for effective performance, this chapter is intended to present an overview of the special educator as a consultant. First, effective communication techniques are presented, followed by communication with parents and school personnel. Finally, a description is provided of models and practices of consultation and collaboration.

Effective Communication

Any situation that requires interpersonal interactions necessitates the use of communication skills. The quality of the communication skills used can determine whether the interactions are successful. Like effective instructional strategies, effective communication skills can be learned and practiced. Communication techniques can be subdivided into several areas, which are described in the next section (see also Ginott, 1993; Gordon, 1987).

Communication Techniques

Active Listening

Whenever a teacher is communicating with another professional or a parent, active listening is important. Active listening means sending messages to the speaker that the listener is interested and concerned with trying to understand the message being conveyed. Active listening involves listener interaction with the speaker and provides the speaker with feedback regarding the listener's understanding. To do this, the listener must first understand the major message and demonstrate to the speaker that he or she is concerned by paying attention to the speaker.

Maintaining eye contact with the speaker conveys that the listener is devoting attention and importance to the speaker and the topic of conversation. The type of body posture displayed by the listener is another nonverbal means of communicating active listening. A listener who leans toward the speaker would be interpreted as someone who is actively listening, whereas a listener who leans back and looks away from the speaker would be interpreted as someone not so concerned. In addition, an active listener devotes all of his or her present attention to the speaker, rather than allowing distractions to interrupt the conversation. Finally, an active listener is able to summarize and restate the other person's major concerns.

Depersonalize Situations

Whenever a conversation occurs, it is critical to depersonalize the situation and orient conversation toward specific goals or possible solutions. In any conversation, it is best to address the situation and not an individual's personality or character. For example, if a student arrives late to class, it is better to state, "It is better to arrive to class on time," than to say, "You are so lazy, you don't care about class. That's why you are late again." In a conversation with a parent of a child who has been delinquent in completing class and homework assignments, it is better to simply state the facts than to insult the child to the parent. Say, for example, "A number of class homework assignments have not been turned in this semester," rather than, "Your child doesn't care about succeeding in my class or he would turn in his work on time." Depersonalization can change the focus of the conversation from negative comments regarding an individual's personality to positive goal-oriented statements that may help solve the problem.

Identify Common Goals

Another major purpose of special educators' conversations with parents, students, and regular educators is to identify common goals or objectives. A special educator can restate problems so that common objectives are seen. For example, during the parent conference mentioned above regarding a student who is obviously not succeeding, the teacher might identify the common goal as "We both want the best for your child. We both would like to see him succeed in school by passing all of his classes." Assume a similar scenario in which a special educator is at a meeting with the general education teacher. The topic of conversation is a special education student, Ed, who has performed poorly on his regular classroom tests, and the general education teacher is questioning the appropriateness of his inclusive placement. The special educator might summarize their common goal by saying, "We both would like to see Ed perform up to his potential." Summarizing the major goals is necessary prior to identifying solutions.

Devising Systematic Procedures for Realizing Goals

Once common goals have been identified and mutually agreed on, systematic steps for realizing those goals must be identified. At first, it is generally a good idea to brainstorm solutions; in this way, no value judgment is placed on the ideas. The special educator should attempt to elicit ideas by initiating statements such as, "What are some possible ways of doing this?" All possible options should be listed. For example, refer back to Ed's problem above and assume that the special educator said the following to the regular educator: "How do you think we should assist Ed in achieving his potential in your class?" The general education teacher would need to identify positive possible solutions, such as, "Perhaps if Ed completed some extra assignments or if he had one of the higher achieving students in my class tutor him. . . ." The special educator should also identify any other possible solutions. If all of the parties involved offer ideas, the problem solving is shared, and several potential alternative solutions are defined.

Selecting the Optimal Solution

The next stage in effective communication is selection of the optimal solution. After all possible solutions to a problem have been identified, it is necessary to prioritize them by considering (a) the most likely to succeed and (b) ease of implementation. Some solutions can be rejected easily; others may need to be reexamined to determine their ultimate feasibility. In fact, it may be decided to try Solution A first because it requires the least amount of extra effort on everyone's part. However, if Solution A does not yield the desired results within a specified time period, then Solution B will be implemented. Finally, if Solution B fails, Solution C will be put into action. At this time, it is also desirable to identify the individuals who will be responsible for specified components during each phase of implementation. Each solution can be briefly described, and each individual's responsibilities can

be listed. In addition, initiation dates can be assigned to each potential solution.

Summarizing the Conversation

Finally, it is important to summarize the major points covered during the conversation. It is generally a good idea to (a) restate the major issues, (b) list the agreed-on solutions, (c) reiterate the persons responsible for implementing the agreed-on solutions, (d) restate what needs to be done, and (e) arrange a tentative follow-up time.

Generally, if the procedures described above are employed during meetings, effective communication will occur. These procedures can be effectively implemented during meetings with parents, students, regular educators, building administrators, or community service personnel. Figure 12.1 summarizes the major components of effective communication, and the following case

Body language	Direct eye contact.
	Upright posture, leaning forward slightly when seated.
	Maintaining attention.
Identifying common goals	Direct conversation toward aspirations for the present and future, not frustration about the past.
	Define the ways in which everyone's goals are similar.
	Provide objective evidence when goals do not match.
Resolve disagreements	In objective terms, identify the exact source of the disagreement.
	Determine that both parties have access to the same information. If different opinions exist regarding the relative importance of information, provide additional objective information. If information is not credible to one party, search for additional verification.
	If all avenues have been attempted without agreement, "agree to disagree" on that particular issue and search for other points of agreement.
Set objectives and determine follow-up	Summarize the meeting with respect to stated objectives of the meeting.
	Identify tasks that must be completed for common goals and objectives to be met.
	Determine who will complete each task and set a date for completion.
	Set a time for a follow-up meeting.

Figure 12.1. Strategies for effective communication. *Note.* Adapted from Ginott (1993) and Gordon (1987).

study presents a sample scenario in which a special educator implements the principles of listening. Special educators are often confronted with problems similar to those described earlier and in the case study. If such issues are handled inappropriately, severe conflicts can arise that can result in breakdowns of effective communi-cation. Ineffective communication can be extremely detrimental for special education and can greatly hinder efforts at facilitating inclusion. The next section presents some suggestions for ensuring effective communication with parents, regular educators, building administrators, and community personnel.

 ## An Active Listening Scenario

Jeff, a high school special education student, has recently been included in Mr. Easton's regular education math class. Jeff storms into Mr. Halleran's (the special education teacher) room after school and the following discussion evolves:

JEFF:	I hate Mr. Easton, and I hate his math class. I am never going back there.
MR. HALLERAN:	Now, Jeff, you sound upset. What happened to make you so upset?
JEFF:	Mr. Easton hates me, and he is unfair to me.
MR. HALLERAN:	But what happened to make you feel this way?
JEFF:	Well, I did my homework and handed it in on time, but Mr. Easton failed me on it.
MR. HALLERAN:	Why do you think you received a failing grade?
JEFF:	He said I didn't follow directions.
MR. HALLERAN:	And did you follow his directions?
JEFF:	Yes, but he doesn't tell me what to do.
MR. HALLERAN:	How could you find out what to do on your homework assignments?
JEFF:	I don't know. He hates me.
MR. HALLERAN:	What do the other students do to find out homework directions?
JEFF:	I don't know; they ask, I guess.
MR. HALLERAN:	I'll tell you what. Next time, you and I will talk to Mr. Easton together about his assignment, and we'll both make sure you know what you have to do.
JEFF:	OK.
MR. HALLERAN:	And later, you will be able to ask him yourself.
JEFF:	OK.

Strategies for Effective Communication

Special educators play many roles throughout their workdays. From the parents' viewpoint, the special educator is the expert and may even seem intimidating. In the regular education teacher's eyes, the special educator is viewed as a colleague who has equal status and position. Building administrators, on the other hand, may see the special educator as one of their teachers who implements and abides by school policies and procedures. Special service administrators, such as school psychologists, may view the special educator as the one who implements IEPs. Community service personnel, such as local mental health center workers and probation officers, tend to see the special educator as a support service delivery person. Given the necessity of dealing with such a wide range of people and backgrounds, special educators must be able to adapt their communication styles to deal effectively with all of the above personnel. Communication strategies appropriate for use with each subgroup are presented in the following sections.

Communicating with Parents

Parents should be viewed as the special educator's primary source of support. Special educators must maintain regular contact with parents, and this open line of communication should be used primarily to disseminate news of students' positive progress. It is good practice to send home "happy grams" and "good day notes" on a regular basis to inform parents of their child's positive growth. It is bad practice to contact parents only when problems arise. Most parents will tend to be more supportive of the school's program if regular positive contact is maintained. Figure 12.2 displays an example of a positive note to a parent.

Many special educators have successfully established monthly parent support meetings. Regular meetings are used to inform parents of the program's goals and objectives, enlist parental support of those goals and objectives, and allow parents to meet one another. Some programs also feature different speakers at their monthly meetings. For example, one month the program might feature special techniques for implementing behavior management plans at home, another session might focus on how to implement appropriate teaching techniques at home, and the next

session might feature a presentation on drugs and their effects. In most instances, parent groups have been very successful and have increased the special educator's communication with parents. Figure 12.3 presents a listing of possible topics to be discussed in parent group meetings.

It is valuable for special educators to establish cooperative working relationships with parents. Many times special educators want parents to do things at home to support the efforts undertaken at school. It is very likely that parents will be asked to do at least one of the following at home: (a) check assignment notebooks, (b) check to ensure homework completion, (c) provide additional guided drill and practice, (d) monitor regular class performance, (e) employ behavior management contracts, and (f) reinforce positive school performance. When any or all of the above are desired, it is necessary to have effective and open communication with parents. When appropriate communication techniques are adhered to and common goals are established, parents will usually follow through and reinforce teaching activities.

Occasionally special problems arise in dealing with parents. If handled properly, these problems can usually be resolved. For example, assume that a parent has said that the special educator has been unfair to his or her child in assigning class grades. In this case, a meeting should be scheduled as soon as possible to show the parent that his or her concern is taken seriously. At the meeting, the special educator should employ the active-listening techniques described earlier. Once the problem has been clearly identified, the special educator can refer to the formative evaluation data documenting the student's performance and progress to determine whether the expectations and grade assignments have been fair. Formative data can be shared with the parent to provide the necessary documentation of the student's grades, progress, or lack of progress. Usually, once such data are shared with parents, they have a better understanding of the attempts that are being made in school to assist their child.

Another problem that can occur in special education is lack of communication with parents.

Dear Mr. and Mrs. Atwood:

   Billy has had an especially good week in school. He has completed all his assignments on time, and he has had a very good attitude toward school.

                              Sincerely,

                              Ms. Westwater
                              Resource Teacher

Figure 12.2. Positive note to parents.

Month	Topic	Speakers
September	Description of Granby's Resource Programs	Ms. M (High School Program)
		Ms. C (Junior High Program)
		Mr. S (Elementary Program)
October	Home tutoring in basic skill areas	Ms. M
November	Drug awareness	Dr. P
December	Behavior management	Ms. C
January	Interpreting test scores	Ms. M
February	Study skills strategies	Mr. S
March	Community support services	Mr. K
April	Vocational awareness	Ms. C
May	Summer placement options	Staff

Figure 12.3. Tentative yearly schedule for parent support meetings.

Some parents do not or cannot make the time to attend parent conferences. Other parents have special concerns themselves, including financial difficulties, several other children, or being single parents. Whatever the reason, some parents seem unable to assist teachers by following through with behavior management plans and/or tutoring activities at home or even by attending parent conferences. Special efforts should be made to maintain contact with these parents, even though they seem unable to reciprocate. Although the teacher may decide not to ask these parents to implement extra work at home, positive notes and phone calls should continue to inform them of their child's progress.

In summary, open lines of communication should be maintained with parents. Conversations with parents should be professional and directly relevant to special education activities. If additional social services are called for, teachers can recommend the services of professional organizations in the community, such as the local mental health center. It should be remembered that special educators are trained as teachers and not anything else.

Communicating with General Education Teachers

Effective communication with general education teachers is a necessary component of special education. With the current emphasis on educational inclusion, it is mandatory for special and regular educators to maintain open lines of communication. Special and regular educators should be viewed as sharing goals—those that will assist students in maximizing their potential. The general education teacher may have made the initial special education referral. By making that referral, the teacher said very clearly that the student did not seem able to maintain the level of performance necessary to succeed independently in his or her classroom. It is, therefore, critical to determine what prerequisite skills the regular educator considers necessary for success in that classroom. Typically, necessary skills can be subdivided into several areas, including (a) social behavior standards, (b) academic survival and study skill standards, and (c) academic performance standards.

Determining Social Behavior Standards

Special educators need to determine the precise standards of social behavior that each regular educator uses to evaluate students. Although every school has guidelines for student behavior, individual teachers may interpret and implement those guidelines differently. For example, Ms. Walker, one fourth-grade teacher, might be exceptionally strict and consistent in implementing the school's rules. She might require students to be seated and prepared for first period prior to the actual ringing of the bell. In addition, she might not allow any out-of-seat behavior or talking unless students first raise their hands for permission. Conversely, Mr. Levi, the other fourth-grade teacher, might not enforce the school's rules as strictly or as consistently. He may allow students to linger in the doorway and hall until the bell rings. He might also allow students to get up to sharpen pencils throughout his class. During class discussions, his students might be encouraged to speak out without raising their hands to be called on. As can be seen from these two illustrations, the standards for acceptable social behavior can and do vary dramatically from teacher to teacher. Although general education students may be able to discern these differences on their own, special education students may need explicit instruction in what standards of behavior are expected in each class. This problem is exacerbated at the secondary level when students may have as many as five to seven different teachers.

Special educators can, however, deal effectively with these differences in social behavior standards by communicating with general education teachers. For instance, special educators can compile a listing of social behavior standards that are enforced by each regular educator. They might, for example, ask regular educators to complete a questionnaire on class rules similar to the one presented in Figure 12.4. This information allows special and regular educators to decide how particular special education students can be most successfully included in those particular classes. If special education students can

---

Name _____

Subject Areas _____

Grade Levels _____

Date _____

1. Briefly describe your classroom rules.

2. Describe the usual type of homework assignment.

3. Describe the usual type and format of in-class quizzes and exams.

4. What do students need to bring to class in order to be considered prepared?

5. How would you describe the behavior of your "best" student?

6. What do you consider prerequisite study skills for students in your classes?

Figure 12.4. Survey of regular educators to determine class rules and expectations.

consistently meet the social behavior standards of a particular inclusive class, they will probably succeed in that class. If, however, students cannot meet those standards, they may require further remediation and practice or additional supports in the inclusive classroom. In summary, special educators must determine the standards of social behavior for each regular classroom. Once these standards have been determined, both teachers can more effectively discuss how inclusive programming can succeed.

Determining Academic Survival and Study Skills Standards

Special educators also must determine the acceptable standards for academic survival and study skills in each regular classroom—in other words, what academically related behaviors students need to be successful in each regular classroom. For instance, Mr. Juarez might expect students to (a) be prepared for class by bringing writing materials, including a pen and pencil; (b) bring a three-ring notebook with dividers and folders for organizing all handouts and assignments; (c) hand in all assignments on time; (d) participate in class discussions by volunteering answers and asking relevant questions; and (e) appear interested in the topics by maintaining eye contact, sitting up straight, and paying attention in class. Ms. Hanson, on the other hand, has extra pencils available for students, accepts late assignments, never asks to see students' notebooks, and does not have a class participation component to her grading system. These two examples illustrate the wide variance in the degree of organization and survival skills in different classrooms. Again, it is necessary for special educators to determine what the particular standards are in each teacher's classroom. Once the standards and expectations are clearly understood, both teachers will be better able to communicate effectively. Special educators can compile a list of these standards using methods similar to those described for standards of social behavior.

Determining Academic Performance Standards

It is also critical for special educators to determine the standards used to evaluate academic performance in regular classrooms. These standards can also vary considerably from teacher to teacher and subject area to subject area. Some teachers may use textbooks that have an especially difficult reading level; others may use texts that are written on lower levels. Some teachers may require additional outside reading and research reports, whereas others require only successful performance on in-class examinations. More important, the types of examinations administered by different teachers can require very different types of studying behavior. Some teachers may administer only identification format tests that require students to select answers from multiple-choice formats. Other teachers may require sentence completion and essay items that force students to produce the answers in writing. The type of questions typically asked by some teachers may be factual recall items that require students to use associative-learning strategies, or the type of questions used might require students to apply learned information to novel instances.

Determining particular standards and requirements for each academic area enables special educators to have more effective, open communication with regular educators. Again, this information could be gathered from survey questionnaires or through individual meetings and conferences with teachers.

In summary, once special educators have clearly identified each regular educator's standards in social behavior, academic survival skills, and academic performance areas, they will be better able to carry on effective communication.

Special Problems

Special educators have reported some common problems that tend to cause breakdowns in communication with regular educators. These problems usually can be circumvented, and they are presented in this section to demonstrate that special educators can use the effective communication skills described earlier to avoid some of the problems that can make communication difficult.

1. *Generalization problems.* Special educators feel that their students can function independently in general education classes when they appear to have mastered all of their instructional objectives. Many times, however, when these students are placed in inclusive settings, they fail to function independently and require more support than anticipated. This failure can be attributed to the student's failure to *generalize* learned skills and behaviors to new settings and situations. If this occurs, two problems arise. First, the general education teacher becomes frustrated because he or she was told the student could function independently in the class. Second, the student becomes frustrated with the situation. To circumvent these problems, special educators need to teach using the table of specifications model presented throughout this text. Recall that the last two cells along the behavioral axis are *application* and *generalization* instructional objectives. When application and generalization objectives have been programmed and mastered, special education students are more likely to succeed.

2. *Curriculum discrepancy problems.* Special educators often make use of specialized instructional materials not used by general educators to address students' special needs. Recall that Chapter 5 emphasized the use of code-emphasis reading series with many special education students. However, prior to entering inclusive settings, special educators should begin to use the same materials that are used in the regular classrooms. Otherwise, students will not have had the exposure to the material used in the general education curriculum. Consequently, students may have difficulties due to the discrepancy in the curriculum materials used rather than due to their skills and abilities. If, for example, the general classroom teacher is using a whole-language or other meaning-emphasis approach to language and literacy development, the special education teacher must ensure that students have sufficient guided practice with this approach to perform to the best of their ability.

3. *Inappropriate placement.* Occasionally, a student with special needs is assigned to an inappropriate inclusive placement. If this occurs, communication between the regular and special educators will be strained. Inappropriate placements may be due to one of many things, including (a) class level, (b) class size, (c) student characteristics, or (d) inappropriate instructional materials or procedures. In other cases, sufficient student support in the inclusive class is not provided or not available. Placement decisions are often difficult to make. Sometimes, the exceptionally good general educator is "rewarded" by being the recipient of many students with special needs in his or her inclusion class. This situation can be very detrimental to teacher morale. Therefore, some placement decisions made by building administrators may address teacher needs rather than student needs. At times, these placement decisions seem inappropriate for particular students; nevertheless, special educators should still attempt to maintain open lines of communication with regular educators.

4. *Inadequate independent* skills. General education teachers typically expect very high levels of independence from students, and on some occasions, newly included students do not exhibit sufficient independent work skills. In some cases, this may be because the special education settings required less independent work habits. When this occurs, effective communication is threatened. However, if special educators meet with these teachers and use the active-listening principles, realistic goals and objectives that will ultimately assist the student in the inclusion efforts can be established.

5. *Inadequate knowledge of general education classroom expectations.* As mentioned previously, lack of knowledge about standards in general education can be especially problematic for special educators. Communication efforts will be

threatened if both regular and special educators do not have a clear understanding of the standards expected for success in the classroom. Special educators should try to keep track of those standards using some of the ideas presented earlier.

This section has presented some of the more commonly encountered problems that can interfere with effective communication between regular and special educators. Many of these problems can be avoided. It is recommended that special educators learn as much as possible about the standards for success in general education programs, as well as the specific scope and sequence and curriculum materials used. Once they know this information, special educators are better equipped to facilitate inclusive placements with their students.

Effective Communication with Other Personnel

The special educator must use the principles described earlier in dealing with all other relevant personnel, ranging from building administrators to community support personnel. Building administrators can often greatly facilitate communication efforts for special education teachers. Inservice programs can be established to explain the entire continuum of special education services to all educators, allowing regular educators to learn about the processes involved in special education and the shared team effort approach required to educate these students. After participation in such programs, regular educators have a better understanding of what special educators do. This understanding usually helps communication efforts later on.

Communication with Students

Finally, it is of utmost importance for special educators to use effective communication with special education students. All of the principles described in this chapter can be applied to communication efforts with the students. This is especially true at the secondary level. Students at this level may participate in their IEP meetings and in their meetings with related service personnel such as psychologists and counselors. The special educators who are most successful tend to apply effective communication skills with their special education students.

For instance, if a student seems to have a problem, the successful educator will use active-listening principles to determine the nature of the problem and to show concern for the student. It is also important to specify objectives for meeting the student's goals and to determine how they will be met. Finally, the student and teacher must agree on what is to be done and who will do it, and a follow-up meeting should be scheduled to determine whether the objectives have been met.

In another instance, a particular student may be having tardiness problems with a general education teacher in an inclusive class. The special education teacher should employ active listening to determine the student's point of view and to communicate concern. The teacher should show the student that both teacher and student want that student to do well and not get into trouble in school. Next, meeting objectives should be discussed—in this case, procedures for arriving to class on time. Perhaps the teacher can help identify the source of the problem (transportation, distance between classes, social exchanges with other students, avoidance, etc.) and suggest means for overcoming the problem. Finally, the necessary steps for solving the problem should be specified, and a follow-up meeting should be scheduled to ensure that objectives have been met. Although it is important to listen to students' problems, it is also necessary for teachers to adopt a businesslike problem-solving attitude in such situations. Simply venting anxieties or frustrations is not likely to be helpful unless problems are identified and solutions are attempted. To this end, keeping a written record of problems expressed, solutions proposed, and follow-up evaluations can be valuable, whether the problem is tardiness, homework completion, fighting, or personal animosity with specific teachers.

Consultation Teacher Models

This section presents several consultation models currently being implemented by schools. The first is a prereferral model, which operates on the assumption that a consulting teacher can assist regular educators in designing interventions as soon as a problem is noticed so that students may not need to be referred for special education services. Next, co-teaching models are described, which involve the creation of partnerships between general and special education teachers to deliver high quality education in inclusive settings.

Prereferral Consultation Models

Some researchers have proposed alternatives to the system of service delivery currently used in special education classrooms. For example, Graden, Casey, and Christenson (1985) proposed that a prereferral intervention model be used as an alternative to traditional service delivery systems. This particular model uses six stages, the first four of which rely on consultation implemented prior to a formal referral step. Stage 1 is the request for consultation and consists of an informal process whereby the referring teacher requests problem-solving assistance from a consultant. This consultant is typically the building special education teacher. Stage 2 is the phase during which the initial consultation occurs. The goals of the consultation are to (a) identify the problem in objective and measurable terms, (b) analyze the problem in terms of current performance and desired performance, (c) design and implement an intervention plan, and (d) evaluate the intervention. Both the re-

ferring teacher and consultant work collaboratively on each of the above steps.

Stage 3 is implemented if Stage 2 is unsuccessful. The purpose of Stage 3 is to collect extensive observational data on the student and characteristics of his or her classroom and peers. Based on the accumulated data, the observer and teacher meet again to design more extensive interventions. Following this, a meeting is scheduled with the student, parents, and teacher to discuss the new intervention, and, finally, the intervention is implemented.

Stage 4 is put into action if Stage 3 is unsuccessful. During Stage 4, a child-study team convenes to share information on all of the behaviors and interventions implemented to date. On the basis of these data, the child-study team can make one of the following decisions: (a) continue the recently implemented intervention, (b) alter the current intervention, or (c) refer the child for assessment and possible special education services.

Stage 5, the final stage, is the implementation of the formal referral process. At this time, all of the previously obtained data are used to assist in selecting assessment devices. Graden, Casey, and Bonstrom (1985) provided some data in support of this model. Their results indicated that, in four of six schools, many teachers did use the consultation stage, and formal referrals for special education services decreased. It is thought that using this type of consultation model opens lines of communication between regular and special educators.

Fuchs, Fuchs, and Bahr (1990) used multidisciplinary "mainstream assistance teams" of general and special education teachers to create and implement prereferral intervention strategies similar to those described by Graden et al. (1985a), including problem identification, problem analysis, implementation of the plan, and evaluation of the problem. Fuchs et al. included student–teacher contracts and self-monitoring on the part of individual students. Students rated themselves on social or academic behavior, as needed, on a regular basis. Using this model, most difficult-to-teach students improved their school performance and remained in the general education class.

Co-Teaching: Partnerships Between Special and General Educators

Co-teaching is practiced across the country in schools to provide special education services to students with disabilities while they are included in general education classrooms. Many different models of co-teaching have evolved, but key elements across models include a special and general educator working together in a single classroom to deliver instruction to students with and without disabilities simultaneously (Cook & Friend, 1995). These partnerships help provide necessary accommodations for students with disabilities within general education classrooms.

Co-teaching models include team teaching, station teaching, parallel teaching, and complementary teaching (see Cook & Friend, 1995, for additional models). Team teaching is an example of two teachers sharing equally in the teaching responsibilities. Station teaching is an example of two teachers splitting responsibilities during a lesson. Each teacher teaches something different at a different "station," and students rotate through the stations in the classroom. Parallel teaching is an example of two teachers teaching simultaneously but each teaching a smaller group rather than the entire class. Complementary teaching refers to the general educator maintaining responsibilities for the instructional content and the special educator maintaining responsibilities over the learning strategies and instructional modifications.

Sufficient time for co-planning appears to be a critical component for any co-teaching model. Teachers who share planning time are able to discuss the lesson content, design any necessary lesson adaptations prior to teaching the class, and discuss respective teaching responsibilities for the class. In a qualitative investigation of two

teachers at the secondary level, Hardy (2001) observed that the biology teacher maintained her responsibilities as the content expert, and the special educator assumed the role of the adaptations and strategies expert. Both teachers shared planning time and worked well together. Some of the modifications designed by the special educator were implemented during lectures, homework assignments, lab activities, and testing situations. She designed vocabulary study guides, video study guide sheets, and review and study sheets, and she made formatting changes, such as changing items to fill-in-the blank responses from longer essay formats and inserted wider lines for responses on worksheets. A particularly useful adaptation during co-teaching included the use of visuals, such as the use of an overhead projector during what had previously been just lecture. For example, the special educator reported the following during an interview:

> We were having a lab and Gwen [the general educator] was saying things like, "I want you to do this and I want you to do that," and it was all auditory. And the kids would be working on the lab and wouldn't hear, so I would get the overhead and start writing it out. (Hardy, 2001, p. 166)

Hardy observed that another major adaptation during the co-teaching was the use of small-group instruction to students who did not understand a concept taught to the entire class. The special education teacher would frequently assemble a small group in the back of the room. The special education teacher reported,

> When I see that the students are confused, then I will work with a couple of tables at a time or have a little group back here . . . I will ask: "Who is still confused on this thing?" . . . And I will say: "OK, if you are confused and you have a question come back here." (Hardy, 2001, p. 171)

Hardy (2001) reported that the co-teaching was generally successful and appeared to benefit all students, but she reported an unsettling finding as well. The general educator indicated that even though she saw the benefits of the instructional modifications, she would cease to implement them if the special educator were not working directly with her in a co-teaching situation.

Although many co-teaching models have been proposed, few have supporting efficacy data. Weiss and Brigham (2000) located more than 700 articles that described co-teaching. However, when those articles were examined more carefully, it was found that only 23 studies provided supporting efficacy data. Out of those 23 studies, most were conducted with teachers at the elementary level, with even fewer appearing at the secondary level. Reported benefits include improved instruction and better communication between general and special education (e.g. Reinhiller, 1996). Walther-Thomas and Carter (1993) also provided evidence of some of the benefits and challenges associated with co-teaching. Given the limited number of co-teaching studies with data, teachers should carefully evaluate any co-teaching situation to determine the effects of the co-teaching—not only on student progress and performance but also on the teachers' abilities to work and teach successfully together. Suggested practices to implement co-teaching include the following:

- determine the goals and objectives of co-teaching

- obtain support from building administrators and from parents

- determine person-specific responsibilities

- build in sufficient co-planning time

- develop procedures for evaluating co-teaching effects on students and teachers

Full Inclusion Models

Some professionals and advocates have proposed full inclusion models of service delivery for students with disabilities. Although there are many different descriptions of exactly what is meant by *full inclusion*, the general notion is that students with disabilities are served completely within the general education classroom, and special education teachers serve entirely as consultants and/or support personnel (e.g., Stainback & Stainback, 1990). *Full inclusion* is generally taken to mean that students with mild disabilities would not receive any instruction in "pull-out" settings, such as resource rooms staffed by special education teachers. Rather, all specialized instruction, when needed, is delivered in the general education classroom by the general education teacher, the special education teacher, instructional aides, classroom peers, or other support personnel. Inclusion models recently have been implemented in a number of locations throughout the country. Advocates for full inclusion maintain that full inclusion is a civil right, similar to racial integration; that all students benefit from fully inclusive environments; that stigma from labeling and more restrictive placements is reduced; that educational efficiency is increased; and that full inclusion promotes equality (see Mastropieri & Scruggs, 2000, for a discussion). As stated by Stainback and Stainback (1990), proponents of full inclusion,

> It is discriminatory that some students, such as those "labeled" disabled, must earn the right to be in the regular education mainstream or have to wait for educational researchers to prove that they can profit from the mainstream, while other students are allowed unrestricted access simply because they have no label. No one should have to pass anyone's test or prove anything in a research study to live and learn in the mainstream of school and community life. This is a basic right, not something one has to earn. (pp. 6–7)

In addition, recent federal legislation provides that students with disabilities should have access to the general education curriculum, and, clearly, inclusive settings offer this access.

We have maintained throughout this book that successful functioning in inclusive environments, both school and community, is the ultimate goal of special education. Nevertheless, many professionals, parents, and individuals with disabilities maintain their support of the variety of educational services made possible by federal law in the Individuals with Disabilities Education Act (Public Law 105-17; U.S. Department of Education, 1998). These individuals are concerned to see that in some schools, different educational settings for service delivery, such as resource rooms, are not service options. They argue that the regular classroom is not the best service alternative in *every* instance; in fact, when direct comparisons have been made based on specific performance data, students with mild disabilities have often learned better with at least some support from special education settings (Fuchs, Fuchs, & Fernstrom, 1993; Marston, 1987–1988; Rudenga, 1992). Furthermore, surveys of special and regular education teachers (e.g., Scruggs & Mastropieri, 1996), surveys of students with mild disabilities (Klingner, Vaughn, Schumm, Cohen, & Forgan, 1998), and observational studies of students with mild disabilities (Rudenga, 1992) have indicated that in many cases, students and school personnel alike prefer having the resource room or special education classroom as a placement option. Although many parents support full inclusion programs, many parents of students with mild disabilities also have expressed satisfaction with current placement and service delivery options (Singer & Butler, 1987), and some have expressed concerns about inclusive schools (Carr, 1993; Green & Shinn, 1995). Finally, analyses of existing regular education classrooms (Baker & Zigmond, 1990) and of the inconsistent ability and willingness of regular education teachers to modify and adapt curriculum and teaching methods (Jenkins & Leicester, 1992) suggest that many of these environments may not be optimal for students with mild disabilities. It is also true that several states do not require any special education coursework for "regular" teacher certification, and this lack of professional preparation may be an important consideration.

It is also important to note that virtually all professional organizations concerned with students with mild disabilities have issued statements expressing support for resource rooms and special education classrooms as placement options, even while emphasizing the desirability of inclusive placements when warranted (Council for Children with Behavior Disorders, 1993; Council for Learning Disabilities, 1993; Division for Learning Disabilities, 1993; Learning Disabilities Association of America, 1993; and National Joint Committee on Learning Disabilities, 1993). It is important and necessary to continue to examine service delivery alternatives in special education and to consider the positive aspects of full inclusion in placement decisions. Nevertheless, in most cases, students were referred initially for special education services because adequate learning did not occur in the regular classroom. When inclusion models are employed, school personnel must collect evidence that appropriate supports are in place and that individual students are meeting important IEP objectives in the regular class setting. Full inclusion can be a positive option if it can be demonstrated that students with disabilities are learning critical academic, social, and life skills optimally in these environments. Effective communication and collaboration between special and general educators can help ensure that progress is being monitored and that students' special needs are being met.

Summary

- Effective communication skills are necessary for effective teachers and can be learned and practiced. Techniques for effective communication include active listening, depersonalizing situations, identifying common goals, devising procedures for realizing goals, selecting the optimal solution, and summarizing the conversation.

- Parents are an invaluable resource for teachers. Regular communication can help establish positive cooperative work efforts such as monitoring homework and assignment completion, providing additional practice, employing behavior management contracts, and reinforcing school achievement. Effective communication techniques can help establish and maintain positive relationships with parents.

- Communicating with general education teachers has become increasingly important in recent years. Determining specific skills and behaviors expected of students in inclusive settings and providing support in these areas can be very helpful in facilitating success in inclusive classrooms. Information-providing activities can be helpful in informing other school personnel of the processes involved in special education and the shared team effort approach necessary for success.

- Prereferral consultation and intervention can help provide assistance to students in need before they are referred to special education. Teams of professionals can work together to identify the problem, analyze the problem, design and implement an intervention plan, and evaluate the effectiveness of the intervention.

- Co-teaching involves partnerships to provide necessary accommodations for students with disabilities within general education classrooms. Co-teaching models include team teaching, station teaching, parallel teaching, and complementary teaching. These models represent different configurations intended to allow for successful learning in inclusive classrooms.

- Full inclusion generally refers to instruction of students with disabilities entirely within general education classroom, with necessary supports provided within the classroom. Although many advantages have been described by proponents of full inclusion, others have expressed concern about the elimination of other service options. As with all placement decisions, educators implementing fully inclusive placements should carefully monitor the progress of students with special needs to ensure that positive and systematic progress is being made on all IEP objectives.

Relevant Research and Resources

Some suggestions for active-listening techniques are provided by Ginott (1993) and Gordon (1987). Information about influencing generalization between classrooms is given by Mastropieri and Scruggs (1984a), Scruggs and Mastropieri (1984c), and Ellis et al. (1987). The development of consultation models in special education is described by Reisberg and Wolf (1986), Friend (1984, 1985), Cook and Friend (1995), and Friend and Cook (1992). Volume 9, Issue 6 (1988) of *Remedial and Special Education (RASE)* is devoted to school consultation practice. Alternative delivery models are described in *RASE* Volume 10, Issue 6 (November/December 1989) and Volume 11, Issue 1 (January/February 1990). In addition to the references cited within this chapter, Volume 11, Issue 3 (May/June 1990) of *RASE* is devoted to inclusion issues. Debate concerning these issues is ongoing (see also Fuchs & Fuchs, 1994; Stainback & Stainback, 1990). Detailed recommendations for adapting instruction in inclusive settings are offered in Scruggs and Mastropieri (1992b); Mastropieri and Scruggs (1994a, 2000); Graden, Casey, and Christenson (1985); and Graden, Casey, and Bonstrom (1985). Information on communicating with parents is discussed by Turnbull and Turnbull (1978). The need for interdisciplinary cooperation is emphasized by results of meta-analysis on medication presented by Kavale and Nye (1983) and by intervention models presented by Hewett and Forness (1984). Helpful information on working with parents is in Gordon (2000).

Forness and his colleagues present procedures for bridging the gap between school psychologists and special educators (Forness, 1970, 1981,

1982; Forness & Kavale, 1987; Sinclair, Forness, & Alexson, 1985). Johnson and Johnson (1975, 1984) and Johnson, Johnson, and Holubec (1991) present suggestions on arranging cooperative learning situations.

Curricular Materials, Computer Software, and Technology

Recently, curricular materials and supporting videotapes have been published in the area of consultation and collaboration. Most of these materials are intended for teachers and teacher trainers. Longman distributes *Interactions: Collaboration Skills for School Professionals*. PRO-ED distributes *Effective Instruction of Difficult-to-Teach Students: An Inservice and Preservice Professional Development Program for Classroom, Remedial, and Special Education Teachers; Collaboration in the Schools: An Inservice and Preservice Curriculum for Teachers, Support Staff, and Administrators* (includes video component); *Teaching: A Venture in Problem Solving* (a videotape program); *What I Need to Know About Special Education: Answers for Parents and Professionals; Special Educator's Consultation Handbook; The Educational Consultant: Helping Professionals, Parents, and Mainstreamed Students* (Heron & Harris, 2001); and *Conferencing Parents of Exceptional Children.* Fuchs et al. (1989) wrote *Mainstream Assistance Teams: A Handbook on Prereferral Intervention.* Longman publishes *Interactions: Collaboration Skills for School Professionals.* Finally, it is recommended that teachers use database software programs and word-processing software programs to document their consultation activities. See Appendix B for a list of addresses of producers and distributors of software and curricular materials.

INCLUSION FEATURE

Partnerships Between Special and General Educators

Partnerships between special and general educators are necessary prerequisites for effective inclusion of students with disabilities. These partnerships involve shared decision making, planning, and co-teaching. Co-teaching is becoming a popular way to deliver instruction in inclusive classes. During co-teaching, a special and general educator are present in the classroom. Many models of co-teaching, such as the ones described by Bauwens, Hourcade, and Friend (1989), include one teacher and one assistant, station teaching, parallel teaching, and team teaching. In one study during which a special and general educator developed excellent co-teaching patterns, teachers demonstrated the following behaviors (Mastropieri et al., 1998):

- expectations of success for all students
- enthusiasm for teaching
- open acceptance of all students
- use of peer assistants when appropriate
- use of effective teaching methods
- use of relevant curriculum
- use of disability-specific adaptations when appropriate
- shared planning time
- excellent communication between teachers

This study documented that students with disabilities learned as well as their peers on science tests during the co-taught units. Although minimal efficacy data exist to date regarding successful co-teaching partnerships, key factors for creating successful partnerships during co-teaching appear to include the following:

- support for co-teaching from building administrators and parents
- effective communication between teachers
- clear goals and objectives for co-teaching
- shared, mutually agreed-upon responsibilities
- shared planning time for instruction
- documentation procedures for recording student learning during co-teaching and the co-teaching process

TECHNOLOGY FEATURE

Communicating Electronically

Electronic communication can help increase communication links among teachers, parents, students, school administrators, and community personnel. Although telephone, in person, and written communication efforts are still very important, the addition of electronic communication via e-mail and postings on Web pages can significantly increase communication efforts. Increased communication between families and teachers helps promote academic and social progress of students with disabilities. Hardy (2001) reported that when high school teachers had telephones installed in their classes, they called families immediately when assistance or communication was necessary. For example, when students did not bring in their homework or acted inappropriately in class, one of the co-teachers immediately contacted parents using the telephone in the classroom. Parents responded positively and helped reinforce the teachers' policies and practices by providing appropriate guidance at home, and students' performance and class behaviors improved significantly. Similar findings might be obtained from using e-mail if parents have easy access to e-mail.

Chapter 13

ᘐ   ᘐ   ᘐ

Epilogue

In this book, we have attempted to describe the best practices in special education as supported by research. Research suggests that teachers can and do make a great difference in the degree to which their students are able to succeed. Some overall suggestions that we hope will be implemented by teachers, regardless of the type of instructional setting, include the following:

1. *Teach directly to relevant objectives.* These objectives should be derived from IEPs and should reflect knowledge and skills that will facilitate student independent functioning in an inclusive setting or a less restrictive environment.

2. *Maximize engaged time-on-task.* Teachers should use all means at their disposal to provide as much engaged, teacher-directed interaction as possible with students in areas that are directly relevant to instructional objectives.

3. *Include the PASS variables.* Remember to prioritize objectives; adapt instructional procedures, curriculum materials, and the environment; use the effective teacher presentation ("SCREAM") variables; and systematically monitor progress.

4. *Provide relevant guided and independent practice activities.* When giving students practice activities, avoid assigning busywork, and ensure that students work only on material that is at the appropriate difficulty level and that is directly relevant to educational objectives.

5. *Use formative evaluation techniques to monitor student progress toward prespecified goals and objectives.* Make frequent, ongoing as-

sessments of learner progress toward meeting IEP objectives throughout the year; do not wait for the end of the school year to determine whether instruction was effective.

6. *Modify instruction in response to outcomes of formative data.* Avoid an overly rigid approach to teaching. Do not be afraid to make changes in instructional procedures or materials if instructional objectives are not being met. Continue to monitor progress and consider additional changes as needed.

7. *Monitor transfer and generalization of learned skills.* Do not assume that students will automatically apply learned skills in new situations (very often they will not). Teach in such a way that students are able to benefit maximally from new skills they have learned.

8. *Make the classroom a positive and pleasant place to be.* Although research on teacher effectiveness has de-emphasized personality as an alterable variable, remember that enthusiasm, warmth, positive expectations, and display of sincere caring about the students are necessary to maximize success in the classroom. Teachers who are enthusiastic about teaching and concerned for the welfare of their students should make sure their students are aware of this. Teachers who are neither enthusiastic nor concerned should consider another profession.

9. *Make school work as meaningful and concrete as possible and encourage students to actively reason through all tasks.* Meaningfulness, concreteness, and active thinking are keys to success.

10. *Remember that acceptable performance in inclusive settings is the final goal of special education.*

Special education teachers should familiarize themselves with the expectations of the general education classroom and direct their teaching activities toward helping their students meet these expectations. The degree to which students are able to function independently in inclusive settings is an important measure of the effectiveness of the special education teacher.

We have presented a number of specific recommendations for effective teaching practices. However, it is difficult to include in one text anything approaching the total amount of information a teacher needs to deal with every situation that may arise. If teachers carefully attend to the 10 major recommendations we have listed above, we do feel that chances for overall success in the classroom will be very high.

Finally, we would like to stress the need for attention to further developments in the field of special education. Given the progress that has been made in recent years, our knowledge of optimal instructional practices is likely to increase in the future. To keep up with future trends and developments in the field, we encourage all practicing special education teachers to join a professional organization in their particular field of interest. Most of these organizations issue professional journals that keep members informed on recent developments in their field and sponsor conferences that provide means for professionals to get together to exchange ideas. Such activities, we feel, are essential components of overall professional development and can help to ensure the continued application of effective instruction for special education.

Appendix A

❧   ❧   ❧

Individualized Education Program

Note. Adapted with permission from Fairfax County Public Schools, Fairfax, VA 22030.

Department of Student Services and Special Education
Individualized Education Program

IEP-1

Page _____ of _____

CONFIDENTIAL	DRAFT UNTIL IEP IS SIGNED

1 Student Name _____ Date of Birth _____ ID No _____

Neighborhood/Base School _____ Current Attending School _____ Grade _____ Family Primary Language _____

Parent/Guardian _____ Home Phone ( ) _____ Work Phone ( ) _____

Parent/Guardian _____ Home Phone ( ) _____ Work Phone ( ) _____

Student Address _____

Number and Street _____ Apartment Number _____ City and State _____ Zip Code _____

2 Most Recent Eligibility Date _____ 3-Year Reevaluation Date _____

Area(s) of Eligibility _____

Date of this IEP Meeting _____ Date this IEP will be Reviewed _____ IEP Addendum ☐ Dismissal ☐

3 [IEP Team]　Who participated in this IEP meeting?

Parent _____ Signature _____ Date _____

Parent _____ Signature _____ Date _____

Student _____ Signature _____ Date _____

Principal/Designee _____ Signature _____ Date _____

Special Education Teacher _____ Signature _____ Date _____

General Education Teacher _____ Signature _____ Date _____

Other _____ Signature/Relationship to Student _____ Date _____

Other _____ Signature/Relationship to Student _____ Date _____

Other _____ Signature/Relationship to Student _____ Date _____

Team member responsible for sharing information in this IEP with all service providers _____

24 [Parent Consent]　Complete this section at the end of the IEP meeting.

I AGREE with the contents of this IEP. I have received a copy of the *Rights and Procedural Safeguards Pertaining to Special Education*. I have had an opportunity to participate in the development of this IEP.

_____ _____
Parent Signature (or student age 18 or older)　　　Date

I DO NOT AGREE with the contents of this IEP. I have received a copy of the *Rights and Procedural Safeguards Pertaining to Special Education*. I have had an opportunity to participate in the development of this IEP.

_____ _____
Parent Signature (or student age 18 or older)　　　Date

CONFIDENTIAL

DRAFT UNTIL
IEP IS SIGNED

Department of Student Services and Special Education

Individualized Education Program
Transition Plan

Complete with student no later than Grade 8 or age 14, whichever comes first.

IEP-2

Page _____ of _____

Student Name	ID Number	Anticipated Graduation Date	Anticipated Diploma

A. Student Participation in Transition Planning

_____ I have participated in drafting my Individualized Transition Plan. All parts include my interests and preferences.
Student's Initials

_____ The student has not been available to provide input into the Transition Plan; therefore, this IEP will be addended in _____ days to include the student's interests, preferences, and goals.
Principal's Designee Initials

B. Anticipated Post-secondary Plan   ✓ Check all that apply

☐ Postsecondary Education/Training   ☐ Employment   ☐ Military   ☐ Other _____

C. Career Information

Interests:

Strengths/Capabilities:

Career Goal:

D. Transition Activities

Includes (a) instruction; (b) related services; (c) community experience; (d) the development of employment and other postschool adult living objectives; and (e) if appropriate, acquisition of daily living skills and functional vocational evaluation

Career: I will

Self-advocacy: I will

Independent Living: I will

CONFIDENTIAL | DRAFT UNTIL IEP IS SIGNED

Department of Student Services and Special Education

Individualized Education Program

Transition Plan

Complete with student no later than Grade 8 or age 14, whichever comes first.

IEP-3

Page _____ of _____

Student Name

ID Number

E. Transition Services: I plan to explore the following options:

School Services: Complete required referral and permission forms

☐ Career/College Guidance

☐ Career/College-Related Course(s) Experiences:

_____

☐ Academy Support Services

☐ Referral for Career Assessment

☐ Referral to Work Awareness & Transition (WAT)

☐ Referral to Office Technology & Procedures (OTP)

☐ Referral to Davis or Pulley Center

☐ Community Work Experience

☐ Referral for Employment Services

☐ Referral for Job Coach Services

☐ Referral to Postsecondary Education Rehabilitation Training (PERT)

☐ Other _____

Postsecondary Services: Complete prior to graduation/program completion.

Include signed Permission for Release of Information with referral

☐ Referral to Virginia Department of Rehabilitative Services (VDRS)

☐ Referral to Fairfax-Falls Church Community Services Board Mental Retardation Programs (CSB-MR)

☐ Referral to Fairfax-Falls Church Community Services Board Mental Health Services (CSB-MH)

☐ Referral to Virginia Department of Visually Handicapped (VDVH)

☐ Other Agency: _____

☐ Other Agency: _____

☐ Other Agency: _____

Postsecondary services were discussed. The student and/or parent does not choose to pursue services at this time.

_____   _____
Student's   Parent's
Initials   Initials

F. Notice of Rights Upon Age of Majority (to be completed at the IEP meeting on or immediately preceding student's 17th birthday.)

_____   _____
Student's Initials   Parent's Initials

The parent and student received the *Age of Majority* brochure and student's rights pertaining to special education upon reaching the age of 18 have been explained.

G. Termination of Services upon Graduation

This student is scheduled to graduate with a regular or advanced studies diploma on _____. At that time, this student will have met all Fairfax County Public Schools and Commonwealth of Virginia requirements for a regular or advanced studies diploma. The awarding of such diploma will terminate all special education and related services for this student in Fairfax County Public Schools.

Department of Student Services and Special Education
Individualized Education Program

| CONFIDENTIAL | DRAFT UNTIL IEP IS SIGNED | IEP-4 |

STUDENT _____ ID # _____ Page _____ of _____

④ Area of Need _____

⑤ **Present Level** — Documentation: _____

How does this area of need impact this student's participation/progress in the general education curriculum or for preschool children, the child's participation in age-appropriate activities?

⑦ **Progress***

How will progress toward this annual goal be measured?

_____ Classroom Participation
_____ Checklists
_____ Classwork
_____ Criterion-referenced Test _____
_____ Homework
_____ Norm-referenced Test _____
_____ Observation
_____ Oral Reports
_____ Special Projects
_____ Tests and Quizzes
_____ Written reports
_____ Other

Date						
Code						

⑥ **Annual Goal** — What does this student need to know or be able to do?

Short-term Objectives — What short-term objectives indicate progress toward this goal?

Progress Comments

*A copy of this form, indicating the student's progress toward this annual goal, will be reported to parents at regular scheduled FCPS reporting periods. **The progress codes are: M** The student has met the criteria for this goal/objective. **SP** The student is making sufficient progress toward achieving this goal/objective within the duration of the IEP. **EP** The student demonstrates emerging skill but may not achieve this goal/objective within the duration of this IEP. **NP** The student has not yet demonstrated progress toward achieving this goal/objective and may not achieve this goal within the duration of this IEP. **NI** This goal/objective has not been introduced.

CONFIDENTIAL

DRAFT UNTIL
IEP IS SIGNED

Department of Student Services and Special Education
Individualized Education Program

IEP-4A

Page _____ of _____

Student Name

ID Number

(8)

CURRICULUM/CLASSROOM ACCOMMODATIONS AND MODIFICATIONS

What accommodations, supplementary aids and services, supports in general education, and/or special education programs or modifications to the general curriculum does this student require because of his/her area(s) of need?

Settings

_____ Preferential Seating
_____ Small Group

Assignment

_____ Reduced Level of Difficulty
_____ Shortened Assignment
_____ Reduced Pencil/Paper Tasks
_____ Extended Time
_____ Opportunity to Respond Orally

Instruction

_____ Shortened Instructions
_____ Assignment Notebook
_____ Oral Exams
_____ Frequent/Immediate Feedback
_____ Dictated Information, Answers on Tape
_____ Individual/Small Group Testing
_____ Taped Lectures
_____ Reduced Language Level/Reading Level
_____ Incorporation of Learning Styles
_____ Peer Tutoring/Paired Working Arrangement

Materials

_____ Taped Text/Material
_____ Highlighted Text/Materials
_____ Manipulatives
_____ Braille
_____ ESL Materials
_____ Calculator
_____ Keyboard Modification
_____ Access to Keyboard/Word Processor

Behavior

_____ Positive Reinforcement
_____ Frequent Breaks
_____ Clearly Defined Limits/Expectations
_____ Quiet Time
_____ Behavior Management Plan

Teacher Supports

_____ Consultation
_____ Information
_____ Other _____
_____ Other _____

Other

_____
_____
_____
_____

CONFIDENTIAL | **DRAFT UNTIL IEP IS SIGNED**

Department of Student Services and Special Education
Individualized Education Program

Page ____ of ____

IEP-5

STUDENT _____ ID # _____

(9) **INFORMATION RELATED TO THE PRESENT LEVEL OF EDUCATIONAL PERFORMANCE**

Record additional important information about the student including, but not limited to, parent/family concerns about the student's education and current academic, behavioral, environmental, social/emotional, and/or medical issues.

CONFIDENTIAL | **DRAFT UNTIL IEP IS SIGNED**

Department of Student Services and Special Education

Individualized Education Program–Elementary

IEP-6

STUDENT _____ ID # _____ Page _____ of _____

---

(10) **SOL/Alternate Assessment**   Which assessment will the student take?

☐ This student is not in a grade/age level that participates in these assessments.

☐ This student will participate in the following SOL assessments:

Check level: ☐ 3 ☐ 4 ☐ 5

For grades 3,* 4, and 5 check all tests that the student will take.

☐ English RL/R ☐ Math ☐ Science ☐ Technology
☐ Writing ☐ Social Studies

*For grade 3 ONLY, student must take both English RL/R and writing or be exempt from both.

☐ This student will participate without accommodations.

☐ This student will participate with accommodations.
(See attached testing accommodations page IEP-6A.)

☐ This student meets the criteria for the Virginia Alternate Assessment Program. (If considering this assessment, the Virginia Alternate Assessment Program Criteria page IEP-6B must be completed.)

Check level ☐ Age 8 ☐ Age 10

---

(11) **State Assessment Program/Stanford 9**

☐ This student is not in a grade level that participates in this assessment.

☐ This student will participate in the Stanford 9 Achievement Tests

Check grade level: ☐ 4 ☐ 6

☐ This student will participate without accommodations.

☐ This student will participate with accommodations.
(See attached testing accommodations page IEP-6A.)

☐ This student is exempt from this assessment. (Complete chart below*)

---

(12) **Districtwide Assessments**

☐ This student is not in a grade level that participates in these assessments.

☐ This student will participate in districtwide assessments using classroom testing accommodations if required and allowed by the test. (See attached testing accommodations page IEP-6A.)

☐ This student is exempt from districtwide assessments. (Complete chart below*)

ARE THERE ANY STATE OR DISTRICTWIDE ASSESSMENTS THAT THIS STUDENT WILL NOT TAKE?   YES ☐   NO ☐   **If yes, complete this section.**

(13) ★

Assessment	Reason	Indicate How the Student Will Be Assessed

---

(14)

The parent (or student age 18 or older) has been informed about the consequences of these decisions and has received written information about graduation requirements and diploma options for students in Fairfax County Public Schools.

If the parent (or student age 18 and older) is not at the IEP meeting, the written information about graduation requirements and diploma options for students in Fairfax County Public Schools was sent to the parent or student.

_____
Parent/student
(age 18 or older) initials

_____
Principal/designee initials

CONFIDENTIAL | **DRAFT UNTIL IEP IS SIGNED**

Department of Student Services and Special Education
Individualized Education Program

IEP-6A

Page _____ of _____

Student _____ ID # _____

Testing Accommodations

The accommodations marked below are required for this student to participate in the assessments indicated. Only those accommodations allowed by the assessment and used by the student during classroom instruction may be considered.

ASSESSMENTS

SOL Accommodation Codes	ELEMENTARY ACCOMMODATIONS	Classroom Testing Accommodations	SOL Grade 3 English R/L and Writing	SOL Grade 3 Math	SOL Grade 3 Science	SOL Grade 3 History/Social Studies	SOL Grade 4 History/Social Studies	SOL Grade 5 English R/L and Research	SOL Grade 5 Math	SOL Grade 5 Science	SOL Grade 5 Technology	SOL Grade 5 Writing Tests	Stanford Accommodation Codes	Stanford 9
1	Flexible schedule												1	**
2	Group size												3	
3	Environmental accommodations												4	
4	Visual aids												6	
5	Amplification equipment												7	
6	Large print or increased size of answer bubbles												8	
7	Assistance with directions												10	
8	Increased space between items or reduced items per page											9		
9	Braille test/Braille answer document													NS
10 or 14	Reading in English of test items		NS					NS					17	*
11 or 15	Audio-cassette version of test items		NS					NS						
12 or 16	Interpreting (e.g., signing, cued speech) test items		NS					NS					19	*
13	Communication board, pictorial presentation												20	NS
17	Bilingual dictionary		L	L	L	L	L	L	L	L	L	L	21	L
18	Mark in test booklet or student responds verbally	■	■											
19	Math aids												25	NS
20	Large diameter pencil, special pencil, pencil grip													
21	Respond by word processor, typewriter, Brailler													
22	Augmentative communication device													
23	Spelling aids, spell checker, spelling dictionary													
24	Tape recorder (prewriting only)											NS		
25	Dictation in English to a scribe												24	NS
26	Use of a calculator or arithmetic tables			NS	NS				NS	NS			2	
27	Preferential seating													
28	Reading/interpreting embedded directions												19	NS

NS Nonstandard Accommodation   ■ Not allowed for this assessment   (L) Limited English Proficient Studies only   *Reading and interpreting (e.g., signing, cued speech) of Reading test items is **NOT** permissible on the Stanford 9. Nonstandard for all other subtests.   **Extended time on entire test or breaks during subtests is nonstandard on the Stanford 9.

CONFIDENTIAL	DRAFT UNTIL IEP IS SIGNED	IEP-6B

Department of Student Services and Special Education
Individualized Education Program–Secondary

STUDENT _____ ID # _____ Page ____ of ____

10 SOL/Alternate Assessment   Which assessment will the student take?

☐ This student is not in a grade/age level that participates in the SOL/Alternate Assessments.

☐ This student will participate in the following SOL assessments

Check grade level: ☐ Grade 8   ☐ End-of-Course Test(s)

For grade 8 check all tests that the student will take:

☐ English RL/R   ☐ Math   ☐ Science   ☐ Technology
☐ Writing   ☐ Social Studies

For end-of-course tests, list all tests that the student will take.

End-of-course test(s): _____

☐ This student will participate without accommodations
☐ This student will participate with accommodations
       (See attached testing accommodations page IEP-6C.)

☐ This student has passed the SOL 8th grade   ☐ Math   ☐ Reading.
☐ This student meets the criteria for The Virginia Alternate Assessment Program.
   (If considering this assessment, the Virginia Alternate Assessment Program
   Criteria page IEP-6D must be completed.)

Check level   ☐ Age 13   ☐ one year prior to leaving High School

11 State Assessment Program/Stanford 9

☐ This student is not in a grade level that participates in this assessment.

☐ This student will participate in the Stanford 9 Achievement Tests grade 9.

   ☐ This student will participate without accommodations

   ☐ This student will participate with accommodations
      (See attached testing accommodations page IEP-6C.)

☐ This student is exempt from this assessment. (Complete chart below)

12 Divisionwide Assessments

☐ This student is not in a grade level that participates in this assessment.

☐ This student will participate in divisionwide assessments using classroom testing
   accommodations if required and allowed by the test. (See attached testing
   accommodations page IEP-6C.)

☐ This student is exempt from divisionwide assessments. (Complete chart below)

ARE THERE ANY STATE OR DIVISIONWIDE ASSESSMENTS THAT THIS STUDENT WILL NOT TAKE?   YES ☐   NO ☐   If yes, complete this section.

13

Assessment	Reason	Indicate how the Student will be Assessed

14

Parent/student (age 18 or older) initials _____

The parent (or student age 18 or older) has been informed about the consequences of these decisions and has received written information about graduation requirements and diploma options for students in Fairfax County Public Schools.

Principal/designee initials _____

If the parent (or student age 18 and older) is not at the IEP meeting, the written information about graduation requirements and diploma options for students in Fairfax County Public Schools was sent to the parent or student.

CONFIDENTIAL | **DRAFT UNTIL IEP IS SIGNED**

Department of Student Services and Special Education
Individualized Education Program

IEP-6C

Page _____ of _____

Student _____ ID # _____

Testing Accommodations

The accommodations marked below are required for this student to participate in the assessments indicated. Only those accommodations allowed by the assessment and used by the student during classroom instruction may be considered.

ASSESSMENTS

SECONDARY ACCOMMODATIONS

SOL Accommodation Codes	Accommodation	Classroom Testing Accommodations	SOL Grade 8 History/Social Studies	SOL Grade 8 English R/L and Research	SOL Grade 8 Math	SOL Grade 8 Science	SOL Grade 8 Technology	SOL EOC Algebra I, Algebra II, Geometry	SOL EOC Biology, Chemistry, Earth Science (Geosystems)	SOL EOC US History, World History I, II	SOL EOC English, R/L R	SOL Writing Tests Grade 8 and EOC	Stanford Accommodation Codes	Stanford 9
1	Flexible schedule												1	**
2	Group size												3	
3	Environmental accommodations												4	
4	Visual aids												6	
5	Amplification equipment												7	
6	Large print												8	
7	Assistance with directions												10	
8	Increased size of answer bubbles												9	
9	Braille test/Braille answer document													NS
10 or 14	Reading in English of test items			NS							NS		17	*
11 or 15	Audio-cassette version of test			NS							NS			■
12 or 16	Interpreting (e.g., signing, cued speech) test items			NS							NS		19	*
13	Communication board, pictorial presentation		L		L	L	L	L	L	L			20	NS
17	Bilingual dictionary		L	L	L	L	L	L	L	L	L	L	21	L
18	Mark in test booklet (Stanford–11 or 23 NS responds verbally)													
19	Math Aids			■			■	■					25	NS
20	Large diameter pencil, special pencil, pencil grip												14	
21	Respond by word processor, typewriter, Brailler											■		
22	Augmentative communication device													
23	Spelling aids, spell checker, spelling dictionary													
24	Tape recorder (pre-writing only)													
25	Dictation in English to a scribe											■		
26	Use of a calculator or arithmetic tables												24	NS
27	Preferential seating												2	
28	Reading/interpreting embedded directions												19	NS

NS Nonstandard Accommodation   ■ Not allowed for this assessment   (L) Limited English Proficient Studies only   *Reading and interpreting (e.g., signing, cued speech) of Reading test items is **NOT** permissible on the Stanford 9. Nonstandard for all other subtests.   **Extended time on entire test or breaks during subtests is non-standard on the Stanford 9.

CONFIDENTIAL | DRAFT UNTIL IEP IS SIGNED

Department of Student Services and Special Education
Individualized Education Program

IEP-6D

Page _____ of _____

STUDENT _____ ID # _____

(16) ### Virginia Alternate Assessment Program (VAAP) Criteria

The IEP team determines participation in alternate assessment. Team members must consider current and historical documentation. The following factors ALONE are not sufficient for determining participation in the VAAP.

- Poor attendance
- Expectations of poor test performance
- Place where the student receives services
- Student's reading level
- Level of intelligence
- Low achievement in general
- English as a Second Language
- Amount of time receiving special education services
- Disruptive behavior
- Categorical disabilities labels
- Social, cultural, and economic difference

The student must meet ALL of the following VAAP participation criteria. If NO is checked for any criteria, this indicates that the student is NOT a candidate for alternate assessment and should be considered for participation in the Standards of Learning (SOL) Assessment.

I. COMPLETE THIS SECTION FOR ALL STUDENTS

☐ Yes ☐ No   This student has a current IEP.

☐ Yes ☐ No   This student demonstrates significant cognitive impairments and adaptive skills deficits that prevent completion of curriculum based on the Standards of Learning (SOL) even with program and testing modifications.

☐ Yes ☐ No   This student's present level of performance indicates the need for extensive direct instruction and/or intervention in a life skills curriculum that may include personal management, recreation and leisure, school and community, vocational, functional academics, communication, social competence, and motor skills to accomplish the application and transfer of life skills.

☐ Yes ☐ No   This student requires intensive, frequent, and individualized instruction in a variety of settings to show progress and acquire, maintain, or generalize life and/or functional academic skills.

II. ADDITIONAL SECTION TO BE COMPLETED FOR STUDENTS IN THE EIGHTH GRADE THROUGH HIGH SCHOOL

☐ Yes ☐ No   This student is working toward educational goals other than those prescribed for a modified standard, standard, or advanced studies diploma.

III. VIRGINIA ALTERNATE ASSESSMENT PROGRAM PARTICIPATION DECISION

After review of the relevant data and consideration of the above factors and criteria statements, the IEP team shall indicate below this student's participation in the Virginia Alternate Assessment Program.

☐ This student meets **ALL** of the criteria above and will participate in the Virginia Alternate Assessment Program and will not participate in other statewide assessments. **OR**

☐ This student does **NOT** meet all of the criteria above and will be considered by the IEP team for participation in other statewide assessments.

This participation decision is supported by current and historical data found in the following documents/data:

☐ Psychological Report ☐ Adaptive Skills Assessment ☐ Pattern of Learning (IEPs) ☐ Parent Observation ☐ Teacher Observation ☐ Anecdotal Records
☐ Other _____

| CONFIDENTIAL | DRAFT UNTIL IEP IS SIGNED | IEP-6E |

Department of Student Services and Special Education
Individualized Education Program

STUDENT _____ ID # _____ Page _____ of _____

This page is to be completed only for those students who entered the ninth grade for the first time during the 1999–2000 school year or earlier.

(17)

VIRGINIA LITERACY PASSPORT TESTING PROGRAM (VLPTP)

☐ This student has passed this/these section(s) of the VLPTP: ☐ Reading ☐ Math ☐ Writing
☐ This student is not scheduled to participate in the VLPTP within the duration of this IEP.
☐ This student will participate in the VLPTP with no accommodations.
☐ This student will participate in the VLPTP with accommodations for section(s):

	READING	MATH	WRITING
Audio-cassette	■		
Braille			
Braille-writer or abacus	■		
Large print, magnification			
Oral administration			
Answers recorded by proctor	N/A	N/A	N/A
Dictation to a scribe	N/A	■	
Electronic calculators	N/A	N/A	N/A
Use of multiplication chart	N/A	N/A	N/A
Interpretation of test directions for student with hearing impairment			
Making response in test booklet		■	
Place keepers, trackers, pointers		■	
Typewriter, word processor, or augmentative communication device			
Written directions	N/A	N/A	N/A
Multiple test sessions			
Testing in separate room			
Other (specify)			

■ = *Nonstandard accommodations that are reflected in student's test records*
N/A = *Not applicable*

☐ This student is not participating in this/these section(s) of the VLPTP this year: ☐ Reading ☐ Math ☐ Writing
☐ This student is EXEMPT from participating in this/these section(s) of the VLPTP. ☐ Reading ☐ Math ☐ Writing
☐ The student's progress toward the annual goals will be assessed as indicated in this IEP.

THE CONSEQUENCES OF THESE DECISIONS AND THE REQUIREMENT THAT THE STUDENT PASS ALL THREE SECTIONS OF THE VLPTP TO RECEIVE A REGULAR DIPLOMA HAVE BEEN FULLY EXPLAINED TO THE PARENT AND/OR STUDENT (18 YEARS OF AGE OR OLDER).

Department of Student Services and Special Education
Individualized Education Program

IEP-7

Page _____ of _____

CONFIDENTIAL   **DRAFT UNTIL IEP IS SIGNED**

STUDENT _____ ID # _____

(18) **Least Restrictive Environment**

To the maximum extent appropriate, students with disabilities must be educated with students without disabilities. This is called the lease restrictive environment. The IEP team must consider all of the factors below and then determine the placement alternative that is the least restrictive environment for the student.

- ☐ The educational needs of the student as reflected in this IEP.

- ☐ Opportunities for education with age-appropriate peers, unless the IEP requires some other arrangement.

- ☐ Unless the IEP requires some other arrangement, the student is educated in the school that he/she would attend if not a student with a disability (neighborhood school).

- ☐ Any potential harmful effect of the placement on the student or on the quality of services that the student needs.

- ☐ The student should not be removed from the general education classroom solely because of needed accommodations or modifications in the general curriculum.

- ☐ Removal from the general education environment occurs only if the nature or severity of the disability is such that education in general education classes with the use of supplementary aids and services cannot be achieved satisfactorily.

Department of Student Services and Special Education

Individualized Education Program

IEP-8

CONFIDENTIAL	DRAFT UNTIL IEP IS SIGNED

Page _____ of _____

Student _____ ID # _____

(19) Areas of Need	Service Delivery Options

Service Delivery Option Codes

A. Consult/monitor/collaboration.

B. Special education services in general education on an intermittent basis.

C. Special education services in general education on a regularly scheduled basis.

D. Special education services in special education setting on an intermittent basis.

E. Special education services in special education setting on a regularly scheduled basis.

F. Preschool special education services in home setting.

Total Special Education Time Required to Meet the Areas of Need = _____ Hours per ☐ Week ☐ Month

Special Education Services Hours Distribution

(20) Primary Special Education Services: _____ Hours per ☐ Week ☐ Month   Begin Date _____ End Date _____
Begin Date _____ End Date _____

Are there areas of need that cannot be met through general education and the primary special education services? If yes, list needs below.   ☐ Yes   ☐ No

(21) Areas of Need	Additional/Related Services	Frequency Week	Month	Hours per	Duration Begin Date	End Date

This student will not participate in the following general education activities: _____

(22) TRANSPORTATION: This student does NOT require special transportation. ☐   This student does require special transportation. ☐
If special transportation is required, give reason: _____

(23) Parent (or student age 18 or older) at initial or annual IEP meeting: I have received a copy of the Extended School Year (ESY) Brochure. Parent (student age 18 or older) initials _____

Appendix B

৵৴   ৵৴   ৵৴

Publishers of Books, Tests, Curricular Materials, and Software

Academic Software
141 Ayers Court
Teaneck, NJ 07666
1-800-227-5816
www.academicsoftwareusa.com

Academic Therapy Publications
20 Commercial Boulevard
Novato, CA 94947
1-800-422-7249
www.academictherapy.com

Addison Wesley Longman Publishing Company
1 Jacob Way
Reading, MA 01867
1-800-552-2499

AIMS Education Foundation
1595 S. Chestnut Street
Fresno, CA 93702
1-559-255-4094
www.aimsedu.org

Allyn & Bacon
60 Gould Street
Needham Heights, MA 02494
1-800-666-9433
www.ablongman.com

American Guidance Service
4201 Woodland Road
Circle Pines, MN 55014
1-800-328-2560
www.agsnet.com

American Speech-Language-Hearing Association
10801 Rockville Pike
Rockville, MD 20852
1-800-638-8255
www.asha.org

Apple Computer, Inc.
1 Infinite Loop
Cupertino, CA 95014
1-800-MYAPPLE
www.apple.com

Argus Communications
P.O. Box 9550
400 West Bethany Drive
Suite 110
Allen, TX 75013-9550
1-800-860-6762
www.argus.com

Aspen Publishers
7201 McKinney Circle
P.O. Box 990
Frederick, MD 21701
1-800-638-8437
www.aspenpub.com

Association for Supervision and Curriculum Development
1703 North Beauregard
Alexandria, VA 22311-1714
1-800-933-ASCD
www.ascd.org

Biological Science Curriculum Study (BSCS)
5415 Mark Dabling Boulevard
Colorado Springs, CO 80918-3842
1-719-531-5550
www.bscs.org

Brookes Publishing Company
P.O. Box 10624
Baltimore, MD 21285-0624
1-410-337-9580
www.pbrooks.com

Brooks/Cole
511 Forest Lodge Road
Pacific Grove, CA 93950
1-800-354-9706
www.brookscole.com

Brookline Books
P.O. Box 1047
Cambridge, MA 02238-1047
1-800-666-BOOK
www.brooklinebooks.com

Cambridge Development Laboratory
86 West Street
Waltham, MA 02154
1-800-637-0047

Carolina Biological Supply
2700 York Road
Burlington, NC 27215

Charles C. Thomas
2600 South First Street
Springfield, IL 62794
1-800-258-8980
www.ccthomas.com

Child Development Media
5632 Van Nuys Boulevard, Suite 286
Van Nuys, CA 91401
1-800-405-8942
www.childdevmedia.com

Center for Multisensory Learning
Lawrence Hall of Science
1 Centennial Drive
Berkeley, CA 94720
1-510-642-5132
www.lawrencehallofscience.org

Compu-Teach
PMB 137
16541 Redmond Way, Suite C
Redmond, WA 98052
1-800-44-TEACH
www.compu-teach.com

Creative Publications
5623 W. 115th Street
Alsip, IL 60803
1-800-624-0822
www.creativepublications.com

The Council for Exceptional Children
1110 North Glebe Road, Suite 300
Arlington, VA 22201-5704
Toll-free: 1-888-CEC-SPED
www.cec.sped.org

Critical Thinking Books & Software
P.O. Box 448
Pacific Grove, CA 93950
1-800-458-4849
www.criticalthinking.com

CTB/McGraw-Hill
20 Ryan Ranch Road
Monterey, CA 93940-5703
1-800-538-9547
www.ctb.ocm

Curriculum Associates
153 Rangeway Road
North Billerica, MA 01862-0901
1-800-225-0248
www.curriculumassociates.com

Dale Seymour Publications
Pearson Learning
299 Jefferson Road
P.O. Box 480
Parsippany, NJ 07054
1-800-526-9907
www.pearsonlearning.com/dsp-publications

Delta Education
80 Northwest Boulevard
P.O. Box 3000
Nashua, NH 03061-3000
1-800-442-5444
www.delta-education.com

Don Johnston Incorporated
26799 West Commerce Drive
Volo, IL 60073
1-800-999-4660
www.donjohnston.com

EBSCO Curriculum Materials
P.O. Box 11521
Birmingham, AL 35202-1591
1-800-633-8623
www.ecmtest.com

Edmark Corporation
P.O. Box 97021
Redmond, WA 98073-9721
1-800-691-2986
www.edmark.com

Education Development Center, Inc.
55 Chapel Street
Newton, MA 02458-1060
1-617-969-7100
www.edc.org

Educational Achievement Systems
319 Nickerson Street, Suite 112
Seattle, WA 98109
1-877-EDPROOF
www.edresearch.com

Educational Activities
P.O. Box 392
Freeport, NY 11520
1-800-645-3739
www.edact.com

Educational Resources
1550 Executive Drive
P.O. Box 1900
Elgin, IL 60123-1900
1-800-860-7004
www.edresources.com

Educators Publishing Service
31 Smith Place
Cambridge, MA 02138
1-800-225-5750
www.epsbooks.com

Edusoft
132 10th Road, Kew
Johannesburg, South Africa
(+2711) 882-1435
www.edusoft.co.za

Encyclopedia Britannica Educational Corporation
425 North Michigan Avenue
Chicago, IL 60611
1-800-621-3900
www.britannica.com

ETA/Cuisenaire
5050 Greenview Court
Vernon Hills, IL 60061
1-800-445-5985
www.etacuisenaire.com

Gamco Industries
Siboney Learning Group
325 N. Kirkwood Road, Suite 200
St. Louis, MO 63122
1-800 351-1404
www.gamco.com

Globe Fearon Educational Publishers
4350 Equity Drive
P.O. Box 2649
Columbus, OH 43216-2649
1-800-321-3106
www.globefearon.com

Harcourt School Publishers
6277 Sea Harbor Drive
Orlando, FL 32887
1-800-225-5425
www.harcourtschool.com

Harcourt, Inc.
6277 Sea Harbor Drive
Orlando, FL 32887-6777
1-800-544-6678
www.harcourtcollege.com

Hawthorne Educational Services
800 Gray Oak Drive
Columbia, MO 65201
1-800-542-1673

Heinemann
88 Post Road West
P.O. Box 5007
Westport, CT 06881
1-800-793-2154
www.heinemann.com

Holt, Rinehart and Winston
1120 S. Capital of Texas Hwy.
Austin, TX 78746-6487
1-800-225-5425
www.hrw.com

Houghton Mifflin Company
13400 Midway Road
Dallas, TX 75244-5165
1-800-733-2828
www.hmco.com

Humanities Software
408 Columbia Street, Suite 222
P.O. Box 950
Hood River, OR 97031
1-541-386-6737
www.humanitiessoftware.com

International Reading Association
800 Barksdale Road
P.O. Box 8139
Newark, DE 19714-8139
1-302-731-1600
www.reading.org

James Stanfield
P.O. Box 41058
Santa Barbara, CA 93140
1-800-421-6534
www.stanfield.com

Kaplan Concepts for Exceptional Children
P.O. Box 609
1310 Lewisville-Clemmons Road
Lewisville, NC 27023-0609
1-800-334-2014
www.kaplanco.com

Knowledge Adventure
4100 W. 190th Street
Torrance, CA 90504
1-800-542-4240
www.knowledgeadventure.com

Kurzweil Educational Systems
52 Third Avenue
Burlington, MA 01803
1-800-894-5374
www.kurzweiledu.com

Lakeshore Learning Materials
2695 East Dominguez Street
P.O. Box 6261
Carson, CA 90749
1-800-421-5354
www.lakeshorelearning.com

Lawrence Hall of Science
1 Centennial Drive
Berkeley, CA 94720
1-510-642-5132
www.lawrencehallofscience.org

Lawrence Productions
1800 S. 35th Street
Galesburg, MI 49053
1-800-556-6195
www.voyager.net/lawrence

The Learning Company
1 Martha's Way
Hiawatha, IA 52233
1-800-395-0277
www.learningco.com

Learning Resources
380 N. Fairway Drive
Vernon Hills, IL 60061
1-847-573-8400
www.learningresources.com

LinguiSystems
3100 4th Avenue
P.O. Box 747
East Moline, IL 61244-9700
1-800-PRO-IDEA
www.linguisystems.com

Longman
1185 Avenue of the Americas
New York, NY 10036
1-800-266-8855
www.ablongman.com

Love Publishing Company
9101 East Canyon Avenue, Suite 2200
Denver, CO 80237
1-303-757-2579

Macmillan Publishing Company
866 3rd Avenue
New York, NY 10022
1-800-257-5755
www.macmillan.com

McGraw-Hill School Division
1221 Avenue of the Americas
New York, NY 10020
1-800-442-9685
www.mmhschool.com

Merrill Education Publishing Company
445 Hutchison Avenue
Columbus, OH 43235-5677
1-800-526-0485
www.merrilleducation.com

MINDPLAY Educational Software
160 W. Ft. Lowell Road
Tucson, AZ 85705
1-520-888-1800
www.mindplay.com

National Education Association Publications
1201 16th Street
Washington, DC 20036
1-202-833-4000
www.nea.org

National Geographic Society
17th and M Streets NW
Washington, DC 20036
1-800-647 5463
www.nationalgeographic.com

National Science Resources Center
Smithsonian Institution
Arts and Industries Building
Room 1201
Washington, DC 20560
1-202-287-2063
www.nsrc.org

National Science Teachers Association
1840 Wilson Boulevard
Arlington, VA 22201-3000
1-703-243-7100

Optimum Resource
18 Hunter Road
Hilton Head Island, SC 29926
1-888-788-2592
www.stickybear.com

Pearson Learning
4350 Equity Drive
P.O. Box 2649
Columbus, OH 43216-2649
1-800-526-9907
www.pearsonlearning.com

Prentice Hall
One Lake Street
Upper Saddle River, NJ 07458
1-800-282-0693
www.prenhall.com

PRO-ED
8700 Shoal Creek Boulevard
Austin, TX 78757-6897
1-512-451-3246
www.proedinc.com

The Psychological Corporation
555 Academic Court
San Antonio, TX 78204-2498
1-800-211-8378
www.hbtpc.com

Research Press
P.O. Box 9177
Champaign, IL 61826
1-800-519-2707
www.researchpress.com

Resources for Educators
Prentice Hall
P.O. Box 362916
Des Moines, IA 50336-2916
1-800-491-0551
www.phdirect.com

Scholastic
P.O. Box 7502
Jefferson City, MO 65102
1-800-724-6527
www.scholastic.com

Scott Forseman/Addison Wesley
School Services
1 Jacob Way
Reading, MA 01867
1-800-552-2259
www.sf.aw.com

Singular Publishing Group
401 West A Street, Suite 325
San Diego, CA 92101
1-800-521-8545
www.singpub.com

Sopris West
P.O. Box 1809
Longmont, CO 80502-1809
1-800-547-6747
www.sopriswest.com

SRA/McGraw-Hill
220 East Danieldale Road
DeSoto, TX 75115-2490
1-888-772-4543
www.sra4kids.com

Steck-Vaughn
8701 North MoPac Expressway
Austin, TX 78759
1-800-531-5015
www.steck-vaughn.com

Summit Learning
P.O. Box 493F
Fort Collins, CO 80522
1-800-777-8817
www.summitlearning.com

Sunburst Communications
101 Castleton Street
P.O. Box 40
Pleasantville, NY 10570
1-800-431-1934
www.sunburst.com

Teachers College Press
1234 Amsterdam Avenue
New York, NY 10027
1-800-488-2665
www.tc-press.tc.columbia.edu

Time Warner/Little, Brown
1271 Avenue of the Americas
New York, NY 10020
www.twbookmark.com

University of Kansas Center for Research on Learning
521 Joseph R. Pearson Hall
1122 West Campus Road
Lawrence, KS 66045
1-785-864-4780
crl@ukans.edu

Wide Range
P.O. Box 3410
15 Ashley Place, Suite 1A
Wilmington DE 19804
1-800-221-9728
www.widerange.com

Words+
1220 W. Avenue J
Lancaster, CA 93534-2902
1-800-869-8521
www.words-plus.com

Zaner-Bloser Educational Publishers
2200 West Fifth Avenue
P.O. Box 16764
Columbus, OH 43216-6764
1-800-421-3018
www.zaner-bloser.com

References

Adams, M. J. (1990). *Beginning to read: Thinking and learning about print*. Cambridge, MA: MIT Press.

Ager, C. L., & Cole, C. L. (1991). A review of cognitive-behavioral interventions for children and adolescents with behavioral disorders. *Behavioral Disorders, 16,* 276–287.

Agran, M., Blanchard, C., & Wehmeyer, M. L. (2000). Promoting transition goals and self-determination through student self-directed learning: The Self-Determined Learning model of instruction. *Education and Training in Mental Retardation and Developmental Disabilities, 35,* 351–364.

Alber, S. R., Heward, W. L., & Hippler, B. J. (1999). Teaching middle school students with learning disabilities to recruit positive teacher attention. *Exceptional Children, 65,* 253–270.

Alberto, P. A., & Troutman, A. C. (1998). *Applied behavior analysis for teachers* (5th ed.). Englewood Cliffs, NJ: Prentice Hall.

Algozzine, B., & Maheady, L. (Eds.). (1986). In search of excellence: Instruction that works in special education classrooms [Special issue]. *Exceptional Children, 52,* 484–590.

Allinder, R. M., Bolling, R. M., Oats, R. G., & Gagnon, W. A. (2000). Effects of teacher self-monitoring on implementation of curriculum-based measurement and mathematics computation achievements of students with disabilities. *Remedial and Special Education, 21,* 219–226.

Alverman, D. E. (1983). Putting the textbook in its place—your students' hands. *Academic Therapy, 18,* 345–351.

Amerikaner, M., & Summerline, M. L. (1982). Group counseling with learning disabled children: Effects of social skills and relaxation training on self-control and classroom behavior. *Journal of Learning Disabilities, 15,* 340–346.

Anderson, L. M., Evertson, C. M., & Brophy, J. E. (1979). An experimental study of effective teaching in first-grade reading groups. *Elementary School Journal, 79,* 193–223.

Anderson, L. M., Evertson, C. M., & Emmer, E. T. (1980). Dimensions in classroom management derived from recent research. *Journal of Curriculum Studies, 12,* 343–346.

Anderson, M. G. (1992). The use of selected theatre rehearsal technique activities with African-American adolescents labeled "behavior disordered." *Exceptional Children, 59,* 132–140.

Anderson, M.G., & Webb-Johnson, G. (1995). Cultural contexts, the seriously emotionally disturbed classifica-tion, and African American learners. In B. A. Ford, F. E. Obiakor, & J. M. Patton (Eds.), *Effective education of African American exceptional learners: New perspectives* (pp. 151–188). Austin, TX: PRO-ED.

Artiles, A. J., & Trent, S. C. (1994). Overrepresentation of minority students in special education: A continuing debate. *Journal of Special Education, 27,* 410–437.

Artiles, A. J., & Zamora-Durán, G. (1997). *Reducing disproportionate representation of culturally diverse students in special and gifted education*. Reston, VA: Council for Exceptional Children.

Asselin, S. B., Todd-Allen, M., & DeFur, S. (1998). Transition coordinators: Define yourselves. *Teaching Exceptional Children, 30*(3), 11–15.

Bacon, E. H., & Carpenter, D. (1989). Learning disabled and nondisabled college students' use of structure in recall of stories and text. *Learning Disability Quarterly, 12,* 108–118.

Baker, J. G., Stanish, B., & Frazer, B. (1972). Comparative effects of a token economy in a nursery school. *Mental Retardation, 10,* 16–19.

Baker, J. M., & Zigmond, N. (1990). Are regular education classes equipped to accommodate students with learning disabilities? *Exceptional Children, 56,* 515–526.

Baker, T., Dixon, N. R., Englebert, B., Kahn, M., Siegel, B. L., & Wood, J. L. (1982). Mainstreaming minimanual: Ten steps to success. *Instructor, 91,* 63–66.

Bakken, J. P., Mastropieri, M. A., & Scruggs, T. E. (1997). Reading comprehension of expository science material and students with learning disabilities: A comparison of strategies. *Journal of Special Education, 31,* 300–324.

Ball, E.W. (1996). Phonological awareness and learning disabilities: Using research to inform our practice. In T. E. Scruggs & M. A. Mastropieri (Eds.), *Advances in learning and behavioral disabilities* (Vol. 10, Part A, pp. 77–100). Stamford, CT: JAI.

Ball, E. W., & Blachman, B. A. (1991). Does phoneme awareness training in kindergarten make a difference in early word recognition and developmental spelling? *Reading Research Quarterly, 26,* 49–66.

Barbe, W. B., Lucas, V. H., Hackney, C. S., Braun, L., & Wasylyk, T. M. (1987). *Zaner-Bloser handwriting: Basic skills and applications*. Columbus, OH: Merrill.

Baroody, A. J. (1989). *A guide to teaching mathematics in the primary grades*. Boston: Allyn & Bacon.

Baroody, A. J., & Hume, J. (1991). Meaningful mathematics instruction: The case for fractions. *Remedial and Special Education, 12,* 54–68.

Baumann, J. R. (1986). The direct instruction of main idea comprehension ability. In J. R. Baumann (Ed.), *Teaching main idea comprehension ability* (pp. 133–178). Newark, DE: IRA.

Bauwens, J., Hourcade, J. J., & Friend, M. (1989). Cooperative teaching: A model for special and general education integration. *Remedial and Special Education, 10*(2), 17–22.

Bay, M., Staver, J. R., Bryan, T., & Hale, J. B. (1992). Science instruction for the mildly handicapped: Direct instruction versus discovery teaching. *Journal of Research in Science Teaching, 29,* 555–570.

Beck, S., Matson, J. L., & Kazdin, A. E. (1983). An instructional package to enhance spelling performance in emotionally disturbed children. *Child and Family Behavior Therapy, 4,* 69–77.

Becker, W. C., Madsen, C. H., & Arnold, C. R. (1967). The contingent use of teacher praise in reducing behavior problems. *Journal of Special Education, 1,* 287–307.

Beirne-Smith, M. (1991). Peer tutoring in arithmetic for children with learning disabilities. *Exceptional Children, 57,* 330–337.

Beirne-Smith, M., Ittenbach, R. F., & Patton, J. R. (1998). *Mental retardation* (7th ed.). Columbus, OH: Merrill.

Bender, M., Brannan, S., & Verhoven, P. (1984). *Leisure education for the handicapped.* San Diego: College-Hill.

Bender, M., & Valletutti, R. J. (1982). *Teaching functional academics: A curriculum guide for adolescents and adults with learning problems.* Baltimore: University Park Press.

Benz, M. R., & Halpern, A. S. (1987). Transition services for secondary students with mild disabilities: A statewide perspective. *Exceptional Children, 53,* 507–513.

Berliner, D. C., & Rosenshine, B. V. (1977). The acquisition of knowledge in the classroom. In R. C. Anderson, E. J. Spiro, & W. E. Montague (Eds.), *Schooling and the acquisition of knowledge* (pp. 375–396). Mahwah, NJ: Erlbaum.

Bickel, W. E., & Bickel, D. D. (1986). Effective schools, classrooms and instruction: Implications for special education. *Exceptional Children, 52,* 489–500.

Biddle, B. J., & Anderson, D. S. (1986). Theory, methods, knowledge and research on teaching. In M. C. Wittrock (Ed.), *Handbook of research on teaching* (3rd ed., pp. 230–252). New York: Macmillan.

Bierman, K. L., & Furman, W. (1984). The effects of social skills training and peer involvement on the social adjustments of preadolescents. *Child Development, 55,* 151–162.

Blackman, L. S., Burger, L. A., Tan, N., & Weiner, S. (1982). Strategy training and the acquisition of decoding skills in EMR children. *Education and Training of the Mentally Retarded, 17,* 83–87.

Blake, C., Wang, W., Cartledge, G., & Gardner, R. (2000). Middle school students with serious emotional disturbances serve as social skills trainers and reinforcers for peers with SED. *Behavioral Disorders, 25,* 280–298.

Blankenship, C. S. (1986). Using curriculum-based assessment data to make instructional decisions. *Exceptional Children, 52,* 233–238.

Bley, N. S., & Thornton, C. A. (1989). *Teaching mathematics to the learning disabled.* Austin, TX: PRO-ED.

Bloom, B. S., Hastings, J. T., & Madaus, G. R. (1971). *Handbook on formative and summative evaluation of student learning.* New York: McGraw-Hill.

Bording, C., McLaughlin, T. F., & Williams, R. L. (1984). Effects of free time on grammar skills of adolescent handicapped students. *Journal of Educational Research, 77,* 312–318.

Borkowski, J. G., & Varnhagen, C. K. (1984). Transfer of learning strategies: Contrast of self-instructional and traditional training formats with EMR children. *American Journal of Mental Deficiency, 88,* 369–379.

Borkowski, J. G., Weyhing, R. S., & Carr, M. (1988). Effects of attributional retraining on strategy-based reading comprehension in learning disabled students. *Journal of Educational Psychology, 80,* 46–53.

Bos, C. S. (1982). Getting past decoding: Assisted and repeated readings as remedial methods for learning disabled students. *Topics in Learning and Learning Disabilities, 1,* 517–555.

Bos, C. S., & Anders, P. L. (1987). Semantic feature analysis: An interactive teaching strategy for facilitating learning from text. *Learning Disabilities Focus, 3,* 55–59.

Bos, C. S., & Anders, R. L. (1990a). Effects of interactive vocabulary instruction on the vocabulary learning and reading comprehension of junior-high learning disabled students. *Learning Disability Quarterly, 13,* 31–42.

Bos, C. S., & Anders, P. L. (1990b). Interactive teaching and learning: Instructional practices for teaching content and strategic knowledge. In T. E. Scruggs & B. Y. L. Wong (Eds.), *Intervention research in learning disabilities* (pp. 116–185). New York: Springer-Verlag.

Bottge, B. A., & Hasselbring, T. S. (1993). A comparison of two approaches for teaching complex, authentic mathematics problems to adolescents in remedial math classes. *Exceptional Children, 59,* 556–566.

Bridge, C. A., & Hiebert, E. H. (1985). A comparison of classroom writing practices, teachers' perception of their writing instruction, and textbook recommendations on writing practices. *The Elementary School Teacher, 86,* 155–172.

Brigham, F. J. (1992a). *Enhancing recall of information presented in maps by students with learning disabilities.* Unpublished doctoral dissertation, Purdue University, West Lafayette, IN.

Brigham, F. J. (1992b). Spatial learning and instruction of students with learning disabilities. In T. E. Scruggs & M. A. Mastropieri (Eds.), *Advances in learning and behavioral disabilities* (Vol. 7, pp. 57–85). Stamford, CT: JAI.

Brigham, F. J., Bakken, J. P., Scruggs, T. E., & Mastropieri, M. A. (1992). Cooperative behavior management: Strategies for promoting a positive classroom environment. *Education and Training of the Mentally Retarded, 27,* 3–12.

Brigham, R. J., Scruggs, T. E., & Mastropieri, M. A. (1992). Teacher enthusiasm in learning disabilities classrooms: Effects on learning and behavior. *Learning Disabilities Research & Practice, 7,* 68–73.

Brigham, F. J., Scruggs, T. E., & Mastropieri, M. A. (1995). Elaborative maps for enhanced learning of historical information: Uniting spatial, verbal, and imaginal information. *Journal of Special Education, 28,* 440–460.

Broden, M., Bruce, C., & Mitchell, M. A. (1970). Effects of teacher attention on attending behavior of two boys at adjacent desks. *Journal of Applied Behavior Analysis, 3,* 199–203.

Brolin, D. E. (Ed.). (1978). *Life-centered career education: A competency-based approach.* Reston, VA: Council for Exceptional Children.

Brolin, D. E. (1989). *Life-centered career education for exceptional children.* Reston, VA: Council for Exceptional Children.

Brophy, J. E. (1979). Teacher behavior and its effects. *Journal of Educational Psychology, 71,* 733–750.

Brophy, J. E. (1981). Teacher praise: A functional analysis. *Review of Educational Research, 51,* 5–32.

Brophy, J. E., & Good, T. L. (1986). Teacher behavior and student achievement. In M. C. Wittrock (Ed.), *Handbook of research on teaching* (3rd ed., pp. 328–375). New York: Macmillan.

Browder, D. M., & Grasso, E. (1999). Teaching money skills to individuals with mental retardation: A research review with practical applications. *Remedial and Special Education, 20,* 297–308.

Brown, A. L., Campione, J. C., & Barclay, C. R. (1979). Training self-checking routines for estimating test readiness: Generalization from list learning to prose recall. *Child Development, 50,* 501–512.

Brown, D. S., & Gerber, P. J. (1992). Introduction to special issue on employment. *Learning Disability Quarterly, 15,* 235–236.

Bruce, H. B., & Chan, L. K. S. (1991). Reciprocal teaching and transenvironmental programming: A program to facilitate the reading comprehension of students with reading difficulties. *Remedial and Special Education, 12,* 44–55.

Bulgren, J., Deshler, D. D., & Schumaker, J. B. (1993). *The content enhancement series: The concept mastery routine.* Lawrence, KS: Edge Enterprises.

Bulgren, J., Deshler, D. D., & Schumaker, J. B. (1997). Use of a recall enhancement routine and strategies in inclusive secondary classes. *Learning Disabilities Research & Practice, 12,* 198–208.

Bulgren, J., Schumaker, J. B., & Deshler, D. D. (1988). Effectiveness of a concept teaching routine in enhancing the performance of LD students in secondary-level mainstream classes. *Learning Disability Quarterly, 11,* 3–17.

Bulgren, J., Schumaker, J. B., & Deshler, D. D. (1994). The effects of a recall enhancement routine on the test performance of secondary students with and without learning disabilities. *Learning Disabilities Research & Practice, 9,* 2–11.

Bullock, J., Pierce, S., & McClelland, L. (1987). *Touch math: Teacher's manual.* Colorado Springs, CO: Touch Learning Concepts.

Bullock, J., Pierce, S., & McClelland, L. (1989). *Touch math.* Colorado Springs, CO: Innovative Learning Concepts.

Bursuck, W. D., Polloway, E. A., Plante, L., Epstein, M. H., Jayanthi, M., & McConeghy, J. (1996). Report card grading and adaptations: A national survey of classroom practices. *Exceptional Children, 62,* 301–318.

Calfee, R., & Drum, P. (1986). Research on teaching reading. In M. C. Wittrock (Ed.), *Handbook of research on teaching* (3rd ed., pp. 804–849). New York: Macmillan.

Canter, L. (1990). *Back to school with Assertive Discipline.* Santa Monica, CA: Lee Canter & Associates.

Canter, L. (2001). *Assertive discipline.* Santa Monica, CA: Lee Canter & Associates.

Canter, L., & Canter, M. (1993). *Succeeding with difficult students: New strategies for reaching your most challenging students.* Santa Monica, CA: Lee Canter & Associates.

Carle, E. (1987). *The very hungry caterpillar.* New York: Philomel.

Carlisle, J. R. (1993). Selecting approaches to vocabulary instruction for the reading disabled. *Learning Disabilities Research & Practice, 8,* 97–105.

Carman, R. A., & Adams, W. R. (1977). *Study skills: A student's guide for survival.* New York: Wiley.

Carnine, D. (1998). Instructional design in mathematics for students with learning disabilities. In D. P. Rivera (Ed.), *Mathematics education for students with learning disabilities: Theory to practice* (pp. 119–138). Austin, TX: PRO-ED.

Carpenter, R. L. (1985). Mathematics instruction in resource rooms: Instruction time and teacher competence. *Learning Disability Quarterly, 8,* 95–100.

Carr, M. N. (1993). A mother's thoughts on inclusion. *Journal of Learning Disabilities, 26,* 590–592.

Cartledge, G. (1996). *Cultural diversity and social skills instruction: Understanding ethnic and gender differences.* Champaign, IL: Research Press.

Cartledge, G., & Milburn, J. F. (Eds.). (1995). *Teaching social skills to children: Innovative approaches* (3rd ed.). Boston: Allyn & Bacon.

Case, L. R., Harris, K. R., & Graham, S. (1992). Improving the mathematical problem solving skills of students with learning disabilities: Self-regulated strategy development. *Journal of Special Education, 26,* 1–19.

Cawley, J. (1994). Science for students with disabilities. *Remedial and Special Education, 15,* 67–71.

Cawley, J. F. (1984). *Developmental teaching of mathematics for the learning disabled.* Rockville, MD: Aspen.

Cawley, J. F., Fitzmaurice-Hayes, A. M., & Shaw, R. A. (1988). *Mathematics for the mildly handicapped.* Boston: Allyn & Bacon.

Chan, L. K. S., Cole, R. G., & Morris, J. N. (1990). Effects of instruction in the use of a visual-imagery strategy on the reading comprehension competence of disabled and average readers. *Learning Disability Quarterly, 13,* 2–11.

Ciborowski, J. (1992). *Textbooks and the students who can't read them: A guide to teaching content.* Cambridge, MA: Brookline.

Clark, F. L., Deshler, D. D., Schumaker, J. B., Alley, G. R., & Warner, M. M. (1984). Visual imagery and self-questioning: Strategies to improve comprehension of written material. *Journal of Learning Disabilities, 17,* 145–149.

Clark, G. M. (1979). *Career education for the handicapped child in the elementary classroom.* Denver, CO: Love.

Clay, M. M., & Watson, B. (1987). *Reading recovery book list.* Auckland, New Zealand: University of Auckland.

Cohen, A. L., Torgesen, J. K., & Torgesen, J. L. (1988). Improving speed and accuracy of word recognition in reading disabled children: An evaluation of two computer variations. *Learning Disability Quarterly, 11,* 333–341.

Condus, M. N., Marshall, K. J., & Miller, S. R. (1986). Effects of the keyword mnemonic strategy on vocabulary acquisition and maintenance by learning disabled children. *Journal of Learning Disabilities, 19,* 609–613.

Connell, D. (1983). Handwriting: Taking a look at the alternatives. *Academic Therapy, 18,* 413–420.

Cook, L., & Friend, M. (1995). Co-teaching: Guidelines for effective practices. *Focus on Exceptional Children, 28*(3), 1–16.

Cook, L. K., & Mayer, R. E. (1988). Teaching readers about the structure of scientific text. *Journal of Educational Psychology, 80,* 448–456.

Cook, S., Scruggs, T. E., Mastropieri, M. A., & Casto, G. C. (1985–1986). Handicapped students as tutors. *Journal of Special Education, 19,* 483–492.

Cooke, T. E., & Apolloni, T. (1976). Developing positive socio-emotional behavior: A study of training and generalization effects. *Journal of Applied Behavior Analysis, 9,* 65–78.

Council for Children with Behavior Disorders. (1993). *CCBD Newsletter November 1993.* Reston, VA: Author.

Council for Learning Disabilities. (1993). Concerns about the full inclusion of all students with learning disabilities in regular education classrooms. *Journal of Learning Disabilities, 26,* 594.

Cronin, M. E., & Patton, J. R. (1993). *Life skills instruction for students with special needs: A practical guide for integrating real life content into the curriculum.* Austin, TX: PRO-ED.

Cullinan, D., Lloyd, J., & Epstein, M. H. (1981). Strategy training: A structured approach to arithmetic instruction. *Exceptional Education Quarterly, 2*(1), 41–49.

Cummins, J. (1989). A theoretical framework for bilingual special education. *Exceptional Children, 56,* 111–119.

Darch, C., & Carnine, D. (1986). Teaching content area material to learning disabled students. *Exceptional Children, 53,* 240–246.

De La Paz, S. (1999). Self-regulated strategy instruction in regular education settings: Improving outcomes for students with and without learning disabilities. *Learning Disabilities Research & Practice, 14,* 92–106.

De La Paz, S., Owen, B., Harris, K. R., & Graham, S. (2000). Riding Elvis's motorcycle: Using self-regulated strategy development to PLAN and WRITE for a state writing exam. *Learning Disabilities Research & Practice, 15,* 101–109.

Delquadri, J., Greenwood, C. R., Whorton, D., Carta, J. J., & Hall, R. V. (1986). Classwide peer tutoring. *Exceptional Children, 52,* 535–542.

Deno, S. (1986). Curriculum-based assessment: The emerging alternative. *Exceptional Children, 52,* 219–323.

Deno, S. L., Marston, D., & Mirkin, P. (1982). Valid measurement procedures for continuous evaluation of written expression. *Exceptional Children, 48,* 368–371.

Deno, S. L., Mirkin, P. K., & Chiang, B. (1982). Identifying valid measures of reading. *Exceptional Children, 49,* 36–45.

Deshler, D. D., Ellis, E. S., & Lenz, B. K. (Eds.). (1996). *Teaching adolescents with learning disabilities* (2nd ed.). Denver, CO: Love.

Deshler, D. D., & Schumaker, J. B. (1990). *Learning strategies model* (Training package). Lawrence: University of Kansas, Institute for Research in Learning Disabilities.

Dev, P. (1997). Intrinsic motivation and academic achievement: What does their relationship imply for the classroom teacher? *Remedial and Special Education, 18,* 12–19.

Devine, T. G. (1981). *Teaching study skills: A guide for teachers.* Boston: Allyn & Bacon.

DiGangi, S. A., & Maag, J. W. (1992). A component analysis of self-management training with behaviorally disordered youth. *Behavioral Disorders, 17,* 181–290.

DiGangi, S. A., Maag, J. W., & Rutherford, R. B., Jr. (1991). Self-graphing of on-task behavior: Enhancing the relative effects of self-monitoring on-task behavior and academic performance. *Learning Disability Quarterly, 14,* 221–230.

Division for Learning Disabilities. (1993). *Inclusion: What does it mean for students with learning disabilities?* Reston, VA: Author.

Donahue, M., & Bryan, T. (1983). Conversational skills and modeling in learning disabled boys. *Applied Psycholinguistics, 4,* 251–278.

Dowis, C. L., & Schloss, P. (1992). The impact of mini-lessons on writing skills. *Remedial and Special Education, 13,* 34–42.

Dowling, D. (1995). *303 dumb spelling mistakes.* Lincolnwood, IL: National Textbook Company.

Doyle, W. (1986). Classroom organization and management. In M. C. Wittrock (Ed.), *Handbook of research on teaching* (3rd ed., pp. 392–431). New York: Macmillan.

Duffie, W. B., Rutherford, T. K., & Schectman, A. J. (1990). *Calculator companions: Classroom activity guide to overhead and student calculators.* Deerfield, IL: Learning Resources.

EBSCO Curriculum Materials. (1990). *IEP generator.* Birmingham, AL: Author.

Edgar, E. (1987). Secondary programs in special education: Are many of them justifiable? *Exceptional Children, 53,* 555–561.

Elksnin, L. K. (1994). Promoting generalization of social skills. *LD Forum, 20*(1), 35–37.

Ellis, E. S., Lenz, B. K., & Sabornie, E. J. (1987). Generalization and adaptation of learning strategies to natural environments: Part I. Critical agents. *Remedial and Special Education, 8,* 6–20.

Engelmann, S., & Bruner, E. (1995). *Reading mastery.* DeSoto, TX: SRA/McGraw-Hill.

Englert, C. S. (1983). Measuring special education teacher effectiveness. *Exceptional Children, 50,* 247–254.

Englert, C. S. (1984). Effective direct instruction practices in special education settings. *Remedial and Special Education, 5,* 38–47.

Englert, C. S. (1990). Unraveling the mysteries of writing through strategy instruction. In T. E. Scruggs & B. Y. L. Wong (Eds.), *Intervention research in learning disabilities* (pp. 186–223). New York: Springer-Verlag.

Englert, C. S., Berry, R., & Dunsmore, K. (2001). A case study of the apprenticeship process: Another perspective on the apprentice and the scaffolding metaphor. *Journal of Learning Disabilities, 34,* 152–171.

Englert, C. S., Culatta, B. E., & Hein, D. G. (1987). Influence of irrelevant information in addition word problems on problem solving. *Learning Disability Quarterly, 10,* 29–36.

Englert, C. S., Hiebert, E. H., & Stewart, S. R. (1985). Spelling unfamiliar words by an analogy strategy. *Journal of Special Education, 19,* 291–306.

Englert, C. S., & Mariage, T. V. (1991). Making students partners in the comprehension process: Organizing the reading POSSE. *Learning Disability Quarterly, 14,* 123–138.

Englert, C. S., & Mariage, T. V. (1996). A sociocultural perspective: Teaching ways-of-thinking and ways-of-talking in a literacy community. *Learning Disabilities Research & Practice, 11,* 157–167.

Englert, C. S., Raphael, T. E., Anderson, L. M., Anthony, H. M., & Stevens, D. D. (1991). Making strategies and self-talk visible: Writing instruction in regular and special education classrooms. *American Educational Research Journal, 28,* 337–372.

Englert, C. S., Tarrant, K. L., Mariage, T. V., & Oxer, T. (1994). Lesson talk as the work of reading groups: The effectiveness of two interventions. *Journal of Learning Disabilities, 27,* 165–185.

Etscheidt, S. (1991). Reducing aggressive behavior and improving self-control: A cognitive behavioral training program for behaviorally disordered adolescents. *Behavioral Disorders, 16,* 107–115.

Evers, W. L., & Schwartz, J. C. (1973). Modifying social withdrawal in preschoolers: The effects of filmed modeling and teacher praise. *Journal of Abnormal Child Psychology, 1,* 248–256.

Ferretti, R. P., MacArthur, C. D., & Okolo, C. M. (2001). Teaching for historical understanding in inclusive classrooms. *Learning Disability Quarterly, 24,* 59–71.

Ferretti, R. P., & Okolo, C. M. (1996). Authenticity in learning: Multimedia design projects in the social studies for students with disabilities. *Journal of Learning Disabilities, 29,* 450–460.

Ferro, S. C., & Pressley, M. G. (1991). Imagery generation by learning disabled and average achieving 11- to 13-year-olds. *Learning Disability Quarterly, 14,* 231–239.

Ferster, C. B., & Skinner, B. F. (1957). *Schedules of reinforcement.* New York: Appleton-Century-Crofts.

Figueroa, R. A., Fradd, S. H., & Correa, V. I. (Guest Eds.). (1989). Meeting the multicultural needs of the Hispanic students in special education [Special issue]. *Exceptional Children, 56*(2).

Fischer, P. E. (1993). *The sounds and spelling patterns of English: Phonics for teachers and parents.* Morrill, ME: Oxton House.

Fisher, E. L., White, J. M., & Fisher, J. H. (1984). Teaching figurative speech. *Academic Therapy, 19,* 403–407.

Five, C. L. (1992). *Special voices.* Portsmouth, NH: Heinemann Educational Books.

Fleischner, J. E., Nuzum, M. B., & Marzola, E. S. (1987). Devising an instructional program to teach arithmetic problem-solving skills to students with learning disabilities. *Journal of Learning Disabilities, 20,* 214–217.

Ford, B. A., Obiakor, F. E., & Patton, J. M. (Eds.). (1995). *Effective education of African American exceptional learners: New perspectives.* Austin, TX: PRO-ED.

Ford, M. E. (1995). Motivation and competence development in special and remedial education. *Intervention in School and Clinic, 31,* 70–83.

Forness, S. R. (1970). Educational prescription for the school psychologist. *Journal of School Psychology, 8,* 96–98.

Forness, S. R. (1981). Concepts of school learning and behavior disorders: Implications for research and practice. *Exceptional Child, 48,* 56–64.

Forness, S. R. (1982). Diagnosing dyslexia: A note on the need for ecologic assessment. *American Journal of Diseases of Children, 136,* 794–799.

Forness, S. R., & Kavale, K. A. (1987). De-psychologizing special education. In R. B. Rutherford, Jr., C. M. Nelson, & S. R. Forness (Eds.), *Severe behavior disorders of children and youth* (pp. 2–14). Boston: Little, Brown.

Forness, S. R., & Kavale, K. A. (1996). Treating social skill deficits in children with learning disabilities: A meta-analysis of the research. *Learning Disability Quarterly, 19,* 2–13.

Forness, S. R., & MacMillan, D. L. (1972). Reinforcement overkill: Implications for the education of the retarded. *Journal of Special Education, 6,* 221–230.

Franklin, M. E. (1992). Culturally sensitive instructional practices for African-American learners with disabilities. *Exceptional Children, 59,* 115–122.

Frase-Blunt, M. (2000). High stakes testing a mixed blessing for special students. *CEC Today, 7*(2), 1, 5, 7, 15.

Friend, M. (1984). Consulting skills for resource teachers. *Learning Disability Quarterly, 7,* 246–250.

Friend, M. (1985). Training special educators to be consultants: Considerations for developing programs. *Teacher Education and Special Education, 8,* 115–120.

Friend, M., & Cook, L. (1992). *Interactions: Collaboration skills for school professionals.* New York: Longman.

Fuchs, D., & Fuchs, L. S. (1994). Inclusive schools movement and the radicalization of special education reform. *Exceptional Children, 60,* 249–309.

Fuchs, D., Fuchs, L. S., & Bahr, M. W. (1990). Mainstream assistance teams: A scientific basis for the art of consultation. *Exceptional Children, 59,* 115–122.

Fuchs, D., Fuchs, L. S., & Burish, P. (2000). Peer-assisted learning strategies: An evidence-based practice to promote reading achievement. *Learning Disabilities Research & Practice, 15,* 85–91.

Fuchs, D., Fuchs, L. S., & Fernstrom, P. (1993). A conservative approach to special education reform: Mainstreaming through transenvironmental programming and curriculum-based measurement. *American Educational Research Journal, 30,* 149–177.

Fuchs, D., Fuchs, L. S., Mathes, P. G., & Simmons, D. C. (1997). Peer-assisted learning strategies: Making classrooms more responsive to diversity. *American Educational Research Journal, 34,* 174–206.

Fuchs, D., Fuchs, L. S., Reeder, P., Gilman, S., Fernstrom, P., Bahr, M., & Moore, P. (1989). *Mainstream assistance teams: A handbook on prereferral intervention.* Nashville, TN: Peabody College of Vanderbilt University, Department of Special Education.

Fuchs, L. S. (1986). Monitoring among mildly handicapped pupils: Review of current practice and research. *Remedial and Special Education, 7,* 5–12.

Fuchs, L. S. (1987). Curriculum-based measurement of instructional program development. *Teaching Exceptional Children, 20,* 42–44.

Fuchs, L. S. (1994). *Connecting performance assessment to instruction.* Reston, VA: Council for Exceptional Children.

Fuchs, L. S., & Deno, S. (1992). Effects of curriculum within curriculum-based measurement. *Exceptional Children, 58,* 232–243.

Fuchs, L. S., Deno, S., & Marston, D. (1983). Improving the reliability of curriculum-based measures of academic skills for psychoeducational decision making. *Diagnostique, 8,* 135–149.

Fuchs, L. S., Deno, S., & Mirkin, P. K. (1984). The effects of frequent curriculum-based measurement and evaluation on pedagogy, student achievement, and student awareness learning. *American Educational Research Journal, 21,* 449–460.

Fuchs, L. S., & Fuchs, D. (1986a). Curriculum-based assessment of progress toward long- and short-term goals. *Journal of Special Education, 20,* 69–82.

Fuchs, L. S., & Fuchs, D. (1986b). Effects of systematic formative evaluation: A meta-analysis. *Exceptional Children, 53,* 199–208.

Fuchs, L. S., Fuchs, D., Allinder, R. M., & Hamlett, C. L. (1992). Diagnostic spelling analysis within curriculum-based measurement: Implications for students with learning and behavioral disabilities. In T. E. Scruggs & M. A. Mastropieri (Eds.), *Advances in learning and behavioral disabilities* (Vol. 7, pp. 35–56). Stamford, CT: JAI.

Fuchs, L. S., Fuchs, D., Hamlett, C. L., Phillips, N. B., & Bentz, J. (1994). Classwide curriculum based measurement: Helping general educators meet the challenge of student diversity. *Exceptional Children, 60,* 518–537.

Fuchs, L. S., Fuchs, D., Hamlett, C. L., & Stecker, P. M. (1991). Effects of curriculum-based measurement and consultation on teacher planning and student achievement in mathematics operations. *American Educational Research Journal, 28,* 617–641.

Fuchs, L. S., Fuchs, D., Hamlett, C. L., & Whinnery, K. (1991). Effects of goal line feedback on level, slope, and stability of performance within curriculum-based measurement. *Learning Disabilities Research & Practice, 6,* 65–74.

Fuchs, L. S., Fuchs, D., Kazdan, S., Karns, K., Calhoon, M. B., Hamlett, C. L., & Hewlett, S. (2000). Effects of workgroup structure and size on student productivity during collaborative work on complex tasks. *Elementary School Journal, 100,* 183–212.

Fulk, B. J. M., & Mastropieri, M. A. (1990). Training positive attitudes: "I tried hard and did well!" *Intervention in School and Clinic, 26*(2), 79–83.

Fulk, B. J. M., Mastropieri, M. A., & Scruggs, T. E. (1992). Mnemonic generalization training for students with learning disabled adolescents. *Learning Disabilities Research & Practice, 7,* 2–10.

Fulk, B. J. M., & Stormont-Spurgin, M. (1995). Spelling interventions for students with learning disabilities: A review. *Journal of Special Education, 28,* 488–513.

Gaffney, J. S. (1984). *LD children's prose recall as a function of prior knowledge, instruction, and context relatedness.* Unpublished doctoral dissertation, Arizona State University, Tempe.

Gagne, R. M. (1965). *The conditions of learning.* New York: Holt, Rinehart & Winston.

Gagne, R. M. (1970). *The conditions of learning* (2nd ed.). New York: Holt, Rinehart & Winston.

Gagne, R. M., & Briggs, L. J. (1974). *Principles of instructional design.* New York: Holt, Rinehart & Winston.

Gajria, M., & Salvia, J. (1992). The effects of summarization instruction on text comprehension of students with learning disabilities. *Exceptional Children, 58,* 508–516.

Galagan, J. E. (1986). Psychoeducational testing: Turn out the lights, the party's over. *Exceptional Children, 52,* 288–298.

Garnett, K. (1992). Developing fluency with basic number facts: Intervention for students with learning disabilities. *Learning Disabilities Research & Practice, 7,* 210–216.

Gaskins, I., & Elliot, T. (1991). *Implementing cognitive strategy training across the school: The Benchmark manual for teachers.* Cambridge, MA: Brookline.

Gaskins, I. W., Downer, M. A., Anderson, R. C., Cunningham, R. M., Gaskins, R. W., Schommer, M., & the teachers of the Benchmark School. (1988). A metacognitive approach to phonics: Using what you know to decode what you don't know. *Remedial and Special Education, 9*(1), 36–41.

Gerber, M. M. (1984). Techniques to teach generalizable spelling skills. *Academic Therapy, 20,* 49–58.

Gerber, R. J. (1992). Personal perspective—At first glance: Employment for people with learning disabilities at the beginning of the Americans-with-Disabilities-Act era. *Learning Disability Quarterly, 15,* 330–332.

Germann, G., & Tindal, G. (1986). An application of curriculum-based assessment: The use of direct and repeated measurement. *Exceptional Children, 52,* 244–265.

Gersten, R., & Dimino, J. (1993). Visions and revisions: A special education perspective on the whole language controversy. *Remedial and Special Education, 14*(4), 5–13.

Gersten, R., Woodward, J., & Darch, C. (1986). Direct instruction: A research-based approach to curriculum design and teaching. *Exceptional Children, 53,* 17–31.

Gettinger, M. (1984). Applying learning principles to remedial spelling instruction. *Academic Therapy, 20,* 41–47.

Gettinger, M., Bryant, N. D., & Fayne, H. R. (1982). Designing spelling instruction for learning-disabled children: An emphasis on unit size, distributed practice, and training for transfer. *Journal of Special Education, 16,* 439–448.

Gickling, E. E., & Thompson, V. R. (1986). A personal view of curriculum-based assessment. *Exceptional Children, 2,* 205–218.

Ginott, H. G. (1993). *Teacher and child.* New York: Macmillan.

Ginsburg, H. P. (1998a). Mathematics learning disabilities: A view from developmental psychology. In D. Rivera (Ed.), *Mathematics education for students with learning disabilities* (pp. 22–58). Austin, TX: PRO-ED.

Ginsburg, H. P. (1998b). Toby's math. In R. J. Sternberg & T. Ben-Zeev (Eds.), *The nature of mathematical thinking* (pp. 175–202). Mahwah, NJ: Erlbaum.

Giordano, G. (1984). Analyzing and remediating writing disabilities. *Journal of Learning Disabilities, 17,* 78–83.

Gleason, M., Carnine, D., & Vala, N. (1991). Cumulative versus rapid introduction of new information. *Exceptional Children, 57,* 353–358.

Goldman, S. R., & Hasselbring, T. S. (1997). Achieving meaningful mathematics literacy for students with learning disabilities. *Journal of Learning Disabilities, 30,* 198–208.

Good, T. L., & Grouws, D. A. (1979). The Missouri mathematics effectiveness program. *Journal of Educational Psychology, 71,* 355–362.

Gordon, J., Vaughn, S., & Schumm, J. S. (1993). Spelling interventions: A review of the literature and implications for instruction for students with learning disabilities. *Learning Disabilities Research & Practice, 8,* 175–181.

Gordon, T. (1987). *T.E.T.: Teacher effectiveness training.* New York: McKay.

Gordon, T. (2000). *Parent effectiveness training: The proven program for raising responsible children.* New York: Three Rivers Press.

Graden, J. L., Casey, A., & Bonstrom, O. (1985). Implementing a prereferral intervention system: Part II: The data. *Exceptional Children, 51,* 487–496.

Graden, J. L., Casey, A., & Christenson, S. L. (1985). Implementing a prereferral system: Part I: The model. *Exceptional Children, 51,* 377–387.

Graham, S. (1982). Composition research and practice: A unified approach. *Focus on Exceptional Children, 14,* 1–16.

Graham, S. (1983). The effect of self-instructional procedures on LD students' handwriting performance. *Learning Disability Quarterly, 6,* 231–234.

Graham, S. (1992). Issues in handwriting instruction. *Focus on Exceptional Children, 25,* 1–14.

Graham, S. (1999). Handwriting and spelling instruction for students with learning disabilities: A review. *Learning Disability Quarterly, 22,* 78–98.

Graham, S., & Harris, K. R. (1987). Improving compositional skills with self-instructional strategy training. *Topics in Language Disorders, 7*(4), 66–77.

Graham, S., Harris, K. R., MacArthur, C. A., & Schwartz, S. (1991). Writing and writing instruction with students with learning disabilities: A review of a program of research. *Learning Disability Quarterly, 14,* 89–114.

Graham, S., & MacArthur, C. A. (1991). Introduction: Research and practice in writing. *Learning Disabilities Research & Practice, 6,* 200.

Graham, S., MacArthur, C. A., Schwartz, S., & Page-Voth, V. (1992). Improving the composition of students with learning disabilities using a strategy involving product and process goal setting. *Exceptional Children, 58,* 322–334.

Graham, S., & Weintraub, N. (1996). A review of handwriting research: Progress and prospects from 1980 to 1994. *Educational Psychology Review, 8,* 7–87.

Graves, A.W. (1986). Effects of direct instruction and metacomprehension training on finding main ideas. *Learning Disabilities Research, 1,* 90–100.

Green, S. K., & Shinn, M. R. (1995). Parent attitudes about special education and reintegration: What is the role of student outcomes? *Exceptional Children, 61,* 269–281.

Greenan, J. P., & Browning, D. A. (1989). Generalizable interpersonal relations skills for students with handicapping conditions: Are assessment strategies and procedures valid? *Journal for Vocational Special Needs Education, 11*(2), 23–28.

Greenwood, C. R., Hops, H., & Delquadri, J. (1974). Group contingencies for group consequences in classroom management: A further analysis. *Journal of Applied Behavior Analysis, 7,* 413–425.

Gresham, F. M. (1981). Social skills training with handicapped children: A review. *Review of Educational Research, 51,* 139–176.

Gresham, F. M. (1982). Misguided mainstreaming: The case for social skills training with handicapped children. *Exceptional Children, 48,* 422–433.

Gresham, F. M. (1984). Social skills and self-efficacy for exceptional children. *Exceptional Children, 51,* 253–261.

Gresham, F. M., & Lemanek, K. L. (1983). Social skills: A review of cognitive-behavioral training procedures with children. *Journal of Applied Developmental Psychology, 4,* 239–261.

Gresham, F. M., Sugai, G., & Horner, R. H. (2001). Outcomes of social skills training for students with high-incidence disabilities. *Exceptional Children, 67,* 331–344.

Griffey, Q. L., Zigmond, N., & Leinhardt, G. (1988). The effects of self-questioning and story structure on the reading comprehension of poor readers. *Learning Disabilities Research, 4*(1), 45–51.

Grobecker, B. (2000). Imagery and fractions in students classified as learning disabled. *Learning Disability Quarterly, 23,* 157–168.

Grossman, P. D. (1992). Employment discrimination law for the learning disabled community. *Learning Disability Quarterly, 15,* 287–329.

Grubb, W. N. (Ed.). (1966). *Education through occupations in American high schools.* New York: Teachers College Press.

Gurney, D., Gersten, R., Dimino, J., & Carnine, D. (1990). Story grammar: Effective literature instruction for high school students with learning disabilities. *Journal of Learning Disabilities, 23*(6), 335–342, 348.

Hachett, R. (1975). In praise of praise. *American Education, 11,* 11–15.

Hagen, R. A. (1983). Write right—or left: A practical approach in handwriting. *Journal of Learning Disabilities, 16,* 266–271.

Hallahan, D. P., Marshall, K. J., & Lloyd, J. W. (1981). Self-recording during group instruction: Effects on attention to task. *Learning Disability Quarterly, 4,* 407–413.

Hammill, D. D., & Larsen, S. (1996). *Test of Written Language–Third Edition.* Austin, TX: PRO-ED.

Hanover, S. (1983). Handwriting comes naturally? *Academic Therapy, 18,* 407–412.

Hardy, S. D. (2001). *A qualitative study of the instructional behaviors and practices of a dyad of educators in self-contained and inclusive co-taught secondary biology classrooms during a nine-week science instruction grading period.* Unpublished doctoral dissertation, George Mason University, Fairfax, VA.

Haring, N., Lovitt, T., Hansen, C., & Eaton, J. (1978). *The fourth R: Research in the classroom.* Columbus, OH: Merrill.

Harris, K. R., & Graham, S. (1996). *Making the writing process work: Strategies for composition and self-regulation.* Cambridge, MA: Brookline.

Harris, V. W., & Sherman, J. A. (1973). Use and analysis of the "Good Behavior Game" to reduce disruptive classroom behavior. *Journal of Applied Behavior Analysis, 6,* 405–417.

Hasselbring, T. S., & Moore, P. R. (1996). Developing mathematical literacy through the use of contextualized learning environments. *Journal of Computing in Childhood Education, 7*(3–4), 199–222.

Haynes, M. C., & Jenkins, J. R. (1986). Reading instruction in special education resource rooms. *American Educational Research Journal, 23,* 161–190.

Hazel, J. S., Schumaker, J. B., Sherman, J. A., & Sheldon, J. (1982). Application of a group training program in social skills and problem solving to learning disabled and nonlearning disabled youth. *Learning Disability Quarterly, 5,* 398–408.

Heinisch, B., & Hecht, J. (1993). A comparison of six programs: Word prediction software. *TAM Newsletter, 8*(3), 4–9.

Hendrickson, J., Roberts, M., & Shores, R. E. (1978). Antecedent and contingent modeling to teach basic sight vocabulary to learning disabled children. *Journal of Learning Disabilities, 11,* 524–528.

Heron, T. E., & Harris, K. C. (2001). *The educational consultant: Helping professionals, parents, and mainstreamed students.* Austin, TX: PRO-ED.

Hewett, F., & Forness, S. R. (1984). *Education of exceptional children* (3rd ed.). Boston: Allyn & Bacon.

Hewett, R. (1968). *The emotionally disturbed child in the classroom.* Boston: Allyn & Bacon.

Higgins, T. S., Jr. (1982). A comparison of two methods of practice on the spelling performance of learning disabled adolescents (Doctoral dissertation, Georgia State University, Atlanta). *Dissertation Abstracts International, 43*(06), 4021B.

Hillocks, G., Jr. (1984). What works in teaching composition: A meta-analysis of experimental treatment studies. *American Journal of Education, 93,* 133–170.

Hine, M. S., Goldman, S. R., & Cosden, M. A. (1990). Error monitoring by learning handicapped students engaged in collaborative microcomputer-based writing. *Journal of Special Education, 23,* 407–422.

Horton, S. V., Lovitt, T. C., & White, O. R. (1992). Teaching mathematics to adolescents classified as educable mentally handicapped: Using calculators to remove the computational onus. *Remedial and Special Education, 13*(3), 36–60.

Howell, K. W., & Davidson, M. R. (1997). Programming: Aligning teacher thought processes with the curriculum. In J. W. Lloyd, E. J. Kameenui, & D. Chard (Eds.), *Issues in educating students with disabilities* (pp. 101–128). Mahwah, NJ: Erlbaum.

Howell, K. W., & Kaplan, J. S. (1980). *Diagnosing basic skills: A handbook for deciding what to teach.* Columbus, OH: Merrill.

Howell, K. W., & Morehead, M. K. (1987). *Curriculum-based measurement for special and remedial education.* Columbus, OH: Merrill.

Howell, K.W., & Nolet, V. (1999). *Curriculum-based evaluation: Teaching and decision making.* Pacific Grove, CA: Wadsworth.

Hudson, P., Lignugaris-Kraft, B., & Miller, T. (1993). Using content enhancements to improve the performance of adolescents with learning disabilities in content classes. *Learning Disabilities Research & Practice, 8,* 106–126.

Hughes, C. (1996). Memory and test-taking strategies. In D. D. Deshler, E. S. Ellis, & B. K. Lenz (Eds.), *Teaching adolescents with learning disabilities* (2nd ed., pp. 209–266). Denver, CO: Love.

Hughes, C., Ruhl, K. L., & Misra, A. (1989). Self-management with behaviorally disordered students in school settings: A promise unfulfilled? *Behavioral Disorders, 14,* 250–262.

Hutchinson, N. L. (1993). Effects of cognitive strategy instruction on algebra problem solving of adolescents with learning disabilities. *Learning Disability Quarterly, 14,* 34–63.

Idol, L. (1987). A critical thinking map to improve content area comprehension of poor readers. *Remedial and Special Education, 8,* 28–40.

Isaacson, S. L. (1984). Evaluating written expression: Issues of reliability, validity, and instructional utility. *Diagnostique, 9,* 96–116.

Isaacson, S. L. (1985a). *Assessing the potential syntax development of third and fourth grade writers.* Unpublished doctoral dissertation, Arizona State University, Tempe.

Isaacson, S. L. (1985b). Assessing written language skills. In S. Simon (Ed.), *Communication skills and classroom success: Assessment methodologies for language-learning disabled students* (pp. 403–424). San Diego: College-Hill.

Isaacson, S. L. (1987). Effective instruction in written language. *Focus on Exceptional Children, 19*(6), 1–12.

Ishii-Jordan, S. R. (2000). Behavioral interventions used with diverse students. *Behavioral Disorders, 25,* 299–309.

Jacobs, A. E., & Hendricks, D. J. (1992). Job accommodations for adults with learning disabilities: Brilliantly disguised opportunities. *Learning Disability Quarterly, 15,* 274–285.

Jenkins, J. R., & Gorrafa, S. (1974). Academic performance of mentally handicapped children as a function of token economies and contingency contracts. *Education and Training of the Mentally Retarded, 9,* 183–186.

Jenkins, J. R., Heliotis, J. D., Stein, M. L., & Haynes, M. C. (1987). Improving reading comprehension by using paragraph restatements. *Exceptional Children, 59,* 421–432.

Jenkins, J. R., & Jewell, M. (1993). Examining the validity of two measures of formative teaching: Reading aloud and maze. *Exceptional Children, 59,* 54–59.

Jenkins, J. R., & Leicester, N. (1992). Specialized instruction within general education: A case study of one elementary school. *Exceptional Children, 58,* 555–563.

Jenkins, J. R., Vadasy, P. F., Firebaugh, M., & Profilet, C. (2000). Tutoring first-grade struggling readers in phonological reading skills. *Learning Disabilities Research & Practice, 15,* 75–84.

Johnson, D. R., Bruininks, R. H., & Thurlow, M. L. (1987). Meeting the challenge of transition service planning through improved interagency cooperation. *Exceptional Children, 53,* 522–530.

Johnson, D. W., & Johnson, R. T. (1975). *Learning together alone: Cooperation, competition, and individualization.* Englewood Cliffs, NJ: Prentice Hall.

Johnson, D. W., & Johnson, R. T. (1984). Building acceptance of differences between handicapped and nonhandicapped students: The effects of cooperative and individualistic instruction. *Journal of Social Psychology, 122,* 257–267.

Johnson, D. W., Johnson, R. T., & Holubec, E. J. (1991). *Cooperation in the classroom* (Rev. ed.). Edina, MN: Interaction Book Company.

Jordan, N., & Montani, T. O. (1996). Mathematical difficulties in young children: Cognitive and developmental perspectives. In T. E. Scruggs & M. A. Mastropieri (Eds.), *Advances in learning and behavioral disabilities* (Vol. 10, Part A, pp. 101–135). Stamford, CT: JAI.

Kavale, K. A., & Forness, S. R. (1985). *The science of learning disabilities.* San Diego: College-Hill.

Kavale, K. A., & Forness, S. R. (1987). The far side of heterogeneity: A critical analysis of empirical subtyping research in learning disabilities. *Journal of Learning Disabilities, 20,* 374–382.

Kavale, K. A., & Forness, S. R. (1995). Social skill deficits and training: A meta-analysis of the research in learning disabilities. In T. E. Scruggs & M. A. Mastropieri, (Eds.), *Advances in learning and behavioral disabilities* (Vol. 10, Part A, pp. 1–45). Stamford, CT: JAI.

Kavale, K. A., Mathur, S. R., Forness, S. R., Rutherford, R. B., & Quinn, M. M. (1997). Effectiveness of social skills training for students with behavior disorders: A meta-analysis. In T. E. Scruggs & M. A. Mastropieri (Eds.), *Advances in learning and behavioral disabilities* (Vol. 11, pp. 1–26). Stamford, CT: JAI.

Kavale, K., & Nye, C. (1983). The effectiveness of drug treatment for severe behavioral disorders: A meta-analysis. *Behavioral Disorders, 9,* 117–130.

Kazdin, A. E., Esveldt-Dawson, K., & Matson, J. L. (1983). The effects of instructional set on social skills performance among psychiatric inpatient children. *Behavioral Therapy, 14,* 413–423.

Kendall, P. C., & Braswell, L. (1985). *Cognitive behavior therapy for impulsive children.* New York: Guilford.

Keogh, B. K. (Ed.). (1981). *Advances in special education: Socialization influences on exceptionality.* Stamford, CT: JAI.

Kerr, M. M., & Nelson, C. M. (1998). *Strategies for managing behavior problems in the classroom* (3rd ed.). Columbus, OH: Merrill.

Kiburz, C. S., Miller, S. R., & Morrow, L. W. (1984). Structured learning using self-monitoring to promote maintenance and generalization of social skills across settings for a behaviorally disordered adolescent. *Behavior Disorders, 10,* 47–55.

Kinder, D., & Bursuck, W. (1993). History strategy instruction: Problem-solution-effect analysis, time, and vocabulary instruction. *Exceptional Children, 59,* 324–335.

King-Sears, M. E., Mercer, C. D., & Sindelar, P. T. (1992). Toward independence with keyword mnemonics: A strategy for science vocabulary instruction. *Remedial and Special Education, 13,* 22–33.

Klingner, J. K., Vaughn, S., Schumm, J. S., Cohen, P., & Forgan, J. W. (1998). Inclusion or pull-out: Which do students prefer? *Journal of Learning Disabilities, 31,* 148–158.

Knowles, M. (1978). *The adult learner: A neglected species* (2nd ed.). Houston: Gulf Publishing.

Knowlton, H. E., & Clark, G. M. (1987). Transition issues for the 1990s. *Exceptional Children, 53,* 562–563.

Kosiewicz, M. M., Hallahan, D. P., Lloyd, J., & Graves, A. W. (1982). Effects of self-instruction and self-correction procedures on handwriting performance. *Learning Disability Quarterly, 5,* 71–78.

Lancioni, G. E. (1982). Normal children as tutors to teach social responses to withdrawn mentally retarded schoolmates: Training, maintenance, and generalization. *Journal of Applied Behavioral Analysis, 15,* 17–40.

Lanford, A. D., & Cary, L. G. (2000). Graduation requirements for students with disabilities. *Remedial and Special Education, 21,* 152–160.

Lang, C. (2001). *The effects of self-instructional strategies on problem solving in algebra for students with special needs.* Unpublished doctoral dissertation, George Mason University, Fairfax, VA.

Lanunziata, L. J., Jr., Hill, D. S., & Krause, L. A. (1981). Teaching social skills in classrooms for behaviorally disordered students. *Behavioral Disorders, 6,* 238–246.

Larrivee, B. (1985). *Effective teaching for successful mainstreaming.* New York: Longman.

Laufenberg, R., & Scruggs, T. E. (1986). Effects of a transformational mnemonic strategy to facilitate digit span recall of mildly handicapped students. *Psychological Reports, 58,* 811–820.

Learning Disabilities Association of America. (1993). Position paper on full inclusion of students with learning disabilities in regular education classes. *Journal of Learning Disabilities, 26,* 595.

Lee, P., & Alley, G. (1981). *Raining junior high LD students to use a test-taking strategy* (Research Rep. No. 38). Lawrence: University of Kansas, Institute for Research in Learning Disabilities.

LeGreca, A. M., & Mesibov, G. B. (1981). Facilitating interpersonal functioning with peers and learning disabled children. *Journal of Learning Disabilities, 14,* 197–299.

Leinhardt, G., Zigmond, N., & Cooley, W. W. (1981). Reading instruction and its effect. *American Educational Research Journal, 18,* 343–361.

Lenz, B. K., Alley, G. R., & Schumaker, J. B. (1987). Activating the inactive learner: Advance organizers in the secondary content classroom. *Learning Disability Quarterly, 10,* 53–68.

Lenz, B. K., Bulgren, J., & Hudson, P. (1990). Content enhancement: A model for promoting the acquisition of content by individuals with learning disabilities. In T. E. Scruggs & B. Y. L. Wong (Eds.), *Intervention research in learning disabilities* (pp. 122–165). New York: Springer-Verlag.

Lenz, B. K., & Hughes, C. A. (1990). A word identification strategy for adolescents with learning disabilities. *Journal of Learning Disabilities, 23*(3), 149–158, 163.

Leon, J. A., & Pepe, H. J. (1983). Self-instructional training: Cognitive behavior modification for remediating arithmetic deficits. *Exceptional Children, 50*, 54–60.

Levendoski, L. S., & Cartledge, G. (2000). Self-monitoring for elementary school children with serious emotional disturbances: Classroom applications for increased academic responding. *Behavioral Disorders, 25*, 211–224.

Lifson, S., Scruggs, T. E., & Bennion, K. (1984). Passage independence in reading achievement tests: A follow-up. *Perceptual and Motor Skills, 58*, 945–946.

Liton, L., & Pumroy, D. K. (1975). A brief review of classroom group-oriented contingencies. *Behavior Research and Therapy, 8*, 341–347.

Lloyd, J., Cullinan, D., Heins, E. D., & Epstein, M. H. (1980). Direct instruction: Effects on oral and written language comprehension. *Learning Disability Quarterly, 3*, 70–76.

Lloyd, J., Saltzman, N. J., & Kauffman, J. M. (1981). Predictable generalization in academic learning as a result of preskills and strategy training. *Learning Disability Quarterly, 4*, 203–216.

Lloyd, J. W., & Landrum, T. (1990). Self-recording of attending to task: Treatment components and generalization of effects. In T. E. Scruggs & B. Y. L. Wong (Eds.), *Intervention research in learning disabilities* (pp. 235–262). New York: Springer-Verlag.

Loomer, B. M. (1982). *The most commonly asked questions about spelling . . . and what the research says.* North Billerica, MA: Curriculum Associates.

Lovitt, T., Rudsit, J., Jenkins, J., Pious, C., & Benedetti, D. (1985). Two methods of adapting science materials for regular and learning disabled seventh graders. *Learning Disability Quarterly, 8*, 275–285.

Lovitt, T., Rudsit, J., Jenkins, J., Pious, C., & Benedetti, D. (1986). Adapting science materials for regular and learning disabled seventh graders. *Remedial and Special Education, 7*(1), 31–39.

Lucangeli, D., Cornoldi, C., & Tellarini, M. (1998). Metacognition and learning disabilities in mathematics. In T. E. Scruggs & M. A. Mastropieri (Eds.), *Advances in learning and behavioral disabilities* (Vol. 12, pp. 219–244). Stamford, CT: JAI.

MacArthur, C. A. (1996). Using technology to enhance the writing processes of students with learning disabilities. *Journal of Learning Disabilities, 29*, 344–354.

MacArthur, C. A. (1998). Word processing with speech synthesis and word prediction: Effects on the dialogue journal writing of students with learning disabilities. *Learning Disability Quarterly, 21*, 151–166.

MacArthur, C. A., Graham, S., & Schwartz, S. (1991). Knowledge of revision and revising behavior among students with learning disabilities. *Learning Disability Quarterly, 14*, 61–73.

MacArthur, C. A., Schwartz, S., & Graham, S. (1991). Effects of a reciprocal peer revision strategy in a special education classroom. *Learning Disabilities Research & Practice, 6*, 201–210.

Maccini, P., & Hughes, C. A. (2000). Effects of a problem-solving strategy on the introductory algebra performance of secondary students with learning disabilities. *Learning Disabilities Research & Practice, 15*, 10–21.

Maccini, P., McNaughton, D. B., & Ruhl, K. (1999). Algebra instruction for students with learning disabilities: Implications from a research review. *Learning Disability Quarterly, 22*, 113–126.

MacMillan, D. L., Forness, S. R., & Trumball, B. M. (1973). The role of punishment in the classroom. *Exceptional Children, 40*, 85–96.

MacMillan, D. L., & Reschly, D. J. (1998). Overrepresentation of minority students: The case for greater specificity or reconsideration of the variables examined. *Journal of Special Education, 32*, 15–24.

Madsen, C. H., Becker, W. C., & Thomas, D. R. (1968). Rules, praise, and ignoring: Elements of elementary classroom control. *Journal of Applied Behavior Analysis, 1*, 139–150.

Mager, R. F. (1962). *Preparing instructional objectives.* Belmont, CA: Fearon.

Majsterek, D. J., Wilson, R., & Mandlebaum, L. (1990). Computerized IEPs: Guidelines for product evaluation. *Journal of Special Education Technology, 10*, 207–219.

Malone, L. D., & Mastropieri, M. A. (1992). Reading comprehension instruction: Summarization and self-monitoring training for students with learning disabilities. *Exceptional Children, 58*, 270–279.

Malouf, D. B., Wizer, D. R., Pilato, V. H., & Grogan, M. M. (1990). Computer assisted instruction with small groups of mildly handicapped students. *Journal of Special Education, 24*, 51–68.

Mariage, T.V. (2000). Constructing educational possibilities: A sociolinguistic examination of meaning-making in "sharing chair." *Learning Disability Quarterly, 23*, 79–103.

Marston, D. (1987–1988). The effectiveness of special education: A time series analysis of reading performance in regular and special education settings. *Journal of Special Education, 21*, 13–26.

Marston, D., & Magnusson, D. (1986). Implementing curriculum-based measurement in special and regular education settings. *Exceptional Children, 52*, 266–276.

Martin, G., & Pear, J. (1998). *Behavior modification: What it is and how to do it* (6th ed.). Columbus, OH: Prentice Hall.

Mastropieri, M. A. (1985). *Increasing learning and memory skills of learning disabled students.* Logan: Utah State University, Developmental Center for Handicapped Persons. (ERIC Document Reproduction Service No. ED 275 278)

Mastropieri, M. A. (1988). Increasing vocabulary acquisition and recall with the keyword method. *Teaching Exceptional Children, 20*(2), 4–8.

Mastropieri, M. A. (1989). Using general education teacher effectiveness literature in the preparation of special education personnel. *Teacher Education and Special Education, 12,* 170–172.

Mastropieri, M. A., Bakken, J. P., & Scruggs, T. E. (1991). Mathematics instruction for individuals with mental retardation: A perspective and research synthesis. *Education and Training in Mental Retardation, 26,* 115–129.

Mastropieri, M. A., Emerick, K., & Scruggs, T. E. (1988). Mnemonic instruction of science concepts. *Behavioral Disorders, 14,* 48–56.

Mastropieri, M. A., Jenne, T., & Scruggs, T. E. (1988). A level system for managing problem behaviors in a high school resource program. *Behavioral Disorders, 13,* 202–208.

Mastropieri, M. A., Leinhart, A., & Scruggs, T. E. (1999). Strategies to increase reading fluency. *Intervention in School and Clinic, 34,* 278–283, 292.

Mastropieri, M. A., & Peters, E. E. (1987). Increasing prose recall of learning disabled and reading disabled students via spatial organizers. *Journal of Educational Research, 80,* 272–276.

Mastropieri, M. A., & Scruggs, T. E. (1984a). Generalization of academic and social behaviors: Five effective strategies. *Academic Therapy, 19,* 427–432.

Mastropieri, M. A., & Scruggs, T. E. (1984b). *Memory strategies for learning disabled students.* Logan: Utah State University, Exceptional Child Center. (ERIC Document Reproduction Service No. ED 246 620)

Mastropieri, M. A., & Scruggs, T. E. (1985–1986). Early intervention for socially withdrawn children. *Journal of Special Education, 19,* 429–442.

Mastropieri, M. A., & Scruggs, T. E. (1988). Increasing the content area learning of learning disabled students: Research implementation. *Learning Disabilities Research, 4*(1), 17–25.

Mastropieri, M. A., & Scruggs, T. E. (1989a). Constructing more meaningful relationships: Mnemonic instruction for special populations. *Educational Psychology Review, 1,* 83–111.

Mastropieri, M. A., & Scruggs, T. E. (1989b). Mnemonic social studies instruction: Classroom applications. *Remedial and Special Education, 10*(3), 40–46.

Mastropieri, M. A., & Scruggs, T. E. (1989c). Reconstructive elaborations: Strategies for adapting content area information. *Academic Therapy, 24*(4), 391–406.

Mastropieri, M. A., & Scruggs, T. E. (1989d). Reconstructive elaborations: Strategies that facilitate content learning. *Learning Disabilities Focus, 4*(2), 73–77.

Mastropieri, M. A., & Scruggs, T. E. (1991). *Teaching students ways to remember: Strategies for learning mnemonically.* Cambridge, MA: Brookline.

Mastropieri, M. A., & Scruggs, T. E. (1992). Science and students with disabilities. *Review of Educational Research, 62,* 377–411.

Mastropieri, M. A., & Scruggs, T. E. (1994a). *A practical guide for teaching science to students with disabilities in inclusive classes.* Austin, TX: PRO-ED.

Mastropieri, M. A., & Scruggs, T. E. (1994b). Text-based vs. activities-oriented science curriculum: Implications for students with disabilities. *Remedial and Special Education, 15,* 72–85.

Mastropieri, M. A., & Scruggs, T. E. (1995). Teaching science to students with disabilities in regular education settings: Practical and proven strategies. *Teaching Exceptional Children, 27,* 10–13.

Mastropieri, M. A., & Scruggs, T. E. (1996). Trends in science education: Implications for special education. In C. Warger & M. Pugach (Eds.), *What's worth knowing: How curriculum trends will affect special education* (pp. 42–52). New York: Teachers College Press.

Mastropieri, M. A., & Scruggs, T. E. (1997a). Best practices in promoting reading comprehension in students with learning disabilities. *Remedial and Special Education, 18,* 197–213.

Mastropieri, M. A., & Scruggs, T. E. (1997b). What's special about special education? A cautious view toward full inclusion. *Educational Forum, 61,* 206–211.

Mastropieri, M. A., & Scruggs, T. E. (1998a). Constructing more meaningful relationships in the classroom: Mnemonic research into practice. *Learning Disabilities Research & Practice, 13,* 138–145.

Mastropieri, M. A., & Scruggs, T. E. (1998b). Enhancing school success with mnemonic strategies. *Intervention in School and Clinic, 33,* 201–208.

Mastopieri, M. A., & Scruggs, T. E. (2000). *The inclusive classroom: Strategies for effective teaching.* Columbus, OH: Prentice Hall/Merrill.

Mastropieri, M. A., Scruggs, T. E., Bakken, J., & Brigham, F. J. (1992). A complex mnemonic strategy for teaching states and capitals: Comparing forward and backward associations. *Learning Disabilities Research & Practice, 7,* 96–103.

Mastropieri, M. A., Scruggs, T. E., Bakken, J. P., & Whedon, C. (1996). Reading comprehension: A synthesis of research in learning disabilities. In T. E. Scruggs & M. A. Mastropieri (Eds.), *Advances in learning and behavioral disabilities: Intervention research* (Vol. 10, Part B, pp. 201–227). Stamford, CT: JAI.

Mastropieri, M. A., Scruggs, T. E., & Bohs, K. (1994). Mainstreaming an emotionally handicapped student in science: A qualitative investigation. In T. E. Scruggs & M. A. Mastropieri (Eds.), *Advances in learning and behavioral disabilities* (Vol. 8, pp. 131–146). Stamford, CT: JAI.

Mastropieri, M. A., Scruggs, T. E., Boon, R., & Carter, K. B. (2001). Correlates of inquiry learning in science: Constructing concepts of density and buoyancy. *Remedial and Special Education, 22,* 130–137.

Mastropieri, M. A., Scruggs, T. E., & Butcher, K. (1997). How effective is inquiry learning for students with mild disabilities? *Journal of Special Education, 31,* 199–211.

Mastropieri, M. A., Scruggs, T. E., & Fulk, B. J. M. (1990). Teaching abstract vocabulary to LD students with the keyword method: Effects on comprehension and recall. *Journal of Learning Disabilities, 23,* 92–107.

Mastropieri, M. A., Scruggs, T. E., & Levin, J. R. (1983). Pictorial mnemonic strategies for special education. *Journal of Special Education Technology, 6,* 24–33.

Mastropieri, M. A., Scruggs, T. E., & Levin, J. R. (1985a). Maximizing what exceptional children can learn: A review of keyword and other mnemonic strategy research. *Remedial and Special Education, 6*(2), 39–45.

Mastropieri, M. A., Scruggs, T. E., & Levin, J. R. (1985b). Memory strategy instruction with learning disabled adolescents. *Journal of Learning Disabilities, 18,* 94–100.

Mastropieri, M. A., Scruggs, T. E., & Levin, J. R. (1986). Direct vs. mnemonic instruction: Relative benefits for exceptional learners. *Journal of Special Education, 20,* 299–308.

Mastropieri, M. A., Scruggs, T. E., & Levin, J. R. (1987a). Mnemonic facilitation of learning-disabled students' memory for expository prose. *American Educational Research Journal, 24,* 505–519.

Mastropieri, M. A., Scruggs, T. E., & Levin, J. R. (1987b). Transformational mnemonic strategies in special education. In M. McDaniel & M. Pressley (Eds.), *Imagery and related mnemonic processes: Theories, individual differences, and applications* (pp. 358–376). New York: Springer-Verlag.

Mastropieri, M. A., Scruggs, T. E., Levin, J. R., Gaffney, J., & McLoone, B. (1985). Mnemonic vocabulary instruction for learning disabled students. *Learning Disability Quarterly, 8,* 57–63.

Mastropieri, M. A., Scruggs, T. E., & Magnusen, M. (1999). Activities-oriented science instruction for students with disabilities. *Learning Disability Quarterly, 22,* 240–249.

Mastropieri, M. A., Scruggs, T. E., Mantzicopoulos, P. Y., Sturgeon, A., Goodwin, L., & Chung, S. (1998). "A place where living things affect and depend on each other": Qualitative and quantitative outcomes associ-ated with inclusive science teaching. *Science Education, 82,* 163–179.

Mastropieri, M. A., Scruggs, T. E., McLoone, B., & Levin, J. R. (1985). Facilitating the acquisition of science classification in LD students. *Learning Disability Quarterly, 8,* 299–309.

Mastropieri, M. A., Scruggs, T. E., & Shiah, R. L. (1991). Mathematics instruction with learning disabled students: A review of research. *Learning Disabilities Research & Practice, 6,* 89–98.

Mastropieri, M. A., Scruggs, T. E., & Shiah, R. L. (1997). Can computers teach problem solving strategies to students with mild mental retardation? A case study. *Remedial and Special Education, 18,* 157–165.

Mastropieri, M. A., Scruggs, T. E., Whittaker, M. E. S., & Bakken, J. P. (1994). Applications of mnemonic strategies with students with mental disabilities. *Remedial and Special Education, 15*(1), 34–43.

Mastropieri, M. A., Spencer, V., Scruggs, T. E., & Talbott, E. (2000). Students with disabilities as tutors: An updated research synthesis. In T. E. Scruggs & M. A. Mastropieri (Eds.), *Educational interventions: Advances in learning and behavioral disabilities* (Vol. 14, pp. 247–279). Stamford, CT: JAI.

Mastropieri, M. A., Sweda, J., & Scruggs, T. E. (2000). Teacher use of mnemonic strategy instruction. *Learning Disabilities Research & Practice, 15,* 69–74.

Mather, N. (1992). Whole language reading instruction for students with learning disabilities: Caught in the cross fire. *Learning Disabilities Research & Practice, 7,* 87–95.

Mathes, P. G., & Fuchs, L. S. (1993). Peer-mediated reading instruction in special education resource rooms. *Learning Disabilities Research & Practice, 8,* 233–243.

Matson, J. L., Esveldt-Dawson, K., Andrasid, F., Ollendick, T. H., Petti, T., & Hersen, M. (1980). Direct, observational, and generalization effects of social skills training with emotionally disturbed children. *Behavior Therapy, 11,* 522–531.

Mayer, R. (1993). Understanding individual differences in mathematical problem solving. *Learning Disability Quarterly, 16,* 2–5.

McGill-Franzen, A. (1979). Beyond illiterate, what can you say? *Learning Disability Quarterly, 2,* 76–80.

McLoone, B. B., Scruggs, T. E., Mastropieri, M. A., & Zucker, S. F. (1986). Memory strategy instruction and training with LD adolescents. *Learning Disabilities Research, 2,* 45–53.

Mellard, D. F., & Hazel, J. S. (1992). Social competencies as a pathway to successful life transitions. *Learning Disability Quarterly, 15,* 251–271.

Mercer, C. D., & Miller, S. R. (1992). Teaching students with learning problems in math to acquire, understand, and apply basic math facts. *Remedial and Special Education, 13*(3), 19–35, 61.

Meyer, L. A. (1982). The relative effects of word-analysis and word-supply correct procedures with poor readers during word-attack training. *Reading Research Quarterly, 17*(4), 544–555.

Miller, S., & Schloss, P. (1983). *Career-vocational education for handicapped youth.* Rockville, MD: Aspen.

Miller, S. P., & Mercer, C. D. (1993). Using a graduated word problem sequence to promote problem-solving skills. *Learning Disabilities Research & Practice, 8,* 169–174.

Minskoff, E. H. (1982). Sharpening language skills in secondary LD students. *Academic Therapy, 18,* 53–60.

Mitchell, D. W., & Crowell, R. J. (1973). Modifying inappropriate behavior in an elementary art class. *Elementary School Guidance and Counseling, 8,* 34–42.

Montague, M. (1992). The effects of cognitive and metacognitive strategy instruction on the mathematical problem solving of middle school students with learning disabilities. *Journal of Learning Disabilities, 25,* 230–248.

Montague, M. (1998). Cognitive strategy instruction in mathematics for students with learning disabilities. In D. P. Rivera (Ed.), *Mathematics education for students with learning disabilities: Theory to practice* (pp. 177–199). Austin, TX: PRO-ED.

Montague, M., & Applegate, B. (1993). Middle school students' mathematical problem solving: An analysis of think aloud protocols. *Learning Disability Quarterly, 16,* 19–33.

Montague, M., Bos, C., & Doucette, M. (1991). Affective, cognitive, and metacognitive attributes of eighth-grade mathematical problem solvers. *Learning Disabilities Research & Practice, 6,* 145–151.

Montague, M., Warger, C., & Morgan, T. H. (2000). Solve it! Instruction to improve mathematical problem solving. *Learning Disabilities Research & Practice, 15,* 110–116.

Moore, G. P., & Hicks, D. M. (1994). Voice disorders. In G. H. Shames, E. H. Wiig, & W. A. Secord (Eds.), *Human communication disorders: An introduction* (4th ed., pp. 292–335). New York: Macmillan.

Moore, R. J., Cartledge, G., & Heckaman, K. (1994). The effects of social skill instruction and self-monitoring on game-related behaviors of adolescents with emotional or behavioral disorders. *Behavioral Disorders, 20,* 253–266.

Moran, M. R. (1983). Learning disabled adolescents' responses to a paragraph-organization strategy. *Pointer, 27,* 28–31.

Morocco, C. C., Hindin, A., Mata-Aguilar, C., & Clark-Chiarelli, N. (2001). Building a deep understanding of literature with middle-grade students with learning disabilities. *Learning Disability Quarterly, 24,* 47–58.

Morsink, C. V., Soar, R. S., Soar, R. M., & Thomas, R. (1986). Research on teaching: Opening door to special education classrooms. *Exceptional Children, 52*(6), 32–40.

Murphy, J., Hern, C., Williams, R., & McLaughlin, T. (1990). The effects of the copy, cover, compare approach in increasing spelling accuracy with learning disabled students. *Contemporary Educational Psychology, 15,* 378–386.

Naglieri, J. A., & Johnson, D. (2000). Effectiveness of a cognitive strategy intervention in improving arithmetic computation based on the PASS theory. *Journal of Learning Disabilities, 33,* 591–597.

National Council of Teachers of Mathematics (NCTM). (2000). *Principles and standards for school mathematics.* Reston, VA: Author.

National Joint Committee on Learning Disabilities. (1993). A reaction to full inclusion: A reaffirmation of the right of students with learning disabilities to a continuum of services. *Journal of Learning Disabilities, 26,* 596.

Neef, N. A., Iwata, B. A., & Page, T. J. (1980). The effects of interpersonal training versus high-density reinforcement of spelling acquisition and retention. *Journal of Applied Behavior Analysis, 13,* 153–158.

Negin, G. A. (1978). Mnemonics and demonic words. *Reading Improvement, 15,* 180–182.

Nelson, J. R., Smith, D. J., Young, R. K., & Dodd, J. M. (1991). A review of self-management outcome research conducted with students who exhibit behavioral disorders. *Behavioral Disorders, 16,* 169–179.

Noble, J. K. (1966). *Better handwriting for you.* New York: Noble & Noble.

Nolet, V., & Tindal, G. (1993). Special education in content area classes: Development of a model and practical procedures. *Remedial and Special Education, 14,* 36–48.

Nutter, N., & Safran, J. (1984). Improving writing with sentence combining exercises. *Academic Therapy, 19,* 449–455.

Obiakor, R. E., Patton, J. M., & Ford, B. A. (Guest Eds.). (1992). Issues in the education of African-American youth in special education settings [Special issue]. *Exceptional Children, 59*(2).

O'Conner, R. E., Jenkins, J. R., Cole, K. N., & Mills, P. E. (1993). Two approaches to reading instruction with children with disabilities: Does program design make a difference? *Exceptional Children, 59,* 312–323.

O'Conner, R. E., Jenkins, J. R., Leicester, N., & Slocum, T. A. (1993). Teaching phonological awareness to young children with learning disabilities. *Exceptional Children, 59,* 532–546.

O'Conner, R. E., Jenkins, J. R., & Slocum, T. A. (1995). Transfer among phonological tasks in kindergarten: Essential instructional content. *Journal of Educational Psychology, 87,* 202–217.

Okolo, C. M. (1988). Instructional environments in secondary vocational education programs: Implications for LD adolescents. *Learning Disability Quarterly, 11,* 136–148.

Okolo, C. M., Bahr, C. M., & Reith, H. J. (1993). A retrospective view of computer-based instruction. *Journal of Special Education Technology, 12,* 1–27.

Okolo, C. M., Cavalier, A. R., Ferretti, R. P., & MacArthur, C. A. (2000). Technology, literacy, and disabilities: A review of the research. In R. M. Gersten, & E. P. Schiller (Eds.), *Contemporary special education research: Syntheses of the knowledge base on critical instructional issues* (pp. 179–250). Mahwah, NJ: Erlbaum.

O'Leary, R. D., Kaufman, K. F., Kass, R. E., & Drabman, R. S. (1970). Effects of loud and soft reprimands on the behavior of disruptive students. *Exceptional Children, 37,* 145–155.

Olson, R. K., Wise, B., Ring, J., & Johnson, M. (1997). Computer-based remedial training in phoneme awareness and phonological decoding: Effects on the post-training development of word recognition. *Scientific Studies of Reading, 1,* 235–253.

O'Melia, M.C., & Rosenberg, M. S. (1997). Effects of cooperative homework teams on the acquisition of mathematics skills by secondary students with mild disabilities. *Exceptional Children, 60,* 538–548.

Orkwis, R., & McLane, K. (1998). *ERIC/OSEP topical brief: A curriculum every student can use: Design principles for student access.* Keston, VA: ERIC/OSEP Special Project. Council for Exceptional Children.

Osguthorpe, R. T., & Scruggs, T. E. (1986). Special education students as tutors: A review and analysis. *Remedial and Special Education, 7*(4), 15–25.

O'Shea, L. J., Sindelar, R. T., & O'Shea, D. J. (1987). The effects of repeated readings and attentional cues on the reading fluency and comprehension of learning disabled readers. *Learning Disabilities Research, 2*(2), 103–109.

Overton, T. (1996). *Assessment in special eduction: An applied approach.* Englewood Cliffs, NJ: Prentice Hall.

Palincsar, A. S., & Brown, A. L. (1984). Reciprocal teaching of comprehension-fostering monitoring activities. *Cognition and Instruction, 1,* 117–175.

Palincsar, A. S., Magnusson, S. J., Collins, K. M., & Cutter, J. (2001). Making science accessible to all: Results of a design experiment in inclusive classrooms. *Learning Disability Quarterly, 24,* 15–32.

Pany, D., & Jenkins, J. R. (1978). Learning word meanings: A comparison of instructional procedures. *Learning Disability Quarterly, 1,* 21–32.

Pany, D., Jenkins, J. R., & Schreck, J. (1982). Vocabulary instruction: Effects on word knowledge and reading comprehension. *Learning Disability Quarterly, 5,* 202–215.

Paris, S., & Oka, E. R. (1989). Strategies for comprehending text and coping with reading difficulties. *Learning Disabilities Research, 12,* 32–41.

Parker, R. I., Tindal, G., & Hasbrouck, J. (1991). Progress monitoring with objective measures of writing performance for students with mild disabilities. *Exceptional Children, 58,* 61–73.

Parmar, R. S., & Cawley, J. F. (1993). Analysis of science textbook recommendations provided for students with disabilities. *Exceptional Children, 59,* 518–531.

Patton, J. R., Cronin, M. E., Bassett, D. S., & Koppel, A. E. (1998). A life skills approach to mathematics instruction: Preparing students with learning disabilities for the real-life math demands of adulthood. In D. P. Rivera (Ed.), *Mathematics education for students with learning disabilities: Theory to practice* (pp. 201–218). Austin, TX: PRO-ED.

Peterson, J., Heistad, D., Peterson, D., & Reynolds, M. (1986). Montevideo individualized prescriptive instructional management system. *Exceptional Children, 52,* 239–243.

Pflaum, S. W., & Bryan, T. H. (1982). Oral reading research and learning disabled children. *Topics in Learning and Learning Disabilities, 1,* 33–42.

Phelps, L. A., & Lutz, R. J. (1977). *Career exploration and preparation for the special needs learner.* Boston: Allyn & Bacon.

Pickering, E., Pickering, A., & Buchanan, M. (1988). LD and nonhandicapped boys' comprehension of cartoon humor. *Learning Disability Quarterly, 10,* 45–51.

Polloway, E. A., Epstein, M. H., Bursuck, W., Jayanthi, M., & Comblad, C. (1994). A national survey of homework practices of general education teachers. *Journal of Learning Disabilities, 27,* 500–509.

Polloway, E. A., Epstein, M. H., Bursuck, W. D., Roderique, T. W., McConeky, J. L., & Jayanthi, M. (1994). Classroom grading: A national survey of policies. *Remedial and Special Education, 15*(3), 162–170.

Polloway, E. A., Foley, R. M., & Epstein, M. (1992). A comparison of the homework problems of students with learning disabilities and nondisabled students. *Learning Disabilities Research & Practice, 7,* 203–209.

Polloway, E. A., & Patton, J. R. (1997). *Strategies for teaching learners with special needs* (6th ed.). Columbus, OH: Prentice Hall/Merrill.

Polloway, E. A., & Smith, T. E. C. (1999). *Language instruction for students with disabilities* (2nd ed., rev.). Denver, CO: Love.

Popham, W. J., & Husek, T. R. (1969). Implications of criterion-referenced measurement. *Journal of Educational Measurement, 6,* 1–9.

Prater, M. A., Joy, R., Chilman, B., Temple, J., & Miller, S. R. (1991). Self-monitoring of on-task behavior by adolescents with learning disabilities. *Learning Disability Quarterly, 14,* 164–177.

Presley, J. A., & Hughes, C. (2000). Peers as teachers of anger management to high school students with behavioral disorders. *Behavioral Disorders, 25,* 114–130.

Pressley, M., & Associates. (1990). *Cognitive strategy instruction that really improves children's academic performance.* Cambridge, MA: Brookline.

Pressley, M., & McCormick, C. (1995). *Advanced educational psychology for educators, researchers, and policy makers.* New York: HarperCollins.

Pressley, M., & Rankin, J. (1994). More about whole language methods of reading instruction for students at-risk for early reading failure. *Learning Disabilities Research & Practice, 9,* 156–168.

Pressley, M., Scruggs, T. E., & Mastropieri, M. A. (1989). Memory strategy instruction for learning disabilities: Present and future directions for researchers. *Learning Disabilities Research, 4,* 68–77.

Ragland, E., Kerr, M. M., & Strain, R. S. (1981). Social play for withdrawn children. *Behavior Modification, 5,* 347–359.

Reid, E. R. (1986). Practicing effective instruction: The Exemplary Center for Reading Instruction. *Exceptional Children, 52*(6), 510–521.

Reiff, H. B., & DeFur, S. (1992). Transition for youths with learning disabilities: A focus on developing independence. *Learning Disability Quarterly, 15,* 237–249.

Reinhiller, N. (1996). Coteaching: New variations on a not so new practice. *Teacher Education and Special Education, 19,* 34–48.

Reisberg, L., & Wolf, R. (1986). Developing a consulting program in special education: Implementation and interventions. *Focus on Exceptional Children, 19*(1), 1–14.

Reith, H. J., Polsgrove, L., & Eckert, R. (1984). A computer-based spelling program. *Academic Therapy, 20,* 49–56.

Rivera, D. P. (1998a). Mathematics education and students with learning disabilities In D. P. Rivera (Ed.), *Mathematics education for students with learning disabilities: Theory to practice* (pp. 1–31). Austin, TX: PRO-ED.

Rivera, D. P. (Ed.). (1998b). *Mathematics education for students with learning disabilities: Theory to practice.* Austin, TX: PRO-ED.

Rivera, D. P., & Smith, D. D. (1987). Influence of modeling on acquisition and generalization computational skills: A summary of research findings from three sites. *Learning Disability Quarterly, 10,* 69–80.

Rivera, D. P., Smith, R. G., Goodwin, M. W., & Bryant, B. R. (1998). Mathematical word problem solving: A synthesis of intervention research for students with learning disabilities. In T. E. Scruggs & M. A. Mastropieri (Eds.), *Advances in learning and behavioral disabilities* (Vol. 12, pp. 245–285). Stamford, CT: JAI.

Robbins, R. (1986). The Napa-Vacaville follow-through project: Qualitative outcomes, related procedures, and implications for practice. *The Elementary School Journal, 87,* 139–157.

Roberts, M., & Deutsch-Smith, D. (1980). The relationship among correct and error oral reading rates and comprehension. *Learning Disability Quarterly, 3,* 54–65.

Robin, A., Armel, S., & O'Leary, K. (1975). The effects of self-instruction on writing deficiency. *Behavior Therapy, 6,* 178–187.

Rojewski, J. W., & Greenan, J. R. (1992). Teacher certification policies and practices for vocational special education personnel: A national study. *Teacher Education and Special Education, 15,* 194–201.

Romberg, T. A., & Carpenter, T. R. (1986). Research on teaching and learning mathematics: Two disciplines of scientific inquiry. In M. C. Wittrock (Ed.), *Handbook of research on teaching* (3rd ed., pp. 850–873). New York: Macmillan.

Rose, M. C., Cundick, B. R., & Higbee, K. L. (1983). Verbal rehearsal and verbal imagery: Mnemonic aids for learning disabled children. *Journal of Learning Disabilities, 16,* 352–354.

Rosenshine, B. (1983). Teaching functions in instructional programs. *Elementary School Journal, 83,* 335–352.

Rosenshine, B. (1997). Advances in research in instruction. In J. W. Lloyd, E. Kameenui, & C. Chard (Eds.), *Issues in educating students with disabilities* (pp. 197–220). Mahwah, NJ: Erlbaum.

Rosenshine, B., & Meister, C. (1994). Reciprocal teaching: A review of the research. *Review of Educational Research, 64,* 479–530.

Rosenshine, B., & Stevens, R. (1986). Teaching functions. In M. C. Wittrock (Ed.), *Handbook of research on teaching* (3rd ed., pp. 376–391). New York: Macmillan.

Rottman, T. R., & Cross, D. R. (1990). Using informed strategies for learning to enhance the reading and thinking skills of children with learning disabilities. *Journal of Learning Disabilities, 23*(5), 270–278.

Rudenga, E. V. A. (1992). *Incompatibility? Ethnographic case studies of learning disabled students in a whole language classroom.* Unpublished doctoral dissertation, Purdue University, West Lafayette, IN.

Ruedy, L. R. (1983). Handwriting instruction: It can be part of the high school curriculum. *Academic Therapy, 18,* 421–429.

Rusch, R. R., & Phelps, L. A. (1987). Secondary special education and transition from school to work: A national priority. *Exceptional Children, 53,* 487–492.

Rutherford, R. B., & Nelson, C. M. (1982). Analysis of the response-contingent time-out literature with behaviorally disordered students in classroom settings. *Behavior Disorders, 5,* 79–105.

Salend, S. L., & Nowak, M. R. (1988). Effects of peer-previewing on LD students' oral reading skills. *Learning Disability Quarterly, 11,* 47–53.

Salvia, J., & Hughes, C. (1990). *Curriculum-based assessment: Testing what is taught.* New York: Macmillan.

Salvia, J., & Ysseldyke, J. E. (1998). *Assessment* (7th ed.). Boston: Houghton Mifflin.

Salzberg, C. L., Lignugaris-Kraft, B., & McCuller, G. L. (1988). Reasons for job loss: A review of employment termination studies of mentally retarded workers. *Research in Developmental Disabilities, 9,* 153–170.

Sarkees-Wircenski, M., & Scott, J. L. (1995). *Vocational special needs.* Homewood, IL: American Technical Publishers.

Schloss, P. J., Schloss, C. N., & Harris, L. (1984). A multiple baseline analysis of an interpersonal skills training program for depressed youth. *Behavioral Disorders, 9,* 182–188.

Schloss, P. J., Smith, M. A., & Schloss, C. N. (1990). *Instructional methods for adolescents with learning and behavior problems.* Boston: Allyn & Bacon.

Schumaker, J. B., Deshler, D. D., Alley, G. R., Warner, M. M., & Denton, P. H. (1982). Multipass: A learning strategy for improving reading comprehension. *Learning Disability Quarterly, 5,* 295-304.

Schumaker, J. B., & Ellis, E. S. (1982). Social skills training of LD adolescents: A generalization study. *Learning Disability Quarterly, 5,* 388–397.

Schwartz, R. G. (1994). Phonological disorders. In G. H. Shames, E. H. Wiig, & W. A. Secord (Eds.), *Human communication disorders: An introduction* (4th ed., pp. 251–290). Columbus, OH: Prentice Hall/Merrill.

Schworm, R. W. (1979). The effects of selective attention on the decoding skills of children with learning disabilities. *Journal of Learning Disabilities, 12,* 639–644.

Scott, K. S. (1993). Multisensory mathematics for children with mild disabilities. *Exceptionality, 4,* 97–111.

Scruggs, T. E. (1985a). *Administration and interpretation of standardized achievement tests with learning disabled and behaviorally disordered elementary school children: Final report.* Logan: Utah State University, Developmental Center for Handicapped Persons. (ERIC Document Reproduction Service No. ED 256 082)

Scruggs, T. E. (1985b). *The administration and interpretation of standardized achievement tests with learning disabled and behaviorally disordered elementary school children: Year 2 final report.* Logan: Utah State University, Developmental Center for Handicapped Persons. (ERIC Document Reproduction Service No. 260 560)

Scruggs, T. E. (1988). The nature of learning disabilities. In K. A. Kavale (Ed.), *Learning disabilities: State of the art and practice* (pp. 22–43). Boston: Little Brown/College-Hill.

Scruggs, T. E. (1992). Single subject research methodology in the study of learning and behavior disorders: Design, analysis, and synthesis. In T. E. Scruggs & M. A. Mastropieri (Eds.), *Advances in learning and behavioral disabilities* (Vol. 7, pp. 223–247). Stamford, CT: JAI.

Scruggs, T. E., Bennion, K., & Lifson, S. (1985a). An analysis of children's strategy use on reading achievement tests. *Elementary School Journal, 85,* 479–484.

Scruggs, T. E., Bennion, K., & Lifson, S. (1985b). Learning disabled students' spontaneous use of test-taking skills on reading achievement tests. *Learning Disability Quarterly, 8,* 205–210.

Scruggs, T. E., & Jenkins, V. (1985). *Improving the test-taking skills of learning disabled students.* Logan: Utah State University, Developmental Center for Handicapped Persons. (ERIC Document Reproduction Service No. ED 172 049)

Scruggs, T. E., & Laufenberg, R. (1986). Transformational mnemonic strategies for retarded learners. *Education and Raining of the Mentally Retarded, 21,* 165–173.

Scruggs, T. E., & Lifson, S. A. (1985). Current conceptions of test-wiseness: Myths and realities. *School Psychology Review, 14,* 339–350.

Scruggs, T. E., & Lifson, S. A. (1986). Are LD students 'testwise'? An inquiry into reading comprehension test items. *Educational and Psychological Measurement, 46,* 1075–1082.

Scruggs, T. E., & Mastropieri, M. A. (1984a). How gifted students learn: Implications from recent research. *Roeper Review, 5,* 183–185.

Scruggs, T. E., & Mastropieri, M. A. (1984b). Improving memory for facts with the 'keyword' method. *Academic Therapy, 20,* 159–166.

Scruggs, T. E., & Mastropieri, M. A. (1984c). Issues in generalization: Implications for special education. *Psychology in the Schools, 21,* 397–403.

Scruggs, T. E., & Mastropieri, M. A. (1984d). Use of content maps to increase children's comprehension and recall. *The Reading Teacher, 37,* 807.

Scruggs, T. E., & Mastropieri, M. A. (1985). Illustrative aids improve reading comprehension. *Reading Horizons, 25,* 107–110.

Scruggs, T. E., & Mastropieri, M. A. (1986). Improving test-taking skills of behaviorally disordered and learning disabled students. *Exceptional Children, 52,* 63–68.

Scruggs, T. E., & Mastropieri, M. A. (1988). Are learning disabled students 'test-wise'? A review of recent research. *Learning Disabilities Focus, 3*(2), 87–97.

Scruggs, T. E., & Mastropieri, M. A. (1989a). Mnemonic instruction of LD students: A field-based evaluation. *Learning Disability Quarterly, 12,* 119–125.

Scruggs, T. E., & Mastropieri, M. A. (1989b). Reconstructive elaborations: A model for content area learning. *American Educational Research Journal, 26,* 311–327.

Scruggs, T. E., & Mastropieri, M. A. (1990a). The case for mnemonic instruction: From laboratory investigations to classroom applications. *Journal of Special Education, 24,* 7–29.

Scruggs, T. E., & Mastropieri, M. A. (1990b). Mnemonic instruction for students with learning disabilities: What it is and what it does. *Learning Disability Quarterly, 13,* 7–32.

Scruggs, T. E., & Mastropieri, M. A. (1992a). Classroom applications of mnemonic instruction: Acquisition, maintenance, and generalization. *Exceptional Children, 58,* 219–229.

Scruggs, T. E., & Mastropieri, M. A. (1992b). Effective mainstreaming strategies for mildly handicapped students. *Elementary School Journal, 92,* 389–409.

Scruggs, T. E., & Mastropieri, M. A. (1992c). Remembering the forgotten art of memory. *American Educator, 16*(4), 31–37.

Scruggs, T. E., & Mastropieri, M. A. (1992d). *Teaching test-taking skills: Helping students show what they know.* Cambridge, MA: Brookline.

Scruggs, T. E., & Mastropieri, M. A. (1993a). Current approaches to science education: Implications for mainstream instruction of students with disabilities. *Remedial and Special Education, 14*(1), 15–24.

Scruggs, T. E., & Mastropieri, M. A. (1993b). The effects of prior field experience on student teacher competence. *Teacher Education and Special Education, 16,* 303–308.

Scruggs, T. E., & Mastropieri, M. A. (1993c). Special education for the 21st century: Integrating learning strategies and thinking skills. *Journal of Learning Disabilities, 26,* 392–398.

Scruggs, T. E., & Mastropieri, M. A. (1994a). Adapting microscope activities for students with disabilities. *Science Scope, 17,* 74–78.

Scruggs, T. E., & Mastropieri, M. A. (1994b). The construction of scientific knowledge by students with mild disabilities. *Journal of Special Education, 28,* 307–321.

Scruggs, T. E., & Mastropieri, M. A. (1994c). The effectiveness of generalization training: A quantitative synthesis of single-subject research. In T. E. Scruggs & M. A. Mastropieri (Eds.), *Advances in learning and behavioral disabilities* (Vol. 8, pp. 259–280). Stamford, CT: JAI.

Scruggs, T. E., & Mastropieri, M. A. (1994d). Successful mainstreaming in elementary science classes: A qualitative investigation of three reputational cases. *American Educational Research Journal, 31,* 785–811.

Scruggs, T. E., & Mastropieri, M. A. (1995a). Science and mental retardation: An analysis of curriculum features and learner characteristics. *Science Education, 79,* 251–271.

Scruggs, T. E., & Mastropieri, M. A. (1995b). Science education for students with behavior disorders. *Education and Treatment of Children, 3,* 322–334.

Scruggs, T. E., & Mastropieri, M. A. (1995c). What makes special education special? An analysis of the PASS variables in inclusion settings. *Journal of Special Education, 29,* 224–233.

Scruggs, T. E., & Mastropieri, M. A. (1996). Teacher perceptions of mainstreaming/inclusion, 1958–1995: A research synthesis. *Exceptional Children, 63,* 59–74.

Scruggs, T. E., & Mastropieri, M. A. (1998). Peer tutoring and students with special needs. In K. Topping & S. Ehly (Eds.), *Peer assisted learning* (pp. 165–182). Mahwah, NJ: Erlbaum.

Scruggs, T. E., & Mastropieri, M. A. (2000). The effectiveness of mnemonic instruction for students with learning and behavioral problems: An update and research synthesis. *Journal of Behavioral Education, 10,* 163–173.

Scruggs, T. E., Mastropieri, M. A., Bakken, J. P., & Brigham, E. J. (1993). Reading vs. doing: The relative effectiveness of textbook-based and inquiry-oriented approaches to science education. *Journal of Special Education, 27,* 1–15.

Scruggs, T. E., Mastropieri, M. A., & Boon, R. (1998). Science for students with disabilities: A review of recent research. *Studies in Science Education, 32,* 21–44.

Scruggs, T. E., Mastropieri, M. A., Brigham, F. J., & Sullivan, G. S. (1992). The effectiveness of mnemonic reconstructions on the spatial learning of students with learning disabilities. *Learning Disability Quarterly, 15,* 154–162.

Scruggs, T. E., Mastropieri, M. A., Cook, S., & Escobar, C. (1986). Early intervention for children with conduct disorders: A quantitative synthesis of single-subject research. *Behavioral Disorders, 11,* 260–271.

Scruggs, T. E., Mastropieri, M. A., & Levin, J. R. (1985). Vocabulary acquisition of retarded students under direct and mnemonic instruction. *American Journal of Mental Deficiency, 89,* 546–551.

Scruggs, T. E., Mastropieri, M. A., & Levin, J. R. (1986). Can children effectively re-use the same mnemonic pegwords? *Educational Communication and Technology Journal, 34,* 83–88.

Scruggs, T. E., Mastropieri, M. A., & Levin, J. R. (1987). Contributions of mnemonic strategy research to a theory of learning disabilities. In H. L. Swanson & K. Gadow (Eds.), *Advances in learning and behavioral disabilities: Memory and learning disabilities* (pp. 225–244). Stamford, CT: JAI.

Scruggs, T. E., Mastropieri, M. A., Levin, J. R., & Gaffney, J. S. (1985). Facilitating the acquisition of science facts in learning disabled students. *American Educational Research Journal, 22,* 575–586.

Scruggs, T. E., Mastropieri, M. A., Levin, J. R., McLoone, B. B., Gaffney, J. S., & Prater, M. (1985). Increasing content area learning: A comparison of mnemonic and visual-spatial direct instruction. *Learning Disabilities Research, 1,* 18–31.

Scruggs, T. E., Mastropieri, M. A., McLoone, B. B., Levin, J. R., & Morrison, C. (1987). Mnemonic facilitation of text-embedded science facts with LD students. *Journal of Educational Psychology, 79,* 27–34.

Scruggs, T. E., Mastropieri, M. A., & Richter, L. L. (1985). Peer tutoring with behaviorally disordered students:

Social and academic benefits. *Behavioral Disorders, 10,* 283–294.

Scruggs, T. E., Mastropieri, M. A., & Sullivan, G. S. (1994). Promoting relational thinking skills: Elaborative interrogation for mildly handicapped students. *Exceptional Children, 60,* 450–457.

Scruggs, T. E., Mastropieri, M. A., Sullivan, G. S., & Hesser, L. S. (1993). Improving reasoning and recall: The relative effects of elaborative interrogation and mnemonic elaboration. *Learning Disability Quarterly, 16,* 233–240.

Scruggs, T. E., Mastropieri, M. A., Tolfa, D., & Jenkins, V. (1985). Attitudes of behaviorally disordered students toward tests. *Perceptual and Motor Skills, 60,* 467–470.

Scruggs, T. E., Mastropieri, M. A., Tolfa, D., & Osguthorpe, R. T. (1986). Behaviorally disordered students as tutors: Effects on social behaviors. *Behavioral Disorders, 12,* 36–44.

Scruggs, T. E., Mastropieri, M. A., & Veit, D. (1986). The effects of coaching on standardized test performances of learning disabled and behaviorally disordered students. *Remedial and Special Education, 7*(5), 37–41.

Scruggs, T. E., Mastropieri, M. A., & Wolfe, S. (1995). Scientific reasoning of students with mental retardation: Investigating preconceptions and conceptual change. *Exceptionality, 5,* 223–244.

Scruggs, T. E., & Osguthorpe, R. T. (1986). Tutoring interventions within special education settings: A comparison of cross-age and peer tutoring. *Psychology in the Schools, 22,* 187–193.

Scruggs, T. E., & Richter, L. L. (1985). Tutoring learning disabled students: A critical review. *Learning Disability Quarterly, 8,* 286–298.

Scruggs, T. E., & Tolfa, D. (1985). Improving the test-taking skills of learning disabled students. *Perceptual and Motor Skills, 60,* 847–850.

Scruggs, T. E., White, K. R., & Bennion, K. (1986). Improving achievement test scores in the elementary grades by coaching: A meta-analysis. *Elementary School Journal, 87,* 69–82.

Shefter, H. (1976). *Six minutes a day to perfect spelling.* New York: Pocket.

Shiah, R. L., Mastropieri, M. A., Scruggs, T. E., & Fulk, B. J. M. (1995). The effects of computer assisted instruction on the mathematical problem solving of students with learning disabilities. *Exceptionality, 5,* 131–161.

Shores, R. E., Gunter, R. L., & Jack, S. L. (1993). Classroom management strategies: Are they setting events for coercion? *Behavioral Disorders, 18,* 92–109.

Simmonds, E. P. M. (1992). The effects of teacher training and implementation of two methods for improving the comprehension skills of students with learning disabilities. *Learning Disabilities Research & Practice, 7,* 194–198.

Simmons, D. C., Kameenui, E. J., & Darch, C. (1988). The effect of textual proximity on fourth- and fifth-grade

LD students' metacognitive awareness and strategic comprehension behavior. *Learning Disability Quarterly, 11,* 380–395.

Sinclair, J., Forness, S., & Alexson, J. (1985). Psychiatric diagnosis: A study of its relationship to school needs. *Journal of Special Education, 19,* 333–344.

Sindelar, R. T., Smith, M. A., Harriman, N. E., Hale, R. L., & Wilson, R. J. (1986). Teacher effectiveness in special education programs. *Journal of Special Education, 20,* 195–207.

Singer, J. D., & Butler, J. A. (1987). The Education for All Handicapped Children Act: Schools as agents of social reform. *Harvard Educational Review, 57,* 125–152.

Skinner, C. H., Bamberg, H. W., Smith, E. S., & Powell, S. S. (1993). Cognitive cover, copy and compare: Subvocal responding to increase rates of accurate division responding. *Remedial and Special Education, 14,* 49–56.

Slavin, R. E. (1997). When does cooperative learning increase student achievement? In E. Dubinsky & D. Mathews (Eds.), *Readings in cooperative learning for undergraduate mathematics* (No. 44, pp. 71–84). Washington, DC: The Mathematical Association of America.

Slavin, R. E., Madden, N. A., & Leavey, M. (1984a). Effects of cooperative learning individualized instruction on mainstreamed students. *Exceptional Children, 50,* 434–443.

Slavin, R. E., Madden, N. A., & Leavey, M. (1984b). Effects of team assisted individualization on the mathematics achievement of academically handicapped and nonhandicapped students. *Journal of Educational Psychology, 76,* 813–819.

Smith, L., & Land, M. (1981). Low inference verbal behaviors related to teacher clarity. *Journal of Classroom Interaction, 17,* 37–42.

Smith, S. W. (1990a). Comparison of individualized education programs (IEPs) of students with behavioral disorders and learning disabilities. *Journal of Special Education, 24,* 85–100.

Smith, S. W. (1990b). Individualized education programs (IEPS) in special education—from intent to acquiescence. *Exceptional Children, 57,* 6–15.

Snell, M. E., & Brown, F. (1993). Instructional planning and implementation. In M. E. Snell (Ed.), *Instruction of students with severe disabilities* (pp. 99–151). Columbus, OH: Prentice Hall.

Snider, V. E. (1989). Reading comprehension performance of adolescents with learning disabilities. *Learning Disability Quarterly, 12,* 86–97.

Snider, V. E. (1997). Transfer of decoding skills to a literature basal. *Learning Disabilities Research & Practice, 7,* 150–159.

Snow, C. E., Burns, M. S., & Griffin, P. (Eds.). (1998). *Preventing reading difficulties in young children.* Washington, DC: National Academy Press.

Speece, D. L., MacDonald, V., Kilsheimer, L., & Krist, J. (1997). Research to practice: Preservice teachers reflect on reciprocal teaching. *Learning Disabilities Research & Practice, 7,* 54–62.

Spencer, R. J., & Gray, D. R. (1973). A time-out procedure for classroom behavioral change within the public school setting. *Child Study Journal, 3,* 29–38.

Stahl, S. (1992). Saying the "p" word: Nine guidelines for exemplary phonics instruction. *The Reading Teacher, 45,* 618–625.

Stahl, S. A., & Miller, R. D. (1989). Whole language and language experience approaches for beginning reading: A quantitative research synthesis. *Review of Educational Research, 59,* 87–116.

Stainback, W., & Stainback, S. (1990). Inclusive schooling. In W. Stainback & S. Stainback (Eds.), *Support networks for inclusive schooling* (pp. 51–63). Baltimore: Paul Brookes.

Stallings, J., & Krasavage, E. M. (1986). Program implementation and student achievement in four-year Madeline Hunter follow through project. *The Elementary School Journal, 87,* 117–138.

Staudacher, C., & Turner, S. (1994). *Practical mathematics for consumers* (2nd ed.). Paramus, NJ: Globe Fearon.

Stein, C. L., & Goldman, J. (1980). Beginning reading instruction for children with minimal brain dysfunction. *Journal of Learning Disabilities, 13,* 52–55.

Stein, M., Silbert, J., & Carnine, D. (1997). *Designing effective mathematics instruction: A direct instruction approach.* (3rd ed.). Columbus, OH: Prentice Hall/Merrill.

Stevens, K. B., & Schuster, J. W. (1987). Effects of a constant time delay procedure on the written spelling performance of a learning disabled student. *Learning Disability Quarterly, 10,* 9–16.

Stokes, T. E., & Baer, D. M. (1977). An implicit technology of generalization. *Journal of Applied Behavior Analysis, 10,* 349–367.

Strain, R. S., & Wiegerink, R. (1976). Effects of sociodramatic activities on social interaction among behaviorally disordered preschool children. *Journal of Special Education, 10,* 71–75.

Suid, M. (1990). *Demonic mnemonics.* New York: Dell.

Sullivan, G. S., & Mastropieri, M. A. (1994). Social competence of individuals with learning disabilities. In T. E. Scruggs & M. A. Mastropieri (Eds.), *Advances in learning and behavioral disabilities* (Vol. 8, pp. 177–214). Stamford, CT: JAI.

Sullivan, G. S., Mastropieri, M. A., & Scruggs, T. E. (1995). Reasoning and remembering: Coaching thinking with students with learning disabilities. *Journal of Special Education, 29,* 310–322.

Suritsky, S. K., & Hughes, C. A. (1996). Notetaking strategy instruction. In D. D. Deshler, E. S. Ellis, & B. K. Lenz (Eds.), *Teaching adolescents with learning disabilities* (2nd ed., pp. 267–312). Denver, CO: Love.

Swanson, H. L., & Hoskyn, M. (2000). Intervention research for students with learning disabilities: A comprehensive meta-analysis of group design studies. In T. E. Scruggs & M. A. Mastropieri (Eds.), *Educational interventions: Advances in learning and behavioral disabilities* (Vol. 14, pp. 1–153). Stamford, CT: JAI.

Swanson, H. L., & Trahan, M. F. (1992). Learning disabled readers' comprehension of computer-mediated text: The influence of working memory, metacognition, and attribution. *Learning Disabilities Research & Practice, 7,* 74–86.

Tateyama-Sniezek, K. M. (1990). Cooperative learning: Does it improve the academic achievement of students with handicaps? *Exceptional Children, 56,* 426–437.

Tawney, J. W., & Gast, D. L. (1984). *Single-subject research in special education.* Columbus, OH: Merrill.

Thomas, C. C., Englert, C. S., & Gregg, S. (1987). An analysis of errors and strategies in the expository writing of learning disabled students. *Remedial and Special Education, 8,* 21–30.

Thorkildsen, R. J. (1984). *An experimental test of a microcomputers videodisk program to develop the social skills of mildly handicapped elementary students.* Unpublished doctoral dissertation, University of Oregon, Eugene.

Thornton, C. A., & Toohey, M. A. (1985). Basic math facts: Guidelines for teaching and learning. *Learning Disabilities Focus, 1,* 44–57.

Thurber, D. N., & Jordan, D. R. (1981). *D'Nealian handwriting.* Glenview, IL: Scott, Foresman.

Tindal, G., & Parker, R. (1989). Assessment of written expression for students in compensatory and special education programs. *Journal of Special Education, 23,* 169–184.

Torgesen, J. K., Waters, M. D., Cohen, A. L., & Torgesen, J. L. (1988). Improving sight word recognition in LD children: An evaluation of three computer program variations. *Learning Disability Quarterly, 11,* 125–132.

Townsend, B. L. (2000). The disproportionate discipline of African American learners: Reducing school suspensions and expulsions. *Exceptional Children, 66,* 381–391.

Trapani, C. (1990). *Transition goals for adolescents with learning disabilities.* Boston: Little, Brown.

Treiman, R. (1985). Onsets and rimes as units of spoken syllables: Evidence from children. *Journal of Experimental Child Psychology, 39,* 161–181.

Trifiletti, J. J., Frith, G. H., & Armstrong, S. (1984). Microcomputer versus resource rooms for LD students: A preliminary investigation of the effects on math skills. *Learning Disability Quarterly, 7,* 69–76.

Tucker, J. A. (Ed.). (1986). Curriculum-based assessment [Special issue]. *Exceptional Children, 52,* 196–299.

Turnbull, A. R., & Turnbull, H. R. (1978). *Parents speak out.* Columbus, OH: Merrill.

U.S. Department of Education. (1998). *Twentieth annual report to Congress on implementation of the Individuals with Disabilities Education Act.* Washington, DC: Author.

Utley, C., Mortweet, S. L., & Greenwood, C. R. (1997). Peer mediated instruction and interventions. *Focus on Exceptional Children, 29*(5), 1–23.

Vadasy, P. E., Jenkins, J. R., Antil, L. R., Wayne, S. K., & O'Conner, R. E. (1997). Community-based early reading intervention for at-risk first graders. *Learning Disabilities Research & Practice, 12,* 29–39.

Vadasy, P., Jenkins, J. R., & Pool, K. (2000). Effects of tutoring in phonological and early reading skills on students at risk for reading disorders. *Journal of Learning Disabilities, 33,* 579–590.

Van Luit, J. E. H., & Schopman, E. A. M. (2000). Improving early numeracy of young children with special educational needs. *Remedial and Special Education, 21,* 27–40.

Vaughn, S., McIntosh, R., & Hogan, A. (1990). Why social skills training doesn't work: An alternative model. In T. E. Scruggs & B. Y. L. Wong (Eds.), *Intervention research in learning disabilities* (pp. 279–303). New York: Springer-Verlag.

Vaughn, S. R., Ridley, C. A., & Cox, J. (1983). Evaluating the efficacy of an interpersonal skills training program with children who are mentally retarded. *Education and Raining of the Mentally Retarded, 18,* 191–196.

Veit, D. T., Scruggs, T. E., & Mastropieri, M. A. (1986). Extended mnemonic instruction with learning disabled students. *Journal of Educational Psychology, 78,* 300–308.

Vellutino, R. R. (1979). *Dyslexia: Theory and research.* Cambridge, MA: MIT Press.

Walberg, H. J. (1986). Syntheses of research on teaching. In M. C. Wittrock (Ed.), *Handbook of research on teaching* (3rd ed., pp. 214–229). New York: Macmillan.

Walker, H. M., Colvin, G., & Ramsey, E. (1995). *Antisocial behavior in school: Strategies and best practices.* Pacific Grove, CA: Brooks/Cole.

Walker, H. M., McConnell, S., Walker, J. L., Clarke, J. Y., Todis, B., Cohen, G., & Rankin, R. (1983). Initial analysis of the ACCEPTS curriculum: Efficacy of instructional and behavior management procedures for improving the social adjustment of handicapped children. *Analysis and Intervention in Developmental Disabilities, 3,* 105–127.

Walmsley, S. A. (1984). Helping the learning disabled child overcome writing disabilities in the classroom. *Topics in Learning and Learning Disabilities, 3,* 81–90.

Walther-Thomas, C. S., & Carter, K. L. (1993). Co-teaching experiences: The benefits and problems that teachers and principals report over time. *Journal of Learning Disabilities, 30,* 397–407.

Weaver, R. L. (1984). *The effects of training strategic behaviors on the spelling performance of learning disabled children.* Unpublished doctoral dissertation, George Peabody College for Teachers, Vanderbilt University, Nashville, TN.

Weinstein, G., & Cooke, N. L. (1992). The effects of two repeated reading interventions on generalization of fluency. *Learning Disability Quarterly, 15,* 21–28.

Weisberg, R. (1988). 1980s: A change in focus of reading comprehension research based upon an interactive model of reading. *Learning Disability Quarterly, 11,* 149–159.

Weiss, M. P., & Brigham, F. J. (2000). Co-teaching and the model of shared responsibility: What does the research support? In T. E. Scruggs & M. A. Mastropieri (Eds.), *Advances in learning and behavioral disabilities* (Vol. 14, pp. 217–245). Stamford, CT: JAI.

Wesson, C. L., & King, R. P. (1996). Portfolio assessment and special education students. *Teaching Exceptional Children, 28*(2), 44–48.

Weygant, A. D. (1981). *The effects of specific instructions and a lesson on the written language expression of learning disabled elementary children.* Unpublished doctoral dissertation, University of Virginia, Charlottesville.

Williams, J. P. (1980). Teaching decoding with an emphasis on phoneme analysis and phoneme blending. *Journal of Educational Psychology, 72,* 1–15.

Wilson, C. L., & Sindelar, P. T. (1991). Direct instruction in math word problems: Students with learning disabilities. *Exceptional Children, 57,* 512–519.

Wilson, R., & Wesson, C. (1986). Making every minute count: Academic learning time in LD classrooms. *Learning Disabilities Focus, 2*(1), 13–19.

Winzer, M. A., & Mazurek, K. (1998). *Special education in multicultural contexts.* Columbus, OH: Prentice Hall.

Wise, B. W., & Olson, R. K. (1995). Computer-based phonological awareness and reading instruction. *Annals of Dyslexia, 45,* 99–122.

Wittrock, M. C. (Ed.). (1986). *Handbook of research on teaching* (3rd ed.). New York: Macmillan.

Wolf, M. M., Hanley, E. L., & King, L. A. (1970). The timer game: A variable interval contingency for the management of out-of-seat behavior. *Exceptional Children, 37,* 113–118.

Wong, B. Y. L. (1979). Increasing retention of main ideas through questioning strategies. *Learning Disability Quarterly, 2,* 42–48.

Wong, B. Y. L. (1980). Activating the inactive learner: Use of questions/prompts to enhance comprehension and retention of implied information in learning disabled children. *Learning Disability Quarterly, 3,* 29–37.

Wong, B. Y. L. (1985). Potential means of enhancing content skills acquisition in learning disabled adolescents. *Focus on Exceptional Children, 17*(5), 1–8.

Wong, B. Y. L. (1986a). A cognitive approach to teaching spelling. *Exceptional Children, 53,* 169–173.

Wong, B. Y. L. (1986b). Metacognition and special education: A review of a view. *Journal of Special Education, 20,* 9–29.

Wong, B. Y. L. (1998). Reflections on current attainments and future directions in writing intervention research in learning disabilities. In T. E. Scruggs & M. A. Mastropieri (Eds.), *Advances in learning and behavioral disabilities* (pp. 127–150). Stamford, CT: JAI.

Wong, B. Y. L., Butler, D. L., Ficzere, S. A., & Kuperis, S. (1997). Teaching adolescents with learning disabilities and low achievers to plan, write, and revise compare and contrast essays. *Learning Disabilities Research & Practice, 12,* 2–15.

Wong, B. Y. L., & Jones, W. (1982). Increasing metacomprehension in learning disabled and normally achieving students through self-questioning training. *Learning Disability Quarterly, 5,* 228–238.

Wong, B. Y. L., & Wong, R. (1986). Study behavior as a function of metacognitive knowledge about critical task variables: An investigation of above average, average, and learning disabled readers. *Learning Disabilities Research, 1,* 101–111.

Wong, B. Y. L., Wong, R., & Blenkinsop, J. (1989). Cognitive and metacognitive aspects of learning disabled adolescents' composing problems. *Learning Disability Quarterly, 12,* 300–322.

Wong, B. Y. L., Wong, R., Darlington, D., & Jones, W. (1991). Interactive teaching: An effective way to teach revision skills to adolescents with learning disabilities. *Learning Disabilities Research & Practice, 6,* 117–127.

Woodward, J., Monroe, K., & Baxter, J. (2001). Enhancing student achievement on performance assessments in mathematics. *Learning Disability Quarterly, 24,* 33–46.

Woodward, J., & Noell, J. (1992). Science instruction at the secondary level: Implications for students with learning disabilities. In D. Carnine & E. Kameenui (Eds.), *Higher order thinking: Designing curriculum for mainstreamed students* (pp. 39–58). Austin, TX: PRO-ED.

Zaner-Bloser Evaluation scale. (1986). Columbus, OH: Author.

Zaragoza, N., & Vaughn, S. (1992). The effects of process writing instruction on three 2nd-grade students with different academic profiles. *Learning Disabilities Research & Practice, 7,* 184–193.

Zaragoza, N., Vaughn, S., & McIntosh, R. (1991). Social skills interventions and children with behavior disorders: A review. *Behavioral Disorders, 16,* 260–275.

Zawaiza, T. R. W., & Gerber, M. M. (1993). Effects of explicit instruction on math word problem solving by community college students with learning disabilities. *Learning Disability Quarterly, 16,* 64–79.

Zigmond, N. (1990). Rethinking secondary school programs for students with learning disabilities. *Focus on Exceptional Children, 23*(1), 1–24.

Zigmond, N., Vallecorsa, A., & Leinhardt, G. A. (1980). Reading instruction for students with learning disabilities. *Topics in Language Disorders, 1,* 89–98.

Index

Business Mathematics

Eighth Edition

R. Robert Rosenberg
Educational Consultant
Former President of Jersey City Junior College

Harry Lewis
Associate Professor
Jersey City State College

Roy W. Poe
Consultant in Business and Career Education

Gregg and Community College Division   McGraw-Hill Book Company

New York   St. Louis   Dallas   San Francisco
Auckland   Düsseldorf   Johannesburg   Kuala Lumpur
London   Mexico   Montreal   New Delhi   Panama
Paris   São Paulo   Singapore   Sydney   Tokyo   Toronto

8 9 10 KPKP 7 8 4 3 2 1 0 9

Cover and Text Design by John Horton
Drawings by Andrew Sprague

Library of Congress Cataloging in Publication Data

Rosenberg, Reuben Robert, date.
  Business mathematics.

  SUMMARY: Introduces the high school student to
various aspects of mathematics that apply to business
including fractions, percentages, discounts, banking
interest, taxes, pricing, and others.
  1. Business mathematics. [1. Mathematics.
2. Business education] I. Lewis, Harry, date.
joint author. II. Poe, Roy W., date. joint
author. III. Title.
HF5691.R6   1975   513'.93   74-20920
ISBN 0-07-053700-3

ABOUT THE EIGHTH EDITION

With this eighth edition, *Business Mathematics* begins its forty-first year as a leading textbook in the field. Over these years, *Business Mathematics* has been the teaching/learning instrument for countless thousands of teachers and students, not only in the United States, but in many other parts of the world.

Aim of the Eighth Edition

As with the preceding editions, the aim of the eighth edition of *Business Mathematics* is to prepare students for today's careers in business—whether in accounting, data processing, distribution, secretarial, or general office duties. And as times have changed, *Business Mathematics* has changed with them. Each edition of the text has reflected the methods (both in business procedures and in teaching/learning techniques), the nomenclature, the government regulations, and the student body of its time. The eighth edition is no exception. This edition has been completely revised to keep abreast of today's developments. New topics have been added; certain areas of the traditional subject matter have received increased attention while other areas of decreasing importance have been eliminated; and a new grouping and sequencing of topics has been instituted, as explained in the "Organization and Sequence" section below. The goal was a leaner, more usable, thoroughly modern program with an emphasis on *doing*.

Organization and Sequence

The text is divided into three parts. Each part is made up of chapters (there are 21 in all). The chapters in turn are broken down into units, with each unit a self-contained learning entity.

Part One, "Basic Skills in Business Mathematics," covers the essential arithmetic skills necessary for most business computations. This part begins with a chapter on the meaning of numbers, emphasizing our decimal system and the use of decimal fractions. The latter is important in today's world of electronic calculators, and the former lays the groundwork for the last chapter of Part One, which introduces the metric, or SI system, of measurement. Throughout the text, where appropriate, problems involving weights and measures alternate between the English and SI systems.

Part Two, "Mathematics Applied to Business Operations," deals with the most common problems requiring computations in business. The chapter on payroll has been expanded to include various methods of computing overtime and of computing commissions and bonuses. Of special interest to students planning to work in accounting are the two chapters on financial statement computations. These emphasize balance sheet ratios, aging accounts receivable, estimating losses from bad debts, estimating merchandise inventory, inventory valuation, accelerated depreciation methods, and allocating overhead costs. Interest computations and banking and banking services are also covered in this part.

Part Three, "Mathematics Applied to Consumer Problems," features new topics that cover special-purpose savings (including Series E bonds), the rate of interest on installment credit with special attention to "truth-in-lending" regulations, and the homeowner's policy in property insurance. This part also covers personal investments, taxes, and automobile and life insurance.

A number of topics have been eliminated from this edition because of their decreasing importance or applicability to modern business situations. Perhaps the most dramatic of these deletions is the 6%, 60-day method of computing interest. Long a favorite shortcut of business people, this method has very limited application today, since interest rates have climbed well above 6% and are not likely to return to that level in the foreseeable future. Other topics that were eliminated because of their decreasing relevance to today's business situations include the currency breakdown in payroll work, time and sight drafts, determining social security benefits, and computing commission sales and commission purchases.

Case Problem Approach

Most units begin with a Case Problem. The main purpose of the Case Problem is to establish a setting to which the student can quickly relate for the presentation of a particular principle of mathematics. Designed to answer the student's frequent question, "Why do I need to know this?" the Case Problems are also aimed at whetting the student's appetite for learning. Each Case Problem is followed by questions for class discussion. In many instances the student can supply the answers from previous study or experience; however, the text material reveals the answers as the student reads further.

Problem Material

The eighth edition is particularly strong on problem material. Each unit contains two types of problems—Exercises and Business Applications—which are graduated in difficulty. The Exercises are basically drill problems for the purpose of skill building (familiarizing students with the mathematical operation under discussion and increasing their speed and accuracy in performing the operation). The Business Applications provide a variety of problems, with emphasis on the narrative type, all of which encourage the students to apply to business situations the principles and skills they have learned.

Each chapter concludes with a set of review problems that covers the material in the entire chapter. These problems can be used to provide reinforcement, to test, to establish a basis for remedial instruction, and to provide additional activity for faster learners. The sequence of these end-of-chapter exercises matches the sequence of the material covered in the chapter.

Teacher's Edition

The text is accompanied by an easy-to-use *Teacher's Edition,* which is identical to the student's edition except that it provides answers to the exercises and problems. The answers are printed in color for easy reference; and, where possible, they are conveniently located at the point where the problem is given. Stimulating teaching suggestions for each chapter in the text and detailed solutions to the problems appear in the last section of the *Teacher's Edition.* Thus, in one volume the teacher has all the material needed to conduct the course.

Workbook and Tests

Additional enrichment problems, closely parallel to those in the text, are provided in the workbook. These give students practice in working with actual business documents and report forms. In addition, topics considered optional for the text are covered in the workbook, and practice exercises are provided. These supplementary projects cover measures of central tendency (particularly the median and the mode) and the interpretation of line, bar, and circle graphs.

Also available is a set of tests, made up of true-false, multiple-choice, completion, and narrative problems. These include tests covering each of the chapters and three comprehensive tests, one for each part. The last of these may be used as a final examination. The individual chapter tests could be used as pretests or post tests, whichever is desired. A *Teacher's Key to Workbook and Tests,* with scripted solutions, is also provided.

Acknowledgments

The authors gratefully acknowledge the assistance of business mathematics teachers and of many people representing business firms and government agencies who have not only supplied up-to-date facts and figures but have also read and commented on portions of the manuscript for appropriateness and accuracy.

The Authors

CONTENTS

viii   Contents

Contents   ix

PART 1
BASIC
SKILLS IN
BUSINESS
MATHEMATICS

CHAPTER 1
THE MEANING OF NUMBERS

When we count, we use a number system based on ten. This is true whether we are counting money, units of merchandise, or the number of people working at a given job.

Actually, it is purely by chance that we count by tens. Early peoples did much of their counting on their fingers. The fact that we have ten fingers led to the development of a number system with ten basic symbols, or *digits*—0, 1, 2, 3, 4, 5, 6, 7, 8, and 9. Such a number system is called the *base-10 system* or the *decimal system* (from the word *decem*, which means "ten"). A number system may be based on any number of symbols. If we had only eight fingers, we would probably be using a number system based on eight symbols—that is, 0, 1, 2, 3, 4, 5, 6, and 7. For now, we will review the decimal system so that you can compute efficiently.

UNIT 1

USING WHOLE NUMBERS

Case Problem Look at the following chart:

| Billions | | | Millions | | | Thousands | | | Hundreds | | |
Hundreds	Tens	Units	Hundreds	Tens	Units	Hundreds	Tens	Units	Hundreds	Tens	Units
											7
								7	0	0	0
					7	0	0	0	0	0	0

Discussion Questions

1. How does the placement of the number 7 indicate its value?
2. How do we indicate the "place" of a number when we do not have a chart?

WHOLE NUMBERS

The *place* of a number determines its value, and each place is ten times that of the place to its right. The same number—for instance, the 7 on this chart—has a value that changes with its location. The 7's first value is seven, its second is seven thousand, and its third is seven million. The purpose of the zeros is to indicate which place the 7 occupies. The numeral 7,003 is really a short way of doing the following arithmetic problem:

$$
\begin{array}{r}
7,000 \\
+\ \ \ 000 \\
+\ \ \ \ \ 00 \\
+\ \ \ \ \ \ 3 \\
\hline
7,003
\end{array}
$$

Each of the digits in the chart makes up a numeral. A *numeral* is a symbol (like 7) or a group of symbols (like 7,000 or 7,000,000) that names a number. To read numerals, we must be able to identify their digit positions. The numeral 847 is made up of three digits. Moving from right to left, we read 7 as seven *units*, 4 as four *tens*, and 8 as eight *hundreds*, or as eight hundred forty-seven.

Example 1:
880 is read as eight hundred eighty. The digit in the hundreds position is 8, the tens digit is 8, and the units digit is 0.

Example 2:
902 is read as nine hundred two. The digit in the hundreds position is 9, the tens digit is 0, and the units digit is 2.

To make large numbers easier to read, we put a comma between every group of three numbers, starting from the right. Commas separate the hundreds from thousands, the thousands from millions, and the millions from billions.

Example:
12,750 is read as twelve thousand, seven hundred fifty. Notice that a comma separates the thousands position in numbers and words.

Whole Numbers as Dollars
To express a number in terms of dollars, simply write the dollar sign directly to the left of the number. Twelve thousand, seven hundred fifty dollars is therefore written $12,750.

Exercises
1. Read the following numerals.

	Billions			Millions			Thousands			Hundreds		
	Hundreds	Tens	Units	Hundreds	Tens	Units	Hundreds	Tens	Units	Hundreds	Tens	Units
a.											2	7
b.										3	7	7
c.									3	2	0	2
d.							5	6	5	1	2	9
e.							7	0	0	2	4	3
f.				4	7	4	1	1	7	8	6	2
g.								1	6	0	0	8
h.					3	7	1	7	9	8	8	4
i.	3	6	2	5	2	1	2	4	2	9	1	6
j.			1	0	2	5	4	4	4	6	9	2

2. Separate by commas the digit positions in the following amounts of money (there are no cents).

a. $3720
b. $42665
c. $129980
d. $356807
e. $3806975
f. $191782040
g. $4840001907
h. $690071357649
i. $207000
j. $1000003
k. $84664
l. $45870000

3. Write the following amounts of money in numerals, inserting commas to separate digit positions.

a. Three thousand, nine hundred forty-two dollars
b. Nineteen thousand, one hundred forty-eight dollars
c. Four hundred eighty-nine thousand, seven hundred seventy-seven dollars
d. One million, six hundred thirty-seven thousand, two hundred twenty-one dollars
e. Sixteen million, five hundred twenty-six thousand, three hundred nineteen dollars
f. Nine billion, four thousand, seven hundred twenty-five dollars
g. Nineteen thousand, three dollars

UNIT 2

USING DECIMAL FRACTIONS

Case Problem Examine the following chart.

	Whole Numbers				Decimal Point	Decimal Fractions			
	Thousands	Hundreds	Tens	Units	.	Tenths	Hundredths	Thousandths	Ten Thousandths
a.		2	3	7	.	5			
b.			6	6	.	8	4		
c.				4	.	1	4	8	
d.			1	9	.	0	0	0	7

Discussion Questions

1. What is the function of the decimal point?
2. How are decimals indicated when they are read aloud?

DECIMAL FRACTIONS

A decimal point is used to separate whole numbers from decimal fractions. A decimal point in front of a number always means that the number following is less than a whole number—that it is a part of a number or a *decimal fraction*. The places after a decimal point are called ten*ths*, hundred*ths*, thousand*ths*, and so on. The chart shows decimal fractions to ten thousand*ths*. (The *ths* in the name distinguishes it from the name of a number at the left of the decimal point.) As the heading of the chart shows, decimal fractions are often called *decimals* for short. Just as with whole numbers, the zero is used to indicate that the place it is filling has no other value.

The decimal point separating whole numbers from fractional numbers is read as "and." The word "point" may also be used to identify the places to the right of the decimal point. Using each of these words, we can read the numeral 4.5 as either *four and five tenths* or *four point five*. The amounts on the chart can be read as follows:

a. Two hundred thirty-seven and five tenths (*or* two-hundred thirty-seven point five)

b. Sixty-six and eighty-four hundredths (*or* sixty-six point eighty-four)

c. Four and one hundred forty-eight thousandths (*or* four point one forty-eight)

d. Nineteen and seven ten-thousandths (*or* nineteen point zero, zero, zero, seven)

Exercises

1. Write the following in word form. Refer to the chart on page 7 if you need to.

a. .06	**b.** 2.78	**c.** .09	**d.** .11
e. .27	**f.** 2.90	**g.** 19.87	**h.** 2.5
i. 7.7	**j.** 96.04	**k.** 176.88	**l.** 67.247
m. 344.42	**n.** 2,472.4	**o.** 731.2275	**p.** 24,572.47
q. 1,412.06	**r.** 717.2125	**s.** 97.008	**t.** .0100

2. Use numerals to write the following in decimal form.
   a. Nine tenths
   b. One tenth
   c. Three and five tenths
   d. Sixteen and eight tenths
   e. One hundred two and two tenths
   f. Six hundredths
   g. Four thousandths
   h. Seventy-seven thousandths

DECIMALS IN BUSINESS

Our money is based on a decimal system just as our system of numbers is. In a dollar there are one hundred cents. Since we rarely deal with amounts of less than one cent, the lowest value we use is $.01 and the highest is $.99. We need only two decimal places to express all money values. (Notice that the decimal point is read as "and" in the following examples.)

Examples:
1. $199.25 is read as one hundred ninety-nine dollars and twenty-five cents.
2. $16.50 is read as sixteen dollars and fifty cents.
3. $16.05 is read as sixteen dollars and five cents.

Occasionally, we may wish to represent fractional parts of a cent. Real estate tax rates and wholesale prices often involve such small amounts. Use the third, fourth, fifth, etc., decimal places to indicate parts of a cent.

Examples:
1. $2.275 The "5" indicates .5 of one cent, and the entire amount represents two dollars and twenty-seven and five-tenths of a cent. This might also be read as two dollars and twenty-seven point five cents.
2. $2.6275 The last two digits indicate .75 of one cent, and the entire amount represents two dollars and sixty-two and seventy-five hundredths of a cent. This might also be read as two dollars and sixty-two point seventy-five cents.

In both these examples, it is convenient to separate the fractional parts of a dollar from whole dollars with the word "and" and the fractional parts of a cent from whole cents with the word "point."

Exercises
1. Go back to the chart at the beginning of this unit, and read the numbers as if they were dollars and cents.
2. Go back to the first exercise on page 8, and write the numerals in word form as though they were dollars and cents.

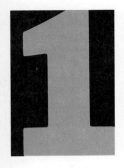

**REVIEW
EXERCISES
FOR
CHAPTER 1**

1. Read the following numerals.
   a. 32
   b. 407
   c. 3,416
   d. 83,792
   e. 121,328
   f. 9,455,201
   g. 38,602,167
   h. 535,716,677

2. Write the following as numerals, inserting commas in the proper places.
   a. Five thousand, six hundred twenty-nine
   b. Twenty-two thousand
   c. Seventy-seven thousand, two hundred seven
   d. Four hundred thirty-three thousand, one hundred nineteen
   e. Two million, nine hundred eighty-eight thousand, four hundred twelve
   f. Sixteen thousand, twelve
   g. Fifty-six million, one hundred fifteen thousand, forty-nine
   h. Eight billion, two hundred twenty million, three hundred sixty-six thousand, four hundred forty-four

3. Write the following numerals, separating groups of digits with commas.
   a. 3721
   b. 14602
   c. 728906
   d. 4889766
   e. 71707104
   f. 831962488
   g. 1606927205
   h. 270400702112

4. Read the following numerals.
   a. .1
   b. .07
   c. .18
   d. .96
   e. .420
   f. 3.3
   g. 6.14
   h. 9.125
   i. 52.2350
   j. 7,162.8
   k. 23,906.15
   l. .107
   m. .0004
   n. 3.0203

5. Write the following as decimals.
   a. Two tenths
   b. Seven hundredths
   c. Four and four tenths
   d. Four and four hundredths

    e. Four and four thousandths

    f. Four and four ten thousandths

    g. Thirty-two and twenty-five thousandths

    h. Eight and six thousandths

6. Write the following in dollars and cents.

    a. Two thousand, three hundred forty-seven dollars and no cents

    b. Twenty dollars and forty cents

    c. Two dollars and thirty-three point four cents

    d. Sixty thousand, nine dollars and fourteen cents

    e. Eight dollars and eighty-two point seventy-five cents

    f. Seventy dollars and thirty-seven and five tenths cents

    g. Three thousand dollars and ninety-five cents

    h. Three dollars and eighty-seven and a half cents

CHAPTER 2
ADDITION
SKILLS

Addition is the most frequently used of all arithmetic skills. As consumers, we constantly count the money in our pockets, add new deposits to our checkbook balances, compute the expenses of a vacation, total the items that go into the cost of remodeling the den, or compute the cost of operating a car. As employees, we use addition to find out how much our employer sells and spends, the total quantity of goods produced, the amount earned by employees, and the taxes that are due the government.

Business people, such as accountants, who add and perform other arithmetic operations constantly, are furnished machines with which to do their computations. Indeed, most office employees have at least some access to adding machines and calculators. Having a machine handy, however, does not eliminate the need for arithmetic skills, even in this age of computers and electronic calculators. Saying that we don't need to know arithmetic because there are machines to do the work for us is like saying that we don't need to know how to write because we have typewriters!

UNIT 1

BUILDING ADDITION SKILLS

ADDING ONE-DIGIT NUMBERS

In addition, the numbers to be added are called *addends;* the answer is the *sum* or *total.* To be skillful in addition, you must be able to recognize *on sight* the sum of two or more numbers.

Adding Two One-Digit Numbers

The following sums of one-digit numbers are sometimes called the "45 addition facts." Practice until you can add all of them in 30 seconds.

	1	2	3	4	5	6	7	8	9
a.	1	2	3	1	2	3	1	2	3
	9	7	5	8	6	4	7	5	3
b.	1	2	1	2	3	6	3	1	2
	6	4	5	3	9	3	8	1	2
c.	3	9	8	1	7	6	9	6	5
	7	2	2	2	6	4	5	6	6
d.	3	4	8	4	5	7	5	9	7
	1	9	5	1	4	4	7	9	9
e.	4	8	5	8	7	8	8	8	6
	4	4	5	9	7	6	8	7	9

Adding Three One-Digit Numbers

Adding three numbers of one digit each should be almost as fast and easy for you as adding two numbers of one digit each. Practice computing the sums below until you can add quickly and accurately.

FIRST GROUP

	1	2	3	4	5	6	7	8	9	10	11
a.	9	8	2	5	1	1	7	1	9	9	9
	4	4	9	5	1	2	1	7	4	8	3
	1	1	2	3	1	8	2	7	9	3	9

b.

6	8	9	8	1	4	1	8	1	6	3
2	2	1	1	6	4	7	3	3	9	3
7	5	2	6	7	8	1	8	5	4	1

c.

9	9	7	6	4	2	6	9	5	8	2
6	5	1	1	4	4	4	7	5	2	4
7	1	4	6	5	2	4	8	7	2	6

d.

5	1	9	4	3	5	3	2	6	5	7
2	2	3	1	7	4	3	7	1	8	8
1	4	3	3	8	1	4	9	2	6	7

e.

8	1	7	2	2	4	2	5	4	8	7
3	4	3	5	4	4	2	4	3	5	1
4	6	3	9	4	4	6	3	4	1	5

SECOND GROUP

	1	2	3	4	5	6	7	8	9	10	11
a.	8	3	1	3	9	3	4	9	3	3	5
	3	1	3	2	4	5	1	2	5	8	5
	1	7	9	1	7	9	4	8	8	3	8
b.	2	1	8	5	5	3	8	3	2	1	2
	1	1	1	2	2	6	4	5	7	3	3
	2	9	1	5	6	8	8	7	8	6	7
c.	9	7	6	4	2	4	8	5	6	7	3
	2	7	6	2	3	7	8	3	2	7	9
	6	2	6	3	3	8	8	3	6	3	6
d.	2	2	4	3	2	4	6	2	7	6	7
	6	3	5	1	4	2	3	9	9	3	7
	8	5	9	1	8	5	2	9	9	4	7
e.	4	1	2	5	9	8	7	2	4	8	5
	4	1	4	6	8	7	9	3	5	4	6
	7	5	7	9	1	8	7	2	6	9	6

	1	2	3	4	5	6	7	8	9	10	11
a.	2	9	5	8	5	6	8	9	9	7	8
	2	9	7	4	5	8	4	6	1	5	2
	2	5	2	6	6	6	5	9	9	7	3
b.	9	3	6	6	5	7	9	9	9	5	7
	3	3	7	3	5	6	8	9	3	7	6
	4	3	6	6	1	3	8	9	7	8	4
c.	7	5	5	5	7	9	2	8	4	9	5
	2	8	1	5	7	7	3	1	6	1	5
	2	9	6	8	4	1	9	7	6	6	9
d.	8	5	6	6	9	2	2	3	8	4	8
	6	7	3	7	6	8	4	4	8	9	6
	7	9	3	7	6	8	9	7	6	4	9
e.	4	4	8	8	5	6	1	5	4	1	3
	1	5	8	9	5	7	2	2	5	6	5
	1	7	1	9	5	5	1	2	5	1	6

Exercises

1. You have practiced with the groups of one-digit numbers below. Now see if you can compute these sums quickly and accurately.

	1	2	3	4	5	6	7	8	9
a.	4	8	5	8	7	8	8	8	6
	4	4	5	9	7	6	8	7	9
b.	3	4	8	4	5	7	5	9	7
	1	9	5	1	4	4	7	9	9
c.	1	2	3	1	2	3	1	2	3
	9	7	5	8	6	4	7	5	3

d. 3	9	8	1	7	6	9	6	5
7	2	2	2	6	4	5	6	6

e. 1	2	1	2	3	6	3	1	2
6	4	5	3	9	3	8	1	2

2. Time yourself. See how long it takes you to compute these sums accurately. You should be able to complete them within 90 seconds.

	1	2	3	4	5	6	7	8	9	10
a.	7	6	4	5	7	4	5	3	8	9
	9	5	6	3	8	8	7	8	6	7
	8	9	8	2	6	3	2	6	5	8
b.	2	7	7	5	2	3	7	5	8	7
	4	8	1	5	3	9	7	6	2	6
	6	7	5	8	7	6	7	6	3	4

ADDING TWO-DIGIT NUMBERS

You can gain speed in adding two-digit numbers by adding first the tens digits and then the units digits. This makes it easier to do the complete sum mentally.

Example 1:
Add 56 and 42.

Solution:
56
42
90 + 8 = 98

First add the tens digits (5 tens and 4 tens are 9 tens, or 90); then add the units digits.

Example 2:
Add 98 and 46.

Solution:
98
46
130 + 14 = 144

First add the tens digits (9 tens and 4 tens are 13 tens, or 130); then add the units digits.

Exercises

Add the following, adding first the tens digits and then the units digits.

	1	2	3	4	5	6	7	8	9	10
a.	21	33	72	45	61	54	27	87	34	66
	37	46	24	52	28	63	32	81	35	32
b.	56	87	78	37	42	84	93	62	26	68
	34	64	94	28	59	29	57	38	74	97
c.	89	64	59	79	71	42	68	84	52	32
	75	83	81	64	38	57	99	22	33	41
d.	55	24	47	35	74	23	56	49	98	53
	38	87	63	67	95	89	68	37	89	31
e.	58	34	97	74	64	85	67	63	76	88
	76	28	56	87	38	27	58	28	42	29

ADDING BY GROUPS WHOSE SUM IS TEN

Another device that can be used to increase your speed in adding a column of numbers is to look for combinations whose sum is 10. The simplest and fastest way of adding the column below, for example,

```
7
8
3
7
2
```

is to note that the 7 and 3 have a sum of 10, and that the 8 and 2 have the same sum. These two combinations of 10 added to the 7 at the top of the column give a total of 27.

```
  7
 ┌8
 │3┐
 │7┘
 └2
 ──
 27
```

Note how the combinations of 10 are grouped in the following columns.

```
 6⎤      ⎡8      1⎤
⎡9⎤     ⎢0      7⎦
⎣1⎦     ⎣2      2
 4⎦      6⎤     ⎡5
 3       4⎦     ⎣5
──      ──      ──
23       20      20
```

In the third column, notice that there can be more than two numbers that make up a group with a sum of ten.

Exercises

1. Find each sum by looking for groupings whose sum is 10.

a	b	c	d	e	f	g	h	i	j
5	6	9	7	3	7	4	9	6	1
3	3	1	4	2	8	6	3	5	9
1	8	8	5	1	3	3	7	5	8
9	4	3	8	8	8	6	8	4	7
6	2	7	9	9	5	7	4	7	6
4	1	5	1	4	7	3	6	3	3
2	6	2	3	6	3	1	9	2	4
							2	6	5
							5	5	6
							3	3	7

2. Add the following columns by looking for groupings whose sum is 10.

a	b	c	d	e	f	g
56	82	27	98	43	57	38
43	19	53	76	86	43	42
21	71	35	54	97	28	96
63	34	86	12	54	86	13
57	56	47	87	83	43	31

3. Add the following columns by looking for groupings whose sum is 10.

a	b	c	d	e	f
327	583	574	943	560	291
642	417	516	155	245	125
897	118	326	864	832	714
263	762	875	319	173	836

Business Applications

1. Paula Matthews was asked to find out how many trucks the Levinson Trucking Company has on hand in six locations. Here is the report she prepared. Find the sum by looking for groupings whose sum is 10.

Factory	Trucks
Daytona Beach	7
Ocala	3
Orlando	8
Pensacola	9
St. Petersburg	6
West Palm Beach	4

2. Fred Mann is a receiving clerk in Liebman's Department Store. Below is a report Fred filled out for a shipment that arrived at the store on June 12. Find the total number of books received from Prime Publishers. Look for groupings whose sum is 10.

Description	Quantity
The Blooming Tree	48
Auto Repair Handbook	26
Treasures of the Louvre	42
Lament for a Soldier	72
The Woof-Woof Book	31
The Magic House	27
Total	

CONDITION: Acceptable ✓   Not Acceptable _____

Received by _Fred Mann_

3. During the week of July 17, Fred Mann received the following items of merchandise. Find each sum, looking for groupings whose sum is 10.

a. Men's White Dress Shirts

Size 14/32	48
Size 14½/32	64
Size 15/32	128
Size 15½/32	96
Size 16/32	72

b. Ruff-Scruff Sneakers

Size 8	144
Size 8½	96
Size 9	160
Size 9½	84
Size 10	72

c. Electric Wall Clocks

Kitchen Queen	48
Westex	60
Precision	70
Master Stroke	32
True Time	67
Perpetual	50

d. Calendar Towels

Mushroom	110
Lady Bug	95
Bless This House	88
Tom Cat	104
Cardinals	175
Zodiac	224

UNIT

ADDING ACCURATELY

Although speed in addition can often be important, speed is never as important as accuracy. The most popular method of checking the accuracy of addition is the *reverse-order check*, which means that if you add "down" the first time, you check your addition by reversing the procedure and adding "up" the second time.

Example:

Add the following; then verify the accuracy of your total by applying the reverse-order check.

```
33
24
62
```

Solution:

```
      119
33                      33
24   First addition—    24   Second addition—
62   add down           62   add up
___
119
```

Accurate addition means finding the correct sum of a column of figures, but it also means having the correct figures in the first place. An error that sometimes occurs when numerals are copied or when they are entered in an adding machine is number *transposition*—the reversal of two digits' places. Avoid this error by checking the numbers that you copy against the original or by adding a column of figures twice (once up, once down) if you are using an adding machine.

Example:
Below are two columns of figures. The column at the right was copied from the original on the left. See if you can detect any transposition errors.

Original	3,457.96	Copy	3,457.96
	4,665.07		4,665.70
	106.54		106.54
	10,221.63		10,221.63
	13.78		31.78
	110.60		110.60

Solution:
If you compared the two columns carefully, you would have found transpositions in lines two and five. Check off those lines and correct them if you haven't already done so.

Exercises
Find the total in each of the following problems, and check your answers by using the reverse-order check.

a	b	c	d	e	f
68	89	17	56	92	18
42	53	35	32	43	52
91	21	79	43	56	48
58	46	26	58	28	67
64	43	58	64	32	54

g	h	i	j	k	l
563	872	832	180	321	41
428	538	568	90	593	54
682	879	589	435	6	187
412	524	426	75	901	1,193
246	216	135	86	45	406
357	974	575	24	339	11
513	236	367	978	67	2,532
849	859	743	132	10	79

Business Applications

1. Jacob Miller, a contractor, supplied the following estimates to a customer while visiting the customer's home. Is Mr. Miller's total correct? If not, supply the correct total.

Retaining wall	$ 642
Sidewalk (flagstone)	188
Patio (20′ × 12′)	1,235
Driveway	377
Barbecue	215
	$2,457

2. Find the totals of the following items on hand in various warehouses. Verify your answers by using the reverse-order check.

	Brass Bolts	Copper Brads	Brass Hinges
Camden	1,206	4,378	14
Newark	8,213	99	432
Bergen	6,339	3,332	3,857
Dover	2,290	666	11,428
Linden	1,111	1,174	7

3. Chris Rizzo is an assistant to the chief accountant of Carson's Big Value Store. The chief accountant says, "Please summarize our monthly profits for the first six months of this year. I need the figures for tomorrow's meeting with the president." Chris refers to the accounting records and records the following:

Month	Profit
January	$ 2,780
February	2,190
March	2,640
April	3,730
May	1,720
June	3,360

What figure should Chris submit as the total profit for the first six months? Verify your answer by using the reverse-order check.

4. Harold McCarthy has been asked to find the total population of the six towns in which Midcontinent Cooperatives has retail stores. The latest figures Mr. McCarthy has obtained are as follows:

Town	Population
Blair	8,887
Colesville	12,133
Danbury	9,695
McGee	4,438
Simsbury	2,481
Tillman	14,790

What is the total population of all the towns in which Mid-continent has stores? Verify your addition by using the reverse-order check.

5. The eight sales representatives for Westover Products Company drove the following number of miles on company business during the past year. What was the total number of miles driven by all representatives? Check the accuracy of your total.

Representative	Miles Driven
Dracapoulos	13,111
Suzuki	9,842
Brady	6,228
Donnelly	8,834
Feinberg	16,660
Laird	7,777
Saputo	3,416
Treadway	11,309

6. Calculating and adding machines are often used for office work. Even though these machines are accurate, it is wise to check the tape on which the entries are printed to be sure that the numbers were entered correctly.

Two tapes follow. Next to them are the entries that should have been made. Check off each entry on the tape if it is correct; write the correct number to replace any that is incorrect. If necessary, find a new corrected total on a separate sheet of paper.

a.
```
   4 2.5 0
   5 8.7 5
   5 6.1 7
   1 2.7 5
   1 8.2 6
     9.3 2
   1 8.5 6
 2 1 6.3 1 T
```

$42.50, $58.75, $56.17
$12.45, $18.26, $14.50
$9.32, $18.56

b.
```
  1 2 7 .2 5
    8 4 .9 6
    1 6 .3 2
    9 5 .5 0
    8 4 .6 2
    7 3 .1 4
  1 0 8 .7 5
    9 8 .0 0
    4 3 .1 7
    5 4 .7 0
    6 7 .2 5
  8 5 3 .6 6  T
```

$127.25, $84.96, $16.23
$95.50, $84.62, $73.14
$108.75, $9.80, $43.17
$54.70, $67.25

UNIT 3

HORIZONTAL AND VERTICAL ADDITION

Many business forms require the office worker to add both *vertically* (up and down) and *horizontally* (across). When you add both ways, you can easily check your accuracy. The sum of the vertical totals must equal the sum of the horizontal totals.

Example:

Complete the following personnel report.

CLARION MANUFACTURING COMPANY
Warehouse Employees
July 31, 19—

Location	Receiving	Shipping	Totals
Morristown	15	17	_____
Bayville	20	22	_____
Lakewood	31	40	_____
Totals	_____	_____	_____

Solution:

CLARION MANUFACTURING COMPANY
Warehouse Employees
July 31, 19—

Location	Receiving	Shipping	Totals
Morristown	15	17	32
Bayville	20	22	42
Lakewood	31	40	71
Totals	66	79	145

In the solution, the totals of the Receiving and Shipping columns are found by adding vertically. The number 66 represents the total number of people who work in the receiving departments at the three locations, and the number 79 represents the total number in the shipping departments. To find the number of warehouse employees at each location, add horizontally. That is, in the Morristown warehouse 15 people work in receiving and 17 in shipping, for a total of 32. The grand total of 145 is the company's total number of warehouse employees. Both the vertical totals and the horizontal totals should have a sum of 145.

Exercises

Find the totals of the columns and the totals of the rows in each of the following exercises. If the sum of the vertical totals equals the sum of the horizontal totals, the additions may be assumed to be correct.

1.   Totals

  26 + 12 = _____

  10 + 16 = _____

Totals ___ + ___ = [_____] Check

2.   Totals

  56 + 37 + 64 = _____

  34 + 26 + 74 = _____

  76 + 84 + 36 = _____

  47 + 93 + 85 = _____

Totals ___ + ___ + ___ = [_____] Check

3.

					Totals
68 +	58 +	92 +	47 +	56 =	_____
42 +	53 +	18 +	63 +	34 =	_____
29 +	76 +	36 +	74 +	65 =	_____
87 +	42 +	78 +	32 +	83 =	_____

Totals ___ + ___ + ___ + ___ + ___ = [ ] Check

4.

			Totals
973 +	355 +	571 =	_____
39 +	932 +	659 =	_____
891 +	628 +	43 =	_____
254 +	274 +	22 =	_____

Totals _____ + _____ + _____ = [ ] Check

Business Applications

1. Complete the following report of books on hand at Stern's Department Store as of May 31.

STERN'S DEPARTMENT STORE
Merchandise on Hand

Book Department   Date: _May 31, 19—_

Classification	On the Sales Floor	In the Stockroom	Totals
Juvenile	147	569	
Art	34	274	
Reference	72	161	
Fiction	304	656	
General	777	430	
Textbooks	219	425	
Totals			

2. Find the total number of pairs of shoes sold by each of the following employees each day, the total sold by each for the week, and the grand total sold by all employees during the week of June 7.

BROWN'S FAMILY SHOE BARN

Sales Record   Week of June 7, 19—

Salesperson	Mon.	Tues.	Wed.	Thurs.	Fri.	Sat.	Totals
Bowen	15	17	21	19	22	30	_____
Carpenter	14	12	0	16	17	21	_____
Coppola	20	19	16	20	14	27	_____
Dudek	15	11	23	23	18	26	_____
Jenkins	12	9	9	8	11	17	_____
Totals	_____	_____	_____	_____	_____	_____	_____

3. Each department in the White and Parker Store supplies the figures for a report of the value of stock on hand every three months. Complete the report.

WHITE AND PARKER STORE

Value of Stock on Hand   First Quarter, 19—

Department	January	February	March	Totals
Rugs	$ 5,415	$ 4,670	$ 4,216	$_____
Furniture	20,732	18,328	22,672	_____
Small Appliances	3,693	2,282	2,108	_____
Fabrics	1,357	1,835	2,074	_____
China	2,548	1,359	2,136	_____
Toys	1,212	2,491	2,917	_____
Totals	$_____	$_____	$_____	$_____

4. A systems analyst called in by Reo-Jay Toy Distributors has asked for a summary of items handled in the first half of the year. Supply the missing totals in the form on the next page.

SUMMARY OF ITEMS HANDLED
Reo-Jay Toy Distributors, Inc.
Beltsville, MD 20705
Date: January to June, 19—

Month	Receiving	Packing	Shipping	Warehousing	Totals
Jan.	316	377	420	497	_____
Feb.	402	223	207	453	_____
Mar.	517	416	333	607	_____
Apr.	317	502	387	329	_____
May	299	199	328	327	_____
June	472	222	380	476	_____
Totals	_____	_____	_____	_____	_____

UNIT 4

ADDING DECIMALS

Phil Rossiter works at the Bedell Service Station. At the end of a day, he has the following credit card receipts from the day's customers:

Credit Card Receipts
   8/7/19—
      $ 8.60
      $ 7.45
      $12.65
      $ 8.20
      $ 9.92
      $22.80
      $19.05
      $ 1.25

Before Rossiter totals the receipts, he should follow two basic rules for adding decimals.

1. If the numbers are arranged in columns, the decimal points should be directly under one another.

Example:

Arrange the following in a column and add: $1.72, $.03, $12.88, $.40, $.15.

Solution:

```
$  1.72
    .03
  12.88
    .40
    .15
$15.18
```

Note that the decimal points are directly under one another. Note also that when you are adding dollars and cents in a column, the dollar sign is written twice only—in front of the first figure in the column and in front of the answer.

2. If dollars and cents are added horizontally (across) to dollars, a decimal point and two zeros should follow the numbers representing dollars only.

Example:

Add $438.71, $832, and $796.65 horizontally.

Solution:

Use a decimal point and two zeros (for cents) after $832 to avoid adding dollars to cents: $832 = $832.00

$$\$438.71 + \$832.00 + \$796.65 = \$2,067.36$$

Many business forms are ruled to separate dollars from cents. In such cases you do not need to use a decimal point in your computations; the rule itself becomes the marker. Note that in the following form the vertical rule separates dollars from cents.

Cranston's Housewares		
Stock Value Report		
Items in Stock	**Value**	
Coffee makers	141	70
Toasters	72	45
Bread warmers	66	35
Hot Trays	244	90
Total	525	40

↑ dollars ↑ cents

Exercises

1. Arrange the following amounts of money vertically; then add.
   a. $1.20 + $.16 + $.75 + $3.60 + $11.40
   b. $42.27 + $38.46 + $95.17 + $58.42
   c. $642.12 + $735.43 + $692.86 + $249.17
   d. $804.65 + $673 + $45.87 + $927.48
   e. $2,467 + $824.58 + $3,006 + $258.12

2. Add the following amounts of money horizontally. Remember to write in the decimal point and zeros whenever they are needed.
   a. $2.76 + $8.03 + $6.77 + $4.36
   b. $26.54 + $12.73 + $7.14 + $8.95
   c. $427.42 + $199.98 + $67 + $432.75
   d. $3,562 + $673.45 + $5,000 + $8,795.95
   e. $14,322 + $62 + $15.94 + $.37 + $162.20

Business Applications

1. Elaine Morris, assistant to the sales manager of Cox Distributors, prepares a weekly summary of sales representatives' expenses. The following figures are taken from the records for the first week in September: Danvers, $203.75; Halleck, $187.50; Isaacs, $185; Meade, $176.85; Munez, $163.90; Wooten, $214.

   Arrange the expenses in a column; then find the total of all representatives' expenses for the week.

2. Roger Pritchard, a dietician, spent the following amounts for food for the employees' lunchroom during a recent week: Monday, $116.72; Tuesday, $112.88; Wednesday, $126; Thursday, $90.90; Friday, $114.95. What was the total amount spent for food during the entire week?

3. Complete the following report of merchandise returned by customers in four branch specialty shops during a recent three-month period.

Store	May	June	July	Totals
Fennel Street	$ 184.95	$ 206.50	$ 193.75	$_____
Elm Terrace	272.30	303.85	194.25	_____
Coles Avenue	177.55	164.85	175.60	_____
King's Highway	182.75	193.80	187.15	_____
Totals	$_____	$_____	$_____	$_____

4. Complete the report below, which shows the telephone expenses of four different departments of a business during a four-month period.

DEPARTMENTAL TELEPHONE EXPENSES
Columbia Plastics, Inc.
January through April, 19—

Department	Jan.	Feb.	Mar.	Apr.	Totals
Office	$ 85.76	$ 123.40	$ 88.92	$ 116.55	$_____
Warehouse	64.27	62.14	80.80	125.19	_____
Factory	69.95	73.85	45.65	98.90	_____
Sales	97.75	246.86	86.98	278.81	_____
Totals	$_____	$_____	$_____	$_____	$_____

5. Bob Gardner, an accounting clerk at Cleverdon Novelties, prepares a deposit slip each day and takes it to the bank along with the cash and checks to be placed on deposit. Two deposit slips that Mr. Gardner prepared follow. Find the total amount to be deposited in the bank on each of the two days.

a.

PLEASE LIST EACH CHECK SEPARATELY	DOLLARS	CENTS
CURRENCY	26	00
COIN	1	34
CHECKS	8	75
	14	98
	125	00
	34	50
	8	29
	2	50
TOTAL $		
CENTRAL NATIONAL BANK		

b.

PLEASE LIST EACH CHECK SEPARATELY	DOLLARS	CENTS
CURRENCY	146	00
COIN	12	78
CHECKS	2385	00
	540	00
	76	82
	251	65
	87	98
	64	50
TOTAL $		
CENTRAL NATIONAL BANK		

REVIEW EXERCISES FOR CHAPTER 2

1. Total each of the following columns. Remember to look for combinations whose sum is ten. Verify your answers by using the reverse-order check.

a	b	c	d	e	f
76	36	756	538	374	6,436
37	84	834	472	645	7,584
53	25	375	384	161	3,125
28	69	917	926	938	2,369
42	11	143	163	582	9,211
65	97	698	859	423	4,643
84	43	521	291	236	1,758
91	12	589	717	694	2,312

g	h	i	j
1,783	$108.60	$ 2,756.84	$ 4,321.70
6,332	86.50	987.16	3,873.33
2,658	90.85	39.73	9,604.10
8,597	95.80	5,864.79	6,517.77
2,013	113.70	546.31	3,146.63
4,375	91.75	694.42	5,472.22
6,936	79.32	6.16	1,378.88
8,684	27.88	2,765.68	2,001.50

2. Complete the sales summary at the top of the next page.

JOHNSON OIL COMPANY
Sales Summary, First Quarter, 19—

Station No.	Tires	Batteries	Parts	Totals
1	$ 1,670	$ 988	$ 765	$_____
2	3,960	1,635	1,895	_____
3	4,225	2,170	1,660	_____
4	1,980	2,010	2,920	_____
5	2,700	1,995	3,640	_____
Totals	$_____	$_____	$_____	$_____

3. Lois Frankel is office manager of the word processing department of Pilgrim Insurance Company. A summary of the pages typed by each employee for the past four months is shown below. For each employee, find (a) the total number of pages typed each month, (b) the total typed in four months, and (c) the grand total for the four-month period.

Employee	September	October	November	December	Totals
Binns	157	196	143	158	_____
Boch	216	193	184	159	_____
Coffey	186	213	173	164	_____
DuBois	167	184	179	152	_____
Linkletter	169	168	196	182	_____
Totals	_____	_____	_____	_____	_____

4. Complete the following salary expense report for the shipping department of the Krueger Company.

SALARY EXPENSE FOR SHIPPING DEPARTMENT
Week of December 11, 19—

Employee	Monday	Tuesday	Wednesday	Thursday	Friday	Totals
Hanson	$ 21.30	$ 21.55	$ 20.85	$ 20.50	$ 21.65	$_____
Lutz	19.90	19.95	21.65	20.35	20.85	_____
Verner	22.10	22.80	21.75	23.25	22.95	_____
White	25.40	26.70	25.85	26.25	26.40	_____
Totals	$_____	$_____	$_____	$_____	$_____	$_____

5. The Lydon Department Store made the following sales during a recent week: household goods, $2,197; furniture, $7,548; children's wear, $2,115; shoes, $3,267; dresses, $3,742; books, $2,412; and toys, $4,147. Find the total sales.

6. The eight supervisors in the Office Services Department of Yankton Supply Company receive the following weekly salaries: $164.18, $176, $178, $179.87, $168.17, $181.27, $180.50, and $179. Find the total salaries paid the supervisors for one week.

7. Henry Manners, a salesman for the Modern Dye Works, is paid a salary of $5,200 a year. Last year, in addition to his salary, he also earned the following monthly commissions: $518.25, $604.86, $833, $499.17, $617.84, $568.24, $751.09, $900.17, $824.35, $714.34, $628.28, and $928.58. Find his total earnings for the year.

8. The postage and mailing expenses for four magazines of the Heritage Publishing Company for the first quarter—the first three-month period in the year—are shown below. Complete the table.

Magazine	January	February	March	Totals
Camera World	$ 287.75	$ 302.02	$ 276.66	$_____
Antiques	141.40	188.88	202.45	_____
Ceramic Age	77.00	88.46	111.18	_____
Science and You	307.10	309.15	299.90	_____
Totals	$_____	$_____	$_____	$_____

9. Check each of the tapes to the left against the original copy at the right. Correct any errors and change the total of the tape where necessary.

a.
```
  2 3 .4 8
1 2 9 .5 0
  1 7 .2 9
3 5 7 .2 0
1 0 5 .8 0
1 3 6 .9 1
7 7 0 .1 8 T
```

	$23.48
	$129.50
	$17.28
	$357.20
	$105.80
	$136.90

b.

5 6 9 .4 0	$596.40
1, 2 5 6 .9 3	$1,256.93
2 .5 3	$2.53
.6 5	$.56
1, 4 7 9 .6 0	$1,479.60
1, 0 3 5 .6 7	$1,035.67
4 5 0 .0 6	$450.06
5 9 7 .3 2	$597.32
5, 3 9 2 .1 6 T	

c.

2 5 .9 7	$25.97
1 2 6 .9 4	$126.94
3, 2 5 8 .7 0	$3,258.70
3, 6 5 0 .0 7	$194.86
2 3 .1 2	$3,650.07
2 .9 8	$23.12
3 5 .7 4	$2.98
3 6 .2 9	$35.74
4, 8 6 5 .9 3	$36.29
1 5 7 .8 0	$4,865.93
1 2, 1 8 3 .5 4 T	$157.80

CHAPTER 3
SUBTRACTION
SKILLS

As an employer or employee, you will use subtraction in many ways. Without subtraction, you could not compute profit, a main goal in business. When you have totaled the sales of a business, you must deduct (subtract) the expenses of making those sales before you can discover the amount of profit earned.

If you have ever received a pay check, you are painfully aware of the role that subtraction plays in the amount you receive or take home. The payroll clerk takes away from your earnings amounts due the federal, state, and local governments for income tax, along with deductions for social security and perhaps for hospital and life insurance.

Subtraction can diminish your funds, but it can also increase them. The individual who pays income tax is allowed to subtract amounts for dependents, for interest paid, for sales and property taxes, and for donations to charities or specific funds. A customer at a supermarket who presents advertisers' coupons or returns empty bottles has the checker subtract the value of the coupons or bottles from the cash register total. On a large scale,

SUBTRACTING NUMBERS WITH MORE THAN ONE DIGIT

Practice subtracting one-digit numbers from two-digit numbers. Time yourself as you practice, and keep track of how long it takes you to complete each row accurately. Try to improve your skill.

	1	2	3	4	5	6	7
a.	18 − 9	16 − 9	17 − 9	16 − 8	16 − 7	15 − 7	14 − 7
b.	16 − 9	15 − 8	15 − 6	14 − 6	13 − 6	15 − 9	14 − 8
c.	13 − 7	14 − 5	13 − 5	12 − 5	11 − 5	14 − 9	13 − 8
d.	12 − 7	11 − 6	13 − 4	12 − 4	11 − 4	13 − 9	12 − 8
e.	11 − 7	12 − 3	11 − 3	12 − 9	11 − 8	11 − 9	11 − 2

Subtracting numbers with more than one digit may become difficult if, for instance, a number in the units place of the subtrahend has a larger value than a number in the minuend in the same place.

$$
\begin{array}{rl}
84 & \text{minuend} \\
-19 & \text{subtrahend} \\
\hline
?? & \text{difference}
\end{array}
$$

We cannot subtract 9 from 4 and be left with an answer that is a whole number. To solve the problem, we can regroup the units and tens in the minuend. Remember that when we regroup numbers that add up to a certain sum (84 in this case), the regrouping does not change the sum.

$$
\begin{array}{rlcrcr}
84 & \text{(minuend)} & = & 80 + 4 & = & 70 + 14 \\
-19 & \text{(subtrahend)} & = & 10 + 9 & = & 10 + 9 \\
\hline
& & & & & 60 + 5 \quad = \quad 65 \quad \text{(difference)}
\end{array}
$$

A shortcut to regrouping can accomplish the same thing.

$$
\begin{array}{r}
\overset{7\;}{8}\overset{14}{4} \\
-19 \\
\hline
65
\end{array}
$$

Regroup the units and tens mentally. As a reminder to yourself, label the 8's place with a small 7 and write a small 1 in front of the 4 to remind yourself that the 4 is now 14. Then subtract 9 from 14 and 1 from 7.

Example:
Subtract these three-digit numbers.

$$763$$
$$-279$$

Solution:

$$\overset{6\;5_1}{\cancel{7}\cancel{6}3}$$
$$-279$$
$$\overline{484}$$

Follow the same regrouping procedure that we used for two-digit numbers, but continue it for one more place. To subtract 9, indicate the regrouping by crossing out the 6 and writing a small five above it and by putting a small 1 in front of the 3; now subtract 9 from 13. To subtract 7, indicate a regrouping by crossing out the 7 and writing a small six above it and by putting a small 1 in front of the small 5; now subtract 7 from 15. Finally, subtract 2 from 6.

Practice regrouping in these subtractions.

	1	2	3	4	5	6	7	8
a.	73	76	98	136	764	880	654	843
	−55	−68	−19	− 68	−316	−112	−425	−535
b.	71	40	75	888	200	9,777	4,008	34,190
	−47	−36	−66	−799	−179	−8,690	−3,886	− 8,702

Exercises
1. Find each difference. Time yourself as you complete the exercises so that you can try to improve your skill.

	1	2	3	4	5	6	7	8	9	10
a.	14	13	12	13	12	13	16	12	14	12
	− 6	− 9	− 9	− 8	− 7	− 7	− 9	− 4	− 7	− 6
b.	15	11	17	16	15	11	11	11	14	12
	− 8	− 2	− 8	− 8	− 6	− 5	− 3	− 7	− 9	− 3

c.

15	13	13	14	18	12	13	16	11	11
− 7	− 4	− 5	− 8	− 9	− 4	− 6	− 7	− 6	− 9

d.

12	17	11	11	15	14	16	13	17	13
− 5	− 9	− 7	− 8	− 9	− 5	− 8	− 5	− 9	− 4

2. Find the difference in each of the following exercises.

	1	2	3	4	5	6	7	8	9	10
a.	28	59	82	36	58	42	67	87	73	89
	−13	−32	−18	−19	−29	−37	−28	−42	−49	−37
b.	64	93	84	59	38	37	83	54	89	87
	−28	−27	−37	−23	−10	−21	−29	−28	−36	−34
c.	49	62	52	71	38	64	89	95	87	83
	−23	−38	−23	−38	−27	−27	−53	−28	−39	−19

3. Find the difference.

	1	2	3	4	5	6	7	8
a.	46	96	84	37	42	47	102	234
	−32	−64	−73	−27	−13	−38	− 77	− 96
b.	198	375	815	798	902	3,007	4,052	2,836
	−139	−208	−407	−239	−623	−1,009	−2,068	−1,999

4. Find the difference in each of the following. Notice that in Problems c through i the word *gross* means "before deductions," and the word *net* means "after deductions."

a.

Amount	$48	00
Less	17	00
Net	$	

b.

Amount	$672	00
Less	247	00
Net	$	

c.

Gross earnings	$131	00
Deductions	32	00
Net pay	$	

d.

Gross earnings	$96	84
Deductions	17	88
Net pay	$	

e. Purchases	$358	40	**f.** Amount	$159	00
Amount paid	174	85	Less	65	00
Due	$		Net	$	

g. Amount	$841	00	**h.** Gross earnings	$187	50
Less	578	00	Deductions	26	40
Net	$		Net pay	$	

i. Gross earnings	$228	63	**j.** Purchases	$2,385	00
Deductions	62	81	Amount paid	985	24
Net pay	$		Due	$	

Business Applications

1. Complete the following purchase order. The discount, or reduction in price, must be subtracted from the total to arrive at the net price.

QUANTITY	CATALOG NO.	DESCRIPTION	PRICE		AMOUNT	
20	276	Cufflinks	5	25	105	00
26	279	Cufflinks	8	88	230	88
		Total				
		Less 30% discount				
		Net				

2. At the beginning of the year the Flynn family estimated they would spend the following amounts during the year: rent, $2,700; food, $4,300; furniture and household needs, $700; clothing, $1,000; car expenses, $2,100; medical expenses, $700; vacation and entertainment, $500; insurance, $1,260; and miscellaneous expenses, $500. Actual expenses for the year amounted to $13,720. (a) Was their estimate of expenses too low or too high? (b) By how much were they "off"?

3. Complete the following purchase orders for Smithvale Jewelers. Note that you must first find the total in Problems c and d before you can find the net price.

a.

Quantity	Description	Amount	
30	Rings, C–14	335	40
45	Bracelets, A–9	412	80
12	Tie pins	19	20
	Total	767	40
	Less 3% discount	23	02
	Net		

b.

Quantity	Description	Amount	
24	Travel clocks	297	78
14	Music boxes	187	82
36	Brass mugs	266	40
	Total	752	00
	Less 6% discount	45	12
	Net		

c.

Quantity	Description	Amount	
80	Silver trays	380	78
112	Bookmarks	336	40
72	Diaries	810	00
60	Lamps	801	00
	Total		
	Less 4% discount	93	13
	Net		

d.

Quantity	Description	Amount	
17	Frames	130	60
25	Figurines	211	25
40 sets	Candle holders	480	80
36	G–87 Compacts	359	28
	Total		
	Less 5% discount	59	10
	Net		

4. While she was on a recent business trip, May C. Carlisle spent the following amounts: hotel, $63; meals, $42.90; laundry, $3.75; tips, $9.50; taxis, $7.85; telephone, $11.30; customer entertainment, $36.60; and supplies, $4.30. If Ms. Carlisle started out with $300 and paid cash while she was away, how much did she have left?

5. Warren Kraus sells automotive parts. At the end of each day, he prepares a daily cash report showing the money he has received from customers. From the total amount received, Mr. Kraus must subtract the cash he started with at the beginning of the day (this is called the "*change fund*"). Complete the daily cash report for August 1, making the necessary additions and subtractions. The form is at the top of the next page.

S. D. HALE & SONS
Daily Cash Report

Department___*Automotive*___

Day___*Monday*___ Date___*Aug. 1, 19 —*___

Pennies		41
Nickels	3	20
Dimes	6	10
Quarters	5	75
Half-Dollars	4	00
Bills	532	00
Checks (List each)	62	50
	20	75
	9	50
	27	39
Total		
Less Change Fund	50	00
Cash Rec'd. from Sales		

UNIT
2
SUBTRACTING ACCURATELY

Accuracy is very important in all business computations, and it is especially important in financial records. Accuracy in subtraction can be checked by adding the subtrahend and the difference; this sum should equal the minuend.

minuend	7	
subtrahend	−4	} sum is 7
difference	3	

44   Chapter 3   Subtraction Skills

Example 1:

Check the accuracy of Cindy Bolton's subtraction on the check stub of July 5.

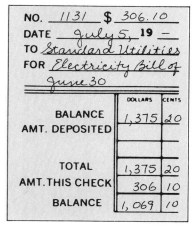

	DOLLARS	CENTS
BALANCE	1,375	20
AMT. DEPOSITED		
TOTAL	1,375	20
AMT. THIS CHECK	306	10
BALANCE	1,069	10

NO. 1131 $ 306.10
DATE July 5, 19 —
TO Standard Utilities
FOR Electricity Bill of June 30

Solution:

Add the subtrahend ($306.10) to the difference ($1,069.10). The sum is $1,375.20, which equals the minuend.

Example 2:

Check the accuracy of the following:

$$
\begin{array}{r}
7{,}518 \\
-\,1{,}964 \\
\hline
5{,}554
\end{array}
$$

Solution:

Add the difference (5,554) to the subtrahend (1,964). The sum should equal the minuend (7,518).

			Check:		
7,518	minuend			1,964	subtrahend
−1,964	subtrahend			+5,554	difference
5,554	difference			7,518	minuend

You can treat the check as a separate example as we did here, or you can extend the subtraction to form part of an addition.

$$
+\left\{
\begin{array}{r}
7{,}518 \\
-\,1{,}964 \\
\hline
5{,}554 \\
\hline
7{,}518
\end{array}
\right.
$$

Exercises

1. Compute the difference in each of the following; then verify your accuracy by adding the subtrahend and the difference to get the minuend.

a. 97
  −23

b. 87
  −46

c. 96
  −53

d. 69
  −28

e. 89
  −19

f. 267
  −148

2. Compute the difference in each of the following. Check your computations.

	1	2	3	4	5	6	7	8
a.	832 −567	586 −368	987 −918	473 −325	935 −876	584 −425	498 −187	732 −614
b.	481 −312	632 −516	511 −243	763 −674	581 −482	613 −417	943 −819	416 −337
c.	5,867 −3,098	6,428 −2,864	3,211 −1,987	5,784 −2,591	3,982 −1,675	2,645 −1,869	7,286 −2,517	9,541 −3,875
d.	3,576 −1,863	4,881 −3,296	2,976 −1,085	3,876 −1,398	5,936 −1,878	8,403 −1,808	2,966 −1,009	5,864 −3,958

3. Complete the following. Verify the accuracy of your work by adding the subtrahend and the difference to get the minuend.

a. Amount $277 85
    Less   27 70
    Net $
        $

b. Amount $462 88
    Less   211 44
    Net $
        $

c. Amount $1,384 47
    Less   138 45
    Net $
        $

d. Amount $640 08
    Less   316 57
    Net $
        $

e. Total charges $4,616 42
    Less payments   1,916 43
    Balance $
        $

f. Total charges $116 35
    Less payments   100 00
    Balance $
        $

g. Total charges $949 99
    Less payments   727 72
    Balance $
        $

h. Total charges $772 22
    Less payments   497 90
    Balance $
        $

i. Gross earnings $275 75
    Deductions   64 40
    Net pay $
        $

j. Gross earnings $303 60
    Deductions   71 75
    Net pay $
        $

k. Gross earnings $788 80
    Deductions   126 92
    Net pay $
        $

l. Gross earnings $1,277 05
    Deductions   204 10
    Net pay $
        $

m. Total purchases $1,287 87
    Less returns   16 90
    Amount due $
        $

n. Total purchases $7,320 44
    Less returns   425 45
    Amount due $
        $

o. Total purchases $721 12
    Less returns   474 12
    Amount due $
        $

p. Total purchases $542 45
    Less returns   78 97
    Amount due $
        $

UNIT

3

HORIZONTAL SUBTRACTION

Just as it was important for you to learn to use horizontal addition, it is necessary that you learn horizontal subtraction. Business forms often require that you use this skill. Suppose you had to complete the following table.

Buyer	Cash on Hand at Beginning of Day	Cash on Hand at End of Day	Amount Spent
Johnson	$567	$213	$ _____
Schultz	$400	$250.75	$ _____

As you probably noticed when you looked at this table, it is a little more difficult to subtract horizontally than vertically. In horizontal subtraction you have to keep a mental image of the digits' place values.

Example:
Subtract: $567 - 213$

Solution:
1. Subtract the units digit from the units digit: 3 from $7 = 4$
2. Subtract the tens digit from the tens digit: 1 from $6 = 5$
3. Subtract the hundreds digit from the hundreds digit: 2 from $5 = 3$
Answer: 354

When you are subtracting numbers that involve dollars and cents from numbers involving only dollars, and vice versa, you must be certain that the decimal point and two zeros follow the numbers representing the dollars.

Example 1:
Subtract: $400 - 250.75

Solution:
Supply two zeros in the minuend ($400) to avoid subtracting units digits from hundreds digits.

$$\$400.00 - \$250.75 = \$149.25$$

Example 2:

Subtract: $604.50 − $117

Solution:

Supply two zeros in the subtrahend ($117).

$$\$604.50 - \$117.00 = \$487.50$$

Exercises

1. In each of the following horizontal subtractions, find the difference.
   Then check the accuracy of each computation.

		Difference	Check
a.	86 − 34	_____	_____
b.	93 − 42	_____	_____
c.	67 − 38	_____	_____
d.	42 − 29	_____	_____
e.	78 − 27	_____	_____
f.	83 − 65	_____	_____
g.	52 − 40	_____	_____
h.	96 − 57	_____	_____
i.	34 − 18	_____	_____
j.	63 − 36	_____	_____

2. Find the difference and check each computation.

		Difference	Check
a.	671 − 321	_____	_____
b.	923 − 871	_____	_____
c.	984 − 956	_____	_____
d.	586 − 397	_____	_____
e.	417 − 324	_____	_____
f.	569 − 187	_____	_____

3. Find the difference in each of the following. Verify the accuracy
   of your work.

		Difference	Check
a.	$ 833 − $ 416	_____	_____
b.	$ 977.45 − $ 608	_____	_____
c.	$ 363 − $ 298.95	_____	_____
d.	$1,444.48 − $ 803	_____	_____
e.	$3,771 − $2,838.55	_____	_____

Business Applications

1. Assume that you are assistant to the national sales manager for Stanton Encyclopedias, which is holding a special sales promotion. The six sales representatives in the Rocky Mountain territory received the following shipments of books for the six-month period of April through September. All representatives returned their unsold books at the end of the period. Find the value of the books sold.

Representative	Value of Books Shipped	Value of Books Returned	Value of Books Sold
Lasser	$ 31,407	$ 6,778	$_____
Moore	16,228	1,803	_____
Myerson	27,772	2,801	_____
Novak	36,696	2,402	_____
Prinz	29,444	860	_____
Rodriguez	24,677	3,462	_____
Totals	$_____	— $_____	= $_____

2. The Evans Cosmetics Company, which sells door-to-door, kept the following record of cosmetics sold by its new representatives during a try-out period of one month. Find the value of each representative's sales.

Rep. No.	Value of Shipments	Value of Returns	Value of Sales Made
1	$ 876.42	$ 81.40	$_____
2	1,717.48	227.68	_____
3	289.95	9.68	_____
4	338.76	8.76	_____
5	3,912.58	684.56	_____
6	2,125.39	517.88	_____
Totals	$_____	$_____	$_____

3. The following tables show the prices a department store charges its customers for certain items of merchandise and the cost of each item to the store. The difference is the amount of profit the store makes on each item. Find the profit on each item and the total profit.

a.

Women's Clothing

Article	Selling Price	Cost to Store	Profit
Coat	$ 55.85	$ 32.36	$ _____
Blouse	8.65	5.87	_____
Dress	28.75	15.38	_____
Hat	9.85	5.39	_____
Scarf	3.85	1.82	_____
Shoes	20.40	11.48	_____
Skirt	10.99	6.42	_____
Slacks	12.95	7.09	_____
Smock	3.10	2.64	_____
Totals	$ _____	$ _____	$ _____

b.

Musical Instruments

Article	Selling Price	Cost to Store	Profit
Banjo	$ 45.50	$ 27.30	$ _____
Cello	97.95	81.39	_____
Drums	110.00	76.40	_____
Flute	50.75	26.87	_____
Guitar	42.50	24.50	_____
Harp	350.00	223.00	_____
Oboe	196.25	140.25	_____
Violin	294.75	176.85	_____
Viola	320.65	208.60	_____
Totals	$ _____	$ _____	$ _____

4. The actual expenses of a personnel department for one month are listed on page 52. Next to them are the estimates made at the beginning of the month. Compute the difference between each actual expense and the estimated expense. Then verify your work by finding the total of each column. The total of the Difference column should equal the difference between the total of the Actual column and the total of the Estimated column.

Expense	Actual	Estimated	Difference
Salaries	$ 4,660	$ 4,400	$ _____
Temporary help	220	160	_____
Employee benefits	940	940	_____
Stationery and supplies	142	100	_____
Repairs and furnishings	220	0	_____
Utilities	229	200	_____
Postage	120	50	_____
Publications	702	648	_____
Totals	$ _____	$ _____	$ _____

UNIT 4

MAKING CHANGE

Case Problem   Phil Torin is cashier at the Vacation Valley Restaurant. Phil receives cash from diners, verifies the totals of the sales checks, and gives the customers their change.

Discussion Questions
1. How can Phil exercise particular care when making change?
2. What are the special skills he needs to learn?

In teaching Phil how to make change correctly, the supervisor stressed two things.
1. When you are handed a bill by a customer, keep it in full view while repeating the cost of the article and the size of the bill. Thus, when a customer gave Phil a $5 bill in payment of a $3 restaurant check, Phil developed the habit of saying "$3 out of $5."
2. In making change, use the largest bills and coins possible. It's easier, and the risk of error is reduced.

Phil also learned to use the *additive method* of subtraction when making change. This means simply adding to the amount of the restaurant check the sum that will equal the amount the customer offers in payment.

Example 1:
A diner's check amounted to $2.95. If he gave the cashier a $10 bill in payment, how will the cashier make change?

Solution:
Add to $2.95 the amount that will equal $10 in the following steps:

1. Add a nickel to $2.95 to make $3.	$ .05
2. To $3, add two one-dollar bills to make $5.	2.00
3. To $5, add a five-dollar bill to make $10.	5.00
	$7.05, change

Example 2:
A shopper in a men's wear store purchased a necktie. The total price, including tax, was $3.79. If he paid with a $5 bill, how would his change be given to him?

Solution:

1. Add one penny to $3.79, to make $3.80.	$ .01
2. To $3.80, add two dimes to make $4.	.20
3. To $4, add one dollar to make a total of $5.	1.00
	$1.21, change

Example 3:
The driver of a car purchased gasoline which amounted to $2.43 on the pump. She gave the service-station attendant a $10 bill in payment. How would the attendant make change?

Solution:

1. Add two pennies to $2.43 to make $2.45.	$ .02
2. To $2.45, add a nickel, to make $2.50.	.05
3. To $2.50, add two quarters to make $3.00.	.50
4. To $3, add two one-dollar bills and a five-dollar bill, to make a total of $10.	2.00
	5.00
	$7.57, change

Exercises

1. Find the change due each of the following customers.

a. Customer Gave $.25

Item Costs	Change
$.22	
$.15	
$.17	
$.13	
$.24	
$.05	
$.14	
$.21	
$.06	
$.20	
$.07	
$.18	

b. Customer Gave $.50

Item Costs	Change
$.26	
$.31	
$.37	
$.42	
$.23	
$.22	
$.19	
$.47	
$.28	
$.35	
$.24	
$.27	

c. Customer Gave $1

Item Costs	Change
$.36	
$.47	
$.86	
$.69	
$.72	
$.85	
$.79	
$.58	
$.44	
$.53	
$.39	
$.67	

d. Customer Gave $2

Item Costs	Change
$1.43	
$1.26	
$1.58	
$1.73	
$1.64	
$1.69	
$1.59	
$1.17	
$1.38	
$1.49	
$1.88	
$1.87	

e. Customer Gave $5

Item Costs	Change
$2.23	
$2.69	
$3.55	
$3.57	
$1.89	
$4.19	
$2.14	
$3.52	
$3.84	
$2.27	
$1.69	
$2.43	

f. Customer Gave $10

Item Costs	Change
$2.28	
$1.67	
$7.53	
$6.48	
$8.35	
$2.69	
$7.48	
$8.67	
$4.35	
$3.18	
$2.64	
$5.49	

2. Examine the change sheet below to see how it is set up.

Amount of Purchase	Bill Given in Payment	Change Due							
		1¢	5¢	10¢	25¢	50¢	$1	$5	$10
$2.43	$10.00	2	1			1	2	1	

Make up a change sheet for each of the following purchases.

	Amount of Purchase	Bill Given in Payment			Amount of Purchase	Bill Given in Payment
a.	$ 3.12	$ 5.00		k.	$ 5.63	$10.00
b.	$ 2.85	$ 5.00		l.	$ 7.14	$20.00
c.	$11.64	$20.00		m.	$ 9.75	$10.00
d.	$ 8.73	$10.00		n.	$18.11	$20.00
e.	$ 4.98	$10.00		o.	$ 1.87	$ 5.00
f.	$ 3.76	$ 5.00		p.	$ 3.38	$ 5.00
g.	$ 5.82	$10.00		q.	$ 4.96	$10.00
h.	$ 2.27	$10.00		r.	$ 5.88	$20.00
i.	$12.58	$20.00		s.	$13.76	$20.00
j.	$14.96	$20.00		t.	$ 8.81	$10.00

Business Applications

1. Tom O'Brien is a checker at the Diamond Supermarket. Tell precisely how he would count out the change due the following customers.

   a. Customer A's total purchases are $16.88. He gives Tom two $10 bills.

   b. Customer B's total purchases are $6.16. She hands Tom a $20 bill.

   c. Customer C's total purchases are $13.40. She wants to write a check for $40, and Tom receives approval to accept it.

   d. Customer D's total purchases are $26.07. She presents coupons worth 80 cents and hands Tom three $10 bills.

   e. Customer E's total purchases are $4.88. He returns soft-drink bottles worth 90 cents and gives Tom a $5 bill.

2. The sales check on the next page was added by the waitress in Big Lou's Pizza Parlor. As the cashier, you must verify the accuracy of all checks before giving customers their change. What will you tell the customer, who hands you a $5 bill and two $1 bills?

BIG LOU'S PIZZA PARLOR
"Home of the Spicy Meatball"
———— Plaza Mall ————

Quantity	Item	Amount	
1	Pizza (reg.)	2	70
1	Spag. w. meatball	2	30
2	Coffee (esp.)		60
2	Pepsi		60
4	Tortoni	2	00
		6	20

CREDIT BALANCE

Case Problem Mrs. Smithers paid her telephone bill by check. The amount of the bill was $14.60. By mistake she sent the company a check for $16.40.

Discussion Questions
1. What error did she make?
2. What is the status of Mrs. Smither's account with the telephone company after she made her payment?
3. How can we find the amount of the overpayment?
4. How will the telephone company indicate the overpayment when she gets her next bill?
5. Can you think of other situations when we might have to subtract backwards?

Sometimes the number to be subtracted is larger than the number it is to be subtracted from—in other words, the subtrahend is larger than the minuend. In such cases, it becomes necessary to subtract the minuend from the subtrahend to find out by how much it is greater. The result we get is called a *negative balance* or a *credit balance*.

Example:

$14.60   minuend
− 16.40   subtrahend

Solution:

It is not necessary to rewrite this problem in order to solve it. Simply subtract $14.60 from $16.40 by working from the top number to the bottom one. You will get an answer of $1.80, which is a negative, or credit balance.

$14.60
− 16.40
$ 1.80 cr

An answer must be labeled as a credit balance so that you will know it means the opposite of the usual answer when you subtract. There are various ways of showing a credit balance. Sometimes it is written in red instead of black ink; sometimes the answer is circled or put in parentheses; sometimes the abbreviation *cr* for "credit" or *cr. bal.* for "credit balance" is written next to it. The abbreviation *cr* is used in the illustration just given. Calculators are usually equipped to print the credit balance in red ink or to write *cr* next to the answer automatically. Electronic display calculators show a credit balance with a minus sign next to it.

Exercises

1. In the following subtraction problems, the answer will sometimes be a "difference" and sometimes a "credit balance." In each case, find the answer. If it is a credit balance indicate that by using one of the methods previously described.

a.
| 2,735 | 34,690 | 694 | 37 | 246 | 1,940 |
| −2,541 | −38,940 | −843 | −59 | −642 | − 950 |

b.
| $129.40 | $87.93 | $ 6.95 | $195.40 | $18.27 |
| − 63.90 | − 92.50 | − 19.23 | − 102.50 | − 28.72 |

c.
| $1,683.49 | $23,013.93 | $16,685.83 | $11,116.40 | $311,009.43 |
| − 27.40 | − 24,031.93 | − 9,820.39 | − 10,115.95 | − 311,019.43 |

2. Find the answer—either a difference or a credit balance—for each of the following horizontal subtraction problems. Label all credit balances.

a. $ 12.93 − $ 63.46 _____

b. $ 129.43 − $ 127.39 _____

c. $ 983.14 − $ 1,083.43 _____

d. $ 1,649.20 − $ 1,692.40 _____

e. $ 1,874.20 − $ 1,784.20 _____

f. $ 2,005.23 − $ 2,015.47 _____

g. $39,400.05 − $37,261.52 _____

h. $ 4,920.56 − $23,940.60 _____

Business Applications

1. Milgrim Manufacturers made expense projections for the month of April. By how much did each expense go below or over the expected amount?

Expense	Expected	Actual	Over	Under
Materials	$ 30,600	$ 30,590	$_____	$_____
Labor	26,000	27,974.50	_____	_____
Supplies	3,900	4,220.10	_____	_____
Factory expenses	2,200	2,182.40	_____	_____
Miscellaneous	800	923.40	_____	_____
Totals	$_____	$_____	$_____	$_____

2. The Universal Book Company sets a quota of $4,000 as the amount of sales each sales representative should make per month. The following are weekly reports of sales made in February by its three representatives. By how much did each one exceed or fail to reach the quota?

Representative	Week 1	Week 2	Week 3	Week 4
Billup	$1,240.50	$970.20	$1,340.90	$1,295.70
Margolies	$1,098.75	$820.82	$1,120.40	$ 845.20
Storch	$1,247.50	$722.80	$1,150.25	$ 870.70

3. A charge customer owed a retail store $14.75 at the beginning of the month. During the month she made purchases of $28.75, $16.34, and $18.70. She made payments of $15, $25, and $50. What was the state of her account at the end of the month?

REVIEW EXERCISES FOR CHAPTER 3

1. Find the difference in each of the following. Check the accuracy of your answers.

a.
```
    68        426        508       4,673       5,376       4,876
  − 39      − 209      − 109     − 2,674     − 1,849     − 2,695
```

b.
```
   5,304     8,206      5,876      $94.01      $620.13     $598.32
 − 2,675   − 3,897    − 3,587    −  53.26    −  264.34   −  368.59
```

c.
```
   $19,743.33       $14,382.00      $45,876.67      $16,000.00
 −  12,869.47     −  11,967.77    −  32,975.58    −   9,110.07
```

2. Perform the following horizontal subtractions.

a. 89 − 36   b. 258 − 138   c. 8,256 − 3,042
d. 94 − 57   e. 467 − 284   f. 7,456 − 3,278
g. 63 − 28   h. 867 − 289   i. $308.46 − $139.78

3. Complete the profit chart below.

Department	Total Sales	Total Cost	Profit
Furniture	$ 68,821	$ 57,845	$_____
Men's shoes	29,158	23,864	_____
Women's shoes	48,014	40,932	_____
Men's ties	3,723	2,847	_____
Bath shop	14,634	13,549	_____
Housewares	20,672	18,396	_____
Totals	$_____	$_____	$_____

4. The monthly totals of new subscribers to *Golden West* magazine are shown on the report below. The report covers a two-year period. Find (a) the monthly increases from year to year and (b) the total number of new subscribers over the two-year period. Verify your results.

Month	19X5	19X6	Increase
January	1,409	2,417	_____
February	1,959	3,005	_____
March	1,322	2,585	_____
April	2,661	3,924	_____
May	2,123	3,536	_____
June	2,817	4,102	_____
July	2,946	4,347	_____
August	1,980	3,368	_____
September	3,141	3,241	_____
October	2,666	2,998	_____
November	1,784	1,937	_____
December	2,102	2,386	_____
Totals	_____	_____	_____

5. Make a change sheet similar to the one below and show the exact change that you would give a customer for each purchase. In each case, record the number of coins and bills of each type needed.

	Amount of Purchase	Bill Given in Payment	Change Due						
			1¢	5¢	10¢	25¢	$1	$5	$10
a.	$ 3.75	$ 5.00							
b.	$ 2.15	$ 5.00							
c.	$ 2.87	$ 5.00							
d.	$ .56	$ 5.00							
e.	$ 8.45	$10.00							
f.	$ 6.12	$10.00							
g.	$ 2.39	$10.00							
h.	$17.10	$20.00							

6. Do the following subtraction problems.

a.
$$\begin{array}{r} 230 \\ -775 \\ \hline \end{array}$$

b.
$$\begin{array}{r} 16,447 \\ -29,480 \\ \hline \end{array}$$

c.
$$\begin{array}{r} \$793.40 \\ -1,275.84 \\ \hline \end{array}$$

d.
$$\begin{array}{r} \$2,943.50 \\ -\ 2,739.06 \\ \hline \end{array}$$

e.
$$\begin{array}{r} \$1,626.49 \\ -\ 1,662.49 \\ \hline \end{array}$$

f.
$$\begin{array}{r} \$18,937.40 \\ -\ 22,400.00 \\ \hline \end{array}$$

7. Complete the following subtractions.

a.   139   —   452   = _____

b. $ 12.73 — $ 17.52 = _____

c. $ 695 — $ 893.70 = _____

d. $ 1,360 — $23,940 = _____

e. $12,560.75 — $22,793.40 = _____

8. Harry Berg decided to put himself on a weekly budget and to keep a record of what he actually spent. The first column shows his budget and the second his actual expenditures.

a. For each item find out by how much he was under or over his budget.

b. How did his budget work out for the week as a whole?

Item	Budget	Actual	Over	Under
Carfares	$ 4.90	$ 4.20	$_____	$_____
Lunches	5.00	5.25	_____	_____
Snacks	4.50	4.00	_____	_____
School supplies	2.00	1.40	_____	_____
Entertainment	6.00	6.30	_____	_____
Savings	3.00	2.50	_____	_____
Totals	$_____	$_____	$_____	$_____

CHAPTER 4
MULTIPLICATION
SKILLS

Multiplication is a quick way to add. If the Jamestown Sporting Goods Store wants to find out how much it would cost to buy two dozen baseball gloves at $2.75 each from a manufacturer, the purchasing manager can either write $2.75 twenty-four times and add, or multiply $2.75 by 24.

You use multiplication every day, maybe without even being aware of it. When the TV sports announcer says that a professional basketball player made 13 field goals, you know that he scored 26 points. If the junior class is raising money by selling soft drinks that cost $2 a case, you know that the cost of 40 cases will come to $80.

The purchasing manager of a business uses multiplication to find the cost of merchandise purchased for resale. Sales representatives use multiplication to arrive at their mileage allowance when they are using their own cars and are paid so much per mile. Secretaries use multiplication to order supplies, payroll clerks use it to find how much hourly-rate employees earn, inventory clerks use it to count stock on hand in the warehouse, and retail salesclerks use it to extend invoices. (To extend an invoice you must multiply the unit cost of each item by the quantity of that item purchased.)

Although most modern adding and calculating machines are capable of performing multiplication, the operation is still performed "by hand" by millions of consumers and employees. Knowing how to multiply will always be important. Besides, machines can help us only after we have determined how and when to multiply.

UNIT

BUILDING MULTIPLICATION SKILLS

Multiplying One-Digit Numbers

When you memorized the multiplication table, you learned that multiplication is really a short way of doing addition. That is, although you memorized that $3 \times 7 = 21$, you knew that the number 21 was the sum of $7 + 7 + 7$.

$$\begin{array}{r} 7 \\ \times 3 \\ \hline 21 \end{array} \quad \begin{array}{l} \text{multiplicand} \\ \text{multiplier} \\ \text{product} \end{array}$$

The multiplier indicates how many times the multiplicand would be added if the product were to be found by addition.

See if you can find the product in all of the following exercises in one minute or less.

	1	2	3	4	5	6	7	8	9	10	11	12
a.	1 ×9	2 ×7	3 ×5	7 ×4	2 ×6	3 ×4	1 ×7	2 ×5	3 ×3	3 ×7	9 ×2	8 ×2
b.	4 ×4	8 ×4	5 ×5	8 ×9	7 ×7	8 ×6	8 ×8	8 ×7	6 ×9	3 ×1	4 ×9	8 ×5

c.	1	2	5	2	7	6	3	1	2	9	6	5
	×6	×4	×4	×3	×9	×3	×8	×1	×2	×5	×6	×6

d.	2	5	9	9	6	8	7	6	9	4	5	0
	×9	×8	×3	×8	×7	×0	×5	×2	×9	×6	×2	×9

Exercises

Find the product in all of the following exercises in one minute or less.

	1	2	3	4	5	6	7	8	9	10	11	12
a.	7	9	5	5	6	9	2	1	3	6	3	2
	×9	×9	×7	×6	×6	×5	×2	×1	×8	×3	×9	×3
b.	1	2	1	7	5	4	8	4	3	6	8	8
	×5	×4	×6	×4	×4	×1	×5	×9	×1	×9	×7	×8
c.	8	7	8	5	8	4	6	7	1	8	9	3
	×6	×7	×9	×5	×4	×4	×4	×6	×2	×2	×2	×7
d.	3	2	1	3	2	1	3	2	1	7	6	4
	×3	×5	×7	×4	×6	×8	×5	×7	×9	×2	×3	×4

Multiplying One-Digit and Two-Digit Numbers

When you multiply two one-digit numbers, you can perform the operation on sight. When you multiply a two-digit number by a one-digit number, you often need to write down each number in the product as you do your computation.

In most of the following exercises, you will have to carry. Carrying in multiplication is similar to carrying in addition, and, as in addition, if you can remember the carry number without writing it down, you can save time. However, if you find it hard to remember the carry number, write it as a small numeral above the next number to be multiplied.

$$
\begin{array}{r}
{}^{2}73 \\
\times 7 \\
\hline
511
\end{array}
$$

Exercises

Multiply the following.

GROUP 1

	1	2	3	4	5	6	7	8	9	10
a.	22 ×2	43 ×3	52 ×6	61 ×5	37 ×2	28 ×8	17 ×4	44 ×9	36 ×3	51 ×7
b.	26 ×6	13 ×3	64 ×5	72 ×2	81 ×9	92 ×4	88 ×6	61 ×8	57 ×7	46 ×3
c.	33 ×4	34 ×6	28 ×8	18 ×3	77 ×7	84 ×5	96 ×2	82 ×9	99 ×5	67 ×3
d.	54 ×8	57 ×5	39 ×4	47 ×2	35 ×9	25 ×6	14 ×4	65 ×3	76 ×7	87 ×4
e.	91 ×6	36 ×4	21 ×6	27 ×7	38 ×2	45 ×8	77 ×5	63 ×3	66 ×9	57 ×4
f.	61 ×7	12 ×8	49 ×3	94 ×6	37 ×9	22 ×7	19 ×2	13 ×4	94 ×8	83 ×5

GROUP 2

	1	2	3	4	5	6	7	8	9	10
a.	64 ×4	72 ×5	49 ×7	57 ×8	80 ×6	96 ×9	86 ×3	59 ×2	52 ×4	83 ×5
b.	13 ×9	57 ×7	66 ×4	89 ×6	58 ×3	65 ×7	32 ×6	57 ×5	27 ×2	35 ×6
c.	54 ×7	42 ×4	27 ×5	79 ×7	69 ×8	72 ×8	24 ×7	45 ×6	52 ×9	92 ×6
d.	37 ×3	34 ×5	52 ×6	14 ×8	24 ×9	94 ×7	21 ×6	73 ×6	43 ×4	75 ×3

Unit 1   Building Multiplication Skills   65

Multiplying Larger Numbers

In multiplying numbers of two or more digits by numbers of two or more digits, make certain that the figures in your computations are properly aligned so that you add accurately.

Right	Wrong
^{3}64	^{3}64
×28	×28
512	512
128	128
1,792	13,312

Exercises

1. Find the product in each of the following. Show the details of your work.

a. 64   b. 36   c. 48   d. 33
  ×28   ×47   ×36   ×44

e. 65   f. 76   g. 37   h. 67
  ×56   ×53   ×46   ×23

i. 25   j. 21   k. 93   l. 94
  ×49   ×34   ×24   ×37

2. Find the product.

a. 188   b. 734   c. 954   d. 662
  ×16   ×12   ×23   ×47

e. 756   f. 901   g. 308   h. 562
  ×38   ×19   ×21   ×44

i. 848   j. 1,205   k. 2,870   l. 4,666
  ×236   ×15   ×29   ×374

Business Applications

1. Jack Frazier works for Presto Business Forms, Incorporated. While he was making a monthly check of the inventory in the warehouse, Jack found that he had several boxes, each containing different quantities of sales ticket pads. Find the total number of pads on hand if his count was as follows:

Number of Boxes	Quantity per Box
3	48
16	36
22	42
16	46
48	24

2. Ray Townsend sold 43 quarts of oil each day during a two-week period (14 days). How many quarts of oil did he sell?

3. On a business trip to Europe, Rachel Perry drove 17 kilometers each day round trip to and from her office. If she worked 22 days in August, how many kilometers did she drive to and from work during the month?

4. In the Lawrence Manufacturing Company, 8 employees produced 16 end tables each during a five-day week, 21 employees produced 23 each, 7 produced 27 each, and 4 produced 29 each. What was the total number of end tables produced by all employees during the week?

5. In counting his stock at the end of the year, Len Nickerson at Casco Sporting Goods discovered that he had several cartons containing handballs from six different manufacturers. How many handballs does he have in stock?

Number of Cartons	Quantity per Carton
16	144
4	162
33	136
19	124
27	96
15	72

UNIT

2 MULTIPLYING DECIMALS

The preceding unit dealt with the multiplication of whole numbers, but you will have to know how to multiply decimals as well in almost any business situation. Simply working with dollars and cents demands that you learn how to handle decimal places.

In most cases, finding the product of two decimals is no different from finding the product of two whole numbers. When you multiply, you should disregard the fact that the numbers contain decimal points. You must determine where the decimal point should be placed only after you have obtained the answer.

MULTIPLYING A DECIMAL AND A WHOLE NUMBER

When you multiply a decimal and a whole number, make sure you mark off as many decimal places in your product as there are places either in the multiplicand or the multiplier.

Example:
Multiply $6.35 by 5.

Solution:

$ 6.35   two decimal places in the multiplicand
  ×5   no decimal places in the multiplier
$31.75   two decimal places in the product

MULTIPLYING A DECIMAL BY A DECIMAL

When you multiply a decimal by a decimal, add the number of decimal places in the multiplicand to the number of decimal places in the multiplier. Then mark off that same number of decimal places in the product.

Example:
Multiply 7.23 by .5.

Solution:

7.23   two decimal places in the multiplicand
 ×.5   one decimal place in the multiplier
3.615   three decimal places in the product

When you mark decimal places, begin counting from the right side of the product. Once you have counted three places in this example, put the decimal point directly in *front* of that place.

Exercises

1. Find the product in each of the following.
   a. $1.57 × 7
   b. $2.39 × 4
   c. $16.44 × 6
   d. $21.08 × 8
   e. $16.66 × 11
   f. $37.62 × 16
   g. $462.95 × 21
   h. $247.75 × 17
   i. $57.48 × 77
   j. $198.75 × 214
   k. $1,402.25 × 7
   l. $2,864.44 × 13

2. Multiply.
   a. 83.4 × 4.76
   b. 5.55 × 3.28
   c. 108.2 × 35.6
   d. 7.714 × 7.8
   e. 6.115 × .08
   f. 8.038 × 2.765
   g. 52.25 × .007
   h. 328.67 × .764
   i. 27.875 × .0125
   j. 4.748 × .913
   k. .03 × 4.3782
   l. .11 × 24.786

Business Applications

1. Do the necessary computations to complete each of the following sales slips.

   a.

Quantity	Article	Total
3	Dress shirts @ $7.99	$ _____
4	Slacks @ $10.98	_____
6	Socks @ $1.50	_____
1	Sweater @ $16.00	_____
1	Belt @ $5.50	_____
8	Knit shirts @ $5.99	_____
1	Gloves @ $4.65	_____
	Total	$ _____

b.

Quantity	Article	Total
4	Sheets @ $3.79	$ _____
12	Towels @ $4.97	_____
6	Pillows @ $2.45	_____
2	Throws @ $9.98	_____
3	Mats @ $6.25	_____
7	Spreads @ $17.75	_____
2	Pads @ $2.49	_____
	Total	$ _____

2. Find the cost of each of the items listed below and the total cost.

Quantity	Item Number	Description	Price	Extension
14	P4468AC	Hedge clipper	$ 9.75	$ _____
18	P4520	Lock set	$ 5.45	_____
25	4684G	Steel bookcase	$19.98	_____
17	4742	Badminton set	$14.80	_____
26	4962W	Basketball	$23.35	_____
28	49630J	Tot table	$18.60	_____
31	5201	Softball	$ 2.35	_____
7	5590	Bench	$57.49	_____
52	5862K	Tennis racquet	$12.75	_____
			Total	$ _____

3. George Rolinson works in the accounting department of Hobby-masters, a wholesale firm that supplies merchandise to retail stores. The company is closing its books at the end of the year, and Mr. Rolinson has recorded the value of merchandise on hand. A form on which he has made a stock count of merchandise in the coin department follows. Make the necessary computations to complete the form.

Stock Count

Hobbymasters

Date _Dec. 31, 19—_

Department _Coin_

Counted by _J.R._

Sheet No. _3_

STOCK NO.	QUANTITY	DESCRIPTION	UNIT PRICE		EXTENSION	
3c - 37	230	De Luxe coin set	12	20		
3c - 41	633	Presidential coin set	1	70		
3c - 42	1,000	Star treasure chest kit	3	10		
3c - 87	2,200	Coin starter set		95		
3c - 101	862	Treasure hunt kit	1	65		
3c - 109	25	Coin viewer	2	80		
3c - 111	644	Rex magnifier	1	95		
3c - 122	480	Battery-lite viewer		70		
3c - 202	2,900	Modern coin album	2	85		
3c - 206	100	World coin album	1	65		
3c - 211	50	United States album	1	75		
3c - 762	400	Bottled Lincoln pennies		25		
			TOTAL			

UNIT 3

MULTIPLYING WHOLE NUMBERS BY 10, 100, AND 1,000

When you multiply whole numbers by 10, 100, or 1,000, simply attach as many zeros to the multiplicand as there are zeros in the multiplier. This shortcut can greatly speed up your multiplication.

Unit 3   Multiplying Whole Numbers by 10, 100, and 1,000   71

Example 1:
Multiply 32 by 10.

Solution:

short way

Since 10 (the multiplier) contains one zero, attach one zero to 32 (the multiplicand). The answer is 320.

long way

$$\begin{array}{r} 32 \\ \times 10 \\ \hline 00 \\ 32 \\ \hline 320 \end{array}$$

Example 2:
Multiply 14 by 100.

Solution:

short way

Since 100 (the multiplier) contains two zeros, attach two zeros to 14 (the multiplicand). The answer is 1,400.

long way

$$\begin{array}{r} 14 \\ \times 100 \\ \hline 00 \\ 00 \\ 14 \\ \hline 1,400 \end{array}$$

Example 3:
Multiply 72 by 1,000.

Solution:

short way

Since 1,000 contains three zeros, attach three zeros to 72. The answer is 72,000.

long way

$$\begin{array}{r} 72 \\ \times 1,000 \\ \hline 00 \\ 00 \\ 00 \\ 72 \\ \hline 72,000 \end{array}$$

Exercises

Multiply the following. Use the shortcut you have just learned.

1. 87×10
2. 87×100
3. $87 \times 1,000$
4. 583×10
5. 826×100
6. 160×100
7. $1,255 \times 10$
8. $3,428 \times 100$
9. $436 \times 1,000$
10. $6,000 \times 100$
11. $20,101 \times 10$
12. $70 \times 1,000$

MULTIPLYING WHOLE NUMBERS BY MULTIPLES OF 10, 100, AND 1,000

To multiply a number by 20, first multiply by 2; then attach one zero to the result.

Example:
Multiply 244 by 20.

Solution:
Step 1 $244 \times 2 = 488$ Step 2 $488 \times 10 = 4,880$

The same principle applies, of course, to 30, 40, etc.
   To multiply a number by 200, first multiply by 2; then attach two zeros to the result.

Example:
Multiply 133 by 200.

Solution:
Step 1 $133 \times 2 = 266$ Step 2 $266 \times 100 = 26,600$

The same principle applies to 300, 400, 800, etc.
   To multiply a number by 2,000, first multiply by 2; then attach three zeros to the result.

Example:
Multiply 424 by 2,000.

Solution:
Step 1 $424 \times 2 = 848$ Step 2 $848 \times 1,000 = 848,000$

Follow a similar procedure when you multiply by 3,000, 6,000, etc.

Exercises
Multiply the following. Use the shortcut you have just learned.

1. 64×20
2. 36×40
3. 48×60
4. 65×80
5. 76×70
6. 217×300
7. 196×200
8. 444×600
9. 388×300
10. 221×900
11. $116 \times 4,000$
12. $212 \times 7,000$
13. $122 \times 9,000$
14. $266 \times 2,000$
15. $1,000 \times 200$
16. $75,010 \times 9,000$

MULTIPLYING DECIMALS BY 10, 100, AND 1,000

When we were multiplying whole numbers, we followed the principle that said: Add a zero to the multiplicand for each zero in the multiplier. This does not work in quite the same way when the multiplicand contains a decimal.

Suppose you were asked to multiply 25.5 by 10. Doing it the long way, you have the following:

$$
\begin{array}{r}
25.5 \\
\times 10 \\
\hline
000 \\
255 \\
\hline
255.0
\end{array}
$$

25.5 one decimal place in the multiplicand
×10 no decimal places in the multiplier

255.0 one decimal place in the product

Notice that we can achieve the same result by moving the decimal point in the multiplicand one place to the right for each zero in the multiplier.

Example 1:
Multiply 29.76 by 10.

Solution:

short way

Move the decimal point *one* place to the right to get 297.6.

long way
$$
\begin{array}{r}
29.76 \\
\times 10 \\
\hline
0000 \\
2976 \\
\hline
297.60
\end{array}
$$

Example 2:
Multiply 29.76 by 100.

Solution:

short way

Move the decimal point *two* places to the right to get 2,976.

long way
$$
\begin{array}{r}
29.76 \\
\times 100 \\
\hline
0000 \\
0000 \\
2976 \\
\hline
2,976.00
\end{array}
$$

Example 3:
Multiply 29.76 by 1,000.

Solution:
Move the decimal point three places to the right to get 29,760.

Explanation:

Here you have to move the decimal point three places to the right, but there are only two decimal places. Add one more decimal place by attaching a zero, so that you have the following result:

$$29.76 \times 1,000 = 29,760$$

— This zero has been added.

Exercises

Multiply the following.

1. 27.4×10
2. 59.673×10
3. 6.59×100
4. 62.594×100
5. 6.2×100
6. $.247 \times 100$
7. $3.799 \times 1,000$
8. $86,743 \times 1,000$
9. $52.92 \times 1,000$
10. $123.4 \times 1,000$
11. $72.3 \times 1,000$
12. $12,003.5 \times 1,000$

MULTIPLYING DECIMALS BY MULTIPLES OF 10, 100, AND 1,000

To multiply 20.72 by 20, multiply by 2 and move the decimal point one place to the right to accommodate the zero in the number 20.

Example:

Multiply 20.72 by 20.

Solution:

1. Multiply by 2:

$$20.72 \times 2 = 41.44$$

2. Move the decimal point one place to the right:

$$41.44 \times 10 = 414.4$$

Exercises

Multiply the following.

1. $\$50.78 \times 20$
2. $\$19.63 \times 70$
3. 3.765×200
4. $63.4 \times 5,000$
5. $\$129.50 \times 60$
6. $\$29.75 \times 4,000$
7. $2.5 \times 6,000$
8. $\$200.50 \times 800$
9. $20.45 \times 6,000$
10. $.06 \times 3,000$
11. $5,302.1 \times 4,000$
12. $\$.04 \times 6,000$

Business Application

Check the amounts on the following order, listing by item number any errors you find.

Quantity	Item Number	Description	Price	Amount
90	455BR	Level, No. 47Y	$ 8.20	$ 73.80
600	741	Monarch plane	$ 9.42	56.52
500	902	Battery lamp	$12.28	61.40
180	1071	Vertical broiler	$17.85	142.80
7,000	3032	3-in-1 appliance	$25.00	175.00
3,400	3077	Rotisserie	$36.70	146.80
1,500	3083	Fireplace set	$41.40	207.00
30	3348	Swift cut power saw	$49.90	149.70
100	3403	Home workshop	$75.50	75.50
			Total	$ 1,088.52

UNIT 4

MULTIPLYING ACCURATELY

Case Problem   Joseph Gibson is a sales representative for Hobby-masters, a large company which supplies hobby shops and other retail stores. When one of his customers phoned recently, Mr. Gibson was asked: "How much will 255 Spitfire model airplane kits cost me, Joe?"

Mr. Gibson made a quick computation and gave the customer a figure: "At $1.21 each, the total would be $299.55."

Discussion Questions
1. How much is 7×5? 5×7?
2. How much is 5×20? 20×5?
3. Is Mr. Gibson's multiplication correct?
4. How might Mr. Gibson check the accuracy of his multiplication?

Sales representatives and others who are asked to make quick computations can easily make errors. Mr. Gibson could verify the accuracy of his multiplication by remultiplying. However, the second time he multiplies, Mr. Gibson should reverse the numbers being multiplied so that he won't be likely to make the same mistake twice. He can do this because the order in which two numbers are multiplied does not affect their product. Notice that $7 \times 5 = 35$ and $5 \times 7 = 35$ are equivalent.

Suppose, for example, Mr. Gibson's first multiplication was as follows:

$$
\begin{array}{r}
255 \\
\times\,\$1.21 \\
\hline
255 \\
420 \\
255 \\
\hline
\$299.55
\end{array}
$$

To verify the accuracy of his work, he multiplies a second time—this time interchanging the positions of the multiplicand and the multiplier.

$$
\begin{array}{r}
\$1.21 \\
\times\,255 \\
\hline
605 \\
605 \\
242 \\
\hline
\$308.55
\end{array}
$$

When the second multiplication does not yield the same answer as the first, Mr. Gibson knows that he has made an error.

Here is another example.

Example:
Multiply 55 by 35.

Solution:

	Interchanging multiplicand and multiplier	
55		35
×35		×55
275		175
165		175
1,925		1,925

Exercises
Multiply the following numbers. Verify each answer by interchanging the multiplicand and the multiplier and again finding the product.

1.	33	2.	67	3.	94	4.	88
	×12		×24		×16		×37

5.	76	6.	745	7.	824	8.	462
	×45		×216		×142		×317

9.	246	10.	435	11.	368	12.	259
	×463		×507		×$1.12		×$3.04

13.	825	14.	936	15.	538
	×$4.16		×$7.25		×$6.22

ANOTHER SHORTCUT IN MULTIPLICATION

Sometimes you can save time by interchanging the multiplier and the multiplicand in the original problem. Suppose you must multiply 900 by 526. You could work it out this way.

900	multiplicand
×526	multiplier
5400	
1800	
4500	
473,400	product

It is much easier, however, to multiply 526 by 9 and add two zeros to the product.

526
×900
─────
4,734   473,400   product

You should choose to do the problem the second way. It is easier and cuts down the possibility of error as well.

Exercises

Do each of the following multiplication problems. Interchange the multiplier and the multiplicand when necessary so that you are doing the multiplication in the easiest way.

1. 600 × 274

2. $15.47 × 20

3. $800 × 2.935

4. 9,000 items @ $2.47 each

5. 22 × 2,946

6. .005 × 16

Business Applications

1. Russell's Hardware Store received the following quotations from a wholesale hardware supply company. If an order were placed according to the quantities and prices given, what would be (a) the amount for each type of item and (b) the total of the order?

Quantity	Description	Cost Price	Amount
900	Bolts	$.12	$_____
450	Saw blades	$.25	_____
2,000	Wood knobs	$.80	_____
625	Hinges	$.28	_____
250	Shelf brackets	$.10	_____
1,500	Toggle bolts	$.155	_____
100	Yardsticks	$.067	_____
3,400	Casters	$.0155	_____
		Total	$_____

2. The price of a Jiffy Queen vacuum cleaner is $125. Find the dollar-value of sales for each of the following sales representatives in one month and the total for all representatives. Verify the accuracy of your work by multiplying the total number of cleaners sold by the price of the vacuum cleaner, and compare your answer with the sum of the Total column.

Representative	Cleaners Sold	Total
Abrams	22	$ _____
Fiscina	18	_____
Mayberry	14	_____
Gilbert	8	_____
Kahn	17	_____
O'Day	23	_____
Muhlenberg	6	_____
Oliver	21	_____
Macklin	17	_____
Moriarty	15	_____
Totals	_____	$ _____

3. Lybrand Brothers owns seven warehouses, which rent various import companies space for storage. The amount received from each renter is based on the location of the warehouse, the number of square meters occupied, and the condition of the building. Following are the square meters in each of the seven warehouses and the rental rate per square meter. Find (a) the annual income for each warehouse and (b) the total annual income. (Multiply square meters of space by amount per square meter.)

Location	Amount of Space in Square Meters	$ Per Square Meter Per Year	Annual Income
Brookside	12,570	$2.16	$ _____
Heatherton	46,875	$1.76	_____
Foley	31,400	$1.82	_____
Monkton	60,420	$1.95	_____
Liberty	6,375	$3.44	_____
Oakmont	11,220	$1.65	_____
Duberville	16,000	$2.00	_____
		Total	$ _____

4. During the past five months, Guard-Rite Rubber Company produced the following products at the manufacturing costs indicated. Find (a) the total cost of manufacturing each product and (b) the total cost of manufacturing for the period.

Product	Quantity Produced	Cost of Production per Unit	Total Cost
Carpet pads	7,250	$12.25	$_____
Belting (rolls)	4,100	$21.80	_____
Tires	8,240	$11.35	_____
Floor runners (rolls)	9,500	$21.88	_____
Sheets	28,950	$ 2.33	_____
Containers	112,238	$ 1.25	_____
		Total	$_____

5. Avery Mandell receives a mileage allowance of 10 cents a mile for the first 500 miles he drives each month and 8 cents a mile for all miles driven over 500. If he drove 800 miles in July, how much did he receive in mileage allowance?

6. The J & L Floor Covering Shop sold the following quantities of carpeting on a recent day. (a) What was the total received for each type of carpeting? (b) What was the total dollar-value of carpeting sales for the day?

Type of Carpeting	Square Yards Sold	Price per Square Yard	Total
Diamond tuft	320	$10.50	$_____
Guild	436	$12.70	_____
Kirk	280	$14.95	_____
Krishna	170	$21.45	_____
Heather	330	$ 8.85	_____
		Total	$_____

REVIEW EXERCISES FOR CHAPTER 4

1. Find the products in the following. Each group should take you one minute or less.

	1	2	3	4	5	6	7	8	9	10	11	12
a.	1 ×9	2 ×7	3 ×5	7 ×4	2 ×6	3 ×4	1 ×7	2 ×5	3 ×3	3 ×7	9 ×2	8 ×2
b.	4 ×4	8 ×4	5 ×5	8 ×9	7 ×7	8 ×6	8 ×8	6 ×9	3 ×1	4 ×9	8 ×5	8 ×7
c.	1 ×6	2 ×4	5 ×4	2 ×3	7 ×9	6 ×3	3 ×8	1 ×1	2 ×2	9 ×5	6 ×6	5 ×6
d.	2 ×9	5 ×8	9 ×3	9 ×8	6 ×7	8 ×0	7 ×5	6 ×2	9 ×9	4 ×6	5 ×2	0 ×9

2. Find the following products in less than two minutes.

   a. 247×10 **b.** $\$34.50 \times 10$

   c. $\$17.90 \times 700$ **d.** $3,760 \times 40$

   e. $16 \times 1,000$ **f.** $\$8.40 \times 2,000$

   g. 160×100 **h.** 750×300

   i. $\$24.50 \times 400$

3. Multiply and verify the accuracy of the product by interchanging the multiplicand and multiplier.

a.	**b.**	**c.**	**d.**
37 ×24	59 ×29	86 ×43	92 ×78

e.	61	f.	264	g.	312	h.	774
	×57		×128		×207		×316

i.	895	j.	637	k.	442	l.	620
	×465		×327		×$1.38		×$5.12

m.	1,842	n.	2,405	o.	7,904
	×$11.16		×$11.28		×$17.62

4. For ten employees in various departments of the Madison Savings and Loan Association, the table below shows the hourly-wage rate and the number of hours worked during a recent week. Find (a) the total earned by each employee and (b) the total earned by all employees.

Employee	Hourly Rate	Hours Worked	Total Earnings
Franklin	$2.50	38	$ _____
Jesurun	$3.05	40	_____
Kirsch	$3.43	40	_____
Morley	$3.25	39	_____
Nofstra	$2.55	40	_____
Quade	$3.70	40	_____
Ralston	$2.50	36	_____
Swinford	$2.62	37	_____
Waters	$3.45	39	_____
Yeary	$3.15	40	_____
		Total	$ _____

5. Ed Owens, a sales representative in Brandman's Paint Store, sold a customer the following: 3 gallons of house paint at $8.65 a gallon; 6 quarts of interior paint at $3.25 a quart; 1 gallon of paint thinner at $.95; 3 rollers at $1.79; 4 paint brushes at $3.80; 6 paint buckets at $.49; and 350 tiles at $.39. Find the total on the sales ticket.

6. Find the value of the stock on the sheet below.

Stock Sheet No. 14

Department Sporting Goods

Counted by B.A.C. **Date** 12/30/19--

Quantity	Article	Cost per Unit		Stock Value	
16	Harry Mackey irons	49	90		
27	Phyllis Monroe irons	24	50		
85	Jack Mowbray woods	82	40		
47	Mac McGrath woods	66	35		
32	Grand Slam racquets	12	95		
16	Lil' Tyke racquets	6	69		
157	Ace tennis balls (3)	1	49		
72	Milt Pate golf balls (12)	6	44		
38	Pat King golf balls (12)	7	80		
		Total			

7. Find the total of the following purchase order.

Purchase Order

To: Miner Candy Mfr.

Durham, N. C.

Order No. 472

Date 10/6/19--

Quantity in Pounds	Description	Amount	
400	Frozen milk caramels @ 59¢		
350	Red & black pectin berries @ 69¢		
475	Miniature fruit slices @ 73¢		
648	Toasted coconut @ 64¢		
1,100	Licorice berries @ 38¢		
176	Crystallized jelly frappe @ 91¢		
506	Chocolate-miniature cherries @ 85¢		
739	Chocolate-large cherries @ $1.07		
	Total		

8. Find the total of the following invoice.

Invoice

Hillsdale Auto Supply Company

Terms: Net Cash   **Date:** ___6/18/19--___

To: Brandt Auto Wholesalers

QUANTITY	DESCRIPTION	UNIT PRICE		AMOUNT
900	Side-view mirrors	$ 5	85	$
636	Black-wall tires	29	75	
756	White-wall tires	36	75	
408	Liquid cleaner	1	35	
240	Deluxe seat cushions	8	60	
1200	Recapped snow tires	14	45	
			Total	

9. Complete the following multiplications. Interchange multiplier and multiplicand whenever that makes a problem easier.

a. $40.50 × 23   **b.** 6,000 × 924

c. 333 × 976   **d.** 654 × $22

e. $40.00 × 273   **f.** 1,222 × 873

10. Complete the following quotation request form.

PRICES QUOTED F.O.B.	TERMS	TO BE SHIPPED VIA	EARLIEST SHIPPING DATE
Brunswick, S.D.	Cash	Parcel Post	5/23/19—

Quantity	Description	Price	Amount
146	Car coats	$13.60	$_____
185	Ski sweaters	$18.45	$_____
300	Terrycloth robes	$ 7.70	$_____
237	Pantsuits	$27.35	$_____
203	All-weather coats	$44.60	$_____
258	Knit coordinates	$18.75	$_____

11. Complete the following.

DATE OF INVOICE	SHIPPED VIA	F.O.B.	TERMS	SALES REP.
6/15/19—	Freight	Chicago, IL	Cash 30 days	F. Bates

Quantity	Description	Price	Amount
38	Portable hair dryers	$24.49	$ _____
54	12-cup automatic percolators	$26.67	_____
126	4-slice toasters	$23.15	_____
200	Chrome toaster-broilers	$25.50	_____
350	Cordless electric knives	$ 8.95	_____
285	4-speed blenders	$26.80	_____
		Total	$ _____

CHAPTER 5
DIVISION
SKILLS

Suppose your club is planning an outing, and the cost of food and soft drinks comes to $27.60, which is to be divided equally among the 12 people who are going. What is each person's share of the expense? You know that you would divide $27.60 by 12 to find that each person owes $2.30. If you want to know what mileage your car is getting per gallon of gas or how much it costs to operate the car for each mile driven, you have to use division. Division, then, is an important arithmetic skill to all consumers.

Division is widely used in business. Business people must use division to set prices. For example, if the total cost of manufacturing 1,000 tennis racquets is $6,000, the manufacturer must divide $6,000 by 1,000 to find the cost of producing each racquet—$6. He can then set a price at which he must sell each racquet in order to make a profit. Division is used to make comparisons of one set of figures with another. For example, an office supervisor reads a report that the average, or typical, salary paid computer programmers in her city is $803.13 per month. To see how the salaries of her programmers compare

with the average for the city, she
divides the total salary expense of
the group for the month ($49,236) by
the number of employees (60) to find
the average amount earned by the
programmers ($820.60). She finds
that her average is slightly higher
than that for the city, and she is
satisfied that she has a fair salary
scale.

UNIT

BUILDING DIVISION SKILLS

DIVISION DRILLS

When you are dividing, you are determining how many times one number is
contained in another. Division is the inverse (opposite) of multiplication.
   Consider this division problem.

$$\underset{\uparrow}{240} \div \underset{\underset{\text{divisor}}{\uparrow}}{12} = 20 \leftarrow \text{quotient}$$

dividend

The number being divided (240) is called the *dividend.* The number doing the
dividing (12) is called the *divisor.* The answer (20) is called the *quotient.*
   The same problem can be written in two other ways.

$$\text{divisor} \rightarrow 12\overline{)240} \qquad \textbf{or} \qquad \frac{240}{12} = 20 \leftarrow \text{quotient}$$

quotient → 20 ... dividend ... dividend ... divisor

   At the top of the next page are 64 division problems. See if you can do them
all mentally in one minute or less.

1	2	3	4	5	6	7	8
a. $2\overline{)8}$	$6\overline{)42}$	$7\overline{)49}$	$4\overline{)20}$	$5\overline{)35}$	$9\overline{)63}$	$2\overline{)4}$	$8\overline{)16}$
b. $9\overline{)72}$	$7\overline{)63}$	$2\overline{)14}$	$9\overline{)81}$	$8\overline{)40}$	$4\overline{)32}$	$5\overline{)45}$	$7\overline{)21}$
c. $7\overline{)35}$	$6\overline{)36}$	$3\overline{)6}$	$2\overline{)10}$	$4\overline{)16}$	$7\overline{)42}$	$4\overline{)12}$	$3\overline{)21}$
d. $4\overline{)8}$	$7\overline{)28}$	$6\overline{)30}$	$8\overline{)32}$	$9\overline{)36}$	$5\overline{)30}$	$2\overline{)18}$	$4\overline{)28}$
e. $6\overline{)18}$	$3\overline{)27}$	$9\overline{)54}$	$2\overline{)6}$	$8\overline{)48}$	$6\overline{)12}$	$9\overline{)27}$	$5\overline{)10}$
f. $3\overline{)9}$	$4\overline{)36}$	$7\overline{)56}$	$8\overline{)72}$	$3\overline{)18}$	$4\overline{)24}$	$8\overline{)64}$	$3\overline{)24}$
g. $5\overline{)20}$	$9\overline{)72}$	$5\overline{)15}$	$6\overline{)54}$	$8\overline{)24}$	$3\overline{)15}$	$5\overline{)40}$	$2\overline{)16}$
h. $7\overline{)14}$	$6\overline{)24}$	$3\overline{)12}$	$5\overline{)25}$	$6\overline{)48}$	$9\overline{)18}$	$9\overline{)45}$	$8\overline{)56}$

Exercises

Divide the following without writing down the quotients. See if you can do all in 30 seconds or less.

1	2	3	4	5	6	7	8
a. $2\overline{)4}$	$5\overline{)45}$	$4\overline{)12}$	$2\overline{)18}$	$9\overline{)27}$	$8\overline{)64}$	$5\overline{)40}$	$9\overline{)45}$
b. $8\overline{)56}$	$7\overline{)14}$	$3\overline{)24}$	$5\overline{)10}$	$4\overline{)28}$	$3\overline{)21}$	$7\overline{)21}$	$8\overline{)16}$
c. $7\overline{)14}$	$6\overline{)24}$	$5\overline{)20}$	$6\overline{)18}$	$4\overline{)8}$	$7\overline{)35}$	$9\overline{)72}$	$2\overline{)8}$
d. $7\overline{)49}$	$2\overline{)14}$	$3\overline{)6}$	$6\overline{)30}$	$9\overline{)54}$	$7\overline{)56}$	$5\overline{)15}$	$3\overline{)12}$
e. $6\overline{)48}$	$8\overline{)24}$	$3\overline{)18}$	$8\overline{)48}$	$9\overline{)36}$	$4\overline{)16}$	$8\overline{)40}$	$5\overline{)35}$

SHORT DIVISION

When you divide by one-digit numbers, you can usually speed up the operation by using short division. In short division, you write only the quotient. For example, examine the divisions at the top of the next page.

```
  short method        long method
     212                 212
  3)636              3)636
                       6
                       ───
                       3
                       3
                       ───
                       6
                       6
                       ───
```

In short division, you often have carry numbers, which represent the amount remaining after a previous partial division. These numbers are written as small numerals to the left of the next digit. In the example below, the 6 with a carry number in front of it becomes 16, and the 2 at the far right becomes 12 when you divide.

```
    3, 81 6
  2)7,¹63¹2
```

Exercises

Divide the following, using short division.

1. 4,688 ÷ 4
2. 8,215 ÷ 5
3. 6,776 ÷ 7
4. 36,972 ÷ 9
5. 9,624 ÷ 8
6. 39,864 ÷ 6
7. 28,887 ÷ 3
8. 412,936 ÷ 4
9. 887,985 ÷ 5
10. 763,467 ÷ 3
11. 53,792 ÷ 4
12. 245,608 ÷ 8

LONG DIVISION

When you divide by two-digit numbers, it is usually necessary to do long division, which means "bringing down" your computations as shown in the following illustration.

Example:
Divide 56,754 by 27.

Solution:

```
      2,102
  27)56,754
     54↓ | |
     ──── 
      2 7 | |
      2 7↓↓
      ────
         54
         54
         ──
```

Note that the quotient (2,102) is written directly above the dividend (56,754) with the digits aligned and that the digits that are brought down are also aligned with the digits in the dividend.

Remainders
In many division problems, you will have a number "left over"—a remainder that cannot be divided by the divisor. This remainder can be expressed as a fractional part of the divisor by writing it over the divisor.

Example:
Divide 9,650 by 17.

Solution:

$$
\begin{array}{r}
567\frac{11}{17} \\
17\overline{)9,650} \\
\underline{8\ 5} \\
1\ 15 \\
\underline{1\ 02} \\
130 \\
\underline{119} \\
11 \text{ remainder}
\end{array}
$$

Notice that the number 11 is left over. This remainder is expressed as a fractional part of the divisor 17, or $\frac{11}{17}$.

Exercises
Find the quotient in each of the following.

1. $36\overline{)23,518}$

2. $84\overline{)56,712}$

3. $76\overline{)64,817}$

4. $108\overline{)76,453}$

5. $252\overline{)172,643}$

6. $315\overline{)95,814}$

7. $96\overline{)42,163}$

8. $312\overline{)98,964}$

9. $804\overline{)317,645}$

10. $7,864\overline{)63,545}$

11. $86\overline{)10,850}$

12. $55\overline{)9,175}$

Business Applications
1. The Mount Tabor Corporation offers on-the-job training to its employees. During the past year 1,240 employees took advantage of these educational opportunities. The expenses of operating the program were as follows: part-time instructions, $114,770; janitorial services, $6,080; books, $12,370; supplies, $4,160; and mis-

cellaneous expenses, $6,150. What was the cost of on-the-job training per employee?

2. The annual salaries for certain jobs in Johnson Products Company are shown below. Complete the form.

Job	Annual Salary	Weekly Salary*	Monthly Salary**
Accountant	$14,200	$_____	$_____
Production supervisor	$12,800	$_____	$_____
Sales representative	$12,200	$_____	$_____
Driver	$11,500	$_____	$_____
Copywriter	$ 8,060	$_____	$_____
Secretary	$ 7,020	$_____	$_____
Typist	$ 5,980	$_____	$_____

* Divide annual salary by 52.
** Divide annual salary by 12.

3. The 39 members of the Outdoor Club collected $1,202 from a white elephant sale for a ski weekend. How much can be allowed each member toward expenses for the weekend?

4. The citizens of Lakeside organized a drive to raise money to build a child-care center. Each contribution to the fund was called "a brick for the center," and a donation of $15 was asked for each "brick." The drive yielded $76,500. How many contributions were received?

5. The Plainview Hotel decided to install color TV in all its rooms. The management announced that the old black-and-white sets would be sold to employees at a very low price. Employees purchased 484 TV sets for which the hotel received $17,628 in cash. What was the price at which the sets were sold to employees?

6. Genevieve Casey is a cost accountant for the Muller Rubber Manufacturing Company. The sales vice-president, John Weaver, walked into her office and said, "Mrs. Casey, those Roadguard tires seem to be priced too high—we're losing sales to our competitors. We've got to find some way to reduce our price. How much exactly does each tire cost us to manufacture?"

   Mrs. Casey assembled various reports and found out that the total cost of materials and production came to $820,600 during the previous 18 months. For this amount, 110,000 tires were manufactured. With these figures, Mrs. Casey could answer Mr. Weaver's question. What would the answer be?

7. Munson Educational Films, Inc., has four branch offices in Oklahoma—Oklahoma City, Tulsa, Lawton, and Ardmore. Each branch office has its own promotion department, which produces letters, advertising brochures, and other promotional literature for its territory. The general advertising manager in the home office of Munson is concerned about the amount of money being spent for direct-mail advertising and asks for a report. Here are the figures of the report.

City	Number of Mailings	Cost
Oklahoma City	40,000	$10,800
Tulsa	26,000	$ 9,620
Lawton	18,000	$ 3,780
Ardmore	16,500	$10,560

Which office spent the most per mailing? Which office spent the least per mailing?

UNIT

DIVIDING ACCURATELY

We mentioned at the beginning of Unit 1 that division is the inverse of multiplication. Just as multiplication is repeated addition, division is repeated subtraction. When we say $20 \div 4 = 5$, we are also saying that 4 can be subtracted from 20 each of 5 times.

We divide all the time and check our divisions automatically. If we paid $20 for 4 tickets, each one would have cost us $5 ($20 \div 4 = $5). To say this another way, if we paid $5 for each of 4 tickets, the total cost would be $20 ($5 \times 4 = $20). Therefore, to verify the accuracy of a division, multiply the quotient by the divisor. The product should equal the dividend.

Example:
Divide 228 by 6 and verify the accuracy of the division.

Solution:

1. $6\overline{)228}$ quotient 38

2. Multiply the quotient (38) by the divisor (6).
3. The product of $38 \times 6 = 228$. This is the same as the dividend, so the division is correct.

If the division is not even—that is, the remainder is not zero—follow these steps:

1. Multiply the divisor by the quotient as above.
2. Add the remainder to the product.

Example:
Divide 769 by 13 and verify your answer.

Solution:

$$
\begin{array}{r}
59 \\
13\overline{)769} \\
65 \\
\hline
119 \\
117 \\
\hline
2 \text{ remainder}
\end{array}
$$

There is a remainder of 2 after you divide 769 by 13. Verify your answer by finding the product of 59×15 and adding the remainder (2).

59 (quotient) $\times$ 13 (divisor) = 767; 767 + 2 (remainder) = 769 (dividend)

Exercises
Find the quotient for each of the following problems. Verify your answer by multiplying the divisor by the quotient and then adding the remainder.

1. $23\overline{)713}$ 2. $57\overline{)1,539}$ 3. $68\overline{)2,992}$

4. $24\overline{)9,680}$ 5. $83\overline{)6,557}$ 6. $96\overline{)4,416}$

7. $23\overline{)2,211}$ 8. $16\overline{)8,920}$ 9. $25\overline{)8,625}$

10. $12\overline{)4,480}$

Business Applications

1. The number of miles by train from Arlington to Maryville is 966. If a train travels at 46 miles an hour, how many hours will be required to make the trip between the two cities? Verify the accuracy of your work.

2. The sales manager of Hill and Brown, Inc., estimated that in the coming year the company will have sales totaling $297,000. For purposes of business operations, the manager wants to break down the total on a month-by-month basis. Assuming that equal sales

will be forecast for each of the 12 months, what will the monthly sales estimate be? Verify your answer.

UNIT 3

DIVIDING DECIMALS

Case Problem   Mrs. Elsie Morris owns the Fabric Shop, a retail store that sells yard goods. Recently Mrs. Morris received a statement from one of her suppliers that showed the following information:

7 yards, Tawny Tweed $12.11

Discussion Questions
1. What was the cost of the material per yard?
2. Why is it important for Mrs. Morris to know the cost per yard?

Mrs. Morris needs to know the cost per yard of the material she buys in order to set the price that she will charge her retail customers. She finds the price per yard by division.

THE WHOLE NUMBER DIVISOR

To find the cost per yard of Tawny Tweed, Mrs. Morris divided a decimal ($12.11) by a whole number (7). When the dividend (the number to be divided) contains a decimal point and the divisor is a whole number, place the decimal point in the quotient directly above the decimal point in the dividend. Then divide normally.

Example:

Divide $12.11 by 7.

Solution:

$$
\begin{array}{r}
\downarrow \\
1.73 \\
7\overline{)12.11} \\
\uparrow
\end{array}
\qquad
\begin{array}{l}
\text{Notice the position} \\
\text{of the decimal points.}
\end{array}
$$

Exercises

Divide the following.

1. 6.93 ÷ 3

2. 29.75 ÷ 5

3. 164.8 ÷ 8

4. 294.84 ÷ 9

5. 22.4 ÷ 16

6. 37.49 ÷ 23

7. 893.52 ÷ 36

8. 192.39 ÷ 121

9. 1,278.75 ÷ 341

10. 475.458 ÷ 109

11. 1,120.56 ÷ 46

12. 709.236 ÷ 81

THE DECIMAL DIVISOR

When the divisor contains a decimal point, we cannot go on until we eliminate it. We do this by multiplying both the divisor *and* the dividend by the same number—10, 100, 1,000, or whatever multiple will get rid of the decimal fraction in the divisor. Remember that when you multiply by 10, 100, or 1,000, you must move the decimal point one place to the right for each zero in the multiplier. This procedure has no effect on the answer; it just makes the division simpler by eliminating a fraction. Multiplying the divisor and dividend by the same number and then completing the division does not change the answer.

Before starting to divide with decimals, follow these steps:

1. Move the decimal point in the divisor as many places to the right as necessary to make it a whole number.

2. Move the decimal point in the dividend the same number of places as you did in the divisor, attaching zeros if necessary. (Adding zeros to the right of a decimal point does not change the value of the decimal fraction.)

3. Place the decimal point for the quotient directly over the decimal point in the dividend.

4. Divide.

When the numbers do not divide evenly and there is a remainder, we have two ways to handle the remainder:

1. Make a fraction out of the remainder, as we suggested in Unit 1. Your answer with a remainder would fall into this pattern: Quotient $\dfrac{\text{Remainder}}{\text{Divisor}}$

2. Add as many zeros as necessary *after the decimal point* in the dividend and continue to divide. This procedure is the one preferred in business. Since we usually work with dollars and cents, it is rarely necessary to carry the answer out to more than three decimal places.

Example:
Divide 48.24 by .225.

Solution:
1. Move the decimal point in the divisor three places to the right, to make the divisor a whole number. The divisor .225 becomes 225.
2. Move the decimal point in the dividend three places to the right, attaching one zero since there are only two places in the dividend. The dividend becomes 48,240.

This is how this division example would look after the first and second steps:

$$.225 \overline{)48.240}$$

3. You are now dividing 48,240 by 225.
4. Place the decimal point for the quotient directly above the new position of the decimal point in the dividend.

$$\downarrow$$
$$225\overline{)48240.}$$
$$\uparrow$$

5. Divide.

```
          214.4    quotient
   225) 48,240.0
        45 0
         3 24
         2 25
           990
           900
            90 0
            90 0
```

Notice that there is a remainder of 90 in this division. To express any remainder as a decimal fraction, add zeros to the dividend *after the decimal point,* and continue to divide.

Exercises

Divide the following.

1. 37.50 by 5
2. 48.30 by 6
3. 123.84 by 16
4. 123.84 by 1.6
5. 3,675 by $.25
6. $25,420 by $8.20
7. 966 by $3.36
8. $5,417.60 by 945
9. 45 by .05
10. 216 by .002
11. .3381 by 4.2
12. 40.404 by .0074

Business Applications

1. Find the cost per can to Murphy's Market of the following purchases of cases of canned goods.

Case No.	No. of Cans in Case	Total Cost	Cost per Can	Case No.	No. of Cans in Case	Total Cost	Cost per Can
1	24	$ 4.80	$ ____	10	36	$13.32	$ ____
2	24	$ 3.60	$ ____	11	36	$14.40	$ ____
3	24	$ 4.32	$ ____	12	36	$12.96	$ ____
4	24	$ 3.36	$ ____	13	48	$ 8.16	$ ____
5	18	$ 4.86	$ ____	14	48	$12.48	$ ____
6	18	$ 5.58	$ ____	15	48	$16.80	$ ____
7	18	$ 7.92	$ ____	16	72	$35.28	$ ____
8	18	$ 9.36	$ ____	17	72	$18.00	$ ____
9	36	$10.80	$ ____	18	86	$23.22	$ ____

2. Yard goods were purchased by The Calico Cat, a neighborhood material store, as follows. What was the cost of each yard of material?

Item No.	No. of Yards	Total Cost	Cost per Yard	Item No.	No. of Yards	Total Cost	Cost per Yard
1	95.5	$ 82.65	$ ____	5	18.375	$ 366.24	$ ____
2	97.25	$103.79	$ ____	6	547.2	$1,263.57	$ ____
3	104.3	$120.64	$ ____	7	82.5	$2,380.18	$ ____
4	108.75	$145.80	$ ____	8	266.125	$5,159.64	$ ____

3. On a recent business trip to Europe, Mary Beth Wakeman flew 1,540 kilometers in 3.5 hours. What was the average speed per hour of the plane?

4. Phil Moorehead is considering buying a new car. The make and model he wants comes to exactly $3,462.20, including taxes and other charges. If he wants to pay for the car in 35 months, what will his monthly payments be?

5. The cost of imported Darjeeling tea to Milford Specialty Store is 98¢ a kilo (kilogram). If the total amount due for Darjeeling tea on the wholesaler's invoice was $348.88, how many kilos did Milford purchase?

6. The Wiggins Piece Goods Company has remnants with which it wants to make cosmetic cases. The remnant lengths measure 3.375 meters, 2.5 meters, 6.275 meters, and 2.2 meters each. If each cosmetic case needs 1.25 meters, how many cases can be made from the remnants?

UNIT

DIVIDING BY 10, 100, AND 1,000

Case Problem Mr. Benjamin Spanswick, a contractor, purchases concrete building blocks in *lots* (or quantities) of 100. On a recent order, Mr. Spanswick purchased 475 blocks at a price of $31 per 100.

Discussion Questions
1. What does $31 per 100 mean?
2. What other expressions are used to indicate that prices are quoted in quantity?
3. How can we make such computations easy to do?

You should learn the following business abbreviations:

Per C means "by the hundred" (in Roman numbers, C = 100).

Per M means "by the thousand" (in Roman numbers, M = 1,000).

Per cwt measures "by the hundredweight."

The prices of many articles are given in lots of 10, 100, 1,000. Wire is often sold in 100-foot lengths. Meat for supermarkets is bought by the hundredweight. Advertising circulars are purchased in lots of 1,000. Stock is generally traded in round lots of 100 shares.

Before we can find the cost in such cases, we must first translate the price given into a price per unit. To find the cost of one unit when the price quoted is 475 blocks at $31 per 100 (or $31 per C), we must first find out how many hundreds of blocks are contained in 475. Divide 475 by 100 to get 4.75.

We will show you how to compute the cost of the blocks a little later. First, let's see how shortcuts can be used when dividing by 10, 100, 1,000.

DIVIDING BY 10

To divide a number by 10, move the decimal point in the dividend one place to the left. If no decimal point appears in a number, its position is at the right of the number; that is, a decimal point is understood at the end of any whole number.

Example 1:

Divide 5,830 by 10.

Solution:

Move the decimal point in the dividend (5,830) one place to the left.

5 8 3 0 .

The quotient is 583. (Since no decimal point appears in the number, its position is at the end of the number.)

Example 2:

Divide $4,240 by 10.

Solution:

Move the decimal point in the dividend one place to the left.

$ 4 2 4 0 .

The quotient is $424.

DIVIDING BY 100

To divide by 100, move the decimal point in the dividend two places to the left.

Example 1:
Divide 5,830 by 100.

Solution:
Move the decimal point in the dividend two places to the left.

5 8 3 0 .

The quotient is 58.30, or 58.3.

Example 2:
Divide $4,240 by 100.

Solution:
Move the decimal point in the dividend two places to the left.

$ 4 2 4 0 .

The quotient is $42.40.

DIVIDING BY 1,000

To divide by 1,000, move the decimal point in the dividend three places to the left.

Example 1:
Divide 5,830 by 1,000.

Solution:
5 8 3 0 .

The quotient is 5.83.

Example 2:
Divide $4,240 by 1,000.

Solution:
$ 4 2 4 0 .

The quotient is $4.24.

COMPUTING THE COST OF ITEMS SOLD IN QUANTITIES

In order for Mr. Spanswick in the problem on page 99 to find the cost of 475 building blocks at a price of $31 per C (100), he would proceed as follows:

1. Divide the quantity of building blocks by 100 in order to find the number of hundreds in the quantity.

$$475 \div 100 = 4.75 \quad \text{(To divide by 100, move the decimal point two places to the left.)}$$

2. Multiply the quotient by the unit price.

$$4.75 \times \$31 = \$147.25, \text{ cost of building blocks}$$

Computing the Cost of Items Sold By the Ton

Some products, such as coal, are sold by the ton (2,000 pounds). To find the cost of an item priced by the ton, proceed as follows:

1. Divide the weight by 2,000 to find the number of tons.
2. Multiply the product by the price per ton.

Example:
Find the cost of 5,000 pounds of chemical fertilizer at $80 a ton.

Solution:
$5,000 \div 2,000 = 2.5$ tons
$2.5 \times \$80 = \$200$, cost

Exercises

1. Divide the following, using the shortcuts you have learned.

   a. $720 \div 10$ b. $638 \div 10$

   c. $976 \div 10$ d. $1,520 \div 10$

   e. $\$882 \div 10$ f. $\$9,240 \div 10$

   g. $\$9,240 \div 100$ h. $\$9,240 \div 1,000$

   i. $32,225 \div 1,000$ j. $\$126,400 \div 100$

   k. $\$87,325 \div 100$ l. $\$495,360 \div 10$

2. Prepare the following for multiplication. You do not have to do the final multiplication itself; just show what numbers you would multiply to arrive at an answer.

   a. 12,750 @ $2.95 per C
   b. 8,200 @ $1.50 per M
   c. 675 @ $3.00 per cwt
   d. 840 @ $2.00 per M
   e. 67 @ $1.95 per C
   f. 50 @ $5.99 per M

   Note: More practice in using measurements (both the English and metric) will be found in Chapter 8.

Business Applications

1. Find the cost of each of the following purchases.
   a. 4,000 articles @ $3.45 per 100
   b. 6,300 articles @ $4.27 per C
   c. 8,000 articles @ $52.25 per 1,000
   d. 4,800 pounds @ $61.90 per cwt.
   e. 7,500 envelopes @ $4.75 per M
   f. 640 pounds @ $1.84 per cwt.
   g. 925 pamphlets @ $2.58 per 100
   h. $6,250 insurance @ 28 cents per $1,000
   i. $575 baggage insurance @ 55 cents per $100
   j. 7,845 pounds @ 69 cents per 1,000 pounds

2. Compute the selling price for the quantities of lumber in the table below.

Quantity in Board Feet	Kind	Price per M	Amount
8,640	Flooring, No. 1	$135	$ _____
6,860	Siding	$ 95	_____
12,600	Floor timbers	$115	_____
6,530	Flooring, No. 2	$ 93	_____
3,750	Scantlings	$107	_____
9,500	Sheathing boards	$ 89	_____
		Total	$ _____

3. Find the cost of business forms on the following section of a purchase order.

No. of Pads	Description	Cost per M	Amount
2,000	Form 523	$ 86.15	$ _____
4,200	Form 437	$ 92.70	_____
3,420	Form 685	$104.85	_____
9,750	Form 126	$ 76.08	_____
12,000	Form 75	$ 53.92	_____
10,500	Form 346	$126.44	_____
		Total	$ _____

4. Purchases of sugar were made at prices that varied slightly during September. Find the total cost of sugar purchased during the month.

Date	Quantity in Kilograms	Cost per 100 Kilograms	Amount
9/5	400	$15.69	$ _____
9/12	720	$15.72	_____
9/17	635	$15.75	_____
9/26	875	$15.70	_____
		Total	$ _____

UNIT 5

COMPUTING AVERAGES

Many computations in business deal with averages—average daily sales, average monthly advertising expenses, average number of miles traveled per hour, and so on.

SIMPLE AVERAGES

To find an average for a set of numbers, do the following:
1. Find the sum of all the items.
2. Divide the sum by the number of items.

Example 1:

During a recent 5-day week, Marie Cotton worked the following hours: Monday, 10; Tuesday, 8; Wednesday, 10; Thursday, 9; Friday, 8. What is the average number of hours Miss Cotton worked each day?

Solution:

1. Find the total hours worked during the week:

$$10 + 8 + 10 + 9 + 8 = 45$$

2. Divide the total hours worked by the number of days:

$$45 \div 5 = 9, \text{ average number of hours worked in a day}$$

Example 2:

The 16 typists in the Mercury Insurance Company word-processing center typed a total of 352 letters during a recent day. How many letters did the average typist produce?

Solution:

Divide 352 (number of letters produced by all typists) by 16 (number of typists):

$$\frac{22}{16)\overline{352}}$$

The average typist produced 22 letters that day.

Exercises

Find the average for each of the following sets of numbers.

1. 36, 42, 38, 40, 34
2. 76, 82, 77, 69, 78, 80
3. 136, 140, 156, 144, 146, 140, 142, 148
4. $562, $593, $644, $608, $528, $581
5. 26.9, 14.6, 12.7, 18.4, 32.7, 16.3
6. 16.1, 18.275, 17.46, 15.3, 19.737

WEIGHTED AVERAGES

Mary Simmons purchased shoes during the year as follows:

> 3 pairs @ $25
> 1 pair @ $13

What was the average cost per pair of shoes?

If we add $25 and $13 and divide by 2, we find that the average cost is $19. ($25 + $13 = $38, ÷ 2 = $19). However, since Mary has purchased more shoes at the higher price, $19 does not give the true picture of her shoe expense. If we say she bought four pairs of shoes at an average of $19 per pair, it would seem that her actual expenditure was $76 (4 × $19). The truth is that her actual expenditure was $88.

> 3 pairs @ $25 = $75
> 1 pair @ $13 = 13
> ――――――――――――――――――――
> 4 pairs $88

Computing the average in this way makes the average price per pair $22 ($88 ÷ 4).

Where there are different numbers of items involved at each amount, we give each amount importance, or weight, in accordance with its numbers by finding a *weighted average*.

Example:
John Dunne makes radio repairs. During one week he repairs 12 radios. To repair six of the radios he spent three hours on each, on four of the radios he spent two hours each, and on the other two he spent one hour each. What was the average time spent on each repair?

Solution:

6 radios @ 3 hours	=	18 hours
4 radios @ 2 hours	=	8 hours
2 radios @ 1 hour	=	2 hours
12		28 hours

$28 \div 12 = 2\frac{1}{3}$ hours, weighted average

Exercises

1. A jeweler had 16 diamonds. Five of them were 2 carats each, eight were $1\frac{1}{2}$ carats each, and three were one-carat. What was the average weight of the diamonds?

2. Martha Adams has a part-time job. On eight days during one month she worked 4 hours a day, on nine days she worked 3 hours, and on three days she worked only 2 hours. What was the average number of hours she spent on the job each day during this month?

Business Applications

1. Nine factory workers produced the following units during a recent week: 135, 187, 86, 57, 203, 153, 126, 144, 115. (a) What was the total number of units produced during the week? (b) What was the average number of items produced per worker?

2. Larry Hinman, a sales representative, earned the following commissions during the first six months of last year: January, $612; February, $560; March, $857; April, $472; May, $708; June, $895.
   a. What were the total commissions earned during the period?
   b. What was the average amount in commissions earned each month?

3. The Wilton Automotive Supply Company publishes a weekly magazine for its 653 employees. The cost of publishing the magazine for the month of August was as follows:

First week $1,474
Second week $1,212
Third week $1,378
Fourth week $1,160

a. What is the average weekly cost of publishing the magazine?

b. What is the average weekly cost per employee?

4. Mr. B. J. Hartman, the president of National Appliances, has learned that the average sales representative of Master Appliances, a competitor, earns $18,000 a year in commissions. He wants to find out how the earnings of his representatives compare with this amount. Mr. Hartman employs 18 representatives and during the past year paid them a total of $288,000 in commissions.

    a. Which company paid its average representative the higher commission?

    b. By how much?

5. The space occupied by various departments in the Blake Insurance Company is shown below. Find the average amount of space occupied by an employee in each of the six departments.

Department	Total Space Occupied Sq Ft	Number of Employees	Average Sq Ft Per Employee
Sales	2,775	15	_____
Records	3,620	20	_____
Adjustments	1,880	10	_____
Accounts	6,586	37	_____
Underwriting	4,941	27	_____
Data Processing	2,280	12	_____

6. Agatha Malm, supervisor of the word-processing department of Hallway Printing Company, wanted to find out how many pages of work the average typist in her department produces. She decided to keep a record for a two-week period. Here is the information she gathered.

Typist	First Week	Second Week
Gordon	206	208
Phipps	180	188
Porter	176	180
Stanislaus	190	178
Tomas	200	200
Zecchi	170	180

a. What was the average number of pages produced by all employees during the first week?
b. During the second week?
c. What was the average for the two-week period?
d. Assuming a five-day week, what was the average number of pages produced each day for the two-week period?

7. Phyllis Lepofsky is Chairwoman of the Community Chest Fund drive for Paulson's, Incorporated. At the end of the drive, Phyllis prepared a report of all contributions. The department that had the highest average contribution per employee was to receive a handsome wall plaque. Complete the report, and answer the following questions:
a. What was the average employee contribution in each department?
b. Which department won the plaque?
c. What was the total amount received in contributions?
d. What was the average contribution of all employees?

Department	Amount of Contributions	Number of Contributors	Average Contribution
Office Services	$ 759.90	85	$ _____
Accounting	683.76	44	_____
Production	903.04	166	_____
Sales	432.12	78	_____
Art and Design	515.37	41	_____
Warehouse/Shipping	287.00	14	_____
Personnel	64.98	9	_____
Totals	$ _____	_____	$ _____

8. Mark Ogilvie, a traveling sales representative, kept the following records on a recent five-day automobile trip. His daily mileage was 269, 280, 195, 140, 275. He bought and used gasoline each day as follows: 16 gallons, 15.4 gallons, 15.9 gallons, 11.3 gallons, 12.7 gallons.
a. What was his average mileage?
b. How many miles per gallon does his car average?

9. During last month a wholesaler bought flour at the following prices:

      100 bags @ $5.75 per bag
      200 bags @ $6.00 per bag
      300 bags @ $5.85 per bag
      400 bags @ $6.30 per bag

What was the weighted average cost per bag?

10. The owner of a fleet of trucks kept the following records on gas consumption.

Number of Trucks	Miles per Gallon
10	10.2
6	9.6
5	9.8
4	10.7

What was the weighted average mileage for his fleet of trucks?

REVIEW EXERCISES FOR CHAPTER 5

1. Divide.
   a. 672 ÷ 3
   b. 875 ÷ 7
   c. 176 ÷ 8
   d. 175 ÷ 25
   e. 2,316 ÷ 4
   f. 9,456 ÷ 8
   g. 7,855 ÷ 5
   h. 8,644 ÷ 4
   i. 67,486 ÷ 9
   j. 39,039 ÷ 13
   k. 6,975 ÷ 75
   l. 27,810 ÷ 54

2. Divide and verify your work by multiplying the quotient by the divisor and then adding the remainder.
   a. 984 ÷ 3
   b. 2,185 ÷ 5
   c. 996 ÷ 4
   d. 3,768 ÷ 6
   e. 4,840 ÷ 24
   f. 6,902 ÷ 17
   g. 18,612 ÷ 36
   h. 14,628 ÷ 46
   i. 24,076 ÷ 52
   j. 34,170 ÷ 85
   k. 73,954 ÷ 6
   l. 765,947 ÷ 8

3. Divide until there is no remainder.
   a. 63.84 ÷ 84
   b. 1.968 ÷ .06
   c. 2.548 ÷ .049
   d. .4134 ÷ 5.3
   e. 5.9784 ÷ 1.06
   f. 75.71 ÷ 6.7
   g. 58 ÷ .08
   h. 8.45 ÷ .26

4. Divide, using the shortcuts you have learned.
   a. 970 ÷ 10
   b. 835 ÷ 10
   c. 6,550 ÷ 100
   d. 1,872 ÷ 100
   e. $46.60 ÷ 10
   f. $372.40 ÷ 100
   g. $4,440 ÷ 100
   h. $54,555 ÷ 1,000

5. Find the cost of each of the following:
   a. 2,750 sheets of cardboard @ $3.00 per C
   b. 16,500 envelopes @ $2.50 per M
   c. 9,650 lbs. @ $1.80 per ton
   d. 380 lbs. @ $4.90 per cwt
   e. 880 circulars @ $1.50 per M

6. Compute averages for the following.
   a. 66, 74, 50, 74, 58, 62
   b. 159, 127, 131, 145, 167, 196, 188
   c. $3.93, $3.11, $3.81, $3.82, $3.47, $3.66, $3.07, $3.29
   d. $141.60, $139.95, $161.38, $172.42, $157.90
   e. 9,807; 7,635; 11,226; 8,841; 10,007

7. The payroll of the Excelsior Company for the last six months of the past year was as follows:

July	$36,220
August	$39,385
September	$42,600
October	$41,855
November	$40,944
December	$46,190

   What was the average monthly payroll? Verify the accuracy of your work.

8. Transportation expenses of various departments in the Raytown Sporting Goods Corporation for a three-month period were as follows:

Field sales	$655
Market research	$385
Direct-mail promotion	$474
Space advertising	$282
Market services	$394

   a. What was the total cost of transportation for all departments for the three-month period?
   b. What was the average cost of transportation for all departments for the period?
   c. What was the average cost per month for transportation?
   d. Verify the accuracy of each answer.

9. A private school has an enrollment of 240 students. The expenses of operating the school during the past year were as follows: instruction, $114,770; materials, $26,870; supplies, $7,320; building maintenance, $6,080; miscellaneous expenses, $6,960.
   a. What were the total expenses for the year?
   b. What is the average cost per student of operating the school for a year?
   c. What is the average monthly cost of operation?
   d. Verify the accuracy of each answer.

10. The sales of the six retail stores of the Red Dragon Merchandising Company for the past two years are shown on the next page.

Store	19X4	19X5
Cushing	$120,300	$146,420
Drumright	$ 88,140	$ 92,774
Easton	$ 96,984	$104,276
Fairfax	$237,774	$234,628
Guthrie	$174,666	$187,902
Shawnee	$299,436	$346,448

a. What were the average yearly sales of all stores for each of the two years?

b. What were the average yearly sales of each store during the two-year period?

c. What were the average monthly sales each year for all stores?

d. Verify the accuracy of each answer.

11. Silver Electronics Corporation had sales income and expenses during a three-year period as tabulated below. From these figures, answer the president's question to the chief accountant: "What were our average annual sales and what were our average expenses during the past three years?"

	First Year	Second Year	Third Year	Total	Average
Sales Income	$46,585	$52,870	$68,017	$ _____	$ _____
Expenses	$38,684	$43,444	$53,385	$ _____	$ _____

12. The costs of operating the Tillman Company employee cafeteria for a six-month period were as follows:

March	$3,871.40	June	$5,763.77
April	$2,979.86	July	$3,470.05
May	$4,201.12	August	$2,643.40

a. What was the average cost per month?

b. If the Tillman Company collected money from employees for food they had purchased at the cafeteria in the amount of $15,465.30, what was the net cost to the company of operating the cafeteria for the six-month period? (The net cost is the difference between the total cost and the amount returned in sales.)

c. What was the average net cost per month to the company?

13. Judy Leeson, a sales representative, drives her car to call on customers. For each mile she drives, the company reimburses her 10¢. In addition, the company pays for parking and tolls.

    During the past year, Miss Leeson drove 11,472 miles. Parking and tolls for the year amounted to $787.44.

    a. How much did it cost the company for Miss Leeson's automobile expenses for the year?

    b. What was the average cost to the company each month?

14. A factory kept records on the number of articles spoiled by each of its workers during the course of a week.

Number of Workers	Spoiled Articles per Worker
14	5
16	6
17	7
3	8

What is the weighted average number of spoiled articles for the week?

CHAPTER 6
SKILLS
WITH FRACTIONS

Too many people who had trouble with fractions when they first learned them said, "Thank goodness that's over" and promptly tried to forget them. Business people and consumers can't afford to forget fractions. The reason, of course, is that we don't always deal in whole numbers. For example, we use fractions in laying carpet, building a sidewalk, or making a bookcase. The homemaker uses fractions in sewing, cooking, decorating, and shopping. The business person uses fractions in producing goods, in buying, pricing, selling, warehousing, shipping, borrowing, and lending. You won't be able to get away from them. As a future employer or employee in a business or government enterprise—and as a consumer—you'll need to know how to add, subtract, multiply, and divide fractions and to perform other computations dealing with fractional parts. In this chapter, you'll be given an opportunity to refresh your knowledge and sharpen your skills.

UNIT

UNDERSTANDING FRACTIONS

THE MEANING OF COMMON FRACTIONS

As you know, expressions of measure and quantity—pound, dozen, foot, mile, gallon, and so on—are called units. A complete unit is expressed as a whole number: 1 dozen oranges, 1 gallon of oil, 1 yard of cloth, and so on. When a single unit is divided into equal parts, each part is expressed as a fraction. A *fraction*, then, is a part of a whole. For example:

1. There are 12 oranges in 1 dozen. A dozen can be expressed as the fraction $\frac{12}{12}$, which has the same value as the whole number 1. The bottom "12" represents the number of parts in the whole unit; the top number represents how many parts of a unit are called for. Thus, 6 oranges can be expressed as $\frac{6}{12}$ of a dozen or $\frac{1}{2}$ dozen.

2. There are four quarts to a gallon. One gallon is equal to the fraction $\frac{4}{4}$, and 3 quarts would be expressed as $\frac{3}{4}$ gallon.

3. If there are 9 employees in a shop and 3 are women, you can say that $\frac{3}{9}$, or $\frac{1}{3}$, of the employees are women.

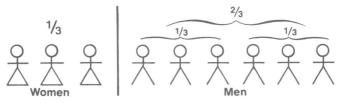

The number below the line in a fraction is called the *denominator*. The number above the line in a fraction is called the *numerator*. Thus, in the fraction $\frac{2}{3}$, 2 is the numerator and 3 is the denominator. The numerator and denominator together make up the *terms* of the fraction. The line between them indicates division.

In the previous unit we learned about decimals, which represent parts of units and are a type of fraction called decimal fractions. The fractions we will work with in this unit, which are expressed by a numerator and a denominator, are known as *common fractions*.

PROPER FRACTIONS

Fractions that express amounts less than one whole unit are called *proper fractions*. In a proper fraction, the numerator is always less than the denominator. The following are proper fractions:

$$\frac{5}{6} \qquad \frac{1}{2} \qquad \frac{3}{4} \qquad \frac{7}{8}$$

IMPROPER FRACTIONS

Often it is necessary to work with fractions in which the numerator is equal to or greater than the denominator. This means that the value of the fraction is equal to or greater than one whole unit. Such fractions are called *improper fractions*. Examples of improper fractions are the following:

$$\frac{5}{5} \qquad \frac{8}{3} \qquad \frac{9}{7} \qquad \frac{15}{13}$$

MIXED NUMBERS

Sometimes you will work with a *mixed number*—that is, a whole number and a fraction. The following are mixed numbers:

$$3\frac{1}{4} \qquad 6\frac{1}{2} \qquad 19\frac{7}{8} \qquad 16\frac{2}{3}$$

TWO FUNDAMENTAL RULES

In working with fractions, it is important for you to understand two rules:
1. The value of a fraction is not changed by multiplying both the numerator and denominator by the same number. The reason for this is simple. If we multiply both the numerator and the denominator by the same number (let's say 2), what we are doing is multiplying $\frac{1}{2} \times \frac{2}{2}$. But, the fraction $\frac{2}{2}$ (or two halves) is equal to one, and multiplying a number by one does not change the value of the number. To complete the problem, $\frac{1}{2} \times \frac{2}{2} = \frac{2}{4}$, which is the same as $\frac{1}{2}$.
2. The value of a fraction is not changed by dividing both the numerator and the denominator by the same number. The reasoning is the same as above.

If we divide each part of the fraction by 3, we are dividing the whole fraction by $\frac{3}{3}$ which is the same as one. Again, this does not change the fraction's value. Thus, when you divide the numerator and the denominator in the fraction $\frac{9}{12}$ by 3, you have the fraction $\frac{3}{4}$. The fraction $\frac{3}{4}$ and the fraction $\frac{9}{12}$ have the same value.

Exercises

1. Identify the following as a proper fraction, an improper fraction or a mixed number.

a. $\frac{3}{4}$ **b.** $\frac{7}{8}$ **c.** $\frac{9}{16}$ **d.** $\frac{5}{3}$ **e.** $\frac{4}{4}$ **f.** $\frac{7}{5}$

g. $\frac{2}{3}$ **h.** $1\frac{1}{2}$ **i.** $93\frac{1}{8}$ **j.** $\frac{12}{11}$ **k.** $\frac{11}{12}$ **l.** $3\frac{31}{45}$

2. Express the following as fractions of a gallon.
   a. 1 quart of milk
   b. 3 quarts of oil
   c. 2 quarts of grape juice

3. Express the following as fractions of a dozen.
   a. 6 eggs
   b. 9 ball-point pens
   c. 3 oranges
   d. 4 writing pads
   e. 2 tennis balls

4. Express the following as fractions of a five-day work week.
   a. 5 days
   b. 3 days
   c. 1 day

5. Indicate whether each of the following statements is true or false.
   a. The number above the line in a fraction is called the numerator.
   b. $\frac{3}{3}$ is a proper fraction.
   c. In a proper fraction, the numerator is always less than the denominator.
   d. In a committee made up of 6 members, 3 were absent from the December meeting. Therefore, $\frac{1}{2}$ of the members were absent.

6. In each of the following shapes, indicate what fractional part the shaded area represents of the whole.

a.

b.

c.

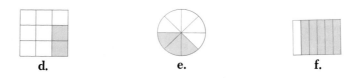

d.   e.   f.

CHANGING AN IMPROPER FRACTION TO A WHOLE OR MIXED NUMBER

An improper fraction is one in which the numerator is equal to or greater than the denominator—$\frac{8}{8}$, $\frac{7}{3}$, $\frac{12}{11}$. Often it is easier to work with such a fraction if it is changed to a whole number or a mixed number.

To change an improper fraction to a whole or a mixed number, *divide the numerator by the denominator.* Any remainder becomes the numerator of a fraction that has the same denominator as the original improper fraction.

What we are accomplishing here is dividing the improper fraction in two parts—the full units (or whole number), and the fractional part of any additional unit. If you were to picture an improper fraction such as $\frac{5}{3}$, it might look like this.

$\frac{3}{3}$ + $\frac{2}{3}$ = $\frac{5}{3}$

Thus, the fraction $\frac{5}{3}$ consists of two fractions—$\frac{3}{3}$ which equals 1 and $\frac{2}{3}$ left over, or a total of $1\frac{2}{3}$.

Example 1:
Change the improper fraction $\frac{8}{8}$ to a whole or mixed number.

Solution:
$\frac{8}{8} = 8 \div 8 = 1$ We divided the numerator (8) by the denominator (8).

Example 2:
Change the improper fraction $\frac{8}{4}$ to a whole or mixed number.

Solution:
$\frac{8}{4} = 8 \div 4 = 2$

Example 3:
Change the improper fraction $\frac{17}{7}$ to a whole or mixed number.

Solution:
$\frac{17}{7} = 17 \div 7 = 2, + 3$ (remainder) $= 2\frac{3}{7}$

Exercises

Change each of the following fractions to whole or mixed numbers.

1. $\frac{24}{3}$ **2.** $\frac{8}{5}$ **3.** $\frac{21}{7}$ **4.** $\frac{28}{9}$ **5.** $\frac{16}{5}$

6. $\frac{58}{9}$ **7.** $\frac{11}{7}$ **8.** $\frac{60}{20}$ **9.** $\frac{56}{6}$ **10.** $\frac{69}{7}$

CHANGING A MIXED NUMBER TO AN IMPROPER FRACTION

When you perform certain operations with fractions, it is often necessary to change a mixed number to an improper fraction. To change a mixed number to an improper fraction do the following:

1. Multiply the whole number by the denominator of the fraction.
2. Add the numerator to the product.
3. Make the result of Step 2 the numerator of a fraction that has the same denominator as the fractional part of the mixed number.

$$\text{Whole No. } \frac{\text{Num.}}{\text{Denom.}} = \frac{\text{Whole No.} \times \text{Orig. Denom.} + \text{Orig. Num.}}{\text{Original Denominator}}$$

Example:

Change the mixed number $5\frac{2}{3}$ to an improper fraction.

Solution:

1. $5 \times 3 = 15$ (whole number $\times$ denominator of fraction)
2. $+2$ (add numerator to product)
3. $\frac{17}{3}$ (improper fraction with same denominator as fractional part of mixed number)

Exercises

Change the following mixed numbers to improper fractions.

1. $7\frac{1}{2}$ **2.** $6\frac{2}{3}$ **3.** $14\frac{4}{5}$

4. $9\frac{7}{16}$ **5.** $7\frac{9}{16}$ **6.** $12\frac{2}{3}$

7. $9\frac{7}{8}$ **8.** $16\frac{3}{7}$ **9.** $20\frac{5}{8}$

10. $8\frac{5}{6}$ **11.** $5\frac{3}{4}$ **12.** $33\frac{1}{3}$

13. $67\frac{11}{12}$ **14.** $102\frac{5}{8}$ **15.** $23\frac{11}{12}$

RENAMING A FRACTION IN SIMPLEST TERMS

A fraction is often easier to work with when it is renamed in its simplest terms. A fraction is renamed in simplest terms by dividing both the numerator and denominator by the largest whole number that will divide both without a remainder. This procedure does not change the value of the fraction.

Example 1:
Rename the fraction $\frac{9}{12}$ in its simplest terms.

Solution:
Find the largest whole number that will divide into both 9 and 12 with no remainder. That number is 3.

$$\frac{9 \div 3 = 3}{12 \div 3 = 4}$$

The fraction $\frac{3}{4}$ is the fraction $\frac{9}{12}$ renamed in simplest terms.

Example 2:
Rename $\frac{15}{20}$ in simplest terms.

Solution:
The largest whole number that will divide into both 15 and 20 with no remainder is 5.

$$\frac{15 \div 5 = 3}{20 \div 5 = 4}$$

The fraction $\frac{3}{4}$ is the fraction $\frac{15}{20}$ renamed in simplest terms.

Example 3:
Rename $\frac{12}{32}$ in simplest terms.

Solution:
The largest whole number that will divide into both 12 and 32 with no remainder is 4.

$$\frac{12 \div 4 = 3}{32 \div 4 = 8}$$

The fraction $\frac{3}{8}$ is the fraction $\frac{12}{32}$ renamed in simplest terms.

Exercises
Rename the following fractions in their simplest terms.

1. $\frac{3}{9}$ 2. $\frac{9}{18}$ 3. $\frac{12}{16}$ 4. $\frac{5}{10}$

5. $\frac{12}{18}$ 6. $\frac{9}{15}$ 7. $\frac{6}{14}$ 8. $\frac{14}{21}$

9. $\frac{12}{20}$ 10. $\frac{12}{30}$ 11. $\frac{10}{16}$ 12. $\frac{12}{32}$

13. $\frac{30}{50}$ 14. $\frac{16}{40}$ 15. $\frac{15}{45}$ 16. $\frac{36}{48}$

17. $\frac{40}{72}$ 18. $\frac{20}{36}$ 19. $\frac{75}{90}$ 20. $\frac{24}{56}$

RENAMING A FRACTION IN HIGHER TERMS

Often it is necessary to rename a fraction in higher terms in order to add, subtract, etc. (Remember that the renamed fraction has the same value as the original fraction.)

If you are dealing with sixteenths, for instance, you may need to be able to express the fraction $\frac{1}{4}$ in terms of sixteenths, that is, to know how many sixteenths are contained in $\frac{1}{4}$.

To change the fraction $\frac{1}{4}$ to an equivalent fraction with a denominator of 16, proceed as follows:

1. Divide the new denominator 16 by the old denominator 4. The quotient is 4.
2. Multiply the quotient 4 by both the old numerator 1 and the old denominator 4. Thus,

$$\frac{1 \times 4}{4 \times 4} = \frac{4}{16}$$

Example 1:

Change the fraction $\frac{7}{8}$ to an equivalent fraction having a denominator of 72.

Solution:

$$\frac{7}{8} = \frac{?}{72}$$

$$72 \div 8 = 9$$

$$\frac{7 \times 9}{8 \times 9} = \frac{63}{72}$$

$$\frac{7}{8} = \frac{63}{72}$$

Example 2:

Change the fraction $\frac{2}{9}$ to an equivalent fraction having a denominator of 45.

Solution:

$$\frac{2}{9} = \frac{?}{45}$$

$$45 \div 9 = 5$$

$$\frac{2 \times 5}{9 \times 5} = \frac{10}{45}$$

$$\frac{2}{9} = \frac{10}{45}$$

Exercises

Change each of the following fractions to an equivalent fraction by finding the numerator of the new fraction.

1. $\frac{3}{4} = \frac{}{48}$ 2. $\frac{1}{6} = \frac{}{78}$ 3. $\frac{5}{8} = \frac{}{56}$

4. $\frac{4}{5} = \frac{}{65}$ 5. $\frac{5}{6} = \frac{}{42}$ 6. $\frac{8}{9} = \frac{}{27}$

7. $\frac{11}{12} = \frac{}{84}$ 8. $\frac{9}{10} = \frac{}{90}$ 9. $\frac{5}{9} = \frac{}{36}$

10. $\frac{7}{12} = \frac{}{96}$ 11. $\frac{3}{16} = \frac{}{48}$ 12. $\frac{2}{3} = \frac{}{54}$

13. $\frac{6}{7} = \frac{}{21}$ 14. $\frac{2}{9} = \frac{}{45}$ 15. $\frac{7}{8} = \frac{}{72}$

16. $\frac{7}{15} = \frac{}{75}$ 17. $\frac{9}{16} = \frac{}{96}$ 18. $\frac{17}{24} = \frac{}{144}$

FRACTIONS AND DECIMALS

We now know two ways of expressing parts of a whole—common fractions and decimal fractions. Since these are two ways of saying the same thing, we must be able to convert easily from one to the other.

CHANGING FRACTIONS TO DECIMALS

The fraction $\frac{1}{2}$ means that we are dividing a unit into two parts. It can therefore be expressed as $1 \div 2$.

$$2\overline{)1.0}^{\ \ .5}$$

Doing this simple division, we get an answer of .5. Therefore, $\frac{1}{2}$ equals .5.

Example:

Express the fraction $\frac{3}{4}$ as a decimal.

Solution:

$$\frac{3}{4} = 3 \div 4 = 4\overline{)3.00}^{\ \ .75}$$

The answer is .75.

Converting common fractions to decimal fractions has two very important uses. (1) If you must perform any mathematical operations with fractions on a calculating machine, you must convert all fractions to decimals before entering them in the machine. (2) Many people find it easier to perform the basic operations with decimal fractions rather than with common fractions. They routinely convert to decimal fractions before making computations, and, if necessary, convert answers back to common fractions.

Exercises

Convert the following fractions into decimals. (If your answer does not come out even, carry it to three decimal places.)

1. $\frac{1}{4}$ 2. $\frac{5}{8}$

3. $\frac{9}{16}$ 4. $\frac{2}{3}$

5. $\frac{3}{5}$ 6. $\frac{7}{12}$

7. $\frac{11}{15}$ 8. $\frac{13}{20}$

9. $\frac{19}{50}$ 10. $\frac{14}{23}$

CHANGING DECIMALS TO FRACTIONS

A decimal can be converted to a fraction simply by writing it as a fraction and then renaming it in simplest terms. Look at these examples:

$$.5 = \frac{5}{10} = \frac{1}{2} \qquad .75 = \frac{75}{100} = \frac{3}{4} \qquad .375 = \frac{375}{1000} = \frac{3}{8}$$

Sometimes the fraction is already in simplest terms. Thus, .51 equals $\frac{51}{100}$; you cannot simplify any further.

You will need a sharp eye and practice with numbers to be able to see quickly whether a fraction is in simplest terms or can be renamed.

Exercises

Convert the following decimals into fractions; rename all answers in simplest terms.

1. .6   2. .7

3. .29   4. .38

5. .16   6. .80

7. .125   8. .245

9. .69   10. .743

Business Applications

1. The Tree Supermarket threw away $\frac{4}{12}$ dozen orange trees because they were diseased. Express the fraction in simplest terms.

2. Manny's Meat Market bought 16 dozen eggs from a farmer. But before the eggs were placed on sale, 9 eggs had been broken. Express in simplest terms the fraction of a dozen that were broken.

3. In unpacking a carton of 48 writing pads, Mildred Amberson discovered that four pads were damaged. Express the damaged pads as a fraction of those in the carton; then rename the fraction in simplest terms.

4. In a shipment of 24 books, 6 had to be returned to the publisher because they were shipped in error. What fraction of the books were shipped in error? (Rename in simplest terms.)

5. Mr. Pavlick draws maps for a living. He gives his specifications in terms of sixteenths of an inch. How should he express these measurements?

   a. $\frac{3}{4}$ in.   **b.** $\frac{1}{2}$ in.   **c.** $\frac{3}{8}$ in.

UNIT

 ADDING FRACTIONS

ADDING PROPER FRACTIONS

We cannot add 5 apples and 6 oranges unless we find some common name for the sum that we will end up with. Since we can decide that they are both types of fruit, we can add them and say we have 11 pieces of fruit. Similarly, we cannot add fractions unless they have the same name, or value. This means that their denominators must be the same before we can add them. To add $\frac{2}{7}$, $\frac{1}{7}$, and $\frac{3}{7}$ (which all have the same denominators) simply add the numerators $2 + 1 + 3 = 6$. The sum of the fractions, then, is $\frac{6}{7}$.

When fractions that contain different denominators are to be added, however, you must change the fractions to equivalent fractions, all having the same denominator. This is done by finding a number into which all the denominators will divide without a remainder.

Example 1:
Add these fractions.

$$\frac{1}{3}$$
$$+\frac{1}{2}$$

Solution:
1. Find the smallest number that can be divided by the different denominators (this number is called the *lowest common denominator*). In the example, this number is 6—there is no lower number of which both 3 and 2 are exact divisors. Now the problem can be stated as follows.

$$\frac{1}{3} = \frac{?}{6}$$

$$+\frac{1}{2} = \frac{?}{6}$$

2. Rename the original fractions to numeric equivalent fractions with a denominator of 6.
   a. Divide the lowest common denominator, 6, by the denominators of the original fractions, 3 and 2.
   b. Multiply the numerators of the original fractions by the quotient of Step 1, thus renaming both original fractions to numeric equivalent fractions with a denominator of 6.

$$\frac{1 \times 2}{3 \times 2} = \frac{2}{6}$$

$$+\frac{1 \times 3}{2 \times 3} = \frac{3}{6}$$

3. Add the renamed fractions.

$$\frac{2}{6}$$

$$+\frac{3}{6}$$

$$\frac{5}{6}$$

Example 2:
Add the fractions $\frac{2}{5}$ and $\frac{15}{20}$.

Solution:
1. The smallest number that can be divided by the denominators 5 and 20 is 20.

$$\frac{2}{5} = \frac{?}{20}$$

$$+\frac{15}{20} = \frac{?}{20}$$

2. $20 \div 5 = 4$
   $20 \div 20 = 1$

   thus
   $$\frac{2 \times 4}{5 \times 4} = \frac{8}{20}$$

   $$+\frac{15 \times 1}{20 \times 1} = \frac{15}{20}$$

3. Add.

$$\begin{array}{r} \dfrac{8}{20} \\[6pt] +\dfrac{15}{20} \\[2pt] \hline \dfrac{23}{20} \end{array}$$

4. Change the improper fraction $\frac{23}{20}$ to a whole or mixed number.

$$23 \div 20 = 1\tfrac{3}{20}$$

Exercises

1. Add the following fractions.

a. $\frac{2}{5} + \frac{1}{5}$

b. $\frac{1}{8} + \frac{3}{8}$

c. $\frac{5}{12} + \frac{7}{12}$

d. $\frac{1}{8} + \frac{5}{8} + \frac{7}{8}$

e. $\frac{3}{10} + \frac{7}{10} + \frac{9}{10}$

f. $\frac{3}{16} + \frac{5}{16} + \frac{7}{16} + \frac{9}{16}$

g. $\frac{2}{3} + \frac{3}{4}$

h. $\frac{2}{5} + \frac{2}{3}$

i. $\frac{5}{9} + \frac{2}{3}$

j. $\frac{3}{8} + \frac{15}{16}$

k. $\frac{3}{4} + \frac{5}{6}$

l. $\frac{7}{8} + \frac{1}{6}$

2. Add the following.

a	b	c	d	e	f	g	h
$\frac{1}{2}$	$\frac{1}{2}$	$\frac{5}{6}$	$\frac{1}{6}$	$\frac{4}{5}$	$\frac{5}{6}$	$\frac{1}{2}$	$\frac{5}{9}$
$\frac{1}{3}$	$\frac{2}{3}$	$\frac{2}{3}$	$\frac{5}{8}$	$\frac{1}{4}$	$\frac{7}{8}$	$\frac{2}{7}$	$\frac{1}{3}$
$\frac{1}{4}$	$\frac{5}{6}$	$\frac{3}{4}$	$\frac{1}{3}$	$\frac{11}{12}$	$\frac{5}{12}$	$\frac{13}{14}$	$\frac{1}{6}$

i	j	k	l	m	n	o	p
$\frac{1}{4}$	$\frac{1}{2}$	$\frac{5}{8}$	$\frac{2}{3}$	$\frac{5}{6}$	$\frac{1}{7}$	$\frac{3}{5}$	$\frac{1}{9}$
$\frac{5}{6}$	$\frac{1}{3}$	$\frac{11}{16}$	$\frac{1}{2}$	$\frac{1}{3}$	$\frac{5}{8}$	$\frac{5}{12}$	$\frac{2}{3}$
$\frac{3}{8}$	$\frac{1}{4}$	$\frac{5}{6}$	$\frac{11}{12}$	$\frac{1}{8}$	$\frac{1}{2}$	$\frac{1}{4}$	$\frac{7}{8}$
$\frac{1}{2}$	$\frac{1}{6}$	$\frac{1}{2}$	$\frac{5}{8}$	$\frac{1}{4}$	$\frac{3}{4}$	$\frac{2}{15}$	$\frac{2}{3}$
				$\frac{11}{12}$	$\frac{3}{14}$	$\frac{5}{6}$	$\frac{7}{12}$

ADDING MIXED NUMBERS

Most fraction problems in business consist of mixed numbers—that is, a combination of a whole number and a fraction. The procedure for adding mixed numbers is as follows:

1. Add the whole numbers.
2. Add the proper fractions.
3. Find the sum of the two answers.

Example 1:

Find the sum of $5\frac{3}{4}$ and $9\frac{7}{8}$.

Solution:

$$5\frac{3}{4} = 5\frac{6}{8}$$
$$+9\frac{7}{8} = 9\frac{7}{8}$$
$$\overline{14\frac{13}{8}} = 14 + \frac{13}{8} = 14 + 1\frac{5}{8} = 15\frac{5}{8}$$

Explanation:

The two proper fractions $\frac{3}{4}$ and $\frac{7}{8}$ were first changed to eighths and then added, for a total of $\frac{13}{8}$. The sum of the whole numbers 5 and 9 is 14. But $14\frac{13}{8}$ represents $14 + \frac{13}{8}$. The value of the improper fraction $\frac{13}{8}$ is $1\frac{5}{8}$. When that number is added to 14, the sum will be $15\frac{5}{8}$.

Example 2:

Find the sum of $17\frac{1}{2}$, $23\frac{2}{3}$, and $15\frac{5}{6}$.

Solution:

$$17\frac{1}{2} = 17\frac{3}{6}$$
$$23\frac{2}{3} = 23\frac{4}{6}$$
$$+15\frac{5}{6} = 15\frac{5}{6}$$
$$\overline{55\frac{12}{6}} = 55 + \frac{12}{6} = 55 + 2 = 57$$

Explanation:

Again, the whole numbers were added separately, for a total of 55. The proper fractions were renamed as sixths and combined, for a total of $\frac{12}{6}$. The value (2) of $\frac{12}{6}$ was added to 55, for a total of 57.

Exercises

1. Add the following mixed numbers.

a. $5\frac{1}{4} + 4\frac{3}{4}$

b. $12\frac{2}{3} + 3\frac{4}{5}$

c. $27\frac{2}{3} + 14\frac{1}{2}$

d. $7\frac{2}{5} + 3\frac{4}{5}$

e. $14\frac{3}{4} + 12\frac{1}{2}$

f. $56\frac{3}{4} + 27\frac{5}{6}$

g. $3\frac{2}{3} + 5\frac{1}{2} + 7\frac{1}{6}$

h. $\frac{2}{3} + 12\frac{1}{2} + 7\frac{3}{4}$

i. $26\frac{5}{16} + 24\frac{7}{8} + 42\frac{3}{4}$

j. $6\frac{3}{4} + 7\frac{5}{8} + 2\frac{1}{2}$

k. $\frac{5}{6} + 6\frac{2}{3} + \frac{3}{4}$

l. $17\frac{5}{12} + 29\frac{3}{4} + 35\frac{2}{3}$

2. Add the following.

a.	b.	c.	d.
$72\frac{5}{6}$	$24\frac{1}{2}$	$46\frac{3}{4}$	$85\frac{2}{5}$
$76\frac{1}{2}$	$56\frac{2}{3}$	$27\frac{1}{2}$	$36\frac{2}{3}$
$35\frac{3}{4}$	$94\frac{1}{4}$	$54\frac{7}{8}$	$72\frac{5}{6}$
$29\frac{2}{3}$	$76\frac{11}{12}$	$68\frac{11}{12}$	$93\frac{9}{10}$

Business Applications

1. A fabric shop ran a special on Orlon material. In one hour the following number of yards were purchased from one bolt of goods: $5\frac{1}{2}$, 8, $4\frac{1}{3}$, $7\frac{3}{4}$, $9\frac{1}{2}$, $10\frac{2}{3}$, and 6. How much material was sold from the bolt in one hour?

2. James Cox built a rectangular mica-top table $38\frac{1}{2}$ inches long and $17\frac{5}{8}$ inches wide. How much metal edging must he buy to go around the table?

3. The top edges of the showcases at a department store were decorated with paper each Christmas. How many feet of paper would be needed to decorate five of the showcases in the children's wear department if the showcases were of the following lengths: $17\frac{1}{2}$ feet, $20\frac{1}{4}$ feet, 22 feet, $23\frac{1}{12}$ feet, $24\frac{5}{6}$ feet?

4. At the outset of each day, one of the butchers in the meat department of a large food store grinds a considerable supply of meat to be sold as chopped meat during the day. The following number of pounds of chopped meat were purchased one day between 10 a. m. and 11 a. m.: $\frac{3}{4}$, 3, $2\frac{1}{2}$, $1\frac{1}{4}$, $5\frac{1}{2}$, 2, $\frac{3}{16}$, 4, $\frac{9}{16}$, $1\frac{1}{2}$, 4. How many pounds of chopped meat were sold during that hour?

5. The material on hand in a section of the drapery materials department of the Sew-and-Save Fabrics Center as of December 31 is shown below.

Sew-and-Save Fabrics Center

Material _Drapery_ Line _Brocade_ Cost _$2.45 per yd._

Pattern	Quantity
Lotus	$47\frac{5}{8}$
Arabesque	92
Queen Bess	$72\frac{7}{8}$
Festival	$61\frac{1}{2}$
Shalimar	$88\frac{7}{8}$
Country Dance	$13\frac{3}{4}$

How many yards of material in the brocade line are on hand?

UNIT

3

SUBTRACTING FRACTIONS

SUBTRACTING PROPER FRACTIONS

In one basic principle, subtraction and addition of fractions are identical: Before either operation is performed, it is necessary to rename the fractions into numerically equivalent fractions that have a common denominator.

Example:

Subtract $\frac{3}{5}$ from $\frac{2}{3}$.

Solution:

1. Find the number into which the denominators 5 and 3 can be divided with no remainder. That number is 15.
2. Convert the fractions $\frac{2}{3}$ and $\frac{3}{5}$ into fractions having a denominator of 15.

$$\frac{2}{3} = \frac{10}{15}$$
$$-\frac{3}{5} = \frac{9}{15}$$

3. Subtract the numerators.

$$\frac{10}{15}$$
$$-\frac{9}{15}$$
$$\frac{1}{15}$$

Exercises

Subtract the following.

1. $\frac{5}{7} - \frac{2}{7}$ 2. $\frac{9}{16} - \frac{5}{16}$ 3. $\frac{5}{8} - \frac{3}{8}$

4. $\frac{3}{4} - \frac{1}{2}$ 5. $\frac{7}{8} - \frac{1}{4}$ 6. $\frac{9}{10} - \frac{3}{5}$

7. $\frac{5}{6} - \frac{5}{12}$ 8. $\frac{2}{3} - \frac{1}{6}$ 9. $\frac{5}{8} - \frac{1}{16}$

10. $\frac{2}{3} - \frac{1}{4}$ 11. $\frac{3}{4} - \frac{2}{3}$ 12. $\frac{5}{6} - \frac{3}{4}$

13. $\frac{5}{8} - \frac{1}{3}$ 14. $\frac{1}{2} - \frac{5}{12}$ 15. $\frac{11}{12} - \frac{3}{8}$

SUBTRACTING A MIXED NUMBER FROM A WHOLE NUMBER

Often it is necessary to subtract a mixed number (a number containing a whole number and a fraction) from a whole number. Follow the three basic steps on the next page.

1. Convert one unit of the minuend into an improper fraction with the same denominator as the fraction in the subtrahend.
2. Reduce the whole number in the minuend by one. (This unit is now in the form of a fraction, so that the total value of the minuend has not been changed.)
3. Subtract.

Example:
Subtract $8\frac{5}{6}$ from 43.

Solution:

$$43 \;=\; 42\frac{6}{6} \quad \text{(Remember that } 42\frac{6}{6} \text{ is equivalent to } 43.\text{)}$$
$$-8\frac{5}{6} = \; 8\frac{5}{6}$$
$$\overline{\phantom{-8\frac{5}{6}} \;\; 34\frac{1}{6}}$$

Exercises
Subtract the following.

1. $12 - 1\frac{1}{2}$ 2. $16 - 9\frac{3}{4}$ 3. $25 - 18\frac{2}{3}$
4. $21 - 15\frac{5}{6}$ 5. $17 - 2\frac{1}{3}$ 6. $29 - 4\frac{7}{8}$
7. $75 - 62\frac{1}{2}$ 8. $28 - 11\frac{13}{16}$ 9. $102 - 50\frac{7}{8}$
10. $277 - 169\frac{7}{8}$ 11. $100 - 9\frac{3}{4}$ 12. $111 - 88\frac{2}{3}$

Business Applications
1. A piece of wood $26\frac{5}{16}$ inches long was cut from a board 36 inches long. How long was the piece of wood that remained?
2. While making a dress, Claudia Lee cut a piece of material $15\frac{3}{4}$ inches wide from a piece that was $42\frac{1}{2}$ inches wide. How wide was the piece of material that remained?
3. Jack Seitz purchased a $2\frac{1}{2}$-pound sirloin steak at a meat market. On returning home, he cut out the bone and weighed it. If the weight of the bone was $\frac{9}{16}$ of a pound, how much actual meat did he purchase?
4. A carpenter had an 18-foot piece of lumber, from which he cut two pieces. One of these pieces was $5\frac{3}{4}$ feet long; the other was $2\frac{5}{12}$ feet long. If the widths of the saw cuts are ignored, how long was the piece that remained?
5. To make a canvas awning, three pieces of material, each $34\frac{3}{4}$ inches long are cut from a bolt of canvas on which 240 inches of material was originally rolled. How much canvas still remained on the bolt?
6. From a piece of broadloom carpeting 12 feet long and 9 feet wide,

two strips of carpeting, each 12 feet long, were cut to be used as runners. If the strips were $2\frac{5}{16}$ feet and $3\frac{1}{4}$ feet wide, respectively, how wide was the piece of carpeting that remained?

SUBTRACTING A MIXED NUMBER FROM A MIXED NUMBER

To subtract a mixed number from a mixed number, proceed as in the following example.

Example:
Subtract $15\frac{3}{4}$ and $22\frac{2}{3}$.

Solution:
1. Where necessary, rename the fractional parts of both the minuend and the subtrahend, so that they have a common denominator.

$$22\frac{2}{3} = 22\frac{8}{12}$$
$$-15\frac{3}{4} = 15\frac{9}{12}$$

2. If the fraction in the subtrahend is *smaller* than the fraction in the minuend, you can now subtract.

but

3. If the fraction in the subtrahend is *greater* than the fraction in the minuend—as it is in this example—do the following:
   a. Convert one unit of the minuend into an improper fraction with the correct denominator, and add this unit to the existing fraction in the minuend. In our example, take one unit from 22 to make $\frac{12}{12}$, and add $\frac{12}{12}$ to $\frac{8}{12}$, yielding $\frac{20}{12}$.
   b. Reduce the whole number in the minuend by one (the unit which is now a fraction). In our example, 22 would become 21.
   c. You are now in a position to subtract.

$$22\frac{2}{3} = 22\frac{8}{12} = 21\frac{20}{12}$$
$$-15\frac{3}{4} = 15\frac{9}{12} = 15\frac{9}{12}$$
$$6\frac{11}{12}$$

Exercises
Subtract the following.

1. $7\frac{3}{4} - 6\frac{1}{4}$
2. $17\frac{2}{3} - 16\frac{1}{3}$
3. $29\frac{5}{7} - 25\frac{3}{7}$
4. $15\frac{3}{4} - 7\frac{5}{8}$
5. $32\frac{2}{3} - 19\frac{2}{5}$
6. $50\frac{7}{8} - 32\frac{1}{4}$
7. $33\frac{1}{3} - 22\frac{1}{2}$
8. $16\frac{3}{5} - 14\frac{7}{8}$
9. $21\frac{4}{5} - 18\frac{7}{8}$
10. $245\frac{11}{16} - 138\frac{9}{16}$

UNIT

4

MULTIPLYING FRACTIONS

MULTIPLYING A WHOLE NUMBER BY A FRACTION

Suppose you were asked to multiply 6 by $\frac{2}{3}$. This is simply an arithmetic way of saying "What is $\frac{2}{3}$ of 6?" Since you are looking for a fractional part of 6, the answer must be less than 6. First you find *one*-third of 6 by dividing by 3. The answer is 2. If $\frac{1}{3}$ of 6 equals 2, then $\frac{2}{3}$ of 6 must equal 4. We can generalize this procedure so that you can multiply any whole number by a fraction; follow these steps:

1. Treat the whole number in the problem as a fraction with a denominator of one. $\left(6 = \dfrac{6}{1}. \text{ You can now rewrite the problem } \dfrac{6}{1} \times \dfrac{2}{3} \text{ or } \dfrac{6 \times 2}{1 \times 3}.\right)$

2. Multiply the numerators and make the product the numerator of the answer. $\left(\dfrac{6 \times 2}{1 \times 3} = \dfrac{12}{}\right)$

3. Multiply the denominators and make the product the denominator of the answer. $\left(\dfrac{6 \times 2}{1 \times 3} = \dfrac{12}{3}\right)$

4. Where the answer is an improper fraction, change this to a proper fraction or a mixed number. $\left(\dfrac{12}{3} = 4\right)$

Example:
Multiply 15 by $\frac{7}{8}$.

Solution:

$$\frac{15}{1} \times \frac{7}{8} = \frac{15 \times 7}{1 \times 8} = \frac{105}{8} = 13\frac{1}{8}$$

Exercises
Multiply the following.

1. $12 \times \frac{3}{4}$	2. $24 \times \frac{7}{8}$	3. $16 \times \frac{2}{3}$
4. $14 \times \frac{3}{5}$	5. $56 \times \frac{3}{7}$	6. $86 \times \frac{3}{4}$
7. $35 \times \frac{6}{7}$	8. $55 \times \frac{2}{3}$	9. $20 \times \frac{1}{16}$
10. $33 \times \frac{1}{4}$	11. $76 \times \frac{13}{16}$	12. $72 \times \frac{5}{6}$

MULTIPLYING A WHOLE NUMBER BY A MIXED NUMBER

To multiply a whole number by a mixed number, change the mixed number to an improper fraction and multiply.

132   Chapter 6   Skills with Fractions

Example:
Multiply 9 by $3\frac{3}{4}$.

Solution:

$$9 \times \frac{15}{4} =$$

$$\frac{9 \times 15}{1 \times 4} = \frac{135}{4} = 33\frac{3}{4}$$

When a multiplication problem involves large numbers, one of which includes a fraction, the solution can sometimes be simplified by dividing the example into two problems.

Example:
Multiply 2,446 by $26\frac{3}{4}$.

Solution:

1. Multiply $\quad 2,446 \times \frac{3}{4} = \frac{7338}{4} = \quad 1,834\frac{1}{2}$
2. Multiply $\quad 2,446 \times 26 \qquad\qquad = 63,596$
3. Add the products together $\qquad 65,430\frac{1}{2}$

MULTIPLYING FRACTIONS AND DECIMALS

Example:
Multiply $1.25 by $3\frac{1}{5}$.

Follow the same rules you learned for multiplication of decimals; that is, do the multiplication first and then mark off as many decimal places in the answer as there are in both the multiplier and the multiplicand.

Solution:
$1.25 \times \frac{16}{5} = \frac{2000}{5} = \$4.00$

Exercises
Multiply the following. (You may omit the decimal points while doing the problem and merely put the decimal point in the proper place in the answer.)

1. $12 \times 5\frac{1}{2}$
2. $16 \times 2\frac{3}{4}$
3. $25 \times 7\frac{3}{5}$
4. $32 \times 8\frac{1}{4}$
5. $18 \times 3\frac{3}{8}$
6. $24 \times 9\frac{2}{3}$
7. $16 \times 7\frac{5}{8}$
8. $22 \times 8\frac{3}{4}$

9. $18 \times 10\frac{3}{4}$

10. $24 \times 4\frac{5}{16}$

11. $20 \times 12\frac{5}{6}$

12. $6 \times 9\frac{2}{3}$

13. $\$2.95 \times 3\frac{1}{5}$

14. $\$16.41 \times 14\frac{2}{3}$

15. $\$127.50 \times 5\frac{1}{2}$

16. $\$62.75 \times 8\frac{1}{4}$

MULTIPLYING A FRACTION BY A FRACTION

To obtain the product of two fractions, do the following:
1. Multiply the numerators to obtain the numerator of the product.
2. Multiply the denominators to obtain the denominator of the product.
3. Rename the product in its simplest terms.

Example:

Multiply $\frac{5}{8}$ by $\frac{2}{5}$.

Solution:

$$\frac{5}{8} \times \frac{2}{5} = \frac{5 \times 2}{8 \times 5} = \frac{10}{40} = \frac{1}{4}$$

Sometimes the multiplication process can be simplified by renaming the fraction in simplest terms before completing the multiplication. Look at the problem we just did, for example.

$$\frac{5}{8} \times \frac{2}{5} = \frac{\overset{1}{\cancel{5}} \times \overset{1}{\cancel{2}}}{\underset{4}{\cancel{8}} \times \underset{1}{\cancel{5}}} = \frac{1}{4}$$

In the fraction $\dfrac{5 \times 2}{8 \times 5}$, the numerator and the denominator were first divided by 5, which changed both 5's to 1. Then both the numerator and the denominator were divided by 2, which changed the 2 to 1 and the 8 to 4. The common practice is to leave the two fractions $\frac{5}{8}$ and $\frac{2}{5}$ as two distinct fractions at the time the numerators and denominators are divided by the same number. Even then, however, they are considered to be a single fraction, so that the principle of dividing the numerator and the denominator by the same number can be applied. To illustrate, the problem could have been completed as follows.

$$\frac{\overset{1}{\cancel{5}}}{\underset{4}{\cancel{8}}} \times \frac{\overset{1}{\cancel{2}}}{\underset{1}{\cancel{5}}} = \frac{1}{4}$$

Exercises

Multiply the following fractions.

1. $\frac{2}{5} \times \frac{7}{9}$

2. $\frac{1}{2} \times \frac{5}{6}$

3. $\frac{3}{4} \times \frac{5}{9}$

4. $\frac{2}{3} \times \frac{7}{8}$

5. $\frac{5}{6} \times \frac{3}{4}$

6. $\frac{2}{5} \times \frac{5}{8}$

7. $\frac{1}{4}$ of $\frac{8}{9}$

8. $\frac{3}{7}$ of $\frac{14}{15}$

9. $\frac{24}{25}$ of $\frac{5}{8}$

10. $\frac{7}{16}$ of $\frac{4}{5}$

11. $\frac{3}{32} \times \frac{8}{9}$

12. $\frac{14}{15} \times \frac{3}{28}$

Business Applications

1. Pamela Cole bought $5\frac{1}{2}$ pounds of chopped meat at a cost of 96 cents a pound. What was the total cost of the purchase?

2. When Jim Tremont repaired his home, he bought $3\frac{3}{4}$ pounds of brads at $5\frac{1}{2}$ cents a pound. What was the total cost of the brads Mr. Tremont used?

3. To complete an end table that she was making, Roberta Sanchez bought a special piece of wood, 18 inches wide and 2 inches thick, for the top. If the cost of each foot was $2.24 and Roberta needed $2\frac{1}{3}$ feet, how much did this piece of lumber cost her?

4. A tract of farmland was divided into $1\frac{3}{4}$-acre plots and sold separately to buyers. If there were 125 of these plots, how many acres were there in the original piece of farmland?

5. When John Valdez died, he left a will dividing his estate of $48,000 among his three children. If Carl received $\frac{1}{4}$ of the estate and Joanna was willed $\frac{3}{8}$ of the estate, how much money was left for Betty, the third child?

6. William Calvin owned a $\frac{2}{3}$ interest in a business valued at $75,000. If he sold $\frac{1}{6}$ of his interest in the business, how much should he have received?

7. Margaret Lester earns $900 a month. During one month she spent $\frac{1}{4}$ of this amount for rent, $\frac{1}{5}$ for food, $\frac{1}{6}$ for clothing, $\frac{1}{8}$ for recreation, and saved the rest. How much money was allotted to rent, food, clothing, recreation, and savings that month?

8. During a recent week, Don Clay worked 38 hours. If his wages are figured at $3.92\frac{1}{2}$ an hour, what were his total earnings for the week?

9. Mrs. Bertha Hall purchased $4\frac{1}{2}$ yards of material at $1.25 a yard and $2\frac{1}{3}$ yards of another material at $2.35 a yard. What was the total amount Mrs. Hall spent for material?

10. Dennis Edwards purchased a house for $24,000, paying $\frac{3}{8}$ of this amount as a down payment. If his mother had given him $\frac{3}{4}$ of

the down payment, how much did Dennis receive from his mother?

11. Complete the following sales slip.

THE BRADLEY STORE

Quantity	Item	Amount
$4\frac{1}{2}$ yd.	Cotton @ $1.28	$ _____
$12\frac{1}{4}$ yd.	Cotton @ $.56	_____
$5\frac{2}{3}$ yd.	Wool @ $3.75	_____
$3\frac{3}{4}$ yd.	Wool @ $2.19	_____
$6\frac{1}{3}$ yd.	Orlon @ $1.79	_____
	Total	$ _____

UNIT

DIVIDING FRACTIONS

DIVIDING PROPER FRACTIONS

To divide one common fraction by another, invert the divisor (the number by which you are to divide) and multiply.

Example:
Divide $\frac{7}{8}$ by $\frac{5}{6}$.

Solution:

$$\frac{7}{8} \div \frac{5}{6} = \frac{7}{8} \times \frac{6}{5} = \frac{42}{40} = 1\frac{1}{20}$$

or

$$\frac{7 \times \overset{3}{\cancel{6}}}{\underset{4}{\cancel{8}} \times 5} = \frac{21}{20} = 1\frac{1}{20}$$

Explanation:
Note that the divisor $\frac{5}{6}$ was inverted and written as $\frac{6}{5}$. The two numerators and the two denominators were then multiplied. The improper fraction was changed to a mixed number.

Exercises

Divide the following fractions.

1. $\frac{5}{6} \div \frac{2}{3}$
2. $\frac{7}{8} \div \frac{3}{16}$
3. $\frac{1}{2} \div \frac{1}{4}$
4. $\frac{2}{3} \div \frac{1}{9}$
5. $\frac{5}{6} \div \frac{5}{12}$
6. $\frac{3}{16} \div \frac{5}{8}$
7. $\frac{4}{5} \div \frac{2}{3}$
8. $\frac{3}{8} \div \frac{1}{3}$
9. $\frac{3}{8} \div \frac{4}{5}$
10. $\frac{2}{3} \div \frac{3}{16}$
11. $\frac{16}{17} \div \frac{4}{5}$
12. $\frac{7}{10} \div \frac{3}{5}$

DIVIDING WHOLE NUMBERS AND FRACTIONS

To divide a whole number by a fraction:

1. Treat the whole number as a fraction with a denominator of one.
2. Invert the divisor.
3. Multiply.

Example:

Divide 24 by $\frac{3}{4}$.

Solution:

$$24 \div \frac{3}{4} = \frac{24}{1} \times \frac{4}{3} = \frac{96}{3} = 32$$

or

$$\frac{\overset{8}{\cancel{24}}}{1} \times \frac{4}{\underset{1}{\cancel{3}}} = \frac{32}{1} = 32$$

To divide a fraction by a whole number, proceed as in the next example.

Example:

Divide $\frac{4}{5}$ by 16.

Solution:

$$\frac{4}{5} \div \frac{16}{1} = \frac{4}{5} \times \frac{1}{16} = \frac{4}{80} = \frac{1}{20}$$

or

$$\frac{\overset{1}{\cancel{4}}}{5} \times \frac{1}{\underset{4}{\cancel{16}}} = \frac{1}{20}$$

Exercises

Divide the following.

1. $14 \div \frac{2}{7}$
2. $24 \div \frac{2}{3}$
3. $30 \div \frac{3}{10}$
4. $28 \div \frac{7}{8}$
5. $15 \div \frac{1}{2}$
6. $32 \div \frac{6}{7}$
7. $100 \div \frac{4}{5}$
8. $120 \div \frac{5}{6}$
9. $\frac{3}{4} \div 4$
10. $\frac{5}{6} \div 8$
11. $\frac{7}{8} \div 14$
12. $\frac{2}{3} \div 6$

DIVIDING A MIXED NUMBER BY A MIXED NUMBER

To divide a mixed number by a mixed number:
1. Change each mixed number to an improper fraction.
2. Invert the divisor.
3. Multiply.

Example:

Divide $15\frac{3}{4}$ by $8\frac{5}{8}$.

Solution:

$$\frac{63}{4} \div \frac{69}{8} = \frac{63}{4} \times \frac{8}{69} = \frac{504}{276} = 1\frac{57}{69} = 1\frac{19}{23}$$

or

$$\frac{\overset{21}{\cancel{63}}}{\underset{1}{\cancel{4}}} \times \frac{\overset{2}{\cancel{8}}}{\underset{23}{\cancel{69}}} = \frac{42}{23} = 1\frac{19}{23}$$

Exercises

Divide the following.

1. $24\frac{1}{4} \div 8\frac{2}{3}$
2. $15\frac{1}{3} \div 2\frac{4}{5}$
3. $33\frac{3}{4} \div 11\frac{1}{4}$
4. $16\frac{2}{3} \div 6\frac{1}{3}$
5. $25\frac{7}{8} \div 6\frac{5}{6}$
6. $14\frac{1}{4} \div 7\frac{1}{8}$
7. $28\frac{3}{4} \div 6\frac{7}{8}$
8. $64\frac{5}{6} \div 30\frac{1}{4}$
9. $17\frac{1}{2} \div 5\frac{3}{16}$
10. $37\frac{3}{4} \div 6\frac{3}{8}$
11. $10\frac{13}{16} \div 5\frac{1}{8}$
12. $10\frac{7}{10} \div 10\frac{7}{20}$

DIVIDING FRACTIONS AND DECIMALS

Since division of fractions is the same as multiplication of fractions once the divisor has been inverted, the rules for decimal places are the same; that is, the number of decimal places in the answer is the sum of the decimal places in the dividend and divisor.

138 Chapter 6   Skills with Fractions

Problem:

Divide $4.50 by $\frac{2}{3}$.

Solution:

$$\$4.50 \div \frac{2}{3} = \frac{450}{1} \times \frac{3}{2} = \frac{1350}{2} = 675 = \$6.75$$

or

$$\frac{\overset{225}{\cancel{450}}}{1} \times \frac{3}{\underset{1}{\cancel{2}}} = \frac{675}{1} = 675 = \$6.75$$

Explanation:

Omit the decimal points completely while solving the problem. When you have found the answer, go back to the original problem and count the number of decimal places. There were 2 in the dividend and none in the divisor, or a total of 2. We therefore marked off 2 places in the answer.

Exercises

Divide the following.

1. $16.25 ÷ $\frac{1}{5}$

2. 102.3 ÷ $\frac{3}{8}$

3. $112.92 ÷ $1\frac{3}{4}$

4. 9.6 ÷ $8\frac{1}{3}$

5. $242.50 ÷ $3\frac{3}{5}$

6. $.24 ÷ $10\frac{2}{3}$

Business Applications

1. A carpenter cut a piece of lumber 24 feet long into sections, each $2\frac{2}{3}$ feet in length. If the widths of the saw cuts are ignored, into how many sections was the entire piece of lumber cut?

2. The owner of a clothing store purchased wire hangers on which to hang his merchandise. How many hangers could he buy for $5 if each hanger cost $2\frac{1}{2}$ cents?

3. A tract of land containing 240 acres was divided into $\frac{3}{4}$-acre plots in order to develop the land for a housing project. If the land needed for roads that are to run through the development is ignored, how many plots will there be in this project?

4. The Diet Sweet Shop advertised a special on summer candy. A $2\frac{1}{2}$-pound box of candy was reduced to $1.95. At this rate, what would be the cost of 1 pound of this candy?

5. William Rabin was sent to the store to buy as many pounds of a certain type of nail as he could for 50 cents. At the store he learned that 1 pound of these nails costs $9\frac{1}{2}$ cents. How many pounds could he buy for the 50 cents?

6. A $7\frac{3}{4}$-ounce can of salmon in the grocery department of a market sells for 73 cents. At this rate, what was the cost per ounce?

7. Two different, but comparable, brands of canned tuna fish were sold in a food store. If the price of a $7\frac{1}{2}$-ounce can of one brand was 57 cents and an $8\frac{1}{4}$-ounce can of the other brand sold for 64 cents, which was the better buy? By how much?

8. Joseph Nunez works in the clock-radio division of the Triden Electronics Company. The operation he performs on each instrument takes $\frac{3}{4}$ of an hour. How many instruments can he process in a five-day week if he works a $7\frac{1}{2}$-hour day?

9. A manufacturer of children's dresses purchased 15 bolts of the same print of cotton material, each bolt containing 35 yards. From these he planned to make children's dresses of the same style. If, including waste, he found that he needed $2\frac{1}{3}$ yards of material for each dress, how many dresses would he be able to cut from the 15 bolts?

10. The Rohmer Development Company buys large tracts of land and subdivides the property into lots suitable for homes. On one project, the owner decided to divide a 30-acre tract into $\frac{3}{4}$-acre lots. How many lots will she have available to sell?

REVIEW EXERCISES FOR CHAPTER 6

1. Change each of the following to a whole or a mixed number.

   a. $\frac{24}{4}$ **b.** $\frac{32}{8}$ **c.** $\frac{48}{6}$ **d.** $\frac{26}{3}$

   e. $\frac{14}{9}$ **f.** $\frac{27}{8}$ **g.** $\frac{36}{5}$ **h.** $\frac{85}{12}$

   i. $\frac{76}{11}$ **j.** $\frac{54}{7}$

2. Change the following mixed numbers to improper fractions.

   a. $2\frac{1}{8}$ **b.** $3\frac{1}{4}$ **c.** $8\frac{1}{9}$ **d.** $6\frac{2}{3}$

   e. $9\frac{3}{4}$ **f.** $12\frac{1}{2}$ **g.** $23\frac{2}{5}$ **h.** $24\frac{2}{3}$

   i. $63\frac{4}{7}$ **j.** $45\frac{8}{9}$

3. Rename the following fractions in simplest terms.

   a. $\frac{5}{15}$ **b.** $\frac{16}{20}$ **c.** $\frac{8}{12}$ **d.** $\frac{22}{33}$

   e. $\frac{16}{34}$ **f.** $\frac{27}{81}$ **g.** $\frac{82}{112}$ **h.** $\frac{55}{120}$

   i. $\frac{64}{96}$ **j.** $\frac{26}{65}$

4. Change each of the following fractions to an equivalent fraction with the given denominator.

   a. $\frac{1}{8} = \frac{}{16}$ **b.** $\frac{1}{9} = \frac{}{27}$ **c.** $\frac{1}{10} = \frac{}{90}$ **d.** $\frac{2}{5} = \frac{}{40}$

   e. $\frac{3}{8} = \frac{}{24}$ **f.** $\frac{7}{16} = \frac{}{32}$ **g.** $\frac{7}{12} = \frac{}{84}$ **h.** $\frac{2}{9} = \frac{}{54}$

5. Convert the following fractions into decimals, carrying the answer to three decimal places where necessary.

   a. $\frac{3}{8}$ **b.** $\frac{7}{16}$ **c.** $\frac{4}{5}$ **d.** $\frac{5}{12}$

   e. $\frac{9}{15}$ **f.** $\frac{23}{40}$ **g.** $\frac{13}{50}$ **h.** $\frac{23}{27}$

6. Convert the following decimals to fractions, renaming in simplest terms.

   a. .3   **b.** .9   **c.** .37   **d.** .54

   e. .625   **f.** .2495   **g.** .900   **h.** .4565

7. Find the sum in each of the following problems.

a. $\frac{1}{4} + \frac{1}{6}$

b. $\frac{2}{3} + \frac{4}{5}$

c. $\frac{5}{6} + \frac{7}{8}$

d. $\frac{7}{15} + \frac{2}{3} + \frac{4}{5}$

e. $\frac{5}{8} + \frac{3}{4} + \frac{1}{2} + \frac{11}{16}$

f. $\frac{3}{4} + \frac{1}{3} + \frac{5}{6} + \frac{1}{2}$

g. $4\frac{7}{9} + 5\frac{4}{9}$

h. $9\frac{5}{8} + 7\frac{3}{4}$

i. $26\frac{5}{6} + 31\frac{3}{8}$

j. $7\frac{3}{4} + 5\frac{7}{8} + 9\frac{2}{3}$

8. Find the difference in each of the following problems.

a. $\frac{11}{12} - \frac{5}{12}$

b. $\frac{5}{8} - \frac{3}{8}$

c. $\frac{1}{4} - \frac{1}{8}$

d. $\frac{4}{5} - \frac{1}{3}$

e. $\frac{5}{6} - \frac{5}{9}$

f. $9\frac{8}{9} - 8\frac{4}{9}$

g. $5\frac{5}{6} - 2\frac{2}{3}$

h. $8\frac{1}{3} - 7\frac{1}{4}$

i. $16\frac{1}{2} - 14\frac{1}{4}$

j. $47\frac{7}{8} - 29\frac{3}{4}$

k. $36 - 7\frac{1}{6}$

l. $54 - 43\frac{2}{3}$

m. $35 - 12\frac{3}{5}$

n. $78\frac{1}{2} - 16\frac{2}{3}$

o. $80\frac{1}{4} - 19\frac{5}{6}$

9. Find the product in each of the following problems.

a. $\frac{7}{8} \times \frac{5}{6}$

b. $\frac{5}{12} \times \frac{7}{15}$

c. $\frac{3}{8} \times \frac{4}{9}$

d. $\frac{1}{5} \times 20$

e. $\frac{3}{4} \times 8$

f. $35 \times \frac{4}{5}$

g. $\frac{3}{8} \times 2\frac{2}{3}$

h. $\frac{7}{12} \times 15\frac{3}{4}$

i. $18\frac{2}{3} \times \frac{3}{4}$

j. $36\frac{5}{6} \times \frac{5}{9}$

k. $36 \times 2\frac{1}{2}$

l. $27 \times 8\frac{5}{6}$

m. $7\frac{1}{4} \times 6$

n. $3\frac{3}{5} \times 5\frac{5}{6}$

o. $12\frac{3}{4} \times 16\frac{2}{3}$

p. $\$27.50 \times \frac{3}{5}$

q. $26.4 \times \frac{1}{4}$

r. $\$23.28 \times \frac{3}{8}$

10. Find the quotient in each of the following problems.

a. $\frac{1}{2} \div \frac{1}{2}$

b. $\frac{3}{4} \div \frac{1}{4}$

c. $\frac{8}{9} \div \frac{2}{3}$

d. $\frac{6}{7} \div \frac{5}{8}$

e. $12 \div \frac{3}{4}$

f. $32 \div \frac{6}{7}$

g. $\frac{3}{4} \div 12$

h. $\frac{8}{9} \div 18$

i. $\frac{5}{6} \div 8\frac{1}{3}$

j. $\frac{7}{8} \div 6\frac{1}{4}$

k. $5\frac{5}{12} \div \frac{5}{6}$

l. $46\frac{3}{8} \div \frac{7}{9}$

m. $36 \div 4\frac{1}{2}$

n. $42 \div 2\frac{2}{5}$

o. $15\frac{3}{4} \div 9$

p. $81\frac{2}{3} \div 24$

q. $8\frac{1}{3} \div 6\frac{1}{4}$

r. $24\frac{3}{5} \div 10\frac{1}{8}$

s. $\$22.50 \div \frac{5}{8}$

t. $132.8 \div \frac{8}{9}$

u. $\$212.28 \div \frac{3}{7}$

11. Solve the following problems.

a. A merchant sold an electronic calculator for $252, making a profit equal to $\frac{1}{6}$ of the selling price. What was the amount of his profit?

b. An estate was divided into 150 plots for a housing development. If each plot was $1\frac{3}{4}$ acres in size, what was the total number of acres in the estate? (Ignore the areas needed for roadways.)

c. A piece of fabric $12\frac{2}{3}$ yards long was cut from a bolt containing $25\frac{1}{2}$ yards of material. How long was the material that remained?

d. The salary of a new accountant in Benson's is $\frac{4}{5}$ of the salary of the senior accountant in the firm. If the weekly salary of the senior accountant is $340, what is the new accountant's weekly salary?

e. Jeffrey Draper earns $12,500 a year. Last year he spent $\frac{1}{4}$ of this amount for taxes, $\frac{1}{5}$ for food, $\frac{1}{3}$ for rent, $\frac{1}{20}$ for clothing, and $\frac{1}{10}$ for recreation. How much money remained?

f. Paul's Open Air Market purchased 240 quarts of strawberries at $47\frac{1}{2}$ cents a quart. How much did he pay for the strawberries?

g. Arlene Fox earns $14,200 a year. Of this amount, $\frac{1}{5}$ was used to pay off a mortgage. If $\frac{1}{20}$ of the mortgage money was for the charge on the debt, how much money did Arlene pay each year on this charge?

h. During a five-day week, Robert J. Nickerson worked the following number of hours each day: $7\frac{1}{2}$, $6\frac{3}{4}$, $8\frac{1}{4}$, $7\frac{1}{3}$, $7\frac{2}{3}$. How many hours did he work during that week?

i. A plot of land containing $487\frac{1}{2}$ acres was broken up into smaller plots, each $3\frac{1}{4}$ acres in size. How many of these smaller plots were formed?

j. Of the 450 freshmen entering a certain high school, only $\frac{2}{3}$ will graduate four years later. Of those that graduate, $\frac{1}{6}$ will receive at least an A average at some time during these four years. How many of the graduating seniors will receive an A average?

k. The Global Food Corporation purchased 4,000 pints of blueberries and repackaged them in plastic containers holding $\frac{2}{3}$ pints each. How many containers were needed?

l. Mildred Durrell owns four vacant lots, each of which is $\frac{5}{6}$ of an acre. How many acres does Ms. Durrell own?

m. Murphy's Remnants purchased several bolts of cloth containing the following yardage:

$3\frac{1}{2}$ yds @ $2.50 per yd.
$5\frac{3}{4}$ yds @ $2.96 per yd.
$4\frac{7}{8}$ yds @ $2.72 per yd.

What was the total cost?

n. Mr. Boke paid $6.45 for $10\frac{3}{4}$ gallons of gasoline. What was the price per gallon?

CHAPTER 7
COMPARISON
OF NUMBERS

There are times when an approximate number can present a clearer picture of a situation than the exact numbers we have been working with up to this point. A speaker at a lecture, for instance, can be fairly certain that an audience will remember a comparison stated in this way: "In our school system of 750,000 pupils, 50,000 had no failures last year." If the speaker used the exact figures of 753,998 and 46,051, the audience would be less likely to remember the numbers correctly. The speaker might have gotten the same idea across by saying that 1 out of every 13 pupils had no failing grades last year.

To compare numbers, we round them off or express them in figures that are related to each other in the same way that the original numbers are. We might also use percents to compare numbers.

One of the most common uses of percent is in sports. A professional basketball team is said to be "hitting 48% of its shots," which means, of course, that out of every 100 tries the team is hitting the basket 48 times. Or a certain player is making 88% of his free throws—88 out of

100. If a TV announcer says that Jones made 9 field goals and 4 free throws in a game, you might think he played pretty well. But you couldn't rate Jones's performance accurately unless you knew how many shots he took at the basket.

Percent helps us to judge performance, whether it be that of a basketball player, sales representative, or a business owner. As a student, you are also judged on a percent basis. If you took a test on which you got 50 correct answers, no one will know how well you did until you say how many items there were on the test. If there were 100, we can assume that you didn't do too well—50%. But if there were 60 items and you got 50 right, you did pretty well—83%.

Comparison of numbers plays an important part in many personal and business activities. It is important that you be able to compare numbers easily and to make decisions based on those comparisons.

UNIT 1

ROUNDING OFF NUMBERS

Case Problem "Ladies and gentlemen," Mr. Bernard Arnold, publisher of the *Baytown News-Sentinel,* said as he began a meeting of the Executive Committee of the newspaper, "last year the *News-Sentinel* contributed nearly $60,000 to local charities, over $7,000 to the Baytown Fresh Air Fund, and nearly $2,500 to the Baytown Symphony. I think that's a very good record for a company whose annual sales volume is around $11,000,000."

The figures that Mr. Arnold recited are not exact. In fact, the *Baytown News-Sentinel* actually gave $59,800 to local charities, $7,312 to the Fresh Air Fund, and $2,487.50 to the Baytown Symphony. The *News-Sentinel*'s actual volume of business last year was $11,261,103.40.

Discussion Questions:
1. Why did Mr. Arnold give approximate figures to his audience instead of reading the exact amounts?
2. Why was this not misleading?
3. When can approximate numbers be justified?

For the purposes of the group to which Mr. Arnold was speaking, the figures he gave were close enough. People often "round off" numbers in speeches and written reports when specific figures are not important and would merely confuse. It's much easier to grasp and remember round figures.

ROUNDING OFF DOLLARS AND CENTS

Consider these procedures for rounding off dollars and cents.

Rounding Off to the Nearest Cent
Look at the *third* decimal place. If this number is less than 5, drop it and also any decimal places that may come after it. If this number is 5 or more, raise the number of cents one higher. Notice that no matter how many decimal places there may be, only the *third* one is of any significance in rounding off to the nearest cent.

$37.83<u>2</u> → $37.83   (The third place is less than 5.)
$37.83<u>8</u> → $37.84   (The third place is more than 5.)
$37.83<u>5</u> → $37.84   (The third place is 5.)
$37.83<u>2</u>6 → $37.83   (The third place is less than 5.)
$37.83<u>4</u>9 → $37.83   (The third place is less than 5.)

Rounding Off to the Nearest Dollar

Look at the number of cents. If there are less than 50 cents, drop the cents. If there are 50 cents or more, round up to the next dollar.

$37.15 → $37.00   (There were less than 50¢, so we dropped them.)
$37.50 → $38.00   (There were exactly 50¢, so we added a unit.)
$37.90 → $38.00   (There were more than 50¢, so we added a unit.)

Exercises

1. Round off to the nearest cent.
   a. $163.439
   b. $16.382
   c. $2.3875
   d. $14.505
   e. $28.497

   f. $.0275
   g. $.0529
   h. $1.006
   i. $2.002
   j. $.0075

2. Round off to the nearest dollar.
   a. $27.25
   b. $108.75
   c. $1,952.50

   d. $248.425
   e. $1,695.833
   f. $62.496

USING ROUNDED DOLLARS AND CENTS

Numbers are rounded off frequently in making forecasts and estimates. A business executive who is trying to predict the amount of company sales two or three years hence will work with round figures rather than try to give exact ones. That is, she or he is more likely to use a figure such as $800,000 than a figure such as $805,677.75. A personnel director who is asked the question, "How many employees do you think we will have five years from now?" will probably answer, "Around 2,000," instead of "2,049." An accountant who is asked to estimate the cost of a new piece of equipment will give a rounded-off figure such as $5,000 instead of the more accurate $4,972.

To develop skill in estimating, you must learn to recognize significant figures in numbers. For example, if the number of square feet in a building is 6,992, the significant figure for general purposes is 7,000. If the cost of leasing a warehouse is $21,750 a year, the significant figure is $22,000. If the selling price of a book is $9.95, the significant figure is $10.

Even in computations where exact figures are required, you must know the rules for rounding off numbers. Suppose, for example, the unit cost of a ball-point pen is $.08657 when it is bought from the manufacturer and you want to find the amount you must pay for 78,375 pens. By multiplying, you get the exact figure of $6,784.92375. You must pay for this, however, in dollars and cents and must therefore "round off" the price to the nearest cent. This would make the payment $6,784.92.

ROUNDING OFF OTHER NUMBERS

Use the following steps when you want to round off a number, either for purposes of estimating an answer before performing computations or to arrive at a final answer. These steps are also used with the repeating decimal that you encountered in the previous unit.

1. Determine the unit you are expected to round off to. For instance, the number 23,182 could be rounded off to the nearest thousand, or to the nearest hundred.
2. Look to the number directly to the *right* of the unit you are rounding off to. This number determines whether you are dropping the portion of the unit it represents or adding an additional unit. Just as with dollars and cents, if the significant unit is less than 5, it means drop; if the significant unit is 5 or more, it means add another unit.

Go back to the numeral 23,182.

If you wish to round it off to the nearest thousand:

$23,\underline{1}82 \rightarrow 23,000$ The significant number is 1. Since this is less than 5, we drop the portion of a thousand which it represents.

If you wish to round off the same number to the nearest hundred:

$23,1\underline{8}2 \rightarrow 23,200$ The significant number is 8, the number after the hundreds position. Since this number is 5 or more, round it up to the next highest hundred.

Additional Examples

Consider the following numeral: 27,653.2175. This can be rounded off as follows, depending on what you are asked to do.

Round Off to	Significant Number (Underscored)		Answer
nearest thousand	27,6̲53.2175	(5 or more)	28,000
nearest hundred	27,65̲3.2175	(5 or more)	27,700
nearest ten	27,653̲.2175	(less than 5)	27,650
nearest unit	27,653.2̲175	(less than 5)	27,653
nearest tenth	27,653.21̲75	(less than 5)	27,653.2
nearest hundredth	27,653.217̲5	(5 or more)	27,653.22
nearest thousandth	27,653.2175̲	(5 or more)	27,653.218

Unless you have instructions to do otherwise, do not round off figures while you work on a problem until you reach the final answer.

Example:

A manufacturer used four materials in making a product. What was the total cost of materials, figured to the nearest cent?

Material 1	$ .763
2	.375
3	.625
4	.2765

Solution: $2.0395 = $2.04

Notice that if you had rounded off the cost of each of the materials, you would have had prices of $.76, $.38, $.63 and $.28, a total of $2.05, which would have been the wrong answer. In figuring many costs where large volumes are involved, every penny counts.

Exercises

1. Round off the following to the places indicated.
   a. Nearest thousand

   (1) 32,609   (3) 215,604   (5) 732,050.7
   (2) 16,375   (4) 192,650   (6) 19,500

   b. Nearest hundred

   (1) 357   (3) 2,923   (5) 1,956
   (2) 821   (4) 23,740   (6) 16,505.8

   c. Nearest ten

   (1) 51   (3) 156   (5) 50.8
   (2) 16   (4) 281   (6) 9.97

   d. Nearest tenth

   (1) 44.037   (3) 3.552   (5) 17.09
   (2) .567   (4) 4.97   (6) .0503

   e. Nearest hundredth

   (1) 553.642   (3) 1.6245   (5) 4.9962
   (2) 19.7957   (4) 3.6952   (6) 427.796

   f. Nearest thousandth

   (1) .07341   (3) 2.07395   (5) 62.9985
   (2) 36.1693   (4) 8.2994   (6) .0095

Business Applications

1. The sales manager for Heathrow British Imports drove a total of 11,475 miles during the past year. In discussing the subject of mileage before a large audience, he wanted to give a rounded-off number rather than the exact number of miles driven. What figure should be used?

2. In figuring a customer's bill, a retailer arrived at the figure of $3.795. What was the charge to the customer?

3. George Harris made purchases at a lumber yard as follows: $7.644, $5.363, $2.75, $8.15, and $4.466. If the sales clerk rounded off the

total of the bill to the nearest cent, what amount will Mr. Harris have to pay?

4. Arleen Murtaugh, advertising director of Moto-Lease Car Rental, has been asked how much the company plans to spend, in thousands of dollars, on advertising in various media during the next five years. Here are the figures Mrs. Murtaugh came up with. Round them off to thousands of dollars.

Media	19X5	19X6	19X7	19X8	19X9
Newspapers and magazines	$350,200	$420,500	$472,160	$500,125	$548,900
Radio and TV	$263,330	$210,490	$344,675	$415,545	$456,600
Direct mail	$111,150	$135,210	$160,666	$224,450	$265,790
Outdoor	$ 75,249	$ 60,440	$ 55,540	$ 60,820	$ 84,515

5. Complete the following stock report, rounding off the total cost of each article to the nearest penny. (Remember, do not round off until each multiplication has been completed.)

Quantity	Item	Unit Cost	Total Cost
64	"Exec" desk sets	$12.644	$ _____
37	Utility desk sets	$ 8.3133	_____
96	Draftsman's drawing kits	$16.279	_____
214	Pens, broad stroke	$ .097	_____
308	Pens, fine line	$ .9992	_____
116	Pens, medium	$ .0861	_____
21	Lighter pens	$ 3.788	_____
		Total	$ _____

UNIT 2

THE MEANING OF PERCENT

You have learned two ways of expressing parts of a whole—decimals and fractions. If you want to express "one part out of a total of two parts," the fraction ½ does this. The decimal .5 does the same thing. If you want to express "five-tenths," which can be written as a fraction $(\frac{5}{10})$, this, renamed in simplest terms, is $\frac{1}{2}$. Thus, .5, .50, .500, $\frac{5}{10}$, $\frac{50}{100}$ are all ways of expressing $\frac{1}{2}$.

A third way to express a part of a whole is through *percent*, which means "for each hundred." Percents are very similar to decimals; we simply replace the decimal point in the hundredths place by a percent sign (%). Thus, .14 (fourteen hundredths) becomes 14% (fourteen percent). Both expressions mean fourteen out of a hundred.

Because decimals, percents, and fractions are simply different ways of expressing the same values, you can easily change percents to decimals, decimals to percents, percents to fractions, and fractions to percents.

CHANGING DECIMALS TO PERCENTS

To change decimals to percents, move the decimal point two places to the right and add the percent sign.

$$.15 \ = .15 \ = 15\%$$
$$.02 \ = .02 \ = \ 2\%$$
$$.125 = .125 = 12.5\%$$

CHANGING PERCENTS TO DECIMALS

To change a percent to a decimal, you reverse the operation. Move the decimal point two places to the left and drop the percent sign.

$$15\% = .15$$
$$2\% = .02$$
$$12.5\% = .125$$

CHANGING FRACTIONS TO PERCENTS

To change a fraction to a percent, change the fraction first to its decimal equivalent. Then move the decimal point two places to the right and add the percent sign.

$$\tfrac{5}{8} = 5 \div 8 = .625 = 62.5\%$$
$$2\tfrac{1}{4} = \tfrac{9}{4} = 9 \div 4 = 2.25 = 225\%$$

CHANGING PERCENTS TO FRACTIONS

To change a percent to a fraction, first write the percent as a decimal; then change the decimal to a fraction and rename in simplest terms.

$$6\% = .06 = \tfrac{6}{100} = \tfrac{3}{50}$$

Unit 2   The Meaning of Percent   **151**

We can easily omit the first step and change the percent directly to a fraction if we remember that *percent* means "for each hundred."

$$6\% = \tfrac{6}{100} = \tfrac{3}{50} \qquad 45\% = \tfrac{45}{100} = \tfrac{9}{20}$$

FRACTION-DECIMAL EQUIVALENTS

Of the three ways of expressing parts of a whole, percent is the one most commonly used to interpret a business's growth or lack of it. But a percent sign cannot be handled arithmetically. Therefore, before you can add, subtract, multiply, or divide using percents, the percent must be changed to either a decimal or a fraction. The question then arises, "Which is better to use—the fraction or the decimal?" The answer is simple—use whichever one is easier in the problem you are solving. But remember, if you are going to use a calculating machine for any computations you must use decimals.

You already know how to convert a decimal to a fraction and vice versa. The problem of deciding which to use in any situation is made much easier if you know instantly their respective values. Many fractional parts are used so frequently in business that their equivalents should be memorized. Just as you know instantly that 8×7 is 56 without having to add 8 seven times, you should know that $\tfrac{1}{4}$ is .25.

Following below is a table of commonly used fractional equivalents that are known as *aliquot parts of 100*. You will find that you already know many

Commonly Used Aliquot Parts of 100

Halves	$\tfrac{1}{2} = 50\%$	Tenths	$\tfrac{1}{10} = 10\%$
Thirds	$\tfrac{1}{3} = 33\tfrac{1}{3}\%$		$\tfrac{3}{10} = 30\%$
	$\tfrac{2}{3} = 66\tfrac{2}{3}\%$		$\tfrac{7}{10} = 70\%$
Fourths	$\tfrac{1}{4} = 25\%$		$\tfrac{9}{10} = 90\%$
	$\tfrac{3}{4} = 75\%$	Twelfths	$\tfrac{1}{12} = 8\tfrac{1}{3}\%$
Fifths	$\tfrac{1}{5} = 20\%$		$\tfrac{5}{12} = 41\tfrac{2}{3}\%$
	$\tfrac{2}{5} = 40\%$		$\tfrac{7}{12} = 58\tfrac{1}{3}\%$
	$\tfrac{3}{5} = 60\%$		$\tfrac{11}{12} = 91\tfrac{2}{3}\%$
	$\tfrac{4}{5} = 80\%$	Sixteenths	$\tfrac{1}{16} = 6\tfrac{1}{4}\%$
Sixths	$\tfrac{1}{6} = 16\tfrac{2}{3}\%$		$\tfrac{3}{16} = 18\tfrac{3}{4}\%$
	$\tfrac{5}{6} = 83\tfrac{1}{3}\%$		$\tfrac{5}{16} = 31\tfrac{1}{4}\%$
Eights	$\tfrac{1}{8} = 12\tfrac{1}{2}\%$		$\tfrac{7}{16} = 43\tfrac{3}{4}\%$
	$\tfrac{3}{8} = 37\tfrac{1}{2}\%$		$\tfrac{9}{16} = 56\tfrac{1}{4}\%$
	$\tfrac{5}{8} = 62\tfrac{1}{2}\%$		$\tfrac{11}{16} = 68\tfrac{3}{4}\%$
	$\tfrac{7}{8} = 87\tfrac{1}{2}\%$		$\tfrac{13}{16} = 81\tfrac{1}{4}\%$
			$\tfrac{15}{16} = 93\tfrac{3}{4}\%$

of them. Those you don't know, you should memorize. In each problem given from now on, you should use this knowledge to choose either the fraction or its decimal equivalent (whichever may be easier to use) before doing the necessary arithmetic computations.

Notice that many fractions have been eliminated. This is because they can be renamed in simpler terms, and the fraction in its simpler terms has already been given. For instance, $\frac{4}{8}$, which is not on the table, can be renamed as $\frac{1}{2}$, which is there.

Only the fractions most commonly used in business are included. Where you have occasion to use others, you can convert them by the methods you have already learned.

Using the knowledge of decimals, percents, and fractions that you already have, you can easily convert the percents given in the table into decimals. You can also easily see that the percents containing a fraction can be written with the fraction converted to a decimal. Thus, $37\frac{1}{2}\%$ is the same as 37.5%, because $\frac{1}{2}$ and .5 express the same thing.

The fractions $\frac{1}{3}$ and $\frac{2}{3}$ are a little more difficult to handle. If you convert these fractions into decimals by division (that is, $1 \div 3$), you will find that the division does not come out evenly. There is always the same remainder, which you can go on dividing indefinitely.

$$\frac{.3333333}{3 \overline{)1.0000000}} \text{ and on and on}$$

Because in business we are usually interested in dollars and cents, which are expressed with two decimal places, for all practical purposes you do not need to carry out repeating decimals for more than three places.

Exercises

1. Interpret each of the following statements without using the word *percent*.
   a. On any given day, 5% of the employees of the Great Lakes Manufacturing Company are late for work.
   b. On the day of a blizzard, 75% of the students of the Alexander School were absent.
   c. During a recent year, 64% of the money spent by the United States government went toward defense.
   d. Of the men over 65 who are still working, 26% are employed as farmers.
   e. In 1900, only 1% of all students were in college; whereas, in a recent year, 8% of those attending school were in college.
   f. During a recent year, the earnings of production workers in the petroleum-refining industry were 142% of what they had been 8 years before.

g. During a recent year, the United States exported to Africa 162% of what it exported in 1970.

h. In one state, student dropouts from high schools are about 28% of the student enrollment.

2. Change each of the following decimals to percents.

a. .43	**b.** .96	**c.** .17	**d.** 1.34
e. 2.08	**f.** .374	**g.** 3	**h.** 3.75
i. .436	**j.** 1.784	**k.** 3.50	**l.** .01

3. Change each of the following percents to decimals.

a. 57%	**b.** 83%	**c.** 14%	**d.** 127%
e. 200%	**f.** 56.4%	**g.** 42.3%	**h.** 8%
i. 4%	**j.** 2.5%	**k.** 100%	**l.** $14\frac{1}{4}$%

4. Change each of the following fractions to percents.

a. $\frac{1}{2}$	**b.** $\frac{3}{4}$	**c.** $\frac{1}{5}$	**d.** $\frac{1}{4}$
e. $\frac{2}{5}$	**f.** $\frac{3}{16}$	**g.** $\frac{7}{8}$	**h.** $\frac{5}{6}$
i. $4\frac{1}{2}$	**j.** $2\frac{2}{3}$	**k.** $3\frac{2}{7}$	**l.** $1\frac{5}{6}$

5. Change each of the following percents to fractions, renaming in simplest terms.

a. 30%	**b.** 60%	**c.** 80%
d. 25%	**e.** 75%	**f.** 50%
g. 35%	**h.** 70%	**i.** $12\frac{1}{2}$%
j. $6\frac{1}{4}$%	**k.** 200%	**l.** 325%

UNIT

3

FINDING THE PERCENTAGE

In a recent personnel survey, the Hampton Gas Company found that 60% of its 500 employees are women. As you know, this means that of every 100 employees at Hampton Gas Company 60 are women.

To find out *how many* of the employees are women, you multiply 500 (the total number of employees) by 60% (the percent that are women, or .60) to arrive at the figure 300. Thus, of 500 employees at Hampton Gas Company, 300 are women.

In the preceding problem each number has a name.

60% is the *rate*
500 is the *base*
300 is the *percentage*

From the method we applied to find the percentage (500 × .60 = 300), this principle can be formulated. The *percentage* is equal to the *base* times the *rate*. Using *P* to represent the word *percentage*, *B* for *base*, and *R* for *Rate*, this principle is usually written as the following formula:

$$P = B \times R$$

Example 1:

Mr. Norton said at a sales meeting: "70% of the television sets sold by our store last year were color sets." If the store sold 300 television sets last year, how many were color TV?

Solution:

In the example, the base is 300, and the rate is 70%. You are to find the percentage. The problem can be outlined as follows:

Outline:

Known: Base   300
Rate   70%

To find: Percentage
Method: $P = B \times R$
$= 300 \times 70\%$
$= 300 \times .70$
$= 210$ color TV sets sold

Example 2:

Find 25% of $2,400

Solution:

Here the base is $2,400 and the rate is 25%. You are asked to find the percentage.

Outline:

Known: Base $2,400
Rate   25%

To find: Percentage
Method: $P = B \times R$
$= \$2,400 \times 25\%$
$= \$2,400 \times \frac{1}{4}$
$= \$600$

Exercises

1. Find the percentage in each of the following problems. First change the percents to either fractions or decimals, depending upon which is easier to use.

a. 50% of 24
b. $66\frac{2}{3}$% of 18
c. 30% of 50
d. 40% of 25
e. $62\frac{1}{2}$% of 32
f. $12\frac{1}{2}$% of 72
g. 75% of 28
h. 50% of 98
i. $37\frac{1}{2}$% of 56
j. 60% of 55
k. $33\frac{1}{3}$% of 90
l. $83\frac{1}{3}$% of 54
m. 80% of 45
n. $16\frac{2}{3}$% of 84
o. 75% of 36
p. $66\frac{2}{3}$% of 60
q. 70% of 80
r. $62\frac{1}{2}$% of 64

2. Find the percentage in each of the following problems. First change the percents to either fractions or decimals, whichever is easier to use.

a. 25% of $1,764
b. $12\frac{1}{2}$% of $2,272
c. 36% of $843
d. $16\frac{2}{3}$% of 3,546 students
e. 52% of 1,879 acres
f. 96% of 2,083 bushels
g. $37\frac{1}{2}$% of 5,768 trees
h. $33\frac{1}{3}$% of 7,347 tires
i. $62\frac{1}{2}$% of 4,360 dresses
j. 86% of 3,264 apples
k. 46% of 14,000 desks
l. $4\frac{1}{2}$% of $425
m. $2\frac{3}{4}$% of 1.375
n. $3\frac{1}{4}$% of $4,350
o. 115% of $37.60
p. 225% of $152.60
q. 200% of $56.84
r. 300% of $235.25
s. 4.2% of $385
t. 16.4% of $4,590
u. 3.05% of $37,000
v. $3\frac{1}{3}$% of $420
w. $4\frac{2}{3}$% of $690
x. $\frac{1}{2}$% of $100,000

Business Applications

In the following problems, change the percents to either fractions or decimals, depending upon which is easier to use in each case.

1. In a certain city, 48.2% of the population are males. If the total population is 62,473 people, how many males are there?

2. If 18% of the 342 employees of Wallington Company live outside the city, how many employees live in the city?

3. During a recent frost, $33\frac{1}{3}$% of a peach crop valued at $3,456,000 was destroyed. How great a loss was this to the peach growers?

4. A recent poll showed that 96% of the employees of Wakeman, Inc. enjoyed reading the employee magazine. The remaining employees did not even know there was a magazine for employees. If there are 750 employees in the company, how many were unaware of the existence of the magazine?

5. An export firm employs 2,200 people. If 85% are sales workers, 7% are office workers, and the remaining employees are administrative, how many employees are in each group?

6. An estimate furnished by a contractor for the construction of a new building was $48,000. Of this amount, 19% was for plumbing, 34% for building materials and supplies, and 36% for labor. The contractor's profits were equal to the remainder. Find the dollar amounts allocated for each expense.

7. Out of an income of $9,260, Jerry Alden spent $26\frac{1}{3}$% for rent, 28% for food, 12% for clothing, $16\frac{2}{3}$% for other items, and the rest he saved.
   a. How much did he spend for each category?
   b. How much money did he save?

8. Mary Roper invested $12\frac{1}{2}$% of her money in real estate, $37\frac{1}{2}$% in corporate stocks, and $16\frac{2}{3}$% in government bonds. The rest she deposited in a savings account. Find the total of each investment if the total amount she began with was $42,000.

UNIT

FINDING THE RATE

Case Problem Janice Kraft operates the Corner Gift Shop. In May Miss Kraft sold $4,000 worth of merchandise on which she made a profit of $600.

Discussion Questions
1. If Miss Kraft wants to compare her results this month with other results in the past, what additional information about the profits would be helpful?
2. How can you use the formula you already know, $P = B \times R$, to get this information?

You can vary the basic formula for finding percentage ($P = B \times R$) to find either the rate or base. Consider this example: 10% of 200 = 20

$$P = 20$$
$$B = 200$$
$$R = 10\%$$

If you knew only the base (200) and the percentage (20), and wanted to find the rate, you would need to know how many times 20 (P) is contained in 200 (B). To find this, you would divide 200 by 20.

Therefore, when the *rate* is the unknown quantity, you can restate the equation as

$$R = P \div B$$

In Miss Kraft's problem, you know the base ($4,000) and the percentage ($600). What you do not know is the rate. To find the rate when the base and percentage are known, divide the percentage by the base. The problem can be outlined as follows.

Outline: *Known:*   Base $4,000
                          Percentage $600
           To find: Rate
           Method: $R = P \div B$
                          $= \$600 \div \$4,000$
                          $= .15$, or 15%

Now test the accuracy of your answer by using the original formula.

$$P = B \times R$$
$$\$600 = 4,000 \times 15\%$$

Since $.15 \times \$4,000 = \$600$, you see that the computation was correct.
Here are other examples.

Example 1:
Gary Woodley earned $45 in December from a part-time job and immediately bought a used tape recorder for $10.35. What percent of his earnings did he spend for the recorder?

Solution:
In this example, $45 is the base and $10.35 is the percentage. You are asked to find the rate or percent.

Outline: *Known:*   Base $45
                          Percentage $10.35
           To Find: Rate
           Method: $R = P \div B$
                          $= \$10.35 \div \$45$
                          $= .23$, or 23%

Example 2:
Cady's Furniture Mart purchased a sofa for $84.25 and sold it for $134.80. What percent of the cost is the selling price?

Solution:

The solution will be easier if the question above is reworded: The selling price ($134.80) is what percent of the cost ($84.25)?

Outline: *Known:* Base $84.25
Percentage $134.80

To Find: Rate

Method: $R = P \div B$
$= \$134.80 \div \$84.25$
$= 1.6$
$= 160\%$

Notice that in this problem the percentage (selling price) is larger than the base (cost). This indicates that the rate must be more than 100%.

Exercises

Find the rate in each of the following problems.

1. $15 is what percent of $60?

2. $75 is what percent of $375?

3. $41 is what percent of $328?

4. $19 is what percent of $114?

5. $13 is what percent of $156?

6. $495 is what percent of $660?

7. $61 is what percent of $427?

8. $51 is what percent of $255?

9. $93 is what percent of $248?

10. $146 is what percent of $219?

11. What percent of $.60 is $.30?

12. What percent of $.75 is $.50?

13. What percent of $.50 is $.02?

14. What percent of $50 is $7.50?

15. What percent of $50 is $75?

Business Applications

1. A merchant sold a tennis racket for $17.85, making a profit of $5.95. The profit was what percent of the selling price?

2. A chemical plant employs 525 people this year. Last year it employed 315 people. The number of employees this year is what percent of the number of employees last year?

3. During the past 5 years, the football team of Morrison High School

played 48 games and won 39 of them. What percent of the games did the team win?

4. The 1970 census of Woodland showed the population to be 5,474 people. In 1973, an aircraft plant was built on the outskirts of the town and the population jumped to 17,797. What percent of the 1970 population was the 1973 population?

5. Fred Egan earns $872 a month. Of this amount, he spends $152.60 each month for rent. What percent of his monthly earnings is needed to pay the rent?

6. Find what percent of sales the selling costs represent for each of the three years of operation of Oceanland Spice Products.

OCEANLAND SPICE PRODUCTS
Sales and Selling Costs 19X3–19X5

	19X3	19X4	19X5
Sales	$700,000	$800,000	$900,000
Selling Costs	$154,000	$168,000	$184,500

7. Of the calls each of the following sales representatives make, what is the percent of sales for each?

Representative	Calls Made	Sales Made	% of Sales per Calls
Auerswald	670	134	
Baker	420	120	
Jurasek	320	116	
Quezon	800	136	

UNIT 5

FINDING PERCENT OF INCREASE OR DECREASE

Case Problem After Clarence Martin graduated from college, his earnings on his first job were $7,500 a year. At present his yearly salary is $10,500. What percent of increase has he received?

Discussion Questions

1. How might you reword the problem to make what we are trying to discover stand out more clearly?
2. In terms of our formulas, $P = B \times R$, or $R = P \div B$, what information do we have? What is missing?

Clarence Martin's problem may be reworded as follows: "The increase in salary is what percent of the original salary?" You can see that the increase is the percentage. The increase can be found by subtracting the original salary from the present salary.

This example calls attention to an important point. Percent of increase or percent of decrease is always based on the original quantity. In this example, the salary that Clarence Martin received on his first job is the original quantity and hence, is the base.

Outline:
    Known: Original salary $7,500, base
                 Present salary $10,500
    To Find: Rate of increase
    Method: Increase $= \$10,500 - \$7,500$
                          $= \$3,000$, percentage amount
                     $R = P \div B$
                          $= \$3,000 \div \$7,500$
                          $= .40$
                          $= 40\%$, percent of increase

Business Applications

Solve the following problems.

1. An article that originally sold for $8 now sells for $10. What is the percent of increase?

2. Two months ago, Elizabeth Foster's typing speed was 32 words a minute. At present she can type at the rate of 48 words a minute. What percent of increase in her typing speed has she achieved in the past two months?

3. In an English class of 32 students, 4 failed the subject. What percent of the class passed?

4. After May Walker was graduated from high school, she went to work as a clerk-typist for an insurance firm at $102.50 a week. After 2 years, her earnings were $133.25 a week. What was the percent of increase in her salary over the two-year period?

5. In a school of 1,460 students, 73 were absent one day. What percent of the students were in attendance that day?

6. The average typist today has to work 20 minutes to earn enough money to buy a monthly magazine. Five years ago he or she had to work 25 minutes. What is the percent of decrease?

7. In the early days of television, 57.8 million dollars were spent in one year on TV advertising. Only 10 years later, 1,563.49 million dollars were spent on this means of advertising. What was the percent of increase during those 10 years?

8. Before retirement, B. L. Sanborn earned a monthly salary of $926.55. His retirement pay, including social security, was $578.40 a month. What percent decrease in his monthly income was this? (Give your answer to the nearest whole-number percent.)

9. In one city, the average beginning salary for a secretary is $6,500 a year. In a rural community, the average beginning salary for a secretary is $5,330 a year. At what percent smaller income does the secretary in the rural community begin?

10. C. D. Mays, whose house was valued at $28,000, insured it for only $20,000 against loss by fire. What percent of the value of the property remained uninsured against this type of loss?

Verify your answers to each of the following problems by finding the sum of the percents. If your work is correct, the total should be 100%. (Although the sum will be an even 100% in these two problems, it will not always be so in other problems. These answers have been rounded off to the nearest whole-number percent.)

11. Factory employees in a certain company number 1,144 women and 616 men.
   a. What percent of the employees are women?
   b. What percent of the employees are men?

12. The total attendance at a movie was 2,660. Of this total, 665 were children, 1,596 were women, and the remainder men. Find the percent of total attendance represented by each group.

UNIT

FINDING THE BASE

Case Problem Alice Morrow pays $195 a month rent for an apartment. After careful calculation, Alice computed that this was 20% of her monthly salary. How much does Alice earn each month?

Discussion Questions

1. Using the formula we have already learned, $P = B \times R$, what is the missing item of information in this case?
2. How can we restate this equation so that we can use it to solve a problem of this sort?

We know the rate (20%) and the percentage ($195). The missing piece of information in this case is the base. To find the base, we apply a third formula based on this principle. To find the *base* when the *rate* and *percentage* are known, divide the *percentage* by the *rate*. Or

$$B = P \div R$$

Here is the way Alice Morrow's problem can be outlined.

Outline: *Known:* Percentage $195, monthly rent
                Rate   20%

To Find: Base   (monthly salary)

Method: $B = P \div R$
           $= \$195 \div 20\%$
           $= \$195 \div .20$
           $= \$975$, monthly salary

Exercises

Find the base in each of the following problems. Round off each answer to the nearest cent.

1. $12 is 20% of what amount?
2. $15 is 6% of what amount?
3. $70 is $12\frac{1}{2}$% of what amount?
4. $90 is $33\frac{1}{3}$% of what amount?
5. $63 is 7% of what amount?
6. $81 is $37\frac{1}{2}$% of what amount?
7. $95 is $62\frac{1}{2}$% of what amount?
8. $72 is 75% of what amount?
9. $84 is 28% of what amount?
10. $18 is $4\frac{1}{2}$% of what amount?
11. $3\frac{3}{4}$% of what amount is $45?
12. $2\frac{1}{4}$% of what amount is $54?
13. 16% of what amount is $4.48?
14. 5% of what amount is $23.95?
15. 72% of what amount is $54.00?

16. 85% of what amount is $108.80?

17. 120% of what amount is $18?

18. 300% of what amount is $45?

19. $72 is 100% of what amount?

20. $52.08 is 4.2% of what amount?

Business Applications

Solve the following problems. If money is involved, round off your answer to the nearest cent. All other answers should be rounded off to the nearest whole number.

1. Frank Jaffee sold a table at a profit of $6. If this was 40% of what he paid for the table, how much did the table cost him?

2. At one school, 5 students failed the first-year accounting course. This was 10% of the students taking the course. How many students were taking first-year accounting?

3. An employment test given by one company was passed by 27 applicants. This number was equal to 75% of the total number who took the test. Find the total number of applicants.

4. The selling expenses of a small musical instrument repair shop last year were 23% of the total sales. If the expenses were $4,991, how much were the total sales?

5. In one year, Ray Mann saved $2,095. If this represented 23% of his total income, what was Ray's annual income?

6. When Charlayne Williams purchased a motorbike, the sales representative asked for a deposit of 20% of the cost of the machine. If she gave $175, what was the total cost of the motorbike?

7. A group of government employees were given an increase in wages of 16 cents an hour. If this was a raise of 5% of the wages they had been receiving, what was their previous hourly wage?

8. The average salary of clerical workers in one manufacturing firm rose 60% during a 10-year period. This rise amounted to $42.50 a week. (a) What was the average weekly salary at the beginning of the 10-year period? (b) What was the average weekly salary at the end of the 10-year period?

9. Employees of the Durable Plastic Company who work on Saturdays receive an hourly rate of 150% of their normal hourly rate. Fred Urban's hourly salary on Saturday is $3.32. What is his normal hourly wage?

10. Each day, $2\frac{1}{2}$% of the employees of the Tarkington Toy Company are absent from work either because of illness or other personal reasons. If the daily absence is 35 employees, how many people work for the company?

11. A sales tax of $4.26 was paid on a purchase in a state having a 3% sales tax. What was the original cost of the purchase?

12. Ricardo Medina paid $27.54 for phonograph records. This price included a 5% city sales tax based on the original price of the records. What was the original price of the records?

13. The total sales of the R. G. Trent Department Store for June 17 amounted to $25,235. This included a 3% state sales tax.
    a. What was the actual selling price of the merchandise sold that day?
    b. What was the amount of the tax that had to be turned over to the state for that day's sales?

14. Mr. Belmont purchased a desk for which he paid $75.40. This price included a city sales tax of 4%. How much of the $75.40 was tax?

UNIT

RATIOS

Case Problem A high school had 336 pupils enrolled in its business math classes. Of these, 224 were girls and 112 were boys. How did the number of girls registered compare with the number of boys?

Discussion Questions

1. What arithmetic process do you already know how to perform that would help answer the question?
2. Why does this process not give you exactly the information you need?

You could find the percent or rate of girls and boys very easily by using a formula you learned earlier.

$$R = P \div B$$
$$R = \tfrac{224}{336} = \tfrac{2}{3} = 66\tfrac{2}{3}\% \text{ girls}$$
$$R = \tfrac{112}{336} = \tfrac{1}{3} = 33\tfrac{1}{3}\% \text{ boys}$$

FINDING THE RATIOS

We want more information than the formula above gives us. We are interested in *comparing* the number of girls to the number of boys. Because the figures in the Case Problem are simple, it is easy to see that there are twice as many girls as boys taking business math ($\tfrac{2}{3}$ is twice as big as $\tfrac{1}{3}$). What we have just found when we speak of "twice as many" is the ratio of girls to boys. A *ratio* is an arithmetic relationship between two amounts, showing the proportion of one to the other. Another way of expressing the idea that there are twice as many girls as boys taking business math is to say that the ratio of girls to boys is 2 to 1 or, as it is often expressed, 2:1. (2:1 is read "2 to 1.")

A ratio can be found in two ways. It can be found by division. We could have found the comparison by dividing the number of girls (224) by the number of boys (112) and expressing the answer (2) in ratio form—2:1. The ratio can also be found by comparing the *numerators* of fractions that have the same *denominator*. Thus in the example given, the ratio of $\tfrac{2}{3}$ (girls) to $\tfrac{1}{3}$ (boys) is, again, 2:1.

Example 1:
An office equipment store found that in a given month it sold 63 electric typewriters and 21 manual typewriters. What was the ratio of sales of electric typewriters to sales of manual typewriters?

Solution 1:
$63 \div 21 = 3$, or a ratio of 3 to 1 (3:1)

Solution 2:
Electric typewriters sold: 63
Manual typewriters sold: <u>21</u>
Total typewriters sold: 84

$\tfrac{63}{84} = \tfrac{3}{4}$ electric typewriters $\left. \right\}$ or

$\tfrac{21}{84} = \tfrac{1}{4}$ manual typewriters $\left. \right\}$ ratio of 3:1

(Use the numerators in a ratio since the denominators are the same.)

Example 2:

In November, a swimsuit manufacturer produced 4,000 synthetic swimsuits, 3,000 cotton ones, and 1,000 made of a wool blend. What was the ratio among the three fabrics used?

Solution:

4,000 synthetic
3,000 cotton
<u>1,000</u> wool blend
8,000 total

$$\frac{4,000}{8,000} = \frac{4}{8} \qquad \frac{3,000}{8,000} = \frac{3}{8} \qquad \frac{1,000}{8,000} = \frac{1}{8}$$

All the denominators are the same (eighths), so we can compare the numerators in the ratio $4:3:1$.

Exercises

1. A survey in a town shows that 2,400 households have color TV sets and 1,600 own black-and-white sets. What is the ratio of color sets to black-and-white sets?

2. A poll taken on a bond issue proposal showed 4,800 for, 3,600 against, and 1,600 with no opinion. What was the ratio among the voters?

3. In a certain suburb, 6,000 families owned two cars, 10,000 had one car, and 2,000 had no car. What is the ratio among them?

USING RATIOS

Example:

Martin Bardy is trying to save money to buy a car. He decides that he must go on a strict budget and put twice as much money into his savings account as he spends on recreation. If the total available for both purposes is $24 per week, how much should he save out of this amount?

Solution:

The proposed relationship between his savings and his recreation is in the ratio of $2:1$. Adding these together, we get a total of 3. Two parts out of the three, or $\frac{2}{3}$, is allocated to savings, and one part out of the three, or $\frac{1}{3}$, goes for recreation.

$\frac{2}{3} \times \$24 = \$16$ for savings

$\frac{1}{3} \times \$24 = \$8$ for recreation

Exercises

1. Candidate A is running for city council. According to a poll, more people like Candidate A than Candidate B by a ratio of 4:3. If it is expected that 14,700 voters will turn out, how many votes does Candidate A expect to receive?

2. Jack Boyle and Frank Skarsky are running a neighborhood tutoring service. They decide to divide their income in proportion to the amount of time they spend in tutoring. Jack spends three hours to every two hours that Frank puts in. If the total amount charged for the week is $35, how much will each one receive?

3. A philanthropist promises that he will donate $3 for every $1 in contributions received to build a new library. If the total cost of the library is estimated to be $520,000, how much must the fund-raisers collect in individual contributions?

4. A vegetable gardener wants to plant three times as many rows of corn and twice as many rows of beans as he uses for carrots. If he has a total of 132 rows available, how many should he put aside for each vegetable?

Business Applications

1. Joan Bosi and David Gordon agree to go into partnership. Bosi invests $24,000 and Gordon $15,000. What is the ratio of their investments?

2. A dealer sells 3,200 tons of Grade A coal and 2,400 tons of Grade B coal. What is the ratio of sales between the two grades?

3. A specialty shop owner has separate departments for handbags, jewelry, and leather accessories. If sales of handbags during the month amount to $6,600, sales of shoes come to $4,200, and sales of leather accessories account for $1,200, what is the ratio of sales among the three departments?

4. A dress shop finds that its sales of dresses run 5:3 as compared with sales of sportswear. If the shop has $4,800 available for new merchandise, how much should be spent for dresses? for sportswear?

5. A real estate development decides that the ratio of space set aside for buildings, recreation areas, and streets and roads should be in the proportion of 3:4:1. If the area to be developed consists of 56 acres, how much should be allotted to each use?

REVIEW EXERCISES FOR CHAPTER 7

A. Do the following problems as indicated.

1. Change each of the following decimals to percents.
   a. .63   **b.** .93   **c.** .389   **d.** .676
   e. 5.2   **f.** 8.9   **g.** 2.74   **h.** .02
   i. .024   **j.** .006

2. Change each of the following percents to decimals.
   a. 37%   **b.** 46%   **c.** 26.3%   **d.** 3%
   e. 3.4%   **f.** 254%   **g.** 150%   **h.** 1.92%
   i. 182.4%   **j.** .3%

3. Change each of the following fractions to percents. (Round off to the nearest tenth of a percent where necessary.)
   a. $\frac{3}{5}$ **b.** $\frac{2}{3}$ **c.** $\frac{1}{6}$ **d.** $\frac{11}{16}$
   e. $2\frac{1}{3}$ **f.** $\frac{5}{8}$ **g.** $\frac{3}{12}$ **h.** $3\frac{5}{6}$
   i. $13\frac{1}{2}$ **j.** $12\frac{9}{10}$

4. Change each of the following percents to fractions, renaming in simplest terms.
   a. 40%   **b.** 90%   **c.** 20%   **d.** 65%
   e. $83\frac{1}{3}$%   **f.** 72%   **g.** $18\frac{3}{4}$%   **h.** 125%
   i. 230%   **j.** 350%

5. Round off each of the following numbers as indicated.
   a. 46.7337—nearest hundredth
   b. $237.941—nearest cent
   c. $9.578—nearest cent
   d. $12,647.29—nearest dollar
   e. $8,253.91—nearest dollar
   f. $46.46—nearest dime
   g. $298.65—nearest dime
   h. 72.59476—nearest thousandth

6. Peggy Bascom is getting ready to prepare a business report from the following figures:

   $76,640.00
   $43,531.60
   $61,407.11
   $53,777.70
   $49,297.00
   $66,151.50

   For the purposes of her report, Ms. Bascom wants to round off all figures to the nearest hundred dollars. Write the figures as they would be rounded.

7. Find the percentage in the following cases, choosing the easiest method in each example.

   a. $33\frac{1}{3}$% of $296
   b. 62% of 150
   c. $87\frac{1}{2}$% of 157.6
   d. $23\frac{1}{2}$% of $184.50
   e. $6\frac{1}{4}$% of $244.80

8. Find the rate in each of the following problems.
   a. $15 is what percent of $75?
   b. 86 is what percent of 215?
   c. 103 is what percent of 824?
   d. What percent of 90 is 24?
   e. What percent of $75 is $100?

9. Find the base in each of the following problems.
   a. 15 is 40% of what amount?
   b. $90 is 2% of what amount?
   c. 6% of what amount is $180?
   d. 15% of what amount is $15?
   e. 50 is 250% of what amount?

B. Solve each of the following problems after analyzing each one to find the missing piece of information—base, rate, or percentage. In each case, round off answers involving money to the nearest cent; round off answers involving percent to the nearest tenth of a percent.

   1. Find the percentage, the base, or the rate, as needed, in each of the following problems.
      a. 25% of $3,516 is what amount?
      b. 17% of $2,375 is what amount?
      c. $4\frac{1}{2}$% of $2,620 is what amount?
      d. $16 is what percent of $64?
      e. $47 is what percent of $94?

f. $1.69 is what percent of $1.30?

g. $15 is 25% of what amount?

h. $75 is $33\frac{1}{3}$% of what amount?

i. $53 is 14% of what amount?

j. What amount is 20% of 127?

k. 18% of how many bushels is 44 bushels?

l. What percent of 75 gallons is 40 gallons?

m. $2,400 is what percent of $1,600?

n. $12\frac{1}{2}$% of 2,576 pints is how many pints?

o. $3.75 is 6% of what amount?

p. How many yards is $16\frac{2}{3}$% of 876 yards?

2. $15 is what percent more than $10?

3. $62 is what percent less than $76?

4. A leather goods dealer purchased an attaché case for $12.50 and sold it for $25.98. The profit on the sale was what percent of the cost?

5. In order to clear out sports jackets that were no longer in style, the owner of a men's wear shop sold them for $6.95, although the cost of each jacket was $20.85. What percent of loss based on his cost was the owner taking?

6. The number of engineers employed by an electronics firm was decreased from 15 to 12. What was the percent of decrease?

7. Arthur North spends 23% of his income on food. If he earns $13,342 a year, how much does Arthur spend for food?

8. A hurricane damaged 20% of the property in the business district of the village of Elmsford. If the damage was estimated at half a million dollars, what was the total value of the property?

9. Hillsbrook High School found that on the average $2\frac{1}{2}$% of its students leave school each year because their parents move out of the city. If the enrollment at Hillsbrook will be 1,296 this year, how many can be expected to leave school for this reason?

10. In a recent poll, 42.7% of the people interviewed said they would vote for Jones as mayor. If 8,500 people were interviewed, how many would not commit themselves or would vote against Jones?

11. The population of Midvale is now 23,756. If this is 140% of what it was when the 1970 census was taken, what was the population of Midvale at that time?

12. Easter sales at Allison's Department Store were 18% better this year than they were last year. If last year's sales amounted to $575,250.00, what were this year's sales?

13. Joanne Brooks offered to sell her one-year-old car to a friend at a $37\frac{1}{2}\%$ reduction from its original cost. If the car cost her $2,984, for how much was she willing to sell it?

14. Harvey Cook, Edna Prescott, and Sherwood Mann bought a dairy bar for $67,500. Cook invested $25,650; Prescott, $21,600; and Mann, $20,250. What percent of the total cost was each person's investment?

15. Out of an income of $12,600, a couple spent 28% for food, 20% for housing, 12% for clothing, 8% for car expenses, $12\frac{1}{2}\%$ for entertainment, 19% for miscellaneous expenses, and saved the rest. (a) How much did they spend in each category? (b) How much did they save?

16. Tugwell Baker had $3,260 on deposit in a savings account. If he received interest of $179.30 for one year, what was the exact percent of interest?

17. In three consecutive years, net profits of the Yoder Brick Company increased as follows: from $24,000 to $28,000 the first year, from $28,000 to $32,000 the second year, and from $32,000 to $40,000 the third year. Find the annual percent of increase for each year.

18. The payroll of a small factory this year amounted to $78,400, which is $12\frac{1}{2}\%$ less than last year's payroll. What was the amount of the payroll last year?

19. Study the table below and answer the questions beneath it.

Kaufman, Inc.
Projected Sales, 19X5–19X7

	19X5		19X6		19X7	
	Amount	% of Sales	Amount	% of Sales	Amount	% of Sales
Present Products						
Men's Clothing	6,500,000	56.2	7,500,000	51.3	8,650,000	48.0
Women's Clothing	3,000,000	26.0	3,750,000	25.7	4,500,000	25.0
Children's Clothing	1,300,000	11.3	1,100,000	8.0	1,000,000	5.5
	10,800,000	93.5	12,350,000	85.0	14,150,000	78.0
New Products						
Infant Wear	500,000	4.3	1,500,000	10.0	2,500,000	14.0
Shoes	250,000	2.2	750,000	5.0	1,500,000	8.3
	750,000	6.5	2,250,000	15.0	4,000,000	22.0
Total Projected Sales	11,550,000	100.0	14,600,000	100.0	18,150,000	100.0

a. Are total projected sales increasing or decreasing each year?
b. What percent of total sales in 19X5 are men's clothing? children's clothing?

c. What percent of total sales in 19X5 are represented by present products? new products?

d. What is the percent of increase in the amount of projected sales of shoes in 19X7 over sales in 19X5?

e. Why are percents valuable in a report like this?

20. In the election for senior class president, Marion Bart received 321 votes and Gregg Burton received 214. What was the ratio of votes cast for Marion as against those cast for Gregg?

21. In an adult education program with 1,200 students, 820 worked full-time, 240 had part-time jobs, and the remainder were not employed. What was the ratio among the three groups?

22. The ratio of sales of men's sport shirts in sizes small, medium, and large were $3:5:2$. If the store was planning to stock 110 shirts, how many should it purchase in each size?

23. Women's housecoats of a certain type come in sizes petite, small, medium, large, and extra large. If a shop planned to stock them in the ratio of $2:3:5:3:2$, how many of each size should it order out of a total order of 120 housecoats?

CHAPTER 8
PRACTICAL
MEASUREMENTS

It is impossible for you to prepare dinner, purchase new curtains for your window, carpet your living room floor, buy gasoline for your car, have a medical prescription filled, or perform any one of a hundred other (give or take a dozen) everyday activities without using some kind of measurement.

You do this so naturally now that you probably do not think about it very often. And the system of measurement that you use (the English system) also seems so natural that you probably have never thought to question it or its efficiency. However, many people who must use very fine measurements or who must deal with measurements in various parts of the world have thought long and hard about the problem of measurement. What they have sought is a uniform, rational, easy-to-use system of measurement. In this chapter, you will learn a bit of the history of the English system of measurement and some of the reasons why this system doesn't meet the needs for uniformity, rationality, and convenience. You will also be introduced to the now worldwide-accepted SI system and to the reasons why this system fulfills these requirements.

The relatively new *Systèms International d'Unites* (International System of Units), or SI system as it is called, is now accepted by most countries, including the United States, in scientific and technical areas. It is a refinement and enlargement of the metric system created in France in 1799, and it offers many advantages over our present English system of measurement.

In this chapter, you will briefly review the English system with which you are so familiar, and then you will be introduced to some of the basic units of the SI system, which you will be hearing more and more about in the near future. It is a very simple system to use (that is the reason for its popularity), and you will find that computations in the SI system are far less complex than they are in the English units.

UNIT 1

THE ENGLISH SYSTEM OF MEASUREMENT

The United States is the only major country in the world that still uses the so-called English system of measurement. (Even England has abandoned it.) This system of measurement is one that you use every day to express measures of length (6 inches, 3 feet, 5 miles); measures of volume (7 cubic feet, 4 pints, 5 gallons, 16 barrels, 2 bushels); and measures of weight (1 ounce, 4 pounds, 15 tons).

BASIC UNITS OF THE ENGLISH SYSTEM

Before the year 1,000, each town seems to have developed its own plan for measuring distance, weight, and volume. People who traveled between towns ran into a good deal of trouble because the weight called a pound in one town was not the same weight called by exactly the same name in another town. Measures of distance, area, and volume were similarly confusing to the traveler.

Some time during the eleventh century, a British king decided to do something about this confusion. He decreed that henceforth the length called one inch would be the distance from the end of his thumb to the first joint of the thumb. Similarly, one foot would be the length of his foot, while one yard would be the distance from the tip of his nose to the end of his middle finger when his arm was stretched to the side.

Although the king had standardized the system of measurement, he created a haphazard assortment of units. Since the length called the inch happened to fit into the unit called the foot exactly 12 times, it was established that there are 12 inches in one foot. Had it fallen 15 times in the foot, then there would be 15 inches in the foot! Similarly, the foot was measured off exactly three times in the distance that the king called the yard, and hence, there are now three feet in one yard. The same process was used to establish that there are $5\frac{1}{2}$ yards in a rod, 40 rods in a furlong, and so on, with absolutely no fixed pattern governing the size of any particular unit and its succeeding unit.

Other countries, including the United States, adopted this system of measurement. Because the English system is probably all that you have ever used, it seems quite simple. Let's review the various units of measurement in the English system.

Measures of Length

In the English system, distance is measured according to the following.

$$12 \text{ inches} = 1 \text{ foot (ft or ')}$$
$$3 \text{ feet} = 1 \text{ yard (yd)}$$
$$16\frac{1}{2} \text{ feet} = 1 \text{ rod (rd)}$$
$$320 \text{ rods} = 1 \text{ mile (mi); 1,760 yards; 5,280 feet}$$

Measures of Area

Surface measure is based on measures of length. A square unit consists of its length times its width.

$$144 \text{ square inches} = 1 \text{ square foot (sq ft)}$$
$$9 \text{ square feet} = 1 \text{ square yard (sq yd)}$$
$$30\frac{1}{4} \text{ square yards} = 1 \text{ square rod (sq rd)}$$
$$160 \text{ square rods} = 1 \text{ acre (A)}$$
$$640 \text{ acres} = 1 \text{ square mile (sq mi)}$$

Measures of Volume

The amount of space that an object occupies is called the volume, and the dimensions are in terms of cubic units based on measures of length. A cubic unit consists of its length times its width times its height.

```
1,728 cubic inches = 1 cubic foot (cu ft)
   27 cubic feet   = 1 cubic yard (cu yd)
  128 cubic feet   = 1 cord (cd) of wood
```

Measures of Capacity

Liquid measures of volume relate to the capacity of containers. There is a distinction between liquid measure and dry measure. Liquid measures are the following:

```
16 fluid ounces (fl oz) = 1 pint (pt)
 2 pints                 = 1 quart (qt)
 4 quarts                = 1 gallon (gal)
31½ gallons              = 1 barrel (bbl)
```

Dry measures include these:

```
2 pints (pt) = 1 quart (qt)
8 quarts     = 1 peck (pk)
4 pecks      = 1 bushel (bu)
```

Measures of Weight

There are three kinds of weights in use in the United States—the *avoirdupois weight*, the *troy weight*, and the *apothecaries' weight*. The most common of these is the avoirdupois weight; it is the type of weight that is meant unless someone specifies otherwise.

Avoirdupois Weight

```
27 11/32 grains (gr) = 1 dram (dr)
16 drams        = 1 ounce (oz)
7,000 grains    = 1 pound (lb)
16 ounces       = 1 pound
100 pounds      = 1 hundredweight (cwt)
2,000 pounds    = 1 ton (T)
2,240 pounds    = 1 long ton
```

Troy Weight
(For weighing precious metals and stones)

```
24 grains        = 1 pennyweight (pwt)
20 pennyweights  = 1 ounce (oz)
12 ounces        = 1 pound (lb)
5,760 grains     = 1 pound
3.086 grains     = 1 carat (k)
```

Apothecaries' Weights
(For weighing drugs and medicines)

```
20 grains (gr) = 1 scruple (sc)
3 scruples     = 1 dram (dr)
8 drams        = 1 ounce (oz)
```

Exercises

1. Change into feet (a) 12 yards; (b) 4 rods; (c) 3 feet, 9 inches.

2. How many square feet are there in 3 acres?

3. How many barrels are there in 189 gallons?

4. How many pecks are there in 360 bushels?

5. How many cubic inches are there in 5 cubic yards?

6. How many ounces are there in 16 pounds? 2 tons?

7. How many ounces (troy weight) does a 2-carat diamond weigh?

8. How many hundredweight are contained in 1 long ton?

9. How many quarts are there in 4 barrels?

10. How many square miles are there in 2,240 acres.

UNIT

THE SI SYSTEM OF MEASUREMENT

Because the English system of measurement is so familiar to you, you naturally accept it as a sensible method. Certainly it works fine for everyday transactions—a quart of milk, 5 gallons of gas, first down and 10 yards to go, etc. In reality, it is a very cumbersome system, particularly when used in science, chemistry, and engineering. It is for this reason that nearly all the nations of the world have abandoned the English system in favor of the SI system.

The *metric system*, of which the SI system is a refinement, was introduced in France in 1799. Since that time it has undergone many revisions. The present *International System of Units*, the *SI* system, was the result of an international agreement in 1960.

The SI or metric system is a decimal (base-10) system. It is designed so that each unit is 10 times greater than the next smaller unit. This makes it easy to convert from one unit to another because you are faced only with the simple process of multiplying and dividing by 10, 100, 1,000, and so on. There is no need to remember that there are 12 inches in a foot, 3 feet in a yard, and 1,760 yards in a mile. All you need be concerned with are 10, 100, 1,000, and the other multiples of ten.

BASIC UNITS OF THE SI SYSTEM

Some basic units of the SI system that you will use in everyday measurement are the following:

> meter (m)—the unit of length
> kilogram (kg)—the unit of weight
> liter (L)—the unit of capacity (liquid)

Note: Because the gram is so small a measurement (an ordinary paper clip weighs about a gram), it is not a practical unit of measurement for everyday use. Instead the *kilogram* or *kilo* (the equivalent of 1,000 grams) is the more commonly used measure of weight. Also, because of long-established usage, the *liter* is taken as the basic unit of capacity; that is, liquid measure. As you will see, cubic meters (cm^3) are the basic units of volume. Liters use the table of prefixes shown below. For purposes of quick reference, the meter is slightly longer than a yard (approximately 1.1 yards), the liter is slightly more than a quart (approximately 1.06 quarts), and the kilogram is slightly more than two pounds (approximately 2.2 pounds).

The SI system combines the basic units listed above with numerical prefixes derived primarily from Latin and Greek roots. To name the other larger and smaller units of the system, consult this table.

Prefix	Derivation	Abbreviation	Meaning
milli	Latin: *thousandth*	m	.001
centi	Latin: *hundredth*	c	.01
deci	Latin: *tenth*	d	.1
deka	Greek: *ten*	da	10
hecto	Greek: *hundred*	h	100
kilo	Greek: *thousand*	k	1,000

In the past few years, two new prefixes have come into common use—*micro* from Latin, indicating one millionth, and *mega*, from Greek, indicating one million.

Notice that the first three prefixes listed in the table (milli, centi, and deci), which come from Latin roots, represent *fractions* of the base unit (the meter), while the others (deka, hecto, and kilo), which are Greek in origin, represent *multiples* of the basic unit.

Measures of Length

With this background, it should be easy to understand how the individual measurements have been put together. Let us illustrate with the *meter*, which is the basic measurement for units of length.

1 millimeter (mm) =	.001 of a meter		1,000 mm = 1 m
	.01 of a decimeter **or**		100 mm = 1 dm
	.1 of a centimeter		10 mm = 1 cm
1 centimeter (cm) =	.01 of a meter	**or**	100 cm = 1 m
	.1 of a decimeter		10 cm = 1 dm
1 decimeter (dm) =	.1 of a meter	**or**	10 dm = 1 m

1 dekameter (dam) = 10 meters

1 hectometer (hm) = 100 meters or 10 dam

1 kilometer (km) = 1,000 meters, = 100 dekameters, = 10 hectometers

In pronouncing the names of the SI units, always put primary stress on the prefix.

Measures of Weight

You would expect that the gram would be the basic unit of weight measurement in the SI system. As we mentioned earlier, however, because it is too small a unit for practical measurement, the kilogram is the basic unit of weight measurement. It is the only basic unit in the SI system to have a numerical prefix.

10 milligrams (mg)	= 1 centigram (cg)
10 centigrams	= 1 decigram (dg)
10 decigrams	= 1 gram (g)
10 grams	= 1 dekagram (dag)
10 dekagrams	= 1 hectogram (hg)
10 hectograms	= 1 kilogram (kg)
1,000 kilograms	= 1 metric ton (t)

Measures of Surface or Area

Just as in the English system, the squares of the units of length are used to measure surface or area in the SI system.

100 square millimeters (mm²)	= 1 square centimeter (cm²)
100 square centimeters	= 1 square decimeter (dm²)
100 square decimeters	= 1 square meter (m²)
100 square meters	= 1 square dekameter (dam²)
100 square dekameters	= 1 square hectometer (hm²)
100 square hectometers	= 1 square kilometer (km²)

Measures of Volume

The measure of volume in the SI system is based, as in the English system, on cubic units of the measure of length.

$$1,000 \text{ cubic millimeters (mm}^3) = 1 \text{ cubic centimeter (cm}^3)$$
$$1,000 \text{ cubic centimeters} = 1 \text{ cubic decimeter (dm}^3)$$
$$1,000 \text{ cubic decimeters} = 1 \text{ cubic meter (m}^3)$$
$$1,000 \text{ cubic meters} = 1 \text{ cubic dekameter (dam}^3)$$
$$1,000 \text{ cubic dekameters} = 1 \text{ cubic kilometer (km}^3)$$

Note: As we explained, the liter is the basic unit of measure of capacity (liquid).

You will notice that the difference between SI units in area is 100 times and between SI units in volume is 1,000 times. As you know, *area = length × width*. Thus the area of an object 1 centimeter long and 1 centimeter wide is $1 \text{ cm} \times 1 \text{ cm} = 1 \text{ cm}^2$. Since 1 centimeter is 10 millimeters, the area of a square centimeter expressed in millimeters is $10 \text{ mm} \times 10 \text{ mm} = 100 \text{ mm}^2 = 1 \text{ cm}^2$.

The same process holds true for volume. *Volume = length × width × height.* A cubic centimeter is $1 \text{ cm} \times 1 \text{ cm} \times 1 \text{ cm} = 1 \text{ cm}^3$. This expressed in millimeters is $10 \text{ mm} \times 10 \text{ mm} \times 10 \text{ mm} = 1,000 \text{ mm}^3 = 1 \text{ cm}^3$.

RELATIONSHIP OF THE UNITS OF MEASUREMENT

Because the units in the SI system use 10, 100, or 1,000, it is quite simple to change from one unit to another.

Example 1:

Change 8,452 centimeters to meters.

Solution:

Since there are 100 centimeters in one meter, divide 8,452 by 100 by moving the decimal point two places to the left.

$$8,452 \text{ cm} = 84.52 \text{ m}$$

Example 2:

Change 3,440 grams to kilograms.

Solution:

Since there are 1,000 grams in a kilogram, divide 3,440 by 1,000 by moving the decimal point three places to the left.

$$3,440 \text{ g} = 3.44 \text{ kg}$$

Example 3:
Change 4.21 hectoliters to liters.

Solution:
Since there are 100 liters in one hectoliter, multiply 4.21 by 100 by moving the decimal point two places to the right.

$$4.21 \text{ hl} = 421 \text{ L}$$

Example 4:
How many grams are there in 5,248 milligrams?

Solution:
Since one gram is 1,000 times larger than one milligram, divide 5,248 by 1,000 by moving the decimal point three places to the left.

$$5,248 \text{ mg} = 5.248 \text{ g}$$

Exercises
Change each of the following to the unit indicated.

1. 15 dam   = _____ m
2. 2 km   = _____ m
3. 7 dag   = _____ dg
4. 2.3 m   = _____ cm
5. .324 dam = _____ cm
6. 56.27 hm = _____ m
7. 4.835 kg = _____ dg
8. 63.8 cm   = _____ mm
9. 426 cg   = _____ g
10. 390 m   = _____ dam
11. 36,000 mm = _____ cm
12. 6,845 dm = _____ dam
13. 537 dag = _____ kg
14. 7,860 cm = _____ hm
15. 9,024 g = _____ kg
16. 46,758 cm = _____ m

UNIT 3

CONVERTING FROM ENGLISH UNITS TO SI UNITS

In converting weights and measures in the English system to their equivalents in the SI system, you need to know the following relationships.

1 meter	= 39.37 inches	1 inch	= 2.54 centimeters
1 square meter	= 10.76 square feet	1 foot	= 30.48 centimeters
1 gram	= 15.43 grains	1 square yard	= 0.84 square meters
1 kilogram	= 2.2 pounds	1 pound	= 453.59 grams

The following conversion tables will permit you to find English and metric equivalents easily. These conversion factors are only approximate. They provide answers that are accurate enough for everyday use.

LENGTHS

To Change From	To	Multiply By
inches	centimeters (cm)	2.54
feet	centimeters (cm)	30.48
yards	meters (m)	0.91
miles	kilometers (km)	1.6
centimeters	inches (in.)	0.39
meters	feet (ft)	3.28
kilometers	miles (mi)	0.63 (or $\frac{5}{8}$)

VOLUMES

To Change From	To	Multiply By
cubic inches	cubic centimeters (cm^3)	16.39
cubic feet	cubic meters (m^3)	0.03
cubic yards	cubic meters (m^3)	0.76
cubic centimeters	cubic inches (cu in.)	0.06
cubic meters	cubic feet (cu ft)	35.31
cubic meters	cubic yards (cu yd)	1.31

LIQUID CAPACITY

To Change From	To	Multiply By
ounces	cubic centimeters (cm^3)	29.57
pints	liters (L)	0.47
quarts	liters (L)	0.95
gallons	liters (L)	3.79
liters	fluid ounces (fl oz)	33.81
liters	quarts (qts)	1.06
liters	gallons (gal)	0.26
cubic centimeters	ounces (oz)	0.034

Unit 3 Converting from English Units to SI Units 183

DRY CAPACITY

To Change From	To	Multiply By
pints	liters (L)	0.55
quarts	liters (L)	1.1
pecks	liters (L)	8.8
bushels	liters (L)	35.24
liters	pints (pts)	1.82
liters	quarts (qts)	0.9
dekaliters	pecks (pk)	1.14
hektoliters	bushels (bu)	2.84

WEIGHTS (AVOIRDUPOIS)

To Change From	To	Multiply By
grains	grams (g)	0.065
ounces	grams (g)	28.35
pounds	kilograms (kg)	0.45
tons	kilograms (kg)	907.18
grams	grains (gr)	15.43
kilograms	pounds (lbs)	2.2
metric tons	pounds (lbs)	2204.62

HOW TO USE THE TABLES OF CONVERSION FACTORS

The following examples illustrate the use of the tables of conversion factors.

Example 1:
Change to centimeters: (a) 6 in., (b) 5 ft, (c) 3 ft 7 in.

Solution:
(a) Refer to the table headed *Lengths*. In the column labeled *To Change From*, find the word "inches," and in the column labeled *To* find the word "centimeters." The number on the same line in the column labeled *Multiply By* is 2.54. Multiply this number by 6, the English length to be converted.

$$2.54 \times 6 = 15.24 \text{ cm}$$

(b) Refer to the table headed *Lengths*. In the column labeled *To Change From*, find the word "feet," and in the column labeled *To* find the word "centimeters." The number on the same line in the column labeled *Multiply By* is 30.48. Multiply this number by 5, the English length to be converted.

$$30.48 \times 5 = 152.4 \text{ cm}$$

(c) Again refer to the table headed *Lengths*. First find the equivalent feet, following the directions in (a) and (b) above; then do the same for equivalent inches. Add the two results.

$$30.48 \times 3 = \quad 91.44$$
$$2.54 \times 7 = \quad \underline{17.78}$$
$$109.22 \text{ cm}$$

Example 2:

Change the following metric measurements to English equivalents: (a) 8 km, (b) 2 kg, (c) 10 g, (d) 15 liters (to gallons)

Solution:

(a) Refer to the table headed *Lengths*. In the column labeled *To Change From*, find the word "kilometers," and in the column labeled *To* find the word "miles." The number on the same line in the column labeled *Multiply By* is 0.63. Multiply this number by 8, the metric length to be converted.

$$0.63 \times 8 = 5.04 \text{ mi}$$

(b) Refer to the table headed *Weights (Avoirdupois)*. In the column labeled *To Change From*, find the word "kilograms," and in the column labeled *To* find the word "pounds." The number on the same line in the column labeled *Multiply By* is 2.2. Multiply this number by 2, the metric length to be converted.

$$2.2 \times 2 = 4.4 \text{ lbs}$$

(c) Refer to the table headed *Weights (Avoirdupois)*. Follow the steps outlined in (a) and (b) above, this time converting grams to grains. The number to be multiplied by 10 is 15.43, thus:

$$15.43 \times 10 = 154.3 \text{ gr}$$

(d) Refer to the table headed *Liquid Capacity*. Follow the steps outlined in (a) and (b) above, this time converting liters to gallons. The number to be multiplied by 15 is 0.26, thus:

$$0.26 \times 15 = 3.90 \text{ gal}$$

Exercises

Using the conversion tables on pages 183 and 184, solve the following problems.

1. Change 620 liters to liquid quarts.
2. Change 44 m to inches.
3. Change 678 cm to feet.
4. Change 316 liters to dry pints.
5. Change 50 kg to pounds.

6. Find the number of cm^3 in 14 cubic inches.

7. Find the number of metric tons in 40 English tons.

8. Find the number of inches in 14 hectometers.

9. How many ounces are there in 180 cm^3?

10. How many feet are there in a meter?

11. How many yards does a runner travel in a 1,000-meter race?

12. How many meters does a sprinter travel in a 100-yard dash?

13. How many centimeters are there in an inch?

14. Elena Perez purchased $4\frac{1}{2}$ yards of material for a dress she plans to make. Under the metric system of measurement, how many meters of material did she buy?

15. According to the conversion table, 1 mile is equivalent to 1.6 km. How many kilometers are there from Philadelphia, Pennsylvania, to Miami, Florida, if the number of miles between the two cities is 1,250?

16. The distance from London to Paris is approximately 360 kilometers. What is the distance in miles?

17. Susan Glover's height is 5 feet, 6 inches. What is her height in meters?

Business Applications

1. The Northeast Textile Co. ships cotton fabrics to its plant in Central America where they are made into children's clothing. The Central American plant asks for a shipment of 2,500 meters of a certain cotton print. How many yards shall the shipping superintendent at Northeast Textile ask the shipping manager to package?

2. The European agent for the Bristol Motor Company reported that she traveled 1,850 kilometers on her last sales survey trip. If the Bristol Company gives its sales people an allowance of 15.6 cents per mile, how much does it owe this agent?

3. The Merx Import Co. is expecting a shipment of Italian knits on a European freighter. The packages, when they arrive, show a total weight of 126 kilograms. If the shipping costs are 8¢ per pound, what will be the freight charge on this shipment?

4. A truck manufacturer finds that its trucks average 10 miles to the gallon of gasoline. It wishes to sell its trucks in the European market, where gas is sold by the liter. In preparing its advertising material, how many kilometers can it say its trucks will average per liter of gasoline?

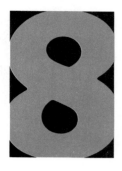

REVIEW EXERCISES FOR CHAPTER 8

1. A manufacturer of a fruit drink prepares its product in barrels and then repackages it into quart jars for sale. How many quarts can be prepared from a total daily production of 25 barrels?

2. A road repair company is repairing and repaving a stretch of road at the rate of 32 feet per hour. If it works an eight-hour day, how long will it take to repair a two-mile stretch of road?

3. The Wilton family's house is situated on a 4-acre plot of land. The county wishes to take 26,000 square feet of their land for a road which will go through their property. How many acres will they have left when the road is finished?

4. A travel agent advertises a tour of the south of France covering 740 kilometers. How many miles will be traveled on the tour?

5. Mrs. Waters wishes to import a French fabric to have drapes made for her home. If she needs a total of 52 yards for the drapes, how many meters of the fabric should she order?

PART 2
MATHEMATICS
APPLIED TO
BUSINESS
OPERATIONS

CHAPTER 9
EMPLOYEE
COMPENSATION

When we hear the word "business," we are likely to think of buildings, offices, machinery, equipment, and articles for sale. Business is all these things. But a business is not merely "things." A business is also the people who perform the work necessary to make it run and keep its doors open—the sales representatives, secretaries, factory workers, buyers, accountants, managers, clerks, maintenance staff, and others. Although people have many reasons for working, one of the most important reasons is to earn the money with which to buy the goods and services necessary for living and enjoyment. It is obvious, then, that no activity in a business or government enterprise is more important than computing employee earnings and making sure workers are paid on time and in the correct amount.

Employees are paid in many ways. Some, such as most office workers and executives, earn a salary that is stated as so much a week, a month, or a year. Others, such as those who work in a factory, are paid an hourly rate, and the number of hours they work determines how much they earn. Still others, such as certain sales representatives, are paid according to how much they sell. Some, on the other hand, are paid according to the number of articles they produce, such as factory workers who make parts for cars, radios, or vacuum cleaners. No matter what the basis for payment, each employee has certain deductions from his or her check each payday—for taxes, insurance, social security, retirement, savings, and so on. Some of these deductions are voluntary; that is, individual employees make the decisions about what they want deducted from their pay; other deductions are required by city, state, and federal government regulations.

In this chapter, you will learn some of the methods of paying workers and how deductions from their earnings are computed.

UNIT 1

COMPUTING HOURLY WAGES

Case Problem Ray Morley is a keypunch operator for Reliable Insurance Company. His earnings are computed at the hourly rate of $3. Ray keeps a time card on which he enters the hours he worked each day. The time card for the week of February 7 is shown on the following page.

Discussion Questions

1. How many hours did Ray work during the week?
2. How will his earnings be computed?

COMPUTING REGULAR TIME EARNINGS

Many employees are paid by the hour. Ray Morley, in the Case Problem, is paid the hourly rate of $3. To find his weekly earnings, you multiply the hours worked (40) by the rate per hour ($3).

$$40 \times \$3 = \$120, \text{ weekly earnings}$$

Time Cards

For each employee who is paid by the hour, it is necessary to keep records that will show the number of hours worked each day. In some businesses, this record is kept by the employee (see the example on this page). At the end of each day the number of hours worked are recorded, and at the end of the week the employee writes in the total hours and turns the card in to a supervisor. When the card is approved by the supervisor, it is given to the payroll department for the purpose of computing the employee's earnings.

In the card illustrated, Ray Morley worked 8 hours a day for 5 days. The total number of hours worked during the week is 40.

In many companies, payroll computations are done by *computers*—electronic machines that can be programmed to process data at high speeds according to a predetermined plan. The time card illustrated is designed for use with a computer, although it may also be used in noncomputer payroll operations.

Exercises

1. Find the total or gross weekly earnings for each employee.

Employee	Hourly Rate	Hours Worked	Gross Weekly Earnings
Abel, T.	$3.50	39	$ _____
Baker, J.	$3.75	40	$ _____
Conroy, J.	$3.60	40	$ _____
Doaks, R.	$3.00	38	$ _____
Dohrman, M.	$4.10	$37\frac{1}{2}$	$ _____
Ehrlich, F.	$3.90	$38\frac{1}{2}$	$ _____

2. Compute the weekly earnings of each employee.

Employee	Hourly Rate	Mon.	Tues.	Wed.	Thurs.	Fri.	Total Hours	Gross Earnings
Parker, H.	$3.75	7	8	7	7	9	_____	$ _____
Porter, C.	$3.95	8	8	8	8	8	_____	$ _____
Quade, D.	$3.80	8	8	7	6	9	_____	$ _____
Rose, M.	$3.20	7	8	9	8	8	_____	$ _____
Sanchez, T.	$3.45	6	8	8	7	7	_____	$ _____

COMPUTING OVERTIME EARNINGS

The standard work week is 40 hours, or 8 hours a day, 5 days a week. Even in companies where employees work a 35-hour week (7 hours a day for 5 days) or a $37\frac{1}{2}$-hour week ($7\frac{1}{2}$ hours a day for 5 days), a 40-hour week is considered standard for purposes of computing earnings. All hours worked up to and including 40 hours during the week are referred to as *regular hours* or *regular time*. The rate per hour for hours worked up to and including 40 is called the *regular rate*.

Companies that do business in more than one state are required by federal law to pay workers $1\frac{1}{2}$ times their regular rate for all hours worked over 40 during the week. Most companies follow this practice even though they are not required to do so. The hours worked over 40 are referred to as *overtime* and the rate as *time and a half*.

Case Problem Bernie Compton's wage rate is $3.60 an hour. During a recent week, he worked 44 hours.

1. Why do many employees like to put in overtime hours?
2. What are some of the disadvantages of overtime work?
3. How can we compute the additional amount earned because of the overtime work?

Many employees like to work overtime because they earn more money for the same amount of time put in. Employers need it in order to meet production schedules, get rush orders out, etc. However, fatigue does set in after a certain amount of work and there may be a drop in efficiency.

METHODS OF COMPUTING TOTAL EARNINGS INVOLVING OVERTIME

1. When an employee works over 40 hours a week, you can find the total earnings for the week in the following manner.

Example:

Bernie Compton worked 44 hours in a recent week. If his regular wage rate was $3.60 an hour, what were his total earnings for the week?

Solution:

a. Multiply the regular hours by the regular rate.

$$40 \times \$3.60 = \$144, \text{ regular earnings}$$

b. Convert the regular rate to an overtime rate by multiplying it by 1.5 ($1\frac{1}{2}$).

$$\$3.60 \times 1.5 = \$5.40, \text{ overtime rate}$$

c. Multiply the overtime hours by the overtime rate.

$$4 \times \$5.40 = \$21.60, \text{ overtime earnings}$$

d. Add the two earnings amounts.

$$\$144.00 \text{ (regular earnings)} + \$21.60 \text{ (overtime earnings)}$$
$$= \$165.60, \text{ gross earnings}$$

2. An alternate method that is frequently used when a company's payroll is to be automated (processed by computers) is to convert overtime hours to their equivalent regular hours.

Example:

Find Bernie Compton's gross weekly earnings by converting overtime hours to regular hours.

194   Chapter 9   Employee Compensation

Solution:

When an employee works overtime, for each overtime hour he puts in he is paid for an additional half hour. You can therefore compute Bernie's earnings as follows:

Total Hrs. Worked	Reg. Hours	Over Hours	Over Prem. Hours	Total Hrs. Paid for	Hourly Rate	Gross Earnings
44	40	4	2	46	$3.60	$165.60

1. Break up the hours worked into regular and overtime hours.
2. Compute the overtime premium (one-half the overtime hours).
3. Add to find the total hours to be paid for: regular hours (40) + overtime hours (4) + overtime premium (2) = 46.
4. Multiply by the hourly rate. 46 hours × $3.60 per hour = $165.60, gross earnings, the same answer as in the first method.

The advantage of this alternate method is that only one wage rate—the regular wage rate—is used. It is, as mentioned earlier, most frequently used for payrolls that are processed by computers.

OVERTIME ON TIME CARDS

Sadie Bellows turned in the following time card during a recent week. Note that the overtime hours are separated from the regular hours on the card. When the card is turned in to the payroll department, Sadie will be paid for 40 regular hours and 4 overtime hours computed by one of the methods already illustrated.

One week, Ralph Mitford submitted the time card that appears on the next page. Mr. Mitford's time card shows that he worked overtime on Monday, Tuesday, and Wednesday. Although his overtime totals 7 hours, he will be given credit for only 5 hours since he did not work a full 40-hour week of regular time. The payroll clerk adds the total hours worked (45) and subtracts the number of hours in the regular work week (40). The difference (5) is the overtime that will be paid at the time and a half rate.

Exercises

1. Find the gross earnings of each of the following employees if time and a half is paid for all hours over 40 each week.

	Employee No.	No. of Hours	Regular Rate	Gross Earnings
a.	085-38-4872	40	$3.80	$_____
b.	543-86-5041	38	$3.75	$_____
c.	400-01-0055	39	$3.87	$_____
d.	862-35-9462	$38\frac{1}{2}$	$3.90	$_____
e.	243-76-5394	$39\frac{1}{4}$	$3.86	$_____
f.	567-02-5000	41	$3.88	$_____
g.	465-92-0521	43	$3.96	$_____
h.	230-22-5261	52	$3.42	$_____
i.	430-27-6664	49	$3.90	$_____
j.	932-43-7243	$42\frac{1}{2}$	$3.24	$_____
k.	861-10-5230	$47\frac{1}{2}$	$4.38	$_____
l.	620-40-1163	$50\frac{1}{2}$	$3.56	$_____

2. Complete the payroll summary on the next page. Assume that time and a half is paid for all hours over 40 during the week.

Employee	M T W T F	Reg. Hours	Reg. Rate	Reg. Pay	Over. Hours	Over. Rate	Over. Pay	Gross Earnings
Armond	10 8 8 8 9	____	$3.00	$_____	____	$____	$_____	$_____
Black	8 7 6 8 8	____	$3.15	$_____	____	$____	$_____	$_____
Camp	9 8 8 9 8	____	$2.90	$_____	____	$____	$_____	$_____
Dillon	7 7 10 5 7	____	$2.98	$_____	____	$____	$_____	$_____

3. Complete the following payroll summary. Assume that time and a half is paid for all hours over 40 during the week. (In computing overtime hours, enter the hours over 40 under *Over. Hours*, then under *Prem. Hours*, enter half the overtime hours.)

Employee	M T W T F	Reg. Hours	Over. Hours	Prem. Hours	Total Hours Paid For	Reg. Rate	Gross Earnings
Figueroa	$7\frac{1}{2}$ 8 8 $7\frac{1}{2}$ 9	____	____	____	____	$3.00	$_____
Hansen	$8\frac{1}{2}$ $9\frac{1}{2}$ 8 $8\frac{1}{2}$ $8\frac{1}{2}$	____	____	____	____	$3.25	$_____
James	$8\frac{1}{2}$ $8\frac{1}{2}$ $8\frac{1}{2}$ 9 9	____	____	____	____	$2.90	$_____
Leonard	$7\frac{1}{2}$ $7\frac{1}{2}$ $7\frac{1}{2}$ $7\frac{1}{2}$ $7\frac{1}{2}$	____	____	____	____	$3.10	$_____
Schwartz	8 7 9 8 10	____	____	____	____	$3.20	$_____

4. Examine the weekly time card for Matthew Coleman below and answer the questions that follow.

a. How many regular hours did Matthew Coleman work during the week?

b. How many overtime hours did he work?

c. What was the total number of hours worked?

d. For how many hours will he be paid at his regular rate?

5. Examine the weekly time card for Renee Barnett below and answer the questions that follow.

Time card — Employee Name: Barnett Renee; Dept. No.: Exec; Supervisor: A. Joyce; Employee Initials: R.B.

	REGULAR	OVERTIME
SAT		
SUN		
MON	7	4
TUE	7	
WED	8	2
THU	6	1
FRI	8	

a. What is the total number of hours worked?

b. How many regular hours will Ms. Barnett get credit for?

c. How many overtime hours will she be paid for?

6. Compute the total number of hours that employees are expected to work weekly in the following situations.

a. A company whose work day is 7 hours and whose standard work week is 5 days.

b. A company whose work day is $7\frac{1}{2}$ hours and whose standard work week is Monday through Friday.

c. A company whose work day is 8 hours and whose standard work week is Monday through Friday.

d. A company whose work day is 7 hours Monday through Friday and 4 hours on Saturday.

SPECIAL COMPUTATIONS FOR OVERTIME

There are several variations of the overtime principles described in the previous section. These include overtime for work on Saturdays, overtime for work on Sundays and holidays, and daily overtime.

Saturday Work

Some companies that operate on a regular 5-day week (Monday through Friday) pay time and a half for work on Saturdays regardless of the number of hours worked during the regular work week.

Example:

Ernest Perry, a janitor, worked 36 hours during a regular 5-day week and 4 hours on Saturday. If the company for which Mr. Perry works pays time and a half for all Saturday work, for how many hours will he be paid during the week?

Solution:

1. Regular hours worked during the week = 36

2. Saturday work at the overtime rate = 4

Thus, Mr. Perry will be paid for 36 hours of regular time and 4 hours of overtime at time and a half. Mr. Perry's 4 hours of overtime is equivalent to 6 hours at regular time. Therefore, he will be paid for a total of 42 hours.

Sundays and Holidays

Many companies pay their employees *double time* (twice the regular rate) for work on Sundays and holidays.

Example:

Bess Bache worked a 40-hour week recently—8 hours each on Monday through Friday. Her regular rate of pay is $3.40 an hour. During that same week, however, she worked 6 hours on Sunday for which she was paid double time. What were her gross earnings for the week?

Solution:

1. Multiply the regular hours worked by the regular rate.

$$40 \times \$3.40 = \$136.00, \text{ regular earnings}$$

2. Multiply the overtime hours by the overtime rate.

$$6 \times \$6.80 \ (\$3.40 \times 2) = \$40.80, \text{ overtime earnings}$$

3. Add the products.

$$
\begin{array}{ll}
\$136.00 & \text{regular earnings} \\
\underline{\quad 40.80} & \text{overtime earnings} \\
\$176.80 & \text{gross earnings}
\end{array}
$$

Daily Time and a Half

In some situations, union contracts require that employees be paid time and a half for every hour worked over 8 hours each day, regardless of the number of hours worked each week.

Example:

Charles Tasker, a lathe operator, works an 8-hour day and is paid at the rate of $3.70 an hour. For every hour over 8 that he works each day, Mr. Tasker receives time and a half. How much did he earn during the week if he worked the following hours?

Monday	8	Wednesday	9	Friday	5
Tuesday	6	Thursday	10		

Solution:

1. Divide each day's work into regular and overtime hours and find the totals for each.

	Regular Hours	Overtime Hours
Monday	8	0
Tuesday	6	0
Wednesday	8	1
Thursday	8	2
Friday	5	0
Totals	35	3

2. Multiply regular hours by regular rate.

$$35 \times \$3.70 = \$129.50$$

3. Multiply overtime hours by overtime rate.

$$3 \times (\$3.70 \times 1.5) = 3 \times \$5.55 = \$16.65$$

4. Add the products.

$129.50   regular earnings
  16.65   overtime earnings
$146.15   gross earnings

Exercises

1. Find the gross weekly earnings for each of the following employees. Assume that all Sunday work is paid at twice the regular rate and all other overtime at $1\frac{1}{2}$ times the regular rate. Also assume that the regular work week is 40 hours and that no overtime is paid for anything over 8 hours any weekday unless the total regular week exceeds 40 hours.

   a. Mary Stone worked 36 hours during the regular week and 2 hours on Saturday. Her regular rate is $3 an hour.

   b. Aaron Ford worked 39 hours during the regular week and 4 hours on Saturday. His regular rate is $2.70 an hour.

   c. Luis Muñez worked 40 hours during the regular week, $1\frac{1}{2}$ hours on Saturday, and 3 hours on Sunday. His regular rate is $3.40 an hour.

   d. Ruby Fulton worked 42 hours during the regular week, 6 hours on Saturday, and 3 hours on Sunday. Her regular rate is $2.96 an hour.

   e. Paul Corey worked $48\frac{1}{2}$ hours during the regular week, $1\frac{1}{2}$ hours on Saturday, and 2 hours on Sunday. His regular rate is $2.88 an hour.

f. Lars Swenson worked $42\frac{1}{2}$ hours during the regular week, $2\frac{1}{2}$ hours on Saturday, and $3\frac{1}{2}$ hours on Sunday. His regular rate is $3.06 an hour.

2. Stacy's Trucking Company pays its drivers time and a half for hours they work over 8 in any one day and time and a half for all Saturday work. Find the earnings of each of the following drivers during a recent week. All receive the regular rate of $4.20 an hour.

Driver	M	T	W	T	F	S	Reg. Hours	Reg. Rate	Reg. Earn.	Over. Hours	Over. Rate	Over. Earn.	Gross Earnings
Abbott	8	8	9	7	6	0	____	$4.20	$_____	____	$____	$____	$_____
Carson	$10\frac{1}{2}$	4	9	9	11	0	____	$4.20	$_____	____	$____	$____	$_____
Casey	5	7	12	4	6	7	____	$4.20	$_____	____	$____	$____	$_____
Day	8	$8\frac{1}{2}$	$9\frac{1}{2}$	$9\frac{1}{2}$	$7\frac{1}{2}$	4	____	$4.20	$_____	____	$____	$____	$_____

3. Find (a) the total number of hours of regular time and total number of hours of overtime for Max Hurlbut, whose time card appears below. Mr. Hurlbut gets time and a half for all Saturday work and double time for Sunday work. (b) If Mr. Hurlbut's hourly rate is $3.06, what were his gross earnings for the week?

4. a. Find the total number of hours of regular time and the total number of hours of overtime for J. R. Lawrence, whose time card appears on the following page. Ms. Lawrence receives time and a half for all hours worked over 8 in one day.

b. If Ms. Lawrence's hourly rate is $2.76, what are her gross earnings for the week?

DP	41						Lawrence J. R.			PAY PERIOD
DEPT. NO.	EMP NO.	HRS.	O/T	SICK	VAC.		EMPLOYEE NAME			

Time clock card (Employee Attendance Card):

D A Y		HOURS WORKED		HOURS LOST				DAILY TOTAL		TO BE COMPLETED BY PERSONNEL DEPARTMENT			
		REGULAR	OVERTIME	SICK	VACATION	OTHER HOURS	REASON			REG	O/T	SICK	VAC
0	SAT												
1	SUN												
	MON	8	2							SUPERVISOR: Lois Purdy			
2	TUE	8	3										
3	WED	8	3							ADJUSTMENTS TO PREVIOUS PAY PERIOD			
	THU	6											
	FRI	5											
4	SAT												
5	SUN												
6	MON												
	TUE												
7	WED												
	THU												
8	FRI												
9	TOT												

Adjustments to previous pay period:

D A Y		HOURS WORKED		HOURS LOST				DAILY TOTAL
		REGULAR	OVERTIME	SICK	VACATION	OTHER HOURS	REASON	
	SAT							
	SUN							
	MON							
	TUE							
	WED							
	THU							
	FRI							
	TOT							

EMPLOYEE INITIALS: JRL

1 2 3 4 5 6 7 8 9 10 11 12 13 14 15 16 17 18 19 20 21 22 23 24 25 26 27 28 29 30 31 32 33 34 35 36 37 38 39 40 41 42 43 44 45 46 47 48 49 50 51 52 53 54 55 56 57 58 59 60 61 62 63 64 65 66 67 68 69 70 71 72 73 74 75 76 77 78 79 80

IBME28650

TIME CLOCK CARDS

A great many business firms use time clocks to record the time that employees arrive at and depart from work. The time clock stamps the "in" time and "out" time daily (morning, afternoon, and overtime) on the employee's weekly time card. At the end of the week, the time cards are collected and the earnings of each employee computed. Following is the time card for Fred Scott.

Employee No. 106-23-7342

Name Fred Scott

Week Ending June 5, 19 —

Days	Regular				Overtime		Hours
	In	Out	In	Out	In	Out	
Mon.	8:00	12:00	1:00	5:00			8
Tues.	8:06	12:01	1:00	5:02			8
Wed.	7:59	12:00	1:03	4:55			8
Thurs.	7:57	11:59	12:58	5:00			8
Fri.	8:10	12:02	1:01	5:04			7¾
Sat.							
Sun.							
				Hours	Rate	Earnings	
		Regular		39¾	2.96	117.66	
		Overtime					
		Total Hours		39¾	Gross Earnings	117.66	

Loss of Time

When the time cards are collected at the end of the week, the payroll clerk computes the number of hours worked by examining the times of arrival and departure each day. Often there is a penalty for arriving several minutes after the morning starting hour or the end of the lunch hour and for departing several minutes before the official closing hour. The policy for charging time for tardiness, early departure, and absences varies from one company to another. Usually, however, charges are made only in full quarter hours (15 minutes).

The work day of the company that employs Fred Scott is from 8:00 a.m. to 5:00 p.m. It has established the following policy concerning loss of time for late arrival. Employees arriving late are penalized a quarter hour if they miss more than half (8 minutes) of any 15 minute period. If they miss less than half the 15 minutes they will be paid for the full quarter hour. Time is not credited for early arrival or late departure unless overtime is authorized.

Arrive at	Consider as
8:01 to 8:07	8:00
8:08 to 8:22	8:15
8:23 to 8:37	8:30
8:38 to 8:52	8:45
8:53 to 9:00	9:00

An employee who arrives after 8:07 and before 8:23 loses $\frac{1}{4}$ hour's pay; after 8:22 and before 8:38, $\frac{1}{2}$ hour's pay; after 8:37 and before 8:53, $\frac{3}{4}$ hour's pay; and after 8:52, 1 hour's pay.

A similar schedule is used for early departure. That is, if employees miss more than half (8 minutes) of any 15-minute period, they are penalized the full quarter hour. If they miss less than half, they are paid for the full quarter hour. Time is not credited for late departure unless overtime is authorized.

1 to 7 minutes early departure	No deduction
8 to 22 minutes early departure	$\frac{1}{4}$ hour deduction
23 to 37 minutes early departure	$\frac{1}{2}$ hour deduction
38 to 52 minutes early departure	$\frac{3}{4}$ hour deduction
53 to 60 minutes early departure	1 hour deduction

Refer to the time card for Fred Scott on opposite page. Why wasn't Fred charged for arriving at 8:06 on Tuesday? Why was he charged on Friday for arriving at 8:10? Was Fred charged for leaving early on Wednesday? Why or why not?

Exercises

1. At what time will Fred Scott be considered to have arrived (see schedules on this page) if he actually arrived at his job at each of the following times?

   a. 8:05 **b.** 8:11 **c.** 8:54 **d.** 8:30
   e. 8:42 **f.** 8:17 **g.** 8:35 **h.** 8:59

2. What deduction (if any) will Fred Scott be charged for leaving at each of the following times? Refer to the schedules on the top of this page.

   a. 4 minutes early   **b.** 10 minutes early
   c. 25 minutes early   **d.** 46 minutes early
   e. 37 minutes early   **f.** 16 minutes early

3. Find the total hours credited to each of the following employees for the week. Assume that late arrivals and early departures are charged according to the schedules on page 203 and that no credit is given for early arrival or late departure. The work day is 8:00 a.m. to 5:00 p.m., and lunch is from 12:00 noon to 1:00 p.m.

a.

Employee No. _354-27-9003_

Name _Noyes, Wilma Jean_

Week Ending _May 16, 19—_

Days	Regular				Overtime		Hours
	In	Out	In	Out	In	Out	
Mon.	8:00	12:00	1:00	5:10			
Tues.	7:58	12:01	12:57	4:45			
Wed.	8:08	11:59	1:00	5:16			
Thurs.	8:12	12:05	1:00	5:02			
Fri.	8:23	12:00	12:55	5:00			
Sat.							
Sun.							

			Hours	Rate	Earnings
	Regular				
	Overtime				
	Total Hours			Gross Earnings	

b.

Employee No. _762-00-2862_

Name _Fellini, John T._

Week Ending _May 16, 19—_

Days	Regular				Overtime		Hours
	In	Out	In	Out	In	Out	
Mon.	7:59	11:58	12:59	5:05			
Tues.	8:14	12:00	1:01	5:02			
Wed.	8:05	12:01	1:02	4:40			
Thurs.	8:00	12:06	1:05	5:08			
Fri.	8:00	11:56	12:58	5:10			
Sat.							
Sun.							

			Hours	Rate	Earnings
	Regular				
	Overtime				
	Total Hours			Gross Earnings	

c.

Employee No. _837-54-8372_

Name _Murphy, R.G._

Week Ending _May 16, 19—_

Days	Regular				Overtime		Hours
	In	Out	In	Out	In	Out	
Mon.	7:56	12:01	12:58	5:01			
Tues.	8:07	12:03	1:02	5:00			
Wed.	8:15	12:00	1:00	5:08			
Thurs.	8:02	11:59	1:15	4:59			
Fri.	8:25	12:02	12:47	5:02			
Sat.							
Sun.							

			Hours	Rate	Earnings
	Regular				
	Overtime				
	Total Hours			Gross Earnings	

d.

Employee No. _931-08-7653_

Name _Rosen, Marcia_

Week Ending _May 16, 19—_

Days	Regular				Overtime		Hours
	In	Out	In	Out	In	Out	
Mon.	8:02	12:02	1:00	5:11			
Tues.	8:21	12:00	1:05	5:00			
Wed.	7:52	12:01	12:48	5:02			
Thurs.	7:58	12:10	1:00	5:05			
Fri.	7:59	12:05	12:59	4:58			
Sat.							
Sun.							

			Hours	Rate	Earnings
	Regular				
	Overtime				
	Total Hours			Gross Earnings	

Business Applications

1. Complete the following. Assume that time and a half is paid for all hours over 40 during the regular week and for all Saturday work.

Employee	M T W T F S	Reg. Hours	Over. Hours	Over. Prem.	Total Hrs. to be Paid For	Rate per Hour	Gross Earnings
North, D.	$7\frac{3}{4}$ 8 $8\frac{1}{4}$ 8 8 4	_____	_____	_____	_____	$3.72	$_____
Peters, R.	$6\frac{1}{2}$ $7\frac{1}{4}$ 8 8 $6\frac{1}{4}$ $5\frac{1}{4}$	_____	_____	_____	_____	$3.92	$_____
Pursell, J.	$5\frac{3}{4}$ $6\frac{1}{2}$ $6\frac{1}{4}$ $7\frac{1}{2}$ 8 8	_____	_____	_____	_____	$3.60	$_____
Reese, M.	6 6 6 $8\frac{3}{4}$ $8\frac{3}{4}$ $6\frac{3}{4}$	_____	_____	_____	_____	$3.68	$_____
						Total	$_____

2. Complete the following payroll computations. Consider all hours over 40 as overtime for which time and a half is paid.

a.

Employee	M T W T F	Reg. Hrs.	Reg. Rate	Amt.	Over. Hours	Over. Rate	Amt.	Gross Earnings
Allan, C.	8 8 8 8 8	_____	$3.40	$_____	_____	$_____	$_____	$_____
Behn, F.	8 8 9 8 8	_____	$2.86	$_____	_____	$_____	$_____	$_____
Eaton, R.	8 8 8 8 8	_____	$2.72	$_____	_____	$_____	$_____	$_____
Hale, S.	6 6 9 8 6	_____	$2.58	$_____	_____	$_____	$_____	$_____
			Totals	$_____			$_____	$_____

b.

Employee	M T W T F	Reg. Hrs.	Reg. Rate	Amt.	Over. Hours	Over. Rate	Amt.	Gross Earnings
Inge, T.	6 6 10 8 $8\frac{1}{2}$	_____	$2.82	$_____	_____	$_____	$_____	$_____
Kling, A.	$7\frac{1}{2}$ 8 $8\frac{1}{2}$ 8 8	_____	$3.20	$_____	_____	$_____	$_____	$_____
Martin, C.	8 $6\frac{1}{2}$ $6\frac{1}{2}$ $6\frac{1}{2}$ 8	_____	$2.88	$_____	_____	$_____	$_____	$_____
Nelson, J.	10 10 $7\frac{1}{2}$ $7\frac{1}{2}$ $7\frac{1}{2}$	_____	$2.64	$_____	_____	$_____	$_____	$_____
			Totals	$_____			$_____	$_____

3. Find the total hours credited to the employees on the next page for the week, then compute the gross weekly earnings of each. The work day begins at 8:00 and ends at 5:00 and lunch is from 12:00 to 1:00. Assume that late arrivals and early departures are charged according to the schedules on page 203 and that time indicated as overtime is authorized. All Saturday work is counted as overtime regardless of the hours worked during the regular week.

a.

Employee No. 422-82-4301

Name Harrison, F.C.

Week Ending Sept. 24, 19—

Days	Regular				Overtime		Hours
	In	Out	In	Out	In	Out	
Mon.	8:00	12:02	1:00	5:00	6:00	8:00	
Tues.	7:59	12:01	1:00	5:00			
Wed.	8:06	12:00	1:05	5:07			
Thurs.	8:04	11:56	12:58	5:13			
Fri.	8:03	12:07	1:07	4:53			
Sat.							
Sun.							

	Hours	Rate	Earnings
Regular		2.75	
Overtime			
Total Hours		Gross Earnings	

b.

Employee No. 927-00-5438

Name Hirsch, Paula

Week Ending Sept. 24, 19—

Days	Regular				Overtime		Hours
	In	Out	In	Out	In	Out	
Mon.	7:58	12:00	1:00	4:02			
Tues.	8:01	12:10	1:00	5:10			
Wed.	7:45	12:01	12:56	4:00			
Thurs.	8:10	11:56	12:59	3:45			
Fri.	8:07	11:30	1:06	4:15			
Sat.					8:03	11:57	
Sun.							

	Hours	Rate	Earnings
Regular		3.17	
Overtime			
Total Hours		Gross Earnings	

4. Aline Gomez, an order clerk, worked $5\frac{3}{4}$ hours beyond the regular 40 hours during a recent week. If she receives $2.92 an hour and time and a half for overtime, what were her gross earnings for the week?

5. Leroy Harmon receives time and a half for all work over 8 hours in a day, time and a half for all Saturday work, and double time for holidays and Sundays. During a recent week, Mr. Harmon worked the following hours.

Monday	$9\frac{1}{2}$	Friday	10
Tuesday	7	Saturday	4
Wednesday	8	Sunday	6
Thursday	$9\frac{1}{2}$		

If his regular hourly rate is $3.60, what were Mr. Harmon's gross earnings for the week?

6. Larry Payson works a 40-hour week at the regular rate of $3.16 an hour. During a recent week, he was charged as follows for tardiness and early departure.

Monday	15 minutes	Wednesday	15 minutes
Tuesday	30 minutes	Friday	45 minutes

a. How many hours will he be given credit for if he worked no more than an 8-hour day?

b. What was his gross weekly earnings?

c. How much did he lose for tardiness and early departure?

UNIT 2

COMPUTING EARNINGS OF SALARIED WORKERS

Case Problem Janice Graham has completed school and is looking for a job. In the newspaper want ads, she notices certain jobs that are advertised as "Wages, $2.70 per hour" and "$3.10 an hour." Other ads indicate "Salary, $130 a week," "$550 per month," and "$6,200 a year." One ad mentioned "Salary, $275 biweekly."

Discussion Questions

1. What is the difference between a wage and a salary?
2. When earnings are stated as weekly, monthly, or annual amounts, how can Janice Graham find the hourly rate?
3. What is meant by the term "biweekly"?

SALARY VERSUS WAGE

There is basically no difference between a wage and a salary. Both refer to earnings. However, it is customary to use the term *wage* when speaking of the earnings of an employee whose pay is stated as an hourly rate and *salary* when speaking of the earnings of an employee whose pay is stated as a weekly, monthly, or annual rate.

COMPUTING MONTHLY SALARY

Some employers pay their employees once a month. If an employee's salary is recorded in the payroll records as an annual amount, the payroll clerk who prepares the checks must determine the amount that is due the employee at the end of the month.

Example:
Kathleen Gorman accepted a position advertised in the newspaper and listed in the payroll records at $12,480 annually. What is her monthly salary?

Solution:
To find her monthly salary, divide the annual salary ($12,480) by 12, the number of months in a year.

$12,480 ÷ 12 = $1,040, monthly salary

COMPUTING WEEKLY SALARY

A great many companies pay their employees weekly. To find the amount of weekly salary due an employee when the salary is stated as an annual rate, divide the annual rate by 52 (the number of weeks in a year).

Example:
Find Ms. Gorman's weekly salary if her annual salary is recorded as $12,480.

Solution:
$12,480 ÷ 52 = $240, weekly salary

When salaries are given as monthly amounts, such as $1,040 per month, and you want to find the weekly salary, first multiply the monthly rate by 12 (months in a year), then divide by 52 (the number of weeks in a year).

$1,040 × 12 = $12,480; $12,480 ÷ 52 = $240, weekly salary

COMPUTING BIWEEKLY SALARY

A large number of companies pay their employees *biweekly*, which means every other week. To find the biweekly salary of an employee, first find the annual salary, then divide by 26 (26 is half of 52, the number of weeks in one year).

Example:
Find Ms. Gorman's biweekly salary if her annual salary is $12,480.

Solution:
$12,480 ÷ 26 = $480, biweekly salary

If you know a weekly salary, you can find the biweekly salary by multiplying the weekly salary by 2.

Be careful when you compute biweekly salaries. Many people think of a month as 4 weeks. This is not so. A year is made up of 12 months and if there were only 4 weeks in a month, we would have only 48 weeks in a year (4 × 12). However, you know that there are 52 weeks in a year; thus, $52 \div 12 = 4\frac{1}{3}$ weeks in a month. Thus, semimonthly (twice a month) means 24 pay periods a year (12 × 2) while biweekly (every other week) means 26 pay periods a year (52 ÷ 2). An employee paid semimonthly receives 24 pay checks a year, while an employee paid biweekly receives 26 pay checks a year.

CONVERTING A SALARY TO AN HOURLY RATE

Often an employee's salary is stated as a weekly, monthly, or annual amount, and for certain computations it must be converted to an hourly rate. To convert a weekly salary rate to an hourly rate, divide the weekly salary by the total hours in the work week.

Example:
What is the hourly rate of Gary Fielding, who earns $118 a week and works a 40-hour week?

Solution:
$118 ÷ 40 = $2.95, hourly rate

To convert a monthly, biweekly, or annual salary to an hourly rate, first find the weekly salary, then proceed as in the example.

Exercises
1. For each annual salary, give the monthly salary.
   - a. $7,800
   - b. $6,756
   - c. $5,664
   - d. $11,208
   - e. $9,420
   - f. $8,340
   - g. $15,600
   - h. $19,740

2. For each annual salary, give the weekly salary.
   - a. $9,100
   - b. $8,424
   - c. $6,604
   - d. $5,980
   - e. $5,824
   - f. $5,148
   - g. $11,492
   - h. $14,508

3. For each annual salary, give the biweekly salary.
   - a. $9,542
   - b. $7,254
   - c. $6,318
   - d. $8,658
   - e. $5,772
   - f. $12,454
   - g. $13,936
   - h. $20,748

4. For each annual salary, give the semimonthly salary.
   - a. $6,480
   - b. $7,080
   - c. $8,412
   - d. $12,246
   - e. $14,652

5. For each weekly salary, give the biweekly salary.
   - a. $118.25
   - b. $237.50
   - c. $190.90

6. Find the hourly rate for each weekly salary.

Employee	Weekly Salary	Hours in Work Week	Hourly Rate
a	$106.00	40	$ _____
b	$131.25	35	$ _____
c	$150.00	$37\frac{1}{2}$	$ _____
d	$220.00	40	$ _____
e	$198.50	$37\frac{1}{2}$	$ _____

Business Applications

The personnel department of Gorham's listed the following jobs in various newspaper want ads, inviting applicants to apply. One of the questions an applicant often asks is, "How much will I earn each payday?" The personnel interviewer wants to convert the annual amounts to monthly, biweekly, and weekly amounts so that she can answer the applicants' questions quickly.

1. Complete the table, rounding off amounts to the nearest penny.

Job	Annual Salary	Monthly Salary	Biweekly Salary	Weekly Salary
Accounting Clerk	$ 6,720	$ _____	$ _____	$ _____
Shipping Supervisor	$ 7,448	$ _____	$ _____	$ _____
Messenger–Clerk	$ 4,996	$ _____	$ _____	$ _____
Executive Secretary	$ 8,360	$ _____	$ _____	$ _____
Systems Analyst	$12,736	$ _____	$ _____	$ _____
Senior Accountant	$14,808	$ _____	$ _____	$ _____
Office Supervisor	$ 9,996	$ _____	$ _____	$ _____
Programmer	$10,420	$ _____	$ _____	$ _____

2. a. If the accounting clerk works a 40-hour week, what is his or her hourly rate of pay?
  b. If the messenger–clerk works a 35-hour week, what is his or her hourly rate of pay?

UNIT

3

COMMISSIONS AND BONUSES

Case Problem Robert Marino sells used cars for Brighton Motor Sales. Mr. Marino receives no salary, but for every car he sells he receives 5% of the selling price of the car. Susan Flowers is a sales clerk in the children's wear department of Faraday's, a large department store. Ms. Flowers receives a salary each week, and, in addition, she is paid 2% of the total sales she makes during the week.

Discussion Questions
1. What kind of compensation plan does Mr. Marino have? Ms. Flowers?
2. What are the advantages of these compensation plans to the employer? to the employee?

COMMISSIONS

Both Mr. Marino and Ms. Flowers in the Case Problem are paid under a commission compensation plan. Mr. Marino's plan is called a *straight commission,* because he receives commission only. Ms. Flowers's plan is called a *salary-plus-commission plan* because she receives a commission in addition to her regular salary. The advantage of commission compensation to salespeople is that the more they sell the more they earn. The employer, on the other hand, feels that a commission plan gives a worker a greater incentive (drive) to succeed.

Straight Commission
The straight-commission sales representative's earnings are usually based on the dollar volume (amount) of his or her sales in a given period. The commission is stated as a percent of sales, and the rate will vary according to the price of the product, the difficulty of selling it, and other factors. To find the earnings of a straight-commission sales representative, multiply the total sales by the commission rate.

Example:
John Turnbull receives a commission of 12% on all of his sales. During a recent month, Mr. Turnbull sold merchandise amounting to $6,500. How much did he earn in commissions?

Solution:
$6,500 (total sales) = 12% (commission rate) = commissions earned
$6,500 × .12 = $780, commissions earned

Salary Plus Commission

Most representatives prefer the salary-plus-commission plan because they are assured a regular income each pay period even though their sales may be low during that period. The commission rate of these representatives is usually lower than that of the straight-commission representative.

Example:
Edward Washington is manager of the record department of Kline's Metropolitan Store. He receives a salary of $85 a week plus a commission of 4% of the selling price of the merchandise he sells. How much will he earn during a week in which he sells $1,750 worth of records?

Solution:
Weekly salary	= $85
Commissions ($1,750 × 4%) =	70
Gross earnings	$155

Commission Plus Override

In some businesses, a sales representative earns commissions on all the sales he makes and, in addition, receives a percent of the amount of sales made by other representatives whom he supervises. The commission earned on the sales of other representatives is called an *override*.

Example:
Margaret Lockhart is a sales supervisor for the Harbor Appliance Manufacturing Company, where she supervises eight commission sales representatives. Ms. Lockhart receives a 10% commission on the merchandise she sells, plus 2% of the value of the merchandise the eight representatives sell. If, during a two-week period, Ms. Lockhart herself sold merchandise valued at $2,000 and the eight representatives sold merchandise valued at $14,000, how much would Ms. Lockhart earn?

Solution:
Personal commissions =	$200 (10% of $2,000, or .10 × $2,000)
Override commissions =	280 (2% of $14,000, or .02 × $14,000)
Gross earnings	= $480

Exercises

1. Find the commission earned on each sale if the commission rate is 4%.

   a. $36,000 **b.** $1,450 **c.** $172,600
   d. $16,420 **e.** $44,148

2. Find the gross monthly earnings for each sales representative. Assume in each case that the commission rate is 8%.

Sales Representative	Monthly Salary	Monthly Sales	Commission Earned	Gross Earnings
Pappas	$400	$1,400	$_____	$_____
Rogers	$375	$2,970	$_____	$_____
Ryerson	$500	$4,470	$_____	$_____
Sacco	$275	$3,420	$_____	$_____
Stimson	$350	$3,350	$_____	$_____
Tong	$200	$6,080	$_____	$_____

3. Find the gross monthly earnings of the following straight-commission sales supervisors. All of them receive 3% on the sales they make plus a 1% override on the sales made by their sales representatives.

Supervisor	Own Sales	Commission	Representatives Sales	Commission	Total Commissions
McVeigh	$25,400	$_____	$ 31,200	$_____	$_____
Myerson	$16,000	$_____	$ 8,800	$_____	$_____
Nabors	$18,250	$_____	$ 57,745	$_____	$_____
Nyland	$ 8,680	$_____	$121,400	$_____	$_____
Ormond	$20,100	$_____	$ 45,500	$_____	$_____

BONUSES

Some sales representatives are paid a regular salary plus an extra amount, called a *bonus*, if they achieve a certain sales goal or quota.

Salary Plus Fixed Bonus

Gregg Gilbert is a representative for the Far East Wholesale Spice Company. He receives a salary of $700 a month. In addition to his salary, Mr. Gilbert receives a bonus based on exceeding a certain sales goal or *quota*. If his sales are under or equal to the quota, he gets no bonus. But if he exceeds the quota, he gets 4% of the amount by which he goes over it. During May, Mr. Gilbert's sales quota was $10,000, but his actual sales amounted to $13,500. The plan under which Mr. Gilbert is paid is called a *salary-plus-fixed-bonus plan*.

Example:

Find Mr. Gilbert's total earnings for the month of May.

Solution:

1. Subtract the sales quota from the total sales.

$13,500   total sales
 10,000   less quota
$ 3,500   base amount for bonus

2. Multiply the base amount for bonus by the percent rate to find the bonus earned.

$3,500   base amount for bonus
×.04   percent rate (4%)
$ 140   bonus earned

3. To the bonus earned add the monthly salary to find total earnings.

$140   bonus earned
 700   add salary
$840   gross earnings for May

Salary Plus Graduated Bonus

Under the *salary-plus-graduated-bonus plan,* the sales representative's bonus is based on a changing percent. That is, the percent increases as sales increase, instead of remaining at a fixed rate.

Example:

Nancy Kosinski sells sporting goods for the Sunny Clime Sporting Goods Company. She receives a base salary of $800 a month, plus a bonus which is based on a graduated scale as follows:

1% of all sales up to and including $10,000
2% of all sales over $10,000, and up to and including $15,000
3% of all sales over $15,000

During the month of October, Ms. Kosinski's sales amounted to $16,500. How much did she earn in October?

Solution:

1% of $10,000 = $ 100   bonus for the first $10,000
2% of $ 5,000 = $ 100   bonus for the next $5,000
3% of $ 1,500 = $ 45   bonus for sales over $15,000
                 $ 245   total bonus
                 $ 800   add monthly salary
                 $1,045   gross earnings

Exercises

1. Find the gross weekly earnings for each sales representative.

Representative	Salary	Sales Quota	% on Sales Over Quota	Actual Sales	Bonus Earned	Gross Earnings
Jarman	$100	$ 3,000	2%	$ 3,300	$_____	$_____
Jessup	$125	$ 500	5%	$ 750	$_____	$_____
Karl	$ 90	$ 1,500	10%	$ 3,000	$_____	$_____
Kimmel	$115	$ 4,000	7%	$ 3,500	$_____	$_____
Loper	$200	$15,000	1%	$16,200	$_____	$_____
Lytel	$150	$ 6,000	$2\frac{1}{2}$%	$ 6,600	$_____	$_____

2. Compute the annual bonus for each sales representative at the Ross Baking Company. Assume the percents given below.

> $1\frac{1}{2}$% of all sales up to and including $50,000
> 2% of all sales over $50,000 and up to and including $75,000
> 5% of all sales over $75,000

    a. Roper: $61,000   **b.** Fernandez $51,000
    c. Ponti: $57,500   **d.** Beck: $72,200
    e. Eggers: $42,800   **f.** Mays: $77,000
    g. Abbott: $39,900   **h.** Maley: $82,300
    i. Ackerman: $49,900

    j. What preliminary work could you have done, so that you did not have to go through the complete computation separately for each salesman?

Business Applications

1. The Excello Corporation sells aluminum cookware through commission sales representatives who call on customers in their homes. A set of the Excello DeLuxe Collection of cookware sells for $220, on which each representative receives a commission of 28%. The purchasers of the cookware are given permission to return their purchase within ten days if they do not wish to keep the set, and these returns must be deducted from the representatives' total sales.

    During the month of September, the five representatives in the Smithfield Region produced the record on the next page. Find the total earnings for each representative for the month.

Representative	DeLuxe Sets Sold	Returns	Net Sales (in Numbers)	Commission Earned per Sale (28% of $220)	Gross Earnings
Abelard	14	4	_____	$ _____	$ _____
Benes	16	3	_____	$ _____	$ _____
Dembofsky	12	0	_____	$ _____	$ _____
Pincus	21	5	_____	$ _____	$ _____
Teachman	27	7	_____	$ _____	$ _____

2. Jerry Windham is a sales representative for the Walk-O-Lite Shoe Store. He receives a weekly salary of $45, plus a commission of 7% of his sales. What were his earnings during a week in which his sales were $972?

3. Olga Gregory receives a salary of $90 a week and a commission of 5% on that part of her weekly sales over $1,200. During the past 3 weeks her sales were as follows: first week, $1,790; second week, $2,167.40; third week, $1,660.60.
   a. How much did she earn in each of the three weeks?
   b. What were her average weekly earnings for the 3-week period?

4. Larry Dobey is a sales supervisor in Montgomery County, Maryland, where he supervises six commission sales representatives. Larry also sells, drawing a commission of 18% on each sale he makes. On all the business produced by his representatives, Larry receives a $1\frac{1}{2}$% override. During the month of February, Larry made sales amounting to $5,400, and his representatives produced $32,490 in business.
   a. How much commission did Larry receive on his own sales?
   b. How much commission did Larry receive on the sales of the six sales representatives?
   c. How much did Larry earn in February?

5. Nilsa Garcia is a sales representative for the Darnell Milling Company. She receives a base salary of $9,200 a year. In addition to her salary, she gets a bonus based on a sales quota. If Nilsa exceeds the quota, she gets $2\frac{1}{2}$% of the amount by which she goes over it. During March, Nilsa's sales quota was $81,500, but her actual sales came to $87,750.
   a. What was Nilsa's base salary for March?
   b. By how much did her sales exceed the March quota?
   c. What was the amount of commission earned by Nilsa in March?
   d. What were her gross earnings in March?

6. Ray Frisch sells advertising space for a magazine for home crafts. He receives a base salary of $4,800 a year. He also has a bonus plan as follows: 4% of all sales up to and including $12,000; 5% of all sales over $12,000 and up to and including $20,000; and 6% of all sales over $20,000 in any one month. During the month of July, Ray's sales amounted to $21,750. What were his gross earnings for the month?

UNIT
4

PIECE-WORK PLANS

Case Problem   Walter Watson works in the Painting Section of the Abilene Farm Equipment Company. It is Mr. Watson's job to spray paint various parts of the farm implements manufactured. Mr. Watson is paid according to the number of articles he paints during the week. The compensation plan under which Mr. Watson is paid is a type of *incentive* compensation. More specifically, it is referred to as a *piece-work plan*.

1. Why might Mr. Watson's compensation plan be referred to as an "incentive" plan?
2. What are the advantages to Mr. Watson of this type of plan? to his employer?
3. Do you know why Mr. Watson's plan is called a "piece-work" plan?

Piece-work wage plans are frequently used in jobs where production can be accurately measured. They get their name from the fact that the employee's earnings are based on the number of items or pieces produced. A typist may be paid according to the number of pages typed, a clerk according to the number of invoices prepared, and a machinist according to the number of metal shafts turned out. To both the employer and the employee, such a plan provides an incentive (an urge to do more) because the greater the number of pieces produced the greater the benefits to both parties.

There are two basic types of piece-work plans—the *straight piece-work plan* and the *differential piece-work plan*.

STRAIGHT PIECE-WORK PLAN

Under the *straight piece-work-wage plan*, the worker receives a given amount for each item or unit produced, regardless of the quantity.

Example:
Gordon McCambridge is a lathe operator in the Lampcraft Corporation. For each lamp base he produces, Mr. McCambridge is paid $3.09. During a recent week, he produced 112 lamp bases. How much did he earn during the week?

Solution:
112 (bases produced) × $3.09 (amount per base) = $346.08, gross weekly earnings.

DIFFERENTIAL PIECE-WORK PLAN

Like the straight piece-work plan, the *differential piece-work plan* is designed to pay a worker according to the number of items produced. However, under the differential piece-work plan, the amount paid per item increases as the production increases in a given period of time, usually one day.

Example:
Myra McIntosh is employed by Gibson Specialties, where she paints designs on various articles of glassware. Ms. McIntosh is paid according to the following differential piece-work schedule.

Articles Completed Per Day	Rate Per Article
12 or less	$2.00
13–14	$2.02
15–16	$2.05
17–18	$2.08
19–20	$2.12
21–22	$2.16
23–24	$2.20
25–26	$2.24
27 or more	$2.29

If Miss McIntosh paints 18 articles in one day, what will be her earnings for the day?

Solution:

Referring to the piece-work schedule above, you will see that the rate per article for 17–18 articles is $2.08. Miss McIntosh completed 18 articles; therefore, to find her earnings, multiply $2.08 by 18.

$2.08 \times 18 = 37.44, earnings for the day

Exercises

1. Find the gross weekly earnings of each of the following employees. Use the straight piece-work plan.

Employee	No. of Articles Produced	Amount per Article	Gross Weekly Earnings
Natali, M.	120	$ 1.11	$_____
Osborne, T.	81	$ 1.91	$_____
Padua, R.	65	$ 2.44	$_____
Quax, R.	214	$ .66	$_____
Reeb, H.	12	$11.125	$_____
Rooney, A.	116	$ 1.015	$_____

2. Find the daily earnings of each of the following employees if their daily production is as shown below. Use the differential piece-work schedule shown at the top of this page.

a. 11   b. 23   c. 16
d. 9   e. 14   f. 21
g. 25   h. 28   i. 19
j. 22   k. 12   l. 27

Business Applications

1. Find the gross earnings of each of the following employees.

Employee	No. of Articles M T W T F	Total Articles	Rate	Gross Weekly Earnings
Adams, J.	17 21 18 20 22	_____	$ .97	$ _____
Cadena, W.	24 23 20 22 19	_____	$ .82½	$ _____
Grant, C.	20 18 16 19 21	_____	$1.36	$ _____
Martin, W.	26 23 20 22 24	_____	$ .95½	$ _____
Moran, S.	19 22 24 25 21	_____	$ .87	$ _____
Pezzuti, H.	27 24 23 28 24	_____	$1.09½	$ _____
Rubin, A.	24 21 19 22 20	_____	$1.08	$ _____
Walsh, H.	18 21 22 19 18	_____	$ .85	$ _____

2. A piece-work employee in Sunburst Electronics has been producing 370 units a day. A systems specialist studies the job and suggests that if certain changes were made the output could be increased by 30%. If this advice is followed, how many units can the employee be expected to produce?

3. Sally Ann Roemer is employed by the Squire Manor Tie Company. For each tie completed and accepted, Sally Ann receives 47½ cents. During a recent week her output in ties was as follows: Monday, 86; Tuesday, 105; Wednesday, 94; Thursday, 97; Friday, 107. During the week, 15 defective ties were rejected. What gross earnings did she receive for the week?

4. Using the schedule of differential rates shown below, find the daily earnings of each of the employees shown in the table on the next page and the gross earnings of each worker for the week.

Units Produced Per Day	Rate Per Article
20 or less	$ .95
21–22	$ .96½
23–24	$ .97
25–26	$ .98½
27–28	$1.00
29–30	$1.01¾
31–32	$1.03¾
33–34	$1.05½
35–36	$1.07

Employee	M	Earnings	T	Earnings	W	Earnings	T	Earnings	F	Earnings	Gross Weekly Earnings
Jacobs, J.	20	$_____	21	$_____	18	$_____	18	$_____	24	$_____	$_____
Ponte, R.	30	$_____	27	$_____	16	$_____	30	$_____	30	$_____	$_____
Rausche, F.	31	$_____	34	$_____	32	$_____	29	$_____	35	$_____	$_____
Tilden, L.	23	$_____	23	$_____	23	$_____	23	$_____	23	$_____	$_____
Valenti, M.	21	$_____	30	$_____	27	$_____	26	$_____	26	$_____	$_____

UNIT 5

PAYROLL DEDUCTIONS—FEDERAL INCOME TAX

Case Problem   Cynthia Holloway is an economist for a large business firm in Washington, D.C. She receives a salary of $12,500 a year. Miss Holloway is not married, but she supports her mother, with whom she shares an apartment.

Following is a stub attached to a recent biweekly paycheck that Miss Holloway received. The stub explains certain deductions that were made from her salary.

Gross Pay	Deductions					Net Amount
	FICA	Fed. WH/Tax	Hosp.	Insur.	D.C. Tax	
$480.77	$28.13	$81.20	$1.50	$3.80	$22.38	$343.76

Discussion Questions

1. Can you explain the various deductions that were made from Miss Holloway's check?
2. Which of the deductions are required by law and which are voluntary (Miss Holloway's decision)?
3. What is Miss Holloway's "take-home pay"?

The deductions made from Miss Holloway's gross pay include the following:

1. FICA, which stands for Federal Insurance Contributions Act but is commonly referred to as social security
2. Federal income tax, which is often called "withholding tax," thus the abbreviation "Fed. WH/Tax"
3. Hospitalization insurance, which is a voluntary deduction and protects Cynthia and her dependents in case of serious illness requiring hospital treatment
4. Insurance, which is a form of *group life insurance* that many employers make available at nominal rates
5. City income tax, which is required by the District of Columbia

Three of the deductions shown on Cynthia's check stub are required by law—FICA, federal income tax, and the city tax. The other two are voluntary. Other deductions that are often made from the pay of employees include union dues, contributions (such as Community Chest), savings bonds, and pensions (retirement). Such deductions are made only upon the request of the employee. When the deductions are made from the employee's gross pay the amount remaining is the *net*, or *take-home*, pay.

The principal computations required in payroll deductions are for taxes and social security. Taxes will be discussed in this unit and social security in the next unit.

INCOME TAX DEDUCTIONS

Nearly everybody who earns money must pay a tax on it to the federal government. Income taxes are the chief source of revenue (money) for operating the United States Government. In addition, some states have an income tax as do a number of cities (you will remember that Cynthia Holloway pays income taxes to Washington, D.C.). The methods of computing these taxes are similar to those of computing federal income taxes.

Rather than wait until the end of the year to collect all the taxes on income, as was the case many years ago, the federal government has a pay-as-you-go system whereby employers must withhold from each employee's earnings a certain amount each pay period. On April 15 of each year everyone who earns a large enough income files a tax return. If too much money has been withheld from the salary, the individual will get a refund. If too little has been withheld, the individual must then pay the balance due.

The income tax withheld from an employee's earnings is remitted by the employer to the federal government (Internal Revenue Service). The amount the employer withholds depends on two things:

1. The amount the employee earns. Therefore, the greater the income the greater the tax. In addition, the tax *rate* itself increases as the income goes up.
2. The number of exemptions allowed. In general, each worker is allowed one exemption for herself or himself and one for each dependent (spouse, child, relative, and others who rely on the employee for their support). Cynthia Holloway has two dependents—herself and her aged mother. A man with three children and a nonworking wife can claim five exemptions—one for himself, one for his wife, and one for each child. The more exemptions a worker is allowed, the less income tax paid. An employee is permitted to claim a "0" exemption. More money will then be withheld from the employee's salary, and the worker can expect a refund after filling out an income tax return for the year.

USING TAX TABLES

The quickest way to find the amount of income tax to be withheld from an employee's earnings is to use withholding tables provided by the Internal Revenue Service. These tables are available for weekly, biweekly, semimonthly, monthly, and daily periods. They have been mathematically constructed so that they take into consideration the tax rates at different levels of income. We will use the biweekly and weekly tables (see this and next three pages).

SINGLE Persons — WEEKLY Payroll Period

And the wages are—		And the number of withholding allowances claimed is—										
At least	But less than	0	1	2	3	4	5	6	7	8	9	10 or more
		The amount of income tax to be withheld shall be—										
100	105	16.50	13.40	10.40	7.80	5.20	2.80	.80	0	0	0	0
105	110	17.50	14.50	11.50	8.70	6.10	3.50	1.50	0	0	0	0
110	115	18.60	15.50	12.50	9.60	7.00	4.40	2.20	.10	0	0	0
115	120	19.60	16.60	13.60	10.50	7.90	5.30	2.90	.80	0	0	0
120	125	20.70	17.60	14.60	11.60	8.80	6.20	3.60	1.50	0	0	0
125	130	21.70	18.70	15.70	12.60	9.70	7.10	4.50	2.20	.20	0	0
130	135	22.80	19.70	16.70	13.70	10.70	8.00	5.40	2.90	.90	0	0
135	140	23.80	20.80	17.80	14.70	11.70	8.90	6.30	3.70	1.60	0	0
140	145	24.90	21.80	18.80	15.80	12.80	9.80	7.20	4.60	2.30	.30	0
145	150	25.90	22.90	19.90	16.80	13.80	10.80	8.10	5.50	3.00	1.00	0
150	160	27.50	24.50	21.40	18.40	15.40	12.30	9.50	6.90	4.30	2.00	0
160	170	29.60	26.60	23.50	20.50	17.50	14.40	11.40	8.70	6.10	3.50	1.40
170	180	31.70	28.70	25.60	22.60	19.60	16.50	13.50	10.50	7.90	5.30	2.80
180	190	33.80	30.80	27.70	24.70	21.70	18.60	15.60	12.60	9.70	7.10	4.50
190	200	35.90	32.90	29.80	26.80	23.80	20.70	17.70	14.70	11.70	8.90	6.30
200	210	38.10	35.00	31.90	28.90	25.90	22.80	19.80	16.80	13.80	10.70	8.10
210	220	40.40	37.10	34.00	31.00	28.00	24.90	21.90	18.90	15.90	12.80	9.90
220	230	42.70	39.30	36.10	33.10	30.10	27.00	24.00	21.00	18.00	14.90	11.90
230	240	45.10	41.60	38.30	35.20	32.20	29.10	26.10	23.10	20.10	17.00	14.00
240	250	47.80	43.90	40.60	37.30	34.30	31.20	28.20	25.20	22.20	19.10	16.10

Unit 5   Payroll Deductions-Federal Income Tax   223

Note that tax rates and tax tables are subject to frequent change. Specific tables and rates cited throughout this book are for purposes of illustration only. You should learn the procedures outlined here so that you can apply these standard methods to new rates and tables.

Example 1:

How much federal income tax will be deducted from Lois Corbin's biweekly salary of $297.85 if she is single and claims herself as her only exemption?

Solution:

In the withholding table for single persons on the next page, find the appropriate figures in the *At least* and *But less than* columns. Since Lois Corbin's salary for the period is at least $290 but less than $300, this is the appropriate line on which to find the tax. The columns to the right of *But less than* indicate the number of exemptions. Lois has only 1 exemption, and you look for the figure in that column, which is $45.80. This is the amount that must be withheld from Lois's biweekly earnings.

Example 2:

How much income tax will be deducted from Peter Marconi's biweekly salary of $386.45? His wife, Peggy, has no income, and the couple has three children. In addition, Peggy's father makes his home with the Marconi family and relies entirely on Peter Marconi's income for his support.

MARRIED Persons—WEEKLY Payroll Period

And the wages are—		And the number of withholding allowances claimed is—										
At least	But less than	0	1	2	3	4	5	6	7	8	9	10 or more
		The amount of income tax to be withheld shall be—										
$100	$105	$14.10	$11.80	$9.50	$7.20	$4.90	$2.80	$.80	$0	$0	$0	$0
105	110	14.90	12.60	10.30	8.00	5.70	3.50	1.50	0	0	0	0
110	115	15.70	13.40	11.10	8.80	6.50	4.20	2.20	.10	0	0	0
115	120	16.50	14.20	11.90	9.60	7.30	5.00	2.90	.80	0	0	0
120	125	17.30	15.00	12.70	10.40	8.10	5.80	3.60	1.50	0	0	0
125	130	18.10	15.80	13.50	11.20	8.90	6.60	4.30	2.20	.20	0	0
130	135	18.90	16.60	14.30	12.00	9.70	7.40	5.10	2.90	.90	0	0
135	140	19.70	17.40	15.10	12.80	10.50	8.20	5.90	3.60	1.60	0	0
140	145	20.50	18.20	15.90	13.60	11.30	9.00	6.70	4.40	2.30	.30	0
145	150	21.30	19.00	16.70	14.40	12.10	9.80	7.50	5.20	3.00	1.00	0
150	160	22.50	20.20	17.90	15.60	13.30	11.00	8.70	6.40	4.10	2.00	0
160	170	24.10	21.80	19.50	17.20	14.90	12.60	10.30	8.00	5.70	3.40	1.40
170	180	26.00	23.40	21.10	18.80	16.50	14.20	11.90	9.60	7.30	5.00	2.80
180	190	28.00	25.20	22.70	20.40	18.10	15.80	13.50	11.20	8.90	6.60	4.30
190	200	30.00	27.20	24.30	22.00	19.70	17.40	15.10	12.80	10.50	8.20	5.90
200	210	32.00	29.20	26.30	23.60	21.30	19.00	16.70	14.40	12.10	9.80	7.50
210	220	34.40	31.20	28.30	25.40	22.90	20.60	18.30	16.00	13.70	11.40	9.10
220	230	36.80	33.30	30.30	27.40	24.50	22.20	19.90	17.60	15.30	13.00	10.70
230	240	39.20	35.70	32.30	29.40	26.50	23.80	21.50	19.20	16.90	14.60	12.30
240	250	41.60	38.10	34.60	31.40	28.50	25.60	23.10	20.80	18.50	16.20	13.90

Solution:

In the withholding table for married persons on page 226, find the appropriate figures in the *At least* and *But less than* columns. Since Peter's salary for the biweekly period is at least $380 but less than $400, this is the appropriate line on which to find the tax. Peter has six exemptions—himself, Peggy, three children, and a dependent father-in-law. Refer to the figure under the 6 column to find the amount to be withheld—$30.20.

SINGLE Persons — BIWEEKLY Payroll Period

And the wages are—		And the number of withholding allowances claimed is—										
At least	But less than	0	1	2	3	4	5	6	7	8	9	10 or more
		The amount of income tax to be withheld shall be—										
180	184	28.10	22.00	16.60	11.50	6.40	2.30	0	0	0	0	0
184	188	28.90	22.90	17.40	12.20	7.00	2.90	0	0	0	0	0
188	192	29.80	23.70	18.10	12.90	7.70	3.40	0	0	0	0	0
192	196	30.60	24.60	18.80	13.60	8.40	4.00	0	0	0	0	0
196	200	31.50	25.40	19.50	14.30	9.10	4.60	.50	0	0	0	0
200	210	32.90	26.90	20.80	15.60	10.40	5.50	1.50	0	0	0	0
210	220	35.00	29.00	22.90	17.40	12.20	7.00	2.90	0	0	0	0
220	230	37.10	31.10	25.00	19.20	14.00	8.80	4.30	.30	0	0	0
230	240	39.20	33.20	27.10	21.10	15.80	10.60	5.70	1.70	0	0	0
240	250	41.30	35.30	29.20	23.20	17.60	12.40	7.20	3.10	0	0	0
250	260	43.40	37.40	31.30	25.30	19.40	14.20	9.00	4.50	.40	0	0
260	270	45.50	39.50	33.40	27.40	21.30	16.00	10.80	5.90	1.80	0	0
270	280	47.60	41.60	35.50	29.50	23.40	17.80	12.60	7.40	3.20	0	0
280	290	49.70	43.70	37.60	31.60	25.50	19.60	14.40	9.20	4.60	.60	0
290	300	51.80	45.80	39.70	33.70	27.60	21.50	16.20	11.00	6.00	2.00	0
300	320	55.00	48.90	42.90	36.80	30.80	24.70	18.90	13.70	8.50	4.10	.10
320	340	59.20	53.10	47.10	41.00	35.00	28.90	22.80	17.30	12.10	6.90	2.90
340	360	63.40	57.30	51.30	45.20	39.20	33.10	27.00	21.00	15.70	10.50	5.70
360	380	67.60	61.50	55.50	49.40	43.40	37.30	31.20	25.20	19.30	14.10	8.90
380	400	71.80	65.70	59.70	53.60	47.60	41.50	35.40	29.40	23.30	17.70	12.50
400	420	76.10	69.90	63.90	57.80	51.80	45.70	39.60	33.60	27.50	21.50	16.10
420	440	80.70	74.10	68.10	62.00	56.00	49.90	43.80	37.80	31.70	25.70	19.70
440	460	85.30	78.70	72.30	66.20	60.20	54.10	48.00	42.00	35.90	29.90	23.80
460	480	90.20	83.30	76.60	70.40	64.40	58.30	52.20	46.20	40.10	34.10	28.00
480	500	95.60	87.90	81.20	74.60	68.60	62.50	56.40	50.40	44.30	38.30	32.20
500	520	101.00	93.30	85.80	79.20	72.80	66.70	60.60	54.60	48.50	42.50	36.40
520	540	106.40	98.70	90.90	83.80	77.20	70.90	64.80	58.80	52.70	46.70	40.60
540	560	112.30	104.10	96.30	88.50	81.80	75.10	69.00	63.00	56.90	50.90	44.80
560	580	118.50	109.60	101.70	93.90	86.40	79.70	73.20	67.20	61.10	55.10	49.00
580	600	124.70	115.80	107.10	99.30	91.50	84.30	77.70	71.40	65.30	59.30	53.20
600	620	130.90	122.00	113.00	104.70	96.90	89.10	82.30	75.70	69.50	63.50	57.40
620	640	137.10	128.20	119.20	110.30	102.30	94.50	86.90	80.30	73.70	67.70	61.60
640	660	143.30	134.40	125.40	116.50	107.70	99.90	92.10	84.90	78.20	71.90	65.80
660	680	149.70	140.60	131.60	122.70	113.70	105.30	97.50	89.70	82.80	76.20	70.00
680	700	156.70	146.80	137.80	128.90	119.90	111.00	102.90	95.10	87.40	80.80	74.20
700	720	163.70	153.60	144.00	135.10	126.10	117.20	108.30	100.50	92.70	85.40	78.80
720	740	170.70	160.60	150.50	141.30	132.30	123.40	114.50	105.90	98.10	90.40	83.40
740	760	177.70	167.60	157.50	147.50	138.50	129.60	120.70	111.70	103.50	95.80	88.00
760	780	184.70	174.60	164.50	154.40	144.70	135.80	126.90	117.90	109.00	101.20	93.40
780	800	191.70	181.60	171.50	161.40	151.30	142.00	133.10	124.10	115.20	106.60	98.80

Unit 5   Payroll Deductions-Federal Income Tax   225

MARRIED Persons—BIWEEKLY Payroll Period

And the wages are—		And the number of withholding allowances claimed is—										
At least	But less than	0	1	2	3	4	5	6	7	8	9	10 or more
		The amount of income tax to be withheld shall be—										
$200	$210	$28.30	$23.60	$19.00	$14.40	$9.80	$5.50	$1.50	$0	$0	$0	$0
210	220	29.90	25.20	20.60	16.00	11.40	6.90	2.90	0	0	0	0
220	230	31.50	26.80	22.20	17.60	13.00	8.40	4.30	.30	0	0	0
230	240	33.10	28.40	23.80	19.20	14.60	10.00	5.70	1.70	0	0	0
240	250	34.70	30.00	25.40	20.80	16.20	11.60	7.10	3.10	0	0	0
250	260	36.30	31.60	27.00	22.40	17.80	13.20	8.60	4.50	.40	0	0
260	270	37.90	33.20	28.60	24.00	19.40	14.80	10.20	5.90	1.80	0	0
270	280	39.50	34.80	30.20	25.60	21.00	16.40	11.80	7.30	3.20	0	0
280	290	41.10	36.40	31.80	27.20	22.60	18.00	13.40	8.80	4.60	.60	0
290	300	42.70	38.00	33.40	28.80	24.20	19.60	15.00	10.40	6.00	2.00	0
300	320	45.10	40.40	35.80	31.20	26.60	22.00	17.40	12.80	8.10	4.10	.10
320	340	48.30	43.60	39.00	34.40	29.80	25.20	20.60	16.00	11.30	6.90	2.90
340	360	52.10	46.80	42.20	37.60	33.00	28.40	23.80	19.20	14.50	9.90	5.70
360	380	56.10	50.30	45.40	40.80	36.20	31.60	27.00	22.40	17.70	13.10	8.50
380	400	60.10	54.30	48.60	44.00	39.40	34.80	30.20	25.60	20.90	16.30	11.70
400	420	64.10	58.30	52.50	47.20	42.60	38.00	33.40	28.80	24.10	19.50	14.90
420	440	68.70	62.30	56.50	50.80	45.80	41.20	36.60	32.00	27.30	22.70	18.10
440	460	73.50	66.60	60.50	54.80	49.00	44.40	39.80	35.20	30.50	25.90	21.30
460	480	78.30	71.40	64.50	58.80	53.00	47.60	43.00	38.40	33.70	29.10	24.50
480	500	83.10	76.20	69.30	62.80	57.00	51.20	46.20	41.60	36.90	32.30	27.70
500	520	87.90	81.00	74.10	67.20	61.00	55.20	49.50	44.80	40.10	35.50	30.90
520	540	92.70	85.80	78.90	72.00	65.00	59.20	53.50	48.00	43.30	38.70	34.10
540	560	97.50	90.60	83.70	76.80	69.80	63.20	57.50	51.70	46.50	41.90	37.30
560	580	102.30	95.40	88.50	81.60	74.60	67.70	61.50	55.70	49.90	45.10	40.50
580	600	107.10	100.20	93.30	86.40	79.40	72.50	65.60	59.70	53.90	48.30	43.70
600	620	111.90	105.00	98.10	91.20	84.20	77.30	70.40	63.70	57.90	52.20	46.90
620	640	116.70	109.80	102.90	96.00	89.00	82.10	75.20	68.30	61.90	56.20	50.40
640	660	121.60	114.60	107.70	100.80	93.80	86.90	80.00	73.10	66.20	60.20	54.40
660	680	127.20	119.40	112.50	105.60	98.60	91.70	84.80	77.90	71.00	64.20	58.40
680	700	132.80	124.70	117.30	110.40	103.40	96.50	89.60	82.70	75.80	68.80	62.40
700	720	138.40	130.30	122.30	115.20	108.20	101.30	94.40	87.50	80.60	73.60	66.70
720	740	144.00	135.90	127.90	120.00	113.00	106.10	99.20	92.30	85.40	78.40	71.50
740	760	149.60	141.50	133.50	125.40	117.80	110.90	104.00	97.10	90.20	83.20	76.30
760	780	155.20	147.10	139.10	131.00	122.90	115.70	108.80	101.90	95.00	88.00	81.10
780	800	160.80	152.70	144.70	136.60	128.50	120.50	113.60	106.70	99.80	92.80	85.90

Exercises

Refer to the withholding tables on pages 225 and 226 and find the federal income tax to be withheld for each of the following biweekly salaries.

No.	Salary	Exemptions	Marital Status	Income Tax		No.	Salary	Exemptions	Marital Status	Income Tax
1	$246.00	1	Single	$_____		11	$206.54	5	Married	$_____
2	$198.70	2	Single	$_____		12	$350.84	6	Married	$_____
3	$377.20	3	Single	$_____		13	$308.52	5	Married	$_____
4	$201.85	4	Married	$_____		14	$254.60	5	Married	$_____
5	$483.12	3	Married	$_____		15	$299.46	3	Single	$_____
6	$309.90	2	Married	$_____		16	$312.54	6	Married	$_____
7	$621.00	5	Married	$_____		17	$576.68	11	Married	$_____
8	$715.90	1	Single	$_____		18	$699.44	0	Single	$_____
9	$505.50	3	Single	$_____		19	$414.25	1	Single	$_____
10	$199.95	0	Single	$_____		20	$696.80	3	Married	$_____

Business Applications

Refer to the withholding tables on pages 225 and 226 to solve the following problems.

1. George Bradley has a biweekly salary of $386.42. For income tax purposes, he claims two exemptions.
   a. If he is single, how much income tax will be withheld from his salary?
   b. If he is married, how much income tax will be withheld from his salary?
   c. How much more would he have to pay as a single person than as a married person?

2. Charles Armond earns $454.84 each biweekly pay period. If he has a wife and three children, how much will be withheld from his salary each biweekly period for income tax?

3. Joanne Warwick, whose husband is in school full time, has two children and two aged parents who also depend on her for support. If Mrs. Warwick's earnings are $685 each biweekly pay period, how much will be withheld from her salary for income tax?

4. Theodore Boyajian and his wife Rachel are both 67 years of age. Mr. Boyajian earns a biweekly salary of $375.24 (Mrs. Boyajian does not work). What will be the income tax withheld from Mr. Boyajian's pay? (Note: An employee over 65 can claim two exemptions for himself and two for his wife if she is also over 65.)

5. An additional exemption can be claimed for a husband or wife for the blindness of either, two exemptions if both are blind. George Stevens is 69 and blind. His wife, Mary, is 61 and earns a biweekly income of $229.66. How much will her income tax deduction be?

UNIT 6

PAYROLL DEDUCTIONS—SOCIAL SECURITY

Case Problem   Roger Blum is a flight engineer for World Route Airlines. His salary is $18,000 a year. Mr. Blum is married and has three children. He claims 5 exemptions for income tax purposes.

Discussion Questions

1. Besides the withholding tax previously discussed, what other deduction will be made from his salary by the federal government?
2. What is the purpose of this tax?
3. How is it computed?

The employer is required to withhold a portion of all employees' salaries each pay period for FICA (social security). FICA stands for Federal Insurance Contributions Act. This money, which is matched dollar for dollar by an equal tax on the employer, will be used to pay employees a pension when they reach retirement age or to supply other benefits. The amount to be withheld is a percent of the gross earnings. At the present time, this rate is 5.85%, but it has been increasing steadily by acts of Congress and can be expected to increase again in the future. Unlike federal income tax, the number of exemptions claimed by a worker does not affect the amount deducted for social security tax.

Example:

Frank Porter's gross earnings for the week of February 7 amounted to $100. How much will the employer deduct from his pay for social security?

Solution:

$100 × 5.85 = $100 × .0585 = $5.85, FICA deduction

The employer may not, however, deduct more than a certain amount during the year from a worker's earnings for FICA. At the present time, when a worker has earned $12,000 from an employer in one year, the employer makes no further deductions for social security for the remainder of that year. This amount, too, may be expected to change through acts of Congress.

Example:

In the Case Problem, our flight engineer's annual salary is $18,000, or $1,500 a month. At what point during the year will his employer stop making deductions for FICA?

Solution:

Since the employer makes FICA deductions only up to $12,000 during the year and Mr. Blum's salary is $1,500 a month, he will have no further FICA deductions after the 8th month, or August, when he will have earned $12,000. At that time, the maximum amount will have been deducted from Mr. Blum's pay.

Frank Porter, in the previous example, will continue to have FICA deductions made from his earnings throughout the year since his total earnings for the year ($5,200) are less than $12,000.

USING A FICA TABLE

Although it is easy to compute the amount to be withheld from an employee's earnings for social security, in many payroll operations it is faster and more convenient to use a social security tax table. These tables are provided by the federal government and show deductions to be made for social security on various earnings. A section of the Social Security Employee Tax Table is shown on pages 229 and 230.

Social Security Employee Tax Table
5.85 percent employee tax deductions

At least	But less than	Tax to be withheld	At least	But less than	Tax to be withheld	At least	But less than	Tax to be withheld	At least	But less than	Tax to be withheld
90.52	90.69	5.30	101.63	101.80	5.95	112.74	112.91	6.60	123.85	124.02	7.25
90.69	90.86	5.31	101.80	101.97	5.96	112.91	113.08	6.61	124.02	124.19	7.26
90.86	91.03	5.32	101.97	102.14	5.97	113.08	113.25	6.62	124.19	124.36	7.27
91.03	91.20	5.33	102.14	102.31	5.98	113.25	113.42	6.63	124.36	124.53	7.28
91.20	91.37	5.34	102.31	102.48	5.99	113.42	113.59	6.64	124.53	124.71	7.29
93.94	94.11	5.50	105.05	105.22	6.15	116.16	116.33	6.80	127.27	127.44	7.45
94.11	94.28	5.51	105.22	105.39	6.16	116.33	116.50	6.81	127.44	127.61	7.46
94.28	94.45	5.52	105.39	105.56	6.17	116.50	116.67	6.82	127.61	127.78	7.47
94.45	94.62	5.53	105.56	105.73	6.18	116.67	116.84	6.83	127.78	127.95	7.48
94.62	94.79	5.54	105.73	105.90	6.19	116.84	117.01	6.84	127.95	128.12	7.49
97.36	97.53	5.70	108.47	108.64	6.35	119.58	119.75	7.00	130.69	130.86	7.65
97.53	97.70	5.71	108.64	108.81	6.36	119.75	119.92	7.01	130.86	131.03	7.66
97.70	97.87	5.72	108.81	108.98	6.37	119.92	120.09	7.02	131.03	131.20	7.67
97.87	98.04	5.73	108.98	109.15	6.38	120.09	120.26	7.03	131.20	131.37	7.68
98.04	98.21	5.74	109.15	109.32	6.39	120.26	120.43	7.04	131.37	131.54	7.69
135.82	135.99	7.95	146.93	147.10	8.60	158.04	158.21	9.25	169.15	169.32	9.90
135.99	136.16	7.96	147.10	147.27	8.61	158.21	158.38	9.26	169.32	169.49	9.91
136.16	136.33	7.97	147.27	147.44	8.62	158.38	158.55	9.27	169.49	169.66	9.92
136.33	136.50	7.98	147.44	147.61	8.63	158.55	158.72	9.28	169.66	169.83	9.93
136.50	136.67	7.99	147.61	147.78	8.64	158.72	158.89	9.29	169.83	170.00	9.94
136.67	136.84	8.00	147.78	147.95	8.65	158.89	159.06	9.30	170.00	170.18	9.95
136.84	137.01	8.01	147.95	148.12	8.66	159.06	159.24	9.31	170.18	170.35	9.96
137.01	137.18	8.02	148.12	148.30	8.67	159.24	159.41	9.32	170.35	170.52	9.97
137.18	137.36	8.03	148.30	148.47	8.68	159.41	159.58	9.33	170.52	170.69	9.98
137.36	137.53	8.04	148.47	148.64	8.69	159.58	159.75	9.34	170.69	170.86	9.99
139.24	139.41	8.15	150.35	150.52	8.80	161.46	161.63	9.45	172.57	172.74	10.10
139.41	139.58	8.16	150.52	150.69	8.81	161.63	161.80	9.46	172.74	172.91	10.11
139.58	139.75	8.17	150.69	150.86	8.82	161.80	161.97	9.47	172.91	173.08	10.12
139.75	139.92	8.18	150.86	151.03	8.83	161.97	162.14	9.48	173.08	173.25	10.13
139.92	140.09	8.19	151.03	151.20	8.84	162.14	162.31	9.49	173.25	173.42	10.14
141.80	141.97	8.30	152.91	153.08	8.95	164.02	164.19	9.60	175.13	175.30	10.25
141.97	142.14	8.31	153.08	153.25	8.96	164.19	164.36	9.61	175.30	175.48	10.26
142.14	142.31	8.32	153.25	153.42	8.97	164.36	164.53	9.62	175.48	175.65	10.27
142.31	142.48	8.33	153.42	153.59	8.98	164.53	164.71	9.63	175.65	175.82	10.28
142.48	142.65	8.34	153.59	153.77	8.99	164.71	164.88	9.64	175.82	175.99	10.29
142.65	142.83	8.35	153.77	153.94	9.00	164.88	165.05	9.65	175.99	176.16	10.30
142.83	143.00	8.36	153.94	154.11	9.01	165.05	165.22	9.66	176.16	176.33	10.31
143.00	143.17	8.37	154.11	154.28	9.02	165.22	165.39	9.67	176.33	176.50	10.32
143.17	143.34	8.38	154.28	154.45	9.03	165.39	165.56	9.68	176.50	176.67	10.33
143.34	143.51	8.39	154.45	154.62	9.04	165.56	165.73	9.69	176.67	176.84	10.34
143.51	143.68	8.40	154.62	154.79	9.05	165.73	165.90	9.70	176.84	177.01	10.35
143.68	143.85	8.41	154.79	154.96	9.06	165.90	166.07	9.71	177.01	177.18	10.36
143.85	144.02	8.42	154.96	155.13	9.07	166.07	166.24	9.72	177.18	177.36	10.37
144.02	144.19	8.43	155.13	155.30	9.08	166.24	166.42	9.73	177.36	177.53	10.38
144.19	144.36	8.44	155.30	155.48	9.09	166.42	166.59	9.74	177.53	177.70	10.39
177.70	177.87	10.40	188.81	188.98	11.05	199.92	200.09	11.70	211.03	211.20	12.35
177.87	178.04	10.41	188.98	189.15	11.06	200.09	200.26	11.71	211.20	211.37	12.36
178.04	178.21	10.42	189.15	189.32	11.07	200.26	200.43	11.72	211.37	211.54	12.37
178.21	178.38	10.43	189.32	189.49	11.08	200.43	200.60	11.73	211.54	211.71	12.38
178.38	178.55	10.44	189.49	189.66	11.09	200.60	200.77	11.74	211.71	211.89	12.39
178.55	178.72	10.45	189.66	189.83	11.10	200.77	200.95	11.75	211.89	212.06	12.40
178.72	178.89	10.46	189.83	190.00	11.11	200.95	201.12	11.76	212.06	212.23	12.41
178.89	179.06	10.47	190.00	190.18	11.12	201.12	201.29	11.77	212.23	212.40	12.42
179.06	179.24	10.48	190.18	190.35	11.13	201.29	201.46	11.78	212.40	212.57	12.43
179.24	179.41	10.49	190.35	190.52	11.14	201.46	201.63	11.79	212.57	212.74	12.44
181.97	182.14	10.65	193.08	193.25	11.30	204.19	204.36	11.95	215.30	215.48	12.60
182.14	182.31	10.66	193.25	193.42	11.31	204.36	204.53	11.96	215.48	215.65	12.61
182.31	182.48	10.67	193.42	193.59	11.32	204.53	204.71	11.97	215.65	215.82	12.62
182.48	182.65	10.68	193.59	193.77	11.33	204.71	204.88	11.98	215.82	215.99	12.63
182.65	182.83	10.69	193.77	193.94	11.34	204.88	205.05	11.99	215.99	216.16	12.64
184.53	184.71	10.80	195.65	195.82	11.45	206.76	206.93	12.10	217.87	218.04	12.75
184.71	184.88	10.81	195.82	195.99	11.46	206.93	207.10	12.11	218.04	218.21	12.76
184.88	185.05	10.82	195.99	196.16	11.47	207.10	207.27	12.12	218.21	218.38	12.77
185.05	185.22	10.83	196.16	196.33	11.48	207.27	207.44	12.13	218.38	218.55	12.78
185.22	185.39	10.84	196.33	196.50	11.49	207.44	207.61	12.14	218.55	218.72	12.79

Social Security Employee Tax Table—Continued

5.85 percent employee tax deductions

Wages At least	But less than	Tax to be withheld	Wages At least	But less than	Tax to be withheld	Wages At least	But less than	Tax to be withheld	Wages At least	But less than	Tax to be withheld
185.39	185.56	10.85	196.50	196.67	11.50	207.61	207.78	12.15	218.72	218.89	12.80
185.56	185.73	10.86	196.67	196.84	11.51	207.78	207.95	12.16	218.89	219.06	12.81
185.73	185.90	10.87	196.84	197.01	11.52	207.95	208.12	12.17	219.06	219.24	12.82
185.90	186.07	10.88	197.01	197.18	11.53	208.12	208.30	12.18	219.24	219.41	12.83
186.07	186.24	10.89	197.18	197.36	11.54	208.30	208.47	12.19	219.41	219.58	12.84
187.10	187.27	10.95	198.21	198.38	11.60	209.32	209.49	12.25	220.43	220.60	12.90
187.27	187.44	10.96	198.38	198.55	11.61	209.49	209.66	12.26	220.60	220.77	12.91
187.44	187.61	10.97	198.55	198.72	11.62	209.66	209.83	12.27	220.77	220.95	12.92
187.61	187.78	10.98	198.72	198.89	11.63	209.83	210.00	12.28	220.95	221.12	12.93
187.78	187.95	10.99	198.89	199.06	11.64	210.00	210.18	12.29	221.12	221.29	12.94
222.14	222.31	13.00	233.25	233.42	13.65	244.36	244.53	14.30	255.48	255.65	14.95
222.31	222.48	13.01	233.42	233.59	13.66	244.53	244.71	14.31	255.65	255.82	14.96
222.48	222.65	13.02	233.59	233.77	13.67	244.71	244.88	14.32	255.82	255.99	14.97
222.65	222.83	13.03	233.77	233.94	13.68	244.88	245.05	14.33	255.99	256.16	14.98
222.83	223.00	13.04	233.94	234.11	13.69	245.05	245.22	14.34	256.16	256.33	14.99
223.00	223.17	13.05	234.11	234.28	13.70	245.22	245.39	14.35	256.33	256.50	15.00
223.17	223.34	13.06	234.28	234.45	13.71	245.39	245.56	14.36	256.50	256.67	15.01
223.34	223.51	13.07	234.45	234.62	13.72	245.56	245.73	14.37	256.67	256.84	15.02
223.51	223.68	13.08	234.62	234.79	13.73	245.73	245.90	14.38	256.84	257.01	15.03
223.68	223.85	13.09	234.79	234.96	13.74	245.90	246.07	14.39	257.01	257.18	15.04
224.71	224.88	13.15	235.82	235.99	13.80	246.93	247.10	14.45	258.04	258.21	15.10
224.88	225.05	13.16	235.99	236.16	13.81	247.10	247.27	14.46	258.21	258.38	15.11
225.05	225.22	13.17	236.16	236.33	13.82	247.27	247.44	14.47	258.38	258.55	15.12
225.22	225.39	13.18	236.33	236.50	13.83	247.44	247.61	14.48	258.55	258.72	15.13
225.39	225.56	13.19	236.50	236.67	13.84	247.61	247.78	14.49	258.72	258.89	15.14
225.56	225.73	13.20	236.67	236.84	13.85	247.78	247.95	14.50	258.89	259.06	15.15
225.73	225.90	13.21	236.84	237.01	13.86	247.95	248.12	14.51	259.06	259.24	15.16
225.90	226.07	13.22	237.01	237.18	13.87	248.12	248.30	14.52	259.24	259.41	15.17
226.07	226.24	13.23	237.18	237.36	13.88	248.30	248.47	14.53	259.41	259.58	15.18
226.24	226.42	13.24	237.36	237.53	13.89	248.47	248.64	14.54	259.58	259.75	15.19
226.42	226.59	13.25	237.53	237.70	13.90	248.64	248.81	14.55	259.75	259.92	15.20
226.59	226.76	13.26	237.70	237.87	13.91	248.81	248.98	14.56	259.92	260.09	15.21
226.76	226.93	13.27	237.87	238.04	13.92	248.98	249.15	14.57	260.09	260.26	15.22
226.93	227.10	13.28	238.04	238.21	13.93	249.15	249.32	14.58	260.26	260.43	15.23
227.10	227.27	13.29	238.21	238.38	13.94	249.32	249.49	14.59	260.43	260.60	15.24
227.27	227.44	13.30	238.38	238.55	13.95	249.49	249.66	14.60	260.60	260.77	15.25
227.44	227.61	13.31	238.55	238.72	13.96	249.66	249.83	14.61	260.77	260.95	15.26
227.61	227.78	13.32	238.72	238.89	13.97	249.83	250.00	14.62	260.95	261.12	15.27
227.78	227.95	13.33	238.89	239.06	13.98	250.00	250.18	14.63	261.12	261.29	15.28
227.95	228.12	13.34	239.06	239.24	13.99	250.18	250.35	14.64	261.29	261.46	15.29
228.12	228.30	13.35	239.24	239.41	14.00	250.35	250.52	14.65	261.46	261.63	15.30
228.30	228.47	13.36	239.41	239.58	14.01	250.52	250.69	14.66	261.63	261.80	15.31
228.47	228.64	13.37	239.58	239.75	14.02	250.69	250.86	14.67	261.80	261.97	15.32
228.64	228.81	13.38	239.75	239.92	14.03	250.86	251.03	14.68	261.97	262.14	15.33
228.81	228.98	13.39	239.92	240.09	14.04	251.03	251.20	14.69	262.14	262.31	15.34
228.98	229.15	13.40	240.09	240.26	14.05	251.20	251.37	14.70	262.31	262.48	15.35
229.15	229.32	13.41	240.26	240.43	14.06	251.37	251.54	14.71	262.48	262.65	15.36
229.32	229.49	13.42	240.43	240.60	14.07	251.54	251.71	14.72	262.65	262.83	15.37
229.49	229.66	13.43	240.60	240.77	14.08	251.71	251.89	14.73	262.83	263.00	15.38
229.66	229.83	13.44	240.77	240.95	14.09	251.89	252.06	14.74	263.00	263.17	15.39
232.40	232.57	13.60	243.51	243.68	14.25	254.62	254.79	14.90	265.73	265.90	15.55
232.57	232.74	13.61	243.68	243.85	14.26	254.79	254.96	14.91	265.90	266.07	15.56
232.74	232.91	13.62	243.85	244.02	14.27	254.96	255.13	14.92	266.07	266.24	15.57
232.91	233.08	13.63	244.02	244.19	14.28	255.13	255.30	14.93	266.24	266.42	15.58
233.08	233.25	13.64	244.19	244.36	14.29	255.30	255.48	14.94	266.42	266.59	15.59
275.99	276.16	16.15	287.10	287.27	16.80	298.21	298.38	17.45	309.32	309.49	18.10
276.16	276.33	16.16	287.27	287.44	16.81	298.38	298.55	17.46	309.49	309.66	18.11
276.33	276.50	16.17	287.44	287.61	16.82	298.55	298.72	17.47	309.66	309.83	18.12
276.50	276.67	16.18	287.61	287.78	16.83	298.72	298.89	17.48	309.83	310.00	18.13
276.67	276.84	16.19	287.78	287.95	16.84	298.89	299.06	17.49	310.00	310.18	18.14
276.84	277.01	16.20	287.95	288.12	16.85	299.06	299.24	17.50			
277.01	277.18	16.21	288.12	288.30	16.86	299.24	299.41	17.51	310.18 and over		
277.18	277.36	16.22	288.30	288.47	16.87	299.41	299.58	17.52	5.85% of wages		
277.36	277.53	16.23	288.47	288.64	16.88	299.58	299.75	17.53			
277.53	277.70	16.24	288.64	288.81	16.89	299.75	299.92	17.54			

Here is how to use the table.

Example:

Rosanne Fiscina's earnings during the last pay period were $204.75. Using the social security employee tax table on page 229, find the amount to be deducted for FICA.

Solution:

Look down the Wages column until you come to *At least* $204.71 *But less than* $204.88. The tax to be withheld is in the next column to the right—$11.98.

The amount deducted from an employee's earnings for FICA is added to an equal amount contributed by the employer, and the total is remitted quarterly (every three months) to an agency of the federal government to be used eventually for pensions and other benefits for which the employee may be eligible upon retirement or disability.

Exercises

1. Find the deductions to be made for social security (FICA) from each of the following paycheck amounts, using the withholding rate of 5.85%. Assume that the employee in each case has not yet paid the maximum yearly tax.

   a. $278   **b.** $214.40   **c.** $295.95
   d. $402.20   **e.** $305.50   **f.** $187.90
   g. $312.34   **h.** $376.75

2. During what month of the year will the last social security tax deduction be made from each of the following monthly earnings?

   a. $2,000   **b.** $1,800   **c.** $1,250

3. Using the Social Security Employee Tax Table on page 229, find the tax to be withheld from each of the following earnings.

   a. $199.95   **b.** $228.80   **c.** $248.95
   d. $225.50   **e.** $249.40   **f.** $233.50
   g. $238.25   **h.** $240.65   **i.** $204.39
   j. $215.49   **k.** $208.45   **l.** $226.03

Business Applications

1. Complete the payroll information on the next page. Assume in each case that the employee has not yet paid the maximum yearly tax. Use the rate of 5.85%.

		Income		Other	Total	Net
Employee	Gross Earnings	Tax	FICA	Deductions	Deductions	Pay
Jacobs, M.	$262.00	$34.00	$ _____	$12.45	$ _____	$ _____
Krause, R.	$346.00	$39.40	$ _____	$ 9.88	$ _____	$ _____
LeQueux, K.	$392.60	$36.70	$ _____	$14.60	$ _____	$ _____
Ronald, T.	$445.55	$64.20	$ _____	$ 8.75	$ _____	$ _____
Ruppert, F.	$336.25	$25.50	$ _____	$11.20	$ _____	$ _____

(Deductions heading spans Income Tax, FICA, Other Deductions, Total Deductions above)

2. Refer to the Social Security Employee Tax Table on page 229 and complete the following payroll information.

		Income		Other	Total	Net
Employee	Gross Earnings	Tax	FICA	Deductions	Deductions	Pay
Aaron, G. H.	$218.48	$23.70	$ _____	$13.12	$ _____	$ _____
Bok, C.	$245.90	$20.50	$ _____	$21.20	$ _____	$ _____
Bragg, J.	$199.92	$ 8.50	$ _____	$18.12	$ _____	$ _____
Crank, Mc. T.	$249.90	$ 4.10	$ _____	$ 9.45	$ _____	$ _____
Croner, W.	$212.45	$15.60	$ _____	$ 8.65	$ _____	$ _____
Dugan, M.	$239.11	$18.50	$ _____	$11.05	$ _____	$ _____
Dugan, W.	$243.70	$28.50	$ _____	$12.25	$ _____	$ _____

3. George Talbot earns $2.96 an hour.
   a. What is his gross income during a week in which he worked $38\frac{1}{4}$ hours?
   b. How much will be withheld from Mr. Talbot's earnings for social security?

4. Ann Millard's hourly rate is $3.48. She receives time and a half for all hours worked over 40 in a week and double time for Sunday work. Last week Ms. Millard worked $47\frac{1}{2}$ hours during the regular week and $4\frac{1}{2}$ hours on Sunday.
   a. What are Ms. Millard's gross earnings for the week?
   b. How much will be withheld from her earnings for FICA?

5. William Reid works as a draftsman at $3.28 an hour plus time and a half for any time he is asked to work over a 40-hour week. He is single, claims one exemption, and is paid biweekly. In order

to finish up a rush job during a recent two-week period, Mr. Reid worked $58\frac{3}{4}$ hours the first week and $47\frac{3}{4}$ hours the second week.

a. What are Mr. Reid's regular earnings?

b. What were his overtime earnings for each of the two weeks?

c. What were gross earnings for two weeks?

d. What was his take-home pay for the two-week period? (Assume that Mr. Reid's only deductions are for federal income tax and FICA.)

THE PAYROLL REGISTER

Case Problem Mary Jane Abel is a payroll clerk in Lofton's Supply Company. It is her job to summarize the information from each employee's time card, to find the gross earnings, to make the deductions, and to compute the net earnings. Ms. Abel uses a form such as the one on the next page, which is called a *payroll register*.

Discussion Questions

1. In the payroll register illustrated, how many exemptions are claimed by A. Lowe? What is his marital status?

2. How many hours did Mr. Lowe work during the regular week? How many overtime hours did he work?

3. What is Mr. Lowe's regular rate? overtime rate?

4. What are the advantages of using a payroll register?

5. What items might the "Other Deductions" consist of?

Employee	Exemptions	M	T	W	T	F	S	Reg. Hrs.	Reg. Rate	Amt.	Over-time Hrs.	Over-time Rate	Amt.	Gross Earnings	Soc. Sec.	Income Tax	Other Deduc.	Total Deduc.	Net Pay
				Hours						Earnings						Deductions			
Lowe, A.	3-M	8	8	8	8	8	3	40	$2.80	$112.00	3	$4.20	$12.60	124.60	$7.29	$10.40	$5.70	$23.39	$101.21
Mays, T.	1-S	8	7	7	8	9	—	39	$2.80	$109.20	—	$4.20	—	109.20	6.39	14.50	6.35	27.24	81.96
Pate, J.M.	4-M	7	7	8	10	8	—	40	$3.40	$136.00	—	$5.10	—	136.00	7.96	12.80	3.88	24.64	111.36
Toby, R.	2-S	8	8	8	8	8	—	40	$3.00	$120.00	—	$4.50	—	120.00	7.02	14.60	7.45	29.07	90.93
													Total	$489.80	$29.66	$52.30	$23.38	$104.34	$385.46

In the payroll register illustrated, observe the information concerning A. Lowe. Mr. Lowe is married and claims three exemptions (3-M in the Exemptions column). He worked 40 hours during the regular week and 3 hours on Saturday. His *gross earnings* are determined by multiplying the regular hours by the regular rate ($2.80) and the overtime (Saturday) hours by the overtime rate ($4.20) and adding the sums. From Mr. Lowe's gross earnings are subtracted the deductions for social security, income tax, and other deductions, which gives the *net pay*. Net pay for Mays, Pate, and Toby are computed similarly. Note that T. Mays is single, claiming one exemption (1-S); Pate is married, claiming four exemptions (4-M); and Toby is single, claiming two exemptions (2-S).

By using this payroll register, Ms. Abel can show all the information relating to the payroll in one place in an organized fashion. Notice, also, that she is able to compute the total amount of the entire payroll and all deductions. "Other Deductions" might consist of hospitalization, insurance payments, bond purchases, etc. There might be a separate column for each deduction instead of lumping them all together as has been done here.

A special type of payroll register is used for employees paid on a straight piece-work basis. A partial register of this type is shown below.

Employee	Exemptions	M	T	W	T	F	S	Total Articles	Rate	Gross Earnings	Soc. Sec.	Income Tax	Other Deduc.	Total Deduc.	Net Pay
				No. of Articles						Earnings			Deductions		
Weld, P.	3-M	19	16	23	24	20		102	$1.25	$127.50	$7.46	$11.20	$4.40	$23.06	$104.44
						Totals	$		$	$	$	$	$	$	

One difference between the payroll register above and the one at the top of the page is that the piece-work payroll register shows the number of *articles produced* each day where the one at the top shows the number of *hours worked* each day. Another difference is that there is no overtime for piece work. P. Weld's gross earnings for the week are found by multiplying the total number of articles produced (102) by the rate per article ($1.25). Net pay was determined by subtracting from gross earnings the various deductions, which in the illustration on the previous page total $21.33.

Business Applications

1. Complete the following payroll registers, referring to the tables on pages 223 and 224 for federal income tax deductions and the tables on pages 229 and 230 for social security deductions. All hours over 40 during the regular week as well as all Saturday work are considered overtime and are paid at the rate for time and a half.

a.

Employee	Exemp-tions	M	T	W	T	F	S	Total Hrs.	Reg. Hrs.	Over. Hrs.	Over. Prem. Hrs.	Total Hrs. Paid for	Rate
				Hours						Earnings			
Stoll, G.	3-M	8	8	8	8	8	—						$3.00
Tifton, C.	2-S	7	9	8	8	8	—						$3.10
Vars, B.	5-M	8	8	8	8	8	—						$3.10
Wight, T.	6-M	7½	8½	8	8	8	—						$3.20

Gross Earnings	Soc. Sec.	Income Tax	Other Deduc.	Total Deduc.	Net Pay
			Deductions		
			$6.40		
			7.15		
			4.25		
			3.80		
Totals $____	$____	$____	$ 21.60	$____	$____

b.

Employee	Exemptions	Hours M	T	W	T	F	S	Total Hrs.	Reg. Hrs.	Over. Hrs.	Over. Prem. Hrs.	Total Hrs. Paid for	Rate
Frost, P.	0-S	8	8	8	8	8	-						$3.60
Gage, Z.	4-M	9	9	9	8	9	-						$3.76
Grubbs, N.	2-S	7½	7½	8	8	8	5						$3.58
Hoy, T.R.	3-S	8	8	8	9	9	-						$3.60

Gross Earnings	Soc. Sec.	Income Tax	Other Deduc.	Total Deduc.	Net Pay
			$7.75		
			8.35		
			4.60		
			6.85		
Totals $____	$____	$____	$27.55	$____	$____

2. Complete the following payroll register.

Employee	Exemptions	M	T	W	T	F	S	Total Articles	Rate	Gross Earnings	Soc. Sec.	Income Tax	Other Deduc.	Total Deduc.	Net Pay
Aalin, W.	7-M	70	72	69	70	71	-		$.45				$6.90		
Vailes, J.	2-S	65	68	66	66	65	-		$.45				7.40		
Weaver, D.	4-M	75	77	74	76	75	-		$.45				6.30		
Wolk, C.	3-M	69	68	69	69	68	-		$.45				6.90		
Totals										$____	$____	$____	$27.50	$____	$____

REVIEW EXERCISES FOR CHAPTER 9

1. Compute the gross weekly earnings in the payrolls below. Time . and a half is to be paid for all overtime hours.

a.

Employee	Total Hours Worked	Regular Hours	Over. Hours	Bonus Hours	Total to be Paid for	Hourly Rate	Gross Earnings
Green	38	40	_____	_____	_____	$2.90	$_____
Gross	42	40	_____	_____	_____	$3.24	$_____
Mc Quade	$45\frac{1}{2}$	40	_____	_____	_____	$4.10	$_____
Valdez	46	40	_____	_____	_____	$3.85	$_____
Walters	39	40	_____	_____	_____	$2.97	$_____

b.

Employee	Regular Hours	Regular Rate	Regular Earnings	Over. Hours	Over. Rate	Over. Earnings	Gross Earnings
Sage	40	$2.76	$_____	3	$_____	$_____	$_____
Thomas	40	$2.80	$_____	$1\frac{1}{2}$	$_____	$_____	$_____
Tisano	40	$2.90	$_____	0	$_____	$_____	$_____
Udell	40	$2.88	$_____	$1\frac{3}{4}$	$_____	$_____	$_____
Vickers	40	$2.80	$_____	2	$_____	$_____	$_____

2. Mary O'Grady recently worked 44 hours during a regular (Monday—Friday) week. In addition, she worked $4\frac{1}{2}$ hours on Saturday and 3 hours on Sunday. Time and a half is paid for all hours worked over 40 during the regular week and for all Saturday work. Double time is paid for all hours worked on Sunday. What were her gross earnings for the week if her regular rate is $3.10 an hour?

3. Find the total hours credited to each of the following employees for the week; then compute the gross weekly earnings of each. The workday is from 8:00 to 5:00. Assume that late arrivals and early departures are charged according to the schedules on page 203 and that time indicated as overtime is authorized. Overtime is at the rate of time and a half, and all Saturday work is counted as overtime regardless of the hours worked during the regular week.

a.

Employee No. _163 - 38 - 4870_

Name _Johnson, Norman F._

Week Ending _Sept. 24, 19 —_

Days	Regular				Overtime		Hours
	In	Out	In	Out	In	Out	
Mon.	8:04	11:59	1:03	5:01			
Tues.	8:00	12:01	1:00	5:00			
Wed.	8:02	12:00	12:59	5:02	5:30	8:00	
Thurs.	8:00	11:58	1:01	5:05	6:00	7:30	
Fri.	8:01	12:02	1:00	5:03			
Sat.							
Sun.							

			Hours	Rate	Earnings
		Regular		3.93	
		Overtime			
		Total Hours		Gross Earnings	

b.

Employee No. _766 - 05 - 7604_

Name _Korshin, Dorothy E._

Week Ending _Sept. 24, 19 —_

Days	Regular				Overtime		Hours
	In	Out	In	Out	In	Out	
Mon.	8:15	12:00	1:03	5:00			
Tues.	8:52	12:01	1:01	5:02			
Wed.	8:12	12:06	1:06	4:00			
Thurs.	8:26	12:02	12:58	4:30			
Fri.	8:17	12:01	12:45	4:15			
Sat.					1:00	6:00	
Sun.							

			Hours	Rate	Earnings
		Regular		2.89	
		Overtime			
		Total Hours		Gross Earnings	

4. Lawrence Kirby's annual salary is $8,432. (Round off uneven amounts to the nearest penny.)
   a. What is his monthly salary?
   b. What is his semimonthly salary?
   c. What is his weekly salary?
   d. What is his biweekly salary?
   e. What is his hourly rate, if he works a 40-hour week?

5. Compute the following sales representatives' gross earnings.

Sales Made	Pay Plan
a. $24,245	8% commission
b. $16,470	$90 salary, plus 5% commission
c. $12,483	$100 salary, plus 8% on all sales over $10,000
d. $23,450	5% commission on first $10,000 sales; 8% on second $10,000; 10% on all additional sales

6. Compute the gross earnings of the following piece-work employees.

	Units Produced	Pay Plan
a.	1,245	12¢ per unit
b.	1,053	15¢ per unit
c.	83	$1.20 for the first 65 units, $1.50 for all others
d.	62	$1.20 for the first 65 units, $1.50 for all others
e.	75	$1.10 for the first 60 units; $1.20 for all others

CHAPTER 10
INTEREST COMPUTATIONS

Phyllis McKay owns The Wood Hut, a retail store that sells modern household furniture. She has just learned that she can purchase the inventory (stock of goods) of a similar store across town. Because the owner of that store is impatient to retire, Miss McKay has been offered the goods for $7,000, which is just half of what she would have to pay if she were purchasing them from the manufacturer. But the terms are cash, and Miss McKay does not have that much money available.

The problem Miss McKay faces is typical of the need of business people to raise cash quickly. Most businesses, both large and small, borrow money frequently. They need funds to expand a "going" business, to buy a new business, to add new product lines, to purchase equipment or a building, to take advantage of special prices on needed merchandise, and to meet unusually heavy expenses.

Although many individuals are embarrassed to borrow money because they think it is a sign of poor financial management, business people are not, nor should they be embarrassed. To them, borrowing money may well be a sign of *good* financial management. A loan often permits them to expand their businesses as well as their profits.

When an individual or a business borrows money, the use of the money must be paid for just as one pays for the use of a house or an apartment one does not own. The amount charged for the use of money is called *interest*. In this chapter you will learn how to compute interest on loans.

FINDING INTEREST ON LOANS

Case Problem Curtis Dunham, who operates a retail sporting goods store, has an opportunity to save $1,000 by purchasing fishing rods, reels, and other equipment from the owner of a boat yard. The boat yard owner is relocating to another part of the country and wants to dispose of his inventory. The cost of the merchandise is $4,000—$1,000 less than it would cost if Mr. Dunham purchased it from a manufacturer.

The owner wants cash. Mr. Dunham, who has recently started his business, is short of cash. He can borrow the money he needs at 8% interest, and he estimates that he could repay such a loan in two years.

Discussion Questions

1. What factors must Dunham consider in making his decision about borrowing?
2. Will he gain or lose if he borrows the $4,000?

There are two main factors business people must consider when making a decision about borrowing money. The first is whether they will be able to repay the money as it comes due. In this case, Mr. Dunham expects to be able to sell the merchandise he will buy with the borrowed money and make a profit on it. He will thus have the funds to repay the loan.

The other important factor to consider is whether the interest on the loan will amount to more than the money made by closing the deal. Once you learn how to make the necessary computations, you will be able to answer the second discussion question yourself.

ANNUAL INTEREST

Interest is always expressed as a percent, and unless it is otherwise stated, the rate given is an *annual* rate. Thus, the term "at 8% interest" means that for each year the money is owed the borrower will pay $8 for each $100 borrowed. Therefore, to find the amount of interest for one year, multiply the amount borrowed by the rate of interest.

Example:

Thelma Conley operates a small restaurant. She has decided to borrow $3,000 in order to remodel the interior and to install new customer booths. She is to repay the loan in one year, with interest at 9%. How much interest will Mrs. Conley have to pay for the use of the $3,000 for one year?

Solution:

$3,000 (amount borrowed) × 9% (interest) × 1 (number of years) = $270, interest for one year

THE INTEREST FORMULA

The method we have just developed can be expressed in a formula, because the same items of information are always present in interest computations.

> *Principal* is the amount borrowed ($3,000).
> *Rate* is the percent of interest being charged (9%).
> *Time* is the number of years for which the money will be borrowed (1).
> *Interest* is the amount paid for the use of money ($270).

The formula for finding interest therefore becomes the following:

$$I = P \times R \times T \text{ (Interest} = \text{Principal} \times \text{Rate} \times \text{Time)}$$

Now let us go back to our Case Problem. Mr. Dunham borrowed $4,000 for a period of two years at 8%.

$$I = P \times R \times T$$
$$= \$4{,}000 \times 8\% \times 2$$
$$= \$640 (4{,}000 \times 8\% = \$320, \$320 \times 2 = \$640)$$

You are now ready to answer the second discussion question about the Case Problem on page 241: Will Mr. Dunham gain or lose if he borrows the $4,000?

Exercises

1. Find the interest on each loan for one year.
   a. $600 at 8%
   c. $750 at 7%
   e. $300 at 8%
   g. $12,000 at $8\frac{3}{4}\%$
   i. $8,600 at $9\frac{1}{4}\%$

   b. $1,500 at 9%
   d. $3,750 at 6%
   f. $9,500 at 10%
   h. $22,500 at $7\frac{1}{2}\%$

2. Find the interest on each loan.
   a. $1,800 at 6% for 2 years
   b. $2,400 at 5% for 3 years
   c. $3,200 at 7% for 2 years
   d. $7,000 at $6\frac{1}{2}\%$ for 4 years
   e. $975 at $5\frac{1}{4}\%$ for 3 years
   f. $1,440 at $3\frac{3}{4}\%$ for 5 years

INTEREST FOR FRACTIONS OF A YEAR

Money is often borrowed for periods of less than a year—that is, for 90 days, 60 days, 4 months, 7 months, and so on. To find interest for such loans, you need to determine the fractional part of the year for which the money is borrowed.

Time Expressed in Months

When the time of a loan is expressed in months, the T in the formula becomes a fraction—the fractional part of twelve months represented. Thus 3 months becomes $\frac{3}{12}$ or $\frac{1}{4}$; 6 months becomes $\frac{6}{12}$ or $\frac{1}{2}$.

Example 1:

Rosa Bronzini borrowed $1,500 from a friend for 3 months at 8% interest. How much interest will Ms. Bronzini pay?

Solution:

Substitute in the formula $I = P \times R \times T.$
$$I = \$1{,}500 \times 8\% \times \tfrac{1}{4}$$
$$= \$120 \times \tfrac{1}{4}$$
$$= \$30$$

Example 2:

R. J. Clarkson borrowed $2,400 for 7 months at 7% interest. How much interest will he pay for the use of the money?

Solution:

$I = P \times R \times T$

$I = \$2,400 \times 7\% \times \frac{7}{12}$

$\quad = \$168 \times \frac{7}{12}$

$\quad = \$98$

Time Expressed in Days

To simplify the computation of interest when time is expressed in days, business people commonly use a *banker's year* of 360 days instead of an actual year of 365 days. (The U.S. Government always uses a 365-day year in computing interest. This is called exact or accurate interest; it is used only infrequently in business.) Thus, to find the interest for 60 days in a banker's year, you would deal with the fraction $\frac{60}{360}$, or $\frac{1}{6}$, instead of the fraction $\frac{60}{365}$, or $\frac{12}{73}$.

Example 1:

Dr. B. J. Simpson borrowed $720 to purchase laboratory equipment. He agreed to pay back the loan in 90 days at 9% interest. How much interest will Dr. Simpson have to pay?

Solution:

1. Find the fractional part of a year represented by 90 days.

$$\frac{90}{360} = \frac{1}{4}$$

2. Use this fraction for the "T" in the formula

$I = \$720 \times 9\% \times \frac{1}{4}$

$\quad = \$64.80 \times \frac{1}{4}$

$\quad = \$16.20$, interest for 90 days

Example 2:

The Swift Line Trucking Company borrowed $10,000 for a period of 72 days at $9\frac{1}{2}\%$ interest. What amount of interest will the company have to pay?

Solution:

$\frac{72}{360} = \frac{1}{5}$

$I = \$10,000 \times 9\frac{1}{2}\%(.095) \times \frac{1}{5}$

$\quad = \$950 \times \frac{1}{5}$

$\quad = \$190$, interest for 72 days

Exercises

1. Find the interest on each loan.
   a. $500 at 8% for 3 months
   b. $450 at 10% for 5 months
   c. $625 at 9% for 8 months
   d. $870 at 10% for 9 months
   e. $1,420 at $8\frac{1}{2}$% for 3 months
   f. $1,840 at $8\frac{1}{4}$% for 6 months
   g. $2,280 at $8\frac{3}{4}$% for 2 months
   h. $3,700 at $10\frac{1}{2}$% for 10 months

2. Find the interest on each loan, using the banker's year.
   a. $600 at 8% for 60 days
   b. $800 at 9% for 90 days
   c. $900 at 10% for 120 days
   d. $450 at 12% for 30 days
   e. $760 at $8\frac{1}{2}$% for 180 days
   f. $520 at $10\frac{1}{4}$% for 40 days
   g. $1,200 at $9\frac{3}{4}$% for 60 days
   h. $1,600 at $10\frac{1}{2}$% for 270 days

Business Applications

1. What interest will be charged on a loan of $5,420 for 120 days at an interest rate of $7\frac{1}{2}$%?

2. How much will it cost a wholesaler to borrow $4,575 for one month at an interest rate of 9%?

3. To take advantage of a special purchase price on typewriters, an office equipment dealer needed to borrow $3,000 for 180 days. If the interest rate was $10\frac{1}{2}$%, how much interest will be charged?

4. Patricia Yoder, a retail store owner, can get a special reduction of $500 in price by paying cash for a line of women's dresses. To do so, she has to borrow $4,800 for eight months at 9% interest.
   a. Find the amount of interest she would have to pay.
   b. How much, if anything, would she save by borrowing the money?

5. By paying a $3,000 bill at once, Alan Graham can save $60. How much would he gain by borrowing the $3,000 for 30 days at 10% to pay the bill?

UNIT 2

COMPUTING THE EXACT NUMBER OF DAYS

Case Problem On March 18, Tom Mandel borrowed $1,200 from his uncle to buy a used car. He agreed to repay the loan as soon as he could save enough money, with interest at 7% annually for the number of days he had use of the money. On July 16, Tom repaid the loan in full, plus interest.

Discussion Questions
1. How would you compute the number of days of the loan?
2. For how many days will Tom Mandel be charged interest?

COMPUTING THE NUMBER OF DAYS

When a loan is made, the exact date on which the borrower is to repay it is not always known. In these instances, the lender and the borrower agree that a charge will be made for each day until the loan is paid. Then when the borrower is ready to pay, the number of days he used the money must be computed.

Example:
In the Case Problem, compute the number of days Tom Mandel will be charged interest.

Solution:
1. Beginning the day *after* the date of the loan, count the days remaining in March.

March 19–31 $= 13$ days

2. Count the actual number of days in the full months (April, May, and June).

April $= 30$ days

May $= 31$ days

June $= 30$ days

3. Count the number of days in July up through the date on which the loan is paid.

July 1–16 $= 16$ days

Total days $\overline{120 \text{ days}}$

Thus, Tom will be charged interest for 120 days.

Now that you have computed the number of days for which Tom Mandel will be charged interest, you are ready to compute the amount of interest he will pay. Use the formula $I = P \times R \times T$.

$$I = \$1200 \times 7\% \times \tfrac{120}{360}$$
$$= \$84 \times \tfrac{1}{3}$$
$$= \$28, \text{ interest for } 120 \text{ days}$$

Exercises

Find the exact number of days from the first date through the second date in each of the following loan periods. Use the calendar provided if it will be helpful to you. (The dates are in the same year unless otherwise noted.)

JANUARY						
S	M	T	W	T	F	S
		1	2	3	4	
5	6	7	8	9	10	11
12	13	14	15	16	17	18
19	20	21	22	23	24	25
26	27	28	29	30	31	

APRIL						
S	M	T	W	T	F	S
		1	2	3	4	5
6	7	8	9	10	11	12
13	14	15	16	17	18	19
20	21	22	23	24	25	26
27	28	29	30			

JULY						
S	M	T	W	T	F	S
		1	2	3	4	5
6	7	8	9	10	11	12
13	14	15	16	17	18	19
20	21	22	23	24	25	26
27	28	29	30	31		

OCTOBER						
S	M	T	W	T	F	S
		1	2	3	4	
5	6	7	8	9	10	11
12	13	14	15	16	17	18
19	20	21	22	23	24	25
26	27	28	29	30	31	

FEBRUARY						
S	M	T	W	T	F	S
						1
2	3	4	5	6	7	8
9	10	11	12	13	14	15
16	17	18	19	20	21	22
23	24	25	26	27	28	

MAY						
S	M	T	W	T	F	S
				1	2	3
4	5	6	7	8	9	10
11	12	13	14	15	16	17
18	19	20	21	22	23	24
25	26	27	28	29	30	31

AUGUST						
S	M	T	W	T	F	S
					1	2
3	4	5	6	7	8	9
10	11	12	13	14	15	16
17	18	19	20	21	22	23
24	25	26	27	28	29	30
31						

NOVEMBER						
S	M	T	W	T	F	S
						1
2	3	4	5	6	7	8
9	10	11	12	13	14	15
16	17	18	19	20	21	22
23	24	25	26	27	28	29
30						

MARCH						
S	M	T	W	T	F	S
						1
2	3	4	5	6	7	8
9	10	11	12	13	14	15
16	17	18	19	20	21	22
23	24	25	26	27	28	29
30	31					

JUNE						
S	M	T	W	T	F	S
1	2	3	4	5	6	7
8	9	10	11	12	13	14
15	16	17	18	19	20	21
22	23	24	25	26	27	28
29	30					

SEPTEMBER						
S	M	T	W	T	F	S
	1	2	3	4	5	6
7	8	9	10	11	12	13
14	15	16	17	18	19	20
21	22	23	24	25	26	27
28	29	30				

DECEMBER						
S	M	T	W	T	F	S
	1	2	3	4	5	6
7	8	9	10	11	12	13
14	15	16	17	18	19	20
21	22	23	24	25	26	27
28	29	30	31			

1. April 5 to June 25

2. November 16 to December 16

3. March 22 to August 11
4. January 17 to April 1
5. January 15 to August 10
6. March 18 to November 29
7. April 30 to September 26
8. February 9 to June 7
9. February 21 to July 7 (a leap year)
10. March 2, 19X4, to February 13, 19X5

USING A TIME TABLE

A quicker way to find the exact number of days from any day in one month to the same day in any other month is with the use of a table. The example shows you how.

Month	Jan.	Feb.	Mar.	Apr.	May	June	July	Aug.	Sept.	Oct.	Nov.	Dec.
January	365	31	59	90	120	151	181	212	243	273	304	334
February	334	365	28	59	89	120	150	181	212	242	273	303
March	306	337	365	31	61	92	122	153	184	214	245	275
April	275	306	334	365	30	61	91	122	153	183	214	244
May	245	276	304	335	365	31	61	92	123	153	184	214
June	214	245	273	304	334	365	30	61	92	122	153	183
July	184	215	243	274	304	335	365	31	62	92	123	153
August	153	184	212	243	273	304	334	365	31	61	92	122
September	122	153	181	212	242	273	303	334	365	30	61	91
October	92	123	151	182	212	243	273	304	335	365	31	61
November	61	92	120	151	181	212	242	273	304	334	365	30
December	31	62	90	121	151	182	212	243	274	304	335	365

Example:
Find the exact number of days between April 5 and September 5 of the same year.

Solution:
1. Follow the *Month* column downward until the name of the month of the first date is found. In this example it is April.
2. Follow the *April* row across until you reach the column headed by the month of the second date. In this example, it is September.
3. The number at which you have stopped—153—represents the exact number of days from April 5 to September 5.

The time table illustrated can also be used to find the exact number of days between two dates when the days of the two months are different.

Example 1:

Find the number of days from April 5 to September 17 of the same year.

Solution:

Proceed exactly as you did in the previous example. According to the table, there are 153 days between April 5 and September 5. However, you want to know the number of days between April 5 and September 17. Therefore, you must add the number of days between September 5 and September 17 (12) to 153. The total is 165 days.

or

April 5 to September 5	153 days
September 5 to September 17	+ 12 days
April 5 to September 17 =	165 days

Example 2:

Find the number of days from April 5, 1975 to September 2, 1975.

Solution:

Again, follow the method used in the first example. The number 153 still represents the number of days from April 5 to September 5. However, since September 2 is 3 days before September 5, it is necessary to subtract 3 days from 153 days, leaving 150 days.

or

April 5 to September 5	153 days
September 2 to September 5	− 3 days
April 5 to September 2 =	150 days

Exercises

Using the time table on page 248, find the exact number of days between each pair of dates. All dates given are in the same year.

1. May 12 to October 12
2. June 14 to October 14
3. February 3 to May 12
4. April 7 to August 23
5. July 12 to September 23
6. June 27 to December 5
7. January 31 to May 17
8. February 20 to September 14
9. June 9 to October 17
10. March 10 to December 31

Business Applications

1. Susan Withers borrowed money from an aunt to pay for her first year's college expenses. She agreed to pay interest on the loan according to the number of days she used the money. If the date on which Miss Withers received the money was August 12 and the date on which she repaid the loan was December 14, for how many days did she pay interest?

2. J. F. Mayberry, who operates a retail appliance store, purchased merchandise from a supplier on credit. He agreed to pay interest on the amount of the purchase for the exact number of days during which the money was owed. If Mr. Mayberry made the purchase on February 26 and paid the amount owed on September 14, for how many days must he pay interest? (Assume it was not a leap year.)

3. Floyd Berman borrowed $3,000 from a business partner to settle some personal debts, agreeing to pay interest for the number of days during which he owed the principal. If the date of the loan was November 12 and the date of payment was June 4 of the following year, for how many days will Mr. Berman pay interest on the loan? (Assume that the year the loan is paid is a leap year.)

4. Joanna Moorman borrowed $2,000 from the credit union where she works, agreeing to pay 9% interest for the actual number of days during which the loan was outstanding. The date on which the money was borrowed was April 12, and the full amount, including interest, was paid on July 11.
   a. For how many days will Mrs. Moorman pay interest?
   b. What is the amount of interest to be paid?
   c. What is the total amount due the credit union?

5. The Harbor Lights Boat Company loaned an employee $3,000 to help toward the down payment on a new house. The employee agreed to pay $9\frac{1}{2}$% interest for the number of days he owed the money. The date of the loan was September 16, and it was repaid on October 31 of the same year.
   a. How many days' interest will the company charge the employee?
   b. What is the amount of interest the company will collect?
   c. What is the total amount the company received from the employee on October 31?

UNIT 3

USING AN INTEREST TABLE

Case Problem Tables such as the one below are often used to compute interest.

SIMPLE-INTEREST TABLE
($100 on a 360-Day-Year Basis)

Time	$2\frac{1}{2}\%$	3%	$3\frac{1}{2}\%$	4%	$4\frac{1}{2}\%$	5%	$5\frac{1}{2}\%$	6%	$6\frac{1}{2}\%$	7%
1 day	.0069	.0083	.0097	.0111	.0125	.0139	.0153	.0167	.0181	.0194
2 days	.0139	.0167	.0194	.0222	.0250	.0278	.0306	.0333	.0361	.0389
3 days	.0208	.0250	.0292	.0333	.0375	.0417	.0458	.0500	.0542	.0583
4 days	.0278	.0333	.0389	.0444	.0500	.0556	.0611	.0667	.0722	.0778
5 days	.0347	.0417	.0486	.0556	.0625	.0694	.0764	.0833	.0903	.0972
6 days	.0417	.0500	.0583	.0667	.0750	.0833	.0917	.1000	.1083	.1167
7 days	.0486	.0583	.0681	.0778	.0875	.0972	.1069	.1167	.1264	.1361
8 days	.0556	.0667	.0778	.0889	.1000	.1111	.1222	.1333	.1444	.1556
9 days	.0625	.0750	.0875	.1000	.1125	.1250	.1375	.1500	.1625	.1750
10 days	.0694	.0833	.0972	.1111	.1250	.1389	.1528	.1667	.1806	.1944
11 days	.0764	.0917	.1069	.1222	.1375	.1528	.1681	.1833	.1986	.2139
12 days	.0833	.1000	.1167	.1333	.1500	.1667	.1833	.2000	.2167	.2333
13 days	.0903	.1083	.1264	.1444	.1625	.1806	.1986	.2167	.2347	.2528
14 days	.0972	.1167	.1361	.1556	.1750	.1944	.2139	.2333	.2528	.2722
15 days	.1042	.1250	.1458	.1667	.1875	.2083	.2292	.2500	.2708	.2917
16 days	.1111	.1333	.1556	.1778	.2000	.2222	.2444	.2667	.2889	.3111
17 days	.1181	.1417	.1653	.1889	.2125	.2361	.2597	.2833	.3069	.3306
18 days	.1250	.1500	.1750	.2000	.2250	.2500	.2750	.3000	.3250	.3500
19 days	.1319	.1583	.1847	.2111	.2375	.2639	.2903	.3167	.3431	.3694
20 days	.1389	.1667	.1944	.2222	.2500	.2778	.3056	.3333	.3611	.3889
21 days	.1458	.1750	.2042	.2333	.2625	.2917	.3208	.3500	.3792	.4083
22 days	.1528	.1833	.2139	.2444	.2750	.3056	.3361	.3667	.3972	.4278
23 days	.1597	.1917	.2236	.2556	.2875	.3194	.3514	.3833	.4153	.4472
24 days	.1667	.2000	.2333	.2667	.3000	.3333	.3667	.4000	.4333	.4667
25 days	.1736	.2083	.2431	.2778	.3125	.3472	.3819	.4167	.4514	.4861
26 days	.1806	.2167	.2528	.2889	.3250	.3611	.3972	.4333	.4694	.5056
27 days	.1875	.2250	.2625	.3000	.3375	.3750	.4125	.4500	.4875	.5250
28 days	.1944	.2333	.2722	.3111	.3500	.3889	.4278	.4667	.5056	.5444
29 days	.2014	.2417	.2819	.3222	.3625	.4028	.4431	.4833	.5236	.5639
30 days	.2083	.2500	.2917	.3333	.3750	.4167	.4583	.5000	.5417	.5833
60 days	.4167	.5000	.5833	.6667	.7500	.8333	.9167	1.0000	1.0833	1.1667
90 days	.6230	.7500	.8750	1.0000	1.1250	1.2500	1.3750	1.5000	1.6250	1.7500
120 days	.8333	1.0000	1.1667	1.3333	1.5000	1.6667	1.8333	2.0000	2.1667	2.3333
150 days	1.0417	1.2500	1.4583	1.6667	1.8750	2.0833	2.2917	2.5000	2.7083	2.9160
180 days	1.2500	1.5000	1.7500	2.0000	2.2500	2.5000	2.7500	3.0000	3.2500	3.5070

Unit 3   Using an Interest Table   251

Discussion Questions
1. What are two advantages of using a table such as the one illustrated?
2. On what amount is the table based? for what period of time?

The advantages of using a table such as the one above is that it speeds up the process of computing interest on loans and it reduces the chance of error. It is based on a $100 loan for a 360-day period.

The following example illustrates how the Simple-Interest Table is used.

Example:
Find the interest on $100 at $5\frac{1}{2}$% for 21 days.

Solution:
In the Time column, find 21 days. Follow this row across until you reach the $5\frac{1}{2}$% column. The number under your pointer will be .3208. This represents the interest on $100 at $5\frac{1}{2}$% for 21 days. It is approximately $.32.

The interest table on page 251 is based on loans of $100, but it can easily be used to find interest on any other principal.

Example 1:
Find the interest on $275 at $5\frac{1}{2}$% for 21 days.

Solution:
Proceed as in the first example above. The number found ($.3208) represents the interest on $100. It is necessary, therefore, to determine how many hundreds there are in $275. To do this, simply divide $275 by 100. This can be done by moving the decimal point in $275 two places to the left. The quotient 2.75 represents the number of hundreds in $275. For each $100, the interest is $.3208; hence, to find the interest for 2.75 hundreds, multiply 2.75 by $.3208. This product ($.8822, or $.88) will be the interest on $275 for 21 days at $5\frac{1}{2}$%.

Outline:
Interest on $100 = $.3208
Interest on $275 = 2.75 × $.3208
         = $.8822, or $.88

Example 2:
Find the interest on $350 at 4% for 124 days.

Solution:
The interest is found on $100 at 4% for 120 days, $1.3333; then on $100 at 4% for 4 days, $.0444. The sum ($1.3777) represents the interest on $100 at 4% for 124 days. To find the interest on $350, you must find the number of hundreds in $350. This is 3.5. Multiplying 3.5 by the interest for $100 ($1.3777) will give $4.82195. Thus, $4.82 is the interest on $350 at 4% for 124 days.

Outline:

$$\$1.3333 = \text{Interest on } \$100 \text{ for } 120 \text{ days}$$
$$\underline{+.0444 = \text{Interest on } \$100 \text{ for } 4 \text{ days}}$$
$$\$1.3777 = \text{Interest on } \$100 \text{ for } 124 \text{ days}$$
$$3.5 \times \$1.3777 = \text{Interest on } \$350 \text{ for } 124 \text{ days}$$
$$\$4.82195, \text{ or } \$4.82 = \text{Interest on } \$350 \text{ for } 124 \text{ days}$$

Exercises

Using the interest table on page 251, find the interest on each loan.

1. $300 @ 3% for 25 days
2. $800 @ $4\frac{1}{2}$% for 20 days
3. $2,400 @ $5\frac{1}{2}$% for 27 days
4. $3,000 @ 7% for 12 days
5. $750 @ $3\frac{1}{2}$% for 28 days
6. $625 @ 4% for 30 days
7. $1,250 @ 6% for 29 days
8. $500 @ $5\frac{1}{2}$% for 61 days
9. $200 @ $4\frac{1}{2}$% for 124 days
10. $550 @ $6\frac{1}{2}$% for 92 days
11. $375 @ 5% for 156 days
12. $2,725 @ 6% for 182 days

Business Applications

Find the interest on each of the following loans by using the interest table on page 251 and the time table on page 248. All dates are in the same year.

No.	Principal	Rate	Period of Loan	No. of Days	Interest
1	$ 600.00	4%	April 5 to May 5	_____	$_____
2	$ 900.00	6%	August 17 to September 15	_____	$_____
3	$ 400.00	5%	February 14 to March 15	_____	$_____
4	$ 300.00	$4\frac{1}{2}$%	June 12 to August 16	_____	$_____
5	$1,400.00	$5\frac{1}{2}$%	March 5 to June 23	_____	$_____
6	$ 350.00	6%	July 24 to November 20	_____	$_____
7	$ 425.00	$3\frac{1}{2}$%	May 27 to September 8	_____	$_____
8	$1,275.00	4%	June 10 to November 18	_____	$_____
9	$ 302.50	$4\frac{1}{2}$%	March 12 to May 15	_____	$_____
10	$ 451.36	7%	April 9 to July 12	_____	$_____

UNIT 4

PROMISSORY NOTES

Case Problem The Phelps Home Laundry recently started business in Springdale. The owner, D. G. Phelps, finds himself short of cash with which to purchase supplies he needs. The Consolidated Chemical Company agreed to sell Mr. Phelps the supplies if Mr. Phelps signs a *promissory note*, which is a written promise to pay a certain amount of money at a specified time.

Following is the promissory note that Mr. Phelps signed.

$ 300.00	Springdale, IL	August 14, *19--*

Ninety days ____ *after date* I *promise to pay to*

the order of ____ Consolidated Chemical Company ____

Three hundred and no/100--- *Dollars*

at ____ 1416 Mariposa Avenue, Springdale ____

Value received with interest at 8%

No. 1 *Due* November 12, 19-- ____ DG Phelps

Discussion Questions

1. For what reason might a seller ask a buyer to sign a promissory note?
2. What interest rate will be charged Mr. Phelps on the note illustrated?

Before anyone—a person in business, a banker, a private individual—lends money, one should be sure, either through one's own knowledge or through investigation, that the debt will be repaid when it falls due. One should also have some evidence that the debt has been acknowledged by the borrower.

A *promissory note* is quite simply a written promise to pay a certain amount at a specified time in the future. It is a clear-cut statement of the amount of the debt, the terms, and the maturity date or due date. And as you will see in a later chapter, there are other uses that can be made of a promissory note.

Sometimes the lender or seller will charge interest on the note (in the note illustrated, the interest rate is 8%), in which case it is called an *interest-bearing* note. When no interest is charged, it is called a *noninterest-bearing* note.

TERMS USED IN PROMISSORY NOTES

Look at the promissory note illustrated on page 254, and learn the following terms:
1. The amount of the note ($300) is called the *face value*.
2. The person who signed the note (D. G. Phelps) is the *maker*.
3. The party to whom payment is promised (Consolidated Chemical Company) is the *payee*.
4. The length of time the money was borrowed (90 days) is the *term*.
5. August 14 is the *date* the note was made.
6. November 12 is the *maturity date* (when the note is to be paid).
7. 8% is the *interest rate*.

COMPUTING THE INTEREST ON A PROMISSORY NOTE

Interest on promissory notes is computed by the same formula you used earlier, $I = P \times R \times T$. In the note signed by Mr. Phelps, compute the interest by substituting in the formula.

$$I = \$300 \times 8\% \times \tfrac{90}{360}$$
$$= \$24 \times \tfrac{1}{4}$$
$$= \$6.00, \text{ interest for 90 days}$$

Finding the Maturity Date
When the time on a note is stated in months, count the exact months from the date of the note.

Example:

Find the maturity date of a 3-month note dated August 12.

Solution:

Count the months until you reach the third month after August.

> August 12 to September 12 = 1 month
> September 12 to October 12 = 1 month
> October 12 to November 12 = <u>1 month</u>
>   3 months

The maturity date is November 12.

If there is no corresponding date because the month in which the note is to become due has fewer days than the month in which the note is dated, use the last day in the month the note comes due. For instance, a two-month note dated December 31 is due on February 28 (or February 29 in a leap year). But a two-month note dated February 28 will be due on April 28 (*not* April 30). If the time is stated in days, you can, of course, use the table on page 248.

Example:

Find the maturity date on a 60-day note dated July 17.

Solution:

Run your finger down the *Month* column until it comes to rest on July. Place a piece of paper along the *July* row. In this row, find the number that is closest to 60. This will be the number 62 that appears in the *September* column. You will recall that the 62 represents the number of days from any date in July to the same date in September. For this problem, the 62 signifies the number of days from July 17 to September 17. Hence, from July 17 to September 15 would be only 60 days. Thus, the maturity date of the note is September 15.

If a time table is not available, you can find the maturity date by subtraction, as in the following example.

Example:

Find the maturity date on a 60-day note dated July 17.

Solution:

1. Subtract from the total number of days the note is to run the days remaining in the month the note is dated.
2. From the difference, subtract the number of days in the following month.

3. Continue subtracting until the number of days left over is contained in the month you have reached:

$$\begin{array}{r}60 \text{ days from July 17} \\ -14 \text{ days left in July} \\ \hline 46 \text{ days left (too many to be reached in August)} \\ -31 \text{ days in August} \\ \hline 15 \text{ days left (Sept., the next month, has enough days.)} \end{array}$$

September 15 is the maturity date.

Note that when you compute interest, you should use the banker's year of 360 days. In the banker's year, interest for thirty days and interest for one month is exactly the same. In computing the term of the note, however, where the time is expressed in days, you must compute the exact number of days from the date of the note until the date of maturity. Thus a one-month note dated May 20 is due on June 20, but a 30-day note dated May 20 is due on June 19.

Exercises

1. Examine the promissory note below and answer the questions.

$ 500.00	Larchmont, NY	June 16,	19--

Seventy-five days *after date* I *promise to pay to the order of* Model Supply Corporation

Five hundred and no/00--- *Dollars*

at Larchmont, NY

Value received with interest at 9½%

No. 12 *Due* August 30, 19-- R.C. Wachener

a. Who is the maker of the note?
b. What is the face value?
c. Who is the payee?
d. What is the date of the note?
e. What is the maturity date?
f. What is the interest rate?

2. Find the maturity date of each of the following notes.

Note	Date of Note	Term	Maturity Date
a	July 5	1 mo.	————
b	Jan. 31	2 mo.	————
c	July 9	3 mo.	————
d	Sept. 12	4 mo.	————
e	Aug. 27	3 mo.	————
f	Oct. 4	6 mo.	————
g	June 3	30 da.	————
h	July 6	30 da.	————
i	Apr. 7	60 da.	————
j	Feb. 25	90 da.	————
k	May 13	120 da.	————
l	Jan. 21	108 da.	————
m	Mar. 3	75 da.	————
n	July 14	180 da.	————
o	Oct. 19	90 da.	————
p	Nov. 22	90 da.	————
q	Jan. 31	1 mo.	————
r	Jan. 31	30 da.	————

Business Applications

For each of the following notes, find (a) the maturity date and (b) the amount of interest.

1.

$ 1,500.00   Erie, PA   July 18,   19--

_____ Sixty days _____ _after date_ I _promise to pay to_

the order of _____ Margaret T. Ellicott _____

One thousand, five hundred and no/100------------------------------- _Dollars_

_at_ _____ Provident Trust Company _____

Value received with interest at 8%

_No._ 74 _Due_ _____   Samuel J. Fletcher

2.

$ 264.00   Atlanta, GA   April 29, *19 --*

       Ninety days   *after date* I *promise to pay to the order of*   George M. Laurel

Two hundred sixty-four and no/100------------------------------------*Dollars*

at   702 Flood Building, Atlanta, GA

Value received with interest at 8½%

No. 183 *Due*   A. J. Hardy

3.

$ 7,200.00   San Rafael, CA   May 23, *19*

     Forty-five days   *after date* I *promise to pay to the order of*   Alden Furniture Co., Inc.

Seventy-two hundred and no/100--------------------------------------- *Dollars*

at   Alden Furniture Co., Inc.

Value received with interest at 12%

No. 47 *Due*   Marcia L. Michaels

4.

$ 3,500.00   Racine, WI   December 16, *19*

     Three months   *after date* I *promise to pay to the order of*   Wilson Supply Co.

Three thousand, five hundred and no/100---------------------------- *Dollars*

at   Badger State Bank

Value received with interest at 10¼%

No. 3 *Due*   R. Clark Stewart

REVIEW
EXERCISES
FOR
CHAPTER 10

1. Find the interest on the following loans.
   a. $2,400 at 8% for 1 year
   b. $1,320 at 9% for 2 years
   c. $8,650 at 10% for 3 years
   d. $4,440 at $8\frac{1}{2}$% for 4 years
   e. $766 at $10\frac{1}{2}$% for 1 year
   f. $961 at $10\frac{1}{4}$% for 2 years

2. Without using a time table, find the number of days between the following dates. All dates, except in problem h, are in the same year.
   a. January 6 to February 11
   b. March 15 to June 11
   c. May 1 to July 31
   d. October 7 to December 4
   e. June 8 to December 9
   f. April 16 to October 19
   g. July 21 to September 29
   h. September 19 to February 28

3. Using the time table on page 248 and the interest table on page 251, find the interest on each of the following loans. All dates are in the same year.

No.	Principal	Rate	Term	No. of Days	Interest
a	$600	4%	August 5 to December 4	_____	$_____
b	$800	6%	September 25 to December 10	_____	$_____
c	$500	$4\frac{1}{2}$%	June 11 to December 14	_____	$_____
d	$725	5%	July 25 to December 26	_____	$_____
e	$650	$5\frac{1}{2}$%	March 12 to September 19	_____	$_____
f	$275	7%	February 3 to November 15	_____	$_____

4. S. P. Grossman, a store owner, paid a loan to a supplier after 4 months. What was the charge if the interest rate was $8\frac{1}{2}$% and the principal was $450?

5. After $2\frac{1}{2}$ years, Dorothy Kingsley paid off a debt of $1,800 on which she was paying interest at the rate of 10%. How much did it cost Ms. Kingsley to borrow the money?

6. Using the interest table on page 251, find the interest on each of the following loans.
  a. $200 at 5% for 25 days
  b. $350 at 7% for 60 days
  c. $1,200 at $4\frac{1}{2}$% for 126 days
  d. $185 at 4% for 90 days
  e. $4,800 at 3% for 30 days
  f. $36,360 at $5\frac{1}{2}$% for 88 days

7. Robert Arnold borrowed $1,330 on May 9 and repaid the loan on August 12 of the same year. Using the appropriate tables, find the interest if the rate was 7%.

8. The Community Service Company loaned $12,500 to Cindy Maestro, an employee, for 90 days at $5\frac{1}{4}$% interest. When the loan was due, Miss Maestro asked that the time of the loan be extended to 120 days, and her request was granted.
  a. How much interest would Miss Maestro have paid if she had paid the loan in the 90-day period?
  b. How much additional interest will Miss Maestro pay for the extra time granted for payment of the loan?

9. Clifford Marple, a sales representative, needed a new car in his job. The model he chose cost $4,255. He had only $2,000 in cash, and was granted a loan by his employer for the balance, agreeing to repay it within $1\frac{1}{2}$ years at 8% interest.
  a. How much interest will Mr. Marple pay for the use of his employer's money?
  b. What amount must he pay when the loan comes due?

10. Find (a) the date of maturity and (b) the amount of interest on the following promissory note.

$4,800.00   Portland, ME   May 31, 19 76

Two years   *after date* I *promise to pay to*

the order of   Whitestone Building Corp.

Four thousand, eight hundred and no/100--------------------------- *Dollars*

at   Penobscot Trust Co.

Value received with interest at 7%

No. 1   *Due*   A.J. Thatcher

CHAPTER 11
BANKING
AND BANKING
SERVICES

No one should leave large amounts of cash around the house or the office. The obvious reason, of course, is that it is not safe. Besides this, however, we need the money to pay our bills and run our businesses, and it is neither practical nor convenient to make most payments in cash. It is also necessary that we have records of the money coming in and going out.

The modern commercial bank serves individuals and businesses by providing a place where they can safely keep their money and through which they can make payments with safety and convenience. This is accomplished primarily through means of the checking account. In addition, the bank performs many other useful services. In this unit, you will study the place of the bank in the financial affairs of individuals and businesses.

OPENING AN ACCOUNT

Case Problem   Martin Miller is ready to open a small dry goods business. He goes to the neighborhood bank, the Eastern City Bank, and asks to open a checking account.

Discussion Questions
1. Why should the bank want to have Mr. Miller as a depositor?
2. What information will the bank want about him?
3. What is the procedure for putting money into the bank?

The bank is interested in Mr. Miller because it can earn money by using Mr. Miller's funds while that money is in the bank. Opening an account is a relatively simple matter. All the bank really needs to know is the name and address of the depositor and the signatures of the people who will be authorized to draw money out.

To open the account and to add money to it, Mr. Miller will have to fill out a deposit slip such as the one illustrated below. We are assuming that Mr. Miller will open his account with an initial deposit of $1,000. The deposit slip is made out in at least two copies. At least one copy is kept by the bank, and a duplicate, which the bank teller stamps at the time the deposit is made, will be kept by Mr. Miller as his receipt for the money on deposit.

		DOLLARS	CENTS
_6/20/—_ Date	Cash	_10_	_0 0_
Deposited In	Checks/Coupons	_1 5 7_	_3 0_
EASTERN CITY BANK New York, NY 10021	"		
	"		
	"		
	"		
Martin Miller Name on Bank Book	"		
	TOTAL	_1 6 7_	_3 0_
119 Sullivan St. Present Address	Cash Returned	_—_	_—_
New York, NY 10012	DEPOSIT	_1 6 7_	_3 0_
030⑈585 2⑈	ALL CHECKS ACCEPTED SUBJECT TO COLLECTION		

Notice the numbers at the bottom of the deposit slip. These have been assigned to Mr. Miller's account and will be used to identify every transaction he has with the bank. The bank will also be glad to have special deposit slips with his name and address printed on them made for him, once he is a regular depositor.

WRITING CHECKS

Once he has money in a checking account, Mr. Miller can use that money to pay his bills. He does this by writing out a check, such as the one illustrated below.

NO. _12_ $_20.00_	Martin Miller	70-2804
DATE _7/1_ 19_	119 Sullivan Street	711
TO _March's_	New York, NY 10012	No.

PAY TO THE ORDER OF _March's_ ——————————— $ _20.00_

Twenty and no/100 ——————————— DOLLARS

EASTERN CITY BANK
New York, NY   10021

Martin Miller

⑆0711⑆2804⑆ 030⑆585 2⑈

	DOLLARS	CENTS
BALANCE	238	00
AMT. DEPOSITED		
TOTAL		
AMT. THIS CHECK	20	00
BALANCE	218	00

Notice that the check is in two parts. The stub is the depositor's (Mr. Miller's) own record so that he has all the facts such as the date and amount of the check, the person to whom the money was paid, what it was for, and the balance remaining in the account. There is also space provided on the stub for him to add any deposits he has made and subtract the amount of this check. Thus he keeps a running record of how much money he has left (his bank balance).

The check is torn off and is given to the person he wishes to pay (called the payee). The payee deposits the check in his own bank, which in turn presents it to the Eastern City Bank. This bank will first see if the signature on the check is an authorized one and if there is enough money in the account to cover the amount of the check. If all is in order, the bank will pay out (or honor) the check and subtract the amount from its own record of how much the depositor has in the bank.

In order to be sure that one doesn't write checks for more money than one has in the bank, it is necessary for each depositor to keep accurate records of all deposits and checks written.

CHECKBOOK RECORDS

Case Problem   Cindy Bolton is treasurer of a boating club. As treasurer, Ms. Bolton keeps a *checkbook record* for the club's bank account, that is, a record of deposits made at the bank and of checks written in payment of bills.

On the next page are the records of the last two checks written.

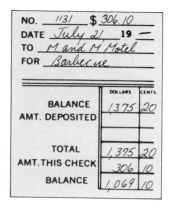

NO. 1130 $ 16.70		
DATE July 11 19 —		
TO Axel Brothers		
FOR Membership cards		
	DOLLARS	CENTS
BALANCE	1,370	50
AMT. DEPOSITED	21	40
TOTAL	1,391	90
AMT. THIS CHECK	16	70
BALANCE	1,375	20

NO. 1131 $ 306.10		
DATE July 21, 19 —		
TO M and M Motel		
FOR Barbecue		
	DOLLARS	CENTS
BALANCE	1375	20
AMT. DEPOSITED		
TOTAL	1,375	20
AMT. THIS CHECK	306	10
BALANCE	1,069	10

Discussion Questions

1. What effect does each deposit and each check drawn have on the balance?
2. How is the new balance found?

In keeping the checkbook record, Ms. Bolton is required to add and subtract. Each time a deposit is made at the bank, the amount is entered on the *Deposits* line and added to the previous balance (*Balance*). The new balance is entered on the *Total* line. From the new total must be subtracted each check that is written; the difference is the new balance.

Exercises

Carl Edgerton made deposits and wrote checks as follows during the week of August 11. Check the stubs for accuracy and list any errors you find.

a.

NO. 416 $ 63.29		
DATE Aug. 11, 19 —		
TO Electronics, Inc.		
FOR New stereo loudspeaker		
	DOLLARS	CENTS
BALANCE	374	64
AMT. DEPOSITED	287	93
TOTAL	662	57
AMT. THIS CHECK	- 63	29
BALANCE	599	28

b.

NO. 417 $ 149.50		
DATE Aug. 12, 19 —		
TO British Imports		
FOR Bicycle		
	DOLLARS	CENTS
BALANCE	599	28
AMT. DEPOSITED	37	89
TOTAL	637	17
AMT. THIS CHECK	-149	50
BALANCE	487	67

c.

NO. _418_ $ _97.50_
DATE _Aug. 12,_ 19 —
TO _Leda's_
FOR _Graduation party_
for Mike

	DOLLARS	CENTS
BALANCE	487	67
AMT. DEPOSITED		
TOTAL		
AMT. THIS CHECK	-97	50
BALANCE	390	07

d.

NO. _419_ $ _378.18_
DATE _Aug. 13_ 19 —
TO _Hellord House_
FOR _Air conditioner_
for store

	DOLLARS	CENTS
BALANCE	390	07
AMT. DEPOSITED	212	20
TOTAL	602	27
AMT. THIS CHECK	-378	18
BALANCE	224	29

e.

NO. _420_ $ _176.42_
DATE _Aug. 15,_ 19 —
TO _Credit Master_
FOR _August charge_
account bill

	DOLLARS	CENTS
BALANCE	224	29
AMT. DEPOSITED	16	36
TOTAL	240	62
AMT. THIS CHECK	-176	42
BALANCE	64	20

f.

NO. _421_ $ _307.77_
DATE _Aug. 16_ 19 —
TO _Leonard Jones_
FOR _4th payment_
on loan

	DOLLARS	CENTS
BALANCE	64	20
AMT. DEPOSITED	446	46
TOTAL	510	66
AMT. THIS CHECK	-307	77
BALANCE	202	89

Business Applications

Audit the following check stubs of Mr. Paul Leslie, listing by check number any errors you find. If the balance at the end of any check stub is incorrect, you will have to correct the balance carried forward to the next check.

a.

NO. _74_ $ _26.53_
DATE _May 17_ 19 —
TO _R. Reisner_
FOR _On account_

	DOLLARS	CENTS
BALANCE	1,313	78
AMT. DEPOSITED		
TOTAL		
AMT. THIS CHECK	26	53
BALANCE	1287	25

b.

NO. _75_ $ _131.48_
DATE _June 1_ 19 —
TO _El. J. Stahle_
FOR _Furniture_

	DOLLARS	CENTS
BALANCE	1287	25
AMT. DEPOSITED	46	72
TOTAL	1,333	97
AMT. THIS CHECK	131	48
BALANCE	1202	49

c.

NO. _76_ $ _65.50_
DATE _June 5_ 19 _—_
TO _Internal Rev. Ser._
FOR _Income Tax, 19-_

	DOLLARS	CENTS
BALANCE	1202	49
AMT. DEPOSITED	481	53
TOTAL	1684	02
AMT. THIS CHECK	65	50
BALANCE	1618	52

d.

NO. _77_ $ _8.00_
DATE _June 6_ 19 _—_
TO _Brookhaven Red Cross_
FOR _Contribution_

	DOLLARS	CENTS
BALANCE	1618	52
AMT. DEPOSITED		
TOTAL		
AMT. THIS CHECK	8	00
BALANCE	1610	52

UNIT

2

BANK RECONCILIATION STATEMENT

Case Problem Martha Dowd keeps her own checkbook. She deposits money which she receives in the Eagle National Bank and pays certain bills by check. Below and on the following page is her check record for the month of October.

NO. _212_ $ _55.20_
DATE _Oct. 3_ 19 _—_
TO _Appliance Center_
FOR _Mixer_

	DOLLARS	CENTS
BALANCE	347	50
AMT. DEPOSITED		
TOTAL	347	50
AMT. THIS CHECK	55	20
BALANCE	292	30

NO. _213_ $ _3.90_
DATE _Oct 9_ 19 _—_
TO _Food Mart_
FOR _Groceries_

	DOLLARS	CENTS
BALANCE	292	30
AMT. DEPOSITED		
TOTAL	292	30
AMT. THIS CHECK	3	90
BALANCE	288	40

NO. 214 $ 29.75	DOLLARS	CENTS
DATE Oct. 12 19 —		
TO G & A Shops		
FOR Sweater		
BALANCE	289	40
AMT. DEPOSITED	150	00
TOTAL	438	40
AMT. THIS CHECK	29	75
BALANCE	408	65

NO. 215 $ 16.40	DOLLARS	CENTS
DATE Oct. 15 19 —		
TO Food Mart		
FOR Groceries		
BALANCE	408	65
AMT. DEPOSITED		
TOTAL	408	65
AMT. THIS CHECK	16	40
BALANCE	392	25

NO. 216 $ 25.00	DOLLARS	CENTS
DATE Oct 18 19 —		
TO Century & Co.		
FOR Books		
BALANCE	392	25
AMT. DEPOSITED		
TOTAL	392	25
AMT. THIS CHECK	25	00
BALANCE	367	25

NO. 217 $ 50.00	DOLLARS	CENTS
DATE Oct. 20 19 —		
TO Cash		
FOR		
BALANCE	367	25
AMT. DEPOSITED		
TOTAL	367	25
AMT. THIS CHECK	50	00
BALANCE	317	25

NO. 218 $ 20.70	DOLLARS	CENTS
DATE Oct 24 19 —		
TO G & A Shops		
FOR Shirts for Andy		
BALANCE	317	25
AMT. DEPOSITED		
TOTAL	317	25
AMT. THIS CHECK	20	70
BALANCE	296	55

NO. 219 $ 47.90	DOLLARS	CENTS
DATE Oct. 31 19 —		
TO Redman Carpets		
FOR Hall runner		
BALANCE	296	55
AMT. DEPOSITED	180	00
TOTAL	476	55
AMT. THIS CHECK	47	90
BALANCE	428	65

Discussion Questions

1. How does Martha know her bank balance at any one time?
2. Who else besides Martha keeps a record of her balance? why?
3. Why might this balance differ from Martha's?

If Martha keeps her records properly, she will automatically know her balance at any time. In the problem presented, her records show a balance on October 31 of $428.65.

Her bank also must keep a record of her balance so that it knows whether she has the money available to cover a check. The bank, therefore, adds to her balance every time it receives a deposit and subtracts from it each time it honors a check.

However, there may be differences on any one day because of the time lag. Martha adds her deposit as soon as she makes it; the bank, however, may not record it until the next day. Also, if a deposit is made by mail there can be two or three days difference in time. Similarly, Martha subtracts a check from her balance as soon as she writes it. The bank, however, doesn't know of the existence of the check until it is presented for payment, which usually takes several days and may sometimes take months, if the payee of the check doesn't deposit it promptly for some reason or other. It is also possible that a check sent by mail may be lost, or that a depositor makes an error in computing a balance, or (more rarely) that the bank makes an error.

To give Martha a report of the status of her account with them, the bank sends her, each month, a bank statement. This statement shows every transaction that has taken place during the month that affects her balance—the deposits the bank has received, the checks it has honored, and any miscellaneous matters. Along with the statement the bank sends her all her canceled checks—the checks which she has written and which have been presented to the bank and honored by it. Martha should preserve these canceled checks carefully, because they are now proof that payment was made.

The statement which Martha received from the Eagle National Bank is presented below. What is the first item that Martha will look at when she receives the statement? How will she compare the correctness of the bank's balance with her own records?

```
┌                          ┐        THE SERVICE CHARGE (S.C.) INDICATED ON THIS STATE-
  MARTHA DOWD                       MENT COVERS ACTIVITY IN YOUR ACCOUNT FOR THE
  52 Redman Drive                   PREVIOUS CALENDAR MONTH.
  Eastport, ID 83826
└                          ┘
```

CHECKS IN DETAIL	DEPOSITS	DATE	BALANCE
BROUGHT FORWARD ☛		Sept. 30	347.50
55.20		Oct. 5	292.30
29.75	150.00	13	412.55
16.40		17	396.15
3.90		18	392.25
20.70		25	371.55
50.00		28	321.55
2.00 SC		31	319.55

PLEASE EXAMINE AT ONCE: IF NO ERROR IS REPORTED IN TEN DAYS
THE ACCOUNT WILL BE CONSIDERED CORRECT

LAST AMOUNT IN THIS
COLUMN IS YOUR BALANCE

Eagle National Bank Co.

Eastport, ID 83826

STATEMENT

KEY

SC–Service Charges	CC–Certified Check
EX–Exchange	DM–Debit Memo.
EC–Error Corrected	CM–Credit Memo.
RT–Returned Item	OD–Overdraft

Martha first looks at the balance the bank gives for her account. You will notice that the bank disagrees with her. Martha's records show a balance of $428.65 at the end of the month, and the bank shows $319.55. Instead of immediately calling the bank to report the error, Martha must first try to see if she can discover the reason or reasons for the difference. She does this by means of a *bank reconciliation statement*. To reconcile means to bring into agreement, and here Martha is trying to bring into agreement the bank balance and her own. She begins with the balance that each shows according to its records.

Depositor *Martha Dowd*

BANK RECONCILIATION STATEMENT

October 31, 19—

BALANCE SHOWN ON BANK STATEMENT $ *319.55*   BALANCE SHOWN ON CHECKBOOK STUB $ *428.65*

Martha's check stubs (page 268) indicate that she made two deposits in October—one on October 12 for $150, and one on October 31 for $180. However, the bank statement has recorded only the first one, probably because the second one was made on the last day of the month and will not be added to her account until the next day. As of October 31, therefore, the bank has $180 less in Martha's account than she really has. She therefore adds this amount to the bank's balance, and the reconciliation statement now looks like this:

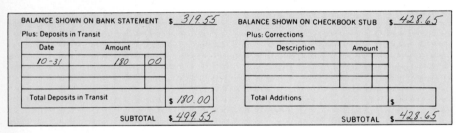

BALANCE SHOWN ON BANK STATEMENT $ *319.55*			BALANCE SHOWN ON CHECKBOOK STUB $ *428.65*		
Plus: Deposits in Transit			Plus: Corrections		
Date	Amount		Description	Amount	
10-31	*180*	*00*			
Total Deposits in Transit	$ *180.00*		Total Additions	$	
	SUBTOTAL $ *499.55*			SUBTOTAL $ *428.65*	

The balances are still not in agreement, so Martha must look further. In examining her checkstubs again, Martha sees that she has written out eight checks in October. The bank, however, has only had six presented to it. (In an actual situation, the six checks themselves would be included with the bank statement). Comparing these checks, which the bank has processed, against her stubs, Martha finds that two checks have not come in—#216 for $25.00 and #219 for $47.90. These are called *outstanding checks* (checks that have not yet been presented to the bank for payment). This means that the bank does not yet know that Martha has taken this money out of her account. Martha therefore adds the two checks together and subtracts the total from the bank balance. Her reconciliation now looks like this:

BALANCE SHOWN ON BANK STATEMENT $ *319.55*			BALANCE SHOWN ON CHECKBOOK STUB $ *428.65*		
Plus: Deposits in Transit			Plus: Corrections		
Date	Amount		Description	Amount	
10-31	180	00			
Total Deposits in Transit			Total Additions		
	$ *180.00*			$	
SUBTOTAL $ *499.55*			SUBTOTAL $ *428.65*		
Less: Checks Outstanding			Less: Charges, Fees, and Corrections		
Number	Amount		Description	Amount	
216	25	00	Service Charge		
219	47	90			
Total Checks Outstanding			Total Deductions		
	$ *72.90*			$	
ADJUSTED BANK BALANCE $ *426.65*			ADJUSTED CHECKBOOK BALANCE $		

Still no agreement, so she keeps looking. On the bank statement, you will notice an "SC" next to a $2.00 item deducted on the last day of the month. If you read the small print on the bank statement, you will see that this represents a service charge that the bank has made and deducted from the account. While Martha is aware of the fact that the bank has a right to make such charges, she often does not know the precise amount until she receives the statement. Therefore, she has not yet deducted this amount from her balance. She must do this now, and her bank reconciliation statement looks as follows:

Depositor *Martha Dowd*

BANK RECONCILIATION STATEMENT

October 31, 19—

BALANCE SHOWN ON BANK STATEMENT $ *319.55*			BALANCE SHOWN ON CHECKBOOK STUB $ *428.65*		
Plus: Deposits in Transit			Plus: Corrections		
Date	Amount		Description	Amount	
10-31	180	00			
Total Deposits in Transit			Total Additions		
	$ *180.00*			$	
SUBTOTAL $ *499.55*			SUBTOTAL $ *428.65*		
Less: Checks Outstanding			Less: Charges, Fees, and Corrections		
Number	Amount		Description	Amount	
216	25	00	Service Charge	2	00
219	47	90			
Total Checks Outstanding			Total Deductions		
	$ *72.90*			$ *2.00*	
ADJUSTED BANK BALANCE $ *426.65*			ADJUSTED CHECKBOOK BALANCE $ *426.65*		

She has reached agreement. She now knows that she and the bank have kept their records correctly. In a short time the bank will record the unrecorded deposit and the outstanding checks will come in.

However, Martha has one further task. Her records still show a balance of $428.65, and we now know that she has only $426.65 available for her use. She must therefore deduct the $2 service charge on her last checkstub, so that her checkbook balance is corrected as of the beginning of the new month.

There are, of course, other items of reconciliation which have not been included in our illustration. Errors can be made by the depositor or by the bank. In each case, however, it becomes necessary to determine which balance is incorrect—the bank statement or the checkbook—and make the adjustment of that balance.

Exercises

Reconcile the bank and checkbook balances for each of the following.

No.	Balance Shown in Bank Statement	Balance Shown in Checkbook	Outstanding Checks	Deposits Not Yet Recorded by Depositor	Adjusted Bank and Checkbook Balances
1	$ 2,176.40	$1,729.00	$197.40	$250.00	$_____
2	$ 908.08	$ 614.58	$125.00	$168.50	$_____
3	$ 5,105.08	$4,919.68	$42.50, $65.00	$ 77.90	$_____
4	$ 2,225.96	$1,877.52	$127.56, $33.92	$186.96	$_____
5	$ 2,244.91	$1,490.86	$12.74, $3.58, $46.39	$691.34	$_____
6	$10,229.73	$7,525.94	$427.32, $695.47, $1,304.25	$276.75	$_____

Business Applications

1. On September 3, Ivan Zukov received his statement from the bank, showing that his balance as of August 31 was $829.22. In going over the statement, he discovered that he had issued two checks of $56.80 and $43.45 that had not yet been returned to his bank. In addition, the bank had made a service charge of $2.50 against his account. His checkbook balance as of August 31 was $731.47. Reconcile the bank statement.

2. On May 31, Bart Harris's checkbook balance was $1,452. His bank statement on that day showed a balance of $1,188.40. Still outstanding was a check for $89.40. On the morning of May 31, he mailed a deposit of $350 to the bank. This, apparently, had not

been received by the bank in time to be recorded on the statement. A service charge of $3 had been deducted from his account that month. Prepare a reconciliation statement, indicating Mr. Harris's available balance.

3. When reconciling his monthly bank statement, Mr. Stan Arben found that he failed to record a deposit he had made of $127.15. A check for $124.50 that he mailed out late in the month had not been returned by the bank. For issuing more checks than his average balance permitted, the bank charged Mr. Arben $3 that month. His checkbook record showed a balance of $1,346.54; the bank's record was $1,595.19. Reconcile the bank statement.

4. The June bank statement for Margaret Wittenmyer showed a balance of $1,189.18. In reconciling this statement against her own checkbook balance of $992.26, Ms. Wittenmyer noticed that the bank had charged her $2.50 for service. She also discovered that she had failed to record a check for $338.64 that she had written while at work. In addition, she had failed to record a deposit of $335.68 made that month. A check for $202.38 issued during the month had not yet been returned to her bank. Prepare a bank reconciliation statement.

UNIT

BORROWING FROM THE BANK

Banks are necessary to a business not only because they provide a checking account, but also because they are a primary source of credit.

When business people need money, they usually go to the institution whose business it is to lend—the bank. Banks and similar lending institutions are willing and eager to make loans to qualified borrowers. Loans are one of the main sources of income for a bank.

DISCOUNTING A PROMISSORY NOTE

When a bank lends money to business people, it usually requires them to sign a promissory note such as that illustrated on the next page. While this looks like the kind of note you studied in the last chapter, there are some important differences.

<table>
<tr><td>$ 2,500.00</td><td>Atlanta, GA</td><td>July 29, 19 --</td></tr>
</table>

<u>Three months</u>   *after date* ^I *promise to pay to*

the order of _____ First National Bank

Twenty-five hundred and no/100--*Dollars*

at _____ First National Bank

Value received

No. ___183___ *Due* October 29, 19--   *George Barnard*

Although there is no mention of interest on the face of this note, nevertheless the bank will charge the borrower, George Barnard, for the use of the principal, $2,500. Banks, however, normally receive their interest in advance; that is, they simply subtract the amount of interest from the face of the note and give the borrower the balance. Following are some terms used in such a transaction:

Bank discount is the interest the bank charges for the use of its money when it is collected in advance.

Discount rate is the percent being charged on the principal.

Proceeds is the amount the borrower receives after the bank discount has been subtracted from the principal.

The procedure of borrowing from a bank in this manner is called discounting a promissory note.

FINDING THE TERM OF DISCOUNT

Case Problem On July 7, Theodore Hopkins borrowed $375 from the Southern States National Bank for a period of two months. The bank discounted his note at 6% and turned the proceeds over to him.

Mr. Hopkins will be charged for the exact number of days between the date of the note and the date of maturity. This period is called the *term of discount*.

To find the *term of discount* (the number of days from the day the bank discounts the note to the day the note becomes due), it is necessary to find first the date of maturity and then the exact number of days from the discount date to the date of maturity. In the note Mr. Hopkins signed, the maturity date is September 7—exactly two months from July 7.

In finding the term of discount, it is important to understand that even though the time in a promissory note is stated in months, the bank always counts the *exact number of days* from the discount date to the date of maturity. The discount date (first day) is not counted, but the date of maturity (last day) is counted.

Example:

Find the term of discount for Mr. Hopkins' note in the Case Problem above.

Solution:

$$\begin{array}{ll} \text{July 7–July 31} = 24 \text{ days (Begin counting on July 8)} \\ \text{Month of August} = 31 \text{ days} \\ \text{September} = \underline{7 \text{ days}} \text{ (September 1–7, the date of maturity)} \\ 62 \text{ days, term of discount} \end{array}$$

FINDING THE PROCEEDS

To find the proceeds (the amount the borrower receives on the discount date), you must compute the bank discount and deduct it from the face value of the note.

The procedure for finding the discount on a promissory note is identical to that for finding interest. Only the terms used in the computation are different. The formula for computing bank discount is exactly like the one you used for interest, except that D (for discount) is substituted for I (for interest).

$$D = P \times R \times T \text{ (Discount} = \text{Principal} \times \text{Rate} \times \text{Time)}$$

Example:

Find the bank discount and the proceeds for Mr. Hopkins' note in the Case Problem.

Solution:

1. Compute the bank discount on Mr. Hopkins' note.

$$\$375 \times 6\% \times \tfrac{62}{360} = \$3.88, \text{ discount}$$

2. Find the proceeds on the note.

$$\$375 \text{ (face value)} - \$3.88 \text{ (discount)} = \$371.12, \text{ proceeds}$$

In our example, Mr. Hopkins will receive $371.12 on the discount date. On September 7, the maturity date, he will repay the bank the face value, $375. In these cases, therefore, the face value and the maturity value are the same.

USING THE INTEREST TABLE TO FIND DISCOUNT

The interest table on page 251 may also be used to find the bank discount on Mr. Hopkins' note.

$1.0000 =$ discount on $100 for 60 days at 6%
$+.0333 =$ discount on $100 for 2 days

$1.0333 =$ discount on $100 for 62 days

3.75 (number of hundreds) $\times$ $1.0333 =$ discount on $375 for 62 days
$3.87 =$ discount on $375 for 62 days

Note that there is often a slight difference in using the tables as against mathematically working the problem out.

Exercises

1. The note shown below was discounted at 5% at the bank on May 17. List the information requested beneath it.

| $ 425.00 | Albany, NY | May 17, *19--* |

Three months — *after date* I *promise to pay to* *the order of* _____ The Commercial Trust Company

Four hundred twenty-five and no/100--- *Dollars*

at _____ The Commercial Trust Company

Value received

No. 537 *Due* August 17, 19-- Raymond Bauer

   a. Maker
   b. Payee

c. Date of note

d. Maturity value

e. Date of maturity

f. Term of discount

g. Bank discount

h. Proceeds

2. Find the maturity date and the term of discount on each of the following notes:

No.	Date of Note	Time to Run	Maturity Date	Term of Discount
a	May 20	3 mo.	_____	_____
b	July 28	60 da.	_____	_____
c	Sept. 14	6 mo.	_____	_____
d	Nov. 30	90 da.	_____	_____
e	Jan. 9	4 mo.	_____	_____
f	Mar. 17	45 da.	_____	_____
g	May 23	30 da.	_____	_____
h	July 6	5 mo.	_____	_____
i	Feb. 15	80 da.	_____	_____
j	Apr. 7	75 da.	_____	_____

Business Applications

1. Using the discount formula $D = P \times R \times T$, find the discount, the proceeds, and the maturity value of each of the following notes. To check each answer, solve each problem again by using the interest table on page 251.

No.	Face of Note	Term of Discount	Discount Rate	Discount	Proceeds	Maturity Value
a	$600	60 da.	6%	$ _____	$ _____	$ _____
b	$400	90 da.	6%	$ _____	$ _____	$ _____
c	$250	30 da.	5%	$ _____	$ _____	$ _____
d	$325	120 da.	$5\frac{1}{2}$%	$ _____	$ _____	$ _____
e	$475	60 da.	4%	$ _____	$ _____	$ _____
f	$255	32 da.	6%	$ _____	$ _____	$ _____

2. Find the proceeds of each of the following notes.

No.	Face of Note	Time to Run	Date of Note	Discount Rate	Term of Discount	Bank Discount	Proceeds
a	$500	1 mo.	June 9	6%	_____	$_____	$_____
b	$300	2 mo.	July 17	6%	_____	$_____	$_____
c	$600	2 mo.	Aug. 4	5%	_____	$_____	$_____
d	$420	3 mo.	Sept. 9	4%	_____	$_____	$_____
e	$250	1 mo.	Mar. 16	6%	_____	$_____	$_____
f	$350	2 mo.	Jan. 22	6%	_____	$_____	$_____
g	$175	3 mo.	Apr. 15	5%	_____	$_____	$_____
h	$600	4 mo.	May 7	$5\frac{1}{2}$%	_____	$_____	$_____

3. Jonathan Arnold discounted his note for $275 at a bank for 30 days at a 6% discount rate. How much money did the bank actually give him?

4. On March 17, Fred Bender discounted his $340 note at a bank for 2 months at a discount rate of $5\frac{1}{2}$%. What were the proceeds?

5. Joanne Black needed $2,000 for 60 days.
   a. If she borrowed this money from a private individual at a 6% interest rate, what would the charge be?
   b. If she borrowed this money from the bank at a discount rate of 6%, what would the charge be?
   c. How much actual cash would she receive from the private individual?
   d. How much actual cash would she receive from the bank?
   e. From which source would it be advisable for her to borrow the money? Why?

UNIT

DISCOUNTING A NONINTEREST-BEARING NOTE

Case Problem Harold Mullens, a wholesaler, sold $1,000 worth of merchandise to J. L. Conklin, accepting Mr. Conklin's 90-day note for that amount. The note was noninterest-bearing and was dated July 10. The note Mr. Conklin signed is shown on the next page.

$ 1,000.00   Olathe, KS   July 10, 19--

_____ Ninety days _____ after date I promise to pay to

the order of _____ Harold Mullens _____

One thousand and no/100--- Dollars

at _____ 406 Southwest Parkway _____

Value received

No. 2 Due October 8, 19-- J L Conklin

You will see that the date of maturity of the note is October 8—90 days from July 10. On August 9, Mr. Mullens found himself short of cash.

Discussion Questions

1. What use might Mr. Mullens make of this promissory note in order to obtain money?
2. Why might the bank be willing to lend him money on the note even though they may not know the maker, J. L. Conklin?
3. What benefit does the bank get from the loan?
4. For what length of time is the bank entitled to interest?
5. How much will Mr. Mullens receive from the bank?
6. Who will the bank expect to get its money back from? when? how much?
7. What happens if Mr. Conklin fails to pay the note when it is due?

Banks are often willing to lend their depositors money by discounting a note which the depositor has received from someone else. Before taking the note, the bank will have the borrower endorse it (sign it on the back). By doing this, the borrower promises to make good on the note in case the original maker does not pay. This gives the bank double protection, because two parties are responsible for payment.

The bank will charge interest (bank discount) for the length of time that it is lending the money (called the *term of discount*). This time runs from the date the note has been discounted until the date of maturity. Just as with discounting

Unit 4 Discounting a Noninterest-Bearing Note 279

a promissory note, the bank subtracts the discount amount from the face of the note and gives the borrower the proceeds. The maker must pay the bank the maturity value of the note, which here is the same as the face value. If the maker doesn't pay, the one who discounted the note is responsible.

STEPS IN DISCOUNTING A NONINTEREST-BEARING NOTE

The general steps taken by a bank in discounting a noninterest-bearing note are outlined in the following example and solution.

Example:
Assume that on August 9 Mr. Mullens discounts the note he received from Mr. Conklin at a discount rate of 5%. What are his proceeds from the note?

Solution:
1. Find the term of discount, the length of time from the date of discount (August 9) to the date of maturity (October 8). The bank discount applies only to the time the note has to run from the *date of discount,* not from the date the note is made. The time from August 9 to October 8 is 60 days, so the bank discounts the note for 60 days at 5%.
2. Determine the value of the note at maturity. Since Mr. Conklin's note is noninterest-bearing, the value of the note at maturity is the same as the face value or principal, $1,000.
3. Apply the discount rate of 5% to the value of the note at maturity, $1,000, for the 60-day period.

$$\$1,000 \times .05(5\%) \times \tfrac{60}{360}(\tfrac{1}{6}) = \$8.333, \text{ or } \$8.33, \text{ discount}$$

4. Subtract from the maturity value the amount of the discount.

$$\$1,000 - \$8.33 = \$991.67, \text{ proceeds}$$

The bank gives Mr. Mullens $991.67 and retains the note. When the note comes due on October 8, the bank will collect the principal, $1,000, from Mr. Conklin. If Mr. Conklin fails to pay, the bank will inform Mr. Mullens, who will then be obliged to pay the bank $1,000 and attempt to collect from Mr. Conklin himself.

Finding the Date of Maturity and Term of Discount
Although you have already learned how to compute time on loans, it is good to review at this point how the date of maturity and term of discount are determined.

Finding the Date of Maturity

Referring to Mr. Conklin's note, you will see that the date of the note is July 10 and the time is 90 days.

	90 days
July 10 to July 31 (21 days)	−21 days
	69 days left
August	−31 days
	38 days left
September	−30 days
	8 days left

October 8 is the date of maturity.

Finding the Term of Discount

The date of maturity of Mr. Conklin's note is October 8 and the date of discount is August 9. We must find the number of days between August 9 and October 8.

August 9 to August 31	22 days
September	30 days
October	8 days
Term of discount	60 days

Exercises

Find the proceeds of each of the following notes.

No.	Face of Note	Term of Note	Date of Note	Discount Date	Discount Rate	Proceeds
1	$ 200	90 days	Aug. 12	Oct. 11	6%	$
2	$ 700	120 days	Mar. 6	Apr. 5	6%	$
3	$1,200	60 days	Sept. 24	Oct. 9	6%	$
4	$ 950	30 days	Dec. 9	Dec. 19	5%	$
5	$2,640	75 days	Feb. 16	Apr. 17	5%	$
6	$3,225	45 days	Jan. 10	Jan. 25	$5\frac{1}{2}\%$	$
7	$ 675	90 days	Apr. 30	May 30	$6\frac{1}{4}\%$	$
8	$1,135	60 days	May 2	May 7	6%	$
9	$1,460	180 days	Apr. 12	May 2	$5\frac{1}{2}\%$	$
10	$ 750	3 mo.	July 17	Aug. 17	7%	$
11	$1,900	6 mo.	Oct. 31	Jan. 31	4%	$
12	$4,400	7 mo.	Nov. 11	May 11	5%	$

Business Applications

1. Sidney Luther had his own 90-day noninterest-bearing note for $775 discounted at his bank. If the discount rate was 6%, find the proceeds.

2. On July 17, S. L. Williams discounted at her bank a customer's 90-day promissory note dated June 5. For how many days was Ms. Williams charged discount by the bank?

3. On July 24, Aaron Baum discounted at 6% a three-month noninterest-bearing note for $725 that he had received from Fargo's Market on June 24. What is the amount that Mr. Baum received from the bank?

4. Find the bank discount at 5% and the proceeds of a 90-day noninterest-bearing note for $5,860 that Edward Ryan received from Clara Lewis on August 18 and discounted on September 2.

5. LeRoy Carter discounted at his bank Louis King's 60-day noninterest-bearing note for $850, dated May 6. If the note was discounted on June 2 at 6%, find the proceeds that Mr. Carter received.

6. On January 25, Nancy Kimball was in need of cash. To obtain it, she discounted Raymond Muir's eight-month noninterest-bearing note for $640, dated September 25. Find the proceeds of the note if the discount rate was $5\frac{1}{2}\%$.

UNIT

5

DISCOUNTING AN INTEREST-BEARING NOTE

Case Problem Gino Parma, owner of Gino's Tile Shop, owes the Riverdale Supply Corporation $2,500 for tile and various other materials used in his business. Because Mr. Parma has been unable to collect what is owed him by two large contractors, he cannot pay the amount due. After discussing the matter with the Riverdale Supply Corporation, Mr. Parma agrees to sign a promissory note for $2,500, with interest at 5%. The note is to be paid in three months.

On September 29, two months after receiving the note, Riverdale Supply Corporation decides to discount the note at its bank. The bank agrees to do so at a 6% discount rate.

$ 2,500.00   Linden, NJ   July 29, *19* --

     Three months   *after date* I *promise to pay to*

the order of   Riverdale Supply Corporation

Twenty-five hundred and no/100----------------------------------- *Dollars*

at   Riverdale Supply Corporation, Linden, NJ

Value received with interest at 5%

No. 12   *Due* October 29, 19--   *Gino Parma*

Discussion Questions

1. Who is the maker of the note?
2. When will he have to pay it?
3. How much will he have to pay at the date of maturity? to whom?
4. Who is discounting the note?
5. On what amount will the bank compute its discount in arriving at the proceeds?
6. How does this differ from discounting the noninterest-bearing note which we discussed in the last unit?

STEPS IN DISCOUNTING AN INTEREST-BEARING NOTE

The situation in the Case Problem differs from the discount examples we considered earlier in that Mr. Parma's note is *interest-bearing* while those in the previous unit were not. As you know, the bank's charge for discounting a note is based on the value of the note at maturity. Since this is an interest-bearing note, the value of the note at maturity will include not only the face value ($2,500) but the interest as well. Thus, the bank will compute its discount on the principal plus the interest.

Example:

Find the proceeds received by Riverdale Supply Corporation when it discounted Mr. Parma's interest-bearing note on September 29. Date of note is July 29, date of maturity is October 29, face of note is $2,500, interest is 5%, and bank discount rate is 6%.

Solution:

1. Determine the value of the note at maturity. Since Mr. Parma has a 3-month note for $2,500 at 5% interest, the value of the note at maturity can be computed as follows:

$$\$2,500 \times 5\% \times \tfrac{3}{12}(\tfrac{1}{4}) = \$31.25, \text{ interest}$$
$$\$2,500 + \$31.25 = \$2,531.25, \text{ maturity value}$$

Note that if the bank had been the lender, it would have computed the exact number of days between July 29 and October 29. However, because the original transaction was between two private individuals, the period of the note remains in terms of months.

2. Find the term of discount. Mr. Parma's note was discounted on September 29. Because the bank computes discount on the exact number of days, you must compute the number of days between September 29 and October 29, the maturity date. The term of discount is 30 days.
3. Compute the discount. This is accomplished by using a slight variation of the formula you learned earlier.

$$Maturity\ value \times Rate \times Time = Discount$$
$$\$2,531.25 \quad \times \quad 6\% \times \tfrac{30}{360}(\tfrac{1}{12}) = \$12.66, \text{ discount}$$

4. Find the proceeds by subtracting from the maturity value of the note the discount to be charged.

$$\begin{aligned} \$2,531.25 & \quad \text{maturity value} \\ -12.66 & \quad \text{discount} \\ \hline \$2,518.59 & \quad \text{proceeds} \end{aligned}$$

The bank gives Riverdale Supply Company the proceeds of the discounted note ($2,518.59), and on October 29 collects from Mr. Parma the full maturity value of the note (including interest) of $2,531.25.

Exercises

Find the proceeds of each note at the top of the next page.

No.	Face of Note	Date of Note	Interest Rate	Term of Note	Discount Date	Discount Rate	Proceeds
1	$ 600	Aug. 3	6%	3 mo.	Sept. 4	6%	$_____
2	$1,200	Nov. 17	4%	6 mo.	Feb. 16	5%	$_____
3	$ 420	Apr. 12	5%	3 mo.	May 13	6%	$_____
4	$3,450	Feb. 11	7%	9 mo.	June 14	6%	$_____
5	$1,900	June 27	8%	120 days	Aug. 26	6%	$_____
6	$2,400	May 5	6%	90 days	June 19	7%	$_____
7	$1,375	Mar. 19	6%	30 days	Apr. 3	6%	$_____

Business Applications

1. On May 17, Douglas Forrester discounted a three-month note for $800 that he had received from a customer. This note bore interest at the rate of 4% per year and was dated April 17. Mr. Forrester's bank charged him a 6% discount rate. Find the proceeds of the discounted note.

2. A 5% interest-bearing note amounting to $620, dated July 28 and due in 90 days, is discounted at the bank on September 11 at 6%. Find the proceeds.

3. On August 11, Fred Ellison received a 120-day $4\frac{1}{2}$% interest-bearing note amounting to $5,870 from Monica Fields and discounted the note on November 9 at 8%. Find the amount that Mr. Ellison received from the bank.

4. Francine Cook discounted on September 29 a nine-month 5% interest-bearing note amounting to $16,800, which she had received from William R. Banker on May 28. If the bank charged a 9% discount rate, how much did Ms. Cook receive for the note?

5. Find the proceeds on the following note if it was discounted January 7 at 6%.

$ 7,200.50   Loomis, NY   December 23, 19 --

_____ Sixty days _____ *after date* I *promise to pay to the order of* _____ Elizabeth Allan _____

Seventy-two hundred and 50/100------------------------------------- *Dollars*

at _____ Manufacturers Banking Company _____

Value received with interest at $5\frac{1}{2}$%

No. 347 *Due* February 21, 19--   *Marcia L. Michaels*

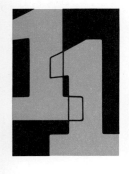

REVIEW
EXERCISES
FOR
CHAPTER 11

1. Complete the checkstubs shown below and find the final balance.

a.
NO. 283	$		
DATE June 3 19 —			
TO Johnson Motors			
FOR Car repairs			
		DOLLARS	CENTS
BALANCE			
AMT. DEPOSITED		60	00
TOTAL			
AMT. THIS CHECK		82	40
BALANCE			

b.
NO. 284	$		
DATE June 5 19 —			
TO "Modern Home"			
FOR 3 year			
subscription			
		DOLLARS	CENTS
BALANCE			
AMT. DEPOSITED			
TOTAL			
AMT. THIS CHECK		17	50
BALANCE			

c.
NO. 285	$		
DATE June 6 19 —			
TO Gentry and Co.			
FOR Slacks			
		DOLLARS	CENTS
BALANCE			
AMT. DEPOSITED			
TOTAL			
AMT. THIS CHECK		20	80
BALANCE			

d.
NO. 286	$		
DATE June 17 19 —			
TO Lois Hendrick			
FOR Repay loan			
		DOLLARS	CENTS
BALANCE			
AMT. DEPOSITED		57	60
TOTAL			
AMT. THIS CHECK		92	89
BALANCE			

2. During June, Arthur Burns made deposits and drew checks as listed on the next page. If he started with a balance of $693.57, how much did he have in the bank on June 30?

286 *Banking and Banking Services*

	Checks Drawn		Deposits Made
June 6	$ 50.00	June 15	$180.00
18	$ 72.40	30	$175.00
19	$ 18.63		
22	$197.50		
28	$ 2.97		
29	$ 13.83		

3. On October 31, a depositor's bank statement showed a balance of $2,065.06. His checkbook balance was $1,488.36. Checks for $206.50 and $290.70 had been issued by the depositor but had not reached the bank. Comparing the bank statement with the checkbook balance, the depositor discovered that he had not recorded either a canceled check for $71.70 nor a deposit of $151.20. Reconcile the balances, indicating the correct checkbook balance.

4. Mary Talmadge's check stubs for the month of March are summarized below.

Bal. For'd	$890.75	Bal. For'd	$900.50
Deposit	———	Deposit	———
Total	890.75	Total	1,060.50
Check #319	64.50	Check #323	116.42
Bal. For'd	$826.25	Bal. For'd	$944.08
Bal. For'd	$826.25	Bal. For'd	$944.08
Deposit	250.00	Deposit	———
Total	1,076.25	Total	944.08
Check #320	27.85	Check #324	67.76
Bal. For'd	$1,048.40	Bal. For'd	$876.33
Bal. For'd	$1,048.40	Bal. For'd	$876.33
Deposit	———	Deposit	———
Total	1,048.40	Total	
Check #321	37.50	Check #325	92.40
Bal. For'd	$1,000.90	Bal. For'd	$783.93
Bal. For'd	$1,000.90	Bal. For'd	$783.93
Deposit	———	Deposit	175.00
Total	1,000.90	Total	958.93
Check #322	100.40	Check #326	100.50
Bal. For'd	$900.50	Bal. For'd	$858.43

At the end of the month, she received her bank statement, as shown below, together with her canceled checks. These checks agreed exactly with the bank statement.

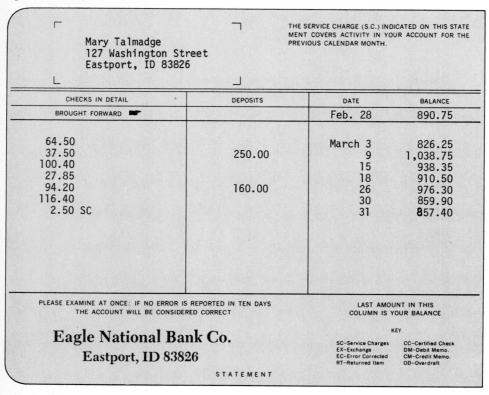

THE SERVICE CHARGE (S.C.) INDICATED ON THIS STATE MENT COVERS ACTIVITY IN YOUR ACCOUNT FOR THE PREVIOUS CALENDAR MONTH.

Mary Talmadge
127 Washington Street
Eastport, ID 83826

CHECKS IN DETAIL	·	DEPOSITS	DATE	BALANCE
BROUGHT FORWARD 🖛			Feb. 28	890.75
64.50			March 3	826.25
37.50		250.00	9	1,038.75
100.40			15	938.35
27.85			18	910.50
94.20		160.00	26	976.30
116.40			30	859.90
2.50 SC			31	857.40

PLEASE EXAMINE AT ONCE: IF NO ERROR IS REPORTED IN TEN DAYS THE ACCOUNT WILL BE CONSIDERED CORRECT

LAST AMOUNT IN THIS COLUMN IS YOUR BALANCE

Eagle National Bank Co.
Eastport, ID 83826

KEY

SC–Service Charges	CC–Certified Check
EX–Exchange	DM–Debit Memo.
EC–Error Corrected	CM–Credit Memo.
RT–Returned Item	OD–Overdraft

STATEMENT

Prepare Miss Talmadge's bank reconciliation statement as of March 31, correcting any errors she might have made on the check stubs.

5. Find the maturity date of a note dated April 17 and due in 90 days.

6. What is the discount period of a note dated August 3 and due in 6 months if the note was discounted at the bank on December 14?

7. Using a promissory note, Bernard Gangi borrowed $8,000 from the bank on April 24 for 9 months at a discount rate of 5%.
a. What is the term of discount?
b. What are the proceeds?

8. On August 24, Priscilla Trogden discounted a $925 noninterest-bearing note at the Middleburg Bank at 5%. If the note was

dated June 15 and was due in 120 days, how much did Miss Trogden receive from the bank?

9. On January 24 F. G. Burns discounted, at 6%, a $1,700 seven-month noninterest-bearing note that he received from Sidney Fields on October 4. How much did Burns receive?

10. Find the bank discount at 5% and the proceeds of a 90-day, 6% note for $5,860 that Luis Rodriguez received from Lewis and Warner, Inc., on August 18 and discounted on August 28.

11. Find the proceeds of the following note, assuming it was discounted November 9 of the same year at the rate of 8%.

$ 5,000.00	Ottumwa, IA October 15, 19--

Ninety days _____ after date I promise to pay to

the order of _____ Mrs. Nancy Mitford Brown

Five thousand and no/100---Dollars

at _____ Ottumwa National Bank

Value received with interest at 6%

No. 411   Due January 13, 19--   Paul G. Bottsford

CHAPTER 12
TRADE
AND CASH
DISCOUNTS

Buying is an important activity in business. The buyer's job is highly specialized. A buyer must have a "sixth sense" about what customers want, when they will want it, and what price they will agree to pay for it. The buyer also has to know where to find the most readily available merchandise at the best price and quality. The success of any business, and particularly of any retail store, depends largely on the buyer's know-how. If the customers' wants are misjudged, the business will be stuck with merchandise it has paid for but cannot sell. On the other hand, if the buying is done wisely, and the stock moves rapidly, the business prospers. This is why the buyer is one of the highest paid executives in retailing.

Those who buy goods for resale are called *buyers,* but those who buy goods to be used exclusively in the business and that are not resold (such as stationery, delivery trucks, typewriters, or janitorial supplies) are called *purchasing managers.*

There are many ways in which buyers and purchasing managers can save money for their companies. One way is to take advantage of the discounts that are allowed them. In this chapter, you will learn what these discounts are and how they are computed.

COMPUTING SINGLE TRADE DISCOUNTS

Case Problem Dennis Webber works in the Shreveport Book Store. Shortly after he came on the job, Dennis was assisting the manager in placing a new order for books. In the publisher's catalog, the price of *Handbook of Skiing* is listed as $8, but on a separate sheet inserted in the catalog, the publisher offers bookstores a "30% trade discount on all sports handbooks."

Discussion Questions
1. What is a trade discount?
2. Why isn't the "real" price of *Handbook of Skiing* ($8 less 30%) shown in the catalog?

THE MEANING OF TRADE DISCOUNT

In business, a *discount* is a reduction in price. A *trade discount* is a reduction in price offered by one business to another business. The name comes from the fact that one business speaks of another as being "in the trade." For example, a publisher of books offers a discount to retail book stores because these stores are in the trade.

All suppliers publish a price list or catalog of the merchandise they sell. The *list price* of an article is the one shown in the catalog.

Yarov, Alex. *Handbook of Skiing.* $8.00.

Buyers in the trade are allowed to deduct a trade discount from the list price. The discount varies—10%, 25%, 30%, $43\frac{1}{2}$%, and so on—but it is always stated as a percent and is called the *discount rate*.

$$\begin{array}{ll} \$8 & \text{list price} \\ \underline{\times .30} & \text{discount rate of 30\%} \\ \$2.40 & \text{trade discount of \$2.40} \end{array}$$

The merchant subtracts the trade discount from the list price to arrive at the price the merchant will actually pay—the *net price*.

$$\begin{array}{ll} \$8.00 & \text{list price} \\ \underline{-2.40} & \text{trade discount} \\ \$5.60 & \text{net price} \end{array}$$

The percent of the list price which the net price represents is called the *net price rate*.

$$\frac{\text{Net price}}{\text{List price}} = \frac{\$5.60}{\$8.00} = 70\%, \text{ net price rate}$$

In all businesses, prices are increased or reduced from time to time. Instead of publishing a new price list or catalog each time a price is changed, businesses merely offer a different discount, which they print on a separate sheet.

COMPUTING SINGLE TRADE DISCOUNTS

Two different methods can be used for finding the net price to a purchaser who is granted a trade discount.

Method 1

In the example that follows, you will learn the first method.

Example:

The Atlas Piano Company manufactures pianos for sale to music stores, department stores, and other retail outlets. In its catalog, Atlas Piano lists Vertichord spinets at $850, less a discount to the trade of 40%. What will Swinford's Music Store have to pay for this piano?

Solution:

1. Multiply the list price by the discount rate to find the trade discount.

$$\$850 \times 40\% = \$340, \text{ discount}$$

2. Subtract the trade discount from the list price to find the net price.

$850 − $340 = $510, net price

Exercises

Find both the trade discount and the net price for each purchase. (Remember that changing the percent to a decimal whenever you multiply a number with a decimal makes the arithmetic easier to do.)

Purchase No.	List Price	Trade Discount Rate	Trade Discount	Net Price
1	$ 60.00	20%	$ _____	$ _____
2	$ 135.00	25%	$ _____	$ _____
3	$ 240.00	18%	$ _____	$ _____
4	$ 475.25	30%	$ _____	$ _____
5	$ 69.98	45%	$ _____	$ _____
6	$ 299.95	35%	$ _____	$ _____
7	$ 798.50	$12\frac{1}{2}$%	$ _____	$ _____
8	$2,376.75	$33\frac{1}{3}$%	$ _____	$ _____
9	$3,584.16	$37\frac{1}{2}$%	$ _____	$ _____
10	$5,850.25	$16\frac{2}{3}$%	$ _____	$ _____

Method 2

The second method of computing single trade discounts calls for finding the net price rate that, when multiplied by the list price, gives the net price.

Example:

Metro Office Equipment Company offers dealers a trade discount of 25% on Speed-Plus Adding Machines. If the list price of the Speed-Plus is $120, what is the net price to the retail merchant?

Solution:

1. If the buyer is getting 25% off the list price, the buyer is paying 75% of the list price. Subtract the discount rate from 100% to get the net price rate.

100% − 25% = 75%, net price rate

2. If we multiply the list price by the net price rate, we get the net price.

$120 × 75% = $90, net price

Unit 1   Computing Single Trade Discounts   **293**

Exercises

Using Method 2, find both the net price rate and the net price for each purchase.

Purchase No.	List Price	Trade Discount Rate	Net Price Rate	Net Price
1	$1,240.00	20%	_____ %	$ _____
2	$ 825.50	25%	_____ %	$ _____
3	$ 62.80	12½%	_____ %	$ _____
4	$ 638.75	30%	_____ %	$ _____
5	$2,940.45	40%	_____ %	$ _____
6	$ 719.90	37½%	_____ %	$ _____
7	$ 500.00	33⅓%	_____ %	$ _____
8	$1,750.50	35%	_____ %	$ _____

FINDING THE DISCOUNT RATE

Case Problem King's Sports Shop ordered merchandise listed at $300. The invoice received showed the net price as $264.

Discussion Questions
1. In what way is this different from the way the price was expressed before?
2. Why might King's Sports Shop want to know the discount rate even if the net price is already known?

Sometimes a wholesaler may list only a list price and a net price. The buyer may want to know the discount rate being offered so that it can be compared with the rate being offered by other suppliers.

Example:
Find the discount rate offered King's Sports Shop in the Case Problem.

Solution:
1. Subtract the net price from the list price to find the discount.

$300 − $264 = $36, discount

2. Divide the discount by the list price to find the discount rate.

$36 ÷ $300 = 12%, discount rate

Exercises

Find both the discount and the discount rate for each purchase in the following table.

Purchase No.	List Price	Net Price	Discount	Discount Rate
1	$ 40	$ 30	$ _____	_____ %
2	$ 75	$ 60	$ _____	_____ %
3	$ 16	$ 12	$ _____	_____ %
4	$155	$124	$ _____	_____ %
5	$770	$439	$ _____	_____ %
6	$520	$325	$ _____	_____ %
7	$960	$840	$ _____	_____ %
8	$333	$222	$ _____	_____ %

Business Applications

1. Using one of the two methods for computing trade discounts described in this unit, find the net price of each purchase.

Item	Quantity	List Price per Item	Total List Price	Discount Rate	Net Price
Power drills	50	$12.00	$ _____	30%	$ _____
Brass pulls	150	$ .45	$ _____	25%	$ _____
Door sets	72	$ 3.20	$ _____	$12\frac{1}{2}$%	$ _____
Planes	16	$ 9.33	$ _____	$37\frac{1}{2}$%	$ _____
Levels	84	$ 2.16	$ _____	20%	$ _____
Scrapers	370	$ .37$\frac{1}{2}$	$ _____	15%	$ _____
Lock sets	64	$ 1.75	$ _____	25%	$ _____

2. The Star Lighting Company purchased 7 floor lamps from a wholesaler at $18.75 each. This purchase was subject to a trade discount of 35%. What was the total net price?

3. Collier and Company, manufacturers of men's sport clothes, sold to one of its dealers a dozen hunting jackets at $39.50 each and 3 dozen pairs of golf slacks at $18.50 each. The entire purchase carried with it a discount rate of $37\frac{1}{2}$%. Find the total net price to the dealer.

4. A manufacturer of transistors offers television repair shops a discount rate of 45% on the CL24A transistor and a discount rate of 33⅓% on the S12R transistor. The list price of the CL24A transistor is $2.60, and the list price of the S12R transistor is $1.98. What would be the net price to a repair shop that purchased 24 boxes (each containing 15 CL24A transistors) and 40 boxes each containing 18 S12R transistors)?

5. A manufacturer offers one brand of golf balls which lists at $84 a gross for $72 a gross, and a second brand which lists at $90 a gross for $75. Compare the discount rates being offered.

6. One dealer in sports shirts offers a dozen at $29 list price, less a 15% discount. A second offers the same shirts for $31.20 a dozen, less a 20% discount. Which is the better offer and by how much?

UNIT

COMPUTING A SERIES OF DISCOUNTS

Case Problem   Paul Schmidt is manager of the Marboro Furniture Mart. Recently he was reading the trade newspaper, *Furniture Retailer,* when he came across this advertisement.

Announcing
Special Discounts
To All Furniture Retailers

25% and 10%

On the Famous "Centennial Celebration" Line

Clarendon—The Sign of Comfort in Home Furnishings

Discussion Questions
1. For what reasons might such a special offer be made to retailers by manufacturers?
2. In what way are the two discounts on each item different from a single discount of 35% on the same item?

MEANING OF A SERIES OF DISCOUNTS

Occasionally, to reduce inventory, a business offers a special trade discount in addition to the one ordinarily given. That is, a company might advertise to its customers that, for the next 30 days, all articles listed in its catalog are subject not only to the usual trade discount of 25% but also to a discount rate of 10%. Sometimes an additional discount may be given to special customers.

The important thing to remember here is that 25% and 10% is not the same as 35%. The two successive rates of 25% and 10% are *less* than the single rate of 35%. A *discount series* of 25% and 10% means that a reduction of 25% is to be taken on the original list price and 10% is to be taken on the balance that remains after the first discount is subtracted from the list price.

You can use two different methods for finding the net price to a dealer who is granted a series of discounts. Examine each of the solutions to the following example.

Example:

Harvey's Food Store purchased a large refrigerator at the list price of $840, less 20% and 10%. What did the store have to pay for the refrigerator?

Solution—Method 1:

1. Multiply the list price by the first discount rate to find the first discount.

   $840 × .20 = $168, first discount

2. Subtract the first discount from the list price to find the first balance.

   $840 − $168 = $672, first balance

3. Multiply the first balance by the second discount rate to find the second discount.

   $672 × .10 = $67.20, second discount

4. Subtract the second discount from the first balance to find the net price.

   $672 − $67.20 = $604.80, net price

Solution—Method 2:

1. Subtract the first discount rate from 100% to find the balance rate (In series discounts, *balance rate* = 100% − discount rate)

   100% − 20% = 80%, first balance rate

2. Multiply the list price by the first rate to find the first balance.

   $840 × .80 = $672, first balance

3. Subtract the second discount rate from 100% to find the second balance rate.

   100% − 10% = 90%, second balance rate

4. Multiply the first balance by the second balance rate to find the net price.

   $672 × .90 = $604.80, net price

Exercises

1. Using Method 1 for computing a discount series, find the net price of each purchase.

Purch.	List Price	Discount Series	Net Price
a	$1,500	20% and 10%	$ _____
b	$2,400	25% and 5%	$ _____
c	$8,750	20% and 20%	$ _____
d	$1,420	10% and 5%	$ _____
e	$1,620	25% and 20%	$ _____
f	$ 840	$16\frac{2}{3}$% and 5%	$ _____

2. Using Method 2 for computing a discount series, find the net price of each purchase.

Purch.	List Price	Discount Series	Net Price
a	$3,250	20% and 10%	$ _____
b	$1,800	20% and 15%	$ _____
c	$4,600	30% and 20%	$ _____
d	$6,200	30% and 10%	$ _____
e	$ 800	20% and 5%	$ _____
f	$2,496	$33\frac{1}{3}$% and $12\frac{1}{2}$%	$ _____

Business Applications

1. The list price of a desk is $600. If this price is subject to discounts of 30% and 10%, what will the net price be?

2. Ace Office Machines purchased a calculator that was listed at $210, less discounts of $12\frac{1}{2}$% and 20%. What was the net price of the calculator to Ace Office Machines?

3. Find the amount due on merchandise listed at $1,268 and subject to discounts of 40%, 20%, and 5%.

4. On men's neckties, listed at $26 a dozen, discounts of $12\frac{1}{2}$% and 10% are allowed. Find the net price of each tie.

5. A furniture dealer bought 12 coffee tables listed at $56.20 each, subject to discount rates of 20% and 10%. If the freight cost was $22.50, how much did the tables cost?

6. M. J. Evans, a purchasing agent for the Durable Life Insurance Company, can buy 36 chairs from a dealer for $14.50 each, less 10%. Similar chairs can be purchased from another firm at $13.75 each, less 10% and 5%. There is a delivery charge of 85 cents a chair, however, if the chairs are purchased from the second firm. How much would Mr. Evans save for his company if he took advantage of the lower price?

FINDING A SINGLE-DISCOUNT EQUIVALENT

Case Problem   Joe Blocker is part-owner of Blocker's Farm Implements. He is studying two advertising circulars. One sent by Midwest Farm Machinery, Inc. features a discount of 20% and 10% on corn planters. Another circular, issued by Bradley Equipment Company, promises discounts of 25% and 5% on corn planters of comparable quality.

Discussion Questions

1. Assuming that the list price of the corn planters advertised is the same ($300), will the net price also be the same?
2. How can Joe find a single discount rate that is equivalent to a series such as 20% and 10% or 25% and 5%?

COMPUTING A SINGLE-DISCOUNT EQUIVALENT

In answer to the first question in the case problem, you know that you cannot make comparisons between two discount series merely by adding the rates in each series. The new price of the corn planters offered by Midwest Farm Machinery, Inc., is not the same as that offered by Bradley Equipment Company, as you will see. Rather than compute each discount separately as in the previous unit, Joe Blocker can speed up the computation by finding a single discount that is equivalent to a series of discounts.

Actually, when there is more than one discount offered (discount series), it doesn't matter which discount is mentioned first. For example, discounts of 20% and 10% on a list price of $300 will give you the same result as discounts of 10% and 20% on $300. (Work it out and see.)

You can multiply the balance rates for each discount (balance rate = 100% − discount) to get the net price rate. Subtracting the net price rate from 100% yields the one discount that is equivalent to the two successive discounts. Let's do the first part of the Case Problem step by step.

Find for Mr. Blocker a single discount rate equivalent to the series of 20% and 10% offered by Midwest Farm Machinery, Inc.

1. Find the balance rate for each of the discounts given.

$$\left.\begin{array}{l} 100\% - 20\% = 80\% \\ 100\% - 10\% = 90\% \end{array}\right\} \text{ balance rates}$$

2. Multiply the balance rates to get the net price rate.

$$80\% \times 90\% = 72\%, \text{ net price rate}$$

3. Subtract the net price rate from 100% to get the single equivalent discount.

$$100\% - 72\% = 28\%, \text{ single equivalent discount}$$

Now apply the same principle to the discount rates of 25% and 5% quoted by the Bradley Equipment Company.

1. $\left.\begin{array}{l} 100\% - 25\% = 75\% \\ 100\% - 5\% = 95\% \end{array}\right\}$ balance rates

2. $75\% \times 95\% = 71\frac{1}{4}\%$, net price rate

3. $100\% - 71\frac{1}{4}\% = 28\frac{3}{4}\%$, single equivalent discount

Which is the better offer?

Midwest Farm Machinery, Inc.	Bradley Equipment Company
Discount rate = 28%	Discount rate = $28\frac{3}{4}\%$
100% − 28% = 72%, percent to be applied to list price	$100\% - 28\frac{3}{4}\% = 71\frac{1}{4}\%$, percent to be applied to list price
$300 × 72% = $216, net price	$300 \times 71\frac{1}{4}\% = \$213.75$, net price

---

As you can see, Joe will get a better price from the Bradley Equipment Company. You will notice that we could simply have used the net price rate which we found in Step 2 to solve the problem, without having to find the single equivalent discount at all. Finding the single equivalent discount, however, is useful in comparing price quotations, and it is important that you know how to do it.

It has probably occurred to you that the same method can be used even if there are three or four discounts in a series. You merely multiply the balance rates of all of them together to find the single equivalent discount.

Exercises

Find a single-discount equivalent for each discount series.

1. 20% and 10%
2. 25% and 20%
3. 25% and 10%
4. 15% and 25%
5. 10% and $12\frac{1}{2}$%
6. $12\frac{1}{2}$% and 15%

USING A DISCOUNT TABLE

In business firms where offering or receiving a series of discounts is common, a discount table such as the one shown below is often used to find the net price rate and also the single-discount equivalent.

DISCOUNT TABLE
Showing Net After Discounts, Shown at Top and Side, Are Taken on $1

Percent	5	$7\frac{1}{2}$	10	15	20	25	30	$33\frac{1}{3}$	40	50
2	.931	.9065	.882	.833	.784	.735	.686	.6533	.588	.49
$2\frac{1}{2}$	.9263	.9019	.8775	.8288	.78	.7313	.6825	.65	.585	.4875
5	.9025	.8788	.855	.8075	.76	.7125	.665	.6333	.57	.475
5 & $2\frac{1}{2}$	.8799	.8568	.8336	.7873	.741	.6947	.6484	.6175	.5558	.4631
$7\frac{1}{2}$	.8788	.8556	.8325	.7863	.74	.6938	.6475	.6166	.555	.4625
$7\frac{1}{2}$ & 5	.8348	.8128	.7909	.7469	.703	.6591	.6151	.5858	.5273	.4394
10	.855	.8325	.81	.765	.72	.675	.63	.60	.54	.45
10 & $2\frac{1}{2}$	.8336	.8117	.7898	.7459	.702	.6581	.6143	.585	.5265	.4388
10 & 5	.8123	.7909	.7695	.7268	.684	.6413	.5985	.57	.513	.4275
10 & 5 & $2\frac{1}{2}$	.7919	.7711	.7503	.7086	.6669	.6252	.5835	.5558	.5002	.4168
10 & 10	.7695	.7493	.729	.6885	.648	.6075	.567	.54	.486	.405
10 & 10 & 5	.7310	.7118	.6926	.6541	.6156	.5771	.5387	.513	.4617	.3848
20 & 5	.722	.703	.684	.646	.608	.57	.532	.5067	.456	.38
20 & 10	.684	.666	.648	.612	.576	.54	.504	.48	.432	.36
25	.7125	.6938	.675	.6375	.60	.5625	.5250	.50	.45	.375
25 & 5	.6769	.6591	.6413	.6056	.57	.5344	.4988	.475	.4275	.3563
25 & 10	.6413	.6244	.6075	.5738	.54	.5063	.4725	.45	.405	.3375
25 & 10 & 5	.6092	.5932	.5771	.5451	.513	.4809	.4489	.4275	.3748	.3206

The *Percent* column at the far left contains discounts taken one, two, or three at a time. The row at the top contains only one discount. Therefore it is possible to find one discount equal to two, three, or four discounts.

Example 1:
Find the net price on an invoice amounting to $300 and subject to discounts of 20% and 5%.

Solution:
At the top of the table, find the first discount rate, 20%, in the horizontal row of figures. Then run your finger down the vertical *Percent* column until you come to the second discount rate, which is 5%. Follow this row across to the 20% column. The number at the intersection of the two columns is .76. This number represents the fact that $.76 must be paid on each dollar of the list price of $300. Therefore, the net price can be found by multiplying $300 by .76, for a product of $228. The single-discount equivalent is 24% (100% − 76%).

Proof: The discount rates of 20% and 5% can be expressed as first and second balance rates of 80% and 95%. When these last two rates are multiplied, we should be left with the net price rate: 80% × 90% = 76%.

Example 2:
Find the net price on an invoice amounting to $200 and subject to discounts of 30%, 10%, and 5%.

Solution:
At the top of the table, find the first discount rate (30) in the horizontal row of figures. Then run your finger down the vertical *Percent* column until you come to the second and third discount rates—10 and 5. Follow the 10 & 5 row across to the number in the 30 column; this number is .5985. Thus, $.5985 is paid on each dollar of the list price of $200. Multiply $200 by .5985. The result is $119.70, the net price.

Exercises
Using the discount table on page 301, find the net price to be shown on each invoice in the table below.

No.	List Price	Discount Series	Net Price
1	$728.00	20% and 10%	$ _____
2	$384.00	10%, 5%, and $2\frac{1}{2}$%	$ _____
3	$176.00	30%, 10%, and 10%	$ _____
4	$280.00	25%, 20%, and 5%	$ _____
5	$ 86.75	15%, 10%, and $2\frac{1}{2}$%	$ _____
6	$263.70	25%, 10%, and $2\frac{1}{2}$%	$ _____
7	$411.90	50%, 25%, and 5%	$ _____

Business Applications

1. A furniture dealer bought 12 redwood lounge chairs listed at $18.50 each, subject to discounts of 20% and 10%. (a) What was the net price of this purchase? (b) If the retailer had to pay a freight charge of $22.50 on the chairs, how much did each chair cost the dealer to place in stock?

2. Which is better and how much better on a bill of merchandise amounting to $360: (a) a discount of 25%, 20%, and 15% or (b) a discount of 50% and 10%?

3. Phil's Appliances purchased a refrigerator for $210, less discounts of 20% and 12½%. What was the amount of the invoice?

4. On men's neckties, listed at $28 a dozen, a discount series of 12½% and 10% is allowed by the manufacturer. What is the net price of each tie?

5. Find the amount paid for the following merchandise bought by Genovese Furniture, Inc. All items are subject to a discount series of 20% and 5%.

> 36 chairs @$84.50
> 18 lamp tables @$21.00
> 24 mirrors @$27.75
> 16 coffee tables @$41.25
> 27 lamps @$18.60
> 12 lamps @$21.75
> 6 bridge tables @$11.40

UNIT

CASH DISCOUNTS

Case Problem Frances Schaum manages the Kentworth Camera Shop. She purchases cameras, film, and other photographic equipment and supplies from various manufacturers and wholesalers. Miss Schaum recently said that she thinks she decreased the store's expenses by nearly a thousand dollars last year by paying her bills promptly.

Discussion Questions
1. Why might paying bills promptly have an effect upon expenses?
2. Why do manufacturers and wholesalers reduce the price of their goods to those who pay promptly?

To encourage the prompt payment of bills and to obtain cash for their operations, businesses offer discounts to those customers who pay their accounts within a specified period of time. Such discounts are called *cash discounts* and are in addition to any trade discounts that may be offered.

When business people sell goods, they send the buyer a bill for the merchandise that is called an *invoice*. The purpose of the invoice is to describe the goods that have been sent, show the unit prices and total amount due, and give the *terms* of payment. These terms indicate when the bill must be paid, and the amount (if any) of cash discount for prompt payment. Both the cash discount rate and the period in which it can be claimed are shown on the invoice. The following is a partial invoice received by the Kentworth Camera Shop from Worldwide Photographic Equipment and Supplies.

Invoice

Worldwide Photographic Equipment and Supplies

312 Vine Street
Cincinnati, OH 45202

To: Kentworth Camera Shop
410 Main Street
Grove City, MN 56243

Terms: 3/10, n/30   Date: May 19, 19--

QUANTITY	DESCRIPTION	UNIT PRICE	AMOUNT
4	Polar Star Light Meters	$ 17 25	$ 69 00

"Terms: 3/10" on the invoice illustrated means that 3% of the net price (*Amount* column) may be deducted if the invoice is paid within 10 days of the date of the invoice. If the Kentworth Camera Shop pays the invoice by May 29 (ten days from May 19), the amount of the cash discount that may be taken can be found by multiplying the amount by the discount rate.

$69 × 3% = $2.07, cash discount

The *net cash price* is then found by subtracting the cash discount from the net price.

$69.00 − $2.07 = $66.93, net cash price

The "n/30" on the invoice means that the net amount shown ($69) must be paid within 30 days of the date of the invoice. If the camera shop chooses not to pay within ten days and claim a discount, it has until June 18 (30 days from May 19) to pay, but it must then remit the full amount of $69.

ALTERNATE CASH DISCOUNTS

Sometimes the terms of sale are more involved. The terms 2/10, 1/30, n/60, for example, mean that 2% of the net price may be deducted if the invoice is paid within 10 days from the date of the invoice and that only 1% may be deducted if the invoice is paid between the 11th day and the 30th day from the date of the invoice. The full price must be paid, however, if the invoice is paid between the 31st day and the 60th day after the date of the invoice.

Example:
The Kentworth Camera Shop ordered 200 photograph albums from Hegel's Photographic Supply Company at a net price of $248. The terms of the invoice were 3/10, 1/30, n/60. Although the invoice is dated March 3, through an oversight it was not paid until March 25. To how much cash discount is the Kentworth Camera Shop entitled?

Solution:
Since the invoice was not paid within 10 days of the date it was prepared, the Kentworth Camera Shop is not entitled to the 3% cash discount. It was, however, paid within 30 days, so the company is entitled to a 1% cash discount (1% of $248 = $2.48). If the invoice had been paid by March 13, the 3% cash discount of $7.44 (3% of $248 = $7.44) could have been deducted.

Here is a list of typical terms of payment which might be offered.

n/30 (or n/60, n/90, etc.)	The invoice must be paid within 30 (60, 90) days of its date. *No* cash discount is offered for prompt payment.
3/10, n/30 (2/20, n/60, 1/30, n/90, etc.)	A 3% (2%, 1%) cash discount is offered if the bill is paid within 10 (20, 30) days of the date of the invoice. If the discount terms are not taken advantage of, the full amount must be paid within 30 (60, 90) days of the date of the invoice.
n/EOM	The abbreviation EOM stands for end of month. The bill must be paid by the last day of the month of the invoice. No cash discount is offered for prompt payment.
2/10 EOM (3/5 EOM, etc.)	Regardless of the date of the invoice, 2% (3%) may be deducted if it is paid within 10 (5) days of the last day of the month of the invoice. (Note: If an invoice is dated on or after the 26th of the month, a month's extension of time is allowed.)

CASH DISCOUNTS AFTER TRADE DISCOUNTS

A cash discount may be offered in addition to a trade discount. In this event, the cash discount is computed *after* the trade discount has been deducted from the list price.

Example:

A florist ordered a lighting fixture listed at $200, less a trade discount of 35%. The terms of the invoice were 2/10, n/30. If the invoice was paid within 10 days of its date, what was the net cost of the fixture?

Solution:

$200 × 35% = $70, trade discount
$200 − $70 = $130, net price
$130 × 2% = $2.60, cash discount
$130 − $2.60 = $127.40, net cost

Exercises

1. Study the invoice and answer the questions that follow.

INVOICE

THE BETTER BUILT FURNITURE COMPANY

Newark, NJ 07100

TO: Atlas Department Store
Paterson, NJ 07500

TERMS: 3/10, n/30   DATE: May 4, 19--

QUANTITY	DESCRIPTION	UNIT PRICE		AMOUNT
3	Sofas No. 467	200	00	

---

   a. What is the total cost of the three sofas?
   b. What are the terms of the invoice?
   c. What is meant by these terms?
   d. By what date must the Atlas Department Store pay this invoice in order to take advantage of the 3% cash discount rate?
   e. What is the last date on which the invoice may be paid?
   f. If a trade discount of 10% was granted and the invoice was paid on May 10, what was the amount of the remittance?

2. Find both the cash discount and the net price computed for each
invoice listed on the table that follows.

Inv.	List Price	Terms	Date of Invoice	Date Paid	Cash Discount	Net Price
a	$2,400.00	5/10, n/30	Oct. 2	Oct. 9	$_____	$_____
b	$1,680.00	2/10, n/30	Jan. 28	Feb. 4	$_____	$_____
c	$3,650.00	5/30, n/60	Aug. 21	Sept. 10	$_____	$_____
d	$1,008.00	4/10, n/30	Dec. 5	Dec. 15	$_____	$_____
e	$3,175.00	3/10, 1/30, n/60	July 15	Aug. 3	$_____	$_____
f	$ 29.95	5/10, 2/30, n/60	Oct. 21	Nov. 1	$_____	$_____

Business Applications

1. An invoice for $725 dated May 15 indicated terms of 3/10 EOM.
   If this invoice is paid on June 8, how large should the check be?

2. The terms of a $1,600 invoice dated June 25 are 5/10, 1/30, n/60.
   What amount of money is needed to pay the invoice on July 20?

3. Alderman's Hardware received an invoice dated May 4 for house-
   wares listed at $720, less a trade discount of 20%. Terms of the
   invoice were 3/10, n/30. What amount will they pay if the bill
   is paid on (a) May 25? (b) May 10?

4. Washington Fabric Shop received an invoice dated July 25 for
   piece goods totaling $390, less a trade discount of 25%. The terms
   were 3/10 EOM.
   a. By what date must the invoice be paid to take advantage of
   the cash discount?
   b. What will be the amount paid on this date?

5. Alfred's Automotive Repair received an invoice on automobile
   parts amounting to $280, less a discount series of 25% and 10%.
   If the invoice was dated July 10 and the terms were 2/10, n/60,
   what was the amount of the payment if: (a) the bill is paid on
   August 1? (b) the bill is paid on July 17?

6. Morton Machines received an invoice dated August 28 for parts
   totaling $525, less discounts of 20% and 10%. The terms of the
   invoice were 2/5 EOM.
   a. By what date must the invoice be paid to take advantage of
   the cash discount?
   b. What amount must be paid on this date?

REVIEW EXERCISES FOR CHAPTER 12

1. Find the net price for each purchase.

Purch.	List Price	Trade Discount	Net Price
a	$ 410.00	15%	$ _____
b	$ 266.80	18%	$ _____
c	$ 977.75	30%	$ _____
d	$1,204.50	$12\frac{1}{2}$%	$ _____
e	$ 63.85	45%	$ _____

2. Find the trade discount and the discount rate for each purchase.

Purch.	List Price	Net Price	Trade Discount	Discount Rate
a	$ 160.00	$128.00	$ _____	_____ %
b	$ 370.00	$323.75	$ _____	_____ %
c	$ 735.00	$490.00	$ _____	_____ %
d	$1,320.40	$858.26	$ _____	_____ %

3. Find the single-discount equivalent for each discount series.
   a. 10% and 20% **b.** 25% and 5%
   c. 25% and 15% **d.** 20% and $12\frac{1}{2}$%
   e. $16\frac{2}{3}$% and $12\frac{1}{2}$% **f.** $12\frac{1}{2}$% and 5%

4. Refer to the discount table on page 301 where possible, and find the net price of each purchase at the top of the next page.

Invoice No.	List Price	Discount Series	Net Price
711	$ 804.00	10% and 20%	$ _____
712	$ 346.25	20% and 25%	$ _____
713	$ 299.48	5%, $12\frac{1}{2}$%, and 5%	$ _____
714	$ 116.15	15%, 10%, and 5%	$ _____
715	$ 962.05	30%, 5%, and $2\frac{1}{2}$%	$ _____
716	$1,103.30	25%, $12\frac{1}{2}$%, and 5%	$ _____
717	$ 626.88	$12\frac{1}{2}$%, 10%, and 5%	$ _____
718	$ 15.70	10%, $12\frac{1}{2}$%, and $12\frac{1}{2}$%	$ _____

5. The catalog price of a sewing machine was $178.50, less 40%. What was the net price?

6. At what net price was a sofa listed at $132, less 25% and 5%, sold?

7. Merchandise was bought for $36. If the terms were 6/10, n/30, and the invoice was paid in 10 days, what was the net price?

8. A discount series of 30% and 5% is equivalent to what single discount rate?

9. What is the amount of cash discount for an invoice of $72, dated January 5 and paid on February 1, if the terms were 7/10, 2/30, n/60?

10. Find the amount due on goods invoiced at $375, subject to discounts of 40% and 20%, terms 5/10, n/30, if the invoice was dated March 12 and was paid on March 21.

11. A. B. Cartwright has the opportunity to purchase a freezer for his store for $2,500, less 15%, from the Freezer Sales Corporation. The Frozen-Aire Corporation offers him similar equipment for $2,350, less 10%, and will charge him $25 for installation. How much will Mr. Cartwright save by accepting the lower of the two offers?

12. The Lester Construction Company purchased equipment invoiced at $7,853.75 from the Sebrook Equipment Company on May 27, terms 8/10, 6/30, n/90. Payment was made June 9.
   a. What discount were they entitled to?
   b. What was the amount of the payment?

CHAPTER 13
ESTABLISHING
RETAIL PRICES

The main reason a person goes into business is to make a profit. Although there are other reasons—to be one's own boss, for example—the primary reason is to earn as much money as one's imagination and hard work warrant. There are many headaches and many risks in running a business, which is why most people prefer to work for someone else rather than strike out on their own. Thousands of businesses close their doors every year because their owners are not making a profit and can't keep the business going.

The biggest cause of failure in business, as you might have guessed, is insufficient sales. And the sales volume a business enjoys is greatly affected by its pricing policies. Here the manager of a business faces a very big challenge. If prices are set very low, the store may pull in lots of customers but lose money in the bargain. If prices are set high enough to cover all expenses and make a reasonable profit, the owner may lose business to competitors.

In this chapter, you will learn how retailers establish prices for their merchandise.

1

ESTABLISHING MARKON

Case Problem   Michael Matthews operates the Country Squire, a men's store. Like all retail store owners, Mr. Matthews is constantly faced with the problem of setting the "right" price for each of the various items of merchandise he sells. If, for example, he pays a wholesaler $40 each for men's topcoats, for how much should he sell each coat?

Discussion Questions
1. What factors help to determine the selling price?
2. Why is intelligent pricing one of the most important challenges a retailer faces?

Every retailer must set prices high enough not only to cover the expenses of doing business—such as advertising, salaries, taxes, rent, and insurance—but also to produce a profit. Many factors play a part in pricing decisions: the cost of goods, the selling prices of comparable articles in competing stores, the expenses of operating the business, and the minimum acceptable profit. Obviously, the retailer who sets prices too high will lose customers to other stores. The retailer who sets them too low may only "break even" or sometimes even lose money.

If a retailer is to pay the expenses of operating the business and still make a profit, merchandise must be priced at a higher amount than the amount that was paid for it. The difference between the selling price of an article and the cost of the article is called *markon*. For example, if Mr. Matthews decides to sell at $65 the topcoats that he bought for $40, $40 is the *cost*; $65 is the *selling price;* and $25 is the *markon* ($65 − $40 = $25).

Note: Some businesses use the term markup for what is now called markon. However, this text uses the now preferred markon. *Markup* in current usage refers to the amount by which the regular or original selling price is increased.

MARKON BASED ON COST

A retailer like Michael Matthews (see the Case Problem on this page) often prices his merchandise at a percent of increase based on what it cost him. This *markon* varies from one department in the store to another. That is, Mr. Matthews may decide to apply an average markon of 30% on men's clothing and an average markon of $33\frac{1}{3}\%$ on men's jewelry and leather goods.

Example:

One line of men's light jackets cost Mr. Matthews $6.50 each. At what price should each jacket be marked for sale if he wants to realize a 30% markon based on the cost?

Solution:

Since the markon is 30% of the cost of $6.50, the markon is found by multiplying $6.50 by 30%. Adding the product ($1.95) to the cost ($6.50) gives the sum of $8.45, which is the selling price.

$6.50 × 30% = $1.95, markon

$6.50 (cost) + $1.95 (markon) = $8.45, selling price

You have probably noticed that prices frequently follow a pattern. A retailer will often mark an article $29.98 rather than $30.00, because it sounds a lot more than 2¢ cheaper. Thus, after the retailer computes what the selling price should be by figuring the necessary markon, he or she may then mark it up or down a few cents to conform to the marking pattern. In the examples you will do, we will consider the answer to be the arithmetically correct one; however, keep in mind the possibility that in an actual situation this price may then be modified.

In determining cost, the costs of transportation, such as freight and trucking charges, are customarily added to the price paid because they are considered to be an essential part of the cost of the merchandise.

Exercises

Find the selling price for each of the following.

No.	Cost	Percent of Markon Based on Cost	Markon	Selling Price
1	$ 60.00	15%	$_____	$_____
2	$ 48.00	33⅓%	$_____	$_____
3	$175.00	45%	$_____	$_____
4	$ 63.50	28%	$_____	$_____
5	$ 99.75	25%	$_____	$_____
6	$128.48	37½%	$_____	$_____
7	$425.00	100%	$_____	$_____
8	$567.50	120%	$_____	$_____

MARKON BASED ON SELLING PRICE

Most retailers prefer to state markon as a percent of selling price rather than as a percent of the cost price because they can state the markon rate at a smaller percent. If, for example, you buy a pair of gloves for $5 and sell them for $6, your markon must be stated as 20% over cost ($6 − $5 = $1; $1 ÷ $5 = .20 = 20%). If you state the same markon ($1) as a percent of the selling price, the markon rate is only $16\frac{2}{3}\%$ ($1 ÷ $6 = .1667, or $16\frac{2}{3}\%$).

MARKON BASED ON COST AND ON SELLING PRICE

Using what you have learned about percents will help you understand the relationship among selling price, cost, and markon. It will then be easy for you to convert markon based on cost to markon based on selling price and vice versa.

Example:
Convert a markon of 25% of cost to a markon based on selling price.

Solution:
The formula you have already learned is:

$$Cost + Markon = Selling\ Price$$

If you know that the markon is 25% of cost, then cost must be 100%. Therefore:

$$100\%\ (cost) + 25\%\ (markon) = 125\%,\ selling\ price$$

To find markon based on selling price, you divide the markon by the selling price:

$$25 ÷ 125 = .20\ or\ 20\%.$$

Using this formula, you can convert any markon based on cost to a markon based on selling price.

Exercises
Convert the following markons based on cost to markons based on selling price.

1. 20%   2. 50%   3. 10%
4. 40%   5. $66\frac{2}{3}\%$

   You can just as easily convert a markon based on selling price to one based on cost.

Example:
Convert a markon of 25% based on selling price to a markon based on cost.

Solution:

If the markon is based on selling price, then selling price must be 100%. Given a markon of 25% of selling price, the following holds true.

$$\text{Cost} + \text{Markon } (25\%) = \text{Selling Price } (100\%)$$
$$\text{Cost} = \text{Selling Price } (100\%) - \text{Markon } (25\%)$$
$$\text{Cost} = 75\% \ (100\% - 25\%)$$

Markon based on cost would therefore be $25\% \div 75\%$.

$$\tfrac{25}{75} = \tfrac{1}{3} = 33\tfrac{1}{3}\%$$

Exercises

Convert the following markons (based on selling price) to markons based on cost.

1. 50%   2. 40%   3. 20%
4. 10%   5. $33\tfrac{1}{3}\%$

The ability to convert markon percents makes solving some problems very easy.

Example:

A stationer purchased word games for $4.50 each and wishes to mark them to make a profit of 25% of selling price. At what price should they be sold?

Solution:

75% (cost) + 25% (markon) = 100%, selling price
$4.50   + $1.50   = $6.00, selling price

Explanation:

Because the markon is based on the selling price, the selling price must be 100%, which leaves 75% for cost. We know that the cost is $4.50. The markon is therefore $\tfrac{1}{3}$ or $33\tfrac{1}{3}\%$ of cost. ($\tfrac{25}{75} = \tfrac{1}{3}$). Our markon is $1.50 ($\tfrac{1}{3}$ of $4.50) and our selling price is $6.00.

Exercises

Complete the following table.

Item	Cost	Markon on Selling Price	Amount of Markon	Selling Price
1	$ 84.00	25%	$ ____	$ ____
2	$114.00	60%	$ ____	$ ____
3	$120.00	20%	$ ____	$ ____
4	$ 90.00	$33\tfrac{1}{3}\%$	$ ____	$ ____
5	$250.00	50%	$ ____	$ ____

USING A CONVERSION TABLE

Many retailers use a conversion table to help them to figure out their selling prices. Below is a typical example of such a table.

MARKON TABLE

Desired Markon (% of Selling Price)	Equivalent % of Cost	Desired Markon (% of Selling Price)	Equivalent % of Cost
4.8%	5.0%	25.0%	33.3%
5.0%	5.3%	26.0%	35.0%
6.0%	6.4%	27.0%	37.0%
7.0%	7.5%	27.3%	37.5%
8.0%	8.7%	28.0%	39.0%
9.0%	10.0%	28.5%	40.0%
10.0%	11.1%	29.0%	40.9%
10.7%	12.0%	30.0%	42.9%
11.0%	12.4%	31.0%	45.0%
11.1%	12.5%	32.0%	47.1%
12.0%	13.6%	33.3%	50.0%
12.5%	14.3%	34.0%	51.5%
13.0%	15.0%	35.0%	53.9%
14.0%	16.3%	35.5%	55.0%
15.0%	17.7%	36.0%	56.3%
16.0%	19.1%	37.0%	58.8%
16.7%	20.0%	37.5%	60.0%
17.0%	20.5%	38.0%	61.3%
17.5%	21.2%	39.0%	64.0%
18.0%	22.0%	39.5%	65.5%
18.5%	22.7%	40.0%	66.7%
19.0%	23.5%	41.0%	70.0%
20.0%	25.0%	42.0%	72.4%
21.0%	26.6%	42.8%	75.0%
22.0%	28.2%	44.4%	80.0%
22.5%	29.0%	46.1%	85.0%
23.0%	29.9%	47.5%	90.5%
23.1%	30.0%	48.7%	95.0%
24.0%	31.6%	50.0%	100.0%

Here is an example of how the table is used.

Example:

The cost of a vase to Mary Tremont, owner-manager of the Ritz Gift Shop, is $4.50. If Miss Tremont wants a 33⅓% markon based on selling price, what will she charge a customer for the vase?

Solution:

In the column *Desired Markon (% of Selling Price)*, find the percent of markon needed (33.3). Move your finger across to the column *Equivalent % of Cost*. The table entry is 50.0, so a 33⅓% markon based on selling price is equivalent to a 50% markon based on cost price. Therefore, multiply the cost ($4.50) by 50% to find the markon.

$4.50 × 50% = $2.25, markon

Add the markon to the cost to find the selling price.

$4.50 + $2.25 = $6.75, selling price

Exercises

Using the markon table on page 315, find the selling price of each article.

No.	Article	Cost	Desired Markon (% of Selling Price)	Selling Price
1	Lamp	$ 37.80	40%	$_____
2	Tire	$ 8.40	25%	$_____
3	Shoes	$ 12.75	33⅓%	$_____
4	Dinette	$ 88.25	30%	$_____
5	Perfume	$ 9.90	50%	$_____
6	China	$124.60	40%	$_____
7	Man's suit	$ 72.00	37½%	$_____
8	Lawn seed	$ 3.75	28%	$_____
9	Golf clubs	$165.00	47½%	$_____
10	Textbook	$ 2.20	35%	$_____

Business Applications

1. Lamps Unlimited purchased a lamp on special order. The cost of the lamp was $24.50, and the shipping charge was $1.10. How much will the store have to charge for this lamp if a 25% profit based on the total cost of the lamp is to be realized?

2. Agnes Lockmiller, owner of a stationery store, purchased cartridge pens at a cost of $19.80 a dozen. At what price will she have to sell each pen in order to realize a profit of 20% on the cost?

3. The Ridgeway Garden Mart paid $264 for 12 hedge trimmers. Trucking fees totaled $12.96. At what price will each hedge trimmer have to be tagged if a 25% profit based on cost is to be realized?

4. David Norris, manager of a produce stand, purchased 12 crates of strawberries at $9.45 a crate. Each crate contains 32 baskets. Before the lot is sold, he estimates that 24 baskets will have to be thrown away because of spoilage. At what price will Mr. Norris have to sell each remaining basket of strawberries in order to make a profit of $33\frac{1}{3}$% on cost?

5. Eggs are packed in crates of 30 dozen to a crate. A purchase of 30 crates was made for Frank's Quik-Way Market at a cost of $14.40 a crate. Breakage will necessitate throwing away 20 dozen eggs. At what price per dozen will the remaining eggs have to be sold so that a profit of 20% on cost can be made?

6. At what price should an office equipment sales representative sell electric typewriters purchased at $325 if the markon rate is 40% based on the selling price?

7. What are the markon and the selling price on desk sets that cost $7.80 if the rate of markon is 35% based on the selling price?

8. Reo Office Interiors, Inc., purchased bookcases for $72.50 each, less a trade discount of 20%. At what price should Reo sell each bookcase in order to realize a profit of 50% based on cost?

9. Ceramic candlesticks were purchased by Cindy's Gift Shoppe at $7.96, less 25%. If the owner wishes to retail the candlesticks at a markon of 35% of the cost, what should the selling price be?

10. Wilson's Fashion Shop purchased women's suits at $40.50, less a trade discount of $33\frac{1}{3}$%. If their markon rate is $16\frac{2}{3}$% of the cost, at what price should these suits be sold?

11. The Shoe Emporium purchased children's shoes at $8.50, less 16%. At what price should the shoes be sold if the 30% markon rate is based on the selling price?

12. A retailer bought throw rugs at $175, less 40%. At what price should they be sold if the markon rate is $47\frac{1}{2}$% and is based on the selling price?

UNIT 2

FINDING RATE OF MARKON

Case Problem Russell Bixby, owner of Pine Palace, an unfinished furniture outlet, purchased desks for $37.50 each. He decided on a selling price of $50 for each desk and arranged a special display outside the store.

Discussion Questions
1. At a selling price of $50, what percent of markon did Mr. Bixby use if based on cost?
2. What percent of markon did he use if based on selling price?

PERCENT OF MARKON BASED ON COST

To find the percent of markon, based on the cost of the merchandise, proceed as follows.

Example:
Find the answer to Discussion Question 1 for the preceding Case Problem.

Solution:
1. Subtract the cost from the selling price. The result is the markon.

$50.00 − $37.50 = $12.50, markon

2. Divide the markon by the cost.

$12.50 ÷ $37.50 = .33$\frac{1}{3}$, or 33$\frac{1}{3}$%, percent of markon

Exercises

Find the markon and the percent of markon based on cost in each of the following. (Compute the percent of markon to the nearest whole-number percent.)

No.	Cost	Selling Price	Markon	% of Markon Based on Cost
1	$ 50.00	$ 60.00	$_____	_____%
2	$ 64.00	$ 80.00	$_____	_____%
3	$ 18.50	$ 24.05	$_____	_____%
4	$137.20	$222.95	$_____	_____%
5	$188.61	$251.48	$_____	_____%

PERCENT OF MARKON BASED ON SELLING PRICE

To find the percent of markon based on the selling price, proceed as follows.

Example:

Find the answer to Discussion Question 2 of the preceding Case Problem.

Solution:

1. Subtract the cost price from the selling price. The result is the markon.

$50.00 - $37.50 = 12.50, markon

2. Divide the markon by the selling price.

$12.50 \div $50.00 = .25$, or 25%, percent of markon

Exercises

Find both the markon and the percent of markon based on the selling price for each item. State the percent of markon as the nearest whole-number percent.

No.	Cost	Selling Price	Markon	% of Markon Based on Selling Price
1	$ 54.00	$ 57.60	$_____	_____%
2	$ 48.60	$ 51.84	$_____	_____%
3	$129.50	$148.00	$_____	_____%
4	$ 45.00	$ 56.25	$_____	_____%
5	$ 67.40	$ 80.88	$_____	_____%

Business Applications

1. A discount store purchased a box of 144 bars of chocolate. If the box cost the store $7.20 and each candy bar was then sold for 10 cents, what was the percent of markon based on the cost?

2. Sid Matson, the owner of a men's store, bought 15 dozen shirts at $60 a dozen. He sold each shirt at $6.50. What was the percent of markon based on the selling price of the shirts?

3. Kingston's Home and Garden Store purchased 25 folding chairs at $8 each, and paid transportation costs of $31 to have the chairs delivered to the store. Ten chairs were sold at $15 each and the remainder at $12 each. What was the percent of markon based on the selling price of the chairs?

4. Rachel Baker bought 500 dresses for Fashion Carousel at $13.20 each. She sold 300 at $18.50 each, 100 at $18.00 each, and the remainder at $16.10 each. Trucking costs to bring the dresses to the shop amounted to $120. What was the percent of markon based on the total cost of the dresses?

5. An appliance dealer bought 30 electric percolators at $9.80 each and sold them for $15.95 each. Freight charges to bring them to the store amounted to $50.50. What was the dealer's percent of markon based on the selling price?

6. A toy dealer purchased 20 dozen dolls at $56.20 per dozen, and paid an additional $12.80 in transportation costs. The dealer wants to sell the dolls to realize 40% on the selling price. At what price should each doll be marked?

UNIT 3

COMPUTING COST PRICE

Case Problem   Peerless Shirt Shop sells men's shirts, neckties, belts, and similar articles. From experience, Fred Pratt, the buyer for the store, knows that many customers will pay no more than $2 for a necktie. The markon Mr. Pratt feels he must have is 30% on selling price.

Discussion Questions

1. Can you think of an article that you are accustomed to buying at a certain price and for which you are determined to pay no more?
2. What problems does Mr. Pratt face in buying neckties to suit his customers?

Through experience, retailers know that most of their customers have an "upper limit" on the amount they are willing to pay for certain articles. Some men, for example, will pay no more than $1.50 for a pair of socks or $7 for a shirt. In these instances, the retailer must look for merchandise to buy at a low enough price to permit the store to continue to sell these articles at the price customers will pay and still clear a reasonable profit.

Example:

Bart Cranford, owner of the Family Shoe Barn, sells sneakers for which his customers will pay no more than $5.95. In order to meet expenses and make a profit, Mr. Cranford must price the shoes at a markon of 30% of the selling price. What is the most Mr. Cranford can pay for a pair of sneakers and still realize a 30% markon on selling price?

Solution:

1. Find the markon by multiplying the selling price by the percent of markon.

    $5.95 \times 30\% = 1.79, markon

2. Subtract the markon from the selling price.

    $5.95 - $1.79 = 4.16, maximum cost price

In the Case Problem presented earlier, the most Mr. Pratt could pay for neckties that must be priced at $2 with a 30% markon on selling price is $1.40.

$2 × 30% = $.60, markon
$2.00 − $.60 = $1.40, maximum cost price

Exercises

Find the maximum cost price for each article that will permit the markon indicated.

No.	Selling Price	Desired Markon	Amount of Markon	Maximum Cost Price
1	$ 3.99	30% on S. P.	$_____	$_____
2	$ 1.29	40% on Cost	$_____	$_____
3	$ 7.95	25% on Cost	$_____	$_____
4	$24.95	33⅓% on Cost	$_____	$_____
5	$ 9.98	35% on S. P.	$_____	$_____
6	$59.95	40% on S. P.	$_____	$_____

Business Applications

1. Lawson's Hobby Shop carries a line of paint sets for which customers are accustomed to paying $3.50 each. For how much must the store purchase the paint sets if it is to maintain that price and realize a 30% markon on selling price?

2. José's Appliance Store sells electric stoves at $215 each. The store uses a markon of 35% based on the selling price. How much can the store's buyer pay for the stoves if they are to sell at the price indicated?

3. Beth Long, owner of a dress shop, features a line of jumpsuits priced at $11.99. If she holds this price and achieves the 40% markon on cost she desires, what is the maximum she can pay for these jumpsuits from a manufacturer?

4. Jill's Card Shop wants to sell personal note paper at $2.40 per box and realize 33 ⅓% markon on cost. How much can be paid for a carton containing a dozen boxes of the paper?

COMPUTING MARKDOWN

Case Problem Gwenn Costello operates Gwenn's Book Nook, a retail book store in Hampton City. Occasionally, Ms. Costello announces a sale in which certain books are offered at a special low price. A recent advertisement in the *Hampton City News* carried this headline:

All Books in **ART TREASURES** Series Now $4.50!

Discussion Questions

1. For what reasons might Ms. Costello sell books at a reduced price?
2. If the books advertised were originally priced at $6, by what percent did she reduce the price?

Retailers often reduce prices on various items in their stores, and they do so for several reasons: to clear out old merchandise that is not selling well, to get rid of shopworn articles, to stimulate more sales by attracting new customers, and to meet the prices of competitors. A reduction in the regular selling price is called a *markdown*.

For inventory purposes the percent of markdown is expressed as a percent of the new reduced price rather than as a percent of the original price.

Example:

Horace Wolff, a retail office supply store manager, offered for sale at $3 staplers that were originally priced at $4.50. Find (a) the markdown and (b) the percent of markdown.

Solution:

1. To find the markdown, subtract the new selling price from the original selling price.

$$\$4.50 - \$3.00 = \$1.50, \text{ markdown}$$

2. To find the percent of markdown, divide the markdown by the new selling price.

$$\$1.50 \div \$3.00 = .50, \text{ or } 50\%, \text{ percent of markdown}$$

In the Case Problem presented earlier, the markdown by which Ms. Costello reduced the price of her art books is $33\frac{1}{3}\%$.

$$\$6.00 - \$4.50 = \$1.50, \text{ markdown}$$
$$\$1.50 \div \$4.50 = .333 \text{ or } 33\frac{1}{3}\%$$

Exercises*

Find both the markdown and the percent of markdown for each article.

No.	Original Price	Reduced Price	Markdown	% of Markdown
1	$50.00	$40.00	$ _____	_____ %
2	$ .65	$ .50	$ _____	_____ %
3	$ 1.98	$ 1.00	$ _____	_____ %
4	$16.90	$13.00	$ _____	_____ %
5	$19.80	$15.00	$ _____	_____ %
6	$ 8.34	$ 6.95	$ _____	_____ %

Business Applications

1. During its January white sale, S. Williams and Sons offered sheets regularly priced at $4.40 each at the reduced price of $3.20. Find both the markdown and the percent of markdown.

2. Sports shirts that regularly sell for $9 could be purchased for $7.50 during the R. J. Murphy storewide sale. What was the percent of markdown?

3. Billfolds that were originally priced at $2.25 were marked down by Bronzini Brothers to $2. Find the markdown and the percent of markdown.

4. A floor lamp originally priced at $70 is marked down to $42. Find both the markdown and the percent of markdown.

5. Carson's had a one-day sale of unfinished book shelves and brackets regularly priced at $17.50 for $12.50. What was the markdown? the percent of markdown?

REVIEW
EXERCISES
FOR
CHAPTER 13

1. An imported wicker armchair cost the T. C. Clark Furniture Store $28.50. At what price will the store have to sell the chair to realize a 25% markon based on the cost?

2. The Consumer Mart purchased car vacuums at $18.50 and sold them at $26.75. (a) What was the percent of markon based on the cost? (b) What was the percent of markon based on the selling price?

3. R. L. Bozier and Company purchased alarm clocks at $4.50 and sold them at $8.98. At what percent of markon based on the selling price is the company operating?

4. The Shoe Department of R. Baxter and Sons operates on a markon of 45% of the cost. On this basis, what is the selling price for shoes purchased at $10.75 a pair?

5. The Houston Comfort Shop purchased fans at $27.50 each and sold them at a markon of 35% of the selling price. What was the selling price?

6. A markon of 40% based on the cost was added to the original cost of a baby bed, which was then sold for $32.20. What was the original cost?

7. Carl's Men's Shop finds that for high sales volume the maximum price at which it can sell Rough 'n Ready tennis shoes is $4.95 a pair. What is the highest price Carl can afford to pay for the shoes if his markon must be at least 25% of the selling price?

8. The Midtown Sleep Shop purchased mattresses at $40, less 10%. At what price will the manager have to sell them in order to obtain 30% on the selling price?

9. During its spring clearance sale, Allison's Bargain Store reduced its cotton sport shirts from $2.99 to $2.50 each. What percent of markdown was the consumer being offered?

10. Boys' coats that regularly sell for $9 each were placed on sale at the special price of $7.20 each. What was the markdown on each coat? What was the percent of markdown?

11. Golf balls that sell for $5.70 a dozen during the summer are marked down to $3.80 a dozen at the end of the season. Compute both the markdown and the percent of markdown.

12. Refer to the markon table on page 315 and find the selling price of the following articles.

	Article	Cost	% Markon Desired Based on Selling Price	Selling Price
a.	Power saw	$29.50	40%	$ _____
b.	Chess set	$16.20	$33\frac{1}{3}$%	$ _____
c.	Belt sander	$22.40	25%	$ _____
d.	Photo album	$ 2.75	30%	$ _____
e.	Scissors	$ 1.10	$37\frac{1}{2}$%	$ _____

CHAPTER 14
FINDING THE RESULTS OF BUSINESS OPERATIONS

We mentioned earlier that one of the main reasons people invest their money in a business is to make a profit. Business owners, however, run the risk of losing money on their investments instead of realizing the profits expected. Every year about half a million new businesses are established in the United States, all owners expecting to gain a profit from their investment, imagination, and hard work. And every year nearly as many businesses close their doors because they are not making money and can no longer afford to operate. Many of those that discontinue operations in a given year are the very same ones that opened for business that year.

There are many reasons why businesses fail. Over half the businesses that fail do so because of inadequate sales. Inadequate sales result from many things. New owners may have a poor location; they may be selling products or services that people either don't want or that are not as good or as well known as those of the competition. They may lack the imagination to advertise and promote their products. Often there is a lack of management know-how.

Another important reason for business failures is inadequate records. Owners must know at all times how much it is costing them to do business. If the cost of the goods they buy and the rent, the salaries, and the other expenses they incur amount to more than their sales, they cannot stay in business. Wise business owners, then, insist on keeping good accounting records. The purposes of accounting records are twofold: to help business owners control costs and to provide them with the information they need to make intelligent decisions. Owners can do neither unless they keep careful records of income and expenses.

One of the most important reports business people (or their accountants) prepare is an *income statement,* which shows the amount of sales, the cost of the goods that were sold, the expenses of operating the business, and the profit earned for the period. (The period may be a month, a quarter, six months, or a year.) But once this report is prepared, it must be analyzed and interpreted. Finding profit is only one objective of the income statement. It should also answer such questions as: Is the cost of the goods sold too high? Are the expenses out of line? Are the expenses increasing or decreasing in proportion to the sales? Is the business achieving a reasonable rate of profit? In this chapter, you will learn how business people deal with the subject of profit and how they prepare the statements they need to interpret the results of their operations.

UNIT

FINDING NET INCOME

Case Problem Arnold Dubroff worked during the summer doing gardening chores for the home owners in his neighborhood. He kept careful records and at the end of his vacation found that he had taken in $850 in gardening fees (revenue) and had paid out $140 for plants and seeds, $83 for small tools, and $50 for insect sprays (expenses). What was his net income for the summer?

Discussion Questions
1. What are the factors that enter into the determination of net income?
2. Work out a formula for finding net income.
3. Under what circumstances would you find that the business sustained a loss?

INCOME FOR A SERVICE BUSINESS

Net income is the difference between *revenues* (what has been earned) and the *expenses* incurred in earning this amount. Thus we can say that

$$Revenue - Expenses = Net\ Income$$

To find out how much Arnold made, we subtract the total of his expenses, $273 ($140 + $83 + $50), from his revenue of $850 to get a net income of $577. Of course, if Arnold's expenses had amounted to more than $850, he would have had a net loss instead of a net income.

Exercises
Find the net income or net loss in each of the following cases.

1. A radio and television repair shop took in $2,300 during the month of April. Its expenses were: rent, $450; salaries, $700; shop expenses, $390; supplies and materials, $240.
2. For the first six months of the year, an accountant charged her clients a total of $29,400. During that period she paid rent of $2,100, salaries of $9,600, office expenses of $2,450, and miscellaneous expenses of $1,740.
3. A window washing service charged its customers $2,390 during its first month of operations. Its expenses were: rent, $400; washing supplies, $370; advertising, $180; salaries, $1,100; and miscellaneous shop expenses, $490.

NET INCOME FOR A MERCHANDISING BUSINESS

Case Problem Anthony Wong has just opened the Maple House, a retail furniture outlet. Mr. Wong purchases furniture from a manufacturer in North Carolina and sells it to his customers unfinished. During the first month of operation, he sold $3,400 worth of furniture—his entire stock. Mr. Wong's costs and expenses for the month were as follows:

$1,900 cost of furniture purchased from manufacturer
$ 250 rental of building
$ 80 heat, light, and water
$ 120 miscellaneous expenses

Discussion Questions

1. In what important way does Mr. Wong's business differ from the service businesses we considered?
2. In a business where merchandise is being sold, what additional piece of information must we have before we can find the profit?
3. Work out a formula to determine net income in a merchandising business.

Mr. Wong sold the merchandise for $3,400 (revenue); it had cost him $1,900 (cost of goods sold). Subtracting, we find that the profit he made just on the difference between the revenue and the cost is $1,500. This is known as the *gross profit* on sales. In order to find Mr. Wong's *net income*, we must now subtract from this gross profit all the costs of doing business, just as we did in the previous examples.

Mr. Wong's net income is found as follows: Add the expenses of doing business (rent, $250; heat, light, and water, $80; and miscellaneous expenses, $120). Then subtract the total of $450 from the gross profit of $1,500 to give a net income of $1,050.

Sometimes customers are able to get adjustments for merchandise they have found unsatisfactory for one reason or another. There are two basic methods of arranging such adjustments. Either customers may send the goods back and get a full refund, which is called a *sales return,* or they may keep the goods at a reduced price, in which case the amount of the reduction is called a *sales allowance.* These sales returns and allowances are then treated as deductions from the sales made to give *net sales.*

You may have noticed that the expenses of doing business, or *operating expenses* as they are also called, differ widely from one business to the next. The nature of the business and the amount of detail the owner wishes to have determine the names of the expenses which are used. Try to think of a typical list of expenses that might be incurred in each of the businesses named below. You will find that some expenses are common to almost all businesses, and some expenses are peculiar to the business under consideration.

1. A florist shop
2. A beauty salon
3. An insurance company
4. A furniture store

The following examples further illustrate how gross profit and net income are determined.

Example 1:

The Bixby High School Choral Group is raising money to buy blazers in the school colors. In October, the members ran the food concession at a football rally, selling pizzas and soft drinks. During the evening the group sold $200 worth of food and drinks. The cost of the pizzas was $75; the cost of the soft drinks was $37. In addition, the members spent $8 for napkins, paper cups, and other supplies, and paid $15 for decorations and signs for the concession stand. What was the gross profit? the net income?

Solution:

To find the gross profit, subtract from the net sales the cost of the goods that were sold—pizzas, $75; soft drinks, $37 ($75 + $37 = $112).

$200   net sales
112   less cost of goods sold
$ 88   gross profit

To find the net income, subtract from the gross profit the operating expenses— paper supplies, $8, and decorations and signs, $15 ($8 + $15 = $23).

$88   gross profit
23   less operating expenses
$65   net income

Example 2:
During the past quarter, Trimble's, Inc., sold carpets and other floor coverings amounting to $9,000. Sales returns and allowances totaled $300. Costs and expenses of operating the business for the period were as follows: Cost of goods sold, $5,200; salaries, $3,000; supplies, $400; and miscellaneous expenses, $700. Find the gross profit and net income for the quarter.

Solution:

$9,000	revenue (income from sales)
300	less sales returns and allowances
$8,700	net sales
5,200	less cost of goods sold
$3,500	gross profit
4,100	less operating expenses
($600)	net loss

As you see, when expenses exceed net income, the result is a loss. In financial statements, negative amounts are often shown by enclosing them in parentheses.

Exercises

1. Find the gross profit and the net income or loss for the following retail stores.
   a. Elmwood Store: revenue from sales, $15,000; sales returns and allowances, $1,000; cost of goods sold, $8,000; operating expenses, $2,000
   b. Lawrenceville Store: revenue from sales, $90,600; sales returns and allowances, $1,800; cost of goods sold, $71,220; operating expenses, $13,140
   c. Kenilworth Store: net sales, $137,500; cost of goods sold, $91,280; operating expenses, $29,800
   d. Mapleton Store: revenue from sales, $64,900; sales returns and allowances, $700; cost of goods sold, $57,100; operating expenses, $12,270

2. Find the gross profit and the net income or loss for each of the following businesses.
   a. Revenue from sales, $16,150; sales returns and allowances, $150; cost of goods sold, $9,600; rent, $800; salaries, $3,200; heat, water, and light, $160; miscellaneous expenses, $575
   b. Net sales, $88,500; cost of goods sold, $61,950; salaries, $9,500; building maintenance, $1,200; telephone, $400; postage, $700; advertising, $3,000; utilities, $770; sales expenses, $6,200; insurance, $220; miscellaneous expenses, $1,440
   c. Revenue from sales, $60,400; sales returns and allowances, $3,200; cost of goods sold, $40,000; salaries, $4,100; rent,

$1,200; telephone, $640; advertising and selling, $8,300; light, heat, and water, $240; delivery expenses, $1,675; miscellaneous expenses, $2,200

FINDING PERCENT OF PROFIT

Case Problem Two friendly competitors decide to compare the results of their operations for the year and present the following:

DuBois	Hendricks	
$150,000	$200,000	net sales
90,000	140,000	cost of goods sold
$ 60,000	$ 60,000	gross profit
45,000	50,000	operating expenses
$ 15,000	10,000	net income

Discussion Questions
1. Which one should be more satisfied with the results?
2. Give your reasons.

Business owners want to know not only the amount of profit in dollars but also the *percent* of gross profit of net sales and the *percent* of net income of net sales. As you learned earlier, percents enable business people to make comparisons more easily than with dollar amounts alone.

To find the percent of gross profit, divide the gross profit by net sales.

	DuBois	Hendricks
$\dfrac{\text{Gross Profit}}{\text{Net Sales}}$	$\dfrac{60,000}{150,000} = 40\%$	$\dfrac{60,000}{200,000} = 30\%$

To find the percent of net income, divide the net income by net sales.

	DuBois	Hendricks
$\dfrac{\text{Net Income}}{\text{Net Sales}}$	$\dfrac{15,000}{150,000} = 10\%$	$\dfrac{10,000}{200,000} = 5\%$

The answer to the discussion question is not simple. Since DuBois is getting a higher rate of profit, he is earning more on the volume of business he is doing. Hendricks, however, is doing more business. If Hendricks had learned how DuBois manages to have lower costs, he would have made a net profit of $20,000 (10% of $200,000). DuBois, on the other hand, might learn something about increasing sales from Hendricks.

The percent of net income varies from one business to another and often from month to month in the same company. In some businesses, a net income of 5% or 6% of net sales is considered good; other businesses insist on 10%; and still others, 15% or more. The percent of net income varies a good deal according to the type of business. The percent of net income for a supermarket, for example, is considerably lower than that of, say, a leather goods store or the cosmetics department of a department store. Because the supermarket owners do a very large volume of business, they can afford to be satisfied with a smaller rate of profit. Stores doing a much smaller volume of business must achieve a higher percent of profit.

Exercises

Find the percent of gross profit of sales and the percent of net income of sales for each business.

No.	Net Sales	Amount of Gross Profit	Percent of Gross Profit	Amount of Net Income	Percent of Net Income
1	$ 40,000	$ 20,000	____%	$ 4,000.00	____%
2	$ 65,000	$ 45,500	____%	$ 9,750.00	____%
3	$180,000	$ 99,000	____%	$22,500.00	____%
4	$ 16,250	$ 4,875	____%	$ 1,137.50	____%
5	$327,500	$157,200	____%	$52,400.00	____%

FINDING THE COST OF GOODS SOLD

In the previous problems, you were given the amount for cost of goods sold, so that finding the gross profit was easy. The determination of the cost of goods sold is in itself, however, a problem. Let us consider various possibilities.

Case Problem Burt McElroy is in the lumber business. He buys a stock of lumber for $3,000. If we know how much he sells it for, we have no difficulty in finding his gross profit. In most cases, however, business people do *not* sell out their complete stock, but arrange always to have some on hand for the next day's business. Let us assume that Mr. McElroy, during the month, made sales amounting to $4,000. At the end of the month, however, he still has some lumber left over.

Discussion Questions

1. How do we know the cost of the merchandise which the owner has not yet sold at the end of the period?
2. What effect does left-over inventory have on the cost of the goods that have been sold?
3. Suppose the owner made additional purchases of merchandise during the period. How would this affect the cost of goods sold?
4. Work out a formula for finding the cost of goods sold.

In order to find out how much has been sold, you actually count the goods that are left over, and obtain the cost by referring back to the purchase price. You then assume that the business has sold the rest of the goods. This process of counting and pricing the goods left over is called *taking inventory*. The cost of goods on hand at any time is called the *merchandise inventory*. If Mr. McElroy finds that he still has $500 worth of lumber left over at the end of the month, you subtract this $500 *ending inventory* from the inventory he started with of $3,000 (*beginning inventory*), and you know that he must have sold $2,500 worth of lumber. His gross profit is therefore his revenue (sales) of $4,000 less $2,500 (the cost of goods sold), or $1,500 (gross profit).

Business people, however, in addition to starting off with a stock of merchandise, keep replacing it during the period, as they need it, by making purchases. Their cost of goods sold is therefore the sum of what they started with, plus their purchases, which gives them the total cost of goods they had available for sale. We subtract from this the goods they *didn't* sell, which they discover by taking inventory of what they have left. We can therefore develop the following formula for finding the cost of goods sold:

Beginning Inventory + Purchases − Ending Inventory = Cost of Goods Sold

To go back to Mr. McElroy, let us add the fact that he purchased $1,000 worth of lumber during the month. Using the above formula, we would then find his cost of goods sold as follows: Beginning inventory $3,000 + Purchases of $1,000 gives us $4,000 goods available for sale. Subtract the ending inventory of $500, and we have a cost of goods sold of $3,500.

Exercises

Find the cost of goods sold for each retail store.

Store No.	Beginning Inventory	Purchases	Ending Inventory	Cost of Goods Sold
1	$ 6,000	$ 1,000	$ 3,800	$_____
2	$ 17,200	$13,700	$ 16,400	$_____
3	$ 33,750	$ 9,780	$ 31,420	$_____
4	$ 1,245	$ 4,650	$ 2,445	$_____
5	$162,000	$47,500	$129,980	$_____

THE INCOME STATEMENT

Case Problem Jerry and Kathleen Newbold, a young married couple, decide to rent a two-story house on Main Avenue and convert the first floor into a small neighborhood grocery store. They use the upstairs as living quarters for themselves and their new baby.

After a few months, Jerry and Kathleen Newbold begin to do well in their new business, which they call the All-Hours Market. In fact, they are doing so much business that they employ part-time help in the store. They also engage a local accounting service to maintain their records and to issue monthly reports on the store's financial operations. The Newbolds are most anxious to know whether they are making a profit and, if so, how much.

Discussion Questions

1. What kinds of costs and expenses might the Newbolds have in operating the All-Hours Market?
2. Some of the customers of the All-Hours Market charge their purchases and pay their bills at the end of the month. At what point should the Newbolds consider that the sale has been made?
3. How should their accountant present the information on revenue and expenses so that they will know the results of their operations for a given period?

At the top of the next page is the statement prepared by Accu-Rapid Accounting Service for the All-Hours Market for the month of April. You will notice that this is just a formal way of putting together the information you have already learned to compute.

As the heading indicates, the report prepared for the All-Hours Market is called an *income statement*. Its purpose is to show business people the results of their operations for a particular period—in this case, the month of April. For ease in referring to the statement as you read the descriptions, the six sections are numbered.

ALL-HOURS MARKET
Income Statement
For the month Ended April 30, 19—

1 {

2 {

Revenue from Sales:		
Sales	$4,200	
Less: Sales Returns and Allowances	80	
Net Sales		$4,120

3 {

Cost of Goods Sold:		
Merchandise Inventory, April 1	$3,600	
Purchases	1,200	
Cost of Goods Available for Sale	$4,800	
Less: Merchandise Inventory, April 30	2,600	
Cost of Goods Sold		2,200

4 { Gross Profit on Sales $1,920

5 {

Operating Expenses:		
Salaries Expense	$ 170	
Utilities Expense	100	
Rent Expense	260	
Telephone Expense	30	
Miscellaneous Expenses	75	
Total Operating Expenses		635

6 { Net Income $1,285

1. The heading of the statement answers three questions: Who? (the All-Hours Market) What? (an income statement) When? (for the month ended April 30, 19—)

2. The revenue from sales during April includes all sales, whether cash or charge; a charge sale is considered revenue when it is made. The amount recorded during this month was $4,200. However, some customers returned merchandise because it was spoiled or otherwise undesirable. They received either a complete refund (return) or a reduction in price (allowance). These sales returns and allowances, amounting to $80 in April, are subtracted from the revenue from sales to arrive at the net sales, $4,120.

3. Once the net sales figure is arrived at, you are ready to find out the cost of the merchandise that was sold. In other words, you can say: Now that I know how much was sold during the period, what did the merchandise that was sold cost? You will notice that the cost of goods sold is computed just as you learned in the previous section.

4. This section shows the *gross profit on sales* which, as is illustrated, is the difference between the cost of goods sold and the net sales. For the All-Hours Market, the gross profit on sales for April was $1,920: $4,120 (net sales) — $2,200 (cost of goods sold) = $1,920, gross profit on sales.

5. Section 5 shows the *operating expenses*—that is, those expenses incurred in operating the All-Hours Market during April. The larger expenses, such as those incurred for wages (or salaries), utilities (gas and electric), rent, and telephone, are listed separately. Small items, such as floor wax, wiping cloths, and laundry, are grouped under the heading Miscellaneous Expense. Total operating expenses were $635.

6. This section shows the *net income*, which is the amount left after the operating expenses have been subtracted from the gross profit on sales. The net income for April is $1,285.

Exercises

Model the income statements following on the one you have just studied.

1. Prepare an income statement for Arthur's Bargain Store for the month ended September 30, 19—, on the basis of the following information.

> Net Sales $11,280
> Merchandise Inventory, September 1 $14,650
> Purchases $4,180
> Merchandise Inventory, September 30 $11,200
> Rent Expense $400
> Salary Expense $1,620
> Telephone Expense $50
> Miscellaneous Expenses $380

2. Prepare an income statement for the Spring Hill Bakery for the month ended April 30, 19—, on the basis of the following information.

> Revenue from Sales $4,400
> Sales Returns and Allowances on Sales $140
> Merchandise Inventory, April 1 $6,500
> Merchandise Inventory, April 30 $5,900
> Purchases during April $2,200
> Salary Expense $750
> Telephone Expense $20
> Rent Expense $125
> Miscellaneous Expenses $45

3. Prepare an income statement for the Marchand Specialty Shop for the month ended November 30, 19—, on the basis of the following information.

> Revenue from Sales $21,430
> Sales Returns and Allowances $1,640

Merchandise Inventory, November 1 $2,970
Merchandise Inventory, November 30 $3,250
Purchases during November $16,840
Salary Expense $1,600
Rent Expense $900
Office Expense $1,050
Miscellaneous Expenses $180

Business Applications

1. Sue Chen and Ken Alaha, seniors at the local high school, organized a summer service to provide baby sitters to neighborhood households. They charged householders $6.00 and workers $3.00 for registration with the service. During the summer 25 householders registered for the service and 20 of their classmates enrolled with them to get jobs. Their expenses in running the business consisted of $67 in telephone bills, $15 for advertisements in the local newspaper, and $10 for miscellaneous expenses. How much did the business earn during the summer?

2. Mamie's Children's Clothing Shop had net sales of $78,500 last year. The merchandise cost $42,700, and the expenses of the business included the following: salaries, $14,200; advertising, $3,700; rent, $2,400; miscellaneous expense, $1,000. What was the gross profit? the net income?

3. McLevin's Sporting Goods Shop started the month of December with an inventory worth $27,300. During the month it made additional purchases of skating goods for $3,940 and ski equipment costing $6,340. Some of the ski equipment was damaged, and $210 worth was returned by McLevin's for credit. At the end of the month the shop had made sales totaling $26,800 and had a merchandise inventory valued at $22,300.
   a. Find the cost of goods sold.
   b. Find the gross profit.

4. Alice Marsh, head of the accounting department at the B-J Specialty Shop finds that the records show the following for the month of May:

   Net Sales $130,000
   Beginning Inventory $ 57,000
   Purchases for the Month $ 63,000

   Because they were short of staff, it is impossible to count the final inventory on May 31. If Ms. Marsh finds from past experience that her gross profit runs about 50% of her net sales, estimate the amount of the final inventory.

ANALYZING THE INCOME STATEMENT

Case Problem Sally Bruckner owns the Southridge Hi-Fi Center. Her accountant has just completed the income statement at the end of August and placed it on Miss Bruckner's desk. As soon as Miss Bruckner sees the statement, she says to the accountant: "Where is the income statement for July?"

Discussion Questions

1. Why do you think the July income statement will be helpful to Miss Bruckner as she examines the August statement?
2. What should Miss Bruckner look for in comparing the two statements?

INCREASE–DECREASE COMPARISONS

No figures in business are as important to owners as those that tell them how much the business is selling, how much it cost to make the sales, and how much the business is making in profits. But to find out whether the business is really progressing, owners must compare the results of operations for one period with the results of operations for another period. They may do this monthly, quarterly, annually, and so on. A report that compares operations for two or more periods is called a *comparative income statement*. Miss Bruckner, in the Case Problem, would find a comparative income statement very helpful in "sizing up" business operations.

One way to compare operations for two or more periods is to show the increase or decrease in the various items on the income statement and the percent of increase or decrease in significant items such as net sales, cost of goods sold, gross profit, operating expenses, and net income.

Here is the income statement for the Southridge Hi-Fi Center showing increase-or-decrease comparisons for July and August of the same year. Note that the figures for the most recent period are presented first.

SOUTHRIDGE HI-FI CENTER
Comparative Income Statement
July and August, 19—

	August	July	Amount of Increase (Decrease)	Percent of Increase (Decrease)
Revenue from Sales:				
Net Sales	$ 7,260	$ 6,600	$660	10%
Cost of Goods Sold:				
Merchandise Inventory, Beginning	$ 6,700	$ 7,100	($400)	
Purchases	3,700	3,200	500	
Cost of Goods Available for Sale	$10,400	$10,300	$100	
Less: Merchandise Inventory, Ending	6,200	6,700	(500)	
Cost of Goods Sold	$ 4,200	$ 3,600	$600	16⅔%
Gross Profit on Sales	$ 3,060	$ 3,000	$ 60	2%
Operating Expenses:				
Salaries Expense	$ 1,200	$ 1,000	$200	
Delivery Expense	200	280	(80)	
Supplies Expense	200	50	150	
Insurance Expense	70	70	—	
Miscellaneous Expenses	250	600	(350)	
Total Operating Expenses	$ 1,920	$ 2,000	(80)	(4%)
Net Income	$ 1,140	$ 1,000	$140	14%

The *Amount of Increase (Decrease)* column shows the amount by which the latest period (in this case, the month of August) is over or under the amount for the previous period (in this case, the month of July). The decrease figures are shown in parentheses.

The *Percent of Increase (Decrease)* column shows the percent of increase or decrease in the amounts of significant items for the two periods.

Example 1:
Net sales for August are greater than for July by $660 ($7,260 − $6,600 = $660), so $660 is entered in the *Increase (Decrease)* column as a positive number or increase. The percent of increase is found by dividing the difference, $660, by the sales for the earlier period $6,600 (or 10%), and this figure is entered in the *Percent* column.

Example 2:

Total operating expenses for August are less than for July by $80, so $80 is entered in parentheses in the *Increase (Decrease)* column as a negative number (decrease). The percent of decrease is found by dividing $80 by $2,000, or 4%, which is entered in parentheses (a decrease) in the percent column.

Exercises

1. In each of the following cases, find the amount of increase or decrease and the percent of the change.

	This Year	Last Year
a.	$180,000	$160,000
b.	$ 25,000	$ 20,000
c.	$ 67,500	$ 75,000
d.	$ 6,400	$ 7,200
e.	$290,000	$210,000

2. Prepare a comparative income statement for the Dreyfus Artificial Flower Shop for the months of August and September, 19—, from the following information. Show increase or decrease in each item for the two periods and percent of increase or decrease for net sales, gross profit, operating expenses, and net income.

August

Net Sales $18,000
Merchandise Inventory, August 1 $18,400
Merchandise Inventory, August 31 $15,800
Purchases $12,400
Rent Expense $300
Salaries Expense $1,200
Miscellaneous Expenses $100

September

Net Sales $18,900
Merchandise Inventory, September 1 $15,800
Merchandise Inventory, September 30 $14,400
Purchases $14,300
Rent Expense $300
Salaries Expense $1,300
Miscellaneous Expenses $250

3. Prepare a comparative income statement for Nelson's Cycle Shop for the years ended December 31, 19X5 and 19X6, based on the information listed on the next page. In addition, (a) show the increase or decrease of each item, using 19X5 as the base year, and (b) show the percent of increase or decrease in net sales, gross profit, and net income.

	19X6	*19X5*
Net Sales	$130,000	$116,000
Beginning Inventory	$ 56,000	$ 53,000
Final Inventory	$ 51,000	$ 56,000
Purchases	$ 87,000	$ 79,000
Operating Expenses	$ 14,000	$ 17,000

PERCENT OF SALES

Case Problem Monroe Auto Glass, Inc., shows a net income for the month of August of $3,200. Mr. Monroe, the owner, is puzzled as to how to interpret this. He knows that he is constantly trying to increase his sales, and wonders whether there isn't some way by which he can measure the results on his income statement in terms of his sales.

Discussion Questions
1. How do we measure two figures in terms of their relation to each other?
2. Of what value would such a measure be?

A very meaningful analysis for business owners to make is to find the percent of net sales that each significant item on the income statement represents. Businesspeople "think sales" constantly and often measure expenses and other important items on the income statement by their relationship to net sales.

On page 344 is an analysis of the income statement of Monroe Auto Glass, Inc., showing the percents of net sales the various items represent.

The percent of sales that each item on the income statement represents can be found by dividing the item by the net sales.

1. The percent of net sales represented by Purchases is found by dividing $4,800 by $20,000 (Net Sales), or 24%.
2. The percent of net sales represented by Cost of Goods Sold is found by dividing $5,300 by $20,000, or 26.5%.
3. The percent of net sales represented by Net Income can be found by dividing $3,200 by $20,000, or 16%.

In the income statement in the example, all items are included in the analysis. Some businesses, however, select only significant items for analysis, such as Cost of Goods Sold, Gross Profit, Operating Expenses, and Net Income.

Having computed percents, owners or managers can more easily compare one business period with another. As you know, percents are often more meaningful than mere dollar amounts. If, for example, ending inventory as a percent of net sales is increasing, owners may well ask whether they are overstocked (excessively large inventories often cause business failures). Or, if cost of goods sold is 46.6%

of net sales this month and it was only 40% last month, they will want to find the reason for the increase—higher cost of merchandise purchased, loss of merchandise from stealing, and so on. If total operating expenses are up 5% or 10%, it is a danger signal to watch expenses more closely.

Most meaningful of all, of course, are the percents of sales that gross profit and net income represent. These percents are excellent barometers for any business. One goal of any business is to increase profits—not just dollars of profit but the percent of profit based on sales.

MONROE AUTO GLASS, INC.
Income Statement
For the Month Ended September 30, 19—

			Percent of Net Sales
Revenue from Sales:			
Sales	$22,400		
Less: Returns and Allowances	2,400		
Net Sales		$20,000	100.0
Cost of Goods Sold:			
Merchandise Inventory, September 1	$ 9,200		46.0
Purchases	4,800		24.0
Cost of Goods Available for Sale	$14,000		70.0
Less: Merchandise Inventory, Sept. 30	8,700		43.5
Cost of Goods Sold		$ 5,300	26.5
Gross Profit on Sales		$14,700	73.5
Operating Expenses:			
Salary Expense	$ 6,200		31.0
Delivery Expense	3,000		15.0
Supplies Used	1,400		7.0
Utilities Expense	800		4.0
Miscellaneous Expenses	100		.5
Total Operating Expenses		$11,500	57.5
Net Income		$ 3,200	16.0

Exercises

1. Find the percent of net sales each item represents if net sales amounted to $4,000.

> Purchases $832
> Ending Merchandise Inventory $1,680
> Cost of Goods Sold $1,260
> Gross Profit on Sales $1,880
> Operating Expenses $1,100
> Net Income $780

2. Prepare an income statement for Jill's Record Center for the month ended July 31, 19—, on the basis of the following information. Indicate along with the amount of gross profit the percent of gross profit to net sales and along with the amount of net income the percent of net income to net sales.

> Revenue from Sales $8,100
> Returns and Allowances on Sales $338
> Merchandise Inventory, July 1 $12,930
> Merchandise Inventory, July 31 $12,390
> Purchases during July $3,225
> Salary Expense $1,800
> Rent Expense $375
> Telephone Expense $40
> Miscellaneous Expenses $340

3. Prepare an income statement for Mason's Used Office Furniture Store for the month ended February 28, 19—. Show the percent of net sales of: Merchandise Inventory, February 28; Cost of Goods Sold; Gross Profit; Operating Expenses; and Net Income.

> Revenue from Sales $12,800
> Returns and Allowances on Sales $800
> Merchandise Inventory, February 1 $11,100
> Purchases during February $2,900
> Merchandise Inventory, February 28 $6,700
> Rent Expense $500
> Salary Expense $600
> Utilities Expense $377
> Telephone and Telegraph Expense $62
> Supplies Used Expense $93
> Miscellaneous Expenses $868

Business Applications

1. The comparative condensed income statement for the Frank Desmond Candy Shop for the months of September and October, 19—, appears below.

	October, 19—	September, 19—
Net Sales	$2,700	$2,400
Cost of Goods Sold	950	900
Gross Profit	$1,750	$1,500
Operating Expenses	800	850
Net Income	$ 950	$ 650

a. How much larger was the net income in October than in September?

b. How much smaller was the gross profit in September than in October?

c. What was the percent of gross profit of net sales for October?

d. What was the percent of gross profit of net sales for September?

e. What was the percent of net income of net sales for September?

f. What was the percent of net income of net sales for October?

2. Paul Michaels operates the Bluejay Grill. In the month of December, sales totaled $1,460. The cost of food served to customers was $640, and operating expenses included the following: supplies, $7; rent, $65; taxes, $12; insurance, $4; telephone, $11; advertising, $20; and repairs to chairs, $18.

a. What was Mr. Michaels' gross profit? the percent of gross profit?

b. What was the net income? the percent of net income?

3. Prepare a comparative income statement for the Oriental Antiques Mart for the years ended December 31, 19X5 and 19X6, based on the information given below. In addition, (a) show the amount of increase or decrease of each item in 19X6 compared with 19X5, and (b) show the percent of increase or decrease for Net Sales, Gross Profit and Net Income. (c) At the bottom of the statement, indicate the percent of Net Sales for the following items for 19X6: Purchases, Cost of Goods Sold, Gross Profit, Operating Expenses, Net Income.

	19X5	19X6
Net Sales	$125,600	$132,700
Merchandise Inventory, Jan. 1	$ 38,450	$ 42,650
Merchandise Inventory, Dec. 31	$ 42,650	$ 46,840
Purchases	$ 92,820	$ 91,820
Salaries Expense	$ 19,480	$ 20,340
Rent Expense	$ 12,400	$ 12,400
Repairs and Maintenance	$ 890	$ 360
Insurance and Office Expense	$ 6,240	$ 4,720

UNIT

SHARING NET INCOME OR NET LOSS IN PARTNERSHIPS

Case Problem Richard Cross and Joan Darcy are real estate agents. After some years of working together for a large real estate firm, they decide to leave their employer and start their own agency. The name is to be the Cross–Darcy Real Estate Agency. It is agreed that each partner will invest $25,000 and that all net income and losses will be shared equally. In its first year the Cross–Darcy Agency earned a net income of $12,500.

Discussion Questions

1. What kind of business organization would you say Cross and Darcy have set up?
2. Can you think of one or more reasons why two or three people would go into business together?
3. What are some of the advantages of this type of organization?

An organization of the type that Cross and Darcy have set up is called a *partnership*. A partnership has two or more partners. There are many reasons why people form partnerships. Two of the most important are (1) two or three people can usually put more money into the business than an individual can, and (2) the work of running the business can be shared. However, since partners must work very closely together, and since each partner is responsible for the business actions of the others, it is necessary to be very careful in one's choice of partner.

Usually when a partnership is set up, the partners sign an agreement that, among other things, states how net income and losses are to be divided. Among the most common ways in which partners share profits or losses are the following:
1. The net income or loss is shared equally among all the partners.
2. The net income or loss is shared by an arbitrary ratio.
3. The net income or loss is shared according to the amount that each partner invested in the business.
4. A portion of the net income is divided according to investment by giving interest on the investment, and the remainder is divided equally.

Can you think of reasons why the partners might not always agree that sharing net income equally is the fairest method of distribution?

NET INCOME OR LOSS DIVIDED EQUALLY

When the partnership agreement states that net income is to be divided equally among the partners, the amounts invested are not a factor in the distribution. Each one gains or loses the same.

Example 1:

Martha Simon, Robert Betts, and William Kyte formed a partnership in which they agreed to share equally in any net income or loss that the business had. The net income for the first year was $25,200. What is each partner's share?

Solution:

Since they are to share equally, each partner will receive $\frac{1}{3}$ of the $25,200, or $8,400. Thus:

$\frac{1}{3} \times \$25,200 = \$8,400$, Simon's share

$\frac{1}{3} \times \$25,200 = \$8,400$, Betts' share

$\frac{1}{3} \times \$25,200 = \$8,400$, Kyte's share

Example 2:

Beth Tate and Lynne Lebeda entered into a partnership agreement to operate the Beth-Lynne Beauty Academy. They agreed to share net income or loss equally. During the first year of operation, net sales from the business amounted to $26,800; expenses totaled $30,000. Find each partner's share of the net income or loss.

Solution:

Since expenses were greater than the net sales, the business had a net loss for the year of $3,200 ($30,000 − $26,800 = $3,200). Each partner will share the loss in the amount of $1,600 ($3,200 ÷ 2 = $1,600).

Exercises

Find the share of the net income or loss for each partner, assuming they agreed to share equally.

No.	Partners	Net Income (Loss)	Share for Each Partner
1	Kim and Ramirez	$42,150	$ _____
2	March, Petty, and Wells	$16,328	$ _____
3	Potts, Clay, Farr, and Dye	$77,784	$ _____
4	Arleigh, Moren, and Batz	($ 3,375)	$ _____
5	LaFarge, Merkle, and Foy	$ 5,460	$ _____

NET INCOME OR LOSS SHARED BY AGREED-UPON RATIO

Sometimes one partner brings more experience or background into the business, or has better business contacts, or is able to devote more of his or her time to operations. In such cases, the partners may agree to a division in a ratio other than equally.

Example:

Martin Kay, who has had ten years experience managing a men's shop in a large department store, opens a haberdashery with Mel Ortise and John O'Brien, both of whom have just finished college. Each partner agrees to invest $15,000, and they will share net income as follows: 50% goes to Kay and 25% to each of the others. The net income for the first year is $21,000. What is the amount of each partner's share?

Solution 1:

50% or $\frac{1}{2}$ of $21,000 =	$10,500	Kay's share
25% or $\frac{1}{4}$ of $21,000 =	5,250	Ortise's share
25% or $\frac{1}{4}$ of $21,000 =	5,250	O'Brien's share
	$21,000	total

Solution 2:

Another way of expressing the same division is to say that net income will be divided 2:1:1. This means that the net income is divided into four parts (2 + 1 + 1), of which Kay will get two parts and the others will each get one part. Thus, $21,000 ÷ 4 = $5,250, each part. Kay's share is two parts ($5,250 × 2 = $10,500) and Ortise's and O'Brien's share is one part each, or 1 × $5,250 = $5,250 each.

Exercises

Find the share of the net income or loss for each partner, assuming they share in the indicated ratios.

	Partners	Net Income (Loss)	Ratio
1.	Bains & Browne	$23,600	3:2
2.	Osamuru & Brook	($17,420)	3:2
3.	Marks, Foy, & Chang	6,800	5:3:2
4.	Blum, O'Connor, Marki, & Lee	$19,480	4:3:2:1
5.	Ruiz & Blackstone	$27,300	5:3

DIVISION OF PROFIT ACCORDING TO INVESTMENT

In some lines of business, technical skill is not as important as the amount of money that has been invested. In such cases, the partners may agree that the fairest division of net income or loss is on the basis of each partner's investment. Investment here is the amount of money or the dollar worth of other property that each partner contributes to the business.

Example:

Catherine Warner, Joan Klein, and Alfreda Drew invested $15,000, $10,000, and $5,000, respectively, in a gift shop. They agreed to share net income according to the amount that each had invested. If the net income is $16,800, what was each partner's share?

Solution:

$15,000 + $10,000 + $5,000 = $30,000, total investment

$\frac{15,000}{30,000}$, or $\frac{1}{2}$, Warner's fraction of net income
$\frac{1}{2} \times$ $16,800 = $8,400, Warner's share of net income

$\frac{10,000}{30,000}$, or $\frac{1}{3}$, Klein's fraction of net income
$\frac{1}{3} \times$ $16,800 = $5,600, Klein's share of net income

$\frac{5,000}{30,000}$, or $\frac{1}{6}$, Drew's fraction of net income
$\frac{1}{6} \times$ $16,800 = $2,800, Drew's share of net income

Exercises

The net incomes of each company below are to be divided according to each partner's investment. Compute each partner's share of the net income.

No.	Investment of Each Partner	Net Income
1	$5,000, $5,000, $10,000	$ 5,200
2	$12,000, $18,000	$ 9,600
3	$10,000, $15,000, $25,000	$12,500
4	$7,000, $9,000	$ 4,000
5	$6,000, $8,500, $8,500	$ 6,900
6	$8,000, $10,000, $15,000	$ 9,500
7	$5,000, $7,500, $10,000, $12,500	$12,800
8	$2,300, $4,200, $5,400, $4,700	$ 8,450

DIVISION OF PROFIT ACCORDING TO INTEREST ON INVESTMENT

If the amount of the investment is considered to be important, but not the only important factor, partners may recognize the different monetary contributions by first giving each partner interest on his or her investment and then sharing any remaining net income equally, or, occasionally, on some other agreed-upon ratio.

Example:
Jacob Kohn and Alfred Campbell entered into a partnership to operate a cleaning and pressing business. Kohn invested $25,000 and Campbell invested $15,000. They agreed that each would receive 6% interest on his investment and that this interest would be deducted from the net income. The remainder of the net income was to be divided equally between them. If the first year's net income amounted to $14,000, what was each partner's share?

Solution:
Interest on Kohn's investment:

$$P \quad \times R \times \quad T \quad = \quad I$$
$$\$25,000 \times 6\% \times 1 \text{ year} = \$1,500$$

Interest on Campbell's investment:

$$\$15,000 \times 6\% \times 1 \text{ year} = \$900$$
$$\$1,500 + \$900 = \$2,400, \text{ total interest}$$
$$\text{Net income (\$14,000)} - \text{Interest (\$2,400)} = \$11,600,$$

remainder to be shared

Division of Profit	Kohn	Campbell	Totals
6% interest in investment	$1,500	$ 900	$ 2,400
Remainder equally shared	5,800	5,800	11,600
Share of net income	$7,300	$6,700	$14,000

Exercises
If the net income of a company is to be divided equally among the partners after the interest on their investments has been deducted

from it, how much will each partner receive of the net incomes indicated?

No.	Investment of Each Partner	Interest Rate	Net Income
1	$5,000, $10,000	6%	$6,000
2	$4,000, $6,000, $7,000	5%	$7,500
3	$9,500, $12,500	7%	$8,600
4	$6,400, $4,800	$5\frac{1}{2}$%	$4,300
5	$7,200, $9,400, $8,500	6%	$7,600
6	$6,600, $8,200, $10,700	$5\frac{1}{2}$%	$8,400

Business Applications

1. Two partners, Ellen Schwartz and Sandy Cramer, invested $11,500 and $17,250, respectively, in an art supply store. The partnership agreement provided for sharing net income according to the original investment. To how much is each partner entitled if the net income for the first year amounted to $7,500?

2. Martin Palmer and Stephen Alvarez invested $46,000 and $34,000, respectively, in a musical instruments business. During the past year the sales of the firm amounted to $240,000, and the net income was 8% of the sales. The partnership agreement provided that they share the net income in proportion to their investments. What was Mr. Alvarez's share of the net income?

3. Sam Nash and Frank Weldon entered into a partnership for a business machine rental service, investing $20,000 and $15,000, respectively. The agreement provided for equal sharing of the net income after 6% interest is paid to each partner on the amount he invested. The business had a net income of $6,400 for the year. Find each partner's share.

4. Investments of $16,000 and $24,000 were made by Morton Higgins and Paula Dumont, respectively, in a bookstore. Each partner was to receive 6% on his or her investment, and what remained of the net income was to be shared equally. Last year's gross profit on sales was $28,500, while expenses came to $6,580.
   a. What was the net income of the business?
   b. What was each partner's share of the net income?

5. Ted Ellinger and David Robertson jointly owned a wholesale hardware company. Last year the net sales of the company amounted to $314,270. The cost of the merchandise that had been

sold was $265,740 and the operating expenses totaled $23,560. If Mr. Ellinger received 55% of the net income, what was his share?

6. Robert Gafney and Rick Medina were partners, having invested $40,000 and $50,000, respectively, in a coffee shop. The partnership agreement provided for the following division of the net income:

   a. Each partner would receive 6% on his investment.
   b. Gafney would receive a bonus of 4% of the net income.
   c. Any remaining net income would be divided equally.

   The net income for the year amounted to $28,600. How should it be divided?

7. Tasker, Kimmel, and Shaw invested $30,000, $18,000, and $12,000, respectively, in a service station. They agreed to share the net income equally after the interest, at the rate of 5% a year, is paid on each partner's original investment. In addition, monthly salaries of $500 were to be paid to Kimmel and Shaw, who managed the station. At the end of the first month, the station produced a net income of $2,400. What was each partner's share?

REVIEW EXERCISES FOR CHAPTER 14

1. Find the net income or net loss for each of the service businesses listed below.

Income	Expenses
a. $16,450	Rent, $1,600; Salaries, $4,700; Office Expense, $2,340; Miscellaneous Expenses, $290
b. $ 7,967	Rent, $950; Wages, $1,175; Supplies, $2,960; Miscellaneous, $640
c. $21,680	Rent, $4,800; Salaries and Wages, $10,500; Office Expense, $2,350; Maintenance of Equipment, $4,720

2. Find the gross profit and the net income for each of the merchandising businesses below.

	Revenue	Returns and Allowances	Cost of Goods Sold	Total Expenses
a.	$ 6,790	—	$ 4,930	$ 1,270
b.	$ 17,650	$ 280	$12,900	$ 5,750
c.	$114,875	$2,950	$76,300	$18,890

3. For each of the following businesses, find the percent gross profit of net sales and the percent net income (loss) of net sales. Carry your answer to the nearest tenth of a percent.

Business	Net Sales	Gross Profit	Net Income (Loss)
a	$56,800	$14,200	$2,840
b	$27,400	$10,960	$3,288
c	$35,300	$10,590	($ 706)
d	$16,950	$ 6,864.75	$2,084.85

4. The Davidson Manufacturing Company sold $607,500 worth of steel products last year. However, customer returns and allowances amounted to $7,500. The cost of materials and labor for these products amounted to $320,000. Operating expenses included the following:

Salary Expense	$110,000
Delivery Expense	$ 12,000
Sales and Advertising Expense	$ 20,000
Rent Expense	$ 15,000
Insurance Expense	$ 4,000
Miscellaneous Expenses	$ 1,000

a. What was the gross profit and the percent of gross profit?
b. What was the net income and percent of net income?

5. In each of the following cases, find the cost of goods sold.

	Beginning Inventory	Purchases for the Period	Ending Inventory
a.	$ 4,750	$ 8,980	$ 3,975
b.	$ 16,950	$ 27,890	$ 17,630
c.	$116,480	$397,500	$125,650
d.	$ 26,400	$ 89,750	$ 25,840

6. Prepare an income statement for Smithvale Used Clothing Store for the quarter ended March 31, 19—, on the basis of the following information. Show the percent of gross profit and the percent of net income.

Revenue from Sales $8,600
Returns and Allowances on Sales $180
Merchandise Inventory, January 1 $7,650
Merchandise Inventory, March 31 $9,540
Purchases during the quarter $6,820
Rent Expense $180
Salary Expense $875
Utilities Expense $36
Supplies Expense $43
Miscellaneous Expenses $40

7. Prepare an income statement for the Sports Toggery for the month ended November 30, 19—, on the basis of the following information. Indicate with the amount of gross profit the percent

of gross profit, and with the amount of net income the percent
of net income.

> Revenue from Sales $5,400
> Returns and Allowances on Sales $225
> Merchandise Inventory, November 1 $8,620
> Merchandise Inventory, November 30 $8,260
> Purchases during November $2,150
> Salary Expense $1,200
> Rent Expense $250
> Telephone Expense $64
> Miscellaneous Expenses $35

8. Prepare an income statement for Ketcham Office Supplies for
the month ended March 31, 19—. Show the percent of net sales
represented by the Merchandise Inventory, March 31; the Cost
of Goods Sold; the Gross Profit on Sales; the Operating Expense;
and the Net Income.

> Revenue from Sales $51,700
> Returns and Allowances on Sales $1,700
> Merchandise Inventory, March 1 $25,500
> Purchases during March $9,000
> Merchandise Inventory, March 31 $14,200
> Rent Expense $2,800
> Salary Expense $10,400
> Postage Expense $2,400
> Supplies Expense $800
> Miscellaneous Expenses $150

9. Prepare an income statement for the Buckeye Garden Store for
the year ended December 31, 19—, on the basis of the following
information. Show the percent of gross profit and the percent
of net income.

> Revenue from Sales $86,580
> Returns and Allowances on Sales $1,370
> Merchandise Inventory, January 1 $57,480
> Merchandise Inventory, December 31 $61,560
> Purchases during the year $58,650
> Salary Expense $21,600
> Building Maintenance Expense $3,600
> Advertising Expense $4,580
> Plant Maintenance Expense $2,740
> Miscellaneous Expenses $320

10. Prepare a comparative income statement for the World Affairs Book Store for the years ended December 31, 19X5 and 19X6, based on the following information. (a) Show the amount of increase or decrease of each item in 19X6 as compared with 19X5 and (b) the percent of increase or decrease for Net Sales, Gross Profit, and Net Income. (c) At the bottom of the statement, indicate the percent of Net Sales of the following items for 19X6: Purchases, Cost of Goods Sold, Gross Profit, Total Operating Expenses, and Net Income.

19X5

Net Sales $58,900
Merchandise Inventory, January 1, 19X5 $38,025
Merchandise Inventory, December 31, 19X5 $45,815
Purchases during the Year $39,200
Salary Expense $17,250
Building Maintenance Expense $1,270
Equipment Rental Expense $475
Miscellaneous Expenses $980

19X6

Net Sales $66,700
Merchandise Inventory, January 1, 19X6 $45,815
Merchandise Inventory, December 31, 19X6 $48,125
Purchases during the Year $38,900
Salary Expense $18,600
Building Maintenance Expense $1,270
Equipment Rental Expense $1,340
Miscellaneous Expenses $390

11. Martin, Nusara, and O'Casey form a partnership in which the net income or loss is shared equally. What would be each one's share in each of the following cases:
a. Net income of $27,000
b. Net income of $37,190
c. Net income of $16,839.50
d. Net loss of $6,300
e. Net loss of $15,937

12. Langston and Friedman invested $66,000 and $44,000, respectively, in a motel, agreeing to share the profits of the business according to the original investment. At the end of the first year, the business yielded a net income of $17,000. What amount will each partner receive of the net income?

13. Frances Wickham and Gene Parker entered into a partnership for the purpose of operating the Char-Flame Restaurant. Mrs. Wickham invested $35,000 and Mr. Parker, $22,500. The partnership contract provided for equal sharing of profits after 6% interest is paid each partner on his or her invested capital. The restaurant produced a profit of $17,600 during the first year. Find each partner's share of the profits, including interest on the investment.

14. Susan Wong and Dolly Watson share profits equally after each receives 8% interest on her investment. Susan invested $35,000 and Dolly invested $20,000. Show the distribution of net income if the business earned $24,200.

CHAPTER 15
FINDING THE
FINANCIAL
POSITION
OF A BUSINESS

In addition to the income statement, business people use another important financial report—the balance sheet. You learned that the income statement summarizes for the owner of a business the results of operations for a particular period of time, such as a month, a quarter, or a year. The *balance sheet,* on the other hand, tells the owner the financial position of the business on a specific date. In other words, the income statement answers the question: "How did I do during the month of April?" The balance sheet answers the questions: "As of April 30th, how much does my business own (assets), how much does it owe (liabilities), and what is the value of my financial interest in the business (owner's equity)?" Obviously, the two statements serve quite different purposes.

The balance sheet is a fairly simple business statement. Let's start with a personal balance sheet. Diana Ortez is a high school student. On one side of a sheet of paper she lists the value of the things she owns. On the other side she lists her debts or the amounts she owes. Then she compares the sums of both lists.

Things Owned:		Debts Owed:	
Clothing	$380.00	Holman's	
Cash	7.70	Appliances	$25.00
Savings	80.00	Dad	15.00
Jewelry	100.00		
Sports Equip.	75.00		
Bicycle	50.00		
Stereo	145.00		
Radio	17.00		
Total	$854.00	Total	$40.00

Although Diana estimates the value of the things she owns as $854.70, she owes $40; and in order to find her personal equity, sometimes referred to as net worth, she must subtract the total of her debts (liabilities) from the total of her assets (things owned). Thus, Diana's personal equity can be stated as $814.70.

Business people prepare balance sheets in much the same manner as that illustrated for Diana Ortez. In this chapter, you will see just how they prepare them and then how they use the information provided in them to make the right business decisions.

UNIT

THE BALANCE SHEET

Case Problem Mrs. Katherine Dunn, owner of the Sew and Save Fabric Center, has decided that she would like to open another store in a nearby suburb. She will need $10,000 to finance this new venture. When Mrs. Dunn talked to an officer at her bank about a loan, the first question she was asked was, "What is the financial position of your business, Mrs. Dunn? Can you supply me with a statement showing what the net worth of the Sew and Save Fabric Center is now?"

Discussion Questions

1. What did the bank officer mean by the question: "What is the financial position of your business?"
2. What was meant by the term "net worth"?
3. Why does the bank officer want this information?

From time to time, a business owner needs to know where the firm stands—that is, what it owns, what it owes, and its net worth. (Net worth is the difference between what the business owns and what it owes. For "net worth" the accountant also uses the term *owner's equity*.)

Banks and other lending agencies will usually ask for a balance sheet—a statement that reveals the financial position of a business—before they will lend money. This gives them some indication of the ability of the business to repay the loan when due. As you know, a balance sheet provides a list of things owned, a list of obligations or debts, and the owner's equity. It may be prepared monthly, quarterly, semiannually, annually, or at any other time the business owner needs to know the financial position of the business.

Examine the various parts of the balance sheet for the Sew and Save Fabric Center at the top of page 362.

Heading. The heading answers three questions: Who? (the Sew and Save Fabric Center) What? (a balance sheet) When? (December 31, 19X5).

Assets. Assets include anything of monetary value the business owns—things that could be exchanged for cash or other property. Mrs. Dunn's assets are listed in the order in which they could be most easily converted into cash.

1. Cash. Cash includes money in the bank as well as that in the cash register. The Sew and Save Fabric Center has $3,800 in cash.
2. Accounts Receivable. The Accounts Receivable are claims against customers who owe the Sew and Save Fabric Center money for merchandise or services

SEW AND SAVE FABRIC CENTER
Balance Sheet
December 31, 19X5

Assets			Liabilities		
Cash		$ 3,800	Notes Payable		$ 2,200
Accounts Receivable:			Accounts Payable:		
E-Z Rest Motel	$1,600		Dura-Style Fabrics	$820	
Lowe Insurance	700	2,300	California Sports	337	
Merchandise Inventory		6,400	Mertz Lighting Co.	63	1,220
Store Equipment		1,200	Total Liabilities		$ 3,420
Office Furn. and Equip.		600	**Owner's Equity**		
			Katherine Dunn, Capital		10,880
Total Assets		$14,300	Total Liab. & O.E.		$14,300

they have purchased but have not yet paid for. Since it is expected that the customers will pay their debts in the near future, these claims have the same value as cash. The Accounts Receivable for the Sew and Save Fabric Center total $2,300 ($1,600 + $700 = $2,300).

3. Merchandise Inventory. The value of the merchandise on hand in the business is $6,400. Mrs. Dunn computes this value by counting the items on the shelves and in the stockroom and multiplying the number of items by the cost per item.

4. Store Equipment. Store equipment includes the cost of the cash register, cutting tools, display cases, and any other equipment used in the store.

5. Office Furniture and Equipment. Mrs. Dunn has a small office that contains such items as a desk, chairs, a typewriter, an electronic calculator, and a postage meter. The cost of these items is included in the balance sheet.

The list of assets of one business may be quite different from that of another. Some businesses, for example, own their own building, which would be listed as an asset. Others have trucks and cars, heavy machinery, tools, cafeteria equipment, books, and so on.

Other examples of frequently used assets are the following two: (1) Notes Receivable. This asset represents claims against customers or others who owe money to the business and who have given a promissory note due in the near future. A promissory note, you will remember, is a written promise to pay. (2) Government Bonds. When a firm has excess cash on hand for a short time, it sometimes invests it in government bonds (or other safe securities) so that additional money can be earned. These securities can readily be sold as soon as the cash is needed again.

Liabilities. Liabilities are amounts owed. The liabilities of the Sew and Save Fabric Center include two items—Notes Payable and Accounts Payable.

1. Notes Payable. Mrs. Dunn had borrowed $2,200 from a local bank in order to take advantage of a special sale of fabrics, and had given the bank her promissory note. The accountant's term for promissory notes given is Notes Payable. This distinguishes them from promissory notes received, which are called Notes Receivable (an asset).

2. Accounts Payable. As you can see from the balance sheet, the Sew and Save Fabric Center owes money to three companies—to two for merchandise (Dura-Style Fabrics and California Sports), and to one for services (the Mertz Lighting Co.). The total Accounts Payable is $1,220.

A firm may also have other liabilities. It may owe money for such items as taxes and salaries. Another liability frequently found on a balance sheet is Mortgage Payable. This represents an amount borrowed on a building or other real estate which is being paid back over a long period of time.

Owner's Equity. The financial interest that an owner has in a business, as we said earlier, is called owner's equity. Other terms, such as capital, proprietorship, and net worth, are also used. The Sew and Save Center is a single proprietorship (a business having just one owner). Mrs. Dunn's equity in the business at any given time is the difference between the assets and liabilities. This relationship is expressed in what is called the *accounting equation.*

THE ACCOUNTING EQUATION

The accounting equation is built upon the three fundamental elements: assets, liabilities, and owner's equity. The assets represent what a business owns. The liabilities and the owner's equity represent the total claims against those assets. The liabilities are the claims of the creditors (those to whom the business owes money), and the owner's equity is the claim of the owner. Whatever is not claimed by the creditors belongs to the owner. As a result, *the total claims against the assets are always equal to the total assets.* The relationship between assets and liabilities and owner's equity is expressed by the accounting equation.

$$Assets = Liabilities + Owner's\ Equity$$

By means of this equation, we were able to determine Mrs. Dunn's equity in the Sew and Save Fabric Center. The total assets of the business are $14,300. Since the total liabilities are $3,420, the owner's equity must be $10,880 because the sum of the total liabilities and the owner's equity must equal the total assets. The relationship of these elements can be illustrated by the accounting equation.

$$Assets\ =\ Liabilities\ +\ Owner's\ Equity$$
$$\$14{,}300\ =\ \ \$3{,}420\ \ +\ \ \ \ \$10{,}880$$

Exercises

1. Compute the amount missing from each accounting equation.

	Assets	=	Liabilities	+	Owner's Equity
a.	$ 2,000	=	$ 200	+	$
b.	$ 2,800	=	$ 240	+	$
c.	$ 2,560	=	$ 720	+	$
d.	$ 3,500	=	$	+	$ 1,640
e.	$ 5,440	=	$	+	$ 3,720
f.	$	=	$ 920	+	$ 3,120
g.	$	=	$ 2,080	+	$ 5,880
h.	$ 17,080	=	$ 4,560	+	$
i.	$ 7,320	=	$	+	$ 4,200
j.	$	=	$ 3,560	+	$ 6,680
k.	$ 7,540	=	$ 0	+	$
l.	$110,500	=	$18,440	+	$

2. Robert Hamden, owner of a motorcycle repair shop, has the assets and liabilities shown below. Find the owner's equity.

Assets		Liabilities	
Cash	$2,250	Accounts Payable	$3,300
Accounts Receivable	$ 750	Notes Payable	$1,800
Merchandise	$6,000		
Shop Equipment	$7,500		
Tools	$2,250		

Assets $_____ = Liabilities $_____ + Owner's Equity $_____

Business Applications

1. Arlene Marcuse, owner of Arlene's Boutique, has the assets and liabilities listed below. List the assets in one column and the liabilities in another column; then find the owner's equity.

Cash	$1,220	Store Equipment	$3,800
Accounts Payable	$ 640	Office Equipment	$ 750
Accounts Receivable	$ 966	Merchandise Inventory	$8,460
Supplies	$ 84	Notes Payable	$1,200

2. Prepare a balance sheet similar to the one on page 362 for Stevens and Rudge, partners in a building supplies business, as of December 31, 19—. Use the following information: Cash, $2,160; Merchandise Inventory, $14,700; Accounts Payable, $1,680; Delivery Trucks, $9,400; Supplies, $1,400; Building, $48,000; Mortgage Payable, $16,250; Accounts Receivable, $3,720; Notes Payable, $4,600.

3. Prepare a balance sheet for Silvertown Office Supplies, C. H. Walters, owner, as of April 30 of the current year, based on the following information: Cash, $3,390; Notes Receivable, $2,905; Accounts Receivable, $8,215; Merchandise Inventory, $23,600; Store Supplies, $720; Store Fixtures, $2,895; Furniture and Equipment, $5,600; Notes Payable, $5,250; Accounts Payable, $4,800.

UNIT 2

THE COMPARATIVE BALANCE SHEET

Case Problem Mrs. Dunn, owner of the Sew and Save Fabric Center, has studied the balance sheet and knows the financial position of her business on December 31, 19X5. But the balance sheet does not answer such questions as: Are the assets increasing or decreasing? How do the liabilities compare with last year's? Is the owner's equity greater this year than it was last year?

Discussion Questions
1. How can Mrs. Dunn obtain the answers to the questions in the Case Problem?
2. What other types of information might be obtained from the balance sheet which would prove useful to Mrs. Dunn?

INCREASE-OR-DECREASE COMPARISONS

A business owner may not be satisfied with just the information provided by a current balance sheet. Although the balance sheet shows the financial position of the business on a given date, the owner also wants to know how the position today compares with the position a year ago, or a month ago, or six months ago. For this reason, the accountant often prepares a *comparative balance sheet*—that is, balance sheet figures for two or more periods. One of the simplest types of comparisons of balance sheet figures is that which shows increases or decreases in one period as compared with another.

On page 366 is the balance sheet you saw in the previous unit, together with figures from the previous year's balance sheet. Note that on a comparative balance sheet the assets and liabilities are listed in a single column (rather than side by side) in order to make comparisons easier.

SEW AND SAVE FABRIC CENTER
Comparative Balance Sheet
December 31, 19X4 and 19X5

	19X5	19X4	Increase or (Decrease)
Assets			
Cash	$ 3,800	$2,750	$1,050
Accounts Receivable	2,300	1,700	600
Merchandise Inventory	6,400	3,200	3,200
Store Equipment	1,200	1,600	(400)
Office Furniture & Equipment	600	500	100
Total Assets	$14,300	$9,750	$4,550
Liabilities			
Accounts Payable	$ 1,220	$1,600	($ 380)
Notes Payable	2,200	—	2,200
Total Liabilities	$ 3,420	$1,600	$1,820
Owner's Equity			
Katherine Dunn, Capital	$10,880	$8,150	$2,730
Total Liab. & O. E.	$14,300	$9,750	$4,550

By studying the balance sheets for the two years, side by side, Mrs. Dunn can get a good idea as to how the business is progressing. Increases in 19X5 amounts over 19X4 amounts are shown in the *Increase or (Decrease)* column; decreases in 19X5 amounts as compared with 19X4 amounts are also shown, but they are placed in parentheses. To find the total of the *Increase or (Decrease)* column sections, add the figures that do not appear in parentheses and subtract from the total the figures that appear in parentheses. The total should equal the difference between the total in the *19X5* column and the total in the *19X4* column.

For example, the Assets items in the *Increase or (Decrease)* column that are greater in 19X5 than 19X4 are: Cash, $1,050; Accounts Receivable, $600; Merchandise Inventory, $3,200; and Office Furniture and Equipment, $100. The sum of these figures is $4,950. Store Equipment, however, was greater in 19X4 than 19X5 and is entered in parentheses. By subtracting the difference ($400) from $4,950, the figure of $4,550 is obtained. The difference between the total of the assets for 19X5 and 19X4 ($14,300 − $9,750) is $4,550; thus, the figures agree.

How does Mrs. Dunn use the information provided by the comparative balance sheet? She notes, for example, that the Accounts Receivable asset is greater in 19X5 than in 19X4 ($600), and she may ask herself whether she is being too lenient in granting credit or whether her customers are slower about paying. An increase in Accounts Receivable could also be a good sign, indicating that she is making more sales. She has a note payable in 19X5 that she did not have in 19X4, so her liabilities are greater. Merchandise Inventory in 19X5 is twice as large as in 19X4, and Mrs. Dunn may wonder whether she is becoming overstocked. Owner's Equity has increased in 19X5 over 19X4 by $2,730, which usually is a sign that the business is growing.

Exercises

The entries in the balance sheet for the West Side Hardware Store (L. S. Miller, owner) for December 31, 19X4 and 19X5 are shown below. Prepare a comparative balance sheet, such as the one on page 366, showing the amount of increase or decrease for each item.

19X5

Assets		Liabilities	
Cash	$ 2,600	Notes Payable	$ 1,600
Accounts Receivable	2,100	Accounts Payable	1,900
Merchandise Inventory	6,300	Total Liabilities	$3,500
Store Supplies	700		
Store Equipment	1,800	**Owner's Equity**	
Office Equipment	600	L. S. Miller, Capital	10,600
Total Assets	$14,100	Total Liab. & O.E.	$14,100

19X4

Assets		Liabilities	
Cash	$ 3,100	Accounts Payable	$ 2,400
Accounts Receivable	1,400		
Merchandise Inventory	4,900		
Store Supplies	1,100		
Store Equipment	1,500	**Owner's Equity**	
Office Equipment	300	L. S. Miller, Capital	9,900
Total Assets	$12,300	Total Liab. & O.E.	$12,300

PERCENT OF CHANGE

Merely knowing the amount of change in each asset and liability gives only partial information. An increase of $1,000 in cash, for instance, may be a significant change to a small business, but may be of no importance at all to a million-dollar company. Finding the *percent of change* gives an idea of the relative importance of what has taken place. In this balance sheet, we have added a column that shows the percent of change for each individual item.

SEW AND SAVE FABRIC CENTER
Comparative Balance Sheet
December 31, 19X4 and 19X5

	19X5	19X4	Increase or (Decrease)	Percent Change
Assets				
Cash	$ 3,800	$2,750	$1,050	38.2
Accounts Receivable	2,300	1,700	600	35.3
Merchandise Inventory	6,400	3,200	3,200	100.0
Store Equipment	1,200	1,600	(400)	(25.0)
Office Furniture & Equip.	600	500	100	20.0
Total Assets	$14,300	$9,750	$4,550	46.7
Liabilities				
Accounts Payable	$ 1,220	$1,600	($ 380)	(23.8)
Notes Payable	2,200	—	2,200	100.0
Total Liabilities	$ 3,420	$1,600	$1,820	113.8
Owner's Equity				
Katherine Dunn, Capital	$10,880	$8,150	$2,730	33.5
Total Liab. & O. E.	$14,300	$9,750	$4,550	46.7

Finding the percent of change is equivalent to finding the rate, which you learned how to do in Chapter 7. The figures for the year 19X4 are the base, the amount of change is the percentage, and the rate is found by dividing the base by the percentage. Thus, to find the percent of increase in Cash in 19X5 as compared with 19X4, divide the amount of increase by the Cash amount for the base year (19X4). The percent of increase is 38.2% ($1,050 ÷ $2,750 = .382, or 38.2%). To find the percent of decrease in Store Equipment in 19X5 as compared with 19X4, divide the amount of decrease by the entry for the base year ($400 ÷ $1,600 = .25, or 25%).

You will notice, of course, that the percent of change for the totals must be independently found and has nothing to do with the individual items in the column.

By studying the percent of change from the base year to the current year, Mrs. Dunn can make more intelligent judgments about her financial position than she would be able to make from the balance sheet alone. She finds out, for example, that her Merchandise Inventory increased 100% in 19X5 over 19X4, which is more revealing than knowing only the dollar increase of $3,200. Owner's Equity is over 33% more in 19X5 than in 19X4, a very important barometer of business growth.

Exercises

The balance sheets for Jiff-Quick Cleaners (Patricia Moss, owner) for December 31, 19X5, and December 31, 19X6, follow. Prepare a comparative balance sheet showing (a) the amount of increase or decrease for each item and (b) the percent of change for each item. Refer to page 368 for an example.

December 31, 19X6

Assets		Liabilities	
Cash	$ 8,000	Accounts Payable	$ 2,300
Accounts Receivable	300	Mortgage Payable	20,000
Supplies	1,200	Total Liabilities	$22,300
Equipment	15,000	**Owner's Equity**	
Building	35,000	Patricia Moss, Capital	37,200
Total Assets	$59,500	Total Liab. & O.E.	$59,500

December 31, 19X5

Assets		Liabilities	
Cash	$ 7,000	Accounts Payable	$ 2,100
Accounts Receivable	500	Mortgage Payable	21,000
Supplies	1,300	Total Liabilities	$23,100
Equipment	11,500	**Owner's Equity**	
Building	35,000	Patricia Moss, Capital	32,200
Total Assets	$55,300	Total Liab. & O.E.	$55,300

PERCENT OF TOTAL ASSETS

Many business people, in analyzing their financial position on a given date, like to know the percent of the total assets represented by each item on the balance sheet. In other words, by using total assets as a base, the owners can understand their financial position better if they can answer such questions as these:

Of the total assets of the business, what percent is represented by cash? by merchandise inventory? by accounts receivable? What is the relationship of the business's liabilities to total assets? What percent of total assets is the owner's equity? To find the answers to these questions, make the total asset amount the base and the amount of each asset the percentage. The rate is found by dividing the percentage (each amount on the balance sheet) by the base (total asset amount).

However, not each asset of a business has the same importance when it is examined for credit purposes. A building worth $50,000 may be a very valuable property, but you cannot pay back a debt with it, because if you have to sell the building, that may be the end of your business. For that reason, it is customary to divide a business's assets into two categories. Those which are cash or which will normally be turned into cash in the near future (and which therefore can be used to pay debts and operating expenses) are called *current assets*. Those which are used in carrying on the business (but which will not normally be sold or used up in the near future) are called *fixed assets*.

Similarly, those liabilities which will have to be paid within a short time are called *current liabilities*, and those which are to be paid over a long period of time are called *long-term liabilities*. Most liabilities, like accounts payable and notes payable, fall due within a short time and are current liabilities. Mortgage payable is an example of a long-term liability because a mortgage is usually paid off over a period of twenty years or more.

SEW AND SAVE FABRIC CENTER
Comparative Balance Sheet
December 31, 19X4 and 19X5

	19X5	% of Total Assets	19X4	% of Total Assets
Assets				
Current Assets:				
Cash	$ 3,800	26.5%	$2,750	28.2%
Accounts Receivable	2,300	16.2%	1,700	17.4%
Merchandise Inventory	6,400	44.7%	3,200	32.9%
Total Current Assets	$12,500	87.4%	$7,650	78.5%
Fixed Assets:				
Store Equipment	$ 1,200	8.4%	$1,600	16.4%
Office Furn. & Equip.	600	4.2%	500	5.1%
Total Fixed Assets	$ 1,800	12.6%	$2,100	21.5%
Total Assets	$14,300	100.0%	$9,750	100.0%
Liabilities				
Current Liabilities:				
Accounts Payable	$ 1,220	8.5%	$1,600	16.4%
Notes Payable	2,200	15.3%	—	0.0%
Total Liabilities	$ 3,420	23.8%	$1,600	16.4%
Owner's Equity				
Katherine Dunn, Capital	$10,880	76.2%	$8,150	83.6%
Total Liab. & O. E.	$14,300	100.0%	$9,750	100.0%

In the comparative balance sheet of the Sew and Save Center on page 370, Cash in 19X5 was 26.5% of the total assets ($3,800 ÷ $14,300 = .265, or 26.5%), while in 19X4 Cash was 28.2% of the total assets ($2,750 ÷ $9,750). In 19X5 Accounts Payable was 8.5% of total assets ($1,220 ÷ $14,300 = .085, or 8.5%) and in 19X4 Accounts Payable was 16.4% of total assets ($1,600 ÷ $9,750 = .164, or 16.4%).

Exercises

Find the percent of total assets each balance-sheet entry represents if total assets amount to $88,000.

1.	Cash	$ 8,184
2.	Merchandise Inventory	$16,368
3.	Accounts Receivable	$13,640
4.	Notes Receivable	$ 2,464
5.	Supplies	$ 3,696
6.	Delivery Equipment	$ 7,920
7.	Furniture and Fixtures	$ 6,160
8.	Office Equipment	$ 5,368
9.	Building	$24,200
10.	Notes Payable	$ 3,520
11.	Accounts Payable	$12,848
12.	Owner's Equity	$71,632

Business Applications

The balance-sheet figures of Mason's Garage (George Mason, owner) for 19X8 and 19X9 are shown below.

19X8	19X9
Cash $1,500	Cash $2,800
Government Bonds $1,000	Government Bonds $2,000
Accounts Receivable $800	Accounts Receivable $1,640
Equipment $5,780	Equipment $7,740
Tools $1,200	Tools $1,670
Notes Payable $950	Notes Payable $600
Accounts Payable $120	Accounts Payable $120
George Mason, Capital $9,210	George Mason, Capital $15,130

Writing lengthwise on your paper, prepare a comparative balance sheet showing (a) the amount of increase or decrease for each item, (b) the percent of increase or decrease for each item, and (c) the percent the following items represent of total assets for 19X9: Total Current Assets, Total Fixed Assets, Total Liabilities, Owner's Equity.

BALANCE SHEET RATIOS

Case Problem   When Mrs. Dunn applied for a bank loan for the Sew and Save Fabric Center, the banker asked for a balance sheet showing the financial position of the business. One of the things the banker was most interested in was the ability of the business to pay back the loan when it falls due.

Discussion Questions

1. What are the resources which the lender can look to for repayment of the loan?
2. Why are these resources not always available for repayment?
3. How might you measure the ability of a business to meet its financial obligations as they fall due?

As you know, current assets are those that can be converted into cash rather quickly. These items are often referred to as "liquid assets." Typical assets listed under the *Current Assets* section of the balance sheet are Cash, Notes Receivable, Accounts Receivable, and Merchandise Inventory. Fixed assets, as you know, are expected to remain in the business for a long time and include such items as building, furniture, equipment, and tools. They are normally not a source of ready cash.

An important reason for separating the current assets from fixed assets and current liabilities for long-term liabilities is to provide the basis for computing certain comparisons and ratios that are important for the business owner to have.

The balance sheet for the Sew and Save Fabric Center as of December 31, 19X5, is shown on the next page. We will use it to illustrate the various comparisons and ratios just mentioned.

SEW AND SAVE FABRIC CENTER
Balance Sheet
December 31, 19X5

Assets			Liabilities		
Current Assets:			Current Liabilities:		
Cash	$ 3,800		Accounts Payable	$ 1,220	
Accounts Receivable	2,300		Notes Payable	2,200	
Merchandise Inventory	6,400		Total Liabilities	$ 3,420	
Total Current Assets	$12,500				
Fixed Assets:					
Store Equipment	$ 1,200				
Office Furn. & Equip.	600		**Owner's Equity**		
Total Fixed Assets	$ 1,800		Katherine Dunn, Capital	10,880	
Total Assets	$14,300		Total Liab. & O.E.	$14,300	

WORKING CAPITAL

One looks to the current assets for the immediate running of the business. The first claim against them are the current liabilities—anything left over represents the funds available to carry on the operations of the firm. This is called *working capital,* and it is simply the difference between current assets and current liabilities. Mrs. Dunn's working capital can be found as follows:

$12,500   current assets
−3,420   current liabilities
$ 9,080   working capital

Thus, Mrs. Dunn has a little over $9,000 on which she can operate the business. Of course, this is not all cash (she has $3,800 in cash), but the other two current assets could be converted into cash rather quickly.

Exercises
1. Find the working capital for each of the following businesses:

	Current Assets	Current Liabilities
a. McCoy's Stationers	$ 17,421	$ 8,230
b. Argo Manufacturing Co.	$136,200	$72,245
c. Mabel's Taxi Service	$ 2,150	$ 1,125
d. Rath's Service Station	$ 8,270	$ 5,240
e. Jill's Quick Burger	$ 1,972	$ 1,900

2. Find the working capital in each of the following cases:

	Cash	Notes Receivable	Accounts Receivable	Merchandise Inventory	Accounts Payable	Notes Payable
a.	$2,900	$2,000	$6,000	$4,250	$3,900	$5,000
b.	$ 629	$1,030	$3,000	$1,690	$2,100	$2,065
c.	$7,250	$5,000	$2,750	$8,240	$6,700	$9,000

CURRENT RATIO

While knowing the amount of working capital is important, this figure alone does not tell us whether the working capital of the business is sufficient to carry on operations successfully. Compare the following two businesses:

	Company A	Company B
Current Assets	$6,000	$508,000
Current Liabilities	3,000	505,000
Working Capital	$3,000	$ 3,000

You will notice that both companies have the same working capital—$3,000. For Company A, which is a small firm, $3,000 would appear to be ample. But Company B owes practically as much as it owns in current assets, and appears to be in serious financial trouble. You can see, therefore, that the relationship between the current assets and the current liabilities is important, and we express that relationship through the current ratio. The *current ratio* is found by dividing current assets by current liabilities.

Example:
What is the amount of working capital available to Sew and Save Fabric Center as of December 31, 19X5?

Solution:
To find the current ratio for the Sew and Save Fabric Center, divide the current assets by the current liabilities.

$$\frac{Current\ assets}{Current\ liabilities} = \frac{\$12,500}{\$\ 3,420} = 3.7,\ or\ 3.7 = \frac{3.7}{1} = 3.7\ to\ 1$$

The current ratio of 3.7 to 1 means that for every $1 of current liabilities, the business possesses $3.70 in current assets. That is, Mrs. Dunn's current assets are almost 4 times greater than current liabilities, a very good ratio. A ratio that most businesses strive for is 2 to 1 ($2 in current assets for every $1 in current liabilities). A ratio of 1 to 1 is not good because the owner barely has enough in current assets to meet current liabilities. Really dangerous is a ratio of 1 to 2 or higher; this means that the owner may not be able to pay current debts when they come due.

Exercises

Find the current ratio for each of the following businesses.

	Current Assets	Current Liabilities
1. Brandt Appliances	$16,660	$10,330
2. Sip 'n Sup Diner	$ 1,420	$ 660
3. Avery Department Store	$21,312	$11,100
4. Guild Book Co.	$77,430	$14,885
5. Wonder-Tread Tire Co.	$17,240	$16,300

ACID-TEST RATIO

The best measure of liquidity (ability to convert assets into cash) of a business is the *acid-test ratio* (which is sometimes called the *quick ratio*). This is similar to the current ratio, but is more conservative in that only assets that can be quickly converted into cash are considered. Among these items are cash, marketable securities (holdings like government bonds that can be converted to cash quickly and without loss) and receivables. The formula for finding the acid-test ratio is as follows:

$$\frac{Cash + marketable\ securities + receivables}{Current\ Liabilities}$$

Example:

Compute the acid-test ratio for Sew and Save Fabric Center as of December 31, 19X5.

Solution:

Sew and Save lists no marketable securities in its balance sheet; therefore, the acid-test ratio is determined as follows:

$$\frac{\$3,800 + \$2,300}{\$3,420} = \frac{\$6,100}{\$3,420} = 1.8,\ \text{acid-test ratio}$$

You will see that in the acid-test ratio only cash assets or assets that can be turned into cash quickly are included; Merchandise Inventory is excluded. The acid-test ratio answers the question, "If all sales were to stop and the business received no sales income, could it pay its debts with 'quick' money?" Most businesses consider an acid-test ratio of 1 to 1 (so that "quick" cash is equal to current debts) satisfactory. Mrs. Dunn, whose acid-test ratio is 1.8 to 1, is in a very good financial position.

Exercises

Find the acid-test, ratio for each of these businesses.

1. Hogarth Hobby Shop: Cash, $3,450; Government Bonds, $10,000; Accounts Receivable, $640. Notes Payable, $2,200; Accounts Payable, $766.

2. Central Office Furniture: Cash, $4,655; Accounts Receivable, $11,200. Accounts Payable, $1,640.

3. Steuben's, Incorporated: Cash, $16,800; Notes Receivable, $4,700; Accounts Receivable, $8,300; Government Securities, $35,000. Accounts Payable, $12,400; Notes Payable, $20,000.

Business Applications

1. The current assets shown on the balance sheet of Lamont and Stone amounted to $58,690; the current liabilities were $29,330. If the inventory was valued at $33,370, what percent of working capital was the inventory? What is the current ratio?

2. The balance sheet of the Morristown Novelty Store is shown below.

MORRISTOWN NOVELTY STORE
Balance Sheet
June 30, 19X6

Assets		Liabilities	
Current Assets:		Current Liabilities:	
Cash	$ 4,272	Notes Payable	$21,100
Accounts Receivable	16,770	Accounts Payable	20,500
Merchandise Inventory	30,600	Total Current Liab.	$41,600
Total Current Assets	$51,642		
Fixed Assets:		**Owner's Equity**	
Store Equipment	8,320	J. R. Lunt, Capital	18,362
Total Assets	$59,962	Total Liab. & O.E.	$59,962

Find the following:
a. Working Capital
b. Current Ratio
c. Acid-test Ratio

Do you think the company is in a good financial position? why or why not?

UNIT 4

DIVIDING ASSETS OF A BANKRUPT BUSINESS

Case Problem   For several years Albert J. Bell has owned Al's Fishing and Boating Pier on a small lake. His business prospered until a year ago, when the lake became polluted and fish could not survive in it. Since the fishing was not good, Mr. Bell's customers stopped coming to the lake. His business failed, and he had to request to be adjudged bankrupt. Mr. Bell has debts totaling $50,000 but only $20,000 in cash and other assets with which to pay off his creditors (those to whom he owes money). For example, Mr. Bell owes M. J. Yardley, owner of a boat sales and repair business, the amount of $2,340.

Discussion Questions
1. What happens when a person or a business is declared bankrupt?
2. Do you feel that this is a fair solution? why?
3. How will the $20,000 Mr. Bell has available be distributed among his creditors?

Unfortunately, every year, thousands of businesses in the United States must close their doors because their owners are not making a profit and can no longer afford to operate them. When owners of such businesses see no way in which to continue, they may have themselves declared bankrupt or insolvent. This means that they don't have enough funds to pay all their debts. In that event, whatever money they have is divided proportionally among all the creditors. Thus, if the total debt is $10,000 and $2,000 is owed to one creditor, this creditor will receive $2,000/$10,000, or 1/5 of the money that is available.

Example:
Determine Mr. Yardley's share of Mr. Bell's available funds.

Solution:
You must begin by finding out how much money is available for each dollar of credit. Since there are $50,000 in debts and only $20,000 available to pay them, each $1 of debt recovers only $2/5 in payment ($20,000 ÷ $50,000 = 2/5 = $.40).

Or if you prefer to treat this without analyzing the method involved, divide the amount available for payment ($20,000) by the total debt ($50,000) to find how much the firm will pay on each dollar that it owes. In this case the $20,000 divided by $50,000 comes to $.40 per dollar of debt.

$$\frac{\$2}{\$5} = \$2 \div \$5 = \$.40, \text{ or } .40 \times \frac{\$1}{\$1} = \$.40 \text{ to } \$1$$

Mr. Yardley, to whom Mr. Bell owes $2,340, will receive $936.

$$\$2,340 \times .40 = \$936$$

Exercises
Each of the following companies was declared bankrupt because of lack of funds to pay debts. Compute the amount that the creditor whose claim is listed in the fourth column will receive.

No.	Total Debts	Total Assets	Creditor's Claim	Paid per $1	Creditor's Share
1	$ 8,400	$ 2,520	$ 1,600	$____	$_____
2	$15,000	$ 4,200	$ 2,780	$____	$_____
3	$16,200	$ 7,614	$ 850	$____	$_____
4	$48,300	$26,082	$ 6,240	$____	$_____
5	$74,420	$18,605	$18,430	$____	$_____
6	$61,350	$28,221	$23,970	$____	$_____

Business Applications

1. When Ms. Shanks filed a petition in bankruptcy, she stated that her assets consisted only of cash amounting to $2,240. Her liabilities, on the other hand, amounted to $5,600. How much money can Mr. Riker, a creditor, expect to receive if he had a claim of $1,725?

2. Mr. Ferguson, a bankrupt, owed debts totaling $32,460. The cash that he had available to his creditors was $11,361. How much money would a creditor who had a claim of $6,251 receive?

3. T. R. Moore and Company had been declared bankrupt. It owed the following amounts of money to its creditors:

Johnson and Wheeler	$4,375
The Spring Corporation	$8,654
K. D. Orson Company	$5,940
Brenner and Brenner	$7,398

The net cash distributed to the creditors above was $12,825. How much money did the K. D. Orson Company receive?

REVIEW EXERCISES FOR CHAPTER 15

1. Kathleen Corcoran, proprietor of The Side Door, a gift shop, has the assets and liabilities shown below. Find the owner's equity.

Assets		Liabilities	
Cash	$ 6,625	Accounts Payable	$1,700
Accounts Receivable	$ 1,875	Notes Payable	$2,000
Merchandise	$15,000		
Store Equipment	$ 3,400		
Office Equipment	$ 1,100		
Supplies	$ 50		

Assets $_____ = Liabilities $_____ + Owner's Equity $_____

2. Prepare a balance sheet for Lambertini, Inc., as of June 30, 19—, from the following information: Cash, $6,480; Merchandise Inventory, June 30, $44,100; Accounts Payable, $5,040; Delivery Trucks, $14,350; Equipment, $3,840; Building, $23,500; Mortgage Payable, $8,450; Accounts Receivable, $9,980; Notes Payable, $6,000.

3. The balance sheet figures for Maynard and Sons Rental Center (Louis A. Maynard, proprietor) for 19X3 and 19X4 are on page 381. Prepare a comparative balance sheet showing for each entry (a) the amount of increase or decrease in assets, liabilities, and owner's equity and (b) the percent of change.

19X4

Assets		Liabilities	
Cash	$ 14,200	Notes Payable	$ 3,500
Notes Receivable	6,300	Accounts Payable	8,680
Accounts Receivable	12,800	Mortgage Payable	12,200
Fixtures	1,320	Total Liabilities	$ 24,380
Equipment	24,600	**Owner's Equity**	
Building	70,500	L. A. Maynard, Capital	105,340
Total Assets	$129,720	Total Liab. & O.E.	$129,720

19X3

Assets		Liabilities	
Cash	$ 12,900	Notes Payable	$ 6,000
Notes Receivable	8,800	Accounts Payable	8,880
Accounts Receivable	9,670	Mortgage Payable	13,200
Fixtures	2,400	Total Liabilities	$ 28,080
Equipment	21,000	**Owner's Equity**	
Building	65,200	L. A. Maynard, Capital	91,890
Total Assets	$119,970	Total Liab. & O.E.	$119,970

4. The balance sheet figures of Fay's Fine Fabrics (Fay Mollini, owner) for last year are shown below. Prepare an analysis showing the percent each entry represents of the total assets.

   Current Assets: Cash, $3,400; Accounts Receivable, $1,640; Merchandise, $8,200

   Fixed Assets: Store Equipment, $4,640; Office Equipment, $1,350
   Current Liabilities: Accounts Payable, $2,700; Notes Payable, $1,000
   Owner's Equity: Fay Mollini, Capital, $15,530

5. Find the working capital for each of the following businesses:

	Current Assets	Current Liabilities
a.	$120,465	$57,140
b.	$ 16,900	$12,200
c.	$ 33,240	$11,110
d.	$ 80,000	$16,000
e.	$ 21,150	$ 3,300

6. Find the current ratio for each of the businesses listed in Exercise 5 on the previous page.

7. What is the amount of working capital of Fay's Fine Fabrics in Exercise 4? the current ratio? the acid-test ratio?

8. Find the acid-test ratio for Centerville Tile Company, which has the following current assets and liabilities: Cash, $7,300; Marketable Securities, $14,200; Accounts Receivable, $2,120; Notes Payable, $1,400; Accounts Payable, $1,850.

9. Herbert Waters, owner of a small motel in a rural community, was declared bankrupt. At the time he filed a bankruptcy petition, he owed the following amounts:

Abe's Laundry	$ 600
Hillsville Lumber Company	$1,400
Maple Leaf Supply Corp.	$3,600
Drumm Furniture Wholesale	$4,200

The net cash available to the creditors above amounted to $2,940. How much should each creditor receive?

CHAPTER 16
FINANCIAL
STATEMENT
COMPUTATIONS

We have emphasized how important it is for owners and managers to know at all times the financial position of their businesses and, periodically, the results of their business operations. As you know, they are not satisfied merely knowing income, costs, expenses, assets, liabilities, and owner's equity; they want to know whether these items are increasing or decreasing and the percent of change in one period compared with another. They also need to know the amount of working capital and the ratio of current assets to current liabilities.

If business people are to make intelligent decisions, they must know more about the individual items that appear on the financial statements. One of these is accounts receivable. Although the accounts receivable records reveal the amount owed by customers who buy on credit, individual accounts must be kept and analyzed with an eye to determining who is likely to pay an account and who is not. (All business people have to expect that there will be some customers who will not pay what they owe.) Business people, therefore, must find methods to determine the true value of their accounts receivable.

The merchandise inventory is another asset that requires close study. Business people have to decide how to place a value on their merchandise inventory when identical items might have been purchased on two different days at two different prices.

Business people also have to analyze the speed with which they sell their merchandise. They must be able to answer such questions as, "Do we have too much money tied up in slow-moving items?" "Will we make a larger profit if we put some items on sale at a lower price to sell them more quickly?"

The financial statement computations which you will learn in this chapter will help you answer these questions.

UNIT

1

CUSTOMER ACCOUNTS

Case Problem Craig Morrison works in the accounts receivable section of the Wolrath Furniture Manufacturing Company. Mr. Morrison keeps the records of those who buy on account. The Wolrath Furniture Manufacturing Company agrees to permit the Turnpike Motel to charge its furniture purchases and pay for them at a later date.

Discussion Questions
1. What effect does a sale to the Turnpike Motel have on the amount which it owes?
2. What effect does a payment made by Turnpike have on the amount owed?
3. How can the Wolrath Furniture Manufacturing Company know how much the Turnpike Motel owes it at any one time?

A separate record, called a *customer's account*, must be kept with each individual customer who purchases on credit. Every time a sale is made, it increases the amount owed (called the balance due); every time the customer makes a payment, the balance is decreased. In order to be able to know at a glance how much is owed at any one time, a separate computation is made each time there is a change in the amount owed. In most businesses of any size, the accounts are kept with the aid of bookkeeping machines or computers. The entire group of accounts is a *ledger*. Here is the customer's account for the Turnpike Motel.

Name _Turnpike Motel_			Acct. No. _37-404_				
Address _Darien, CT 06850_							
Date	Explanation	Charges		Payments		Balance	
Aug 11	Furniture	1,402	18			1,402	18
20	Check #327			1,000	00	402	18
27	Luggage racks	360	20			762	38

When a customer purchases merchandise on credit, Mr. Morrison writes the amount in the *Charges* column. When the customer pays on the account, the amount is written in the *Payments* column. Each time a number is written in one of these two columns, the entry in the *Balance* column must be changed.

On August 11 the Turnpike Motel bought furniture for $1,402.18. This amount was written in both the *Charges* column and the *Balance* column. The number in the *Balance* column is simply the amount of money that the customer owes at any particular time. On August 20 the motel paid $1,000 of the amount it owed, so this amount was written in the *Payments* column. By subtracting the payment ($1,000) from the balance ($1,402.18), Mr. Morrison obtained a new balance of $402.18 and wrote this amount in the *Balance* column. On August 27 the Turnpike Motel purchased luggage racks for $360.20, so this amount was written in the *Charges* column. It was then added to the previous balance of $402.18, for a new balance of $762.38. As you see, all charges for purchases are added to the customer's balance and all payments are subtracted from the customer's balance.

Charges − Payments = Balance

The records for the Turnpike Motel illustrate what is called a *running balance*, which means that the amount in the *Balance* column always shows how much a customer owes. That is, each time a customer buys something on credit or makes a payment on the account, a new amount is written in the *Balance* column.

Exercises

Prepare customer accounts for each of the following customers of Dalton Stationers.

1. Customer—Janet Barwell, 151 State Street, Trenton, NJ 08608; Account No. A1947.

March	1	Sold 12 boxes of stationery	$87.50
	4	Received a check on account	$50.00
	9	Sold one gross file folders	$15.95
	15	Sold 10 typewriter ribbons	$14.70
	21	Received a check on account	$37.50

2. Customer—Barnett Stern, 1640 Rosemont Street, Trenton, NJ 08618; Account No. B2320.

March	1	February 28 balance forward	$67.50
	8	Received check on account	$67.50
	17	Sold 10 boxes stationery	$72.50
	22	Sold one case duplicating paper	$37.49
	25	Received check on account	$50.00

Business Applications

1. a. Draw up account forms and prepare the accounts kept with three customers of the Kraft Specialty Shops during the month of June, 19X4.

Customers

Mrs. Marjorie Lewin, 60 Gardon Street, Hopewell Junction, NY 12533; Acct. No. 14-73

Mr. James Bernstein, 16 Morton Lane, Claverack, NY 12513; Acct. No. 14-74

Ms. Marie O'Hara, 12 North Avenue, Rhinebeck, NY 12572; Acct. No. 14-75

Transactions

June	1	Sold three pairs of shoes to Mrs. Lewin for $68.85.
	4	Sold a sports suit and jacket to Mr. Bernstein for $188.95.
	8	Mrs. Lewin paid $50 on her account
	10	Sold two handbags to Ms. O'Hara for $47.75
	12	Mr. Bernstein mailed in a check for $100.00
	15	Sold two blouses to Mrs. Lewin for $16.95
	18	Sold three scarves to Ms. O'Hara for $14.75
	19	Mrs. Lewin paid the balance of her June 1 purchase
	22	Mr. Bernstein sent a check for $50.00
	25	Received a check for $25.00 from Ms. O'Hara
	29	Mr. Bernstein purchased two pairs of shoes for $52.78

b. What was the total amount due from these three customers on June 30?

2. Sections of six customer accounts are shown below. Check them for missing or incorrect entries. On a separate sheet of paper, show any corrected accounts.

a.

Date	Charges	Payments	Balance
May			
12	114.00		114.00
27	96.50		210.50
30		114.00	96.50

b.

Date	Charges	Payments	Balance
Feb.			
6	14.35		14.35
9	143.70		
23		158.05	

c.

Date	Charges	Payments	Balance
Oct.			
1			200.95
16		100.00	100.95
21	74.20		

d.

Date	Charges	Payments	Balance
July			
6	432.60		432.60
15		350.00	
19		52.60	

e.

Date	Charges	Payments	Balance
Mar.			
11	673.95		
11	561.40		
20	428.83		
31		1,500.00	

f.

Date	Charges	Payments	Balance
Dec.			
1			516.00
5		437.00	
7	721.40		
17	300.00		

UNIT 2

AGING ACCOUNTS RECEIVABLE

Case Problem Byron Patton, owner of Patton's Building Supply, recently met with his accountant to decide on the amount of cash that will be needed during the coming year not only to operate the business but also to make some expansions. "Although we receive a good deal of cash from our customers for their purchases, more and more of them are charging what they buy," the accountant remarked. "Besides," she continued, "too many of our charge customers delay paying their accounts."

"Let's see," said Mr. Patton. "We have $3,500 in Accounts Receivable on our balance sheet. How good are those accounts?"

Discussion Questions

1. How does the way customers settle their accounts affect a business person's need for cash?
2. What did Mr. Patton mean by the question, "How good are those accounts?"

You have already learned that the accounts of customers who buy on credit and still owe for their purchases are called accounts receivable. Business people study these accounts very carefully when they forecast their cash requirements, since the promptness with which charge customers settle their accounts may determine whether or not the business must borrow money in order to continue its operations. If a large number of customers are slow in paying, and many customers refuse to pay at all, there may be little cash to work with. Then a business person may have to obtain a bank loan to pay salaries, rent, and other operating expenses. On the other hand, if a great majority of customers can be counted on to pay their bills, they fit Mr. Patton's idea of "good" acounts. These accounts supply the business with sufficient cash to maintain operations without the necessity of borrowing and, naturally, paying interest charges on the money borrowed.

AGING THE ACCOUNTS RECEIVABLE

From time to time, the accountant makes a careful study of the accounts receivable, classifying them as to "age"—not yet due, 30 days past due, 31 to 60 days past due, and so on. This process is called *aging the accounts receivable.* Some businesses age accounts receivable every month; others, only once or twice a year.

When the accounts receivable are aged, a schedule, or list, similar to the one on page 389 is prepared.

By looking at this schedule, Mr. Patton can determine the "shape" of his accounts receivable—that is, how his customers are paying, which ones need extra collection effort, and whether to stop giving certain ones credit. Sometimes, when a business owner or manager wants to borrow money, the bank asks for a schedule such as the one prepared for Patton's Building Supply.

To find the date on which payment becomes due, the business person must take into account (1) the terms of sale and (2) the date of the invoice.

PATTON'S BUILDING SUPPLY
Age of Accounts Receivable
As of September 30, 19—

Customer	Total	Not Yet Due	Past Due			
			1–30 Days	31–60 Days	61–90 Days	Over 90 Days
Aaron, S.	$202.50	$102.00	$100.50			
Brandt, C.	146.20		146.20			
Bunyan, McA.	19.50				$19.50	
Coleman, G.	90.00			$90.00		
Gaines, T.	224.85	124.00	50.85	50.00		
Heiman, S.	73.70					$73.70
Hoyer, N.	100.00	80.50			19.50	
Young, L.	56.10		40.00	16.10		
Yu, C.	129.40			100.00	29.40	
Zabor, M.	70.00	70.00				
TOTALS	$6,920.00	$3,420.00	$2,520.00	$560.00	$280.00	$140.00
Percent	100	50	36	8	4	2

Example:

Patton's Building Supply sold merchandise to White Castle Inn on an invoice dated June 10, terms n/30. When is payment due on the invoice?

Solution:

Of the 30 days permitted for payment, 20 will be used up in June. This leaves 10 days for July. The due date is July 10.

The schedule at the top of this page is prepared from the individual accounts of the charge customers. The account of S. Aaron, the first name shown in the schedule, appears at the top of page 390.

Note that Mr. Aaron's balance ($202.50) is entered in the Total column of the schedule on this page. His balance was 0 after the June 10 payment of $105.00. However, his purchase of July 12, due to be paid in 60 days, or by September 11, has not been paid; therefore, on September 30 it is overdue by 19 days, and the amount is entered in the 1–30 Days column. The purchase on September 16, payable in 60 days is not yet due, and the amount of $102 is entered in the Not Yet Due column.

When all the accounts have been entered in the schedule, the various columns are added and a percent of the total accounts receivable is calculated for each age category.

Name _Aaron, S_			Acct. No. _473_		

Address _507 W. Peachtree Street, Atlanta, GA 30308_

Date		Explanation	Charges		Payments		Balance	
May	15	INV. 63T496	105	00			105	00
June	10				105	00	—	—
July	12	INV. 63T964	100	50			100	50
Sept	16	" 63T1235	102	00			202	50

Refer to the schedule on page 389. Note that 50% of the accounts receivable are not yet due, 36% are 1 to 30 days past due, 8% are 31 to 60 days past due, 4% are 61 to 90 days past due, and 2% are over 90 days past due. The percent that each category represents is found by dividing the total of that category by the total accounts receivable. Thus, to find the percent that the accounts over 90 days past due represent, divide $140 by $6,920 to find 2%.

The percent each category represents of the total is particularly useful for comparing the ages of accounts receivable for different periods. For example, in the schedule on page 389, 36% of the accounts are 1 to 30 days past due, while only 4% are 61 to 90 days past due. If in the coming year Mr. Patton finds that only 15% of the accounts receivable are 1 to 30 days past due, and 20% are 61 to 90 days past due, he may reach the conclusion that either he is not properly screening charge customers or the collection procedures are not effective. Then he can take the action that is necessary to reduce the age of his receivables.

Exercises

Accounts receivable in the ledger of Nathan Wholesale Hardware Company are being aged as of June 30. On a sheet of paper, find the ages of the following accounts that are still unpaid, assuming that the terms of all sales are net 60 days.

No.	Date of Invoice	Due Date	Not Yet Due	Past Due			
				1–30 Days	31–60 Days	61–90 Days	Over 90 Days
0	April 8	June 7					
1	March 3	May 2					
2	January 14	March 15					
3	April 19	June 18					
4	May 2	July 1					
5	February 28	April 29					

6	February 16	April 17						
7	March 1	April 30						
8	January 29	March 30						
9	April 24	June 23						
10	June 1	July 31						
11	May 17	July 16						
12	April 30	June 29						

Business Applications

1. Rule a schedule of accounts receivable such as the one on page 389 and (a) enter the amounts of the following customer accounts in the appropriate columns; (b) find the totals. The date of the schedule is June 30 and the terms of all sales are net 30 days.

	Customer	Date of Invoice	Amount of Invoice	Payments	Balance
a.	W. J. Bailey	January 2	$ 70.00		$ 70.00
		January 22		$65.00	$ 5.00
		March 16		$ 5.00	0
		April 12	$ 35.00		$ 35.00
		April 17	$ 40.00		$ 75.00
		May 10	$ 10.00		$ 85.00
		June 29	$ 63.00		$148.00
b.	Soloman Berman	April 29	$104.50		$104.50
c.	Rose Cass	June 14	$ 16.40		$ 16.40
d.	A. E. Lowe	January 15	$ 6.75		$ 6.75
		February 10	$ 8.80		$ 15.55
		March 16		$ 6.75	$ 8.80
		April 14	$ 19.60		$ 28.40
		May 12	$ 12.25		$ 40.65
		June 6	$ 3.30		$ 43.95
e.	D. R. Schulz	February 8	$ 77.70		$ 77.70
		March 2		$77.70	0
		June 1	$ 16.20		$ 16.20
		June 15		$10.00	$ 6.20

2. The totals of the schedule of aged accounts receivable for Powers Produce, Inc., as of March 31 are shown on the next page. Find the percent that each age category represents.

Total	Not Yet Due	Past Due			
		1–30 Days	31–60 Days	61–90 Days	Over 90 Days
$94,000	$42,300	$30,080	$14,100	$4,700	$2,820
100%	___%	___%	___%	___%	___%

3. The terms of sale of Mackie Distributors, Inc., are n/30. Find the due date of each invoice.

a. January 11
b. March 16
c. February 1
d. September 10
e. April 2
f. December 23
g. May 8
h. July 29

UNIT

ESTIMATING LOSS FROM BAD DEBTS

Case Problem   Martin Barrow owns the Lehigh Diamond Center, which he has operated for about 3 years. He is now considering expanding the store and has invited an experienced jewelry store manager, Ray Thomas, to join him in a partnership. In examining the store's accounting records, Mr. Thomas is struck by the amount of credit business the store does. He asks Mr. Barrow, "How much of the sum your customers owe you do you really expect to collect?"

Discussion Questions

1. How did Mr. Thomas know how much was owed to Mr. Barrow?
2. Of what importance is the fact that some customers might not pay?

3. What information would help Mr. Barrow in estimating how much he might lose?

Nearly every business that offers credit to its customers must expect that some of these customers will not pay the amounts they owe. These uncollectible accounts are, in the accountant's language, *bad debts,* and from time to time the accountant must "write off" (cancel) customer accounts that are uncollectible.

Loss from bad debts reduces profits. In some businesses the total of bad debts runs very high—so high, in fact, that many companies have failed because they could not collect from their customers. This is the reason Mr. Thomas wants to know the amount of loss from bad debts each year.

Business people usually estimate in advance what their bad debt loss will be for the year because losses from bad debts are as much an expense of running the business as rent or salaries. (Bad debt expenses are included in the income statement as an operating expense.) In trying to establish the amount of bad debt loss, business people must *estimate;* they cannot know in advance which customers will pay and which will not. Estimates of loss from bad debts may be based on sales or on accounts receivable.

BAD DEBT LOSS ESTIMATED ON SALES

The most common method of estimating bad debt loss is to write off a percent of net credit sales. The rate to be applied is based mainly on the past experience of the business. It should be applied to net credit sales (credit sales minus returns) only, since there is no problem of collection from cash sales.

Example 1:
The net credit sales for the Lehigh Diamond Center for the coming year are estimated to be $100,000. Based on experience, the accountant expects that the loss from bad debts will be 3% of net credit sales. (1) How much will be charged to bad debt expense for the year? (2) How much will be charged to bad debt expense each month?

Solution:
1. Multiply the net credit sales by the percent of bad debt expense.

   $100,000 × 3% = $3,000, estimate of bad debt loss for the year

2. Divide the annual estimate by 12 (months in a year).

   $3,000 ÷ 12 = $250, amount to be charged to bad debt expense monthly

Exercises
Find the annual and monthly amounts to be charged to loss from bad debts. Round off to the nearest dollar.

Store	Net Sales	Percent	Annual Charge	Monthly Charge
a	$480,000	2%	$_____	$_____
b	$ 88,800	1%	$_____	$_____
c	$125,000	$\frac{3}{4}$%	$_____	$_____
d	$626,000	$1\frac{1}{2}$%	$_____	$_____
e	$212,500	$\frac{1}{2}$%	$_____	$_____
f	$ 78,000	3%	$_____	$_____
g	$182,000	$2\frac{1}{2}$%	$_____	$_____
h	$710,000	$\frac{1}{4}$%	$_____	$_____
i	$422,600	$4\frac{1}{4}$%	$_____	$_____
j	$555,400	$3\frac{3}{4}$%	$_____	$_____

BAD DEBT LOSS ESTIMATED ON ACCOUNTS RECEIVABLE

There is a drawback to estimating bad debt loss as a percent of estimated sales for the year. It involves considerable guesswork. In the first place, accountants do not know in advance what the sales will be. And even if they could predict sales accurately, they would still be left with the problem of applying the appropriate percent for estimating the expense from bad debts.

A more accurate method of estimating loss from bad debts is one that is based on accounts receivable. By this method, accountants work from an actual, rather than an estimated, base—the accounts of customers actually "on the books." In estimating loss from bad debts based on accounts receivable, accountants first prepare a schedule of aged accounts receivable such as that illustrated on page 389. After the schedule is completed, they estimate the percent of each age group that will be uncollectible. This percent varies from one age group to another—the longer an account has been past due the more difficult it is to collect. For example, 50% of the accounts over 90 days past due might be considered uncollectible, and 5% in the 1–30 days age group might be considered uncollectible.

Example:
The accounts receivable past due for Patton's on September 30 are below.

Age Group	Totals
Over 90 days past due	$ 140
61–90 days past due	$ 280
31–60 days past due	$ 560
1–30 days past due	$2,520
Not yet due	$3,420

What amount should be written off as bad debt expense for September?

Solution:

By applying a percent to each group, the accountant can estimate loss from bad debts for the month. (Note: For purpose of illustration, certain totals have been rounded off to give whole dollar amounts in the *Estimated Loss* column.)

Age Group	Total	Estimated Percent	Estimated Loss
Over 90 days	$ 140	50%	$ 70
61–90 days	280	20%	56
31–60 days	550	10%	55
1–30 days	2,500	4%	100
Not yet due	3,450	2%	69
Totals	$6,920		$350

The total amount to be written off as bad debt expense for September is $350.

Exercises

The schedule of accounts receivable for Larry's Men's Wear contained the following totals. The accountant's percent estimates of uncollectible accounts are included. Complete the table.

Age Group	Total	Estimated Percent Uncollectible	Estimated Loss
Over 90 days	$ 400	40%	$ _____
61–90 days	800	25%	$ _____
31–60 days	1,600	10%	$ _____
1–30 days	2,300	4%	$ _____
Not yet due	4,100	1%	$ _____
Totals	$9,200		$ _____

Business Applications

1. Miller Supply Corporation, a wholesale distributor of office furniture, estimates loss from uncollectible accounts at $\frac{1}{4}$% of net credit sales. Net credit sales for the coming year are expected to be $16,765,000. If this estimate proves to be correct, what will the bad debt expense be for the coming year?

2. Allen and Pogue, partners, operate Moto-Mile Car Rental. During the past year, the partners accepted $732 in checks that proved later to be worthless. If their income from car rentals was $366,000 last year, what was the percent of loss from bad checks?

3. Ricardo's Moving and Storage estimated that loss from bad debts for the current year would amount to $\frac{3}{4}$% of net credit sales. Net credit sales for the year amounted to $78,600, and bad debts came to $820. Did the company underestimate or overestimate the loss from bad debts? by how much? What would be your advice to Ricardo's Moving and Storage for next year's bad debt policy?

4. **a.** In aging its accounts receivable at the end of the current year, Bagget's Department Store compared the totals in each age category with the totals of the previous year.

Age Group	Current Year	Last Year
Over 90 days past due	$ 3,000	$ 1,000
61–90 days past due	3,000	1,500
31–60 days past due	5,000	2,500
1–30 days past due	6,000	5,000
Not yet due	8,000	10,000
	$25,000	$20,000

Find the percent of total accounts receivable that each age category represents for each year. Would you say the accounts receivable are in better condition in the current year as compared with last year?

b. If the percent of expected loss from bad debts is as shown below, what would have been the estimate of loss from bad debts for each year.

Over 90 days past due	35%
61–90 days past due	25%
31–60 days past due	8%
1–30 days past due	5%
not yet due	2%

UNIT

ESTIMATING THE MERCHANDISE INVENTORY

Case Problem Mildred Tabor operates the Gift Attic at a beach resort. At the end of October, Miss Tabor is getting ready to prepare her income statement and balance sheet for the season. She has discovered a problem. Usually, in getting ready to make up the financial statements, she takes a physical *inventory*, or actual count, of all the merchandise in stock. However, October has been an unusually busy month, and Miss Tabor has been unable to make an actual count of the stock.

Discussion Questions

1. Why is it important to have an accurate inventory figure at the time financial statements are prepared?
2. How can Miss Tabor estimate her October inventory without taking a physical inventory?

Most businesses take a physical inventory at least once a year. The latest inventory is used in determining the cost of goods sold on the income statement and in arriving at total assets on the balance sheet. Some businesses take a physical inventory every month. Often, however, a physical inventory is a huge task, requiring a near-shutdown of operations while it is being completed, and for that reason some business people estimate the value of the inventory during certain periods.

THE GROSS-MARGIN METHOD

The method most often used to estimate inventory is called the *gross-margin method*. (Gross margin means the same thing as gross profit.) Using this method, you assume that the gross margin (the net sales less the cost of goods sold) for the period will represent a certain percent of net sales. This percent can be estimated fairly accurately from previous income statements.

Examples:

During October the Gift Attic had net sales of $6,000. The inventory at the beginning of the month was valued at $3,000 based on cost price, and purchases during the month totaled $2,800. Based on a 30% gross margin, what is the estimated cost price value of the inventory at the end of the month?

Solution:

1. First find the value of merchandise available for sale.

$3,000   beginning inventory
<u>2,800</u>   add purchases
$5,800   cost value of goods available for sale

2. Then estimate the value of the cost of goods sold, using gross margin as a percent of net sales.

> Gross margin = 30% of net sales
> 100% − 30% = 70%, cost-of-sales percent
> $6,000 (net sales) × 70% = $4,200, cost of goods sold

3. Subtract cost of goods sold from cost of goods available for sale.

$5,800	cost of goods available for sale
4,200	less cost of goods sold
$1,600	value of ending inventory based on cost prices

Outline:

Beginning inventory	$3,000	
Add purchases	2,800	
Cost of goods available for sale		$5,800
Estimated gross margin (30%)		
Cost-of-sales percent (100% − 30% = 70%)		
Net sales for the month		$6,000
Cost of goods sold (70% of $6,000)		4,200
Estimated value of ending inventory		$1,600

When the gross-margin method of estimating inventory is used, it is usually applied separately to each department, since the percent of gross margin often varies by department. This method can give a fairly accurate estimate for the purpose of preparing monthly financial statements.

Exercises

Estimate the value of the ending inventory for each of the following departments of the Metropolitan Center Discount Store.

Dept.	Net Sales	Cost of Goods Available for Sale	Percent of Gross Margin	Estimated Value of Ending Inventory
1	$ 15,000	$ 15,000	30%	$_____
2	$ 40,000	$ 36,400	28%	$_____
3	$ 12,000	$ 10,650	25%	$_____
4	$ 400,000	$ 302,600	$42\frac{1}{2}$%	$_____
5	$6,742,500	$4,315,200	36%	$_____

Business Applications

1. Estimate the value of the ending inventory in the Bismark Superette from the following information: sales, $11,700; sales returns and allowances, $255; beginning inventory, $12,300; purchases, $4,500; percent of gross margin, 20%.

2. Estimate the value of the ending inventory for the Plaza Artificial Flower Shop for the month of October from the following information: net sales, $7,800; beginning inventory, $4,600; purchases, $3,000; percent of gross margin, 40%.

3. Estimate the value of the inventory at the end of January for Nelson's Cycle Shop from the following information: net sales, $72,600; beginning inventory, $30,156; purchases, $28,300; percent of gross margin, 45%.

4. Estimate the value of the inventory on April 30 for Ketcham Office Supplies from the following information: sales, $12,900; sales returns and allowances, $360; beginning inventory, $9,540; purchases, $10,230; returned purchases, $1,580; percent of gross margin, 35%.

UNIT

INVENTORY VALUATION

Case Problem The Monarch Wholesale Supply Company is taking inventory on June 30, the end of the second quarter. Among the articles to be counted are Sure-Time wall clocks, and it is found that there are 500 on hand. As the inventory clerk prepares to make the *extensions* (to make an extension, you multiply the cost price by the number of items), he remembers that the price charged by the clock manufacturer has increased several times during the past few months. He wonders which of these prices he should use in recording the cost value of the clocks on hand. He decides to look at the purchase and inventory records, and here is what he finds:

	Quantity	Cost per Clock
On hand January 1	300	$ 8.00
February 10 purchase	400	$ 9.50
March 16 purchase	500	$10.00
May 8 purchase	400	$11.00

Discussion Questions

1. Why is it important to know as precisely as possible the cost value of the clocks on hand?
2. Can you think of different ways that can be used to compute the cost value of clocks on hand?

Business people are very careful to arrive at an accurate value of the merchandise they have in stock. If the value of the final inventory is understated, the gross profit and net income shown will be understated; if the value of the final inventory is overstated, the gross profit and net income shown will be overstated.

Inventory Understated

Net sales		$30,000
Beginning inventory	$15,000	
Add purchases	10,000	
Cost of goods avail. for sale	$25,000	
Less ending inventory	12,000	
Cost of goods sold		$13,000
Gross profit		$17,000
Less operating expenses		8,000
Net income		$ 9,000

Inventory at Actual Value

Net sales		$30,000
Beginning inventory	$15,000	
Add purchases	10,000	
Cost of goods avail. for sale	$25,000	
Less ending inventory	14,000	
Cost of goods sold		$11,000
Gross profit		$19,000
Less operating expenses		8,000
Net income		$11,000

As this comparison shows, the greater inventory value of $2,000 yielded a higher gross profit of $2,000 and a higher net income of $2,000.

As the cost of purchases increases, the value of the merchandise inventory increases; as the cost of purchases decreases, the value of the merchandise inventory decreases. This is why it is important, when valuating an inventory, to take into consideration the changes that occur from time to time in the cost prices of the merchandise.

Three methods may be used for inventory valuation: the *average cost method;* the *first-in, first-out method;* and the *last-in, first-out method.*

AVERAGE COST METHOD

In the *average cost method* of inventory valuation, the cost prices of the beginning inventory and all purchases made are averaged. The result, or *average cost* is used to compute the value of the new inventory.

To find the average cost per clock and the value of the inventory in the Case Problem, the inventory clerk would compute as follows:

	Quantity	Cost per Clock	Extension
On hand January 1	300	$ 8.00	$ 2,400.00
February 10 purchase	400	$ 9.50	3,800.00
March 16 purchase	500	$10.00	5,000.00
May 8 purchase	400	$11.00	4,400.00
Total	1,600		$15,600.00

(15,600 (total cost) ÷ 1,600 (total quantity) = $9.75, average cost

You will notice that a weighted average (as discussed in Unit 5 of Chapter 5) is used in making this computation.

To find the value of the inventory, multiply the quantity on hand by the average cost. The value of the inventory of Sure-Time wall clocks as of June 30 is $4,875 (500 × $9.75 = $4,875).

Exercises

1. The National Paper Company is taking inventory. Among the items to be counted are ruled writing pads. A count reveals that there are 2,000 of these pads on hand on March 31. The purchase and inventory records show the information listed at the top of the following page.

	Quantity	Cost per Pad	Extension
On hand January 1	2,500	$.08	$_____
January 10 purchase	2,400	$.085	_____
February 16 purchase	3,000	$.09	_____
March 12 purchase	1,500	$.095	_____
March 29 purchase	2,400	$.10	_____
Totals	_____		$_____

Find the value of the March 31 inventory of ruled writing pads by the average cost method.

2. The Motor-Cade Auto Supply Company is taking inventory for the quarter ending June 30. It discovers that it has 150 cans of Q-56 motor oil on hand. Records reveal the following information:

	Quantity	Cost per Can
Inventory, April 1	130	$.36
Purchase, April 15	100	$.365
Purchase, May 23	180	$.40
Purchase, June 29	120	$.425

Find the value of this item in their inventory, using the average cost method.

FIRST-IN, FIRST-OUT METHOD

Many business people insist that the average cost method of inventory valuation is not really accurate. These business people assume that as each sale is made to a customer, the oldest merchandise in stock is always supplied before any new stock is opened. Thus, the stock on hand would be from the latest purchase. This stock should, therefore, be valued according to the latest cost price. Approaching inventory valuation in this way is called the *first-in, first-out method* of inventory valuation, or FIFO for short.

Apply the FIFO method to the valuation of the inventory of 500 Sure-Time wall clocks on hand as of June 30.

	Quantity	Cost per Clock
On hand January 1	300	$ 8.00
February 10 purchase	400	$ 9.50
March 16 purchase	500	$10.00
May 8 purchase	400	$11.00

Since there are 500 clocks on hand and by the FIFO method the first clocks received are always the first ones supplied to customers, 400 of the 500 clocks on hand are assumed to be the 400 purchased on May 8, the last ones received, at a cost price of $11. The remaining 100 are assumed to be from the next-to-last purchase, or that made March 16, at a cost price of $10 each. By the FIFO method, the value of the inventory as of June 30 is computed as follows:

$$\begin{array}{lll}
400 \text{ clocks from May 8 purchase @ } \$11 & = \$4,400 \\
\underline{100} \text{ clocks from March 16 purchase @ } \$10 & = \underline{\ 1,000} \\
500 & \$5,400, \text{ value of} \\
& \text{June 3 inventory}
\end{array}$$

Exercises

1. Beacon Novelties, in its inventory for the third quarter ending September 30, found that there were 4,200 music boxes on hand. The purchase and inventory records concerning music boxes revealed the following information:

	Quantity	Cost per Music Box
On hand July 1	3,000	$6.40
July 19 purchase	4,000	$6.90
August 16 purchase	2,500	$6.95
September 1 purchase	4,000	$7.05
September 20 purchase	3,500	$7.10

Find the value of the music box inventory as of September 30 by the FIFO method.

2. Refer to the exercises under Average Cost Method (page 401) and compute the value of the final inventory for these problems, using the FIFO method.

LAST-IN, FIRST-OUT METHOD

Still other business people prefer a third method of inventory valuation. They contend that in some cases when new merchandise is purchased, it is placed on top or in front of older merchandise, so that when an item is sold, it must be from the business's latest purchase. That is, the oldest stock is the last to be used and the newest stock is the first to be used. Their inventory valuation is based on the cost of the oldest merchandise in stock. This is called the *last-in, first-out method* of inventory valuation, or LIFO for short. There are accounting and tax considerations that make this a popular method for inventory valuation.

Apply the LIFO method of inventory valuation to the 500 Sure-Time wall clocks on hand as of June 30.

	Quantity	Cost per Clock
On hand January 1	300	$ 8.00
February 10 purchase	400	$ 9.50
March 16 purchase	500	$10.00
May 8 purchase	400	$11.00

On the assumption that the latest clocks received were sold before the older ones, the inventory is valued as follows:

300 clocks on hand January 1 @ $8.00	= $2,400
200 clocks from February 10 purchase @ $9.50 =	1,900
500	$4,300, value of
	June 30 inventory

Exercises

1. Panhandle Leather Goods Company, in its fourth-quarter inventory on December 31, found that there were 550 western saddles on hand. Details concerning inventories and purchases are as follows:

	Quantity	Cost per Saddle
Inventory, Oct. 1	275	$65
October 21 purchase	200	$68
November 30 purchase	250	$72
December 15 purchase	300	$75

   Find the value of the inventory of western saddles as of December 31, using the LIFO method.

2. Refer to the exercises under Average Cost Method (page 401), and compute the value of the final inventory for these problems, using the LIFO method.

COMPARISON OF THE THREE METHODS

For the same 500 wall clocks, three different methods were used to compute the value of the June 30 inventory. Each, as you have seen, yields a different cost value of the inventory.

Method of Valuation	Value of Inventory
Average cost	$4,875
FIFO	$5,400
LIFO	$4,300

A business may use any *one* of the three methods. Once it chooses a method of inventory valuation, it should use it consistently.

Business Applications

1. The Bunyan Wholesale Hardware Company is taking an inventory on June 30. Among the items on hand are 4,200 Pro-Speed No. 4 paint brushes. The purchase and inventory records reveal the following information.

	Quantity	Cost per Brush
On Hand January 1	1,500	$.32
February 20 purchase	2,500	$.33
March 12 purchase	2,000	$.35
May 9 purchase	5,000	$.40
June 15 purchase	4,000	$.42

Find the value of the final inventory using each of the following three methods you have learned.
a. Average Cost
b. FIFO
c. LIFO

2. The Magic-Voice Radio Supply Company is taking inventory at the end of the year. One of the items on stock is their #84A tubes. Records for these tubes show the following:

	Quantity	Cost per Tube
Inventory, January 1	800	$.252
Purchase of March 3	2,000	$.247
Purchase of June 5	1,500	$.262
Purchase of October 13	900	$.27
Purchase of November 25	600	$.272

If the quantity of these tubes on hand is 1,700, what would be the value of the inventory using each of the following methods?
a. Average Cost
b. FIFO
c. LIFO

UNIT

MERCHANDISE TURNOVER

Case Problem Henry Leopold owns a men's clothing store. He buys a certain brand of suit for $100 and has a markon of 60%, making his selling price $160. He finds that he sells an average of five of these suits per week. Mr. Leopold notices that a competitor with the same type of merchandise is underselling him. Mr. Leopold is afraid to cut his prices to meet the competition for fear that he will not make enough money to carry on his business.

Discussion Questions

1. What might happen to the volume of his business if he cut his prices?
2. What effect would a change in volume have on his total profits?

A cut in prices very often results in an increase in the number of sales. Mr. Leopold estimates that if he reduced his markon to 25%, he would double his weekly sales of this brand of suit. He does not, however, wish to invest more than the $500 it costs him to purchase the five suits he has been able to sell per week.

Let's do some computing. As things stand now, Mr. Leopold's selling price is $160 per suit.

Sales per week	5 @ $160 =	$800
Cost of sales	5 @ $100 =	500
Gross profit for the week		$300

Suppose he reduces his markon to 40% and doubles his sales.

First half week

Sales	5 @ $140 = $700	
Cost	5 @ $100 = 500	
Gross profit ½ week		$200

Second half week

Sales	5 @ $140 = $700	
Cost	5 @ $100 = 500	
Gross profit ½ week		200
Gross profit entire week		$400

Notice that with the same $500 which he puts into the purchase of these suits he would earn $400 at the reduced price as compared with $300 at the higher price. The reason for this is that he would sell his merchandise more quickly and use the money he makes on the first sales to buy merchandise for the second half of the week. The speed with which he sells his merchandise, or, more precisely, the number of times during a given period that a merchant will sell all the merchandise he has bought is called the *merchandise turnover*. In the first case, in one week his turnover was one—all the merchandise was bought and sold once during the week. In the second case, in one week his turnover was two—the merchandise was bought and sold twice during one week. Or, to put it another way, on an annual basis a turnover of four means the merchandise is in the store an average of three months (12 months ÷ 4 turnovers). A turnover of six means that the merchandise is on the shelves an average of two months (12 months ÷ 6 turnovers).

The rate of turnover is very important to the business owner for several reasons. In the first place, if he has a low turnover rate, it means he is not selling the stock quickly and may therefore need to borrow money to meet current expenses, such as rent and salaries. The rate of turnover as we have just seen also has an effect on the rate of markon. A supermarket that turns over its stock, say, ten times a year can place a smaller markon on its merchandise than a jewelry store that turns over stock only once a year.

AVERAGE INVENTORY

In computing merchandise turnover, you must be familiar with the term *average inventory*. The average inventory is the average of the total of inventories taken during the year. For example, if you take inventory only at the end of the year, you add the inventory at the beginning of the year to the year-end inventory and divide by two. If, however, you take inventory twice a year, you have three inventory figures to add—the one at the beginning of the year, the inventory at the end of six months, and the year-end inventory. Here you will divide by three. If you take inventory at the end of every month, you will have 13 figures to add—the inventory at the beginning of the year plus the inventory for each of the 12 months in the year.

Example:
Riddle's Toy Store takes a physical inventory at the end of each quarter—March 31, June 30, September 30, and December 31. The values of the inventories for last year, based on cost, were as follows:

January 1 (beginning)	$27,800
March 31	$34,200
June 30	$29,500
September 30	$37,900
December 31	$32,100

Find the average inventory for the year.

Solution:
1. Find the total of all inventories. The total is $161,500
2. Divide the total of all inventories by the number of inventories.

$161,500 ÷ 5 = $32,300, average inventory

Some retailers place a value on the inventory at the cost of the merchandise when they purchased it. Others carry their inventory at the selling price—that is, cost price plus markon.

Exercises

Find the average inventory for each branch store of a 5-and-10 chain.

Branch No.	Inventory					Average Inventory
	January	March	June	September	December	
1	$16,200	—	—	—	$14,100	$_____
2	$26,750	—	$31,444	—	$29,980	$_____
3	$ 6,320	$ 7,575	—	$ 6,776	$ 7,833	$_____
4	$53,380	$46,773	$49,907	$51,119	$56,119	$_____

MERCHANDISE TURNOVER RATE

Merchandise turnover measures the speed with which merchandise is purchased, sold out, and then replenished. If, on the average, a merchant keeps $1,000 in goods on stock, and during the period sells goods that cost $5,000, the *merchandise turnover rate* is five ($5,000 ÷ $1,000). This means that the merchant has started out with $1,000 in stock and then sold out and replenished it, and sold out and replenished it again five times during the period.

Use the following formula to find the merchandise turnover rate:

$$\frac{Cost\ of\ Goods\ Sold}{Average\ Inventory} = Merchandise\ Turnover\ Rate$$

Example:

The Brock Shoe Palace takes inventory three times a year, computing the value of the merchandise at cost. The inventory figures for the year just ended were as follows:

January 1 (beginning)	$50,000
April 30	$72,000
August 31	$66,000
December 31	$45,000

Find the rate of turnover to the nearest thousandth if the cost of goods sold during the year was $127,900.

Solution:

1. Find the total of the inventories.

$50,000 + $72,000 + $66,000 + $45,000 = $233,000

2. Divide the total of the inventories by the number of inventories.

$233,000 ÷ 4 = $58,250, average inventory

3. Divide the cost of goods sold by the average inventory.

$$\$127,900 \div \$58,250 = 2.1957, \text{ or } 2.196, \text{ turnover rate}$$

Exercises

Find the turnover rate in each store.

Store	Average Inventory	Cost of Goods Sold	Merchandise Turnover Rate
1	$16,000	$ 48,000	_____
2	$57,500	$143,750	_____
3	$83,800	$653,640	_____
4	$27,840	$125,280	_____
5	$ 6,740	$ 75,488	_____

COST OF GOODS SOLD NOT GIVEN

In Chapter 15 we learned that the cost of goods sold was found by adding the purchases to the beginning inventory and subtracting the final inventory. We often must first find the cost of goods sold before we can find the merchandise turnover rate.

Example:
The following figures were taken from the records of Martin's Appliance Store:

        Beginning Inventory $16,000
        Purchases $58,000
        Final Inventory $14,000

What is the rate of merchandise turnover?

Solution:
1. Find the average inventory.

$16,000 + $14,000 ÷ 2 = $15,000, average inventory

2. Find the cost of goods sold.

Beginning Inventory + Purchases − Final Inventory = Cost of Goods Sold
    $16,000   + $58,000 − $14,000   = $60,000

3. Find the merchandise turnover rate.

Cost of Goods Sold ÷ Average Inventory = Merchandise Turnover Rate
    $60,000   ÷ $15,000   =   4 times

Exercises

Find the merchandise turnover rate in each of the following cases.

	Beginning Inventory	Purchases	Final Inventory
1.	$ 2,900	$ 21,200	$ 3,100
2.	$26,450	$112,900	$32,550
3.	$ 8,640	$ 27,480	$ 9,220
4.	$11,970	$ 63,490	$12,030

Business Applications

1. The Stillwater Drug Store takes inventory twice a year—June 30 and December 31. Last year's inventories were as follows: January 1 (beginning), $36,000; June 30, $44,000; December 31, $40,000. Find the rate of merchandise turnover if the cost of goods sold during the year amounted to $120,000.

2. Kupperman's Food Market takes inventory every three months. The inventories during the past year were: January 1, $29,200; March 31, $37,400; June 30, $26,600; September 30, $29,900; December 31, $44,700. Find the rate of merchandise turnover if the cost of goods sold for the year was $251,700.

3. Pierre, manager of a jewelry store, computes his inventory at selling prices. On December 31, the value of the inventory, based on selling price, was $34,770. If Pierre's average markon is $33\frac{1}{3}\%$, what is the value of his inventory at cost?

4. Nancini Sporting Goods takes inventory quarterly. Its inventories were as follows: January 1, $67,450; March 31, $73,980; June 30, $56,390; September 30, $82,440; December 31, $61,390. If purchases for the year amounted to $379,865, what was the rate of merchandise turnover for the year?

REVIEW
EXERCISES
FOR
CHAPTER 16

1. The totals of the schedule of aged accounts receivable for the Tarrytown Electric Supply Company as of August 31 are shown below. Find the percent that each age category represents.

Total accounts receivable $12,450

Not yet due	$5,727	____%
1–30 days past due	$2,988	____%
31–60 days past due	$1,992	____%
61–90 days past due	$1,245	____%
Over 90 days past due	$ 498	____%

2. Find the amount to be charged off to loss from bad debts in the following:

Net Sales	Percent Charged to Bad Debts	Amount
a. $85,000	$\frac{1}{2}$%	$_____
b. $44,500	$\frac{3}{4}$%	$_____
c. $94,720	1%	$_____
d. $63,440	$1\frac{1}{4}$%	$_____
e. $21,200	$\frac{1}{4}$%	$_____
f. $45,500	$\frac{3}{5}$%	$_____
g. $37,200	$1\frac{1}{5}$%	$_____

3. The schedule of accounts receivable for the Lafayette Furniture Store contained the totals below. The accountant's estimates of percents that will not be collected in each group are also shown. Complete the table.

Age Group	Total	Estimated Percent Uncollectible	Estimated Loss
Over 90 days	$ 1,000	45%	$ _____
61–90 days	1,200	20%	$ _____
31–60 days	1,400	10%	$ _____
1–30 days	3,200	3%	$ _____
Not yet due	8,600	1%	$ _____
Totals	$15,400		$ _____

4. Estimate the cost value of the ending inventory for each department of the Lakeside Suburban Store.

Dept.	Net Sales	Cost of Goods Available for Sale	Percent of Gross Margin	Estimated Value of Ending Inventory
a	$12,200	$11,480	25%	$ _____
b	$80,000	$76,700	30%	$ _____
c	$ 9,600	$ 7,960	$33\frac{1}{3}$%	$ _____
d	$21,000	$16,450	40%	$ _____
e	$ 6,400	$ 4,600	$37\frac{1}{2}$%	$ _____

5. Pinson's Wholesale Hardware Company is taking a year-end inventory of all merchandise on hand. Among the items to be counted are steel bolts. There are 44,000 of these bolts on hand by actual count on December 31. The purchase and inventory records reveal the following information:

	Quantity	Cost per M
January 1 (beginning inventory)	27,000	$6.00
March 12 purchase	50,000	$6.50
September 11 purchase	35,000	$7.00
December 3 purchase	40,000	$7.50

Find the value of the December 31 inventory by (a) the average cost method, (b) the FIFO method, and (c) the LIFO method.

6. The Maple Avenue Card Shop takes inventory twice a year—June 30 and December 31. The inventories were as follows: January 1, $12,000; June 30, $14,600; December 31, $13,000. Find the rate of merchandise turnover if the cost of goods sold during the year amounted to $42,900.

7. The El Centro Suburban Grocery Store takes inventory every three months. The inventories during the past year were as follows: January 1, $14,600; March 31, $18,700; June 30, $13,300; September 30, $14,950; December 31, $22,350. Find the rate of merchandise turnover if the cost of goods sold for the year amounted to $209,750.

8. The Monticello Gift Shop computes its inventory at selling price. On December 31, the value of the inventory, based on selling price, was $5,954. If the store's average markon is $37\frac{1}{2}\%$, what is the value of the inventory at cost?

9. The Galveston Fishing Tackle Company has the following merchandise records:

Inventory:	January 1	$ 29,450
	June 30	$ 38,370
	December 31	$ 26,840
Purchases for the year:		$224,500

What is its annual merchandise turnover rate?

CHAPTER 17
DEPRECIATION AND OTHER OVERHEAD EXPENSES

You know that fixed assets are those that are required to operate a business and are expected to have a relatively long life. Examples of such assets are furniture, equipment, and buildings.

These assets, however, decrease in value as time goes on, mainly for two reasons. The first one is the actual wear and tear of use. A desk, for example, becomes scarred through years of constant use, and its value declines year by year. A delivery truck wears out.

The second reason for a decrease in value is obsolescence; that is, equipment becomes outmoded or out of date. Older equipment often needs to be replaced by newer, more efficient models. A large mechanical adding machine, for instance, loses value when a small electronic model is offered at a lower price and promises greater efficiency.

A decrease in value of a fixed asset for either of these two reasons is called *depreciation.* Not only does depreciation affect the value of the asset that is shown on the balance sheet, it also affects the income statement because depreciation must be considered an operating expense.

The asset is paid for when purchased, and after a certain number of years it will have little or no value. Its cost, therefore, must be recognized by the business as an expense during its period of use, or the net income of the business will be overstated.

In addition, most larger businesses make it a practice to determine as accurately as possible the cost of operating each of their various departments. Only by knowing these costs can the owner or manager decide whether a certain department is profitable or not. Some expenses, such as the salaries of the people who work in that department or the supplies and postage used, are easily identified and charged to the department. There are, however, many expenses which are not directly identifiable with any one department, and this creates a problem. How much of the total rent paid should be charged or allocated to each department? How much of the costs of running the employee's cafeteria or the medical department should be charged?

In this chapter you will learn how to compute depreciation by various methods and how to allocate overhead expenses to different departments.

UNIT

DEPRECIATION—THE STRAIGHT-LINE METHOD

Case Problem Stuart Nystrom operates Dew-Fresh Cleaners in Riverdale. When he opened the shop three years ago, he purchased new cleaning and pressing equipment for $13,200. When he was asked what his expenses were for operating the business, Mr. Nystrom listed rent on the building he occupies; the salary of his helper; the cost of chemicals and other cleaning supplies he uses in the business; light, water, and heat; hangers, plastic garment bags, and miscellaneous supplies.

Discussion Questions

1. Can you think of any expense that Mr. Nystrom has overlooked in his list?
2. How might he be overstating his profits by this oversight?

IMPORTANCE OF DEPRECIATION

Perhaps by looking at the title of this chapter you've decided that Mr. Nystrom has overlooked the expense of depreciation on his cleaning and pressing equipment. All business people know that their machines, furniture, tools, office equipment, and other similar assets will decline in value with the passing of time. Some of this loss in value is due to wear and tear, but *obsolescence* (becoming outdated) also causes an asset to decrease in value. For example, last year's car, even though it has not been driven, decreases in value when a later model appears.

Depreciation must be taken into account in computing the expense of operating a business. Thus, if Stuart Nystrom does not include in his operating expenses the depreciation of his cleaning and pressing equipment, he is overstating his net income.

There are several methods of computing depreciation of assets. Three of the most commonly used are the *straight-line method,* the *declining-balance method,* and the *sum-of-the-years-digits method.* The second two methods are also known as *accelerated depreciation* methods and will be discussed later in this chapter.

COMPUTING DEPRECIATION BY THE STRAIGHT-LINE METHOD

In the *straight-line method* of computing depreciation, the annual amount of depreciation to be charged off to operating expenses is distributed evenly over the expected number of years the asset will be in use. In order to apply the straight-line method, the owner of the asset must first make two estimates:

1. The number of years the asset is expected to last before it is sold, traded in, or scrapped. This is known as the *life of the asset*.

2. The value of the asset at the time it is replaced. This is known as *disposal, residual, scrap,* or *salvage value*.

Once these two estimates have been made, the annual depreciation is computed as follows:

1. From the original cost of the asset (purchase price) subtract the disposal value. The difference is the total depreciation of the asset.

2. Divide the total depreciation by the number of years the asset is expected to be in use. The quotient is the annual depreciation.

> *Cost − Disposal Value = Total Depreciation*
> *Total Depreciation ÷ Estimated Years of Use = Annual Depreciation*
> *Annual Depreciation ÷ 12 = Monthly Depreciation*

Example:

The purchase price of Stuart Nystrom's cleaning and pressing equipment (see the Case Problem) was $13,200. Mr. Nystrom estimates that the equipment will last for 15 years and that at the end of that time it will have a disposal value of $1,500. What is the annual depreciation?

Solution:

1. From the original cost (purchase price) subtract the disposal value of the asset. The difference is the total depreciation.
2. Divide the total depreciation by the number of years the asset is expected to be used. The quotient is the annual depreciation.

$13,200   cost
−1,500   disposal value
$11,700   total depreciation

$11,700 ÷ 15 = $780, annual depreciation

Each year Mr. Nystrom will charge $780 to operating expenses for depreciation of the cleaning and pressing equipment. If he prepares an income statement each month, the amount to be charged as depreciation for the month is $65 ($780 ÷ 12 = $65).

Exercises

Find the annual depreciation of each asset.

No.	Asset	Cost	Disposal Value	Life of Asset	Annual Depreci- ation
1	Wood lathe	$ 850.00	$ 70	12	$ _____
2	Metal lathe	$ 7,400.00	$ 600	10	$ _____
3	Electric motor	$ 625.00	$ 75	8	$ _____
4	Outboard motor	$ 329.00	$ 150	3	$ _____
5	Typewriter	$ 176.75	$ 35	7	$ _____
6	Metal desk	$ 109.95	$ 15	15	$ _____
7	Gas furnace	$ 627.50	$ 0	18	$ _____
8	Refrigerator	$ 399.98	$ 25	16	$ _____
9	Power mower	$ 117.25	$ 55	4	$ _____
10	Factory building	$124,000.00	$2,000	25	$ _____

BOOK VALUE

The original cost of an asset minus any accumulated depreciation is called the asset's *book value*. Thus, an asset which cost $5,500 when bought and which carries an annual depreciation of $1,000 will have a book value as follows:

First Year:
Cost $5,500
Depreciation   1,000
Book Value $4,500

Second Year:
Cost $5,500
Accumulated Depreciation   2,000   ($1,000 for each of two years)
Book Value $3,500

Third Year:
Cost $5,500
Accumulated Depreciation   3,000   ($1,000 for each of three years)
Book Value $2,500

Exercises

Find the book value at the end of the first, second, third and fourth years for each of the fixed assets on the next page.

	Cost	Annual Depreciation
1.	$ 35,000	$ 5,000
2.	$120,000	$25,000
3.	$ 6,000	$ 800
4.	$ 18,450	$ 1,200

FINDING THE RATE OF DEPRECIATION

Accountants often wish to report not only the amount of annual depreciation of an asset but also the *annual rate* of depreciation. The rate, expressed as a percent, is based on the original cost of the asset. It is found by dividing the annual depreciation amount by the original cost of the asset.

Example:

A metal lathe that cost $10,000 when it was new is estimated to have a disposal value of $400 after 12 years. (a) What is the annual depreciation? (b) What is the annual rate of depreciation?

Solution:

1. Find the annual depreciation.
2. Divide the annual depreciation by the original cost of the asset. The quotient is the annual rate of depreciation.

$10,000
-400
$ 9,600, total depreciation
$9,600 ÷ 12 = $800, annual depreciation
$800 ÷ $10,000 = .08 or 8%, annual rate of depreciation

Exercises

1. Find the annual rate of depreciation of each asset. Round off each amount to the nearest tenth of a percent.

Asset	Original Value	Annual Depreciation	Annual Rate of Depreciation
a	$3,100	$248.00	_____ %
b	$2,720	$272.00	_____ %
c	$1,100	$ 71.50	_____ %
d	$ 650	$ 97.50	_____ %
e	$ 325	$ 75.00	_____ %
f	$ 975	$128.70	_____ %

2. Find the annual depreciation and annual rate of depreciation of each asset.

Asset	Cost	Scrap Value	Life of Asset	Annual Depreciation	Annual Rate of Depreciation
a	$ 800	$ 200	10	$_____	_____%
b	$2,400	$ 800	15	$_____	_____%
c	$1,600	$ 400	5	$_____	_____%
d	$1,200	$ 300	6	$_____	_____%
e	$ 380	$ 80	4	$_____	_____%
f	$3,650	$1,000	10	$_____	_____%
g	$2,860	$ 500	12	$_____	_____%
h	$ 560	$ 0	8	$_____	_____%

Business Applications

1. Bill Green bought a new motorcycle for $700 three years ago. Bill figures he can get $300 on a trade-in when he disposes of it now. (a) What is the annual depreciation? (b) What is the annual rate of depreciation?

2. Clifton Martin bought a new car five years ago. He paid $5,300 for it. Today the car is worth $1,200. Find (a) the annual depreciation and (b) the annual rate of depreciation.

3. The New Products Chemical Corporation purchased $350,000 worth of equipment for its new plant. If the equipment will be completely worthless because of obsolescence at the end of eight years, at what annual rate is it depreciating? What is the annual amount of depreciation? What is the book value of the equipment at the end of the second year?

4. The Business Education Department of Edison High School bought 24 new typewriters at a cost of $350 each. Assuming that the estimated life of the typewriters is four years, after which they are expected to have a disposal value of $75 each, (a) what is the annual depreciation for each typewriter? (b) the monthly depreciation for each? (c) the annual rate of depreciation for each? (d) the book value of each at the end of the third year?

5. Melton Manufacturers can buy a machine for $12,000 which will have a disposal value of $2,000 after four years of use or of $1,000 after five years of use. By how much will the annual amount of depreciation change if they decide to keep it for five years instead of four years?

UNIT 2

DEPRECIATION—ACCELERATED DEPRECIATION METHODS

Case Problem   Cloverdale Farms recently purchased a refrigerated milk truck for $10,000. Judy Tisdale, the owner, has set up her records to charge off depreciation each year by the straight-line method. When a new accountant was hired recently, he told her, "I think your method of charging depreciation is not the best one you could use. Equipment such as a delivery truck doesn't depreciate the same amount every year. You know that when you buy an automobile the amount of depreciation is more in the first year than in the second, more in the second year than in the third, and so on. Why don't you take advantage of that fact?"

Discussion Questions

1. What is the advantage of the method of depreciation suggested by the accountant?
2. How will such a method affect profits during the first year in which it is used?

DECLINING-BALANCE METHOD

The method of computing depreciation discussed in the last unit is called the "straight-line" method because the depreciation expense is the same each period, and the book value of the asset, if we plot it on a graph, decreases in a straight line. An alternate view is that an asset depreciates at a faster or "accelerated" rate during its earlier years, and that therefore more depreciation expense should be taken during these earlier years. One method of computing accelerated depreciation is the *declining-balance method.*

Under this method, the rate of depreciation is applied not to the original cost, as in the straight-line method, but to the book value (original cost minus accumulated depreciation), which is a constantly decreasing amount. Thus the depreciation will be greatest in the first year and will decrease each succeeding year. Under this method of computing depreciation, the rate of depreciation must be fixed in advance.

For tax purposes, the federal government allows an adjusted depreciation rate in the declining-balance method of no more than double the straight-line depreciation rate. The straight-line rate of depreciation for this purpose is computed by finding the decimal equivalent of a fraction composed of 1 over the number of years in the life of the asset. For instance, for an asset expected to last for ten years, the straight-line depreciation rate would be $\frac{1}{10}$, or .10, or 10% per year. Thus, the declining-balance rate could be any rate up to 20%.

Example:

Creative Photographers, Inc., purchased a specialized camera for $2,000, on which the accountant decided to use the declining-balance method of depreciation. What will the annual depreciation be the first, second, and third years if the rate of depreciation is fixed at 10% a year?

Solution:

First year
1. Multiply the original cost by the fixed rate of depreciation. The product is the amount of depreciation during the first year.

$$\$2,000 \times 10\% = \$200, \text{ amount of depreciation}$$

2. Subtract the amount of depreciation from the original cost of the asset. The difference is the book value of the asset at the end of the first year.

$$\$2,000 - \$200 = \$1,800, \text{ book value at the end}$$
$$\text{of the first year}$$

Second year
1. Multiply the book value of the asset at the end of the first year by the fixed rate of depreciation. The product is the amount of depreciation during the second year.

$$\$1,800 \times 10\% = \$180, \text{ amount of depreciation}$$

2. Subtract the amount of depreciation from the book value of the asset. The difference is the book value at the end of the second year.

$$\$1,800 - \$180 = \$1,620, \text{ book value at the end}$$
$$\text{of the second year}$$

Third year
1. The depreciation for the third year is computed on the book value of the camera at the end of the second year, so the third year's depreciation is $162 ($1,620 × 10% = $162).

2. The book value of the camera at the end of the third year is $1,458 ($1,620 − $162 = $1,458). These depreciation computations will continue for the life of the camera. You note, however, that the full cost of the camera can never be depreciated under this method, which is why it is not necessary to deduct an estimated disposal value from the cost.

Notice that, although the rate of depreciation remains the same (10%), the amount of annual depreciation becomes smaller each year. This is true because the rate is based on an ever-declining balance. By using the declining-balance method, business people can charge off a greater amount to expense in the early years and thus pay less income tax because their net income will be less.

Exercises

Using the declining-balance method, find the annual depreciation and the book value for the first three years of the life of each asset.

No.	Property	Cost	Fixed Depreciation Rate
1	Fork truck	$ 3,600	20%
2	Factory building	$200,000	5%
3	Photocopier	$ 850	15%
4	Office furniture	$ 14,000	8%
5	Printing press	$ 25,000	6%
6	Multilith	$ 5,975	7%
7	Cutting machine	$ 3,745	10%
8	Electric baggage cart	$ 850	$4\frac{1}{2}$%

SUM-OF-THE-YEARS-DIGITS METHOD

Another method of achieving the advantages of accelerated depreciation is called the *sum-of-the-years-digits* method. Like the declining balance method, this method is based on the assumption that depreciation of an asset is greater in the first year than in the second, greater in the second year than in the third year, and so on. However, in computing depreciation by the sum-of-the-years-digits method, the number of years an asset is expected to be used becomes the base for finding annual depreciation.

The Bay State Realty Company purchased a new car for $6,400. It is expected that the car will be in use for five years and at the end of that time will have a disposal value of $1,900.

Since the automobile purchased by Bay State Realty Company is expected to be in use five years, the first step in applying the sum-of-the-years-digits method is to add the numbers 1 through 5. Thus:

$$1 + 2 + 3 + 4 + 5 = 15$$

With this sum in mind, the first year's depreciation is computed as $\frac{5}{15}$ of the total depreciation. The second year's depreciation is $\frac{4}{15}$, the third, $\frac{3}{15}$; the fourth, $\frac{2}{15}$; and the fifth, $\frac{1}{15}$.

In applying the sum-of-the-years-digits method, you must estimate the disposal value of the asset, as in the straight-line method. The automobile purchased by Bay State Realty is estimated to have a trade-in value of $1,900 at the end of five years, so that the total depreciation is $4,500 ($6,400 − $1,900 = $4,500).

The depreciation of the Bay State Realty Company car is computed by the sum-of-the-years-digits method as follows:

Total depreciation = $6,400 − $1,900 = $4,500
Sum of the years digits = 5 + 4 + 3 + 2 + 1 = 15

1st year's depreciation $= \frac{5}{15} \times \$4,500 = \$1,500$

2nd year's depreciation $= \frac{4}{15} \times \$4,500 = 1,200$

3rd year's depreciation $= \frac{3}{15} \times \$4,500 = 900$

4th year's depreciation $= \frac{2}{15} \times \$4,500 = 600$

5th year's depreciation $= \frac{1}{15} \times \$4,500 = 300$

Total depreciation $\overline{\$4,500}$

As you can see, the greatest depreciation of the automobile occurs in the first year, when the asset drops $1,500 in book value. During the fifth year, however, the loss in book value is only $300.

COMPARISON OF THE METHODS

Using the automobile owned by Bay State Realty Company, let's compare the annual depreciation amounts yielded by the straight-line and declining-balance methods with the computations for the sum-of-the-years-digits method above.

Straight-Line Method

$6,400 (original cost) − $1,900 (trade-in value) = $4,500, total depreciation
$4,500 ÷ 5 (years) = $900, annual depreciation each of the five years

Declining-Balance Method

Fixed rate $= 2 \times \frac{1}{5} = 2 \times .20 = .40$ or 40%

1st year's depreciation	$= \$6,400.00 \times 40\% =$	$2,560.00
2nd year's depreciation	$= \$3,840.00 \times 40\% =$	1,536.00
3rd year's depreciation	$= \$2,304.00 \times 40\% =$	921.60
4th year's depreciation	$= \$1,382.40 \times 40\% =$	552.96
5th year's depreciation	$= \$\ 829.44 \times 40\% =$	331.78
Total depreciation		$5,902.34

Total depreciation, $5,902.34; final book value, $497.66. Note that the total depreciation figure assumes that there is no disposal value for the asset. If a disposal value is assigned to the asset (the $1900 used in the other methods), the rate would be fixed to end with that amount of book value in the fifth year.

Exercises

Using the sum-of-the-years-digits method, find the annual depreciation on each of the following assets for the first three years.

No.	Cost	Disposal Value	No. of Years Held	1st Year	2nd Year	3rd Year
1	$1,200	$300	5	$_____	$_____	$_____
2	$1,500	$240	6	$_____	$_____	$_____
3	$1,100	$110	9	$_____	$_____	$_____
4	$ 600	$125	4	$_____	$_____	$_____
5	$3,450	$400	7	$_____	$_____	$_____
6	$8,500	$875	8	$_____	$_____	$_____
7	$5,240	$100	10	$_____	$_____	$_____
8	$2,654	$250	12	$_____	$_____	$_____

Business Applications

1. The depreciation rate on a bulldozer that cost $12,800 was 8% on the declining balance. Find the annual depreciation and the book value each year for the first five years.

2. The depreciation charge on a machine costing $640 was computed at 12% on the decreasing annual value. Find the amount at which the machine was carried on the books at the beginning of the fourth year.

3. Machinery and equipment costing $23,800 were installed in the new plant of a manufacturing business. The accountant established an annual depreciation rate of $12\frac{1}{2}\%$ of the declining value. Find the annual depreciation for each of the first four years.

4. The City of Meadville computes depreciation on its sanitation trucks by the declining-balance method. The rate of depreciation was established at $9\frac{1}{2}\%$ annually. If the original value of each truck was $9,200, what was the book value of each truck at the end of the second year?

5. The Guaranteed Life Insurance Company charges depreciation on its calculators at the rate of 15% a year on the declining balance. If ten calculators in the claims adjustment department were purchased for $4,800, what will be the book value of each calculator at the end of three years? What will be the depreciation expense for each of these years?

6. A delivery truck that originally cost $7,800 is expected to have a disposal value of $2,800 at the end of four years when it will be traded in. Find the annual depreciation on the truck, using the sum-of-the-years-digits method.

7. The J. R. Banks Company purchased a garden tractor for $9,850. It is estimated that the tractor will be used for 10 years at which time it will have a disposal value of $1,600. In computing depreciation, the firm's accountant uses the sum-of-the-years digits method.
   a. What is the depreciation during the first year?
   b. What is the depreciation during the fifth year?
   c. What is the depreciation during the tenth year?

8. The Trent Construction Company uses the sum-of-the-years-digits method for computing the depreciation on all its equipment. One of these assets was purchased for $1,500 and is expected to have a disposal value of $50 at the end of eight years.
   a. What is the book value of the asset at the end of the fourth year?
   b. What is the book value of the asset at the end of the seventh year?

9. The rate department of the Mid-America Freight Company purchases 10-key adding machines for its rate clerks at a cost of $195 each. At the end of five years, these machines will be traded in for new ones. The disposal value of the old machines will be $85 each.
   a. Using the straight-line method of depreciation, what is the depreciation on each machine during the first year? the last year?
   b. Using the sum-of-the-years-digits method of depreciation, what is the depreciation on each machine during the first year? the last year?
   c. Find the book value for each of the five years, assuming depreciation is computed by the declining-balance method and the annual rate is 15.3%.

UNIT

ALLOCATING OVERHEAD COSTS

Case Problem Colonial Age Corporation leases a building on King's Highway for the purpose of manufacturing unfinished furniture, which is sold to local retail stores and other outlets. There are five departments in the company: sales, design, production, finishing, and administrative.

In the past, separate financial records were not kept for each of the five departments. A new chief accountant, however, insists that only by maintaining separate records for each department can management know how efficient the department is and thus be in a position to control the various expenses of operation.

Many businesses maintain separate financial records for each department for the reasons given by the new chief accountant and charge each department with its share of all *overhead*—a term that accountants often use for all expenses incurred in operating the business.

Discussion Questions

1. On what basis might an overhead expense such as rent be allocated to each of the five departments of Colonial Age Corporation?
2. What other expenses can you think of that might be difficult to allocate?

Some expenses can be accurately allocated because the amount spent by each department can be easily identified. These include salaries, telephone, supplies used, postage, and depreciation on furniture. However, overhead expenses such as rent, electricity, taxes, insurance, and janitorial services cannot be easily identified according to use. A bill for electricity, for example, gives only a total amount for the entire business—not a separate amount for each department. The company must therefore find some other way of allocating certain overhead expenses to the various departments. The guiding principle is that a department should be charged with an expense because of the relative benefit it receives or because of its responsibility for causing the expense.

ALLOCATING OVERHEAD ACCORDING TO SPACE OCCUPIED

The most common method of allocating overhead expenses to each department is according to the amount of space it occupies in the building.

Example 1:

Colonial Age Corporation occupies a building containing 40,000 square feet of space. The company pays an annual rent at the rate of $2 a square foot, or $80,000 a year. The rental expense is to be charged to each of its five departments according to the amount of space the department occupies. The space occupied by the five departments is as follows:

Design	10,000 square feet
Production	10,000 square feet
Finishing	8,000 square feet
Sales	8,000 square feet
Administrative	4,000 square feet

How much will each department be charged for annual rent?

Solution (Method 1):

One method of allocating rent to each department is to multiply the number of square feet occupied by the cost per square foot.

Design	10,000 × $2 =	$20,000
Production	10,000 × $2 =	20,000
Finishing	8,000 × $2 =	16,000
Sales	8,000 × $2 =	16,000
Administrative	4,000 × $2 =	8,000
	40,000	$80,000

Solution (Method 2):

Another method of allocating rent expense among the various departments is to find the percent each department's floor space represents of the total space and then multiply the total cost by that rate.

1. You will remember (Chapter 7) that to find the rate when you know the base and the percentage, you use the formula $R = \dfrac{P}{B}$. Here the base is the total space (40,000 square feet) and the percentage is the amount of space each department occupies.

2. To find the amount allocated to each department, you take the rate you found in Step 1, and multiply it by the total expenses ($80,000), thus using the formula $P = B \times R$, where P is the amount of expense allocated to each department, B is the total expense ($80,000), and R is the rate you found in Step 2. For convenience, use an arrangement like the table at the top of the next page.

Department	Percent of Space Occupied by Department $R = \dfrac{P}{B}$	Amount of Expense Allocated to Department $P = B \times R$
Design	$R = \dfrac{10,000}{40,000} = .25 = 25\%$	$P = \$80,000 \times 25\% = \$20,000$
Production	$R = \dfrac{10,000}{40,000} = .25 = 25\%$	$P = \$80,000 \times 25\% = 20,000$
Finishing	$R = \dfrac{8,000}{40,000} = .20 = 20\%$	$P = \$80,000 \times 20\% = 16,000$
Sales	$R = \dfrac{8,000}{40,000} = .20 = 20\%$	$P = \$80,000 \times 20\% = 16,000$
Administrative	$R = \dfrac{4,000}{40,000} = .10 = 10\%$	$P = \$80,000 \times 10\% = 8,000$
Totals	100%	$80,000

Example 2:

The five departments of Colonial Age Corporation occupy space as follows: design, 25% of the total; production, 25%; finishing, 20%; sales, 20%; and administrative, 10%. The accountant charges each department for taxes, insurance, heat, water, and janitorial services according to the space occupied. These expenses for the month of April were as follows:

Taxes	$ 800
Insurance	200
Heat	300
Water	100
Janitorial services	900
Total	$2,300

a. What amount will each department be charged for each of the expenses?
b. What is the total amount that each department is charged for expenses?

Solution:

In this allocation of expenses, the total of each overhead expense was multiplied by the percent that each department's space represents of the total space. Because the design department occupies 25% of the total space, it is charged with 25%

of the expenses for taxes, insurance, heat, water, and janitorial services. The sales department is charged 20%; and so on. The total of all departments' allocated expenses must equal the total overhead expenses to be charged for the month, and the total of the percents for all departments must equal 100%. This is a way of verifying that your computations are correct.

		Amount of Expense					
Department	Percent of Total Space	Taxes $800	Insurance $200	Heat $300	Water $100	Janitorial Services $900	Totals
Design	25	$200	$ 50	$ 75	$ 25	$225	$ 575
Production	25	$200	$ 50	$ 75	$ 25	$225	$ 575
Finishing	20	$160	$ 40	$ 60	$ 20	$180	$ 460
Sales	20	$160	$ 40	$ 60	$ 20	$180	$ 460
Administrative	10	$ 80	$ 20	$ 30	$ 10	$ 90	$ 230
Totals	100%	$800	$200	$300	$100	$900	$2,300

Exercises

1. Using Method 1 to allocate overhead, find the rent expense to be charged to each department. The annual rent expense of the building occupied is $3.50 a square foot.

Department	Space Occupied (Square Feet)	Rent Expense
a	1,000	$ _____
b	1,400	$ _____
c	2,000	$ _____
d	1,800	$ _____
e	1,200	$ _____
f	820	$ _____
g	1,160	$ _____
h	780	$ _____

2. Using Method 2, find the rent expense to be charged to each department. The annual rent is $20,000 and the total space occupied is 24,000 square feet.

Department	Space Occupied (Square Feet)	Percent of Total Space	Rent Expense
a	3,000	_____ %	$ _____
b	6,000	_____ %	$ _____
c	2,000	_____ %	$ _____
d	9,000	_____ %	$ _____
e	4,000	_____ %	$ _____
Totals	24,000	_____ %	$ _____

3. Find the amount of rent, taxes, maintenance, and utilities expense to be distributed to each department in May.

Department	Percent of Total Space	Rent $3,000	Taxes $300	Maintenance $740	Utilities $240	Totals
Finance	$12\frac{1}{2}$%	$ _____	$ _____	$ _____	$ _____	$ _____
Executive	$6\frac{1}{4}$%	$ _____	$ _____	$ _____	$ _____	$ _____
Production	25%	$ _____	$ _____	$ _____	$ _____	$ _____
Marketing	$31\frac{1}{4}$%	$ _____	$ _____	$ _____	$ _____	$ _____
Research	$18\frac{3}{4}$%	$ _____	$ _____	$ _____	$ _____	$ _____
Personnel	$6\frac{1}{4}$%	$ _____	$ _____	$ _____	$ _____	$ _____
Totals		$ _____	$ _____	$ _____	$ _____	$ _____

ALLOCATING OVERHEAD ACCORDING TO NUMBER OF EMPLOYEES

Certain personnel expenses may be allocated to each department in a business according to the number of employees in the department. Such expenses include safety, employee activities, and the salary and office expense of the personnel manager. These expenses have a direct relationship to the number of employees involved. When expenses are to be allocated to departments according to the number of employees, you will again use the percent formulas as you just did in allocating rent expense.

Example:

The number of employees in each of the five departments of Colonial Age Corporation is as follows: design, 5; production, 40; finishing, 20; sales, 5; and administrative, 10. The expenses to be distributed to these departments in July are: employee activities, $400; safety, $640; and salary and office expense of the personnel manager, $3,200. How will the expenses be allocated to each department according to the number of employees in that department?

Solution:

1. Find the total number of employees.

$$5 + 40 + 20 + 5 + 10 = 80, \text{ total number of employees}$$

2. Using the formula $R = \dfrac{P}{B}$, find the percent each department's number of

employees represents of the total number of employees. Here the base is the total number of employees (40), and the percentage is the number of employees in each department.

3. Find the total expenses for the month.

$$\$400 + \$640 + \$3,200 = \$4,240, \text{ total expenses in July}$$

4. To find the amount of expense allocated to each department, multiply the total expense by the rate you found in Step 2, thus using the formula $P = B \times R$ where P is the amount of expense allocated to each department, B is the total amount of expenses to be allocated, and R is the rate you found in Step 2.

For convenience, use a table like the one below.

Department	Percent of Total Employees $R = \dfrac{P}{B}$	Amount of Expense to Each Department $P = B \times R$			
		Employee Activities $400	Safety $640	Personnel Department $3,200	Totals
Design	$R = \dfrac{5}{80} = 6\dfrac{1}{4}\%$	$ 25	$ 40	$ 200	$ 265
Production	$R = \dfrac{40}{80} = 50\%$	200	320	1,600	2,120
Finishing	$R = \dfrac{20}{80} = 25\%$	100	160	800	1,060
Sales	$R = \dfrac{5}{80} = 6\dfrac{1}{4}\%$	25	40	200	265
Administrative	$R = \dfrac{10}{80} = 12\dfrac{1}{2}\%$	50	80	400	530
Totals	100%	$400	$640	$3,200	$4,240

Exercises

In the Jay-Dee Company certain personnel expenses are allocated to departments according to the number of employees. The four departments and the number of employees in each are: purchasing, 5; inventory, 20; sales, 15; and management, 10. The expenses to be allocated are recreation, $320; cafeteria, $1,640; and administrative, $960. With this information, complete the following schedule.

Department	Percent of Total Employees $R = \dfrac{P}{B}$	Recreation $320	Cafeteria $1,640	Administrative $960	Totals
		Amount of Expense to Each Department $P = B \times R$			
Purchasing	_____ %	$_____	$_____	$_____	$_____
Inventory	_____ %	$_____	$_____	$_____	$_____
Sales	_____ %	$_____	$_____	$_____	$_____
Management	_____ %	$_____	$_____	$_____	$_____
Totals	_____ %	$_____	$_____	$_____	$_____

Business Applications

1. The Conar Supply Company leased a warehouse building for a three-year period. The warehouse contains 62,500 square feet, and the lease stipulates that the tenant is to pay annual rent of $2 a square foot, plus taxes and insurance. If the taxes amounted to $12,000 a year and the insurance is $400, what is the cost of occupancy for (a) one year? (b) three years?

2. Find the annual rent expense to be allocated to each department of Prospero Printers if the space cost per square foot is $5.40 annually.

Department	No. of Square Feet	Annual Rent Allocation
Composition	2,000	$_____
Proofreading	3,100	_____
Platemaking	5,000	_____
Printing	15,000	_____
Binding	10,600	_____
Marketing	8,450	_____
Administrative	7,750	_____
Totals	_____	$_____

3. Find the share of the monthly rent of $3,160 charged to each department of the Pottsville Manufacturing Company on the basis of the square *Meters* of space occupied.

Department	No. of Square Meters	Monthly Rent Allocation
Raw materials	2,500	$ _____
Manufacturing	5,000	_____
Finished goods	2,000	_____
Administrative	500	_____
Totals	_____	$ _____

4. The Chamberlin Manufacturing Company allocates overhead to each of its six departments on the basis of the space occupied in the building. Overhead expenses for the month of February were as follows: rent, $4,000; taxes, $600; insurance, $100; utilities, $250; cleaning and maintenance, $750. The space occupied by the various departments is as follows:

Raw materials 1,200 m²   Finishing 2,000 m²
Processing 2,400 m²   Storage 3,000 m²
Assembling 1,800 m²   Offices 1,600 m²

What is the amount that each department will be charged for overhead for the month?

5. Marcal Distributors allocates certain monthly expenses to each of four departments according to the number of employees in the department. The expenses in October were: president's salary and office expense, $2,520; recreation and welfare of employees, $840; safety, $420. The number of employees in the four departments is as follows: planning and scheduling, 24; manufacturing, 42; warehousing and shipping, 12; office, 6. How much will each department be charged for overhead during the month?

UNIT

ALLOCATING OVERHEAD COSTS— RETAIL APPLICATIONS

Case Problem Lloyd Gibson, owner of Gibson's Giant Jewelry Store, has organized his store into four departments: jewelry, watches, giftware, and china. Although Mr. Gibson has been allocating overhead to the departments according to the amount of space each occupies, he is not satisfied with this method and is looking for a way to distribute overhead expenses more fairly.

Discussion Questions

1. Why might Mr. Gibson not be satisfied with distributing overhead expenses to the four departments on the basis of the store space each occupies?
2. What different method might he use to distribute these expenses so that each department is charged with its fair share?

EXPENSE ALLOCATION BASED ON SALES VOLUME

Some retail store owners feel that allocation of overhead expenses should not be based solely on the amount of space a department occupies. One department might require less space than any other and still sell more merchandise. For example, in a dime store, the lamp shade department may require far more space than the pet supplies department; yet the sales volume of pet supplies may be much greater than that of lamp shades. Also, location of space in retail stores often has a bearing on the amount of goods sold, and many retailers take this into account when distributing overhead.

Many retailers therefore favor basing their allocation of expenses on the sales volume of each department. This can be accomplished in two ways. First, the retailer might relate the department's contribution to expenses directly to the department's sales. Second, a retailer might assign a percent of the expenses to a department based on the desirability of that department's location in the store, a department with a more desirable location, naturally, being assigned a higher rate than one with a less desirable location.

When expenses are to be allocated to departments directly on the basis of sales volume, you can compute the expenses for each department using the methods you have already learned.

Example:

The manager of The Hobby Mart, a retail store, has organized the store into five departments as follows: models, stamp collecting, hobby supplies, games, and coin collecting. Rent, advertising, utilities, and other overhead expenses, totaling $1,575 during February, are to be allocated according to the sales volume of each department. Sales volumes for each department during February were as follows:

Models	$ 4,250
Stamp collecting	2,500
Hobby supplies	2,000
Games	1,250
Coin collecting	500
Total	$10,500

How should the overhead expenses of $1,575 be allocated to the five departments based on sales volume?

Solution:

1. Find the percent that total expenses represent of total sales. To do this, divide the total expenses by the total sales.

$$\$1,575 \div \$10,500 = .15 \text{ or } 15\%$$

2. Multiply each department's sales by 15% to find the amount of expense to be allocated to that department.

Models	$ 4,250 × 15% =	$ 637.50
Stamp collecting	2,500 × 15% =	375.00
Hobby supplies	2,000 × 15% =	300.00
Games	1,250 × 15% =	187.50
Coin collecting	500 × 15% =	75.00
Totals	$10,500	$1,575.00

Explanation:

With this method, you use only one rate rather than a separate rate for each department. Basically, you find the percent that total expenses are of total sales. Step 1 shows this to be 15%. This means that 15% of the sales of each department should be charged off to meet expenses, which you found in Step 2. As a verification of your answers, check that the total of expenses to all departments equals the total expenses you were given.

Exercises

1. Find the amount to be charged each department in the following store if overhead expenses totaled $16,000 for the month.

Department	Sales Volume	Percent of Expenses to Sales	Share of Overhead
a	$16,200	_____ %	$ _____
b	$32,700	_____ %	$ _____
c	$18,300	_____ %	$ _____
d	$22,500	_____ %	$ _____
e	$15,250	_____ %	$ _____
f	$12,350	_____ %	$ _____
g	$10,700	_____ %	$ _____
		Total	$ _____

2. The June sales of the five departments of a retail store were as follows:

Accessories	$15,100
Leather goods	$10,400
Outerwear	$31,500
Sportswear	$25,700
Shoes	$13,300

The overhead expenses for the month amounted to $12,000. If these expenses are allocated to each department according to the sales volume of that department, how much expense will be charged to each department?

3. The March Sales of the seven departments of the Fancy Kitchen Market were as follows:

Fresh produce	$1,600
Canned goods	$1,200
Bakery	$1,800
Meat	$1,100
Household supplies	$ 800
Frozen foods	$ 700
General merchandise	$ 300

The overhead expenses for the month amounted to $1,350. How much expense was charged each department?

REVIEW EXERCISES FOR CHAPTER 17

1. The Transamerica Insurance Company recently bought 40 type-writers at a cost of $480 each. These typewriters are to be traded in for new models after four years, and it is estimated that the disposal value of each will be $200.
   a. What is the annual depreciation of each machine by the straight-line method?
   b. What is the annual rate of depreciation?
   c. What is the book value of each machine at the end of the second year?
   d. If the company were to use the declining-balance method at an annual rate of $12\frac{1}{2}\%$, what would be the book value of each typewriter at the end of the second year?

2. Find the book value for the first three years of an oil burner that cost $2,400 if the depreciation was computed at the rate of $12\frac{1}{2}\%$ on the decreasing value.

3. The Curtis-Beck Corporation uses the sum-of-the-years-digits method for computing depreciation on all its equipment. A bull-dozer that the company purchased at $15,500 will have a trade-in value of $2,600 after five years. What is the book value of this machine at the end of each of the first three years? What is the depreciation for each year?

4. A garden tractor owned by Wildwood Nurseries cost $2,400. It is expected to have a useful life of four years and a resale value of 30% of its original cost. Using the straight-line method, find (a) the annual depreciation and (b) the rate of depreciation.

5. A postage machine that cost $3,210 has an estimated life of eight years. At the end of that period, it is estimated that the machine will have a disposal value of $600. Using the straight-line method, find (a) the annual depreciation, (b) the annual rate of depreciation, and (c) the book value at the end of the third year.

6. Complete the following table. (Use the straight-line method.)

Property	Cost	Disposal Value	Estimated Life	Yearly Depreciation	Rate of Depreciation
Machinery	$24,000	$6,000	12 years	$_____	_____ %
Furniture	$ 9,500	$ 500	15 years	$_____	_____ %
Tools	$13,200	$ 0	10 years	$_____	_____ %
Car	$ 5,700	$1,200	5 years	$_____	_____ %
Tow truck	$16,500	$4,500	4 years	$_____	_____ %

7. An industrial floor polisher was purchased at a cost of $1,800 and is expected to have a disposal value of $600 at the end of five years. If the sum-of-the-years-digits method is used to compute depreciation, what is the book value of the machine at the start of the third year? What is the annual depreciation during each of the first three years?

8. Find the amount of monthly overhead chargeable to each department in the Wonder King Electrical Company, based on the information in the following table. The charges are computed on the basis of square feet of space occupied by each department.

Department	Square Feet of Space Occupied	Percent of Total Space	Amount of Expenses						Totals
			July $6,400	Aug. $5,700	Sept. $7,200	Oct. $7,000	Nov. $4,400	Dec. $6,100	
Raw materials	3,600	_____	_____	_____	_____	_____	_____	_____	_____
Parts	1,800	_____	_____	_____	_____	_____	_____	_____	_____
Assembly	2,400	_____	_____	_____	_____	_____	_____	_____	_____
Finished goods	1,000	_____	_____	_____	_____	_____	_____	_____	_____
Office	1,200	_____	_____	_____	_____	_____	_____	_____	_____
Totals	10,000	_____	_____	_____	_____	_____	_____	_____	_____

9. The December sales in the six departments of Lansburgh's Discounts were as follows:

Accessories	$1,800		Leather goods	$3,000
Children's shoes	$2,400		Men's shoes	$3,600
Hosiery	$1,200		Women's shoes	$4,000

The overhead expenses of $2,800 for the month are to be charged to each department on the basis of its sales volume. How much will each department be charged?

PART 3
MATHEMATICS
APPLIED TO
CONSUMER
PROBLEMS

CHAPTER 18
PERSONAL INVESTMENTS

When you put your money to work so that it earns additional money, you have made an *investment*. Many millions of people invest in a savings account at a bank or at a savings and loan company. Others purchase U.S. savings bonds. Still others purchase stock in corporations or buy corporate, municipal (city), or state bonds. A great many people use all of these methods of investing their money as well as others, such as buying real estate, purchasing an interest in a business, and so on.

No matter where they invest their money, all investors have a common objective—to earn money on their investments. Some types of investments, such as savings accounts and U.S. savings bonds, are popular because they pay a good rate of interest and are safe. Safety means that investors can be certain to receive back not only the amount they have invested but interest as well. Other investments, such as stocks, are not always safe, but these offer investors the opportunity to earn a great deal more money on their investments than they would if they purchased, say, U.S. savings bonds. Where such an opportunity exists for making substantial amounts of money on an investment, it is usually accompanied by risk. That is, investors may, in their attempt to get the highest possible returns on their money, lose not only any return they may have expected but also their original investment.

In this chapter, you will study the more common types of investments selected by individuals and learn how to compare the advantages and disadvantages of the various types of investments from which you may choose.

UNIT

SAVINGS ACCOUNTS—COMPUTING COMPOUND INTEREST

Case Problem Upon graduation from high school three years ago, Brad Alden obtained a job as salesman for Grossman Automotive Sales. Shortly after Brad received his first pay check, he established a checking account with a bank near his home. At first, Brad used all his earnings for clothes, entertainment, and other things, but in a few months he began to have money left over from his pay check. It wasn't long before he realized that he had a checking account balance of nearly $1,000.

Discussion Questions
1. Why is Brad's checking account not the best place in which to keep his savings?
2. How might Brad put his money to "work"?

Although a checking account is a safe place for Brad Alden to keep his savings, the money does not "work" for him there. That is, it earns no interest. Millions of people who have money they do not need to meet immediate day-to-day expenses put it in a *savings account* where it will earn interest.

As you know, interest is always expressed as an annual percent. This means that if Brad Alden left $1,000 in a savings account for one year with interest at 5%, he would have earned $50 *simple* interest $(I = P \times R \times T$ or $50 = $1,000 \times 5\%)$. However, all savings institutions *compound* interest at least semi-annually. This means that twice a year the interest earned is added to the previous balance so that the base amount on which interest is paid becomes greater and greater. The principal plus the compound interest is called the *compound amount*.

INTEREST COMPOUNDED SEMIANNUALLY

As you know, interest rates are stated in terms of one year. Therefore, the bank that advertises "Interest at 5%, compounded semiannually" is simply saying that every half year its savings account depositors will receive interest on their deposits at the rate of $2\frac{1}{2}\%$ $(\frac{1}{2} \times 5\% = 2\frac{1}{2}\%)$.

Example:
Morris and Karen Shatz received a check for $10,000 from his grandparents as a wedding present. They decided to deposit the money in a savings and loan association, which pays interest at 5%. If interest is compounded semiannually and the Shatzes leave the $10,000 in savings for 2 years, how much will they have on deposit?

Solution:
An annual interest rate of 5% is the same as a semiannual rate of $2\frac{1}{2}\%$. Hence, at the end of the first half year, interest on the Shatzs' deposit is found by multiplying $10,000 by $2\frac{1}{2}\%$. The product ($250) is added to the original deposit of $10,000, making the new principal $10,250 at the end of the first half year. Interest for the second half of the first year is computed on $10,250. The same process is repeated for the first half of the second year and the second half of the second year. The table below shows the results.

Period	Interest	Principal
Start of year		$10,000.00
First half year ($2\frac{1}{2}\% \times $10,000)	$250.00	$10,250.00
Second half year ($2\frac{1}{2}\% \times $10,250)	$256.25	$10,506.25
Third half year ($2\frac{1}{2}\% \times $10,506)	$262.65	$10,768.90
Fourth half year ($2\frac{1}{2}\% \times $10,768)	$269.20	$11,038.10

At the end of the second year, the Shatzes will have $11,038.10 on deposit, having earned $1,038.10 on their savings.

Note: Compound interest is not computed by most banks on amounts less than $1. Thus, in computing interest on $10,506.25, for example, the rate is multiplied by $10,506.00—not $10,506.25.

Exercises

Assume that each depositor neither adds money to his savings account nor withdraws from it and that interest is compounded semiannually. Compute his savings at the end of the period indicated. (Since compound interest is not computed on amounts less than $1 by most banks, do not compute it in this way for the problems in this unit.)

No.	Original Deposit	Interest Rate	Period of Deposit	Compound Amount
1	$4,000	4%	2 yrs.	$ _____
2	$3,500	$4\frac{1}{2}$%	2 yrs.	$ _____
3	$4,500	3%	3 yrs.	$ _____
4	$ 500	$4\frac{1}{2}$%	3 yrs.	$ _____

INTEREST COMPOUNDED QUARTERLY

When interest is credited four times a year, it is referred to as being compounded *quarterly*. The procedure for finding the interest earned and the value of a savings deposit for quarterly periods is very similar to that used in computations involving interest for semiannual periods. The only difference is that you are dealing with four periods a year instead of two. That is, the savings institution that advertises its interest as being compounded quarterly at 5% means that every three months its depositors will receive interest on their deposits at the rate of $1\frac{1}{4}$% ($\frac{1}{4} \times$ 5% = $\frac{5}{4}$%, or $1\frac{1}{4}$% per quarter).

Example:

Morris and Karen Shatz deposited $10,000 in a savings account at 5%. If interest is compounded quarterly, what will the amount of their deposit be at the end of two years?

Solution:

An annual interest rate of 5% is the same as a quarterly rate of $1\frac{1}{4}$%. At the end of the first quarter (three months), interest on the Shatz's deposit is found by multiplying $10,000 by $1\frac{1}{4}$%. The product ($125) is added to the original deposit of $10,000, making the compound amount $10,125 at the end of the first quarter. Interest for the second quarter is computed on $10,125. The same is repeated for the third and fourth quarters of the first year and for each of four quarters in the next year.

At the end of	Interest	Principal
First quarter	$125.00	$10,125.00
Second quarter	$126.56	$10,251.56
Third quarter	$128.14	$10,378.70
Fourth quarter (1 year)	$129.74	$10,509.44
Fifth quarter	$131.36	$10,640.80
Sixth quarter	$133.00	$10,773.80
Seventh quarter	$134.66	$10,908.46
Eighth quarter (2 years)	$136.35	$11,044.81

Notice that, when the interest on the Shatz's $10,000 was compounded quarterly, the deposit earned $6.71 more than when it was compounded semiannually. Why do you think this is so?

Exercises

Find the amount on deposit at the end of the period indicated for each of the following depositors. Assume that none of the depositors added to or withdrew money during the period and that interest is compounded quarterly.

No.	Original Deposit	Interest Rate	Period of Deposit	Compound Amount
1	$ 400	4%	1 quarter	$ _____
2	$1,000	4%	6 mo.	$ _____
3	$2,000	5%	1 yr.	$ _____
4	$3,600	5%	$1\frac{1}{2}$ yrs.	$ _____
5	$ 840	6%	2 yrs.	$ _____

Business Applications

1. How much interest will accumulate on an $800 deposit over three years if interest is compounded semiannually at 5%?

2. A $5,000 check is deposited in a savings and loan association at a 4% interest rate and allowed to remain there for three years.
   a. How much will a depositor gain in three years on the $5,000 if interest is compounded semiannually?
   b. How much will he gain in three years if interest is compounded quarterly?

3. When Mary-Jane Bates completed the eighth grade, an aunt gave her $2,000 as a college fund. Mary-Jane and her parents decided to deposit the money in a savings bank that offered interest at 5% compounded quarterly. If Mary-Jane left the money in the

bank and neither added to it nor withdrew from it, how much money will she have for college four years later?

4. Ben Allison invested $1,000 in a savings account at 6%. The interest was compounded monthly. How much will Mr. Allison have on deposit at the end of five months?

UNIT 2

USING A COMPOUND-INTEREST TABLE

Case Problem Pamela Medina is a clerk at the Guaranteed Savings Bank. It is her job to compute interest on the savings accounts of depositors.

Discussion Questions
1. How might the work of computing interest for large numbers of accounts be simplified?
2. What are the advantages of using a compound-interest table?

The interest for various sums of money invested for long periods of time can be found more easily by using a *compound-interest table*. A compound-interest table enables Miss Medina to compute interest more quickly and with greater accuracy. In addition, banks make use not only of interest tables but also of computers. Many banks compound interest daily, and these computations are feasible only with a computer.

To find the compound interest on an investment, locate the rate, expressed as a percent, and the number of years. Go down the column and across the row to find the interest payment on every dollar of the investment.

COMPOUND INTEREST
Amount on $1 Compounded Annually

Years	1%	$1\frac{1}{4}$%	$1\frac{1}{2}$%	2%	$2\frac{1}{4}$%	$2\frac{1}{2}$%	3%	$3\frac{1}{2}$%	4%	5%	$5\frac{1}{2}$%	6%
1	1.0100	1.0125	1.0150	1.0200	1.0225	1.0250	1.0300	1.0350	1.0400	1.0500	1.0550	1.0600
2	1.0201	1.0252	1.0302	1.0404	1.0455	1.0506	1.0609	1.0712	1.0816	1.1025	1.1130	1.1236
3	1.0303	1.0380	1.0457	1.0612	1.0690	1.0769	1.0927	1.1087	1.1249	1.1576	1.1742	1.1910
4	1.0406	1.0509	1.0614	1.0824	1.0931	1.1038	1.1255	1.1475	1.1699	1.2155	1.2388	1.2625
5	1.0510	1.0641	1.0773	1.1041	1.1177	1.1314	1.1593	1.1877	1.2167	1.2763	1.3070	1.3382
6	1.0615	1.0774	1.0934	1.1262	1.1428	1.1597	1.1941	1.2293	1.2653	1.3401	1.3788	1.4185
7	1.0721	1.0909	1.1098	1.1487	1.1685	1.1887	1.2299	1.2723	1.3159	1.4071	1.4547	1.5036
8	1.0329	1.1045	1.1265	1.1717	1.1948	1.2184	1.2668	1.3168	1.3686	1.4775	1.5347	1.5938
9	1.0937	1.1183	1.1434	1.1951	1.2217	1.2489	1.3048	1.3629	1.4233	1.5513	1.6191	1.6895
10	1.1046	1.1323	1.1605	1.2190	1.2492	1.2801	1.3439	1.4106	1.4802	1.6289	1.7081	1.7908
11	1.1157	1.1464	1.1779	1.2434	1.2773	1.3121	1.3842	1.4600	1.5395	1.7103	1.8021	1.8983
12	1.1268	1.1608	1.1956	1.2682	1.3060	1.3449	1.4258	1.5111	1.6010	1.7959	1.9012	2.0122
13	1.1381	1.1753	1.2136	1.2936	1.3354	1.3785	1.4685	1.5640	1.6651	1.8856	2.0058	2.1329
14	1.1495	1.1900	1.2318	1.3195	1.3655	1.4130	1.5126	1.6187	1.7317	1.9799	2.1161	2.2609
15	1.1610	1.2048	1.2502	1.3459	1.3962	1.4483	1.5580	1.6753	1.8009	2.0789	2.2325	2.3966
16	1.1726	1.2199	1.2690	1.3728	1.4276	1.4845	1.6047	1.7340	1.8730	2.1829	2.3553	2.5404
17	1.1843	1.2351	1.2880	1.4002	1.4597	1.5216	1.6528	1.7947	1.9479	2.2920	2.4848	2.6928
18	1.1961	1.2506	1.3063	1.4282	1.4926	1.5597	1.7024	1.8575	2.0258	2.4066	2.6215	2.8543
19	1.2081	1.2662	1.3270	1.4568	1.5262	1.5987	1.7535	1.9225	2.1068	2.5270	2.7656	3.0256
20	1.2202	1.2820	1.3469	1.4859	1.5605	1.6386	1.8061	1.9898	2.1911	2.6533	2.9178	3.2071
21	1.2324	1.2981	1.3671	1.5157	1.5956	1.6796	1.8603	2.0594	2.2788	2.7860	3.0782	3.3996
22	1.2447	1.3143	1.3876	1.5460	1.6315	1.7216	1.9161	2.1315	2.3699	2.9253	3.2475	3.6035
23	1.2572	1.3307	1.4084	1.5769	1.6682	1.7646	1.9736	2.2061	2.4647	3.0715	3.4262	3.8197
24	1.2697	1.3474	1.4295	1.6084	1.7085	1.8087	2.0328	2.2833	2.5633	3.2251	3.6146	4.0489
25	1.2824	1.3642	1.4509	1.6406	1.7441	1.8539	2.0938	2.3632	2.6658	3.3864	3.8134	4.2919

INTEREST COMPOUNDED ANNUALLY

Example:

Jim Hurley deposited $2,000 in a savings account at 4%. If the interest is compounded annually, how much will he have on deposit at the end of three years?

Solution:

Jim Hurley left his money for three years. Locate 3 in the *years* column. Now follow that line across until you come to the interest rate that Jim was earning,

4%. The entry 1.1249 represents the value of $1 at the end of three years at 4%. In order to find the amount Jim has on deposit, multiply that entry by the amount on deposit during that time. The product is the compound amount. In this case, the product is $2,249.80 (1.1249 × $2,000 = $2,249.80).

INTEREST COMPOUNDED SEMIANNUALLY

Example:
Joan Portola deposited $3,500 in a savings account, with interest at 5%. The interest was compounded semiannually. How much will she have on deposit at the end of two years?

Solution:
1. Divide the annual interest rate by 2, to find the interest rate for a half year. In this case, the semiannual interest rate is $2\frac{1}{2}\%$ ($5\% \div 2 = 2\frac{1}{2}\%$).
2. Determine the number of years the savings have been on deposit, and multiply it by 2 to yield the number of semiannual periods. In this case, the result is 4 ($2 \times 2 = 4$).
3. To apply Steps 1 and 2, look down the *Years* column to find the number of semiannual interest periods, in this case, 4; then look across to find the semiannual interest rate, in this case, $2\frac{1}{2}\%$. The number you find there (1.1038) represents the value of $1 at the end of the specified period.
4. Multiply the amount on deposit by this entry to find the compound amount. $3,500 at 5% interest compounded semiannually for two years is $3,863.30 ($3,500 × 1.1038 = $3,863.30).

INTEREST COMPOUNDED QUARTERLY

Example:
Ralph and Jennifer Doby deposited $5,000 in a savings bank that pays 5% interest compounded quarterly. How much will they have on deposit at the end of four years?

Solution:
1. Divide the annual interest rate by 4, to find the interest rate for one quarter (3 months); in this case, $1\frac{1}{4}\%$ is the result ($5\% \div 4 = 1\frac{1}{4}\%$).
2. Determine the number of years the savings have been on deposit and multiply it by 4 to yield the number of quarters in the period. In this case, the result is 16 ($4 \times 4 = 16$).
3. To apply Steps 1 and 2, look down the *Years* column to find the number of interest periods (16) and across to find the quarterly interest rate ($1\frac{1}{4}\%$). The entry you find there (1.2199) represents the value of $1 at the end of the specified period.

4. Multiply the amount on deposit by this entry to find the compound amount. $5,000 at 5% interest compounded quarterly is $6,099.50 ($5,000 × 1.2199 = $6,099.50).

Exercises

In each exercise below, assume that the depositor neither adds any money to his account nor withdraws any from it. Use the table on page 448 to compute the savings at the end of the period.

Depositor	Original Deposit	Interest Rate	Compounded	Period of Deposit	Compound Amount
1	$ 400	4%	Semiannually	2 yrs.	$_____
2	$1,000	$4\frac{1}{2}$%	Semiannually	2 yrs.	$_____
3	$2,000	4%	Quarterly	1 yrs.	$_____
4	$3,600	5%	Semiannually	3 yrs.	$_____
5	$4,000	$4\frac{1}{2}$%	Semiannually	$2\frac{1}{2}$ yrs.	$_____
6	$4,500	4%	Semiannually	3 yrs.	$_____
7	$ 800	5%	Quarterly	4 yrs.	$_____
8	$7,500	5%	Quarterly	5 yrs.	$_____

INTEREST COMPOUNDED DAILY

Many savings institutions now advertise savings accounts with interest that is compounded daily. (The computations in this case are so complicated they are done by computer.) The table below was issued recently by a savings and loan association. Similar tables are available at varying rates of interest.

How Savings Grow	$5 Monthly	$10 Monthly	$15 Monthly	$20 Monthly	$25 Monthly	$50 Monthly	$100 Monthly
1 yr.	61.67	123.33	185.00	246.67	308.34	616.67	1233.35
2 yrs.	126.50	252.99	379.49	505.99	632.50	1264.98	2529.97
3 yrs.	194.66	389.30	583.96	778.62	973.28	1946.54	3893.11
4 yrs.	266.32	532.60	798.92	1065.23	1331.55	2663.07	5326.17
5 yrs.	341.65	683.25	1024.90	1366.55	1708.20	3416.35	6832.76
10 yrs.	780.40	1560.68	2341.08	3121.48	3901.88	7803.64	15607.40
15 yrs.	1343.84	2687.47	4031.32	5375.16	6719.01	13437.80	26875.81
20 yrs.	2067.42	4134.50	6201.92	8269.34	10336.76	20673.19	41346.72

This schedule is based on our passbook rate of 5% a year on savings, with earnings added to the account and compounded daily.

Example:

How much interest is paid on a $5 monthly deposit in a one-year period?

Solution:

Refer to the *$5 Monthly* column down and the *1 Year* column across. You will find the sum $61.67. This represents the total value of the monthly deposits at the end of the year. Thus:

$61.67   value at the end of the year
60.00   amount deposit ($5 × 12 months)
$ 1.67   interest

Exercises

1. If Jonas Brehm deposits $100 monthly for 20 years, what will the value of his savings account be at the end of that time?

2. Monica Tarleton deposits $10 each month over a 10-year period. How much are her interest earnings?

3. Joseph Kolt deposits $50 a month for 15 years. What will be his savings bank account balance at the end of that time? How much of this is principal? How much is interest?

Business Applications

1. Solve each problem, using the compound-interest table on page 448.

   a. On July 1, 19X4 Fred Delcott deposited $540 in a bank that pays interest at the rate of 4% per year, compounded semi-annually. If Mr. Delcott made no other deposits or any withdrawals, how much money did he have on deposit on January 2, 19X5?

   b. On July 1, 19X4, A. B. Clyne opened an account in a savings bank with a deposit of $750. The bank pays interest every six months at an interest rate of $4\frac{1}{2}$% per year. How much did Mr. Clyne have in the bank on July 1, 19X5 if he made no deposits or withdrawals during the year?

   c. George Curtis deposited $1,200 in a savings and loan association on April 1, 19X2. Starting with the first of the year, the association pays interest compounded quarterly at 4%. If Mr. Curtis made no other deposits or withdrawals in 19X2, how much did he have on deposit on January 2, 19X3?

   d. A depositor had $10,000 on deposit in a bank that pays interest at 5% twice a year. How much more interest would the depositor gain during the first year if the bank compounded interest quarterly rather than semiannually?

2. Use the table on page 450 for the following.

  a. Kim Yong deposited $25 a month in a savings bank that compounds interest daily at 5%. What amount is on deposit after three years? How much is principal? How much is interest?

  b. If, as indicated in the explanation beneath the table, 5% interest a year is paid on savings, how do you account for the fact that a person who deposits $600 a year ($50 monthly) receives only $16.67 in interest rather than $30 ($600 @ 5%)?

UNIT

3

SPECIAL-PURPOSE SAVINGS

Case Problem Gilbert Shannon and his wife Eileen both work. Together they earn a total of $1,400 a month. Both are water sports enthusiasts, and they have their hearts set on a new sailboat. At a recent boat show they found exactly what they wanted—a day sailer priced at $3,000. The Shannons decide to start saving money in order to make the purchase.

Discussion Questions

1. If the Shannons put their money in a savings account that pays 5% interest compounded quarterly, how much money will they have to save each month in order to have enough in five years to buy the boat?

2. What other methods of saving might the Shannons choose?

FINDING MONTHLY SAVINGS TO REACH A CERTAIN GOAL

The Shannons can use a table such as the one below to find out how much they will need to save each month to have enough in five years to buy their boat.

Monthly Savings Needed to Yield $1,000
(Interest Compounded Quarterly)

Time	4%	5%	6%	7%
5 years	$15.05	$14.70	$14.40	$13.95
10 years	$ 6.80	$ 6.45	$ 6.10	$ 5.80
15 years	$ 4.10	$ 3.75	$ 3.45	$ 3.15
20 years	$ 2.75	$ 2.45	$ 2.20	$ 1.95

Example:
How much per month will the Shannons have to save at 5% interest to have $3,000 in five years?

Solution:
1. Using the schedule above, find the specified period in the *Time* column. For the Shannons it is five years—the top row.
2. Find the column labeled with the specified interest rate. In this case, it is 5%, so look for the amount in the 5% column that is on the row labeled "5 years"—$14.70. This is the amount that the Shannons must deposit each month in order to have $1,000 at the end of five years.
3. Divide the amount desired ($3,000) by $1,000. Then multiply the entry found in Step 2 by this result. The amount the Shannons must deposit monthly is $44.10 ($3,000 ÷ $1,000 = $3; $14.70 × 3 = $44.10).

Exercises
Refer to the schedule above and complete the table below.

No.	Amount Desired	Years	Annual Rate of Interest	Monthly Savings Required
1	$2,000	5	5%	$_____
2	$1,500	10	4%	$_____
3	$3,000	5	6%	$_____
4	$2,500	15	4%	$_____
5	$1,000	5	5%	$_____

BUYING U.S. SAVINGS BONDS

Another method of saving the Shannons might have used is the purchase of *U.S. savings bonds*. When you purchase a bond, the government, in effect, is borrowing money from you and pays you interest while it is using your money. A bond issued by the federal government may be purchased at a bank, a post office, or through the company by which you are employed.

Hundreds of thousands of Americans buy *Series E bonds* on the bond-a-month plan. Under this plan, the employer deducts from an employee's pay the purchase price of the savings bond denomination he or she selects and periodically turns the bonds purchased over to the employee. (The denomination was the maturity value of the bond at the time it was first issued. The government, however, has since raised interest rates, so the denomination has no real meaning any more except to identify the bond. As you will soon see, a $25 bond, now held to maturity, yields $25.73.)

Denomination	Purchase Price
$ 25	$ 18.75
$ 50	$ 37.50
$ 75	$ 56.25
$ 100	$ 75.00
$ 200	$150.00
$ 500	$375.00
$1,000	$750.00

The issue price (cost price) is always 75% of the value of the bond when it matures. For example, a bond with a denomination of $25 sells for $18.75 ($25 × 75% = $18.75). All Series E bonds now mature in 5 years and 10 months.

The advantage of Series E bonds is that they are completely safe and pay up to $5\frac{1}{2}$% interest if held to maturity. The following table shows the *redemption value* of Series E bonds (the amount they are worth when cashed in) in half-year periods. The redemption value increases at the end of each period by the amount of interest which the government is paying at that time.

From the table, you will see that the interest rate on Series E bonds gradually increases until it reaches the maximum of $5\frac{1}{2}$% at maturity date (5 years and 10 months from issue date).

REDEMPTION VALUES OF
BONDS BEARING ISSUE DATES BEGINNING JUNE 1, 1970

Period After Issue Date	Redemption values during each $\frac{1}{2}$-year period						Annual Interest
	($25 Bond)	($50 Bond)	($75 Bond)	($100 Bond)	($200 Bond)	($500 Bond)	
First $\frac{1}{2}$ year	$18.75	$37.50	$56.25	$ 75.00	$150.00	$375.00	0.00%
$\frac{1}{2}$ to 1 year	$19.05	$38.10	$57.15	$ 76.20	$152.40	$381.00	3.20%
1 to $1\frac{1}{2}$ years	$19.51	$39.02	$58.53	$ 78.04	$156.08	$390.20	4.01%
$1\frac{1}{2}$ to 2 years	$19.95	$39.90	$59.85	$ 79.80	$159.60	$399.00	4.18%
2 to $2\frac{1}{2}$ years	$20.40	$40.80	$61.20	$ 81.60	$163.20	$408.00	4.26%
$2\frac{1}{2}$ to 3 years	$20.88	$41.76	$62.64	$ 83.52	$167.04	$417.60	4.35%
3 to $3\frac{1}{2}$ years	$21.39	$42.78	$64.17	$ 85.56	$171.12	$427.80	4.44%
$3\frac{1}{2}$ to 4 years	$21.93	$43.86	$65.79	$ 87.72	$175.44	$438.60	4.53%
4 to $4\frac{1}{2}$ years	$22.53	$45.06	$67.59	$ 90.12	$180.24	$450.60	4.64%
$4\frac{1}{2}$ to 5 years	$23.16	$46.32	$69.38	$ 92.64	$185.28	$463.20	4.75%
5 to $5\frac{1}{2}$ years	$23.82	$47.64	$71.46	$ 95.28	$190.56	$476.40	4.84%
$5\frac{1}{2}$ years to 5 years and 10 months	$24.51	$49.02	$73.53	$ 98.04	$196.08	$490.20	4.93%
MATURITY VALUE (5 yrs. & 10 mos. from issue date)	$25.73	$51.46	$77.19	$102.92	$205.84	$514.60	5.50%

The Treasury Department publishes tables showing how investments in Series E bonds grow. Such tables are shown here.

SERIES E SAVINGS BONDS

Weekly Savings	Accumulated value at end of:			
	1 yr.	3 yrs.	5 yrs. 10 mos.	15 yrs. 10 mos.
$ 1.25	$ 66	$ 205	$ 429	$ 1,600
$ 2.50	$131	$ 412	$ 861	$ 3,211
$ 3.75	$197	$ 618	$1,295	$ 4,824
$ 5.00	$263	$ 825	$1,726	$ 6,432
$ 6.25	$328	$1,031	$2,160	$ 8,047
$ 7.50	$395	$1,237	$2,593	$ 9,657
$12.50	$657	$2,063	$4,323	$16,103
$18.75	$987	$3,095	$6,489	$24,167

Monthly Savings	Accumulated value at end of:			
	1 yr.	3 yrs.	5 yrs. 10 mos.	15 yrs. 10 mos.
$ 3.75	$ 45	$ 142	$ 296	$ 1,102
$ 6.25	$ 76	$ 237	$ 494	$ 1,842
$ 7.50	$ 91	$ 284	$ 595	$ 2,212
$12.50	$151	$ 474	$ 993	$ 3,689
$18.75	$228	$ 714	$1,493	$ 5,556
$25.00	$303	$ 951	$1,987	$ 7,398
$37.50	$455	$1,428	$2,986	$11,112
$56.25	$683	$2,142	$4,480	$16,669
$75.00	$910	$2,856	$5,973	$22,225

Example:
Tom Byram authorized his employer to withhold the cost of a $50 bond ($37.50) from his pay check each month. (a) How much will Mr. Byram have saved at the end of three years? (b) How much will he have saved at the end of 5 years and 10 months? (c) How much of the answer in "b" is interest?

Solution:
1. Refer to the table above. In the *Monthly Savings* column find the amount deducted from Mr. Byram's pay ($37.50). On the same line in the *3 yrs.* column

is the figure $1,428. This is the amount Mr. Byram will have saved in three years.

2. To find the total amount saved at the end of 5 years and 10 months, look in the 5 *yrs., 10 mos.* column. The figure on the $37.50 line in the *Monthly Savings* column is $2,986. This is the amount Mr. Byram will have saved at the end of 5 years and 10 months.

3. To find the amount of interest Mr. Byram earned on the $50 bonds after 5 years and 10 months, do the following:

   a. Multiply the amount saved each month by the number of months. The product of this operation is the principal, or total amount Mr. Byram saved.

   5 (years) × 12 (months per year) + 10 (months) = 70 months
   70 (months) × $37.50 (per month) = $2,625 (principal)

   b. Subtract the principal from the accumulated value shown in the table. The difference is the interest earned.

   Accumulated Value − Principal = Interest
   $2,986   − $2,625 = $361

Series H Bonds

Series H bonds are issued in denominations of $500, $1,000, and $5,000. All mature in 10 years. The interest rates paid on these bonds are the same as for Series E bonds. A difference in the handling of these two types of government bonds is that twice a year interest checks are mailed to purchasers of Series H bonds by the Treasury Department, beginning six months from issue date. Many buyers of E bonds convert them to H bonds when their E bond investment reaches $500.

Exercises

1. Refer to the table on page 455 and determine the redemption values of each of the following Series E bonds if they are cashed during the periods indicated.
   a. A $25 denomination bond if redeemed within $3\frac{1}{2}$ to 4 years
   b. A $75 denomination bond if held to maturity
   c. A $50 denomination bond if cashed within 5 to $5\frac{1}{2}$ years
   d. A $200 denomination bond if redeemed within six months after purchase
   e. A $100 denomination bond if held to maturity

2. Turn to the tables on page 456, showing the accumulated value of Series E savings bonds, and answer the following questions.
   a. How much will weekly savings of $7.50 be worth at the end of three years?

b. How much will an investor have at the end of 5 years and 10 months if he buys the lowest denomination Series E bond each week?

c. If Lois Landry were able to purchase a $75 denomination bond each month, how much would she accumulate (a) at the end of one year? (b) three years?

d. Aaron Webb purchased a $50 denomination bond through monthly savings. At the end of 5 years and 10 months, how much would Mr. Webb have accumulated?

Business Applications

1. Refer to the Redemption Value Table on page 455.

   a. How much more would a bondholder have if she bought a $100 bond and held it to maturity rather than if she bought a $75 bond? How much of this would be additional interest?

   b. Marian Dix owned a $100 Series E bond. How much more would she have if she kept it for five years instead of cashing it in at the end of four years?

2. Refer to the Series E Savings Bonds tables on page 456 and answer the following questions.

   a. Ed Wilcher has been purchasing Series E bonds at the rate of $6.25 a month. If the bonds are held to maturity, how much cash will he need to convert to a Series H bond?

   b. Ted Logan and his wife Myra have each been buying a $100 Series E bond a month for the past three years. How much did they accumulate in that period?

UNIT 4

BUYING STOCK

Case Problem On reaching the age of 25, Warren Holliday inherits $25,000 that had been willed to him by an uncle several years earlier. He thinks about various ways in which he can use this inheritance to earn additional money. Among the investments he considers are a savings account and U.S. savings bonds. He also considers buying stock in a corporation.

Discussion Questions

1. What do we mean by buying stock in a corporation?
2. What advantages might this have over investing the money in U.S. government bonds or depositing it in a savings account? what disadvantages?
3. How would Mr. Holliday purchase stock in a corporation?
4. How can he keep up to date on the prices of various stocks that are bought and sold each day?

One of the most common ways in which people invest their money is by buying stock in a corporation. When an individual purchases certificates of stock (*shares*) issued by a corporation, that person becomes a part owner of the corporation. A part owner may share in any profits that the corporation makes available through dividends. *Dividends* are payments a corporation makes to its stockholders out of its profits. Moreover, if the corporation prospers, the shares will also probably increase in value, so that an investment is worth more. There is a risk in being a stockholder, however; if the corporation does not do well, the value of the stock may decrease. Also, the corporation may not have enough profit to declare a dividend. With government bonds or savings accounts you are assured a safe and steady return; with stocks, you have an opportunity to make more money, but there is the risk of substantial loss.

HOW STOCKS ARE BOUGHT AND SOLD

Most stocks are bought and sold through agents called *stockbrokers* or simply *brokers*. Brokers act as agents in the buying and selling of stock; that is, they buy and sell stock for other people. Unlike other types of commission agents, brokers deal only in stock and similar investments. People who want to buy shares of stock in a certain company get in touch with a broker. The broker, in turn, makes the stock purchases through a central agency where other brokers gather to buy and sell stock. The largest of these agencies is the New York Stock

Exchange. Another large agency is the American Stock Exchange. Although exchanges are located in only a few major cities, in most cities you can buy stock from brokers who are associated with one of these exchanges.

Brokers charge a fee for their services in buying and selling stock. This fee is called a *commission,* or *brokerage,* and it is regulated by the stock exchanges. Buyers of stock on the New York and American Stock exchanges must also pay a tax to the State of New York. Commissions and taxes are not included in the discussion of stocks and bonds in this book.

STOCK MARKET QUOTATIONS

Because so many people are interested in the value of stock, the financial pages of large city newspapers print the daily transactions that take place at the major exchanges. The following is a sample listing as it might appear in a newspaper.

Yesterday's sales, 15,040,000; previous day, 13,983,460; year ago, 10,981,240; two years ago, 11,366,950; Jan. 1 to date, 2,012,412,585; 19X3 to date, 1,292,986,210; 19X2 to date, 1,342,277,413.

19X4		Stocks and Div.	Sales					
High	Low	in Dollars	100s	Open	High	Low	Last	Chg.
16⅞	11¼	Geiger Bak	44	15¾	15¾	14¼	14⅞	−⅝
34	25½	Gela-Finch 1.24 . .	26	33	33	32¾	32⅞	−⅛
88¼	50	Gelb Glass .90 . .	40	80¾	83	80¾	83	+1½
59	53⅝	Gem Instr pf 3.50 .	10	56	56	56	56	+⅛
37⅜	21⅞	Gemini Prop .80 .	478	32¼	32¼	30⅝	30⅝	−1⅞
16½	11	Gendr-Films 1.16 .	69	12	12¼	12	12⅛	+⅜
19⅝	13⅝	Gen Crfts .30 . .	32	13⅝	13⅞	13⅝	13¾	+¼
42⅜	28	Gen Transp .80 . .	80	36⅞	37⅜	36½	37	+1⅛
13⅞	6	Gen Serv	73	10⅝	10⅝	10⅜	10½	. . .
25½	18⅜	Gentry App 1.23 .	76	25	25⅜	24¾	25	. . .
44⅞	35	Georg Fash 1.50 .	31	44¼	44⅜	43½	44	−⅛
67¾	44⅝	Georgia Min 2.40 .	11	56⅜	57¾	56¼	57¾	+¾
60⅝	27⅞	Gerar Mov 1.20 .	34	45⅞	46	45⅝	45⅝	+⅞
25⅛	17⅛	Gertz Ins 1 . . .	50	22⅛	22⅜	22⅛	22¼	+¼
34¾	20	Giant Air .20 . .	1	21½	21½	21½	21½	+½
32½	21⅜	Giant Ind .25 . .	27	23⅝	24¼	23½	23½	+⅛
85⅜	70	Gibr Constr 1.60 .	66	74⅞	74⅞	74	74⅝	+⅜
30⅝	24¾	Gibson Cam 1.30 .	144	26	26¼	25¾	25¾	−¼
38¼	30¼	Gideon Mot 1.60 .	4	31½	31⅝	31½	31½	. . .
27⅛	12⅛	Gilco Dair I . . .	39	23¾	24¼	23¼	23¼	−¼
65¾	47½	Gilb Comp 2 . .	20	47¾	47¾	47	47½	−¾
42⅜	28	Gypsy Oil	80	36⅞	37⅜	36½	37	. . .
45½	22½	Harrig Tir 1.20 . .	38	36⅝	36⅝	35¼	35⅞	−⅜
119¼	97½	Hoyer Chem 2 . .	54	109	110⅜	108½	108⅝	−⅜
27¼	22¼	Hygrade Bro 1.20 .	36	25⅜	25⅜	25¼	25½	−⅛
48¼	37⅜	Hyman Gas 1.85 .	4	45½	46	45½	45½	. . .
24¼	17⅞	Ideal Sup .50 . .	24	20⅝	20⅝	20⅛	20¼	−½
27¼	22¼	Inter RR 1.10 . .	36	25⅜	25⅜	25¼	25½	−⅛
11¾	5⅞	Ivy-Dolman .30 . .	4	8	8⅛	8	8	. . .
34	25½	Jaynes Fab 1.24 .	26	33	33	32¾	32⅞	. . .
14⅞	7½	Joyden Meat . . .	424	7⅞	8⅜	7⅞	8¼	+¼
30¾	19	Kroyden Eng .80 .	16	31½	31⅝	31⅛	31⅝	+¼
64¼	43½	Kyser Paint 1.20 .	11	44½	44½	43¼	43¾	−1¼
16½	11	Lomb Syst	69	12	12¼	12	12⅛	+⅜
28⅞	25⅝	Lothr Ent .90 . .	7	27⅞	27⅞	27¾	27¾	−⅛
45⅜	35	Luder Asso 1.30 .	6	37⅞	39⅞	39¼	39⅞	−⅛
28⅛	20	Lyden Steel .70 . .	22	27	27	26⅝	26⅝	. . .
27	22½	Magee Data 1.20 .	10	22¾	23⅛	22⅝	23⅛	+⅝
52¼	43	Meyer Hot 2.55 . .	10	52½	52½	52½	52½	+¼
10⅝	8	Moss Ins 2	8	10	10	9⅞	9⅞	−⅛
42¼	33½	Motta Graph 1.50 .	6	40½	40½	40⅛	40⅛	. . .
79¾	72	Mourse Mills 4 . .	20	73	73	73	73	+1

Sample Stock Market Quotations

Let's look at the stock transactions of Gemini Properties (find the row labeled Gemini Prop in the left-hand column of the listing).

1. The first two entries in each row, labeled *High* and *Low*, represent the highest and the lowest prices at which stock was sold during the year to the current date. Thus, until the current date, the highest price that a buyer had had to pay for each share of Gemini Properties was $37\frac{3}{8}$, or $37.375; the lowest was $21\frac{7}{8}$, or $21.875.

2. The number .80 (80 cents) that appears immediately after the words Gemini Prop is the dividend amount (the stockholder's share of profits) that the company is expected to declare on each share of stock that year.

3. The number 478 that appears as the next entry under the *Sales 100s* column indicates that 47,800 ($478 \times 100 = 47,800$) shares of stock were sold that day.

4. Under *Open*, $32\frac{1}{4}$ means that the first sale of Gemini Properties stock that day was at $32.25 a share.

5. Under *High*, $32\frac{1}{4}$ signifies that the highest price paid by a buyer that day was $32.25 a share.

6. Under *Low*, $30\frac{1}{8}$ indicates that the lowest price paid for a share of Gemini Properties stock that day was $30.125.

7. Under *Last*, $30\frac{5}{8}$ signifies that the last purchaser of the day paid $30.625.

8. Under *Change (Chg.)*, $-1\frac{7}{8}$ indicates that the last price of the day was $1\frac{7}{8}$, or $1.875, lower than the closing price *on the previous day*.

Notice that the fractional parts of quotations are in eighths, fourths, and halves of a dollar. These are the only fractional parts of a dollar at which shares of stock are sold.

Example:

Refer to the stock listing and find the cost of 200 shares of General Services Corporation (Gen Serv) if they were purchased at the low for the day.

Solution:

The day's low for General Services Corporation was $10\frac{3}{8}$, or $10.375.

$$200 \times \$10.375 = \$2,075, \text{ cost of 200 shares}$$
$$\text{of General Services Corporation}$$
$$\text{stock}$$

Before multiplying, the fractional parts of a dollar should be expressed as a decimal fraction ($\frac{3}{8} = \$.375$).

Exercises

1. Find the cost of each of the following purchases by referring to the stock quotations on page 460.

	No. of Shares

a. If purchased at the opening price:
- (1) Gerardi Moving and Storage (Gerar Mov) — 300
- (2) Interstate Railroad (Inter RR) — 100
- (3) Giant Aircraft Company (Giant Air) — 700

b. If purchased at the lowest price:
- (1) Moss Insurance Company (Moss Ins) — 100
- (2) Gendreau Films, Inc. (Gendr Films) — 600
- (3) Hoyer Chemicals, International (Hoyer Chem) — 300

c. If purchased at the last price:
- (1) Geiger Baking Company (Geiger Bak) — 900
- (2) Gilbreth Computers (Gilb Comp) — 2,300
- (3) Lyden Steel Corporation (Lyden Steel) — 2,700

2. On the basis of the stock quotations illustrated, what was the highest price paid for a share of each of the following stocks that year?

a. Gelb Glass   **b.** Gilco Dairies

c. Gideon Motors   **d.** Kyser Paints

e. Harrigan Tires   **f.** Georgia Mining

g. Gela-Finch   **h.** Gem Instruments

Business Applications

1. Refer to the stock quotations on page 460 and answer the following questions:

a. What is the highest price paid for Hyman Gas stock this year?

b. What was the total number of shares of Gibson Cameras sold today?

c. What was the closing price on Mourse Mills stock?

d. What was the lowest price paid this year for Meyer Hotels?

e. What was today's high for Luder Associates?

f. What was the price at which Lomb Systems opened for the day?

g. What was the lowest price paid during the day for General Crafts, Inc.?

h. What was the change in price of Gibraltar Construction today compared with yesterday?

2. R. F. Scanlon purchased 300 shares of Magee Data stock at the high of the day and 400 shares of Giant Industrials at the low of the day. What was the total cost of Mr. Scanlon's purchase?

3. Alice Kemp purchased 500 shares of Ivy-Dolman Corporation at the high of the day. How much would she have saved if she had been able to purchase them at the low instead?

4. Refer to the top of the transaction listing to answer these questions.
   a. How many more shares of stock were traded on the exchange yesterday than on the previous day? on the same day a year ago? on the same day two years ago?
   b. How many shares of stock have been traded on the exchange from January 1 to date? How many more than on the previous year to date?

UNIT

STOCK DIVIDENDS

Case Problem Thomas Kleinert purchased 80 shares of 5% preferred stock of the Commercial Transport Corporation at $83.50 a share. The par value of the stock is $100. The year in which Mr. Kleinert bought the stock the company earned enough profit to distribute a quarterly divided among its 5% preferred stockholders.

Discussion Questions
1. What is the difference between preferred and common stock?
2. What do we mean by par value?
3. How is the amount of a dividend computed?

TYPES OF STOCK

The following is an illustration of a stock certificate.

You will notice that this certificate represents common stock. (Find the notation in the right hand corner of the certificate). Although all shares of stock represent ownership in a corporation, many corporations issue two classes of stock—preferred and common.

Preferred stock carries a certain stated dividend rate, and, provided the company makes sufficient profits, the holders of this stock can expect to receive this amount regularly as a return on their investment. For preferred stock, the dividend is usually stated as a percentage of the par value. *Par value* is the price that was placed on the stock by the corporation when it was originally issued. Thus, a 6% annual dividend (paid once a year) on a share of preferred stock with a par value of $100 would amount to $6 (6% × $100 = $6). If the dividend were paid semiannually (every six months), it would be $3 ($\frac{1}{2}$ × $6 = $3), and if it were paid quarterly (every three months), it would be $1.50 ($\frac{1}{4}$ × $6 = $1.50).

You must remember that the par value of a stock may bear no relationship to the *market value* of the stock; that is, the price it can be sold for on the market at any given time. A share of the preferred stock mentioned above with a par value of $100, for instance, might be purchased by an investor for $82.50. However, the dividend of 6% would be applied against the par value, not the purchase price of $82.50.

Common stock is the base stock of the corporation and usually carries no guarantee that dividends will be paid. In addition, holders of common stock do not receive any dividends until the guaranteed dividend on the preferred stock has been paid. After the preferred stock dividend has been paid, the remaining profit to be paid out as dividends, if any, is usually divided equally among the outstanding shares of common stock. For instance, if a corporation had $1,500 to be allocated as dividends among 10,000 shares of common stock, it would declare a dividend of 15 cents per share ($1,500 ÷ 10,000 = $.15). This means that the owner of 100 shares would receive $15 (100 × $.15). Notice that in this method of declaring dividends, the par value of the stock plays no part. In fact, because par value has very little meaning with respect to common stock (remember that the value of stock at any given time is what someone will pay you for it), many corporations issue no-par stock (stock without a par value), or they assign a purely token par value (say $1 or $2) to the stock. This just acknowledges the fact that the value of a stock is what it will bring on the open market.

Let's now go back to Mr. Kleinert in the Case Problem. Since the dividends are stated on the par value ($100) of the stock, the dividend on one share of stock would be 5% of $100, or $5. Hence, Mr. Kleinert's 80 shares would earn $400 (80 × $5 = $400) for the *entire year*. His quarterly dividend, therefore, would have been one-fourth of this amount, or $100.

$100 × 5% = $5, yearly dividend on one share
80 × $5 = $400, yearly dividend on 80 shares
$400 × $\frac{1}{4}$ = $100, quarterly dividend on 80 shares

To find the dividend, the *par value* of the preferred stock was used, not the purchase price of $83.50.

Assume that after distributing the dividends on the preferred stock, the Commercial Transport Corporation found that it had enough profit left over to distribute a quarterly dividend of $18\frac{1}{2}$ cents on each share of common stock.

Example:

If Mr. Kleinert owned 65 shares of common stock, what were his dividends?

Solution

$65 \times \$.18\frac{1}{2}$ (dividend per share) = $12.025, or $12.03, quarterly dividend

Exercises

1. Find the total dividend payment that each owner of common stock would receive.

Owner	No. of Shares	Dividend and Period	Total Dividends for the Period
a	50	25¢ quarterly	$ _____
b	75	30¢ semiannually	$ _____
c	250	$1.40 annually	$ _____
d	125	1\frac{1}{2}$ quarterly	$ _____
e	385	3\frac{3}{4}$ annually	$ _____
f	350	62$\frac{1}{2}$¢ quarterly	$ _____
g	250	$\frac{3}{4}$ extra dividend	$ _____
h	2,340	37$\frac{1}{2}$¢ extra dividend	$ _____

2. Find the total dividend payment that each owner of preferred stock would receive.

Owner	Percent on Preferred	Par Value	No. of Shares	Period	Total Dividends for the Period
a	5%	$100	60	Semiannually	$ _____
b	4%	$100	200	Quarterly	$ _____
c	3%	$ 80	75	Semiannually	$ _____
d	7%	$ 50	250	Quarterly	$ _____
e	4$\frac{1}{2}$%	$ 50	100	Annually	$ _____
f	5$\frac{1}{2}$%	$ 20	375	Semiannually	$ _____
g	6$\frac{1}{4}$%	$ 25	2,000	Quarterly	$ _____
h	5$\frac{3}{4}$%	$ 10	925	Semiannually	$ _____

Business Applications

Use the stock quotations on page 460 to solve Exercises 1 and 2.

1. Jonathan Wright owns 500 shares of Kroyden Engineering stock. How much can he expect to receive in dividends for the year?

2. How much can Agnes Duquesne, who owns 85 shares of Jaynes Fabrics stock, expect to receive in dividends for the year?

3. Elaine Porter bought 100 shares of $4\frac{1}{2}\%$ preferred stock of the Transcontinental Transport Company at $92.75 a share. If the par value of the stock is $100 a share, what quarterly dividends does she receive?

4. Gilbert Thomas owned 75 shares of Mid-Ocean Oil common stock and 135 shares of its 5% $50 par-value preferred stock. If the company paid its regular dividend on the preferred stock and a 35-cent dividend on each share of common stock, what was the total amount in dividends that Mr. Thomas received on his investment?

5. General Allied Corporation paid the semiannual dividend on its $5\frac{3}{4}\%$ preferred stock, par value $100, and also declared a dividend of $1.60 on its common stock. How much would Ann Bricker receive on 975 shares of preferred stock and 352 shares of common stock?

6. Tomás Torres owned 350 shares of Colgate Products $1 par-value common stock which he had purchased at $56.75 per share. The company paid a quarterly dividend of $1.20 per share, and an extra year-end dividend of 30¢ per share because it had had a profitable year. What was Mr. Torres' total income from this stock for the year?

UNIT

BUYING BONDS

Case Problem Arthur Peterson at the age of 60 has accumulated $25,000 through wise investments in stock. He thinks that now it would be advisable for him to sell his stock and put the money to work in a way that involves less risk. After careful study, Mr. Peterson decides to buy 10% first mortgage bonds of the All-American Metals Corporation. He buys these bonds through his broker at $108\frac{3}{5}\%$ of their par value of $1,000.

Discussion Questions

1. What are corporation bonds?
2. In what respect are corporation bonds a safer investment than stocks?
3. Why would someone pay more for a bond than its par value?

FINDING INTEREST ON BONDS

A corporation can raise large sums of money in two ways. Either it can issue stock or it can borrow money. Often the amount needed is so large that a single individual or institution is unwilling or unable to lend it, so the corporation must instead borrow money from the public. If a corporation wants to borrow 5 million dollars, for example, it may issue 5,000 certificates worth $1,000 each and promise to return the money in, say, 25 years. These certificates are called *bonds*. A bond is a promissory note in which the time for repayment covers a great many years. As was the case with other notes, the borrower—in this case, the corporation—may give some sort of security to guarantee that the bondholder will not lose the invested money. The payment of interest to bondholders is an obligation the corporation must meet, or the bondholders may have the property that has been pledged as security sold to meet the payments. Note that a corporation *must* meet its obligation to pay interest on its bonds; it has no obligation to pay dividends on its common stock.

You know that the amount borrowed on a promissory note is called the face value of the note. In the case of a bond, this amount is known as the *par value* of the bond. During the 25 or more years before the debt is paid, a bond may be sold many times by its various owners. The *market value* of a bond is the price at which it can be purchased at any particular time during this period.

Mr. Peterson, in the Case Problem, felt that investing in All-American Metals bonds was wise because it offered less risk than his holdings in stocks and still yielded a high interest rate (10%). For these reasons, he was willing to buy the bonds for more than their par value.

As with dividends on preferred stock, interest on a bond is determined on the basis of the par value of the bond, not on the purchase price. Interest on a $5\frac{1}{2}$% bond purchased at $987.50 and having a par value of $1,000 is computed on $1,000—not on $987.50. The $5\frac{1}{2}$% represents the rate of interest the corporation is paying on its debt.

Example:

James Kemper owns a $5\frac{1}{2}$% bond whose par value is $1,000. The bond was purchased at $987.50. How much did Mr. Kemper receive on his semiannual interest payment?

Solution:

$I = P \times R \times T$ (Time is expressed as a fraction of a year.)
= $1,000 $\times 5\frac{1}{2}$% $\times \frac{1}{2}$ year
= $27.50, semiannual interest payment

With some bonds, the corporation sends checks to its bondholders when the interest is due. Other bonds, known as coupon bonds, have coupons attached to them. Each coupon represents one interest payment. As the interest payment falls due, the bondholder clips the coupon from the bond and deposits it in his bank, just as he would deposit a check.

Exercises

For each bond, compute the interest for the period shown.

No.	Market Value	Par Value	Interest Rate	Period	Interest
1	$ 981.25	$1,000	5%	Annually	$_____
2	$ 975.00	$1,000	7%	Annually	$_____
3	$ 327.50	$ 500	$8\frac{1}{4}$%	Annually	$_____
4	$ 785.00	$1,000	6%	Semiannually	$_____
5	$ 307.50	$ 500	$9\frac{1}{2}$%	Semiannually	$_____
6	$ 677.50	$1,000	$4\frac{1}{4}$%	Semiannually	$_____
7	$1,040.00	$1,000	$5\frac{3}{4}$%	Semiannually	$_____
8	$ 495.00	$ 500	5%	Quarterly	$_____
9	$ 977.50	$1,000	$6\frac{1}{2}$%	Quarterly	$_____
10	$ 886.25	$1,000	$5\frac{3}{4}$%	Quarterly	$_____

BOND MARKET QUOTATIONS

Newspapers print bond quotations in their financial sections just as they do stock quotations. A sample section of a bond market trading report as it might appear in your daily newspaper is shown below. You might compare it with the stock market listing on page 460 before reading on.

Bonds	Sales in $1,000	High	Low	Last	Net Chg.
	Current Yields				
Albans 5s 96 cv	54	111⅞	111¼	111⅞	+ ⅞
Alcord Cp 9s 88	6	100⅝	100⅝	100⅝	. . .
Aleppa Ch 8⅞s 87 cv . . .	1	95½	95½	95½	. . .
Alden Can 7⅞s 84	7	93½	93⅜	93⅜	− ⅛
Alpine Rub 6s 83 cv	15	81⅞	81¾	81¾	− ⅛
Am Furn 4¼s 88	3	99⅛	99⅛	99⅛	. . .
Am Gas 8s 90	3	98½	98½	98½	. . .
Am Hot 7⅛s 90	8	102¼	102¼	102¼	− ⅛
Am Ind 6s 2030	53	59	58¼	59	+ ¼
Am Lime 4.80s 93	30	52½	52	52½	. . .
Am M T 5s 83 cv	1	354½	354½	354½	+ ¾
Am Toy 8½s 9	9	99⅝	99⅝	99⅝	− ⅛
Argyris Med 3s 78	7	92⅞	92⅞	92⅞	+ ⅛
Atwater Inv 7.35s 90 . . .	1	98¼	98¼	98¼	+ ¼
Aultmans 5s 90	40	86	85⅜	85½	− ½
Avery Mf 5⅛s 85	3	104⅝	104⅝	104⅝	. . .
Avion Tex 8s 90	9	102⅝	102¼	102⅝	. . .
Axel Ref 8¾s 99	10	93¼	93	93	− ¼
Axiom Pt 6⅞s 99	4	89	89	89	+ 1
Ayers Con 5s 90	2	100¼	100¼	100¼	− ¼
Ayres Stl 8.7s 93 cv	5	104½	104½	104½	+ ½
Azor Met 5s 85	169	127¼	125	125	. . .
Balt Ut 3¼s 79 cv	1	82¼	82¼	82¼	+ ¾
Benson Fin 5¼s 88	3	99⅛	99⅛	99⅛	. . .
Bethes G&E 7½s 90	10	78¼	78¼	78¼	. . .
Borg-Rex 5s 85 cv	14	96¾	96½	96½	. . .
Bos Co 7⅛s 79	3	104⅝	104⅝	104⅝	. . .
Brazil Cp 7⅛s 87 cv . . .	29	86¾	86⅝	86¾	. . .
Bunje Cp 9¼s 86 cv . . .	13	130	130	130	. . .
Byrom El 8¼s 93	3	38½	38½	38½	+ ⅜
Byzan Cst 7½s 90 cv . . .	41	103½	102¼	103½	+ 1
Can West 5s 83	10	102⅜	102⅜	102⅜	. . .
Cap Mf 9½s 98 cv	11	107½	107½	107½	+ ⅜
Carlson Sh 6½s 86	129	97½	97	97⅜	+ ⅞
Cent Paper 6s 90	10	78¼	78¼	78¼	. . .
Cent Ref 8s 93	1	104¼	104¼	104¼	− ¾
Chamb & T 6½s 80	11	72⅜	71¾	71¾	− ¼
Chem Cp A 9s 82	18	81¼	80¾	81	+ ¼
Chi P&L 8⅞s 88	3	111½	111½	111½	. . .
Cryst Pl 7s 84	41	103½	102¼	103½	+ 1
Culp Stl 4¾s 81	3	89	89	89	. . .
Cumb W cv 6⅝s 89 . . .	18	81¼	80¾	81	+ ¼
Cymb Rad 7⅛s 89	5	102	102	102	+ ½
Damon Cp 2⅞s 83	10	96	96	96	− 1¼
Danv L&P 6s 87 cv	1	95½	95½	95½	. . .
Delmon Ref 9¾s 79	1	83¼	83¼	83¼	. . .
Draper Ind 8⅛s 87 cv . . .	3	99⅛	99⅛	99⅛	. . .
Dykstra Cem 5.90s 79 . . .	10	86½	86½	86½	+ ½
Dylan Fab 6½s 84	2	100¼	100¼	100¼	− ¼
Dynam Cp 9⅛s 94	8	19⅞	18⅝	19⅞	+ ⅞

Sample Domestic Bond Quotations

Interpreting bond quotations is much the same as interpreting stock quotations. There are, however, a few major differences that will be apparent if you examine the Alpine Rubber Company (Alpine Rub) quotations.

Bonds	Sales in $1,000	High	Low	Last	Net Chg.
Alpine Rub 6s 83 cv	15	$81\frac{7}{8}$	$81\frac{3}{4}$	$81\frac{3}{4}$	$-\frac{1}{8}$

1. The 6s follows the name of the corporation represents the current yield (rate of interest) that the company is paying on these bonds—6%.
2. The 83 that follows the symbol 6s shows that the bonds will mature in 1983. The company will have to pay the par value of these bonds to the owners in that year.
3. Some listings contain the abbreviation cv. This means that the bond is convertible to common stock; that is, the owner may trade in the bond to purchase common stock.
4. The number 15 indicates that fifteen $1,000 bonds were sold that day.
5. Unlike stock quotations, the number $81\frac{7}{8}$ under *High* does not mean that the highest price paid for a bond of this company was $81.875. Instead, it means that the highest price paid for a bond of this company on that day was $81\frac{7}{8}$% of its par value of $1,000. The par value of all bonds sold on the New York Stock Exchange is $1,000, and quotations are always given as a percent of the par value. Bonds that are not sold on the New York Stock Exchange and that have a par value other than $1,000 are always quoted in exact dollars and cents, not as a percent of the par value.
6. As with the high, the low figure of $81\frac{3}{4}$ means that the lowest price paid for an Alpine Rubber bond that day was $81\frac{3}{4}$% of its par value.
7. The net change of $-\frac{1}{8}$ signifies that the closing price that day was $\frac{1}{8}$% of the par value lower that day than it had been on the previous day.

Example 1:

Find the market value of two Avion Textile Company 8% bonds if they were purchased at the high for the day. The par value of each bond is $1,000.

Solution:

The quotation $102\frac{5}{8}$ means $102\frac{5}{8}$%; this can be expressed as 1.02625.

1. Multiply the par value of the bonds by the purchase price to find the market value of one bond.

$1,000 × 1.02625 = $1,026.25, market value of one bond

2. Multiply the market value of one bond by the number of bonds purchased.

$1,026.25 × 2 = $2,052.50, market value of two bonds

Example 2:

What was the market value of three Aultmans bonds (par value of $1,000 each) that were sold at the low of the day?

Solution:

$1,000 × .85375 (85⅜%) = $853.75, market value of one bond
$853.75 × 3 = $2,561.25, market value of three bonds

Example 3:

If the net change of a bond with a par of $1,000 is $-\frac{1}{8}$, how much will the bond have decreased in value from the previous day's closing price?

Solution:

$-\frac{1}{8}\% = -.00125$
$1,000 × -.00125 = -$1.25$, net change in market value

Exercises

Refer to the bond market quotations on page 469 to solve each of these problems.

1. For each bond, find the date of maturity, the rate of interest, and the net change in dollars.

No.	Company	Date of Maturity	Rate of Interest	Net Change
a	Alden Can	_____	_____ %	$ _____
b	Aultmans	_____	_____ %	$ _____
c	Ayres Stl	_____	_____ %	$ _____
d	Bethes G&E	_____	_____ %	$ _____
e	Byzan Cst	_____	_____ %	$ _____
f	Can West	_____	_____ %	$ _____
g	Cent Ref	_____	_____ %	$ _____
h	Cymb Rad	_____	_____ %	$ _____

2. Using the table on page 469, find the market value of each of the following purchases:

No.	Company	Price Range	No. of Bonds	Market Value
a	Alcord Cp	Low	2	$ _____
b	Am Hot	Last	3	$ _____
c	Atwater Inv	High	4	$ _____
d	Balt Ut	Last	3	$ _____
e	Borg-Rex	Last	8	$ _____
f	Bunje Cp	Last	4	$ _____
g	Cap Mf	Low	2	$ _____
h	Cent Paper	Low	3	$ _____
i	Chem Cp A	High	2	$ _____
j	Cryst Pl	Low	5	$ _____

3. Using the table on page 469, find the interest paid for the period indicated.

No.	Company	Par Value	No. of Bonds	Period	Interest
a	Albans	$1,000	2	Annually	$ _____
b	Alden Can	$1,000	3	Semiannually	$ _____
c	Carlson Sh	$1,000	2	Semiannually	$ _____
d	Bunje Cp	$1,000	4	Quarterly	$ _____
e	Cumb W	$1,000	2	Semiannually	$ _____
f	Byrom El	$1,000	4	Quarterly	$ _____
g	Atwater Inv	$1,000	3	Semiannually	$ _____
h	Bos Co	$1,000	5	Semiannually	$ _____

Business Applications

1. Lois Barton owned five Standard Mining Company $8\frac{1}{2}$% bonds, which she purchased at $955 each. If the par value of each of these bonds is $1,000, how large were the interest payments that Miss Barton received each year?

2. On July 19, Paul Ciolli received his semiannual interest payment on the three Western Railroad $5\frac{1}{4}$% bonds that he bought for

$1,016.25 each. The par value of each bond is $1,000. What was the amount of interest that he received?

3. On March 1, the Atlantic Union Corporation mailed its quarterly interest checks to the owners of its $7\frac{3}{4}\%$ bonds. If each bond had a par value of $500, how large a check would the owner of eight bonds receive?

4. Mrs. Rita Valdez owned six Hudson Gas Company $9\frac{1}{8}\%$ coupon bonds. Although the par value of these bonds was $500, she had purchased them for $375 each. On the date that the annual interest fell due, Mrs. Valdez clipped the coupons from the bonds and presented the coupons at her bank for payment. How large an amount did Mrs. Valdez receive?

UNIT

ACCRUED INTEREST ON BONDS

Case Problem Herbert Wallace holds six $7\frac{1}{2}\%$ $1,000 corporate bonds issued by Linkmeyer Associates. The interest dates on the bonds are May 1 and November 1. On June 18, Mr. Wallace, who needed cash, sold one of the bonds.

Discussion Questions
1. Why is Mr. Wallace entitled to interest on the bond that was sold?
2. For how many days will the interest be computed? How much will he receive?

A bond is in reality a long-term note on which interest is being accumulated continuously. This interest is paid to bondholders annually, semiannually, or quarterly. If payments, for example are made semiannually, the corporation may send out checks on May 1 and November 1 each year. However, if a bondholder were to sell one of the corporation bonds on, say, June 18, it would be unfair to him if he did not receive the interest that had accumulated on the bond from May 1 to June 18. Therefore, the buyer of Mr. Wallace's bond in the Case Problem must pay Mr. Wallace not only the market value of the bond but also all the interest that has accumulated from the date on which interest was last paid until the date the bond is sold. This accumulated interest is called *accrued interest.*

Although the buyer pays the accrued interest to Mr. Wallace at the time of the purchase, this money should not be considered part of the cost of purchase.

Because the buyer receives interest for the *entire* period on the next interest date, he is reimbursed for the accrued interest he paid.

Interest on the bond sold by Mr. Wallace would have accrued from May 1 to June 18, or 48 days (May 1 to May 31 is 30 days plus 18 days in June). The accrued interest the buyer will have to pay can be found as follows:

$$I = P \times R \times T$$

$$I = \$1,000 \times 7\tfrac{1}{2}\% \times \frac{48 \text{ days}}{360 \text{ days in banker's year}}$$

$$= \$75 \times \frac{48}{360}$$

$$= \$75 \times \frac{2}{15}$$

$$= \$10, \text{ accrued interest}$$

Exercises

1. Find the accrued interest on each bond transaction.

Trans- action	Par Value	Interest Rate	Interest Dates	Sale Date	No. of Bonds	Accrued Interest
a	$1,000	6%	May 1 and Nov. 1	June 28	1	$ _____
b	$1,000	8%	Apr. 1 and Oct. 1	July 6	2	$ _____
c	$1,000	$7\tfrac{1}{2}\%$	Apr. 1 and Oct. 1	May 30	4	$ _____
d	$ 500	9%	June 1 and Dec. 1	Oct. 29	1	$ _____
e	$ 500	$8\tfrac{1}{2}\%$	May 1 and Nov. 1	Dec. 17	2	$ _____
f	$1,000	$6\tfrac{3}{4}\%$	Feb. 1 and Aug. 1	May 19	3	$ _____

2. Referring to the quotations on page 469, find the accrued interest on each bond sale. Assume that each transaction took place on November 3 and that all the companies cited have been paying their interest regularly.

Trans- action	Company	Par Value	Interest Dates	No. of Bonds	Accrued Interest
a	Albans	$1,000	Feb. 1 and Aug. 1	1	$ _____
b	Danv L&P	$1,000	Apr. 1 and Oct. 1	2	$ _____
c	Carlson Sh	$1,000	June 1 and Dec. 1	1	$ _____
d	Cumb W	$1,000	May 1 and Nov. 1	3	$ _____
e	Draper Ind	$1,000	Mar. 1 and Sept. 1	5	$ _____

Business Applications

1. Patsy Emery purchased three Union Gas Corporation 6% bonds ($1,000 par) at 93 on June 25. If the interest dates on these bonds are May 1 and November 1, what was the total of the accrued interest and the cost of the bonds?

2. On April 4, R. W. Thornton purchased two Wheeling Steel $7\frac{3}{4}$% bonds ($1,000 par) at $94\frac{1}{2}$. Interest on these bonds is payable June 1 and December 1 each year. What was the total cost of these bonds to Mr. Thornton including the accrued interest?

3. Wilbur Towne sold five World Hotel 8% bonds ($1,000 par) at $102\frac{1}{2}$ on September 17. These bonds bear interest on April 1 and October 1 of each year. What was the total of the accrued interest and the selling price on the bonds?

UNIT 8

FINDING RATE OF RETURN ON INVESTMENTS

Case Problem   Marilyn Loeffler has several investments, including corporation stock, series H bonds, corporation bonds, and a savings account in the Home State National Bank.

Discussion Questions

1. How can Miss Loeffler find out which of her investments is the most profitable?
2. What other factors besides profitability will determine the type of investment to choose?

The safest place to invest money is in a savings account. The savings bank pays a definite rate of interest. Deposits up to $40,000 are insured through the federal government. And you always know just what your money is earning.

Investments in government bonds, Series E and Series H, also give a definite rate of return and are guaranteed by the government. Secured bonds are generally almost as safe as savings accounts. However, should you need money quickly, it is sometimes difficult to sell them, and there is a chance that the selling price may change somewhat from the price you paid for the bond. In general, it is wise to invest in bonds only if they earn a better rate than you can get in a savings account. Some bonds may also have income tax advantages.

Stocks are the investment involving the most risk because stock prices may go sharply up or down. Investors often buy stocks not only for the income which they hope to receive through dividends but also for the profit they expect to make if the price per share goes up. If investors can sell stocks at a higher price than the one they paid per share, they have made a profit over and above the dividend payment. Of course, there is also the possibility that a stock may neither make its interest payment nor increase in price.

RATE OF RETURN

In order to be able to invest wisely, an investor must know the rate of return on his investment. The *rate of return* is a percent determined by dividing the number of dollars profit by the number of dollars invested.

Rate of Return on Savings Accounts

The percent of interest on a savings account is always stated by the bank. However, because savings bank interest is compounded, you actually earn more than the stated percent. You may have noticed savings banks advertising an interest rate of 5% which yields, or gives, a return of 5.27% because interest is compounded from the date of deposit until the date of withdrawal.

Rate of Return on Stock Investments

The rate of return on stocks is found by dividing the amount earned by the amount invested. Notice that the par value is of no consequence here. The question is, "What percent is the money you have actually put into the purchase of the stock earning for you?" Thus, if a person invested $200 in stocks that paid $14 in annual dividends, the rate of return would be 7%.

$$\frac{\$14}{\$200} = \frac{\$7}{\$100} = .07 = 7\%$$

Example 1:

Janice Conrad purchased 100 shares of General Baking Company stock at $9\frac{3}{8}$. If Ms. Conrad received a 60-cent yearly dividend on each share, what rate of return was she receiving on her investment?

Solution:

Divide the dividend per share by the cost per share.

$.60 ÷ $9.375 = .064, or 6.4%, rate of return

Explanation:

Notice that the 100 shares purchased were not used in the solution. Since dividends are always declared on the basis of one share, the cost of one share is all that is needed to determine the rate of return.

In the purchase of preferred stock, the investor can usually predict what his rate of return will be. When these stocks are issued, the company pledges itself to pay a certain fixed rate of the par value of the stock if the earnings permit the payment of a dividend. On the basis of the rate pledged, the purchaser can determine the actual rate of return that he will receive.

Example 2:

Robert Brant purchased 75 shares of Samuels Corporation $4\frac{1}{2}$% preferred stock at $45\frac{1}{4}$ a share. What rate of return was he receiving on this investment if the par value of the stock was $50?

Solution:

1. Multiply the par value of the stock by the preferred rate to find the dividend per share.

$$\$50 \times 4\frac{1}{2}\% = \$2.25, \text{ dividend per share}$$

2. Divide the dividend per share by the purchase price to find the rate of return.

$$\$2.25 \div \$45.25 = .0497, \text{ or } 4.97\%, \text{ rate of return}$$

Exercises

1. Find the rate of return to the nearest tenth of a percent on each stock purchase.

Purchase	Price per Share	Yearly Dividend	Rate of Return
a	$75	$2.50	_____ %
b	$19	$1.25	_____ %
c	58\frac{1}{2}$	$3.35	_____ %
d	16\frac{3}{4}$	$1.20	_____ %
e	18\frac{1}{8}$	$1.60	_____ %
f	12\frac{3}{8}$	$1.00	_____ %
g	$ 8$\frac{7}{8}$	$ .60	_____ %
h	62\frac{5}{8}$	$ .90	_____ %

2. Find the rate of return to the nearest tenth of a percent on each preferred stock purchase.

Purchase	Price per Share	Par Value	Dividend Percent	Dividend Amount	Rate of Return
a	$ 91	$100	$4\frac{1}{2}$	$_____	_____%
b	$ 42	$ 50	$2\frac{1}{4}$	$_____	_____%
c	$154	$100	7	$_____	_____%
d	$ 47\frac{1}{2}	$ 50	$3\frac{1}{2}$	$_____	_____%
e	$ 45\frac{1}{4}	$ 50	$4\frac{1}{2}$	$_____	_____%
f	$ 93\frac{3}{8}	$100	4.2	$_____	_____%

3. Using the stock quotations in the table on page 460, find the rate of return to the nearest tenth of a percent on each stock purchase.

Purchase	Company	Purchase Range	Price per Share	Dividend That Year	Rate of Return
a	Ivy-Dolman	Low	$_____	$_____	_____%
b	Gem Instr	Low	$_____	$_____	_____%
c	Lyden Steel	First	$_____	$_____	_____%
d	Hygrade Bro	High	$_____	$_____	_____%
e	Gerar Mov	Low	$_____	$_____	_____%
f	Harrig Tir	High	$_____	$_____	_____%

Rate of Return on Bond Investments

Bonds carry a stated rate of interest. However, to find the rate of return, just as with stock investments, the investor wishes to know what percent he is earning on the amount of money that has been invested. The rate of return is therefore computed by dividing the amount earned (interest for the year) by the amount invested (market price, *not* par).

Example:

Walter Blass recently purchased three $5\frac{1}{2}$% bonds at $95\frac{3}{4}$. The par value of the bonds is $1,000. What rate of return is Mr. Blass receiving?

Solution:

You found out earlier that the interest on bonds is found by multiplying the par value by the annual guaranteed rate of interest. After you find the actual yearly return, find the rate of return by dividing the annual interest by the purchase price.

$$I = P \times R \times T$$
$$= \$1{,}000 \times 5\tfrac{1}{2}\% \times 1 \text{ year}$$
$$= \$1{,}000 \times .055 \times 1$$
$$= \$55, \text{ yearly interest per bond}$$

$$\text{Rate of return} = \text{Interest} \div \text{Purchase price}$$
$$= \$55 \div \$957.50$$
$$= .057, \text{ or } 5.7\%, \text{ rate of return}$$

The total bond purchase of three bonds did not enter into the computation because the rate of return on one bond is the same as the rate of return on all the bonds.

Exercises

Find the rate of return to the nearest tenth of a percent on each bond purchase.

No.	Par Value	Market Value	Guaranteed Annual Interest	Rate of Return
1	$1,000	94	4%	_____ %
2	$1,000	102	$5\tfrac{1}{2}\%$	_____ %
3	$1,000	$97\tfrac{1}{2}$	$6\tfrac{1}{2}\%$	_____ %
4	$1,000	$105\tfrac{3}{4}$	$5\tfrac{1}{4}\%$	_____ %
5	$1,000	$84\tfrac{1}{4}$	4%	_____ %
6	$1,000	$86\tfrac{1}{4}$	$4\tfrac{1}{2}\%$	_____ %
7	$1,000	$113\tfrac{1}{4}$	$7\tfrac{1}{2}\%$	_____ %
8	$1,000	$66\tfrac{1}{2}$	8%	_____ %
9	$1,000	$78\tfrac{1}{4}$	$7\tfrac{7}{8}\%$	_____ %
10	$1,000	$92\tfrac{3}{4}$	4.60%	_____ %

Business Applications

1. L. G. Cartwright purchased preferred stock at a total cost of $60 a share. The company paid an annual dividend of 6% on the par value of $50. What rate of return did Mr. Cartwright receive on his investment? Express your answer to the nearest tenth of a percent.

2. A share of preferred stock in the Tempered Steel Corporation costs a buyer $62. The company pays an annual dividend of 5% on the

par value of $50. What rate of return to the nearest tenth of a percent will a purchaser make on an investment in Tempered Steel stocks?

3. During a recent year, Ruth Conley received dividends of $48, $64, $82.50, and $90 from stock that she held in four different companies. If her total investment was $12,450, what percent of the investment did the dividends represent? Give your answer to the nearest tenth of a percent.

4. Charles Darby purchased 30 shares of stock for $1,440. During the three years that he had the stock, he received a quarterly dividend of 65 cents a share. At the end of the three years, he sold the stock and received $1,827 from his broker. All charges on the sale had already been deducted. What was Mr. Darby's total gain during the three years?

5. On June 15, Paul Kernan purchased two National Ore Corporation $6\frac{3}{4}\%$ bonds ($1,000 par) at $88\frac{3}{4}$. What rate of return did Mr. Kernan expect on his investment?

6. What rate of return would the purchaser of 3% municipal bonds receive on his investment if he purchased them at $46\frac{1}{2}$ and the par value of each bond is $1,000?

7. Adam Parker bought five $4\frac{3}{4}\%$ bonds at $82\frac{3}{4}$. What rate of return did he receive if the par value of these bonds is $1,000?

8. Edith O'Shea has the choice of buying a $6\frac{1}{4}\%$ $1,000 bond at 98, or 10 shares of 6% preferred stock par valued at $100 each at 101. (a) Which would give her the greater rate of return? (b) by how much?

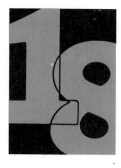

REVIEW EXERCISES FOR CHAPTER 18

1. Complete the table below, using the compound-interest table on page 448.

Depositor	Amount on Deposit	Interest Rate	Time on Deposit	Compounded	Compound Amount
a	$ 600	6%	2 years	Annually	$_____
b	$ 1,800	7%	5 years	Semiannually	$_____
c	$15,000	6%	6 years	Quarterly	$_____
d	$ 6,400	6%	4 years	Semiannually	$_____
e	$ 4,800	5%	6 years	Quarterly	$_____

2. Find the dividends that the owners of the following shares of common stock would receive per year.

Owner	No. of Shares	Dividend	Total Dividends
a	200	35¢ quarterly	$_____
b	52	62½¢ semiannually	$_____

3. How large would the quarterly dividend be for the owner of 100 shares of $5\frac{1}{2}$% preferred stock having a par value of $25?

4. Matthew Carr loaned John Fleming $2,500 for one year with interest at 6%. In computing the following, use the table on page 448 where possible.
   a. If the interest is computed semiannually and added to the loan, how much will be due Mr. Carr at the end of the year?
   b. How much more would Mr. Carr receive at the end of the year if the interest were computed quarterly and added to the loan?

5. The sum of $5,000 is loaned for a period of three years at an interest rate of 8%.

a. How much interest will the lender receive during the three-year period if simple interest is paid on the loan?

b. If the interest is compounded annually and paid in one amount at the end of the three-year period, how much interest will the lender receive?

c. How much will the lender receive at the end of the three-year period if the interest is computed semiannually?

d. How much will be needed to repay the loan at the end of the three-year period if the interest is compounded quarterly?

6. Lorna Townsend purchased 60 shares of Mabley-Davis at 80½. If the company has been paying a yearly dividend on stock of $3, what rate of return can Miss Townsend look forward to on her investment?

7. A 5½% preferred stock having a par value of $50 is selling for 52¾. What rate of return would a purchaser of this stock receive?

8. George Swenson purchased 60 shares of stock at $32 per share. During the three years he kept the stock, the company paid a quarterly dividend of 30 cents per share. When Mr. Swenson sold the stock, he received $2,896 after all expenses were deducted. What was Mr. Swenson's rate of return on his original investment?

9. Find the interest for the period shown for each bond.

No.	Market Value	Par Value	Interest Rate	Period	Interest
a	97¾	$1,000	4%	Annually	$_____
b	105	$1,000	4½%	Semiannually	$_____
c	101⅝	$1,000	3¾%	Quarterly	$_____

10. How much annual interest is collected by the owner of five 5⅞% bonds with a par value of $1,000 that were purchased at 92¾?

11. What is the accrued interest on two 6% bonds with a par value of $1,000 that were purchased on July 16 if the interest is paid semiannually on May 1 and November 1?

12. Assuming that the transactions recorded on page 469 took place on November 3, find the accrued interest on all the Ayres Steel Company bonds that were sold that day. The interest dates were February 1 and August 1.

13. What rate of return will Jean Romano receive on the purchase of a 6½% North American Corporation bond at 87¼? The par value of the bond is $1,000.

CHAPTER 19
CONSUMER
CREDIT

Charles and Mary Gibson, newlyweds, are gradually replacing the hand-me-down furniture donated by various relatives. Money, however, is a problem. Although both Gibsons have good jobs, they have very little money at their disposal. They recently bought a co-op apartment and are paying off a $4,000 loan they needed for the down payment.

"Look at this advertisement, Charlie," says Mary as she studies the Sunday newspaper supplements. "Here's the mod den chair we want, and it's on sale. We can pay for it in a year for only $15 a month."

"What's the cash price?" asks her husband.

"$149.95."

Some day you will probably have to make the decision whether to buy something "on time" or to wait until you have enough money to pay cash. This decision faces nearly every consumer who wants a new car, a trip to Europe, a refrigerator, a set of encyclopedias, or a new Easter outfit.

Several different names are given to *deferred-payment plans*—revolving charge account, installment account, budget account, easy-payment plan, modernizing credit plan, and so on. All operate under the same principle, however; the buyer pays extra for the buy-now-pay-later privilege. What he pays may be called a *finance charge, carrying charge,* or *service charge.* But whatever it's called, the amount is based on the cost of the purchase and the length of time the buyer takes to pay for it.

In effect, then, the buyer is paying interest because he is using the seller's money instead of his own. The seller also charges more because it costs him more to provide this service—not only must he hire additional people to handle the credit accounts, but the cost of making collections and absorbing the bad debts of those who do not pay can be considerable.

Before you sign a contract for the purchase of goods or services on a deferred-payment plan, read it carefully. The seller is required to show the annual interest rate you are being charged in the contract. This regulation comes under the Truth-in-Lending law enacted by the federal government.

UNIT

THE COST OF INSTALLMENT CREDIT

Case Problem Sara Weber is shopping for a new sofa for her apartment. One that she especially likes was advertised at the price of $280. Upon inquiry at the store, Miss Weber learns that she can buy the sofa under the store's "easy-payment" plan by paying $40 down and $18 a month for 15 months.

Discussion Questions

1. What is the advantage to Miss Weber of buying the sofa "on time"? the disadvantage?
2. How much would Miss Weber save by paying cash?

The advantage to Miss Weber of buying the sofa "on time" is that she can have the use of it while she is paying for it. The disadvantage, of course, is that she will have to pay more under the easy-payment, or installment, plan than if she paid cash.

FINDING THE FINANCE CHARGE

The regular selling price of a unit of merchandise is the *cash price*. The amount a buyer pays for a purchase over the cash price is called the *finance charge*. To find the finance charge:
1. Add the down payment to the sum of the monthly payments. The result is the *installment price*.
2. Subtract from the installment price the cash price of the article. The difference is the finance charge.

How much will the finance charge to Sara Weber be if she buys the sofa on the store's easy-payment plan?

1. Add the down payment to the sum of monthly payments to find the installment price.

  $ 40 down payment
  _270_ add the sum of the monthly payments ($18 × 15)
  $310 installment price

2. Subtract the cash price from the installment price to find the finance charge.

$310
$\underline{280}$ less cash price
$ 30 finance charge

Miss Weber is paying $30 more for the sofa under the installment plan than she would have paid if she bought it for cash.

Exercises

Find the finance charge on each of the purchases in the following table.

No.	Merchandise	Cash Price	Down Pay-ment	No. of Pay-ments	Amount of Each Payment	Finance Charge
1	Jacket	$ 55.00	$20.00	8	$5.00	$_____
2	Clock radio	$ 30.00	$ 8.00	6	$4.00	$_____
3	Bike	$ 47.00	$ 7.50	7	$6.00	$_____
4	Ski equipment	$ 62.50	$10.50	10	$5.50	$_____
5	Typewriter	$112.75	$12.75	12	$8.75	$_____
6	Tape player	$163.40	$25.00	18	$8.25	$_____

FINDING THE PERCENT OF FINANCE CHARGE

In comparing the cost of an installment purchase with the cash price, it is often important to know the percent of finance charge, or more properly, by what *percent* the installment price exceeds the cash price. This is determined by dividing the finance charge by the cash price.

Example:

George Carver purchased a power lawn mower on the installment plan. The installment price was $115, and the cash price was $100. (a) What was the finance charge? (b) By what percent did the installment price exceed the cash price?

Solution:

$115 installment price
$\underline{100}$ less cash price
$ 15 finance charge

$15 (finance charge) ÷ $100 (cash price) = 15%, percent by which
the installment price exceeds the cash price

Exercises

Find the finance charge and the percent by which the installment price exceeds the cash price (to the nearest tenth of a percent) on each purchase.

No.	Merchandise	Cash Price	Down Payment	No. of Payments	Amount of Payment	Finance Charge	Percent in Excess
1	Set of encyclopedias	$350.00	$ 40.00	24	$15.00	$_____	_____%
2	Sewing machine	$225.00	$ 24.00	14	$16.50	$_____	_____%
3	Coat	$ 40.00	$ 11.20	7	$ 5.00	$_____	_____%
4	Television set	$188.00	$ 44.40	12	$13.22	$_____	_____%
5	Used car	$575.00	$ 57.50	10	$63.25	$_____	_____%
6	Piano	$800.00	$120.00	20	$38.48	$_____	_____%

FINDING THE INSTALLMENT PAYMENT

Often, the terms of an installment sale require a certain percentage as down payment. The amount of the installment payment for the remainder depends upon three factors:
1. the purchase price still to be paid
2. the amount of the finance charge
3. the number of installments to be made

The greater the number of installments, the larger will be the finance charge. This is so because a large part of the finance charge consists of interest, and time, as you already know, is one of the factors involved in computing interest. In addition, the longer the debt is outstanding, the more bookkeeping costs retailers have and the greater the risk that they will not collect all the money outstanding.

Example:

Edna Towan purchases a stereo set on the installment plan. The cash price is $150, and she is required to pay $33\frac{1}{3}\%$ as a down payment. If the finance charges amount to $10.50, and she wishes to pay the amount outstanding in ten monthly installments, what would be the amount of each installment?

Solution:

Down payment: $33\frac{1}{3}\% \times \$150 = \$50$
Still to be paid:

$$\begin{array}{ll} \$150.00 - \$50.00 = \$100.00 & \text{balance of cash price} \\ \underline{\hspace{1.3cm} 10.50} & \text{finance charges} \\ \$110.50 & \text{total due} \end{array}$$

$110.50 \div 10$ (the number of installments) $= \$11.05$ each installment

Exercises

Find the installment payment for each of the following articles.

	Cash Price of Article	Down Payment	Finance Charge	No. of Payments	Amount of Each Payment
1.	$120.00	25%	$ 8.50	10	$_____
2.	$250.00	30%	$24.00	12	$_____
3.	$ 67.50	40%	$ 5.25	15	$_____
4.	$480.00	33⅓%	$37.50	18	$_____
5.	$375.00	35%	$47.50	24	$_____

Business Applications

1. Amanda Kitt bought a boat for $75 down and $40 a month for six months. If she had paid cash, it would have cost her $300. What was the finance charge on the purchase?

2. Lawrence Brothers Furniture advertised a dining room suite for $335.50. The suite may be purchased on the installment plan for 25 monthly payments of $15.45 each. No down payment is required. What is the finance charge?

3. A storage shed can be purchased for $399.95 cash or $49.95 down and $12.25 a month for 36 months. How large is the finance charge? By what percent does the installment price exceed the cash price? (Round off to the nearest tenth of a percent.)

4. Burt's Cycle Shop offered to sell a $275 used motorcycle for 10% down and $18.20 a month for 18 months. Find (a) the finance charge and (b) the percent, to the nearest tenth of a percent, by which the installment price exceeds the cash price.

5. Holmes Appliances advertised a color television-stereo combination at $895 cash or 15% down and 30 months to pay. Prospective buyers were told that the monthly payments would amount to $29.42. If the set is purchased on the deferred-payment plan, what finance charge will the buyer have to pay?

6. Arthur Durant can purchase a patio set for $250 cash. If he prefers, however, he can buy this same set by paying $60 down and making 12 monthly payments of $18 each. To the nearest tenth of a percent, by what percent will the installment price exceed the cash price?

7. R. B. Dudley purchased a used car listed at a selling price of $720. He paid 30% down and agreed to pay the remaining balance, plus a carrying charge of $60.48, in 12 equal monthly installments. What was the amount of each monthly installment?

8. Ann Gorman bought wall-to-wall carpeting at a selling price of $1,240. She paid one-fourth down at the time of purchase and agreed to pay the remainder, plus a carrying charge of $139.50, in 15 equal monthly installments. How large was each installment?

9. A freezer can be purchased for $375 cash or bought on the installment plan by paying 10% extra. An installment purchaser made a down payment of $120 and agreed to pay $9.75 each month. How many months will she have to pay for this purchase?

UNIT

FINDING THE ANNUAL RATE OF INTEREST

Case Problem Josh Richards has just purchased a Miracle Sound electronic organ from the Carleton Music Company. The cash price of the organ is $495. However, Mr. Richards did not have that much money, and he decided to purchase the organ on the store's deferred-payment plan. This plan required a down payment of $45 and 20 payments of $26 each.

Discussion Questions
1. What is the amount Mr. Richards is being charged to buy the organ "on time"?
2. What is the annual rate of interest?

As you know, Mr. Richards can determine the finance charge as follows:

$ 45 down payment
 520 add the sum of the monthly payments (20 × $26)
$565 installment price
 495 less cash price
$ 70 finance charge

Mr. Richards is paying Carleton Music Company $70 for the use of their money. To find the annual rate of interest, you must first determine how much he is actually borrowing; this amount is called the *principal of original debt*. The principal is found by subtracting the down payment from the cash price.

$495 cash price
−45 less down payment
$450 principal of original debt

The principal of original debt, $450, can be considered a loan made by Carleton Music Company to Mr. Richards.

The Truth-in-Lending law, which became effective in 1969, requires that the seller reveal to the buyer the annual percent of interest he is being charged. To assist business people in computing annual interest rates under this law, the federal government provides the necessary tables. The partial table on the facing page applies to equal monthly payment plans.

HOW TO USE THE TABLE

To use the table for computing annual percent rates for equal monthly payments, proceed as follows:

1. First find the rate being charged on the principal.

$$Rate = \frac{Percentage}{Base}$$

$$Rate = \frac{70}{450} = .1556$$

For purposes of convenience in using the table, we multiply this by 100 to find the finance charge per $100.

.1556 × $100 = $15.56, finance charge per $100 of amount financed

2. Follow down the left-hand column of the table to the line for 20 months. Move your finger across this row until you find the number nearest $15.56. In this instance, it is $15.54. At the top of the column under which $15.54 appears is the annual percent—17%—that Mr. Richards is paying on his purchase. This is often called the *true interest rate*.

Number of Payments	Annual Percent (Finance Charge per $100 of Amount Financed)															
	14.00%	14.25%	14.50%	14.75%	15.00%	15.25%	15.50%	15.75%	16.00%	16.25%	16.50%	16.75%	17.00%	17.25%	17.50%	17.75%
1	1.17	1.19	1.21	1.23	1.25	1.27	1.29	1.31	1.33	1.35	1.37	1.40	1.42	1.44	1.46	1.48
2	1.75	1.78	1.82	1.85	1.88	1.91	1.94	1.97	2.00	2.04	2.07	2.10	2.13	2.16	2.19	2.22
3	2.34	2.38	2.43	2.47	2.51	2.55	2.59	2.64	2.68	2.72	2.76	2.80	2.85	2.89	2.93	2.97
4	2.93	2.99	3.04	3.09	3.14	3.20	3.25	3.30	3.36	3.41	3.46	3.51	3.57	3.62	3.67	3.73
5	3.53	3.59	3.65	3.72	3.78	3.84	3.91	3.97	4.04	4.10	4.16	4.23	4.29	4.35	4.42	4.48
6	4.12	4.20	4.27	4.35	4.42	4.49	4.57	4.64	4.72	4.79	4.87	4.94	5.02	5.09	5.17	5.24
7	4.72	4.81	4.89	4.98	5.06	5.15	5.23	5.32	5.40	5.49	5.58	5.66	5.75	5.83	5.92	6.00
8	5.32	5.42	5.51	5.61	5.71	5.80	5.90	6.00	6.09	6.19	6.29	6.38	6.48	6.58	6.67	6.77
9	5.92	6.03	6.14	6.25	6.35	6.46	6.57	6.68	6.78	6.89	7.00	7.11	7.22	7.32	7.43	7.54
10	6.53	6.65	6.77	6.88	7.00	7.12	7.24	7.36	7.48	7.60	7.72	7.84	7.96	8.08	8.19	8.31
11	7.14	7.27	7.40	7.53	7.66	7.79	7.92	8.05	8.18	8.31	8.44	8.57	8.70	8.83	8.96	9.09
12	7.74	7.89	8.03	8.17	8.31	8.45	8.59	8.74	8.88	9.02	9.16	9.30	9.45	9.59	9.73	9.87
13	8.36	8.51	8.66	8.81	8.97	9.12	9.27	9.43	9.58	9.73	9.89	10.04	10.20	10.35	10.50	10.66
14	8.97	9.13	9.30	9.46	9.63	9.79	9.96	10.12	10.29	10.45	10.62	10.78	10.95	11.11	11.28	11.45
15	9.59	9.76	9.94	10.11	10.29	10.47	10.64	10.82	11.00	11.17	11.35	11.53	11.71	11.88	12.06	12.24
16	10.20	10.39	10.58	10.77	10.95	11.14	11.33	11.52	11.71	11.90	12.09	12.28	12.46	12.65	12.84	13.03
17	10.82	11.02	11.22	11.42	11.62	11.82	12.02	12.22	12.42	12.62	12.83	13.03	13.23	13.43	13.63	13.83
18	11.45	11.66	11.87	12.08	12.29	12.50	12.72	12.93	13.14	13.35	13.57	13.78	13.99	14.21	14.42	14.64
19	12.07	12.30	12.52	12.74	12.97	13.19	13.41	13.64	13.86	14.09	14.31	14.54	14.76	14.99	15.22	15.44
20	12.70	12.93	13.17	13.41	13.64	13.88	14.11	14.35	14.59	14.82	15.06	15.30	15.54	15.77	16.01	16.25
21	13.33	13.58	13.82	14.07	14.32	14.57	14.82	15.06	15.31	15.56	15.81	16.06	16.31	16.56	16.81	17.07
22	13.96	14.22	14.48	14.74	15.00	15.26	15.52	15.78	16.04	16.30	16.57	16.83	17.09	17.36	17.62	17.88
23	14.59	14.87	15.14	15.41	15.68	15.96	16.23	16.50	16.78	17.05	17.32	17.60	17.88	18.15	18.43	18.70
24	15.23	15.51	15.80	16.08	16.37	16.65	16.94	17.22	17.51	17.80	18.09	18.37	18.66	18.95	19.24	19.53
25	15.87	16.17	16.46	16.76	17.06	17.35	17.65	17.95	18.25	18.55	18.85	19.15	19.45	19.75	20.05	20.36
26	16.51	16.82	17.13	17.44	17.75	18.06	18.37	18.68	18.99	19.30	19.62	19.93	20.24	20.56	20.87	21.19
27	17.15	17.47	17.80	18.12	18.44	18.76	19.09	19.41	19.74	20.06	20.39	20.71	21.04	21.37	21.69	22.02
28	17.80	18.13	18.47	18.80	19.14	19.47	19.81	20.15	20.48	20.82	21.16	21.50	21.84	22.18	22.52	22.86
29	18.45	18.79	19.14	19.49	19.83	20.18	20.53	20.88	21.23	21.58	21.94	22.29	22.64	22.99	23.35	23.70
30	19.10	19.45	19.81	20.17	20.54	20.90	21.26	21.62	21.99	22.35	22.72	23.08	23.45	23.81	24.18	24.55

There are two reasons why the true interest rate is different from the .1556 rate which we originally computed. One is that Mr. Richards has 20 months to pay, and we did our computation on the basis of one year. The longer period of time would lower the interest rate. The second reason is that Mr. Richards is not borrowing $450 for the full 20 months. Every time he makes an installment payment, he reduces his principal, so the average amount borrowed is a great deal less than $450. This would raise the rate.

Exercises

To the nearest tenth of a percent, what annual rate of interest will an installment purchaser have to pay for each of the following purchases?

No.	Article	Cash Price	Down Payment	Principal of Original Debt	Number of Payments	Monthly Payment	Finance Charge	Rate of Interest
1	Refrigerator	$280.00	$40.00	$ _____	16	$16.75	$ _____	_____ %
2	Boat	$760.00	$90.00	$ _____	15	$50.00	$ _____	_____ %
3	Color TV	$270.00	$65.00	$ _____	20	$11.75	$ _____	_____ %
4	Silverware	$ 97.50	$14.25	$ _____	6	$14.50	$ _____	_____ %
5	Diamond ring	$479.00	$20.00	$ _____	10	$49.00	$ _____	_____ %

Business Applications

1. Kenneth Stillman bought a used car at $300 down and $40 a month for 24 months. If he had paid cash, the car would have cost him $1,120. What annual rate of interest did Mr. Stillman have to pay? Refer to the table on page 491 to compute the annual rate.

2. Gloria Atwater purchased an electric guitar on a deferred-payment plan. She paid $14.95 down and agreed to pay $10 a month for 8 months. If Miss Atwater had bought the guitar for cash, she would have paid $90.50. What annual rate of interest is she paying? Use the table on page 491.

3. The Shopper's Mart advertised a desk at the cash price of $125. An installment buyer, however, could buy the desk with a down payment of $16.25 and $7.50 a month for 16 months. What rate of interest will Brenda Mayhew pay if she buys the desk on the installment plan?

4. Mrs. Emily Hogarth saw an advertisement for carpeting at the cash price of $150. The advertisement also stated that on the deferred-payment plan, the purchaser would make no down payment and could have the carpeting for 18 payments at $9.50. If she bought the carpeting on the deferred-payment plan, what annual rate of interest would Mrs. Hogarth pay?

REVIEW EXERCISES FOR CHAPTER 19

1. Find the amount by which the installment price exceeds the cash price for each purchase.

No.	Cash Price	Down Payment	No. of Payments	Monthly Payment	Installment Price	Finance Charge
a	$498.00	$ 74.60	18	$26.36	$_____	$_____
b	$133.20	$ 54.00	8	$10.96	$_____	$_____
c	$135.00	$ 26.00	10	$12.40	$_____	$_____
d	$706.60	$141.00	36	$17.60	$_____	$_____
e	$ 96.00	$ 18.00	8	$12.50	$_____	$_____

2. Refer to the table on page 491 to find the annual rate of interest on each purchase.

No.	Cash Price	Down Payment	No. of Payments	Monthly Payment	Rate of Interest
a	$240.00	$ 30.00	12	$19.00	_____%
b	$165.00	$ 25.00	13	$11.80	_____%
c	$530.00	$ 60.00	24	$22.56	_____%
d	$690.00	$100.00	30	$23.50	_____%

3. A lamp can be purchased with $120 cash or with an easy-payment plan for $15 down and $2.50 a week for 46 weeks. What is the finance charge on this purchase?

4. Harvey Michaelson bought a garbage disposal unit on the following terms: $27.50 down and $9.95 a month for 12 months. He could have purchased the unit for $129.95 cash. How much lower was the cash price than the installment price?

5. Jim and Pat Thompson purchased a piano for $547.50, paying 20% down. The seller added 20% to the remainder for installment charges. If the contract stipulated that the debt be paid off in 36 months, what will be the amount of each monthly payment?

6. One retailer charges $1\frac{1}{2}$% interest per month on the unpaid balance of each customer's account. Under Truth-in-Lending regulations, what must the retailer indicate on the sales contract as the annual interest rate?

7. The Breton Falls Department Store charges customers $1\frac{1}{2}$% interest each month on the unpaid balance. Mrs. Hazel Wirtz's unpaid balance from last month amounted to $162.40. How much will be added to her balance for interest?

CHAPTER 20
TAXES

Everybody complains about taxes, and it is true that each year the taxes we pay seem to increase. But taxes have always been one of the favorite gripes of people since history was first recorded. The fact is that people have found no better way to obtain money needed to finance the needs of government than through taxation. Today we pay a tax on most of the things we buy. Taxes are sometimes imposed by three different governments—federal, state, and local (city). We may pay a tax on our property, both *real* (land and buildings, for example) and *personal* (cars, for example). The largest tax of all, and the one from which the federal government derives the greatest portion of the money it needs, is the *income tax*. More and more states and cities are levying taxes on income.

Because tax rates are liable to change frequently, the specific tax tables used in this chapter are cited only for the sake of illustration. Once you understand the procedures used in computing taxes and tax rates, you can apply the procedures to any new rates or tables.

Taxes are very much a part of our daily lives and will continue to be. In this chapter, you will learn how the various taxes that you pay or can expect to pay in the future are computed.

UNIT

1

SALES TAXES

Case Problem   Floyd and Jo Lindley live in Norwalk, Connecticut, about 45 miles away from New York City. Recently they purchased a set of redwood patio furniture priced at $230 from a department store in New York City. The sales ticket that accompanied the furniture showed exactly the amount of $230, which the Lindleys paid by check.

Jim and Leta Morris, who live in New York City, purchased the same set of furniture from the same department store for their apartment terrace. However, the sales ticket that accompanied the furniture upon delivery was in the amount of $246.10.

Discussion Questions

1. How much more did the Morrises have to pay for the same furniture than the Lindleys paid?
2. What do you think accounts for the difference in price?

Most of the 50 states have some form of sales tax on goods and services purchased by consumers and businesses; increasingly, local city governments have also begun to levy sales taxes. The rate of the tax, expressed as a percent, varies both from state to state and from community to community. Sales taxes are charged on most of the articles you purchase at local stores; in addition, they are charged on water and gas bills, telephone service, hotel and motel services, airplane tickets, and so on. Computing the sales tax is simply an application of the principles you studied earlier in this course.

Example 1:
S. H. Tabler purchased a bedroom suite for $485. If the state sales tax is $3\frac{1}{2}\%$ and there is no local tax, what is the actual amount Mr. Tabler will have to pay for the suite?

Solution:
Cost of suite ($485) × tax rate ($3\frac{1}{2}\%$) = $16.975, or $16.98
Total price = $485 + $16.98
$\qquad\qquad$ = $501.98

Example 2:
The tag on a power lawn mower shows the selling price to be $189.50. If the state sales tax is 2% and the city tax is 3%, how much will George Lutz have to pay for the mower?

Solution:
2% + 3% = 5%, total tax rate
$189.50 × 5% = $9.475, or $9.48, sales tax
$189.50 + $9.48 = $198.98, total price

TAX ZONES

In general, a sales tax is charged only on purchases made and delivered within a *tax area*. In the Case Problem on page 496, Floyd and Jo Lindley are exempt from the combined New York State and New York City sales tax because they live in Connecticut and their redwood patio furniture was delivered outside the tax area. Jim and Leta Morris, however, live in the tax area; they are therefore subject to the 7% tax, which amounted to $16.10.

TAX TABLES

For purposes of speed and accuracy, retail salespeople use a printed tax chart, which they keep near the cash register. Here is a sales tax chart issued by one state. Note that both the local tax and the state tax are included.

4% COMBINED STATE AND LOCAL SALES & USE TAX CHART

SALES	TAX	SALES	TAX	SALES	TAX	SALES	TAX
0— .09	.00	12.88—13.12	.52	25.88—26.12	1.04	38.88—39.12	1.56
.10— .29	.01	13.13—13.37	.53	26.13—26.37	1.05	39.13—39.37	1.57
.30— .59	.02	13.38—13.62	.54	26.38—26.62	1.06	39.38—39.62	1.58
.60— .84	.03	13.63—13.87	.55	26.63—26.87	1.07	39.63—39.87	1.59
.85— 1.12	.04	13.88—14.12	.56	26.88—27.12	1.08	39.88—40.12	1.60
1.13— 1.37	.05	14.13—14.37	.57	27.13—27.37	1.09	40.13—40.37	1.61
1.38— 1.62	.06	14.38—14.62	.58	27.38—27.62	1.10	40.38—40.62	1.62
1.63— 1.87	.07	14.63—14.87	.59	27.63—27.87	1.11	40.63—40.87	1.63
1.88— 2.12	.08	14.88—15.12	.60	27.88—28.12	1.12	40.88—41.12	1.64
2.13— 2.37	.09	15.13—15.37	.61	28.13—28.37	1.13	41.13—41.37	1.65
2.38— 2.62	.10	15.38—15.62	.62	28.38—28.62	1.14	41.38—41.62	1.66
2.63— 2.87	.11	15.63—15.87	.63	28.63—28.87	1.15	41.63—41.87	1.67
2.88— 3.12	.12	15.88—16.12	.64	28.88—29.12	1.16	41.88—42.12	1.68
3.13— 3.37	.13	16.13—16.37	.65	29.13—29.37	1.17	42.13—42.37	1.69
3.38— 3.62	.14	16.38—16.62	.66	29.38—29.62	1.18	42.38—42.62	1.70
3.63— 3.87	.15	16.63—16.87	.67	29.63—29.87	1.19	42.63—42.87	1.71
3.88— 4.12	.16	16.88—17.12	.68	29.88—30.12	1.20	42.88—43.12	1.72
4.13— 4.37	.17	17.13—17.37	.69	30.13—30.37	1.21	43.13—43.37	1.73
4.38— 4.62	.18	17.38—17.62	.70	30.38—30.62	1.22	43.38—43.62	1.74
4.63— 4.87	.19	17.63—17.87	.71	30.63—30.87	1.23	43.63—43.87	1.75
4.88— 5.12	.20	17.88—18.12	.72	30.88—31.12	1.24	43.88—44.12	1.76
5.13— 5.37	.21	18.13—18.37	.73	31.13—31.37	1.25	44.13—44.37	1.77
5.38— 5.62	.22	18.38—18.62	.74	31.38—31.62	1.26	44.38—44.62	1.78
5.63— 5.87	.23	18.63—18.87	.75	31.63—31.87	1.27	44.63—44.87	1.79
5.88— 6.12	.24	18.88—19.12	.76	31.88—32.12	1.28	44.88—45.12	1.80
6.13— 6.37	.25	19.13—19.37	.77	32.13—32.37	1.29	45.13—45.37	1.81
6.38— 6.62	.26	19.38—19.62	.78	32.38—32.62	1.30	45.38—45.62	1.82
6.63— 6.87	.27	19.63—19.87	.79	32.63—32.87	1.31	45.63—45.87	1.83
6.88— 7.12	.28	19.88—20.12	.80	32.88—33.12	1.32	45.88—46.12	1.84
7.13— 7.37	.29	20.13—20.37	.81	33.13—33.37	1.33	46.13—46.37	1.85
7.38— 7.62	.30	20.38—20.62	.82	33.38—33.62	1.34	46.38—46.62	1.86
7.63— 7.87	.31	20.63—20.87	.83	33.63—33.87	1.35	46.63—46.87	1.87
7.88— 8.12	.32	20.88—21.12	.84	33.88—34.12	1.36	46.88—47.12	1.88
8.13— 8.37	.33	21.13—21.37	.85	34.13—34.37	1.37	47.13—47.37	1.89
8.38— 8.62	.34	21.38—21.62	.86	34.38—34.62	1.38	47.38—47.62	1.90
8.63— 8.87	.35	21.63—21.87	.87	34.63—34.87	1.39	47.63—47.87	1.91
8.88— 9.12	.36	21.88—22.12	.88	34.88—35.12	1.40	47.88—48.12	1.92
9.13— 9.37	.37	22.13—22.37	.89	35.13—35.37	1.41	48.13—48.37	1.93
9.38— 9.62	.38	22.38—22.62	.90	35.38—35.62	1.42	48.38—48.62	1.94
9.63— 9.87	.39	22.63—22.87	.91	35.63—35.87	1.43	48.63—48.87	1.95
9.88—10.12	.40	22.88—23.12	.92	35.88—36.12	1.44	48.88—49.12	1.96
10.13—10.37	.41	23.13—23.37	.93	36.13—36.37	1.45	49.13—49.37	1.97
10 38—10.62	.42	23.38—23.62	.94	36.38—36.62	1.46	49.38—49.62	1.98
10.63—10.87	.43	23.63—23.87	.95	36.63—36.87	1.47	49.63—49.87	1.99
10.88—11.12	.44	23.88—24.12	.96	36.88—37.12	1.48	49.88—50.12	2.00
11.13—11.37	.45	24.13—24.37	.97	37.13—37.37	1.49	50.13—50.37	2.01
11.38—11.62	.46	24.38—24.62	.98	37.38—37.62	1.50	50.38—50.62	2.02
11.63—11.87	.47	24.63—24.87	.99	37.63—37.87	1.51	50.63—50.87	2.03
11.88—12.12	.48	24.88—25.12	1.00	37.88—38.12	1.52	50.88—51.12	2.04
12.13—12.37	.49	25.13—25.37	1.01	38.13—38.37	1.53	51.13—51.37	2.05
12.38—12.62	.50	25.38—25.62	1.02	38.38—38.62	1.54	51.38—51.62	2.06
12.63—12.87	.51	25.63—25.87	1.03	38.63—38.87	1.55	51.63—51.87	2.07

Such a chart is very easy to use. For example, if a customer bought goods amounting to $25.95, you would look for that amount in the *Sales* column and charge the tax indicated at the right. In this case, $25.95 falls in the range $25.88–$26.12, so the sales tax is $1.04.

Exercises

1. Determine the sales tax and actual price of each purchase.

Purchase	Selling Price	Tax Rate	Sales Tax	Actual Price
a	$2,000.00	5%	$_____	$_____
b	$ 65.00	4%	$_____	$_____
c	$ 4.98	$4\frac{1}{2}$%	$_____	$_____
d	$ 79.95	6%	$_____	$_____
e	$ 125.00	$5\frac{1}{4}$%	$_____	$_____
f	$2,400.00	7%	$_____	$_____
g	$ 368.00	$3\frac{3}{4}$%	$_____	$_____
h	$5,625.00	$5\frac{1}{2}$%	$_____	$_____

2. Using the chart on page 498, find the tax on each of the following sales:

a. $50.00

b. $37.40

c. $26.95

d. $40.88

e. $2.63

f. $.05

Business Applications

1. A large city levies a 3% sales tax, and the state in which the city is located has a $2\frac{1}{2}$% sales tax rate. What is the tax that an office manager will have to pay on a used filing cabinet that costs $60?

2. Roger Reinhardt can purchase blackwall tires on sale at $33.15 a pair. The total sales tax in Mr. Reinhardt's community is $5\frac{1}{2}$%. How much will it cost him to purchase four tires in this special sale?

3. Merchants in one state pay a sales tax rate of 44/100% on their gross sales. If The Burns Company sold $42,750 worth of merchandise in a week, how much tax will the company have to pay?

4. In one state, the gross sales of a retail merchant are taxed on the following scale:

For the first $20,000 in sales, no tax
For sales between $20,000 and $100,000, $\frac{1}{2}$%
For sales over $100,000, $\frac{1}{4}$%

a. How much tax would a merchant have to pay if his gross sales were $18,427?

b. How much tax would a merchant have to pay if his gross sales were $46,420?

c. How much tax would a merchant have to pay if his gross sales were $123,584?

5. In one state, restaurant meals priced at one dollar or more are taxed at the state sales tax rate of 3%. Mr. and Mrs. Edward Warren and their two children stopped at a restaurant for dinner one evening. The cost of their meals was $6.75, $5.50, $2.35, and $1.95. What was the total amount, excluding tips, that the Warrens had to pay if:
a. only one check was issued for the meals?
b. four separate checks were issued?

6. Refer to the sales tax chart on page 498 and find the tax due on each purchase.

a. $17.70	**b.** $50.00	**c.** $26.07
d. $.13	**e.** $6.10	**f.** $43.88
g. $39.99	**h.** $41.98	**i.** $38.11

7. In one large city in the East, water is sold to homeowners by the cubic foot, and bills are mailed every six months. The rates are as follows:

Minimum charge: $15.31 for up to and including 3,600 cubic feet
$.15 for each 100 cubic feet over 3,600

The Ralph Jefferson family received a statement from the water department showing they had used 35,700 cubic feet of water over a six-month period. The local tax is 4%. How much will the Jeffersons' water bill amount to?

8. The water rates in the city of Rosement are as follows:

First 30,000 gallons = 60¢ per 1,000 gallons
Over 30,000 gallons = 55¢ per 1,000 gallons

During one three-month period, the Chamberlain family consumed 48,600 gallons of water. The local sales tax rate is $3\frac{1}{2}$%. What was the total of the Chamberlains' water bill for the quarter?

UNIT

PROPERTY TAXES—COMPUTING THE RATE

Case Problem The expenses of the town of Davenport for the coming year are budgeted at $5,000,000. This amount includes expenses of operating the schools, providing police protection, maintaining sanitation services, and running libraries, parks, playgrounds, and welfare programs. The way the money is spent is shown below.

TOWN OF DAVENPORT
Distribution of Tax Revenue

Item	Percent of Tax
Local and state schools	38.56
County tax	14.71
Police and fire departments	18.34
Debt	1.75
Road, sewer, light, sanitation departments, and public grounds maintenance	9.32
Central administration and reserves	12.53
Library	1.87
Health and charity	2.92

Discussion Questions

1. How can the town of Davenport obtain the money it needs to provide the services shown in the table?
2. On what basis can the residents and business people be charged their share of the expenses?

The major source of revenue to local governments with which they pay for the services to residents and business establishments is a tax on buildings and land, called a *real estate tax*, or a *real property tax*.

In order to determine each person's or business's share of the community's expenses, the total amount in taxes that must be raised is divided among all the property owners in accordance with the value of the property each one owns.

The percentage of the total tax that each property owner must pay is called the *tax rate*. For the purpose of computing taxes, a value is given to the property by a local *tax assessor;* this value is called the *assessed value*, or *assessed valuation*, of the property. The assessed value of property is generally far less than its market value. A house having a market value of $20,000 may be assessed for as little as 10% of that amount, or $2,000, in some communities. Nevertheless, it is on the total assessed value of a community's property that the tax rate is determined—*not* on the market value.

TAX RATE EXPRESSED IN CENTS PER DOLLAR

In some communities, the tax rate is expressed in cents per dollar of assessed valuation. For example, if the total value of the property in the village of Ashton is assessed at $500,000 and the total expenses budgeted for the year are $25,000, then for each dollar value of property, each property owner would have to pay 5 cents in taxes. The amount of 5 cents was found by dividing the expenses by the total assessed value of the property ($25,000 ÷ $500,000 = $.05). A person who owns $10,000 worth of property will have to pay $500 as his share of the taxes, since he must pay 5 cents for each $1 of the assessed value of his property ($10,000 × $.05 = $500). Similarly, a person who owns $15,000 worth of property will have to pay $750 in taxes ($15,000 × $.05 = $750).

Example:

The total expenses the city of Batesville will have to meet during the coming year are estimated at $3,022,600, and the assessed valuation of all the property in the city is $63,500,000. Find the tax rate.

Solution:

Total expenses ÷ total assessed valuation = tax rate
$3,022,600 ÷ $63,500,000 = $.0476, tax rate

TAX RATE EXPRESSED IN DOLLARS PER $100

More commonly, the tax rate is expressed in dollars per $100 of assessed valuation. In order to compare the tax rate of one community with that of another when different bases are used, you must change the base of one rate or the other. Thus, if a tax rate of $.0476 per $1 is compared with one of $4.53 per $100, the first base must be changed from $1 to $100 or the second base from $100 to $1 before a comparison can be made.

Example:

Express the tax rate of $.0476 per $1 as an equivalent rate in dollars per $100.

Solution:

Since the base we are given ($1) must be multiplied by 100 to obtain the new base of $100, the same must be done with the number $.0476. The quickest way of multiplying this number by 100 is to move the decimal point two places to the right. Thus, a rate of $.0476 per $1 is the same as a rate of $4.76 per $100.

TAX RATE EXPRESSED IN DOLLARS PER $1,000

Sometimes, the tax rate is expressed in dollars per $1,000 of assessed valuation, and to make comparisons with a different base the bases must be equivalent.

Example:

Express the tax rate of $57.20 per $1,000 as an equivalent rate in cents per $1.

Solution:

Move the decimal point three places to the left in the tax rate per thousand, $57.20, to find the tax rate per hundred, $.0572.

Exercises

1. Express each tax rate below as an equivalent rate of the new base.

	Tax Rate		New Rate
a.	$.0347 per $1	$_____	per $100
b.	$.0562 per $1	$_____	per $100
c.	$.0473 per $1	$_____	per $1,000
d.	$6.84 per $100	$_____	per $1,000
e.	$7.39 per $100	$_____	per $1,000
f.	$5.74 per $100	$_____	per $1,000
g.	$45.80 per $1,000	$_____	per $100
h.	$8.66 per $100	$_____	per $1
i.	$5.03 per $100	$_____	per $1
j.	$.67 per $1,000	$_____	per $100

2. Find the tax rate in dollars per $100 for each community.

Town	Total Assessed Value	Total Expenses for Coming Year	Tax Rate per $100
a	$ 15,300,000	$ 483,000	$_____
b	$ 87,900,000	$ 5,714,000	$_____
c	$214,000,000	$16,050,000	$_____
d	$176,400,000	$ 6,703,200	$_____
e	$ 93,400,000	$ 4,436,500	$_____

Business Applications

1. The tax rate of one town was $5.23 per $100 and that of another was 6 cents per $1. Which town had the greater tax rate?

2. In a city whose total assessed property valuation was $70,000,000, the amount of money that had to be raised for the school budget was $2,000,000. How much of the tax rate in dollars per $100 was devoted to education?

3. During a recent year, the budget requirements of a large city called for the following departmental expenditures:

Office of the Mayor	$ 248,846
Department of Public Works	$5,408,795
Police Department	$4,510,268
Fire Department	$2,952,575
Department of Health and Welfare	$5,166,762

In dollars per $100, what part of the tax rate was needed for the budget of each of these departments? The assessed value of property in this city was $701,000,000.

4. A town has to raise $262,680 to meet its expenses for the coming year. If the total assessed value of property in the town is $7,462,500, what will the tax rate have to be in dollars per $1,000?

5. The budget of the village of Lynbrook calls for expenditures of $125,626.79 for the current year. Through fines, issuing of licenses, and other sources, the village expects to raise $4,256.30. If the total assessed valuation of the property is $2,697,112, what will the tax rate have to be in dollars per $1,000?

6. The total assessed valuation of property in the town of Minona is $6,250,000. If $360,000 has to be raised for educational purposes and $115,000 for health and welfare needs, how much in dollars per $100 of the tax rate will be needed for each?

UNIT

PROPERTY TAXES—COMPUTING THE TAX

Case Problem   Basil and Pamela Waldron had been married four years before they felt that they could afford to purchase their own house. After several months of search, they found two houses that seemed to offer everything they were looking for. The houses were located in well-kept sections of neighboring communities, where the residents took pride in the appearance of their homes. The price of each house was $25,000. In fact, there seemed to be no feature that made one house more desirable than the other. They were faced with the problem of choosing between two equally attractive dwellings.

Discussion Questions

1. In such a situation, what other factors should be considered that might make one house more desirable than the other?
2. Why might one community have a larger tax rate than another?

REAL AND PERSONAL PROPERTY TAXES

Two different kinds of property are taxed:

1. Real property: land or anything attached to it, such as a building
2. Personal property: furniture in a house or office, cars, trailers, and so on

Some communities have only a real property tax. In those communities which levy both taxes—both real and personal property—a homeowner must pay both. However, a person who does not own real estate in such a community pays only the personal property tax. In most communities, the tax rate is the same for both types of property; in others, the rate is different. Both are determined on the total assessed value of the property, whether it is real or personal.

Example 1:

Find the tax paid by Cyrus Ming on his house that is assessed for $17,300 if the tax rate is $3.83 per $100.

Solution:

Since Mr. Ming must pay $3.83 on each $100 of the assessed value of the property, it is necessary to find the number of hundreds in $17,300. Divide $17,300 by 100, giving a quotient of 173. On each of these 173 hundreds, the owner must pay $3.83. Thus, he will pay 173 times $3.83, or $662.59, in tax.

$$173 \times \$3.83 = \$662.59, \text{ property tax}$$

Example 2:

Find the personal property tax paid by Mr. Ming, if his personal property (his car and the furniture in his house) had an assessed valuation of $2,500. The tax rate is the same as for real property.

Solution:

There are 25 hundreds in $2,500. The tax rate is $3.83 per $100 of assessed valuation.

$$25 \times \$3.83 = \$95.75, \text{ personal property tax}$$

COMPARING PROPERTY TAXES

There is often a considerable difference in tax rates between different communities, which might make a substantial difference in the cost of living in a house there. A community with a high tax rate, however, may be giving its residents more and better services in the form of better police and fire protection, garbage disposal, library facilities, and schools.

Often a low tax rate is confused with a low tax. The tax itself, as you saw in the preceding example, depends on two factors—the tax rate and the assessed value of the property. If the tax rate is low, the tax may still be comparatively high because property in that community may be assessed rather high. It was not enough for the Waldrons in the Case Problem to compare only the tax rates. If property is assessed much higher in the community in which they decided to buy the house than in the community in which they turned the house down, they find that their actual taxes are higher in spite of the lower tax rate.

Example:

Let us go back to the Case Problem and the decision facing the Waldrons in deciding upon which house to buy. The tax rate in Community A is $3.42 per $100 of assessed valuation; in Community B it is $5.76 per $100 of assessed valuation. The market value of both houses is $25,000. The assessed value in the first community, however, is based on 60% of the market value; in the second community it is based on 35%. Compare the taxes of each community on each of the houses.

Solution:

Assessed value of house in Community A = 60% of $25,000
$$= \$15,000$$

Assessed value of house in Community B = 35% of $25,000
$$= \$8,750$$

Tax on house in Community A = ($15,000 ÷ 100) × $3.42
$$= \$150 \times \$3.42$$
$$= \$513.00, \text{ tax in Community A}$$

Tax on house in Community B = ($8,750 ÷ 100) × $5.76
$$= \$87.50 \times \$5.76$$
$$= \$504.00, \text{ tax in Community B}$$

The second house will therefore cost $9.00 less in taxes ($513.00 − $504.00 = $9.00) than the first house. This is not a very large difference, but if the Waldrons felt that there was no difference in community services, this might help them to decide to locate in Community B.

Exercises

Find the tax on each of the properties in the table at the top of the next page.

Property	Assessed Value	Tax Rate	Tax
1	$ 6,000	$4.27 per $100	$_____
2	$ 7,400	$5.36 per $100	$_____
3	$12,300	$4.98 per $100	$_____
4	$15,650	$2.27 per $100	$_____
5	$ 7,800	$54.20 per $1,000	$_____
6	$10,500	$85.70 per $1,000	$_____
7	$25,400	$17.60 per $1,000	$_____
8	$ 8,700	$.057 per $1	$_____
9	$11,450	$.0628 per $1	$_____
10	$33,500	$.072 per $1	$_____

Business Applications

1. Property in Marysville is assessed at 65% of its market value. If the tax rate is $4.57 per $100, what is the tax on a house that can be sold for $18,400?

2. The personal property in the branch office of a large insurance company is assessed at $125,000. If the tax rate is $7.24 per $100, how much tax will be paid on the property?

3. The total assessed value of all personal property in a large city during a recent year was $128,794,800. If the tax rate was $8.43 per $100, how much should the city expect to collect in personal property taxes alone?

4. Thomas Verner lived in a town where 28% of the property tax was passed along to the county government to help it meet its expenses. If Mr. Verner's property was assessed for $17,400 and the tax rate in the town was $24.90 per $1,000, how much of his tax was turned over to the county?

5. Lillian Fein owns two buildings in a town where the tax rate is $43.72 per $1,000. The market value of each is $17,000 and $25,000, respectively. The properties, however, are assessed at only 75% of these values. How much real estate tax does Ms. Fein have to pay?

6. George Okada purchased a home for $28,750 in Garden Town, where homes are assessed at approximately 38% of their market value. The tax rate in Garden Town is $8.42 per $100.
   a. If about 47% of the community's taxes is spent on schools, approximately how much of Mr. Okada's tax will go toward the education of his children that year?

b. There are three children of school age in the Okada family. What will the education of each child cost Mr. Okada for that year?

7. To support education in Riverdale, the school tax rate is $31.48 per $1,000 of assessed valuation. Mrs. Stuart owns a house valued at $27,000 and assessed at 60% of its value. What is Mrs. Stuart's school tax?

8. The real and personal property in a town was assessed at $2,600,000. The budget for the town amounted to $68,000.
   a. Find the tax rate in dollars per $100.
   b. How much tax will the owner of an office building have to pay if the building and the land were assessed at $35,000 and the furniture in the building was assessed at $5,200?

UNIT 4

FEDERAL INCOME TAX

Case Problem   Angela DuPree is a computer programmer trainee in the data processing department of Walston Insurance Company. Angela is single and lives at home with her parents, both of whom work. During the past year, Angela's earnings were $8,400, and each pay period her employer made a deduction from her salary for federal withholding tax.

Discussion Questions

1. What is the purpose of the federal withholding tax which is deducted from Angela's salary?

2. What further responsibility does Angela have with regard to this tax?

When you studied compensation plans and payroll procedures, you learned that an employee's earnings are subject to federal withholding tax, which is another term for *federal income tax*. The employer is required to deduct these taxes from the employee's check each pay period. Although income taxes were withheld from Angela DuPree's salary, Angela is required to submit an income tax return to the Internal Revenue Service (IRS) on or before April 15 of each year covering earnings for the previous year. We speak of this as *filing* a return. On this return Angela will compute the actual amount of tax she owes for federal income taxes. The tax which is being withheld each pay period represents an advance payment of the total tax which is due on her earnings for the year. Most people who earn over $1,700 for the year are required to file a return.

FORM W-2

At the end of the year, employers are obligated by law to furnish every person in their employ for any period of time during the year a statement of taxes withheld from his or her pay. This statement, known by its government form number *Form W–2*, is shown below for Angela DuPree.

	Wage and Tax Statement 19—

EMPLOYER'S STATE IDENTIFYING NUMBER | **Copy B** To be filed with employee's FEDERAL tax return

TYPE OR PRINT EMPLOYER'S FEDERAL IDENTIFYING NUMBER, NAME, ADDRESS AND ZIP CODE ABOVE

	FEDERAL INCOME TAX INFORMATION				SOCIAL SECURITY INFORMATION		
1 Federal income tax withheld	2 Wages, tips and other compensation	3 FICA employee tax withheld	4 Total FICA wages	5 Uncollected employee FICA tax tips
$1287.00	$8,400.00	$491.40	$8,400.00	

EMPLOYEE'S social security number ▶	000-00-000	6 State income tax withheld	7 State wages paid	8 Name of State

Angela DuPree

| 9 City income tax withheld | 10 City wages paid | 11 Name of City |

STATUS 1. SINGLE 2. MARRIED | OTHER INFORMATION (SEE CIRCULAR E) | Cost of group term life insurance included in box 2 | Excludable sick pay included in box 2

TYPE OR PRINT EMPLOYEE'S NAME, ADDRESS AND ZIP CODE ABOVE.
AN "X" IN THE UPPER LEFT CORNER INDICATES THIS IS A CORRECTED FORM.
Form **W-2** THIS INFORMATION IS BEING FURNISHED TO THE INTERNAL REVENUE SERVICE AND APPROPRIATE STATE OFFICIALS
Department of the Treasury–Internal Revenue Service

As you see, the W–2 shows Angela DuPree's total earnings during the year, the amount of income tax withheld, and deductions for F.I.C.A. (Federal Insurance Contributions Act, which is more commonly known as social security). In those localities where state or local income taxes are levied, the amounts withheld for these taxes would also be shown.

Form 1040

Department of the Treasury—Internal Revenue Service

US Individual Income Tax Return

19—

For the year January 1–December 31, 19 , or other taxable year beginning .... 19 , ending .... , 19.......

Name (If joint return, give first names and initials of both)	Last name	COUNTY OF RESIDENCE	Your social security number

Please print or type

Present home address (Number and street, including apartment number, or rural route)

Spouse's social security no.

City, town or post office, State and ZIP code

Occu-pation — Yours ▶
Spouse's ▶

Filing Status—check only one:

1 ☐ Single
2 ☐ Married filing joint return (even if only one had income)
3 ☐ Married filing separately. If spouse is also filing give spouse's social security number in designated space above

and enter full name here ▶ _____

4 ☐ Unmarried Head of Household
5 ☐ Widow(er) with dependent child (Year spouse died ▶ 19)

Exemptions

Regular / 65 or over / Blind

6a Yourself . . ☐ ☐ ☐
b Spouse . . . ☐ ☐ ☐

Enter number of boxes checked ▶

c First names of your dependent children who lived with you _____

Enter number ▶

d Number of other dependents (from line 27) . . . ▶
7 Total exemptions claimed . . . . ▶

8 **Presidential Election Campaign Fund.**—Check ☐ if you wish to designate $1 of your taxes for this fund. If joint return, check ☐ if spouse wishes to designate $1. **Note:** *This will not increase your tax or reduce your refund.* **See note below.**

Income

9	Wages, salaries, tips, and other employee compensation. (Attach Forms W–2. If unavailable, attach explanation)	9
10a	Dividends (See instructions on page 6.) $.................., 10b Less exclusion $............., Balance ▶	10c
10d	(Gross amount received, if different from line 10a . . . . $....................)	
11	Interest income	11
12	Income other than wages, dividends, and interest (from line 38)	12
13	Total (add lines 9, 10c, 11, and 12)	13
14	Adjustments to income (such as "sick pay," moving expenses, etc. from line 43) .	14
15	Subtract line 14 from line 13 (adjusted gross income)	15

● If you do not itemize deductions and line 15 is under $10,000, find tax in Tables and enter on line 16.
● If you itemize deductions or line 15 is $10,000 or more, go to line 44 to figure tax.
● CAUTION. If you have unearned income and can be claimed as a dependent on your parent's return, check here ▶ ☐ and see instructions on page 7.

Tax, Payments and Credits

16	Tax, check if from: Tax Tables 1–12 / ☐ Schedule D / ☐ Schedule G / Tax Rate Schedule X, Y, or Z / ☐ Form 4726 **OR** ☐ Form 4972	16
17	Total credits (from line 54)	17
18	Income tax (subtract line 17 from line 16)	18
19	Other taxes (from line 61)	19
20	Total (add lines 18 and 19)	20
21a	Total Federal income tax withheld (attach Forms W–2 or W–2P to front)	21a
b	1973 estimated tax payments (include amount allowed as credit from 1972 return)	b
c	Amount paid with Form 4868, Application for Automatic Extension of Time to File U.S. Individual Income Tax Return	c
d	Other payments (from line 65)	d
22	Total (add lines 21a, b, c, and d)	22

Balance Due or Refund

23	If line 20 is larger than line 22, enter **BALANCE DUE IRS** Pay in full with return. Make check or money order payable to Internal Revenue Service ▶ (Check here ▶ ☐ , if Form 2210, Form 2210F, or statement is attached. See instructions on page 8.)	23
24	If line 22 is larger than line 20, enter amount **OVERPAID** . . . . ▶	24
25	Amount of line 24 to be **REFUNDED TO YOU** . . . . ▶	25
26	Amount of line 24 to be credited on 1974 estimated tax . . . . ▶ 26	

Note: 1972 Presidential Election Campaign Fund Designation.—Check ☐ if you did not designate $1 of your taxes on your 1972 return, but now wish to do so. If joint return, check ☐ if spouse did not designate on 1972 return but now wishes to do so.

Sign here

Under penalties of perjury, I declare that I have examined this return, including accompanying schedules and statements, and to the best of my knowledge and belief it is true, correct, and complete. Declaration of preparer (other than taxpayer) is based on all information of which he has any knowledge.

Your signature ▶ _____ Date
Preparer's signature (other than taxpayer) _____ Date

Spouse's signature (if filing jointly, BOTH must sign even if only one had income) ▶
Address (and ZIP Code) Preparer's Emp. Ident. or Soc. Sec. No.

Write soc. sec. no. on Check or Money Order. Attach here
Please attach Copy B of Forms W–2 here

Chapter 20 Taxes

FORM 1040

Angela DuPree filed her tax return with the IRS on *Form 1040*, a specimen copy of which is shown on page 510. When Angela sends in this form, she must accompany it with a copy of the W-2 form illustrated. On the basis of her entries on Form 1040, Angela can determine whether she owes the government additional money or the government owes her a refund because of an overpayment. Angela can partially fill in the form and let the IRS (Internal Revenue Service) complete it for her. Angela elects to prepare her own return so that she can see for herself whether she has underpaid or overpaid her income tax.

For most young people like Angela DuPree, preparing an income tax return is a simple process. She has only one source of income—her $8,400 salary from her job as a computer programmer trainee.

Unlike sales and property taxes, for which the tax rate is the same for everyone, income tax rates can vary from individual to individual—even among those earning the same salary. The tax for most people whose earnings consist solely of their salaries depends on three factors:
1. The total amount earned.
2. Exemptions. Generally speaking, you are allowed an exemption for each person who depends on you for support. (The amount allowed for each exemption in 1973 was $750.) You may take yourself as one exemption, one for your spouse (if he or she has no income), one for each child, dependent parent, etc. Angela DuPree has one exemption—herself.
3. Deductions. The federal government permits expenditures for certain items, such as heavy medical costs, taxes, interest, and charitable contributions to be deducted from each taxpayer's income before figuring the income tax owed. A deduction of 15% of income, up to a maximum of $2,000, is permitted for these purposes without any proof of the expenditure actually having to be given. This 15% deduction is called the *standard deduction*. A taxpayer who has made expenditures for these allowable purposes in excess of the standard deduction is permitted to *itemize* or list them separately. In such case, the taxpayer must be prepared to furnish proof of the expenditure should it be demanded of him. Because most new workers do not have many of these deductions, they are usually better off taking the standard deduction and not itemizing expenses. Angela DuPree is allowed $1,260 ($8,400 × 15% = $1,260), which is more than she could claim if she itemized deductions.

Form 1040, which the IRS mails to taxpayers each year after they have once filed a return, can also be obtained at an IRS office, a U.S. Post Office, and at many banks. The form itself is contained in a booklet with instructions for preparing and filing the return. In the booklet are tax tables of two types: (1) tables for persons who earn less than $10,000 and do not itemize deductions and (2) tables for persons who choose to itemize deductions. Angela DuPree will use the table of the first type. Following is a section of the table for people like Angela who claim only one exemption.

If line 15 (adjusted gross income) is—		And you are—			
				Married filing separate return claiming—	
At least	But less than	Single, not head of household	Head of household	Low income allowance	%Standard deduction
		Your tax is—			
$6,250	$6,300	$737	$703	$883	$818
6,300	6,350	748	712	894	828
6,350	6,400	758	722	905	837
6,400	6,450	769	731	916	846
6,450	6,500	779	741	927	856
6,500	6,550	790	750	938	865
6,550	6,600	800	760	949	875
6,600	6,650	811	769	960	884
6,650	6,700	821	779	971	894
6,700	6,750	832	788	982	905
6,750	6,800	842	798	993	916
6,800	6,850	853	807	1,004	927
6,850	6,900	863	817	1,015	938
6,900	6,950	874	826	1,026	949
6,950	7,000	884	836	1,037	960
7,000	7,050	895	845	1,048	971
7,050	7,100	905	855	1,059	982
7,100	7,150	916	864	1,070	993
7,150	7,200	926	874	1,081	1,004
7,200	7,250	937	883	1,092	1,015
7,250	7,300	947	893	1,103	1,026
7,300	7,350	958	902	1,114	1,037
7,350	7,400	968	912	1,125	1,048
7,400	7,450	979	921	1,136	1,059
7,450	7,500	989	931	1,149	1,070
7,500	7,550	1,000	940	1,161	1,081
7,550	7,600	1,010	950	1,174	1,092
7,600	7,650	1,021	959	1,186	1,103
7,650	7,700	1,031	969	1,199	1,114
7,700	7,750	1,042	978	1,211	1,125
7,750	7,800	1,052	988	1,224	1,136
7,800	7,850	1,063	997	1,236	1,149
7,850	7,900	1,073	1,007	1,249	1,161
7,900	7,950	1,084	1,016	1,261	1,174
7,950	8,000	1,094	1,026	1,274	1,186
8,000	8,050	1,105	1,035	1,286	1,199
8,050	8,100	1,116	1,046	1,299	1,211
8,100	8,150	1,128	1,057	1,311	1,224
8,150	8,200	1,140	1,068	1,324	1,236
8,200	8,250	1,152	1,079	1,336	1,249
8,250	8,300	1,164	1,090	1,349	1,261
8,300	8,350	1,176	1,101	1,361	1,274
8,350	8,400	1,188	1,112	1,374	1,286
8,400	8,450	1,200	1,123	1,386	1,299
8,450	8,500	1,212	1,134	1,399	1,311
8,500	8,550	1,224	1,145	1,411	1,324
8,550	8,600	1,236	1,156	1,424	1,336
8,600	8,650	1,248	1,167	1,436	1,349
8,650	8,700	1,260	1,177	1,449	1,361
8,700	8,750	1,270	1,187	1,461	1,374
8,750	8,800	1,280	1,196	1,474	1,386
8,800	8,850	1,290	1,205	1,486	1,399
8,850	8,900	1,301	1,215	1,499	1,411
8,900	8,950	1,311	1,224	1,511	1,424
8,950	9,000	1,321	1,233	1,524	1,436
9,000	9,050	1,331	1,243	1,536	1,449
9,050	9,100	1,341	1,252	1,549	1,461
9,100	9,150	1,352	1,261	1,561	1,474
9,150	9,200	1,362	1,271	1,574	1,486
9,200	9,250	1,372	1,280	1,586	1,499
9,250	9,300	1,382	1,289	1,599	1,511
9,300	9,350	1,392	1,299	1,611	1,524
9,350	9,400	1,403	1,308	1,624	1,536
9,400	9,450	1,413	1,317	1,637	1,549
9,450	9,500	1,423	1,327	1,651	1,561

To find the tax that is due the federal government, you look first at Form 1040, line 15 (adjusted gross income). Adjusted gross income is the total of all income received less certain expenses and payments that are allowed by the IRS in special situations. Like most people, Angela DuPree has no income other than her salary and can claim no special expenses; therefore, her adjusted gross income and her annual earnings ($8,400) are the same.

Now on the tax table in the section headed "If line 15 (adjusted gross income) is—," look at the columns *At least* and *But less than.* Angela's adjusted gross income is $8,400; therefore, you find the figure $8,400 in the *At least* column and the figure $8,450 in the *But less than* column. Angela is single and not the head of a household,° so the column *Single, not head of household* is the appropriate one to find the amount of tax. You will see that Angela's federal income tax for the year amounts to $1,200.

Now refer back to the W-2 on page 509. You will see that during the past year Angela's employer withheld $1,287 from her salary for federal income tax. According to the tax table, however, Angela's federal income tax for the year amounts to $1,200. Her employer has therefore deducted $87 too much, and Angela asks for a refund on lines 24 and 25 of Form 1040. She then signs the return, attaches her W-2 form, and mails it to the district office of the IRS. Her refund check will be sent to her within a few weeks of filing. Should the amount withheld have been *less* than the total tax due, Angela would have had to include a check for the difference along with the tax return.

Exercises

1. Using the tax table on page 512, find the income tax each individual owes the federal government. Assume that each is single and not the head of a household.

Name	Adjusted Gross Income	Tax Due
Susan Yeary	$6,670.00	$_____
Mary Beth Clarkson	$9,145.55	$_____
Robert St. Clair	$7,231.20	$_____
Michael McNaughton	$9,212.85	$_____
Hanna Bethel	$8,862.00	$_____

2. Using the federal tax table on page 512, complete the following chart. Each individual is single and not the head of a household.

° Unmarried taxpayers who maintain a household for themselves and a dependent can generally file as "head of household." The tax for these people is somewhat less than that for unmarried people who do not maintain such a home.

Married persons may file what is called a *joint return* (a single return representing both husband and wife), even though one may have no income or deductions. It is generally advantageous to do this.

Name	Adjusted Gross Income	Tax Withheld During Year	Tax Due from Tax Table	Amount Owed to Government	Amount Owed to Employee
Cox, A. N.	$6,400.00	$ 830.60	$_____	$_____	$_____
Brehm, M.	$8,960.40	$1,422.20	$_____	$_____	$_____
Mann, J. T.	$6,370.85	$ 693.00	$_____	$_____	$_____
Love, S. J.	$7,200.40	$1,011.15	$_____	$_____	$_____
Mahr, B. C.	$9,490.90	$1,394.60	$_____	$_____	$_____

3. Using the tax table on page 512, find the income tax due the federal government in each of the following instances:
   a. A single person, head of household, one exemption. Adjusted gross income is $9,187.80
   b. A single person, not head of household, one exemption. Adjusted gross income is $9,000.
   c. A married person, filing separate return, one exemption, claiming standard deduction. Adjusted gross income is $8,188.85.

4. Jacob Lefkowitz is married, has three children of ages 3, 7, and 12, and a dependent mother. His wife has no income. What is the maximum number of exemptions that Mr. Lefkowitz can claim?

5. Sarah Appleby is a widow who maintains a home for herself, her two high-school-aged children, and her dependent father.
   a. What filing status should she claim?
   b. How many exemptions is she allowed?

ITEMIZED DEDUCTIONS

The tax table we have been using states the tax with the standard deduction already taken off. Taxpayers who chose to itemize their deductions because they are larger than the standard deduction permitted by the tax law have a somewhat more complicated computation to do in order to determine their tax. This computation consists of two parts.

1. Find the taxable income. (Special forms accompanying Form 1040 provide space in which to do this.)

2. Compute the tax due on this amount.

Example 1:

Luis Montez earned $11,400 for the year and has allowable deductions totaling $2,000. He has one exemption—himself.

Solution:

1. Luis should itemize his deductions because the standard deduction permits him to take off $1,710 (15% of $11,400), and he has deductions of $2,000. He therefore computes his taxable income as follows:

$11,400   adjusted gross income
−2,000   less itemized deductions
$ 9,400
  −750   less exemptions ($750 × 1)
$ 8,650   taxable income

2. Luis then turns to the tax table for single taxpayers who choose to itemize deductions, a portion of which is reproduced below.

SCHEDULE X—Single Taxpayers Not Qualifying for Rates in Schedule Y or Z

If the amount on Form 1040, line 48, is: Enter on Form 1040, line 16:

Not over $500....14% of the amount on line 48.

Over—	But not over—		of excess over—
$500	$1,000	$70+15%	$500
$1,000	$1,500	$145+16%	$1,000
$1,500	$2,000	$225+17%	$1,500
$2,000	$4,000	$310+19%	$2,000
$4,000	$6,000	$690+21%	$4,000
$6,000	$8,000	$1,110+24%	$6,000
$8,000	$10,000	$1,590+25%	$8,000
$10,000	$12,000	$2,090+27%	$10,000
$12,000	$14,000	$2,630+29%	$12,000
$14,000	$16,000	$3,210+31%	$14,000
$16,000	$18,000	$3,830+34%	$16,000
$18,000	$20,000	$4,510+36%	$18,000
$20,000	$22,000	$5,230+38%	$20,000
$22,000	$26,000	$5,990+40%	$22,000
$26,000	$32,000	$7,590+45%	$26,000

Looking at the table, you see that Luis' taxable income of $8,650 falls into this line:

	But not	of excess
Over—	over—	over—
$8,000	$10,000	$1,590 + 25%	$8,000

Luis' tax is computed as follows:

$1,590.00	tax on $8,000
162.50	25% tax on $650 (amount in excess of $8,000)
$1,752.50	total tax on taxable income of $8,650

Example 2:

Mr. and Mrs. Bernard McGuiness have two children. Mr. McGuiness earned a total of $14,500 and Mrs. McGuiness, who works part time, earned $7,250. They compute their allowable itemized deductions at $2,500. They wish to file a joint return. What is their federal income tax?

Solution:

1. Find the taxable income.

$14,500	Mr. McGuiness' income
7,250	Mrs. McGuiness' income
$21,750	adjusted gross income
−2,500	less itemized deductions
$19,250	
−3,000	exemptions ($750 × 4)
$16,250	taxable income

2. Find the tax. At the top of the facing page is a section of the tax table to be used by married taxpayers filing a joint return.

   Their taxable income of $16,250 falls within the line which reads

	But not	of excess
Over—	over—	over—
$16,000	$20,000	$3,260 + 28%	$16,000

The tax is computed as follows:

$3,260	tax on income of $16,000
70	28% tax on $250 (amount in excess of $16,000)
$3,330	total tax on taxable income of $16,250

Married Taxpayers Filing Joint Returns and Certain Widows and Widowers (See page 5)			

If the amount on Form 1040, line 48, is: — **Enter on Form 1040, line 16:**

Not over $1,000...14% of the amount on line 48.

Over—	But not over—		of excess over—
$1,000	$2,000	$140+15%	$1,000
$2,000	$3,000	$290+16%	$2,000
$3,000	$4,000	$450+17%	$3,000
$4,000	$8,000	$620+19%	$4,000
$8,000	$12,000	$1,380+22%	$8,000
$12,000	$16,000	$2,260+25%	$12,000
$16,000	$20,000	$3,260+28%	$16,000
$20,000	$24,000	$4,380+32%	$20,000
$24,000	$28,000	$5,660+36%	$24,000
$28,000	$32,000	$7,100+39%	$28,000
$32,000	$36,000	$8,660+42%	$32,000
$36,000	$40,000	$10,340+45%	$36,000

Exercises

1. Find the income tax due from the following people. Use the tax table on page 515.

Name	Deductions	Adjusted Gross Income	Exemp.	Tax Due
Paula Preston	$3,000	$14,750	1	$_____
Joseph Milne	$2,100	$14,200	2	$_____
Maddie DeGroat	$1,000	$ 6,821	2	$_____
Linda Strauss	$ 900	$ 4,520	1	$_____
Fidor Malenkov	$1,120	$ 5,786	1	$_____

2. Using the tax rate schedule for married taxpayers filing joint returns which appears on page 517, find the taxable income and the federal income tax.

	Adjusted Gross Income	Itemized Deductions	No. of Exemp.	Taxable Income	Federal Income Tax
a.	$26,380	$2,400	3	$_____	$_____
b.	$19,650	$2,720	2	$_____	$_____
c.	$41,290	$4,200	5	$_____	$_____
d.	$21,850	$2,350	3	$_____	$_____
e.	$36,400	$2,900	4	$_____	$_____

Business Applications

1. Martin Duber claims one exemption and uses the standard deduction. He earned $9,357 during the year, and his W–2 form showed a federal withholding tax of $1,397. Will he have to pay on April 15 or is he entitled to a refund? how much?

2. Sally Benson, a widow, runs a home for herself and her 23-year old daughter who is self-supporting. She files as head of household, claims the standard deduction, has earned $9,140 during the year, and has a W-2 form that shows federal withholding taxes of $1,380. Will she have to pay on April 15 or can she get a refund? how much?

3. Merle Masters earned $21,000 during the year and has allowable itemized deductions of $2,800. She supports her widowed mother who lives alone.
   a. What is her taxable income?
   b. What is her federal income tax?

4. Sandra Bennett supports her disabled husband and three children. She earns $26,300. Her husband does some work at home from which he earned $3,200 during the year. They have itemized deductions amounting to $3,100. They wish to file a joint return.
   a. What is their taxable income?
   b. What is their federal income tax?

REVIEW
EXERCISES
FOR
CHAPTER 20

1. Doris Wong purchased an evening gown for $89.95. If the state sales tax was $3\frac{1}{2}$%, what was the total amount that Doris had to pay for the gown?

2. D. C. Temple purchased the components for a stereo set for $684.75. The state tax amounted to 4% and the city tax was 2%. Mr. Temple could have purchased the same components for $698.50 in an adjoining state where neither of these taxes existed. How much less would the cost have been had Mr. Temple made this purchase outside the state in which he lived?

3. Change each of the tax rates below to an equivalent rate in terms of the new base indicated.

	Tax Rate	New Rate
a.	$.0327 per $1	$_____ per $1,000
b.	$6.25 per $100	$_____ per $1,000

4. In a community where property is assessed at $45,000,000, the anticipated expenses for the coming year amount to $1,800,000. What should the tax rate be in dollars per $100 for the coming year?

5. What is the tax on a beach cottage assessed at $9,200 if the tax rate is $6.54 per $100?

6. In a city where manufacturing plants are assessed at 48% of their actual value, a new factory was erected at a cost of $450,000. If the tax rate in that city is $8.64 per $100, how much tax will have to be paid on this building?

7. Which tax rate is the greater, $4.37 per $100 or $41.56 per $1,000? Explain.

8. Using the tax table on page 512, find the income tax due the federal government from each of these people. Assume that each individual is single and not the head of a household.

Name	Adjusted Gross Income	Tax Due
Willard L. Wade	$8,770.00	$ _____
Patricia von Staden	$6,345.55	$ _____
Harold T. Tsu	$7,999.90	$ _____
Charlotte Valenti	$9,306.65	$ _____
Lawrence Webber	$6,762.20	$ _____

9. Refer to the tax rate schedule on page 512. Find the income tax due or refund for each of the following people who chose the standard deduction and have one exemption.

Name	Status*	Adjusted Gross Income	Amount Withheld	Refund (R) Tax Due (T)
Louis Poznanski	S	$9,210	$1,370	$ _____
Marjorie Prior	HH	$9,320	$1,246	$ _____
John Preston	M–S	$6,747	$ 920	$ _____
Alice Pyn	S	$6,660	$ 835	$ _____
Stewart Ramel	HH	$8,850	$1,201	$ _____

* S—single; HH—head of household; M–S—married but filing separately

10. Refer to the tax rate schedule for single persons who choose to itemize deductions (page 515), and find the income tax due from each person.

Name	Exemp.	Adjusted Gross Income	Itemized Deductions	Tax Due
Bruce Jacobus	1	$16,500	$2,710	$ _____
Marcia Jasko	2	$22,650	$3,640	$ _____
Rita Juraschek	3	$31,100	$2,753	$ _____
Paul E. Cordazzo	2	$17,820	$2,940	$ _____
David Schwann	1	$ 6,772	$1,500	$ _____

11. Income information for the following married taxpayers filing jointly is given below.

Refer to the tax table on page 517, and find the income tax due for each couple.

Name	Exemp.	Adjusted Gross Income	Itemized Deductions	Tax Due
Angela and Edward Monrovia	3	$14,500	$2,100	$_____
Amy and Werner Wolfson	4	$25,400	$3,750	$_____
Joan and Oscar Voth	2	$ 5,775	$1,600	$_____
Mildred and Paul Feingold	5	$33,705	$2,840	$_____
Ann and Lloyd Russell	2	$17,211	$2,600	$_____

CHAPTER 21
INSURANCE

The major purpose of all insurance is to protect people against unexpected financial loss. So that no one person will have to bear a loss alone, many people join together, each person contributing a small share, to cover a large loss that any one of them may suffer.

For example, assume that in a community of 200 families each family owns its own home. Over the years, it was found that, on an average, fire damaged only one house each year to an extent of $10,000. Hence, each family agreed to contribute $50 ($10,000 ÷ 200 = $50) annually to a common fund to cover a fire loss that might be incurred that year. In this way, the family whose home was burned would not suffer a $10,000 loss, but merely a $50 loss, the amount of its contribution.

Basic to all insurance—whether on a building, household goods, a car, or a person's life—are two factors:
1. uncertainty about exactly who will suffer the loss
2. certainty that the loss will occur to someone in a large group

If Edward Bryant, a resident of the community referred to above, knew that his home would not burn during the coming year, he would not need to join the other residents in insuring his house against loss from fire. Because he can't make such a prediction with absolute certainty, however, he would be wise to pay the $50. Although he will be $50 poorer, he realizes this is better than the possibility of being $10,000 poorer.

Insurance, then, is protection against large financial losses. People take risks every day of their lives—their houses may burn down, their cars may be stolen or damaged, they may suffer serious injury, they may injure someone else and have to pay the hospital bill, and so on. This is why people need insurance of one form or another.

UNIT

1

FINDING THE COST OF FIRE INSURANCE

Case Problem Joe Underwood owns a house in the small town of Cloverleaf Junction. His brother Tom owns a house in Hartsdale, a city some 200 miles away. Both brothers have insured their houses for $25,000. Recently, when they were discussing the cost of home ownership, Joe asked Tom, "How much do you pay a year for your $25,000 policy?"

Tom replied, "I think my annual premium is a little over $65."

"Sixty-five dollars!" exclaimed Joe. "How do you get that kind of rate? Do you realize that the insurance on my house costs me over $100 a year?"

1. Can you account for the difference in the premiums paid by the Underwood brothers?
2. What determines the amount a property owner pays for insurance?

BASES FOR ESTABLISHING PREMIUM RATES

The *insured* is the person who is protected; the company selling the protection is the *insurer*. The contract covering the terms of the protection is the *policy*. The *premium* is the amount the insured pays for protection. The amount of the premium for a fire insurance policy depends on three things: (1) the risk the insurance company takes, (2) the number of perils (tornadoes, for example) the policy covers, and (3) the dollar amount the property is insured for, the *face* of the policy.

In establishing fire insurance rates, insurance companies consider two basic risk factors:

1. The material with which the house is constructed—brick, frame (wood), or mixed construction (brick and frame).
2. The degree of fire protection in the community—that is, the fire-fighting equipment available, the efficiency of the fire department personnel, the dependability of the fire alarm system, and the nearness of a water supply.

It is likely that the major difference in the amount of premium paid by each of the Underwood brothers lies in the two risk factors mentioned. However, the number of perils a person insures against also influences the amount of the premium. The most common perils against which homeowners insure their property are fire or lightning, windstorm or hail, explosion, and riot or civil commotion. Other perils include damage from falling objects, weight of ice and snow, aircraft, vehicles, smoke, vandalism, theft, and breakage.

Finally, the dollar amount for which the property is insured affects the premium. That is, the man who insures a house for $35,000 pays a higher premium than his neighbor who carries only $18,000 insurance.

COMPUTING THE PREMIUM

Although insurance companies sell insurance to individuals and business firms, the amount they may charge in premiums is regulated carefully by the various states in which insurance is sold. Insurance laws differ from one state to another, and the method of computing premiums often varies as well. All states, nevertheless, use the two risk factors mentioned previously—that is, the material the house is made of and the adequacy of fire protection—in establishing rates.

The table on page 526 is adapted from a rate booklet published by the Insurance Rating Bureau of one midwestern state. This table is only for one-family dwellings (the rates for two-family dwellings are higher), and applies to residences only. Separate tables are published for farm houses and buildings, mobile homes (or trailers), apartments, rooming houses, factory and store buildings, motels, restaurants, and so on.

Note that the state has classified its towns into five categories—A, B, C, D, and E—depending on the efficiency of fire protection in each.

How to Use the Rate Table

The following examples illustrate the use of the rate table.

Example 1:

Find the annual premium on a brick one-family dwelling insured for $20,000 and located in a Class C town.

Solution:

Refer to the *Amount of Insurance* column and find the amount of the policy ($20,000). Locate *Class C* under *Brick One-Family Dwellings* in the same row. The entry $50.35 is the annual premium.

Example 2:

Find the annual premium on a frame one-family dwelling insured for $30,000 and located in a Class A town.

Solution:

Refer to the *Amount of Insurance* column and find the amount of the policy ($30,000). Locate *Class A* under *Frame One-Family Dwellings* in the same row. The entry $54.10 is the annual premium.

Example 3:

Find the annual premium on a frame one-family dwelling insured for $22,500 and located in a Class B town.

ANNUAL PREMIUM RATES FOR FIRE INSURANCE

Amount of Insurance	Brick One-Family Dwellings Class of Town					Frame One-Family Dwellings Class of Town				
	A	B	C	D	E	A	B	C	D	E
$ 5,000	$16.65	$18.35	$20.35	$ 25.35	$ 28.85	$19.10	$20.60	$24.10	$ 29.60	$ 32.60
$ 6,000	$18.15	$19.95	$22.35	$ 38.35	$ 32.55	$20.50	$22.30	$26.50	$ 33.10	$ 36.70
$ 7,000	$19.45	$21.55	$24.35	$ 31.35	$ 36.25	$21.90	$24.00	$28.90	$ 36.60	$ 40.80
$ 8,000	$20.75	$23.15	$26.35	$ 34.35	$ 39.95	$23.30	$25.70	$31.30	$ 40.10	$ 44.90
$ 9,000	$22.05	$24.75	$28.35	$ 37.35	$ 43.65	$24.70	$27.40	$33.70	$ 43.60	$ 49.00
$10,000	$23.35	$26.35	$30.35	$ 40.35	$ 47.35	$26.10	$29.10	$36.10	$ 47.10	$ 53.10
$11,000	$24.65	$27.95	$32.35	$ 43.35	$ 51.05	$27.50	$30.80	$38.50	$ 50.60	$ 57.20
$12,000	$25.95	$29.55	$34.35	$ 46.35	$ 54.75	$28.90	$32.50	$40.90	$ 54.10	$ 61.30
$13,000	$27.25	$31.15	$36.35	$ 49.35	$ 58.45	$30.30	$34.20	$43.30	$ 57.60	$ 65.40
$14,000	$28.55	$32.75	$38.35	$ 52.35	$ 62.15	$31.70	$35.90	$45.70	$ 61.10	$ 69.50
$15,000	$29.85	$34.35	$40.35	$ 55.35	$ 65.85	$33.10	$37.60	$48.10	$ 64.60	$ 73.60
$20,000	$36.35	$42.35	$50.35	$ 70.35	$ 84.35	$40.10	$46.10	$60.10	$ 82.10	$ 94.10
$25,000	$42.85	$50.35	$60.35	$ 85.35	$102.85	$47.10	$54.60	$72.10	$ 99.60	$114.60
$30,000	$49.35	$58.35	$70.35	$100.35	$121.35	$54.10	$63.10	$84.10	$117.10	$135.10
For each $100 not shown add:	$ .13	$ .16	$ .20	$ .30	$ .37	$ .14	$ .17	$ .24	$ .35	$ .41

Solution:

Refer to the *Amount of Insurance* column and find the amount $20,000. The annual premium for this amount of insurance is $46.10.

$22,500	insurance coverage desired
−20,000	insurance shown on table
$ 2,500	additional insurance to be charged on this amount

To find the premium on the additional $2,500, refer to the last line of the table. The rate for Class B frame homes is shown on this line as 17 cents for every $100.

There are 25 $100 in $2,500 ($2,500 ÷ $100 = 25)
25 × $.17 = $4.25, premium on additional $2,500

Add to find the total insurance premium.

$46.10	insurance on $20,000
4.25	insurance on $2,500
$50.35	insurance on $22,500

Cost for Longer Periods

Most people purchase insurance policies for a period longer than one year. To compute such premiums, multiply the annual rate by the number of years of protection.

Example:

Martin Boucher purchased a three-year $20,000 policy on a brick one-family dwelling in a Class E town. What is the premium?

Solution:

Find the premium for a $20,000 policy for one year ($84.35) and multiply by the total number of years (3).

$84.35 × 3 = $253.05, premium for the three-year policy

To encourage owners of *commercial property* to buy insurance for a period of time longer than one year, insurance companies offer discount rates on periods of two, three, four, or five years. The schedule below gives the insurance rates for commercial property for periods greater than one year.

Period	Rate
2 years	1.85 times annual premium
3 years	2.70 times annual premium
4 years	3.55 times annual premium
5 years	4.40 times annual premium

Example:

The annual premium for fire insurance on the Jamestown Motel amounted to $1,440 for $300,000 worth of insurance. Based on the schedule on page 527, what will the insurance for three years be?

Solution:

To find the insurance premium for three years, multiply $1,440 (annual premium) by 2.70.

$1,440 × 2.70 = $3,888, premium for a three-year policy

Exercises

1. Refer to the rate table on page 526 to compute the annual premium on each insurance policy.

Policy	Amount of Insurance	Type of Dwelling	Class of Town	Annual Premium
a	$ 6,000	Brick	B	$_____
b	$12,000	Frame	A	$_____
c	$12,000	Brick	A	$_____
d	$25,000	Frame	C	$_____
e	$25,000	Frame	E	$_____
f	$30,000	Brick	D	$_____
g	$35,000	Brick	B	$_____
h	$27,500	Frame	C	$_____
i	$16,200	Brick	E	$_____
j	$ 8,800	Frame	A	$_____

2. Find the difference in annual premiums.

| Amount of Insurance | Brick Dwelling | | | Frame Dwelling | | |
	Class A Town	Class E Town	Difference	Class A Town	Class E Town	Difference
a. $15,000	$_____	$_____	$_____	$_____	$_____	$_____
b. $30,000	$_____	$_____	$_____	$_____	$_____	$_____
c. $10,000	$_____	$_____	$_____	$_____	$_____	$_____
d. $22,500	$_____	$_____	$_____	$_____	$_____	$_____

3. Find the difference in annual premiums on a $20,000 policy on the following.

Policy	Class of Town	Brick Dwelling	Frame Dwelling	Difference
a	B	$_____	$_____	$_____
b	D	$_____	$_____	$_____
c	E	$_____	$_____	$_____
d	A	$_____	$_____	$_____

4. Find the commercial property insurance premium for each of the following. (Refer to the schedule on page 527.)

Annual Premium	Period of Coverage
$2,420	3 years
$1,670	5 years
$2,640	4 years

Business Applications

1. Mrs. Amy Vandercook lives in a Class B town, Oakmont, where she owns a frame house which she has insured for $24,000. R. F. Schuyler owns a frame house in Livermore, a Class A town, which is insured for the same amount. (a) Who pays the greater annual premium? (b) how much greater?

2. Sidney Seidel lives in a Class A town and carries a $30,000 insurance policy on his brick house. Sybil Dartnell lives in the same city, and carries a $30,000 insurance policy on her frame house. (a) Who pays the greater annual premium? (b) how much greater?

3. Lewiston and Monohan, partners, own a factory building that is insured for $75,000. The annual insurance premium on the property is $270. Refer to the schedule on page 527, and decide how much the partners save each year by buying (a) a three-year policy? (b) a four-year policy? (c) a five-year policy?

UNIT 2

THE HOMEOWNER'S POLICY

Case Problem Bernard and Gertrude Fine carry an insurance policy on their home. The house was assessed, or valued, at $30,000 but was insured for only $20,000. When fire damaged the attached garage to the amount of $3,000, the Fines expected the insurance company to pay the entire amount of the damage. The company, however, took the position that the maximum that could be paid on this claim was $2,000.

Discussion Questions
1. Why do you think the Fines could not collect the full amount of the damage, $3,000?
2. Do you think the Fines could have collected more if their home had been insured for $25,000 instead of $20,000?

ADVANTAGES OF THE HOMEOWNER'S POLICY

You can buy a *standard* fire policy that insures your home and its contents against fire and lightning only. For a little more money, you can have *extended coverage,* which includes damage from wind, hail, smoke, explosion, riot, vehicles, and falling aircraft. You can buy another policy that protects you against burglary and theft, and another for injuries suffered by people on your property or damage you might do to their property. You can also buy insurance against all these perils in one policy, which is called the *homeowner's policy.*

Essentially, there are two advantages to having a homeowner's policy: You have only one policy and so only one premium to worry about; and the cost of a homeowner's policy is less than you would pay for comparable protection in separate policies.

The basic homeowner's policy covers the following risks:
1. Living quarters and attached structures (for example, a garage that was constructed as part of the dwelling).
2. "Appurtenant" structures, which means nearby property such as a tool shed, a guest house, a detached garage.
3. Personal property; that is, household contents and personal belongings.
4. Additional living expenses. If the house is damaged by fire and the owners must move to temporary quarters, the homeowner's policy reimburses the insured for these additional living expenses.

Note that our discussion of the homeowner's policy is restricted to property owned by the insured. There is a special homeowner's policy for those who rent an apartment or a house, which covers personal belongings such as furniture and clothing.

DEDUCTIBLES

About one-third of all losses for damage to houses and their contents amount to less than $50. In most forms of the homeowner's policy, the *deductible* is $50. This means that the insured is responsible for all losses up to the deductible amount. If fire breaks out in the kitchen, causing damage to a built-in cabinet in the amount of $44.50, the insured pays the full amount. For losses of over $50 and up to and including $500, the insured pays a gradually reduced portion of the loss and the insurance company pays the rest. When the loss is over $500, the company pays the entire amount.

For a little less money, a person can buy a policy with a basic deductible of $100 or more. The principle is the higher the deductible, the less the insurance company is responsible for and hence the premium is lower.

AMOUNTS OF COVERAGE

The amount of each type of protection in a homeowner's policy is based on a percent of the amount of insurance on the dwelling itself.

Property Coverage	Insured Value
Dwelling	100%
Appurtenant private structures	10% of dwelling
Personal property	50% of dwelling
Additional living expenses	20% of dwelling

Example:
Clarence Putnam owns a house that has an assessed value of $25,000. If he has purchased a $25,000 homeowner's policy, how much coverage does he have for each type of risk? What is the maximum he could receive as an allowance for additional living expenses?

Solution:

$25,000	dwelling (100%)
2,500	appurtenant private structures (10% of $25,000)
12,500	personal property (50% of $25,000)
5,000	additional living expenses (20% of $25,000)
$45,000	total amount of coverage

You must understand that the amounts listed are maximum amounts. If the actual cost of damage is less than the maximum amount, the lower amount will be paid. It is impossible to make money on an insured loss. Remember, insurance is for protection only.

THE 80% CO-INSURANCE CLAUSE

Although insurance companies recommend that the homeowner insure his dwelling for its full value, many people do not do so, because either they want to save money on premiums or they neglect to increase their insurance when the property increases in value. The insurance company pays only up to the face value, or total amount, of the insurance policy regardless of the assessed value of the house. For example, the owner of a house assessed at $30,000 but insured at $25,000 receives only $25,000 in case of total loss by fire.

Many policies require that in order to receive full payment for any *partial loss*, the homeowner must insure his dwelling for at least 80% of its replacement value. This is known as the *80% co-insurance clause*. If the property is insured for less than 80% of its value, the owner must share part of the loss or damage caused by fire. If, for example, an owner insures his property for only 60% of its assessed value and the dwelling is partially damaged by fire, the insurance company pays only 60% of the loss and no more.

Example:

Bruce Levine's house is valued at $18,000 and is insured against fire for $15,000. If fire destroys a bedroom to the extent of $3,500, how much of the loss must the insurance company pay?

Solution:

80% of $18,000 = $14,400
Amount of insurance = $15,000

Since 80% of the assessed value of the house is $14,400 and the house is insured for more than that amount ($15,000), the insurance company must pay the full cost of the damage ($3,500).

If the homeowner insures his property for less than 80% of its assessed value, he must agree to share part of any loss to the property.

Example:

Cynthia Salton owns a house assessed at $20,000, on which she carries insurance in the amount of $12,000. A recent damage by fire to the attached garage amounted to $5,000. How much of the loss must the insurance company pay? How much must Miss Salton pay?

Solution:

Amount of insurance required for full coverage (80% × $20,000) is $16,000.
Amount of insurance carried is $12,000.

Portion of loss which insurance company will pay is 12,000/16,000 or $\frac{3}{4}$.
Loss paid by insurance company is $\frac{3}{4}$ or 75% of $5,000 or $3,750.
Loss paid by Miss Salton is $\frac{1}{4}$ or 25% of $5,000 or $1,250.

This can be stated in the following formula for computing the amount paid on losses by the insurance company under an 80% clause:

$$\text{Amount paid out} = \frac{\text{Amount of coverage}}{80\% \text{ of the value of the property}} \times \text{Loss}$$

Substituting the figures from the problem, we have the following:

$$\text{Amount paid out} = \frac{\$12,000}{80\% \times \$20,000} \times \$5,000$$

$$= \frac{\$12,000}{\$16,000} \times \$5,000$$

$$= \$3,750, \text{ amount paid by insurance company}$$

In no event may an insured receive more from the insurance company than the amount of the loss or the face value of the policy.

Exercises

1. Find the amount of insurance coverage in the following. (Refer to the table on page 531.)

	Assessed Value	Amount of Insurance	Dwelling	Appurtenant Structures	Personal Property	Additional Living Expenses
a.	$40,000	$40,000	$_____	$_____	$_____	$_____
b.	$27,500	$27,500	$_____	$_____	$_____	$_____
c.	$16,000	$16,000	$_____	$_____	$_____	$_____
d.	$21,000	$21,000	$_____	$_____	$_____	$_____
e.	$35,500	$35,500	$_____	$_____	$_____	$_____

2. For what amount must each house be insured in order to meet the minimum 80% coverage requirement.

	Assessed Value	Amount of Insurance
a.	$17,500	$_____
b.	$22,800	$_____
c.	$41,500	$_____
d.	$35,200	$_____
e.	$15,000	$_____

3. What fraction of the loss will the insurance company have to pay in each of the following situations under an 80% clause?

	Assessed Value	80% of Assessed Value	Amount of Insurance	Percent of Loss Paid
a.	$60,000	$_____	$24,000	_____
b.	$25,000	$_____	$15,000	_____
c.	$35,000	$_____	$21,000	_____
d.	$15,000	$_____	$10,000	_____
e.	$25,000	$_____	$ 5,000	_____

4. Each of the following policies contains an 80% clause. Use the formula for computing amount paid on losses to find the amount the insurance company will have to pay for fire loss in each case.

	Valuation	80% of Assessed Value	Amount of Insurance	Percent	Loss	Amount Paid by Ins. Co.
a.	$37,500	$_____	$20,000	_____	$2,500	$_____
b.	$45,000	$_____	$16,000	_____	$8,000	$_____
c.	$22,500	$_____	$20,000	_____	$9,300	$_____
d.	$62,500	$_____	$40,000	_____	$1,200	$_____
e.	$15,000	$_____	$13,000	_____	$2,750	$_____

Business Applications

1. A. G. Morrall has a $100 deductible homeowner's policy. Recently a fire in the basement of his home destroyed property amounting to $800. Assuming that Mr. Morrall has 100% coverage, how much will he receive from the insurance company for his loss?

2. Carolyn Matson has a $50 deductible homeowner's policy. A fire in the attic of her home destroyed personal property amounting to $37. How much will Miss Matson receive from the insurance company in payment for the damage?

3. The value of the land on which a house is situated is not covered in fire insurance policies. Millie and Paul Johannsen paid $32,700 for their house and land. They estimated that the land is worth $5,500 and decided to insure the house at 80% of its estimated value. How much insurance will they purchase?

4. Complete the following table for a house which has an assessed value of $30,000 but which is insured for 80% of the assessed value.

Property Coverage	Insurance Coverage
Dwelling (100%)	$ _____
Appurtenant structures (10%)	$ _____
Personal property (50%)	$ _____
Additional living expenses (20%)	$ _____
Total	$ _____

5. L. B. Sing insures his house valued at $45,000 for $36,000 under an 80% co-insurance clause. If he suffers a fire loss of $10,500, what portion of the loss must he bear?

UNIT

AUTOMOBILE INSURANCE—BODILY INJURY AND PROPERTY DAMAGE

Case Problem James Montgomery and his family were on the way home from a two-week skiing vacation. The roads on one mountain pass were icy, and on a sharp turn Mr. Montgomery skidded into an oncoming car. The driver of the other car, a Mr. Thorssen, was thrown from his vehicle and badly injured. As Mr. Montgomery reported the accident to the state police and watched the ambulance leave to take Mr. Thorssen to the hospital, he wondered about his insurance coverage.

Unit 3   Automobile Insurance—Bodily Injury and Property Damage   **535**

1. Why is automobile insurance a "must" for every car owner?
2. Do you think Mr. Montgomery could have purchased insurance that would have paid the hospital bills for Mr. Thorssen?

Recent figures tell us that over 40 automobile accidents occur in the United States every minute, with one traffic death every ten minutes. Obviously, then, anyone who drives a car runs the risk of having an accident—an accident that may result in a smashed car that will cost hundreds of dollars to repair, or more important, in serious injury to one or more people.

The risk of accident is so great, and the losses so heavy, that most states by law require drivers to purchase automobile insurance of one kind or another. The purchase of an insurance policy is not a matter of choice in such states, although the *amount* of insurance coverage one carries above the required minimum may be left to one's discretion.

As a driver or potential driver, you should understand the four major types of insurance coverage that a car owner can consider buying:
1. Bodily injury
2. Property damage
3. Collision
4. Comprehensive coverage

BODILY INJURY INSURANCE

Bodily injury insurance covers risks of injuring or killing pedestrians, passengers in the insured's car, and persons riding in other cars. The three bodily injury coverages are *bodily injury liability, medical payments,* and protection against *uninsured motorists.*

1. *Bodily Injury Liability.* Bodily injury liability insurance protects the driver of a car against the cost of injuries that might be inflicted on other people through the use of his or her car. This is the type of insurance that can protect Mr. Montgomery in the Case Problem. The basic bodily injury insurance coverage limits are commonly known as 10-and-20. These numbers are abbreviations for $10,000 and $20,000. The owner of a 10-and-20 liability policy is protected to a maximum payment of $10,000 to any one person and to a maximum payment of $20,000 for any one accident.

In the Case Problem, if Mr. Thorssen sues Mr. Montgomery for $12,000 and is awarded this amount by the court, the insurance company will pay only $10,000. The remaining $2,000 would have to be paid by Mr. Montgomery. If Mr. Thorssen is awarded $8,500 by the court, the insurance company would pay the entire $8,500. If four persons were injured in the accident and all four were awarded a total of $24,000 for injuries, the insurance company would pay only $20,000. The remaining $4,000 would have to be paid by the insured.

In most states, 10-and-20 is sufficient coverage, but minimum limits are higher in some states. For a little more money, the driver can buy a 25-and-50, a 50-and-100, or a 100-and-300 liability policy. The first amount in each case is the maximum payment, in thousands of dollars, to be made by the insurance company for the injuries to any one person in any one accident. The second amount is the maximum payment to be made for all of the injuries sustained in any one accident.

2. *Medical Payments*. This coverage pertains to medical expenses resulting from injuries suffered by the insured and all members of his immediate family while riding in his car or someone else's car, or when struck by a car while walking. It also applies to guests in the insured's car. Under medical payments coverage, the insurance company agrees to pay all reasonable medical expenses incurred in the accident and reported within one year from the date of the accident. Such expenses include medical, surgical, X-ray, dental, ambulance, hospital, etc.

3. *Uninsured Motorists*. This type of coverage is designed to protect the insured and other members of his family if they are injured by a hit-and-run driver or by a motorist who carries no liability insurance.

PROPERTY DAMAGE INSURANCE

Property damage insurance applies when the car of the insured damages the property of others. More often than not the property damaged is another car, but the insured is also covered for damages to other property such as a house, a lawn, a bicycle, a lamp post, or a telephone pole. Such coverage can be purchased in amounts from $5,000 to $50,000 or more.

COLLISION AND COMPREHENSIVE COVERAGE INSURANCE

These policies, which cover damages to the insured's car as opposed to one that belongs to another, are discussed in the next unit.

HOW ARE PREMIUMS DETERMINED?

The cost of automobile insurance depends primarily on what insurance companies must pay on claims resulting from automobile accidents. That is, the more accidents there are, the more claims insurance companies must pay; and the higher the cost of the claims, the higher the cost of insurance. The state regulates not only the amount of coverage a driver must buy but also the rates that insurance companies can charge.

Three things are taken into account by the state and the insurance company in determining the amount a person must pay for car insurance.

1. *Where the driver lives and how he uses his car*. Each state is divided into "rating territories." A rating territory may be a large city, a suburb, or a rural

area. For each territory, insurance companies compile statistics on claims relating to cars garaged in that area. If the insured lives in a territory that has a high accident rate, he will pay more for car insurance.

2. *The classification of the driver.* Factors in driver classification include age, sex, marital status, and driving record.
3. *The kind of car.* The year, make, and model of the car to be insured are all factors that help to determine the amount of the premium.

Discounts

If the insured has completed a driver education course, he is eligible to receive a discount on car insurance premiums. In some states, this discount applies to drivers through age 24; in others, through age 20 only.

Many companies offer a "good student" discount of up to 25% on car insurance rates. To get this discount, the insured must be at least 16, a junior or senior in high school, or a full-time college student. The student must also rank in the upper 20% of the class, or have a "B" average or better, or be on an honor roll or "dean's list."

In this unit we will consider the cost of premiums on bodily injury insurance and property damage liability. The premiums on comprehensive and collision insurance will be discussed in the next unit.

BASE PREMIUMS

As we mentioned, each state is divided into rating territories according to the number of accidents that occur there, and *base premiums* are established for the territory in which the car is garaged. Table A shows base premium rates for bodily injury, property damage, and medical payments in one state. (Naturally, the figures in this and the following tables in this unit would be different in each state.)

TABLE A
BASE PREMIUM SCHEDULE

Terr.	Bodily Injury				Property Damage			Medical Payments			
	10–20	25–50	50–100	100–300	$5,000	$10,000	$25,000	$500	$1,000	$2,000	$5,000
01	$42	$52	$57	$63	$45	$47	$49	$6	$8	$10	$13
02	$53	$65	$72	$79	$45	$47	$49	$7	$9	$11	$14
03	$31	$38	$42	$46	$41	$43	$44	$4	$6	$ 8	$11
04	$30	$37	$41	$45	$39	$41	$42	$4	$6	$ 8	$11
05	$41	$50	$55	$61	$41	$43	$44	$6	$8	$10	$13
06	$40	$49	$54	$60	$35	$37	$38	$6	$8	$10	$13

In Table A, the base premium on a 10-and-20 bodily injury policy in the 05 territory is $41; the base premium on $25,000 property damage insurance is $44; and on $2,000 in medical payments coverage, $10.

OPERATOR FACTORS

The base premium schedule is merely a starting point for finding the cost of car insurance. An insurance agent must also consult the following tables.

TABLE B-1
FACTORS FOR YOUTHFUL OPERATOR

	Age	Pleasure or Farm Use	Drive to Work or Business Use*
Female (Married or Unmarried), Under 21			
WITHOUT DRIVER TRAINING	17 or less	1.75	1.90
	18	1.60	1.75
	19	1.50	1.65
	20	1.25	1.40
WITH DRIVER TRAINING	17 or less	1.60	1.75
	18	1.50	1.65
	19	1.40	1.55
	20	1.20	1.35
Female (Married or Unmarried), 21 and Over			
WITH OR WITHOUT DRIVER TRAINING	21	1.15	1.30
	22	1.10	1.25
	23	1.05	1.20
	24	1.00	1.15
Married Male, Under 21			
WITHOUT DRIVER TRAINING	17 or less	1.95	2.10
	18	1.85	2.00
	19	1.75	1.90
	20	1.65	1.80
WITH DRIVER TRAINING	17 or less	1.70	1.85
	18	1.65	1.80
	19	1.60	1.75
	20	1.55	1.70
Married Male, 21 and Over			
WITH OR WITHOUT DRIVER TRAINING	21	1.50	1.65
	22	1.40	1.55
	23	1.30	1.45
	24	1.20	1.35

* Less than 10 miles

TABLE B-2
FACTORS FOR YOUTHFUL OPERATOR

		Not Owner or Principal Operator		Owner or Principal Operator	
	Age	Pleasure or Farm Use	Drive to Work or Business Use*	Pleasure or Farm Use	Drive to Work or Business Use*
		Unmarried Male, Under 21			
WITHOUT DRIVER TRAINING	17 or less	2.75	2.90	3.50	3.65
	18	2.55	2.70	3.30	3.45
	19	2.40	2.55	3.10	3.25
	20	2.25	2.40	2.85	3.00
WITH DRIVER TRAINING	17 or less	2.30	2.45	3.10	3.25
	18	2.15	2.30	2.90	3.05
	19	2.05	2.20	2.70	2.85
	20	1.95	2.10	2.55	2.70
		Unmarried Male, 21 and Over			
WITH OR WITHOUT DRIVER TRAINING	21	1.90	2.05	2.50	2.65
	22	1.70	1.85	2.35	2.50
	23	1.55	1.70	2.20	2.35
	24	1.35	1.50	2.05	2.20

° 10 miles or less

FACTORS FOR NO YOUTHFUL OPERATOR

Age and Other Factors	Pleasure	Business	Farm	Drive to or from Work (miles)	
				Less than 10	10 or More
Only operator is female, age 30–64	.90	1.35	.75	1.05	1.30
Principal operator is 65 or over	.95	1.40	.80	1.10	1.35
All other	1.00	1.45	.85	1.15	1.40

An insurance agent applies determinants called *factors* to the base premium to arrive at the actual cost of insurance coverage. These determinants are the following:

1. The age and marital status of the driver; the purpose for which the car is used; and whether, in the case of a youthful operator, the driver has had driver training.
2. The accident record of the driver.

The first of these is shown in Tables B-1 and B-2 on pages 539 and 540. For each type of driver on these tables, a figure is given by which an insurance agent multiplies the base premium.

ACCIDENT FACTORS

The final determinant of the cost of car insurance is the factor that relates to the driving record of the operator—that is, the number of accidents he or she has had over the past three years. The accident factors in one state are shown in Table C.

TABLE C
ACCIDENT FACTORS

Number of Accidents	Factor
0	.00
1	.40
2	.90
3	1.50
4	2.20

You will see that a driver who has had no accidents over the past three years pays no penalty. If he has had one accident, he is charged with a factor of .40; two, a factor of .90; and so on.

HOW THE TABLES ARE USED

Example 1:

Ruth Boswell, 17, lives in territory 04 and uses the family car occasionally—for transportation to school, for shopping, and for pleasure. She has had no driver training and has had one accident since she began driving a year ago. What will be the cost of a 50-and-100 bodily injury policy?

Solution:

The base premium for 50-and-100 bodily injury insurance in territory 04 is $41 (see Table A). The factor for a youthful operator (Table B-1) for a 17-year-old female without driver training who uses the car for pleasure is 1.75. The factor for one accident (Table C) is .40. The total factor for Ruth Boswell is 2.15 (1.75 + .40). This total factor figure multiplied by the base premium gives the total premium.

1.75	operator factor	Total Factor × Base Premium = Total Premium
.40	accident factor	2.15 × $41 = $88.15, or $88
2.15	total factor	All premiums are rounded off to the nearest dollar.

Example 2:

Harold Tabor, 18, drives the family car in territory 02, using it for pleasure only. Harold has had driver training, is unmarried, and has had no accidents. What is the cost of insurance with 100-and-300 bodily injury, $25,000 property damage, and $2,000 medical payments coverage?

Solution:

The base premiums in 02 territory are as follows:

$ 79	bodily injury
49	property damage
11	medical payments
$139	total base premium

The factor for pleasure use for an 18-year-old unmarried male with driver training is 2.15. Since Harold has had no accidents, his accident factor is .00. To find the total premium for one year, multiply the total factor (2.15) by the total base premium ($139).

2.15 × $139 = $298.85, or $299 (rounded), total premium for one year

Example 3:

Paul Goldblatt, 19, bought a car of his own shortly after graduating from high school. He works at a garage seven miles from his home and drives to and from work each day. Paul is unmarried and lives with his family in territory 06. He has had driver training and has had two accidents since he received his license at age 16. What will be the amount of premium Paul will pay for 25-and-50 bodily injury, $25,000 property damage, and $5,000 medical payments coverage?

Solution:

Base premiums in 06 territory:

$ 49	bodily injury
38	property damage
13	medical payments
$100	total base premium
2.85	operator factor
.90	accident factor
3.75	total factor

$100 × 3.75 = $375, total annual premium

Example 4:

Walter O'Kane, 65, lives in 01 territory and uses his car for business. (He is an insurance salesman.) What will be the cost for 100-and-300 bodily injury, $25,000 property damage, and $5,000 medical payments coverage if he has had two accidents within the past three years?

Solution:

The base premium amounts are as follows:

$$
\begin{aligned}
&\$\ 63 \quad \text{bodily injury} \\
&\quad 49 \quad \text{property damage} \\
&\underline{\quad 13} \quad \text{medical payments} \\
&\$125 \quad \text{total base premium} \\
\\
&1.40 \quad \text{operator factor} \\
&\underline{\ .90} \quad \text{accident factor} \\
&2.30 \quad \text{total factor}
\end{aligned}
$$

$125 \times 2.30 = \$287.50$, or $288 (rounded), cost of insurance

Exercises

1. Find the total base premium for each type of coverage.

		Bodily Injury		Property Damage		Medical Payments		
	Terr.	Type	Amount	Type	Amount	Type	Amount	Total
a.	05	10/20	$_____	$10,000	$_____	$1,000	$_____	$_____
b.	02	50/100	$_____	$ 5,000	$_____	$ 500	$_____	$_____
c.	06	100/300	$_____	$25,000	$_____	$5,000	$_____	$_____
d.	03	25/50	$_____	$25,000	$_____	$2,000	$_____	$_____
e.	01	10/20	$_____	$ 5,000	$_____	$1,000	$_____	$_____

2. Find the total factor for each driver.

	Operator	Driver Training	Use of Car	Acci-dents	Operator Factor	Accident Factor	Total Factor
a.	Female, 23	Yes	Pleasure	1	_____	_____	_____
b.	Male, 20, unmarried	No	Business	2	_____	_____	_____
c.	Male, 23, married	No	Work, 9 miles	0	_____	_____	_____
d.	Female, 37, only driver	No	Pleasure	3	_____	_____	_____
e.	Male, 18, single, owner	Yes	Pleasure	0	_____	_____	_____

3. Find the cost of each of the following. (Bodily injury is abbreviated b.i.; property damage, p.d.; and medical payments, m.p.) Complete the table on the next page.

Unit 3   Automobile Insurance—Bodily Injury and Property Damage   543

	Operator	Driver Training	Use of Car	Terri-tory	Acci-dents	Coverage	Cost
a.	Male, 42	No	Business	02	1	50-and-100 b.i.	$_____
b.	Female, 17, unmarried	Yes	Work, 6 miles	06	0	$10,000 p.d.	$_____
c.	Male, 17, unmarried, owner	Yes	Pleasure	06	0	$10,000 p.d.	$_____
d.	Female, 46, only operator	No	Business	05	0	$5,000 m.p.	$_____
e.	Male, 24, married	No	Work, 8 miles	03	3	25-and-50 b.i.	$_____
f.	Male, 67	No	Farm	04	2	$25,000 p.d.	$_____

Business Applications

1. John Baggett, 17, is one of the drivers of a car that is used by the family only for pleasure. The family has had no accidents, and the car is garaged in 04 territory. How much would John's father save on the cost of a 25-and-50 bodily injury and a $10,000 property damage policy if John had taken a course in driver training?

2. George Bailey, 23 and single, owns a car and lives in 03 territory. He uses his car for business and has had no accidents. To protect himself, George carries 100-and-300 bodily injury, $25,000 property damage, and $5,000 medical payments insurance. If George were married, how much would he save on the cost of automobile insurance in one year?

3. Clarence and Adele Robbins, both just over age 30, were in three automobile accidents in a three-year period. They carry 50-and-100 bodily injury, $10,000 property damage, and $2,000 medical payments coverage. They live in 02 territory. Mr. Robbins uses the car for business. How much would the couple save on their car insurance premiums this year if they had had no accidents?

4. T. J. Waldenheim injured two persons in an automobile accident. They sued and were awarded $6,000 and $4,000 by the court. If Mr. Waldenheim carries a 5-and-10 bodily injury policy, how much did each injured person collect from the insurance company?

5. While driving, Lori Dixon lost control of her car. It went over a curb, knocking down a boy standing on the sidewalk and demolishing the front porch of his parents' house. The family sued Miss

Dixon and were awarded $5,600 for injuries to the boy and $875.26 for damages to the house. If Miss Dixon's insurance coverage is a 5-and-10 bodily injury policy and a $5,000 property damage policy, how much did she have to pay?

6. As a result of a blowout, Bill Gratz's car swerved and struck another car, injuring five persons. Through court action, he was required to pay them amounts of $27,000, $14,000, $6,000, $5,000, and $2,700. If Bill carries 50-and-100 bodily injury insurance, how much did his insurance company have to pay?

UNIT 4

AUTOMOBILE INSURANCE—COLLISION AND COMPREHENSIVE COVERAGE

Case Problem Anthony Searles had been saving for two years to purchase a car. Finally, he was able to buy a nearly new hardtop model for $2,700. Anthony immediately purchased 10-and-20 liability insurance and $10,000 property damage insurance.

Discussion Questions
1. What risks has Anthony insured himself against?
2. What are some of the other risks involved in car ownership for which Anthony is *not* insured?

As you know, bodily injury insurance covers the owner's liability for injury to other persons, and property damage insurance covers damage to the property of other people. Neither covers damage to the insured's own car. The two basic types of coverage for one's own car are *comprehensive physical damage* and *collision insurance.*

COMPREHENSIVE PHYSICAL DAMAGE

Comprehensive physical damage insurance protects the insured against financial loss resulting from such perils as fire, theft, glass breakage, flood, falling objects, explosion, and hail. Comprehensive physical damage insurance, which applies only to the insured's car, fails to apply when the car is damaged in a collision with another car or object, or is damaged due to upset.

COLLISION

If the insured's car is damaged as a result of colliding with a vehicle or other object or as a result of upset, collision insurance covers the damage to the insured's car regardless of who was responsible. This coverage does not apply to personal injuries suffered in automobile accidents or to damage the car may do to the property of others. It is intended *only* for the insured's car.

Collision insurance is usually written on a $50 or $100 deductible basis. This means that the insured pays the first $50 or $100 of damage and the insurance company pays the rest. The higher the deductible, the lower the premium.

The base premium schedule for comprehensive physical damage and $50 and $100 deductible collision insurance for one state follows on the next page.

BASE PREMIUM SCHEDULE

Territory. The first column in the table shows the territory in which the car is garaged. As in bodily injury and property damage insurance, the base premium for collision and comprehensive coverage varies by territory in a given state.

Age Group. Age group refers to the age of the car. That is, 0–1 means the car is new or not more than one year old; 2–3, at least two but not more than three years old, and so on.

Symbol Group. The symbol number in the Symbol Group column represents the group into which a car is placed according to the cost of the car when it was new; the larger the symbol number, the greater the original price of the car and the greater the base premium.

Using the Table
The following example demonstrates how the base premium schedule is used.

Example:
A three-year old car classified as symbol 1 is garaged in an 03 territory. The owner of the car, Fred Engel, is 24 years old and unmarried. What is the cost of both comprehensive and $50-deductible collision insurance if Fred had one accident last year and uses his car for business?

BASE PREMIUM SCHEDULE

Terr.	Age Group	COMPREHENSIVE					$50 DEDUCTIBLE					$100 DEDUCTIBLE				
		Symbol Group					Symbol Group					Symbol Group				
		1	2	3	4	5	1	2	3	4	5	1	2	3	4	5
01	0–1	$29	$38	$48	$ 65	$ 84	$116	$132	$155	$186	$217	$ 71	$ 81	$ 95	$114	$133
	2–3	22	29	36	48	63	87	99	116	140	163	53	61	71	86	100
	4–5	16	21	26	36	46	76	85	101	121	141	47	52	62	74	86
	6	13	17	22	29	38	64	73	85	102	119	39	45	52	63	73
02	0–1	44	59	74	100	130	159	180	212	254	297	108	122	144	173	202
	2–3	33	44	56	75	97	119	136	159	191	223	81	92	108	130	151
	4–5	24	33	41	55	71	104	117	138	165	193	71	79	94	112	131
	6	20	27	33	45	58	87	100	117	140	163	59	68	79	95	111
03	0–1	15	20	25	34	44	81	92	108	130	151	69	78	92	110	129
	2–3	11	15	19	25	33	60	69	81	97	113	52	59	69	83	97
	4–5	8	11	14	19	24	53	59	70	84	98	45	51	60	72	84
	6	7	9	11	15	20	44	51	59	71	83	38	43	51	61	71
04	0–1	19	25	31	42	54	102	115	136	163	190	67	76	89	107	125
	2–3	14	19	23	31	41	76	87	102	122	143	50	57	67	80	93
	4–5	10	14	17	23	30	67	75	88	106	124	44	49	58	69	81
	6	8	11	14	19	24	56	64	75	90	105	36	42	49	59	69
05	0–1	20	27	34	46	60	80	91	107	128	150	68	77	91	109	127
	2–3	15	20	26	34	45	60	68	80	96	112	51	58	68	82	96
	4–5	11	15	19	25	33	52	59	70	83	97	45	50	59	71	83
	6	9	12	15	21	27	44	50	59	71	82	37	43	50	60	70
06	0–1	22	29	36	49	63	86	98	115	138	161	74	83	98	118	137
	2–3	16	22	27	36	47	64	74	86	104	121	55	63	74	88	103
	4–5	12	16	20	27	35	56	63	75	90	105	48	54	64	76.	89
	6	10	13	16	22	28	47	54	63	76	89	40	46	54	65	75

Solution:

2.20   operator factor (page 540)

  .40   accident factor (page 541)

2.60   total factor

Comprehensive base premium is $11

Comprehensive premium = 2.60 × $11 = $28.60, or $29 (rounded)

$50 deductible base premium is $60

$50-deductible collision premium = 2.60 × $60 = $156

Total comprehensive and collision premium = $29 + $156 = $185

Unit 4   Automobile Insurance—Collision and Comprehensive   547

Exercises

1. Find the base premium for each.

	Age Group	Car Symbol	Territory	Policy	Base Premium
a.	New	5	04	$50 deductible	$_____
b.	2–3	2	06	Comprehensive	$_____
c.	4–5	4	02	$100 deductible	$_____
d.	0–1	3	05	$50 deductible	$_____
e.	6	1	03	Comprehensive	$_____

2. Find the cost of each.

	Operator	Use of Car	Accidents	Age Group	Car Symbol	Territory	Policy	Cost
a.	Male, 45	Business	0	New	3	04	$50 ded.	$_____
b.	Female, 36, only operator	Pleasure	1	2 yrs.	5	05	Comp.	$_____
c.	Male, 24, married	Work, under 10 mi	2	6 yrs.	2	01	Comp.	$_____
d.	Male, 68	Pleasure	0	4 yrs.	4	06	$100 ded.	$_____
e.	Female, 22	Business	3	3 yrs.	1	02	Comp.	$_____
f.	Male, 19, unmarried, owner°	Farm	1	5 yrs.	3	03	$50 ded.	$_____
g.	Female, 17°	Work, under 10 mi	0	New	5	04	Comp.	$_____

° Has had driver education

Business Applications

1. Find the total cost of automobile insurance for Gerald McCready from this information.

> Personal information:
> Male, age 18
> Owner of his own car
> Uses car only for pleasure
> Has had one accident in the past year
> Car is kept in territory 03
> Has had driver training
> Car is six years old and in symbol group 3

Insurance coverage:
  50-and-100 bodily injury
  $5,000 property damage
  $5,000 medical payments
  Comprehensive
  $100-deductible collision

2. In an accident, Louis Harding damaged Rachel Stargill's car to the extent of $265.73 and his own car to the extent of $273.76. How much must Mr. Harding's insurance company pay if he carries $50-deductible collision and $5,000 property damage?

3. During a strike at the factory where he works, Mr. Wolk's car was overturned causing damage amounting to $346.50. Although Mr. Wolk carried $50-deductible collision insurance, he did not have comprehensive coverage on the car. How much did the insurance company pay for the damage?

4. Irene Johnson, 34, uses her new car for business. She drives a car that is classified as symbol 5 and is garaged in an 06 territory. She has had no accidents until recently when, through no fault of her own, her car was damaged. The cost of repairs was $100. How much would Miss Johnson have gained or lost if she had purchased $100-deductible collision insurance rather than $50-deductible insurance?

5. When Miss Johnson's previous car was four years old (see Problem 4), she purchased 50-and-100 bodily injury insurance, $10,000 property damage insurance, and comprehensive coverage. What was the total cost for her car insurance if she had had no accidents during the previous three-year period?

6. Fred Rigley, age 24 and unmarried, is the owner of a two-year-old car. He uses the car to drive to work, a distance of $7\frac{1}{2}$ miles, round trip, and keeps it in 03 territory. During the past three years, Fred was in one car accident. How much would he save on both $100-deductible collision insurance and comprehensive coverage if he drove a car classified as symbol 1 rather than symbol 5?

7. As the result of an accident, Kenneth Cartwright's automobile injured three passengers of another car, badly damaging that car and smashing the front end of his own car. Through court action, Mr. Cartwright was required to pay $12,500, $2,300, and $1,500 to the injured persons, as well as $1,240 for the damage to the car he struck. Repairs for the damage to his own car cost $810. He carried 10-and-20 bodily injury, $5,000 property damage, $100-deductible collision, and comprehensive coverage insurance. Explain how and through what coverages the claims were paid.

LIFE INSURANCE

Case Problem Edward Vaughan, 22, graduated from college, obtained his first job, and married, all in the same year. As a management trainee in personnel administration, Edward earns a modest salary but anticipates higher earnings when he completes his training. The Vaughans know that their finances will be touch-and-go for the next several years while they are establishing themselves.

Discussion Questions
1. For what reasons might the Vaughans buy life insurance now?
2. How might their having children affect their need for life insurance in the future?

Anyone with dependents feels the need for some kind of life insurance. If the number of dependents increases, (if a couple has more children, for instance), the need for life insurance increases. Life insurance offers financial protection to the insured's dependents if he or she dies. This is the major purpose of life insurance, although many people also invest in life insurance as a form of savings that will assure them an income during their retirement years.

Life insurance policies can be divided into four major types: term; whole, or straight life; limited payment; and endowment.

TERM INSURANCE

Term insurance gets its name from the fact that it is purchased for a certain period of time or *term*, such as 5, 10, or 20 years. Under a 10-year term policy, for example, the insured agrees to pay premiums until his death or for 10 years, whichever occurs first. If the insured is still living at the end of 10 years, he or she will no longer be insured, nor will the *beneficiary* of the policy (the person to whom the money is paid in the event the insured dies) receive any money from the insurance company. If the insured should die at any time during the 10-year term, the beneficiary will receive the face value of the policy.

Because term insurance provides only protection against loss (it has no cash value if the insured lives until the policy expires), it is the least expensive form of life insurance. Often term insurance is purchased for a special purpose, such as for an airplane trip; thus, a term insurance policy can be obtained for almost any period of time the insured desires it. Young people often buy term insurance during their time of lowest earnings, with the provision that this be converted to some other type of insurance later on when they can afford it.

WHOLE LIFE INSURANCE

Under a whole life policy, the insured agrees to pay premiums for his entire life, whether he lives one day or ninety years. At the time of the insured's death, the beneficiary will receive the face value of the policy. The basic difference between whole life insurance and term insurance is that whole life insurance has a *cash value* while term insurance does not. That is, if the insured cancels the whole life policy after, say, 12 years, he or she is entitled to a certain sum of money from the insurance company, the amount depending on how much was paid in. Term insurance, as mentioned previously, has no cash value.

LIMITED-PAYMENT LIFE INSURANCE

Like whole life insurance, limited-payment insurance provides permanent protection. The difference is that a limited-payment policyholder pays premiums for a fixed period of time, the most common periods being 20 and 30 years. At the end of the period, the insured no longer makes any payments but is insured for the remainder of his life. The beneficiary will receive the face value of the policy at the time of the insured's death whether it occurs during or following the period covered by the policy.

ENDOWMENT INSURANCE

Endowment insurance is an insured savings plan. It is purchased for a fixed period of time, usually 20 or 30 years. At the end of that time, the cash value of the policy (the amount the insurance company will pay the insured) is equal to its face value and the insurance expires. The insured may take the money as a lump sum payment, as a series of monthly payments for a specified number of years, or for life. If the insured dies before completing payment of his endowment policy, the face value is paid to the beneficiary.

RATE TABLE

The following table shows typical rates that are charged by life insurance companies for the four types of policies just discussed.

ANNUAL PREMIUMS PER $1,000 OF INSURANCE

Age at Issue	Term 10-Yr.	Term 15-Yr.	Whole Life	Limited-Payment 20-Yr.	Limited-Payment 30-Yr.	Endowment 20-Yr.	Endowment 30-Yr.
15	...	...	$10.11	$17.97	$13.80	$42.47	$25.90
20	$ 4.99	$ 5.42	$11.55	$19.84	$15.26	$42.55	$26.15
25	$ 5.19	$ 5.63	$13.35	$22.07	$17.03	$42.69	$26.50
30	$ 5.77	$ 6.20	$15.65	$24.73	$19.20	$43.01	$26.92
35	$ 7.09	$ 7.42	$18.61	$27.93	$21.93	$43.63	$27.50
40	$ 9.18	$ 9.67	$22.55	$31.80	$25.38	$44.76	$29.85
45	$12.74	$13.44	$27.58	$36.49	$29.79	$46.67	$33.33
50	$18.59	$19.03	$33.61	$42.19	$35.52	$49.65	$37.77
55	$24.89	...	$41.57	$42.25	...	$54.14	...
60	...	...	$52.71	$58.68	...	$61.26	...

Example:

Find the annual premium on a $1,000 30-payment life policy purchased at age 35.

Solution:

Find the number 35 in the *Age at Issue* column and follow this row across to the *30-Yr.* column under the heading *Limited-Payment*. The entry $21.93 at the intersection of the columns represents the annual premium on the $1,000 policy.

Notice that term insurance is the least expensive of the various types of insurance shown on the table; endowment insurance is the most expensive. A person would select term insurance if he or she is interested primarily in protection; the person would select endowment insurance if he or she is interested primarily in savings. The majority of people prefer whole life and limited-payment life policies. Under these policies, they are insured for their entire lives at a cost that is much less than the cost of an endowment policy.

Example:

Find the annual premium on a $25,000 20-year endowment policy issued at age 30.

Solution:

Premium for $1,000 = $43.01
Premium for $25,000 = 25 × $43.01
                         = $1,075.25, annual premium

PERIODIC PREMIUM PAYMENTS

Premiums on life insurance may be paid annually, semiannually, quarterly, monthly, or weekly. The more frequently premiums are paid, the greater the cost of the insurance—primarily because the insurance company's administrative costs are higher. The following table is used by many insurance companies for computing premiums on semiannual, quarterly, and monthly premiums. (Weekly payment plans are omitted since they are relatively rare.)

PERIODIC PREMIUM TABLE

If Period Is:	Multiply Annual Premium by:
Semiannual	.51
Quarterly	.26
Monthly	.087

Example:

Find the annual premium on a $5,000 whole life policy issued at age 15 for premiums payable semiannually, quarterly, and monthly.

Solution:

1. Find the annual premium for $1,000 of insurance.

      Annual premium for $1,000 = $10.11

2. Find the annual premium on the face value of the policy by multiplying the annual premium for $1,000 by the number of 1,000's in the face value of the policy.

      Annual premium for $5,000 = $10.11 × 5
                             = $50.55

Semiannual premium payment:

1. Multiply the annual premium for the face value of the policy by .51 (see the Periodic Premium Table). The result is the semiannual premium.

      $50.55 × .51 = $25.78, semiannual premium

2. Multiply the semiannual premium by the number of periods in the year; in this case, two. The result is the annual premium when paid semiannually.

$25.78 × 2 = $51.56, annual premium if paid semiannually

Quarterly premium payment:
1. Multiply the annual premium for the face value of the policy by .26 (see Periodic Premium Table). The result is the quarterly premium.

$50.55 × .26 = $13.14, quarterly premium

2. Multiply the quarterly premium by the number of periods in the year; in this case, 4. The result is the annual premium when paid quarterly.

$13.14 × 4 = $52.56, annual premium if paid quarterly

Monthly premium payment:
1. Multiply the annual premium for the face value of the policy by .087 (see Periodic Premium Table). The result is the monthly premium.

$50.55 × .087 = $4.397, or $4.40, monthly premium

2. Multiply the monthly premium by the number of periods in the year; in this case, 12. The result is the annual premium when paid monthly.

$4.40 × 12 = $52.80, annual premium if paid monthly

Exercises
1. Find the annual premiums for each policy.

	Policy	Age at Issue	Face Value	Premium per $1,000	Annual Premium
a.	10-year term	30	$ 5,000	$_____	$_____
b.	20-payment life	45	$10,000	$_____	$_____
c.	30-year endowment	25	$20,000	$_____	$_____
d.	Whole life	40	$ 2,000	$_____	$_____
e.	20-year endowment	20	$24,000	$_____	$_____
f.	15-year term	30	$ 5,000	$_____	$_____
g.	30-payment life	45	$ 7,000	$_____	$_____
h.	Whole life	30	$12,000	$_____	$_____
i.	30-year endowment	20	$15,000	$_____	$_____
j.	10-year term	45	$25,000	$_____	$_____

2. Find the periodic payment on each policy.

	Policy	Age at Issue	Face Value	Period	Premium
a.	Whole life	25	$ 1,000	Semiannually	$_____
b.	20-payment life	30	$20,000	Semiannually	$_____
c.	30-year endowment	20	$ 4,000	Semiannually	$_____
d.	15-year term	40	$ 8,000	Semiannually	$_____
e.	30-payment life	45	$14,000	Semiannually	$_____
f.	10-year term	25	$ 9,000	Quarterly	$_____
g.	20-year endowment	30	$16,000	Quarterly	$_____
h.	Whole life	15	$ 5,000	Quarterly	$_____
i.	20-year endowment	20	$15,000	Monthly	$_____
j.	30-payment life	25	$18,000	Monthly	$_____

Business Applications

1. How much more will the premiums be on a $5,000 20-payment life policy issued at age 25 than on a 30-payment life policy?

2. Sue Jacovina is 20. How much less will she pay each year if she purchases a $4,000 whole life policy than if she purchases a $4,000 20-year endowment policy?

3. Perry Thorberg purchased a $10,000 20-payment life policy at age 30. If he had purchased the policy at age 20, how much less would his annual premiums have been?

REVIEW EXERCISES FOR CHAPTER 21

In order to solve many of the problems below, you will need to refer to the tables in this chapter.

1. Find the premium on an $18,500 three-year ordinary fire insurance policy on a brick house in a class C town.

2. Fire caused $12,400 in damage to property assessed at $25,000. Although the policy contained an 80% clause, the owner had insured it for only $15,000. How much of the loss did the fire insurance company pay?

3. Perry Sanger, age 22 and unmarried, bought a used car strictly for pleasure. His insurance coverage includes both 25-and-50 bodily injury liability and $10,000 property damage liability insurance. If he lives in an 04 territory and has no record of accidents, what is the cost of his coverage?

4. Perry Sanger (see Problem 3) accidentally struck another car, resulting in $875 in damage to that car and serious injury to two of its passengers. Lawsuits against Perry required him to pay injured Party A $27,000 and injured Party B $5,000. How much of the indemnity was paid by the insurance company to each of these persons? How much was paid by the insurance company for damages to the other car?

5. Silas Greenwood, who is 35 years old and the owner of a new symbol-5 car in an 06 territory, plans to take out collision insurance. He has a record of one accident with his previous car. How much more will he have to pay for a $50-deductible policy than for a $100-deductible policy if he uses the new car for business?

6. When Agatha Morrison was 30, she purchased a $5,000 20-payment life policy. If she survived beyond that period and paid premiums annually, how much less did she pay the insurance company than her beneficiaries will receive at the time of her death?

7. How much will A. L. Baxter save each year on his $5,000 20-year endowment policy by making annual payments rather than quarterly payments? The policy was issued to him at age 25.

8. How much less will Ed Rupert pay each year if he purchases a $10,000 whole life policy at age 20 than Michael Bowman who purchases a $10,000 20-year endowment policy at the same age?

INDEX